The
Canadian
Oxford
Spelling
Dictionary

The
Canadian
Oxford
Spelling
Dictionary

Edited by
Robert Pontisso and Eric Sinkins

OXFORD
UNIVERSITY PRESS

OXFORD

UNIVERSITY PRESS

70 Wynford Drive, Don Mills, Ontario M3C 1J9
www.oupcan.com

Oxford   New York

Athens   Auckland   Bangkok   Bogotá   Buenos Aires   Calcutta
Cape Town   Chennai   Dar es Salaam   Delhi   Florence
Hong Kong   Istanbul   Karachi   Kuala Lumpur   Madrid
Melbourne   Mexico City   Mumbai   Nairobi   Paris   São Paulo
Singapore   Taipei   Tokyo   Toronto   Warsaw

with associated companies in Berlin   Ibadan

Oxford is a trade mark of Oxford University Press
in the UK and in certain other countries

Published in Canada
By Oxford University Press

Canadian Cataloguing in Publication Data

Main entry under title:

The Canadian Oxford spelling dictionary

ISBN 0-19-541456-X

1. English language—Orthography and spelling—Dictionaries.
2. English language—Canada—Orthography and spelling—
Dictionaries.

I. Pontisso, Robert, 1968–   .   II. Sinkins, Eric, 1970–   .
PE1146.C345 1999   423'.1   C99-931598-6

1 2 3 4 - 02 01 00 99

This book is printed on permanent (acid-free) paper ∞.

Printed in Canada

Introduction

A standard entry in *The Canadian Oxford Spelling Dictionary* consists of up to four parts: the headword, the gloss, the forms, and the pointer.

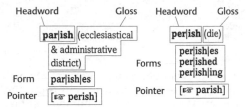

I. HEADWORDS

I-1. Organization

The entries in *The Canadian Oxford Spelling Dictionary* are arranged alphabetically by the headword. Capitalized headwords come before lower-case headwords of the same spelling. Strict alphabetical order is followed even when the headword consists of more than one word or of a hyphenated word:

> ice
> ices
> iced
> icing
> ice bag +s
> iceberg +s
> iceblink +s
> ice-blue +s
> iceboat +s +ed +ing

Because this dictionary is meant to be a spelling guide rather than a source for meanings, there is normally only one entry for each spelling; homographs—different words that are spelled the same—are usually treated in a single entry. For example, the entry

> converse
> converses
> conversed
> conversing

covers both the verb meaning 'engage in conversation' and the noun and adjective meaning 'opposite', since anyone looking for either of these words should recognize this spelling as the one sought. Furthermore, a single headword is used even when there are differing sets of forms for the various meanings of a word. In such cases each set of forms is introduced by a bullet (•) and identified with a short gloss:

> antenna
> • (aerial) *plural* antennas
> • (*Zoology*) *plural* antennae
> hide
> • *verb* (conceal)
> hides

> hid
> hidden
> hiding
> • *verb* (flog)
> hides
> hided
> hiding
> • *noun*
> hides

However, if the difference between homographs is such that it necessitates different word breaks or could lead to confusion, the words are listed as separate entries marked by superscript numbers immediately following the headword:

> re|fuse[1] *verb*
> re|fus|es
> re|fused
> re|fus|ing
> ref|use[2] *noun*
> tear[1] (rip)
> tears
> tore
> torn
> tear|ing
> tear[2] +s +ed +ing (liquid from eyes)
> tuber|ose[1] (of, like, or covered with tubers)
> tube|rose[2] (plant)

Entries for geographical names are treated like standard entries, with each distinct spelling listed only once:

> **London** (cities, England & Canada)

Words indicating a type of geographical feature, such as *Lake*, *River*, and *Desert*, are not normally included in a headword for a geographical entry unless they form part of the name of a city or town:

> **Laberge** (lake, Canada)
> **Cold Lake** (town & lake, Canada)

In biographical entries the headword normally consists of the surname followed by the given name(s), so individuals who share a surname are given separate entries. Exceptions include those who are commonly known by a first name, title, etc., and members of a single family identifiable by a single gloss:

> **James** (kings of Scotland & England; saints)
> **James, Henry** (US novelist)
> **James, Jesse Woodson** (US outlaw)
> **Dionne, Cécile, Yvonne, Émilie, Annette, & Marie** (Cdn quintuplets)
> **Dionne, Marcel** (Cdn hockey player)

I-2. Spelling

The Canadian Oxford Spelling Dictionary features all spellings commonly used by Canadians. The selection of words is based on *The Canadian Oxford Dictionary*, with additional items included on grounds of spelling difficulty or possible confusion. Spellings were determined by examining a database of almost twenty million words of text taken from over 8,000 Canadian publications, including works of fiction and non-fiction, newspapers, magazines, and catalogues.

If a word has more than one acceptable spelling, e.g. *rac(c)oon*, the spelling most often used by Canadians in edited text is recommended:

racoon +s (*use* raccoon)

No such preference is normally given among variants that differ more than slightly in pronunciation; these are treated as synonyms, e.g. *brontosaur* and *brontosaurus*. A milder recommendation, signified by '=', is used in certain cases to assure the user that two words with similar spellings but different pronunciations are in fact synonyms, and indicates that the word following '=' is favoured. Such words are entered thus:

sovereignist +s
sovereigntist +s (= sovereignist)
iced tea +s
ice tea +s (= iced tea)

The milder recommendation '=' is also used in entries for variant spellings and transliterations of foreign names:

Dostoyevsky, Fyodor (= Dostoevsky)
Posen (= Poznań, Poland)

(For more information on spelling recommendations, see section II: GLOSSES.)

Capital initial letters

Pairs of words beginning with capital and lower-case letters are given separate entries if they have different meanings:

Afghan +s (of Afghanistan; hound)
afghan +s (blanket, coat)
Brier +s (bonspiel)
brier +s (plants; pipe)

However, a lower-case word that may be capitalized when used as a title, e.g. *prime minister*, *brigadier general*, or *mademoiselle*, is normally shown only in the lower case. Rules concerning the capitalization of titles vary widely from publisher to publisher; we recommend that titles be capitalized only when they are placed directly before a name and are not set off by commas, thus:

She spoke with Prime Minister Jean Chrétien.

but

She spoke with the prime minister, Jean Chrétien.

She spoke with Jean Chrétien, prime minister of Canada.

One exception to this rule is the word *queen*, which is always capitalized when used to refer to the Queen of England and Canada.

Compounds

This dictionary contains a large number of compound expressions written as one word or with a hyphen, so that the reader is left in no doubt as to the recommended form. (Syntactic hyphenated compounds, such as *mud-spattered*, being almost unlimited in number, are only given if they are extremely common, e.g. *panic-stricken*, or if there could be doubt about the spelling of one of their elements, e.g. *storm-stayed*.)

Compounds that are written as separate words are not included unless:

• there is evidence of variation in their spelling, as with *living room*, which is also, but not as frequently, written as *living-room* or *livingroom*;

• there is variation in their spelling depending on the part of speech, as with *French Canadian* (*noun*) and *French-Canadian* (*adjective*), or *face off* (*verb*) and *faceoff* (*noun*);

• they could be confused with particular single-word or hyphenated compounds, e.g. *all together* (compare *altogether*).

In addition, there are many open compounds which take a hyphen when used adjectivally immediately preceding the noun they modify. For example, *emerald green* is written as two words in *her slippers were emerald green*, but with a hyphen in *she wore emerald-green slippers*. Such words are entered thus:

emerald green (emerald-green *when preceding a noun*)

I-3. Word Division

In handwriting and typing, it is safest (and often neatest) not to divide words at all; however, in word processing and typesetting that is justified, the overall appearance can often be improved by dividing a word at the end of a line to keep word spacing even.

A vertical bar (|) indicates a point at which a word can be divided under almost any circumstances. The word divisions shown in this text are based on a combination of etymological and phonological considerations, since relying on either principle exclusively can result in misleading or inelegant divisions, such as *auto-nomous*, *minc-ing*, and *not-able*, or *arse-nic*, *plane-tary*, and *medi-cable*.

Division of regular inflections

In regular inflections, the endings are separable as follows:

+ed: only in narrow-measure work and then only if the word is of at least six letters and the ending is pronounced as a separate syllable, e.g. *heat-ed* or *land-ed*; compare *acted* and *calmed*.

+ing: always, if the word is of more than six letters, e.g. *calm-ing* or *sharpen-ing*, but otherwise only in narrow-measure work, e.g. *try-ing*.

+er: only in narrow-measure work and then only if the word is of at least six letters, e.g. *calm-er* or *sharp-er*; compare *odder*.

+est: always, if the word is of more than six letters, as in *calm-est* or *shallow-est*, but otherwise only in narrow-measure work, e.g. *odd-est*.

Division of compounds and derivatives

Composite words, which include compounds such as *wintertime* and derivatives such as *winterize*, can be divided between their constituent elements under almost any circumstances; the only proviso is that when two composite words are differentiated only by the presence or absence of a hyphen, as with *redress* ('rectify') and *re-dress* ('dress again'), breaking either of them between the two elements should be avoided if doing so results in ambiguity.

The user will find that, in many cases, a word that is shown with recommended division points when it appears on its own, such as *fin|ger*, is not shown with the same breaks when it appears as part of a composite word, e.g. *fore|finger*, *finger|nail*. This is because the user is encouraged to divide the word between its elements rather than break the elements themselves. If absolutely necessary, however, an element of a composite word may be broken according to the recommendations found at the entry for the element itself: *forefin-ger*, *fin-gernail*. The most important consideration in doing so would be to avoid an unacceptably obtrusive or misleading result, such as *cher-rystone* or *mon-keywrench*.

The same rule applies to hyphenated compounds, with the exception that words are not usually divided within six letters of a hyphen. Thus *stu|dent* can be broken on its own but not in the compound *student-at-law*, and only one of the division points in *gov|ern|ment* can be used in *self-govern|ment*.

II. GLOSSES

Words are only glossed in *The Canadian Oxford Spelling Dictionary* if they can be mistaken for something else. In such cases the glosses include only what is necessary to identify the word and distinguish it from others similar to it. Instead of complete definitions, then, glosses often consist merely of a single sense indicator, subject field, or part of speech:

> **llama** (animal)
> **lama** (monk)
> **pistil** (*Botany*)
> **pistol** (gun)
> **hemophiliac** *noun*
> **hemophilic** *adjective*

A gloss may also include a reference to a preferred spelling variant:

> **racoon** +s (*use* raccoon)
> **sovereignlist** +s (= sovereignist)

(For more information about entries like these and other variants, see section I-2: **Spelling**.)

Glosses are also used in entries where the headword is the preferred spelling for some, but not all, senses of the word. For example, the entry

> **loony** (crazy; *for* dollar *use* **loonie**)

indicates that while *loony* can be used to mean both 'crazy' and 'dollar', the preferred spelling for 'dollar' is *loonie*.

III. FORMS

All plural forms of nouns, conjugated forms of verbs, and comparative and superlative forms of adjectives and adverbs are indicated in this dictionary.

If all inflected forms of a word are regular, i.e. are formed by adding -s, -ed, -ing, -er, or -est to the unaltered headword, only the endings are given, and they appear immediately after the headword:

> **warm** +er +est +s +ed +ing (slightly hot)
> **ex|pect** +s +ed +ing

Otherwise all forms are written in full and appear after any gloss:

stare (look fixedly)
stares
stared
star|ing

Verb forms are given in the order:

3rd person singular of the present tense
past tense
past participle
present participle

If the past tense and the past participle have the same form, it is given only once:

make
makes
made
mak|ing

If a word is both a noun and a verb, and the plural and the 3rd person singular present have the same form, it is given only once:

crash
crash|es
crashed
crash|ing

When an inflection has more than one possible spelling or form, the first one given is recommended:

banjo
ban|jos or ban|joes
spec|trum
spec|tra or spec|trums

Like headwords, inflections are printed with word divisions indicated. See section I-3: **Word Division**.

IV. POINTERS (☞)

To help users find desired spellings more easily, words for which a headword may be mistaken are included in square brackets at the end of the entry, marked with the symbol ☞. These pointers are intended to draw users' attention to spellings they may not have considered when looking for a word, and can be taken to mean 'Also consider...' or 'Do not confuse with...'.

Several factors have been considered in determining where to include pointers, including phonetic similarity between words, e.g.

cygnet +s (young swan)
[☞ signet]
signet +s (seal)
[☞ cygnet]

Graphic similarity has been taken into account when words do not sound the same:

crochet (*Needlework*)
crochets
crocheted
crocheting
[☞ crotchet]
crotchet +s (*Music*; fancy)

Note in this example that the pointer is included only at the entry for *crochet*, which could conceivably be mistaken for the word *crotchet*, but not at the entry for *crotchet*, which is not likely to be mistaken for *crochet*.

Pointers are also included to alert users to words that are neither phonetically identical nor graphically similar but may be confused because their senses are closely related:

> **Philippine** *adjective* (of the Philippines)
> [☞ Filipino]
> **Filipino** +s (native of the Philippines)

Pointers also appear in entries for compounds that share a common element spelled differently:

> **Stoney Creek** (city, Canada)
> [☞ Stony Plain]
> **Stony Plain** (town, Canada)
> [☞ Stoney Creek]

When there are three or more consecutive entries for the same surname, an entry has been included in addition to these to represent them all; all necessary pointers are included at this entry only, which is glossed simply as 'surname':

> **Reid** (surname)
> [☞ Read, Reade, Reed, rede]
> **Reid, (Daphne) Kate** (Cdn actress)
> **Reid, George Agnew** (Cdn painter)
> **Reid, Thomas** (Scottish philosopher)
> **Reid, William Ronald** (Cdn sculptor)

Pointers may be omitted if the entries involved are within one or two headwords of each other.

NOTE ON PROPRIETARY STATUS

This dictionary includes some words which have, or are asserted to have, proprietary status as trademarks or otherwise. Their inclusion does not imply that they have acquired for legal purposes a non-proprietary or general significance, nor is any other judgment implied concerning their legal status. In cases where the editors have some evidence that a word has proprietary status this is indicated in the entry for that word but no judgment concerning the legal status of such words is made or implied thereby.

Acknowledgements

Producing a reference book like *The Canadian Oxford Spelling Dictionary* would have been unthinkable were it not for the years of scrupulous research and analysis already conducted by the Dictionary Department at Oxford University Press Canada. To all our colleagues, whose labours in producing *The Canadian Oxford Dictionary* continue to bear fruit in new publications based on its unchallenged authority, we owe the utmost thanks. We are especially indebted to Katherine Barber, editor-in-chief of *The Canadian Oxford Dictionary*, and senior lexicographer Alex Bisset for their invaluable assistance and support through all stages of this project. We would also like to express our gratitude to Maurice Waite, whose *Oxford Colour Spelling Dictionary* inspired our own efforts.

R.P.
E.S.

A

A
• (letter; music note; mark)
A's
• (blood type; ampere)
Å (angstrom)
A1
a
• (letter)
a's
• (*indefinite article*; are, metric unit)
[☞ **aye, eh**]
AA (battery, classification, rating, anti-aircraft)
AAs
aa (lava)
AAA (battery, classification, rating)
AAAs
Aachen (city, Germany)
Aal|borg (city, Denmark)
Aalst (city, Belgium)
Aalto, Alvar (Finnish architect)
aard|vark +s
aard|wolf
aard|wolves
Aar|hus (city, Denmark)
Aaron (*Bible*)
[☞ **Aran, Arran, Erin**]
Aaron, Henry Louis ('Hank') (US baseball player)
Aaron's rod +s
AB (blood, degree)
ab +s
aba +s (= abaya)
aba|ca +s
aback
aba|cus
aba|cus|es
Aba|dan (port, Iran)
Abad|don (hell; the devil)
abaft
Aba|kan (city, Russia)
aba|lone +s
aban|don +s +ed +ing
aban|doned *adjective*
aban|don|er +s
aban|don|ment +s

abase
abas|es
abased
abas|ing
abase|ment +s
abash
abash|es
abashed
abash|ing
abashed *adjective*
abash|ment +s
abate
abates
abat|ed
abat|ing
abate|ment +s
aba|tis
plural aba|tis or aba|tis|es
abat|toir +s
ab|axial +s
abaya +s
ab|bacy
ab|ba|cies
Ab|bado, Clau|dio (Italian conductor)
Ab|bas|id +s
ab|ba|tial
Abbe, Ernst (German physicist)
abbé +s (priest)
ab|bess
ab|bess|es
Abbe|vil|lian
ab|bey +s (monastery)
[☞ **abbé**]
ab|bot +s
Abbots|ford (city, Canada)
abbot|ship +s
Ab|bott, Bud (US comedian)
Ab|bott, Sir John Jo|seph Cald|well (Cdn prime minister)
ab|brevi|ate
ab|brevi|ates
ab|brevi|at|ed
ab|brevi|at|ing
ab|brevi|a|tion +s
ABC (alphabet, rudiments; Dutch Caribbean islands)
ABC's
ABD (all but dissertation)
ABDs
ab|di|cate
ab|di|cates
ab|di|cat|ed
ab|di|cat|ing
ab|di|ca|tion +s
ab|di|ca|tor +s

ab|domen +s
ab|dom|in|al +s
ab|dom|in|al|ly
ab|duct +s +ed +ing
ab|duc|tion +s
ab|duct|or +s
Abduh, Muham|mad (Egyptian Islamic scholar)
Abdul Hamid II (sultan of Turkey)
Abdul-Jabbar, Kar|eem (US basketball player)
Ab|dul|lah, Sheik Muham|mad (Kashmiri Muslim leader)
Ab|dul|lah ibn Hus|sein (Jordanian king)
Abdul Rah|man, Tunku (Malayan leader)
abeam
abed
Abed|nego (*Bible*)
Abeg|weit (Aboriginal people; name for PEI)
plural Abeg|weit or Abeg|weits
Abel (*Bible*)
[☞ **able**]
Abel, Niels Hen|rik (Norwegian mathematician)
Abel|ard, Peter (French theologian & philosopher)
Abel|ian group +s
Aben|aki
plural Aben|aki or Aben|akis
Abeo|kuta (city, Nigeria)
Aber|deen (lake, Canada; city, Scotland)
Aber|deen, George Ham|il|ton Gor|don, 4th Earl of (British prime minister)
Aber|deen, Ish|bel Maria Gor|don, Count|ess of (British social reformer)
Aberdeen, John Camp|bell Gor|don, 7th Earl of (governor general of Canada)
Aber|deen Angus
Aber|deen Angus|es

Aber|deen|shire (former county, Scotland)
Aber|don|ian +s
Aber|fan (village, Wales)
Aber|hart, Wil|liam ('Bible Bill') (Cdn politician)
aber|rance +s
aber|rancy
aber|ran|cies
aber|rant
aber|ra|tion +s
abet
abets
abet|ted
abet|ting
abet|ment +s
abet|tor +s
abey|ance +s
abey|ant
abhor
ab|hors
ab|horred
ab|hor|ring
ab|hor|rence +s
ab|hor|rent
ab|hor|rer +s
abid|ance +s
abide
abides
abid|ed
abid|ing
abid|ing *adjective*
abid|ing|ly
Abi|djan (port, Ivory Coast)
Abi|gail (*Bible*)
abil|ity
abil|ities
ab initio
abio|gen|esis
abio|genic
Abi|ola, Mos|hood Kashi|mawo Ola|wale (Nigerian politician)
Abi|tibi (lake, river, administrative region, Canada)
Abitibi-Témisca|mingue (= Abitibi: administrative region, Canada)
ab|ject
ab|ject|ly
ab|jec|tion +s
ab|ject|ness
ab|ject|ness|es
ab|jur|a|tion +s

ab|jure
  ab|jures
  ab|jured
  ab|jur|ing
Ab|khazia (territory, Republic of Georgia)
Ab|khaz|ian +s
ab|late
  ab|lates
  ab|lat|ed
  ab|lat|ing
ab|la|tion +s
abla|tive +s
ab|laut +s
ablaze
able (having ability)
  abler
  ablest
  [☞ Abel]
able-bodied
abloom
ab|lu|tion +s
ab|lu|tion|ary
ably
ABM (anti-ballistic missile)
  ABMs
Ab|naki (use Abenaki)
  plural Ab|naki or Ab|nakis
ab|neg|ate
  ab|neg|ates
  ab|neg|at|ed
  ab|neg|at|ing
ab|neg|a|tion +s
ab|neg|ator +s
ab|nor|mal
ab|nor|mal|ity
  ab|nor|mal|ities
ab|nor|mal|ly
Abo +s (offensive)
aboard
abode +s
aboi|teau
  aboi|teaux
abol|ish
  abol|ish|es
  abol|ished
  abol|ish|ing
abol|ish|able
abol|ish|er +s
abol|ish|ment +s
Abo|li|tion (against slavery or capital punishment)
abo|li|tion (in general use)
abo|li|tion|ism
abo|li|tion|ist +s
abo|ma|sum
  abo|masa
A-bomb +s

Abo|mey (town, Benin)
abom|in|able
abom|in|ably
abom|in|ate
  abom|in|ates
  abom|in|at|ed
  abom|in|at|ing
abom|in|a|tion +s
abom|in|ator +s
ab|oral
Ab|orig|in|al +s (peoples, Canada & Australia)
ab|orig|in|al +s (native)
ab|orig|in|al|ity
ab|orig|in|al|ly
Ab|orig|ine +s (Australian Aboriginal)
ab|orig|ine +s (original inhabitant)
aborn|ing
abort +s +ed +ing
abor|ti|fa|cient +s
abor|tion +s
abor|tion|ist +s
abor|tive
abor|tive|ly
abor|tu|ary
  abor|tu|aries
Abou|kir (bay, off Egypt)
abou|lia (use abulia)
abou|lic (use abulic)
abound +s +ed +ing
about
about-face
  about-faces
  about-faced
  about-facing
about-turn +s +ed +ing verb & noun
about turn interjection
above
above board (above-board when preceding a noun)
above ground (above-ground when preceding a noun)
above-mentioned
ab ovo
abra|ca|dab|ra +s
abrade
  abrades
  abrad|ed
  abrad|ing
abrad|er +s
Abra|ham (Bible)
abra|sion +s
abra|sive +s

ab|react +s +ed +ing
ab|reac|tion +s
ab|react|ive
abreast
abridge
  abridg|es
  abridged
  abridg|ing
abridge|able
abridge|ment +s
abridg|er +s
abridg|ment +s (use abridgement)
abroad
ab|ro|gate
  ab|ro|gates
  ab|ro|gat|ed
  ab|ro|gat|ing
ab|ro|ga|tion +s
ab|ro|ga|tor +s
abrupt
abrupt|ly
abrupt|ness
Ab|ruz|zi (region, Italy)
Absa|llom (Bible)
ab|scess
  ab|scess|es
ab|scessed
ab|scis|ic acid
ab|scis|sa
  ab|scis|sae or ab|scis|sas
ab|scis|sion +s
ab|scond +s +ed +ing
ab|scond|er +s
ab|seil +s +ed +ing
ab|sence +s
ab|sent adjective, preposition & verb
  ab|sents
  ab|sent|ed
  ab|sent|ing
ab|sen|tee +s
ab|sen|tee|ism
ab|sent|ly
absent-minded
absent-minded|ly
absent-minded|ness
ab|sinth +s (plant; for liqueur use absinthe)
ab|sinthe +s (liqueur)
absit omen
ab|so|lute +s
ab|so|lute|ly
ab|so|lute|ness
ab|so|lu|tion +s
ab|so|lut|ism
ab|so|lut|ist +s
ab|solve
  ab|solves
  ab|solved
  ab|solv|ing

ab|solv|er +s
ab|sorb +s +ed +ing
ab|sorb|abil|ity
ab|sorb|able
ab|sorbed adjective
ab|sorb|ed|ly
ab|sorb|ency
  ab|sorb|en|cies
ab|sorb|ent
ab|sorb|er +s
ab|sorb|ing adjective
ab|sorb|ing|ly
ab|sorp|tion +s
ab|sorp|tive
ab|stain +s +ed +ing
ab|stain|er +s
ab|stemi|ous
ab|stemi|ous|ly
ab|stemi|ous|ness
ab|sten|tion +s
ab|stin|ence
ab|stin|ent
ab|stin|ent|ly
ab|stract +s +ed +ing
ab|stract|ed adjective
ab|stract|ed|ly
ab|strac|tion +s
ab|strac|tion|ism
ab|strac|tion|ist +s
ab|stract|ly
ab|stract|ness
ab|stract|or +s
ab|struse
ab|struse|ly
ab|struse|ness
ab|surd
ab|surd|ism
ab|surd|ist +s
ab|surd|ity
  ab|surd|ities
ab|surd|ly
ab|surd|ness
Abu-Bakr (Islamic caliph)
Abu-Bekr (= Abu-Bakr, Islamic caliph)
Abu Dhabi (state & its capital, UAE)
Abuja (capital of Nigeria)
abu|lia
abu|lic
Abu Musa (island, Persian Gulf)
abun|dance +s
abun|dant
abun|dant|ly
abuse
  abus|es
  abused
  abus|ing
abus|er +s

Abu Sim|bel (ancient site, Egypt)
abu|sive
abu|sive|ly
abu|sive|ness
abut (adjoin)
  abuts
  abut|ted
  abut|ting
  [☞ abbot]
abut|ment +s
abuzz
abysm +s (archaic = abyss)
abys|mal
abys|mal|ly
abyss
  abyss|es
abys|sal
Abys|sinia (former name for Ethiopia)
Abys|sin|ian +s
AC (ante Christum)
a/c (air conditioning)
aca|cia +s
aca|deme +s
aca|demia
aca|dem|ic +s
aca|dem|ic|ally
aca|demi|cian +s
aca|demi|cism
aca|dem|ics
Aca|dé|mie fran|çaise
acad|em|ism
Acad|emy (of Plato)
acad|emy (in general use)
  acad|em|ies
Acadia (French Maritimes)
Acad|ian +s (francophone people)
  [☞ Accadian, Akkadian]
acan|thus
  acan|thus|es
a cap|pella
Aca|pul|co full name **Aca|pul|co de Juá|rez** (resort, Mexico)
acari|cide +s
aca|rid +s
Ac|cad|ian +s (Mesopotamian people, language: use Akkadian)
  [☞ Acadian]
ac|cede (take up office; agree)

ac|cedes
acced|ed
acced|ing
  [☞ exceed]
ac|cel|er|ando +s
ac|cel|er|ate
  ac|cel|er|ates
  ac|cel|er|at|ed
  ac|cel|er|at|ing
ac|cel|er|at|ed adjective
ac|cel|er|a|tion +s
ac|cel|er|a|tive
ac|cel|er|ator +s
ac|cel|er|om|eter +s
ac|cent +s +ed +ing
ac|cen|tor +s
ac|cen|tual
ac|cen|tu|ate
  ac|cen|tu|ates
  ac|cen|tu|at|ed
  ac|cen|tu|at|ing
ac|cen|tu|a|tion +s
ac|cept +s +ed +ing (receive)
  [☞ except]
ac|cept|abil|ity
ac|cept|able
ac|cept|able|ness
ac|cept|ably
ac|cept|ance +s
ac|cept|ant
ac|cep|ta|tion +s
ac|cept|or +s
ac|cess
  ac|cess|es
  ac|cessed
  ac|cess|ing
ac|cess|ibil|ity
ac|cess|ible
ac|cess|ibly
ac|ces|sion +s +ed +ing
ac|ces|sor|ial
ac|ces|sor|ize
  ac|ces|sor|iz|es
  ac|ces|sor|ized
  ac|ces|sor|iz|ing
ac|ces|sory
  ac|ces|sor|ies
acciac|ca|tura +s
ac|ci|dence +s
ac|ci|dent +s
ac|ci|dent|al +s
ac|ci|dent|al|ly
accident-prone
ac|ci|die
ac|cip|iter +s
ac|cipi|trine
ac|claim +s +ed +ing
ac|claimed adjective
ac|claim|er +s

ac|clam|a|tion +s (election; oral vote or praise)
  [☞ acclimation]
ac|clim|ate
  ac|clim|ates
  ac|clim|ated
  ac|clim|at|ing
ac|clim|a|tion (familiarization)
  [☞ acclamation]
ac|clima|tiz|a|tion
ac|clima|tize
  ac|clima|tiz|es
  ac|clima|tized
  ac|clima|tiz|ing
ac|clivi|tous
ac|cliv|ity
  ac|cliv|ities
ac|col|ade +s
ac|com|mo|date
  ac|com|mo|dates
  ac|com|mo|dat|ed
  ac|com|mo|dat|ing
ac|com|mo|dat|ing adjective
ac|com|mo|dat|ing|ly
ac|com|mo|da|tion +s
ac|com|mo|da|tion|ist +s
ac|com|pani|ment +s
ac|com|pan|ist +s
ac|com|pany
  ac|com|pan|ies
  ac|com|pan|ied
  ac|com|pany|ing
ac|com|plice +s
ac|com|plish
  ac|com|plish|es
  ac|com|plished
  ac|com|plish|ing
ac|com|plished adjective
ac|com|plish|ment +s
ac|cord +s +ed +ing
ac|cord|ance
ac|cord|ant
ac|cord|ant|ly
ac|cord|ing adverb
ac|cord|ingly
ac|cor|dion +s
ac|cor|dion|ist +s
ac|cost +s +ed +ing
ac|couche|ment +s
ac|cou|cheur +s
ac|count +s +ed +ing
ac|count|abil|ity
ac|count|abil|ities
ac|count|able
ac|count|ably
ac|count|ancy

ac|count|ant +s
ac|count|ing noun
ac|count pay|able
  ac|counts pay|able
ac|count re|ceiv|able
  ac|counts re|ceiv|able
ac|coutre
  ac|coutres
  ac|coutred
  ac|cout|ring
ac|coutred adjective
ac|coutre|ment +s
Accra (capital of Ghana)
ac|credit +s +ed +ing
ac|credit|ation +s
ac|credit|ed adjective
ac|crete
  ac|cretes
  ac|cret|ed
  ac|cret|ing
ac|cre|tion +s
ac|cre|tive
ac|crual +s
ac|crue
  ac|crues
  ac|crued
  ac|cru|ing
ac|crued adjective
ac|cul|tur|ate
  ac|cul|tur|ates
  ac|cul|tur|at|ed
  ac|cul|tur|at|ing
ac|cul|tur|a|tion +s
ac|cul|tur|a|tive
ac|cumu|late
  ac|cumu|lates
  ac|cumu|lat|ed
  ac|cumu|lat|ing
ac|cumu|la|tion +s
ac|cumu|la|tive
ac|cumu|la|tive|ly
ac|cumu|la|tor +s
ac|cur|acy
  ac|cur|acies
ac|cur|ate
ac|cur|ate|ly
ac|cursed
ac|curst (archaic = accursed)
ac|cusal +s
ac|cus|a|tion +s
ac|cusa|tival
ac|cusa|tive +s
ac|cusa|tive|ly
ac|cusa|tor|ial
ac|cusa|tory
ac|cuse
  ac|cuses
  ac|cused
  ac|cus|ing

ac|cused *noun &*
adjective:
plural ac|cused
ac|cus|er +s
ac|cus|ing|ly
ac|cus|tom +s +ed
+ing
ac|cus|tomed
adjective
AC/DC (alternating
current/direct
current; bisexual)
ace
aces
aced
acing
acedia
acel|lu|lar
aceph|al|ous
acerb
acer|bic
acer|bic|ally
acer|bity
acer|bit|ies
acer|ola +s
acet|abu|lum
acet|abula
acet|al +s (organic
compound)
[☞ acetyl]
acet|alde|hyde +s
aceta|mino|phen +s
acet|anil|ide +s
acet|ate +s
acetic
acet|one +s
acet|ous
acetyl (radical of
acetic acid)
[☞ acetal]
acetyl|ated
acetyl|a|tion +s
acetyl|choline +s
acetyl|ene +s
acetyl|ide +s
acetyl|sali|cylic acid
Achaea (region,
ancient Greece)
Achae|an +s
Achae|men|ian +s
Achae|menid +s
Acha|tes (*Roman
Myth*; in '*fidus
Achates*')
ache
aches
ached
ach|ing
Achebe, Chinua
(Nigerian writer)
achene +s
Acher|nar (star)

Acher|on (mythical
river)
Ache|son, Dean
Gooder|ham (US
statesman)
Acheu|lean +s (*use*
Acheulian)
Acheu|lian +s
achier
achiest
achiev|able
achieve
achieves
achieved
achiev|ing
achieve|ment +s
achiev|er +s
achil|lea +s
Achil|les (*Greek Myth*)
Achil|les heel +s
Achil|les ten|don +s
aching|ly
achoo
achro|mat +s
achro|mat|ic
achro|mat|ic|ally
achro|ma|ti|city
achro|ma|tism
achy
achier
achiest
acid +s
acid|ic
acid|head +s
acid|ifi|ca|tion
acid|ify
acid|ifies
acid|ified
acid|ify|ing
acid|ity
acid|ities
acid|ly
acid|ness
acido|phil|ic
acid|oph|ilus
acid|o|sis
acid|otic
acidu|late
acidu|lates
acidu|lat|ed
acidu|lat|ing
acidu|la|tion +s
acidu|lous
acin|us
acini
ack-ack +s
ackee +s
ac|know|ledge
ac|know|ledg|es
ac|know|ledged
ac|know|ledg|ing
ac|know|ledge|able

ac|know|ledge|ment
+s
ac|know|ledg|ment
+s (*use*
acknowledgement)
aclin|ic
acme +s
acne
acned
aco|lyte +s
Acon|cagua
(mountain, Andes)
acon|ite +s
acon|itic
acon|it|ine
Acorn, Mil|ton (Cdn
poet)
acorn +s
acous|tic +s
acous|tic|al
acous|tic|al|ly
acous|ti|cian +s
acous|tics
ac|quaint +s +ed
+ing
ac|quaint|ance +s
ac|quaint|ance|ship
+s
ac|qui|esce
ac|qui|es|ces
ac|qui|esced
ac|qui|es|cing
ac|qui|es|cence +s
ac|qui|es|cent
ac|quir|able
ac|quire
ac|quires
ac|quired
ac|quir|ing
ac|quired im|mune
de|fi|ciency
syn|drome
ac|quire|ment +s
ac|qui|si|tion +s
ac|quisi|tive
ac|quisi|tive|ly
ac|quisi|tive|ness
ac|quisi|tor +s
ac|quit
ac|quits
ac|quit|ted
ac|quit|ting
ac|quit|tal +s
ac|quit|tance +s
Acre (town, Israel;
state, Brazil)
acre +s
acre|age +s
acred
acre-foot
acre-feet
acrid
acrid|ine +s

acrid|ity
acrid|ly
acri|flavine
Acri|lan *proprietary*
acri|moni|ous
acri|moni|ous|ly
acri|mony
acri|mon|ies
acro
acro|bat +s
acro|bat|ic
acro|bat|ic|ally
acro|bat|ics
acro|meg|alic
acro|meg|aly
acro|nym +s
acrop|etal
acrop|etal|ly
acro|phobia +s
acro|phob|ic
Acrop|olis (citadel,
Athens)
acrop|olis (citadel)
acrop|olis|es
across
acros|tic +s
Acrux (star)
acryl|ic +s
act +s +ed +ing
act|abil|ity
act|able
Ac|taeon (*Greek Myth*)
ACTH
(adrenocorticotrophic
hormone)
actin
[☞ Acton]
act|ing *noun &
adjective*
ac|tinia
ac|tin|iae
ac|tin|ic
actin|ide +s
actin|ism
ac|tin|ium
actin|oid +s
ac|tino|lite +s
actin|om|eter +s
ac|tino|morph|ic
ac|tino|my|cete +s
ac|tion +s +ed +ing
action|able
action|ably
Ac|tion Di|recte
action|er +s
Ac|tion Fran|çaise
action-packed
Ac|tium (promontory,
Greece)
acti|vate
acti|vates

acti|vat|ed
acti|vat|ing
acti|va|tion +s
acti|va|tor +s
act|ive +s
act|ive|ly
active-matrix
active|ness
active|wear
ac|tiv|ism +s
ac|tiv|ist +s
ac|tiv|ity
ac|tiv|ities
Acton (community, Canada)
[☞ actin]
Acton, John Emer|ich Ed|ward Dal|berg, 1st Baron (English historian)
[☞ actin]
ac|tor +s
ACTRA (Alliance of Canadian Cinema, Television and Radio Artists)
ac|tress
ac|tress|es
Acts (New Testament)
Acts of the Apos|tles (= Acts)
ac|tual
ac|tu|al|ity
ac|tu|al|ities
ac|tual|iz|a|tion +s
ac|tual|ize
ac|tual|iz|es
ac|tual|ized
ac|tual|iz|ing
ac|tual|ly
ac|tu|arial
ac|tu|arial|ly
ac|tu|ary
ac|tu|aries
ac|tu|ate
ac|tu|ates
ac|tu|at|ed
ac|tu|at|ing
ac|tu|a|tion +s
ac|tu|ator +s
actus reus
acu|ity
acu|ities
acu|leate
acu|men
acu|min|ate
acu|pres|sure
acu|punc|ture
acu|punc|tur|ist +s
acute
acute|ly
acute|ness
acyclo|vir

acyl
AD (Anno Domini)
ad +s
Ada
ad|age +s (maxim)
adage +s (Dance)
ada|gio +s
Adam (Bible; drug)
Adam, Adolphe (French composer)
Adam, James (Scottish architect)
Adam, Rob|ert (Scottish architect)
ada|mant +s
ada|mant|ine
ada|mant|ly
Adams (mountains, US)
Adams (surname)
[☞ Addams]
Adams, Ansel (US photographer)
Adams, Bryan (Cdn singer & songwriter)
Adams, Henry (Brooks) (US writer)
Adams, John (1735–1826; US president)
Adams, John Couch (English astronomer)
Adams, John Quin|cy (1767–1848; US president)
Adams, Rich|ard (British novelist)
Adams, Sam|uel (US revolutionary)
Adam's ale
Adam's ap|ple +s
Adam's Bridge (shoals between Sri Lanka & India)
Adam's Peak (mountain, Sri Lanka)
Adana (province & its capital, Turkey)
adapt +s +ed +ing
adapt|abil|ity
adapt|able
adapt|ably
adap|ta|tion +s
adapt|er +s
adap|tion +s
adapt|ive
adapt|ive|ly
adapt|or +s (use adapter)
Adas|kin, Harry (Cdn musician)
Adas|kin, John (Cdn musician)

Adas|kin, Mur|ray (Cdn musician)
ad|axial
ADC (aide-de-camp; analog-digital converter)
ADCs
ADD (attention deficit disorder)
add +s +ed +ing verb
Ad|dams, Jane (US social reformer)
[☞ Adams]
addax
ad|dax|es
added adjective
ad|den|dum
ad|den|da
ad|der +s
adder's tongue +s
ad|dict +s +ed +ing
ad|dict|ed adjective
ad|dic|tion +s
ad|dict|ive
add-in +s
Ad|ding|ton, Henry (1st Viscount Sidmouth, British prime minister)
Addis Ababa (capital of Ethiopia)
Ad|di|son, Jo|seph (English writer)
Ad|di|son, Thom|as (English physician)
Addison's dis|ease
addi|tion +s
addi|tion|al
addi|tion|al|ly
addi|tive +s
addle
ad|dles
ad|dled
ad|dling
ad|dled adjective
Addo (national park, South Africa)
add on verb
adds on
added on
adding on
add-on +s noun
ad|dress
ad|dress|es
ad|dressed
ad|dress|ing
ad|dress|able
ad|dres|see +s
ad|dress|er +s
Ad|dresso|graph +s proprietary

ad|duce
ad|du|ces
ad|duced
ad|du|cing
ad|du|cible
ad|duct +s +ed +ing
ad|duc|tion +s
ad|duct|or +s
Adel|aide (city, Australia; peninsula, Canada)
Adélie (land & coast, Antarctica; penguin)
Aden (port, Yemen; gulf, Arabian Sea)
Aden|auer, Kon|rad (German chancellor)
ad|en|ine +s
ad|en|oid|al
ad|en|oid|al|ly
ad|en|oids
ad|en|oma
ad|en|omas or ad|en|omata
adeno|sine
adept +s
adept|ly
adept|ness
ad|equa|cy
ad|equate
ad|equate|ly
à deux
ad fin.
Ad|hara (star)
ad|here
ad|heres
ad|hered
ad|her|ing
ad|her|ence
ad|her|ent +s
ad|hesion +s
ad|hes|ive +s
ad|hes|ive|ly
ad|hes|ive|ness
ad hoc
ad homi|nem
adia|bat|ic +s
adia|bat|ic|ally
adieu
adieus or adieux
Adi Granth (Sikhism)
ad in|fin|itum
ad in|ter|im
adios
adi|po|cere
adi|pose
adi|pos|ity
Adi|ron|dack +s (mountain range, N America; chair)
Adis Abeba (= Addis Ababa, Ethiopia)
adit +s

Adi|vasi +s
ad|ja|cency
ad|ja|cent
ad|jec|tival
ad|jec|tival|ly
ad|jec|tive +s
ad|join +s +ed +ing
ad|join|ing *adjective*
ad|journ +s +ed +ing
ad|journ|ment +s
ad|judge
  ad|judg|es
  ad|judged
  ad|judg|ing
ad|judge|ment +s
  (*use* adjudgment)
ad|judg|ment +s
ad|judi|cate
  ad|judi|cates
  ad|judi|cat|ed
  ad|judi|cat|ing
ad|judi|ca|tion +s
ad|judi|ca|tive
ad|judi|ca|tor +s
ad|junct +s
ad|junct|ive
ad|junct|ive|ly
ad|jur|ation +s
ad|jura|tory
ad|jure
  ad|jures
  ad|jured
  ad|jur|ing
ad|just +s +ed +ing
ad|just|abil|ity
ad|just|able
ad|just|er +s
ad|just|ment +s
ad|ju|tancy
  ad|ju|tan|cies
ad|ju|tant +s
ad|ju|vant +s
Adler, Al|fred
  (Austrian
  psychologist)
Adler|ian +s
ad lib
  ad libs
  ad libbed
  ad lib|bing
ad lib|itum
ad litem
ADM (Assistant
  Deputy Minister)
  ADMs
adman
  admen
ad|mass
  ad|mass|es
ad|meas|ure
  ad|meas|ures
  ad|meas|ured
  ad|meas|ur|ing

ad|measure|ment +s
Ad|metus (*Greek*
  Myth)
admin +s
ad|min|icle +s
ad|min|icu|lar
ad|min|is|ter +s +ed
  +ing
ad|min|is|trable
ad|min|is|trate
  ad|min|is|trates
  ad|min|is|trat|ed
  ad|min|is|trat|ing
ad|min|is|tra|tion +s
ad|min|is|tra|tive
ad|min|is|tra|tive|ly
ad|min|is|tra|tor +s
ad|min|is|tra|tor|ship
  +s
ad|min|is|tra|trix
  ad|min|is|tra|tri|ces
  or
  ad|min|is|tra|trix|es
ad|mir|able
ad|mir|ably
ad|miral +s
ad|miral|ship +s
Ad|miral|ty (islands,
  Pacific;
  administrative
  department)
ad|miral|ty (*Law*)
ad|mir|a|tion +s
ad|mire
  ad|mires
  ad|mired
  ad|mir|ing
ad|mir|er +s
ad|mir|ing *adjective*
ad|mir|ing|ly
ad|mis|si|bil|ity
ad|mis|sible
ad|mis|sion +s
admit
  ad|mits
  ad|mit|ted
  ad|mit|ting
ad|mit|tance +s
ad|mit|ted|ly
admix
  ad|mixes
  ad|mixed
  ad|mix|ing
ad|mix|ture +s
ad|mon|ish
  ad|mon|ish|es
  ad|mon|ished
  ad|mon|ish|ing
ad|mon|ish|ment +s
ad|mon|ition +s
ad|moni|tory
ad nau|seam
ad|nom|inal

ado
adobe +s
ado|les|cence +s
ado|les|cent +s
Adonai (name for
  God)
Adonis (*Greek Myth*;
  handsome young
  man)
  Adonis|es
adopt +s +ed +ing
adopt|able
adop|tee +s
adopt|er +s
adop|tion +s
adopt|ive
adopt|ive|ly
ador|able
ador|ably
ador|ation
adore
  adores
  adored
  ador|ing
ador|er +s
ador|ing *adjective*
ador|ing|ly
adorn +s +ed +ing
adorn|ment +s
Ador|no, Theo|dor
  Wiesen|grund
  (German
  philosopher)
ad per|sonam
ADR (alternative
  dispute resolution)
  ADRs
Adrar des Iforas
  (Saharan region)
ad rem
adrenal
ad|rena|lin
ad|rena|line (*use*
  adrenalin)
ad|reno|cortico|
            troph|ic
ad|reno|cortico|
            troph|in
ad|reno|cortico|
            trop|ic
  (= adrenocortico-
  trophic)
Adrian, Edgar
  Doug|las, 1st Baron
  (English
  neurophysiologist)
Adrian (popes)
Adri|atic (sea,
  Mediterranean)
adrift
adroit
adroit|ly
adroit|ness

ad|sorb +s +ed +ing
ad|sorb|able
ad|sorb|ate +s
ad|sorb|ent +s
ad|sorb|tion (*use*
  adsorption)
ad|sorp|tion
ad|suki +s (*use*
  adzuki)
adu|late
  adu|lates
  adu|lat|ed
  adu|lat|ing
adu|la|tion +s
adu|la|tor +s
adu|la|tory
adult +s
adul|ter|ant +s
adul|ter|ate
  adul|ter|ates
  adul|ter|at|ed
  adul|ter|at|ing
adul|ter|a|tion
adul|ter|ator +s
adul|ter|er +s
adul|ter|ess
  adul|ter|esses
adul|ter|ine
adul|ter|ous
adul|ter|ous|ly
adul|tery
  adul|ter|ies
adult|hood
adult|ly
ad|um|brate
  ad|um|brates
  ad|um|brat|ed
  ad|um|brat|ing
ad|um|bra|tion +s
ad|um|bra|tive
ad val|orem
ad|vance
  ad|van|ces
  ad|vanced
  ad|van|cing
ad|vanced *adjective*
ad|vance|ment +s
ad|van|cer +s
ad|van|tage
  ad|van|tages
  ad|van|taged
  ad|van|ta|ging
ad|van|taged
  adjective
ad|van|ta|geous
ad|van|ta|geous|ly
ad|vec|tion
ad|vec|tive
Ad|vent (*Christianity*)
ad|vent +s (arrival)
Ad|vent|ism
Ad|vent|ist +s
ad|ven|ti|tious

ad|ven|ti|tious|ly
ad|ven|ture
  ad|ven|tures
  ad|ven|tured
  ad|ven|tur|ing
ad|ven|tur|er +s
ad|ven|ture|some
ad|ven|tur|ess
  ad|ven|tur|ess|es
ad|ven|tur|ism
ad|ven|tur|ist +s
ad|ven|tur|ous
ad|ven|tur|ous|ly
ad|ven|tur|ous|ness
ad|verb +s
ad|verb|ial +s
ad|ver|sar|ial
ad|ver|sary
  ad|ver|sar|ies
ad|ver|sa|tive
ad|ver|sa|tive|ly
ad|verse
  (unfavourable;
  hurtful)
  [☞ averse]
ad|verse|ly
ad|verse|ness
ad|ver|sity
  ad|ver|sit|ies
ad|vert +s +ed +ing
ad|ver|tise
  ad|ver|tis|es
  ad|ver|tised
  ad|ver|tis|ing
ad|ver|tise|ment +s
ad|ver|tis|er +s
ad|ver|tor|ial +s
ad|vice +s noun
  [☞ advise]
ad|vis|abil|ity
ad|vis|able
ad|vis|ably
ad|vise verb
  ad|vis|es
  ad|vised
  ad|vis|ing
  [☞ advice]
ad|vised adjective
ad|vis|ed|ly
ad|vise|ment
ad|vis|er +s
ad|vis|or +s (use
  adviser)
ad|vis|ory
  ad|vis|ories
ad|vo|caat +s
  (liqueur)
  [☞ advocate]
ad|vo|cacy
ad|vo|cate
  (spokesperson;
  support)

ad|vo|cates
ad|vo|cat|ed
ad|vo|cat|ing
  [☞ advocaat]
ad|vo|ca|tory
ad|vow|son
ady|tum
  adyta
adze
  adzes
  adzed
  adz|ing
ad|zuki +s
ae|dile +s
ae|dile|ship +s
Ae|gean
  (Mediterranean sea
  & islands)
Ae|geus (Greek Myth)
Aegir (Scandinavian
  Myth)
aegis
  aegis|es
Aegis|thus (Greek
  Myth)
aegro|tat +s
Ael|fric (Anglo-Saxon
  writer)
Ae|neas (Greek &
  Roman Myth)
Ae|olian (islands off
  Italy; musical mode)
ae|olian (of wind;
  harp)
Ae|olus (Greek Myth)
aeon +s (use eon)
aepy|or|nis
  aepy|or|nis|es
aeradio (use air radio)
aer|ate
  aer|ates
  aer|at|ed
  aer|at|ing
aer|ation
aer|ator +s
aer|en|chyma
aer|ial +s (pertaining
  to air; antenna;
  freestyle skiing)
  [☞ areal]
aer|ial|ist +s
aer|ial|ity
aer|ial|ly
aerie +s (nest; lofty
  position)
aero (aerodynamic)
  [☞ arrow]
aero|bat +s
aero|bat|ic
aero|bat|ic|ally
aero|bat|ics
aer|obe +s
aer|ob|ic

aer|ob|ic|ally
aer|ob|ics
aero|biol|ogy
aero|drome +s
aero|dy|nam|ic
aero|dy|nami|ic|ally
aero|dy|nami|cist +s
aero|dy|nam|ics
aero|gel +s
aero|gram +s
aero|gramme +s (use
  aerogram)
aero|lite +s
aero|logic|al
aer|ol|ogy
aero|naut|ic
aero|naut|ic|al
aero|naut|ics
aeron|omy
aero|plane +s Brit.
aero|sol +s
aero|space
  (technology &
  industry of air &
  space travel)
aero|stat +s
Aes|chines (Greek
  statesman)
Aes|chylus (Greek
  dramatist)
Aes|cu|lap|ian
Aes|cu|lap|ius (Roman
  Myth)
Aesir (Scandinavian
  Myth)
Aesop (Greek author
  of fables)
Aesop|ian
Aesop|ic
aes|thete +s
Aes|thet|ic (19th-c.
  artistic movement)
aes|thet|ic +s (in
  general use)
aes|thet|ic|ally
aes|thet|ician +s
aes|theti|cism
aes|thet|ics
aes|tival
aes|tiv|ate
  aes|tiv|ates
  aes|tiv|at|ed
  aes|tiv|at|ing
aes|tiv|a|tion
aetatis
aether (sky, substance
  permeating space:
  use ether)
  [☞ ether]
afar
affa|bil|ity
af|fable
af|fably

af|fair +s (business;
  event; sexual liaison)
  [☞ affaire]
af|faire +s
  (controversy,
  scandal)
  [☞ affair]
af|faire de cœur
af|faires de cœur
af|fect
 • verb (have an effect
  on; feign)
  af|fects
  af|fect|ed
  af|fect|ing
 • noun (Psychology)
  af|fects
  [☞ effect]
af|fect|ation +s
af|fect|ed adjective
  (artificial)
  [☞ effected]
af|fect|ed|ly
af|fect|ing adjective
  (touching, moving)
  [☞ effecting]
af|fect|ing|ly
af|fec|tion +s
af|fec|tion|al
af|fec|tion|al|ly
af|fec|tion|ate
af|fec|tion|ate|ly
af|fect|ive
  (concerning
  emotion)
  [☞ effective]
af|fec|tiv|ity
  (emotional
  susceptibility)
  [☞ effectivity]
affen|pin|scher +s
af|fer|ent
af|fianced
af|fi|dav|it +s
af|fili|ate
  af|fili|ates
  af|fili|at|ed
  af|fili|at|ing
af|fili|at|ed adjective
af|fili|a|tion +s
af|fined
af|fin|ity
  af|fin|ities
af|firm +s +ed +ing
af|firm|a|tion +s
af|firma|tive +s
af|firma|tive|ly
af|firma|tory
affix
  af|fix|es
  af|fixed
  af|fix|ing
af|fix|a|tion +s

af|fla|tus
af|flict +s +ed +ing
af|flic|tion +s
af|flict|ive
af|flu|ence
af|flu|ent
af|flu|ent|ly
af|flux
  af|flux|es
af|ford +s +ed +ing
af|ford|abil|ity
af|ford|able
af|for|est +s +ed
  +ing
af|for|est|a|tion +s
af|fran|chise
  af|fran|chis|es
  af|fran|chised
  af|fran|chis|ing
af|fray +s
af|fri|cate +s
af|front +s +ed +ing
  (insult)
  [☞ effrontery]
Af|ghan +s (of
  Afghanistan; hound)
af|ghan +s (blanket,
  coat)
Af|ghani +s (of
  Afghanistan)
af|ghani +s (currency
  of Afghanistan)
Af|ghan|istan
  (country, central
  Asia)
afi|cion|ado +s
afield
afire
aflame
af|la|toxin +s
afloat
aflut|ter
afoot
afore
afore|thought
a for|ti|ori
afoul
afraid
A-frame +s
af|reet +s
afresh
Af|ri|ca (continent)
Af|ri|can +s
  [☞ Afrikaans,
  Afrikaner]
Af|ri|cana
African-American +s
African-Canadian +s
Af|ri|kaans (language)
Af|ri|ka Korps
Af|ri|kan|er +s
  (person)
afrit +s (use afreet)

Afro +s
Afro-American +s
Afro-Asiatic +s
Afro-Caribbean +s
Afro|cen|tric
af|ror|mo|sia +s
aft
after
after|birth +s
after|burn|er +s
after-care
after|deck +s
after-effect +s
after|glow +s
after-hours
after|image +s
after|life
after|market +s
after|math +s
after|most
after|noon +s
after|pains
afters
after|shave +s
after|shock +s
after|taste +s
after|thought +s
after|touch
  after|touch|es
after|ward
  (= afterwards)
  [☞ afterword]
after|wards (later)
after|word +s
  (concluding remarks)
  [☞ afterward]
AG (Attorney General;
  Auditor General)
  AGs
ag (agriculture)
Aga +s proprietary
  (stove)
aga +s (Muslim chief)
Aga|dir (seaport,
  Morocco)
again
against
Aga Khan +s (Islam)
Aga|mem|non
  (Mycenaean king)
agam|ic
Agaña (capital of
  Guam)
aga|pan|thus
  aga|pan|thus|es
agape[1] (gaping)
aga|pe[2] +s (fellowship;
  feast)
agar
agar-agar
aga|ric +s
Agar|tala (city, India)

Agas|si, André (US
  tennis player)
Agas|siz, Jean Louis
  Ro|dolphe (Swiss-
  born scientist)
Agas|siz (former
  glacial lake,
  N America)
ag|ate +s
agave +s
Agawa (bay &
  archaeological site,
  Lake Superior)
age
  ages
  aged
  aging or age|ing
aged adjective
Agee, James (US
  writer)
age|ing noun &
  adjective (use aging)
age|ism
age|ist +s
age|less
age-long
agency
  agen|cies
agen|da +s
agent +s
agent gen|er|al
  agents gen|er|al
agen|tial
Agent Or|ange
agent pro|voca|teur
  agents
  pro|voca|teurs
agent|ry
age-old
ager|atum +s
ag|gie +s
ag|glom|er|ate
  ag|glom|er|ates
  ag|glom|er|at|ed
  ag|glom|er|at|ing
ag|glom|er|a|tion +s
ag|glom|era|tive
ag|glu|tin|ate
  ag|glu|tin|ates
  ag|glu|tin|at|ed
  ag|glu|tin|at|ing
ag|glu|tin|a|tion +s
ag|glu|tina|tive
ag|glu|tin|in +s
ag|grand|ize
  ag|grand|iz|es
  ag|grand|ized
  ag|grand|iz|ing
ag|grand|ize|ment +s
ag|grand|iz|er +s
ag|gra|vate
  ag|gra|vates

ag|gra|vat|ed
ag|gra|vat|ing
ag|gra|va|tion +s
ag|gre|gate
  ag|gre|gates
  ag|gre|gat|ed
  ag|gre|gat|ing
ag|gre|ga|tion +s
ag|gres|sion +s
ag|gres|sive
ag|gres|sive|ly
ag|gres|sive|ness
ag|gres|siv|ity
ag|gres|sor +s
ag|grieved
ag|griev|ed|ly
aggro (trouble,
  troublemaking)
  [☞ agro]
agha +s (use aga)
aghast
agile
agile|ly
agil|ity
agin
Agin|court (battle site,
  France)
aging noun & adjective
agio +s
agism (use ageism)
agist +s (use ageist)
agi|tate
  agi|tates
  agi|tat|ed
  agi|tat|ing
agi|tat|ed adjective
agi|tat|ed|ly
agi|ta|tion +s
agi|tato
agi|ta|tor +s
Agit|prop (Soviet
  agency)
agit|prop (propaganda
  generally)
Ag|laia (Greek Myth)
ag|let +s
agley
ag|loo +s
aglow
aglu +s (use agloo)
AGM (annual general
  meeting; air-to-
  ground missile)
  AGMs
agma +s
ag|nail +s
ag|nate +s
ag|nat|ic
ag|na|tion
Agnes (saint)
Agnesi, Maria
  Gae|tana (Italian
  mathematician)

Agnew, Spiro Theo|dore (US vice-president)
Agni (*Hinduism*)
agnol|otti
Agnon, Shmuel Yosef (Israeli writer)
ag|no|sia
ag|nos|tic +s
ag|nos|ti|cism
Agnus Dei +s
ago
agog
à gogo
agon +s
ag|on|ic
agon|is|tic
agon|is|tic|ally
ag|on|ize
   ag|on|iz|es
   ag|on|ized
   ag|on|iz|ing
ag|on|ized *adjective*
ag|on|iz|ing *adjective*
ag|on|iz|ing|ly
agony
   ag|on|ies
ag|ora +s
agora|phobe +s
agora|phobia
agora|phob|ic +s
Ag|os|tini, Gia|como (Italian motorcycle racer)
agouti +s
AGR (advanced gas-cooled reactor)
   AGRs
Agra (city, India)
agrar|ian +s
agree
   agrees
   agreed
   agree|ing
agree|able
agree|able|ness
agree|ably
agree|ment +s
ag rep +s
Agri|bi|tion
agri|busi|ness
   agri|busi|ness|es
Agric|ola, Gnaeus Jul|ius (Roman general)
agri|cul|tur|al
agri|cul|tur|al|ist +s
agri|cul|tur|al|ly
agri|cul|ture +s
agri|cul|tur|ist +s
agri-food
agri|mony
   agri|mon|ies

Agrip|pa (Middle Eastern kings)
Agrip|pa, Mar|cus Vip|san|ius (Roman general)
Ag|rip|pina (mother of Caligula; mother of Nero)
agro +s (agriculture student)
   [☞ **aggro**]
agro|chem|ical +s
agro|forest|ry
agro|nom|ic
agro|nom|ic|al
agro|nom|ic|al|ly
agron|o|mist +s
agron|omy
aground
Aguas|ca|lien|tes (state & its capital, Mexico)
ague +s
agued
aguish
Agul|has (cape, South Africa; current off E Africa)
AH (*anno Hegirae*, of the Muslim era)
ah *interjection*
AHA (alpha-hydroxy acid)
   AHAs
aha *interjection*
Ahab (*Bible*)
Ahag|gar (mountain range, Algeria)
ahead
ahem
ahim|sa
ahis|tor|ic
ahis|tor|ic|al
ahis|tor|ic|al|ly
ahis|tori|cism
Ah|mada|bad (city, India)
Ah|meda|bad (= Ahmadabad)
Ahou|saht (*use* Ahousat)
   plural **Ahou|saht** *or* **Ahou|sahts**
Ahou|sat
   plural **Ahou|sat** *or* **Ahou|sats**
ahoy
Ahri|man (*Zoroastrianism*)
à huis clos
Ahura Mazda (*Zoroastrianism*)
Ahvaz (city, Iran)

Ahwaz (= Ahvaz, Iran)
AI (artificial intelligence; artificial insemination)
   AIs
ai +s (three-toed sloth)
AID (artificial insemination by donor)
aid +s +ed +ing (help)
aide +s (assistant)
aide-de-camp
   aides-de-camp
aide-mémoire
   aides-mémoire
AIDS (acquired immune deficiency syndrome)
AIDS-related *adjective*
aig|rette +s (tuft; plume)
   [☞ **egret**]
Aigues-Mortes (town, France)
ai|guille +s
ai|guil|lette +s
Aiken, Con|rad Pot|ter (US writer)
ai|kido
ail +s +ed +ing (trouble; be ill)
   [☞ **ale**]
ai|lan|thus
   ai|lan|thus|es
ail|eron +s
ail|ing *adjective*
ail|ment +s
aim +s +ed +ing
aim|less
aim|less|ly
aim|less|ness
ain't
Ain|tab (*former name for* Gaziantep)
Ain|tree (racetrack, England)
Ainu
   plural **Ainu** *or* **Ainus**
aïoli
air +s +ed +ing (atmosphere; breeze; aura; tune)
   [☞ **heir, err, are, Ayer**]
air bag +s
air base +s
air|borne
air|brush
   air|brush|es
   air|brushed
   air|brush|ing

air-conditioned *adjective*
air con|di|tion|er +s
air con|di|tion|ing *noun*
air-cool +s +ed +ing
air-cooled *adjective*
air|craft
   plural **air|craft**
air|craft|man
   air|craft|men
air|craft|woman
   air|craft|women
air|crew
   • (crew of an aircraft)
   plural **air|crews**
   • (member of a crew)
   plural **air|crew**
Air|drie (city, Canada)
air|drop
   air|drops
   air|dropped
   air|drop|ping
air-dry
   air-dries
   air-dried
   air-drying
Aire|dale +s (district, England; dog)
airer +s
air|fare +s
air|field +s
air|flow +s
air|foil +s
air|frame +s
air freight *noun*
air|freight +s +ed +ing *verb*
air|glow
air|head +s
air|i|er
air|i|est
air|i|ly
air|i|ness
air|ing +s *noun*
air|less (without air)
   [☞ **heirless**]
air|less|ness
air|lift +s +ed +ing
air line +s (conduit)
air|line +s (company operating aircraft)
air|liner +s
air|lock +s
air|mail +s +ed +ing
air|man
   air|men
air mile +s (unit of distance)
Air Miles *proprietary* (points for air travel)
air-mobile
air|plane +s

air|play
air|port +s
air radio
air raid +s (air-raid
when preceding a
noun)
air|screw +s
air-sea rescue +s
air|ship +s (aircraft)
air show +s
air|sick
air|sick|ness
air|some
air space (pocket of
trapped air; Real
Estate)
[☞ airspace]
air|space (Aviation)
[☞ air space,
aerospace]
air|speed +s
air|stream +s
air|strip +s
air|tight
air time +s
air-to-air
air-to-ground
air-to-surface
air|waves
air|way +s
air|woman
air|women
air|worthy
Airy, Sir George
Bid|dell (English
geophysicist)
[☞ aerie, eyrie]
airy (breezy; like air)
air|i|er
air|i|est
[☞ aerie, eyrie]
airy-fairy
Aisha (wife of
Muhammad)
aisle +s (passage)
[☞ isle]
aisled adjective
aitch
aitches
aitch|bone +s
Ait|ken, Rob|ert
Mor|ris (Cdn flutist)
Ait|ken, Wil|liam
Max|well (Lord
Beaverbrook)
Aivi|lik
plural Aivi|lik or
Aivi|liks
Aix-en-Provence
(city, France)
Aix-la-Chapelle
(French name for
Aachen)

Aizawl (city, India)
Ajac|cio (city, Corsica)
Ajan|ta (caves, India)
ajar
Ajax (town, Canada;
Greek Legend)
Ajman (emirate & its
capital, UAE)
Ajmer (city, India)
AK-47
AK-47s
a.k.a. (also known as)
Akan +s
Akbar, Jalal|udin
Muham|mad (Mogul
emperor of India)
akee +s (use ackee)
Akela +s
Akhe|naten (pharaoh)
Akhe|taten (ancient
capital of Egypt)
Akh|mat|ova, Anna
(Russian poet)
Aki|hito (emperor of
Japan)
akim|bo
Aki|miski (island,
Canada)
akin
Akita +s
Akkad (city &
kingdom,
Mesopotamia)
Ak|kad|ian +s
(Mesopotamian
people, language)
[☞ Acadian]
Akko (= Acre, Israel)
Akron (city, US)
Aksai Chin
(Himalayan region)
Aksum (town,
Ethiopia)
Aksum|ite +s
akva|vit +s (use
aquavit)
Ak|we|sasne (Indian
reserve, N America)
à la
Ala|bama (state, US)
Ala|baman +s
ala|bas|ter
ala|bas|trine
à la carte
alack
alack-a-day
alac|rity
Alad|din
Aladdin's cave +s
Aladdin's lamp +s
Ala|goas (state, Brazil)
Alain-Fournier
(French novelist)

à la king
Alamo (mission, US)
à la mode
Åland (islands, Gulf of
Bothnia)
alan|ine
Alar proprietary
(growth-regulating
chemical)
alar (of wings)
Alar|cón, Pedro
An|tonio de
(Spanish writer)
Al|aric (Visigothic
king)
alarm +s +ed +ing
alarm|ing adjective
alarm|ing|ly
alarm|ism
alarm|ist +s
alar|um +s
alas
Al|as|ka (state, US;
gulf, Pacific; dessert)
Al|as|kan +s
alate
alb +s
Alba, Duke of
(= Duke of Alva)
Alba|cete (province &
city, Spain)
alba|core +s
Alba Iulia (city,
Romania)
Alban (British saint)
Al|bani, Dame Emma
(Cdn soprano)
[☞ Albany]
Al|ban|ia (republic,
Europe)
Al|bany (city, US;
river, Canada)
[☞ Albani]
alba|tross
alba|tross|es
al|bedo +s
Albee, Ed|ward
Frank|lin (US
playwright)
[☞ Albi]
al|beit
Al|bena (resort,
Bulgaria)
Al|béniz, Isaac
(Spanish composer)
Al|bers, Josef (US
artist)
Al|bert (husband of
Queen Victoria;
Belgian kings; lake,
Africa)
al|bert +s (watch-
chain)

Al|berta (province &
mountain, Canada)
Al|ber|tan +s
Al|berti, Leon
Bat|tis|ta (Italian
architect)
al|ber|tite +s
al|berto|saur|us
al|berto|saur|us|es
Al|ber|tus Mag|nus
(medieval
philosopher)
al|bes|cent
Albi (town, France)
[☞ Albee]
Al|bi|gen|ses
Al|bi|gen|sian +s
al|bin|ism
al|bino +s
Al|bin|oni, Tom|aso
(Italian composer)
al|bin|otic
Al|binus (= Alcuin,
English theologian)
Al|bion (England;
Britain)
al|bite +s
Al|boin (Lombard
king)
Ål|borg (= Aalborg,
Denmark)
album +s
al|bu|men (egg white;
endosperm)
al|bu|min (protein)
al|bu|min|oid +s
al|bu|min|ous
al|bu|min|uria
album-oriented
Albu|quer|que (city,
US)
Albu|quer|que,
Al|fonso de
(Portuguese
statesman)
Albu|quer|quean +s
al|bur|num
Al|caeus (Greek poet)
al|ca|hest (use
alkahest)
al|caic
al|caics
Al|calá de He|nares
(city, Spain)
al|calde +s
Alcan (highway,
N America)
Alca|traz (island, US)
Al|ces|tis (Greek Myth)
al|chem|ic
al|chem|ical
al|chem|ist +s

al|chem|ize
al|chem|iz|es
al|chem|ized
al|chem|iz|ing
al|chemy
al|chem|ies
Al|ci|bi|ades (Greek general)
alcid +s (bird)
[☞ alkyd]
Al|cin|dor, Fer|di|nand Lewis ('Lew') (Kareem Abdul-Jabbar)
Al|cin|oüs (Greek Myth)
Alc|mene (Greek Myth)
Al|cock, Sir John Wil|liam (English aviator)
al|co|hol +s
al|co|hol|ic +s
al|co|hol|ism
al|co|hol|om|eter +s
al|co|hol|om|etry
al|cool +s
Al|cott, Lou|isa May (US novelist)
al|cove +s
Al|cuin (English theologian)
Al|cyone (Greek Myth)
Al|dabra (islands, Indian Ocean)
Al|deb|aran (star)
alde|hyde +s
alde|hydic
al dente
alder +s
alder|fly
  alder|flies
alder|man
  alder|men
alder|man|ic
alder|man|ship
Alder|ney (Channel Island; cattle)
alder|person +s
alder|woman
  alder|women
Al|dine
Aldis lamp +s
Al|drin, Edwin Eu|gene, Jr. ('Buzz') (US astronaut)
al|drin (insecticide)
Aldus Manu|tius (Italian printer)
ale +s (beer)
[☞ ail]
alea|tor|ic
alea|tory

Alecto (Greek Myth)
alee
ale|house +s
Alei|chem, Sho|lem (Russian writer)
Ale|khine, Alex|an|der (Russian-born chess player)
Alek|san|dro|pol (former name for Gyumri, Armenia)
Alek|san|drovsk (former name for Zaporizhzhya, Ukraine)
Alemán, Mateo (Spanish novelist)
alem|bic +s
Alen|tejo (region, Portugal)
aleph +s
Alep|po (city, Syria)
Alert (Cdn Forces Station)
alert +s +ed +ing
Alert Bay (bay & village, Canada)
alert|ly
alert|ness
Aletsch|horn (mountain, Switzerland)
aleuron (use aleurone)
aleur|one
Aleut
  plural Aleut or Aleuts
Aleu|tian +s (islands off Alaska; people; language)
alevin +s
ale|wife
  ale|wives
Alex|an|der
• (Greek general; Scottish kings; Russian emperors; popes; archipelago off Alaska)
• (drink)
Alex|an|ders
Alex|an|der Nevski (Russian saint)
Alex|an|der of Tunis, Har|old Ru|pert Leof|ric George, 1st Earl (governor general of Canada)
alex|an|ders (plant)
Alex|an|der tech|nique +s

Alex|an|dra (waterfall, Canada; Russian czarina)
Alex|an|dret|ta (former name for Iskenderun)
Alex|an|dria (port, Egypt)
Alex|an|drian +s (of Alexandria)
alex|an|drine +s (line of verse)
alex|an|drite +s (mineral)
Alex|an|dro|pol (= Aleksandropol, Armenia)
alexia
alexic
Alexis Mikh|ail|ovich (Russian czar)
Alex|ius I
Com|nenus (Byzantine emperor)
al|fal|fa
Al|fieri, Count Vit|torio (Italian writer)
Al|fonso (Spanish kings)
Al|fred (king of Wessex)
al|fredo
al|fresco
Al Fu|jay|rah (emirate & its capital, UAE)
Alf|vén, Hannes Olof Gösta (Swedish physicist)
alga
  algae
algal
Al|garve (province, Portugal)
al|ge|bra +s
al|ge|bra|ic
al|ge|bra|ic|al
al|ge|bra|ic|al|ly
al|ge|bra|ist +s
Alge|ciras (resort, Spain)
Alger, Hor|atio (US writer)
Al|geria (republic, Africa)
Al|ger|ian +s
algi|cide +s
algid
algid|ity
Al|gieba (star)
Al|giers (capital of Algeria)

al|gin|ate +s
al|gin|ic
Algol (star; computing language)
al|go|lag|nia
al|go|lag|nic +s
al|go|logic|al
al|gol|o|gist +s
al|gol|ogy
Al|gon|kian (= Algonquian)
  plural Al|gon|kian or Al|gon|kians
• Although Algonquian & Algonquin are currently more common in Cdn usage, some users insist on Algonkian & Algonkin.
[☞ Algonkin]
Al|gon|kin (= Algonquin people, dialect)
  plural Al|gon|kin or Al|gon|kins
• See Usage Note at Algonkian.
[☞ Algonkian, Algonquin]
Al|gon|quian (language group; group of Aboriginal peoples including Algonquin, Cree, Mi'kmaq, etc.)
  plural Al|gon|quian or Al|gon|quians
• See Usage Note at Algonkian.
[☞ Algonquin]
Al|gon|quin
• (Algonquian people living along the Ottawa River; Algonquian dialect)
  plural Al|gon|quin or Al|gon|quins
• See Usage Note at Algonkian.
• (snowshoe)
  plural Al|gon|quins
[☞ Algonquian]
al|go|rism
al|go|rithm +s
al|go|rith|mic
Al|gren, Nel|son (US novelist)
al|gua|cil +s
al|gua|zil +s (use alguacil)
Al|ham|bra (palace, Spain)

Ali (Islamic caliph)
Ali, Muham|mad (US boxer)
alias
alias|es
aliased
alias|ing
Ali Baba
alibi
alibis
alibied
alibi|ing
Ali|cante (port, Spain)
Alice-in-Wonder|land adjective
Alice Springs (town, Australia)
ali|cyclic
ali|dade +s
alien +s
alien|abil|ity
alien|able
alien|age
alien|ate
alien|ates
alien|at|ed
alien|at|ing
alien|at|ed adjective
alien|a|tion
alien|ator +s
alien|ist +s
alien|ness
ali|form
Ali|garh (city, India)
Ali|ghieri, Dante (Italian poet)
alight +s +ed +ing
align +s +ed +ing
align|ment +s
alike
ali|ment +s
ali|men|tal
ali|men|tary
ali|men|ta|tion
ali|mony
A-line
Alioth (star)
ali|phat|ic
ali|quot +s
A-list +s
alit|eracy
(disinclination to read)
[☞ illiteracy]
alit|er|ate +s
(disinclined to read)
[☞ illiterate, alliterate]
alive
alive|ness
aliyah
aliz|arin

Al Jizah (= Giza, Egypt)
al|ka|hest
Al|kaid (star)
al|kali +s
al|ka|lim|eter +s
al|ka|lim|etry
al|ka|line
al|ka|line earth +s
(alkaline-earth when preceding a noun)
al|ka|lin|ity
al|ka|loid +s
al|ka|loid|al
al|ka|losis
al|kane +s
al|kanet +s
al|kene +s
alky
alkies
alkyd +s (resin; paint)
alkyl +s
alkyl|ate
alkyl|ates
alkyl|at|ed
alkyl|at|ing
al|kyne +s
all (everything, everyone, etc.)
[☞ awl]
alla breve
alla cap|pel|la
Allah (Islam)
Allah|abad (city, India)
all-American +s
Allan, Sir Hugh (Cdn railway financier)
[☞ Allen]
Allan Cup
al|lan|toic
al|lan|tois
al|lan|to|ides
all around adverb
all-around adjective
preceding a noun
allay +s +ed +ing
(alleviate, relieve)
[☞ allée, ally]
all-Canadian +s
all-candidates meet|ing +s
all-clear +s
all-day adjective
preceding a noun
all-dressed
Al|lec|to (Greek Myth: use Alecto)
allée +s (garden path)
[☞ allay, alley]
al|leg|a|tion +s

al|lege
al|leges
al|leged
al|leging
al|leged adjective
al|leged|ly
Al|leghe|ny (mountain range, US)
Al|leghe|nies
al|le|giance
al|le|gian|ces
al|legor|ic
al|legor|ic|al
al|legor|ic|al|ly
al|legor|ist +s
al|legor|iz|a|tion +s
al|legor|ize
al|legor|iz|es
al|legor|ized
al|legor|iz|ing
al|legory
al|legor|ies
al|le|gret|to +s
Al|leg|ri, Gre|gorio (Italian composer)
al|leg|ro +s
al|lele +s (Genetics)
[☞ allyl]
al|lel|ic
al|lelo|morph +s
al|lelo|morph|ic
al|le|luia +s
alle|mande +s (Dance)
all-embracing
Allen (surname; key, wrench, screw)
[☞ Allan]
Allen, Ethan (US revolutionary)
Allen, Ralph (Cdn journalist)
Allen, Woody (US filmmaker)
Al|len|by, Ed|mund Henry Hyn|man, 1st Vis|count (English field marshal)
Al|lende, Sal|va|dor (Chilean president)
al|ler|gen +s
al|ler|gen|ic
al|ler|gic
al|ler|gist +s
al|lergy
al|ler|gies
al|levi|ate
al|levi|ates
al|levi|at|ed
al|levi|at|ing
al|levi|a|tion +s
al|levia|tive

al|levi|ator +s
al|levia|tory
al|ley +s (lane; Sports; garden path; marble)
[☞ allée, allay, ally]
alley-oop +s
alley|way +s
All Fools' Day
All Hal|lows
al|li|aceous
al|li|ak +s
Al|li|ance (church)
al|li|ance
al|li|an|ces (in general use)
al|lied adjective
Al|lier (river, France)
al|li|ga|tor +s
all-import|ant
all-in adjective
preceding a noun
all-inclusive
Al|line, Henry (Cdn evangelist)
Al|ling|ham, Mar|gery (English novelist)
all-in-one +s
Al|li|son (mountain pass, Canada)
al|lit|er|ate (contain or use alliteration)
al|lit|er|ates
al|lit|er|at|ed
al|lit|er|at|ing
[☞ aliterate, illiterate]
al|lit|er|a|tion +s
al|lit|era|tive
al|lium +s
all-new
all-night adjective
preceding a noun
all-nighter +s
al|loc|able
al|lo|cate
al|lo|cates
al|lo|cat|ed
al|lo|cat|ing
al|lo|ca|tion +s
al|lo|ca|tor +s
al|loch|thon +s
al|loch|thon|ous
al|lo|cu|tion +s
al|log|amy
allo|morph +s
allo|morph|ic
allo|path +s
allo|path|ic
allo|path|ist +s
allo|pathy
allo|pat|ric
allo|phone +s

allo|phon|ic
allot (apportion, allocate)
al|lots
al|lot|ted
al|lot|ting
[☞ a lot]
al|lot|ment +s
allo|trope +s
allo|trop|ic
allo|trop|ic|al
al|lot|ropy
al|lot|tee +s
all out adverb
all-out adjective preceding a noun
all-over adjective preceding a noun
al|low +s +ed +ing (permit, set aside, admit)
al|low|able
al|low|ably
al|low|ance
al|low|an|ces
al|low|anced
al|low|an|cing
al|lowed conjugated form of allow [☞ aloud]
al|low|ed|ly
al|loy +s +ed +ing
all-points bul|letin +s
all-purpose
all ready (entirely ready) [☞ already]
all right
all round adverb
all-round adjective preceding a noun
all-rounder +s
All Saints' Day
all|sorts
All Souls' Day
all|spice
all-star +s
All|ston, Wash|ing|ton (US painter)
all-terrain adjective preceding a noun
all-time adjective & adverb
all to|geth|er (all in one place, all at once) [☞ altogether]
all told
al|lude (refer indirectly)

al|ludes
al|lud|ed
al|lud|ing
[☞ elude]
all-up adjective preceding a noun
al|lure
al|lures
al|lured
al|lur|ing
al|lure|ment +s
al|lur|ing adjective
al|lur|ing|ly
al|lu|sion +s (indirect reference) [☞ elusion, illusion]
al|lu|sive (pertaining to allusion) [☞ elusive, illusive]
al|lu|sive|ly (with allusion) [☞ elusively]
al|lu|sive|ness (allusive nature) [☞ elusiveness]
al|luv|ial +s
al|luv|ion
al|luv|ium
al|luvia or al|luv|iums
all-weather adjective
all-wheel drive
ally (partner)
al|lies
al|lied
ally|ing
[☞ alley]
allyl +s (Chemistry) [☞ allele]
Alma (city, Canada)
Alma-Ata (= Almaty, Kazakhstan)
alma|can|tar +s (use almucantar)
Alma|gest (Ptolemy's treatise)
alma|gest (in general use)
alma mat|er +s
al|ma|nac +s
al|man|dine (gemstone) [☞ amandine]
Alma-Tadema, Sir Law|rence (English painter)
Al|maty (former capital of Kazakhstan)
Al|meria (city & province, Spain)
al|mighty

Al|mir|ante Brown (city, Argentina)
Almo|dó|var, Pedro (Spanish filmmaker)
Almo|had +s
Almo|hade +s (use Almohad)
al|mond +s (nut) [☞ allemande, almandine, amandine]
al|mon|er +s
Al|monte (town, Canada)
Al|mora|vid +s
Al|mora|vide +s (use Almoravid)
al|most
alms
alms|giver +s
alms|giving
alms|house +s
almu|can|tar +s
Al|ni|lam (star)
Al|ni|tak (star)
aloe +s
aloe vera +s
aloft
alogic|al
aloha
alone
alone|ness
along
along|shore
along|side
aloof
aloof|ly
aloof|ness
alo|pecia
Alor Setar (city, Malaysia)
a lot (much) [☞ allot]
aloud (audibly) [☞ allowed]
Alou|ette +s (CFL team)
alow (below, in a ship) [☞ allow]
Aloy|sius Gon|zaga (saint)
alp +s (any high mountain) [☞ Alps]
al|paca +s
alpen|glow
alpen|horn +s
alpen|stock +s
al|pha +s
alpha|bet +s
alpha|bet|ic
alpha|bet|ic|al
alpha|bet|ic|al|ly

alpha|bet|iz|a|tion +s
alpha|bet|ize
alpha|bet|iz|es
alpha|bet|ized
alpha|bet|iz|ing
alpha-blocker +s
Alpha Cen|tauri (star)
alpha-hydroxy acid +s
alpha|num|er|ic
alpha|num|er|ic|al
Al|phard (star)
alpha test +s +ed +ing
alp|horn +s
Alp|ine (of the Alps)
alp|ine +s (of high mountains; an alpine plant)
alpin|ism
alpin|ist +s
Alps (mountain ranges, Europe & elsewhere)
al|ready (beforehand; as early or as soon as this; as an intensifier) [☞ all ready]
al|right (use all right)
ALS (amyotrophic lateral sclerosis)
Al|sace (region, France)
Al|sa|tian +s
al|sike
also
also-ran +s
al|stroe|meria +s
Alt
Altai (territory, Russia; mountain system, central Asia)
Al|taic
Al|tair (star)
Alta|mira (paleolithic site, Spain; town, Brazil)
al|tar +s (Religion) [☞ alter]
altar|piece +s
Altay (territory, Russia: use Altai)
alt|azi|muth +s
Alt|dor|fer, Al|brecht (German painter)
al|ter +s +ed +ing (change) [☞ altar]
alter|able
alter|a|tion +s
alter|cate
alter|cates

alter|cat|ed
alter|cat|ing
alter|ca|tion +s
alter ego +s
alter|nate
alter|nates
alter|nat|ed
alter|nat|ing
alter|nate|ly
alter|na|tion +s
al|terna|tive +s
al|terna|tive|ly
alter|na|tor +s
alt|horn +s
al|though
Alt|house, John
George (Cdn
educator)
Alt|hus|ser, Louis
(French philosopher)
al|tim|eter +s
alti|plano +s
alti|tude +s
alti|tud|inal
Alt|man, Rob|ert (US
filmmaker)
alto +s
[☞ Aalto]
alto|cumu|lus
al|to|geth|er
(completely; on the
whole; in total)
[☞ all together]
alto|ist +s
alto-relievo +s
alto-rilievo +s (use
alto-relievo)
alto|strat|us
al|tru|ism +s
al|tru|ist +s
al|tru|is|tic
al|tru|is|tic|ally
alum +s
alum|ina
alum|in|iz|a|tion +s
alum|in|ize
alum|in|iz|es
alum|in|ized
alum|in|iz|ing
alum|in|ium Brit.
alum|ino|sili|cate +s
alum|inum
alumna
alum|nae
alum|nus
alumni
Alva, Duke of
(Spanish general)
Al|varez, Luis Wal|ter
(US physicist)
al|veo|lar
al|veo|late

al|veo|lus
al|veoli
Al|ver|stone
(mountain peak,
Yukon–Alaska
border)
al|ways
alys|sum +s
Alz|heimer's
dis|ease or
Alz|heimer
dis|ease
• Although
Alzheimer's disease is
more common in
general Cdn usage, it
is the official policy
of some groups to
use the form
Alzheimer disease.
AM (amplitude
modulation; Master
of Arts)
am conjugated form of
be
a.m. (before noon)
Amad|juak (lake,
Canada)
ama|dou
amah +s
Amal|fi (port, Italy)
amal|gam +s
amal|gam|ate
amal|gam|ates
amal|gam|at|ed
amal|gam|at|ing
amal|gam|a|tion +s
Amal|thea (Greek
Myth; moon of
Jupiter)
aman|dine (garnished
with almonds)
[☞ almandine]
amanu|en|sis
amanu|en|ses
Amapá (state, Brazil)
am|ar|anth +s
amar|anth|ine
amar|etti (biscuits)
[☞ amoretti]
amar|etto +s (liqueur)
[☞ amoretto]
Amar|one +s
ama|ryl|lis
ama|ryl|lis|es
amass
amass|es
amassed
amass|ing
amass|er +s
Ama|ter|asu
(Shintoism)
ama|teur +s
ama|teur|ish

ama|teur|ish|ly
ama|teur|ish|ness
ama|teur|ism
Amati (family of
Italian violin makers)
ama|tory
amaur|o|sis
amaur|o|ses
amaur|otic
amau|ti +s
amau|tik +s
amaze
amaz|es
amazed
amaz|ing
amaze|ment
amaz|ing adjective
amaz|ing|ly
amaz|ing|ness
Ama|zon +s (river &
region, S America;
Greek Myth)
ama|zon +s (athletic
woman; parrot)
Ama|zon|as (state,
Brazil)
Ama|zonia (region,
S America; national
park, Brazil)
Ama|zon|ian +s
am|bas|sa|dor +s
am|bassador-at-
large
am|bassadors-at-
large
am|bas|sa|dor|ial
am|bas|sa|dor|ship
+s
am|bas|sa|dress
am|bas|sa|dres|ses
Am|bato (town,
Ecuador)
am|ber +s
amber|gris
amber|jack
plural amber|jack or
amber|jacks
am|bi|ance +s (use
ambience)
ambi|dex|ter|ity
ambi|dex|trous
ambi|dex|trous|ly
ambi|dex|trous|ness
am|bi|ence +s
am|bi|ent
ambi|gu|ity
ambi|gu|ities
am|bigu|ous
am|bigu|ous|ly
am|bigu|ous|ness
ambi|son|ics
ambit +s
am|bi|tion +s

am|bi|tious
am|bi|tious|ly
am|bi|tious|ness
am|biva|lence +s
am|biva|lency
am|biva|lent
am|biva|lent|ly
ambi|ver|sion
ambi|vert +s
amble
am|bles
am|bled
am|bling
Am|bler, Eric (US
novelist)
am|bly|opia
am|bly|opic
ambo
ambos or ambo|nes
Am|boina (= Ambon,
Indonesia)
[☞ amboyna]
Ambon (island & port,
Indonesia)
am|boyna (wood)
[☞ Amboina]
Am|brose (saint)
am|bro|sia
am|bro|sial
Am|bro|sian
(pertaining to St.
Ambrose)
am|bro|sian
(delectable; divine)
ambry
am|bries
ambu|lance +s
ambu|lant
ambu|la|tory
ambu|la|tor|ies
am|bus|cade
am|bus|cades
am|bus|cad|ed
am|bus|cad|ing
am|bush
am|bush|es
am|bushed
am|bush|ing
amel|ior|ate
amel|ior|ates
amel|ior|at|ed
amel|ior|at|ing
amel|ior|ation
amel|ior|ative
amel|ior|ator +s
amen +s
amen|abil|ity
amen|able
amen|able|ness
amen|ably
amend +s +ed +ing
(improve)
[☞ emend]

amend|able
amende honor|able
amendes honor|ables
amend|er +s
amend|ment +s
amends
Amen|hotep
(pharaohs)
amen|ity
amen|ities
Amen|ophis (*Greek name for* Amenhotep)
amen|or|rhea
amen|or|rhoea (*use* amenorrhea)
ament +s
amen|tia
amen|tum
amenta
Amer|asian +s
amerce
amer|ces
amerced
amer|cing
amerce|ment +s
amer|ci|able
Amer|ica +s (country, continents)
Amer|ican +s
Amer|icana
Amer|ican|ism +s
Amer|ican|iz|a|tion
Amer|ican|ize
Amer|ican|iz|es
Amer|ican|ized
Amer|ican|iz|ing
America's Cup
ameri|cium
Amer|ind +s
Amer|in|dian +s
Ames, Sir Her|bert Brown (Cdn politician)
Ames test +s
am|ethyst +s
am|ethyst|ine
AMEX (American Stock Exchange)
Am|haric
Am|herst (town, Canada)
Am|herst, Jef|fery, 1st Baron (British general)
Am|herst of Arakan, Wil|liam Pitt, Earl (British colonial administrator)
Am|herst|burg (town, Canada)
ami|abil|ity
ami|able

ami|able|ness
ami|ably
ami|an|thus
ami|an|tus (*use* amianthus)
am|ic|abil|ity
am|ic|able
am|ic|able|ness
am|ic|ably
amice +s
ami|cus curiae
amici curiae
amid
amide +s
amid|ship (= amidships)
amid|ships
amidst
Amiens (city, France)
amigo +s
Amin, Idi *full name* Idi Amin Dada (Ugandan head of state)
Amin|divi (island group, Indian Ocean)
amine +s
amino +s
Ami|rante (islands, Indian Ocean)
Amis, Sir Kings|ley (English writer) [☞ Amos, amiss]
Amis, Mar|tin (English writer) [☞ Amos, amiss]
Amish
Amish|man
Amish|men
amiss (out of order; wrong)
ami|tosis
ami|trip|tyl|ine
amity
Amman (capital of Jordan)
am|meter +s
ammo
Ammon *Egyptian Myth* (= Amun) [☞ Amman]
am|mo|nia
am|mo|niac|al
am|mo|ni|ated
am|mon|ite +s
am|mo|nium
am|mu|ni|tion +s
am|nesia
am|nes|iac +s *noun* (person suffering from amnesia)
am|nes|ic +s *adjective* & *noun* (of amnesia;

person suffering from amnesia)
am|nesty
am|nes|ties
am|nes|tied
am|nesty|ing
amnio +s
amnio|cen|tesis
amnio|cen|teses
am|nion
amnia
am|niot|ic
amoeba
amoe|bas *or* amoe|bae
amoeb|ia|sis
amoeb|ic
amoeb|oid
amok
among
amongst
amon|til|lado +s
amoral
amoral|ism
amoral|ist +s
amoral|ity
amor|etto (cupid)
amor|etti [☞ amaretto, amaretti]
amor|ist +s
Am|or|ite +s
amor|oso +s
amor|ous
amor|ous|ly
amor|ous|ness
amor|phous
amor|phous|ly
amor|phous|ness
amor|tiz|a|tion
amor|tize
amor|tiz|es
amor|tized
amor|tiz|ing
Amos (town, Canada; *Bible*) [☞ Amis]
amount +s +ed +ing
amour +s
amour-propre
am|oxi|cil|lin
am|oxy|cil|lin (*use* amoxicillin)
Amoy (= Xiamen, China)
amp +s
ampel|op|sis
amper|age +s
Am|père, André-Marie (French physicist)
am|pere +s (unit)
am|per|sand +s

am|pheta|mine +s
am|phib|ian +s
am|phib|ious
am|phib|ious|ly
am|phi|bole +s
am|phi|bol|ogy
am|phi|bol|o|gies
am|phi|mic|tic
am|phi|mixis
amphi|mixes
amphi|oxus
amphi|path|ic
amphi|pod +s
am|phip|ro|style +s
am|phis|baena +s
am|phi|the|ater +s (*use* amphitheatre)
am|phi|the|atre +s
Amphi|trite (*Greek Myth*)
Am|phit|ryon (*Greek Myth*)
am|phora
am|phorac *or* am|phoras
ampho|teric
ampi|cil|lin
ample
ampler
amplest
ample|ness
ampli|fi|ca|tion +s
ampli|fier +s
ampli|fy
ampli|fies
ampli|fied
ampli|fy|ing
ampli|tude +s
amply
am|poule +s
am|pul|la
am|pul|lae
am|pu|tate
am|pu|tates
am|pu|tat|ed
am|pu|tat|ing
am|pu|ta|tion +s
am|pu|ta|tor +s
am|pu|tee +s
Am|rit|sar (city, India)
Am|ster|dam (capital of the Netherlands)
am|trac +s (amphibious vehicle) [☞ Amtrak]
Am|trak *proprietary* (US train) [☞ amtrac]
am|trak +s (amphibious vehicle: *use* amtrac) [☞ Amtrak]
amuck (*use* amok)

Amu Darya (river, Asia)
amu|let +s
Amun (*Egyptian Myth*)
Amund Ring|nes (island, Canada)
Amund|sen (gulf, Canada)
Amund|sen, Roald (Norwegian explorer)
Amur +s (river, Asia; maple)
amuse
  amuses
  amused
  amus|ing
amuse|ment +s
amus|ing *adjective*
amus|ing|ly
amyg|dal|oid
amyl
amyl|ase +s
amyl|oid
amyo|troph|ic
  lat|eral scler|o|sis
Amy|tal *proprietary*
an
ana
• *plural noun* (rumours or anecdotes)
• *singular noun* (collection of sayings)
  plural anas
Ana|bap|tism
Ana|bap|tist +s
ana|batic
ana|bio|sis
  ana|bio|ses
ana|biot|ic
ana|bol|ic
anab|ol|ism
an|achron|ism +s
an|achron|is|tic
an|achron|is|tic|ally
ana|co|lu|thic
ana|co|lu|thon
  ana|co|lu|tha
ana|conda +s
Anac|reon (Greek poet)
Anac|re|on|tic +s
ana|cru|sis
  ana|cru|ses
anad|ro|mous
an|aer|obe +s
an|aer|obic
anaes|the|sia
anaes|the|si|ol|o|gist +s (*use* anesthesiologist)
anaes|the|si|ol|ogy (*use* anesthesiology)

anaes|thet|ic +s
an|aes|the|tist +s
an|aes|the|tiz|a|tion
an|aes|the|tize
  an|aes|the|tiz|es
  an|aes|the|tized
  an|aes|the|tiz|ing
ana|glyph +s
ana|glyph|ic
ana|gram +s
ana|gram|mat|ic
ana|gram|mat|ic|al
ana|gram|ma|tize
  ana|gram|ma|tiz|es
  ana|gram|ma|tized
  ana|gram|ma|tiz|ing
Ana|heim (city, US)
anal (of the anus)
  [☞ annal]
ana|lecta (= analects)
ana|lects
ana|lep|tic +s
an|al|gesia
an|al|gesic +s
anal|ly
ana|log (*Computing*; *Electronics*)
  [☞ analogue]
ana|logic|al
ana|logic|al|ly
an|alo|gize
  an|alo|giz|es
  an|alo|gized
  an|alo|giz|ing
an|alo|gous
an|alo|gous|ly
ana|logue +s (an analogous thing)
  [☞ analog]
an|alogy
  an|alo|gies
anal-retentive
ana|lys|able (*use* analyzable)
an|aly|sand +s
ana|lyse (*use* analyze)
  ana|lys|es
  ana|lysed
  ana|lys|ing
ana|lys|er +s (*use* analyzer)
an|aly|sis
  an|aly|ses
ana|lyst +s (a person who analyzes)
  [☞ annalist]
ana|lytic
ana|lytic|al
ana|lytic|al|ly
ana|lyz|able
ana|lyze
  ana|lyz|es

ana|lyzed
ana|lyz|ing
ana|lyz|er +s
an|am|nesis
  an|am|neses
ana|morph|ic
ana|morph|osis
  ana|morph|oses
an|an|drous
Ana|nias (*New Testament*)
ana|paest +s (*use* anapest)
ana|paes|tic (*use* anapestic)
ana|pest +s
ana|pes|tic
ana|phase +s
anaph|ora +s
ana|phor|ic
an|aphro|dis|iac +s
an|aphyl|actic
an|aphyl|axis
  ana|phyl|axes
anap|tyc|tic
anap|tyxis
  anap|tyxes
an|arch|ic
an|arch|ic|al
an|arch|ic|al|ly
an|arch|ism
an|arch|ist +s
an|arch|is|tic
an|archy
  an|arch|ies
Ana|sazi
  plural Ana|sazi or Ana|saz|is
ana|stig|mat +s
ana|stig|mat|ic
anas|to|mose
  anas|to|mos|es
  anas|to|mosed
  anas|to|mos|ing
anas|to|mo|sis
  anas|to|mo|ses
anas|tro|phe +s
anath|ema +s
anath|ema|tize
  anath|ema|tiz|es
  anath|ema|tized
  anath|ema|tiz|ing
Ana|to|lia (peninsula forming most of Turkey)
Ana|to|lian +s
ana|tom|ic
ana|tom|ic|al
ana|tom|ic|al|ly
anato|mist +s
anato|mize
  anato|miz|es

anato|mized
anato|miz|ing
anat|omy
  anat|omies
Anax|ag|oras (Greek philosopher)
Anaxi|man|der (Greek philosopher)
Anax|im|enes (Greek philosopher)
An|cas|ter (town, Canada)
an|ces|tor +s
an|ces|tral
an|ces|tress
  an|ces|tress|es
an|ces|try
  an|ces|tries
An|chi|ses (*Greek Myth*)
an|cho +s
an|chor +s +ed +ing
  [☞ Angkor]
An|chor|age (city, US)
an|chor|age +s (*Nautical*)
an|chor|ess
  an|chor|ess|es
anchor-ice
an|chor|ite +s
an|chor|itic
anchor|man
  anchor|men
anchor|person
  anchor|persons or anchor|people
anchor|woman
  anchor|women
an|cho|veta +s
an|chovy
  an|cho|vies
an|chusa +s
an|chyl|ose (*use* ankylose)
an|chyl|os|es
an|chyl|osed
an|chyl|os|ing
an|chyl|o|sis (*use* ankylosis)
an|chyl|o|ses
an|cien ré|gime
an|ciens ré|gimes
an|cient +s
ancient|ness
an|cil|lary
  an|cil|lar|ies
ancon
  an|co|nes
An|cona (port, Italy)
and
Anda|lu|sia (region, Spain)
Anda|lu|sian +s

Anda|man (island group off India)
an|dan|te +s
an|dan|tino +s
An|de|an
An|der|sen, Hans Chris|tian (Danish writer)
[☞ Anderson]
An|der|son (river, Canada; surname)
[☞ Andersen]
An|der|son, Carl David (US physicist)
An|der|son, Eliza|beth Gar|rett (English physician)
An|der|son, James Thom|as Mil|ton (Cdn politician)
An|der|son, Dame Jud|ith (Australian actress)
An|der|son, Lind|say (English filmmaker)
An|der|son, Mar|ian (US singer)
An|der|son, Phil|ip War|ren (US physicist)
An|der|son, Sher|wood (US writer)
Andes (mountain system, S America)
andes|ite +s
An|dhra Pra|desh (state, India)
and|iron +s
and/or
An|dorra (principality, Europe)
An|dor|ran +s
André ('Brother André', Cdn religious)
André, John (English officer)
An|drea del Sarto (Italian painter)
An|dret|ti, Mario Gab|ri|ele (race-car driver)
An|drew (apostle; English prince)
An|drews, Julie (English actress)
An|drews, Thom|as (Irish chemist)
An|drić, Ivo (Yugoslav writer)
andro|cen|tric
andro|cen|trism

An|dro|cles (Roman Legend)
an|droe|cium
an|droe|cia
andro|gen +s (male hormone)
[☞ androgyne]
andro|gen|ic
andro|gyne +s (hermaphrodite)
[☞ androgen]
an|dro|gyn|ous
an|dro|gyny
an|droid +s
An|drom|ache (Greek Myth)
An|drom|eda (Greek Myth; galaxy)
An|drop|ov (former name for Rybinsk)
An|drop|ov, Yuri Vlad|imir|ovich (Soviet president)
andro|stene|dione
anec|dot|age
anec|dotal
anec|dotal|ist +s
anec|dote +s
anec|dotic
anec|dot|ist +s
an|echo|ic
an|emia +s
an|emic
anemo|graph +s
anemo|graph|ic
an|emom|eter +s
anemo|met|ric
an|emom|etry
anem|one +s
an|emoph|il|ous
an|er|oid +s
anes|the|sia (use anaesthesia)
anes|the|si|ol|o|gist +s US (a doctor who administers anaesthetics)
anes|the|si|ol|ogy
anes|thet|ic +s (use anaesthetic)
an|es|the|tist +s (use anaesthetist)
an|es|the|tiz|a|tion (use anaesthetization)
an|es|the|tize (use anaesthetize)
an|es|the|tiz|es
an|es|the|tized
an|es|the|tiz|ing
an|eur|ism +s (use aneurysm)

an|eur|is|mal (use aneurysmal)
an|eur|ysm +s
an|eur|ys|mal
anew
an|frac|tu|os|ity
an|frac|tu|os|ities
an|frac|tu|ous
an|ga|kok +s
an|gary (Law)
[☞ angry]
Angel (waterfall, Venezuela)
[☞ Angell, Angle]
an|gel +s (heavenly being)
[☞ angle]
An|gel|eno +s
angel|fish
plural angel|fish or angel|fish|es
angel food cake +s
an|gel|ic
an|gel|ica
an|gel|ic|al
an|gel|ic|al|ly
An|gel|ico, Fra (Italian painter)
An|gell, Sir Nor|man (English economist)
[☞ Angel, Angle]
An|ge|lou, Maya (US writer)
angels-on-horseback
an|gelus
an|ger +s +ed +ing
An|gers (city, France)
An|gers, Fé|li|cité (Cdn writer)
An|ge|vin +s
an|gina
an|gina pec|tor|is
angio|gram +s
angio|graph|ic
angio|graph|ic|ally
angi|og|raphy
angi|og|raph|ies
angi|oma
angi|omas or angi|oma|ta
angio|plasty
angio|plas|ties
angio|sperm +s
angio|sperm|ous
Ang|kor (ancient city, Cambodia)
Angle +s (Germanic people)
[☞ Angel, Angell]
angle (corner, slant; to fish)

angles
angled
an|gling
[☞ angel]
angled adjective
angle-park +s +ed +ing
an|gler +s
angler|fish
plural angler|fish or angler|fish|es
Angle|sey (island off Wales)
Angli|an
Angli|can +s
Angli|can|ism
an|glice
angli|cism +s
angli|cize
angli|ciz|es
angli|cized
angli|ciz|ing
an|gling noun
An|glo +s
Anglo-American +s
Anglo-Canadian +s
Anglo-Catholic +s
Anglo-Catholi|cism
Anglo|cen|tric
Anglo-French
Anglo-Indian +s
Anglo-Irish
Anglo-Latin
Anglo|mania
Anglo-Norman
anglo|phile +s
anglo|philia
anglo|phobe +s
anglo|phobia
anglo|phob|ic
anglo|phone +s
Anglo-Saxon +s
An|gola (country, Africa)
An|go|lan +s
An|gora (former name of Ankara)
an|gora (fabric, wool; cat, goat, rabbit)
Angos|tura (former name of Ciudad Bolívar)
angos|tura (flavouring)
Angos|tura Bit|ters proprietary
angri|ly
angry (mad)
angri|er
angri|est
[☞ angary]
angst

Ång|ström, An|ders
Jonas (Swedish
physicist)
ang|strom +s (unit)
An|guil|la (island,
Caribbean)
An|guil|lan +s
an|guine
an|guish
an|guished
angu|lar
angu|lar|ity
angu|lar|ities
angu|lar|ly
Angus (former county,
Scotland; cattle)
Anguses
An|halt, Ist|ván (Cdn
composer)
an|hed|ral
Anhui (province,
China)
[☞ Anouilh, ennui]
An|hwei (province,
China: use Anhui)
an|hyd|ride +s
an|hyd|rite
an|hyd|rous
Anik
anil|ine
ani|ma +s
anim|ad|ver|sion +s
anim|ad|vert +s +ed
+ing
ani|mal +s
ani|mal|cu|lar
ani|mal|cule +s
ani|mal|ism
ani|mal|is|tic
ani|mal|ity
ani|mal|iz|a|tion +s
ani|mal|ize
ani|mal|iz|es
ani|mal|ized
ani|mal|iz|ing
ani|mate
ani|mates
ani|mat|ed
ani|mat|ing
ani|mat|ed adjective
ani|mat|ed|ly
anima|teur +s
(coordinator)
[☞ animator]
ani|ma|tion +s
ani|ma|tor +s (maker
of animated films; for
coordinator use
animateur)
anima|tron|ic
adjective
anima|tron|ics noun
animé

ani|mism
ani|mist +s
ani|mis|tic
ani|mos|ity
ani|mos|ities
ani|mus
an|ion +s
an|ion|ic
anise
ani|seed
ani|sette
Anishi|nabe
plural Anishi|nabe
Anish|nabe (use
Anishinabe)
plural Anish|nabe
an|iso|trop|ic
an|iso|trop|ic|ally
an|isot|ropy
an|isot|rop|ies
Anjou (region, France;
city, Canada; pear)
[☞ Angevin]
Anka, Paul Al|bert
(Cdn singer-
songwriter)
An|kara (capital of
Turkey)
ankh +s
an|kle +s
ankle-biter +s
ank|let +s
an|kyl|ose
an|kyl|os|es
an|kyl|osed
an|kyl|os|ing
an|kyl|o|sis
an|kyl|o|ses
an|kyl|otic
anna +s
An|naba (port,
Algeria)
an|nal +s (record,
narrative, journal)
an|nal|ist +s (writer of
annals)
[☞ analyst]
an|nal|is|tic
an|nal|is|tic|ally
Annam (part of
French Indochina)
An|nam|ese
An|nand, Wil|liam
(Cdn politician)
An|nap|olis (river,
Canada; city, US)
An|nap|olis Royal
(town, Canada)
An|na|purna
(mountain ridge,
Nepal)
an|nates
an|nat|to

Anne (mother of
Virgin Mary; English
queens; English
princess; French
queen)
Anne of Cleves
(English queen)
an|neal +s +ed +ing
an|neal|er +s
an|nel|id +s
an|nel|id|an +s
annex
an|nex|es
an|nexed
an|nex|ing
an|nex|a|tion +s
an|nex|a|tion|ism
an|nex|a|tion|ist +s
An|ni|goni, Pietro
(Italian painter)
an|nihi|late
an|nihi|lates
an|nihi|lat|ed
an|nihi|lat|ing
an|nihi|la|tion +s
an|nihi|la|tor +s
an|ni|ver|sary
an|ni|ver|sar|ies
Anno|bón (island,
Equatorial Guinea)
Anno Dom|ini
an|no|tat|able
an|no|tate
an|no|tates
an|no|tat|ed
an|no|tat|ing
an|no|ta|tion +s
an|no|ta|tive
an|no|ta|tor +s
an|nounce
an|noun|ces
an|nounced
an|noun|cing
an|nounce|ment +s
an|noun|cer +s
an|noy +s +ed +ing
an|noy|ance +s
an|noy|er +s
an|noy|ing adjective
an|nual +s
an|nu|al|ized
an|nu|al|ly
an|nu|it|ant +s
an|nu|it|ize
an|nu|it|iz|es
an|nu|it|ized
an|nu|it|iz|ing
an|nu|ity
an|nu|ities
annul (declare invalid;
cancel)
an|nuls

an|nulled
an|nul|ling
[☞ annal]
an|nu|lar
an|nu|lar|ly
an|nu|late (having
rings)
[☞ annulet]
an|nu|la|tion +s
an|nu|let +s
(Architecture; small
ring)
[☞ annulate]
an|nul|ment +s
an|nu|lus
an|nuli
annum (in 'per
annum')
an|nun|ci|ate
an|nun|ci|ates
an|nun|ci|at|ed
an|nun|ci|at|ing
An|nun|ci|a|tion
(Christianity)
an|nun|ci|a|tion
(generally)
an|nun|ci|ator +s
annus mira|bi|lis
anni mira|bi|les
annus hor|ri|bi|lis
anni hor|ri|bi|les
anoa +s
anod|al
an|ode +s
anod|ic
ano|dize
ano|diz|es
ano|dized
ano|diz|ing
ano|diz|er +s
ano|dyne +s
anoint +s +ed +ing
anoint|er +s
anom|al|is|tic
anom|al|ous
anom|al|ous|ly
anom|al|ous|ness
anom|aly
anom|alies
anom|ic
an|omie
anomy (use anomie)
anon
ano|nym +s
ano|nym|ity
an|onym|ous
an|onym|ous|ly
anoph|eles
plural anoph|eles
ano|rak +s
an|or|ec|tic +s
an|or|ex|ia
an|or|ex|ia ner|vosa

an|or|ex|ic +s
an|ortho|site +s
an|osmia
an|osmic
an|other
Anouilh, Jean
(French dramatist)
[☞ Anhui, ennui]
ANOVA (analysis of
variance)
ANOVAs
an|ovu|lant +s
an|ovu|la|tory
an|oxia
an|oxic
An|schluss
An|selm (saint)
an|ser|ine
An|shan (city, China)
an|swer +s +ed +ing
an|swer|abil|ity
an|swer|able
an|swer|phone +s
ant +s
ant|acid +s
An|taeus (Greek Myth)
an|tag|on|ism
an|tag|on|ist +s
an|tag|on|is|tic
an|tag|on|is|tic|ally
an|tag|on|iz|a|tion
an|tag|on|ize
antagon|iz|es
antagon|ized
antagon|iz|ing
ant|alkali +s
An|tall, Jozsef
(Hungarian prime
minister)
An|talya (port,
Turkey)
Anta|nana|rivo
(capital of
Madagascar)
Ant|arc|tic (region,
ocean, peninsula)
Ant|arc|tica
(continent)
An|tares (star)
ante (wager)
antes
anted
ante|ing
[☞ anti]
ant|eater +s
ante|bellum
ante|cedence
ante|cedent +s
ante|cedent|ly
ante|chamber +s
ante|date
ante|dates

ante|dated
ante|dat|ing
ante|dilu|vian
ante|lope
plural ante|lope or
ante|lopes
ante|natal
an|ten|na
• (aerial)
plural an|ten|nas
• (Zoology)
plural an|ten|nae
an|ten|nal
an|ten|nary
ante|nuptial
ante|pendium
ante|pendia
ante|penult +s
ante|penul|ti|mate
+s
an|ter|ior
an|ter|ior|ity
an|ter|ior|ly
ante|room +s
anthe|li|on
anthe|lia
anthel|min|thic +s
(use anthelmintic)
anthel|min|tic +s
an|them +s
an|the|mion
an|the|mia
An|the|mius of
Tralles (Greek
architect)
an|ther +s
an|ther|al
an|ther|idium
an|ther|idia
ant|hill +s
antho|cyanin +s
an|thol|o|gist +s
an|thol|o|gize
an|thol|o|giz|es
an|thol|o|gized
an|thol|o|giz|ing
an|thol|ogy
an|thol|o|gies
An|thony, Susan
Brow|nell (US
feminist)
An|thony of Egypt
(saint)
An|thony of Padua
(saint)
an|tho|zoan +s
an|thra|cene
an|thra|cite
an|thra|cit|ic
an|thrac|nose
an|thrax
an|thro
an|throp|ic

an|thropo|cen|tric
an|thropo|
    cen|tric|ally
an|thropo|cen|trism
an|thropo|gen|ic
an|thropo|gen|ic|ally
an|thro|pogeny
an|thro|poid +s
an|thropo|logic|al
an|thro|pol|o|gist +s
an|thro|pol|ogy
an|thropo|metric
an|thro|pom|etry
an|thropo|morph|ic
an|thropo|
    morph|ic|ally
an|thropo|morph|ism
an|thropo|morph|ize
an|thropo|
    morph|izes
an|thropo|
    morph|ized
an|thropo|
    morph|ous
an|thro|poph|a|gous
an|thro|poph|agy
an|thropo|soph|ical
an|thro|poso|phy
an|thur|ium +s
anti +s (against;
opposer)
[☞ ante]
anti-abortion
anti-abortion|ist +s
anti-aircraft
anti-ballistic mis|sile
+s
An|tibes (resort,
France)
anti|bio|sis
anti|bio|ses
anti|biot|ic +s
anti|body
anti|bodies
antic +s
anti|cathode +s
anti-choice
anti-choicer +s
Anti|christ +s
an|tici|pate
an|tici|pates
an|tici|pat|ed
an|tici|pat|ing
an|tici|pa|tion
an|tici|pa|tive
an|tici|pa|tor +s
an|tici|pa|tory
anti|clerical
anti|clerical|ism
anti|climac|tic

anti|climac|tic|ally
anti|climax
anti|climax|es
anti|clinal
anti|cline +s
anti|clock|wise
anti|coagu|lant +s
anti|codon +s
anti|convul|sant +s
An|ti|costi (island,
Canada)
anti|cyclone +s
anti|cyclon|ic
anti|depres|sant +s
anti|diur|etic
anti|dotal
anti|dote +s
anti|freeze
anti-g
anti|gen +s
anti|genic
An|tig|one (Greek
Legend)
Antig|onish (town,
Canada; co-op
movement)
An|tig|onus
(Macedonian king)
anti-gravity
An|tigua (island,
Caribbean; town,
Guatemala)
An|ti|guan +s
anti-hero
anti-heroes
anti|hista|mine +s
anti-inflam|ma|tory
anti-
    inflam|ma|tor|ies
anti-knock
Anti-Lebanon
(mountains, Middle
East)
An|til|lean +s
An|til|les (islands,
Caribbean)
anti-lock brake +s
anti|log +s
anti|loga|rithm +s
an|til|ogy
an|til|o|gies
anti|macas|sar +s
anti|matter
anti|metab|ol|ite +s
anti|monial
anti|monic
anti|moni|ous
anti|mony (chemical
element)
[☞ antinomy]
anti|node +s
Anti|nomian +s noun
anti|nomian adjective

anti|nomian|ism
an|tin|omy (paradox; conflict between laws)
an|tin|omies [☞ antimony]
anti|novel +s
anti-nuclear
An|tioch (cities, Turkey & Phrygia)
An|tio|chus (Seleucid king)
An|tio|chus IV Epiph|anes (Seleucid King)
anti|oxidant +s
anti|par|ticle +s
anti|pasto
  anti|pastos or anti|pasti
An|tip|ater (Macedonian general)
anti|path|etic
anti|path|etic|al
anti|path|etic|al|ly
anti|path|ic
an|tip|athy
  an|tip|athies
anti-person|nel
anti|perspir|ant +s
anti|phlo|gis|tic +s
anti|phon +s
an|tiph|on|al +s
an|tiph|on|al|ly
an|tiph|on|ary
  an|tiph|on|aries
an|tiph|ony
  an|tiph|onies
an|tip|odal
anti|pode +s (opposite)
An|tipo|dean +s (Australasian)
an|tipo|dean +s (of opposites)
An|tipo|des (islands, Pacific; Australia & New Zealand)
anti|pope +s
anti|proton +s
anti|prur|itic +s
anti|pyr|etic +s
an|ti|quar|ian +s
an|ti|quar|ian|ism
an|ti|quary
  an|ti|quar|ies
an|ti|quat|ed
an|tique
  an|tiques
  an|tiqued
  an|tiquing
an|tiquing noun

an|tiquity
  an|tiqui|ties
anti-racism
anti-racist +s
an|tir|rhinum +s
anti|scor|bu|tic +s
anti-Semite +s
anti-Semitic
anti-Semitism
anti|sep|sis
anti|sep|tic +s
anti|sep|tic|ally
anti|serum
  anti|sera
anti-social
anti-static
An|tis|thenes (Greek philosopher)
an|tis|tro|phe +s
an|tith|esis
  an|tith|eses
anti|thet|ic
anti|thet|ic|al
anti|thet|ic|al|ly
anti|toxic
anti|toxin +s
anti|trades
anti|trust
anti|tus|sive +s
anti|type +s
anti|typical
anti|venin +s
anti|venom +s
anti|viral
anti|vivi|sec|tion|ism
anti|vivi|sec|tion|ist +s
ant|ler +s
ant|lered
ant|ler|less
ant-lion +s
An|to|fa|gasta (port & region, Chile)
An|to|nine +s
An|to|ni|nus Pius (Roman emperor)
An|toni|oni, Michel|angelo (Italian filmmaker)
An|to|nius, Mar|cus (Mark Antony)
an|tono|masia
An|tony, Mark (Roman general)
an|tonym +s
an|tonym|ous
an|tonymy
An|tony of Egypt (= Anthony of Egypt)

An|tony of Padua (= Anthony of Padua)
an|tral
An|trim (town & county, Northern Ireland)
an|trum
  antra
antsi|ness
antsy
  antsi|er
  antsi|est
An|tung (former name for Dandong, China)
Ant|werp (port & province, Belgium)
Anu|bis (Egyptian Myth)
Anura|dha|pura (city, Sri Lanka)
anur|an +s
anus
  anus|es
anvil +s
anx|iety
  anx|ieties
anx|ious
anx|ious|ly
anx|ious|ness
any
any body (any one body)
any|body (anyone)
any|how
any more
any one (any single one)
any|one (anybody)
any place (any one place)
any|place (anywhere)
any|thing
any time
any way (any one way)
any|way (in any case)
any|ways (= anyway)
any|where
any|wise
Anzac (Australian & New Zealand Army Corps)
Anzus (Australia, New Zealand, US)
A-OK (all systems OK)
Aor|angi (= Mount Cook, New Zealand)
aor|ist +s
aor|is|tic
aorta +s
aor|tic
Aosta (city, Italy)

Aou|zou Strip (region, Africa)
apace
Apa|che (Aboriginal people; language) plural Apache or Apaches
apa|che +s (street ruffian)
apan|age +s (use appanage)
apart
apart|heid
apart|ment +s
apart|ness
apa|thet|ic
apa|thet|ic|ally
apathy
apa|tite +s (mineral) [☞ appetite]
APB (all-points bulletin)
  APBs
APC (armoured personnel carrier)
  APCs
ape
  apes
  aped
  aping
Apel|doorn (city, the Netherlands)
Apel|les (Greek painter)
Apen|nines (mountain range, Italy)
aper|çu +s
aperi|ent +s
aperi|od|ic
aperi|od|icity
aperi|tif +s
aper|ture +s
apery
  aper|ies
apet|al|ous
Apex (advanced purchase excursion)
apex (point)
  api|ces or apex|es
Apgar score +s
aphaer|esis (use apheresis)
  aphaer|eses
apha|sia
apha|sic +s
apheli|on
  aphelia
apher|esis
  apher|eses
aphes|is
  aphes|es
aphet|ic
aphet|ic|ally

aphid +s
aphis
  aphi|des
aphon|ia
aphon|ic
aphony (= aphonia)
aphor|ism +s
aphor|ist +s
aphor|is|tic
aphor|is|tic|ally
aphor|ize
  aphor|iz|es
  aphor|ized
  aphor|iz|ing
aphro|dis|iac +s
Aphro|dis|ias (ancient
  city, Turkey)
Aphro|dite (Greek
  Myth)
aphyl|lous
API (application
  program interface)
  APIs
Apia (capital of
  Western Samoa)
  [☞ Via Appia]
apian (of bees)
  [☞ Appian Way]
api|ar|ist +s
api|ary
  api|aries
apical
apical|ly
api|ces
api|cul|tur|al
api|cul|ture
api|cul|tur|ist +s
apieçe
Apis (Egyptian Myth)
apish
apish|ly
apish|ness
apla|nat +s
apla|nat|ic
apla|sia
aplas|tic
aplen|ty
aplomb
ap|nea +s
Apoca|lypse (New
  Testament)
apoca|lypse (in
  general use)
apoca|lyp|tic
apoca|lyp|tic|ally
apo|car|pous
apo|chro|mat +s
apo|chro|mat|ic
apo|cope +s
apo|crine
Apoc|rypha (Bible)

apoc|rypha (spurious
  writings)
apoc|ryph|al
apod|al
apo|deic|tic (use
  apodictic)
apo|dic|tic
apod|o|sis
  apod|o|ses
apo|gean
apo|gee +s
apolit|ical
Apol|li|naire,
  Guil|laume (French
  poet)
Apol|lo (Greek &
  Roman Myth; US
  space program)
Apol|lo|nian
Apol|lon|ius of Perga
  (Greek
  mathematician)
Apol|lon|ius of
  Rhodes (Greek poet)
Apol|lyon (New
  Testament)
apolo|get|ic +s
apolo|get|ic|ally
apo|lo|gia +s
apolo|gist +s
apolo|gize
  apolo|giz|es
  apolo|gized
  apolo|giz|ing
apo|logue +s
apol|ogy
  apol|o|gies
apo|lune +s
apo|mic|tic
apo|mixis
  apo|mixes
apoph|thegm +s
  (maxim)
  [☞ apothem]
apoph|theg|mat|ic
apo|plec|tic
apo|plec|tic|ally
apo|plexy
apor|ia +s
apo|sem|atic
apos|tasy
  apos|tas|ies
apos|tate +s
apos|tat|ical
apos|ta|tize
  apos|ta|tiz|es
  apos|ta|tized
  apos|ta|tiz|ing
a pos|teri|ori
apos|tle +s
Apostles' Creed
apostle|ship
apos|tol|ate +s

apos|tol|ic
apos|tro|phe +s
apos|tro|phize
  apos|tro|phiz|es
  apos|tro|phized
  apos|tro|phiz|ing
apoth|ecaries'
  meas|ure +s
apoth|ecaries'
  weight +s
apoth|ecary
  apoth|ecar|ies
apo|thegm +s
  (maxim: use
  apophthegm)
  [☞ apothem]
apo|theg|mat|ic (use
  apophthegmatic)
apo|them +s
  (Geometry)
  [☞ apothegm,
  apophthegm]
apo|theo|sis
  apo|theo|ses
apo|theo|size
  apo|theo|siz|es
  apo|theo|sized
  apo|theo|siz|ing
apo|tro|paic
app +s
appal (use appall)
  appals
  ap|palled
  ap|pal|ling
Ap|pa|la|chia (region,
  US)
Ap|pa|la|chian +s
  (mountain system,
  N America)
  [☞ appellation]
ap|pall +s +ed +ing
ap|pal|ling adjective
ap|pal|ling|ly
Ap|pa|loosa +s
ap|pan|age +s
ap|pa|rat +s
ap|pa|rat|chik +s
ap|par|at|us
  ap|par|at|us|es
ap|par|at|us crit|icus
ap|par|el
  ap|par|els
  ap|par|elled
  ap|par|el|ling
ap|par|ent
ap|par|ent|ly
ap|par|ition +s
ap|peal +s +ed +ing
ap|peal|able
ap|peal|ing adjective
ap|peal|ing|ly
ap|pear +s +ed +ing
ap|pear|ance +s

ap|pease
  ap|peas|es
  ap|peased
  ap|peas|ing
ap|pease|ment
ap|peas|er +s
Appel, Karel (Dutch
  artist)
ap|pel|lant +s
ap|pel|late
ap|pel|la|tion +s
  (name, title)
  [☞ Appalachian]
ap|pel|la|tion
  con|trôlée
ap|pel|la|tive
ap|pend +s +ed +ing
ap|pend|age +s
ap|pend|ant +s
ap|pen|dec|tomy
  ap|pen|dec|to|mies
ap|pen|di|cec|tomy
  (Brit.)
  ap|pen|di|
    cec|to|mies
ap|pen|di|citis
ap|pen|dix
  ap|pen|di|ces or
  ap|pen|dix|es
ap|per|ceive
  ap|per|ceives
  ap|per|ceived
  ap|per|ceiv|ing
ap|per|cep|tion +s
ap|per|cep|tive
ap|per|tain +s +ed
  +ing
ap|pe|tence +s
ap|pe|tency
  ap|pe|ten|cies
ap|pe|tite +s (hunger,
  desire)
  [☞ apatite]
ap|peti|tive
ap|pe|tiz|er +s
ap|pe|tiz|ing
ap|pe|tiz|ing|ly
Ap|pian Way (ancient
  Roman road)
  [☞ apian]
ap|plaud +s +ed +ing
ap|plause
apple +s (fruit etc.)
  [☞ Appel]
Apple|baum, Louis
  (Cdn composer)
apple-cheeked
apple green +s
  (apple-green when
  preceding a noun)
apple|jack +s
apple pan|dowdy
  apple pan|dow|dies

apple pie +s (apple-
pie *when preceding a
noun*)
apple|sauce
Apple|seed, John|ny
(US orchardist)
apple seed +s
Apple|ton, Sir
Ed|ward Vic|tor
(English physicist)
Apple|yard, Peter
(Cdn musician)
ap|pli|ance +s
ap|plic|abil|ity
ap|plic|able
ap|plic|ably
ap|pli|cant +s
ap|pli|ca|tion +s
ap|pli|ca|tor +s
ap|plied *adjective*
ap|pli|er +s
ap|pli|qué
ap|pli|qués
ap|pli|quéd
ap|pli|qué|ing
apply
ap|plies
ap|plied
ap|ply|ing
ap|pog|gia|tura +s
ap|point +s +ed +ing
ap|point|ed *adjective*
ap|poin|tee +s
ap|point|er +s
ap|point|ive
ap|point|ment +s
Ap|po|mat|tox (battle
site, US)
ap|por|tion +s +ed
+ing
ap|por|tion|able
ap|por|tion|ment +s
ap|pos|ite
ap|pos|ite|ly
ap|pos|ite|ness
ap|pos|ition +s
ap|posi|tive +s
ap|prais|able
ap|prais|al +s
ap|praise
ap|prais|es
ap|praised
ap|prais|ing
ap|prais|er +s
ap|prais|ing|ly
ap|pre|cia|ble
ap|pre|cia|bly
ap|pre|ci|ate
ap|pre|ci|ates
ap|pre|ci|at|ed
ap|pre|ci|at|ing
ap|pre|ci|a|tion +s
ap|pre|cia|tive

ap|pre|cia|tive|ly
ap|pre|cia|tive|ness
ap|pre|ci|ator +s
ap|pre|cia|tory
ap|pre|hend +s +ed
+ing
ap|pre|hen|si|bil|ity
ap|pre|hen|sible
ap|pre|hen|sion +s
ap|pre|hen|sive
ap|pre|hen|sive|ly
ap|pre|hen|sive|ness
ap|pren|tice
ap|pren|ti|ces
ap|pren|ticed
ap|pren|ti|cing
ap|pren|tice|ship +s
ap|prise (inform)
ap|pris|es
ap|prised
ap|pris|ing
[☞ apprize]
ap|prize (esteem;
appraise)
ap|priz|es
ap|prized
ap|priz|ing
[☞ apprise]
appro
ap|proach
ap|proach|es
ap|proached
ap|proach|ing
ap|proach|abil|ity
ap|proach|able
ap|pro|ba|tion
ap|pro|ba|tive
ap|pro|ba|tory
ap|pro|pri|ate
ap|pro|pri|ates
ap|pro|pri|at|ed
ap|pro|pri|at|ing
ap|pro|pri|ate|ly
ap|pro|pri|ate|ness
ap|pro|pri|a|tion +s
ap|pro|pri|ator +s
ap|prov|al +s
ap|prove
ap|proves
ap|proved
ap|prov|ing
ap|prov|ing|ly
ap|proxi|mate
ap|proxi|mates
ap|proxi|mat|ed
ap|proxi|mat|ing
ap|proxi|mate|ly
ap|proxi|ma|tion +s
Apps, Charles
Jo|seph Syl|van|us
('Syl') (Cdn hockey
player)
[☞ apse]

ap|pur|ten|ance +s
ap|pur|ten|ant
APR (annual or
annualized
percentage rate)
APRs
après-ski
apri|cot +s
April +s
April Fool's Day
a pri|ori
apri|or|ism +s
apron +s
aproned
apro|pos
apse +s
[☞ Apps]
ap|sidal
apsis
ap|si|des
apt +er +est
ap|ter|ous
ap|teryx
ap|teryx|es
ap|ti|tude +s
aptly
apt|ness
Apu|leius (Roman
writer)
Apu|lia (region, Italy)
Aqaba (port, Jordan;
gulf, Red Sea)
aqua
aqua|cul|ture
aqua|cul|tur|ist +s
aqua for|tis
aqua|lung +s
aqua|marine +s
aqua|naut +s
aqua|plane
aqua|planes
aqua|planed
aqua|plan|ing
aqua regia
aqua|relle +s
Aquar|ian +s
aquar|ist +s
aquar|ium
aquar|iums or
aquar|ia
Aquar|ius
(constellation;
Zodiac)
aqua|tic +s
aqua|tics
aqua|tint +s
aqua|vit +s
aqua vitae
aque|duct +s
aque|ous
aqui|fer +s

Aquila (city, Italy;
constellation)
aqui|legia +s
aquil|line
Aquin, Hu|bert (Cdn
writer)
Aqui|nas, Thom|as
(saint)
Aqui|no, Cora|zón
(president of the
Philippines)
Aqui|taine (region,
France)
aquiv|er
Arab +s
ara|besque +s
Arab|ia (peninsula,
Asia)
Arab|ian +s
Arab|ic
arab|ica +s
arabi|dop|sis
ar|abis
Arab|ist +s
ar|able
Araby (*literary*
= Arabia)
Ara|cajú (port, Brazil)
Ar|achne (*Greek Myth*)
arach|nid +s
arach|nid|an +s
arach|noid +s
arach|no|phobia
Ara|fat, Yas|ser
(Palestinian leader)
Ara|fura (sea north of
Australia)
Ara|gon (region,
Spain)
Ara|gon, Louis
(French writer)
arag|on|ite
arak
Aral (sea, central Asia)
Ara|maic
Aran (islands off
Ireland; knitwear)
[☞ Aaron, Arran,
Erin]
Ar|an|da
plural Ar|an|da or
Ar|an|das
Ara|nyaka +s
Arap|aho
plural Arap|aho or
Arap|ahos
Arap|ahoe (*use*
Arapaho)
plural Arap|ahoe or
Arap|ahoes
Ara|rat (mountain,
Turkey)
aration|al

Arau|can|ian +s
arau|caria +s
Ara|wak
  plural Ara|wak or
  Ara|waks
Ara|wakan
arba|lest +s
arba|list +s (*use*
  arbalest)
arbi|ter +s
arbi|ter ele|gan|tiae
  (= arbiter
  elegantiarum)
arbi|ter
  ele|gan|ti|arum
arbi|trage
arbi|trager +s (*use*
  arbitrageur)
arbi|tra|geur +s
arbi|tral
ar|bitra|ment +s
arbi|trar|i|ly
arbi|trar|i|ness
arbi|trary
arbi|trate
  arbi|trates
  arbi|trat|ed
  arbi|trat|ing
arbi|tra|tion +s
arbi|tra|tor +s
arbi|tra|tor|ship +s
arbi|tress
  arbi|tress|es
arbor +s (spindle; *for*
  bower *use* arbour)
arbor|aceous
Arbor Day
ar|bor|eal
ar|bored (having a
  bower: *use*
  arboured)
ar|bor|eous
arbor|es|cence
arbor|es|cent
arbor|etum
  arbor|etums or
  arbor|eta
ar|bori|cul|tur|al
ar|bori|cul|ture
ar|bori|cul|tur|ist +s
ar|borio
arbor|ist +s
Arbor|ite *proprietary*
arbor|iz|a|tion
arbor|vitae +s
arbour +s (bower)
  [☞ arbor]
ar|boured
Arbus, Diane (US
  photographer)
Ar|buth|not, John
  (Scottish satirist)

ar|bu|tus
ar|bu|tus|es
arc +s +ed +ing
  (curve; *Electricity*)
  [☞ ark]
ar|cade +s
ar|cad|ed
Ar|cadia (district,
  Greece; pastoral
  paradise)
Ar|cad|ian +s
Ar|cad|ian|ism
Ar|cand, Denys (Cdn
  filmmaker)
ar|cane
ar|cane|ly
ar|canum
  ar|cana
arch
  arch|es
  arched
  arch|ing
Ar|chaean (*use*
  Archean)
ar|chaeo|logic
ar|chaeo|logic|al
ar|chae|olo|gist +s
ar|chae|olo|gize
  ar|chae|olo|giz|es
  ar|chae|olo|gized
  ar|chae|olo|giz|ing
ar|chae|ol|ogy
ar|chae|op|teryx
Ar|chaeo|zoic (*use*
  Archeozoic)
Ar|chaic (early
  cultural period in
  Greece or
  N America)
ar|chaic (*in general
  use*)
ar|chaic|ally
ar|cha|ism +s
ar|cha|ist +s
ar|cha|is|tic
ar|cha|ize
  ar|cha|iz|es
  ar|cha|ized
  ar|cha|iz|ing
Arch|angel (port,
  Russia)
arch|angel +s
  (*Religion*)
arch|angel|ic
arch|bishop +s
arch|bishop|ric +s
arch|deacon +s
arch|deacon|ry
  arch|deacon|ries
arch|deacon|ship +s
arch|dio|cesan
arch|dio|cese +s

arch|ducal
arch|duch|ess
  arch|duch|ess|es
arch|duchy
  arch|duch|ies
arch|duke +s
Ar|chean
arched *adjective*
arche|gon|ium
  arche|gonia
arch-enemy
  arch-enemies
ar|cheo|logic (*use*
  archaeologic)
ar|cheo|logic|al (*use*
  archaeological)
ar|che|olo|gist +s (*use*
  archaeologist)
ar|che|olo|gize (*use*
  archaeologize)
ar|che|olo|giz|es
ar|che|olo|gized
ar|che|olo|giz|ing
ar|che|ol|ogy (*use*
  archaeology)
Ar|cheo|zoic
arch|eparch +s
arch|eparchy
  arch|eparch|ies
Arch|er (constellation;
  Zodiac)
arch|er +s (*in general
  use*)
arch|ery
arche|typal
arche|type +s
arche|typ|ical
archi *plural of* arco
Archi|bald, Sir
  Adams George (Cdn
  politician)
archi|diac|onal
archi|diac|on|ate +s
archi|epis|copal
archi|epis|cop|ate +s
archil +s (*use* orchil)
archi|man|drite +s
Archi|med|ean
Archi|med|ean
  screw +s
Archi|medes (Greek
  mathematician)
Archi|medes'
  prin|ciple
Archi|medes' screw
  +s (= Archimedean
  screw)
archi|pel|ago
  archi|pel|agos or
  archi|pel|agoes
Archi|pen|ko,
  Alek|sandr
  Por|fir|evich

(Russian-born
  sculptor)
archi|tect +s
archi|tec|tonic
archi|tec|tonics
archi|tec|tur|al
archi|tec|tur|al|ly
archi|tec|ture +s
archi|trave +s
ar|chiv|al
ar|chive +s
ar|chiv|ist +s
archi|volt +s
arch|ly
arch|ness
ar|chon +s
ar|chon|ship +s
arch|way +s
arco
  archi
Arc|tic (north polar
  region; ocean; in
  names of animals &
  plants)
arc|tic +s (very cold;
  designed for cold
  weather; boot)
Arc|tic Bay (harbour
  & hamlet, Canada)
Arc|tic Cir|cle
Arc|tic Red River
  (river, Canada)
Arc|turus (star)
ar|cu|ate
arc weld|ing
Arden, Eliza|beth
  (Cdn-born
  businesswoman)
ar|dency
Ar|dennes (region,
  NW Europe)
ar|dent
ar|dent|ly
Ardna|mur|chan
  (peninsula, Scotland)
ardor (*use* ardour)
ar|dour
ardox
ar|du|ous
ar|du|ous|ly
ar|du|ous|ness
are
  • *conjugated form of* be
  • *noun* (metric unit)
  ares
  [☞ Ayer]
area +s
areal (pertaining to
  area)
  [☞ aerial]
area|way +s
areca +s
areg (sand dunes)

arena +s
ar|en|aceous
Ar|endt, Han|nah (US philosopher)
aren't
areola (*Anatomy*)
areo|lae or areo|las [☞ aureole]
areo|lar
Areop|agus (Greek council)
Are|quipa (city, Peru)
Ares (*Greek Myth*) [☞ Aries]
arête +s
Are|thusa (*Greek Myth*)
Are|tino, Pietro (Italian writer)
arf
ar|gali
  plural ar|gali
ar|gent
argen|tif|er|ous
Argen|tina (country, S America)
Argen|tine +s (Argentinian; Argentina)
argen|tine (of silver)
Argen|tin|ian +s
argh
argil (clay) [☞ argyle]
ar|gil|la|ceous
ar|gil|lite +s
ar|gin|ine +s
Ar|give +s
argol +s
argon
Argo|naut +s (*Greek Legend*; CFL team)
Argos (city, ancient Greece) [☞ Argus]
ar|gosy
  ar|go|sies
argot +s
argu|able
argu|ably
argue
  argues
  argued
  argu|ing
argu|er +s
argu|ment +s
argu|men|ta|tion
argu|men|ta|tive
argu|men|ta|tive|ly
argu|men|ta|tive|
                    ness

Argus (Ulysses' dog; monster; watchful guardian) [☞ Argos]
argus (butterfly; pheasant)
ar|guses
Argus-eyed
argy-bargy
argy-bargies
argy-bargied
argy-bargying
ar|gyle +s (pattern) [☞ argil]
ar|gyll +s (pattern: *use* argyle) [☞ argil]
Argyll|shire (former county, Scotland)
Århus (= Aarhus, Denmark)
aria +s
Ari|adne (*Greek Myth*)
Arian +s (of Arius; of the zodiac sign Aries) [☞ Aryan]
Arian|ism
Arias Sán|chez, Oscar (Costa Rican president)
arid
arid|ity
arid|ly
arid|ness
Ariel (Shakespearean character; satellites)
Aries (constellation; Zodiac) *plural* Aries [☞ Ares]
ari|et|ta +s
aright
Arik|ara
  plural Arik|ara or Arik|aras
aril +s (*Botany*) [☞ aryl]
aril|late
Arima|thea (town, ancient Palestine)
ari|oso +s
Ari|osto, Ludo|vico (Italian poet)
arise
  arises
  arose
  arisen
  aris|ing
Aris|tar|chus of Samos (Greek astronomer)

Aris|tar|chus of Samo|thrace (Greek librarian)
Aris|tide, Jean-Bertrand (Haitian president)
Aris|tides (Greek statesman)
Aris|tip|pus (Greek philosophers)
aristo +s
aris|toc|racy
  aris|toc|ra|cies
aris|to|crat +s
aris|to|crat|ic
aris|to|crat|ic|ally
Aris|topha|nes (Greek playwright)
Aris|to|tel|ian +s
Aris|to|tel|ian|ism
Aris|totle (Greek philosopher)
Arita
arith|met|ic
arith|met|ic|al
arith|met|ician +s
Arius (Christian theologian)
Ari|zona (state, US)
Ari|zon|an +s
Ar|juna (*Hinduism*)
Ark (in 'Ark of the Covenant', 'Holy Ark', 'Ark of the Law')
ark +s (Noah's boat; box) [☞ arc]
Arkan|san +s
Arkan|sas (state, US)
Arkhan|gelsk (= Archangel, Russia)
Ark|wright, Sir Rich|ard (English inventor)
Arles (city, France)
Ar|ling|ton (city & cemetery, US)
Arlon (town, Belgium)
arm +s +ed +ing
Ar|mada (Spanish naval fleet)
ar|mada +s (*in general use*)
arma|dillo +s
Arma|ged|don
Ar|magh (county, Northern Ireland)
Ar|ma|gnac +s (area, France; brandy)
arma|ment +s

arma|men|tar|ium
arma|men|taria
Ar|mani, Gior|gio (Italian designer)
ar|ma|ture +s
arm|chair +s
armed *adjective*
Armed For|ces (Cdn military)
armed for|ces (military generally)
Ar|menia (country and region, Caucasus)
Ar|men|ian +s (of Armenia) [☞ Arminian]
arm|ful +s
arm|hole +s
armi|ger +s
ar|mi|ger|ous
ar|mil|lary sphere +s
Ar|mini|an +s (of Jacobus Arminius) [☞ Armenian]
Ar|mini|an|ism
Ar|min|ius (Germanic chieftain)
Ar|min|ius, Jaco|bus (Dutch theologian)
armis|tice +s
arm|less
arm|let +s
arm|load +s
ar|moire +s
ar|mor +s +ed +ing (*use* armour)
ar|mored *adjective* (*use* armoured)
ar|mor|er +s (*use* armourer)
ar|mor|ial
ar|mory (*use* armoury)
ar|mor|ies
ar|mour +s +ed +ing
ar|moured *adjective*
ar|mour|er +s
armour-plate
ar|moury
  ar|mour|ies
arm|pit +s
arm|rest +s
arm's length (arm's-length *when preceding a noun*)
Arm|strong, Edwin How|ard (US engineer)
Arm|strong, Louis ('Satch|mo') (US musician)

Arm|strong, Neil Alden (US astronaut)
arm-twisting
arm-wrestle *verb*
arm-wrestles
arm-wrestled
arm-wrestling
arm wrest|ling *noun*
army
ar|mies
army-navy store +s
Arne, Thom|as (English composer)
Arn|hem (city, the Netherlands)
Arn|hem Land (peninsula & Aboriginal reservation, Australia)
ar|ni|ca
Arno (river, Italy)
Ar|nold, Ben|edict (American military officer)
Ar|nold, Sir Mal|colm Henry (English composer)
Ar|nold, Mat|thew (English writer)
Ar|nold, Thom|as (English educator)
Ar|nold|ian
Arn|pri|or (town, Canada)
aroid
aro|ma +s
aroma|thera|peut|ic
aroma|ther|apist +s
aroma|ther|apy
aro|mat|ic +s
aro|mat|ic|ally
aroma|ti|city
aroma|tiz|a|tion
aroma|tize
aroma|tiz|es
aroma|tized
aroma|tiz|ing
Aroo|stook (river, Canada)
arose
around
arous|able
arous|al +s
arouse
arous|es
aroused
arous|ing
arous|er +s
Arp, Jean (or Hans) (French artist)
ar|peg|giat|ed
ar|peg|gio +s

ar|pent +s
ar|que|bus (*use* harquebus)
ar|que|bus|es
ar|rack (*use* arak)
ar|raign +s +ed +ing
ar|raign|ment +s
Arran (island off Scotland)
[☞ Aaron, Aran, Erin]
ar|range
ar|ran|ges
ar|ranged
ar|ran|ging
ar|range|able
ar|ranged *adjective*
ar|range|ment +s
ar|ran|ger +s
ar|rant (utter)
[☞ errant, knight errant]
ar|rant|ly
Arras (city, France)
arras (tapestry)
ar|ras|es
[☞ arris]
Arrau, Clau|dio (Chilean pianist)
ar|ray +s +ed +ing
ar|rear|age +s
ar|rears
ar|rest +s +ed +ing
ar|rest|er +s (*use* arrestor)
ar|rest|ing *adjective*
ar|rest|ing|ly
ar|rest|or +s
Ar|rhen|ius, Svante Au|gust (Swedish chemist)
ar|rhyth|mia +s
ar|rhyth|mic
arrière-pensée +s
arris (*Architecture*)
ar|ris|es
[☞ arras]
ar|riv|al +s
ar|rive
ar|rives
ar|rived
ar|riv|ing
ar|riv|iste +s
ar|ro|gance
ar|ro|gant
ar|ro|gant|ly
ar|ro|gate
ar|ro|gates
ar|ro|gat|ed
ar|ro|gat|ing
ar|ro|ga|tion
ar|ron|disse|ment +s

Arrow, Ken|neth Jo|seph (US economist)
ar|row +s (long dart; pointer)
[☞ aero]
arrow grass
arrow|head +s
arrow|root +s
arrow worm +s
ar|rowy
ar|royo +s
arse +s
arse|hole +s
arse-licking
ar|sen|al +s
ar|sen|ic
ar|sen|ic|al +s
ar|sen|ious
ars|ine
arsis
arses
ar|son +s
ar|son|ist +s
ars|phena|mine +s
art +s *noun & archaic conjugated form of* be
Ar|taud, An|tonin (French dramatist)
Arta|xerxes (kings of Persia)
art deco
arte|fact +s (*use* artifact)
Arte|mis (*Greek Myth*)
arte|misia +s
ar|ter|ial (of an artery)
[☞ arteriole]
ar|ter|ial|iz|a|tion
ar|ter|ial|ize
ar|ter|ial|iz|es
ar|ter|ial|ized
ar|ter|ial|iz|ing
ar|teri|ole +s (branch of an artery)
[☞ arterial]
ar|terio|scler|o|sis
ar|terio|scler|otic
ar|ter|itis
ar|tery
ar|ter|ies
ar|tesian
art film +s
art form +s
art|ful
art|ful|ly
art|ful|ness
art house +s
arth|rit|ic
arth|ritis
arth|ro|pod +s
arth|ro|scope +s

arth|ro|scop|ic
arth|ros|copy
arth|ros|cop|ies
Ar|thur (legendary king)
Ar|thur, Ches|ter Alan (US president)
Ar|thur|ian
arti|choke +s
arti|cle
arti|cles
arti|cled
artic|ling
arti|cled *adjective*
ar|ticu|lacy
ar|ticu|lar
ar|ticu|late
ar|ticu|lates
ar|ticu|lat|ed
ar|ticu|lat|ing
ar|ticu|lat|ed *adjective*
ar|ticu|late|ly
ar|ticu|late|ness
ar|ticu|la|tion +s
ar|ticu|la|tor +s
arti|fact +s
arti|fac|tual
arti|fice +s
arti|ficer +s
arti|fi|cial
arti|fi|ci|al|ity
arti|fi|ci|al|ities
arti|fi|cial|ly
ar|ti|gi +s (*use* atigi)
ar|til|ler|ist +s
ar|til|lery
ar|til|ler|ies
ar|til|lery|man
ar|til|lery|men
arti|san +s
arti|san|al
artisan|ship +s
art|ist +s (practitioner of fine or performing arts etc.)
ar|tiste (pretentiously artistic person; *for* professional performer *use* artist)
art|is|tic
art|is|tic|ally
art|istry
art|less
art|less|ly
art nou|veau
Ar|tois (region, France)
art|sie +s *noun*
[☞ artsy]
artsi|ness

artsy *adjective*
art|si|er
art|si|est
[☞ artsie]
artsy-craftsy
artsy-fartsy
art the|atre +s
art|work +s
arty *adjective*
art|i|er
art|i|est
arty-crafty
Aruba (island, Caribbean)
aru|gula
arum +s
Aru|nachal Pra|desh (state, India)
Ar|vi|at (hamlet, Canada)
Arya|bhata I (Indian mathematician)
Ary|an +s (people; language)
[☞ Arian]
aryl +s (*Chemistry*)
[☞ aril]
as
• *adverb, conjunction & pronoun*
• *noun* (Roman coin)
asses
ASA (acetylsalicylic acid)
asa|fet|ida
asa|foet|ida (*use* asafetida)
asa|na +s
Asan|sol (city, India)
As|ante (*use* Ashanti)
plural As|ante
ASAP (as soon as possible)
as|bes|tine
As|bes|tos (town, Canada)
as|bes|tos (mineral, insulation)
as|bes|to|sis
as|carid +s
as|cend +s +ed +ing
as|cend|ancy
as|cend|an|cies
as|cend|ant +s
as|cend|ency (*use* ascendancy)
as|cend|en|cies
as|cend|er +s
As|cen|sion (*Christianity*; Atlantic island)
as|cen|sion +s (act of ascending)

as|cen|sion|al
As|cen|sion|tide
as|cent +s (rise)
[☞ assent]
as|cer|tain +s +ed +ing
as|cer|tain|able
as|cer|tain|ment
as|cet|ic +s
as|cet|ic|ally
as|ceti|cism
Asch, Sho|lem (US writer)
As|cham, Roger (English scholar)
as|cid|ian +s
ASCII (American Standard Code for Information Interchange)
as|ci|tes
plural a|sci|tes
As|clep|ius (*Greek Myth*)
as|cor|bic
Ascot (municipality, Canada; town & racetrack, England)
as|cot +s (tie)
as|crib|able
as|cribe
as|cribes
as|cribed
as|crib|ing
as|crip|tion +s
asdic
asep|sis
asep|tic
asex|ual
asex|u|al|ity
asex|ual|ly
As|gard (*Scandinavian Myth*)
ash
ashes
[☞ Ashe]
ashamed
asham|ed|ly
Ashan|ti (region, people & language, Ghana)
plural Ashan|ti
ash|can +s
Ash|croft, Dame Peggy (English actress)
Ash|dod (seaport, Israel)
Ashe, Ar|thur Rob|ert (US tennis player)
ashen
Asher (*Bible*)

Ash|ga|bat (capital of Turkmenistan)
ash|i|er
ash|i|est
Ash|kelon
(= Ashqelon, Israel)
Ash|ken|azi (Jew)
Ash|ken|azim
[☞ Ashkenazy]
Ash|ken|azic
Ash|ken|azy, Vlad|i|mir David|ovich (Russian-born pianist)
[☞ Ashkenazi]
Ash|kha|bad
(= Ashgabat, Turkmenistan)
ash|lar +s
ash-leaf maple +s
ash-leaved maple +s
Ash|ley, Laura (Welsh designer)
Ash|more (reef, Indian Ocean)
Ash|mole, Elias (English antiquary)
ashore
ash|pan +s
Ash|qelon (city, Israel)
ash|ram +s
ash|rama +s
Ash Shari|qah
(= Sharjah: state & its capital, UAE)
Ash|ton, Sir Fred|erick Wil|liam (British choreographer)
Ash|tor|eth (*Bible*)
ash|tray +s
Ashur (Mesopotamian city, Assyrian god: *use* Assur)
Ashur|bani|pal (Assyrian king)
Ash Wed|nes|day
ashy
ash|i|er
ash|i|est
Asia (continent)
Asi|ago
Asia Minor
Asian +s
Asiat|ic +s
• *Offensive* when used of people.
ASIC (application-specific integrated circuit)
ASICs
A-side +s (first side)

aside +s (to one side; incidental comment)
Asi|mov, Isaac (Russian-born author)
asin|ine
asin|in|ity
Asir (mountain range, Saudi Arabia)
ask +s +ed +ing
askance
as|kari
plural as|kari or as|karis
ask|er +s
askew
aslant
asleep
aslope
ASM (air-to-surface missile)
ASMs
As|mara (capital of Eritrea)
As|mera (= Asmara)
As|mo|deus (demon)
asocial
Asoka (emperor of India)
asp +s
as|para|gus
as|par|tame
as|par|tic
As|pasia (Greek courtesan)
as|pect +s
as|pec|tual
Aspen (resort, US)
aspen +s (tree)
As|per|ity (mountain, Canada)
as|per|ity
as|per|ities
as|perse
as|pers|es
as|persed
as|pers|ing
as|per|sion +s
as|phalt +s
as|phalt|er +s
as|phalt|ic
as|pho|del +s
as|phyxia
as|phyx|ial
as|phyxi|ant +s
as|phyxi|ate
as|phyxi|ates
as|phyxi|at|ed
as|phyxi|at|ing
as|phyxi|a|tion
as|phyxi|a|tor +s
aspic
as|pi|dis|tra +s

aspir|ant +s
aspir|ate
aspir|ates
aspir|at|ed
aspir|at|ing
aspir|a|tion +s
aspir|a|tor +s
as|pire
as|pires
as|pired
as|pir|ing
As|pir|in proprietary:
plural As|pir|in or
As|pir|ins
as|pir|ing adjective
as|quint
As|quith, Her|bert
Henry (British prime
minister)
ass
asses
Assad, Hafez al-
(president of Syria)
as|sa|gai +s (use
assegai)
assai (Music)
[☞ assay]
as|sail +s +ed +ing
as|sail|able
as|sail|ant +s
Assam (state, India;
tea)
As|sam|ese
plural As|sam|ese
As|sas|sin +s (History
Ismaili Muslim
sectarian)
as|sas|sin +s (in
general use)
as|sas|sin|ate
as|sas|sin|ates
as|sas|sin|at|ed
as|sas|sin|at|ing
as|sas|sin|a|tion +s
as|sault +s +ed +ing
as|sault|er +s
as|sault|ive
assay +s +ed +ing
(test; analyze)
[☞ assai]
assay|er +s
as|se|gai +s
as|sem|blage +s
as|sem|ble
as|sem|bles
as|sem|bled
as|sem|bling
as|sem|bler +s
as|sem|bly
as|sem|blies
as|sembly|man
as|sembly|men

as|sent +s +ed +ing
(agree)
[☞ ascent]
as|sent|er +s
as|sent|or +s (use
assenter)
as|sert +s +ed +ing
as|sert|er +s (use
assertor)
as|ser|tion +s
as|sert|ive
as|sert|ive|ly
as|sert|ive|ness
as|ser|tor +s
asses plural of as &
ass
[☞ assess]
as|sess (evaluate;
penalize)
as|sess|es
as|sessed
as|sess|ing
as|sess|able
as|sess|ment +s
as|ses|sor +s
as|ses|sor|ial
asset +s
asset-stripping
as|sever|ate
as|sever|ates
as|sever|at|ed
as|sever|at|ing
as|sever|a|tion +s
ass|hole +s
as|sibi|late
as|sibi|lates
as|sibi|lat|ed
as|sibi|lat|ing
as|sibi|la|tion +s
assi|du|ity
assi|du|ities
as|sidu|ous
as|sidu|ous|ly
as|sidu|ous|ness
as|sign +s +ed +ing
as|sign|able
as|sig|na|tion +s
as|sign|ee +s
as|sign|er +s (in legal
contexts use
assignor)
as|sign|ment +s
as|sign|or +s (Law)
[☞ assigner]
as|simil|able
as|simi|late
as|simi|lates
as|simi|lat|ed
as|simi|lat|ing
as|simi|la|tion +s
as|simi|la|tion|ism
as|simi|la|tion|ist +s
as|simi|la|tive

as|simi|la|tor +s
as|simi|la|tory
As|sini|boia (former
district, Canada)
As|sini|boian +s
(resident of
Assiniboia)
[☞ Assiniboine]
As|sini|boine
(mountain & river,
Canada; Aboriginal
people; language)
plural As|sini|boine
or As|sini|boines
[☞ Assiniboian]
As|sisi (town, Italy)
as|sist +s +ed +ing
as|sist|ance
as|sist|ant +s
as|sist|er +s
as|size +s
ass-kissing
ass-licking
as|so|ci|ate
as|so|ci|ates
as|so|ci|at|ed
as|so|ci|at|ing
as|so|ci|ate|ship +s
as|so|ci|a|tion +s
as|so|ci|a|tion|al
as|so|ci|ative
as|so|ci|ator +s
as|so|cia|tory
As|somp|tion sash
As|somp|tion
sash|es
as|son|ance +s
as|son|ant
as|son|ate
as|son|ates
as|son|at|ed
as|son|at|ing
as|sort +s +ed +ing
as|sorta|tive
as|sort|ed adjective
as|sort|ment +s
as|suage
as|sua|ges
as|suaged
as|sua|ging
as|suage|ment
as|sua|ger +s
As Sulay|ma|ni|yah
(= Sulaymaniyah,
Iraq)
as|sum|able
as|sume
as|sumes
as|sumed
as|sum|ing
as|sum|ed|ly
As|sump|tion
(Catholicism)

[☞ Assomption
sash, L'Assomption]
as|sump|tion +s (act
of assuming etc.)
[☞ Assomption
sash, L'Assomption]
as|sump|tive
Assur (city,
Mesopotamia;
Assyrian god)
as|sur|able
as|sur|ance +s
Assur|banipal
(= Ashurbanipal,
Assyrian king)
as|sure
as|sures
as|sured
as|sur|ing
as|sured adjective
as|sur|ed|ly
as|sur|er +s
As|syr|ia (ancient
country)
As|syr|ian +s
As|syri|ol|o|gist +s
As|syri|ol|ogy
As|taire, Fred (US
dancer)
As|tana (capital of
Kazakhstan)
As|tarte (Phoenician
Myth)
astat|ic
asta|tine
aster +s (plant)
[☞ astir, Astor]
aster|isk +s +ed +ing
aster|ism +s
astern
aster|oid +s
aster|oid|al
as|the|nia
as|then|ic +s
as|theno|sphere
asth|ma
asth|mat|ic +s
asth|mat|ic|ally
Asti +s
astig|matic
astig|ma|tism
as|tilbe +s
astir (awake; in
motion)
[☞ aster, Astor]
Asti Spu|mante
Aston, Fran|cis
Wil|liam (English
physicist)
as|ton|ish
as|ton|ish|es
as|ton|ished
as|ton|ish|ing

as|ton|ish|ing
adjective
as|ton|ish|ing|ly
as|ton|ish|ment +s
Astor, Nancy
Witcher,
Vis|count|ess
(English politician)
[☞ aster]
astound +s +ed +ing
astound|ing *adjective*
astound|ing|ly
astrad|dle
as|tra|gal +s
as|trag|alus
as|trag|ali
As|tra|khan (city,
Russia)
as|tra|khan (*Textiles*)
as|tral
as|tral|ly
astray
astride
astrin|gency
astrin|gen|cies
astrin|gent +s
astrin|gent|ly
astro|chem|istry
Astro|dome (stadium,
US)
astro|dome +s
(domed observing
window)
astro|hatch
astro|hatch|es
astro|labe +s
as|trol|oger +s
astro|logic|al
as|trol|o|gist +s
as|trol|ogy
astro|naut +s
astro|naut|ics
as|tron|omer +s
astro|nomic
astro|nomic|al
astro|nomic|al|ly
as|tron|omy
astro|physic|al
astro|physi|cist +s
astro|phys|ics
Astro|turf *proprietary*
As|tur|ias (region,
Spain)
As|tur|ias, Mi|guel
Ángel (Guatemalan
novelist)
as|tute
as|tute|ly
as|tute|ness
As|tya|nax (*Greek
Legend*)
Asun|ción (capital of
Paraguay)

asun|der
Asur (= Assur,
Mesopotamia)
asura +s
Aswan (city & dam,
Egypt)
asy|lum +s
asym|met|ric
asym|met|ric|al
asym|met|ric|al|ly
asym|metry
asym|met|ries
asymp|tom|atic
asymp|tote +s
asymp|tot|ic
asymp|tot|ic|ally
asyn|chron|ous
asyn|chron|ous|ly
asyn|det|ic
asyn|deton
asyn|deta
at
Ata|balipa
(= Atahualpa, Inca
ruler)
Ata|cama (desert,
Chile)
Ata|hualpa (Inca
ruler)
Ata|lanta (*Greek
Myth*)
[☞ Atlanta]
ata|rac|tic +s
ata|raxia (*use*
ataraxy)
ata|raxic +s
(= ataractic)
ata|raxy
Ata|türk, Kemal
(Turkish president)
atav|ism
atav|is|tic
atav|is|tic|ally
ataxia
ataxic
ATB (all-terrain
bicycle)
ATBs
at-bat +s
Ate (*Greek Myth*)
ate *past tense of* eat
atel|ier +s
a tempo
Aten (*Egyptian Myth*)
Atha|basca (river,
lake, drainage basin,
pass & district,
Canada)
Atha|bas|can
(language group,
people: *use*
Athapaskan)

plural Atha|bas|can
or Atha|bas|cans
Atha|bas|kan
(language group,
people: *use*
Athapaskan)
plural Atha|bas|kan
or Atha|bas|kans
Atha|na|sian Creed
Atha|na|sius (saint)
Atha|pas|kan
(language group;
people)
plural Atha|pas|kan
or Atha|pas|kans
Atharva-Veda
athe|ism
athe|ist +s
athe|is|tic
athe|is|tic|al
athel|ing +s
Athel|stan (Anglo-
Saxon king)
athem|atic
Athe|na (*Greek Myth*)
athen|aeum +s
Athe|ne (*Greek Myth*:
use Athena)
athen|eum +s (*use*
athenaeum)
Athen|ian +s
Ath|ens (capital of
Greece)
ath|ero|scler|o|sis
ath|ero|scler|ot|ic
Ather|ton Table|land
(in Australia)
athirst
ath|lete +s
ath|lete's foot
ath|let|ic
ath|let|ic|ally
ath|leti|cism
ath|let|ics
Ath|lone, Alex|an|der
Au|gus|tus
Fred|erick
Cam|bridge, Earl of
(governor general of
Canada)
at-home +s
Atho|nite +s
Athos (mountainous
monastic peninsula,
Greece)
athwart
ati|gi +s
At|lan|ta (city, US)
At|lan|tan +s (of
Atlanta)
At|lan|tean (of Atlas;
of Atlantis)

at|lan|tes
(*Architecture*)
At|lan|tic (ocean; Cdn
provinces)
At|lan|ti|cist +s
At|lan|tis (*Greek
Legend*)
Atlas (*Greek Myth*;
mountain range,
Africa)
atlas (map book;
vertebra)
at|las|es
at|latl +s
Atli (*Scandinavian
Myth*)
Atlin (lake, Canada)
ATM (automated teller
machine)
ATMs
atman
atmos|phere +s
atmos|pher|ic
atmos|pher|ic|al
atmos|pher|ic|al|ly
atmos|pher|ics
at|oll +s
atom +s
atom|ic
atom|ic|ally
atom|icity
atom|ism
atom|ist +s
atom|is|tic
atom|iz|a|tion
atom|ize
atom|iz|es
atom|ized
atom|iz|ing
atom|iz|er +s
atom-smasher +s
Aton (*Egyptian Myth*:
use Aten)
aton|al
aton|al|ity
aton|al|ities
atone
atones
atoned
aton|ing
Atone|ment
(*Christianity*)
atone|ment +s (*in
general use*)
aton|ic
atony
atop
atop|ic
atopy
ato|pies
ATP (adenosine
triphosphate)
atra|bil|ious

atra|zine
Atre|us (*Greek Myth*)
atri|al
atri|um
  atri|ums or atria
atro|cious
atro|cious|ly
atro|cious|ness
atroci|ty
  atroci|ties
atroph|ic
atro|phy
  atro|phies
  atro|phied
  atro|phy|ing
atro|pine
Atro|pos (*Greek Myth*)
At|sina
  plural At|sina
atta|boy
at|tach
  at|tach|es
  at|tached
  at|tach|ing
at|tach|able
at|ta|ché +s
at|tach|er +s
at|tach|ment +s
at|tack +s +ed +ing
at|tack|er +s
at|tain +s +ed +ing
at|tain|abil|ity
at|tain|able
at|tain|able|ness
at|tain|der +s
at|tain|ment +s
at|taint +s +ed +ing
At|ta|lid +s
at|tar +s
At|tawa|pis|kat (river, Canada)
at|tempt +s +ed +ing
at|tempt|able
At|ten|bor|ough, Rich|ard (English filmmaker)
at|tend +s +ed +ing
at|tend|ance +s
at|tend|ant +s
at|ten|dee +s
at|tend|er +s
at|ten|tion +s
at|ten|tion defi|cit dis|or|der
at|ten|tive
at|ten|tive|ly
at|ten|tive|ness
at|tenu|ate
  at|tenu|ates
  at|tenu|at|ed
  at|tenu|at|ing
at|tenu|at|ed *adjective*
at|tenu|a|tion +s

at|tenu|ator +s
at|test +s +ed +ing
at|test|able
at|test|a|tion
at|test|or +s
Attic (of Attica; language)
at|tic +s (room in roof)
At|tica (promontory, Greece)
At|tika|mek
  plural At|tika|mek or At|tika|meks
At|tila (king of the Huns)
at|tire
  at|tires
  at|tired
  at|tir|ing
at|tired *adjective*
Attis (*Greek & Roman Myth*)
at|ti|tude +s
at|ti|tud|inal
at|ti|tud|in|ize
  at|ti|tud|in|iz|es
  at|ti|tud|in|ized
  at|ti|tud|in|iz|ing
Att|lee, Clem|ent Rich|ard, 1st Earl (British prime minister)
at|tor|ney +s
  at|tor|neys gen|er|al
attorney|ship +s
at|tract +s +ed +ing
at|tract|able
at|tract|ant +s
at|trac|tion +s
at|tract|ive
at|tract|ive|ly
at|tract|ive|ness
at|tract|or +s
at|trib|ut|able
at|trib|ute
  at|trib|utes
  at|trib|ut|ed
  at|trib|ut|ing
at|tri|bu|tion +s
at|tribu|tive
at|tribu|tive|ly
at|tri|tion
at|tri|tion|al
at|tune
  at|tunes
  at|tuned
  at|tun|ing
ATV (all-terrain vehicle)
ATVs

At|wood, Mar|garet Elea|nor (Cdn writer)
atyp|ical
atyp|ical|ly
au|bade +s
Auber, Dan|iel Fran|çois Es|prit (French composer)
au|berge +s
auber|gine +s
au|bre|tia +s (*use* aubrietia)
Aub|rey, John (English antiquarian)
au|brie|ta +s (*use* aubrietia)
au|brie|tia +s
au|burn
Au|bus|son +s
Auck|land (city, New Zealand)
au con|traire
au cou|rant
auc|tion +s +ed +ing
auc|tion|eer +s
auc|tion|eer|ing
au|da|cious
au|da|cious|ly
au|da|cious|ness
au|da|city
  au|da|ci|ties
Auden, Wys|tan Hugh (English-born poet)
audi|bil|ity
aud|ible +s
aud|ible|ness
aud|ibly
audi|ence +s
aud|ile
audio
audio-confer|ence +s
audi|ol|o|gist +s
audi|ol|ogy
audi|om|eter +s
audio|phile +s
audio tape +s *noun*
audio|tape *verb*
  audio|tapes
  audio|taped
  audio|tap|ing
audio|vis|ual
aud|it +s +ed +ing
au|di|tion +s
aud|it|or +s
aud|it|or gen|er|al
  aud|it|ors gen|er|al
audi|tor|ial
audi|tor|ium
  audi|tor|iums or audi|toria
audi|tory

Audu|bon, John James (US naturalist & artist)
[☞ autobahn]
Auer, Carl, Baron von Wels|bach (Austrian chemist)
Auer|bach, Frank (German-born painter)
au fait
au fond
Au|gean
Au|geas (*Greek Myth*)
aug|er +s (tool)
[☞ augur]
aught (anything; in 'for aught I know')
[☞ ought]
aug|ite +s
aug|ment +s +ed +ing
aug|men|ta|tion +s
aug|menta|tive
aug|ment|ed *adjective*
aug|ment|er +s
Au|gra|bies (waterfalls, South Africa)
au gra|tin
Augs|burg (city, Germany)
Augs|burg Con|fes|sion (*Lutheranism*)
aug|ur +s +ed +ing (portend; interpreter of signs)
[☞ auger]
aug|ur|al
aug|ury
  aug|ur|ies
Aug|ust +s (month)
au|gust (venerable)
Au|gusta (cities, US; mountain peak, Yukon–Alaska border)
Au|gus|tan +s (of Augustus; literary period)
Au|gus|tine +s (saints; *for* member of religious order *use* Augustinian)
Aug|us|tin|ian +s (member of a religious order)
[☞ Augustine]
au|gust|ly
au|gust|ness
Au|gus|tus (Roman emeror)

au jus
auk +s
auk|let +s
auld
auld lang syne
aum|bry (*use* ambry)
aum|bries
au natu|rel
Aung San (1914–47;
Burmese leader)
Aung San Suu Kyi
(b.1945; Burmese
leader, Nobel
laureate)
aunt +s
aunt|ie +s
aunty (*use* auntie)
aunt|ies
au pair +s
aura +s
aural (of the ear;
pertaining to an
aura)
[☞ oral]
aur|al|ly (by means of
the ear)
[☞ orally]
Aur|ang|zeb (Mogul
emperor of
Hindustan)
aur|eate
Aurel|ian (Roman
emperor)
Aurel|ius, Mar|cus
(Roman emperor)
aur|eo|la +s (halo,
corona: *use* aureole)
[☞ areola]
aur|eole +s (halo;
corona)
[☞ oriole, areola]
Aur|eo|mycin
proprietary
au re|voir +s
Auric, Georges
(French composer)
auric (of an aura)
aur|icle (*Anatomy*)
[☞ oracle]
aur|ic|ula +s
aur|icu|lar
aur|icu|lar|ly
aur|icu|late
aur|if|er|ous
Auriga (constellation)
Aurig|na|cian
aur|ochs
plural aur|ochs
Au|rora (town,
Canada; *Roman
Myth*)

au|rora (atmospheric
lights; dawn; trout)
au|roras or au|rorae
au|rora aus|tral|is
au|rora bor|eal|is
au|ror|al
Ausch|witz
(concentration
camp)
aus|cul|ta|tion
aus|cul|ta|tory
Aus|lese
aus|pice +s
aus|pi|cious
aus|pi|cious|ly
aus|pi|cious|ness
Aus|sie +s (Australian)
[☞ Ossi]
Aus|ten, Jane (English
novelist)
[☞ Austin]
aus|tere
aus|ter|er
aus|ter|est
aus|tere|ly
aus|ter|ity
aus|ter|ities
Aus|ter|litz (battle
site, Napoleonic
Wars)
Aus|tin +s (city, US;
Augustinian)
[☞ Austen]
Aus|tin, John (1790–
1859; English jurist)
Aus|tin, John
Lang|shaw (1911–
60; English
philosopher)
Aus|tral
• (of Australia or
Australasia)
• (= Tubai Islands,
French Polynesia)
aus|tral (southern)
Austral|asia
Austral|asian +s
Aus|tralia (country)
Aus|tral|ian +s
Aus|tral|ian cat|tle
dog +s
Aus|tral|ian|ism +s
Aus|tral|ian Rules
Aus|tral|oid +s
aus|tralo|pith|ecine
+s
Aus|tralo|pith|ecus
Aus|tria (country,
Europe)
Austria-Hungary
(former empire,
central Europe)
Aus|trian +s

Austro-Hungar|ian
Austro|nesian +s
aut|arch|ic (of
autarchy)
[☞ autarkic]
aut|arch|ic|al (of
autarchy)
[☞ autarkical]
aut|archy (absolute
sovereignty)
aut|arch|ies
[☞ autarky]
aut|ark|ic (of autarky)
[☞ autarchic]
aut|ark|ic|al (of
autarky)
[☞ autarchical]
aut|ark|ist +s
aut|arky (self-
sufficiency)
aut|ark|ies
[☞ autarchy]
au|teur +s (film
director)
[☞ hauteur]
au|then|tic
au|then|tic|ally
au|then|ti|cate
au|then|ti|cates
au|then|ti|cat|ed
au|then|ti|cat|ing
au|then|ti|ca|tion +s
au|then|ti|ca|tor +s
au|then|ti|city
au|then|ti|ci|ties
auth|or +s +ed +ing
author|ess
author|ess|es
author|ial
au|thori|tar|ian +s
au|thori|tar|ian|ism
au|thori|ta|tive
au|thori|ta|tive|ly
au|thori|ta|tive|ness
au|thor|ity
au|thor|ities
au|thor|iz|a|tion +s
au|thor|ize
au|thor|iz|es
au|thor|ized
au|thor|iz|ing
au|thor|ship
aut|ism
au|tis|tic
auto +s (automobile;
automatic)
[☞ otto]
auto|bahn +s
(highway)
[☞ Audubon]
auto|biog|raph|er +s
auto|bio|graph|ic
auto|bio|graph|ic|al

auto|biog|raphy
auto|biog|raph|ies
auto|ceph|al|ous
au|toch|thon
au|toch|thons or
au|toch|thones
au|toch|thon|ous
auto|clave +s
au|toc|racy
au|toc|ra|cies
auto|crat +s
auto|crat|ic
auto|crat|ic|ally
auto|cross
auto-da-fé
autos-da-fé
auto|didact +s
auto|didac|tic
auto-erotic
auto-eroticism
auto-erotism
(= auto-eroticism)
auto|focus
au|tog|am|ous
au|tog|amy
auto|genic
au|togen|ous
auto|giro +s (*use*
autogyro)
auto|graft +s
auto|graph +s +ed
+ing
auto|graph|ic
au|tog|raphy
auto|gyro +s
auto|harp +s
auto|immune
auto|immun|ity
auto|intoxi|ca|tion
au|tol|o|gous
au|toly|sis
auto|lytic
auto|maker +s
Auto|mat +s
au|tom|ata
auto|mate
auto|mates
auto|mat|ed
auto|mat|ing
auto|matic +s
auto|matic|ally
auto|mati|city
auto|mation +s
au|toma|tism +s
au|toma|tiz|a|tion
au|toma|tize
au|toma|tiz|es
au|toma|tized
au|toma|tiz|ing
au|tom|aton
au|tom|ata or
au|tom|atons
auto|mobile +s

auto|motive
auto|nomic
au|tono|mist +s
au|tono|mous
au|tono|mous|ly
au|ton|omy
au|ton|omies
Auto|pac (insurance)
Auto Pact (Canada-
US Automotive
Products
Agreement)
auto|pilot +s
aut|opsy
aut|opsies
auto|radio|graph +s
auto|radio|graphic
auto|radi|og|raphy
auto|route +s
auto|strada
auto|stradas or
auto|strade
auto|sugges|tion +s
auto|telic
au|tot|omy
auto|toxic
auto|toxin +s
auto|troph|ic
auto work|er +s
aut|oxi|dation
au|tumn +s
autum|nal
Au|vergne (region,
France)
aux|iliary
aux|iliar|ies
auxin +s (plant
hormone)
Auyu|it|tuq (national
park, Canada)
avail +s +ed +ing
avail|abil|ity
avail|abil|ities
avail|able
avail|able|ness
avail|ably
Ava|lanche (peak,
Canada)
ava|lanche
ava|lanch|es
ava|lanched
ava|lanch|ing
Ava|lon (peninsula,
Canada; Arthurian
Legend; Welsh Myth)
avant-garde +s
avant-gardism
avant-gardist +s
Avar +s
avar|ice
avar|icious
avar|icious|ly
avar|icious|ness

avast
ava|tar +s
avaunt
ave +s (Hail Mary;
welcome)
Ave|bury (prehistoric
site, England)
Ave Maria +s
avenge
aven|ges
avenged
aven|ging
aven|ger +s
avens
plural avens
aven|tur|ine
av|enue +s
aver
avers
averred
aver|ring
aver|age
aver|ages
aver|aged
aver|aging
aver|age|ly
aver|ment +s
Aver|nus (lake, Italy)
Aver|roës (Islamic
philosopher)
averse (disinclined)
[☞ adverse]
aver|sion +s
avert +s +ed +ing
(turn away; prevent)
[☞ evert]
avert|ible
Aves|ta
Aves|tan
avgas
avian
avi|ary
avi|ar|ies
avi|ation
avi|ator +s
avia|trix
avia|tri|ces or
avia|trix|es
Avi|cen|na (Islamic
philosopher)
avi|cul|ture
avi|cul|tur|ist +s
avid
avid|ity
avid|ly
avi|fauna
Avi|gnon (city, France)
avi|onic
avi|on|ics
Avi|son, Mar|garet
(Cdn poet)
avita|min|osis
avo|cado +s

avo|ca|tion +s
avo|cet +s
Avo|gadro, Ama|deo
(Italian physicist)
Avo|gadro's
con|stant
Avo|gadro's law
Avo|gadro's num|ber
avoid +s +ed +ing
avoid|able
avoid|ably
avoid|ance
avoid|er +s
avoir|du|pois
Avon (county,
England; rivers,
England & Canada)
avouch
avouch|es
avouched
avouch|ing
avouch|ment +s
avow +s +ed +ing
avow|al +s
avowed adjective
avow|ed|ly
avul|sion
avun|cular
aw interjection
AWACS (airborne
warning and control
system)
plural AWACS
await +s +ed +ing
awake
awakes
awoke
awoken
awak|ing
awak|en +s +ed +ing
awak|en|ing +s noun
& adjective
award +s +ed +ing
award|er +s
aware
aware|ness
awash
away (to or at a
distance etc.)
[☞ aweigh]
Awdry, Wil|bert Vere
(English writer)
awe (wonder; amaze)
awes
awed
awing
aweigh (of an anchor)
awe-inspiring
awe|some
awe|some|ly
awe|some|ness
awe|stricken
awe|struck

awful (terrible)
[☞ offal]
aw|ful|ly
aw|ful|ness
awhile
awk|ward
awk|ward|ly
awk|ward|ness
awl +s (tool)
awn +s
awned
awn|ing +s
awn|inged
awoke
awoken
AWOL (absent without
leave)
awry
aw-shucks adjective
axe
axes
axed
axing
Axel +s (Figure
Skating)
[☞ axle, axil]
Axel Hei|berg (island,
Canada)
Axel|rod, Jul|ius (US
biochemist)
axe|man
axe|men
axes plural of axe &
axis
axial
axi|al|ity
axi|al|ly
axil +s (Botany)
[☞ Axel, axle]
ax|il|la
ax|il|lae
ax|il|lary
axi|ology
axiom +s
axio|mat|ic
axio|mat|ic|ally
Axis (WWII German
alliance)
axis (imaginary line
around which a body
turns etc.)
axes
axle +s (rod
connecting wheels)
[☞ Axel, axil]
Ax|min|ster +s
axo|lotl +s
axon +s
Axum (= Aksum,
Ethiopia)
Axum|ite +s
(= Aksumite)

ay +s (yes: *use* aye)
[☞ **aye**]
Aya|cucho (city, Peru)
ayah +s
aya|tol|lah +s
Ayck|bourn, Alan
(English playwright)
aye +s
• (yes; vote)
• (always; in 'for aye')
[☞ **eye, eh**]
aye aye (*Nautical* yes)
aye-aye +s (lemur)
Ayer, Sir Al|fred Jules
(English philosopher)
[☞ **Eyre**]
Ayers Rock (in
Australia)
[☞ **Eyre**]
Ayesha (= Aisha, wife
of Muhammad)
Ayles|bury +s (town,
England; duck)
Ayl|mer (city & town,
Canada)
**Ayl|ward, Gladys
May** (English
missionary)
Ay|mara
plural **Ay|mara** or
Ay|maras
Ayr|shire +s (former
county, Scotland;
cattle)
Ayur|veda
Ayur|vedic
Azad Kash|mir (state,
Pakistan)
aza|lea +s
Azan|ia (South Africa)
Azan|ian +s
Azazel (demon)
azeo|trope +s
azeo|trop|ic
Azer|bai|jan (country,
Europe)
Azer|bai|jani +s
Azeri +s
azide +s
Azil|ian
azi|muth +s
azi|muth|al
azine +s
azoic
Azores (Atlantic
islands)
Azov (sea)
Az|rael (angel)
AZT (azidothymidine)
Aztec +s
azuki +s (*use* adzuki)
azure +s
azy|gous

B

....

B
• (letter; music note;
mark)
B's
• (blood type; pencil
softness; magnetic
flux density; bel)
b
• (letter)
b's
• (*Physics* barn)
B.A. (Bachelor of Arts)
B.A.'s
B.A.A. (Bachelor of
Applied Arts)
B.A.A.'s
baa (bleat)
baas
baaed
baaing
**Baade, Wil|helm
Hein|rich Wal|ter**
(US astronomer)
Baal (fertility god)
Baal|bek (town,
Lebanon)
Baal Shem Tob
(= Baal Shem Tov)
Baal Shem Tov
(Jewish religious
leader)
baas *South Africa*
(boss)
baas|es
baas|skap
Baath (pan-Arabic
socialist movement)
[☞ **Bath**]
Ba'ath (pan-Arabic
socialist movement:
use Baath)
[☞ **Bath**]
Bab (Persian religious
leader)
baba +s
(grandmother, old
woman; father, holy
man; cake)
baba gha|nouj
Babar (= Baber,
Mogul emperor of
India)
Bab|bage, Charles
(English inventor)
Bab|bitt +s (metal;
complacent business
person)

**Bab|bitt, Mil|ton
Byron** (US
composer)
bab|bitt +s (lining for
bearings)
Bab|bit|try
bab|ble (chatter)
bab|bles
bab|bled
bab|bling
[☞ **babel**]
babble|ment
bab|bler +s
babe +s
Babel (Biblical tower)
[☞ **Bebel**]
babel (commotion)
[☞ **babble, Bebel**]
Baber (Mogul emperor
of India)
Babi +s
ba|biche
Ba|bine (lake, Canada)
Bab|ism
babka +s
ba|boon +s
Ba|bruisk (city,
Belarus)
Ba|bruysk
(= Babruisk,
Belarus)
Babur (= Baber,
Mogul emperor of
India)
ba|bush|ka +s
Babu|yan (islands, the
Philippines)
baby
babies
babied
baby|ing
baby blue +s (baby-
blue *when preceding*
a noun)
baby blue eyes
(plant)
baby boom +s
baby boom|er +s
baby bot|tle +s
baby buggy
baby bug|gies
baby doll +s (baby-
doll *when preceding a*
noun)
baby farm +s
baby-farming
baby|hood
baby|ish
baby|ish|ly
baby|ish|ness
Baby|lon
(Mesopotamian city;

any decadent city;
white society)
Baby|lonia (ancient
Mesopotamia)
Baby|lon|ian +s
baby's breath (plant)
baby|sit
baby|sits
baby|sat
baby|sit|ting
baby|sit|ter +s
baby|sit|ting noun
baby's tears (plant)
baby talk
baby tears (= baby's
tears)
baby tooth
baby teeth
baca|lao (dried salt
cod, Spanish)
baca|lhau (dried salt
cod, Portuguese)
bac|ca|la (dried salt
cod, Italian)
bac|ca|laure|ate +s
bac|ca|lieu bird +s
bac|cara (*use*
baccarat)
bac|carat
bac|cate
Bac|chae
bac|cha|nal +s
Bac|cha|nalia
(Roman festival)
bac|cha|nalia +s
(drunken revelry)
bac|cha|nal|ian +s
bac|chant
bac|chants or
bac|chan|tes
bac|chan|te +s
(female bacchant)
bac|chan|tic
Bac|chic
Bac|chus (*Roman &*
Greek Myth)
baccy
Bach (surname)
[☞ **Back**]
**Bach, Carl Phil|ipp
Eman|uel** (German
composer)
**Bach, Jo|hann
Chris|tian** (German
composer)
**Bach, Jo|hann
Sebas|tian** (German
composer)
**Bach, Wil|helm
Friede|mann**
(German composer)
Bacha|rach, Burt (US
songwriter)

bach|elor +s
bach|elor but|ton +s
bachelor|ette +s
bachelor|hood
bachelor's but|ton +s (= bachelor button)
Bach|ian
ba|cil|lary
ba|cil|li|form
ba|cil|lus
ba|cil|li
ba|cil|lus thur|in|gien|sis
Back (river, Canada; surname) [☞ Bach]
Back, Fré|dé|ric (Cdn animator)
Back, Sir George (English explorer)
back +s +ed +ing
back|ache +s
back al|ley +s (back-alley when preceding a noun)
back|bar +s
back|beat +s
back|bench
back|bench|es
back|bench|er +s
back bend +s
back|biter +s
back|biting
back|blocks
back|board +s
back|bone +s
back-breaker +s
back-breaking
back burn|er +s noun
back-burner +s +ed +ing verb
back cast +s
back|catch|er +s
back chan|nel +s (back-channel when preceding a noun)
back|chat +s
back|check +s +ed +ing
back|check|er +s
back|check|ing noun
back|cloth +s
back|comb +s +ed +ing
back|country
back|coun|tries
back|court +s
back|cross
back|cross|es
back|crossed
back|cross|ing

back|date
back|dates
back|dated
back|dating
back door +s noun (rear door; indirect method)
back|door adjective (alternative, clandestine; Basketball)
back|draft +s
back|drop +s
back eddy
back ed|dies
back end +s (back-end when preceding a noun)
back|er +s
back|fat
back|field (Football)
back|field|er +s
back|fill +s +ed +ing
back|fire
back|fires
back|fired
back|firing
back|flip +s
back-formation +s
back|gam|mon
back|ground +s
back|ground|er +s
back|hand +s +ed +ing
back|hand|ed adjective
back|hand|er +s
back|hoe +s
back|house +s
back|ing +s noun
back|lands
back lane +s
back|lash
back|lash|es
back|less
back|light
back|lights
back|lit or back|light|ed
back|light|ing
back|light|ing noun
back|liner +s
back|list +s
back|lit adjective
back|log
back|logs
back|logged
back|log|ging
back|lot +s
back mat|ter +s
back|most
back or|der +s

back|pack +s +ed +ing
back|pack|er +s
back|pack|ing noun
back|pedal
back|pedals
back|ped|alled
back|ped|al|ling
back|plate +s
back-projec|tion +s
back|rest +s
back ribs
back road +s
back|room +s
back|room|er +s
back rub +s
back|saw +s
back|scat|ter
back|scat|ter|ing
back-scratch|er +s
back-scratch|ing
back seat +s (back-seat when preceding a noun)
back|sheesh (use baksheesh)
back|side +s
back sight +s
back slang
back|slap
back|slaps
back|slapped
back|slap|ping
back|slap|per +s
back|slap|ping noun
back|slash
back|slash|es
back|slide
back|slides
back|slid
back|slid|ing
back|slid|er +s
back|space
back|spaces
back|spaced
back|spacing
back|spin +s
back|splash
back|splash|es
back|split +s
back|stab|ber +s
back|stab|bing
back|stage
back stairs (back|stairs when preceding a noun)
back|stay +s
back|stitch
back|stitch|es
back|stitched
back|stitch|ing

back|stop
back|stops
back|stopped
back|stop|ping
back street +s (back|street when preceding a noun)
back|stretch
back|stretch|es
back|stroke +s
back|swing +s
back|talk
back to back adverb
back-to-back adjective
back to front
back-to-nature adjective preceding a noun
back-to-school adjective preceding a noun
back-to-work adjective preceding a noun
back|track +s +ed +ing
back up verb
backs up
backed up
back|ing up
back|up +s noun & adjective
back|ward
back|ward|a|tion
back|ward|ness
back|wards
back|wash
back|wash|oo
back|washed
back|wash|ing
back|water +s
back|woods
back|woods|man
back|woods|men
back|yard +s
Ba|co|lod (city, the Philippines)
Bacon, Sir Fran|cis (English philosopher)
Bacon, Fran|cis (Irish-born painter)
Bacon, Roger (English scholar)
bacon (cured pork)
Bacon|ian +s
bac|teria plural of bacterium
bac|ter|ial
bac|teri|cid|al
bac|teri|cide +s
bac|terio|logic|al
bac|terio|logic|al|ly

bac|teri|ol|o|gist +s
bac|teri|ol|ogy
bac|teri|oly|sis
 bac|teri|oly|ses
bac|terio|lytic
bac|terio|phage +s
bac|terio|stat +s
bac|terio|stat|ic
bac|ter|ium
 bac|teria
bac|teri|uria
Bac|tria (ancient
 country, central Asia)
Bac|trian (camel)
bad
• (inferior, harmful,
 evil, etc.)
 worse
 worst
• *slang* (excellent)
bad|der
bad|dest
 [☞ bade]
bad|ass
 bad|asses
bad boy +s (bad-boy
 when preceding a
 noun)
Bad|deck (village,
 Canada)
bad|die +s
baddy (*use* baddie)
 bad|dies
bade *archaic past tense*
 of bid
Baden (town, Austria)
 [☞ Badon Hill]
Baden-Baden (town,
 Germany)
Baden-Powell,
 Rob|ert (founder of
 Scouting movement)
Baden-
 Württem|berg
 (state, Germany)
Bader, Sir Doug|las
 (British fighter pilot)
badge +s
badg|er +s +ed +ing
bad guy +s (bad-guy
 when preceding a
 noun)
Bad|ham (mountain
 peak, Canada)
bad|in|age
bad|lands
badly
 worse
 worst
bad|min|ton
bad-mouth +s +ed
 +ing
bad|ness

bad news (bad-news
 when preceding a
 noun)
Badon Hill (battle site,
 Britain)
bad-tempered
bad-tempered|ly
Baeck, Leo (German
 rabbi)
Baed|eker +s
Baer, Karl Er|nest
 von (German
 biologist)
Baeyer, Adolf von
 (German chemist)
Baez, Joan (US
 folksinger)
Baf|fin (island,
 Canada; bay,
 N Atlantic)
Baf|fin, Wil|liam
 (English navigator)
baf|fle
 baf|fles
 baf|fled
 baf|fling
baffle|gab
baffle|ment +s
baf|fler +s
baf|fling *adjective*
baf|fling|ly
bag
 bags
 bagged
 bag|ging
ba|gasse
baga|telle +s
Bage|hot, Wal|ter
 (English economist &
 journalist)
bagel +s
bag|ful +s
bag|gage +s
bag|gata|way
Bag|gie +s *proprietary*
 (plastic bag)
bag|gi|ly
bag|gi|ness
baggy (loose, puffy)
 bag|gi|er
 bag|gi|est
Bagh|dad (capital of
 Iraq)
bag lady
 bag ladies
bag|man
 bag|men
bagnio +s
Bagot, Sir Charles
 (Cdn governor
 general)
bag|pipe +s
bag|piper +s

ba|guette +s
bah
Baha'i +s
Baha'ism
Ba|ha|mas (country,
 W Indies)
Ba|ha|mian +s
Ba|hasa
Baha'ullah (Persian
 founder of Baha'ism)
Ba|hawal|pur (city,
 Pakistan)
Bahia (state & city,
 Brazil)
Bahía Blanca (port,
 Argentina)
Bah|rain (sheikdom,
 Persian Gulf)
Bah|raini +s
baht (Thai currency)
 plural baht
bai|dar +s
 (= baidarka)
bai|dar|ka +s
Baie-Comeau (city,
 Canada)
Baie des Cha|leurs
 (= Chaleur Bay,
 Canada)
Bai|kal (lake, Siberia)
Baiko|nur (space
 launch site,
 Kazakhstan)
bail +s +ed +ing
 (security against
 released prisoner,
 release; deliver
 goods; typewriter
 bar, cricket
 crosspiece; part of
 castle; scoop water;
 jump out, abandon)
 [☞ bale]
bail|able
bailee +s (*Law* person
 to whom goods are
 entrusted)
 [☞ bailey, bailie,
 Baily's beads]
bail|er +s (water
 scoop)
 [☞ bailor, baler]
Bailey, Don|ovan
 (Cdn sprinter)
Bailey, Ir|vine
 Wal|lace ('Ace')
 (Cdn hockey player)
Bailey, Nathan (or
 Na|than|iel) (English
 lexicographer)
bail|ey +s (part of
 castle)
 [☞ bailie, bailee,
 Baily's beads]

Bailey bridge +s
bailie +s (Scottish
 magistrate)
 [☞ bailey, bailee,
 Baily's beads]
bail|iff +s
baili|wick +s
bail|ment +s
bail|or +s (*Law*)
 [☞ bailer, baler]
bail out *verb*
 bails out
 bailed out
 bail|ing out
bail|out +s *noun*
bails|man
 bails|men
Baily's beads
 [☞ bailee, bailie,
 bailey]
bain-marie
 bains-marie
Bai|ram (*Islam*)
Baird (peninsula,
 Canada)
Baird, John Logie
 (Scottish inventor)
bairn +s
bait +s +ed +ing
bait and switch (bait-
 and-switch *when*
 preceding a noun)
bait|cast|er +s
bait|cast|ing
bait|ed *adjective* (set
 with bait)
 [☞ bated]
bait|fish
 plural bait|fish or
 bait|fish|es
baize
Baja Cali|for|nia
 (peninsula, Mexico)
Baja Cali|for|nia
 (Norte) (state,
 Mexico)
Baja Cali|for|nia Sur
 (state, Mexico)
Bajan +s
bake
 bakes
 baked
 bak|ing
bake|apple +s
baked-apple berry
 baked-apple
 ber|ries
bake|house +s
Bake|lite *proprietary*
Bake-Off +s
 proprietary
Baker, Car|roll (Cdn
 singer)

Baker, Chet (US musician)
Baker, Dame Janet (English singer)
Baker, Jo|seph|ine (French entertainer)
Baker, Peggy Laur|ayne (Cdn dancer)
Baker, Sir Sam|uel White (English explorer)
baker +s (one who bakes; baking appliance)
Baker Lake (lake & hamlet, Canada)
baker's doz|en +s
bakery
  baker|ies
bake sale +s
bake|shop +s
bake|ware
Bake|well, Rob|ert (English agriculturist)
Bake|well +s (tart)
bak|ing +s adjective & noun
bak|la|va +s
bak|sheesh
Bakst, Léon (Russian stage designer)
Baku (capital of Azerbaijan)
Baku|nin, Mikh|ail Alek|san|dro|vich (Russian anarchist)
Balaam (Bible)
bala|clava +s
bala|fon +s
Bala|ki|rev, Mily Alex|sey|evich (Russian composer)
bala|lai|ka +s
Bal|ance (zodiac sign, constellation)
bal|ance (in general use)
  bal|an|ces
  bal|anced
  bal|an|cing
bal|ance|able
bal|anced adjective
bal|an|cer +s
bal|ance sheet +s
Bal|an|chine, George (Russian-born choreographer)
bal|ata +s
Bala|ton (lake, Hungary)

Bal|boa, Vasco Núñez (Spanish explorer)
bal|boa +s (Panamanian currency)
Bal|brig|gan +s
bal|con|ied
bal|cony
  bal|con|ies
bald (hairless)
  bald|er
  bald|est
  [☞ Cape Bauld]
bal|da|chin +s
bal|da|quin +s (use baldachin)
Bal|der (Scandinavian Myth)
bal|der|dash
bald-faced
bald|head|ed
bald|ie +s
bald|ing
bald|ish
bald|ly
bald|ness
bald|pate +s
bal|dric +s
Bald|win (king of Jerusalem)
Bald|win, James Ar|thur (US writer)
Bald|win, Rob|ert (Cdn politician)
Bald|win, Stan|ley (British prime minister)
Bald|win, Wil|liam War|ren (Cdn politician)
bale (bundle; evil; woe; for scoop, jump out, or abandon use bail)
  bales
  baled
  baling
  [☞ bail]
Bale|ar|ic +s (Mediterranean islands)
ba|leen
bale|ful
bale|ful|ly
bale|ful|ness
baler +s (machine for baling hay etc.; twine; for water scoop use bailer)
  [☞ bailer, bailor]

Bal|four, Ar|thur James (British politician
Bali (island, Indonesia)
Bali|nese
  plural Bali|nese
balk +s +ed +ing (hesitate; frustrate; miss; shirk; beam; hindrance; plowing ridge; Baseball; Billiards)
  [☞ bawk, bock]
Bal|kan +s (countries, peninsula & mountains, S Europe)
bal|kan|iz|a|tion
bal|kan|ize
  bal|kan|iz|es
  bal|kan|ized
  bal|kan|iz|ing
balk|er +s
Bal|khash (= Lake Balqash, Kazakhstan)
balk|i|ness
Bal|kis
balky
  balk|i|er
  balk|i|est
Ball, John (English rebel)
Ball, Lu|cille (US actress)
ball +s +ed +ing (sphere; dance)
  [☞ bawl]
bal|lad +s (narrative poem or song; love song)
  [☞ ballade]
bal|lade +s (poetic form; piano piece)
  [☞ ballad]
bal|lad|eer +s
bal|lad|ry
  bal|lad|ries
ball-and-socket
Bal|lan|tyne, Rob|ert Mi|chael (Scottish author)
Bal|la|rat (town, Australia)
Bal|lard, James Gra|ham (British writer)
bal|last +s
ball bear|ing +s
ball|boy +s
ball-breaker +s
ball-buster +s
ball club +s
ball|cock +s

bal|ler|ina +s
Bal|le|steros, Sev|eri|ano ('Sevvy') (Spanish golfer)
bal|let +s
bal|let|ic
bal|leto|mane +s
bal|leto|mania
ball field +s
ball game +s
ball|girl +s
balli|cat|ter
bal|lista
  bal|lis|tae
bal|lis|tic
bal|lis|tic|ally
bal|lis|tics
bal|locks (use bollocks)
bal|lon (Dance)
bal|loon +s +ed +ing (inflatable bag or pouch; wineglass; swell; increase)
bal|loon|ing noun & adjective
bal|loon|ist +s
bal|lot +s +ed +ing
bal|lot|ing noun
ball|park +s
ball-peen ham|mer +s
ball|player +s
ball|point +s
ball|room +s
balls-up +s noun
ballsy
  balls|i|er
  balls|i|est
bally (Brit. slang)
  [☞ Bali]
bally|hoo +s +ed +ing
bally|hooed adjective
Bally|mena (town, Northern Ireland)
balm +s (ointment; fragrance; herb)
  [☞ bomb, bombe, Baum]
Bal|main, Pierre Alex|andre Claud|ius (French designer)
balm|i|er
balm|i|est
balm|i|ly
balm|i|ness
balm of Gil|ead
Bal|moral (castle, Scotland)

bal|moral +s (hat; boot)
balmy
balm|i|er
balm|i|est
bal|neo|logic|al
bal|ne|ol|o|gist +s
bal|ne|ol|ogy
ba|loney +s (luncheon meat; nonsense)
Bal|qash (lake, Kazakhstan)
balsa
bal|sam +s
bal|sam|ic
balsam|root +s
balsa wood
Balt +s
Bal|tha|sar (one of the Magi)
Bal|tic (sea; states, Europe; language)
Bal|ti|more (city, US)
Bal|ti|mor|ean +s
Bal|ti|stan (Himalayan region)
Ba|luch|istan (region, W Asia; province, Pakistan)
bal|us|ter +s
bal|us|trade +s
Bal|zac, Hon|oré de (French writer)
Bal|zac|ian
bam
Bam|ako (capital of Mali)
bam|bino
bam|binos or bam|bini
bam|boo +s
bam|boozle
bam|boo|zles
bam|boo|zled
bam|booz|ling
bam|boozle|ment +s
bam|booz|ler +s
Bamian (city, Afghanistan)
ban (prohibit; prohibition; curse)
bans
banned
ban|ning
[☞ banns]
Banaba (island, Kiribati)
banal
ban|al|ity
ban|al|ities
ban|al|ly
ba|nana +s
ba|nanas

ban|ausic
Ban|bury (town, England; tart)
banc (Law)
banco (Law)
band +s +ed +ing
Banda (sea)
ban|dage
ban|da|ges
ban|daged
ban|da|ging
Band-Aid +s proprietary
ban|dana +s
ban|danna +s (use bandana)
Ban|da|ra|naike, Siri|mavo Rat|watte Dias (Sri Lankan prime minister)
Band|ar Seri Be|ga|wan (capital of Brunei)
B & B (bed & breakfast; bilingualism & biculturalism)
B & Bs
band|box
band|boxes
B and E (breaking & entering)
B and Es
ban|deau
ban|deaus or ban|deaux
band|ed adjective
ban|der|illa +s
ban|derol +s (use banderole)
ban|der|ole +s
bandi|coot +s
band|i|er
band|i|est
band|ing +s noun
ban|dit +s
ban|dit|ry
Band|jar|masin (= Banjarmasin, Indonesia)
band|leader +s
band|master +s
band|mate +s
band|do|leer +s (use bandolier)
ban|do|lier +s
band|pass
band|pass|es
band saw +s
band|shell +s
bands|man
bands|men
band|stand +s

Ban|dung (city, Indonesia)
ban|dura +s
ban|dur|ist +s
band|wagon +s
band|width +s
bandy (curved legs; spread a rumour; Sport)
ban|dies
ban|died
bandy|ing
ban|di|er
ban|di|est
bandy-legged
bane +s
bane|berry
bane|ber|ries
bane|ful
bane|ful|ly
Banff (town & national park, Canada)
Banff|shire (former county, Scotland)
bang +s +ed +ing (loud sound; hair fringe; slam; etc.)
[☞ bhang]
Banga|lore (city, India)
bang-bang adjective
bang|belly
bang|bel|lies
bang|er +s
Bang|kok (capital of Thailand)
Ban|gla|desh (country, Asia)
Ban|gla|deshi +s
ban|gle +s
bang|tail +s
Ban|gui (capital of the Central African Republic)
bang up verb
bangs up
banged up
bang|ing up
bang-up adjective
ban|ish
ban|ish|es
ban|ished
ban|ish|ing
ban|ish|ment
ban|is|ter +s (handrail)
[☞ Bannister]
Ban|jar|masin (port, Indonesia)
banjo
ban|jos or ban|joes
banjo|ist +s

Ban|jul (capital of Gambia)
bank +s +ed +ing (slope; heap; rebound; row; rely; Finance)
[☞ banc]
bank|able
bank book +s
bank|er +s
banker's hours
Bank|head, Tal|lu|lah (US actress)
bank|ing noun
bank|note +s
bank|roll +s +ed +ing
bank|rupt +s +ed +ing
bank|rupt|cy
bank|rupt|cies
Banks (W Arctic island)
Banks, Sir Jo|seph (English naturalist)
bank|sia +s
ban|ner +s
ban|nered
ban|ner|et +s
Ban|nis|ter, Sir Roger Gil|bert (English runner)
[☞ banister]
ban|nis|ter +s (handrail: use banister)
ban|nock +s
ban|nock ball
Ban|nock|burn (battle site, Scotland)
banns (of marriage)
ban|quet +s +ed +ing (feast)
[☞ banquette]
ban|quet|er +s
ban|quette +s (bench; raised step)
[☞ banquet]
ban|shee +s
ban|tam +s
bantam|weight +s
ban|ter +s +ed +ing
ban|ter|er +s
Ban|ting, Sir Fred|erick Grant (Cdn co-discoverer of insulin)
Bantu
plural Bantu or Bantus
Bantu|stan +s
ban|yan +s

ban|zai (battle cry; greeting)
[☞ bonsai]
bao|bab +s
Bao|tou (city, China)
bap +s
bap|tism +s
bap|tis|mal
Bap|tist +s (denomination)
bap|tist +s (person who baptizes)
bap|tis|tery
bap|tis|ter|ies
bap|tis|try (use baptistery)
bap|tis|tries
bap|tize
bap|tiz|es
bap|tized
bap|tiz|ing
bar (rod; barrier; counter; pub; unit of pressure; Music; Law; fasten; prohibit; except)
bars
barred
bar|ring
[☞ barre]
Bar|ab|bas (New Testament)
bara|chois
plural bara|chois
Baraka, Imamu Amiri (LeRoi Jones)
bara|thea +s
barb +s +ed +ing
Bar|bad|ian +s
Bar|bados (Caribbean island)
bar|bar|ian +s
bar|bar|ic
bar|bar|ic|ally
bar|bar|ism +s
bar|bar|ity
bar|bar|ities
bar|bar|iz|a|tion +s
bar|bar|ize
bar|bar|iz|es
bar|bar|ized
bar|bar|iz|ing
Bar|ba|rossa (Barbary pirate; German king)
bar|bar|ous
bar|bar|ous|ly
bar|bar|ous|ness
Bar|bary (Saracen states; ape)
Bar|beau (mountain, Canada)

Bar|beau, (Charles) Mar|ius (Cdn folklorist)
Bar|beau, Jean (Cdn dramatist)
bar|be|cue
bar|be|cues
bar|be|cued
bar|be|cu|ing
barbed adjective
barbed wire
bar|bel +s (fish)
[☞ barbell]
bar|bell +s (weights)
[☞ barbel]
bar|be|que (use barbecue)
bar|be|ques
bar|be|qued
bar|be|qu|ing
Bar|ber, Sam|uel (US composer)
[☞ Barbour]
bar|ber +s +ed +ing
bar|berry
bar|ber|ries
barber|shop +s
bar|bet +s (bird)
[☞ barbette]
bar|bette +s (gun platform or mount)
[☞ barbet]
bar|bi|can +s
Bar|bie +s
• proprietary (doll)
• (young woman)
bar|bie +s (barbecue)
Bar|bi|rolli, Sir John (English conductor)
bar|bi|tal
bar|bi|tone
bar|bit|ur|ate +s
bar|bit|ur|ic
Bar|bi|zon school
barb|less
bar|bot +s (catfish: use barbotte)
[☞ barbotte]
bar|botte +s (catfish; gambling game)
Bar|bour, Doug|las (Cdn poet)
[☞ Barber]
Bar|bour, John (Scottish poet)
[☞ Barber]
Bar|buda (island, W Indies)
barb|ule +s
barb|wire (informal = barbed wire)
bar|ca|role +s

bar|ca|rolle +s (use barcarole)
Bar|ce|lona (city, Spain)
Bar-Cochba (Jewish rebel)
bar code +s
bar-coded
bar-coding
bard +s +ed +ing
Bar|deen, John (US physicist)
bard|ic
Bar|dot, Bri|gitte (French actress)
bare (uncovered, mere, uncover, etc.)
bares
bared
baring
barer
barest
[☞ bear]
bare|back
bare|boat +s
bare bones noun
bare-bones adjective
Bare|bones Par|lia|ment (English History)
bare|faced
bare|faced|ly
bare|faced|ness
bare|foot
bare|foot|ed (= barefoot)
ba|rège +s
bare-handed
bare-headed
Ba|reilly (city, India)
bare-knuckle
bare-knuckled (= bare-knuckle)
bare|ly
Baren|boim, Dan|iel (Israeli musician)
bare|ness
Bar|ents (sea)
Bar|ents, Wil|lem (Dutch explorer)
barer comparative of bare
[☞ bearer]
barf +s +ed +ing
bar|fly
bar|flies
bar|gain +s
bar|gain|er +s
barge
bar|ges
barged
bar|ging
barge|board +s

bar|gee +s
barge pole +s
bar|goon +s
bar graph +s
bar-hop
bar-hops
bar-hopped
bar-hopping
Bari (seaport, Italy)
Bari|loche (= San Carlos de Bariloche, Argentina)
baring conjugated form of bare
[☞ bearing, Bering, Behring]
Bari|sal (port, Bangladesh)
bar|ite +s
bari|tone +s
bar|ium
bark +s +ed +ing (dog's cry, call out; on trees, scrape; ship, boat)
[☞ barque]
bar|keep +s
bar|ken|tine +s (use barquentine)
Bar|ker, Wil|liam George ('Billy') (Cdn fighter pilot)
bark|er +s (person who calls out; dog that barks)
Bar|ker|ville (historic town, Canada)
Bark|ley Sound (off Vancouver Island)
Bark|ly Table|land (Australia)
bar|ley +s
barley|corn +s
bar line +s
barm
bar|maid +s
bar|man
bar|men
barm|brack +s
Bar|me|cide +s
barm|i|ly
barm|i|ness
bar mitz|vah
bar mitz|vahs or bar mitz|voth
bar mitz|vahed
barmy
barm|i|er
barm|i|est
barn +s
Bar|na|bas (saint)
bar|nacle +s

bar|nacled
Bar|nard (surname)
[☞ Bernard, St.
Bernard]
Bar|nard, Chris|tiaan
Neeth|ling (South
African surgeon)
Bar|nard, Ed|ward
Emer|son (US
astronomer)
Bar|nar|do, Thom|as
John (British
philanthropist)
Bar|naul (city, Russia)
barn|board +s
barn|brack +s
(= barmbrack)
barn|burn|er +s
barn dance +s
bar|ney +s
barn rais|ing +s
Barns|ley (town,
England)
barn|storm +s +ed
+ing
barn|storm|er +s
Bar|num, Phin|eas
Tay|lor (US circus
impresario)
barn|wood
barn|yard +s
Bar|oda
• (former state, India)
• (former name for
Vadodara)
baro|graph +s
Ba|roja, Pio full name
Pio Ba|roja y Nessi
(Spanish novelist)
Ba|ro|lo +s
bar|om|eter +s
baro|met|ric
baro|met|ric|al
bar|om|etry
bar|on +s (member of
nobility; powerful
person)
[☞ barren,
Behrens]
baron|age
baron|ess (female
baron)
baron|ess|es
[☞ barrenness]
bar|on|et +s
baron|et|age
baron|etcy
baron|et|cies
bar|on|ial
bar|ony
bar|on|ies
bar|oque
bar|ouche +s

barque +s (ship, boat)
[☞ bark]
bar|quen|tine +s
Bar|quisi|meto (city,
Venezuela)
bar|rack +s +ed +ing
bar|ra|cuda
plural bar|ra|cuda or
bar|ra|cudas
bar|rage
bar|ra|ges
bar|raged
bar|ra|ging
bar|ra|mundi
plural bar|ra|mundi
or bar|ra|mun|dis
Bar|ran|quilla (port,
Colombia)
bar|ra|tor +s
bar|ra|trous
bar|ra|try
Bar|rault, Jean-Louis
(French filmmaker)
Barr Col|onist +s
barre (Dance)
[☞ bar, barré]
barré (Music)
barred adjective
bar|rel (container,
cylindrical body,
measure of capacity;
move quickly)
bar|rels
bar|relled
bar|rel|ling
[☞ beryl]
barrel-chested
barrel|head +s
barrel|house +s
barrel-jumping
Bar|ren +s (Arctic
region, Canada)
[☞ Behrens]
bar|ren +er +est +s
(infertile; treeless
land, marsh, muskeg)
[☞ baron]
bar|ren ground
cari|bou
plural bar|ren
ground cari|bou
bar|ren|ly
barren|ness
(infertility etc.)
[☞ baroness]
Bar|rès, (Au|guste)
Mau|rice (French
writer)
Bar|rett, Eliza|beth
(Elizabeth Barrett
Browning)
bar|rette +s (hair clip)
[☞ beret]

bar|ri|cade
bar|ri|cades
bar|ri|cad|ed
bar|ri|cad|ing
Bar|rie (city, Canada)
[☞ Barry, Berry]
Bar|rie, Sir James
Mat|thew (Scottish
writer)
[☞ Barry, Berry]
bar|rier +s
bar|ring preposition
bar|rio +s
bar|ris|ter +s
barrister-at-law
barristers-at-law
bar|room +s
bar|row +s
Barry, Sir Charles
(English architect)
[☞ Barrie, Berry]
Barry|more, Ethel
(US actress)
Barry|more, John
(US actor)
Barry|more, Lionel
(US actor)
Bar|sac +s
bar stool +s
Bart, Lionel (English
composer)
[☞ Barth, Barthes]
bar|tend +s +ed +ing
bar|tend|er +s
bar|tend|ing noun
bar|ter +s +ed +ing
bar|ter|er +s
bar|ter shop +s
Barth, John
Sim|mons (US
novelist)
Barth, Karl (Swiss
theologian)
Barthes, Ro|land
(French literary
critic)
Bar|tholdi, Fré|dé|ric
Au|guste (French
sculptor & architect)
Bar|tholo|mew
(apostle)
bar|ti|zan +s
bar|ti|zaned
Bart|lett pear +s
Bar|tók, Béla
(Hungarian
composer)
Bar|tolom|meo, Fra
Baccio della Porta
(Florentine painter)
Bar|ton, Sir Derek
Har|old Rich|ard
(English chemist)

Bar|ton, Sir Ed|mund
(Australian
statesman)
Bar|uch (Apocrypha)
bary|on +s
bary|on|ic
Barysh|nikov,
Mikh|ail (Soviet-
born dancer)
bary|sphere
baryta
baryte +s (use barite)
ba|rytes Brit. (use
barite)
ba|ryt|ic
basal (forming a base)
[☞ basil, Basel]
bas|alt +s
bas|alt|ic
bas|cule +s
base
• noun (foundation,
basis, Military,
Chemistry, Math,
Baseball, Heraldry)
bases
• verb (establish,
station)
bases
based
bas|ing
• adjective (cowardly,
impure, debased)
baser
bas|est
[☞ bass]
base|ball +s
base|board +s
Basel (city,
Switzerland)
[☞ Basil, basal]
base|less
base|less|ly
base|less|ness
base|line +s
base|load +s
base|ly
base|man
base|men
base|ment +s
base|ness
base pair +s
base|path +s
base|run|ner +s
base|run|ning +s
bases plural of base,
basis
bash
bashes
bashed
bash|ing
bash|er +s
bash|ful

bash|ful|ly
bash|ful|ness
bash|ing +s *noun*
Basho (Japanese poet)
BASIC (*Computing*)
basic +s (of a base; fundamental)
basic|ally
bas|icity
bas|ici|ties
ba|sid|ium
ba|sidia
Basie, Wil|liam ('Count') (US musician)
Basil (saint)
[☞ Basel]
bas|il +s (herb)
basi|lar
Ba|sil|ian +s
ba|sil|ica +s
ba|sil|ican
Ba|sili|cata (region, Italy)
basi|lisk +s
basin +s
basin|ful +s
basip|etal
basip|etal|ly
basis
bases
bask +s +ed +ing (laze in the sun etc.)
[☞ basque]
Bas|ka|tong (reservoir, Canada)
Bas|ker|ville, John (English printer)
bas|ket +s
basket|ball +s
basket case +s
basket|ful +s
Bas|ket Maker +s (people)
basket-of-gold
bas|ketry
bas|ket sled +s
bas|ket sleigh +s
bas|ket weave
basket|work
bask|ing shark +s
bas|mati
Basov, Niko|lai Gen|nediy|evich (Russian physicist)
Basque +s (people, language; regions, Spain & France)
basque +s (bodice, waistline)
[☞ bask]
Basra (port, Iraq)
bas-relief +s

Bass (strait, Australia)
bass[1] (*Music*, deep-sounding)
bass|es
[☞ base]
bass[2] (fish, tree, wood) *plural* bass or bass|es
Bas|sein (port, Burma)
Basse-Norman|die (region, France)
bas|set +s (hound)
Basse|terre (capital of St. Kitts and Nevis)
[☞ Basse-Terre]
Basse-Terre (capital & island, Guadeloupe)
[☞ Basseterre]
bas|set horn +s
bas|si|net +s
bass|ist +s
basso
bas|sos or bassi
bas|soon +s
bas|soon|ist +s
basso pro|fun|do
basso pro|fun|dos or bassi pro|fundi
basso-rilievo
basso-rilievos
bass|wood +s
bast
bas|tard +s
bas|tard|iz|a|tion +s
bas|tard|ize
bas|tard|iz|es
bas|tard|ized
bas|tard|iz|ing
bas|tardy
baste
bastes
basted
bast|ing
bast|er +s
Bas|tet (*Egyptian Myth*)
Bas|tia (port, Corsica)
Bas|tille (fortress, Paris)
bas|tin|ado
• *noun*
bas|tin|ados
• *verb*
bas|tin|adoes
bas|tin|adoed
bas|tin|ado|ing
bas|tion +s
Ba|suto|land (*former name of* Lesotho)

bat (stick, club; hit; blink; flying mammal)
bats
bat|ted
bat|ting
[☞ batt]
Bata (seaport, Equatorial Guinea)
Bata, Thom|as John (Cdn shoe manufacturer)
Batan (islands, the Philippines)
ba|tard +s
Ba|tavia (*former name of* Djakarta, Indonesia)
bat boy +s
batch
batch|es
batched
batch|ing
ba|teau
ba|teaux
bated *adjective* (in 'with bated breath')
[☞ baited]
Bate|man, Rob|ert Mc|Lel|lan (Cdn painter)
Bates, Henry Wal|ter (English naturalist)
Bates, Her|bert Er|nest (English writer)
Bath (town, England)
bath +s +ed +ing (tub; wash)
bathe (wash; swim; immerse; expose to sunlight etc.)
bathes
bathed
bath|ing
bath|er +s
ba|the|tic
bath|house +s
bath|ing *noun*
bath|ing suit +s
bath mat +s
batho|lith +s
Bath Oli|ver +s
ba|thos
bath|robe +s
bath|room +s
bath salts
Bath|sheba (*Bible*)
bath|tub +s
Bath|urst (city, island & inlet, Canada; *former name for* Banjul, Gambia)

bath|water
ba|thym|eter +s
bathy|met|ric
ba|thym|etry
bathy|scaphe +s
bathy|sphere +s
batik +s
ba|tiked
Bat|ista, Ful|gen|cio *full name* Ful|gen|cio Bat|ista y Zal|vidar (Cuban dictator)
bat|iste +s (cloth)
[☞ Saint-Jean-Baptiste Day]
bat|man (officer's assistant)
bat|men
bat mitz|vah
bat mitz|vahs or bat mitz|voth
Ba|toche (battle site, Canada)
baton +s (*Music; Sport*; truncheon; staff of authority)
[☞ batten]
bâton|nier +s
Baton Rouge (city, US)
bat|ra|chian +s
bats (crazy)
bats|man
bats|men
bats|man|ship
batt (sheet of insulation; wadding)
bat|tal|ion +s
Bat|tam|bang (province & its capital, Cambodia)
bat|teau (*use* bateau)
bat|teaux
bat|tels (Oxford college account)
Bat|ten, Jean (New Zealand aviator)
[☞ Baton Rouge]
bat|ten +s +ed +ing (fastening strip; fasten; 'batten down the hatches'; cotton wadding; thrive)
[☞ baton]
Batten|berg (cake; lace)
bat|ter +s +ed +ing
bat|tered *adjective*
bat|ter|er +s
bat|tery
bat|ter|ies
Bat|tica|loa (city, Sri Lanka)

bat|ti|er
bat|ti|est
bat|ti|ly
bat|ti|ness
bat|ting noun (cotton
    wadding; Baseball)
bat|tle (fight)
    bat|tles
    bat|tled
    bat|tling
    [☞ battels]
battle-axe +s
    (weapon)
battle|axe +s
    (formidable woman)
bat|tle cruis|er +s
bat|tle cry
    bat|tle cries
battle|dore +s
battle|dress
battle|field +s
battle|ground +s
battle|ment +s
battle|ment|ed
bat|tler +s
bat|tle royal
    bat|tles royal
battle-scarred
battle|ship +s
battle-weary
bat|tue +s
batty
    bat|ti|er
    bat|ti|est
bat|wing adjective
bau|ble +s (trinket;
    jester's baton)
    [☞ bobble]
Bau|cis (Greek Myth)
baud (Computing)
    [☞ bawd]
Baude|laire, Charles
    (French writer)
Baude|lair|ean
Bau|douin (Belgian
    king)
Bau|dril|lard, Jean
    (French sociologist)
Bauer, David
    Wil|liam (Cdn priest
    & hockey coach)
Bau|haus
Bauld (cape, Canada)
Baum, Lyman Frank
    (US writer)
baux|ite
baux|it|ic
Bav|aria (state,
    Germany)
Bav|arian +s
bawd +s (prostitute)
    [☞ baud]
bawd|i|ly

bawd|i|ness
bawdy (lewd)
    bawd|i|er
    bawd|i|est
bawk +s (shearwater)
    [☞ bock, balk]
bawl +s +ed +ing
    (yell; weep)
bawl|er +s
bawn +s (meadow;
    place for drying cod)
    [☞ Cape Bon,
    Bonn]
Bax, Sir Ar|nold
    (English composer)
Bax|ter, John
    Bab|ing|ton
    Mac|aulay (Cdn
    politician)
Bay (the Hudson's Bay
    Company)
bay (cove; recess;
    window; tree; horse;
    howl)
    [☞ bey]
Bay|ard, Pierre du
    Ter|rail, Sei|gneur
    de (French soldier)
bay|berry
    bay|ber|ries
bay boat +s
Bay d'Espoir (inlet,
    Canada)
Bay|field, Henry
    Wol|sey (British
    surveyor)
bay|front +s
Bay|kal (= Lake
    Baikal, Russia)
Bayko|nyr
    (= Baikonur,
    Kazakhstan)
Bayle, Pierre (French
    philosopher)
bay leaf
    bay leaves
Bay|lis, Lil|lian Mary
    (English theatre
    manager)
Bay man (employee of
    the Hudson's Bay
    Company)
    Bay men
bay|man (person
    living in an outpost
    or near a bay)
    bay|men
bay-noddy
    bay-noddies
bay|on|et
    bay|on|ets
    bay|on|et|ted
    bay|on|et|ting
bayou +s

Bay|reuth (town,
    Germany)
Bay Rob|erts (town,
    Canada)
bay rum
Bay|side (around
    Hudson Bay)
bay|side (in general
    use)
Bay Street (in
    Toronto)
bay|wop +s
ba|zaar +s (market)
    [☞ bizarre]
ba|zooka +s
ba|zoom +s
bazz
    bazz|es
    bazzed
    bazz|ing
BB (pellet)
    BBs
BBQ (barbecue)
    BBQs
BBS (bulletin board
    service)
    BBSs
BC (British Columbia)
BC (before Christ)
BCD (Computing)
    BCDs
BCE (before the
    Common Era)
BCG (Bacillus
    Calmette-Guérin)
B.Com. (Bachelor of
    Commerce)
    B.Com.'s
B.Comm. (Bachelor of
    Commerce: use
    B.Com.)
    B.Comm.'s
bdel|lium +s
be verb
    am
    are
    is
    was
    were
    been
    being
beach (shore)
    beach|es
    beached
    beach|ing
    [☞ beech]
beach ball +s
beach bird +s
beach|comb +s +ed
    +ing
beach|comb|er +s
beached adjective
beach|front

beach grass
    beach grass|es
beach|head +s
Beach-la-mar
beach pea +s
beach plum +s
bea|con +s
Bea|cons|field (city,
    Canada)
bead +s +ed +ing
    (Jewellery; drop; tire
    edge; gunsight)
    [☞ Bede]
bead|ed adjective
bead|i|er
bead|i|est
bead|i|ly
bead|i|ness
bead|ing noun
Bea|dle, George
    Wells (US geneticist)
bea|dle (usher; church
    officer)
beadle|ship +s
beads|man
    beads|men
bead|work
beady
    bead|i|er
    bead|i|est
beady-eyed
Bea|gle (channel,
    Tierra del Fuego)
bea|gle (dog; spy;
    hunt)
    bea|gles
    bea|gled
    beag|ling
beag|ler +s
beag|ling noun
beak +s
beaked adjective
beak|er +s
Beak|er Folk
beaky
beal +s
Beale, Doro|thea
    (English
    educationist)
beal|ing +s
be-all and end-all
Beals, Car|lyle Smith
    (Cdn astronomer)
beam +s +ed +ing
beamed adjective
Bea|mon, Rob|ert
    ('Bob') (US athlete)
beamy
    beam|i|er
    beam|i|est
bean +s +ed +ing
    (food plant & seed;

hit on the head)
[☞ been]
bean|bag +s
bean|ball +s
bean-counter +s
bean-counting
bean curd
bean|ery
  bean|eries
bean|feast +s
beanie +s
beano +s
bean|pole +s
bean sprout +s
bean|stalk +s
Bean|town (Boston)
bear (animal; carry;
  yield; give birth to;
  endure; veer)
  bears
  bore
  borne
  bearing
  • See Usage Note at
  born.
[☞ bare]
bear|abil|ity
bear|able
bear|able|ness
bear|ably
bear-baiting
bear|berry
  bear|ber|ries
beard +s +ed +ing
beard|ed adjective
beard|less
Beard|more (glacier,
  Antarctica)
Beards|ley, Aub|rey
  Vin|cent (English
  artist)
beard|tongue +s
bear|er +s (one who
  brings or presents)
[☞ barer]
bear|grass
bear hug +s
bear|ing +s noun
  (demeanour;
  relevance;
  endurability;
  position; machine
  part)
[☞ baring, Bering,
  Behring]
bearing-rein +s
bear|ish
bear|ish|ly
bear|ish|ness
Bear Lake (people;
  language)
Béar|naise (sauce)
bear|paw +s

bear root
bear's breech
  bear's breech|es
bear's ear +s
bear's foot +s
bear|skin +s
Beas (river, India)
beast +s
beast|ie +s
beast|li|ness
beast|ly
  beast|li|er
  beast|li|est
beat (strike; defeat;
  migrate; rhythm;
  route; exhausted;
  beatnik)
  beats
  beat
  beat|en
  beat|ing
[☞ beet]
beat|able
beat box
  beat boxes
beat|en adjective
beat|er +s
bea|tif|ic
bea|tif|ic|ally
be|ati|fi|ca|tion
be|ati|fy (Catholicism;
  please)
  be|ati|fies
  be|ati|fied
  be|ati|fy|ing
[☞ beatify]
beat|ing +s noun
be|ati|tude +s
beat|nik +s
Bea|ton, Sir Cecil
  Wal|ter Hardy
  (English
  photographer)
Bea|trice (Dante's
  inspiration)
Bea|trix (queen of the
  Netherlands)
Beat|ty, (Henry)
  War|ren (US actor)
beat up verb
  beats up
  beat up
  beat|en up
  beat|ing up
beat-up adjective
beau (boyfriend; fop)
  beaux or beaus
[☞ bo tree, bow]
Beau|fort (sea; scale)
Beau|fort, Henry
  (adviser to
  Plantagenet kings)

beau geste
  beaux gestes
Beau|har|nais,
  Jo|séph|ine de (wife
  of Napoleon)
Beau|har|nois (town,
  Canada)
Beau|har|nois (de La
  Boische), Charles
  de (governor of New
  France)
Beau|har|nois (de La
  Chaus|saye, Baron
  de Beau|ville),
  Fran|çois de
  (intendant of New
  France)
beau ideal
  beaux ideals
Beau|jo|lais (district,
  France; wine)
  plural Beaujolais
Beau|mar|chais,
  Pierre Au|gus|tin
  Caron de (French
  dramatist)
beau monde
Beau|mont (town,
  Canada)
Beau|mont, Fran|cis
  (English dramatist)
Beaune +s (town,
  France; wine)
Beau|port (city,
  Canada)
Beau|sejour (town,
  Manitoba)
[☞ Fort
  Beauséjour]
beaut +s (beautiful
  thing; excellent)
[☞ butte, Bute]
beaut|eous
beaut|ician +s
beauti|fi|ca|tion
beauti|fi|er
beauti|ful
beauti|ful|ly
beauti|fy (make
  beautiful)
  beauti|fies
  beauti|fied
  beauti|fy|ing
beauty
  beaut|ies
beauty|bush
  beauty|bush|es
beauty mark +s
beauty spot +s
Beau|voir, Si|mone
  de (French writer)
beaux plural of beau
beaux arts

Bea|ver
  • (Aboriginal people;
  language)
  plural Bea|ver or
  Bea|vers
  • (Scouting)
  plural Bea|vers
bea|ver
  • (animal)
  plural bea|ver or
  bea|vers
  • (hat etc.)
  plural bea|vers
Beaver|board +s
  proprietary
Beaver|brook,
  Wil|liam Max|well
  Ait|ken, 1st Baron
  (Cdn-born
  entrepreneur &
  politician)
Bea|ver Dams (Cdn
  battle site, War of
  1812)
bea|ver pond +s
Bea|ver Tail +s
  proprietary (food)
bea|ver tail +s (tail of
  a beaver)
beaver|tail (paddle,
  canoe)
Bebb's wil|low +s
  (= Bebb willow)
Bebb wil|low +s
Bebel, (Fer|di|nand)
  Aug|ust (German
  socialist)
[☞ Babel]
bebop
bebop|per +s
be|calmed
be|came
Bé|can|cour (town,
  Canada)
be|cause
bé|cha|mel
bêche-de-mer
  plural bêche-de-mer
  or
  bêches-de-mer
Bech|uana|land
  (former name of
  Botswana)
beck +s (in 'beck and
  call'; stream)
[☞ Baeck]
Becken|bauer, Franz
  (German soccer
  player & manager)
Beck|er, Boris
  (German tennis
  player)

Beck|et, Thom|as (à) (saint)
[☞ Beckett]
beck|et +s (*Nautical*)
Beck|ett, Sam|uel Bar|clay (Irish-born dramatist)
[☞ Becket]
Beck|ford, Wil|liam (English writer)
Beck|mann, Ernst Otto (German chemist)
Beck|mann, Max (German artist)
beck|on +s +ed +ing
beck|on|ing *adjective*
Beck|with, John (Cdn musician)
be|cloud +s +ed +ing
be|cloud|ed *adjective*
be|come
  be|comes
  be|came
  be|come
  be|com|ing
be|com|ing *adjective*
be|com|ing|ly
be|com|ing|ness
Bec|querel, Antoine-Henri (French physicist)
bec|querel +s (unit of radioactivity)
B.Ed. (Bachelor of Education)
B.Ed.'s
bed
  beds
  bed|ded
  bed|ding
bedad
bed and break|fast +s
be|daub +s +ed +ing
be|dazzle
  be|daz|zles
  be|daz|zled
  be|daz|zling
be|dazzle|ment +s
bed|bug +s
bed|chamber +s
bed|clothes
bed|covers
bed|dable
bed|der +s
bed|ding +s *noun*
Bed|does, Thom|as Lov|ell (English poet)
beddy-bye +s
Bede (saint, historian)
be|deck +s +ed +ing

be|devil
  be|devils
  be|dev|illed
  be|devil|ling
be|devil|ment +s
be|dew +s +ed +ing
bed|fellow +s
Bed|ford (urban community & basin, Canada)
Bed|ford, Duke of (protector of England & regent of France)
Bed|ford cord
Bed|ford|shire (county, England)
be|dight
bedim
  be|dims
  be|dimmed
  be|dim|ming
be|dizen +s +ed +ing
bed|lam +s
bed|lam|er +s
bed|lam|ite +s
bed lin|en +s
bed|liner +s
Bed|ling|ton +s
bed|mate +s
Bed|ouin
  plural Bed|ouin
bed|pan +s
bed|plate +s
bed|post +s
be|drag|gled
bed|rest
bed|rid|den
bed|rock
bed|roll +s
bed|room +s
bed|sheet +s
bed|side
bed|sit +s (*Brit.*)
bed-sitter +s
bed-sitting room +s
bed|skirt +s
bed|sock +s
bed|sore +s
bed|spread +s
bed|spring +s
bed|stead +s
bed|straw +s
bed|time +s
Bed|uin (*use* Bedouin)
  plural Bed|uin
bed|wet|ter +s
bed|wet|ting
bee +s
Beeb
bee balm +s
bee bread

beech (tree)
beech|es
[☞ beach]
Bee|cham, Thom|as (British conductor)
Bee|cher, Har|riet Eliza|beth (Harriet Beecher Stowe)
Bee|cher, Henry Ward (US minister)
Bee|chey (island, Canada)
Bee|chey, Fred|erick Wil|liam (English explorer)
beech|mast
  plural beech|mast
beech|nut +s
beech|wood
bee-eater +s
beef
• *noun* (cow, steer, bull)
  plural beeves
• *noun* (complaint)
  plural beefs
• *verb* (complain; in 'beef up')
  beefs
  beefed
  beef|ing
beef|alo
  plural beef|alo or beef|aloes
beef|burger +s
beef|cake +s
beef|eat|er +s
beef|i|ly
beef|i|ness
beef|steak +s
beefy
  beef|i|er
  beef|i|est
bee|hive +s
bee|keep|er +s
bee|keep|ing
bee|line +s
Beel|ze|bub (Satan)
been *past participle of* be
[☞ bean]
beep +s +ed +ing
beep|er +s
beep|er|less
beer (drink)
  plural beer or beers
[☞ bier]
beer-bellied
beer belly
  beer bel|lies
Beer|bohm, Sir (Henry)

Max|imil|ian (English writer)
beer gar|den +s
beer hall +s
beer|i|er
beer|i|est
beer|i|ly
beer|i|ness
beer mat +s
beer|nut +s
Beers, Wil|liam George (Cdn lacrosse promoter & dentist)
Beer|sheba (city, Israel)
beery
  beer|i|er
  beer|i|est
bee-stung
bees|wax
  bees|wax|es
  bees|waxed
  bees|wax|ing
beet +s (plant)
[☞ beat]
Beethov|en, Lud|wig van (German composer)
Beethov|en|ian +s
bee|tle (insect, scurry; tool, machine; crush; overhang, project)
  bee|tles
  bee|tled
  bee|tling
[☞ beadle, betel]
beetle-browed
bee|tling *adjective*
beet|root +s
beeves
be|fall
  be|falls
  be|fell
  be|fall|en
  be|fall|ing
befit
  be|fits
  be|fit|ted
  be|fit|ting
be|fit|ting *adjective*
be|fit|ting|ly
befog
  be|fogs
  be|fogged
  be|fog|ging
be|fool +s +ed +ing
be|fore
be|fore|hand
be|foul +s +ed +ing
be|foul|ment +s
be|friend +s +ed +ing

be|fuddle
be|fud|dles
be|fud|dled
be|fud|dling
be|fuddle|ment +s
beg
begs
begged
beg|ging
begad
began *past tense of*
begin
[☞ Begin, Bégon]
begat
Beg|bie, Sir Mat|thew
Bail|lie (English-
born Cdn judge)
beget
be|gets
begat *or* begot
be|got|ten
be|get|ting
be|get|ter +s
beg|gar +s +ed +ing
beg|gar|li|ness
beg|gar|ly
beggar-my-
neighbour
(= beggar-thy-
neighbour)
beggar-thy-
neighbour
beg|gary
Begin, Men|achem
Wolf|ovitch (Israeli
prime minister)
[☞ Bégon]
begin (start)
be|gins
began
begun
be|gin|ning
be|gin|ner +s
be|ginner's luck
be|gin|ning +s
Bégon (de La
Picar|dière), Michel
(intendant of New
France)
[☞ Begin]
be|gone
be|gonia +s
be|gorra
begot *past tense of*
beget
be|got|ten *past
participle of* beget
be|grimed
be|grudge
be|grudg|es
be|grudged
be|grudg|ing
be|grudg|ing|ly

be|guile
be|guiles
be|guiled
be|guil|ing
be|guile|ment +s
be|guil|er +s
be|guil|ing *adjective*
be|guil|ing|ly
be|guine +s
Begum (title of
Muslim woman)
begum +s (high-
ranking Muslim
woman)
begun
be|half
Behan, Bren|dan
Fran|cis (Irish
writer)
be|have
be|haves
be|haved
be|hav|ing
be|hav|ior +s (*use*
behaviour)
be|hav|ior|al (*use*
behavioural)
be|hav|ior|al|ist +s
(*use* behaviouralist)
be|hav|ior|ism (*use*
behaviourism)
be|hav|ior|ist +s (*use*
behaviourist)
be|hav|ior|is|tic (*use*
behaviouristic)
be|hav|iour +s
be|hav|iour|al
be|hav|iour|al|ist +s
be|hav|iour|ism
be|hav|iour|ist +s
be|hav|iour|is|tic
be|head +s +ed +ing
be|head|ing +s *noun*
be|held
be|he|moth +s
be|hest +s (command,
request)
[☞ bequest]
be|hind +s
behind|hand
Behn, Aphra (English
author)
be|hold
be|holds
be|held
be|hold|ing
be|hold|en
be|hold|er +s
be|hoof
be|hoove
be|hooves
be|hooved
be|hoov|ing

be|hove (*use* behoove)
be|hoves
be|hoved
be|hov|ing
Behr|ens, Peter
(German architect)
Behr|ing, Emil Adolf
von (German
immunologist)
Beider|becke, Leon
Bis|marck ('Bix')
(US musician)
beige +s
bei|gnet +s
Beijing (capital of
China)
be|ing +s
Beira (port,
Mozambique)
Bei|rut (capital of
Lebanon)
be|jab|bers
be|jabers
(= bejabbers)
Béjart, Mau|rice
(French-born
choreographer)
be|jasus
be|jesus
be|jew|elled
Bekaa (valley,
Lebanon)
Bel (fertility god)
[☞ Bell]
bel +s (ten decibels)
[☞ bell, belle]
be|labor +s +ed +ing
(*use* belabour)
be|labour +s +ed
+ing
Bela|fonte, Har|old
George ('Harry')
(US singer)
Bel and the Drag|on
(*Apocrypha*)
Bel|aney, Archi|bald
Stans|feld (Grey
Owl)
Bela|rus (country,
Europe)
Bela|ru|sian +s (of
Belarus; language)
[☞ Belorussian,
Byelorussian]
Bela|rus|sian +s (*use*
Belarusian)
be|lated
be|lated|ly
be|lated|ness
Belau (= Palau)
be|lay +s +ed +ing
[☞ Bellay]
bel canto

belch
belch|es
belched
belch|ing
Bel|cher +s (islands,
Canada)
Bel|cher, Jona|than
(Cdn lawyer & judge)
bel|dam +s
bel|dame +s (*use*
beldam)
be|lea|guer +s +ed
+ing
be|lea|guered
adjective
Belém (city, Brazil)
belem|nite +s
bel es|prit
beaux es|prits
Bel|fast (capital of
Northern Ireland)
bel|fry
bel|fries
Bel|gae
Bel|gaum (city, India)
Bel|gian
Bel|gic
Bel|gium (country,
Europe)
Bel|gorod (city,
Russia)
Bel|grade (capital of
Yugoslavia)
Belial (*Bible*)
belie
be|lies
be|lied
be|lying
be|lief +s
be|liev|abil|ity
be|liev|able
be|liev|ably
be|lieve
be|lieves
be|lieved
be|liev|ing
be|liev|er +s
be|like
Beli|sar|ius
(Byzantine general)
Be|li|sha bea|con +s
be|little
be|lit|tles
be|lit|tled
be|lit|tling
be|little|ment +s
be|lit|tler +s
be|lit|tling|ly
Be|li|tung (island,
Indonesia)
Béli|veau, Jean (Cdn
hockey player)

Bel|ize (country & its former capital, Central America)
Beliz|ean +s
Bell (island, Canada)
[☞ Bel]
Bell, Acton (Anne Brontë)
Bell, Alex|an|der Gra|ham (inventor of telephone)
Bell, Cur|rer (Charlotte Brontë)
Bell, Ellis (Emily Brontë)
Bell, Mari|lyn (Cdn swimmer)
Bell, Van|essa (English painter & designer)
bell +s +ed +ing (object that rings, etc.; cry of a stag)
[☞ bel, belle]
Bella Bella (= Heiltsuk)
plural Bella Bella
Bella Coola (= Nuxalk)
plural Bella Coola
bella|don|na +s
Bella|trix (star)
Bel|lay, Joa|chim du (French poet)
[☞ belay]
bell|bird +s
bell-bottom +s
bell-bottomed
bell|boy +s (bellhop)
bell buoy +s (buoy equipped with a bell)
bell|cast
bell curve +s
belle +s (beautiful woman)
[☞ bell, bel]
belle époque
belles époques
Belle Isle (strait, Canada)
Bel|lero|phon (Greek Myth)
belles let|tres
bell|let|rism
bell|let|rist +s
bell|let|ris|tic
Belle|ville (city, Canada)
bell|flower +s
bell glass
bell glass|es
bell|hop +s
bell|li|cose

bell|li|cos|ity
bell|lied adjective (in 'pot-bellied' etc.)
[☞ belied]
bel|liger|ence
bel|liger|ency
bel|liger|ent +s
bel|liger|ent|ly
Bel|lings|hau|sen (sea)
Bel|lini, Gen|tile (Venetian painter)
Bel|lini, Gio|van|ni (Venetian painter)
Bel|lini, Jac|opo (Venetian painter)
Bel|lini, Vin|cen|zo (Italian composer)
bell|man
bell|men
Bel|loc, Hil|aire (French-born writer)
Bel|lona (Roman Myth)
Bel|lot (strait, Canada)
Bel|low, Saul (Cdn-born US novelist)
bell|low +s +ed +ing (roar)
[☞ below]
bell|lows (for blowing air; Music; Optics)
plural bell|lows
bell pull +s
bell push
bell push|es
bell-ringer +s
bell-ringing +s
Bell's palsy
bell|wether +s
bell|wort +s
belly
bell|lies
bell|lied
belly|ing
belly|ache
belly|aches
belly|ached
belly|ach|ing
belly|acher +s
belly|band +s
belly but|ton +s
belly dance +s
belly dan|cer +s
belly dan|cing
belly flop +s noun
belly-flop verb
belly-flops
belly-flopped
belly-flopping
belly|ful +s
belly land|ing +s
belly laugh +s

belly up adjective & verb
bell|lies up
bell|lied up
belly|ing up
Bel|mont Stakes
Bel|mo|pan (capital of Belize)
Belœil (city, Canada)
Belo Hori|zonte (city, Brazil)
be|long +s +ed +ing
be|long|ing noun
be|long|ing|ness
be|long|ings noun
Belo|rus|sia (a former name for Belarus)
Belo|rus|sian +s (of Belorussia; for language use Belarusian)
[☞ Belarusian]
Belo|stok (= Białystok, Poland)
be|lov|ed (beneath)
below (beneath)
[☞ bellow]
Bel Paese proprietary
Bel|sen (concentration camp, Germany)
Bel|shazzar (king of Babylon)
bel|snickle +s
belt +s +ed +ing
Bel|tane
belt|ed adjective
belt|er +s
belt|line +s
Belt|way (Washington, DC)
belt|way +s (highway)
be|luga +s
bel|ve|dere +s
bely|ing present participle of belie
Bembo
be|med|alled
be|mire
be|mires
be|mired
be|mir|ing
be|moan +s +ed +ing
be|muse
be|muses
be|mused
be|mus|ing
be|mused adjective
be|mus|ed|ly
be|muse|ment
ben +s (mountain)
[☞ Behn]

Ben|ares (former name for Varanasi, India)
Bena|vente y Mar|tínez, Ja|cin|to (Spanish writer)
Ben Bella, Moham|med Ahmed (Algerian statesman)
bench
bench|es
benched
bench|ing
bench-clearing
bench|er +s
bench|land +s
bench|mark +s
bench press noun
bench press|es
bench-press verb
bench-presses
bench-pressed
bench-pressing
bench test +s +ed +ing
bench|warm|er +s
bench-warming
bench war|rant +s
bend
bends
bent
bend|ing
bend|able
bend|er +s
Ben|digo (town, Australia)
bend|i|ness
bends (decompression sickness)
bend sin|is|ter
bends sin|is|ter
bendy
bend|i|er
bend|i|est
be|neath
bene|di|cite +s
Bene|dict (saint; popes)
Bene|dict|ine +s
• (monk or nun)
• proprietary (liqueur)
Bene|dic|tion +s (Roman Catholic service)
bene|dic|tion +s (utterance of a blessing; blessedness)
Bene|dic|tus
bene|fac|tion +s
bene|fac|tor +s
bene|fac|tress
bene|fac|tress|es

bene|fice +s
bene|ficed
be|nefi|cence
be|nefi|cent
be|nefi|cent|ly
bene|fi|cial
bene|fi|cial|ly
bene|fici|ary
  bene|fici|aries
bene|fit
  bene|fits
  bene|fit|ed or
  bene|fit|ted
  bene|fit|ing or
  bene|fit|ting
Bene|lux (Belgium, the Netherlands, Luxembourg)
Beneš, Ed|vard (Czechoslovak politician)
Benesh (dance notation)
Benét, Ste|phen Vin|cent (US writer)
be|nevo|lence
be|nevo|lent
be|nevo|lent|ly
Ben|gal (region, India; bay, Indian Ocean; tiger)
Ben|gali +s
ben|ga|line
Ben|ghazi (port, Libya)
Ben|guela (port, Angola)
Ben-Gurion, David (Israeli prime minister)
be|night|ed
be|night|ed|ness
be|nign
be|nig|nancy
be|nig|nant
be|nig|nant|ly
be|nig|nity
  be|nig|ni|ties
be|nign|ly
Benin (country & bight, Africa)
Benin|ese
  plural Benin|ese
beni|son +s
Ben|ja|min (Bible)
Ben|ja|min, Wal|ter (German literary critic)
ben|ja|mina ficus (= Ficus benjamina)
Ben|jamin's fig +s

Ben|nett, (Enoch) Ar|nold (English novelist)
Ben|nett, James Gor|don (US newspaper editor)
Ben|nett, Rich|ard Bed|ford, Vis|count (Cdn prime minister)
Ben|nett, Rich|ard Rod|ney (English composer)
Ben|nett, Wil|liam An|drew Cecil ('Wacky') (1900–79; Cdn politician)
Ben|nett, Wil|liam Rich|ards ('Bill') (b.1932; Cdn politician)
Ben|nett buggy
  Ben|nett bug|gies
Ben Nevis (mountain, Scotland)
Benny, Jack (US comedian)
benny (amphetamine)
  ben|nies
Be|noît, Jehane ('Madame') (Cdn chef)
Be|noît de Sainte-Maure (French trouvère)
ben|omyl
Ben|oni (city, South Africa)
bent +s adjective & noun
bent grass
  bent grass|es
Ben|tham, Jer|emy (English philosopher)
Ben|tham|ism
Ben|tham|ite +s
ben|thic
ben|thos
Ben|tinck, Wil|liam Henry Cav|en|dish (3rd Duke of Portland, English statesman)
Bent|ley, Ed|mund Cleri|hew (English writer)
Ben|ton, Thom|as Hart (US painter)
ben|ton|ite
bent|wood
be|numb +s +ed +ing
Benxi (city, China)
Benz, Karl Fried|rich (German automobile pioneer)

Ben|ze|drine proprietary
ben|zene
  [☞ benzine]
ben|zene ring +s
ben|zen|oid
ben|zine
  [☞ benzene]
benzo|di|azep|ine +s
ben|zo|ic
ben|zo|in
ben|zol
ben|zole (use benzol)
ben|zoyl
ben|zyl
Beo|grad (= Belgrade, Yugoslavia)
Beo|thuck (use Beothuk)
  plural Beo|thuck or Beo|thucks
Beo|thuk
  plural Beo|thuk or Beo|thuks
Beo|wulf (Scandinavian Myth)
be|queath +s +ed +ing
be|queath|able
be|queath|al +s
be|queath|er +s
be|quest +s (legacy; act of bequeathing)
  [☞ behest]
be|rate
  be|rates
  be|rat|ed
  be|rat|ing
Ber|ber +s (people; language)
ber|ber +s (carpet)
Ber|bera (port, Somalia)
ber|beris
ber|ceuse +s
Berch|tes|gaden (town, Germany)
Berczy, Wil|liam (Cdn painter)
ber|dache +s
ber|dach|ism
ber|dash (use berdache)
  ber|dash|es
Ber|dya|yev, Niko|lai Alek|san|dro|vich (Russian philosopher)
be|reave
  be|reaves
  be|reaved or bereft
  be|reav|ing

be|reaved adjective (saddened by loss)
be|reave|ment +s
be|reft adjective (deprived)
bereft|ness
Beren|son, Ber|nard (US art historian)
Beres|ford (town, Canada)
Beresford-Howe, Con|stance (Cdn novelist)
beret +s (hat)
  [☞ Barrett, barrette]
Berg, Alban (Austrian composer)
berg +s (iceberg)
  [☞ burg]
ber|ga|mot +s
Ber|gen (port, Norway)
Bergen-Belsen (concentration camp, Germany)
ber|genia +s
Ber|ger, Hans (German psychiatrist)
  [☞ burger, burgher]
Ber|gerac (region & town, France)
Ber|gerac, Cyr|ano de (French soldier & writer)
Ber|gius, Fried|rich Karl Ru|dolf (German chemist)
Berg|man, Ing|mar (Swedish filmmaker)
Berg|man, Ing|rid (Swedish actress)
berg|schrund +s
Berg|son, Henri (French philosopher)
Berg|son|ian
bergy bit +s
Beria, Lav|renti Pav|lo|vich (head of Soviet secret police)
be|ribboned
beri|beri
Ber|ing, Vitus Jonas|sen (Danish explorer)
  [☞ Behring]
Ber|ing (N Pacific sea & strait)
  [☞ Behring]
be|ringed

Berio, Lu|ciano
(Italian composer)
berk +s (fool)
[☞ Burke]
Berke|ley (city,
California)
Berke|ley, Busby (US
choreographer)
Berke|ley, George
(Irish-born
philosopher)
Berke|ley, Sir
Len|nox Ran|dall
Fran|cis (English
composer)
ber|kel|ium
Berk|shire (county,
England)
Berle, Mil|ton (US
comedian)
[☞ birl, burl]
Ber|lin (capital of
Germany)
Ber|lin, Irv|ing (US
songwriter)
Ber|lin, Sir Isaiah
(British philosopher)
Ber|lioz, Hec|tor
(French composer)
berm +s
Ber|muda +s
(country; shorts;
grass; onion)
Ber|mud|an +s
(= Bermudian)
Ber|mud|ian +s
Bern (= Berne,
Switzerland)
[☞ Burne-Jones,
bourn, burn]
Ber|na|dette (French
saint)
Ber|na|dotte, Folke,
Count (Swedish
statesman)
Ber|na|dotte, Jean
Bap|tiste Jules (King
Charles of Sweden)
Ber|nanos, George
(French writer)
Ber|nard (saints)
[☞ Barnard]
Ber|nard, Claude
(French physiologist)
[☞ Barnard]
Ber|nardi, Mario
(Cdn conductor)
Berne (capital of
Switzerland)
[☞ Burne-Jones,
bourn, burn]
Bern|ese (of Bern)
plural Bern|ese
[☞ Béarnaise]

Bern|hardt, Sarah
(French actress)
Ber|nières
(community,
Canada)
Bernières-Saint-
Nicolas
(city, Canada)
Ber|nini,
Gian|lor|enzo
(Italian artist)
Ber|noulli, Dan|iel
(Swiss
mathematician)
Ber|noulli, Jakob
(Swiss
mathematician)
Ber|noulli, Jo|hann
(Swiss
mathematician)
Bern|stein, Leon|ard
(US musician)
Berra, Law|rence
Peter ('Yogi') (US
baseball player)
ber|ried (having
berries; egg-bearing)
[☞ buried]
Berry (former
province of France)
[☞ Barrie, Barry]
Berry, Charles
Ed|ward ('Chuck')
(US musician)
[☞ Barrie, Barry]
berry (fruit)
ber|ries
[☞ bury]
berry|ing noun
(gathering berries)
[☞ burying]
Berry|man, John (US
poet)
berry spoon +s
ber|serk +s
ber|serk|er +s
berth +s +ed +ing
(bunk; position;
Nautical; Sport;
Forestry)
[☞ birth]
bertha +s
Ber|to|lucci,
Ber|nar|do (Italian
filmmaker)
Ber|ton, Pierre (Cdn
writer)
[☞ Burton]
Ber|wick|shire
(former county,
Scotland)
Berwick-upon-
Tweed
(town, England)

beryl +s (precious
stone)
beryl|lium
Ber|zel|ius, Jöns
Jakob (Swedish
chemist)
Bes (Egyptian Myth)
Besan|çon (city,
France)
Bes|ant, Annie
(English social
reformer)
be|seech
be|seech|es
be|sought or
be|seeched
be|seech|ing
be|seech|ing adjective
be|seech|ing|ly
beset
besets
beset
beset|ting
beset|ment +s
beset|ting adjective
be|side
be|sides
be|siege
be|sieges
be|sieged
be|sieging
be|sieger +s
be|smear +s +ed
+ing
be|smirch
be|smirch|es
be|smirched
be|smirch|ing
besom +s
be|sot|ted (infatuated;
stupefied)
be|sought past & past
participle of beseech
be|spatter +s +ed
+ing
be|speak
be|speaks
be|spoke
be|spoken
be|speak|ing
be|spec|tacled
be|spoke adjective &
past tense of bespeak
be|spoken past
participle of bespeak
be|sprinkle
be|sprinkles
be|sprinkled
be|sprink|ling
Bes|sar|abia (region,
Europe)
Bes|sar|abian +s
Bess|bor|ough, Vere
Brab|azon

Pon|son|by, 9th Earl
of (governor general
of Canada)
Bes|sel, Fried|rich
Wil|helm (German
astronomer)
Bes|semer (converter;
process)
Bes|semer, Sir Henry
(English engineer)
Bes|sette, Gé|rard
(Cdn writer)
Best, Charles
Her|bert (Cdn co-
discoverer of insulin)
best +s +ed +ing
best-before date +s
best boy +s
bes|tial
bes|ti|al|ity
bes|ti|al|ities
bes|tial|ize
bes|tial|iz|es
bes|tial|ized
bes|tial|iz|ing
bes|tial|ly
bes|ti|ary
bes|ti|aries
be|stir
be|stirs
be|stirred
be|stir|ring
best man
best men
be|stow +s +ed +ing
be|stow|al +s
be|strew
be|strews
be|strewed
be|strewed or
be|strewn
be|strew|ing
be|stride
be|strides
be|strode
be|strid|den
be|strid|ing
best-seller +s
best|seller|dom
best-selling
bet
bets
bet or betted
bet|ting
Beta (= Betamax)
[☞ Bethe]
beta +s (Greek letter)
beta block|er +s
beta car|ot|ene
be|take
be|takes
be|took
be|taken
be|tak|ing

Beta|max *proprietary*
Beta|maxes
beta par|ticle +s
beta radi|ation
beta ray +s
beta re|cep|tor +s
beta test +s *noun*
beta-test +s +ed +ing
verb
beta|tron +s
beta ver|sion +s
betel +s (leaf)
Betel|geuse (star)
betel nut +s
bête noire
bêtes noires
Bethe, Hans
Al|brecht (US
physicist)
be|think
be|thinks
be|thought
be|think|ing
Beth|le|hem (town,
Israel)
Beth|mann Holl|weg,
Theo|bald von
(German chancellor)
Be|thune, Henry
Nor|man (Cdn
surgeon)
be|tide
be|times
bêt|ise +s
Betje|man, Sir John
(English poet)
be|token +s +ed +ing
bet|ony
bet|onies
be|took
be|tray +s +ed +ing
be|tray|al +s
be|tray|er +s
be|troth +s +ed +ing
be|troth|al +s
be|trothed *noun &*
adjective:
plural be|trothed
Bet|tel|heim, Bruno
(US psychologist)
bet|ter +s +ed +ing
(comparative of
good or well; a
better thing;
improve)
[☞ bettor]
better|ment
Bet|ter|ton, Thom|as
(English actor)
Betti, Ugo (Italian
writer)
bet|ting *noun*

bet|tor +s (one who
bets)
[☞ better]
be|tween
be|twixt
Beur|ling, George
Fred|erick ('Buzz')
(Cdn pilot)
beurre blanc
Beuys, Jo|seph
(German sculptor)
[☞ Boyce]
Bevan, An|eurin
('Nye') (English
politician)
bevel
bev|els
bev|elled
bevel|ling
bev|er|age +s (drink)
[☞ Beveridge]
Bev|er|idge, Wil|liam
Henry, 1st Baron
(British economist)
[☞ beverage]
Bev|er|ly Hills (city,
California)
Bevin, Er|nest
(English statesman)
bevy
bev|ies
be|wail +s +ed +ing
be|wail|er +s
be|ware
be|whis|kered
Bew|ick, Thom|as
(English artist)
be|wil|der +s +ed
+ing
be|wil|dered *adjective*
be|wil|dered|ly
be|wil|der|ing
adjective
be|wil|der|ing|ly
bew|il|der|ment
be|witch
be|witch|es
be|witched
be|witch|ing
be|witch|ing *adjective*
be|witch|ing|ly
be|witch|ment
bey +s (Ottoman
governor)
[☞ bay]
Bey|non, Wil|liam
(Cdn ethnographer)
be|yond
bez|ant +s
bez|el +s
bez|ique +s
be|zoar +s

BGH (bovine growth
hormone)
Bhagavad-Gita
bhajan +s
bhaji +s
bhakti
Bhakti|vedan|ta,
Abhay
Chara|na|ra|vinda
(Hare Krishna
leader)
bhang (drug)
bhan|gra
bhar|al +s
Bha|ra|tiya Jan|ata
Party
Bhar|at|pur (bird
sanctuary, India)
Bhav|nagar (port,
India)
Bho|pal (city, India)
b.h.p. (brake
horsepower)
BHT (butylated
hydroxytoluene)
Bhuba|nesh|war (city,
India)
Bhu|tan (kingdom,
Himalayas)
Bhu|tan|ese
plural Bhu|tan|ese
Bhut|to, Bena|zir
(Pakistani president)
Bhut|to, Zul|fikar Ali
(Pakistani president)
bi +s (bisexual;
bilingualism;
biculturalism)
BIA (business
improvement
association)
BIAs
Bi|afra (former state,
Africa)
Bi|af|ran +s
Biały|stok (city,
Poland)
bi|annu|al (twice a
year)
[☞ biennial]
bi|annu|al|ly (twice a
year)
[☞ biennially]
Biar|ritz (resort,
France)
bias
bias|es
biased
bias|ing
biased *adjective*
bias-ply
bi|ath|lete +s
bi|ath|lon +s

bi|axial
bib (clothing covering,
chest patch; fish; to
drink)
bibs
bibbed
bib|bing
[☞ bibb]
bibb +s (lettuce)
[☞ bib]
bib|ber +s
bib|bing *noun*
bib|cock +s
bibe +s
bibe|lot +s
Bible +s (Jewish or
Christian scriptures)
bible +s (any
authoritative book)
Bible bash|er +s
Bible bash|ing
Bible belt +s
Bible col|lege +s
Bible oath +s
Bible school +s
Bible-thumper +s
Bible-thumping
Bib|lical (of the Bible)
bib|lical
bib|lical|ly
bibli|og|raph|er +s
bib|lio|graph|ic
bib|lio|graph|ic|al
bib|lio|graph|ic|al|ly
bibli|og|raphy
bibli|og|raph|ies
bib|lio|mancy
bib|lio|mania
bib|lio|maniac +s
bib|lio|phile +s
bib|lio|phil|ic
bibli|oph|ily
bib|lio|pole +s
bibu|lous
bibu|lous|ly
bibu|lous|ness
Bic +s *proprietary*
bi|cam|eral
bi|cam|eral|ism
bi|carb
bi|car|bon|ate +s
bi|cen|ten|ary
bi|cen|ten|aries
bi|cen|ten|nial +s
bi|cep +s (*use* biceps)
• Although *bicep* is
becoming more
common in informal
use, *biceps* remains
standard as the
singular noun.
bi|ceph|al|ous

bi|ceps
  plural bi|ceps
bick|er +s +ed +ing
bick|er|er +s
Bick|ert, Ed|ward
  Isaac (Cdn guitarist)
bi|coast|al
bi|col|our +s
bi|col|oured
bi|con|cave
bi|con|vex
bi|cultur|al
bi|cultur|al|ism
bi|cus|pid +s
bi|cus|pid|ate
bi|cycle
  bi|cycles
  bi|cycled
  bi|cyc|ling
bi|cycler +s
bi|cyclic
bi|cyc|list +s
bid
• (state what one
  would pay or charge;
  Cards)
  bids
  bid
  bid|ding
• (command, invite)
  bids
  bid or bade
  bid or bid|den
  bid|ding
• (utter)
  bids
  bade or bid
  bid|den or bid
  bid|ding
bid|dabil|ity
bid|dable
bid|den *conjugated
form of* bid
bid|der +s
bid|ding *noun*
Bid|dle, John (English
  theologian)
biddy
  bid|dies
bide
  bides
  bided
  biding
bi|det +s
bi|direc|tion|al
Bid|well, Mar|shall
  Spring (Cdn
  politician)
Bieder|meier
Blele|feld (city,
  Germany)
Bi|en|nale +s
  (Venetian festival)

bi|en|nale +s (any
  biennial exhibition or
  festival)
bi|enni|al +s (every
  two years; lasting
  two years)
  [☞ biannual]
bi|enni|al|ly (every
  two years; lasting
  two years)
  [☞ biannually]
bi|enni|um
  bi|enni|ums or
  bi|ennia
bien pen|sant +s
bier +s (stand for
  coffin)
Bierce, Am|brose
  Gwin|nett (US
  writer)
bier|wurst +s
bi|face +s
bi|facial
bi|facial|ly
biff +s +ed +ing
bif|fin +s
biffy
  bif|fies
bifid
bi|focal +s
bi|fold +s
bi|fur|cate
  bi|fur|cates
  bi|fur|cat|ed
  bi|fur|cat|ing
bi|fur|ca|tion +s
big
  big|ger
  big|gest
biga|mist +s
biga|mous
big|amy
  biga|mies
Big Bear (Cree leader)
Big Dip|per
  (constellation)
Big|foot
big|gie +s
big|gish
big head +s
big-headed
big-headed|ness
big-hearted
big|horn +s
big house +s
bight +s (inlet; loop)
  [☞ bite, byte]
big|leaf maple +s
big league +s *noun*
big-league *adjective*
big-leaguer +s
big|mouth +s
big|ness

big noise +s
Bigot, Fran|çois
  (intendant of New
  France)
big|ot +s
big|ot|ed
big|otry
  big|ot|ries
bigs
big shot +s
big-ticket
big time +s *noun*
big-time *adjective*
big-timer +s
big|tooth aspen +s
big top +s
bi|guine +s (*use*
  beguine)
big wheel +s
big|wig +s
Bihar (state, India)
Bi|hari +s
bijou
  bi|joux
bike
  bikes
  biked
  bik|ing
bik|er +s
bike|way +s
Bi|kini (atoll, Pacific)
bi|kini +s (bathing suit
  etc.)
bi|ki|nied
Biko, Ste|phen (South
  African activist)
bi|labi|al
bi|lat|eral
bi|lat|eral|ly
bi|layer +s
Bil|bao (city, Spain)
bil|berry
  bil|ber|ries
bilbo (sword)
  plural bil|bos or
  bil|boes
  [☞ bilboes]
bil|boes (ankle
  shackles)
  [☞ bilbo]
Bil|dungs|roman
  Bil|dungs|romane or
  Bil|dungs|romans
bile
bi-level +s
bilge
  bilges
  bilged
  bil|ging
bil|har|zia
bil|har|zia|sis
bili|ary
bi|lin|gual +s

bi|lin|gual|ism
bi|lin|gual|ize
  bi|lin|gual|iz|es
  bi|lin|gual|ized
  bi|lin|gual|iz|ing
bi|lin|gual|ly
bil|ious
bil|ious|ly
bil|ious|ness
bili|rubin
bilk +s +ed +ing
bilk|er +s
bill +s +ed +ing
bill|able
bill|la|bong +s
bill|board +s
billed *adjective*
bil|let
  bil|lets
  bil|let|ed
  bil|let|ing
billet-doux
  billets-doux
bil|let|ee +s
bil|let|er +s
bill|fish
  plural bill|fish or
  bill|fish|es
bill|fold +s
bill|hook +s
bil|liard +s
bill|ing +s *noun*
Bil|lings|gate (market,
  London)
bil|lion
  plural bil|lion or
  bil|lions
bil|lion|aire +s
bil|lionth +s
Bill of Rights (of a
  specific country)
bill of rights (any
  statement of rights)
  bills of rights
bil|lon
bil|low +s +ed +ing
bil|lowy
bill|post|er +s
bill|post|ing
billy
  bil|lies
billy|can +s
billy club +s
billy goat +s
billy-oh
Billy the Kid (US
  outlaw)
bi|lob|ate
bi|lobed
bima +s (*usc* bimah)
bimah +s
bi|manu|al
bim|bette +s

bim|bo +s
bi|metal (of two metals)
bi|metal|lic (of two metals; *Currency*)
bi|metal|lism
bi|mil|len|ary
  bi|mil|len|aries
bi|modal
bi|modal|ity
  bi|modal|ities
bi|molecu|lar
bi|month|ly
  bi|month|lies
bin (receptacle; store)
  bins
  binned
  bin|ning
  [☞ been]
bi|nary
  bi|nar|ies
bi|nate
bi|nation|al
bin|aural
bind
  binds
  bound
  bind|ing
bind|er +s
bind|er twine +s
bind|ery
  bind|eries
bind|ing +s *noun & adjective*
bind|weed +s
bine +s
Binet, Al|fred (French psychologist)
Binet-Simon test +s
Binet test +s
Bing (cherry)
Bing, Sir Ru|dolph (manager of Metropolitan Opera)
  [☞ Byng]
bing *interjection*
binge
  bin|ges
  binged
  binge|ing or bin|ging
bin|ger +s
bingo +s
bin|nacle +s
bin|ocu|lar +s
bin|ocu|lars
bi|nom|ial +s
bi|nom|ial|ly
bint +s
bio +s
bio|ac|cumu|late
  bio|ac|cumu|lates

bio|ac|cumu|lat|ed
bio|ac|cumu|lat|ing
bio|assay +s
bio|avail|abil|ity
bio|avail|able
bio|cen|o|sis (*use* biocoenosis)
  bio|cen|o|ses
bio|cen|tric
bio|cen|trism
bio|cen|trist +s
bio|chem|ical +s
bio|chem|ical|ly
bio|chem|ist +s
bio|chem|istry
bio|cide +s
bio|coen|o|sis
  bio|coen|o|ses
bio|com|pat|ibil|ity
bio|com|pat|ibil| ities
bio|com|pat|ible
bio|degrad|abil|ity
  bio|degrad|abil|ities
bio|degrad|able
bio|deg|rad|a|tion +s
bio|degrade
  bio|degrades
  bio|degrad|ed
  bio|degrad|ing
bio|divers|ity
bio|dynam|ic
bio|dynam|ics
bio|ener|get|ics
bio|engin|eer +s
bio|engin|eer|ing
bio|ethic|al
bio|ethi|cist +s
bio|ethics
bio|feed|back
bio|flavon|oid +s
bio|gas
bio|gen|esis
bio|gen|etic
bio|genic
bio|geo|graph|ic
bio|geo|graph|ic|al
bio|geog|raphy
biog|raph|er +s
bio|graph|ic
bio|graph|ic|al
biog|raphy
  biog|raph|ies
bio|haz|ard +s
Bioko (island, Equatorial Guinea)
bio|logic
bio|logic|al
bio|logic|al|ly
biol|o|gist +s
biol|ogy
  biol|o|gies

bio|lumin|es|cence
bio|lumin|es|cent
bio|mass
  bio|mass|es
bio|math|emat|ics
bi|ome +s
bio|mech|an|ical
bio|mech|an|ical|ly
bio|mech|an|ics
bio|med|ical
bio|medi|cine
bio|met|ric
bio|met|ric|al
bio|met|ri|cian +s
bio|met|rics
biom|etry
bio|morph +s
bio|morph|ic
bi|on|ic
bi|on|ic|ally
bi|on|ics
bio|nom|ic
bio|nom|ics
bio|physic|al
bio|physi|cist +s
bio|phys|ics
bio|pic
bi|op|sy
  bi|op|sies
  bi|op|sied
  bi|op|sy|ing
bio|region +s
bio|region|al
bio|rhythm +s
bio|rhyth|mic
bio|rhyth|mic|ally
BIOS (basic input output system)
bio|sphere +s
bio|statis|tical
bio|statis|ti|cian +s
bio|statis|tics
bio|synth|esis
  bio|synth|eses
bio|syn|thet|ic
biota +s
bio|tech +s
bio|tech|no|logic|al
bio|tech|nol|ogy
  bio|tech|nol|o|gies
biot|ic
bio|tin
bio|tite +s
bio|type +s
bi|par|tisan
bi|par|tisan|ship
bi|part|ite
bi|ped +s
bi|pedal
bi|pedal|ism
bi|pedal|ity
bi|phenyl +s

bi|pin|nate
bi|plane +s
bi|polar
bi|polar|ity
birch
  birch|es
birch|bark +s
birch broom +s
birch|en
Birch|er +s
birch rod +s
birch|wood
bird +s (animal etc.)
  [☞ Byrd]
bird bath +s
bird|brain +s
bird|brained
bird|cage +s
bird call +s
bird course +s
bird|er +s
bird feed|er +s
bird|house +s
bird|ie
  bird|ies
  bird|ied
  birdie|ing
bird|ing *noun*
bird|life
bird|lime
bird|seed +s
Bird|sell, San|dra (Cdn author)
bird's-eye +s (maple)
bird's-eye prim|rose +s
bird's-eye view +s
bird's-foot (plant)
  bird's-foots
bird|shot
bird's nest (fern; soup)
bird|song +s
bird strike +s
bird|watch|er +s
bird|watch|ing
bi|refrin|gence
bi|refrin|gent
bi|reme +s
bir|etta +s
Bir|gitta (Saint Bridget of Sweden)
biri|ani +s (*use* biryani)
Bir|ken|stock +s *proprietary*
Birks, Henry (Cdn jeweller)
birl +s +ed +ing (spin a floating log)
  [☞ burl, Berle]
birl|ing *noun*

Bir|ming|ham (cities, England & US)
Bir|ney, Earle (Cdn poet)
Biro +s *proprietary*
birr (Ethiopian currency)
plural birr or birrs
[☞ burr, brr]
birth +s +ed +ing (being born; origin; give birth)
[☞ berth]
birth con|trol pill +s
birth|date +s
birth|day +s
birth|ing +s *noun*
birth|mark +s
birth|place +s
birth rate +s
birth|right +s
birth|stone +s
birth weight +s
birth|wort
Birt|wistle, Sir Har|ri|son Paul (English musician)
biry|ani +s
Bis|cay (N Atlantic bay)
bis|cotti
bis|cuit +s
bis|cuity
bi|sect +s +ed +ing
bi|sec|tion +s
bi|sect|or +s
bi|sex|ual +s
bi|sex|u|al|ity
bish
bishes
Bish|kek (capital of Kyrgyzstan)
Bish|op, Eliza|beth (US poet)
Bish|op, Will|iam Avery ('Billy') (Cdn pilot)
bish|op +s
bish|op|ric +s
Bishop's (university, Canada)
Bis|la|ma
Bis|marck (city, US; sea)
Bis|marck, Otto Ed|uard Leo|pold, Prince von (German statesman)
bis|marck +s (doughnut)
bis|muth
bison
plural bison

bisque +s
Bis|sagos (islands off W Africa)
Bis|sau (capital of Guinea-Bissau)
Bis|soon|dath, Neil (Cdn author)
bi|stable
bis|ter +s (*use* bistre)
bis|tort +s
bistre +s
bis|tro +s
bi|sul|fate +s (*use* bisulphate)
bi|sul|phate +s
bit (small piece or part etc.; tool; bridle part; provide with a bit; *Computing*)
bits
bit|ted
bit|ting
[☞ bitts]
bitch
bitch|es
bitched
bitch|ing
bitch|ery
bitch|eries
bitch|i|ly
bitch|i|ness
bitchy
bitch|i|er
bitch|i|est
bite (cut or grip with teeth; be swindled; be bad or unpleasant; *Curling*)
bites
bit
bit|ten
bit|ing
[☞ byte, bight]
biter +s
bite-size (= bite-sized)
bite-sized
Bi|thynia (ancient region, Asia Minor)
bit|ing *adjective*
bit|ing|ly
bit|map +s
bit|mapped
bit|ten
bit|ter +s +er +est
bitter|brush
bit|ter cress
bit|ter|ly
bit|tern +s
bit|ter|ness
bitter|nut +s
bitter|root +s
bitter|sweet +s

bitts (*Nautical*)
bitty
bit|ti|er
bit|ti|est
bitu|men
bitu|min|iz|a|tion
bitu|minize
bitu|min|iz|es
bitu|min|ized
bitu|min|iz|ing
bi|tu|min|ous
bi|valence
bi|valent +s
bi|valve +s
biv|ou|ac
biv|ou|acs
biv|ou|acked
biv|ou|ack|ing
bi|week|ly
bi|week|lies
bi|year|ly
biz
Bi|zard (island, Canada)
bi|zarre (strange)
bi|zarre|ly
bi|zarre|ness
bi|zar|rerie +s
bi|zar|ro
Bi|zerta (port, Tunisia)
Bi|zerte (= Bizerta)
Bizet, Georges (French composer)
Bjerk|nes, Vil|helm Fri|mann Koren (Norwegian meteorologist)
Bjørn|son, Bjørn|stjerne Mar|tin|ius (Norwegian writer)
blab
blabs
blabbed
blab|bing
blab|ber +s
blabber|mouth +s
blab|by
blab|bi|er
blab|bi|est
Black (hills, US; sea)
Black, Con|rad Mof|fat (Cdn newspaper magnate)
Black, David|son (Cdn anthropologist)
Black, Jo|seph (Scottish chemist)
Black, Shir|ley Tem|ple (Shirley Temple)

black +s +ed +ing (colour; person)
black Af|ri|ca
black|amoor +s
black An|gus
black An|gus|es
black|ball +s +ed +ing
Black|beard (English pirate)
black|berry
black|ber|ries
black|ber|ried
black|berry|ing
black|bird +s
black|board +s
black|body
black|bodies
black|buck
plural black|buck
Black|burn (town, England)
black|cap +s
black-capped chick|a|dee +s
Black|comb (mountain, Canada)
black|currant +s
black damp
Black Death
black|en +s +ed +ing
black|ened *adjective*
black Eng|lish
Black|ett, Pat|rick May|nard Stu|art, Baron (English physicist)
black eye +s
black-eyed pea +s
black-eyed Susan +s
black|face
black|fish
plural black|fish
black|fly
black|flies
Black|foot
plural Black|foot or Black|feet
• (group of Aboriginal peoples including Siksika, Blood & Peigan; their language)
• (Blackfoot people living in central Alberta, their language: *use* Siksika)
black-footed alba|tross
black-footed alba|tross|es

Black For|est (region, Germany; cake, torte; ham)
black|guard +s
black|guard|ly
black|head +s
black|ing *noun*
black|ish
black|jack +s
black|lead +s +ed +ing
black|leg
black|legs
black|legged
black|leg|ging
black let|ter (typeface)
black light +s
black|list +s +ed +ing
black lung
black|ly
black|mail +s +ed +ing
black|mail|er +s
Black Maria +s
Black Mass
Black Mass|es
Black|more, Rich|ard Dod|dridge (English author)
Black Moun|tain (writers)
Black Mus|lim +s
black|ness
black out *verb*
blacks out
blacked out
black|ing out
black|out +s *noun*
Black Pan|ther +s
black|poll +s
Black|pool (resort, England)
black pow|der
Black Prince (Edward Plantagenet)
black robe +s
Black Rod
black rot
black|shirt +s
black|smith +s
black|smith|ing
black spot
Black|stone, Sir Wil|liam (English jurist)
black|strap (molasses)
black|tail +s
black|thorn +s

black tie +s (black-tie *when preceding a noun*)
black|top
black|tops
black|topped
black|top|ping
Black Watch (Royal Highland Regiment; tartan)
black|water fever
Black|wood, Fred|erick Tem|ple Ham|il|ton (1st Marquess of Dufferin and Ava, governor general of Canada
Black|wood, David Lloyd (Cdn artist)
blad|der +s
bladder|nut +s
bladder|wort +s
bladder|wrack +s
blade
blades
blad|ed
blad|ing
blad|ed *adjective*
blad|er +s
blad|ing *noun*
blag
blags
blagged
blag|ging
blag|ger +s
blah (nonsense; bland; lethargic)
blah-blah (nonsense)
blah blah blah *interjection*
blahs (depression)
blain +s
Blain|ville (city, Canada)
Blair, An|drew George (Cdn politician)
[☞ **blare**]
Blair, An|thony Charles Lyn|ton ('Tony') (British prime minister)
[☞ **blare**]
Blais, Marie-Claire (Cdn author)
[☞ **Blaise**]
Blaise, Clark (Cdn author)
[☞ **Blais, blaze**]
Blake, Ed|ward (Cdn politician)

Blake, Hec|tor ('Toe') (Cdn hockey player & coach)
Blake, James Huber ('Eubie') (US musician)
Blake, Rob|ert (English parliamentarian commander)
Blake, Wil|liam (English poet & artist)
Blak|ean
Blake|ian (*use* Blakean)
Blake|ney, Allan Emrys (Cdn politician)
Blakey, Ar|thur ('Art') (US drummer)
blam
blams
blammed
blam|ming
blam|able (deserving blame: *use* blameable)
blame
blames
blamed
blam|ing
blame|able
blamed *adjective*
blame|ful
blame|ful|ly
blame|less
blame|less|ly
blame|less|ness
blame|worthi|ness
blame|worthy
blanc de blancs
plural blanc de blancs
blanch
blanch|es
blanched
blanch|ing
Blan|chard, Jean Pierre Fran|çois (French balloonist)
blanc|mange +s
bland +er +est
blan|dish
blan|dish|es
blan|dished
blan|dish|ing
blan|dish|ment +s
bland|ly
bland|ness
blank +s +ed +ing +er +est

blan|ket +s +ed +ing (cover)
[☞ **blanquette**]
blan|ket stitch
blan|ket stitch|es
blan|kety
blankety-blank
blan|kie +s
blank|ly
blank|ness
blan|quette +s (stew)
[☞ **blanket**]
Blan|tyre (city, Malawi)
blare
blares
blared
blar|ing
[☞ **Blair, Port Blair**]
blar|ney +s +ed +ing
Blas|co Ibá|ñez, Vi|cente (Spanish novelist)
blasé
blas|pheme
blas|phemes
blas|phemed
blas|phem|ing
blas|phem|er +s
blas|phem|ous
blas|phem|ous|ly
blas|phemy
blas|phem|ies
blast +s +ed +ing
blast|ed *adjective &*
adverb
blast|er +s
blast|hole +s
blast off *verb*
blasts off
blast|ed off
blast|ing off
blast-off +s *noun*
blas|tula
blas|tu|las or
blas|tu|lae
blasty
blat
blats
blat|ted
blat|ting
bla|tancy
bla|tant
bla|tant|ly
blath|er +s +ed +ing
blath|er|ing +s *noun*
blather|skite +s
Bla|vat|sky, Helen Pet|rovna (Russian spiritualist)
blax|ploit|a|tion

blaze
  blaz|es
  blazed
  blaz|ing
  [☞ Blaise]
blaz|er +s
blaz|ing adjective
blaz|ing|ly
blaz|on +s +ed +ing
blaz|on|er +s
blazon|ment
blaz|onry
bleach
  bleach|es
  bleached
  bleach|ing
bleach|er +s
bleak +er +est +s
bleak|ly
bleak|ness
blear +s +ed +ing
blear|i|ly
blear|i|ness
bleary
  blear|i|er
  blear|i|est
bleary-eyed
bleat +s +ed +ing
bleat|er +s
bleat|ing|ly
bleb +s
blech
bleed
  bleeds
  bled
  bleed|ing
bleed|er +s
bleed|ing adjective &
  adverb
bleep +s +ed +ing
bleep|er +s
blem|ish
  blem|ish|es
  blem|ished
  blem|ish|ing
blench
  blench|es
  blenched
  blench|ing
blend +s +ed +ing
  (mix, mixture,
  combine, etc.)
  [☞ blende]
blende +s
  (Mineralogy)
  [☞ blend]
blend|er +s
Blen|heim (palace,
  England; battle site,
  Bavaria; town,
  Canada)
blen|ny
  blen|nies

blent
bleph|ar|itis
bleph|aro|plasty
  bleph|aro|plas|ties
Blé|riot, Louis
  (French aviator)
bles|bok
  plural bles|bok or
  bles|boks
bles|buck (use
  blesbok)
  plural bles|buck or
  bles|bucks
bless
  bless|es
  blessed
  bless|ing
Bless|ed adjective
  (beatified)
blessed adjective
  (revered, fortunate,
  blissful)
bless|ed|ly
bless|ed|ness
Bless|ed Sac|ra|ment
bless|ing +s noun
blest archaic
  (= blessed)
bleth|er +s +ed +ing
  (= blather)
bleth|er|ing +s noun
  (= blathering)
bleu +s (Quebec
  Conservative)
blew past tense of
  blow
blew|its
  plural blew|its
Bligh, Wil|liam
  (captain of The
  Bounty)
blight +s +ed +ing
blight|er +s
Bligh|ty (Britain)
blimey
Blimp +s
  (reactionary)
blimp +s (airship; fat
  person; camera
  cover)
blimp|ery
blimp|ish
blind +s +ed +ing
  +er +est
blind|er +s noun
blind|fold +s +ed
  +ing
blind gut +s
blind|ing +s noun &
  adjective
blind|ing|ly
blind|ly
blind man's bluff

blind man's buff
  (= blind man's
  bluff)
blind|ness
blind side +s noun
blind|side verb
  blind|sides
  blind|sid|ed
  blind|sid|ing
blind spot +s
blind|stitch
  blind|stitch|es
  blind|stitched
  blind|stitch|ing
blind|worm +s
blini
  plural blini or blinis
blink +s +ed +ing
blink|er +s +ed +ing
blink|ered adjective
blink|ing adjective &
  adverb
blintz
  blintz|es
blintze +s (use blintz)
blip
  blips
  blipped
  blip|ping
Bliss, Sir Ar|thur
  (English composer)
bliss
blissed-out adjective
bliss|ful
bliss|ful|ly
bliss|ful|ness
bliss out verb
  bliss|es out
  blissed out
  bliss|ing out
blis|ter +s +ed +ing
blis|ter|ing adjective
blis|ter|ing|ly
blis|ter pack +s
blis|tery
blithe
  blith|er
  blith|est
blithe|ly
blithe|ness
blith|er +s +ed +ing
blith|er|ing adjective
Blitz (World War II)
blitz
  blitz|es
  blitzed
  blitz|ing
blitzed adjective
blitz|er +s
blitz|krieg +s
Blix|en, Baron|ess
  Karen (Isak Dinesen)
bliz|zard +s +ed +ing

bliz|zardy
bloat +s +ed +ing
bloat|ed adjective
bloat|er +s
blob +s
blobby
  blob|bi|er
  blob|bi|est
Bloc (= Bloc
  Québécois)
bloc +s (coalition,
  alliance)
  [☞ block]
Bloch, Er|nest (US
  composer)
Bloch, Felix (Swiss-
  born physicist)
Bloch, Kon|rad Emil
  (German-born
  biochemist)
block +s +ed +ing (in
  all senses except
  coalition, alliance)
  [☞ bloc, Bloc
  Québécois, Bloc
  populaire canadien]
block|ade
  block|ades
  block|ad|ed
  block|ad|ing
block|ad|er +s
blockade-runner +s
blockade-running
block|age +s
block|board +s
block|bust|er +s
blocked adjective
block|er +s
block|head +s
block|head|ed
block heat|er +s
block|house +s
block|ish
blocky
  block|i|er
  block|i|est
Bloc popu|laire
  cana|dien
Bloc Qué|bé|cois
Bloem|fon|tein
  (judicial capital of
  South Africa)
bloke +s
Blom|idon (cape,
  Canada)
blond +s +er +est
  female or male
blonde female
  blondes
  blond|er
  blond|est
Blon|din, Charles
  (French acrobat)

blond|ish
blond|ness
Blood (people,
language)
plural Blood
blood +s +ed +ing
blood bank +s
blood|bath +s
blood brother +s
blood count +s
blood-curdling
blood|ed *adjective*
blood feud +s
blood group +s
blood|hound +s
blood|i|ly
blood|i|ness
blood|less
blood|less|ly
blood|less|ness
blood|let|ting
blood|line +s
blood lust +s
blood meal
blood money
blood poi|son|ing
blood pres|sure +s
blood pud|ding +s
blood-red
blood|root +s
blood saus|age +s
blood|shed
blood|shot
blood sport +s
blood|stain +s
blood|stained
blood|stock
blood|stone +s
blood|stream +s
blood|suck|er +s
blood|suck|ing
blood sugar
blood test +s
blood|thirst|i|ly
blood|thirst|i|ness
blood|thirsty
 blood|thirst|i|er
 blood|thirst|i|est
blood type +s
blood ves|sel +s
blood work
blood|worm +s
blood-wort +s
bloody
 blood|i|er
 blood|i|est
 blood|ies
 blood|ied
 bloody|ing
Bloody Caesar +s
Bloody Falls (rapids,
Canada)

Bloody Mary +s
 (Mary Tudor; drink)
bloody-minded
bloody-minded|ly
bloody-minded|ness
bloom +s +ed +ing
 (flower, iron, etc.)
 [☞ Blum]
bloom|er +s
bloom|ers
bloom|ery
 bloom|eries
Bloom|field,
 Leon|ard (US
 linguist)
Bloom|field|ian +s
bloom|ing *adjective &
 adverb*
Blooms|bury (area,
 London; group of
 writers etc.)
bloop +s +ed +ing
bloop|er +s
Bloore, Ron|ald (Cdn
 painter)
Blo|quiste +s
blos|som +s +ed +ing
blos|somy
blot
 blots
 blot|ted
 blot|ting
blotch
 blotch|es
 blotched
 blotch|ing
blotchy
 blotch|i|er
 blotch|i|est
blot|ter +s
blot|ting paper
blot|to
blouse
 blous|es
 bloused
 blous|ing
blous|on +s
blow
 blows
 blew
 blown
 blow|ing
blow-by-blow
blow down *verb*
 blows down
 blew down
 blown down
 blowing down
blow|down +s *noun*
blow-dried *adjective*
blow-dry
 blow-dries

blow-dried
blow-drying
blow-dryer +s
blow|er +s
blow|fish
 plural blow|fish
blow|fly
 blow|flies
blow|gun +s
blow|hard +s
blow|hole +s
blow|i|er
blow|i|est
blow job +s
blow|lamp +s
blown
blow out *verb*
 blows out
 blew out
 blown out
 blowing out
blow|out +s *noun*
blow|pipe +s
blows|i|ly
blows|i|ness
blowsy
 blows|i|er
 blows|i|est
blow|torch
 blow|torch|es
blow up *verb*
 blows up
 blew up
 blown up
 blowing up
blow-up +s *noun &
 adjective*
blowy
 blow|i|er
 blow|i|est
blowz|i|ly (*use*
 blowsily)
blowz|i|ness (*use*
 blowsiness)
blowzy (*use* blowsy)
 blowz|i|er
 blowz|i|est
BLT (sandwich)
 BLTs
blub
 blubs
 blubbed
 blub|bing
blub|ber +s +ed +ing
blub|ber|er +s
blub|bery
Blü|cher, Geb|hard
 Lebe|recht von
 (Prussian
 commander)
blu|chers (boots)

bludge
 bludges
 bludged
 bludg|ing
bludg|eon +s +ed
 +ing
bludg|er +s
Blue (mountains,
 Australia, Jamaica &
 US; Nile headwater)
blue (colour etc.)
 blues
 blued
 blu|ing or blue|ing
 bluer
 blu|est
 [☞ *bleu*]
blue|back
 plural blue|back or
 blue|backs
blue-bead lily
 blue-bead lil|ies
Blue|beard +s (fairy-
 tale character;
 murderer)
blue|bell +s
blue beret +s
blue|berry
 blue|ber|ries
blue|bird +s
blue-black
blue blood (noble
 birth)
blue|blood +s
 (aristocrat)
blue-blooded
Blue Bomb|er +s (pro
 football team)
Blue Book +s (record
 of Cdn government
 expenditures)
blue book (British
 Privy Council report;
 index of people or
 cars; exam booklet)
blue|bottle +s
blue box
 blue boxes
blue chip +s (blue-
 chip *when preceding
 a noun*)
blue chip|per +s
blue-collar *adjective*
Blue En|sign
blue-eyed
blue-eyed Mary +s
Blue|fields (port,
 Nicaragua)
blue|fin
 plural blue|fin or
 blue|fins
blue|fish
 plural blue|fish

blue|gill
plural blue|gill or
blue|gills
blue|grass
blue-green
blue hel|met +s
blue|jacket +s
blue jay +s
blue-jeaned
blue jeans
blue-joint
blue line +s
blue|liner +s
blue|ness
Blue|nose +s (Nova
Scotian)
blue|nose +s (prude)
Blue|nos|er +s
(= Bluenose)
blue note +s
blue pages
blue-pencil
blue-pencils
blue-pencilled
blue-pencil|ling
blue peter +s
blue|print +s +ed
+ing
blue rib|bon (blue-
ribbon when
preceding a noun)
Blue Ridge
(mountains, US)
blue rinse noun
blue-rinse adjective
(= blue-rinsed)
blue-rinsed
blues (glum state;
Music)
blue shift
blue|shift|ed
blues|i|er
blues|i|est
blue-sky adjective
blues|man
blues|men
blue|stem +s
blue|stock|ing +s
blue|stone +s
bluesy
blues|i|er
blues|i|est
bluet +s
blue tit +s
blue|tongue
blue|weed
blue-winged
bluey
bluff +s +ed +ing +er
+est
bluff|er +s
bluff|ly
bluff|ness

blu|ing noun
blu|ish
Blum, Léon (French
statesman)
Blumen|bach,
Jo|hann Fried|rich
(German
physiologist)
Blun|den, Ed|mund
Charles (English
poet)
blun|der +s +ed +ing
blunder|buss
blunder|buss|es
blun|der|er +s
blun|der|ing|ly
Blunt, An|thony
Fred|erick (English
art historian & spy)
blunt +s +ed +ing
+er +est
blunt|ly
blunt|ness
blur
blurs
blurred
blur|ring
blurb +s +ed +ing
blur|ri|ness
blur|ry
blur|ri|er
blur|ri|est
blurt +s +ed +ing
blush
blush|es
blushed
blush|ing
blush|er +s
blus|ter +s +ed +ing
blus|te|rer +s
blus|tery
Bly|ton, Enid (English
writer)
BM (British Museum;
Bachelor of
Medicine; bowel
movement)
BMs
BMI (body mass
index)
BMIs
B movie +s
BMX (Cycling)
BMXs
B'nai B'rith
B.O. (body odour; box
office)
boa +s
Boab|dil (sultan of
Granada)
Boa|di|cea (British
tribal queen: use
Boudicca)

boar +s (pig)
[☞ bore, boor,
Boer, Bohr]
board +s +ed +ing
(plank; provision of
meals; load, embark;
lodge)
[☞ bored]
board|er +s (lodger;
person boarding a
ship)
[☞ border]
board foot
board feet
board game +s
board|ing noun
board|ing house
(boarding-house
when preceding a
noun)
board|room +s
board|sail|er +s (use
boardsailor)
board|sail|ing
board|sail|or +s
board|walk +s
boart +s (use bort)
Boas, Franz (US
anthropologist)
[☞ Boaz]
boast +s +ed +ing
boast|er +s
boast|ful
boast|ful|ly
boast|ful|ness
boast|ing|ly
boat +s +ed +ing
boatel +s
boat|er +s
boat|ful +s
boat|hook +s
boat|house +s
boat|ing noun
boat|load +s
boat|man
boat|men
boat neck +s
boat shoe +s
boat|swain +s
boat|swain's chair
+s
boat|yard +s
Boa Vista (city, Brazil)
Boaz (Bible husband of
Ruth)
[☞ Boas]
bob
bobs
bobbed
bob|bing
bob|ber +s
bob|bin +s
bob|binet +s

bob|ble (bob; fumble;
pompom)
bob|bles
bob|bled
bob|bling
[☞ bauble]
bob|bled adjective
bobby
bob|bies
bobby pin +s
bobby socks
bobby soxer +s
Bob|Cat +s
proprietary (front-
end loader)
bob|cat +s (lynx)
bobo|link +s
Bo|bruisk
(= Babruisk,
Belarus)
Bo|bruysk
(= Babruisk,
Belarus)
bob|skate +s
bob|sled
bob|sleds
bob|sled|ded
bob|sled|ding
bob|sled|der +s
bob|sleigh +s +ed
+ing
bob|stay +s
bob|tail +s
bob|white +s
Boc|caccio,
Gio|van|ni (Italian
writer)
bocce
Boc|cher|ini, Luigi
(Italian composer)
bocci (use bocce)
boccie (use bocce)
Boccio|ni, Um|ber|to
(Italian artist)
boc|con|cini
Boche +s offensive
(German)
[☞ Bosch, bosh,
botch]
Bochum (city,
Germany)
bock +s (beer)
[☞ balk, bawk]
BOD (biochemical
oxygen demand)
bod +s (body)
[☞ baud, bawd]
bo|da|cious
bode
bodes
boded
bod|ing
bo|dega +s

Bode's law
Bodh|gaya (village, India)
Bodhi|sat|tva +s
bodh|ran +s (Irish drum)
bod|ice +s
bodice-ripper +s
bod|ied
bod|i|less
bod|i|ly
bod|ing noun
bod|kin +s
Bod|ley, Sir Thom|as (English librarian)
Bo|doni, Giam|bat|tista (Italian printer)
Bod|rum (town, Turkey)
body (Anatomy; mass; group; etc.)
bod|ies
bod|ied
body|ing
[☞ bawdy]
body bag +s
body blow +s
body|build|er +s
body|build|ing
body|check +s +ed +ing
body clock +s
body count +s
body|guard +s
body|man
body|men
body paint +s
body perm +s
body rub +s (body-rub when preceding a noun)
body search
body search|es
body shop +s
body snatch|er +s
body|snatch|ing
body|suit +s
body|surf +s +ed +ing
body|surf|er +s
body|surf|ing noun
body wave +s
body|work
body wrap +s
Boehme, Jakob (= Böhme)
Boe|otia (region of Greece)
Boe|otian +s
Boer +s (Dutch South African)
[☞ Bohr]

Bo|eth|ius (Roman philosopher)
boff +s +ed +ing
bof|fin +s
boffo
Bo|fors gun +s
bog
bogs
bogged
bog|ging
bogan +s
Bo|garde, Sir Dirk (English filmmaker)
Bo|gart, Hum|phrey ('Bogey') (US actor)
bog|bean +s
bogey +s +ed +ing (Golf; evil spirit; nasal mucus)
[☞ bogie]
bogey|man
bogey|men
bog|gi|ness
bog|gle (baffle; hesitate)
bog|gles
bog|gled
bog|gling
[☞ bogle]
boggy (like a bog)
bog|gi|er
bog|gi|est
[☞ bogy]
bogie +s (wheeled undercarriage; cart)
[☞ bogey, boogie]
bog|land +s
bogle +s (scarecrow; evil spirit; nasal mucus)
[☞ boggle]
Bo|gotá (capital of Colombia)
bog-standard
bog|trot|ter +s offensive
bogus
bogus|ly
bogus|ness
bogy (evil spirit, nasal mucus: use bogey)
bogies
[☞ boggy, bogie]
bogy|man (use bogeyman)
bogy|men
Bo Hai (inlet, China)
Bo|hem|ia (region, Czech Republic)
Bo|hem|ian +s (from Bohemia; waxwing)
bo|hem|ian +s (socially

unconventional person)
bo|hem|ian|ism
Böhme, Jakob (German mystic)
boho +s
Bohol (island, the Philippines)
Bohr, Niels Hen|drik David (Danish physicist)
bo|hunk +s offensive
Boi|ar|do, Mat|teo Maria, conte di Scan|diano (Italian poet)
boil +s +ed +ing
Boi|leau, Nico|las full name Nico|las Boileau-Despréaux (French writer)
boil|er +s
boiler|maker +s
boiler|plate +s
boil|ing adjective
boing +s
boing-boing +s
boink +s +ed +ing
Bois|briand (city, Canada)
bois-brûlé +s
Bois-des-Filion (town, Canada)
Boise (city, US)
bois|ter|ous
bois|ter|ous|ly
bois|ter|ous|ness
boîte +s
Boito, Ar|rigo (Italian composer)
Bo|kas|sa, Jean Bédel (African statesman)
bok choy
Bo|khara (= Bukhoro, Uzbekistan)
Boky, Col|lette (Cdn soprano)
bolas (weapon) plural bolas
[☞ bolus]
bold +er +est +s +ed +ing
Bol|den, Charles ('Buddy') (US musician)
bold|er comparative of bold
[☞ boulder]
bold|face
bold|faces
bold|faced
bold|facing

bold|faced adjective
bold|ly
bold|ness
bole +s (stem, trunk; clay)
[☞ boll]
bol|ero +s
bol|ete +s
bol|etus
bol|etus|es or bol|eti
Bol|eyn, Anne (wife of Henry VIII)
Bol|ger, James Bren|dan (New Zealand prime minister)
Bol|ling|broke, Henry St. John, 1st Vis|count (English politician)
Boli|var, Simón (Venezuelan leader)
boli|var +s (Venezuelan currency)
Bo|livia (country, S America)
Bo|liv|ian +s
bo|liv|iano +s
Böll, Hein|rich (German writer)
boll +s (capsule containing seeds; weevil)
[☞ bole]
Bol|land|ists
bol|lard +s
bol|lix
• verb
bol|lix|es
bol|lixed
bol|lix|ing
• plural noun (= bollocks)
bol|lock|ing +s
bol|locks plural noun
[☞ bollix]
boll wee|vil +s
bolo +s
Bol|ogna (city, Italy)
[☞ Boulogne]
bol|ogna +s (luncheon meat)
[☞ Boulogne]
Bol|ognese (of Bologna) plural Bol|ognese
bol|ognese (sauce)
bo|lom|eter +s
bolo|met|ric
bo|lom|etry
Bol|she|vik +s
Bol|she|vism

Bol|she|vist +s
Bol|shie +s
(Bolshevik)
bol|shie +s (left-wing;
rebellious)
bol|shi|ness
Bol|shoi (ballet;
theatre)
Bol|shy (*use* Bolshie)
Bol|shies
bol|ster +s +ed +ing
bol|ster|er +s
Bolt, Rob|ert Oxton
(English dramatist)
[☞ Boult]
bolt +s +ed +ing
bolt|er +s
bolt hole +s (hole for
a bolt)
bolt-hole +s (means
of escape; refuge)
Bol|ton (city, England;
town, Canada)
bolt on *verb*
bolts on
bolt|ed on
bolt|ing on
bolt-on +s *noun &*
adjective
Boltz|mann, Lud|wig
(Austrian physicist)
bolus (soft mass; pill;
pharmaceutical
dose)
bo|lus|es
[☞ bolas]
Bol|zano (city, Italy)
bomb +s +ed +ing
(explosive device;
failure; aerosol can;
long shot; move
quickly)
[☞ bombe, balm,
Baum]
bom|bard +s +ed
+ing (attack with
bombs, etc.)
bom|barde +s (*Music*)
Bom|bar|dier, J.
Ar|mand (Cdn
inventor)
Bom|bar|dier +s
proprietary (vehicle)
bom|bar|dier +s
(*Military*)
bom|bard|ment +s
bom|bar|don +s
bom|bast
bom|bas|tic
bom|bas|tic|ally
Bom|bay (*former name*
for Mumbai, India)

[☞ bomb bay,
bombé]
Bom|bay duck +s
bom|ba|zine +s
bomb bay +s
(compartment in
aircraft)
bombe +s (frozen
dessert)
[☞ bomb]
bom|bé (curved,
rounded)
[☞ Bombay]
bombed *adjective*
bombed-out
bomb|er +s
bomb|er jack|et +s
bomb|let +s
bom|bora +s
bomb|proof
bomb|shell +s
bomb shel|ter +s
bomb|sight +s
(device for aiming
bombs)
bomb site +s (area
devastated by
bombing)
bomb squad +s
Bon (cape, Tunisia)
[☞ Bonn, bawn]
bona fide *adjective &*
adverb
bona fides *noun*:
plural bona fides
Bon|aire (island,
Netherlands Antilles)
bon|an|za +s
Bona|parte (family of
European rulers)
Bona|parte's gull +s
Bona|part|ism
Bona|part|ist +s
bon ap|pé|tit
bona va|can|tia
Bona|ven|ture (saint;
island, Canada)
Bona|vista (town,
cape, bay &
peninsula, Canada)
bon|bon +s
bonce +s
Bond, Ed|ward
(English dramatist)
bond +s +ed +ing
bond|able
bond|age
bond|ed *adjective*
bond|hold|er +s
Bondi (resort,
Australia)
bonds|man
bonds|men

bond store +s
Bône (*former name for*
Annaba, Algeria)
bone (*Anatomy*)
bones
boned
bon|ing
[☞ Beaune]
bone|bed +s
bone-chilling
boned *adjective*
bone-dry
bone|fish
plural bone|fish or
bone|fish|es
bone|head +s
bone|head|ed
bone lazy
bone|less
bone mar|row +s
bone meal
bon|er +s
bone|set +s
bone-setter +s
bone|shak|er +s
bone-tired
bone-weary
bone|yard +s
bon|fire +s
Bon|fire Night
bong +s
bongo
● (drum)
plural bon|gos
● (antelope)
plural bongo or
bon|gos
Bon|heur, Rosa
(French artist)
bon|homie
bon|hom|ous
bon|i|er
bon|i|est
Boni|face (saint;
popes)
bon|i|ness
bon|ito +s
bonk +s +ed +ing
bonk|er +s
bonk|ers
bon mot
bons mots
Bonn (city, Germany)
[☞ Bon, bawn]
Bon|nard, Pierre
(French artist)
bon|net +s
bon|net|ed
bon|net mon|key +s
Bon|ney, Wil|liam H.
(Billy the Kid)
Bon|nie Prince
Char|lie (Charles

Edward Stuart, 'the
Young Pretender')
bon|ni|ly
bon|ni|ness
bonny
bon|ni|er
bon|ni|est
Bonny|ville (town,
Canada)
Bono (Irish musician)
bon|sai +s
(*Horticulture*)
[☞ banzai]
bon|spiel +s
bont|bok
(= bontebok)
plural bont|bok or
bont|boks
bon|te|bok
plural bon|te|bok or
bon|te|boks
bonus
bo|nus|es
bo|nus|ing
bon vi|vant
bon vi|vants or
bons vi|vants
bon vi|veur
bon vi|veurs or
bons vi|veurs
bon voy|age
bony
bon|i|er
bon|i|est
bonze +s
bon|zer
boo
boos
booed
boo|ing
boob +s +ed +ing
boo-bird +s
boo|boo +s
boob tube +s
booby
boob|ies
booby prize +s
booby trap +s *noun*
booby-trap *verb*
booby-traps
booby-trapped
booby-trapping
boo|dle +s
boog|er +s
boogey|man
boogey|men
boog|ie (dance, music)
boog|ies
boog|ied
boogy|ing
[☞ bogie, bougie]
Boog|ie Board +s
proprietary

boog|ie board|ing
boogie-woogie
boo hoo *interjection*
boo-hoo *noun & verb*
boo-hoos
boo-hooed
boo-hooing
boo hoo hoo
   interjection (= boo
   hoo)
book +s +ed +ing
book|able
book|bag +s
book|bind|er +s
book|bind|ing
book|case +s
book club +s
book|end +s +ed
   +ing
book|er +s
Book|er Prize +s
book|ie +s
book|ish
book|ish|ly
book|ish|ness
book|keep|er +s
book|keep|ing
book|let +s
book-louse
   book-lice
book|maker +s
book|making
book|man
   book|men
book|mark +s +ed
   +ing
book|mobile +s
book|plate +s
book|rest +s
book|sell|er +s
book|shelf
   book|shelves
book|shop +s
book-signing +s
book|stall +s
book|stand +s
book|store +s
book val|ue +s
book|worm +s
Boole, George
   (English
   mathematician)
   [☞ boule, buhl]
Bool|ean
boom +s +ed +ing
boom box
   boom boxes
boom chain +s
boom|er +s
boom|er|ang +s +ed
   +ing

boom|ing *noun &
   adjective*
boom|let +s
boom|stick +s
boom town +s
boomy
   boom|i|er
   boom|i|est
boon +s
boon|docks
boon|dog|gle
   boon|dog|gles
   boon|dog|gled
   boon|dog|gling
Boone, Dan|iel (US
   folk hero)
boon|ies
boor +s (rude or
   clumsy person)
   [☞ boar, bore,
   Boer, Bohr]
boor|ish
boor|ish|ly
boor|ish|ness
boost +s +ed +ing
boost|er +s
boost|er cable +s
boost|er|ish
boost|er|ism
boot +s +ed +ing
boot|able
boot|black +s
boot camp +s
boot|ed *adjective*
boot|ee +s (shoe: *use*
   bootie)
   [☞ booty]
Bo|ötes (constellation)
Booth, Edwin
   Thom|as (US actor)
Booth, John Wilkes
   (US assassin)
Booth, Jun|ius
   Bru|tus (US actor)
Booth, Wil|liam
   (Salvation Army
   founder)
booth +s (small
   enclosed area)
Booth|ia (gulf &
   peninsula, Canada)
boot|ie +s (shoe)
   [☞ booty]
boot|jack +s
boot|lace +s
boot|leg
   boot|legs
   boot|legged
   boot|leg|ging
boot|leg|ger +s
boot|less
boot|lick|er +s
boot|lick|ing

boot|strap
boot|straps
boot|strapped
boot|strap|ping
booty (plunder)
   [☞ bootie, bootee]
booze
   booz|es
   boozed
   booz|ing
booze can +s
booze|hound +s
booz|er +s
booze up *verb*
   booz|es up
   boozed up
   booz|ing up
booze-up +s *noun*
booz|i|ly
booz|i|ness
boozy
   booz|i|er
   booz|i|est
bop
   bops
   bopped
   bop|ping
Bophu|tha|tswa|na
   (former homeland,
   South Africa)
bop|per +s
bora +s
Bora-Bora (island,
   French Polynesia)
bor|acic
bor|age +s
bor|ane +s (*Chemistry*)
   [☞ bodhran]
Borås (city, Sweden)
bor|ate +s
borax
bora|zon
bor|boryg|mic
bor|boryg|mus
   bor|boryg|mi
Bor|deaux (city,
   France; wine)
   plural Bor|deaux
bor|del|lo +s
Bor|den (island &
   peninsula, Canada)
Bor|den, Liz|zie
   An|drew (suspected
   murderer)
Bor|den, Rob|ert
   Laird (Cdn prime
   minister)
bor|der +s +ed +ing
   (edge; adjoin)
   [☞ boarder,
   bordure]
bor|der col|lie +s
bor|der cross|ing +s

bor|der|er +s
border|land +s
border|less
border|line +s
Bor|ders
   (administrative
   region, Scotland)
Bor|det, Jules
   (Belgian
   immunologist)
Bor|duas, Paul-Émile
   (Cdn painter)
bor|dure +s
   (*Heraldry*)
bore (hole; to weary;
   tiresome person;
   wave; past tense of
   bear)
   bores
   bored
   bor|ing
   [☞ boar, Boer,
   Bohr, boor]
bor|eal
Bor|eas (*Greek Myth*)
bored *adjective &
   conjugated form of
   bore*
   [☞ board]
bore|dom
bore|hole +s
bor|er +s
Borg, Bjorn (Swedish
   tennis player)
Borges, Jorge Luis
   (Argentinian writer)
Borgia, Cesare
   (Italian statesman)
Borgia, Lu|cre|zia
   (Italian noblewoman)
Bor|glum, (John)
   Gut|zon (US
   sculptor)
boric
bor|ing *adjective*
bor|ing|ly
bor|ing|ness
Bor|laug, Nor|man
   Er|nest (US
   agronomist)
Bor|mann, Mar|tin
   (German Nazi)
Born, Max (German
   physicist)
born (used only in
   reference to birth:
   was born in July)
   [☞ borne, bourn]
born-again
borne (*past participle
   of* bear: *was borne on
   their shoulders*)
   [☞ born, bourn]
Born|ean

Bor|neo (island, Malay Archipelago)
Born|holm (Danish island)
Boro|bu|dur (Buddhist monument, Java)
Boro|din, Alex|an|der (Russian composer)
Boro|dino (Napoleonic battle site, Russia)
boron
bor|onia +s
boro|sili|cate +s
bor|ough +s
Boro|vets (resort, Bulgaria)
Bor|ro|mini, Fran|cesco (Italian architect)
Bor|row, George (English writer)
bor|row +s +ed +ing
bor|row|er +s
bor|row|ing +s *noun*
bor|row pit +s
borscht
Bor|stal +s
bort +s
bor|zoi +s
bosc|age
Bosch, Hier|ony|mus (Dutch painter)
[☞ Boche, bosh]
Bosc pear +s
Bose, Sir Jag|dis Chan|dra (Indian scientist)
Bose, Sat|yen|dra Nath (Indian scientist)
bosh (nonsense)
[☞ Bosch, Boche]
bosk|age (*use* boscage)
Bos|kop (town, South Africa)
bosky
bosk|i|er
bosk|i|est
bo's'n +s (*use* boatswain)
Bos|nia (region, Bosnia and Herzegovina)
Bos|nia and Herze|go|vina (country, Europe)
Bosnia-Herzego|vina (= Bosnia and Herzegovina)
Bos|nian +s

bosom +s
bos|omed
bos|omy
boson +s (*Physics*)
[☞ bosun, bo'sun, bo's'n, boatswain]
Bos|phorus (= Bosporus)
Bos|porus (strait, Turkey)
boss (manager etc.)
boss|es
bossed
boss|ing
[☞ baas]
bossa nova +s
boss-eyed
boss|i|er
boss|i|est
boss|i|ly
boss|i|ness
boss man
boss men
Bos|suet, Jacques Bé|nigne (French writer)
Bossy, Mi|chael ('Mike') (Cdn hockey player)
bossy
boss|i|er
boss|i|est
bossy-boots
Bos|ton (city, US; rocker; in names of flora, fauna & foods)
Bos|ton|ian +s
Bos|ton Tea Party
bo'sun +s (*use* boatswain)
bosun +s (*use* boatswain)
Bos|well, James (Scottish biographer)
Bos|worth Field (battle site, England)
bot +s (botfly larva)
[☞ baht]
bo|tan|ic
bo|tan|ic|al +s
bo|tan|ic|al|ly
bot|an|ist +s
bot|an|ize
bot|an|iz|es
bot|an|ized
bot|an|iz|ing
Bot|any (bay, Australia; wool)
bot|any (study of plants)
botch
botch|es

botched
botch|ing
botch|er +s
botch up *verb*
botch|es up
botched up
botch|ing up
botch-up +s *noun*
botel +s (*use* boatel)
bot|fly
bot|flies
both
Botha, Louis (South African statesman)
Botha, Pieter Wil|lem (South African statesman)
both|er +s +ed +ing
bother|a|tion
bother|some
Both|nia (gulf, Baltic Sea)
Both|well, 4th Earl of (husband of Mary, Queen of Scots)
bothy
both|ies
bo tree +s
botry|oid|al
botry|tis
botry|tised
Bot|swana (country, Africa)
Bot|swan|an +s
bott +s (botfly larva: *use* bot)
[☞ baht]
Bot|ti|celli, San|dro (Florentine painter)
bot|tle
bot|tles
bot|tled
bot|tling
bot|tle blond +s
bottle|brush
bottle|brush|es
bot|tled *adjective*
bottle-feed
bottle-feeds
bottle-fed
bottle-feeding
bottle|ful +s
bot|tle green +s (bottle-green *when preceding a noun*)
bottle|neck +s
bottle|nosed dol|phin +s (= bottlenose dolphin)
bottle|nose dol|phin +s
bot|tler +s

bottle-washer +s
bot|tom +s +ed +ing
bottom-feeder +s
bottom-feeding
bottom|land +s
bottom|less
bottom|most
bot|tom|ry
bot|tom|ries
bot|tom|ried
bot|tomry|ing
bot|toms up (toast)
bot|tom up (upside down)
bottom-up (non-hierarchical)
botu|lism +s
Bou|chard, Lu|cien (Cdn politician)
Bou|cher, Fran|çois (French artist)
Bou|cher, Gaëtan (Cdn speed skater)
Boucher|ville (city, Canada)
Bou|ci|cault, Dion (Irish-born playwright)
bou|clé
Bou|dicca (British tribal queen)
bou|doir +s
Boud|reau, Wal|ter (Cdn composer)
bouf|fant +s
Bou|gain|ville (S Pacific island)
Bou|gain|ville, Louis-Antoine de (French explorer)
bou|gain|vil|lea
plural
bou|gain|vil|lea or bou|gain|vil|leas
bough +s (branch)
[☞ bow]
bought *past & past participle of* buy
[☞ bot]
bought|en *adjective*
bou|gie +s (surgical instrument)
[☞ boogie]
bouil|la|baisse +s
bouil|lon +s (broth)
[☞ bullion]
Bou|lan|ger, Georges Er|nest Jean Marie (French general & war minister)
Bou|lan|ger, Nadia Juli|ette (French composer)

boul|der +s (large stone)
boul|der|ing
boul|dery
boule +s (lawn bowling; Greek council; *for* inlay *use* buhl)
[☞ Boole]
boule|vard +s
boule|vard|ed
boule|var|dier +s
Bou|lez, Pierre (French composer)
boulle (inlay: *use* buhl)
Bou|logne (port, France)
[☞ Bologna]
Boult, Sir Ad|rian Ced|ric (English conductor)
[☞ Bolt]
boult +s +ed +ing (sift: *use* bolt)
bounce
boun|ces
bounced
boun|cing
boun|cer +s
boun|ci|ly
boun|ci|ness
boun|cing *adjective*
boun|cing Bet +s
bouncy
boun|ci|er
boun|ci|est
bound +s +ed +ing
bound|ary
bound|aries
bound|en
bound|er +s
bound|less
bound|less|ly
bound|less|ness
boun|teous
boun|teous|ly
boun|teous|ness
boun|ti|ful
boun|ti|ful|ly
Bounty (mutiny ship)
bounty (reward; abundance; generosity)
boun|ties
bou|quet +s
bou|quet garni
bou|quets gar|nis
Bou|ras|sa, Henri (Cdn politician)
Bou|ras|sa, Rob|ert (Cdn politician)

Bour|baki, Nico|las (mathematicians' pseudonym)
Bour|bon +s (French dynasty)
bour|bon +s (whiskey)
Bour|bon|nais (former province, France)
bour|don +s (low-pitched bell or organ stop; bagpipe drone)
[☞ burden]
Bour|geois, Léon Vic|tor Au|guste (French statesman)
[☞ Bourgeoys]
bour|geois
plural bour|geois
bour|geoi|sie +s
bour|geoi|si|fi|ca|tion
bour|geoi|si|fy
bour|geoi|si|fies
bour|geoi|si|fied
bour|geoi|si|fy|ing
Bour|geoys, Mar|guer|ite (saint)
[☞ Bourgeois]
Bour|get, Ignace (Cdn bishop)
bour|gui|gnon
Bouri|not, Sir John George (Cdn parliamentary clerk)
Bourke-White, Mar|garet (US photojournalist)
bourn +s (stream; goal; limit)
[☞ born, borne, Berne, Burne-Jones]
bourne +s (goal, limit: *use* bourn)
[☞ bourn]
Bourne|mouth (port, England)
Bour|non|ville, Au|guste (Danish choreographer)
bour|rée +s
bourse +s
bous|tro|phedon
bout +s
bou|tique +s
bouton|niere +s
Boutros-Ghali, Bou|tros (UN secretary-general)
Bou|troue d'Aubigny, Claude de (intendant of New France)

Bou|vet (S Atlantic island)
Bou|vier +s
Bou|vier des Flan|dres
Bou|viers des Flan|dres
bou|zouki +s
Bovet, Dan|iel (Swiss physiologist)
bo|vine
bo|vine|ly
Bov|ril *proprietary*
bov|ver
bov|ver boot +s
bov|ver boy +s
Bow (river, Canada)
Bow, Clara (US actress)
bow[1] +s +ed +ing (knot; ribbon; *Archery*; *Music*)
[☞ beau, bo tree]
bow[2] +s +ed +ing (bend downward; submit; withdraw; usher; *Nautical*)
[☞ bough]
bowd|ler|ism
bowd|ler|iz|a|tion
bowd|ler|ize
bowd|ler|iz|es
bowd|ler|ized
bowd|ler|iz|ing
bow drill +s
bowel +s (*Anatomy* etc.)
[☞ Bowell]
Bow|ell, Sir Mac|ken|zie (Cdn prime minister)
[☞ bowel]
Bowen (island, Canada)
bower +s +ed +ing
[☞ Bauer]
bower|bird +s
Bow|er|ing, George (Cdn writer)
Bow|er|ing, Mari|lyn (Cdn poet)
Bow|ery (community, US)
bow|ery
bow|fin +s
bow front +s
bow-fronted
bow|head +s
bow|hunt +s +ed +ing
bow|hunt|er +s
bow|hunt|ing *noun*

Bowie, David (English singer-songwriter)
Bowie, James ('Jim') (US frontiersman)
bowie knife
bowie knives
bow|ing *noun*
bowl +s +ed +ing (basin; stadium; *Sport*; overwhelm)
[☞ bole, boll]
bow|legged
bow legs
bowl|er +s
Bowles, Paul Fred|erick (US writer & composer)
bowl|ful +s
bowl|line +s
bowl|ing *noun*
bowls (lawn bowling)
[☞ Bowles]
Bow|man, Wil|liam Scott ('Scot|ty') (Cdn hockey coach)
bow|man (archer; rower)
bow|men
Bow|man|ville (community, Canada)
bow|saw +s
bow|ser +s
bow|shot
bows|man (rower: *use* bowman)
bows|men
bow|sprit +s
Bow Street run|ner +s
bow|string +s
bow tie +s
bow-tied
bow-wow +s
bow|yer +s
box
boxes
boxed
box|ing
box ball
box|board
box|car +s
box elder +s
Boxer +s (Chinese secret society member)
box|er +s (pugilist; dog; shorts)
box|ful +s
box|i|er
box|i|est
box|ing *noun*
Box|ing Day

Box|ing Week
boxla
box|like
box of|fice +s (box-
office *when preceding
a noun*)
box score +s
box spring +s
box|wood +s
boxy
box|i|er
box|i|est
boy +s (young male
etc.)
[☞ buoy]
boyar +s
Boyce, Wil|liam
(English composer)
[☞ Beuys]
boy|cott +s +ed +ing
Boyd, Liona (Cdn
guitarist)
Boyd Orr, John (1st
Baron Boyd Orr of
Brechin Mearns,
Scottish nutritionist)
Boyer, Charles
(French actor)
boy|friend +s
boy|hood
boy|ish
boy|ish|ly
boy|ish|ness
Boyle, Rob|ert (Irish-
born scientist)
Boyle's law
Boyne (river & battle
site, Ireland)
boyo +s
Boy Scout +s
boysen|berry
boysen|ber|ries
boy toy +s
Boz (Charles Dickens)
bozo +s
BP (boiling point;
blood pressure)
BP (before the present
era)
bps (bits per second)
bra +s
Bra|bant (former
duchy, Europe)
brace
braces
braced
bracing
Brace|bridge (town,
Canada)
brace|let +s
bracer +s
bra|chial

brachi|ate
brachi|ates
brachi|at|ed
brachi|at|ing
brachi|a|tion
brachi|ator +s
brachio|pod +s
brachio|saur +s
brachio|saur|us
brachio|saur|us|es
bra|chis|to|chrone +s
brachy|ceph|alic
brachy|ceph|al|ous
bracing *adjective*
bracing|ly
Brack|en, John (Cdn
politician)
brack|en
plural brack|en
brack|et +s +ed +ing
brack|ish
brack|ish|ness
bract
brac|teal
brac|te|ate
brad +s
brad|awl +s
Brad|bury, Mal|colm
Stan|ley (English
writer)
Brad|bury, Ray
Doug|las (US
author)
Brad|ford (city,
England)
Brad|ford West
Gwil|lim|bury
(town, Canada)
Brad|ley, Fran|cis
Her|bert (English
philosopher)
Brad|ley, James
(English astronomer)
Brad|street, Anne
Dud|ley (US poet)
brady|car|dia
brae +s (hillside)
[☞ bray]
brag
brags
bragged
brag|ging
Braga (city, Portugal)
Bra|ganza (city,
Portugal; Portuguese
& Brazilian dynasty)
Bragg, Sir Wil|liam
Henry (English
physicist)
brag|ga|do|cio
brag|gart +s
brag|ger +s
brag|ging|ly

braggy
brag|gi|er
brag|gi|est
Brahe, Tycho (Danish
astronomer)
Brah|ma +s (Hindu
god; cattle)
[☞ Bramah,
Brahman, brahma]
brah|ma +s (fowl: *use*
brahmaputra)
Brah|man +s
(member of highest
Hindu caste; *for*
cattle *use* Brahma)
[☞ Brahmin,
Brahmana,
Brahma]
Brah|mana +s
(commentary on
Vedas)
[☞ Brahman,
Brahmin]
Brah|man|ic
Brah|man|ic|al
Brah|man|ism
Brah|ma|putra (river,
S Asia)
brah|ma|putra +s
(fowl)
Brah|min +s (superior
person; *for* member
of Hindu caste *use*
Brahman)
[☞ Brahma,
Brahmana,
Brahman]
Brah|min|ic
Brah|min|ic|al
Brahms, Jo|han|nes
(German composer)
braid +s +ed +ing
braid|ed *adjective*
braid|er +s
braid|ing *noun*
Brăila (city, Romania)
Braille, Louis
(inventor of writing
system)
Braille (writing system
for the blind)
brain +s +ed +ing
brain|case +s
brain|child
brain|chil|dren
brain dam|age
brain-damaged
brain-dead
brain death
brain drain +s
Braine, John Ger|ard
(English novelist)
brain fever

brain food
brain|i|er
brain|i|est
brain|i|ly
brain|i|ness
brain|less
brain|pan +s
brain|power
brain scan +s
brain stem +s
brain|storm +s +ed
+ing
brain|storm|ing *noun*
brains trust +s (*use*
brain trust)
brain|teas|er +s
brain trust +s
brain-twister +s
brain|wash
brain|wash|es
brain|washed
brain|wash|ing
brain|wash|ing *noun*
brain|wave +s
brainy
brain|i|er
brain|i|est
braise (cook)
brais|es
braised
brais|ing
[☞ braze]
brake (stopping
device; stop, slow
down; crush flax or
hemp; harrow;
thicket; bracken;
archaic past tense of
break)
brakes
braked
brak|ing
[☞ break]
brake block +s
brake drum +s
brake flu|id +s
brake light +s
brake lining +s
brake|man
brake|men
brake pad +s
brake shoe +s
brakes|man (*use*
brakeman)
brakes|men
brake van +s
bra|less
Bram|ah, Jo|seph
(English inventor)
[☞ Brahma]
Bra|mante, Do|nato
(Italian architect)
bram|ble +s

bram|bling
bram|bly
Bram|ley +s
Bramley's seed|ling +s (= Bramley)
Bramp|ton (city, Canada)
bran
Bran|agh, Ken|neth Charles (British filmmaker)
branch
branch|es
branched
branch|ing
branched *adjective*
bran|chia (gills) [☞ bronchi]
bran|chiae (= branchia: lungs)
bran|chi|al (of gills) [☞ bronchial]
bran|chi|ate
branch|i|er
branch|i|est
branch|let +s
branch|like
branch line +s
branch plant +s *noun*
branch-plant *adjective preceding a noun*
branchy
branch|i|er
branch|i|est
Bran|cusi, Con|stan|tin (Romanian sculptor)
brand +s +ed +ing
bran|dade +s
Bran|den|burg (state, Germany; concertos; gate, Berlin)
brand|er
bran|died
brand|ing *adjective*
bran|dish
bran|dish|es
bran|dished
bran|dish|ing
bran|dish|er +s
brand|ling +s
brand name +s
brand new
Bran|do, Mar|lon (US actor)
Bran|don (city, Canada)
Brandt, Willy (German statesman) [☞ Brant]
brandy
bran|dies

brandy glass
brandy glass|es
brandy snap +s
Brandy|wine (waterfall, Canada)
brank-ursine +s
Brant, Jo|seph (Mohawk chief) [☞ Brandt]
Brant, Mary ('Molly') (Mohawk leader) [☞ Brandt]
brant +s
Brant|ford (city, Canada)
Bran|ting, Karl Hjal|mar (Swedish statesman)
Braque, Georges (French painter)
Bras D'Or (lake, Canada)
brash +er +est
brash|ly
brash|ness
Bra|silia (capital of Brazil)
Bra|şov (city, Romania)
brass
brass|es
bras|sard +s
brassed off
bras|serie +s
Bras|sey, Thom|as (English engineer) [☞ brassy, brassie]
brass hat +s
bras|sica +s
brass|ie +s (*Golf*) [☞ brassy, Brassey]
bras|siere +s (bra)
brass|i|ly
brass|i|ness
brassy (impudent; showy; loud; like brass; *for* golf club *use* brassie)
brass|i|er
brass|i|est
brass|ies [☞ Brassey]
brat +s
Brati|slava (capital of Slovakia)
brat pack +s
brat pack|er +s
brat|tice +s
brat|ti|ness
brat|tish
brat|tish|ness

bratty
brat|ti|er
brat|ti|est
brat|wurst +s
Brau|del, Fer|nand Paul (French historian)
Braun (surname) [☞ Brown, Browne]
Braun, Eva (Hitler's mistress)
Braun, Karl Fer|di|nand (German physicist)
Braun, Wern|her Mag|nus Max|imil|ian von (German rocket designer)
brava
bra|vado
brave
braves
braved
brav|ing
brav|er
brav|est
brave|ly
brave|ness
brav|ery
brav|eries
bravo
• (interjection) *plural* bra|vos
• (ruffian) *plural* bra|voes or bra|vos
bra|vura
brawl +s +ed +ing
brawl|er +s
brawn
brawn|i|ness
brawny
brawn|i|er
brawn|i|est
Brax|ton Hicks con|trac|tion +s
bray +s +ed +ing (cry of donkey; crush) [☞ brae]
Bra|yon +s
braze (solder; make of or with brass)
braz|es
brazed
braz|ing [☞ braise]
braz|en +s +ed +ing
brazen-faced
braz|en|ly
braz|en|ness

bra|zier +s (cooking grill, heater; brass worker) [☞ brassiere]
bra|ziery
Bra|zil (country, S America)
Bra|zil|ian +s
Bra|zil nut +s
brazil|wood
Braz|za|ville (capital of the Republic of the Congo)
breach (break a law, contract, etc.; leap out of water; gap)
breach|es
breached
breach|ing [☞ breech]
bread +s +ed +ing (food; coat with bread crumbs) [☞ bred]
bread and but|ter *noun*
bread-and-butter *adjective*
bread|basket +s
bread bin +s
bread|board +s
bread|box
bread|boxes
bread crumb +s
bread flour
bread|fruit *plural* bread|fruit or bread|fruits
bread|knife bread|knives
bread|line +s
bread pud|ding +s
bread|root
bread sauce +s
bread stick +s
breadth +s
breadth|ways
breadth|wise
bread|win|ner +s
bread|win|ning
break (fracture; interrupt; cause to yield; pause; dash; carriage frame; etc.)
breaks
broke
broken
break|ing [☞ brake]
break|able +s
break|age +s

break away *verb*
breaks away
broke away
brok|en away
break|ing away
break|away +s *noun & adjective*
break|dance
break|dan|ces
break|danced
break|dan|cing
break|dan|cer +s
break|dan|cing *noun*
break down *verb*
breaks down
broke down
brok|en down
break|ing down
break|down +s *noun*
break|er +s
break even *verb*
breaks even
broke even
brok|en even
break|ing even
break-even +s *noun & adjective*
break|fast +s +ed +ing
break|fast|er +s
break|front +s
break in *verb*
breaks in
broke in
brok|en in
break|ing in
break-in +s *noun*
break|ing *adjective*
break|ing ball +s
break|ing pitch
break|ing pitch|es
breaking-point +s
break|neck
break open *verb*
breaks open
broke open
brok|en open
break|ing open
break-open +s *noun & adjective*
break out *verb*
breaks out
broke out
brok|en out
break|ing out
break|out +s *noun*
break point +s
(interruption; breaking-point; *Tennis*)
break|point +s
(*Computing*)

Break|spear, Nicho|las (Pope Adrian IV)
break through *verb*
breaks through
broke through
brok|en through
break|ing through
break|through +s *noun*
break-through bleed|ing
break up *verb*
breaks up
broke up
brok|en up
break|ing up
break|up +s *noun*
break|wall +s
break|water +s
Bream, Jul|ian Alex|an|der (English musician)
bream (fish)
plural bream or breams
breast +s +ed +ing
[☞ Brest]
breast-beating
breast|bone +s
breast|ed *adjective*
breast-feed
breast-feeds
breast-fed
breast-feeding
breast|less
breast|plate +s
breast pump +s
breast|stroke +s
breast|strok|er +s
breast|work +s
breath +s *noun*
[☞ breathe]
breath|abil|ity
breath|able
breath|alyze
breath|alyz|es
breath|alyzed
breath|alyz|ing
Breath|alyz|er +s *proprietary*
breathe *verb*
breathes
breathed
breath|ing
[☞ breath]
breath|er +s
breath|i|er
breath|i|est
breath|i|ly
breath|i|ness
breath|ing *noun*
breath|less

breath|less|ly
breath|less|ness
breath mint +s
breath|taking
breath|taking|ly
breath test +s
breathy
breath|i|er
breath|i|est
Bré|beuf, Jean de (missionary in New France)
brec|cia (*Geology*)
brec|cias
[☞ Brescia]
brecci|ate
brecci|ates
brecci|at|ed
brecci|at|ing
brecci|at|ed *adjective*
brecci|a|tion +s
Brecht, Ber|tolt (German dramatist)
Brecht|ian
Breck|nock|shire (= Breconshire)
Brecon|shire (former county, Wales)
bred *past & past participle of* breed
[☞ bread]
Breda (city, the Netherlands)
breech (gun part; birth; buttocks)
breech|es
breeched
breech|ing
[☞ breach]
breech|block +s
breech|cloth +s
breech|clout +s
breech|es (pants)
breech-loader +s
breech-loading
breed
breeds
bred
breed|ing
breed|er +s
breed|ing +s *noun*
breed|ing ground +s
breeks
breeze
breez|es
breezed
breez|ing
breeze-block +s
breeze|way +s
breez|i|ly
breez|i|ness

breezy
breez|i|er
breez|i|est
Bre|genz (city, Austria)
brek|kie
Brel, Jacques (Belgian singer)
Bre|men (state & its capital, Germany)
brems|strah|lung
Bren +s (gun)
Bren|dan (saint)
Bren|del, Al|fred (Austrian pianist)
Bren|ner (mountain pass, the Alps)
brent +s (*use* brant)
Bre|scia (city, Italy)
[☞ breccia]
Bres|lau (*former name of* Wrocław)
Bres|son, Rob|ert (French filmmaker)
Brest (cities, France & Belarus)
[☞ breast]
breth|ren
Bre|ton, André (French writer)
Bret|on +s (cape, Canada; person & language of Brittany)
Breuer, Mar|cel Lajos (Hungarian-born designer)
Breuer chair +s
Breu|ghel (family of painters: *use* Bruegel)
Breuil, Henri Édouard Pros|per (French archaeologist)
breve +s
brevet
brev|ets
brev|et|ed or brev|et|ted
brev|et|ing or brev|et|ting
brevi|ary
brevi|aries
brev|ity
brev|ities
brew +s +ed +ing
brew|er +s
brewer's yeast
brew|ery
brew|eries
brewis
brew|master +s
brew pub +s

brew|ski
  brew|skis or
  brew|skies
Brew|ster, Sir David
  (Scottish physicist)
brew up *verb*
  brews up
  brewed up
  brew|ing up
brew-up +s *noun*
Brezh|nev, Leo|nid
  Ilich (Soviet
  statesman)
Brian Boru (king of
  Ireland)
Briand, Aristide
  (French politician)
Bri|ansk (= Bryansk,
  Russia)
briar +s (plants, pipe:
  use brier)
  [☞ **Brier**]
brib|able
bribe
  bribes
  bribed
  brib|ing
brib|er +s
brib|ery
  brib|er|ies
bric-a-brac
Brice, Fanny (US
  performer)
brick +s +ed +ing
brick|bat +s
brickie +s
brick|lay|er +s
brick|lay|ing
brick red (brick-red
  when preceding a
  noun)
brick|work +s
brick|yard +s
brico|lage +s
bridal (of a bride)
  [☞ **bridle**]
Bridal Veil Falls (in
  Canada)
Bride (Saint Bridget of
  Ireland)
bride +s
bride|groom +s
bride price +s
brides|maid +s
bride|well +s
Bridge, Frank
  (English composer)
bridge
  bridg|es
  bridged
  bridg|ing
bridge|able
bridge-builder +s

bridge-building
bridge|head +s
bridge loan +s
bridge mix (= Bridge
  Mixture)
Bridge Mix|ture
  proprietary
bridge roll +s
Bridg|es, Rob|ert
  Sey|mour (English
  writer)
Bridget (Swedish &
  Irish saints)
Bridge|town (capital
  of Barbados)
Bridge|water (town,
  Canada)
bridge|work +s
bridg|ing loan +s
  Brit.
Bridg|man, Percy
  Wil|liams (US
  physicist)
bridie +s
bridle (horse's
  headgear; restraint;
  mooring cable; curb;
  show offence)
  bri|dles
  bri|dled
  brid|ling
  [☞ **bridal**]
bridle path +s
bridle|way +s
bri|doon +s
brie +s
brief +er +est +s +ed
  +ing
brief|case +s
brief|er +s
brief|ing +s *noun*
brief|ly
brief|ness
Brier +s (bonspiel)
brier +s (plants; pipe)
briery
brig +s
brig|ade
  brig|ades
  brig|ad|ed
  brig|ad|ing
briga|dier +s
briga|dier gen|er|al
  +s
bri|gand +s
bri|gand|age
bri|gand|ry
bri|gan|tine +s
Briggs, Henry
  (English
  mathematician)
Bright, John (English
  politician)

bright +s +er +est
bright|en +s +ed
  +ing
bright|en|er +s
bright-eyed
bright|ish
bright|ly
bright|ness
  bright|ness|es
Bright|on (city,
  England)
Bright's dis|ease
bright|work
Brigid (Saint Bridget
  of Ireland)
Brigus (town, Canada)
brill
  plural brill
Brillat-Savarin,
  (Jean) An|thelme
  (French gourmet)
bril|liance
bril|lian|cy
bril|liant +s
bril|liant|ine
bril|liant|ly
Brillo +s *proprietary*
Brillo pad +s
  proprietary
brim
  brims
  brimmed
  brim|ming
brim|ful
brim-full (*use*
  brimful)
brim|less
  brimmed *adjective*
brim|stone
brin
brin|dle (= brindled)
brin|dled
brine
  brines
  brined
  brin|ing
bring
  brings
  brought
  bring|ing
bring|er +s
brin|i|er
brin|i|est
brin|i|ness
Brink, André (South
  African writer)
brink +s
brink|man|ship
brinks|man|ship
  (= brinkmanship)
briny
  brin|i|er
  brin|i|est

brio
bri|oche +s
bri|quet +s (*use*
  briquette)
bri|quette +s
bris
Bris|bane (city,
  Australia)
Bris|bane, Sir
  Thom|as
  Mak|doug|all
  (Scottish soldier &
  astronomer)
brisk +er +est +s +ed
  +ing
bris|ket +s
brisk|ly
brisk|ness
bris|ling (fish)
  plural bris|ling or
  bris|lings
  [☞ **bristling**]
bris|tle (stiff hair;
  show irritation; be
  abundant with)
  bris|tles
  bris|tled
  brist|ling
  [☞ **Bristol, bristols,**
  bristol board]
bristle|cone pine +s
bristle|tail +s
brist|ly
  brist|li|er
  brist|li|est
Bris|tol (city &
  channel, England)
bris|tol board
bris|tols (breasts)
Brit +s
Brit|ain (island off
  W Europe)
  [☞ **Briton, Britten**]
Britan|nia
Britan|nic
britch|es
Briti|cism +s
Brit|ish
Brit|ish Col|um|bia
  (province, Canada)
Brit|ish Col|um|bian
  +s
Brit|ish|er +s
Brit|ish|ism +s
  (= Briticism)
Brit|ish|ness
Briton +s (people)
  [☞ **Britain, Britten**]
Brit|tany (region,
  France)
Brit|ten, (Ed|ward)
  Ben|jam|in (Lord

Britten of Aldeburgh,
English composer)
[☞ Britain, Briton]
brit|tle
brittle|ly
brittle|ness
brittle|star +s
Brit|ton|ic (use
Brythonic)
Brno (city, Czech
Republic)
bro +s
broach (bring up;
open; surface; veer)
broach|es
broached
broach|ing
[☞ brooch]
broad +s +er +est
broad|axe +s
broad|band
broad bean +s
Broad|bent, (John)
Ed|ward ('Ed') (Cdn
politician)
broad-brush
broad|cast
broad|casts
broad|cast or
broad|cast|ed
broad|cast
broad|cast|ing
broad|cast|er +s
broad|cast|ing noun
Broad Church
broad|cloth
broad|en +s +ed +ing
broad jump +s
broad|leaf adjective &
noun
broad|leaves
broad-leafed
adjective
(= broadleaf)
broad-leaved
adjective
(= broadleaf)
broad|loom
broad|loomed
broad|ly
broad-minded
broad-minded|ly
broad-minded|ness
broad|ness
Broads (region,
England)
broad|sheet +s
broad|side
broad|sides
broad|sid|ed
broad|sid|ing
broad|sword +s
broad|tail

Broad|way (street,
US; Theatre)
broad|ways
broad|wise
Brob|ding|nag|ian +s
bro|cade
bro|cades
bro|cad|ed
bro|cad|ing
bro|cad|ed adjective
broc|coli
broch +s (tower)
[☞ brock, broach,
brooch]
broch|ette +s
bro|chure +s
Brock, Sir Isaac
(English military
commander)
brock +s (badger)
[☞ broch]
Brock|en (mountain,
Germany)
brock|et +s
Brock|ville (city,
Canada)
bro|de|rie an|glaise
Bro|deur (peninsula,
Canada)
Brod|sky, Jo|seph
(US poet)
bro|gan +s
brogue +s
broil +s +ed +ing
broil|er +s
broil|ing adjective
broke adjective
bro|ken adjective
broken-down
broken-hearted
broken-hearted|ness
Bro|ken Hill (town,
Australia; former
name for Kabwe,
Zambia)
broken|ly
broken|ness
bro|ken wind
broken-winded
brok|er +s +ed +ing
broker|age +s
brok|ing
brol|ga +s
brol|ly
brol|lies
bro|mate +s
brome +s
brome grass
brome grass|es
bro|melia +s
(= bromeliad)
bro|meli|ad +s
bro|mic

bro|mide +s
bro|mine
Bromp|ton Cock|tail
+s
bronc +s
bron|chi (plural of
bronchus: air
passage in the lungs)
bron|chi|al (of the
bronchi)
[☞ bronchiole]
bron|chi|ol|ar
bron|chi|ole +s
(division of a
bronchus)
[☞ bronchial]
bron|chit|ic +s
bron|chitis
bron|cho|cele +s
bron|cho|dila|tor +s
bron|cho|
pneu|monia
bron|cho|scope +s
bron|chos|copy
bron|chos|cop|ies
bron|chus
bron|chi
bron|co +s
bronco|bust|er +s
bronco|bust|ing
Bron|të, Anne
(English novelist)
Bron|të, Char|lotte
(English novelist)
Bron|të, Emily
(English novelist)
bron|to|saur +s
bron|to|saur|us
bron|to|saur|us|es
Bronx (borough, US)
bronze
bronz|es
bronzed
bronz|ing
Bronze Age
Bron|zino, Agnolo
(Italian painter)
bronzy
brooch (Jewellery)
brooch|es
[☞ broach]
brood +s +ed +ing
brood|er +s
brood|i|ly
brood|i|ness
brood|ing adjective
brood|ing|ly
broody
brood|i|er
brood|i|est
Brook, Peter Ste|phen
Paul (English theatre

director)
[☞ Brooke]
brook +s +ed +ing
(stream; tolerate)
Brooke, Ru|pert
Chaw|ner (English
poet)
[☞ Brook]
brook|ie +s
Brook|lands
(racetrack, England)
brook|let +s
Brook|lyn (borough,
US)
Brook|ner, Anita
(English writer)
[☞ Bruckner]
Brooks (town,
Canada; mountain
range, US)
Brooks, Cle|anth (US
literary critic)
Brooks, Mel (US
filmmaker)
broom +s (brush;
shrub)
[☞ brume,
brougham]
broom|ball
broom|ball|er +s
broom|rape +s
broom|stick +s
Bros|sard (city,
Canada)
Bros|sard, Ni|cole
(Cdn writer)
broth +s
broth|el +s
broth|er
• (sibling; friend; union
member; fellow
human being)
plural broth|ers
• (Religion; member or
associate in a
common cause)
plural broth|ers or
breth|ren
broth|er ger|man
broth|ers ger|man
brother|hood +s
brother-in-law
brothers-in-law
brother|less
brother|li|ness
brother|ly
broth|er uter|ine
broth|ers uter|ine
Brott, Boris (Cdn
conductor)
brougham +s
(carriage;
automobile)
[☞ brume]

brought *conjugated form of* bring
[☞ Brott]
Brough|ton Island (hamlet & island, Canada)
brou|haha +s
Brou|wer, Adri|aen (Flemish painter)
brow +s
brow|beat
brow|beats
brow|beat
brow|beat|en
brow|beat|ing
brow|beat|er +s
browed
brow log +s
Brown (surname)
[☞ Browne, Braun]
Brown, Sir Ar|thur Whit|ten (Scottish aviator)
Brown, Ford Madox (English painter)
Brown, George (Cdn journalist & politician)
Brown, James (US singer-songwriter)
Brown, John (US abolitionist)
Brown, Lan|ce|lot ('Cap|abil|ity') (English landscape gardener)
Brown, Rob|ert (Scottish botanist)
brown +s +ed +ing
brown bag
brown bags
brown bagged
brown bag|ging
brown bag|ger +s
brown Betty +s
Browne, Sir Thom|as (English writer)
[☞ Brown, Braun]
browned off
brown|er +s
Brown|ian
Brown|ie +s (Scouting)
brown|ie +s (food; elf)
[☞ browny]
brown|ie point +s
Brown|ing, Eliza|beth Bar|rett (English poet)
Brown|ing, Kurt (Cdn figure skater)
Brown|ing, Rob|ert (English poet)

brown|ing *noun*
brown|ish
Brown|lee, John Ed|ward (Cdn politician)
brown|ness
brown-nose
brown-noses
brown-nosed
brown-nosing
brown-noser +s
brown-nosing *noun*
brown|out +s
Brown Owl +s (Scouting)
brown owl +s (bird)
Brown|shirt +s (Nazi storm trooper)
brown|shirt +s (any fascist)
brown-shirted
brown|stone +s
browny (somewhat brown)
[☞ brownie, Brownie]
brows|able
browse
brows|es
browsed
brows|ing
browse line +s
brows|er +s
Broz, Josip (Tito)
brr (expressing cold)
Bru|beck, David War|ren ('Dave') (US jazz musician)
Bruce (peninsula, Canada)
Bruce, James ('the Abys|sin|ian') (Scottish explorer)
Bruce, Rob|ert the (king of Scotland)
bru|cel|lo|sis
Bruch, Max (German composer)
bru|cite +s
Bruck|ner, (Josef) Anton (Austrian composer)
[☞ Brookner]
Brue|gel, Jon ('Vel|vet') (Flemish painter)
Brue|gel, Pieter ('the Elder') (Flemish painter)
Brue|gel, Pieter ('Hell') ('the Young|er') (Flemish painter)

Brue|ghel (= Bruegel: Flemish painters)
Bruges (city, Belgium)
bruin +s
bruise
bruis|es
bruised
bruis|ing
bruis|er +s
bruit +s +ed +ing (spread rumours)
[☞ brut, brute]
Brû|lé, Étienne (explorer, New France)
brume (mist)
[☞ broom, brougham]
Brum|ma|gem
Brum|mell, George Bryan ('Beau') (English dandy)
Brum|mie +s
Brummy (use Brummie)
Brum|mies
brunch
brunch|es
brunched
brunch|ing
brunch|er +s
Brundt|land, Gro Har|lem (Norwegian stateswoman)
Bru|nei (sultanate, Borneo)
Bru|nei|an
Bru|nei Darus|salam (official name of Brunei)
Bru|nel, Isam|bard King|dom (English engineer)
Bru|nel, Sir Marc Isam|bard (English engineer)
Bru|nel|les|chi, Filip|po (Italian architect)
brun|ette +s
Brun|hild (Germanic Myth)
Brunn|hilde (= Brunhild)
Bruno (saint)
Bruno, Frank|lin Ray (English boxer)
Bruno, Gior|dano (Italian philosopher)
Bruns|wick (city and former duchy & state, Germany)
brunt +s
brus|chet|ta +s

brush
brush|es
brushed
brush|ing
brush|back +s
brush cut +s
brush|cut|ter +s
brushed *adjective*
brush fire +s
brush|i|er
brush|i|est
brush|land +s
brush|less
brush|like
brush off *verb*
brush|es off
brushed off
brush|ing off
brush-off +s *noun*
brush stroke +s
brush wolf
brush wolves
brush|wood
brush|work
brushy
brush|i|er
brush|i|est
brusque
brus|quer
brus|quest
brusque|ly
brusque|ness
brus|querie
Brus|sels (capital of Belgium)
Brus|sels sprout +s
brut (of wine)
[☞ brute, bruit]
brutal
brutal|ism
brutal|ist +s
bru|tal|ity
bru|tal|ities
brutal|iz|a|tion +s
brutal|ize
brutal|iz|es
brutal|ized
brutal|iz|ing
brutal|ly
brute +s (brutal person; animal-like; etc.)
[☞ brut, bruit]
brut|ish
brut|ish|ly
brut|ish|ness
Bru|ton, John Ger|ard (Irish statesman)
Bru|tus (legendary Trojan)
Bru|tus, Lu|cius Jun|ius (legendary

founder of Roman
Republic)
Bru|tus, Mar|cus
Jun|ius (Roman
senator)
brux|ism
Bryan, Wil|liam
Jen|nings (US
presidential
candidate & Scopes
Trial prosecutor)
Bry|ansk (city, Russia)
Bryl|creem
proprietary
Bryn|hild
(*Scandinavian Myth*)
bryo|logic|al
bry|ol|o|gist +s
bry|ol|ogy
bry|ony
bry|on|ies
bryo|phyte +s
bryo|phyt|ic
bryo|zoan +s
bryo|zo|ology
Bry|thon|ic
BS (bullshit)
　BS's
　BS'd
　BS'ing
B.Sc. (Bachelor of
Science)
　B.Sc.'s
BSE (breast self-
examination; bovine
spongiform
encephalopathy)
BSer
　BSers
B-side +s
BST (bovine
somatotropin)
BT (*bacillus
thuringiensis*)
BTU (British thermal
unit)
　BTUs
bub +s
bub|ba +s (redneck)
bub|be +s (Jewish
grandmother)
bub|bie +s (= bubbe)
bub|ble
　bub|bles
　bub|bled
　bub|bling
bub|ble bath +s
bub|ble cham|ber +s
bub|ble gum
bubble|head +s
bubble|head|ed
Bub|ble Jet +s
proprietary

bub|ble pack +s
bub|ble wrap
bub|bly
　bub|bli|er
　bub|bli|est
　bub|blies
Buber, Mar|tin (Israeli
philosopher)
bubo
　bu|boes
bu|bon|ic
buc|cal (of the mouth
or cheek)
　[☞ buckle]
buc|can|eer +s +ed
　+ing
buc|can|eer|ing noun
　& adjective
buc|can|eer|ish
buc|cin|ator +s
Bu|ceph|alus (horse
of Alexander the
Great)
Buch|an, John, 1st
Baron Tweeds|muir
(governor general of
Canada & novelist)
Bu|chan|an, James
(US president)
Bucha|rest (capital of
Romania)
Buchen|wald
(concentration
camp)
Buch|ner, Ed|uard
(German organic
chemist)
Buck, Pearl
Syden|strick|er (US
writer)
buck +s +ed +ing
buck and doe +s
buck|a|roo +s
buck|bean +s
buck|board +s
buck|brush
　buck|brush|es
buck|er +s
buck|et +s +ed +ing
buck|et brig|ade +s
bucket|ful +s
bucket|mouth +s
buck|et seat +s
buck|et shop +s
buck|eye +s
Buck|ing|ham
(palace, England;
town, Canada)
Buck|ing|ham,
George Vil|liers, 1st
Duke of (1592–1628;
English courtier &
statesman)

Buck|ing|ham,
George Vil|liers,
2nd Duke of (1628–
87; English courtier
& writer)
Buck|ing|ham|shire
(county, England)
Buck knife proprietary
　Buck knives
Buck|land, Wil|liam
(English geologist)
buckle (fastener;
fasten; give way
under pressure)
　buckles
　buckled
　buck|ling
　[☞ buccal]
buck|ler +s
buck|ling +s noun
buck|min|ster|ful|ler|
　ene +s
buck-naked
bucko
　buck|oes
buck off verb
　bucks off
　bucked off
　buck|ing off
buck-off +s noun
buck-passer +s
buck-passing +s
buck|ram
buck|saw +s
buck|shot
buck|skin +s
buck|tail +s
buck|thorn +s
buck|tooth
　buck|teeth
buck|toothed
buck|wheat
bucky|ball +s
bu|col|ic +s
bu|col|ic|ally
bud
　buds
　bud|ded
　bud|ding
Buda|pest (capital of
Hungary)
Bud|dha +s (founder
of Buddhism; statue
etc.)
Buddh Gaya (village,
India: use
Bodhgaya)
Bud|dhism
Bud|dhist +s
Bud|dhis|tic
bud|dleia +s

buddy
　bud|dies
　bud|died
　buddy|ing
buddy-buddy
Budge, John Don|ald
('Don') (US tennis
player)
budge
　budges
　budged
　budg|ling
budg|eri|gar +s
budget +s +ed +ing
budget|ary
budgie +s
bud vase +s
bud|worm +s
Buena|ven|tura (port,
Colombia)
Buenos Aires (capital
of Argentina)
buff +s +ed +ing
Buf|falo (city, US)
buf|falo (animal)
　plural buf|falo or
　buf|fa|loes
buf|falo bean +s
buf|falo berry
　buf|falo ber|ries
Buf|falo Bill (US
showman)
buf|fa|loed
buf|falo grass
buf|fer +s +ed +ing
buf|fet[1] +s (meal;
table; cabinet)
buf|fet[2] +s +ed +ing
(strike repeatedly)
buf|fet|ing +s noun
buffle|head +s
buf|fo +s
Buf|fon, Georges-
Louis Le|clerc,
Comte de (French
naturalist)
buf|foon +s
buf|foon|ery
　buf|foon|eries
buf|foon|ish
bug
　bugs
　bugged
　bug|ging
Buga|boo +s
(mountains, Canada)
buga|boo +s (object
of fear)
Bu|gan|da (former
kingdom, Africa)
bug|bear +s
bug-eyed
bug|ger +s +ed +ing

bug|gery
buggy
  bug|gies
  bug|gi|er
  bug|gi|est
bug|house +s
bugle
  bugles
  bugled
  bugling
bugler +s
bugle|weed +s
bu|gloss
  bu|gloss|es
buhl (inlay)
  [☞ boule, Boole]
build
  builds
  built
  build|ing
build|able
build|er +s
build in verb
  builds in
  built in
  build|ing in
build|ing +s noun
build|ing block +s
build up verb
  builds up
  built up
  build|ing up
build|up +s noun
built adjective
built-in +s adjective &
  noun
built-up adjective
Bu|jum|bura (capital
  of Burundi)
Bu|khara
  (= Bukhoro)
Bu|kha|rin, Niko|lai
  Ivan|ovich (Russian
  revolutionary)
Bu|khoro (city,
  Uzbekistan)
Buko|vina (region,
  Europe)
Buko|vin|ian +s
Bula|wayo (city,
  Zimbabwe)
bulb +s
bul|bil +s (small bulb)
  [☞ bulbul]
bul|bous
bul|bul +s (bird)
  [☞ bulbil]
Bul|ga|nin, Niko|lai
  Alek|san|dro|vich
  (Soviet statesman)
Bul|gar +s (people)
bul|gar (wheat: use
  bulgur)

Bul|garia (country,
  Europe)
Bul|gar|ian +s
bulge
  bulges
  bulged
  bul|ging
bul|ghur (wheat: use
  bulgur)
bul|ging|ly
bul|gur (wheat)
bulgy
  bulgi|er
  bulgi|est
bu|lima|rex|ia
bu|lima|rex|ic
bu|limia
bu|limia ner|vosa
bu|lim|ic +s
bulk +s +ed +ing
bulk|er +s
bulk|head +s
bulk|i|ly
bulk|i|ness
bulky
  bulk|i|er
  bulk|i|est
Bull (zodiac sign;
  constellation)
bull +s +ed +ing
bul|lace +s
bull block +s
bull buck|er +s
bull|cook +s
bull|dog +s
bull|dog|ger +s
bull|dog|ging
bull|doze
  bull|doz|es
  bull|dozed
  bull|doz|ing
bull|doz|er +s
bull-dyke +s
bul|let +s
bul|letin +s
bullet|proof +s +ed
  +ing
bul|ley +s (boat: use
  bully)
bull|fight +s
bull|fight|er +s
bull|fight|ing
bull|finch
  bull|finch|es
bull|frog +s
bull|head +s
bull|head|ed
bull|head|ed|ly
bull|head|ed|ness
bull|horn +s
bul|lion (bulk metal)
  [☞ bouillon]
bull|ish

bull|ish|ly
bull|ish|ness
bull-necked
bull-nose
bull-nosed (= bull-
  nose)
bull|lock +s
bull|pen +s
bull rid|er +s
bull rid|ing
bull|ring +s
bull's eye +s
bull|shit
  bull|shits
  bull|shit|ted
  bull|shit|ting
bull|shit|ter +s
bull snake +s
bull team +s
bull trout
  plural bull trout
bull|whip
  bull|whips
  bull|whipped
  bull|whip|ping
bull work (strenuous
  labour)
  [☞ bulwark]
bully
  bul|lies
  bul|lied
  bully|ing
bully boat +s
bully boy +s
bully|rag
  bully|rags
  bully|ragged
  bully|rag|ging
Bülow, Prince
  Bern|hard von
  (German statesman)
bul|rush
  bul|rush|es
Bult|mann, Ru|dolf
  Karl (German
  theologian)
bul|tow +s
bul|wark +s
  (defensive wall;
  Nautical)
  [☞ bull work]
Bulwer-Lytton,
  Ed|ward George
  Earle (1st Baron
  Lytton)
bum
  bums
  bummed
  bum|ming
bum|bag +s
bum-bailiff +s

bum|ble
  bum|bles
  bum|bled
  bum|bling
bumble|bee +s
bumble|berry
bum|bler +s
bum|bling adjective
bum|boat +s
bum|boy +s
bumf (use bumph)
bum|malo
  plural bum|malo
bummed adjective
bummed out
bum|mer +s
bump +s +ed +ing
bump|er +s
bump|er boat +s
bump|er car +s
bump|er pad +s
bump|er stick|er +s
bumph
bump|i|er
bump|i|est
bump|i|ly
bump|i|ness
bump|kin +s
bump|tious
bump|tious|ly
bump|tious|ness
bumpy
  bump|i|er
  bump|i|est
bum steer +s
bun +s
Bun|bury (town,
  Australia)
bunch (cluster etc.)
  bunch|es
  bunched
  bunch|ing
  [☞ Bunche]
bunch|berry
  bunch|ber|ries
Bunche, Ralph
  John|son (US
  diplomat)
bunch|er +s
bunch grass
  bunch grass|es
bunchy
  bunch|i|er
  bunch|i|est
bun|co
 • noun
  bun|cos
 • verb
  bun|coes
  bun|coed
  bun|co|ing
bun|combe (use
  bunkum)

Bundes|rat
Bundes|tag
bun|dle
  bun|dles
  bun|dled
  bund|ling
bun|dle buggy
  bun|dle bug|gies
bund|ler +s
Bundt *proprietary* (*Cooking*)
bun|fight +s
bung +s +ed +ing
bun|ga|low +s
bunged up
bun|gee cord +s
bun|gee jump +s +ed +ing
bun|gee jump|er +s
bun|gee jump|ing *noun*
bung|hole +s
bun|gle
  bun|gles
  bun|gled
  bun|gling
bun|gler +s
Bunin, Ivan Alek|se|evich (Russian writer)
bun|ion +s (callus) [☞ Bunyan]
bunk +s +ed +ing
bunk bed +s
bun|ker +s
Bun|ker Hill (battle, American Revolution)
bunk|house +s
bunk|ie +s
bun|kum
bunny
  bun|nies
bunny hug +s
Bun|sen, Rob|ert Will|helm Eber|hard (German chemist)
Bun|sen burn|er +s
bunt +s +ed +ing (*Baseball*; butt; baggy part of a sail etc.; wheat disease) [☞ Bundt]
bunt|er +s
bunt|ing +s *noun*
bunt|line +s
Bu|ñuel, Luis (Spanish filmmaker)
Bun|yan, John (English writer) [☞ bunion]

Bun|yan, Paul (US folk hero) [☞ bunion]
bun|yip +s
Buona|parte (*Italian name for* Bonaparte)
Buon|ar|roti, Michel|angelo (Italian artist)
buoy +s +ed +ing (float; keep afloat; uplift)
buoy|age
buoy|ancy
  buoy|an|cies
buoy|ant
buoy|ant|ly
bup|pie +s
bur +s (clinging seed case, rough edge, dentist's drill, millstone, whetstone: *use* burr) [☞ burr, birr, brr]
burb +s
Bur|bage, Rich|ard (English actor)
Bur|bank (city, US)
bur|ble
  bur|bles
  bur|bled
  burb|ling
burb|ler +s
bur|bot
  plural bur|bot *or* bur|bots
bu|rden +s +ed +ing (load; duty; chorus, refrain; theme) [☞ bourdon]
bur|den|some
bur|dock +s
bur|eau +s
bureau|cracy
  bureau|cra|cies
bureau|crat +s
bureau|crat|ese
bureau|crat|ic
bureau|crat|ic|ally
bureau|crat|iz|a|tion
bureau|crat|ize
  bureau|crat|iz|es
  bureau|crat|ized
  bureau|crat|iz|ing
buret +s (*use* burette)
bur|ette +s
burg +s (town) [☞ berg]
bur|gage +s
Bur|gas (port, Bulgaria)
bur|gee +s

Bur|gen|land (state, Austria)
bur|geon +s +ed +ing
bur|geon|ing *adjective*
bur|ger +s (food) [☞ burgher, Berger]
Bur|gess, An|thony (English writer)
Bur|gess, Guy (Fran|cis de Moncy) (British spy)
bur|gess
  bur|gess|es
Bur|gess Shale
bur|gher +s (citizen) [☞ burger, Berger]
Burgh|ley, Will|iam Cecil, 1st Baron (English statesman)
bur|glar +s
bur|glar|ious
bur|glar|ize
  bur|glar|iz|es
  bur|glar|ized
  bur|glar|iz|ing
bur|glary
  bur|glar|ies
bur|gle
  bur|gles
  bur|gled
  bur|gling
burgo|master +s
Bur|gos (city, Spain)
Bur|goyne, John ('Gentle|man John|ny') (English general & playwright)
Bur|gundy (region, France)
bur|gundy (wine; colour)
bur|gun|dies
bur|ial +s
bur|ied *past & past participle of* bury
Burin (peninsula, Canada)
burin +s (tool)
burk +s (fool: *use* berk) [☞ Burke]
burka +s
Burke (surname) [☞ berk]
Burke, Ed|mund (British politician & writer)
Burke, John (Irish genealogist)
Burke, Rob|ert O'Hara (Irish explorer)

Burke, Will|iam (Irish murderer)
Bur|kina (country, Africa)
Bur|kina Faso (*official name for* Burkina)
Bur|kinan +s
Bur|kitt's lymph|oma
burl +s (knotty tree growth; knot in wool; *for* a swirled pattern in wood grain *or* the base of an antler *use* burr) [☞ birl, Berle]
bur|lap
burled
Bur|leigh, Will|iam Cecil, 1st Baron (= Burghley)
bur|lesque
  bur|lesques
  bur|lesqued
  bur|les|quing
bur|les|quer +s
bur|li|ness
Bur|ling|ton (city, Canada)
Bur|ling|ton bun +s
burly
  bur|li|er
  bur|li|est
Burma (country, Asia)
Bur|man +s
Burm|ese
  plural Burm|ese
burn (scorch etc.)
  burns
  burned *or* burnt
  burn|ing [☞ Burne-Jones, Berne]
Bur|naby (city, Canada)
Burne-Jones, Sir Ed|ward Coley (English artist) [☞ Berne]
burn|er +s
bur|net +s (plant) [☞ Burnett]
Bur|nett, Fran|ces Eliza Hodg|son (US novelist) [☞ burnet]
Bur|ney, Fran|ces ('Fanny') (English novelist)
burn|ing *adjective*
burning-glass
  burning-glasses
burn|ing|ly

bur|nish
  bur|nish|es
  bur|nished
  bur|nish|ing
bur|nish|er +s
bur|noose +s
bur|nous (use burnoose)
  bur|nous|es
burn out verb
  burns out
  burned out
  or burnt out
  burn|ing out
burn|out +s noun
Burns, George (US comedian)
Burns, Pat|rick (Cdn rancher & businessman)
Burns, Rob|ert (Scottish poet)
Burns Night
burnt adjective
burnt-out adjective
burnt si|en|na +s (burnt-sienna when preceding a noun)
bur oak +s (use burr oak)
burp +s +ed +ing
bur|pee +s
burp gun +s
Burr, Aaron (US statesman)
burr +s +ed +ing (clinging seed case; rough edge; dentist's drill; millstone; whetstone; whirring sound; rough sounding r; swirled pattern in wood grain; base of an antler) [☞ birr, brr]
Bur|rard (inlet, Canada)
bur reed +s
bur|rito +s
burro +s (donkey) [☞ burrow]
burr oak +s
Bur|roughs, Edgar Rice (US writer)
Bur|roughs, Wil|liam Seward (US writer)
bur|row +s +ed +ing (tunnel; search) [☞ burro]
bur|row|er +s
Bursa (city, Turkey)
bursa (Anatomy)
  bur|sae or bur|sas

bur|sal
bur|sar +s
bur|sar|ial
bursar|ship +s
bur|sary
  bur|sar|ies
bur|sitis
burst
  bursts
  burst
  burst|ing
Bur|ton (surname) [☞ Berton]
Bur|ton, Rich|ard (Welsh actor)
Bur|ton, Sir Rich|ard Fran|cis (English explorer)
Bur|ton, Rob|ert (English scholar & writer)
bur|ton +s (two-block tackle; 'go for a burton') [☞ Berton]
Bur|undi (country, Africa)
Bur|und|ian +s
bury (to inter)
  bur|ies
  bur|ied
  bury|ing
  [☞ berry]
bus (transportation vehicle; clear dishes; Electricity; Computing)
  buses
  bused
  bus|ing
  [☞ buss]
bus|boy +s
busby
  bus|bies
Bush, George Her|bert Walk|er (US president)
bush
  bush|es
bush baby
  bush babies
bush|buck +s
bush camp +s
bush|craft
bushed adjective
bushel +s
bushel|ful +s
bush|fire +s
bu|shido
bush|i|er
bush|i|est
bush|i|ly
bush|i|ness

bush|ing +s noun
bush|land
bush league +s (bush-league when preceding a noun)
bush leaguer +s
bush|lot +s
Bush|man (African people; language)
Bush|men
bush|man (a logger etc. living in the bush)
  bush|men
bush|master +s
bush plane +s
bush|ranger +s
bush|whack +s +ed +ing
bush|whack|er +s
bush work
bush|work|er +s
bushy
  bush|i|er
  bush|i|est
  bush|ies
bushy-tailed
busi|er
busi|est
busi|ly
busi|ness (commercial enterprise; job; affair; patronage; etc.)
  busi|ness|es
  [☞ busyness]
busi|ness class
busi|ness|like
busi|ness|man
  busi|ness|men
busi|ness per|son
  busi|ness people
busi|ness|woman
  busi|ness|women
busk +s +ed +ing
busk|er +s
bus|kin +s
bus|kined
busk|ing noun
bus lane +s
bus|load +s
bus|man
  bus|men
busman's holi|day
Bu|soni, Fer|ruc|cio Ben|ven|uto (Italian composer)
buss (kiss)
  buss|es
  bussed
  buss|ing
  [☞ bus]

bust
  busts
  bust|ed or bust
  bust|ing
bus|tard +s
bust|ed adjective
bus|tee +s
bust|er +s
bus|tier^1 +s (bodice)
busti|er^2 comparative of busty
busti|est
busti|ness
bus|tle
  bus|tles
  bus|tled
  bust|ling
bust|ler +s
bust up verb
  busts up
  bust|ed up
  or bust up
  bust|ing up
bust-up +s
busty
  busti|er
  busti|est
busy
  busi|er
  busi|est
  busies
  busied
  busy|ing
busy|body
  busy|bod|ies
busy Liz|zie +s
busy|ness (state of being busy) [☞ business]
busy|work
but +s (however, except, only, etc.; 'but me no buts'; objection; room) [☞ butt]
bu|ta|di|ene
bu|tane
butch
  butch|es
Butch|art Gar|dens (in Canada)
butch|er +s +ed +ing
butch|er bird +s
butch|er block +s
butch|er paper +s
butcher's (look)
butcher's broom +s
butch|ery
  butch|eries
Bute (inlet, Canada) [☞ beaut, butte]

Bute, 3rd Earl of
(British prime
minister)
[☞ beaut, butte]
Buten|andt, Adolf
Fred|erick Jo|hann
(German biochemist)
buteo +s
Buthe|lezi, Chief
Man|go|suthu
Gatsha (South
African Inkatha
leader)
butle (use buttle)
butles
butled
butling
[☞ butyl]
But|ler, Sam|uel
(1612–80; English
poet)
But|ler, Sam|uel
(1835–1902; English
novelist)
but|ler +s
bu|toh
butt +s +ed +ing
(push; joint; target;
cigarette; buttocks;
meat; thick end;
cask)
[☞ but, butte]
butte +s (hill)
[☞ beaut, butt,
Bute]
butt end +s noun
butt-end +s +ed +ing
verb
butt-ending noun
but|ter +s +ed +ing
butter-and-eggs
plural butter-and-
eggs
butter|ball +s
but|ter bean +s
butter|bur +s
butter|cream +s
butter|cup +s
butter|fat
Butter|field, Wil|liam
(English architect)
butter|fingered
butter|fingers
plural butter|fingers
butter|fish
plural butter|fish or
butter|fish|es
butter|flied adjective
butter|fly
butter|flies
butter|flied
butter|fly|ing

butter|fly fish
plural butter|fly fish
or butter|fly fish|es
butter|head +s
butter|horn +s
butter|i|ness
but|ter knife
but|ter knives
butter|milk
butter|nut +s
butter|scotch
but|ter tart +s
butter|wort +s
but|tery
but|ter|ies
butt|in|ski +s (use
buttinsky)
butt|in|sky
butt|in|skies
but|tle
but|tles
but|tled
but|tling
butt-naked
but|tock +s
but|ton +s +ed +ing
button-back +s
button|ball +s
but|ton blan|ket +s
button|bush
button|bush|es
button-down (of a
collar or shirt)
[☞ buttoned-
down]
but|toned adjective
buttoned-down
(formal,
conservative)
[☞ button-down]
buttoned-up
button|hole
button|holes
button|holed
button|hol|ing
button|hol|er +s
button|hook +s
button|less
button|wood +s
but|tress
but|tress|es
but|tressed
but|tress|ing
butt|stock +s
butt weld +s
butty
but|ties
butyl (Chemistry)
butyl|ated
hy|droxy|tolu|ene
buty|rate +s
bu|tyr|ic acid
buxom

buxom|ness
Bux|te|hude,
Diet|rich (Danish
musician)
buy (purchase, etc.)
buys
bought
buy|ing
[☞ by, bi, bye]
buy back verb
buys back
bought back
buy|ing back
buy|back +s noun
buy-down +s
buy|er +s
buy out verb
buys out
bought out
buy|ing out
buy|out +s noun
buzz
buzz|es
buzzed
buzz|ing
buz|zard +s
buzz|bait +s
buzz bomb +s
buzz cut +s
buzzed adjective
buzz|er +s
buzz saw +s
buzz|word +s
buzzy
buzz|i|er
buzz|i|est
bwana
BWR (boiling water
reactor)
BWRs
By, John (British
military engineer)
by preposition & adverb
[☞ bye, bi, buy]
Byatt, An|tonia Susan
(English writer)
Byb|los (ancient
seaport, Lebanon)
by-blow +s
by-boat +s
by|catch
by|catch|es
Byd|goszcz (city,
Poland)
bye +s (goodbye;
Sports; in 'by the
bye')
[☞ by, bi, buy]
bye-boat +s (use by-
boat)
bye-bye +s (goodbye;
sleep)
bye-byes (sleep)

bye-law +s (use
bylaw)
by-election +s
Byelo|rus|sia (a
former name for
Belarus)
Byelo|rus|sian +s (of
Byelorussia; for
language use
Belarusian)
[☞ Belarusian]
by-form +s
by|gone +s
by|law +s
by|line +s
Bylot (island, Canada)
by|name +s
Byng, Jul|ian
Hed|worth George
(Viscount Byng of
Vimy, governor
general of Canada)
[☞ Bing]
by|pass
by|pass|es
by|passed
by|pass|ing
by|play +s
by-product +s
Byrd, Rich|ard
Eve|lyn (US
explorer)
Byrd, Wil|liam
(English composer)
byre +s
by|road +s
Byron, George
Gor|don, Lord
(English poet)
By|ron|ic
bys|sal
bys|sus
bys|sus|es or byssi
by|stand|er +s
byte +s (Computing)
[☞ bite, bight]
by the by (use by the
bye)
by the bye
Bytom (city, Poland)
By|town (former name
for Ottawa)
by|way +s
by|word +s
by-your-leave +s
noun
Byzan|tine +s
Byzan|tium (ancient
Istanbul)

C

c
• (letter; music note; mark; battery)
C's
• (Celsius, Centigrade; coulomb; capacitance; computing language)
c
• (letter)
c's
• (speed of light)
c. (century)
c. (*circa*)
CA (chartered accountant)
CAs
Caaba (*use* Kaaba)
cab
cabs
cabbed
cab|bing
ca|bal +s
Ca|bala (*Judaism: use* Kabbalah)
ca|bala (general mysticism: *use* cabbala)
Ca|bal|lé, Mont|ser|rat (Spanish soprano)
ca|bal|lero +s
ca|bana +s
ca|bane à sucre
ca|banes à sucre
caba|ret +s
cab|bage +s
cab|bage roll +s
cab|bagy
Cab|bala (*Judaism: use* Kabbalah)
cab|bala (general mystic interpretation; *for Judaism sense use* Kabbalah)
Cab|bal|ism (*Judaism: use* Kabbalism)
cab|bal|ism (*generally*)
Cab|bal|ist +s (*Judaism: use* Kabbalist)
cab|bal|ist +s (*generally*)
Cab|bal|is|tic (*Judaism: use* Kabbalistic)
cab|bal|is|tic (*generally*)

cab|bie +s
cabby (*use* cabbie)
cab|bies
caber +s
Cab|er|net +s
Cab|er|net Franc +s
Cab|er|net Sau|vi|gnon +s
cab|in +s +ed +ing
cabin boy +s
cabin class
cabin crew +s
cabin cruis|er +s
Cab|inda (region & its capital, Angola)
Cab|inet +s (*Politics*)
[☞ Kabinett]
cab|inet +s (cupboard; furniture)
[☞ Kabinett]
cabinet|maker +s
cabinet|making
cab|in|etry
cable
cables
cabled
cab|ling
cable car +s
cable|cast
cable|casts
cable|cast
cable|cast|ing
cable|cast|er +s
cable|gram +s
cable-knit +s
cable-laid
cable length +s
cable stitch
cable stitch|es
cable|vision
cable|way +s
cab|ling *noun*
cabo|chon +s
Ca|bon|ga (reservoir, Canada)
ca|boo|dle +s
ca|boose +s
Ca|bora Bassa (lake, Mozambique)
Cabot (strait & trail, Canada)
Cabot, John (Venetian explorer)
Cabot, Sebas|tian (Venetian cartographer)
cabo|tage
cab|ri|ole +s (*Furniture, Dance*)
cab|rio|let +s (carriage; car)
caca (nonsense)
[☞ kaka]

ca'canny
ca|cao +s (tree; seeds used to make cocoa)
[☞ cocoa]
caccia|tore
cacha|lot +s
cache (store)
cach|es
cached
cach|ing
ca|chec|tic
cache|pot +s
ca|chet +s
ca|chex|ia
ca|chex|ic
ca|chexy (= cachexia)
cach|in|nate
cach|in|nates
cach|in|nat|ed
cach|in|nat|ing
cach|in|na|tion +s
cach|in|na|tory
ca|chou +s (lozenge; vegetable extract)
ca|chu|cha +s
ca|cique +s
cack-handed
cack-handed|ly
cack-handed|ness
cackle
cackles
cackled
cack|ling
caco|daemon +s (*use* cacodemon)
caco|demon +s
caco|dyl
caco|dyl|ic
caco|ethes
caco|mistle +s
cac|oph|on|ous
cac|oph|ony
cac|oph|onies
cac|ta|ceous
cac|tus
cacti or cac|tus|es
ca|cu|min|al
CAD (computer-aided design)
cad +s (dishonourable person)
cad|as|tral
cad|av|er +s
cad|av|er|ic
cad|av|er|ous
Cad|boro|saur|us
Cad|bury, George (English manufacturer & reformer)
CAD/CAM (computer-aided

design and computer-aided manufacturing)
cad|die +s (*Golf: use* caddy)
cad|dis
cad|dis|es
cad|dis fly
cad|dis flies
cad|dish (typical of a cad)
[☞ Kaddish]
cad|dish|ly
cad|dish|ness
caddis|worm +s
Caddo
plural Caddo or Cad|dos
Cad|do|an
Caddy (Cadborosaurus)
caddy (container; *Golf*)
cad|dies
cad|died
caddy|ing
[☞ qadi]
Cade, John ('Jack') (Irish rebel)
ca|dence +s
ca|denced
ca|den|tial
ca|den|za +s
ca|det +s
cadet|ship
cadge (beg)
cadges
cadged
cadg|ling
cadg|er +s
cadi +s (judge: *use* qadi)
[☞ caddy]
Cadiz (city, Spain)
cad|mium
Cad|mus (*Greek Myth*)
cadre +s
ca|du|ceus (staff)
ca|ducei
[☞ caducous]
ca|du|city
ca|du|cous (*Botany & Zoology*)
[☞ caduceus]
cae|cil|ian +s (animal)
cae|cum (*use* cecum)
caeca
Caed|mon (English poet)
Caen (city, France)
Caeno|zoic (*use* Cenozoic)

Caer|nar|fon (town, Wales)

Caer|nar|von (= Caernarfon, Wales)

Caer|philly

Caer|phil|lies

Caesar, (Gaius)

Jul|ius (Roman general & statesman)

Caesar +s (Roman emperors; autocrat; salad; drink)

Caesa|rea (ancient port, Israel)

Caes|ar|ean +s

Caesa|rea Phil|ip|pi (city, ancient Palestine)

Caes|ar|ian +s (use Caesarean)

caes|ious

caes|ium (use cesium)

caes|ura +s

caes|ur|al

caf +s (cafeteria; café) [☞ calf]

ca|fard

café +s

café au lait

cafés au lait [☞ caffe latte]

café noir

cafés noirs

cafe|teria +s

cafe|tor|ium +s

caff +s (= caf)

caf|fein|at|ed

caf|feine

caffe latte

plural caffe latte [☞ café au lait]

caf|tan +s

Caga|yan (islands, the Philippines)

Cage, John (US composer)

cage (enclosure)

cages

caged

caging [☞ cadge]

cage bird +s

cager +s

cagey

cagier

cagi|est

cagey|ness (use caginess)

cagier

cagi|est

cagily

cagi|ness

Ca|glia|ri (city, Sardinia)

Cagli|os|tro, Count Ales|san|dro di (Italian adventurer & swindler)

Cag|ney, James (US actor)

ca|goule +s

cagy (use cagey)

cagier

cagi|est

ca|hoots

cai|man +s (reptile) [☞ Cayman]

Cain (Bible) [☞ Caine, Kain, cane, Kane]

Caine, Mi|chael (English actor) [☞ Cain, Kain, cane, Kane]

Caino|zoic

ca|ique +s

cairn +s

Cairn|gorm +s (mountains, Scotland)

cairn|gorm +s (mineral)

Cairo (capital of Egypt)

caisse popu|laire

caisses popu|laires

cais|son +s

Caith|ness (former county, Scotland)

cai|tiff +s

Caius (= Gaius, Roman jurist)

ca|jole

ca|joles

ca|joled

ca|jol|ing

ca|jole|ment

ca|jol|ery

Cajun +s

cake

cakes

caked

cak|ing

cake|walk +s +ed +ing

cal +s (calorie)

Cala|bar (port, Nigeria; bean)

cala|bash

cala|bash|es

cala|bogus (use callibogus)

cala|boose +s

cala|brese

Ca|lab|ria (region, Italy)

Ca|lab|rian +s

ca|la|di|um

plural ca|la|di|um or ca|la|di|ums

Calais (port, France)

cala|man|der +s

cala|mari (food) [☞ calamary]

cala|mary (animal)

cala|mar|ies [☞ calamari]

cala|mata +s (use kalamata)

cal|ami

cala|mine

cala|mint +s

ca|lami|tous

ca|lami|tous|ly

ca|lam|ity

ca|lam|ities

Ca|lam|ity Jane (US frontierswoman)

cala|mon|din +s

cala|mus

calami

ca|lan|do

ca|lash

ca|lash|es

cala|thea +s

cal|ca|neum (= calcaneus)

cal|ca|nea

cal|ca|neus

cal|ca|nei

cal|car|eous

cal|ceo|laria +s

cal|ceo|late

cal|ces

cal|cif|erol

cal|cif|er|ous

cal|cif|ic

cal|ci|fi|ca|tion

cal|ci|fy

cal|ci|fies

cal|ci|fied

cal|ci|fy|ing

cal|cin|a|tion

cal|cine

cal|cines

cal|cined

cal|cin|ing

cal|cite +s

cal|ci|tonin

cal|cium

cal|crete

calc|spar +s

cal|cul|abil|ity

cal|cul|able

cal|cul|ably

cal|cu|late

cal|cu|lates

cal|cu|lat|ed

cal|cu|lat|ing

cal|cu|lat|ed adjective

cal|cu|lat|ed|ly

cal|cu|lat|ing adjective

cal|cu|lat|ing|ly

cal|cu|la|tion +s

cal|cu|la|tive

cal|cu|la|tor +s

cal|cu|lous adjective (Medicine)

cal|cu|lus noun (Math; Medicine)

cal|culi or cal|cu|lus|es

Cal|cutta (port, India)

Cal|der, Alex|an|der (US artist)

cal|dera +s

Cal|de|rón de la Barca, Pedro (Spanish writer)

Cald|well, Ers|kine (US novelist)

ca|lèche +s

Cal|edon (town, Canada)

Cal|edon|ian +s (canal; of Scotland; Geology)

cal|en|dar +s +ed +ing (almanac; schedule, timetable; register) [☞ calender, Callander]

cal|en|der +s +ed +ing (Textiles) [☞ calendar, Callander]

ca|len|dric

ca|len|dric|al

cal|ends

cal|len|dula

plural ca|llen|dula or ca|llen|dulas

cal|en|ture

calf (young animal; part of leg; floating ice)

calves

calf|hood

calf|like

calf|skin

Cal|gar|ian +s

Cal|gary (city, Canada)

Cali (city, Colombia) [☞ Kali]

cali|brate
cali|brates
cali|brat|ed
cali|brat|ing
cali|bra|tion +s
cali|bra|tor +s
cali|bre +s
cali|bred
cali|ces *plural of* calix
[☞ calluses]
cal|li|che +s
cal|ico
cal|icoes or cal|icos
Cali|cut (port, India)
Cali|for|nia (state, US; gulf, Pacific; poppy; sea lion)
Cali|for|nian +s
cali|for|nium
Ca|lig|ula (Roman emperor)
cali|per +s +ed +ing
ca|liph +s
ca|liph|ate +s
cal|is|then|ic
cal|is|then|ics
Cal-Ital
calix (*use* calyx)
cali|ces or calix|es
call +s +ed +ing (summon; phone; visit; name; etc.)
[☞ col, caul, Coll]
calla +s
Cal|laghan, (Leon|ard) James (Baron Callaghan of Cardiff, British prime minister)
Cal|laghan, Mor|ley Ed|ward (Cdn writer)
calla lily
calla lil|ies
cal|la|loo
Cal|lan|der (community, Canada)
[☞ calendar, calender]
Cal|lao (port, Peru)
Cal|las, Maria (US soprano)
call back *verb*
calls back
called back
call|ing back
call|back +s *noun*
call box
call box|es
call boy +s
call dis|play

call|er +s (one who calls etc.)
[☞ collar, choler]
call|er ID
call for|ward|ing
call girl +s
calli|bogus
Cal|lic|ra|tes (Greek architect)
Cal|lière, Louis-Hector de (governor of Montreal & New France)
Cal|lières, Louis-Hector de (= Callière)
cal|lig|raph|er +s
cal|li|graph|ic
cal|lig|raph|ist +s
cal|lig|raphy
Cal|lima|chus (Greek sculptor; Greek poet)
call in *verb*
calls in
called in
call|ing in
call-in +s *noun*
call|ing +s *noun*
Call|ing Card +s *proprietary* (telephone credit card)
call|ing card +s (business card; distinctive feature)
Cal|liope (*Greek & Roman Myth*)
cal|liope +s
cal|lis|then|ic (*use* calisthenic)
cal|lis|then|ics (*use* calisthenics)
Cal|listo (*Greek Myth*; *Astronomy*)
cal|los|ity
cal|los|ities
cal|lous
• *adjective* (insensitive; hardened)
• *noun* (area of hardened skin: *use* callus)
cal|lous|es
cal|loused
cal|lous|ly
cal|lous|ness
call out *verb*
calls out
called out
call|ing out
call-out +s *noun*
cal|low
cal|low|ly

Cal|lo|way, Cabell ('Cab') (US bandleader)
call|low|ness
call sign +s
cal|luna +s
call up *verb*
calls up
called up
call|ing up
call-up +s *noun*
cal|lus *noun* (area of hardened skin)
cal|lus|es
[☞ callous]
cal|lused (*use* calloused)
cal|lus|es *plural of* callus
[☞ calices]
call wait|ing
Call|wood, June (Cdn journalist)
[☞ Colwood]
calm +er +est +s +ed +ing
calma|tive +s
calm|ly
calm|ness
calo|mel +s
Calor gas *proprietary*
ca|lor|ic +s
cal|orie +s
cal|or|if|ic
cal|or|if|ic|ally
cal|or|im|eter +s
cal|ori|met|ric
cal|or|im|etry
calque
calques
calqued
cal|quing
cal|trap +s (*use* caltrop)
cal|trop +s
calu|met +s
calum|ni|ate
calum|ni|ates
calum|ni|at|ed
calum|ni|at|ing
calum|ni|a|tion
calum|ni|ator +s
calum|ni|a|tory
calum|ni|ous
cal|um|ny
cal|um|nies
cal|um|nied
cal|um|ny|ing
Cal|va|dos (region, France; brandy)
Cal|vary (Crucifixion site)

calve
calves
calved
calv|ing
Cal|vert, Sir George, 1st Baron Bal|ti|more (English statesman)
Cal|vert, Leon|ard (English statesman)
Cal|vin, John (Protestant theologian)
Cal|vin, Mel|vin (US biochemist)
Cal|vin|ism
Cal|vin|ist +s
Cal|vin|is|tic
Cal|vino, Italo (Italian writer)
calx (*Chemistry*)
cal|ces
caly|ces
Ca|lyp|so (*Greek Myth*)
ca|lyp|so +s (West Indian music; orchid)
calyp|son|ian
calyx (*Botany*; *Biology*)
caly|ces or calyx|es
cal|zone +s
cam +s
cama|rad|erie
Cam|argue (region, France)
cama|rilla +s
camas
Cam|bay (gulf, Arabian Sea)
cam|ber +s +ed +ing
Camber|well beauty
Camber|well beaut|ies
cam|bial
cam|bium
cam|bia or cam|biums
Cam|bo|dia (country, Asia)
Cam|bo|dian +s
cam|boose +s
Cambo|zola *proprietary*
Cam|brian
cam|bric +s
Cam|bridge (cities, England, US & Canada)
Cam|bridge Bay (bay & hamlet, Canada)
Cam|bridge blue +s (Cam|bridge-blue

when preceding a noun)
Cam|bridge|shire (county, England)
Cam|by|ses (Persian king)
cam|corder +s
came *past tense of* come
[☞ kame]
camel +s
camel|back +s
camel|eer +s
camel hair
camel|lia +s
cam|elo|pard +s
Cam|elo|par|dalis (constellation)
Cam|elot (*Arthurian Legend*)
camel's hair (*use* camel hair)
Camem|bert +s (village, France; cheese)
cameo +s
cam|era +s
cam|era lu|cida +s
camera|man
camera|men
cam|era ob|scura +s
camera|person +s
camera-ready
camera|woman
camera|women
Cam|eron, Julia Mar|garet (English photographer)
Cam|eron High|lands (resort, Malaysia)
Cam|er|oon (country, Africa) ·
Cam|er|oon|ian +s
cami +s
cami|knick|ers
cami|sole +s
camo +s
Camo|ëns, Luis Vaz de (= Camões)
Cam|ões, Luis Vaz de (Portuguese poet)
camo|mile
Cam|orra
cam|ou|flage
cam|ou|flages
cam|ou|flaged
cam|ou|fla|ging
Camp, Dal|ton Kings|ley (Cdn political adviser)
camp +s +ed +ing +er +est

cam|paign +s +ed +ing
cam|paign|er +s
Cam|pa|nia (region, Italy)
cam|pa|nile +s
cam|pano|logic|al
cam|pan|ol|o|gist +s
cam|pan|ol|ogy
cam|pan|ula +s
cam|panu|late
camp bed +s
Camp|bell, Sir Alex|an|der (1822–92; Cdn politician)
Camp|bell, Alex|an|der Brad|shaw (b.1933; Cdn politician)
Camp|bell, (Avril) Kim (Cdn prime minister)
Camp|bell, Clar|ence (NHL president)
Camp|bell, Doug|las Lloyd (Cdn politician)
Camp|bell, Jo|seph (US mythologist)
Camp|bell, Mrs. Pat|rick (English actress)
Camp|bell, Thane Alex|an|der (Cdn politician)
Camp|bell, Thom|as (Scottish poet)
Campbell-Bannerman, Sir Henry (British prime minister)
Camp|bell River (municipality, Canada)
Camp|bell|ton (city, Canada)
camp|craft
Cam|peche (state & its capital, Mexico)
camp|er +s
campe|sino +s
camp|fire +s
camp|ground +s
cam|phor
cam|phor|ate
cam|phor|ates
cam|phor|at|ed
cam|phor|at|ing
cam|phor|ic
camp|i|er
camp|i|est
camp|i|ly

Cam|pin|as (city, Brazil)
camp|i|ness
camp|ing *noun*
Cam|pion, Ed|mund (English priest)
Cam|pion, Jane (New Zealand filmmaker)
Cam|pion, Thom|as (English poet & composer)
cam|pion +s
Campo|basso (city, Italy)
Campo|bello (island, Canada)
Campo Gran|de (city, Brazil)
camp out *verb*
camps out
camped out
camp|ing out
camp-out +s *noun*
camp|site +s
camp stove +s
cam|pus
cam|pus|es
campy
camp|i|er
camp|i|est
cam|pylo|bac|ter +s
Cam|rose (city, Canada)
cam|shaft +s
Camus, Al|bert (French writer)
cam|wood
can
• *auxiliary verb* (be able)
 present can
 past could
• *noun & verb* (metal container etc.; preserve; fire; record)
cans
canned
can|ning
[☞ khan, Cannes]
Cana (ancient town, Galilee)
[☞ canna]
Canaan (*early name for* Palestine; any promised land; heaven)
Canaan|ite +s
Can|ada +s (country, N America; in names of animals & plants)
[☞ Kannada]
Canad|arm
proprietary

Can|ad|ian +s
Can|adi|ana
Can|ad|ian|ism +s
Can|ad|ian|ist +s
Can|ad|ian|iz|a|tion
Can|ad|ian|ize
Can|ad|ian|iz|es
Can|ad|ian|ized
Can|ad|ian|iz|ing
Can|ad|ian|ness
Can|ad|ian Shield
Can|ad|ian whisky
Can|ad|ian whis|kies
Cana|dien +s (a French Canadian; NHL team)
[☞ Canadian]
Cana|dienne +s (a French-Cdn woman or girl)
ca|naille
Can|ajan +s (*use* Canajun)
Can|ajun +s
can|al +s
canal boat +s
Cana|letto (Italian painter)
can|al|iz|a|tion
can|al|ize
can|al|iz|es
can|al|ized
can|al|iz|ing
canal rays
Canal Zone (territory surrounding the Panama Canal)
Can-Am
can|apé +s (food; sofa)
[☞ canopy]
can|ard +s
Can|ar|ese (*use* Kanarese)
plural Can|ar|ese
Can|ary (Atlantic islands)
Can|aries
[☞ Cannary]
can|ary (bird; wine)
can|aries
[☞ cannery]
can|ary yel|low (canary-yellow *when preceding a noun*)
can|asta +s
Can|av|eral (cape & space centre, US)
Can|berra (capital of Australia)
can|can +s

can|cel
can|cels
can|celled
can|cel|ling
can|cel|late
can|cel|lat|ed
can|cel|la|tion +s
can|cel|ler +s
can|cel|lous
Can|cer +s
(constellation;
Zodiac)
can|cer +s
Can|cer|ian +s
(Astronomy &
Astrology)
can|cer|ous (of a
cancer)
canc|er stick +s
Can|Con
Can|Cult
Can|cún (resort,
Mexico)
can|dela +s
can|del|abra
plural can|del|ab|ras
can|del|ab|rum
(= candelabra)
plural can|del|abra
can|des|cence
can|des|cent
Can|diac (town,
Canada)
can|did
can|dida +s
can|di|dacy
can|di|da|cies
can|di|date +s
can|di|da|ture +s
can|di|dia|sis
can|did|ly
can|did|ness
can|died adjective
can|dle
can|dles
can|dled
cand|ling
can|dled ice
(= candle ice)
candle|fish
plural candle|fish
can|dle hold|er +s
can|dle ice
candle|light
candle|lit
Candle|mas
candle|power
cand|ler +s
candle|stick +s
candle|wick +s
can-do (enthusiastic,
efficient)
[☞ CANDU]

Can|dolle, Au|gus|tin
Pyr|ame de (Swiss
botanist)
Can|dom|blé
can|dor (use candour)
can|dour
CANDU (nuclear
reactor)
CANDUs
candy (confection)
can|dies
can|died
candy|ing
[☞ Kandy]
candy apple +s
candy-apple red
candy-ass
candy-asses
candy-assed
candy bar +s
candy cane +s
candy-coloured
candy col|ours
candy corn
candy floss
candy stripe +s
candy-striped
candy|striper +s
candy|tuft +s
cane (reed; walking
stick)
canes
caned
caning
[☞ Kane, Cain,
Caine, Kain]
cane|brake +s
cane chair +s
caner +s
cane sugar
cane toad +s
Can|etti, Elias
(novelist &
playwright)
CANEX
CANEXes
can|id +s
ca|nine +s
caning noun
Canis Major
(constellation)
Canis Minor
(constellation)
can|is|ter +s
can|ker +s
can|ker|ous
can|ker sore +s
canker|worm +s
Can|Lit
Can|more (town,
Canada)
can|na +s (plant)
[☞ Cana]

can|na|bis
Can|nary, Mar|tha
Jane (Calamity Jane)
[☞ cannery]
canned adjective
can|nel
can|nel coal
can|nel|loni
can|nel|ure +s
can|ner +s
can|nery (factory)
can|ner|ies
[☞ canary,
Cannary]
Cannes (resort,
France; film festival)
can|ni|bal +s
can|ni|bal|ism
can|ni|bal|is|tic
can|ni|bal|is|tic|ally
can|ni|bal|iz|a|tion
+s
can|ni|bal|ize
can|ni|bal|iz|es
can|ni|bal|ized
can|ni|bal|iz|ing
can|ni|er
can|ni|est
can|ni|kin +s
can|ni|ly
can|ni|ness
Can|ning, Charles
John, 1st Earl
(governor general of
India)
Can|ning, George
(British prime
minister)
can|ning noun
Can|niz|zaro,
Stan|is|lao (Italian
chemist)
can|noli
can|non
• noun (gun; Billiards;
Mechanics)
plural can|non or
can|nons
• verb (collide;
Billiards)
can|nons
can|noned
can|non|ing
[☞ canon]
can|non|ade
can|non|ades
can|non|ad|ed
can|non|ad|ing
cannon|ball +s +ed
+ing
can|non bone +s
can|non fod|der +s

can|not (can not)
[☞ canot du
maître, canot du
nord]
can|nula
can|nu|lae or
can|nu|las
can|nu|late
can|nu|lates
can|nu|lat|ed
can|nu|lat|ing
can|nu|la|tion +s
canny
can|ni|er
can|ni|est
canoe
ca|noes
ca|noed
canoe|ing
canoe|able
canoe camp|er +s
canoe-camping
canoe|ing noun
canoe|ist +s
canoe|man
canoe|men
can|ola
can|on +s (rule;
Religion; recognized
list; Music)
[☞ cannon]
canon|ess
canon|ess|es
ca|non|ic
ca|non|ic|al +s
ca|non|ic|al|ly
can|on|icity
can|on|ist +s
can|on|iz|a|tion +s
can|on|ize
can|on|iz|es
can|on|ized
can|on|iz|ing
can|onry
can|on|ries
ca|noo|dle
ca|noo|dles
ca|noo|dled
ca|nood|ling
Ca|no|pic
Ca|no|pus (star)
can|opy (covering)
can|opies
can|opied
can|opy|ing
[☞ canapé]
can|opy bed +s
can|or|ous
canot du maître
ca|nots du maître
canot du nord
ca|nots du nord

Ca|nova, An|tonio (Italian sculptor)
Canso (town & strait, Canada)
canst
cant +s +ed +ing (language; talk; slant, tilt) [☞ can't, Kant]
can't (cannot) [☞ cant]
can|ta|bile +s
Can|tab|ria (region, Spain)
Can|tab|rian +s
Can|ta|brig|ian +s
can|ta|loup +s (use cantaloupe)
can|ta|loupe +s
can|tan|ker|ous
can|tan|ker|ous|ly
can|tan|ker|ous|ness
can|tata +s
can|teen +s
can|ter +s +ed +ing
Can|ter|bury (city & cathedral, England; region, New Zealand)
can|thari|des
cant hook +s
can|thus
   can|thi
can|ticle +s
Can|ticle of Can|ticles
Can|ticles (= Canticle of Canticles)
can|ti|lena +s
can|ti|lever +s +ed +ing
can|ti|levered adjective
can|til|late
   can|til|lates
   can|til|lat|ed
   can|til|lat|ing
can|til|la|tion +s
can|tina +s
can|tle +s
can|to +s (section of a poem) [☞ Kanto]
Can|ton (= Guangzhou, China)
can|ton +s +ed +ing
can|ton|al
Can|ton|ese plural Can|ton|ese
can|ton|ment +s

Can|tor, Georg (Russian-born mathematician)
can|tor +s
can|tor|ial
can|toris
can|trip +s
Can|uck +s
Ca|nute (king of England, Denmark & Norway)
can|vas (cloth, painting; cover with canvas)
   can|vas|es
   can|vassed
   can|vas|sing [☞ canvass]
canvas|back +s
can|vass (solicit etc.)
   can|vass|es
   can|vassed
   can|vass|ing [☞ canvas]
can|vass|er +s
can|yon +s
canyon|land +s
CAO (chief administrative officer)
   CAOs
Caou|ette, (Joseph-David) Réal (Cdn politician)
caou|tchouc
cap
   caps
   capped
   cap|ping
Capa, Rob|ert (Hungarian-born US photographer) [☞ kappa]
ca|pabil|ity
   ca|pabil|ities
ca|pable
ca|pably
cap|acious
cap|acious|ly
cap|acious|ness
cap|aci|tance +s
cap|aci|tate
   cap|aci|tates
   cap|aci|tat|ed
   cap|aci|tat|ing
cap|aci|ta|tive
cap|aci|tive
cap|aci|tor +s
cap|acity
   cap|aci|ties
ca|pari|son +s

Cap-de-la-Madeleine (city, Canada)
Cape (= Cape of Good Hope or Cape Province, South Africa)
cape +s (garment; promontory)
Cape Ann +s
Cape Bret|on (regional municipality, Canada)
Cape Bret|on Coun|ty (former name for Cape Breton)
Cape Bret|on|er +s
Cape Bret|on Island (in Canada)
Cape Can|av|eral (space centre, US)
Cape Cod (peninsula, US)
Cape Cod|der +s
Cape Col|ony (former name for Cape Province, South Africa)
Cape Col|oured +s
caped adjective
Cape Dor|set (hamlet, Canada)
Cape goose|berry
   Cape goose|ber|ries
Cape Island boat +s
Cape Island|er +s
Cape John|son Depth
Čapek, Karel (Czech writer)
cape|let +s
cape|lin (= caplin) plural cape|lin or cape|lins
Ca|pella (star)
cap|el|lini
Cape of Good Hope (promontory, South Africa)
Cape Prov|ince (former province, South Africa)
caper +s +ed +ing
caper|cail|lie +s
caper|cail|zie +s (use capercaillie)
caper|er +s
Cape Sable (island, Canada)
cape|skin

Capet, Hugh or Hugues (French king)
Cap|etian +s
Cape Town (legislative capital of South Africa)
Cape Verd|ean +s
Cape Verde Islands (country, Atlantic Ocean)
cap|ful +s
capi|as
cap|iche
capi|col|la (= capicollo)
capi|col|lo
Capi|lano
cap|il|lar|ity
ca|pil|lary
   ca|pil|lar|ies
cap|ita (in 'per capita')
cap|ital +s (government city; money; letter; principal, leading; of death) [☞ Capitol]
capital-intensive
cap|ital|ism
cap|ital|ist +s
cap|ital|is|tic
cap|ital|is|tic|ally
cap|ital|iz|a|tion +s
cap|ital|ize
   cap|ital|iz|es
   cap|ital|ized
   cap|ital|iz|ing
cap|ital|ly
capi|ta|tion +s
Cap|itol +s (legislative building) [☞ capital]
Cap|itol Hill
Cap|ito|line (hill, Rome)
ca|pitu|lar
ca|pitu|late
   ca|pitu|lates
   ca|pitu|lat|ed
   ca|pitu|lat|ing
ca|pitu|la|tion +s
ca|pitu|la|tor +s
ca|pitu|la|tory
ca|pitu|lum
   ca|pitu|la
cap|let +s
cap|lin plural cap|lin
cap'n +s
capo +s (Music; crime boss)
ca|pon +s

Ca|pone, Al|phonse ('Al') (US gangster)
capon|ize
  capon|iz|es
  capon|ized
  capon|iz|ing
ca|pot +s (use capote)
capo tasto
  capo tas|tos
Ca|po|te, Tru|man (US writer)
ca|pote +s
Capp, Al (US cartoonist)
Cap|pa|do|cia (ancient region, Asia Minor)
Cap|pa|do|cian +s
capped adjective
cap|pel|la
cap|per +s
cap|ping +s noun
cap|puc|cino +s (coffee) [☞ capuchin]
Capra, Frank (US filmmaker)
Capra|esque
Capri (island off Italy)
ca|pri +s
ca|pric|cio +s
ca|pric|cio|so
ca|price +s
ca|pri|cious
ca|pri|cious|ly
ca|pri|cious|ness
Cap|ri|corn +s (constellation; Zodiac)
Cap|ri|corn|ian +s
Cap|ri|corn|us (the constellation Capricorn)
cap|rine
cap|ri|ole
  cap|ri|oles
  cap|ri|oled
  cap|ri|ol|ing
Ca|pri|vi Strip (region, Namibia)
cap|rock +s
Cap-Rouge (town, Canada)
cap|sai|cin
Cap|si|an
cap|si|cum +s
cap|sid +s
cap|siz|al +s
cap|size
  cap|siz|es
  cap|sized
  cap|siz|ing
cap sleeve +s

cap|stan +s
cap|stone +s
cap|su|lar
cap|su|late
  cap|su|lates
  cap|su|lat|ed
  cap|su|lat|ing
cap|su|lat|ed adjective
cap|sule +s
cap|su|lize
  cap|su|liz|es
  cap|su|lized
  cap|su|liz|ing
cap|tain +s +ed +ing
cap|tain|cy
  cap|tain|cies
captain's bed +s
captain's chair +s
captain|ship +s
cap|tion +s +ed +ing
cap|tious
cap|tious|ly
cap|tious|ness
cap|tiv|ate
  cap|tiv|ates
  cap|tiv|at|ed
  cap|tiv|at|ing
cap|tiv|at|ing|ly
cap|tiv|a|tion +s
cap|tive +s
captive-bred
cap|tiv|ity
  cap|tiv|ities
cap|tor +s
cap|ture
  cap|tures
  cap|tured
  cap|tur|ing
cap|tur|er +s
Capu|chin +s (friar)
capu|chin +s (monkey; cloak) [☞ cappuccino]
capy|bara +s
car +s (vehicle) [☞ Carr, Kars]
cara|bi|neer +s (soldier using carbine) [☞ carabiner, carabiniere]
cara|biner +s (Mountaineering) [☞ carabineer, carabiniere]
cara|bi|nier +s (soldier using carbine: use carabineer) [☞ carabiniere, carabiner]

cara|bi|niere (Italian police officer) cara|bi|nieri [☞ carabineer, carabiner]
cara|cal +s (lynx) [☞ caracole, karakul]
Cara|calla (Roman emperor)
cara|cara +s
Ca|ra|cas (capital of Venezuela)
cara|cole (Equestrian)
  cara|coles
  cara|coled
  cara|col|ing [☞ caracal, karakul]
cara|cul +s (sheep: use karakul) [☞ caracal, caracole]
ca|rafe +s
cara|gana +s
Cara|jás (region, Brazil)
caram|bola +s
cara|mel +s (confectionery) [☞ Carmel]
cara|mel|iz|a|tion
cara|mel|ize
  cara|mel|iz|es
  cara|mel|ized
  cara|mel|iz|ing
cara|pace +s
Cara|quet +s (town, Canada; oyster)
carat +s (unit of weight for gems; for measure of purity of gold use karat) [☞ caret]
Cara|vag|gio, Michel|angelo Merisi da (Italian painter)
cara|van
  cara|vans
  cara|vanned
  cara|van|ning
cara|van|ner +s
cara|van|sary (use caravanserai)
  cara|van|sar|ies
cara|van|serai +s
cara|vel +s (ship) [☞ carvel-built]
cara|way
carb +s
car|ba|mate +s
car barn +s
car|bide +s

car|bine +s
car|bo +s
carbo|hy|drate +s
car|bol|ic
carbo-load +s +ed +ing
carbo-loading noun
car bomb +s
car|bon +s
carbon-12
carbon-14
car|bon|aceous
car|bon|ado +s
car|bon|ara
car|bon|ate
  car|bon|ates
  car|bon|at|ed
  car|bon|at|ing
car|bon|at|ed adjective
car|bon|a|tion
Car|bon|ear (town, Canada)
car|bon|ic
Car|bon|if|er|ous (geological era)
car|bon|if|er|ous (producing carbon or coal)
car|bon|iz|a|tion
car|bon|ize
  car|bon|iz|es
  car|bon|ized
  car|bon|iz|ing
car|bon|nade +s
car|bonyl +s
car boot sale +s
car|bor|un|dum
carb|oxyl +s
carb|oxyl|ic
car|boy +s
car|bun|cle +s
car|bun|cu|lar
car|bur|a|tion
car|bur|et
  car|bur|ets
  car|bur|et|ed or
  car|bur|et|ted
  car|bur|et|ing or
  car|bur|et|ting
car|bur|etor +s
car|bur|et|tor +s (use carburetor)
car|ca|jou +s
car|cass
  car|cass|es
Car|cas|sonne (city, France)
Car|che|mish (ancient city, Syria)
car|cino|gen +s
car|cino|gen|esis
car|cino|gen|ic

car|cino|gen|icity
car|cin|oma
car|cin|omas or
car|cin|omata
car|cin|oma|tous
car coat +s
card +s +ed +ing
Car|da|mom
(mountains,
Cambodia)
car|da|mom (plant)
car|da|mon
(= cardamom)
card|board +s
card-carrying
card|ed *adjective*
Cár|denas, Láz|aro
(Mexican president)
card|er +s
card game +s
card|holder +s
car|diac +s
Car|diff (capital of
Wales)
car|di|gan +s
Cardigan|shire
(former county,
Wales)
Car|din, Pierre
(French designer)
Car|din|al, Doug|las
Jo|seph (Cdn
architect)
Car|din|al, Har|old
(Cdn Indian leader)
car|din|al +s
car|din|al|ate +s
car|din|al|ly
car|din|al|ship +s
card index *noun*
card in|dex|es
card-index *verb*
card-indexes
card-indexed
card-indexing
car|dio
cardio|gram +s
cardio|graph +s
cardi|og|raph|er +s
cardi|og|raphy
cardi|ol|o|gist +s
cardi|ol|ogy
cardio|myop|athy
cardio|myop|athies
cardio|pulmon|ary
cardio|vascu|lar
car|doon +s
card shark +s
card sharp +s *noun*
card-sharp +s +ed
+ing *verb*
card sharp|er +s
card table +s

Car|ducci, Gio|suè
(Italian poet)
care
cares
cared
caring
ca|reen +s +ed +ing
ca|reer +s +ed +ing
career|ism
career|ist +s
care|free
care|free|ness
care|ful
care|ful|ly
care|ful|ness
care|giver +s
care|giving
Care|less, James
Mau|rice Stock|ford
(Cdn historian)
care|less
care|less|ly
care|less|ness
carer +s
ca|ress
ca|ress|es
ca|ressed
ca|ress|ing
ca|ress|ing|ly
caret +s (insertion
mark)
[☞ carat, karat]
care|taker +s
care|taking
Carew, Thom|as
(English poet)
[☞ Karoo]
care|worn
Carey, George
Leon|ard
(Archbishop of
Canterbury)
[☞ Cary]
car|fare +s
car|ful +s
cargo
car|goes or car|gos
car|hop +s
Caria (ancient region,
SW Asia)
Carian +s
[☞ carrion]
Carib +s
Carib|bean +s (sea;
islands; people)
Cari|boo (mountains,
Canada; gold rush)
[☞ Caribou Inuit]
cari|boo (deer: *use*
caribou)
plural cari|boo

cari|bou (deer; drink;
moss)
plural cari|bou
Cari|bou Inuit
[☞ Cariboo]
cari|ca|tu|ral
cari|ca|ture
cari|ca|tures
cari|ca|tured
cari|ca|tur|ing
cari|ca|tur|ist +s
caries (bone decay)
plural caries
Car|ignan (town,
Canada)
Car|ignan, Jean ('Ti-
Jean', Cdn fiddler)
Car|illon (canal,
Canada)
car|illon +s (*Music*)
car|illon|neur +s
Carina (constellation)
carina +s (*Biology*)
carin|al
carin|ate
car|ing *adjective*
car|ing|ly
Car|in|thia (state,
Austria)
Car|in|thian +s (of
Carinthia)
[☞ Corinthian]
Cari|oca +s (native of
Rio de Janeiro)
cari|oca +s (samba-
like dance & music)
[☞ karaoke]
cario|gen|ic
cari|ole +s (*use*
carriole)
cari|ous
car|jack +s +ed +ing
car|jack|er +s
car|jack|ing +s *noun*
car jock|ey +s
cark|ing
carl +s
Carl XVI Gus|taf
(king of Sweden)
[☞ Karl, Carle]
Carle, Gilles (Cdn
filmmaker)
Carle|ton, Guy, 1st
Baron Dor|ches|ter
(British colonial
administrator in
Canada)
Carle|ton, Thom|as
(lieutenant-governor
of New Brunswick)
Carle|ton Place
(town, Canada)
car|line +s

Car|ling, Sir John
(Cdn brewer)
Car|lisle (town,
England)
[☞ Carlyle]
car|load +s
Car|los, Don (Spanish
prince)
Car|lota (empress of
Mexico)
Car|lo|vin|gian +s
Car|low (county &
town, Ireland)
Car|lyle, Thom|as
(Scottish writer)
[☞ Carlisle]
car|maker +s
Car|man, (Wil|liam)
Bliss (Cdn writer)
Car|mar|then|shire
(former county,
Wales)
Car|mel (mountains,
Israel)
[☞ caramel]
Car|mel|ite +s
Car|michael,
Frank|lin (Cdn
painter)
Car|michael,
Hoag|land How|ard
('Hoagy') (US
musician)
car|mina|tive +s
car|mine +s
Car|naby Street (in
London)
Car|nac (monument
site, France)
[☞ Karnak]
car|nage
car|nal
car|nal|ity
car|nal|ize
car|nal|iz|es
car|nal|ized
car|nal|iz|ing
car|nal|ly
Car|nap, Ru|dolf (US
philosopher)
car|nas|sial +s
car|na|tion +s
car|nauba +s
Car|negie, An|drew
(US entrepreneur)
car|nel|ian +s
(mineral)
[☞ cornelian
cherry)]
carn|et +s (permit)
car|ney +s (carnival
worker: *use* carny)
[☞ carnet]

car|nie +s (*use* carny)
car|ni|val +s
car|ni|val|esque
car|ni|vore +s
car|niv|or|ous
car|niv|or|ous|ly
car|niv|or|ous|ness
Car|not, La|zare
  Nico|las
  Mar|guer|ite (French
  military engineer)
Car|not, (Nico|las
  Léo|nard) Sadi
  (French scientist)
carny
  car|nies
carob +s
Carol (king of
  Romania)
  [☞ Carroll, Carrel]
carol (song; sing)
  car|ols
  car|olled
  car|ol|ling
  [☞ carrel]
Caro|lean
Caro|lina +s (states,
  US)
Caro|line +s (islands,
  W Pacific; of Charles
  I or II of England)
Caro|lin|gian +s (of
  the second Frankish
  dynasty; *Calligraphy*)
Caro|lin|ian +s (of
  the Carolinas; forest
  region)
carol|ler +s
carom +s +ed +ing
Caron, Louis (Cdn
  writer)
car|ot|ene +s (orange
  plant pigment)
car|ot|en|oid +s
Ca|roth|ers, Wal|lace
  Hume (US chemist)
ca|rotid +s
ca|rous|al +s
  (drunken revel)
  [☞ carousel]
ca|rouse
  ca|rous|es
  ca|roused
  ca|rous|ing
car|ou|sel +s (merry-
  go-round; conveyor;
  rotating tray;
  tournament)
  [☞ carousal]
ca|rous|er +s
carp
 • (fish)
  plural carp

• (complain)
  carps
  carped
  carp|ing
Car|pac|cio, Vit|tore
  (Italian painter)
car|pac|cio (food)
car|pal +s (bone)
  [☞ carpel]
car|pal tun|nel
  syn|drome
car park +s
Car|path|ian
  (mountains, Europe)
carpe diem
car|pel +s (*Botany*)
  [☞ carpal]
car|pel|lary
Car|pen|taria (gulf,
  Australia)
car|pen|ter +s +ed
  +ing
car|pen|try
carp|er +s
car|pet +s +ed +ing
car|pet bag +s
carpet|bag|ger +s
car|pet bomb|ing
car|pet bowl|ing
carpet|ing noun
car|pet sweep|er +s
car phone +s
car|pol|ogy
car pool +s noun
car|pool +s +ed +ing
  verb
car|pool|er +s
car|pool|ing noun
car|port +s
car|pus
  carpi
Carr, Emily (Cdn
  painter)
Car|racci, Agos|tino
  (Italian painter)
Car|racci, Anni|bale
  (Italian painter)
Car|racci, Ludo|vico
  (Italian painter)
car|rack +s (merchant
  ship)
  [☞ carrick bend,
  Carrick-on-
  Shannon]
car|ra|geen
car|ra|geen|an +s
car|ra|geen|in +s (*use*
  carrageenan)
car|ra|gheen (*use*
  carrageen)
Car|rara (town, Italy)

Car|rel, Alexis
  (French surgeon)
  [☞ Carroll, Carol]
car|rel +s (cubicle)
  [☞ carol]
Car|reras, José
  (Spanish tenor)
car|riage +s
carriage|way +s
car|rick bend +s
  (knot)
  [☞ carrack]
Carrick-on-Shannon
  (town, Ireland)
Car|ri|er, Roch (Cdn
  writer)
Car|ri|er (people;
  language)
  plural Car|rier or
  Car|riers
car|ri|er +s (person or
  thing that carries)
car|ries *conjugated*
  form of carry
  [☞ caries]
Car|ring|ton, Dora de
  Hough|ton (English
  painter)
car|ri|ole +s
car|rion (carcass;
  crow; flower)
Car|roll, Lewis
  (English writer)
  [☞ Carrel, Carol]
car|rot +s (vegetable;
  enticement)
  [☞ caret, carat,
  karat, carotene]
carrot-and-stick
  adjective
car|rot cake +s
car|rot top +s
carrot-topped
car|roty
carry (lift etc.)
  car|ries
  car|ried
  carry|ing
  [☞ Cary, Carey,
  Kerry]
carry|all +s
carry|cot +s
carrying-on noun
carryings-on
carry on verb
  car|ries on
  car|ried on
  carry|ing on
carry-on +s noun
carry out verb
  car|ries out
  car|ried out
  carry|ing out
carry-out adjective

carry over verb
  car|ries over
  car|ried over
  carry|ing over
carry-over +s noun
cars plural of car
  [☞ Kars]
car seat +s
car|sick
car|sick|ness
Car|son,
  Chris|to|pher ('Kit')
  (US frontiersman)
Car|son, John
  Wil|liam ('John|ny')
  (US TV personality)
Car|son, Rachel
  Lou|ise (US
  zoologist)
Car|son City (city, US)
car|spiel +s
cart +s +ed +ing
  (vehicle; convey)
  [☞ go-kart]
cart|age +s
Car|ta|gena (cities,
  Spain & Colombia)
carte blanche
car|tel +s
car|tel|ize
  car|tel|iz|es
  car|tel|ized
  car|tel|iz|ing
Car|ter, Sir Fred|erick
  Bow|ker
  Ter|ring|ton (Cdn
  statesman)
Car|ter, How|ard
  (English
  archaeologist)
Car|ter, James Earl
  ('Jimmy') (US
  president)
Car|ter, Wil|fred
  Ar|thur Charles
  ('Wilf') (Cdn singer)
cart|er +s
Car|ter|et, John, 1st
  Earl Gran|ville
  (English statesman)
Car|tesian +s
Car|tesian|ism
cart|ful +s
Car|thage (ancient
  city, N Africa)
Car|tha|gin|ian +s
cart horse +s
Car|thu|sian +s
Car|tier (islands,
  Indian Ocean)
  [☞ quartier]

Car|tier, Sir George-
Étienne (Cdn
statesman)
[☞ quartier]
Car|tier, Jacques
(French explorer)
[☞ quartier]
Cartier-Bresson,
Henri (French
photographer)
car|ti|lage +s
car|ti|la|gin|oid
car|ti|la|gin|ous
Cart|land, Dame
(Mary) Bar|bara
Ham|il|ton (English
novelist)
cart|load +s
carto|gram +s
car|tog|raph|er +s
carto|graph|ic
carto|graph|ic|al
car|tog|raphy
carto|mancy
car|ton +s
car|toon +s +ed +ing
car|toon|ish
car|toon|ish|ly
car|toon|ist +s
cartoon-like
car|toony
car|touche +s
car|tridge +s
cart track +s
cart trail +s
cart|wheel +s +ed
+ing
Cart|wright,
Ed|mund (English
inventor)
cart|wright +s
car|uncle +s
car|uncu|lar
Ca|ruso, En|rico
(Italian tenor)
carve
carves
carved
carv|ing
car|vel +s (= caravel)
carvel-built
carv|en archaic
conjugated form of
carve
Car|ver, George
Wash|ing|ton (US
educator &
agricultural chemist)
carv|er +s
carv|ery
carv|eries

carve up verb
carves up
carved up
carv|ing up
carve-up +s noun
carv|ing +s noun
car wash
car wash|es
Cary, (Ar|thur) Joyce
Lunel (English
novelist)
[☞ Carey, Kerry,
carry]
cary|atid
cary|atids or
cary|ati|des
cary|op|sis
cary|op|ses
ca|saba +s
Casa|blanca (city,
Morocco)
Ca|sals, Pablo (or
Pau) (Spanish
musician)
Casa|nova,
Gio|van|ni Jac|opo
(Italian adventurer)
Casa|nova +s
(seducer)
cas|bah +s (use
kasbah)
CASBY (Cdn pop
music award)
CASBIES
Cas|cade (mountains,
N America)
cas|cade
cas|cades
cas|cad|ed
cas|cad|ing
cas|cara
cas|cara sag|rada
(= cascara)
case
cases
cased
cas|ing
case|book +s
case|bound
case-harden +s +ed
+ing
case-hardened
adjective
ca|sein
case|load +s
case lot +s
case|mate +s
Case|ment, Sir Roger
David (Irish
nationalist)
case|ment +s
case study
case stud|ies
case|work

case|work|er +s
Cas|grain, Thé|rèse
(Cdn feminist &
politician)
Cash, John|ny (US
singer-songwriter)
cash
• (money; cash
register; redeem)
cash|es
cashed
cash|ing
• (Asian coin)
plural cash
[☞ cache]
cash|able
cash and carry
cash and car|ries
cash bar +s
cash|book +s
cash box
cash boxes
cash card +s
cash cow +s
cash crop +s
cash crop|per +s
cash crop|ping
cash desk +s
cash dis|pen|ser +s
cash|ew +s (nut &
tree)
[☞ cachou]
cash flow +s
cash|ier +s +ed +ing
cash|less
cash|mere +s (wool)
[☞ Kashmir]
cash on de|liv|ery
cash|point +s
cash-poor
cash|spiel +s
cash-strapped
cas|ing +s noun
ca|sino +s
cask +s (container)
[☞ casque]
cask|et +s
Cas|lon, Wil|liam
(English
typographer)
Cas|par (one of the
Magi)
Cas|pian (sea, Asia)
casque +s (helmet)
Cas|san|dra +s (Greek
Myth; disregarded
prophet)
cas|sata +s
cas|sa|tion +s
Cas|satt, Mary (US
artist)
cas|sava +s

casse-croûte
plural casse-croûte
cas|ser|ole +s
cas|sette +s
cas|sia +s
Cas|siar (mountain
range, Canada)
Cas|sini, Gio|van|ni
Domen|ico (Italian-
born astronomer)
Cassin's auk|let +s
Cas|sio|dor|us,
Fla|vius Mag|nus
Aurel|ius (Roman
writer)
cas|sio|pe +s
Cas|sio|peia (Greek
Myth; constellation)
Cas|sir|er, Ernst
(German
philosopher)
cas|sis
cas|sit|er|ite +s
Cas|sius, Gaius full
name Gaius Cas|sius
Lon|gi|nus (Roman
general)
cas|sock +s
cas|socked
Cas|son, Al|fred
Jo|seph (Cdn
painter)
Cas|son, Sir Hugh
Max|well (English
architect)
cas|sou|let +s
cas|so|wary
cas|so|war|ies
cast (throw etc.; mould
etc.; Drama)
casts
cast
cast|ing
[☞ caste]
cas|ta|nets
cast|away +s
caste +s (social class
etc.)
[☞ cast]
caste|ism
Cas|tel Gan|dol|fo
cas|tel|lan +s
cas|tel|lat|ed
cas|tel|la|tion +s
caste mark +s
cast|er +s (person
who casts; swivelled
wheel; perforated
container)
[☞ castor]
cast|ered
cast|er sugar

cas|ti|gate
  cas|ti|gates
  cas|ti|gat|ed
  cas|ti|gat|ing
cas|ti|ga|tion +s
cas|ti|ga|tor +s
cas|ti|ga|tory
Cas|ti|glione, Count
  Bal|das|sare (Italian
  writer)
Cas|tile (region,
  Spain)
Cas|til|ian +s
Castilla-La Man|cha
  (region, Spain)
Castilla-León (region,
  Spain)
cast|ing +s noun
cast iron (cast-iron
  when preceding a
  noun)
castle (fortified
  building; Chess)
  cas|tles
  cas|tled
  cast|ling
  [☞ Kassel]
Castle|bar (town,
  Ireland)
Castle|gar (city,
  Canada)
Castle Hill (historic
  site, Canada)
Castle|reagh, Rob|ert
  Stew|art, Vis|count
  (British statesman)
cast net +s
cast off verb
  casts off
  cast off
  cast|ing off
cast-off adjective
cast|off +s noun
Cas|tor (Greek Myth;
  star)
cas|tor +s (oily
  substance; for wheel
  or perforated jar use
  caster)
cas|tor bean +s
cas|tor|eum
cas|tor gras
cas|tor oil
cas|tor oil bean +s
cas|tor oil plant +s
cas|tor sugar (use
  caster sugar)
cas|trate
  cas|trates
  cas|trat|ed
  cas|trat|ing
cas|tra|tion +s

cas|trato
  cas|trati
cas|tra|tor +s
Cas|tries (capital of
  St. Lucia)
Cas|tro, Fidel full
  name Fidel Cas|tro
  Ruz (Cuban
  statesman)
cas|ual +s
cas|ual|ly
cas|ual|ness
cas|ual|ty
  cas|ual|ties
cas|uar|ina +s
casu|ist +s
casu|is|tic
casu|is|tic|al
casu|is|tic|al|ly
casu|istry
casus belli
  plural casus belli
CAT (computerized
  axial tomography)
Cat +s proprietary
  (Caterpillar vehicle)
cat (animal; cool
  person; boats;
  Nautical)
  cats
  cat|ted
  cat|ting
cata|bol|ic
ca|tab|ol|ism
cata|chres|is
  cata|chres|es
cata|chres|tic
cata|clysm +s
cata|clys|mic
cata|clys|mic|ally
cata|comb +s
ca|tad|ro|mous
cata|falque +s
Cata|lan +s
cata|lase +s
cata|lepsy
  cata|lep|sies
cata|lep|tic +s
cata|logne
cata|logue
  cata|logues
  cata|logued
  cata|loguing
cata|loguer +s
cata|logue rai|son|né
  cata|logues
  rai|son|nés
Cata|lonia (region,
  Spain)
ca|tal|pa +s
cata|lyse (use
  catalyze)

cata|lys|es
cata|lysed
cata|lys|ing
cat|aly|sis
  cat|aly|ses
cata|lyst +s
cata|lytic
cata|lytic|ally
cata|lyze
  cata|lyz|es
  cata|lyzed
  cata|lyz|ing
cata|ma|ran +s
cata|mite +s
cata|mount +s
cat and mouse noun
  (cat-and-mouse
  when preceding a
  noun)
Ca|tania (city, Italy)
cata|plec|tic
cata|plexy
  cata|plex|ies
cata|pult +s +ed +ing
cata|ract +s
Cata|raqui (former
  name for Kingston,
  Canada)
ca|tarrh
  (inflammation;
  discharge)
  [☞ Qatar]
ca|tar|rhal
cat|ar|rhine +s
catas|tro|phe +s
cat|as|troph|ic
cat|as|troph|ic|ally
catas|troph|ism
catas|troph|ist +s
cata|tonia
cata|ton|ic
cata|wam|pus
Ca|taw|ba (people &
  language)
  plural Ca|taw|ba or
  Ca|taw|bas
ca|taw|ba +s (grape;
  wine; tree)
cat|bird +s
cat|boat +s
cat|brier +s
cat burg|lar +s
cat|call +s
catch
  catch|es
  caught
  catch|ing
Catch-22
  Catch-22s
catch|able
catch-all +s
catch-and-release
catch|er +s

catch|fly
  catch|flies
catch|i|er
catch|i|est
catch|i|ly
catch|i|ness
catch|ing adjective
catch|ment +s
catch|penny
catch|phrase +s
catch up verb
  catch|es up
  caught up
  catch|ing up
catch-up noun
catch|word +s
catchy
  catch|i|er
  catch|i|est
cate +s
cat|echet|ic
cat|echet|ic|al
cat|echet|ic|al|ly
cat|echet|ics
cat|ech|ism +s
cat|ech|is|mal
cat|ech|ist +s
cat|ech|ize
  cat|ech|iz|es
  cat|ech|ized
  cat|ech|iz|ing
cat|ech|iz|er +s
cat|echol|amine +s
cat|echu +s
cat|echu|men +s
cat|egor|ial
cat|egor|ic
cat|egor|ic|al
cat|egor|ic|al|ly
cat|egor|iz|a|tion +s
cat|egor|ize
  cat|egor|iz|es
  cat|egor|ized
  cat|egor|iz|ing
cat|egory
  cat|egor|ies
ca|tena
  ca|tenae or ca|tenas
cat|en|ary
  cat|en|aries
cat|en|ate
  cat|en|ates
  cat|en|at|ed
  cat|en|at|ing
cat|en|a|tion +s
cater +s +ed +ing
cat|eran +s
cater-corner
  (= cater-cornered)
cater-cornered
cater|er +s
cater|ing noun

Cater|pil|lar +s
proprietary (vehicle
with steel treads)
cater|pil|lar +s (larva;
articulated steel
tread)
cater|waul +s +ed
+ing
cat|face +s
cat fight +s
cat|fish
plural cat|fish
cat flap +s
cat|gut
Cath|ar (medieval
sectarian)
Cath|ars or Cath|ari
[☞ Cather]
cathar|an|thus
plural
cathar|an|thus
Cath|ar|ism
Cath|ar|ist +s
cath|ar|sis
cath|ar|ses
cath|ar|tic +s
cath|ar|tic|ally
Ca|thay (*former name
for* China)
Cath|cart, Charles
Mur|ray, 2nd Earl
(governor general of
BNA)
cat|head +s
cath|ec|tic
cath|edra
cath|edral +s
Cather, Willa Sibert
(US writer)
[☞ Cathar]
Cath|er|ine (name)
[☞ St. Catharines]
Cath|er|ine (Russian
empresses; saint)
Cath|er|ine de'
Med|ici (queen of
France)
Cath|er|ine of
Ara|gon (wife of
Henry VIII)
Cath|er|ine of
Bra|ganza (wife of
Charles II)
Cath|er|ine wheel +s
cath|eter +s
cath|eter|iz|a|tion +s
cath|eter|ize
cath|eter|iz|es
cath|eter|ized
cath|eter|iz|ing
cath|eter|ized
adjective

cath|exis
cath|exes
cath|odal
cath|ode +s
cath|ode ray +s
cath|od|ic
Cath|olic +s (Roman
Catholic)
cath|olic (of the
Church before the
Great Schism or the
Western Church after
this; all-embracing,
universal)
Cath|oli|cism
Cath|ol|icity
(affiliation with the
Roman Catholic
Church)
cath|ol|icity
(universality)
Cath|oli|cize (make
Roman Catholic)
Cath|oli|cizes
Cath|oli|cized
Cath|oli|ciz|ing
cath|oli|cize (make
catholic)
cath|oli|cizes
cath|oli|cized
cath|oli|ciz|ing
cath|olic|ly
cat|house +s
cat ice
Cati|line (Roman
nobleman)
cat|ion +s
cat|ion|ic
cat|kin +s
cat|like
cat|lin|ite
cat|mint
cat|nap
cat|naps
cat|napped
cat|nap|ping
cat|nip
Cato, Mar|cus
Por|cius ('the Elder'
or 'the Cen|sor')
(Roman statesman)
Cato, Mar|cus
Por|cius ('the
Young|er') (Roman
statesman)
cat-o'-nine-tails
cat|op|tric
cat|op|trics
CAT scan +s
CAT scan|ner +s
cat's cradle
cat's ear +s (plant)

Cat's Eye +s
proprietary
(reflective lane
marker)
cat's-eye +s
(gemstone)
cat's-foot (plant)
cat's-foots or
cat's-feet
Cats|kill +s
(mountains, US)
cat|skin|ner +s
cat's-paw +s (breeze;
dupe)
cat spruce
plural cat spruce or
cat spru|ces
cat|suit +s
cat|tail +s
cat|tery
cat|ter|ies
cat|ti|er
cat|ti|est
cat|ti|ly
cat|ti|ness
cat|tish
cat|tish|ly
cat|tish|ness
cat|tle
cat|tle cake +s
cat|tle call +s
cat|tle grid +s
cat|tle guard +s
cattle|man
cattle|men
catt|leya +s
cat train +s
catty
cat|ti|er
cat|ti|est
catty-corner
catty-cornered
(= catty-corner)
Catul|lus, Gaius
Valer|ius (Roman
poet)
cat|walk +s
Cau|ca|sia
(= Caucasus)
Cau|ca|sian +s
Cau|cas|oid
Cau|casus (region,
SE Europe)
Cauchy, Au|gus|tin
Louis, Baron
(French
mathematician)
cau|cus (*Politics*)
cau|cus|es
cau|cused
cau|cus|ing
[☞ coccus]
cau|dal

cau|dal|ly
cau|date
cau|dillo +s
caught *past & past
participle of* catch
[☞ cot, khat]
caul +s (amnion;
ometum; headdress)
[☞ col, Coll]
caul|dron +s
cauli|flower +s
caulk +s +ed +ing (fill
cracks; sealing
compound; spike;
boot)
caulk|er +s
caulk|ing +s *noun*
caus|able
caus|al
caus|al|ity
caus|al|ly
caus|a|tion
caus|a|tive
caus|a|tive|ly
cause (reason, motive;
make happen)
caus|es
caused
caus|ing
[☞ Kos]
'cause (because)
cause cé|lèbre
causes cé|lèbres
cause|less
caus|er +s
caus|erie +s
cause|way +s
caus|tic
caus|tic|ally
caus|ti|city
caut|er|iz|a|tion +s
caut|er|ize
caut|er|iz|es
caut|er|ized
caut|er|iz|ing
caut|ery
caut|eries
cau|tion +s +ed +ing
cau|tion|ary
cau|tious
cau|tious|ly
cau|tious|ness
Cau|very (river, India)
Ca|vafy,
Con|stan|tine Peter
(Greek poet)
caval|cade +s
Cava|lier +s
(supporter of
Charles I)
cava|lier +s
(gentleman;

horseman;
supercilious)
cava|lier|ly
cav|al|ry
cav|al|ries
cav|alry|man
cav|alry|men
cav|al|ry twill
Cavan (county &
town, Ireland)
cava|tina +s
cave
caves
caved
cav|ing
ca|veat +s
ca|veat emp|tor
cave dwell|er +s
cave in verb
caves in
caved in
cav|ing in
cave-in +s noun
cave|like
Cav|ell, Edith Lou|isa
(English nurse)
[☞ cavil]
cave|man
cave|men
Cav|en|dish
(community,
Canada)
Cav|en|dish, Henry
(English chemist &
physicist)
caver +s
cav|ern +s
cav|ern|ous
cav|ern|ous|ly
cavi|ar +s
cavil
cavils
cav|illed or cav|iled
cavil|ling or
cavil|ing
[☞ Cavell]
cavil|ler +s
cav|ing noun
cavi|ta|tion
cav|ity
cav|ities
ca|vort +s +ed +ing
Ca|vour, Cam|illo
Benso, Conte di
(Italian prime
minister)
cavy
cavies
caw +s +ed +ing
(crow's cry)
[☞ ka]
Cawn|pore
(= Kanpur, India)

Cax|ton, Wil|liam
(English printer)
cay +s (bank, reef)
[☞ Kay, Kaye]
Cay|enne (capital of
French Guiana)
cay|enne +s (pepper)
Cay|ley, Ar|thur
(English
mathematician)
[☞ ceilidh]
Cay|ley, Sir George
(English engineer)
[☞ ceilidh]
Cay|man +s
(Caribbean islands)
cay|man +s (reptile:
use caiman)
Cay|uga
plural Cay|uga or
Cay|ugas
cay|use +s
CB (radio)
CBs
cc (cubic centimetre;
carbon copy)
cc's
CCD (charge-coupled
device)
CCDs
CCFer (Co-operative
Commonwealth
Federation member)
CCFers
C clef +s
CD (compact disc; CD-
ROM)
CDs
CD-I (compact disc-
interactive)
CD-ROM (Computing)
CD-ROMs
CD video +s
CE (Common Era)
cea|noth|us
cea|noth|us|es
Ceará (state, Brazil)
cease
ceas|es
ceased
ceas|ing
cease|fire +s
cease|less
cease|less|ly
Ceau|şescu, Nico|lae
(Romanian
statesman)
Cebu (island & port,
the Philippines)
cecal
Cec|chet|ti, En|rico
(Italian dancer)

Cec|chet|ti (dance
method)
Cecil, Rob|ert full
name Rob|ert
Ar|thur Tal|bot
Gas|coigne-Cecil,
3rd Mar|quess of
Salis|bury (British
prime minister)
Cecil, Wil|liam, 1st
Baron Burgh|ley
(English statesman)
Ce|ci|lia (saint)
cecum
ceca
Cedar (lake, Canada)
cedar +s
cedar shake +s
cedar|strip
cedar|wood
cedary
cede (give up)
cedes
ceded
ced|ing
[☞ seed]
cedi (Ghanaian
currency)
plural cedi or cedis
ced|illa +s (diacritic
mark)
[☞ sedile]
Cee|fax
CEGEP (school)
CEGEPs
cei|lidh +s (party,
concert)
ceil|ing +s (upper
surface or limit)
ceil|inged
ceil|ing fan +s
cein|ture flé|chée
cein|tures flé|chées
cel +s (celluloid sheet)
cela|don +s
Ce|laeno (Greek Myth)
celan|dine +s
celeb +s
Cell|ebes (sea; former
name for Sulawesi)
cele|brant +s
cele|brate
cele|brates
cele|brat|ed
cele|brat|ing
cele|brat|ed adjective
cele|bra|tion +s
cele|bra|tor +s
cele|bra|tory
ce|leb|rity
ce|leb|ri|ties
ce|leb|rity|hood
ce|leri|ac

ce|ler|ity
cel|ery
ce|lesta +s
ce|leste +s (use
celesta)
ce|les|tial
ce|les|tial|ly
ce|li|ac
celi|bacy
celi|bate +s
Cé|line, Louis-
Ferdin|and (French
novelist)
cell +s (chamber,
compartment;
faction; battery;
Biology; Computing;
Telecommunications;
Meteorology)
[☞ cel]
cel|lar +s +ed +ing
(basement; wine
stock; store)
[☞ seller]
cellar|age
cellar-dweller +s
cellar-dwelling
cellar|er +s
cel|lar|et +s
cell|block +s
Cell|ini, Ben|ven|uto
(Italian sculptor)
cel|list +s
cell|mate +s
cello +s
Cello|phane
proprietary
cell|phone +s
cel|lu|lar +s
cel|lule +s
cel|lu|lite
cel|lu|litis
cel|lu|loid +s
cel|lu|lose
cel|lu|losic
celom (use coelom)
plural celoms or
cel|omata
celom|ate +s (use
coelomate)
celom|ic (use
coelomic)
Cel|sius, An|ders
(temperature scale
inventor)
Cel|sius (denoting
temperature)
Celt +s (people)
celt +s (prehistoric
implement)
[☞ kelt]
Celt|ic (sea; of the
Celts)

Celti|cism
ce|ment +s +ed +ing
ce|men|ta|tion
ce|ment|er +s
ce|ment mixer +s
ce|men|tum
cem|etery
  cem|eter|ies
ceno|bite +s
ceno|bit|ic
ceno|bit|ic|al
ceno|taph +s
Ceno|zoic
cens (feudal payment)
  plural cens
cense (direct smoke)
  cens|es
  censed
  cens|ing
cens|er +s (vessel in
  which incense is
  burned)
  [☞ censor,
  censure, sensor]
cen|si|taire +s
cen|sor +s +ed +ing
  (expurgator,
  expurgate; Roman
  magistrate;
  Psychology)
  [☞ censer, censure,
  sensor]
cen|sor|ial
cen|sor|ious
cen|sor|ious|ly
cen|sor|ious|ness
cen|sor|ship
cen|sur|able
cen|sure (criticize;
  disapproval)
  cen|sures
  cen|sured
  cen|sur|ing
  [☞ censor, censer,
  sensor]
cen|sus
  cen|sus|es
  cen|sused
  cen|sus|ing
cent +s (monetary
  unit (not of Estonia);
  in 'per cent')
  [☞ scent, sent]
cen|taur +s
Cen|taur|us
  (constellation)
cen|taury
  cen|taur|ies
cen|tavo +s
cen|ten|ar|ian +s
cen|ten|ary
  cen|ten|aries
cen|ten|nial +s

cen|ter +s +ed +ing
  (*use* centre)
cen|ter bit +s (*use*
  centre bit)
center|board +s (*use*
  centreboard)
cen|tered *adjective*
  (*use* centred)
centered|ness (*use*
  centredness)
cen|ter field (*use*
  centre field)
cen|ter field|er +s
  (*use* centre fielder)
center|fire (*use*
  centrefire)
center|fold +s (*use*
  centrefold)
cen|ter for|ward +s
  (*use* centre forward)
cen|ter half (*use*
  centre half)
cen|ter halves
cen|ter ice (*use* centre
  ice)
center|man (*use*
  centreman)
center|men
center|most (*use*
  centremost)
center|piece +s (*use*
  centrepiece)
cen|ter spread +s
  (*use* centre spread)
cen|ter stage (*use*
  centre stage)
cen|tes|imal
cen|tes|imal|ly
cen|tési|mo +s
centi|grade
centi|gram +s
centi|litre +s
cen|time +s
centi|metre +s
centimetre-gram-
  second
cen|timo +s
centi|pede +s
cen|to +s
cen|tral +s
Cen|tral Af|ri|can
  Re|pub|lic (country,
  Africa)
cen|tral|ism
cen|tral|ist +s
cen|tral|ity
  cen|tral|ities
cen|tral|iz|a|tion
cen|tral|ize
  cen|tral|iz|es
  cen|tral|ized
  cen|tral|iz|ing
  cen|tral|iz|er +s

cen|tral|ly
Centre (region,
  France)
centre
  cen|tres
  cen|tred
  cen|tring
centre bit +s
centre|board +s
cen|tred *adjective*
centred|ness
centre field
centre field|er +s
centre|fire
centre|fold +s
centre for|ward +s
centre half
  centre halves
centre ice
centre|man
  centre|men
centre|most
centre|piece +s
centre spread +s
centre stage
cen|tric
cen|tric|al
cen|tri|city
  cen|tri|ci|ties
cen|tri|fu|gal
cen|tri|fu|gal|ly
cen|tri|fu|ga|tion +s
cen|tri|fuge
  cen|tri|fu|ges
  cen|tri|fuged
  cen|tri|fu|ging
cen|tri|ole +s
cen|trip|etal
cen|trip|etal|ly
cen|trism
cen|trist +s
cen|troid +s
cen|tro|mere +s
cen|tro|mer|ic
cen|tro|some +s
cen|trum
  cen|tra
cen|tuple
  cen|tuples
  cen|tupled
  cen|tup|ling
cen|tur|ion +s
cen|tury
  cen|tur|ies
CEO (chief executive
  officer)
  CEOs
cep +s
ceph|alic
ceph|alo|met|ric
ceph|al|om|etry
Cepha|llonia (island,
  Greece)

ceph|alo|pod +s
ceph|alo|spor|in +s
ceph|alo|thor|ax
  ceph|alo|thor|aces
  or
  ceph|alo|thor|ax|es
Ceph|eid +s
Ceph|eus
  (constellation)
Ceram (sea, W Pacific)
cer|am|ic +s
cer|ami|cist +s
cer|am|ics
cer|am|ist +s
cer|as|tes
  plural cer|as|tes
Cer|ber|us (*Greek
  Myth*; protector)
cer|caria
  cer|car|iae
cer|cus (*Zoology*)
  cerci
  [☞ circus]
cere +s (*Ornithology*)
  [☞ sear, seer, sere,
  Cyr]
cer|eal +s (grain;
  breakfast food)
  [☞ serial]
cere|bel|lar
cere|bel|lum
  cere|bel|lums or
  cere|bella
ce|re|bral
ce|re|bral|ly
ce|re|bral palsy
cere|brate
  cere|brates
  cere|brat|ed
  cere|brat|ing
cere|bra|tion +s
ce|re|bro|spin|al
ce|re|bro|vascu|lar
ce|re|brum
  ce|re|bra
cere|cloth +s
cere|ment +s
cere|mon|ial +s
cere|mon|ial|ism
cere|mon|ial|ist +s
cere|mon|ial|ly
cere|moni|ous
cere|moni|ous|ly
cere|moni|ous|ness
cere|mony
  cere|mon|ies
Ceren|kov radi|ation
  [☞ Cherenkov]
Ceres (*Roman Myth*;
  asteroid)
ce|rise +s (red)
cer|ium
cer|met +s

cert +s
cer|tain
cer|tain|ly
cer|tain|ty
cer|tain|ties
cer|ti|fi|able
cer|ti|fi|ably
cer|tifi|cate
cer|tifi|cates
cer|tifi|cat|ed
cer|tifi|cat|ing
cer|tifi|cat|ed
adjective
cer|tifi|ca|tion +s
cer|ti|fied adjective
cer|tify
cer|ti|fies
cer|ti|fied
cer|ti|fy|ing
cer|tior|ari
cer|ti|tude +s
ceru|lean +s
ceru|men
ceru|min|ous
cer|use
Cer|van|tes, Mi|guel
de full name Mi|guel
de Cer|van|tes
Saav|edra (Spanish
writer)
cer|vic|al
cer|vine
cer|vi|ces
Cesar|ean +s (use
Caesarean)
Cesar|ian +s (use
Caesarean)
ces|ium
České Budě|jo|vice
(city, Czech
Republic)
cess
cess|es
ces|sa|tion +s
ces|sion +s (ceding;
territory ceded)
[☞ session]
cess|pit +s
cess|pool +s
ces|tode +s
cet|acean +s
cet|aceous
cetane
cet|eris pari|bus
cetol|o|gist +s
cetol|ogy
Cetus (constellation)
Ceuta (Spanish
enclave, N Africa)
Cé|vennes
(mountains, France)
ce|viche

Cey|lon (former name
for Sri Lanka; tea;
moss; satinwood)
Cey|lon|ese
plural Cey|lon|ese
Ceyx (Greek Myth)
Cé|zanne, Paul
(French painter)
CFA (come from away)
CFAs
CFB (Canadian Forces
Base)
CFC
(chlorofluorocarbon)
CFCs
CFO (chief financial
officer)
CFOs
CFS (Chronic Fatigue
Syndrome)
CGA (certified general
accountant)
CGAs
CGT (capital gains tax)
Chablis
plural Chablis
cha-cha
cha-chas
cha-chaed or
cha-cha'd
cha-chaing or
cha-cha'ing
cha-cha-cha
cha-cha-chas
cha-cha-chaed or
cha-cha-cha'd
cha-cha-chaing or
cha-cha-cha'ing
Chaco (= Gran
Chaco)
cha|conne +s
Chad (country & lake,
Africa)
Chad|ian +s
chad|or +s
Chad|wick, Sir James
(English physicist)
chae|bol
plural chae|bol or
chae|bols
chaet|og|nath +s
chafe
chafes
chafed
chaf|ing
chaf|er +s (beetle)
chaff +s +ed +ing
chaf|fer +s +ed +ing
(haggle)
chaf|fer|er +s
chaf|finch
chaf|finch|es
chaffy

chaf|ing dish
chaf|ing dish|es
Cha|gall, Marc
(Russian-born artist)
Chagas' dis|ease
Cha|gos (archipelago,
Indian Ocean)
cha|grin +s +ed +ing
cha|grined adjective
chai +s
Chain, Sir Ernst Boris
(English biochemist)
[☞ Cheyne-Stokes]
chain +s +ed +ing
[☞ Cheyne-Stokes]
chain drive +s
chain|er +s
chain fern +s
chain gang +s
chain let|ter +s
chain-link
chain mail
chain|man
chain|men
chain|saw
chain|saws
chain|sawed
chain|saw|ing
chain-smoke
chain-smokes
chain-smoked
chain-smoking
chain-smoker +s
chain-smoking noun
chain stitch
chain stitch|es
chair +s +ed +ing
chair|lift +s
chair|man
chair|men
chair|man|ship +s
chair|person
chair|persons or
chair|people
chair|woman
chair|women
chaise +s
chaise longue
chaise longues or
chaises longues
chaise lounge +s
(= chaise longue)
chak|ra +s
cha|laza
cha|lazae or
cha|lazas
Chal|ce|don (former
city, Bosporus)
Chal|ce|don|ian +s
chal|ce|don|ic
chal|ce|dony
chal|cid +s
Chal|cis (city, Greece)

chal|co|lith|ic
chal|co|pyr|ite +s
Chal|dea (ancient
country, Babylonia)
[☞ Chaldee]
Chal|dean +s
Chal|dee (Chaldean
language)
cha|let +s
Cha|leur (bay,
Canada)
Cha|lia|pin, Feo|dor
Ivan|ovich (Russian
singer)
chal|ice +s (cup)
[☞ challis]
chalk +s +ed +ing
(calcium carbonate;
writing instrument,
etc.)
[☞ choc, chock]
chalk|board +s
chalk|i|er
chalk|i|est
chalk|i|ness
chalk line +s
chalk pit +s
chalk|stone
chalk-stripe +s
chalk-striped
chalk talk +s
chalky
chalk|i|er
chalk|i|est
chal|lah
chal|lahs or
chal|loth
chal|lenge
chal|len|ges
chal|lenged
chal|len|ging
chal|lenge|able
chal|lenged adjective
chal|len|ger +s
chal|len|ging adjective
chal|lis (textile)
[☞ chalice]
Chal|mers, Floyd
Sher|man (Cdn arts
patron)
cha|lyb|eate
chamae|phyte +s
cham|ber +s
cham|bered
Cham|ber|lain, Sir
(Jo|seph) Aus|ten
(English statesman)
Cham|ber|lain,
Jo|seph (English
statesman)
Cham|ber|lain,
(Ar|thur) Nev|ille

(British prime
minister)
Cham|ber|lain, Owen
(US physicist)
cham|ber|lain +s
cham|ber|lain|ship
+s
chamber|maid +s
cham|ber pot +s
Cham|bly (city &
canal, Canada)
cham|bray +s (cloth)
[☞ chambré]
cham|bré (denoting
wine at room
temperature)
[☞ chambray]
cha|meleon +s
cha|mele|on|ic
cham|fer +s +ed +ing
cham|ois (leather;
mammal)
plural cham|ois
chamo|mile (use
camomile)
Chamo|nix (resort,
France)
Chamonix-Mont-
Blanc
(= Chamonix,
France)
champ +s +ed +ing
Cham|pagne +s
(region, France)
Cham|pagne, Claude
(Cdn composer)
cham|pagne
(sparkling wine;
colour)
[☞ champaign]
Champagne-
-Ardenne
(region, France)
cham|paign +s (open
country)
[☞ champagne]
cham|pers
cham|per|tous
cham|perty
cham|per|ties
Cham|pigny, Jean
Bo|chart de
(intendant of New
France)
cham|pion +s +ed
+ing
cham|pion|ship +s
Cham|plain (lake,
N America)
Cham|plain, Sam|uel
de (governor of New
France)
champ|levé

Cham|pol|lion, Jean-
François (French
Egyptologist)
Champs Élysées
(street, France)
chance
chan|ces
chanced
chan|cing
chan|cel +s
chan|cel|lery
chan|cel|ler|ies
chan|cel|lor +s
chan|cel|lor|ship +s
chance-medley +s
Chan|cery (Lord
Chancellor's court)
chan|cery (embassy
or consulate office;
Catholic
administrative office;
record office; court
of equity)
chan|cer|ies
Chan Chan (ancient
city, Peru)
chan|ci|ly
chan|ci|ness
chan|cre +s
chan|croid
chancy
chan|ci|er
chan|ci|est
chan|de|lier +s
chan|de|liered
Chan|di|garh
(territory & city,
India)
Chand|ler, Ed|ward
Baron (Cdn
politician)
Chand|ler, Ray|mond
Thorn|ton (US
writer)
chand|ler +s
chand|lery
chand|ler|ies
Chan|dra|gupta
Maurya (Indian
emperor)
Chan|dra|sekhar,
Sub|rah|man|yan
(Indian-born
astronomer)
Cha|nel, Gab|ri|elle
Bon|heur ('Coco')
(French designer)
[☞ Channel]
Cha|nel jack|et +s
Chaney, Alon|so
('Lon') (US actor)
Chaney, Creigh|ton
('Lon, Jr.') (US actor)

Chang|an (former
name for Xian,
China)
Chang|chun (city,
China)
change
chan|ges
changed
chan|ging
change|abil|ity
change|able
change|able|ness
change|ably
change|ful
change|less
change|less|ly
change|less|ness
change|ling +s
change over verb
chan|ges over
changed over
chan|ging over
change|over +s noun
change purse +s
chan|ger +s
change room +s
change table +s
change up verb
chan|ges up
changed up
chan|ging up
change|up +s noun
Chan|ging of the
Guard
Chang|sha (city,
China)
Cha|nia (port, Crete)
Chan|nel (= English
Channel)
[☞ Chanel]
chan|nel
chan|nels
chan|nelled
chan|nel|ling
Chan|nel Coun|try
(region, Australia)
chan|nel|iz|a|tion
chan|nel|ize
chan|nel|iz|es
chan|nel|ized
chan|nel|iz|ing
Channel-Port aux
Basques (town,
Canada)
chan|son +s
chan|son de geste
chan|sons de geste
chan|son|nier +s
(singer)
chan|son|ni|ère +s
(female singer)
chant +s +ed +ing
chant|er +s

chan|ter|elle +s
chant|euse +s
chan|ti|cleer +s
Chan|tilly
chan|try
chan|tries
chanty (song: use
shanty)
chan|ties
[☞ shanty]
Cha|nu|kah +s
(Judaism: use
Hanukkah)
Chao Phra|ya
(waterway, Thailand)
Chaos (Greek Myth)
chaos (in general use)
cha|ot|ic
cha|ot|ic|ally
chap
chaps
chapped
chap|ping
Cha|pais, Jean-
Charles (Cdn
politician)
chapa|rajos
chap|ar|ral +s
cha|pati +s
chap|book +s
chape +s
chap|eau
chap|eaux
chap|el +s (place of
worship)
[☞ chappal]
chap|el royal
chap|els royal
chap|er|on|age
chap|er|one
chap|er|ones
chap|er|oned
chap|er|on|ing
chap|fallen
chap|lain +s
chap|lain|cy
chap|lain|cies
Chap|leau, Sir
Joseph-Adolphe
(Cdn politician)
chap|let +s
chap|let|ed
Chap|lin, Sir Charles
Spen|cer ('Char|lie')
(English actor)
Chap|man, George
(English writer)
chap|man
chap|men
chap|pal +s (sandal)
[☞ chapel]
Chappa|quid|dick
(island, US)

chapped *adjective*
chap|pie +s
chaps
Chap Stick +s
  proprietary
chap|tal|iz|a|tion
chap|tal|ize
  chap|tal|iz|es
  chap|tal|ized
  chap|tal|iz|ing
chap|ter +s
Chap|ter 11
chap|ter house +s
char
• (burn; charwoman; tea)
  chars
  charred
  char|ring
• (fish)
  plural char
  [☞ charr]
chara|banc +s
chara|cin +s
char|ac|ter +s +ed +ing
char|ac|ter|ful
char|ac|ter|is|tic +s
char|ac|ter|is|tic|ally
char|ac|ter|iz|a|tion +s
char|ac|ter|ize
  char|ac|ter|iz|es
  char|ac|ter|ized
  char|ac|ter|iz|ing
char|ac|ter|less
char|ac|ter|o|logic|al
cha|rade +s
charas
char|broil +s +ed +ing
char|broiled *adjective*
char|coal +s
char|coal grey +s
Char|cot, Jean-Martin (French neurologist)
char|cu|terie +s
chard +s (vegetable)
  [☞ charred]
Char|don|nay +s
Cha|rente (river, France)
charge
  char|ges
  charged
  char|ging
char|gé +s (= chargé d'affaires)
charge|able
charge card +s
charge-coupled de|vice +s

charged *adjective*
char|gé d'affaires
  char|gés d'affaires
char|ger +s
charge sheet +s
char|ging *noun*
char|i|er
char|i|est
char|i|ly
char|i|ness
char|iot +s +ed +ing
char|iot|eer +s
char|is|ma
  cha|ris|mata
char|is|matic
char|is|matic|ally
char|it|able
char|it|able|ness
char|it|ably
char|ity
  char|ities
chari|vari +s
char|lady
  char|ladies
char|la|tan +s
char|latan|ism
char|latan|ry
Charle|bois, Rob|ert (Cdn singer-songwriter)
Charle|magne (King of the Franks; town, Canada)
Charle|roi (city, Belgium)
Charles (British, French, Spanish & Swedish kings; Holy Roman emperors; English prince)
Charles, Ray (US singer-songwriter)
Charles|bourg (city, Canada)
Charles' Law
Charles Mar|tel (Frankish ruler)
Charles's Law (*use* Charles' Law)
Charles's Wain (constellation)
Charles|ton +s +ed +ing (cities, US; dance)
char|ley horse +s
char|lock
Char|lotte (city, US)
char|lotte +s (dessert)
Char|lotte Ama|lie (capital of the US Virgin Islands)
char|lotte russe

Char|lottes (= Queen Charlotte Islands, Canada)
Char|lotte|town (city, Canada)
charm +s +ed +ing
charm|er +s
charm|euse
charm|ing *adjective*
charm|ing|ly
charm|less
charm|less|ly
charm|less|ness
char|nel house +s
Char|ny (town, Canada)
Charo|lais
  plural Charo|lais
Charon (*Greek Myth & Astronomy*)
  [☞ Sharon]
char|poy +s
charr (fish: *use* char)
  plural charr
charred *past & past participle of* char
  [☞ chard]
chart +s +ed +ing
chart|bust|er +s
Char|ter (Canadian Charter of Rights and Freedoms)
char|ter +s +ed +ing
  (*in general use*)
char|tered *adjective*
char|ter|er +s
Chart|ism
Chart|ist +s
Char|tres (city, France)
Char|treuse +s
  proprietary (liqueur)
char|treuse +s
  (colour)
char|woman
  char|women
chary
  char|i|er
  char|i|est
Cha|ryb|dis (*Greek Myth*)
chase
  chas|es
  chased
  chas|ing
chas|er +s
Chasid (*use* Hasid)
Chasid|im
Chasid|ic (*use* Hasidic)
Chasid|ism (*use* Hasidism)

chasm +s
chas|mic
chas|sé
  chas|sés
  chas|séd
  chas|sé|ing
Chas|sid (*use* Hasid)
Chas|sid|im
Chas|sid|ic (*use* Hasidic)
Chas|sid|ism (*use* Hasidism)
chas|sis
  plural chas|sis
chaste
chaste|ly
chas|ten +s +ed +ing
chas|tened *adjective*
chas|ten|er +s
chaste|ness
chas|ten|ing *adjective*
chas|tise
  chas|tis|es
  chas|tised
  chas|tis|ing
chas|tise|ment +s
chas|tis|er +s
chas|tity
chas|uble +s
chat
  chats
  chat|ted
  chat|ting
châ|teau
  châ|teaux
Cha|teau|briand, François-René, Vi|comte de (French writer)
cha|teau|briand +s (steak)
Châ|teau Clique
Châ|teau|guay (city, Canada)
Châ|teau style
chat|el|aine +s
Chat|ham (city, Canada; SW Pacific islands)
Chat|ham, Wil|liam, 1st Earl of (English statesman)
chat line +s
chat show +s
chat|tel +s
chat|ter +s +ed +ing
chatter|box
  chatter|boxes
chat|ter|er +s
Chat|ter|ton, Thom|as (English poet)
chat|tery

chat|ti|ly
chat|ti|ness
chatty
chat|ti|er
chat|ti|est
Chatty Cathy
Chatty Cath|ies
Chau|cer, Geof|frey
(English poet)
Chau|cer|ian +s
chaud-froid +s
Chau|dière (river,
Canada)
chauf|feur +s +ed
+ing (driver)
[☞ shofar]
chauf|feuse +s
chaul|moo|gra +s
chau|tau|qua +s
Chau|veau, Pierre-
Joseph-Olivier (Cdn
politician & writer)
chau|vin|ism +s
chau|vin|ist +s
chau|vin|is|tic
chau|vin|is|tic|ally
Cha|vez, Cesar
Es|tra|da (US labour
organizer)
Cha|vín
chaw +s (chewing
tobacco)
chay|ote +s
cheap +er +est
(inexpensive etc.)
[☞ cheep]
cheap|en +s +ed +ing
cheap|ie +s
cheap|ish
cheap|jack +s
cheap|ly
cheap|ness
cheapo +s
cheap shot +s
cheap|skate +s
cheat +s +ed +ing
cheat|er +s
cheat|ing|ly
cheat sheet +s
Cheb|ok|sary (city,
Russia)
Chech|en +s
(autonomous
republic, Russia;
people, language)
Chech|nya
(= Chechen
Republic)
check +s +ed +ing
(verify; stop; restrain;
mark; pattern;
Hockey; Chess;

restaurant bill; ticket)
[☞ cheque, Czech]
check|able
checked adjective
check|er +s +ed +ing
checker|berry
checker|ber|ries
checker|board
check|ered
check|er lily
check|er lil|ies
check|ers (game)
check in verb
checks in
checked in
check|ing in
check-in +s noun
check|list +s
check mark +s
check|mate
check|mates
check|mat|ed
check|mat|ing
check out verb
checks out
checked out
check|ing out
check|out +s noun
check|point +s
check|rein +s
check|room +s
check|stop +s
check|sum +s
check up verb
checks up
checked up
check|ing up
check|up +s noun
check valve +s
ched|dar +s (cheese)
che|der +s (Jewish
school)
chee|chako +s
Chee Chee,
Ben|ja|min (Cdn
artist)
cheek +s +ed +ing
cheek|bone +s
cheek|i|ly
cheek|i|ness
cheeky
cheek|i|er
cheek|i|est
cheep +s +ed +ing
(bird cry)
[☞ cheap]
cheer +s +ed +ing
cheer|ful
cheer|ful|ly
cheer|ful|ness
cheer|i|er
cheer|i|est
cheer|i|ly

cheer|i|ness
Cheer|io +s
proprietary (cereal)
cheer|io +s interjection
cheer|lead|er +s
cheer|lead|ing
cheer|less
cheer|less|ly
cheer|less|ness
cheery
cheer|i|er
cheer|i|est
cheese
chees|es
cheesed
chees|ing
cheese|board +s
cheese|burger +s
cheese|cake +s
cheese|cloth +s
cheese cut|ter +s
cheese|monger +s
cheese-paring
cheese plant +s
cheese straw +s
chees|i|ness
cheesy
chees|i|er
chees|i|est
chee|tah +s
Chee|ver, John (US
writer)
chef +s
chef de cui|sine
chefs de cui|sine
chef de mis|sion
chefs de mis|sion
chef-d'œuvre
chefs-d'œuvre
chef's knife
chef's knives
Chekh|ov, Anton
Pav|lo|vich (Russian
writer)
Che|khov|ian
Che|kiang
(= Zhejiang, China)
chela
• (Zoology)
plural che|lae
• (Hinduism)
plural che|las
che|late
che|lates
che|lat|ed
che|lat|ing
che|la|tion +s
che|la|tor +s
Chel|lean
Chelms|ford (city,
England)
chelo|nian +s

Chel|sea (district of
London, England;
city, Canada)
Chel|sea bun +s
Chel|ten|ham (town,
England)
Chel|ya|binsk (city,
Russia)
chem
Che|main|us
(community,
Canada)
chem|ical +s
chem|ical|ly
chemi|
lumin|es|cence
chemi|lumin|es|cent
che|min de fer
che|mins de fer
che|mise +s
chemi|sorp|tion +s
chem|ist +s
chem|istry
chem|is|tries
Chem|nitz (city,
Germany)
chemo
chemo|synth|esis
chemo|tac|tic
chemo|taxis
chemo|thera|peut|ic
chemo|ther|apist +s
chemo|ther|apy
Che|nab (river, India &
Pakistan)
Cheng|chow
(= Zhengzhou,
China)
Cheng|du (city, China)
Ché|nier, Jean-
Olivier (Cdn Patriote
leader)
che|nille +s
Che|nin Blanc +s
cheong|sam +s
Che|ops (pharaoh)
cheque +s (Banking,
Finance)
[☞ check, Czech]
cheque book +s noun
cheque|book adjective
preceding a noun
chequing ac|count
+s
Cher (river, France)
Cher|bourg (city,
France)
Cher|en|kov, Pavel
Alek|sey|evich
(Soviet physicist)
Cher|en|kov
radi|ation (use
Cerenkov radiation)

Cher|epo|vets (city, Russia)
cher|ish
cher|ish|es
cher|ished
cher|ish|ing
Cher|kassy (city, Ukraine)
Cher|kessk (city, Russia)
Cher|nenko, Kon|stan|tin Ustin|ovich (Soviet statesman)
Cher|ni|gov (city, Ukraine)
Cher|niv|tsi (city, Ukraine)
Cher|nobyl (city, Ukraine)
Cher|no|reche (former name for Dzerzhinsk, Russia)
cher|no|zem
Chero|kee
plural Chero|kee or Chero|kees
che|root +s
cherry
cher|ries
cherry-pick +s +ed +ing
cherry pick|er +s
cherry|stone +s
cherry|wood +s
Cher|so|nese (ancient region by Hellespont)
chert +s
cherty
cher|ub
• (Theology heavenly being)
plural cher|ub|im
• (Art winged child; beautiful child)
plural cher|ubs
che|rub|ic
che|rub|ic|ally
Cheru|bini, (Maria) Luigi Carlo Zeno|bio Sal|va|tore (Italian composer)
cher|vil
Cher|well, Fred|erick Alex|an|der Linde|mann, 1st Vis|count (German-born physicist)
Chesa|peake (bay, US)
Chesh|ire (county, England; cheese; cat)

Chesil (shingle beach, England)
chess
chess|board +s
chess|man
chess|men
chest +s
Ches|ter (town, England; village, Canada)
Ches|ter|field (inlet, Canada)
Ches|ter|field, Phil|ip Dor|mer Stan|hope, 4th Earl of (English statesman & writer)
ches|ter|field +s
Ches|ter|ton, Gil|bert Keith (English writer)
chest|i|ly
chest|i|ness
chest|nut +s
chesty
chest|i|er
chest|i|est
Chet|nik +s
Chetu|mal (city, Mexico)
che|val glass
che|val glass|es
Che|va|lier, Mau|rice (French entertainer)
cheva|lier +s
che|vet +s
Chev|iot +s (hills, Britain; sheep)
chev|iot (wool)
chèvre +s
chev|ron +s
chev|ro|tain +s
chev|ro|tin +s (use chevrotain)
chevy (use chivvy)
chev|ies
chev|ied
chevy|ing
chew +s +ed +ing
chew|able
chew|er +s
chew|i|ness
chewy
chew|i|er
chew|i|est
Chey|enne (city, US; people & language)
plural Chey|enne or Chey|ennes
Cheyne-Stokes
chez
chi +s (Greek letter; for vital life source use qi)

ch'i (vital life source: use qi)
Chiang Kai-shek (Chinese general & statesman)
Chiang|mai (city, Thailand)
Chi|anti +s
Chi|apas (state, Mexico)
chiaro|scuro +s
chi|asma
chi|as|mata
chi|as|mus
chi|as|mi
chi|as|tic
Chiba (city, Japan)
Chi|bou|ga|mau (town, Canada)
chi|bouk +s
chi|bouque +s (use chibouk)
chic +er +est (stylish) [☞ chick]
Chi|ca|go (city, US)
Chi|ca|go|an +s
Chi|cana +s
chi|cane
chi|canes
chi|caned
chi|can|ing
chi|can|ery
chi|can|eries
Chi|cano +s
Chic-Chocs (mountains, Canada)
Chi|ches|ter (city, England)
chi-chi
chick +s (young bird) [☞ chic]
chick|a|dee +s
Chick|a|saw
plural Chick|a|saw or Chick|a|saws
chick|en +s +ed +ing
chicken-and-egg adjective
chick|en coop +s
chick|en feed
chicken-fried steak +s
chick|en hawk +s
chicken-hearted
chick|en Kiev
chicken-livered
chick|en pox
chick|en scratch
chick|en scratch|es
chicken|shit +s
chick|en wire +s
chick|pea +s
chick|weed +s

chicle
chic|ly
chic|ness
chic|ory
chic|ories
Chi|cou|timi (city, Canada)
chide
chides
chid|ed or chid
chid|ed or chid|den
chid|ing
chid|er +s
chid|ing|ly
Chid|ley (cape, Canada)
chief +s
chief|dom +s
chief|est
Chief Fac|tor +s
chief|ly
chief|tain +s
chief|tain|cy
chief|tain|cies
chief|tain|ess
chief|tain|ess|es
chief|tain|ship +s
Ch'ien-lung (= Qian Long, Chinese emperor)
chiff|chaff +s
chif|fon +s
chif|fon|ier +s
chig|ger +s
Chig|nec|to (cape & bay, Canada)
chi|gnon +s
chig|oe +s
Chihli, Gulf of (= Bo Hai, China)
Chi|hua|hua (state & its capital, Mexico)
chi|hua|hua +s (dog)
chil|blain +s
chil|blained
Chil|cotin (region & river, Canada; for people & language use Tsilhqot'in)
plural Chil|cotin or Chil|cotins
Child, Julia (US cooking instructor)
child
chil|dren
[☞ childe]
child abuse
child-bearing
child|bed
child|birth
child care
childe (youth of noble birth)

Chil|der|mas
child|hood +s
child|ish
child|ish|ly
child|ish|ness
child|less
child|less|ness
child|like
child|mind|er +s
child|proof +s +ed +ing
chil|dren
Children's Aid
child's play
Chile (country, S America; nitre; pine; saltpetre)
[☞ Gulf of Chihli]
chile +s (in 'chile relleno'; for spicy dish, pepper, powder, etc. use chili)
[☞ chilly]
Chil|ean +s
chile con carne (use chili con carne)
chile pep|per +s (use chili pepper)
chile pow|der +s (use chili powder)
chile rel|leno
chile rel|lenos or chiles rel|lenos
chili (spicy dish; pepper)
chil|ies
[☞ chile relleno, chilly, Chile, Gulf of Chihli]
chili|ad +s
chili|asm
chili|ast +s
chili|as|tic
chili con carne
chili dog +s
chili pep|per +s
chili pow|der +s
Chil|kat +s
Chil|kat blan|ket +s
Chil|koot (mountain pass, N America)
chill +s +ed +ing
chill|er +s
chill|i|ness
chill|ing|ly
Chil|li|wack (people & language; district municipality, Canada)
plural Chil|li|wack or Chil|li|wacks
chill|ness

chilly (cold)
chill|i|er
chill|i|est
[☞ chili, chile, Chile]
Chil|pan|cingo (city, Mexico)
Chil|tern +s (hills, England)
Chil|tern Hun|dreds
chi|maera +s (use chimera)
chi|maer|ic (use chimeric)
chi|maer|ic|al (use chimerical)
chi|maer|ic|al|ly (use chimerically)
Chim|bo|razo (mountain, Ecuador)
chime (bell; rim; in 'chime in')
chimes
chimed
chim|ing
[☞ chyme]
chim|er +s
chi|mera +s
chi|mer|ic
chi|mer|ic|al
chi|mer|ic|al|ly
chimi|chan|ga +s
chim|ney +s
chim|ney piece +s
chim|ney sweep +s
chimp +s
chim|pan|zee +s
Chin
• (hills, Burma)
• (= Jin, Chinese dynasties AD 265–420 & 1115–1234)
[☞ Qin]
Ch'in (Chinese dynasty 221–206 BC: use Qin)
[☞ Chin, Jin]
chin
chins
chinned
chin|ning
China (country, Asia; sea)
china +s (ceramic)
China aster +s
china|berry
china|ber|ries
china clay
China|man offensive
China|men
China tea +s
China|town +s
china|ware

China White (heroin)
[☞ Chinese white]
chinch (bug; fill seams or cracks)
chinch|es
chinched
chinch|ing
chin|cherin|chee +s
chin|chilla +s
chin-chin
Chin|dit +s
Chin|dwin (river, Burma)
chine
chines
chined
chining
Chi|nese
plural Chi|nese
Chi|nese New Year
Chi|nese wall +s
Chi|nese white (pigment)
[☞ China White]
Ch'ing (= Qing, Chinese dynasty 1644–1912)
ching +s (ringing sound)
[☞ Qing]
Chini|quy, Charles Paschal-Télesphore (Cdn ecclesiastic)
Chink +s offensive (Chinese person)
chink +s +ed +ing (crack; seal a crack; ring, clink)
chink|ing noun
chin|less
chino +s
chi|nois|erie +s
Chi|nook (people; language)
plural Chi|nook or Chi|nooks
chi|nook
• (wind)
plural chi|nooks
• (salmon)
plural chi|nook or chi|nooks
chi|nook arch
chi|nook arch|es
Chi|nook Jar|gon
chin|qua|pin +s
chinse (fill seams or cracks)
chins|es
chinsed
chins|ing
[☞ chintz]
chin|strap +s

chintz (Textiles)
chintz|es
[☞ chinse]
chintz|i|ly
chintz|i|ness
chintzy
chintz|i|er
chintz|i|est
Chinua|lum|gu, Al|bert (Chinua Achebe)
chin up interjection
chin-up +s noun
chin|wag
chin|wags
chin|wagged
chin|wag|ging
chi|ono|doxa +s
Chios (island, Aegean)
chip
chips
chipped
chip|ping
chip|board +s
Chipe|wyan (Athapaskan people of NW Canada; language)
plural Chipe|wyan or Chipe|wyans
[☞ Chippewa]
chip|maker +s
chip|making
chip|munk +s
chipo|lata +s
chi|potle +s
Chip|pen|dale, Thom|as (English cabinetmaker)
Chip|pen|dale (style of furniture)
chip|per +s
Chip|pe|wa (Ojibwa living east, south & southwest of the Great Lakes; language)
plural Chip|pe|wa or Chip|pe|was
[☞ Chipewyan]
chip|pi|ness
chip|py
chip|pi|er
chip|pi|est
chip|pies
chip set +s
chip shot +s
chip wag|on +s
Chirac, Jacques René (French prime minister)
chiral
chiral|ity

Chiri|aeff, Lud|milla (Cdn ballet director)
Chi|rico, Gior|gio de (Italian painter)
chiro|graph|ic
chir|og|raphy
chiro|mancy
Chiron (*Greek Myth* centaur; asteroid)
chi|ron|omid +s
chi|rop|odist +s
chi|rop|ody
chiro|prac|tic
chiro|prac|tor +s
chir|op|ter|an +s
chirp +s +ed +ing
chirp|er +s
chirp|i|ly
chirp|i|ness
chirpy
  chirp|i|er
  chirp|i|est
chirr +s +ed +ing
chir|rup +s +ed +ing
chir|rupy
chis|el
  chis|els
  chis|elled
  chis|el|ling
chis|elled *adjective*
chis|el|ler +s
Chişi|năn (capital of Moldova)
chi-square test +s
chit +s
chital +s
chit-chat
  chit-chats
  chit-chatted
  chit-chatting
chi|tin (fungal & exoskeletal polysaccharide)
  [☞ chiton]
chitin|ous
chit|lin +s (= chitterling)
chit|ling +s (= chitterling)
chi|ton +s (tunic; mollusk)
  [☞ chitin]
Chit|ta|gong (city, Bangladesh)
chit|ter +s +ed +ing
chitter|ling +s
chiv|al|ric
chiv|al|rous
chiv|al|rous|ly
chiv|al|ry
chiv|aree +s (noisy gathering, serenade: *use* shivaree)

chive +s
chiv|vy
  chiv|vies
  chiv|vied
  chivvy|ing
Chka|lov (*former name for* Orenburg, Russia)
chla|myd|ia
  chla|myd|iae
chla|myd|ial
chlor|acne
chlor|al
chlor|am|pheni|col
chlor|ate +s
chlor|dane
chlor|ella +s
chlor|ic
chlor|ide +s
chlor|in|ate
  chlor|in|ates
  chlor|in|ated
  chlor|in|at|ing
chlor|in|a|tion
chlor|in|ator +s
chlor|ine +s
chlor|ite +s
chlor|itic
chloro|
  fluoro|car|bon +s
chloro|form +s +ed +ing
chloro|phenol +s
chloro|phyll +s
chloro|phyl|lous
chloro|plast +s
chloro|quine
chlor|osis
chlor|otic
chlor|ous
chlor|proma|zine
choc +s (chocolate)
  [☞ chock, chalk]
chock +s +ed +ing (block, wedge; ring, hook; secure; cram full)
  [☞ choc, chalk]
chock|a|block
chock full
choco|hol|ic +s
choc|o|late +s
chocolate-box *adjective preceding a noun*
choc|o|late brown +s (chocolate-brown *when preceding a noun*)
choc|o|latey
choc|ola|tier +s
Choc|taw
  • (people; language)

plural Choc|taw or Choc|taws
  • (*Figure Skating*)
  plural Choc|taws
choice
  choices
  choicer
  choicest
choice|ly
choice|ness
choir +s (musical group; part of a church)
  [☞ quire]
choir|boy +s
choir|girl +s
choir loft +s
choir|master +s
choke
  chokes
  choked
  chok|ing
choke|berry
  choke|ber|ries
choke chain +s
choke|cherry
  choke|cher|ries
choked *adjective*
choke|damp
choke point +s
chok|er +s
choker|man
  choker|men
choker|set|ter +s
chok|ey +s (prison: *use* choky)
choky (prison; tending to choke)
  chok|ies
  chok|i|er
  chok|i|est
chol|angi|og|raphy
chole|cal|cif|erol
chole|cyst|ec|tomy
chole|cyst|
  ec|to|mies
chole|cyst|og|raphy
chol|ent
choler (anger; bile)
  [☞ collar]
chol|era
chol|er|aic (of cholera)
chol|er|ic (irascible)
chol|er|ic|ally
chol|es|terol
choli +s
choli|amb +s
choli|am|bic
cho|line +s
cholin|ergic
cholla +s
cholo +s

chomp +s +ed +ing
Chom|sky, (Avram) Noam (US linguist & activist)
chon|drite +s
chon|drit|ic
Chong|jin (port, North Korea)
Chong|qing (city, China)
choo-choo +s
choose
  choos|es
  chose
  chosen
  choos|ing
choos|er +s
choos|i|ly
choos|i|ness
choosy
  choos|i|er
  choos|i|est
chop
  chops
  chopped
  chop|ping
chop-chop
chop|house +s
Cho|pin, Fré|dé|ric Fran|çois (French composer)
Cho|pin, Kate O'Flaher|ty (US writer)
chop|per +s +ed +ing
chop|pi|ly
chop|pi|ness
choppy
  chop|pi|er
  chop|pi|est
chop shop +s
chop-socky
  chop-sockies
chop|stick +s
chop suey +s
chor|al +s (of a choir or chorus; *for* hymn tune *or* choir *use* chorale)
  [☞ corral, coral]
chor|ale +s (hymn tune; choir)
  [☞ choral, corral]
chor|al|ly
chor|al so|ci|ety
  chor|al so|ci|eties
chord +s +ed +ing (*Music; Math; Aviation;* horizontal beam of a truss; *for Anatomy senses use* cord)
  [☞ cord]
chord|al

chord|ate +s (animal)
[☞ cordate]
chore +s
chorea (medical disorder)
chore|boy +s
choreo|graph +s +ed +ing
chor|eog|raph|er +s
choreo|graph|ic
choreo|graph|ic|ally
chor|eog|raphy
chor|eog|raph|ies
chor|eol|o|gist +s
chor|eol|ogy
chori|amb +s
chori|am|bic
choric
chor|ine +s
chor|ion +s
chori|onic
chor|is|ter +s
cho|rizo +s
chor|oid +s
chor|tle
    chor|tles
    chor|tled
    chort|ling
chor|us
    chor|us|es
    chor|used
    chor|us|ing
chor|us boy +s
chor|us girl +s
chor|us line +s
chose
chosen
Chou (= Zhou, Chinese dynasty)
Chou En-lai (= Zhou Enlai, Chinese prime minister)
chough +s (bird)
[☞ chuff]
choux (pastry)
chow +s +ed +ing (food; eat; dog)
[☞ ciao]
chow chow +s (dog)
chow|der +s
chowder|head +s
chow mein +s
Chré|tien, (Joseph-Jacques) Jean (Cdn prime minister)
Chré|tien de Troyes (French poet)
chrism (oil)
[☞ chrisom]
chris|om +s (robe)
[☞ chrism]
chris|om cloth +s
(= chrisom)

Chris|sake
Chris|sakes
(= Chrissake)
Christ +s (title or a representation of Jesus)
Christ|adelph|ian +s
Christ child
Christ|church (city, New Zealand)
chris|ten +s +ed +ing
Chris|ten|dom
chris|ten|er +s
chris|ten|ing +s noun
Christ|hood
Chris|tian, Fletch|er (Bounty mutineer)
Chris|tian +s (island, Canada; follower of Christ)
Chris|ti|ania (former name for Oslo, Norway)
Chris|ti|an|ity
Chris|tian|iz|a|tion
Chris|tian|ize
    Chris|tian|iz|es
    Chris|tian|ized
    Chris|tian|iz|ing
Chris|tian|ly
Chris|tie, Dame Aga|tha Mary Clar|issa (English writer)
[☞ Corpus Christi]
Chris|tie +s (Skiing)
[☞ Corpus Christi]
Chris|tie stiff +s (hat)
Chris|tina (queen of Sweden)
Christ|like
Christ|ly
    Christ|li|er
    Christ|li|est
Christ|mas (holiday; island, Indian Ocean; former name for Kiritimati, Pacific island)
Christ|mas|es
Christ|mas Eve +s
Christ|mas|tide
Christ|mas|time
Christ|masy
Christ|o|logic|al
Christ|ol|ogy
Chris|tophe, Henri (Haitian revolutionary leader)
Chris|to|pher (saint)
Christy (Skiing: use Christie)
Chris|ties

[☞ Corpus Christi, Christie]
Christy stiff +s (use Christie stiff)
chroma
chroma-key +s +ed +ing
chro|mate +s
chro|mat|ic
chro|mat|ic|ally
chro|mati|cism
chro|ma|ti|city
    chro|ma|ti|ci|ties
chro|ma|tid +s
chro|ma|tin
chro|mato|graph +s
chro|mato|graph|ic
chro|ma|tog|raphy
chro|mato|phore +s
chrome +s
chromed
chrome dome +s
chrome-domed
chrome-moly
chrome steel
chrom|ic
chro|min|ance
chro|mite +s
chro|mium
chromo|genic
chromo|litho|graph +s
chromo|litho|graph|er +s
chromo|litho|graph|ic
chromo|litho|graphy
chromo|phore +s
chromo|som|al
chromo|some +s
chromo|sphere +s
chromo|spher|ic
chron|ic
chron|ic|ally
chron|icity
chron|icle
    chron|icles
    chron|icled
    chron|ic|ling
chron|ic|ler +s
Chron|icles (Bible)
chrono|biol|o|gist +s
chrono|biol|ogy
chrono|graph +s
chrono|graph|ic
chrono|logic|al
chrono|logic|al|ly
chron|ol|o|gist +s
chron|ol|o|gize
chron|ol|o|giz|es

chron|ol|o|gized
chron|ol|o|giz|ing
chron|ol|ogy
chron|ol|o|gies
chron|om|eter +s
chrono|met|ric
chrono|met|ric|al
chrono|met|ric|al|ly
chron|om|etry
chrys|alis
chrys|alis|es or chrys|al|ides
chrys|an|the|mum +s
chrys|ele|phant|ine
Chrys|ler proprietary (automaker)
[☞ Crysler's Farm, Kreisler]
chryso|beryl +s
chryso|lite +s
chryso|prase +s
Chrys|os|tom, John (saint)
chryso|tile
chthon|ian
(= chthonic)
chthon|ic
chub
• (fish)
    plural chub or chubs
• (sausage)
    plural chubs
chub|bi|ly
chub|bi|ness
chubby
    chub|bi|er
    chub|bi|est
Chubu (region, Japan)
chuck +s +ed +ing
chuck driv|er +s
chucker-out
    chuckers-out
chuck|hole +s
chuckle
    chuckles
    chuckled
    chuck|ling
chuckle|head +s
chuckle|head|ed
chuck|ler +s
chuck|wagon +s
chuck|wal|la +s
chuff +s +ed +ing (puff)
[☞ chough]
chuffed adjective
chug
    chugs
    chugged
    chug|ging
chug|a|lug
    chug|a|lugs

chug|a|lugged
chug|a|lug|ging
Chu|go|ku (region, Japan)
chu|kar +s
Chuk|chi (people & language; sea)
 plural Chuk|chi
chum
• noun (friend)
 plural chums
• noun (salmon)
 plural chum or chums
• noun (fish refuse)
• verb
 chums
 chummed
 chum|ming
Chu|mash
 plural Chu|mash or Chu|mash|es
Chu|mash|an
chum|mi|ly
chum|mi|ness
chummy
 chum|mi|er
 chum|mi|est
chump +s
chun|der +s +ed +ing
Chung|king
 (= Chongqing)
chunk +s +ed +ing
chunk|i|ness
chunky
 chunk|i|er
 chunk|i|est
chun|ter +s +ed +ing
chup|pa (use chuppah)
 chup|pot or chup|pas
chup|pah
 chup|pot or chup|pahs
Chu|qui|saca (former name for Sucre, Bolivia)
Church (body of Christians)
church (building; service; bring to church)
 church|es
 churched
 church|ing
church|goer +s
church|going
church|i|er
church|i|est
Church|ill (city & rivers, Canada)

Church|ill, John (Duke of Marlborough)
Church|ill, Ran|dolph Henry Spen|cer (English politician)
Church|ill, Sir Win|ston Leon|ard Spen|cer (British prime minister)
Church|ill Falls (falls & community, Canada)
Church|ill|ian
church|i|ness
church key +s
church|ly
church|man
 church|men
church|warden +s
church|woman
 church|women
churchy
 church|i|er
 church|i|est
church|yard +s
chur|inga
 chur|inga or chur|in|gas
churl +s
churl|ish
churl|ish|ly
churl|ish|ness
churn +s +ed +ing
churr +s +ed +ing
 (= chirr)
Chur|ri|guer|esque
chur|ro +s
chute +s (channel, passage; pen; rapid; parachute)
 [☞ shoot, Shute]
Chute Ouiat|chou|ane (waterfall, Canada)
Chu Teh (= Zhu De, Chinese military leader)
chut|ist +s (parachutist)
 [☞ shootist]
chut|ney +s
chutz|pah
chyle
chyl|ous
chyme (Physiology)
 [☞ chime]
chymo|tryp|sin
chym|ous
chypre +s
Ciano, Galeaz|zo (Italian statesman)

ciao interjection (hello; goodbye)
Cib|ber, Col|ley (English dramatist)
ci|bor|ium
 ci|boria
ci|cada +s
cica|trice
 cica|tri|ces
cica|tri|cial
cica|trix (= cicatrice)
 cica|tri|ces
cica|triz|a|tion +s
cica|trize
 cica|triz|es
 cica|trized
 cica|triz|ing
ci|cely (plant)
 ci|cel|ies
 [☞ Sicily, Sisley]
Ci|cero, Mar|cus Tul|lius (Roman statesman & writer)
ci|cer|one
 ci|cer|oni
Cl|cero|nian
cich|lid +s
Cid, El (Spanish soldier)
CIDA (Canadian International Development Agency)
cider +s
ci-devant
cig +s (cigarette)
 [☞ sig]
cigar +s
ciga|rette +s
ciga|ril|lo +s
cigar-store In|di|an +s
cig|gie +s
cil|an|tro
cilia
cili|ary
cili|ate
 cili|ates
 cili|at|ed
 cili|at|ing
cili|at|ed adjective
cili|ation +s
Cili|cia (ancient region, Asia Minor)
Cili|cian
Cili|cian Gates (mountain pass, Turkey)
cil|ium (hair)
 cilia
 [☞ psyllium]
Cima|bue, Gio|van|ni (Italian artist)

cim|ba|lom +s
cimet|idine
Cim|mer|ian +s
C.-in-C. (commander-in-chief)
C.-in-C.'s
cinch (easy task; certainty; firm hold; girth)
 cinch|es
 cinched
 cinch|ing
 [☞ chinch]
cin|cho|na +s
cin|chon|ic
cin|chon|ine +s
Cin|cin|nati (city, US)
Cin|cin|nat|us, Lu|cius Quinc|tius (Roman statesman)
cinc|ture +s
cin|der +s
cin|der block +s
 (cinder-block when preceding a noun)
cin|der cone +s
Cin|der|ella +s
cin|dery
cine|aste +s
cin|ema +s
Cinema|Scope proprietary
cine|ma|theque +s
cine|mat|ic
cine|mat|ic|ally
cine|ma|tog|raph|er +s
cine|mato|graph|ic
cine|mato|graph|ic|ally
cine|ma|tog|raphy
cinéma-vérité
cine|phile +s
Cine|plex proprietary
 Cine|plex|es
cin|er|aria +s (plant)
cin|er|ari|um +s
 (place for urn)
cin|er|ary
cin|er|eous
cin|gu|late
cin|gu|lum
 cin|gula
cin|na|bar +s
cin|na|mon +s
cin|que|cen|tist +s
cin|que|cento
cinque|foil +s
Cinque Ports (in England)
Cin|tra (= Sintra, Portugal)
ci|paille +s

ci|pher +s +ed +ing
circa
cir|cad|ian
Cir|cas|sian +s
Circe (*Greek Myth*)
cir|cin|ate
cir|cle
  cir|cles
  cir|cled
  circ|ling
circ|ler +s
circ|let +s
circs (circumstances)
  [☞ cirques]
cir|cuit +s
cir|cuit board +s
cir|cuit break|er +s
cir|cu|it|ous
cir|cu|it|ous|ly
cir|cu|it|ous|ness
cir|cuit rid|er +s
cir|cuit|ry
  cir|cuit|ries
cir|cu|lar
circu|lar|ity
circu|lar|iz|a|tion +s
circu|lar|ize
  circu|lar|iz|es
  circu|lar|ized
  circu|lar|iz|ing
cir|cu|lar|ly
cir|cu|late
  cir|cu|lates
  cir|cu|lat|ed
  cir|cu|lat|ing
circu|la|tion +s
circu|la|tive
circu|la|tor +s
circu|la|tory
circum|ambi|ence
circum|ambi|ency
circum|ambi|ent
circum|ambu|late
  circum|ambu|lates
  circum|ambu|lat|ed
  circum|ambu|lat|ing
circum|ambu|la|tion +s
circum|ambu|la|tory
circum|bor|eal
cir|cum|cise
  cir|cum|cis|es
  cir|cum|cised
  cir|cum|cis|ing
cir|cum|cision +s
cir|cum|fer|ence +s
cir|cum|fer|en|tial
cir|cum|fer|en|tial|ly
cir|cum|flex
  cir|cum|flex|es
cir|cum|flu|ence
cir|cum|fluent

cir|cum|fuse
  cir|cum|fus|es
  cir|cum|fused
  cir|cum|fus|ing
circum|locu|tion +s
circum|locu|tion|al
circum|locu|tion|ary
circum|locu|tion|ist +s
circum|locu|tory
circum|lunar
circum|navi|gate
  circum|navi|gates
  circum|navi|gat|ed
  circum|navi|gat|ing
circum|navi|ga|tion +s
circum|navi|ga|tor +s
cicum|polar
cir|cum|scrib|able
cir|cum|scribe
  cir|cum|scribes
  cir|cum|scribed
  cir|cum|scrib|ing
cir|cum|scrib|er +s
cir|cum|scrip|tion +s
circum|solar
cir|cum|spect
cir|cum|spec|tion +s
cir|cum|spect|ly
cir|cum|stance +s
cir|cum|stanced
cir|cum|stan|tial
cir|cum|stan|ti|al|ity
cir|cum|stan|tial|ly
circum|terres|trial
circum|val|late
  circum|val|lates
  circum|val|lat|ed
  circum|val|lat|ing
circum|val|la|tion +s
cir|cum|vent +s +ed +ing
cir|cum|ven|tion +s
circum|volu|tion +s
cir|cus (travelling show, performance; chaos; open space; Roman arena)
  cir|cus|es
  [☞ cercus]
ciré
Ciren|ces|ter (town, England)
cirque +s (hollow; ring; arena)
  [☞ circs]
cir|rho|sis (liver disease)
  [☞ sorosis]
cir|rhot|ic
cir|ri|ped +s

cir|ri|pede +s (*use* cirriped)
cirro|cumu|lus
cirro|strat|us
cir|rus (cloud)
  [☞ scirrhus, scirrhous, serous]
cis|alpine
Cis|alpine Gaul (ancient region, Europe)
cis|atlan|tic
cisco
  cis|coes
Cis|kei (former homeland, South Africa)
cis|lunar
cist +s (coffin, burial chamber; box for sacred articles)
  [☞ cyst]
Cis|ter|cian +s
cis|tern +s
cis|tus
  cis|tus|es
cit|able
cita|del +s
cit|a|tion +s
cite (quote; commend; summon)
  cites
  cited
  cit|ing
  [☞ site]
citi|fied
cit|izen +s
cit|izen|hood +s
cit|izen|ry
citizen's ar|rest +s
citizens' band
cit|izen|ship +s
Cit|izen|ship Court
Cit|lal|té|petl (mountain, Mexico)
cit|rate +s
cit|ric
cit|rine +s
cit|ron +s
cit|ron|ella
cit|rous *adjective*
cit|rus *noun*:
  plural cit|rus
cit|rusy
cit|tern +s
city
  cit|ies
city|fied (*use* citified)
city|scape +s
city slick|er +s
city state +s
city-wide

Ciu|dad Bolí|var (city, Venezuela)
Ciu|dad Tru|jillo (*former name for* Santo Domingo, Dominican Republic)
Ciu|dad Vic|toria (city, Mexico)
civ|et +s
civet cat +s
civic
civic|ally
civic holi|day
civ|ics
civil
civil|ian +s
civil|ian|iz|a|tion
civil|ian|ize
  civil|ian|iz|es
  civil|ian|ized
  civil|ian|iz|ing
civil|ity
  civil|ities
civil|iz|able
civil|iz|a|tion +s
civil|ize
  civil|iz|es
  civil|ized
  civil|iz|ing
civil|ized *adjective*
civil|iz|er +s
civil list
civil|ly
civ|vies (civilian clothes)
civvy (a civilian)
  civ|vies
civvy street
clack +s +ed +ing (sharp sound; chatter)
  [☞ claque]
clack|er +s (person etc. that clacks)
  [☞ claqueur]
clad
  • *adjective* (clothed)
  • *verb* (provide with cladding)
  clads
  clad|ded or clad
  clad|ding
clad|ding +s *noun*
clade +s
clad|ism
clad|is|tic
clad|is|tics
clad|ode +s
clado|gram +s
cla|fou|tis
claim +s +ed +ing
claim|able

claim|ant +s (person making a claim) [☞ clamant]
claim|er +s
Clair, René (French filmmaker) [☞ Claire, Clare,]
Claire (lake, Canada) [☞ Clair, Clare, St. Clair River, Lake St. Clair]
clair|voy|ance
clair|voy|ant +s
clair|voy|ant|ly
clam
  clams
  clammed
  clam|ming
cla|mant (insistent) [☞ claimant]
cla|mant|ly
Cla|mato +s proprietary
clam|bake +s
clam|ber +s +ed +ing (climb) [☞ clammer, clamour]
clam|mer +s (person who digs for clams) [☞ clamour, clamber]
clam|mi|ly
clam|mi|ness
clam|my
  clam|mi|er
  clam|mi|est
clamor +s +ed +ing (shout: use clamour) [☞ clammer]
clam|or|ous
clam|or|ous|ly
clam|or|ous|ness
clam|our +s +ed +ing (shout) [☞ clammer]
clamp +s +ed +ing
clamp down verb
  clamps down
  clamped down
  clamp|ing down
clamp|down +s noun
clamp|er +s
clam|shell +s
clan +s (family; tribe; group) [☞ Ku Klux Klan]
Clan|cy, Fran|cis Mi|chael ('King') (Cdn hockey player)
clan|des|tine
clan|des|tine|ly
clan|des|tin|ity

clang +s +ed +ing
clang|er +s (mistake) [☞ clangour]
clang|or (clanging sound, uproar: use clangour) [☞ clanger]
clang|or|ous
clang|or|ous|ly
clang|our (clanging sound; uproar) [☞ clanger]
clank +s +ed +ing
clank|ing|ly
clanky
clan|nish
clan|nish|ly
clan|nish|ness
clans|man (member of a clan) clans|men [☞ Klansman]
clans|woman (member of a clan) clans|women [☞ Klanswoman]
clap
  claps
  clapped
  clap|ping
clap|board +s (siding)
clap|board|ed
clapped out (clapped-out when preceding a noun)
clap|per +s
clapper|board +s (Film)
clap|per load|er +s
Clap|ton, Eric (English guitarist)
clap|trap
claque +s (hired audience) [☞ clack]
cla|queur +s (member of a claque) [☞ clacker]
Clare (county, Ireland; saint) [☞ Clair, Claire, St. Clair River, Lake St. Clair]
clar|ence +s
Clar|en|don, Ed|ward Hyde, Earl of (English statesman & historian)
Clare of As|sisi (saint)
clar|et +s
clari|fi|ca|tion +s
clari|fied adjective

clari|fi|er +s
clari|fy
  clari|fies
  clari|fied
  clari|fy|ing
clari|net +s
clari|net|ist +s
Clar|ing|ton (municipality, Canada)
clar|ion +s
clar|ity
  clar|ities
Clark (surname) [☞ Clarke]
Clark, Charles Jo|seph ('Joe') (Cdn prime minister)
Clark, Paras|keva (Russian-born Cdn painter)
Clark, Wil|liam (US explorer)
Clarke, Ar|thur Charles (English writer) [☞ Clark]
clar|kia +s
clary
  clar|ies
clash
  clash|es
  clashed
  clash|ing
clash|er +s
clasp +s +ed +ing
clasp|er +s
clasp-knife
  clasp-knives
class
  class|es
  classed
  class|ing
class ac|tion +s (class-action when preceding a noun)
class-conscious
class-conscious|ness
clas|sic +s
clas|sic|al
clas|sic|al|ism
clas|sic|al|ist +s
clas|sic|al|ity
clas|sic|al|ly
clas|si|cism
clas|si|cist +s
clas|si|cize
  clas|si|ciz|es
  clas|si|cized
  clas|si|ciz|ing
clas|si|ciz|ing adjective
clas|si|er

clas|si|est
clas|si|fi|able
clas|si|fi|ca|tion +s
clas|si|fi|ca|tory
clas|si|fied +s adjective & noun
clas|si|fi|er +s
clas|si|fy
  clas|si|fies
  clas|si|fied
  clas|si|fy|ing
class|i|ly
class|i|ness
class|ism
class|ist +s
class|less
class|less|ness
class|mate +s
class|room +s
class|work
classy
  class|i|er
  class|i|est
clas|tic
clath|rate +s
clat|ter +s +ed +ing
Claudel, Ca|mille Rosa|lie (French sculptor)
Claudel, Paul Louis Charles Marie (French writer)
Claude Lor|rain (French painter)
claudi|ca|tion
Claud|ius (Roman emperors)
claus|al
clause +s
Clause|witz, Karl von (Prussian soldier & writer)
Claus|ius, Ru|dolf (German physicist)
claus|tral
claus|tro|phobia
claus|tro|phob|ic
claus|tro|phob|ic|ally
cla|vate
clave +s
clavi|chord +s
clav|icle +s
cla|vicu|lar
cla|vier +s
clavi|form
claw +s +ed +ing
claw back verb
  claws back
  clawed back
  claw|ing back
claw|back +s noun
clawed adjective

claw foot
claw feet
claw-footed
claw|less
Clay, Cas|sius
Mar|cel|lus
(Muhammad Ali)
[☞ Klee]
Clay, Henry (US
politician)
[☞ Klee]
clay +s
Clay Belt (region,
Canada)
clay|ey
clay|ish
clay|like
clay|mation
clay|more +s
Clayo|quot Sound
(inlet, Canada)
clay-pan +s
clay pi|geon +s
clean +s +ed +ing
+er +est
clean|able
clean-cut
clean|er
clean|ish
clean|li|ness
clean-living
clean|ly adverb &
adjective
clean|li|er
clean|li|est
clean|ness
clean out verb
cleans out
cleaned out
clean|ing out
clean|out +s noun
clean room +s
cleanse
cleans|es
cleansed
cleans|ing
cleans|er +s
clean-shaven
clean|skin +s
Cle|anth|es (Greek
philosopher)
clean up verb
cleans up
cleaned up
clean|ing up
clean|up +s noun
clear +er +est +s +ed
+ing
clear|able
clear|ance +s
clear-cut
clear-cuts

clear-cut
clear-cutting
clear-cutter +s
clear-cutting noun
clear|er +s
clear-eyed
Clear Grit +s
clear-headed
clear|ing +s noun
clear|ing house +s
clear|ly
clear|ness
clear-sighted
Clear|water (river,
Canada)
clear|way +s
cleat +s
cleat|ed
cleav|able
cleav|age +s
cleave
• (break apart)
cleaves
cleaved or clove or
cleft
clo|ven or cleft or
cleaved
cleav|ing
• (adhere)
cleaves
cleaved
cleav|ing
cleav|er +s (tool)
cleav|ers (plant)
plural cleav|ers
cleaves conjugated
form of cleave
[☞ Anne of Cleves]
Cleese, John
Mar|wood (English
comedian)
clef +s
cleft +s
cleg +s
Cleis|the|nes
(Athenian statesman)
cleis|to|gam|ic
clem|atis
plural clem|atis
Cle|men|ceau
(mountain, Canada)
Cle|men|ceau,
Georges Eu|gène
Ben|ja|min (French
prime minister)
clem|ency
Clem|ens, Sam|uel
Lang|horne (Mark
Twain)
Clem|ent (saints;
popes)
clem|ent
clem|en|tine +s

clench
clench|es
clenched
clench|ing
cle|ome +s
Cleon (Athenian
leader)
Cleo|patra (Egyptian
queen)
clep|syd|ra +s
cleres|tory
cleres|tor|ies
clergy
cler|gies
clergy|man
clergy|men
clergy|person
clergy|persons
clergy|woman
clergy|women
cler|ic +s
cler|ic|al
cler|ic|al|ism
cler|ic|al|ist +s
cler|ic|al|ly
cleri|hew +s
cler|isy
cler|is|ies
clerk +s +ed +ing
[☞ de Klerk]
clerk|ish
clerk|ly
clerk|ship +s
Clermont-Ferrand
(city, France)
Cleve|land (city, US;
county, England)
Cleve|land,
(Ste|phen) Gro|ver
(US president)
clev|er +er +est
(smart)
[☞ cleaver,
cleavers]
clev|er Dick +s
clev|er|ly
clev|er|ness
clev|is
clev|is|es
clew +s +ed +ing
(Nautical; ball of
thread)
[☞ clue]
cli|ché +s
cli|chéd
click +s +ed +ing
(sound; engage,
press)
[☞ klick]
click|able
click|er +s
cli|ent +s
clien|tele +s

client-server
client|ship +s
cliff +s
cliff-hanger +s
cliff-hanging
cliff|like
cliff|side +s
cliff|top +s
cliffy
cliff|i|er
cliff|i|est
Clift, (Ed|ward)
Mont|gom|ery (US
actor)
cli|mac|ter|ic +s
cli|mac|tic (of a
climax)
clim|ac|tic|ally
cli|mate +s
cli|mate con|trol
climate-controlled
cli|mat|ic (of climate)
cli|mat|ic|ally
cli|mato|logic|al
clima|tol|o|gist +s
clima|tol|ogy
cli|max
cli|max|es
cli|maxed
cli|max|ing
climb +s +ed +ing
(ascend, ascent;
increase, etc.)
[☞ clime]
climb|able
climb down verb
climbs down
climbed down
climb|ing down
climb|down +s noun
climb|er +s
clime +s (region;
climate)
[☞ climb]
clinal
clinch
clinch|es
clinched
clinch|ing
clinch|er +s
Cline, Patsy (US
singer)
[☞ Klein, Kline]
cline +s
cling
clings
clung
cling|ing
cling|er +s
cling film +s
cling|i|ness
cling|ing|ly
cling|stone +s

clingy
  cling|i|er
  cling|i|est
clin|ic +s
clin|ic|al
clin|ic|al|ly
clin|ician +s
clink +s +ed +ing
clink|er +s
clinker-built
clin|om|eter +s
Clin|ton, Wil|liam
  Jef|fer|son ('Bill')
  (US president)
clin|tonia +s
Clio (Greek Myth)
clio|met|ric
clio|met|ri|cian +s
clio|met|rics
cli|om|etry
clip
  clips
  clipped
  clip|ping
clip art
clip|board +s
clip-clop
  clip-clops
  clip-clopped
  clip-clopping
clip joint +s
clip on verb
  clips on
  clipped on
  clip|ping on
clip-on +s noun
clip|pable
clip|per +s
clip|ping +s noun
clique +s (exclusive
  group)
cliquey
cliquish
cliquish|ness
cliquism
Clis|the|nes
  (= Cleisthenes,
  Athenian statesman)
clit +s
clit|ic +s
cliti|ciz|a|tion +s
clit|oral
clit|ori|dec|tomy
  clit|ori|dec|to|mies
clit|or|is
  clit|or|is|es
Clive, Rob|ert (1st
  Baron Clive of
  Plassey, English
  general & colonial
  administrator)
cliv|ers (use cleavers)
  plural clivers

clo|aca
  clo|acae
clo|acal
cloak +s +ed +ing
cloak-and-dagger
cloak|room +s
clob|ber +s +ed +ing
cloche +s
clock +s +ed +ing
clock|er +s
clock|maker +s
clock|making
clock-watcher +s
clock-watching
clock|wise
clock|work +s
clod +s
clod|dish
clod|dish|ly
clod|dish|ness
clod|hop|per +s
clod|hop|ping
clog
  clogs
  clogged
  clog|ging
clog dance
  clog dan|ces
  clog danced
  clog dan|cing
clog dan|cer +s
clog|ger +s
cloi|son|né
clois|ter +s +ed +ing
clois|tered adjective
clois|tral
clomp +s +ed +ing
clon|al
clone
  clones
  cloned
  clon|ing
clon|ic
clonk +s +ed +ing
Clon|mel (town,
  Ireland)
clo|nus
  clo|nus|es
clop
  clops
  clopped
  clop|ping
clo|qué +s
clos|able
close[1] (near etc.;
  street, enclosed
  space)
  clos|er
  clos|est
  clos|es
close[2] (shut etc.;
  conclusion)

clos|es
closed
clos|ing
  [☞ cloze, clothes]
close-cropped
closed adjective
closed cap|tion +s
closed-captioned
closed-caption|ing
closed-circuit
  adjective
closed door +s
  (closed-door when
  preceding a noun)
closed-end adjective
closed-minded
closed-minded|ness
close-fisted
close-fitting
close-grained
close-hauled
close-knit
close|ly
closely-knit
close-mouthed
close|ness
close-quarter
  adjective preceding a
  noun
close quar|ters (in 'at
  close quarters', 'in
  close quarters')
close-quarters
  (= close-quarter)
clos|er +s noun
close-set
clos|et +s +ed +ing
clos|et|ed adjective
close up adverb (as in
  'wanted to view the
  players close up')
close-up +s adjective
  & noun (as in 'a
  close-up view'; 'a
  close-up of the
  players')
clos|ing +s noun
clos|ing time +s
clos|trid|ial
clos|ure
  clos|ures
  clos|ured
  clos|ur|ing
clot
  clots
  clot|ted
  clot|ting
clot|bur +s
cloth (woven material
  etc.)
  cloths
  [☞ clothe, clothes]
cloth-bound

cloth-cap
clothe (put clothes on
  etc.)
  clothes
  clothed (or formal
  clad)
  cloth|ing
  [☞ cloth]
clothes noun
  (garments)
  [☞ close, cloze,
  cloths]
clothes horse +s
clothes|line +s
clothes moth +s
clothes peg +s
clothes|pin +s
cloth|ier +s
cloth|ing noun
Clo|tho (Greek Myth)
cloths plural of cloth
  [☞ clothes]
clot|ted cream
clo|ture
  clo|tures
  clo|tured
  clo|tur|ing
cloud +s +ed +ing
cloud base
cloud|berry
  cloud|ber|ries
cloud|burst +s
cloud cham|ber +s
cloud-cuckoo-land
  +s
cloud|i|er
cloud|i|est
cloud|i|ly
cloud|i|ness
cloud|land +s
cloud|less
cloud|less|ly
cloud|let +s
cloud|scape +s
cloudy
  cloud|i|er
  cloud|i|est
clout +s +ed +ing
clout|er +s
clove
  • noun
    cloves
  • past tense of cleave
clove hitch
  clove hitch|es
clo|ven adjective
cloven-footed
cloven-hoofed
clo|ver +s
clo|ver leaf (leaf)
  clo|ver leaves

clover|leaf (highway intersection)
clover|leafs
Clo|vis (Frankish king)
clown +s +ed +ing
clown|ery
clown|ish
clown|ish|ly
clown|ish|ness
cloy +s +ed +ing
cloy|ing adjective
cloy|ing|ly
clo|za|pine
cloze +s (test)
[☞ close, clothes]
CLSC (health clinic)
CLSCs
club
clubs
clubbed
club|bing
club|babil|ity
club|bable
club|bable|ness
club|ber +s
club|bi|ness
club|bing noun
clubby
club|bi|er
club|bi|est
club car +s
club foot
club feet
club-footed
club|head +s
club|house +s
club|land
club|man
club|men
club|mate +s
club|moss
club|moss|es
club|root
club|woman
club|women
cluck +s +ed +ing
cluck-cluck +s +ed +ing
cluck|er +s
clue (evidence; hint)
clues
clued
cluing or clue|ing
[☞ clew]
clue|less
clue|less|ly
clue|less|ness
Cluj (= Cluj-Napoca, Romania)
Cluj-Napoca (city, Romania)
clump +s +ed +ing
clum|per +s

clum|pet +s
clumpy
clump|i|er
clump|i|est
clum|si|ly
clum|si|ness
clumsy
clum|si|er
clum|si|est
clung
Clun|iac +s
clunk +s +ed +ing
clunk|er +s
clunk|ing adjective
clunky
clunk|i|er
clunk|i|est
clus|ter +s +ed +ing
clus|ter fly
clus|ter flies
clutch
clutch|es
clutched
clutch|ing
clutch bag +s
Clu|tha (river, New Zealand)
clut|ter +s +ed +ing
clut|tered adjective
Clwyd (county, Wales)
Clyde (river & firth, Scotland)
Clydes|dale +s
clyp|eal
clyp|eate
clyp|eus
clypei
clys|ter +s
Clytem|nes|tra (Greek Myth)
CMA (certified management accountant)
CMAs
CMV (cytomegalovirus)
C-note +s
CNS (central nervous system)
Cnut (= Canute, Danish king)
Co. (company)
c/o (care of)
co-accused
plural co-accused
coach
coach|es
coached
coach|ing
coach|able
coach box
coach boxes
coach house +s

coach|ing noun
coach|man
coach|men
coach|work +s
coady (sweet sauce)
[☞ Cody]
co|agul|able
co|agu|lant +s
co|agu|late
co|agu|lates
co|agu|lat|ed
co|agu|lat|ing
co|agu|la|tion
co|agu|la|tive
co|agu|la|tor +s
co|agu|lum
co|agula
Coa|huila (state, Mexico)
coal +s +ed +ing (rock; fuel)
[☞ cole, kohl]
coal-black +s
Coal|dale (town, Canada)
co|alesce
co|ales|ces
co|alesced
co|ales|cing
co|ales|cence
co|ales|cent
coal face +s
coal|field +s
coal-fired
coal gas
co|ali|tion +s
co|ali|tion|ist +s
coal oil
Coal|sack (Astronomy)
coal tar (coal-tar when preceding a noun)
coam|ing +s
co-anchor +s +ed +ing
coarse (rough; crude)
coars|er
coars|est
[☞ corse, course]
coarse fish
plural coarse fish or coarse fish|es
coarse grain +s
coarse-grained
coarse|ly
coars|en +s +ed +ing
coarse|ness
coars|er comparative of coarse
[☞ courser]

Coast (Pacific coast of N America; mountains, Canada)
coast +s +ed +ing
coast|al
coast|er +s
coast guard +s
coast|land +s
coast|line +s
Coast Sal|ish (= Sne Nay Muxw)
plural Coast Sal|ish
coast-to-coast
Coast Tsim|shian
plural Coast Tsim|shian
coast|ward
coast|wise
coat +s +ed +ing (garment; fur; membrane; cover, layer)
[☞ cote]
coat check +s
coat dress
coat dress|es
coat|ed adjective
coat hang|er +s
coati +s
Co|ati|cook (town, Canada)
coati|mundi +s
coat|ing +s noun
coat of arms
coats of arms
coat rack +s
coat|room +s
Coats (island, Canada)
Coats Land (region, Antarctica)
coat stand +s
coat|tail +s
co-author +s +ed +ing
coax[1] (persuade; manipulate)
coax|es
coaxed
coax|ing
coax[2] (coaxial; coaxial cable)
coax|er +s
co|axial
co|axial|ly
coax|ing noun
coax|ing|ly
cob +s (of corn; of coal etc.; of bread; horse; swan; hazelnut)
[☞ kob, Cobb]

Co|bain, Kurt
Don|ald (US singer-
songwriter)
Co|balt (town,
Canada)
co|balt
cobalt-60
co|balt blue +s
(cobalt-blue *when
preceding a noun*)
co|balt|ic
co|balt|ous
Cobb, Tyrus
Ray|mond ('Ty')
(US baseball player)
cob|ber +s
Cob|bett, Wil|liam
(English political
reformer)
cob|ble (stone; pave;
mend shoes)
cob|bles
cob|bled
cob|bling
[☞ coble]
cob|bled *adjective*
cob|bler +s
cobble|stone +s
Cob|den, Rich|ard
(English political
reformer)
co-belliger|ence
co-belliger|ency
co-belliger|ent +s
Cobe|quid
(mountains, Canada)
cobia
coble +s (boat)
[☞ cobble]
cob|nut +s
COBOL (*Computing*)
Co|bourg (town,
Canada)
cobra +s
cob|web +s
cob|webbed
cob|web|by
coca +s
co|caine
coc|cal
coc|ci|di|osis
coc|ci|di|oses
coc|coid
coc|cus (bacterium;
Botany)
cocci
[☞ caucus]
coc|cy|geal
coc|cyx
coc|cy|ges or
coc|cyx|es
Cocha|bam|ba (city,
Bolivia)

co-chair +s +ed +ing
co-chairman
co-chairmen
co-chair|person +s
Co|chin +s (port,
India; fowl)
Co|chin China +s
(fowl = Cochin)
Cochin-China
(former region,
Vietnam)
coch|in|eal +s
Co|chise (Apache
chief)
coch|lea
coch|leae
coch|lear
Coch|ran, Ed|ward
('Eddie') (US singer-
songwriter)
[☞ Cochrane]
Coch|rane (towns,
Canada)
[☞ Cochran]
cock +s +ed +ing
(male bird, clam,
etc.; gun lever;
Curling; *Plumbing*;
friend; nonsense;
penis; pile of hay
etc.; raise, tilt)
[☞ coq au vin,
caulk, cox]
cock|ade +s
cock|ad|ed
cock-a-doodle-doo
+s
cock-a-hoop
cock-a-leekie
cocka|lorum +s
cocka|mamie
cocka|mamy (*use
cockamamie*)
cock-and-bull
cocka|poo +s
cocka|teel +s (*use
cockatiel*)
cocka|tiel +s
cocka|too +s
cocka|trice +s
cock|boat +s
Cock|burn, Bruce
(Cdn singer-
songwriter)
Cock|burn, James
(Cdn politician)
cock|chafer +s
Cock|croft, Sir John
Doug|las (English
physicist)
cock crow
cock|erel +s
cock|er span|iel +s

cock|eyed
cock|fight +s
cock|fight|ing
cock|i|er
cock|i|est
cock|i|ly
cock|i|ness
cock|le
cock|les
cock|led
cock|ling
cockle|bur +s
cockle|shell +s
cock|ney +s
cock|ney|ism +s
cock-of-the-rock +s
cock of the walk
cocks of the walk
cock|pit +s
cock|roach
cock|roach|es
cocks|comb +s (crest
or comb of a rooster;
plant)
[☞ coxcomb]
cocks|foot +s
cock|shy
cock|shies
cock|suck|er +s
cock|suck|ing
cock|sure
cock|sure|ly
cock|sure|ness
cock|tail +s
cocktail-length
cock|teas|er +s
cock|teas|ing
cock up *verb*
cocks up
cocked up
cock|ing up
cock-up +s *noun*
cocky
cock|i|er
cock|i|est
cock|ies
coco +s (tree bearing
coconuts)
[☞ cocoa]
cocoa +s (chocolate;
hot chocolate; *for*
coconut tree *use*
coco)
[☞ cacao]
cocoa bean +s
cocoa but|ter
coco-de-mer +s
coco mat|ting
co-conspira|tor +s
coco|nut +s
co|coon +s +ed +ing
co|coon|er +s
co|coon|ing *noun*

Cocos (islands, Indian
Ocean)
co|cotte +s
Coc|teau, Jean
(French writer)
COD (collect (or cash)
on delivery)
cod
plural cod
coda +s
cod|dle
cod|dles
cod|dled
cod|dling
cod|dler +s
code
codes
coded
cod|ing
codec +s
co-defend|ant +s
co|deine
code name +s *noun*
code-name *verb*
code-names
code-named
code-naming
cod end +s
co|depend|ency
co|depend|ent +s
coder +s
code-share
code-shares
code-shared
code-sharing
code-sharing *noun*
code-switch|ing
co-determin|a|tion
codex
co|dices
cod|fish
plural cod|fish
codg|er +s
co|di|cil +s
codi|cil|lary
codi|fi|ca|tion +s
codi|fi|er +s
codi|fy
codi|fies
codi|fied
codi|fy|ing
cod|lin +s (apple,
moth: *use* codling)
cod|ling +s (apple;
moth; small cod)
cod-liver oil
co|domain +s
codon +s
cod|piece +s
co-driver +s
cods|wallop
cod tongue +s
cod trap +s

Cody, Wil|liam Fred|erick (Buffalo Bill) [☞ coady]
coe|cil|ian +s (use caecilian)
coed +s
co-edit +s +ed +ing
co-editor +s
co|educa|tion
co|educa|tion|al
co|effi|cient +s
coela|canth +s
coel|enter|ate +s
coel|iac (use celiac)
coelom
  coel|oms or coel|omata
coel|om|ate +s
coel|om|ic
coeno|bite +s (use cenobite)
co|enzyme +s
co|equal +s
co|equal|ity
co|equal|ly
co|erce
  co|er|ces
  co|erced
  co|er|cing
co|er|cible
co|er|cion +s
co|er|cive
co|er|cive|ly
co|er|cive|ness
co|er|civ|ity
Coet|zee, John Mi|chael (South African novelist)
Coeur de Lion (Richard I)
co|eval +s
co|ev|al|ity
co|eval|ly
co-evolution
co-evolve
  co-evolves
  co-evolved
  co-evolving
co|exist +s +ed +ing
co|exist|ence
co|exist|ent
co-extensive
co|fac|tor +s
cof|fee +s
cof|fee bar +s
cof|fee bean +s
cof|fee break +s
cof|fee cake +s
cof|fee grind|er +s
cof|fee hour +s
cof|fee house +s

cof|fee klatch
cof|fee klatch|es
cof|fee klatsch (use coffee klatch)
cof|fee klatsch|es
cof|fee maker +s
cof|fee mill +s
cof|fee morn|ing +s
cof|fee pot +s
cof|fee shop +s
cof|fee spoon +s
cof|fee table +s
coffee-table book +s
cof|fer +s (box; treasury; Architecture) [☞ cougher]
cof|fer|dam +s
cof|fered
cof|fin +s
cof|fined
cof|fle +s
co-found +s +ed +ing
co-founder +s
cog +s
co|gen|cy
co|gener|a|tion
co|gent
co|gent|ly
cogged
cogit|able
cogi|tate
  cogi|tates
  cogi|tat|ed
  cogi|tat|ing
cogi|ta|tion +s
cogi|ta|tive
cogi|ta|tor +s
cogi|to
co|gnac +s
cog|nate +s
cog|nate|ly
cog|nate|ness
cog|ni|tion +s
cog|ni|tion|al
cog|ni|tive
cog|ni|tive|ly
cog|niz|able
cog|niz|ably
cog|ni|zance +s
cog|ni|zant
cog|nom|en +s
cogno|scen|te
  cogno|scen|ti
cogno|scen|ti plural of cognoscente
cog|wheel +s
co|habit
  co|hab|its
  co|habit|ed
  co|habit|ing

co|habit|ant +s
co|habit|a|tion +s
co|hab|itee +s
co|habit|er +s
Cohen, Leon|ard (Cdn writer & musician) [☞ Cohn]
Cohen, Matt (Cdn writer) [☞ Cohn]
co|here
  co|heres
  co|hered
  co|her|ing
co|her|ence +s
co|her|ency
co|her|ent
co|her|ent|ly
co|hesion +s
co|hesive
co|hesive|ly
co|hesive|ness
Cohn, Fer|di|nand Jul|ius (German botanist) [☞ Cohen]
coho +s
co|hort +s
co|hosh
  co|hosh|es
co-host +s +ed +ing
coif (hairstyle; cap)
  coifs
  coiffed
  coif|fing [☞ quaff]
coiffed adjective
coif|feur +s (hairdresser) [☞ coiffure, quaffer]
coif|feuse +s
coif|fure (hairstyle)
  coif|fures
  coif|fured
  coif|fur|ing [☞ coiffeur]
coif|fured adjective
coign of van|tage
  coigns of van|tage
coil +s +ed +ing (wound rope etc.; spiral, helix; in 'mortal coil') [☞ Koil]
coil spring +s
Co|im|ba|tore (city, India)
Co|im|bra (city, Portugal)
coin +s +ed +ing (money; devise)

[☞ quoin, coign of vantage]
coin|age +s
coin box
  coin boxes
co|incide
  co|incides
  co|incid|ed
  co|incid|ing
co|inci|dence +s
co|inci|dent
co|inci|dent|al
co|inci|dent|al|ly (at the same time or place, esp. by chance)
co|inci|dent|ly (at the same time or place; in agreement)
coin|er +s
coin-op +s
coin-operat|ed
Coin|treau +s proprietary
coir (fibre) [☞ choir]
coit|al
coit|al|ly
co|ition
coit|us
coit|us inter|rup|tus
cojon|es
Coke, Sir Ed|ward (English jurist)
Coke +s proprietary (drink)
coke (form of coal; cocaine)
  cokes
  coked
  cok|ing
Coke-bottle adjective preceding a noun
coke|head +s
col +s (Geology; Meteorology) [☞ caul, Coll]
COLA (cost-of-living adjustment)
  COLAs
cola +s (drink; tree) [☞ Kola]
col|an|der +s
cola nut +s
co-latitude +s
Col|bert, Jean Bap|tiste (French statesman)
Col|borne, Sir John, 1st Baron Sea|ton (British colonial administrator in BNA)

colby
  col|bies
col|can|non
Col|ches|ter (town, England)
col|chi|cine +s
col|chi|cum +s
Col|chis (ancient region, Caucasus)
cold +er +est +s
cold-blooded
cold-blooded|ly
cold-blooded|ness
cold call +s *noun*
cold-call *verb*
  cold-calls
  cold-called
  cold-calling
cold-cock
  cold-cocks
  cold-cocked
  cold-cocking
cold cream +s
cold cuts
cold frame +s
cold-hearted
cold-hearted|ly
cold-hearted|ness
cold|ish
Cold Lake (town & lake, Canada)
cold|ly
cold|ness
cold room +s
cold shoul|der +s *noun*
cold-shoulder *verb*
  cold-shoulders
  cold-shouldered
  cold-shoulder|ing
cold snap +s
cold sore +s
cold spell +s
Cold|stream (town, Canada)
cold-water *adjective preceding a noun*
cold wave +s
Cold|well, Major James Wil|liam ('M.J.') (Cdn politician)
Cole, Nat King (US entertainer)
  [☞ Kohl]
cole (cabbage)
  [☞ kohl, coal]
Cole|man, Or|nette (US musician)
Cole|man lamp +s *proprietary*
Cole|man lan|tern +s *proprietary*

Cole|man stove +s *proprietary*
col|eop|ter|an +s
col|eop|ter|ist +s
col|eop|ter|ous
col|eop|tile +s
Cole|ridge, Sam|uel Tay|lor (English poet)
Coles, George (Cdn politician)
cole|slaw
Colet, John (English scholar)
  [☞ Colette, collet]
Col|ette (French novelist)
  [☞ Colet, collet]
co|leus
  co|leus|es
col|ic +s
col|icky
Coli|cos, John (Cdn actor)
coli|form +s
Co|ligny, Gas|pard de (French soldier)
Co|li|ma (state & its capital, Mexico)
coli|seum +s (any large amphitheatre etc.)
  [☞ Colosseum]
col|itis
Coll (island, Scotland)
  [☞ col, caul]
col|lab|or|ate
  col|lab|or|ates
  col|lab|or|at|ed
  col|lab|or|at|ing
col|lab|or|a|tion +s
col|lab|or|a|tion|ist +s
col|lab|or|a|tive
col|lab|or|a|tive|ly
col|lab|or|ator +s
col|lage (*Art*)
  col|lages
  col|laged
  col|la|ging
  [☞ college]
col|la|gen +s
col|la|gist +s
col|lapse
  col|laps|es
  col|lapsed
  col|laps|ing
col|laps|ibil|ity
col|laps|ible
col|lar +s +ed +ing (neckband; restraining ring; rope

for mooring; rolled meat; seize etc.)
  [☞ caller, choler]
col|lar beam +s
collar|bone +s
col|lard +s (cabbage)
  [☞ collared]
col|lard greens
col|lared *adjective* (having a collar)
  [☞ collard]
col|lared lem|ming +s
collar|less
col|late
  col|lates
  col|lat|ed
  col|lat|ing
col|lat|eral +s
col|lat|er|al|ity
col|lat|eral|ize
  col|lat|eral|iz|es
  col|lat|eral|ized
  col|lat|eral|iz|ing
col|lat|eral|ly
col|la|tion +s
col|la|tor +s
col|league +s
col|lect +s +ed +ing
col|lect|able +s (*use* collectible)
col|lect|ed *adjective*
col|lect|ed|ly
col|lect|ible +s
col|lec|tion +s
col|lect|ive +s
col|lect|ive|ly
col|lect|ive|ness
col|lec|tiv|ism
col|lec|tiv|ist +s
col|lec|tiv|is|tic
col|lec|tiv|ity
  col|lec|tiv|ities
col|lec|tiv|iz|a|tion +s
col|lec|tiv|ize
  col|lec|tiv|iz|es
  col|lec|tiv|ized
  col|lec|tiv|iz|ing
col|lect|or +s
col|lector's item +s
col|leen +s
col|lege +s (school)
col|lège clas|sique
  col|lèges clas|siques
col|legial
col|legi|al|ity
col|legial|ly
col|legian +s
col|legi|ate +s (of a college; school)
col|len|chyma

col|let +s (*Machinery; Jewellery*)
  [☞ Colet, Colette]
col|lide
  col|lides
  col|lid|ed
  col|lid|ing
col|lid|er +s
col|lie +s (dog)
  [☞ Cali, Kali]
col|lier +s
col|liery
  col|lier|ies
col|li|gate (join, link)
  col|li|gates
  col|li|gat|ed
  col|li|gat|ing
  [☞ collegiate]
col|li|ga|tion +s
col|li|mate
  col|li|mates
  col|li|mat|ed
  col|li|mat|ing
col|li|ma|tion +s
col|li|ma|tor +s
col|linear
col|linear|ity
Col|ling|wood (town, Canada)
Col|lins, Joan Hen|ri|etta (English actress)
Col|lins, Mi|chael (Irish nationalist)
Col|lins, (Wil|liam) Wil|kie (English writer)
Col|lins, Wil|liam (English poet)
Col|lins (drink)
  Col|lins|es
Col|lip, James Ber|tram ('Bert') (Cdn co-discoverer of insulin)
  [☞ collop]
col|li|sion +s
col|li|sion|al
col|lo|cate
  col|lo|cates
  col|lo|cat|ed
  col|lo|cat|ing
col|lo|ca|tion +s
col|lo|dion +s
col|logue
  col|logues
  col|logued
  col|loguing
col|loid +s
col|loid|al
col|lop +s (slice of meat)
  [☞ Collip]
col|lo|qui|al

col|lo|qui|al|ism +s
col|lo|qui|al|ly
col|lo|qui|um
  col|lo|quia
col|lo|quy
  col|lo|quies
col|lo|type +s
col|lude
  col|ludes
  col|lud|ed
  col|lud|ing
col|lud|er +s
col|lu|sion +s
col|lu|sive
colly|wobbles
colo|bus
  colo|bus|es
colo|cynth +s
Co|logne (city,
  Germany)
co|logne +s
Co|lom|bia (country,
  S America)
  [☞ Columbia,
  British Columbia]
Co|lom|bian +s
Co|lom|bo (capital of
  Sri Lanka)
Colón (port, Panama)
co|lon +s (punctuation
  mark; Anatomy)
colón (currency)
  co|lon|es
col|onel +s (officer)
Col|onel Blimp +s
col|onel|cy
  col|onel|cies
col|oni|al +s
col|oni|al|ism
col|oni|al|ist +s
col|oni|al|iz|a|tion +s
col|oni|al|ize
  col|oni|al|iz|es
  col|oni|al|ized
  col|oni|al|iz|ing
col|oni|al|ly
col|onic
col|onist +s
col|oniz|a|tion
col|onize
  col|oniz|es
  col|onized
  col|oniz|ing
col|oniz|er +s
col|on|nade +s
col|on|nad|ed
co|lono|scope +s
co|lono|scop|ic
colon|os|copy
  colon|os|cop|ies
col|ony
  col|onies
colo|phon +s

col|or +s +ed +ing
  (use colour)
color|able (use
  colourable)
color|ably (use
  colourably)
Col|o|rado (state &
  river, US; beetle;
  spruce)
color|ant +s (use
  colourant)
color|a|tion +s
col|ora|tura +s
color-blind (use
  colour-blind)
color-blindness (use
  colour-blindness)
color code +s noun
  (use colour code)
color-code verb (use
  colour-code)
  color-codes
  color-coded
  color-coding
color-coded adjective
  (use colour-coded)
color-coding noun
  (use colour-coding)
colo|rectal
col|ored +s (use
  coloured).
  • Offensive when
  used of people.
color|fast (use
  colourfast)
color|fast|ness (use
  colourfastness)
color|ful (use
  colourful)
color|ful|ly (use
  colourfully)
color|ful|ness (use
  colourfulness)
color|ific
color|im|eter +s
col|ori|met|ric
col|ori|met|ric|ally
color|im|etry
col|or|ing +s noun
  (use colouring)
col|or|ing book +s
  (use colouring book)
color|ist +s (use
  colourist)
color|is|tic (use
  colouristic)
color|iz|a|tion +s (use
  colourization)
color|ize (use
  colourize)
color|iz|es
color|ized
color|iz|ing

color|less (use
  colourless)
color|less|ly (use
  colourlessly)
color scheme +s (use
  colour scheme)
color wash noun (use
  colour wash)
  color wash|es
color-wash verb (use
  colour-wash)
  color-washes
  color-washed
  color-washing
color|way +s (use
  colourway)
col|os|sal
col|os|sal|ly
Col|os|seum (in
  Rome)
  [☞ coliseum]
Col|os|sians (New
  Testament)
col|os|sus
  col|os|si
col|os|tomy
  col|os|to|mies
col|os|trum
col|our +s +ed +ing
colour|able
colour|ably
colour|ant +s
colour|a|tion +s (use
  coloration)
colour-blind
colour-blindness
col|our code +s noun
colour-code verb
  colour-codes
  colour-coded
  colour-coding
colour-coded
  adjective
colour-coding noun
col|oured +s
  • Offensive when
  used of people.
colour|fast
colour|fast|ness
colour|ful
colour|ful|ly
colour|ful|ness
col|our|ing +s noun
col|our|ing book +s
col|our|ist +s
col|our|is|tic
col|our|iz|a|tion +s
col|our|ize
  col|our|iz|es
  col|our|ized
  col|our|iz|ing
colour|less
colour|less|ly

col|our scheme +s
col|our wash noun
  colour wash|es
colour-wash verb
  colour-washes
  colour-washed
  colour-washing
colour|way +s
col|po|scope +s
col|pos|copy
  col|pos|cop|ies
Colt, Sam|uel (US gun
  manufacturer)
colt +s
col|ter +s (use
  coulter)
colt|hood +s
colt|ish
colt|ish|ly
colt|ish|ness
Col|trane, John
  Wil|liam (US
  musician)
colts|foot +s
colu|brid +s
colu|brine
Colum, Pad|raic
  (Irish-born writer)
  [☞ column]
Col|um|ba (saint)
col|um|bar|ium
  col|um|bar|iums or
  col|um|bar|ia
Col|um|bia (district &
  city, US; mountains
  & cape, Canada;
  river, N America)
  [☞ Colombia]
Col|um|bine
  (pantomime
  character)
col|um|bine +s (plant)
col|um|bite
col|um|bium
Col|um|bus (city, US)
Col|um|bus,
  Chris|to|pher
  (Italian-born Spanish
  explorer)
Col|um|bus Day
col|umn +s
  (Architecture etc.)
  [☞ Colum]
col|um|nar
col|umned
col|umn inch
  col|umn inch|es
col|um|nist +s
colure +s (Astronomy)
Col|vile, Eden
  (governor of
  Rupert's Land)

Col|ville, Alex|an|der (Cdn painter)

Col|wood (city, Canada) [☞ Callwood]

colza

coma
• (unconsciousness) plural comas
• (Astronomy; Botany) plural comae [☞ comma]

Com|an|che plural Com|an|che or Com|an|ches

Comä|neci, Nadia (Romanian gymnast)

coma|tose

comb +s +ed +ing

com|bat com|bats com|bat|ted or com|bat|ed com|bat|ting or com|bat|ing

Com|bat|ant (mountain, Canada)

com|bat|ant +s

com|bat|ive

com|bat|ive|ly

com|bat|ive|ness

combe +s (valley: use coomb) [☞ cwm, khoum]

combed adjective

comb|er +s

combi +s

com|bin|able

com|bin|a|tion +s

com|bin|a|tion|al

com|bin|a|tive

com|bin|a|tor|ial

com|bin|a|tory

com|bine com|bines com|bined com|bin|ing

com|bined adjective

com|bin|er +s

comb|ings

combo +s

com|bust +s +ed +ing

com|bust|ibil|ity

com|bust|ible +s

com|bus|tion

com|bus|tive

come verb & noun comes came come com|ing [☞ cum]

come along verb comes along came along come along com|ing along

come-along +s noun

come back verb comes back came back come back com|ing back

come|back +s noun

Come-by-Chance (town, Canada)

Com|econ (Council for Mutual Economic Assistance)

com|ed|ian +s

com|ed|ic

com|edi|enne +s

com|ed|ist +s

com|edo com|edo|nes

come down verb comes down came down come down com|ing down

come|down +s noun

com|edy com|ed|ies

come from away +s

come-hither

come|li|ness

come|ly come|li|er come|li|est

Com|en|ius, John Amos (Czech educational reformer)

come on verb comes on came on come on com|ing on

come-on +s noun

com|er +s

com|est|ible +s

comet +s

comet|ary

come|uppance +s

com|fi|er

com|fi|est

com|fi|ly

com|fi|ness

com|fit +s

Com|fort, Charles Fraser (Cdn painter)

com|fort +s +ed +ing

com|fort|able

com|fort|able|ness

com|fort|ably

Com|fort|er (the Holy Spirit)

com|fort|er +s (quilt; scarf; one who comforts)

com|fort|ing adjective

com|fort|ing|ly

com|fort|less

com|frey +s

comfy com|fi|er com|fi|est

com|ic +s (funny; comedian; comic book or strip) [☞ kamik]

comic|al

comic|al|ity

comic|al|ly

comic book +s

comic strip +s

Co|mines, Phil|ippe de (French chronicler)

com|ing +s adjective & noun

co|min|gle (use commingle) co|min|gles co|min|gled co|min|gling

com|ing of age (coming-of-age when preceding a noun)

Com|ino (island, Malta)

Com|in|tern

com|ity com|ities

comma +s (punctuation mark; butterfly) [☞ coma, Kama]

com|mand +s +ed +ing

com|mand|ant +s

com|mand|ant|ship +s

com|man|deer +s +ed +ing

com|mand|er +s

com|mander-in-chief com|manders-in-chief

com|mand|er|ship +s

com|mand|ing adjective

com|mand|ing|ly

com|mand|ment +s

com|mando +s

Com|mand Paper +s

com|mand post +s

comme ci, comme ça

com|media dell'arte

comme il faut

com|mem|or|ate com|mem|or|ates com|mem|or|at|ed com|mem|or|at|ing

com|mem|or|a|tion +s

com|mem|or|a|tive

com|mem|or|ator +s

com|mence com|men|ces com|menced com|men|cing

com|mence|ment +s

com|mend +s +ed +ing

com|mend|able

com|mend|ably

com|men|da|tion +s

com|men|da|tory

com|men|sal +s

com|men|sal|ism

com|men|sal|ity

com|men|sur|abil|ity

com|men|sur|able

com|men|sur|ably

com|men|sur|ate

com|men|sur|ate|ly

com|ment +s +ed +ing

com|men|tary com|men|tar|ies

com|men|tate com|men|tates com|men|tat|ed com|men|tat|ing

com|men|ta|tor +s

com|ment|er +s

com|merce

com|mer|cial

com|mer|cial|ism

com|mer|ci|al|ity

com|mer|ci|al|iz|a|tion

com|mer|cial|ize com|mer|cial|iz|es com|mer|cial|ized com|mer|cial|iz|ing

com|mer|cial|ized adjective

com|mer|cial|ly

com|mie +s (communist) [☞ commis]

com|min|a|tion +s

com|min|a|tory

Com|mines, Phil|ippe de (= Comines)

com|min|gle
  com|min|gles
  com|min|gled
  com|min|gling
com|min|ute
  com|min|utes
  com|min|ut|ed
  com|min|ut|ing
com|min|ut|ed
  adjective
com|minu|tion +s
com|mis (junior chef
  or waiter)
  plural com|mis
  [☞ commie]
com|miser|ate
  com|miser|ates
  com|miser|at|ed
  com|miser|at|ing
com|miser|a|tion +s
com|miser|a|tive
com|miser|ator +s
com|mish
  com|mish|es
com|mis|sar +s
com|mis|sar|ial
com|mis|sar|iat +s
com|mis|sary
  com|mis|sar|ies
com|mis|sary|ship
  +s
com|mis|sion +s +ed
  +ing
com|mis|sion|aire +s
com|mis|sion|er +s
Com|mis|sion|er for
  Oaths
  Com|mis|sion|ers
  for Oaths
com|mis|sur|al
com|mis|sure +s
com|mit
  com|mits
  com|mit|ted
  com|mit|ting
com|mit|ment +s
com|mit|table
com|mit|tal +s
com|mit|ted *adjective*
com|mit|tee +s
com|mit|tee|man
  com|mit|tee|men
com|mit|tee woman
  com|mit|tee women
com|mit|ter +s
com|mix
  com|mix|es
  com|mixed
  com|mix|ing
com|mix|ture +s
com|mode +s
com|modi|fi|ca|tion
  +s

com|mod|ify
  com|modi|fies
  com|modi|fied
  com|modi|fy|ing
com|modi|ous
com|modi|ous|ly
com|modi|ous|ness
com|mod|ity
  com|mod|ities
com|mo|dore +s
Com|mo|dus, Lu|cius
  Ael|ius Aurel|ius
  (Roman emperor)
com|mon +er +est +s
com|mon|age
com|mon|al|ity
  com|mon|al|ities
com|mon|alty
  com|mon|al|ties
com|mon|er +s
Com|mon Era
com|mon|ly
Com|mon Mar|ket
com|mon|ness
com|mon|place +s
com|mon|place|ness
Com|mon Prayer
com|mon room +s
Com|mons (legislative
  body)
com|mon sense *noun*
common|sens|ical
com|mon weal (the
  general good)
com|mon|weal
  (commonwealth; *for*
  the general good *use*
  common weal)
com|mon|wealth +s
com|mo|tion +s
com|mun|al
com|mun|al|ism
com|mun|al|ist +s
com|mun|al|is|tic
com|mun|al|ity
  com|mun|al|ities
com|mun|al|iz|a|tion
  +s
com|mun|al|ize
  com|mun|al|iz|es
  com|mun|al|ized
  com|mun|al|iz|ing
com|mun|al|ly
com|mu|nard +s
com|mune
  com|munes
  com|muned
  com|mun|ing
com|munic|abil|ity
com|munic|able
com|munic|ably
com|muni|cant +s

com|muni|cate
  com|muni|cates
  com|muni|cat|ed
  com|muni|cat|ing
com|muni|ca|tion +s
com|muni|ca|tion|al
com|muni|ca|tion
  sat|el|lite +s
  (= communications
  satellite)
com|muni|ca|tions
  sat|el|lite +s
com|muni|ca|tive
com|muni|ca|tive|ly
com|muni|ca|tor +s
com|muni|ca|tory
Com|mun|ion
  (Eucharist)
com|mun|ion +s
  (fellowship, sharing;
  body of Christians)
com|muni|qué +s
Com|mun|ism
  (specific movement
  or party)
com|mun|ism
  (political theory)
Com|mun|ist +s
  (member of party)
com|mun|ist +s
  (advocate of system)
com|mun|is|tic
com|muni|tar|ian +s
com|muni|tar|ian|
           ism
com|mun|ity
  com|mun|ities
com|mun|iz|a|tion
com|mun|ize
  com|mun|iz|es
  com|mun|ized
  com|mun|iz|ing
com|mut|abil|ity
com|mut|able
com|mu|tate
  com|mu|tates
  com|mu|tat|ed
  com|mu|tat|ing
com|mu|ta|tion
com|mu|ta|tive
com|mu|ta|tor +s
com|mute
  com|mutes
  com|mut|ed
  com|mut|ing
com|mut|er +s
com|muter|shed +s
Como (lake, Italy)
Como|doro
  Riva|davia (port,
  Argentina)
Com|or|an +s (of
  Comoros)

Com|or|in (cape,
  India)
Com|or|os (island
  country, Indian
  Ocean)
co|mose
Comox (town,
  Canada; people &
  language)
  plural Comox or
  Co|mox|es
comp +s +ed +ing
com|pact +s +ed
  +ing
com|pact disc +s
com|pact|er +s (*use*
  compactor)
com|pac|tion +s
com|pact|ly
com|pact|ness
com|pact|or +s
com|padre +s
com|pan|ion +s +ed
  +ing
com|pan|ion|abil|ity
com|pan|ion|able
com|pan|ion|able|
           ness
com|pan|ion|ably
com|pan|ion|ate
com|pan|ion|ship
com|pan|ion|way +s
com|pany
  com|pan|ies
com|par|abil|ity
com|par|able
com|par|able|ness
com|par|ably
com|para|tive +s
com|para|tive|ly
com|para|tor +s
com|pare (note
  similarities &
  differences)
  com|pares
  com|pared
  com|par|ing
  [☞ compère]
com|pari|son +s
com|part|ment +s
  +ed +ing
com|part|ment|al
com|part|ment|al|
           iz|a|tion +s
com|part|ment|al|ize
  com|part|ment|al|
             iz|es
  com|part|ment|al|
             ized
  com|part|ment|al|
             iz|ing
com|part|ment|al|ly
com|part|ment|
          a|tion +s

com|pass
  com|pass|es
  com|passed
  com|pass|ing
com|pass|able
com|pas|sion
com|pas|sion|ate
com|pas|sion|ate|ly
com|pat|ibil|ity
  com|pat|ibil|ities
com|pat|ible +s
com|pat|ibly
com|patri|ot +s
com|patri|ot|ic
com|peer +s
com|pel
  com|pels
  com|pelled
  com|pel|ling
com|pel|lable
com|pel|ling adjective
com|pel|ling|ly
com|pen|di|ous
com|pen|di|ous|ly
com|pen|di|ous|ness
com|pen|dium
  com|pen|diums or
  com|pen|dia
com|pen|sate
  com|pen|sates
  com|pen|sat|ed
  com|pen|sat|ing
com|pen|sa|tion +s
com|pen|sa|tion|al
com|pen|sa|tive
com|pen|sa|tor +s
com|pen|sa|tory
com|père (act as MC)
  com|pères
  com|pèred
  com|pèr|ing
com|pete
  com|petes
  com|pet|ed
  com|pet|ing
com|pe|tence +s
com|pe|tency
  com|pe|ten|cies
com|pe|tent
com|pe|tent|ly
com|pe|ti|tion +s
com|peti|tive
com|peti|tive|ly
com|peti|tive|ness
com|peti|tor +s
com|pil|a|tion +s
com|pile
  com|piles
  com|piled
  com|pil|ing
com|pil|er +s

com|pla|cence +s
  (self-satisfaction;
  tranquil pleasure)
  [☞ complaisance]
com|pla|cency
  com|pla|cen|cies
com|pla|cent (self-
  satisfied; calmly
  content)
  [☞ complaisant]
com|pla|cent|ly
com|plain +s +ed
  +ing
com|plain|ant +s
com|plain|er +s
com|plain|ing|ly
com|plaint +s
com|plai|sance +s
  (deference;
  acquiescence)
  [☞ complacence]
com|plai|sant
  (deferential;
  acquiescent)
  [☞ complacent]
com|pleat (proficient)
  [☞ complete]
com|plec|ted
com|ple|ment +s +ed
  +ing (something that
  completes; full
  number needed;
  Grammar;
  Biochemistry; Math;
  Geometry; complete,
  go well with)
  [☞ compliment]
com|ple|ment|al
com|ple|men|tar|i|ly
  (completing,
  complementing)
  [☞
  complimentarily]
com|ple|men|
        tar|i|ness
com|ple|men|tar|ity
com|ple|men|
        tar|ities
com|ple|ment|ary
  (completing,
  complementing)
  [☞
  complimentary]
com|ple|ment|ary
  angle +s
com|ple|ment|ary
  col|our +s
com|plete
  • verb
    com|pletes
    com|plet|ed
    com|plet|ing
  • adjective (entire;
    finished; absolute; for

proficient use
  compleat)
com|plet|ed adjective
com|plete|ly
com|plete|ness
com|plet|er +s
com|ple|tion +s
com|plet|ist +s
com|plex
  com|plex|es
com|plex|ion +s
com|plex|ioned
com|plex|ity
  com|plex|ities
com|plex|ly
com|pli|ance
com|pli|ant
com|pli|ant|ly
com|pli|cate
  com|pli|cates
  com|pli|cat|ed
  com|pli|cat|ing
com|pli|cat|ed
  adjective
com|pli|cat|ed|ly
com|pli|cat|ed|ness
com|pli|ca|tion +s
com|plicit
com|plici|tous
com|plici|ty
  com|plici|ties
com|pli|ment +s +ed
  +ing (praise;
  greeting)
  [☞ complement]
com|pli|men|tar|i|ly
  (with praise; freely)
  [☞
  complementarily]
com|pli|ment|ary
  (praising; free)
  [☞
  complementary]
com|pli|ment|ary
  clos|ing +s
com|pline +s
com|ply
  com|plies
  com|plied
  com|ply|ing
compo +s
com|pon|ent +s
com|pon|en|tial
com|pon|en|try
com|port +s +ed
  +ing
com|port|ment
com|pose
  com|pos|es
  com|posed
  com|pos|ing
com|posed adjective
com|pos|ed|ly

com|pos|er +s
com|pos|ite +s
com|pos|ite|ly
com|pos|ite|ness
com|pos|ition +s
com|pos|ition|al
com|pos|ition|al|ly
com|posi|tor +s
com|pos men|tis
com|post +s +ed
  +ing
com|post|able
com|post|er +s
com|po|sure
com|pote +s
com|pound +s +ed
  +ing
com|pound|able
com|pra|dor +s
com|pra|dore +s (use
  comprador)
com|pre|hend +s +ed
  +ing
com|pre|hend|er +s
com|pre|hen|si|bil|ity
com|pre|hen|sible
com|pre|hen|sibly
com|pre|hen|sion
com|pre|hen|sive
com|pre|hen|sive|ly
com|pre|hen|sive|
        ness
com|press
  com|press|es
  com|pressed
  com|press|ing
com|press|ibil|ity
com|press|ible
com|pres|sion +s
com|pres|sive
com|pres|sor +s
com|pris|able
com|prise
  com|pris|es
  com|prised
  com|pris|ing
com|prom|ise
  com|prom|is|es
  com|prom|ised
  com|prom|is|ing
com|prom|ised
  adjective
com|prom|is|er +s
com|prom|is|ing|ly
Comp|ton, Ar|thur
  Holly (US physicist)
comp|trol|ler +s
  (financial affairs
  executive)
  [☞ controller]
com|pul|sion +s
com|pul|sive
com|pul|sive|ly

com|pul|sive|ness
com|pul|sor|i|ly
com|pul|sor|i|ness
com|pul|sory
com|pul|sor|ies
com|punc|tion +s
com|punc|tious
com|punc|tious|ly
com|pur|ga|tion +s
com|pur|ga|tor +s
com|pur|ga|tory
com|put|abil|ity
com|put|able
com|pu|ta|tion +s
com|pu|ta|tion|al
com|pute
  com|putes
  com|put|ed
  com|put|ing
com|put|er +s
com|put|er|ese
com|puter|i|za|tion
com|puter|ize
  com|puter|iz|es
  com|puter|ized
  com|puter|iz|ing
com|puter|ized
  adjective
computer-literate
com|puter|phobe +s
com|puter|phobia
com|puter|phob|ic
com|put|ing noun
com|rade +s
  [☞ camaraderie]
comrade-in-arms
  comrades-in-arms
com|rade|ly
com|rade|ship
Comte, Au|guste
  (French philosopher)
  [☞ conte]
Comt|ean
con (cheat, trick;
  against; convict;
  steer a ship; study)
  cons
  conned
  con|ning
  [☞ khan]
Con|acher, Lionel
  Pre|toria (Cdn
  athlete)
Con|akry (capital of
  Guinea)
con amore
Conan, Laure (Félicité
  Angers)
Conan Doyle, Sir
  Ar|thur (Scottish
  novelist)
con art|ist +s
con brio

CONCACAF
  (Confederation of
  North, Central
  American &
  Caribbean
  Association Football)
con|cat|en|ate
  con|cat|en|ates
  con|cat|en|at|ed
  con|cat|en|at|ing
con|ca|ten|a|tion +s
con|cave
con|cave|ly
con|cav|ity
  con|cav|ities
con|ceal +s +ed +ing
con|ceal|er +s
con|ceal|ment +s
con|cede
  con|cedes
  con|ced|ed
  con|ced|ing
con|ced|er +s
con|ceit +s
con|ceit|ed
con|ceit|ed|ly
con|ceit|ed|ness
con|ceiv|abil|ity
con|ceiv|able
con|ceiv|ably
con|ceive
  con|ceives
  con|ceived
  con|ceiv|ing
con|cele|brant +s
con|cele|brate
  con|cele|brates
  con|cele|brat|ed
  con|cele|brat|ing
con|cele|bra|tion +s
con|cen|trate
  con|cen|trates
  con|cen|trat|ed
  con|cen|trat|ing
con|cen|trat|ed
  adjective
con|cen|trat|ed|ly
con|cen|tra|tion +s
con|cen|tra|tive
con|cen|tra|tor +s
con|cen|tre
  con|cen|tres
  con|cen|tred
  con|cen|tring
con|cen|tric
con|cen|tric|ally
con|cen|tri|city
Con|cep|ción (city,
  Chile)
con|cept +s
con|cep|tion +s
  [☞ Concepción]
con|cep|tion|al

Con|cep|tion Bay (in
  Canada)
Con|cep|tion Bay
  South (town,
  Canada)
con|cep|tual
con|cep|tual|ism
con|cep|tual|ist +s
con|cep|tual|iz|a|tion
  +s
con|cep|tual|ize
  con|cep|tual|iz|es
  con|cep|tual|ized
  con|cep|tual|iz|ing
con|cep|tual|ly
con|cern +s +ed +ing
con|cerned adjective
con|cern|ed|ly
con|cern|ing
  preposition
con|cert +s +ed +ing
con|cert band +s
con|cert|ed adjective
concert-goer +s
con|cert hall +s
con|cer|tina (musical
  instrument; collapse
  like a concertina)
  con|cer|tinas
  con|cer|tinaed or
  con|cer|tina'd
  con|cer|tina|ing
  [☞ concertino]
con|cer|tina wire
con|cer|tino +s (short
  concerto; instrument
  playing a concerto)
  [☞ concertina]
con|cert|ize
  con|cert|iz|es
  con|cert|ized
  con|cert|iz|ing
con|cert|master +s
con|certo
  con|cer|tos or
  con|certi
con|certo grosso
  con|certi grossi or
  con|certo grossos
con|ces|sion +s
con|ces|sion|aire
con|ces|sion|al
con|ces|sion|ary
con|ces|sive
conch (gastropod;
  shell; domed roof; for
  external ear or shell-
  shaped part use
  concha)
  conch|es or conchs
  [☞ conk]

concha (external ear;
  shell-shaped part)
con|chae
Con|cho|bar (Irish
  Myth)
con|choid|al
con|cho|logic|al
con|chol|o|gist +s
con|chol|ogy
con|cierge +s
con|cil|iar
con|cili|ate
  con|cili|ates
  con|cili|at|ed
  con|cili|at|ing
con|cili|a|tion +s
con|cili|a|tive
con|cili|a|tor +s
con|cili|a|tor|i|ness
con|cili|a|tory
con|cise
con|cise|ly
con|cise|ness
con|ci|sion +s
con|clave +s
con|clude
  con|cludes
  con|clud|ed
  con|clud|ing
con|clu|sion +s
con|clu|sive
con|clu|sive|ly
con|clu|sive|ness
con|coct +s +ed +ing
con|coct|er +s
con|coc|tion +s
con|coct|or +s (use
  concocter)
con|comi|tance
con|comi|tancy
con|comi|tant +s
con|comi|tant|ly
Con|cord (city &
  town, US; grape)
  [☞ Concorde]
con|cord +s
con|cord|ance
  con|cord|an|ces
  con|cord|anced
  con|cord|an|cing
con|cord|an|cer +s
con|cord|an|cing +s
  noun
con|cord|ant
con|cord|ant|ly
con|cordat +s
Con|corde +s
  (airplane)
  [☞ Concord]
con|cours
  (competition)
  plural con|cours
  [☞ concourse]

con|course +s (open area in a large building; lower-level shopping area; gathering) [☞ concours]
con|cres|cence
con|cres|cent
con|crete
  con|cretes
  con|cret|ed
  con|cret|ing
con|crete|ly
con|crete|ness
con|cre|tion +s
con|cre|tion|ary
con|cret|iz|a|tion
con|cret|ize
  con|cret|iz|es
  con|cret|ized
  con|cret|iz|ing
con|cu|bin|age
con|cu|bin|ary
con|cu|bine +s
con|cu|pis|cence
con|cu|pis|cent
con|cur
  con|curs
  con|curred
  con|cur|ring
con|cur|rence +s
con|cur|rent
con|cur|rent|ly
con|cuss
  con|cuss|es
  con|cussed
  con|cuss|ing
con|cus|sion +s
con|cus|sive
Condé, Prince de (French general)
con|demn +s +ed +ing
con|dem|nable
con|dem|na|tion +s
con|dem|na|tory
con|demned adjective
con|dens|able
con|den|sate +s
con|den|sa|tion +s
con|dense
  con|dens|es
  con|densed
  con|dens|ing
con|densed adjective
con|dens|er +s
con|des|cend +s +ed +ing
con|des|cend|ing adjective
con|des|cend|ing|ly
con|des|cen|sion +s
con|dign

con|dign|ly
con|di|ment +s
con|di|tion +s +ed +ing
con|di|tion|al +s
con|di|tion|al|ity
  con|di|tion|al|ities
con|di|tion|al|ly
con|di|tioned adjective
con|di|tion|er +s
con|di|tion|ing noun & adjective
con|do +s
con|dola|tory
con|dole
  con|doles
  con|doled
  con|dol|ing
con|dol|ence +s
con|dom +s
con|do|min|ium +s
con|don|ation +s
con|done
  con|dones
  con|doned
  con|don|ing
con|don|er +s
con|dor +s
Con|dor|cet, Mar|quis de (French philosopher)
con|dot|tiere
  con|dot|tieri
con|duce
  con|du|ces
  con|duced
  con|du|cing
con|du|cive
con|duct +s +ed +ing
con|duct|ance +s
con|duct|ibil|ity
con|duct|ible
con|duc|tion
con|duct|ive
con|duct|ive|ly
con|duc|tiv|ity
  con|duc|tiv|ities
con|duct|or +s
con|ductor|ship +s
con|duc|tress
  con|duc|tress|es
con|duit +s
con|dyl|ar
con|dyle +s
con|dyl|oid
cone
  cones
  coned
  coning
cone|flower +s

Con|eglia|no, Em|man|uele (Lorenzo Da Ponte)
cone-shell +s
Con|es|toga wag|on +s
co|ney +s (use cony)
Coney Island (resort, US)
con|fab
  con|fabs
  con|fabbed
  con|fab|bing
con|fabu|late
  con|fabu|lates
  con|fabu|lat|ed
  con|fabu|lat|ing
con|fabu|la|tion +s
con|fabu|la|tory
con|fect +s +ed +ing
con|fec|tion +s
con|fec|tion|ary (adjective: of or like confections; for noun use confectionery)
  con|fec|tion|aries
con|fec|tion|er +s
con|fec|tioner's sugar
con|fec|tion|ery noun (candy; store; art of making candy)
  con|fec|tion|eries [☞ confectionary]
con|fed|er|acy
  con|fed|er|acies
con|fed|er|al
con|fed|er|al|ism
con|fed|er|ate +s
con|fed|er|at|ed
Con|fed|er|a|tion (Cdn union)
con|fed|er|a|tion +s
con|fed|er|a|tion|ist +s
con|fer
  con|fers
  con|ferred
  con|fer|ring
con|feree +s
con|fer|ence +s
  con|fer|en|ces
  con|fer|enced
  con|fer|en|cing
con|fer|ment +s
con|fer|rable
con|fer|ral +s
con|fess
  con|fess|es
  con|fessed
  con|fess|ing
con|fess|ed|ly
con|fes|sion +s

con|fes|sion|al +s
con|fes|sion|al|ism
con|fes|sor +s
con|fetti
con|fi|dant +s (trusted person) [☞ confidante, confident]
con|fi|dante +s (trusted female) [☞ confident]
con|fide
  con|fides
  con|fid|ed
  con|fid|ing
con|fi|dence +s
con|fi|dent (self-assured) [☞ confidant, confidante]
con|fi|den|tial
con|fi|den|ti|al|ity
con|fi|den|tial|ly
con|fi|dent|ly
con|fid|ing|ly
con|fig|ur|abil|ity
con|fig|ur|able
con|fig|ur|a|tion +s
con|fig|ur|a|tion|al
con|fig|ure
  con|fig|ures
  con|fig|ured
  con|fig|ur|ing
con|fine
  con|fines
  con|fined
  con|fin|ing
con|fine|ment +s
con|firm +s +ed +ing
con|firm|and +s
con|firm|a|tion +s (act of confirming; Religion) [☞ conformation]
con|firm|a|tive
con|firm|a|tory
con|firmed adjective
con|fis|cable
con|fis|cate
  con|fis|cates
  con|fis|cat|ed
  con|fis|cat|ing
con|fis|ca|tion +s
con|fis|ca|tor +s
con|fis|ca|tory
con|fit
Con|fit|eor
con|flag|ra|tion +s
con|flate
  con|flates
  con|flat|ed
  con|flat|ing
con|fla|tion

con|flict +s +ed +ing
con|flict|ing *adjective*
con|flic|tion +s
con|flict|ive
con|flict of in|ter|est
  con|flicts of
  in|ter|est
con|flic|tual
con|flu|ence +s
con|flu|ent +s
con|form +s +ed
  +ing
con|form|abil|ity
con|form|able
con|form|ably
con|form|al
con|form|ance +s
con|form|a|tion +s
  (shape, structure,
  arrangement)
  [☞ confirmation]
con|form|a|tion|al
con|form|ism
con|form|ist +s
con|form|ity
  con|form|ities
con|found +s +ed
  +ing
con|found|ed
  adjective
con|found|ed|ly
con|fra|ter|nity
  con|fra|ter|ni|ties
con|frere +s
con|front +s +ed
  +ing
con|fron|ta|tion +s
con|fron|ta|tion|al
Con|fu|cian +s
Con|fu|cian|ism
Con|fu|cian|ist +s
Con|fu|cius (Chinese
  philosopher)
con|fus|abil|ity
con|fus|able +s
con|fuse
  con|fus|es
  con|fused
  con|fus|ing
con|fused *adjective*
con|fus|ed|ly
con|fus|ing *adjective*
con|fus|ing|ly
con|fu|sion +s
con|fu|ta|tion +s
con|fute
  con|futes
  con|fut|ed
  con|fut|ing
conga
  con|gas
  con|gaed
  conga|ing

con|gé +s (dismissal;
  leave-taking)
  [☞ congee]
con|geal +s +ed +ing
con|gealed *adjective*
con|gee +s (soup)
  [☞ congé]
con|gel|a|tion +s
con|gen|er +s
con|gen|er|ic
con|gen|ial
con|geni|al|ity
con|gen|ial|ly
con|gen|ital
con|gen|ital|ly
con|ger +s (eel)
  [☞ conjure]
con|ger|ies
  plural con|ger|ies
con|gest +s +ed +ing
con|ges|tion +s
con|gest|ive
con|glom|er|ate
  con|glom|er|ates
  con|glom|er|at|ed
  con|glom|er|at|ing
con|glom|era|teur +s
con|glom|er|a|tion +s
Congo (river and
  countries, Africa)
  [☞ Kongo]
  • Congo is now
  commonly used for
  either of two African
  states: the Republic
  of the Congo,
  known until 1990 as
  the People's Republic
  of the Congo, and
  the Democratic
  Republic of the
  Congo, known until
  1997 as Zaire.
Con|go|lese
  plural Con|go|lese
con|grats
con|gratu|late
  con|gratu|lates
  con|gratu|lat|ed
  con|gratu|lat|ing
con|gratu|la|tion +s
con|gratu|la|tor +s
con|gratu|la|tory
con|gre|gant +s
con|gre|gate
  con|gre|gates
  con|gre|gat|ed
  con|gre|gat|ing
con|gre|ga|tion +s
Con|gre|ga|tion|al (of
  Congregationalism)
con|gre|ga|tion|al (of
  a congregation)

Con|gre|ga|tion|al|
          ism
Con|gre|ga|tion|al|ist
  +s
con|gress
  con|gress|es
con|gres|sion|al
con|gress|man
  con|gress|men
con|gress|person
  con|gress|persons
  or con|gress|people
con|gress|woman
  con|gress|women
Con|greve, Wil|liam
  (English dramatist)
con|gru|ence +s
con|gru|ency
  (= congruence)
  con|gru|en|cies
con|gru|ent
con|gru|ent|ly
con|gru|ity
  con|gru|ities
con|gru|ous
con|gru|ous|ly
Coni|bear +s
con|ic +s
con|ic|al
con|ic|al|ly
co|nid|ium
  co|nidia
con|ifer +s
con|ifer|ous
coni|ine
con|jec|tur|able
con|jec|tur|al
con|jec|tur|al|ly
con|jec|ture
  con|jec|tures
  con|jec|tured
  con|jec|tur|ing
con|join +s +ed +ing
con|joined *adjective*
  (joined)
con|joint *adjective*
  (associated, joint)
con|joint|ly
con|ju|gal
con|ju|gal|ity
con|ju|gal|ly
con|ju|gate
  con|ju|gates
  con|ju|gat|ed
  con|ju|gat|ing
con|ju|ga|tion +s
con|ju|ga|tion|al
con|ju|ga|tive
con|junct +s
con|junc|tion +s
con|junc|tion|al

con|junc|tiva
  con|junc|tivas or
  con|junc|tivae
con|junc|tival
con|junc|tival
con|junct|ive +s
con|junct|ive|ly
con|junc|tiv|itis
con|junc|ture +s
con|jur|a|tion +s
con|jure (produce by
  magic)
  con|jures
  con|jured
  con|jur|ing
con|jur|er +s (*use*
  conjuror)
con|jur|ing *noun*
con|jur|or +s
conk +s +ed +ing (in
  'conk out'; head; a
  blow; hit; fungus)
  [☞ conch]
conk|er +s (horse
  chestnut; children's
  game)
  [☞ conquer]
con man
  con men
con moto
Con|nacht (province,
  Ireland)
con|nate
con|nat|ur|al
con|nat|ur|al|ly
Con|naught
  (= Connacht,
  Ireland)
Con|naught and
  Strath|earn,
  Ar|thur Wil|liam
  Pat|rick Al|bert, 1st
  Duke of (governor
  general of Canada)
con|nect +s +ed +ing
con|nect|able
con|nect|ed *adjective*
con|nect|ed|ly
con|nect|ed|ness
Con|necti|cut (state,
  US)
con|nec|tion +s
con|nec|tion|al
con|nect|ive +s
con|nect|iv|ity
con|nect|or +s
Con|ne|mara (region,
  Ireland)
con|ner +s
Con|nery, Sean
  (Scottish actor)
con|ning tower +s
con|nip|tion +s
con|niv|ance +s

con|nive
con|nives
con|nived
con|niv|ing
con|niv|er +s
con|niv|ing *adjective*
con|nois|seur +s
con|nois|seur|ship
Con|nolly, James
 (Irish nationalist &
 union leader)
con|nor +s (*use*
 conner)
Con|nors, James
 Scott ('Jimmy') (US
 tennis player)
con|no|ta|tion +s
con|no|ta|tive
con|note
con|notes
con|not|ed
con|not|ing
con|nubi|al
con|nubi|al|ity
con|nubi|al|ly
con|odont +s
con|oid +s
con|oid|al
con|quer +s +ed +ing
 (overcome)
 [☞ conker]
con|quer|able
con|quer|or +s
Con|quest (British
 conquest of French
 N America in 1763;
 Norman Conquest)
con|quest +s (*in
 general use*)
con|quis|ta|dor
con|quis|ta|dores or
con|quis|ta|dors
Con|rad, Jo|seph
 (English novelist)
Con|rad|ian
con rod +s
con|san|guin|eal
con|san|guin|eous
con|san|guin|ity
con|san|guin|ities
con|science +s
con|science|less
con|science-stricken
con|scien|tious
con|scien|tious|ly
con|scien|tious|ness
con|scious
con|scious|ly
con|scious|ness
con|scious|ness-
 raising
con|script +s +ed
 +ing

con|scrip|tion +s
con|se|crate
con|se|crates
con|se|crat|ed
con|se|crat|ing
con|se|crat|ed
 adjective
con|se|cra|tion +s
con|se|cra|tor +s
con|se|cra|tory
con|se|cu|tion +s
con|secu|tive
con|secu|tive|ly
con|secu|tive|ness
con|sen|sual
con|sen|sual|ly
con|sen|sus
con|sen|sus|es
con|sent +s +ed +ing
con|sen|tient
con|sent|ing *adjective*
con|se|quence +s
con|se|quent +s
con|sequen|tial
con|sequen|tial|ism
con|sequen|tial|ist
 +s
con|sequen|ti|al|ity
con|sequen|tial|ly
con|sequent|ly
con|serv|an|cy
con|serv|an|cies
con|serv|a|tion +s
con|serv|a|tion|al
con|serv|a|tion|ist +s
con|serv|a|tism
Con|serv|a|tive +s (of
 the Progressive
 Conservative Party;
 Judaism)
con|serv|a|tive +s (*in
 general use*)
con|serv|a|tive|ly
con|ser|va|toire +s
con|serv|ator +s
con|serv|atory
con|serv|ator|ies
con|serve
con|serves
con|served
con|serv|ing
con|sid|er +s +ed
 +ing
con|sider|able
con|sider|ably
con|sider|ate
con|sider|ate|ly
con|sider|a|tion +s
con|sid|ered *adjective*
con|sider|ing
 preposition
con|si|gliere
con|si|glieri

con|sign +s +ed +ing
con|sign|ee +s
con|sign|ment +s
con|signor +s
con|sist +s +ed +ing
con|sist|ence +s
con|sist|ency
con|sist|en|cies
con|sist|ent
con|sist|ent|ly
con|sis|tor|ial
con|sis|tory
con|sis|tor|ies
con|so|ci|a|tion +s
con|so|ci|a|tion|al
con|sol|able
con|sol|a|tion +s
con|sol|a|tory
con|sole (panel of
 switches; cabinet;
 comfort)
con|soles
con|soled
con|sol|ing
 [☞ consul]
con|sol|er +s
con|soli|date
con|soli|dates
con|soli|dat|ed
con|soli|dat|ing
con|soli|dat|ed
 adjective
con|soli|da|tion +s
con|soli|da|tor +s
con|soli|da|tory
con|sol|ing|ly
con|som|mé +s (clear
 soup)
con|son|ance
con|son|ant +s
con|son|ant|al
con|son|ant|ly
con|sort +s +ed +ing
con|sor|tium
con|sor|tiums or
con|sor|tia
con|specif|ic +s
con|spec|tus
con|spec|tus|es
con|spicu|ity
con|spicu|ous
con|spicu|ous|ly
con|spicu|ous|ness
con|spir|acy
con|spir|acies
con|spir|ator +s
con|spira|tor|ial
con|spira|tor|ial|ly
con|spire
con|spires
con|spired
con|spir|ing

Con|stable, John
 (English painter)
con|stable +s
con|stabu|lary
con|stabu|lar|ies
Con|stance (lake,
 Germany)
con|stancy
con|stan|cies
Con|stant, Ben|ja|min
 (French novelist)
con|stant +s
Con|stan|ţa (port,
 Romania)
con|stan|tan
Con|stan|tine (Roman
 emperor; Greek
 kings; city, Algeria)
Con|stan|tin|ople
 (*former name for*
 Istanbul)
con|stant|ly
Con|stan|za
 (= Constanţa,
 Romania)
con|stel|late
con|stel|lates
con|stel|lat|ed
con|stel|lat|ing
con|stel|la|tion +s
con|ster|nate
con|ster|nates
con|ster|nat|ed
con|ster|nat|ing
con|ster|na|tion
con|sti|pate
con|sti|pates
con|sti|pat|ed
con|sti|pat|ing
con|sti|pat|ed
 adjective
con|sti|pa|tion
con|stitu|en|cy
con|stitu|en|cies
con|stitu|ent +s
con|sti|tute
con|sti|tutes
con|sti|tut|ed
con|sti|tut|ing
con|sti|tu|tion +s
con|sti|tu|tion|al
con|sti|tu|tion|al|ism
con|sti|tu|tion|al|ist
 +s
con|sti|tu|tion|al|ity
con|sti|tu|tion|al|ize
con|sti|tu|tion|al|
 iz|es
con|sti|tu|tion|al|
 ized
con|sti|tu|tion|al|
 iz|ing
con|sti|tu|tion|al|ly
con|sti|tu|tive

con|sti|tu|tive|ly
con|sti|tu|tor +s
con|strain +s +ed
  +ing
con|strained *adjective*
con|strain|ed|ly
con|straint +s
con|strict +s +ed
  +ing
con|stric|tion +s
con|stric|tive
con|strict|or +s
con|stru|able
con|stru|al +s
con|struct +s +ed
  +ing
con|struc|tion +s
con|struc|tion|al
con|struc|tion|al|ly
con|struc|tion|ism
con|struc|tion|ist +s
con|struct|ive
con|struct|ive|ly
con|struct|ive|ness
con|struc|tiv|ism
con|struc|tiv|ist +s
con|struct|or +s
con|strue
  con|strues
  con|strued
  con|stru|ing
con|sub|stan|tial
con|sub|stan|ti|al|ity
con|sub|stan|ti|a|tion
con|sue|tude +s
con|sue|tud|in|ary
con|sul +s (official;
  magistrate)
  [☞ console]
con|sul|ar
Con|sul|ate (French
  government 1799–
  1804)
con|sul|ate +s (*in
  general use*)
con|sul|ship +s
con|sult +s +ed +ing
con|sult|ancy
  con|sult|an|cies
con|sult|ant +s
con|sul|ta|tion +s
con|sul|ta|tive
con|sult|ing *adjective*
con|sum|able +s
con|sume (eat, use up)
  con|sumes
  con|sumed
  con|sum|ing
  [☞ consommé]
con|sum|er +s
con|sumer|ism
con|sumer|ist +s

con|sum|er price
  index
con|sum|ing|ly
con|sum|mate
  con|sum|mates
  con|sum|mat|ed
  con|sum|mat|ing
con|sum|mate|ly
con|sum|ma|tion +s
con|sum|ma|tive
con|sum|ma|tor +s
con|sump|tion +s
con|sump|tive
con|sump|tive|ly
con|tact +s +ed +ing
con|tact|able
con|ta|gion +s
con|ta|gious
con|ta|gious|ly
con|ta|gious|ness
con|tain +s +ed +ing
con|tain|able
con|tained *adjective*
con|tain|er +s
con|tainer-grown
con|tain|er|iz|a|tion
con|tain|er|ize
  con|tain|er|iz|es
  con|tain|er|ized
  con|tain|er|iz|ing
con|tain|er ship +s
con|tain|ment +s
con|tam|in|ant +s
con|tam|in|ate
  con|tam|in|ates
  con|tam|in|at|ed
  con|tam|in|at|ing
con|tam|in|a|tion +s
con|tam|in|ator +s
con|tango +s
Conté (pencil etc.)
conte +s (story)
  [☞ Comte]
con|temn +s +ed
  +ing
con|tem|ner +s
con|tem|plate
  con|tem|plates
  con|tem|plat|ed
  con|tem|plat|ing
con|tem|pla|tion +s
con|tem|pla|tive
con|tem|pla|tive|ly
con|tem|pla|tor +s
con|tem|por|an|eity
con|tem|por|an|eous
con|tem|por|an|eous|
  ly
con|tem|por|an|eous|
  ness
con|tem|por|ar|i|ly
con|tem|por|ar|i|ness

con|tem|por|ary
  con|tem|por|ar|ies
con|tempt +s
con|tempt|ibil|ity
con|tempt|ible
con|tempt|ibly
con|temp|tu|ous
con|temp|tu|ous|ly
con|tend +s +ed +ing
con|tend|er +s
con|tent +s +ed +ing
con|tent|ed *adjective*
con|tent|ed|ly
con|tent|ed|ness
con|ten|tion +s
con|ten|tious
con|ten|tious|ly
con|ten|tious|ness
con|tent|ment +s
con|ter|min|ous
con|ter|min|ous|ly
con|tes|sa +s
con|test +s +ed +ing
con|test|able
con|test|ant
con|test|a|tion +s
con|test|a|tory
con|test|ed *adjective*
con|text +s
con|text|ual
con|text|ual|ism
con|text|ual|ist +s
con|text|ual|iz|a|tion
  +s
con|text|ual|ize
  con|text|ual|iz|es
  con|text|ual|ized
  con|text|ual|iz|ing
con|text|ual|ly
con|tigu|ity
con|tigu|ous
con|tigu|ous|ly
con|tin|ence
Con|tin|ent +s
  (mainland Europe)
con|tin|ent +s
Con|tin|ent|al +s (of
  mainland Europe)
con|tin|ent|al +s
con|tin|ent|al
  break|fast +s
con|tin|ent|al|ism
con|tin|ent|al|ist +s
con|tin|ent|al|ly
con|tin|ent|ly
con|tin|gency
  con|tin|gen|cies
con|tin|gent +s
con|tin|gent|ly
con|tin|ual
con|tinu|al|ly
con|tinu|ance +s

con|tinu|ant +s
con|tinu|a|tion +s
con|tinue
  con|tinues
  con|tinued
  con|tinu|ing
con|tinu|ity
  con|tinu|ities
con|tinuo +s
con|tinu|ous
con|tinu|ous|ly
con|tinu|ous|ness
con|tinu|um
  con|tinua
con|tort +s +ed +ing
con|tort|ed *adjective*
con|tor|tion +s
con|tor|tion|ist +s
con|tour +s +ed +ing
con|toured *adjective*
Con|tra +s
  (Nicaraguan
  guerrilla)
con|tra +s (dance; in
  'per contra')
con|tra|band
con|tra|band|ist +s
contra|bass
  contra|bass|es
contra|bass|ist +s
con|tra|cep|tion
con|tra|cep|tive +s
con|tract +s +ed
  +ing
con|tract|ible
con|tract|ile
con|tract|ility
con|trac|tion +s
con|trac|tion|al
con|tract|ive
con|tract|or +s
con|trac|tual
con|trac|tual|ly
con|tract|ure +s
con|tra|dict +s +ed
  +ing
con|tra|dic|tion +s
con|tra|dic|tor|ily
con|tra|dict|ori|ness
con|tra|dict|ory
contra|dis|tinc|tion
  +s
contra|dis|tin|guish
  contra|
    dis|tin|guish|es
  contra|
    dis|tin|guished
  contra|
    dis|tin|guish|ing
contra|flow +s
con|trail +s

contra|indi|cate
contra|indi|cates
contra|indi|cat|ed
contra|indi|cat|ing
contra|indi|ca|tion
+s
con|tral|to +s
contra|pos|ition +s
contra|posi|tive +s
con|trap|posto +s
con|trap|tion +s
contra|pun|tal
contra|pun|tal|ly
contra|pun|tist +s
con|trar|ian +s
con|trar|ian|ism
con|trar|iety
con|trar|ieties
con|trar|i|ly
con|trar|i|ness
con|trar|i|wise
con|trary
con|trar|ies
con|trast +s +ed +ing
con|trast|ing adjective
con|trast|ing|ly
con|trast|ive
con|trast|ive|ly
con|trasty
con|trast|i|er
con|trast|i|est
con|tra|vene
con|tra|venes
con|tra|vened
con|tra|ven|ing
con|tra|ven|er +s
con|tra|ven|tion +s
Contre|cœur
(municipality,
Canada)
contre|danse +s
contre|temps
plural contre|temps
con|trib|ute
con|trib|utes
con|trib|ut|ed
con|trib|ut|ing
con|trib|ut|ing
adjective
con|tri|bu|tion +s
con|tribu|tive
con|tribu|tor +s
con|tribu|tory
con|trite
con|trite|ly
con|trite|ness
con|tri|tion
con|triv|able
con|triv|ance +s
con|trive
con|trives
con|trived
con|triv|ing

con|trived adjective
con|triv|er +s
con|trol
con|trols
con|trolled
con|trol|ling
con|trol|labil|ity
con|trol|lable
con|trolled-release
adjective
con|trol|ler +s
(person or thing that
controls; board of
control member; for
financial affairs
executive use
comptroller)
con|troller|ship
con|trol rod +s
con|trol top +s
con|tro|ver|sial
con|tro|ver|sial|ist +s
con|tro|ver|sial|ly
con|tro|versy
con|tro|ver|sies
con|tro|vert +s +ed
+ing
con|tro|vert|ed
adjective
con|tro|vert|ible
con|tu|ma|cious
con|tu|macy
con|tu|ma|cies
con|tu|meli|ous
con|tume|ly
con|tume|lies
con|tu|sion +s
con|un|drum +s
con|urba|tion +s
con|ure +s
con|va|lesce
con|va|les|ces
con|va|lesced
con|va|les|cing
con|va|les|cence
con|va|les|cent +s
con|vec|tion +s
con|vec|tion|al
con|vec|tive
con|vec|tor +s
con|vene
con|venes
con|vened
con|ven|ing
con|ven|er +s (use
convenor)
con|ven|ience +s
con|ven|ient
con|ven|ient|ly
con|ven|or +s
con|vent +s
con|ven|ticle +s
con|ven|tion +s

con|ven|tion|al
con|ven|tion|al|ity
con|ven|tion|al|ities
con|ven|tion|al|ize
con|ven|tion|al|iz|es
con|ven|tion|al|ized
con|ven|tion|al|
        iz|ing
con|ven|tion|al|ly
con|ven|tion|eer +s
con|ven|tual
con|verge
con|ver|ges
con|verged
con|ver|ging
con|ver|gence +s
con|ver|gency
con|ver|gen|cies
con|ver|gent
con|ver|sancy
con|ver|sant
con|ver|sa|tion +s
con|ver|sa|tion|al
con|ver|sa|tion|al|ist
+s
con|ver|sa|tion|al|ly
con|ver|sa|zione
con|ver|sa|zioni or
con|ver|sa|ziones
con|verse
con|vers|es
con|versed
con|vers|ing
con|verse|ly
con|ver|sion +s
con|vert +s +ed +ing
con|vert|er +s
con|vert|ibil|ity
con|vert|ible +s
con|vex
con|vex|ity
con|vex|ities
con|vex|ly
con|vey +s +ed +ing
con|vey|able
con|vey|ance +s
con|vey|an|cer +s
con|vey|an|cing
con|vey|or +s
con|vey|or belt +s
con|vict +s +ed +ing
con|vic|tion +s
con|vince
con|vin|ces
con|vinced
con|vin|cing
con|vinced adjective
con|vin|cer +s
con|vin|cible
con|vin|cing adjective
con|vin|cing|ly
con|viv|ial
con|vivi|al|ity

con|vivi|al|ly
con|vo|ca|tion +s
con|vo|ca|tion|al
con|voke
con|vokes
con|voked
con|vok|ing
con|vo|lut|ed
con|vo|lut|ed|ly
con|vo|lu|tion +s
con|vo|lu|tion|al
con|volve
con|volves
con|volved
con|volv|ing
con|volvu|lus
con|volvu|lus|es or
con|volvu|li
con|voy +s +ed +ing
con|vul|sant +s
con|vulse
con|vuls|es
con|vulsed
con|vuls|ing
con|vul|sion +s
con|vul|sion|ary
con|vul|sive
con|vul|sive|ly
cony
co|nies
COO (chief operating
officer)
COOs
coo (murmur)
coos
cooed
coo|ing
[☞ coup]
coochy-coo
Cook (mountain,
N America;
mountain & strait,
New Zealand; Pacific
islands)
Cook, James (English
explorer)
Cook, Peter Ed|ward
(English comedian)
cook +s +ed +ing
cook|able
cook|book +s
cook-chill
cooked adjective
cook|er +s
cook|ery
cook|er|ies
cook|house +s
cook|ie +s
cookie cut|ter
(cookie-cutter when
preceding a noun)
cookie jar +s
cook|ing noun

cook-off +s
cook|out +s
cook|shack +s
Cook's tour +s
cook|stove +s
cook tent +s
cook|top +s
cook|ware
cool +er +est +s +ed
  +ing
coola|bah +s
cool|ant +s
cool down *verb*
  cools down
  cooled down
  cool|ing down
cool-down +s *noun*
cool|er +s
cool-headed
cooli|bah +s (*use*
  coolabah)
Cool|idge, (John)
  Cal|vin (US
  president)
coo|lie +s (unskilled
  labourer)
  [☞ coolly, coulis,
  coulee]
coo|lie hat +s
cooling-off per|iod
  +s
cool|ish
cool|ly (in a cool
  manner)
  [☞ coolie, coulis,
  coulee]
cool|ness
coolth
coomb +s (valley)
  [☞ cwm, khoum]
coon +s (raccoon;
  offensive black
  person)
  [☞ Kun]
coon-can
coon dog +s
coon|hound +s
coon|shit
coon|skin +s
coop +s +ed +ing
  (cage, pen)
  [☞ coupe, co-op]
co-op +s (co-operative
  enterprise or
  apartment)
Coop|er, Gary (US
  actor)
  [☞ Cowper]
Coop|er, James
  Feni|more (US
  novelist)
  [☞ Cowper]
coop|er +s +ed +ing

coop|er|age +s
co-operant
co-operate
  co-operates
  co-operat|ed
  co-operat|ing
co-operation
co-operative
co-operative|ly
co-operative|ness
co-operativ|ism
co-operator +s
co-opt +s +ed +ing
co-optation +s
co-option +s
co-optive
co|ordin|ate
  co|ordin|ates
  co|ordin|at|ed
  co|ordin|at|ing
co|ordin|at|ed
  adjective
co|ordin|ate|ly
co|ordin|a|tion +s
co|ordin|a|tive
co|ordin|ator +s
coot +s
cootie +s
cop (police officer; ball
  of thread)
  cops
  copped
  cop|ping
  [☞ copse]
Copa|ca|bana Beach
  (resort, Brazil)
copa|cet|ic
copal
Copán (ancient Mayan
  city)
co|partner +s
co|partner|ship +s
co|pay|ment +s
cope
  copes
  coped
  cop|ing
Copen|hagen (capital
  of Denmark)
co|pepod +s
Coper|ni|can
Coper|ni|cus,
  Nico|laus (Polish
  astronomer)
copi|able
copi|er +s
co-pilot +s
cop|ing +s *noun*
cop|ing saw +s
copi|ous
copi|ous|ly
copi|ous|ness
co|planar

co|planar|ity
Cop|land, Aaron (US
  composer)
  [☞ Coupland]
Cop|ley, John
  Single|ton (US
  painter)
co|polymer +s
co|polymer|ize
  co|polymer|iz|es
  co|polymer|ized
  co|polymer|iz|ing
cop out *verb*
  cops out
  copped out
  cop|ping out
cop-out +s *noun*
cop|per +s +ed +ing
cop|peras
cop|per beech
  cop|per beech|es
Copper|belt (region,
  Zambia)
copper-bottomed
copper|head
Cop|per Inuit
Copper|mine (River,
  Canada; *former name
  for* Kugluktuk)
copper|plate +s
copper|smith +s
cop|pery
cop|pice
  cop|pices
  cop|piced
  cop|picing
cop|piced *adjective*
Cop|pola, Fran|cis
  Ford (US filmmaker)
copra
co|proces|sor +s
co-produce
  co-produces
  co-produced
  co-producing
co-producer +s
co-product +s
co-produc|tion +s
copro|lite +s
cop|roph|a|gous
cop|roph|agy
copro|philia
cops and rob|bers
  (cops-and-robbers
  *when preceding a
  noun*)
copse +s (thicket;
  small wood)
cop shop +s
copsy
Copt +s
'copter +s
Cop|tic

cop|ula +s
copu|lar
copu|late
  copu|lates
  copu|lat|ed
  copu|lat|ing
copu|la|tion +s
copu|la|tive
copu|la|tive|ly
copu|la|tory
copy (duplicate etc.;
  Journalism; jump
  from an ice floe)
  cop|ies
  cop|ied
  copy|ing
  [☞ kopje, koppie]
copy|book +s
copy|cat +s
copy-edit +s +ed
  +ing
copy edi|tor +s
copy|ist +s
copy pro|tect|ed
copy|read
  copy|reads
  copy|read
  copy|read|ing
copy|read|er +s
copy|right +s +ed
  +ing (right to use
  original artistic
  material)
  [☞ copywriter,
  copywriting]
copy|writer +s (one
  who prepares
  newspaper copy etc.)
copy|writ|ing
  (preparation of
  newspaper copy etc.)
  [☞ copyrighting]
coq au vin (chicken
  stew)
co|quet|ry
  co|quet|ries
co|quette +s
co|quet|tish
co|quet|tish|ly
co|quet|tish|ness
co|quilles St.
  Jacques
co|quina
Co|quit|lam
  (municipality,
  Canada)
co|quito +s
cor *interjection*
  [☞ corps, core]
cor|acle +s
cora|coid +s
Coral (sea)

coral (hard accumulated secretions of aquatic organisms; colour)
[☞ corral, choral]
coral|bells
plural coral|bells
coral|berry
coral|ber|ries
coral|line +s
coral|lite +s
coral|loid +s
coral reef +s
coral root +s
coral snake +s
cor an|glais
cors an|glais
cor|bel
cor|bels
cor|belled
cor|bel|ling
cor|bie +s
cor|bie steps
cor blimey
Cor|co|vado (mountain, Brazil)
Cor|cyra (former name for Corfu, Greece)
cord +s +ed +ing (rope, cable, tie; Anatomy; Textiles; measure of wood)
[☞ chord]
cord|age
cor|date (heart-shaped)
[☞ chordate]
Cor|day (d'Armont), (Marie Anne) Char|lotte (assassin of Jean Paul Marat)
corded adjective
cord|grass
cord|grass|es
cor|dial (polite; drink)
[☞ entente cordiale)]
cor|di|al|ity
cor|dial|ly
cor|dil|lera +s
Cor|dil|ler|an (physiographic region, Canada)
cor|dil|ler|an
cord|ing noun
cord|ite
cord|less
cord|like
Cor|doba (cities, Spain & Argentina)
cor|doba +s (Nicaraguan currency)

cor|don +s +ed +ing
cor|don bleu
cor|dons bleus
cor|don sani|taire
cor|dons sani|taires
Cor|dova (= Cordoba, Spain & Argentina)
[☞ cordoba]
cor|do|van +s
Cor|dura proprietary
cor|du|roy +s
cor|du|roy road +s
cord|wood
core (centre; Archaeology)
cores
cored
cor|ing
[☞ corps, cor]
core lanes
co-religion|ist +s
cor|ella +s
Cor|elli, Arc|angelo (Italian composer)
core|op|sis
plural core|op|sis
corer +s
co-respond|ent +s (in divorce)
[☞ correspondent]
Corfu (Greek island)
corgi +s
cori|aceous
cori|an|der
Cor|inth (city, gulf, isthmus & canal, Greece)
Cor|inth|ian +s (of Corinth; columns)
[☞ Carinthian]
Cor|inth|ians (New Testament)
Corio|lanus, Gaius (or Gnaeus) Mar|cius (Roman general)
Cori|olis effect +s
cor|ium
coria
Cork (county & town, Ireland)
cork +s +ed +ing
cork|age
cork|board +s
cork boot +s
corked adjective
cork|er +s
cork|ing adjective
cork|like
cork oak +s
cork|screw +s +ed +ing

cork|wood +s
corky
cork|i|er
cork|i|est
corm +s
Cor|mier, Er|nest (Cdn architect)
cor|mor|ant +s
corn +s +ed +ing
corn|ball
corn belt
corn boil +s
corn|bread +s
corn broom +s
corn chip +s
corn|cob +s
corn cock|le +s
corn|crake +s
corn|crib +s
corn dog +s
corn dolly
corn doll|ies
cor|nea +s
cor|neal
corn ear|worm +s
corned beef
Cor|neille, Pierre (French dramatist)
cor|nel +s (dogwood)
[☞ Cornell]
cor|nel|ian (= carnelian: mineral)
cor|nel|ian cherry
cor|nel|ian cher|ries
Cor|nell, Ezra (US entrepreneur)
[☞ cornel]
cor|neous
cor|ner +s +ed +ing
corner|back +s
Cor|ner Brook (city, Canada)
cor|ner kick +s
corner|stone +s
cor|net +s (Music; ice cream cone; officer)
[☞ coronet]
cornet|cy
cornet|cies
cor|net|ist +s
cor|net|tist +s (use cornetist)
cor|netto
cor|netti
corn|field +s
corn|flake +s
corn flour (flour made from corn)
[☞ cornflour, cornflower]
corn|flour Brit. (cornstarch)

[☞ corn flour, cornflower]
corn|flower +s (plant)
[☞ corn flour, cornflour]
cor|nice +s
cor|niced
cor|niche +s (road)
[☞ Cornish]
cor|ni|chon +s
corn|i|er
corn|i|est
corn|i|ly
corn|i|ness
Cor|nish (of Cornwall; language; game hen; pasty)
[☞ corniche]
corn lily
corn lil|ies
corn|meal
corn on the cob
corn pone +s (corn-pone when preceding a noun)
corn roast +s
corn|row +s +ed +ing
corn|silk +s
corn snow
corn|stalk +s
corn|starch
corn syr|up
cor|nu|co|pia +s
cor|nu|co|pian
Corn|wall (city & Sverdrup Island, Canada; county, England)
Corn|wal|lis (Parry Island, Canada)
Corn|wal|lis, Charles, 1st Mar|quess and 2nd Earl (English general)
Corn|wal|lis, Ed|ward (governor of Nova Scotia)
corny
corn|i|er
corn|i|est
cor|olla +s
cor|ol|lary
cor|ol|lar|ies
Coro|man|del (coast, India)
cor|ona
• (halo; chandelier; Anatomy; Botany; Architecture)
plural cor|onae or

cor|onas
• (cigar)
plural cor|onas
[☞ krona, krone]
cor|ona|graph +s
cor|on|al +s
cor|on|ary
cor|on|aries
Cor|on|a|tion (gulf, Canada)
cor|on|a|tion +s
cor|oner +s
coroner|ship
cor|onet +s (crown; on a deer's antler or horse's pastern)
[☞ cornet]
cor|on|et|ed
Corot, (Jean-Baptiste) Ca|mille (French painter)
cor|ozo +s
corozo-nut +s
cor|pora *plural of* corpus
cor|por|al +s
cor|por|al|ity
cor|por|al|ities
cor|por|al|ly
cor|poral's guard +s
cor|por|ate
cor|por|ate|ly
cor|por|a|tion +s
cor|pora|tism
cor|pora|tist +s
cor|pora|tive
cor|pora|tiv|ism
cor|pora|tiz|a|tion +s
cor|pora|tize
cor|pora|tiz|es
cor|pora|tized
cor|pora|tiz|ing
cor|por|eal
cor|por|eal|ity
cor|por|eal|ly
cor|por|eity
corps (*Military*; body of people)
plural corps
[☞ core, cor, corpse]
corps de bal|let
plural corps de bal|let
corps dip|lo|ma|tique corps dip|lo|ma|tiques
corpse +s (dead body)
[☞ corps]
corps|man
corps|men
cor|pu|lence
cor|pu|lency

cor|pu|lent
cor|pus
cor|pora or
cor|pus|es
cor|pus cal|lo|sum
cor|pora cal|losa
Cor|pus Chris|ti (Christian festival; city, US)
cor|puscle +s
cor|pus|cu|lar
cor|pus de|licti
cor|pus lu|teum
cor|pora lu|tea
cor|ral (pen, enclosure; enclose)
cor|rals
cor|ralled
cor|ral|ling
[☞ coral, choral, chorale]
cor|ra|sion +s
cor|rect +s +ed +ing
cor|rect|able
cor|rect|ible (*use* correctable)
cor|rec|tion +s
cor|rec|tion|al
cor|rec|ti|tude
cor|rect|ive +s
cor|rect|ive|ly
cor|rect|ly
cor|rect|ness
cor|rect|or +s
Cor|reg|gio, An|tonio Al|legri da (Italian painter)
cor|rel|ate
cor|rel|ates
cor|rel|at|ed
cor|rel|at|ing
cor|rel|a|tion +s
cor|rel|a|tion|al
cor|rela|tive +s
cor|rela|tive|ly
cor|rela|tiv|ity
cor|res|pond +s +ed +ing
cor|res|pond|ence +s
cor|res|pond|ent +s (letter writer; *Journalism*)
[☞ co-respondent]
cor|res|pond|ing
adjective
cor|res|pond|ing|ly
cor|rida +s
cor|ri|dor +s
cor|rie +s
cor|ri|gen|dum
cor|ri|gen|da
cor|ri|gible
cor|ri|gibly

cor|rob|or|ate
cor|rob|or|ates
cor|rob|or|at|ed
cor|rob|or|at|ing
cor|rob|or|a|tion +s
cor|rob|ora|tive
cor|rob|or|ator +s
cor|rob|ora|tory
cor|rob|oree +s
cor|rode
cor|rodes
cor|rod|ed
cor|rod|ing
cor|rod|ed *adjective*
cor|rod|ible
cor|ro|sion +s
cor|ro|sive +s
cor|ro|sive|ly
cor|ro|sive|ness
cor|ru|gate
cor|ru|gates
cor|ru|gat|ed
cor|ru|gat|ing
cor|ru|gat|ed *adjective*
cor|ru|ga|tion +s
cor|rupt +s +ed +ing
cor|rupt|er +s
cor|rupt|ibil|ity
cor|rupt|ible
cor|rup|tion +s
cor|rupt|ive
cor|rupt|ly
cor|rupt|ness
cor|sage +s
cor|sair +s
corse +s (corpse)
[☞ coarse, course]
corse|let +s (armour)
cor|sel|ette +s (underwear)
cor|set +s +ed +ing
cor|set|ed *adjective*
cor|setry
Cor|sica (island, Mediterranean)
Cor|si|can +s
cor|tège +s
Cor|tes (Spanish legislative assembly)
Cor|tés, Her|nan|do (Spanish conquistador)
cor|tex
cor|ti|ces
Cor|tez, Her|nan|do (= Cortés)
Corti (in 'organ of Corti')
cor|ti|cal
cor|ti|cal|ly
cor|ti|cate
cor|ti|cat|ed
cor|ti|ca|tion +s

cor|ti|ces
cor|ti|coid +s
cor|ti|co|ster|oid +s
cor|ti|sol
cor|ti|sone +s
Cort|land +s
cor|un|dum +s
Cor|uña, La (= Corunna, Spain)
Cor|un|na (city, Spain)
cor|us|cant
cor|us|cate
cor|us|cates
cor|us|cat|ed
cor|us|cat|ing
cor|us|ca|tion +s
cor|vée +s
cor|vette +s
cor|vine
cory|ban|tic
coryd|alis
coryd|alis|es
cor|ymb +s
cor|ymbed
cory|phée +s
co|ryza
Cos (= Kos, Greece)
cos (lettuce; cosine; because)
plural cos
Cosa Nos|tra
cosec
co|secant +s
co|set +s (*Math*)
[☞ cosset]
cosh
• (heavy weapon)
cosh|es
coshed
cosh|ing
• (*Math*)
cosi|er (*use* cozier)
cosi|est (*use* coziest)
co-sign +s +ed +ing (sign jointly)
[☞ cosine]
co-signer +s
Cos|imo de' Med|ici (Florentine statesman)
co|sine +s (*Math*)
cos|met|ic
cos|met|ic|ally
cos|met|ician +s
cos|meti|cize
cos|meti|ciz|es
cos|meti|cized
cos|meti|ciz|ing
cos|met|ol|o|gist +s
cos|met|ol|ogy
cos|mic
cos|mic|al
cos|mic|al|ly

cosmo|gon|ic
cosmo|gon|ic|al
cos|mog|on|ist +s
cos|mog|ony
  cos|mog|on|ies
cos|mog|raph|er +s
cosmo|graph|ic
cosmo|graph|ic|al
cosmo|graph|ic|al|ly
cos|mog|raphy
  cos|mog|raph|ies
cosmo|logic|al
cosmo|logic|al|ly
cos|mol|o|gist +s
cos|mol|ogy
  cos|mol|o|gies
cosmo|naut +s
cos|mop|olis
  cos|mop|olis|es
cosmo|pol|itan +s
cosmo|pol|itan|ism
cosmo|pol|itan|ize
  cosmo|pol|itan|iz|es
  cosmo|pol|itan|ized
  cosmo|pol|itan|
    iz|ing
cos|mopo|lite +s
cos|mos
• (universe; ordered
  system)
  plural cos|mos|es
• (plant)
  plural cos|mos
Cos|sack +s (people)
cos|sack +s (pullover)
cos|set +s +ed +ing
  (pamper)
  [☞ coset]
cost
• (have as a price, etc.)
  costs
  cost
  cost|ing
• (fix or estimate price
  of)
  costs
  cost|ed
  cost|ing
Costa Blanca (region,
  Spain)
Costa Brava (region,
  Spain)
Costa del Sol (region,
  Spain)
cos|tal
co-star
  co-stars
  co-starred
  co-starring
cos|tard +s
Costa Rica (country,
  Central America)
Costa Rican +s

cost-benefit adjective
cost-conscious
cost-cutting
cost-effect|ive
cost-effect|ive|ly
cost-effect|ive|ness
cost-efficien|cy
  cost-efficien|cies
cost-efficient
cost-efficient|ly
Cos|tel|lo, Lou (US
  comedian)
cos|ter +s
coster|monger +s
cost|ing +s noun
cos|tive
cos|tive|ly
cos|tive|ness
cost|li|ness
cost|ly
  cost|li|er
  cost|li|est
cost|mary
  cost|mar|ies
cost of liv|ing (cost-
  of-living when
  preceding a noun)
cost-plus
cost price +s
cost-push in|fla|tion
cos|tume
  cos|tumes
  cos|tumed
  cos|tum|ing
cos|tum|er +s
cos|tum|ing noun
cosy (use cozy)
  cosi|er
  cosi|est
  cos|ies
  cos|ied
  cosy|ing
cot +s (bed, crib;
  shelter; cottage;
  cotangent)
  [☞ caught, khat]
co|tan|gent +s
co|teau +s
co|terie +s
co|termin|ous
Côte-Saint-Luc (city,
  Canada)
Côtes du Rhône
coth
co-tidal line +s
co|til|lion +s
co|tin|ga +s
coto|ne|as|ter +s
Coto|nou (city, Benin)
Coto|paxi (volcano,
  Ecuador)

Cots|wolds (hills,
  England)
cot|ta +s
cot|tage
  cot|tag|es
  cot|taged
  cot|tag|ing
cot|tag|er +s
cot|tagey
cot|tar +s (Scottish
  labourer; cottier)
  [☞ cotter]
Cott|bus (city,
  Germany)
cot|ter +s (pin, bolt;
  for Scottish labourer
  use cottar)
  [☞ cottar]
cotter|less
cot|ti|er +s (Irish
  peasant)
cot|ton +s +ed +ing
cot|ton bat|ten
  (= cotton batting)
cot|ton bat|ting
cot|ton cake +s
cot|ton candy
  cot|ton can|dies
cot|ton grass
  cot|ton grass|es
cotton-pickin'
cotton-picking
cotton|seed
cotton|tail +s
cot|ton waste
cotton|wood +s
cot|ton wool
cot|tony
coty|ledon +s
coty|ledon|ary
coty|ledon|ous
couch
  couch|es
  couched
  couch|ing
couch|ant
couch|ette +s
couch grass
Cou|chi|ching (lake,
  Canada)
couch po|ta|to
  couch po|ta|toes
Coué, Émile (French
  psychologist)
Coué|ism
cou|gar +s
cough +s +ed +ing
cough drop +s
cough|er +s (one who
  coughs)
  [☞ coffer]
cough syr|up +s

could
couldn't
cou|lee +s (ravine;
  stream)
  [☞ coulis, coolie]
cou|lis (thin purée)
  plural cou|lis
  [☞ coulee, coolie,
  coulisse]
cou|lisse +s (Theatre)
  [☞ coulis]
coul|oir +s
Cou|lomb, Charles-
  Augustin de (French
  physicist)
cou|lomb +s (unit of
  electric charge)
Coulomb's Law
coul|ter +s
Coul|thard, Jean
  (Cdn composer)
cou|ma|rin +s
cou|ma|rone
coun|cil +s (assembly)
  [☞ counsel]
coun|cil cham|ber +s
coun|cil house +s
coun|cil|lor +s
  (member of a
  council)
  [☞ counsellor]
coun|cil|lor|ship +s
council|man
  council|men
council|woman
  council|women
coun|sel
• noun (advice;
  consultation; plan)
  plural coun|sels
• noun (lawyer)
  plural coun|sel
• verb (advise; give
  guidance to;
  recommend)
  coun|sels
  coun|selled
  coun|sel|ling
  [☞ council]
coun|sel|ling noun
coun|sel|lor +s
  (adviser; camp
  supervisor; barrister;
  diplomat)
  [☞ councillor]
counselor-at-law US
  counselors-at-law
count +s +ed +ing
count|able
count|back
count down verb
  counts down
  count|ed down
  count|ing down

count|down +s *noun*
coun|ten|ance
  coun|ten|an|ces
  coun|ten|anced
  coun|ten|an|cing
count|er[1] +s (person or thing that counts or is used in keeping score)
coun|ter[2] +s +ed +ing (flat working surface etc.; oppose, opposite; countermove; part of horse, ship or shoe)
counter|act +s +ed +ing
counter|action +s
counter|active
counter-argument +s
counter|attack +s +ed +ing
counter-attrac|tion +s
counter|balance
  counter|balan|ces
  counter|balanced
  counter|balan|cing
counter|blast +s
counter|charge
  counter|char|ges
  counter|charged
  counter|char|ging
coun|ter cheque +s
counter|claim +s +ed +ing
counter-clockwise
counter|cultur|al
counter|culture +s
counter-espionage
counter-example +s
counter|feit +s +ed +ing
counter|feit|er +s
counter|feit|ing *noun*
counter|foil +s
counter|force +s
counter-insurgen|cy
counter-intelli|gence
counter|intui|tive
counter|irri|tant +s
counter|irri|ta|tion
counter|man
  counter|men
counter|mand +s +ed +ing
counter|march
  counter|march|es
  counter|marched
  counter|march|ing
counter|measure +s

counter|move
  counter|moves
  counter|moved
  counter|mov|ing
counter|offen|sive
counter-offer +s
counter|pane +s
counter|part +s
counter|plot
  counter|plots
  counter|plot|ted
  counter|plot|ting
counter|point +s +ed +ing
counter|poise
  counter|pois|es
  counter|poised
  counter|pois|ing
counter|product|ive
counter|punch
  counter|punch|es
  counter|punched
  counter|punch|ing
counter|punch|er +s
Counter-Reform|a|tion (16th–17th-c. Catholic Church reform)
counter-reform|a|tion +s (*in general use*)
counter-revolu|tion +s
counter-revolu|tion|ary
  counter-revolu|tion|aries
counter|scarp +s
counter|shaft +s
counter|sign +s +ed +ing
counter-signature +s
counter|sink
  counter|sinks
  counter|sunk
  counter|sink|ing
counter|suit +s
counter-tenor +s
counter|terror|ism
counter|top +s
counter-transfer|ence
counter|vail +s +ed +ing
counter|weight +s
coun|tess
  coun|tess|es
count|ing house +s
count|less
count *noun* +s

Count Pala|tine (in the Roman or German Empire)
  Counts Pala|tine
count pala|tine (in England or Ireland)
  counts pala|tine
coun|tri|fied
coun|try
  coun|tries
coun|try and west|ern
coun|try club +s
country|fied (*use* countrified)
coun|try house +s
country|ish
country|man
  country|men
country|side
country|wide
country|woman
  country|women
coun|ty
  coun|ties
coun|ty pala|tine
  coun|ties pala|tine
coun|ty town +s
coup +s (notable move; *coup d'état*; touching an enemy in battle)
  [☞ coo, coupe, coop]
coup de foudre
  coups de foudre
coup de grâce
  coups de grâce
coup de main
  coups de main
coup d'état
  coups d'état
coup de thé|âtre
  coups de thé|âtre
coup d'oeil
  coups d'oeil
coupe +s (car, carriage; dish for fruit or ice cream)
  [☞ coup]
Coupe|rin, Fran|çois (French composer)
Coup|land, Doug|las (Cdn writer)
  [☞ Copland]
couple
  couples
  coupled
  coup|ling
couple|dom
coup|ler +s
coup|let +s
coup|ling +s *noun*

cou|pon +s
cour|age
cour|age|ous
cour|age|ous|ly
cour|age|ous|ness
cou|rante +s (*Dance; Music*)
  [☞ au courant]
Cour|bet, Gus|tave (French painter)
Cour|celle, Dan|iel de Rémy de (governor of New France)
cour|eur de bois
  cour|eurs du bois
cour|gette +s
cour|ier +s (person who conveys or transports documents etc.; font; guide; send by courier)
  [☞ currier, Currier]
Cour|règes, André (French designer)
course (path, track; *Golf; Education*; part of a meal; *Architecture*; sail; flow; hunt)
  cours|es
  coursed
  cours|ing
  [☞ coarse, corse]
course|book +s
cours|er +s (horse; dog; bird)
  [☞ coarser]
course|ware
course|work
court +s +ed +ing
court bouil|lon
  courts bouil|lons
court card +s
Courte|nay (city, Canada)
cour|te|ous
cour|te|ous|ly
cour|te|ous|ness
cour|tesan +s
cour|tesy
  cour|tes|ies
court|house +s
court|ier +s
court|li|ness
court|ly
  court|li|er
  court|li|est
court mar|tial *noun*
  courts mar|tial

court-martial *verb*
court-martials
court-martialled
court-martial|ling
court or|der +s
court|room +s
court|ship +s
court shoe +s
court|yard +s
cous|cous (food)
[☞ cuscus]
cous|in +s (relative)
[☞ cozen]
cousin-german
cousins-german
cousin|hood
cousin|ly
cousin|ship
Cous|teau, Jacques-
Yves (French
oceanographer)
couth
Coul|ture, Guil|laume
(Cdn composer)
cou|ture
cou|tur|ier +s
(clothing designer)
cou|turi|ère +s
(female clothing
designer)
cou|vade
couver|ture
co|valence
co|valen|cy
(= covalence)
co|valent
co|valent|ly
cove
coves
coved
cov|ing
cov|en +s
Coven|ant (*Bible*)
coven|ant +s +ed
+ing (*in general use*)
coven|ant|al
coven|ant|ed *adjective*
Coven|ant|er +s
(17th-c. supporter of
Presbyterianism)
coven|ant|er +s (one
who covenants: *use*
covenantor)
coven|ant|or +s (one
who covenants)
[☞ Covenanter]
Cov|ent Gar|den
(area & opera house,
England)
Cov|en|try (city,
England)
cov|er +s +ed +ing
cover|able

cover|age +s
cover|all +s
cover charge +s
cover crop +s
Cov|er|dale, Miles
(English Bible
translator)
cov|ered *adjective*
cov|er|er +s
cover girl +s
cov|er|ing +s *noun*
cov|er|ing let|ter +s
cov|er|let +s
cover let|ter +s
(= covering letter)
cover plate +s
cover price +s
cover slip +s
cover story
cover stor|ies
co|vert +s
co|vert|ly
cover up *verb*
cov|ers up
cov|ered up
cov|er|ing up
cover-up +s *noun*
cov|et +s +ed +ing
cov|et|ed *adjective*
cov|et|ous
cov|et|ous|ly
cov|et|ous|ness
covey +s
cov|ing +s *noun*
cow +s +ed +ing
cowa|bunga
cow|age +s
Cow|ans|ville (town,
Canada)
Cow|ard, Sir Noël
Pierce (English
playwright)
cow|ard +s
cow|ard|ice
cow|ard|li|ness
cow|ard|ly
cow|bane +s
cow|bell +s
cow|berry
cow|ber|ries
cow|bird +s
cow|boy +s
cow|boy|ing
cow-calf *adjective*
cow camp +s
cow|catch|er +s
cow|er +s +ed +ing
Cowes (town,
England)
cow|fish
plural cow|fish
cow flop +s

cow|girl +s
cow|hage +s (*use*
cowage)
cow|hand +s
cow|herd +s
cow|hide +s
Cowi|chan (people;
language)
plural Cowi|chan
Cowi|chan sweat|er
+s
cowl +s
cowled
Cow|ley, Abra|ham
(English writer)
cow|lick +s
cow|like
cowl|ing +s
cowl neck +s
co-worker +s
cow pat +s
cow patty
cow pat|ties
cow|pea +s
Cow|per, Wil|liam
(English poet)
[☞ Cooper]
cow-pie +s
cow|poke +s
cow|pox
cow|punch|er +s
cow|rie +s (mollusc,
shell)
[☞ kauri]
co-write
co-writes
co-wrote
co-written
co-writing
co-writer +s
cowry (*use* cowrie)
cow|ries
[☞ kauri]
cow|shed +s
cow|slip +s
Cow|town (Calgary)
cow|town +s
cow-wheat +s
Cox (apple)
Coxes
cox (coxswain)
coxes
coxed
cox|ing
coxa
coxae
coxal
cox|comb +s (dandy)
[☞ cockscomb]
cox|combry
cox|comb|ries
cox|less

Cox's Bazar (town,
Bangladesh)
Cox's or|ange
pip|pin +s (apple)
cox|swain +s
cox|swain|ship
coy (shy, reticent)
coyer
coy|est
[☞ koi]
coyau
coy|dog +s
coyly
coy|ness
coy|ote +s
coy|pu +s
coz (because; cousin)
coz|en +s +ed +ing
(cheat)
[☞ cousin]
cozen|age
cozi|ly
cozi|ness
Cozu|mel (resort
island, Mexico)
cozy
cozi|er
cozi|est
coz|ies
coz|ied
cozy|ing
CP (cerebral palsy;
command post)
CPI (consumer price
index)
cpi (characters per
inch)
CPP (Canada Pension
Plan)
CPR (cardiopulmonary
resuscitation;
Canadian Pacific
Railway)
cps (characters per
second; cycles per
second)
CPU (central
processing unit)
CPUs
Crab (constellation;
Zodiac)
crab
crabs
crabbed
crab|bing
crab|apple +s
crabbed *adjective*
crab|bed|ly
crab|bed|ness
crab|ber +s
crab|bi|ly
crab|bi|ness

crabby
  crab|bi|er
  crab|bi|est
crab|grass
  crab|grass|es
crab|like
crab louse
  crab lice
crab|meat
crab pot +s
crab tree +s
crab|wise
crack +s +ed +ing
crack baby
  crack babies
crack-brained
crack co|caine
crack down verb
  cracks down
  cracked down
  crack|ing down
crack|down +s noun
cracked adjective
crack|er +s
cracker-barrel
  adjective
cracker|berry
  cracker|ber|ries
cracker|jack +s
crack|ers adjective
crack|head +s
crack house +s
crack|ie +s (dog)
  [☞ cracky]
crack|i|er
crack|i|est
crack|ing adjective &
  adverb
crackle
  crackles
  crackled
  crack|ling
crack|ling +s noun
crack|ly
crack|nel +s
crack|pot +s
crack up verb
  cracks up
  cracked up
  crack|ing up
crack-up +s noun
cracky (like cracks; in
  'by cracky')
crack|i|er
crack|i|est
  [☞ crackie]
Cra|cow (city, Poland)
cradle
  cradles
  cradled
  crad|ling
cradle|board +s
cradle cap

cradle-hill +s
cradle-robber +s
cradle-snatch|er +s
cradle song +s
cradle-to-grave
  adjective
crad|ling +s noun
Craft (Freemasonry)
craft
• noun (trade, art; skill;
  product; activity;
  trade union)
  plural crafts
• noun (boat, vessel,
  spacecraft, etc.)
  plural craft
• verb (make etc.)
  crafts
  craft|ed
  craft|ing
  [☞ kraft]
craft|er +s
craft|i|er
craft|i|est
craft|i|ly
craft|i|ness
craft shop +s
crafts|man
  crafts|men
crafts|man|ship
crafts|person
  crafts|people
craft store +s
crafts|woman
  crafts|women
crafty
  craft|i|er
  craft|i|est
crag +s
crag|gi|ly
crag|gi|ness
craggy
  crag|gi|er
  crag|gi|est
crags|man
  crags|men
Craig (mountain,
  Canada)
Craig, Ed|ward
  Gor|don (English
  director & stage
  designer)
Craig, Sir James
  Henry (British
  colonial
  administrator in
  BNA)
Craig|el|lachie (site of
  CPR last spike)
Crai|gie, Sir Wil|liam
  Alex|an|der
  (Scottish
  lexicographer)

Craio|va (city,
  Romania)
crake +s
cram
  crams
  crammed
  cram|ming
cram|mer +s
cramp +s +ed +ing
cramp bark +s
cramped adjective
cram|pon +s
crampy
Cran|ach, Lucas ('the
  Elder') (German
  painter)
cran|apple +s
cran|berry
  cran|ber|ries
Cran|brook (city,
  Canada)
Crane, (Har|old) Hart
  (US poet)
Crane, Ste|phen (US
  writer)
crane
  cranes
  craned
  cran|ing
crane fly
  crane flies
cranes|bill +s
cra|nial
cra|niate +s
cra|nio|logic|al
crani|ol|o|gist +s
crani|ol|ogy
cra|nio|met|ric
crani|om|etry
crani|ot|omy
  crani|ot|o|mies
cra|nium
  cra|niums or cra|nia
crank +s +ed +ing
crank|bait +s
crank call +s
crank|case +s
crank|i|er
crank|i|est
crank|i|ly
crank|i|ness
Cran|ko, John (South
  African
  choreographer)
crank|pin +s
crank|shaft +s
cranky
  crank|i|er
  crank|i|est
Cran|mer, Thom|as
  (English Protestant
  reformer)
cran|nog +s

cranny
  cran|nies
Cran|ston, Tol|ler
  (Cdn skater)
crap
  craps
  crapped
  crap|ping
crape (black fabric; for
  generic wrinkled
  fabric use crepe)
  [☞ crepe]
crape myr|tle +s
crap|ola
crap|per +s
crap|pie +s (fish)
  [☞ crappy]
crappy (inferior;
  nasty)
  crap|pi|er
  crap|pi|est
  [☞ crappie]
crap|shoot
crap|shoot|er +s
crapu|lence
crapu|lent
crapu|lous
craque|lure
crash
  crash|es
  crashed
  crash|ing
Crash|aw, Rich|ard
  (English poet)
crash-dive
  crash-dives
  crash-dived
  crash-diving
crash|ing adjective
crash-land verb
  crash-lands
  crash-landed
  crash-landing
crash land|ing +s
  noun
crash pad +s
crash test
  crash tests
  crash test|ed
  crash test|ing
crass
  crass|er
  crass|est
crass|ly
crass|ness
Cras|sus, Mar|cus
  Li|cin|ius (Roman
  general & politician)
crate (box)
  crates
  crat|ed
  crat|ing
  [☞ krait]
Cra|ter (lake, US)

cra|ter +s
cra|tered
crater|ous
C ra|tion +s
cra|ton +s
cra|ton|ic
cra|vat +s
cra|vat|ted
crave
  craves
  craved
  crav|ing
cra|ven +s
cra|ven|ly
craven|ness
crav|er +s
crav|ing +s *noun*
craw +s (bird's crop;
  in 'stick in one's
  craw')
  [☞ Kra]
craw|dad +s
craw|daddy
  craw|dad|dies
craw|fish
  plural craw|fish
Craw|ford, Isa|bel|la
  Val|ancy (Cdn
  writer)
Craw|ford, Joan (US
  actress)
crawl +s +ed +ing
crawl|er +s
crawl space +s
crawly
cray|fish
  plural cray|fish
cray|on +s +ed +ing
craze
  craz|es
  crazed
  craz|ing
crazed *adjective*
craz|i|ly
craz|i|ness
craz|ing +s *noun*
crazy
  craz|i|er
  craz|i|est
  craz|ies
crazy car|pet +s
crazy eights
Crazy Horse (Sioux
  chief)
crazy pav|ing
crazy quilt +s
crazy|weed +s
creak +s +ed +ing
  (noise; move stiffly,
  show strain)
  [☞ creek]
creak|i|ly
creak|i|ness

creak|ing|ly
creaky
  creak|i|er
  creak|i|est
cream +s +ed +ing
  (dairy product;
  choicest part; colour;
  creamy substance;
  produce cream; *for*
  non-dairy filling *etc.*
  use creme)
  [☞ creme, creme
  rinse]
cream cheese +s
creamed *adjective*
cream|er +s
cream|ery
  cream|eries
cream|i|er
cream|i|est
cream|i|ly
cream|i|ness
cream pie +s
cream puff +s
cream sauce +s
cream soda
cream|ware
creamy
  cream|i|er
  cream|i|est
crease (fold, wrinkle;
  Hockey; graze)
  creas|es
  creased
  creas|ing
  [☞ kris]
cre|at|able
cre|ate
  cre|ates
  cre|at|ed
  cre|at|ing
cre|a|tine
Cre|ation (*Religion*)
cre|ation +s (*in*
  general use)
cre|ation|ism
cre|ation|ist +s
cre|ative
cre|ative|ly
cre|ative|ness
crea|tiv|ity
Cre|ator (*Religion*)
cre|ator +s (*in general*
  use)
crea|ture +s
crea|ture|ly
crèche +s
Crécy (battle, France)
cred
cre|dal
cre|dence +s
cre|dence table +s
cre|den|tial +s

cre|den|tialed
cre|den|tial|ing
cre|den|za +s
cred|ibil|ity
cred|ible (believable,
  convincing)
cred|ibly
cred|it +s +ed +ing
credit|abil|ity
credit|able (that
  brings credit to; that
  can be credited)
  [☞ credible]
credit|ably
credit card +s
credit course +s
Crédi|tiste +s
credit line +s
credit note +s
credit|or +s
credit union +s
credit|worthi|ness
credit|worthy
Credo +s (*Christianity*)
credo +s (set of
  principles; *Music*)
credu|lity
credu|lous
credu|lous|ly
credu|lous|ness
Cree (lake, Canada;
  people; language)
  plural Cree or Crees
Creed +s (*Christianity*)
creed +s (*in general*
  use)
creed|al (*use* credal)
Creek (people;
  language)
  plural Creek or
  Creeks
creek +s (stream; bay)
  [☞ creak]
creel +s (basket)
  [☞ creole]
creep
  creeps
  crept
  creep|ing
creep|er +s
creep|i|ly
creep|i|ness
creep|ing *adjective*
creep|ing char|lie +s
creep|ing Jenny
  creep|ing Jen|nies
creepy
  creep|i|er
  creep|i|est
creepy-crawly
  creepy-crawlies

cre|mate
  cre|mates
  cre|mat|ed
  cre|mat|ing
cre|ma|tion +s
cre|ma|tor +s
crema|tor|ium
  crema|toria or
  crema|tor|iums
crema|tory
  crema|tor|ies
Créma|zie, Oc|tave
  (Cdn poet)
creme (*in commercial*
  use: non-dairy
  dessert filling; *for*
  lotions *use* cream)
  [☞ crème]
crème an|glaise
crème brû|lée
  crèmes brû|lées
crème cara|mel +s
crème de cacao
  crèmes de cacao
crème de cas|sis
  crèmes de cas|sis
crème de la crème
crème de menthe
  crèmes de menthe
crème fraîche
creme rinse +s
cre|mini
  plural cre|mini
Cre|mona (city, Italy)
Cremon|ese
  plural Cremon|ese
cre|nate
cre|nat|ed
cre|na|tion +s
crenel +s
crenel|ate (*use*
  crenellate)
  crenel|ates
  crenel|at|ed
  crenel|at|ing
crenel|a|tion +s (*use*
  crenellation)
crenel|late
  crenel|lates
  crenel|lat|ed
  crenel|lat|ing
crenel|la|tion +s
Cre|ole +s (people;
  their language;
  pertaining to the
  Creoles)
cre|ole +s (any pidgin)
  [☞ creel]
creol|iz|a|tion
creol|ize
  creol|iz|es
  creol|ized
  creol|iz|ing

Creon (*Greek Myth*)
creo|sote
creo|soted
crepe +s (fine wrinkled fabric; thin pancake; paper; rubber)
[☞ **crape**]
crepe de Chine
crepe paper
crêp|erie +s
crepe rub|ber
crepe Su|zette
  crepes Su|zette
crepey
crep|i|ness
crepi|tant
crepi|tate
  crepi|tates
  crepi|tat|ed
  crepi|tat|ing
crepi|ta|tion +s
crepi|tus
crept
cre|pus|cu|lar
Crerar, Henry Dun|can Gra|ham (Cdn army officer)
cre|scendo
• *noun*
  cre|scen|dos or cre|scendi
• *verb*
  cre|scen|does
  cre|scen|doed
  cre|scendo|ing
Cres|cent (world of Islam)
cres|cent (shape)
cres|cent|ic
cresol +s *noun*
[☞ **cresyl**]
cress
  cress|es
cres|set +s
Cres|sida (legendary lover of Troilus)
crest +s +ed +ing
crest|ed *adjective*
crest|fallen
crest|less
cresyl *adjective*
[☞ **cresol**]
Cre|ta|ceous (geological period)
cre|ta|ceous (chalky)
Cret|an +s (of Crete)
Crete (Greek island)
cret|in +s (sufferer of a thyroid deficiency; idiot)
cret|in|ism

cret|in|ize
  cret|in|iz|es
  cret|in|ized
  cret|in|iz|ing
cret|in|ous
cre|tonne (*Textiles*)
[☞ **cretons**]
cre|tons (pork spread)
[☞ **cretonne**]
Creutzfeldt–Jakob dis|ease
cre|vasse +s (deep open crack in glacier etc.)
[☞ **crevice**]
crev|ice +s (narrow fissure in rock or building etc.)
[☞ **crevasse**]
crew +s +ed +ing (team, gang, company; past tense & past participle of crow)
[☞ **Crewe, cru, Kru**]
crew|cut +s
Crewe (town, England)
crewel (yarn)
crewel work
crew|man
  crew|men
crew|neck +s
crib
  cribs
  cribbed
  crib|bing
crib|bage
crib|ber +s
crib|bing *noun*
crib death +s
cribri|form
crib sheet +s
Crich|ton, James (Scottish adventurer)
Crick, Fran|cis Harry Comp|ton (English biophysicist)
crick +s +ed +ing (neck pain)
[☞ **creek**]
crick|et +s +ed +ing
crick|et|er +s
cri|coid +s
cri de cœur
  cris de cœur
cried
crier +s
crikey
crime +s
Cri|mea (peninsula, Ukraine)

Cri|mean
crime fight|er +s
crime-fighting
crim|in|al +s
crim|in|al|is|tic
crim|in|al|ity
crim|in|al|iz|a|tion
crim|in|al|ize
  crim|in|al|iz|es
  crim|in|al|ized
  crim|in|al|iz|ing
crim|in|al|ly
crim|in|o|logic|al
crim|in|ol|o|gist +s
crim|in|ol|ogy
crimp +s +ed +ing
crimp|er +s +ed +ing
crimp|i|ly
crimp|i|ness
crimpy
crim|son +s +ed +ing
cringe
  crin|ges
  cringed
  crin|ging
crin|ger +s
crin|kle
  crin|kles
  crin|kled
  crink|ling
crinkle-cut
crinkle|root +s
crink|ly
crin|oid +s
crin|oid|al
crino|line +s
crino|lined
cripes
crip|ple
  crip|ples
  crip|pled
  crip|pling
crip|pled *adjective*
crip|pler +s
crip|pling *adjective*
crip|pling|ly
crisis
  crises
crisis cen|tre +s
crisp +s +ed +ing +er +est
crisp|ate
crisp|bread +s
crisp|er +s
Cris|pin +s (saint; apple)
crisp|i|ness
crisp|ly
crisp|ness
crispy
  crisp|i|er
  crisp|i|est

criss-cross
  criss-crosses
  criss-crossed
  criss-crossing
crista
  cris|tae
cris|tate
cris|to|bal|ite +s
crit +s
cri|ter|ial
cri|ter|ion
  cri|ter|ia
crit|ic +s
crit|ic|al
crit|ic|al|ity
crit|ic|al|ities
crit|ic|al|ly
crit|ic|al|ness
criti|cism +s
criti|ciz|able
criti|cize
  criti|ciz|es
  criti|cized
  criti|ciz|ing
criti|ciz|er +s
cri|tique
  cri|tiques
  cri|tiqued
  cri|tiquing
crit|ter +s
croak +s +ed +ing
croak|er +s
croak|i|ly
croak|i|ness
croaky
  croak|i|er
  croak|i|est
Croat +s (= Croatian)
Cro|atia (country, Europe)
Cro|atian +s
croc +s (crocodile)
[☞ **crock, croque monsieur**]
Croce, Bene|detto (Italian philosopher)
cro|chet (*Needlework*)
  cro|chets
  cro|cheted
  cro|chet|ing
[☞ **crotchet**]
cro|cheter +s
cro|cido|lite
crock +s (pot or jar; old person or thing; lie)
[☞ **croc, Crock-Pot, croque monsieur**]
crocked
crock|ery

crock|et +s
(*Architecture*)
[☞ Crockett]
Crock|ett, David
('Davy') (US
frontiersman)
[☞ crocket]
Crock-Pot +s
proprietary (slow
cooker)
croco|dile +s
croco|dil|ian +s
cro|cus
cro|cus|es
Croe|sus (Lydian king;
rich man)
Croe|sus|es
croft +s +ed +ing
croft|er +s
Crohn's dis|ease
crois|sant +s
croki|nole
Cro-Magnon +s
Crom|arty Firth
(inlet, Scotland)
crom|lech +s
Cromp|ton, Sam|uel
(English inventor)
Crom|well, Oli|ver
(English general &
statesman)
Crom|well|ian +s
crone +s (old woman)
[☞ krone]
Cronen|berg, David
(Cdn filmmaker)
Cro|nin, Archi|bald
Jo|seph (Scottish
novelist)
Cro|nin, James
Wat|son (US
physicist)
Cro|nus (*Greek Myth*)
crony
cron|ies
crony|ism
crook +s +ed +ing
crook-back +s
crook|ed *adjective*
crook|ed|er
crook|ed|est
crook|ed|ly
crook|ed|ness
crook|ery
Crookes, Sir Wil|liam
(English scientist)
crook|neck squash
crook|neck
squash|es
croon +s +ed +ing
(*Music*)
[☞ kroon]
croon|er +s

croony
crop
crops
cropped
crop|ping
crop cir|cle +s
crop-duster +s
crop-dusting
crop-eared
crop|land +s
crop|per +s
crop top +s
croque mon|sieur +s
cro|quet (game)
cro|quets
cro|queted
cro|quet|ing
[☞ croquette]
cro|quette +s (food)
crore +s
Cros|bie, John
Car|nell (Cdn
politician)
Cros|by, Harry Lil|lis
('Bing') (US
entertainer)
cro|sier +s (*use*
crozier)
cross (two intersecting
lines, etc.; blend;
angry)
cross|es
crossed
cross|ing
cross|er
cross|est
[☞ crosse]
cross|able
cross|bar +s
cross|beam +s
cross-bed +s
cross-bedded
cross-bedding
cross-bench
cross-benches
cross-bencher +s
cross|bill +s
cross|bones
cross-border
cross|bow +s
cross|bow|man
cross|bow|men
cross|breed
cross|breeds
cross|bred
cross|breed|ing
cross-check +s +ed
+ing
cross-country
cross-countries
cross-court
cross-cultur|al
cross-cultur|al|ly

cross-current +s
cross-curricu|lar
cross|cut
cross|cuts
cross|cut
cross|cut|ting
cross|cut saw +s
cross-dating +s
cross-dress
cross-dresses
cross-dressed
cross-dressing
cross-dresser +s
cross-dressing *noun*
crosse (lacrosse stick)
[☞ cross]
cross-examin|a|tion
+s
cross-examine
cross-examines
cross-examined
cross-examin|ing
cross-examin|er +s
cross-eyed
cross-fade
cross-fades
cross-faded
cross-fading
cross-fertiliz|a|tion
+s
cross-fertil|ize
cross-fertil|iz|es
cross-fertil|ized
cross-fertil|iz|ing
cross|fire
cross fox
cross foxes
cross-grained
cross|hair +s
cross-hatch
cross-hatches
cross-hatched
cross-hatching
cross-hatching *noun*
cross-head +s
cross-heading +s
cross-ice
cross-index
cross-indexes
cross-indexed
cross-indexing
cross|ing +s *noun*
cross|ing guard +s
cross-legged
cross-link +s +ed
+ing
cross-linkage +s
cross|ly
cross|match
cross|match|es
cross|matched
cross|match|ing
cross|match|ing *noun*

cross|ness
cross|over +s
cross-ownership +s
cross|patch
cross|patch|es
cross|piece +s
cross|ply
cross-pollin|ate
cross-pollin|ates
cross-pollin|at|ed
cross-pollin|at|ing
cross-pollin|a|tion
+s
cross-question +s
+ed +ing
cross-react +s +ed
+ing
cross-reaction +s
cross-refer
cross-refers
cross-referred
cross-referring
cross-reference
cross-referen|ces
cross-referenced
cross-referen|cing
cross-rhythm +s
cross rib +s
cross|road +s (road
that crosses another)
cross|roads
(intersection; critical
point)
plural cross|roads
cross-ruff +s +ed
+ing
cross-section +s
cross-section|al
cross-stitch
cross-stitch|es
cross-stitched
cross-stitch|ing
cross-
subsid|iz|a|tion +s
cross-subsid|ize
cross-subsid|iz|es
cross-subsid|ized
cross-subsid|iz|ing
cross-subsidy
cross-subsid|ies
cross|talk
cross|town
cross-train +s +ed
+ing
cross-trainer +s
cross-training *noun*
cross|walk +s
cross|ways
cross|wind +s
cross|wise
cross|word +s
cros|tini

crotch
crotch|es
crotch|et +s (*Music*; fancy)
crotch|et|i|ness
crotch|ety
crotch|less
cro|ton +s (plant)
[☞ crouton]
crouch
crouch|es
crouched
crouch|ing
croup +s
croup|ier +s
croupy
crou|ton +s (bread cube)
[☞ croton]
Crow (people & language)
plural Crow or Crows
crow
crows
crowed (or crew)
crowed
crow|ing
crow|bar +s
crow|berry
crow|ber|ries
crowd +s +ed +ing
crowd|ed *adjective*
crowded|ness
crowd-pleaser +s
crowd-pleasing
crow duck +s
Crow|foot (Blackfoot chief)
crow|foot +s (plant)
[☞ crow's feet]
Crown (monarchy)
crown +s +ed +ing
Crown at|tor|ney +s
crown col|ony
crown col|onies
Crown cor|por|a|tion +s
Crown coun|sel
plural Crown coun|sel
Crown Court +s
crown fire +s
crown im|per|ial +s
crown jew|el +s
crown land +s
crown of thorns
crown prince +s
crown prin|cess
crown prin|cess|es
Crown pros|ecu|tor +s

Crown re|serve +s
crown roast +s
crown wheel +s
Crown wit|ness
Crown wit|ness|es
Crow rate
crow's feet (wrinkles)
[☞ crowfoot]
crow's nest +s
Crows|nest Pass (pass & municipality, Canada)
crow steps
Cro|zet (islands, Indian Ocean)
cro|zier +s
CRT (cathode ray tube)
CRTs
cru +s (vineyard; wine)
[☞ crew, Kru]
cru|ces *plural of* crux
cru|cial
cru|ci|al|ity
cru|ci|al|ities
cru|cial|ly
cru|ciate liga|ment +s
cru|cible +s
cruci|fer +s
cru|cifer|ous
cruci|fi|er +s
cruci|fix
cru|ci|fix|es
Cruci|fix|ion (*Christianity*)
cruci|fix|ion +s
cruci|form +s
cru|cify
cruci|fies
cruci|fied
cruci|fy|ing
cruck +s
crud +s
cruddy
crud|di|er
crud|di|est
crude
cruder
crud|est
crudes
crude|ly
crude|ness
cru|di|tés (raw vegetables)
cru|dity (crude remarks or actions)
cru|di|ties
cruel (causing pain; harsh)
cruel|ler or cruel|er

cruel|lest or cruel|est
[☞ crewel]
cruel|ler *comparative of* cruel
[☞ cruller]
cruel|ly
cruel|ness
cruelty
cruel|ties
cruelty-free
cru|et +s
Cruik|shank, George (English artist)
cruise (voyage etc.)
cruis|es
cruised
cruis|ing
[☞ cruse]
cruise mis|sile +s
cruis|er +s
cruiser|weight +s
crul|ler +s (doughnut)
[☞ crueller]
crumb +s +ed +ing
crumble
crum|bles
crum|bled
crum|bling
crum|bli|ness
crum|bly
crum|bli|er
crum|bli|est
crum|blies
crumby (like or covered with crumbs; *for* dirty, inferior *etc. use* crummy)
crumb|i|er
crumb|i|est
[☞ crummy]
crum|horn +s
crum|mi|ly
crum|mi|ness
crum|my (dirty, inferior; logging vehicle)
crum|mi|er
crum|mi|est
crum|mies
[☞ crumby]
crump +s +ed +ing
crum|pet +s
crum|ple
crum|ples
crum|pled
crum|pling
crum|ple zone +s
crum|ply
crum|pli|er
crum|pli|est

crunch
crunch|es
crunched
crunch|ing
crunch|er +s
crunch|i|ly
crunch|i|ness
crunchy
crunch|i|er
crunch|i|est
crunch|ies
crup|per +s
crural
cru|sade
cru|sades
cru|sad|ed
cru|sad|ing
cru|sad|er +s
cruse +s (jar)
[☞ cruise]
crush
crush|es
crushed
crush|ing
crush|able
crush|er +s
crush|ing *adjective*
crush|ing|ly
crush|proof
crust +s +ed +ing
crus|ta|cean +s
crus|ta|ceol|ogy
crus|ta|ceous
crust|al
crust|ed *adjective*
crust|i|ly
crust|i|ness
crust|less
crust|ose
crusty
crust|i|er
crust|i|est
crutch
crutch|es
Crutched Fri|ars
Crux (constellation)
crux
crux|es or cru|ces
cru|zado +s
cru|zeiro +s
cry (weep, shout)
cries
cried
cry|ing
[☞ krai]
cry|baby
cry|babies
cry|ing *adjective*
cry|ing room +s
cryo|bio|logic|al
cryo|biol|o|gist +s
cryo|biol|ogy
cryo|gen +s

cryo|gen|ic
cryo|gen|ic|ally
cryo|gen|ics
cryo|lite +s
cry|on|ic
cry|oni|cist +s
cry|on|ics
cryo|pres|er|va|tion
cryo|pre|served
cryo|pro|tect|ant +s
cryo|stat +s
cryo|sur|gery
crypt +s
crypt|analy|sis
crypt|ana|lyst +s
crypt|ana|lytic
crypt|ana|lytic|al
cryp|tic
cryp|tic|ally
crypto|analy|sis (use
  cryptanalysis)
crypto|ana|lyst +s
  (use cryptanalyst)
crypto|ana|lytic (use
  cryptanalytic)
crypto|ana|lytic|al
  (use
  cryptanalytical)
crypto|coc|cal
crypto|coc|co|sis
crypto|crys|tal|line
crypto|gam +s (plant)
crypto|gam|ic
cryp|tog|am|ous
crypto|gram +s
  (enciphered text)
crypto|gram|mic
cryp|tog|raph|er +s
crypto|graph|ic
crypto|graph|ic|ally
cryp|tog|raphy
crypto|logic|al
cryp|tol|o|gist +s
cryp|tol|ogy
crypto|meria +s
Crysler's Farm
  (battle site, Canada)
  [☞ Chrysler,
  Kreisler]
crys|tal +s
crys|tal gaz|er +s
crys|tal gaz|ing
crys|tal|line
crys|tal|lin|ity
crys|tal|lite +s
crys|tal|liz|able
crys|tal|liz|a|tion +s
crys|tal|lize
  crys|tal|liz|es
  crys|tal|lized
  crys|tal|liz|ing

crys|tal|log|raph|er
  +s
crys|tal|lo|graph|ic
crys|tal|log|raphy
crys|tal|loid +s
CSB (Canada Savings
  Bond)
CSBs
C-section +s
CS gas
CSIS (Canadian
  Security Intelligence
  Service)
CT (computerized
  tomography)
cten|oid
cteno|phore +s
Ctesi|phon (ancient
  city near Baghdad)
CT scan +s
Cub +s (Scouting)
cub
  cubs
  cubbed
  cub|bing
Cuba (country,
  Caribbean)
Cu|ban +s
Cu|bango
  (= Okavango River,
  Africa)
cubby
  cub|bies
cubby|hole +s
cube
  cubes
  cubed
  cubing
cubeb +s
cuber +s
cube root +s
cube van +s
cubic
cubic|al (cube-
  shaped)
  [☞ cubicle]
cubic|al|ly
cu|bicle +s
  (partitioned space)
  [☞ cubical]
cubi|form
cub|ism
cub|ist +s
cub|is|tic
cubit +s
cu|bit|al
cu|boid +s
cu|boid|al
Cu|chul|ain (Irish
  Myth)
cuck|ing stool +s
cuck|old +s +ed +ing
cuck|old|ry

cuckoo +s
cuckoo bee +s
cuckoo clock +s
cuckoo pint +s
cuckoo-spit
cuckoo wasp +s
cu|cum|ber +s
cu|cumber-root
cu|cur|bit +s
cu|cur|bit|aceous
cud
cud|dle
  cud|dles
  cud|dled
  cud|dling
cud|dler +s
cuddle|some
cud|dli|ness
cud|dly
  cud|dli|er
  cud|dli|est
cuddy
  cud|dies
cudgel
  cudg|els
  cudg|elled
  cudgel|ling
cud|weed +s
cue (signal; Billiards;
  hint; fast-forward)
  cues
  cued
  cue|ing or cuing
  [☞ queue, Kew
  Gardens]
cue ball +s
cue-bid +s
cue card +s
cue|ist +s
Cuen|ca (city,
  Ecuador)
Cuer|na|vaca (town,
  Mexico)
cues|ta +s
cuff +s +ed +ing
cuff|able
cuffed adjective
cuff|link +s
Cufic (use Kufic)
Cuia|bá (city & river,
  Brazil)
cui bono?
cui|rass
  cui|rass|es
cui|ras|sier +s
Cui|sin|art +s
  proprietary
cui|sine +s
cuisse +s
cuke +s
Cul|bert|son, Ely (US
  bridge player)
cul|chie +s

Cul|dee +s
cul-de-sac
  cul-de-sacs or
  culs-de-sac
Culia|cán Ros|ales
  (city, Mexico)
culin|ar|i|ly
culin|ary
cull +s +ed +ing
Cul|len, Mau|rice
  Gal|braith (Cdn
  painter)
cull|er +s (one who
  culls)
  [☞ colour]
cul|let
Cul|loden (battle site,
  Scotland)
culm +s
culm|if|er|ous
cul|min|ant
cul|min|ate
  cul|min|ates
  cul|min|at|ed
  cul|min|at|ing
cul|min|a|tion +s
cu|lottes
culpa
culp|abil|ity
culp|able
culp|ably
cul|prit +s
cul|shie +s (use
  culchie)
cult +s
cult|ic
cul|ti|gen +s
cult|ish
cult|ish|ness
cult|ism
cult|ist +s
cul|tiv|able
cul|ti|var +s
cul|ti|vat|able
cul|ti|vate
  cul|ti|vates
  cul|ti|vat|ed
  cul|ti|vat|ing
cul|ti|vat|ed adjective
cul|ti|va|tion +s
cul|ti|va|tor +s
cul|tur|al
cul|tur|al|ly
cul|ture
  cul|tures
  cul|tured
  cul|tur|ing
culture-bound
cul|tured adjective
cul|ture shock +s
cul|tus
cul|verin +s
Cul|ver's root

cul|vert +s
cum (combined with)
  [☞ Qom]
cum|ber +s +ed +ing
Cum|ber|land (city,
  sound & peninsula,
  Canada; former
  county, England)
cum|ber|some
cum|ber|some|ly
cum|ber|some|ness
cum|bia +s
Cum|bria (county,
  England)
Cum|brian +s
cum|brous
cum|brous|ly
cum|brous|ness
cumin
cummer|bund +s
Cum|mings, Bur|ton
  (Cdn singer-
  songwriter)
cum|mings, e. e. born
  Ed|ward Est|lin
  Cum|mings (US
  poet & artist)
cumu|late
  cumu|lates
  cumu|lat|ed
  cumu|lat|ing
cumu|la|tion +s
cumu|la|tive
cumu|la|tive|ly
cumu|la|tive|ness
cumu|lo|nim|bus
cumu|lus
Cu|nard, Sir Sam|uel
  (Cdn-born
  shipowner)
cune|ate
cu|nei|form +s
Cu|nene (river,
  Angola)
cunni|lin|gus
cun|ning
  cun|ning|er
  cun|ning|est
Cun|ning|ham,
  Merce (US
  choreographer)
cun|ning|ly
cun|ning|ness
Cuno|bel|in|us
  (= Cymbeline,
  British chieftain)
cunt +s
cup
  cups
  cupped
  cup|ping
cup|bear|er +s
cup|board +s

cup|cake +s
CUPE (Cdn Union of
  Public Employees)
  [☞ kewpie]
cupel
  cupels
  cu|pelled
  cupel|ling
cupel|la|tion
cup|ful +s
Cu|pid +s
cu|pid|ity
Cu|pids (town,
  Canada)
Cupid's bow +s
cu|pola +s
cu|po|laed
cup|pa +s
cu|pram|mo|nium
cu|pre|ous
cu|pric
cu|prif|er|ous
cu|prite +s
cupro-nickel
cu|prous
cu|pule +s
CUPW (Cdn Union of
  Postal Workers)
cur +s (dog)
  [☞ Coeur de Lion;
  affaire de cœur, cri
  de cœur]
cur|abil|ity
cur|able
Cura|çao (island,
  Netherlands Antilles)
  [☞ curassow]
cura|çao +s (liqueur)
  [☞ curassow]
cura|çoa +s
  (= curaçao)
cur|acy
  cur|acies
cur|are +s
cur|as|sow +s (bird)
  [☞ curaçao]
cur|ate
  cur|ates
  cur|at|ed
  cur|at|ing
cur|a|tion
cur|a|tive
cur|ator +s
cur|a|tor|ial
cur|ator|ship +s
curb +s +ed +ing
curb|side +s
curb|stone +s
cur|cuma +s
curd +s (food)
  [☞ Kurd]
curd cheese +s

cur|dle
  cur|dles
  cur|dled
  curd|ling
curd|ler +s
curdy
cure (remedy;
  preserve; etc.)
  cures
  cured
  cur|ing
curé +s (French priest)
cure-all +s
curer +s
cur|et|tage
cur|ette
  cur|ettes
  cur|et|ted
  cur|et|ting
cur|few +s
Curia
Cur|ial
Curie, Marie (French
  physicist)
  [☞ Currie]
Curie, Pierre (French
  physicist)
  [☞ Currie]
curie +s (unit of
  radioactivity)
  [☞ curry]
curio +s
curi|osa
curi|os|ity
  curi|os|ities
curi|ous
curi|ous|ly
curi|ous|ness
Curi|tiba (city, Brazil)
cur|ium
curl +s +ed +ing
curl|er +s
cur|lew
  plural cur|lew or
  cur|lews
curl|i|cue +s
curl|i|ness
curl|ing *noun*
curl|ing iron +s
curly
  curl|i|er
  curl|i|est
  curl|ies
curly-grass fern +s
curly kale +s
cur|mudg|eon +s
cur|mudg|eon|li|ness
cur|mudg|eon|ly
Cur|noe, Greg|ory
  Rich|ard ('Greg')
  (Cdn painter)
cur|rach +s

Cur|ragh (plain,
  Ireland)
cur|ragh +s (*use*
  currach)
cur|rant +s (fruit;
  plant)
  [☞ current, au
  courant, courante]
cur|ren|cy
  cur|ren|cies
cur|rent +s (present;
  airflow, stream;
  trend; *Electricity*)
  [☞ currant, au
  courant, courante]
cur|rent|ly
cur|rent|ness
cur|ricle +s
cur|ricu|lar
cur|ricu|lum
  cur|ric|ula
cur|ricu|lum vitae
  cur|ric|ula vitae or
  cur|ric|ula vitarum
Cur|rie, Sir Ar|thur
  Wil|liam (Cdn army
  officer)
  [☞ Curie]
Cur|rier, Na|than|iel
  (US lithographer)
cur|rier +s (person
  who colours leather)
  [☞ courier]
curry (spicy dish;
  groom, treat; thrash;
  in 'curry favour')
  cur|ries
  cur|ried
  curry|ing
  [☞ Currie, Curie,
  curie]
curry comb +s
curse
  curs|es
  cursed
  curs|ing
cursed *adjective*
curs|ed|ly
curs|ed|ness
curs|er +s (one who
  curses)
  [☞ cursor]
curs|es *interjection*
cur|sillo +s
cur|sive
cur|sive|ly
cur|sor +s (*Computing*;
  Math)
  [☞ curser]
cur|sor|ial
cur|sor|ily
cur|sor|i|ness
cur|sor key +s
cur|sory

curst (archaic
  = cursed)
curt
cur|tail +s +ed +ing
cur|tail|ment +s
cur|tain +s +ed +ing
cur|tain call +s
cur|tained adjective
cur|tain|less
cur|tain rais|er +s
cur|tain rod +s
cur|tana +s
cur|til|age +s
curt|ly
curt|ness
curt|sey +s +ed +ing
  (use curtsy)
curt|sy
  curt|sies
  curt|sied
  curtsy|ing
cur|ule
curv|aceous
curva|ture +s
curve
  curves
  curved
  curv|ing
curve|ball +s
curved adjective
cur|vet
  cur|vets
  cur|vet|ted
  cur|vet|ting
curvi|foli|ate
curvi|form
curvi|linear
curvi|linear|ly
curv|i|ness
curvy
  curv|i|er
  curv|i|est
cus|cus (root;
  marsupial)
  cus|cus|es
  [☞ couscous]
cu|sec +s
Cush (region of
  ancient Nubia; son of
  Ham)
  [☞ Hindu Kush]
cush|i|er
cush|i|est
cush|i|ness
Cush|ing, Har|vey
  Wil|liams (US
  neurosurgeon)
Cushing's dis|ease
Cushing's syn|drome
cush|ion +s +ed +ing
cush|ioned adjective
cush|ion|ing noun
cush|iony

Cush|itic
cushy
  cush|i|er
  cush|i|est
cusk
  plural cusk
cusp +s
cus|pate
cusped
cus|pi|dor +s
cuss
  cuss|es
  cussed
  cuss|ing
cuss|ed adjective
cuss|ed|ly
cuss|ed|ness
cuss word +s
cus|tard +s
cus|tardy
Cus|ter, George
  Arm|strong (US
  cavalry general)
cus|tod|ial
cus|tod|ian +s
cus|tod|ian|ship
cus|tody
cus|tom +s
cus|tom|ar|i|ly
cus|tom|ary
custom-built
cus|tom|er +s
cus|tom house +s
  (= customs house)
cus|tom|iz|able
cus|tom|iz|a|tion
cus|tom|ize
  cus|tom|iz|es
  cus|tom|ized
  cus|tom|iz|ing
cust|om|ized adjective
custom-made
cus|toms house +s
cut
  cuts
  cut
  cut|ting
cut-and-paste
cu|ta|neous
cut away verb
  cuts away
  cut away
  cut|ting away
cut|away adjective
cut back verb
  cuts back
  cut back
  cut|ting back
cut|back +s noun
cut|bank +s
cut down verb
  cuts down

cut down
  cut|ting down
cut-down adjective
cute
  cuter
  cutest
cute|ly
cute|ness
cutesy
  cute|si|er
  cute|si|est
cutesy-poo
cut glass
cu|ticle +s
cu|ticu|lar
cutie +s
cutie-pie +s
cut in verb
  cuts in
  cut in
  cut|ting in
cut-in +s noun
cutis
Cut Knife (battle site,
  Canada)
cut|lass
  cut|lass|es
cut|ler +s
cut|lery
cut|let +s
cut|line +s
cut off verb
  cuts off
  cut off
  cut|ting off
cut-off +s noun &
  adjective
cut out verb
  cuts out
  cut out
  cut|ting out
cut-out +s noun &
  adjective
cut over verb
  cuts over
  cut over
  cut|ting over
cut|over +s noun &
  adjective
cut-price adjective
cut|purse +s
cut-rate adjective
cut|ter +s
cut|throat +s
cut time
cut|ting +s noun &
  adjective
cut|ting edge
  (cutting-edge when
  preceding a noun)
cut|ting|ly
cut|ting room +s
cut|tle +s

cuttle|bone +s
cuttle|fish
  plural cuttle|fish or
  cuttle|fish|es
cutty
  cut|ties
cut up verb
  cuts up
  cut up
  cut|ting up
cut-up +s noun
cut|water +s
cut|work
cut|worm +s
cu|vée +s
cu|vette +s
Cu|vier, Georges
  Jean Léo|pold
  Nico|las Fré|dé|ric,
  Baron (French
  naturalist)
Cuzco (city, Peru)
c.v. (curriculum vitae)
c.v.'s
CWAC (Cdn Women's
  Army Corps
  member)
  CWACs
cwm +s (valley;
  cirque)
  [☞ coomb, khoum]
cyan +s
cy|ana|mide +s
cy|an|ic
cyan|ide +s
cyano|bac|teria
  plural of
  cyanobacterium
cyano|bac|ter|ium
  cyano|bac|teria
cyano|co|bal|amin
  +s
cy|ano|gen +s
cy|ano|gen|ic
cyan|o|sis
  cyan|o|ses
cyan|otic
Cybele (Myth)
cyber|nate
  cyber|nates
  cyber|nat|ed
  cyber|nat|ing
cyber|na|tion
cyber|net|ic
cyber|net|ician +s
cyber|neti|cist +s
cyber|net|ics
cyber|punk +s
cyber|space +s
cy|borg +s
cycad +s
Cycla|des (islands,
  Aegean)

Cy|clad|ic
cycla|mate +s
cycla|men +s
cycle
cycles
cycled
cyc|ling
cyclic
cyclic|al +s
cyclic|al|ly
cyc|ling +s *noun*
cyc|list +s
cyclo|alkane +s
cyclo|cross
cyclo|hex|ane +s
cyc|loid +s
cyc|loid|al
cyc|lom|eter +s
cy|clone +s
cy|clon|ic
cyclo|paedia +s (*use*
  cyclopedia)
cyclo|paed|ic (*use*
  cyclopedic)
cyclo|par|af|fin +s
Cyclo|pean (of or like
  a Cyclops)
cyclo|pean (of
  masonry)
cyclo|pedia +s
cyclo|ped|ic
Cyclo|pi|an (*use*
  Cyclopean)
cyclo|pi|an (*use*
  cyclopean)
cyclo|pro|pane +s
Cy|clops (one-eyed
  giant)
  plural Cy|clops or
  Cy|clops|es or
  Cy|clo|pes
cy|clops (crustacean)
  cy|clops or
  cy|clo|pes
cyclo|rama +s
cyclo|ram|ic
cyclo|sporin
cy|clos|tom|ate
cyclo|stome +s
cyclo|thymia
cyclo|thym|ic
cyclo|tron +s
cyg|net +s (young
  swan)
  [☞ signet]
Cyg|nus
  (constellation)
cylin|der +s
cylin|dric|al
cylin|dric|al|ly
cyma +s

cym|bal +s
  (percussion
  instrument)
  [☞ symbol]
cym|bal|ist +s
  (cymbal player)
  [☞ symbolist]
Cym|bel|ine (British
  chieftain)
cym|bid|ium +s
cyme +s
cym|ose
Cym|ric
Cyne|wulf (Anglo-
  Saxon poet)
Cyn|ic +s (*Greek
  Philosophy*)
cyn|ic +s (cynical
  person)
cyn|ic|al
cyn|ic|al|ly
cyni|cism +s
cyno|sure +s
cy|pher +s +ed +ing
  (*use* cipher)
cy pres (*Law*)
cy|press (tree)
  cy|press|es
  [☞ Cyprus]
Cy|press Hills
  (region, Canada)
Cyp|ri|an (saint)
cyp|rin|oid +s
Cyp|ri|ot +s
Cyp|ri|ote +s (*use*
  Cypriot)
cypri|ped|ium +s
Cy|prus (island,
  Mediterranean)
  [☞ cypress]
cyp|sela
  cyp|selae
Cyr, Louis (Cdn
  strongman)
Cyr|ano de
  Ber|gerac,
  Savi|nien (French
  writer)
Cyre|na|ica (region,
  Libya)
Cy|rene (ancient city,
  N Africa)
Cyril (saint)
Cyr|il|lic
Cyrus, 'the Great'
  (Persian king)
Cyrus, 'the Young|er'
  (Persian prince)
cyst +s (*Medicine*;
  Biology; *Botany*)
  [☞ cist]

cyst|eine +s (amino
  acid)
  [☞ cystine, Sistine]
cyst|ic
cyst|ic fi|bro|sis
cyst|ine +s (dimer of
  cysteine)
  [☞ cysteine,
  Sistine]
cyst|itis
cysto|scope +s
cysto|scop|ic
cyst|os|copy
  cyst|os|cop|ies
cyti|dine
cyto|chrome +s
cyto|gen|etic
cyto|gen|etic|al
cyto|gen|etic|al|ly
cyto|gen|eti|cist +s
cyto|gen|etics
cyto|kine +s
cyto|logic|al
cyto|logic|al|ly
cy|tol|o|gist +s
cy|tol|ogy
cyto|meg|alo|virus
  cyto|meg|alo|virus|
  es
cyto|plasm +s
cyto|plas|mic
cyto|sine
cyto|skel|etal
cyto|skel|eton +s
cyto|toxic
cyto|tox|icity
czar +s
czar|das
  plural czar|das
czar|dom
czar|evich
  czar|evich|es
czar|ina +s
czar|ism
czar|ist +s
Czech +s (of the
  Czech Republic or
  Czechoslovakia)
Czecho|slo|vak +s (of
  Czechoslovakia)
Czecho|slo|vakia
  (former country,
  Europe)
Czecho|slo|vak|ian
  +s (of
  Czechoslovakia)
Czech Re|pub|lic
  (country, Europe)
Czerny, Karl
  (Austrian musician)
Często|chowa (city,
  Poland)

D

D (letter; note; mark;
  shape; battery)
D's
d (letter)
d's
DA (district attorney)
DAs
da +s (dad)
  [☞ dah, daw]
dab
dabs
dabbed
dab|bing
dab|ber +s
dab|ble
dab|bles
dab|bled
dab|bling
dab|bler +s
dab|bling duck +s
dab hand +s
DAC (digital to analog
  converter)
DACs
da capo
Dacca (= Dhaka,
  Bangladesh)
dace
  plural dace
dacha +s
Dachau
  (concentration camp,
  Germany)
dachs|hund +s
Dacia (ancient
  country, Europe)
Dacian
da|cite +s
da|coit +s
Dac|ron +s
  proprietary
dac|tyl +s
dac|tyl|ic +s
dad +s
Dada (*Art*)
dada +s (father)
Dada|ism
Dada|ist +s
Dada|is|tic
daddy
  dad|dies
daddy-long-legs
  plural daddy-long-
  legs
dado +s
Daeda|lus (*Greek
  Myth*)

dae|mon +s
(*Computing; for* spirit
use demon)
dae|mon|ic (*use*
demonic)
daff +s
daf|fi|ly
daf|fi|ness
daf|fo|dil +s
daffy
  daf|fi|er
  daf|fi|est
daft
daft|ly
da Gama, Vasco
(Portuguese
explorer)
dag|ger +s
dago +s *offensive*
Dagon (*Bible*)
Da|guerre, Louis
(French
photographic
innovator)
da|guerre|otype +s
dah +s (dash)
[☞ da, daw]
Dahl, Roald (British
writer)
[☞ dhal, dal, Dall
sheep]
dahl|ia +s
Da|homey (*former
name for* Benin)
dai|kon +s
Dáil
Dáil Éire|ann (= Dáil)
daili|ness
d'Aille|boust (de
Cou|longe et
d'Ar|gen|te|nay),
Louis (governor of
New France)
daily
  dai|lies
daily double +s
dai|mio (*use* daimyo)
  plural dai|mio or
  dai|mios
Daim|ler, Gott|lieb
(German auto
engineer)
dai|mon +s (demon)
[☞ daemon]
dai|mon|ic (demonic)
dai|myo
  plural dai|myo or
  dai|myos
dain|ti|ly
dain|ti|ness
dainty
  dain|ti|er

dain|ti|est
dain|ties
dai|quiri +s
Dai|ren (*former name
for* Dalian, China)
dairy (milk products
etc.)
  dair|ies
[☞ Derry]
dairy farm +s
dairy farm|er +s
dairy farm|ing
dairy|ing
dairy|maid +s
dairy|man
  dairy|men
dais
  dais|es
daisy
  dais|ies
daisy chain +s *noun*
daisy-chain *verb*
  daisy-chains
  daisy-chained
  daisy-chaining
daisy-chained
  adjective
daisy|wheel +s
Dakar (capital of
Senegal)
Da|kota
• (states, US)
  plural Da|kotas
• (people; language)
  plural Da|kota or
  Da|kotas
dal +s (lentil)
[☞ Dall sheep,
Dahl]
Dala|dier, Édouard
(French statesman)
Dalai Lama +s
(*Buddhism*)
[☞ Dalai]
da|lasi
  plural da|lasi or
  da|lasis
Dale, Sir Henry
Hal|lett (English
physiologist &
pharmacologist)
dale +s
d'Alem|bert, Jean le
Rond (French
philosopher)
dales|man
  dales|men
Dal|housie (town,
Canada)
Dal|housie, George
Ram|say, 9th Earl of
(British colonial
administrator in
BNA)

Dal|housie, James
An|drew Broun
Ram|say, 1st
Mar|quis of (British
colonial
administrator)
Dali, Sal|va|dor
(Spanish painter)
[☞ Dalai Lama]
Da|lian (port, China)
Dali|esque
Dal|las (city, US)
dal|li|ance +s
Dall sheep
  plural Dall sheep
[☞ Dahl, dal]
Dall's sheep (= Dall
sheep)
  plural Dall's sheep
dally
  dal|lies
  dal|lied
  dally|ing
Dal|ma|tia (region,
Croatia)
Dal|ma|tian +s
dal|mat|ic +s
Dal|ri|ada (ancient
Gaelic kingdom)
dal segno
Dal|ton, John (English
chemist)
dal|ton +s (atomic
mass unit)
dal|ton|ism
dam (barrier; obstruct;
mother)
dams
dammed
dam|ming
[☞ damn]
dam|age
dam|ages
dam|aged
dam|ag|ing
dam|aged *adjective*
dam|ag|ing *adjective*
dam|ag|ing|ly
Da|mara
  plural Da|mara or
  Da|maras
Da|mara|land (region,
Namibia)
dam|as|cene
  dam|as|cenes
  dam|as|cened
  dam|as|cen|ing
Da|mas|cus (capital of
Syria)
dam|ask +s +ed +ing
dame +s
dame-school +s
Da|mien (Belgian
missionary)

Dami|etta (port,
Egypt)
dam|mar +s
dammed *past & past
participle of* dam
[☞ damned]
dam|ming *conjugated
form of* dam
[☞ damning]
dam|mit
damn +s +ed +ing
(curse; condemn;
negligible amount)
[☞ dam]
dam|nable
dam|nably
dam|na|tion
dam|na|tory
damned *adjective &
adverb* (cursed;
extremely)
[☞ dammed]
damned|est
dam|ni|fi|ca|tion
dam|ni|fy
  dam|ni|fies
  dam|ni|fied
  dam|ni|fy|ing
damn|ing *adjective*
(proving the guilt of)
[☞ damming]
damn|ing|ly
Damo|cles (legendary
courtier of
Dionysius)
Damon (legendary
Syracusan)
damp +er +est +s
+ed +ing
damp|en +s +ed +ing
damp|en|er +s
damp|er +s
Dam|pier, Wil|liam
(English explorer)
damp|ish
damp|ly
damp|ness
dam|sel +s
damsel|fish
  plural damsel|fish
damsel|fly
  damsel|flies
dam|son +s
Dan (*Bible*)
dan +s (*Martial Arts;*
buoy)
Dana, James Dwight
(US mineralogist)
Danae (*Greek Myth*)
Dana|ids (*Greek Myth*)
Dana|kil
De|pres|sion
(region, Africa)

Da Nang (city, Vietnam)
Dana|us (*Greek Myth*)
dan buoy +s
dance (rhythmic movement etc.)
dan|ces
danced
dan|cing
[☞ *danse macabre*]
dance|able
dance band +s
dance card +s
dance floor +s
dance hall +s
dance|mak|er +s
dance|making
dan|cer +s
dan|cer|cise
dan|cer|cize (*use* dancercise)
dance|wear
dan|cey
D. and C. (dilation & curettage)
D. and C.'s
dan|de|lion +s
dan|der +s
dan|di|fied *adjective*
dan|di|fy
dan|di|fies
dan|di|fied
dan|di|fy|ing
dan|dle
dan|dles
dan|dled
dandl|ing
Dan|dong (port, China)
dan|druff
dandy
dan|dies
dan|di|er
dan|di|est
dandy brush
dandy brush|es
dandy|ish
dandy|ism
Dane +s (of Denmark)
[☞ deign]
Dane|geld
Dane|law
dang
dan|ger +s
dan|ger|ous
dan|ger|ous|ly
dan|ger|ous|ness
dan|gle
dan|gles
dan|gled
dan|gling
dan|gler +s
dan|gling *adjective*

dan|gly
Dan|iel (*Bible*)
[☞ Daniell cell]
Dan|iel, Sam|uel (English writer)
[☞ Daniell cell]
Dan|iell cell +s
Dan|ish
• (of Denmark)
• (pastry)
Dan|ish|es
dank
dank|ly
dank|ness
d'Annun|zio, Gab|ri|ele (Italian writer)
dan|sak (*use* dhansak)
danse ma|cabre
danses ma|cabres
dan|seur +s (male ballet dancer)
dan|seur noble
dan|seurs nobles
dan|seuse +s (female ballet dancer)
Dante *full name* Dante Ali|ghieri (Italian poet)
Dan|te|an +s
Dan|tesque
dan|thonia
Dan|ton, Georges Jacques (French revolutionary)
Dan|ube (river, Europe)
Dan|ub|ian
Dan|zig (= Gdańsk, Poland)
dap
daps
dapped
dap|ping
Daph|ne (nymph pursued by Apollo)
daph|ne +s (shrub)
daph|nia (crustacean)
plural daph|nia
Daph|nis (Sicilian shepherd)
Da Ponte, Lor|enzo (Italian poet & librettist)
dap|per
dap|per|ly
dap|per|ness
dap|ple
dap|ples
dap|pled
dap|pling
dap|pled *adjective*

dap|ple grey +s
Dap|sang (= K2: mountain, Asia)
Da|qing (city, China)
Darby, Abra|ham (English iron manufacturer)
[☞ Derby]
Darby and Joan
Dar|dan|elles (strait, Turkey)
Dar|danus (*Greek Myth*)
dare
dares *or* dare
dared
dar|ing
dare|devil +s
dare|devil|ry
Dar es Sa|laam (port, Tanzania)
Dar|fur (region, Sudan)
d'Argen|son, Pierre de Voyer (governor of New France)
Dar|ien (province, Panama)
dar|ing *noun* & *adjective* (courage; courageous)
[☞ derring-do]
dar|ing|ly
Dario, Rubén (Nicaraguan writer)
dari|ole +s
Dar|ius (Persian kings)
Dar|jee|ling (town, India; tea)
Dar|ji|ling (= Darjeeling, India)
dark +er +est +s
Dark Age +s
dark|en +s +ed +ing
dark|en|er +s
Dar|khan (city, Mongolia)
dark horse +s
dark|ie +s *offensive*
dark|ish
dark|ling
dark|ly
dark|ness
dark|ness|es
dark|room +s
dark|some
darky *offensive*
dark|ies
Dar|ling (river, Australia)
dar|ling +s
Dar|ling|ton (town, England)

Darm|stadt (town, Germany)
darn +s +ed +ing
darndest
darned *adjective* & *adverb*
darned|est (*use* darndest)
dar|nel +s
darn|er +s
darn|ing *noun*
darn|ing nee|dle +s
Darn|ley, Lord (Scottish nobleman)
darn tootin'
Dar|row, Clar|ence (US lawyer)
Dart, Ray|mond Ar|thur (South African anthropologist)
dart +s +ed +ing
dart|board +s
dart|er +s
Dart|moor (region & prison, England; pony)
Dart|mouth (city, Canada; port, England)
Dar|win (city, Australia)
Dar|win, Charles Rob|ert (English evolutionist)
Dar|win|ian +s
Dar|win|ism
Dar|win|ist +s
dash
dash|es
dashed
dash|ing
dash|board +s
da|sheen +s
dash|er +s
dash|er board +s
da|shiki +s
dash|ing *adjective*
dash|ing|ly
das|tard|li|ness
das|tard|ly
dasy|ure +s
DAT (digital audio tape)
DATs
data *singular noun* & *plural of* datum
data bank +s
data|base +s
dat|able
data cap|ture
data glove +s
data link +s

data pro|cess|ing
data pro|ces|sor +s
date
 dates
 dated
 dat|ing
date|book +s
dated adjective
date|less
Date Line
 (= International
 Date Line)
date|line (Journalism)
date|lines
date|lined
date|lin|ing
date palm +s
date rape +s
date square +s
date stamp +s noun
date-stamp +s +ed
 +ing verb
dat|ing noun
dativ|al
dat|ive +s
Da|tong (city, China)
datum
 data
da|tura +s
daub +s +ed +ing
 (spread, smear;
 paint, plaster, etc.)
 [☞ dob, daube]
daube +s (stew)
 [☞ daub]
daub|er +s
Dau|bigny, Charles
 Fran|çois (French
 landscape painter)
Dau|det, Al|phonse
 (French writer)
daugh|ter +s (relative)
 [☞ dodder]
daughter-in-law
 daughters-in-law
daugh|ter|ly
Dau|mier, Hon|oré
 (French artist)
daunt +s +ed +ing
daunt|ing adjective
daunt|ing|ly
daunt|less
daunt|less|ly
daunt|less|ness
Dau|phin (town,
 Canada)
dau|phin +s (sons of
 French kings)
Dau|phiné (region,
 France)
Davao (port, the
 Philippines)
daven +s +ed +ing

Dav|enant, Sir
 Wil|liam (English
 writer)
daven|port +s
David (Bible; Scottish
 kings; saint)
David, Jacques-Louis
 (French painter)
Davies, Sir Peter
 Max|well (English
 composer)
Davies, (Wil|liam)
 Robert|son (Cdn
 writer)
da Vinci, Leo|nar|do
 (Italian artist)
Davis (Arctic strait;
 surname)
 [☞ Sir Peter
 Maxwell Davies]
Davis, Bette (US
 actress)
Davis, Jef|fer|son
 (president of the
 Confederate States)
Davis, John (English
 explorer)
Davis, Miles Dewey
 (US musician)
Davis, Wil|liam
 Gren|ville ('Bill')
 (Cdn politician)
Davis Inlet
 (community,
 Canada)
Davis|son, Clin|ton
 Jo|seph (US
 physicist)
davit +s
Davos (resort,
 Switzerland)
Davy, Sir Hum|phry
 (English chemist)
Davy (lamp)
 Davies
Davy Jones
Davy Jones's lock|er
Davys, John
 (= Davis)
daw +s (jackdaw)
 [☞ dah, da]
daw|dle
 daw|dles
 daw|dled
 dawd|ling
dawd|ler +s
Dawes, Charles
 Gates (US vice-
 president)
Daw|kins, Rich|ard
 (English zoologist)
dawn +s +ed +ing
 (daybreak; start)
 [☞ don]

dawn|ing noun
Daw|son (town,
 Yukon)
 [☞ Dawson Creek]
Daw|son, George
 Mer|cer (Cdn
 geologist)
Daw|son, Sir John
 Wil|liam (Cdn
 geologist &
 university
 administrator)
Daw|son City
 (= Dawson, Yukon)
Daw|son Creek (city,
 BC)
Day, Doris (US
 entertainer)
day +s
Dayak
 plural Dayak or
 Day|aks
Dayan, Moshe (Israeli
 statesman)
day|bed +s
day|book +s
day boy +s
day|break +s
day camp +s
day|care +s
day|dream +s +ed
 +ing
day|dream|er +s
day|dream|ing noun
day|dreamy
day girl +s
Day-Glo proprietary
day job +s
Day-Lewis, Cecil
 (Irish-born poet)
Day-Lewis, Dan|iel
 (English actor)
day|light +s
day|light sav|ings
 time (= daylight
 saving time)
day|light sav|ing
 time
day lily
 day lil|ies
day|long
day pack +s
day pass
 day pass|es
day re|lease
day re|turn +s
day room +s
day sack +s
day school +s
day stu|dent +s
day|time
Day|tim|er +s
 proprietary

day-to-day
Day|ton (city, US)
 [☞ Deighton]
day trip +s
day trip|per +s
day|wear
day|work
daze
 dazes
 dazed
 daz|ing
dazed adjective
daz|ed|ly
daz|zle
 daz|zles
 daz|zled
 daz|zling
daz|zled adjective
dazzle|ment
daz|zler +s
daz|zling adjective
daz|zling|ly
DBS (direct-broadcast
 satellite)
DCC (digital compact
 cassette)
DCCs
D-Day
ddC (dideoxycytidine)
ddI (dideoxyinosine)
DDT
 (dichlorodiphenyl-
 trichloroethane)
de|acces|sion +s +ed
 +ing
dea|con +s +ed +ing
deacon|ate +s
deacon|ess
 deacon|ess|es
deacon|ship
de|acti|vate
 de|acti|vates
 de|acti|vat|ed
 de|acti|vat|ing
de|acti|va|tion +s
de|acti|va|tor +s
dead +er +est
dead air
dead beat (exhausted)
dead|beat +s
 (someone who
 avoids paying; loafer)
dead|bolt +s
dead-cat bounce +s
dead centre
dead cert +s
dead duck +s
dead|en +s +ed +ing
dead end +s (dead-
 end when preceding a
 noun)
dead|en|er +s
dead|eye +s

dead|fall +s
dead|head +s +ed +ing
dead heat +s *noun*
dead-heat *verb*
dead-heats
dead-heated
dead-heating
dead|li|er
dead|li|est
dead lift +s *noun*
dead|lift +s +ed +ing *verb*
dead|line +s
dead|li|ness
dead|lock +s +ed +ing
dead|locked *adjective*
dead loss
dead loss|es
dead|ly
dead|li|er
dead|li|est
dead|man (of a safety mechanism)
dead man's (= deadman: of a safety mechanism)
dead man's fin|gers
deadman's float
dead march
dead march|es
dead meat
dead|ness
dead net|tle +s
dead-on
dead|pan
dead|pans
dead|panned
dead|pan|ning
dead ring|er +s
Dead Sea (Israel–Jordan border)
dead set *adjective*
dead time +s
dead|water +s
dead weight +s
dead|wood
de-aerate
de-aerates
de-aerated
de-aerating
de-aeration +s
de-aerator +s
deaf (unable to hear)
[☞ def]
deaf-blind
deaf|en +s +ed +ing
deaf|en|ing *adjective*
deaf|en|ing|ly
deaf|ly
deaf-mute +s
deaf|ness

deal
• (take appropriate measures; treat; distribute; agreement; timber)
deals
dealt
deal|ing
• (in 'wheel and deal')
deals
dealed
deal|ing
[☞ dele]
de-alcohol|ized
deal|er +s
dealer|ship +s
deal|ing +s *noun*
dealt
Dean (river, Canada)
Dean, Chris|to|pher (English skater)
Dean, James Byron (US actor)
dean +s (university or church official; senior member)
[☞ dene]
dean|ery (dean's office etc.)
dean|eries
[☞ denary]
dean's list +s
dear +s +er +est (beloved etc.; expensive)
[☞ deer, Deere]
dear|ie +s
Dear John +s (letter)
dear|ly
dear|ness
dearth +s
deasil (clockwise)
[☞ diesel]
death +s
death ad|der +s
death|bed +s
death blow +s
death camp +s
death cap +s
death knell +s
death|less
death|less|ness
death|like
death|ly
death|li|er
death|li|est
death mask +s
death metal
death rate +s
death rat|tle +s
death row +s
death's head +s
death squad +s

death star +s
death toll +s
death trap +s
Death Val|ley (desert, US)
death war|rant +s
death watch
death watch|es
death-watch bee|tle +s
death wish
death wish|es
deb +s
de|bacle +s
debag
de|bags
de|bagged
de|bag|ging
debar
de|bars
de|barred
de|bar|ring
de|bark +s +ed +ing
de|bark|a|tion +s
de|bar|ment +s
de|base
de|bas|es
de|based
de|bas|ing
de|base|ment +s
de|bas|er +s
de|bat|able
de|bat|ably
de|bate
de|bates
de|bat|ed
de|bat|ing
de|bat|er +s
de|bauch (corrupt; seduce; indulgence)
de|bauch|es
de|bauched
de|bauch|ing
[☞ debouch]
de|bauched *adjective*
de|bau|chee +s
de|bauch|er +s
de|bauch|ery
de|bauch|eries
de Beau|voir, Si|mone (French writer)
de|ben|ture +s
de|bili|tate
de|bili|tates
de|bili|tat|ed
de|bili|tat|ing
de|bili|tat|ing *adjective*
de|bili|tat|ing|ly
de|bili|ta|tion +s
de|bili|ta|tive

de|bil|ity
de|bil|ities
deb|it +s +ed +ing
debit card +s
deb|on|air
deb|on|air|ly
de|bone
de|bones
de|boned
de|bon|ing
Deb|or|ah (Bible)
de|bouch (emerge; flow out)
de|bouch|es
de|bouched
de|bouch|ing
[☞ debauch]
de|bouch|ment +s
Deb|recen (city, Hungary)
De|brett, John (English publisher)
de|bride|ment +s
de|brief +s +ed +ing
de|brief|ing +s *noun*
deb|ris
de Brog|lie, Louis-Victor, Prince (French physicist)
Debs, Eu|gene Vic|tor (US labour organizer)
debt +s
debt|or +s
de|bug
de|bugs
de|bugged
de|bug|ging
de|bug|ger +s
de|bug|ging +s *noun*
de|bunk +s +ed +ing
de|bunk|er +s
De|bussy, (Achille) Claude (French composer)
debut
debuts
debuted
debut|ing
debu|tante +s
Debye, Peter Jo|seph Wil|liam (Dutch-born physicist)
dec|ad|al
dec|ade +s
deca|dence
deca|dent +s
deca|dent|ly
de|caf +s
de|caf|fein|ate
de|caf|fein|ates
de|caf|fein|at|ed
de|caf|fein|at|ing

de|caf|fein|at|ed
adjective
de|caf|fein|a|tion
deca|gon +s
dec|ag|on|al
deca|hed|ral
deca|hed|ron
deca|hed|rons or
  deca|hedra
dec|al +s (transferable
  picture)
[☞ deckle]
de|calci|fi|ca|tion +s
de|calci|fi|er +s
de|calci|fy
  de|calci|fies
  de|calci|fied
  de|calci|fy|ing
de|calco|mania +s
deca|litre +s
Deca|logue +s
deca|metre +s
de|camp +s +ed +ing
de|camp|ment +s
de|can|al
de|cani
de|cant +s +ed +ing
de|cant|er +s
de|capi|tate
  de|capi|tates
  de|capi|tat|ed
  de|capi|tat|ing
de|capi|ta|tion +s
deca|pod +s
de|capod|an
de|carbon|iz|a|tion
  +s
de|carbon|ize
  de|carbon|iz|es
  de|carbon|ized
  de|carbon|iz|ing
de|carb|oxyl|ase
de|carb|oxyl|ate
  de|carb|oxyl|ates
  de|carb|oxyl|at|ed
  de|carb|oxyl|at|ing
de|carb|oxyl|a|tion
  +s
deca|syllab|ic
deca|sylla|ble +s
dec|ath|lete +s
dec|ath|lon +s
De|catur, Ste|phen
  (US naval officer)
de|cay +s +ed +ing
decay|able
Dec|can (plateau,
  India)
de|cease
  dec|ceas|es
  de|ceased
  de|ceas|ing

de|ceased
  plural de|ceased
de|ced|ent +s
de|certi|fi|ca|tion
  (remove
  certification)
[☞ desertification]
de|certi|fy
  de|certi|fies
  de|certi|fied
  de|certi|fy|ing
de|ceit +s
de|ceit|ful
de|ceit|ful|ly
de|ceit|ful|ness
de|ceiv|able
de|ceive
  de|ceives
  de|ceived
  de|ceiv|ing
de|ceiv|er +s
de|celer|ate
  de|celer|ates
  de|celer|at|ed
  de|celer|at|ing
de|celer|a|tion +s
de|celer|ator +s
de|celer|om|eter +s
De|cem|ber +s
De|cem|brist +s
de|cency
  de|cen|cies
de|cen|nial
de|cen|nial|ly
de|cent (proper etc.)
[☞ descent,
  dissent]
de|cent|ly
de|cen|tral|ist +s
de|cen|tral|iz|a|tion
  +s
de|cen|tral|ize
  de|cen|tral|iz|es
  de|cen|tral|ized
  de|cen|tral|iz|ing
de|cen|tral|ized
  adjective
de|centre
  de|cen|tres
  de|cen|tred
  de|cen|tring
de|cep|tion +s
de|cep|tive
de|cep|tive|ly
de|cep|tive|ness
de|cere|brate
deci|bel +s
de|cid|able
de|cide
  de|cides
  de|cid|ed
  de|cid|ing
de|cid|ed *adjective*

de|cid|ed|ly
de|cid|ed|ness
de|cid|er +s
de|cidu|ous
de|cidu|ous|ness
deci|gram +s
decile +s
deci|litre +s
deci|mal +s
deci|mal|iz|a|tion +s
deci|mal|ize
  deci|mal|iz|es
  deci|mal|ized
  deci|mal|iz|ing
deci|mal|ly
deci|mate
  deci|mates
  deci|mat|ed
  deci|mat|ing
deci|ma|tion +s
deci|ma|tor +s
deci|metre +s
de|cipher +s +ed
  +ing
de|cipher|able
de|cipher|ment +s
de|ci|sion +s
decision-making
de|ci|sive
de|ci|sive|ly
de|ci|sive|ness
De|cius (Roman
  emperor)
deck +s +ed +ing
deck chair +s
deck|er (in 'double-
  decker' etc.)
[☞ Dekker]
deck|hand +s
deckle +s
  (*Papermaking*)
[☞ decal]
deckle edge +s *noun*
deckle-edged
  adjective
deck shoe +s
de|claim +s +ed +ing
de|claim|er +s
dec|lam|a|tion +s
de|clama|tory
de|clar|able
de|clar|ant +s
dec|lar|a|tion +s
de|clara|tive
de|clara|tive|ly
de|clara|tory
de|clare
  de|clares
  de|clared
  de|clar|ing
de|clared *adjective*
de|clar|ed|ly
de|clar|er +s

de|class
  de|class|es
  de|classed
  de|class|ing
dé|classé
de|classi|fi|ca|tion +s
de|classi|fy
  de|classi|fies
  de|classi|fied
  de|classi|fy|ing
de|claw +s +ed +ing
de|clen|sion +s
de|clen|sion|al
de|clin|able
dec|lin|a|tion +s
dec|lin|a|tion|al
de|cline
  de|clines
  de|clined
  de|clin|ing
de|clin|er +s
de|cliv|itous
de|cliv|ity
  de|cliv|ities
dc|clutch
  de|clutch|es
  de|clutched
  de|clutch|ing
Deco (= art deco)
[☞ dekko]
de|coc|tion +s
de|cod|able
de|code
  de|codes
  de|cod|ed
  de|cod|ing
de|cod|er +s
dé|col|le|tage +s
dé|col|leté +s
de|col|oniz|a|tion
de|col|onize
  de|col|oniz|es
  de|col|onized
  de|col|oniz|ing
de|color|iz|a|tion
de|color|ize
  de|color|iz|es
  de|color|ized
  de|color|iz|ing
  adjective
de|colour|iz|a|tion
  (*use* decolorization)
de|colour|ize (*use*
  decolorize)
  de|colour|iz|es
  de|colour|ized
  de|colour|iz|ing
de|colour|iz|ing
  adjective (*use*
  decolorizing)
de|com|mis|sion +s
  +ed +ing

de|com|pen|sa|tion +s
de|com|pos|abil|ity
de|com|pos|able
de|com|pose
de|com|pos|es
de|com|posed
de|com|pos|ing
de|com|pos|er +s
de|com|pos|ition +s
de|com|press
de|com|press|es
de|com|pressed
de|com|press|ing
de|com|pres|sion
de|com|pres|sor +s
de|con|gest|ant +s
de|con|se|crate
de|con|se|crates
de|con|se|crat|ed
de|con|se|crat|ing
de|con|se|cra|tion +s
de|con|struct +s +ed +ing
de|con|struc|tion +s
de|con|struc|tion|ism
de|con|struc|tion|ist +s
de|con|struct|ive
de|con|tam|in|ate
de|con|tam|in|ates
de|con|tam|in|at|ed
de|con|tam|in|at|ing
de|con|tam|in|a|tion
de|context|ual|iz|a|tion
de|context|ual|ize
de|context|ual|iz|es
de|context|ual|ized
de|context|ual|iz|ing
de|context|ual|ized adjective
de|con|trol
de|con|trols
de|con|trolled
de|con|trol|ling
decor +s
decor|ate
decor|ates
decor|ated
decor|at|ing
decor|at|ed adjective
Decor|at|ed style
decor|a|tion +s
decor|a|tive
decor|a|tive|ly
decor|a|tive|ness
decor|ator +s
dec|or|ous
dec|or|ous|ly
dec|or|ous|ness

de|cor|ti|cate
de|cor|ti|cates
de|cor|ti|cat|ed
de|cor|ti|cat|ing
de|cor|ti|ca|tion +s
de|cor|um +s
De Cos|mos, Amor (Cdn politician)
de|coup|age +s
de|couple
de|couples
de|coupled
de|coup|ling
de|coupled adjective
de|coup|ling noun
de|coy +s +ed +ing
de|crease
de|creas|es
de|creased
de|creas|ing
de|creas|ing|ly
de|cree
de|crees
de|creed
de|cree|ing
dec|re|ment +s
dec|re|ment|al
de|creol|iz|a|tion
de|crep|it
de|crepi|tate
de|crepi|tates
de|crepi|tat|ed
de|crepi|tat|ing
de|crepi|ta|tion
de|crepi|tude
de|crescen|do +s
de|cretal +s
de|crier +s
de|crim|in|al|iz|a|tion
de|crim|in|al|ize
de|crim|in|al|iz|es
de|crim|in|al|ized
de|crim|in|al|iz|ing
de|cry
de|cries
de|cried
de|cry|ing
de|crypt +s +ed +ing
de|cryp|tion +s
de|cum|bent
de|cus|sate
de|cus|sates
de|cus|sat|ed
de|cus|sat|ing
de|cus|sa|tion +s
Dede|kind, (Jul|ius Wil|helm) Rich|ard (German mathematician)
dedi|cate
dedi|cates

dedi|cat|ed
dedi|cat|ing
dedi|cat|ed adjective
dedi|catee +s
dedi|ca|tion +s
dedi|ca|tor +s
dedi|ca|tory
de|duce
de|duces
de|duced
de|ducing
de|ducible
de|duct +s +ed +ing
de|duct|ibil|ity
de|duct|ible +s
de|duc|tion +s
de|duct|ive
de|duct|ive|ly
de Duve, Chris|tian René (Belgian biochemist)
Dee (rivers, UK)
Dee, John (English translator & alchemist)
dee +s
deed +s +ed +ing
deed poll
dee|jay +s +ed +ing (= DJ)
deem +s +ed +ing (regard; consider) [☞ deme]
de-emphasis
de-emphasize
de-emphasiz|es
de-emphasized
de-emphasiz|ing
deep +er +est +s
deep-dish adjective
deep|en +s +ed +ing
deep fat fryer +s
deep-freeze
deep-freezes
deep-froze
deep-frozen
deep-freezing
deep-fried adjective
deep-fry
deep-fries
deep-fried
deep-frying
deep fryer +s
deep-laid
deep|ly
deep|ness
deep-pocket|ed
Deep River (town, Canada)
deep-rooted
deep sea +s (deep-sea when preceding a noun)

deep-seated
deep-set
deep-six
deep-sixes
deep-sixed
deep-sixing
deep space
deep water +s (deep|water when preceding a noun)
Deer (island, Canada) [☞ Deere]
deer (animal) plural deer [☞ dear]
deer|berry
deer|ber|ries
Deere, John (US manufacturer) [☞ Deer]
deer fly
deer flies
deer|hound +s
Deer Lake (lake & town, Canada)
deer mouse
deer mice
deer|skin +s
deer|stalk|er +s
deer tick +s
deer tongue +s
deer yard +s
de-escalate
de-escalates
de-escalat|ed
de-escalat|ing
de-escala|tion
DEET
def (excellent) [☞ deaf]
de|face
de|faces
de|faced
de|facing
de|face|able
de|face|ment +s
de|facer +s
de facto
de|fal|cate
de|fal|cates
de|fal|cat|ed
de|fal|cat|ing
de|fal|ca|tion +s
de|fal|ca|tor +s
de Falla, Man|uel (Spanish composer)
def|am|a|tion +s
de|fama|tory
de|fame
de|fames
de|famed
de|fam|ing
de|fam|er +s

de|famil|iar|iz|a|tion
de|famil|iar|ize
  de|famil|iar|iz|es
  de|famil|iar|ized
  de|famil|iar|iz|ing
de|fang +s +ed +ing
de|fat
  de|fats
  de|fatted
  de|fat|ting
de|fault +s +ed +ing
de|fault|ed *adjective*
de|fault|er +s
de|feas|ance +s
de|feas|ibil|ity
de|feas|ible
de|feas|ibly
de|feat +s +ed +ing
de|feat|ism
de|feat|ist +s
defe|cate
  defe|cates
  defe|cated
  defe|cat|ing
defe|ca|tion
de|fect +s +ed +ing
de|fec|tion +s
de|fect|ive
de|fect|ive|ly
de|fect|ive|ness
de|fect|or +s
de|fence +s
de|fence|less
de|fence|less|ly
de|fence|less|ness
de|fence|man
  de|fence|men
de|fend +s +ed +ing
de|fend|able
de|fend|ant +s
de|fend|er +s
de|fen|es|trate
  de|fen|es|trates
  de|fen|es|trat|ed
  de|fen|es|trat|ing
de|fen|es|tra|tion +s
de|fense +s (*use*
  defence)
de|fense|less (*use*
  defenceless)
de|fense|less|ly (*use*
  defencelessly)
de|fense|less|ness
  (*use*
  defencelessness)
de|fense|man (*use*
  defenceman)
  de|fense|men
de|fens|ibil|ity
de|fens|ible
de|fens|ibly
de|fen|sive
de|fen|sive|ly

de|fen|sive|ness
defer (postpone; yield,
  give way)
  de|fers
  de|ferred
  de|fer|ring
  [☞ differ]
def|er|ence (respect;
  compliance)
  [☞ vas deferens,
  difference]
def|er|en|tial
  (showing deference)
  [☞ differential]
def|er|en|tial|ly
  (respectfully)
  [☞ differentially]
de|fer|ment +s
de|fer|ral +s
de|ferred *adjective*
de|fi|ance
de|fi|ant
de|fi|ant|ly
de|fib|ril|la|tion
de|fib|ril|la|tor +s
de|fi|cien|cy
  de|fi|cien|cies
de|fi|cient
de|fi|cient|ly
defi|cit +s
def|il|ade
  def|il|ades
  def|il|ad|ed
  def|il|ad|ing
de|file
  de|files
  de|filed
  de|fil|ing
de|file|ment
de|fil|er +s
de|fin|able
de|fine
  de|fines
  de|fined
  de|fin|ing
de|fined *adjective*
de|fin|er +s
def|in|ite +s
def|in|ite|ly
def|in|ite|ness
def|in|ition +s
def|in|ition|al
de|fin|itive
de|fin|itive|ly
def|la|grate
  def|la|grates
  def|la|grat|ed
  def|la|grat|ing
def|la|gra|tion +s
de|flate
  de|flates
  de|flat|ed
  de|flat|ing

de|flat|ed *adjective*
de|fla|tion +s
de|fla|tion|ary
de|fla|tion|ist +s
de|fla|tor +s
de|flect +s +ed +ing
de|flec|tion +s
de|flect|or +s
de|flor|a|tion +s
de|flower +s +ed
  +ing
de|focus
  de|focus|es
  de|focused or
  de|focussed
  de|focus|ing or
  de|focus|sing
Defoe, Dan|iel
  (English writer)
de|fog
  de|fogs
  de|fogged
  de|fog|ging
de|fog|ger +s
de|foli|ant +s
de|foli|ate
  de|foli|ates
  de|foli|at|ed
  de|foli|at|ing
de|foli|a|tion
de|foli|ator +s
De For|est, Lee (US
  electrical engineer)
de|forest +s +ed +ing
de|forest|a|tion
de|forest|ed *adjective*
de|form +s +ed +ing
de|form|able
de|forma|tion +s
de|forma|tion|al
de|formed *adjective*
de|form|ity
  de|form|ities
de|fraud +s +ed +ing
de|fraud|er +s
de|fray +s +ed +ing
de|fray|able
de|fray|al +s
de|fray|ment +s
de|frock +s +ed +ing
de|frost +s +ed +ing
de|frost|er +s
de|frost|ing *noun*
deft
deft|ly
deft|ness
de|funct
de|fuse (remove the
  fuse from; reduce the
  tension or danger of)
  de|fus|es
  de|fused

de|fus|ing
  [☞ diffuse]
defy
  de|fies
  de|fied
  defy|ing
dé|gagé
Degas, (Hil|aire
  Ger|main) Edgar
  (French artist)
degas
  de|gases
  de|gassed
  de|gas|sing
de Gaulle, Charles
  An|dré Jo|seph
  Marie (French
  president)
de|gauss
  de|gauss|es
  de|gaussed
  de|gauss|ing
de|gauss|er +s
de|gen|er|acy
  de|gen|er|acies
de|gen|er|ate
  de|gen|er|ates
  de|gen|er|at|ed
  de|gen|er|at|ing
de|gen|er|ate|ly
de|gen|er|a|tion +s
de|gen|er|a|tive
de|glaci|a|tion +s
de|glaze
  de|glaz|es
  de|glazed
  de|glaz|ing
de|grad|abil|ity
de|grad|able
deg|rad|a|tion +s
de|grad|a|tive
de|grade
  de|grades
  de|grad|ed
  de|grad|ing
de|grad|ed *adjective*
de|grad|ing *adjective*
de|grad|ing|ly
de|grease
  de|greas|es
  de|greased
  de|greas|ing
de|greas|er +s
de|gree +s
de|gree day +s
degree|less
de|gres|sive (at
  successively lower
  rates; reducing)
  [☞ digressive]
de|hair +s +ed +ing
de haut en bas

de Hav|il|land, Sir
  Geof|frey (English
  aircraft designer)
de Hav|il|land,
  Oliv|ia Mary (US
  actress)
de|hisce
  de|his|ces
  de|hisced
  de|his|cing
de|his|cence
de|his|cent
de Hooch, Pieter
  (Dutch painter)
de Hoogh, Pieter
  (= de Hooch)
de|horn +s +ed +ing
de|human|iz|a|tion
  +s
de|human|ize
  de|human|iz|es
  de|human|ized
  de|human|iz|ing
de|humidi|fi|ca|tion
de|humidi|fi|er +s
de|humidi|fy
  de|humidi|fies
  de|humidi|fied
  de|humidi|fy|ing
de|hy|drate
  de|hy|drates
  de|hydrat|ed
  de|hydrat|ing
de|hydrat|ed *adjective*
de|hydra|tion +s
de|hydra|tor +s
de|hydro|gen|ase +s
de|hydro|gen|ate
  de|hydro|gen|ates
  de|hydro|gen|at|ed
  de|hydro|gen|at|ing
de|hydro|gen|a|tion
  +s
Deia|nira (*Greek
  Myth*)
de-ice
  de-ices
  de-iced
  de-icing
de-icer +s
dei|cide +s
deic|tic +s
deic|tic|ally
deifi|ca|tion +s
deify
  dei|fies
  dei|fied
  deify|ing
Deigh|ton, Len
  (English writer)
  [☞ Dayton]
deign +s +ed +ing
Dei gra|tia

Dei|mos (*Greek Myth*;
  moon of Mars)
de-index
  de-indexes
  de-indexed
  de-indexing
de-indexa|tion +s
**de|indus|tri|al|iz|
  a|tion** +s
de|indus|tri|al|ize
  de|indus|tri|al|iz|es
  de|indus|tri|al|ized
  de|indus|tri|al|iz|ing
de|indus|tri|al|ized
  adjective
de-ink +s +ed +ing
**de|insti|tu|tion|al|iz|
  a|tion** +s
de|insti|tu|tion|al|ize
  de|insti|tu|tion|al|
    iz|es
  de|insti|tu|tion|al|
    ized
  de|insti|tu|tion|al|
    iz|ing
**de|insti|tu|tion|al|
    ized**
  adjective
de|ioniz|a|tion +s
de|ionize
  de|ioniz|es
  de|ionized
  de|ioniz|ing
de|ionized *adjective*
de|ioniz|er +s
Deir|dre (*Irish Myth*)
deism
deist +s
deis|tic
deis|tic|al
deity
  dei|ties
déjà vu
de|ject +s +ed +ing
de|ject|ed *adjective*
de|ject|ed|ly
de|jec|tion +s
de jure (rightful,
  rightfully)
  [☞ *du jour*]
deke
  dekes
  deked
  dek|ing
Dek|ker, Thom|as
  (English dramatist)
dek|ko +s (look)
  [☞ Deco]
de Klerk, Fred|erik
  Wil|lem (South
  African president)

de Koo|ning, Wil|lem
  (Dutch-born US
  painter)
De|la|croix,
  Fer|di|nand Vic|tor
  Eu|gène (French
  painter)
de la Mare, Wal|ter
  John (English writer)
de|lamin|ate
  de|lamin|ates
  de|lamin|at|ed
  de|lamin|at|ing
de|lamin|a|tion +s
De la Roche, Mazo
  (Cdn novelist)
de|late
  de|lates
  de|lat|ed
  de|lat|ing
de|la|tion +s
de|la|tor +s
De|lau|nay, Rob|ert
  (French painter)
Dela|ware (state &
  river, US; people &
  language)
  plural Dela|ware or
  Dela|wares
De La Warr, Baron
  (English colonial
  administrator)
de|lay +s +ed +ing
de|lay|able
delayed-action
  *adjective preceding a
  noun*
de|lay|er +s
delay line +s
Del|brück, Max
  (German-born US
  biologist)
dele (delete; deletion)
  deles
  deled
  dele|ing
  [☞ deal]
de|lect|able +s
de|lect|ably
de|lect|a|tion
De|led|da, Gra|zia
  (Italian novelist)
del|eg|able
del|eg|acy
  del|eg|acies
dele|gate
  dele|gates
  dele|gat|ed
  dele|gat|ing
delegate-general
  del|egates-general
dele|ga|tion +s
de|legit|im|iz|a|tion
  +s

de|legit|im|ize
  de|legit|im|iz|es
  de|legit|im|ized
  de|legit|im|iz|ing
de Les|seps,
  Fer|di|nand Marie,
  Vi|comte (French
  diplomat)
de|lete
  de|letes
  de|let|ed
  de|let|ing
dele|teri|ous
dele|ter|ious|ly
de|letion +s
Delft (town,
  Netherlands;
  pottery)
Delft|ware
Delhi (union territory
  & city, India)
deli +s (delicatessen)
Del|ian +s
de|lib|er|ate
  de|lib|er|ates
  de|lib|er|at|ed
  de|lib|er|at|ing
de|lib|er|ate|ly
de|lib|er|ate|ness
de|lib|er|a|tion +s
de|lib|era|tive
de|lib|era|tive|ly
de|lib|era|tive|ness
de|lib|er|ator +s
De|libes, (Clé|ment
  Phili|bert) Léo
  (French composer)
deli|cacy
  deli|ca|cies
deli|cate
deli|cate|ly
deli|cate|ness
deli|ca|tes|sen +s
De|li|cious (apple)
  plural De|li|cious
de|li|cious
de|li|cious|ly
de|li|cious|ness
delict +s
de|light +s +ed +ing
de|light|ed *adjective*
de|light|ed|ly
de|light|ful
de|light|ful|ly
de|light|ful|ness
De|lilah (*Bible*)
de|limit +s +ed +ing
de|limit|a|tion +s
de|lin|eate
  de|lin|eates
  de|lineat|ed
  de|lineat|ing
de|linea|tion +s

de|linea|tor +s
de|lin|quency
  de|lin|quen|cies
de|lin|quent +s
de|lin|quent|ly
deli|quesce
  deli|ques|ces
  deli|quesced
  deli|ques|cing
deli|ques|cence
deli|ques|cent
de|liri|ous
de|liri|ous|ly
de|lir|ium +s
de|lir|ium trem|ens
de|list +s +ed +ing
De|lius, Fred|erick
  (English composer)
de|liv|er +s +ed +ing
de|liv|er|abil|ity
de|liv|er|able
de|liv|er|ance +s
de|liv|er|er +s
de|liv|ery
  de|liv|eries
dell +s
Della (waterfall,
  Canada)
della Rob|bia,
  An|drea (Italian
  ceramicist)
della Rob|bia, Luca
  (Italian ceramicist)
de|local|iz|a|tion +s
de|local|ize
  de|local|iz|es
  de|local|ized
  de|local|iz|ing
De|lorme, Phili|bert
  (French architect)
Delors, Jacques
  Lu|cien Jean
  (French statesman)
Delos (island, Greece)
de los An|gel|es,
  Vic|toria (Spanish
  soprano)
de|louse
  de|lous|es
  de|loused
  de|lous|ing
Del|phi (site of oracle,
  ancient Greece)
Del|phic
del|phin|ium +s
del|phin|oid +s
del Sarto, An|drea
  (Italian painter)
Del|son (town,
  Canada)
delt +s
Delta (municipality,
  Canada)

del|ta +s
del|taic
delta rays
delta wave +s
delta wing +s
del|ti|ol|o|gist +s
del|ti|ol|ogy
del|toid +s
de|lude
  de|ludes
  de|lud|ed
  de|lud|ing
de|lud|er +s
del|uge
  del|ug|es
  del|uged
  del|ug|ing
de|lu|sion +s
de|lu|sion|al
de|lu|sive
de|lu|sive|ly
de|lu|sive|ness
de|lu|sory
de|luxe
delve
  delves
  delved
  delv|ing
delv|er +s
de|magnet|iz|a|tion
  +s
de|magnet|ize
  de|magnet|iz|es
  de|magnet|ized
  de|magnet|iz|ing
de|magnet|iz|er +s
dema|gogic
dema|gogue +s
dema|goguery
dema|gogy
de|mand +s +ed +ing
de|mand|er +s
de|mand|ing adjective
de|mand|ing|ly
demand-pull
  in|fla|tion
demand-side
de|man|toid +s
de|mar|cate
  de|mar|cates
  de|mar|cat|ed
  de|mar|cat|ing
de|mar|ca|tion +s
de|mar|ca|tor +s
dé|marche
  dé|marches
de|materi|al|iz|a|tion
  +s
de|materi|al|ize
  de|materi|al|iz|es
  de|materi|al|ized
  de|materi|al|iz|ing

deme +s (Greek
  political division;
  population group)
  [☞ deem]
de|mean +s +ed +ing
  (debase; behave)
  [☞ demesne]
de|mean|ing adjective
de|mean|or +s (use
  demeanour)
de|mean|our +s
de' Med|ici,
  Cath|er|ine (French
  queen)
de' Med|ici, Cos|imo
  (Florentine
  statesman)
de' Med|ici,
  Gio|van|ni (Pope
  Leo X)
de' Med|ici, Lor|enzo
  (Florentine
  statesman and arts
  patron)
de' Med|ici, Maria
  (= Marie de
  Médicis)
de Mé|di|cis, Marie
  (French queen)
de|men|ted adjective
de|men|ted|ly
de|men|ted|ness
de|men|tia +s
de|men|tia prae|cox
Dem|er|ara (river &
  former Dutch colony,
  S America)
dem|er|ara (sugar)
de|merge
  de|mer|ges
  de|merged
  de|mer|ging
de|mer|ger +s
de|merit +s
de|meri|tori|ous
Dem|er|ol proprietary
de|mer|sal
de|mesne +s
  (territory; domain)
  [☞ demean]
Dem|eter (Greek Myth)
demi-glace +s
demi|god +s
demi|god|dess
  demi|god|dess|es
demi|john +s
de|mili|tar|iz|a|tion
  +s
de|mili|tar|ize
  de|mili|tar|iz|es
  de|mili|tar|ized
  de|mili|tar|iz|ing

de Mille, Agnes
  George (US
  choreographer)
  [☞ deMille]
de|Mille, Cecil Blount
  (US filmmaker)
  [☞ de Mille]
demi|mon|daine +s
demi|monde +s
de|min|er|al|iz|a|tion
  +s
de|min|er|al|ize
  de|min|er|al|iz|es
  de|min|er|al|ized
  de|min|er|al|iz|ing
de|min|er|al|ized
  adjective
demi-pension +s
de|mise
  de|mis|es
  de|mised
  de|mis|ing
demi|semi|quaver +s
de|mis|sion +s
de|mist +s +ed +ing
de|mist|er +s
demit
  de|mits
  de|mit|ted
  de|mit|ting
demi|tasse +s
demi|urge +s
demi|urgic
demi|urgic|al
demo +s
demob
  de|mobs
  de|mobbed
  de|mob|bing
de|mobil|iz|a|tion +s
de|mobil|ize
  de|mobil|iz|es
  de|mobil|ized
  de|mobil|iz|ing
dem|oc|racy
  dem|oc|ra|cies
Demo|crat +s
  (supporter of US
  party)
demo|crat +s (in
  general use)
Demo|crat|ic (of US
  party)
demo|crat|ic (in
  general use)
demo|crat|ic|ally
dem|oc|ra|tiz|a|tion
  +s
dem|oc|ra|tize
  dem|oc|ra|tiz|es
  dem|oc|ra|tized
  dem|oc|ra|tiz|ing

De|moc|ri|tus (Greek
philosopher)
dé|mo|dé
de|modu|late
de|modu|lates
de|modu|lat|ed
de|modu|lat|ing
de|modu|la|tion +s
de|modu|la|tor +s
Demo|gor|gon
dem|og|raph|er +s
demo|graph|ic
demo|graph|ic|al
demo|graph|ic|al|ly
demo|graph|ics
dem|og|raphy
dem|oi|selle +s
de|mol|ish
de|mol|ish|es
de|mol|ished
de|mol|ish|ing
de|mol|ish|er +s
demo|li|tion +s
demo|li|tion|ist +s
de|mon +s (spirit etc.)
[☞ daemon]
de|monet|iz|a|tion +s
de|monet|ize
de|monet|iz|es
de|monet|ized
de|monet|iz|ing
de|mon|iac +s
de|mon|iac|al
de|mon|iac|al|ly
de|mon|ic
de|mon|ic|ally
demon|ism
demon|iz|a|tion +s
demon|ize
demon|iz|es
demon|ized
demon|iz|ing
demon|ol|atry
de|mono|logic|al
demon|ol|o|gist +s
demon|ol|ogy
demon|ol|o|gies
de|mon|stra|bil|ity
de|mon|strable
de|mon|strably
dem|on|strate
dem|on|strates
dem|on|strat|ed
dem|on|strat|ing
dem|on|stra|tion +s
dem|on|stra|tion|al
de|mon|stra|tive +s
de|mon|stra|tive|ly
de|mon|stra|tive|
                 ness
dem|on|stra|tor +s

de Monts, Pierre Du
Gua (French
explorer)
de|moral|iz|a|tion +s
de|moral|ize
de|moral|iz|es
de|moral|ized
de|moral|iz|ing
de|moral|iz|ing
adjective
de|moral|iz|ing|ly
De|mos|then|es
(Athenian statesman)
de|mote
de|motes
de|mot|ed
de|mot|ing
dem|otic
de|mo|tion +s
de|motiv|ate
de|motiv|ates
de|motiv|at|ed
de|motiv|at|ing
de|motiv|at|ing
adjective
de|motiv|a|tion +s
de|mount +s +ed
+ing
de|mount|able
Demp|sey, Wil|liam
Har|ri|son ('Jack')
(US boxer)
de|mul|cent +s
demur verb
de|murs
de|murred
de|mur|ring
de|mure adjective
de|mur|er
de|mur|est
de|mure|ly
de|mure|ness
de|mur|er comparative
of demure
[☞ demurrer]
de|mur|rage +s
de|mur|ral +s
de|mur|rer +s (Law)
[☞ demurrer]
de|mysti|fi|ca|tion +s
de|mysti|fy
de|mysti|fies
de|mysti|fied
de|mysti|fy|ing
de|myth|olo|gize
de|myth|olo|giz|es
de|myth|olo|gized
de|myth|olo|giz|ing
den
dens
denned
den|ning
Den|ali (= Mount
McKinley, US)

den|ar|ius
den|arii
den|ary (of ten)
[☞ deanery]
de|nation|al|iz|a|tion
+s
de|nation|al|ize
de|nation|al|iz|es
de|nation|al|ized
de|nation|al|iz|ing
de|natur|al|iz|a|tion
+s
de|natur|al|ize
de|natur|al|iz|es
de|natur|al|ized
de|natur|al|iz|ing
de|natur|ant +s
de|natur|a|tion
de|nature
de|natures
de|natured
de|natur|ing
de|natured adjective
de-nazifi|ca|tion
de-nazify
de-nazifies
de-nazified
de-nazify|ing
Den|bigh|shire
(former county,
Wales)
Dench, Dame Jud|ith
Oliv|ia ('Judi')
(English actress)
den|drite +s
den|drit|ic
den|drit|ic|ally
den|dro|bium +s
den|dro|
          chrono|logic|al
den|dro|
          chron|ol|o|gist +s
den|dro|chron|ol|ogy
den|droid
den|dro|logic|al
den|drol|o|gist +s
den|drol|ogy
Dene (people)
plural Dene
[☞ Dean]
dene +s (valley, vale)
[☞ dean]
Deneb (star)
Denen|deh (proposed
name for NWT)
De|neuve, Cath|er|ine
(French actress)
den|gue
Deng Xiao|ping
(Chinese statesman)
deni|abil|ity
deni|able
de|nial +s

de|nier¹ +s (one who
denies)
den|ier² +s (unit of
weight)
deni|grate
deni|grates
deni|grat|ed
deni|grat|ing
deni|gra|tion
deni|gra|tor +s
deni|gra|tory
denim +s
De Niro, Rob|ert (US
actor)
Denis (saint)
de|nitri|fi|ca|tion
de|nitri|fy
de|nitri|fies
de|nitri|fied
de|nitri|fy|ing
deni|zen +s
deni|zen|ship
Den|mark (country,
Europe)
den moth|er +s
de|nomin|ate
de|nomin|ates
de|nomin|at|ed
de|nomin|at|ing
de|nomin|a|tion +s
de|nomin|a|tion|al
de|nomin|a|tion|al|
                    ism
de|nomin|a|tion|al|
                    ist +s
de|nomin|a|tive
de|nomin|ator +s
Denon|ville,
Jacques-René de
Brisay, Mar|quis de
(governor general of
New France)
de|nota|tion +s
de|nota|tive
de|note
de|notes
de|not|ed
de|not|ing
de|noue|ment +s
de|nounce
de|noun|ces
de|nounced
de|noun|cing
de|nounce|ment +s
de|noun|cer +s
de novo
Den|pasar (city, Bali)
dense
dens|er
dens|est
dense|ly
dense|ness
densi|tom|eter +s

dens|ity
dens|ities
dent +s +ed +ing
den|tal (of teeth)
[☞ dentil]
den|tal floss
den|tal floss|es
den|tal|ium
den|talia
den|tal|ize
den|tal|iz|es
den|tal|ized
den|tal|iz|ing
den|tate
denti|care
den|ticle +s
den|ticu|late
denti|frice +s
den|til +s
(Architecture)
[☞ dental]
denti|lin|gual
den|tin|al
den|tine +s
den|tist +s
dent|istry
den|ti|tion +s
den|ture +s
den|tur|ism
den|tur|ist +s
de|nuclear|iz|a|tion
de|nuclear|ize
de|nuclear|iz|es
de|nuclear|ized
de|nuclear|iz|ing
de|nud|a|tion +s
de|nud|a|tive
de|nude
de|nudes
de|nud|ed
de|nud|ing
de|numer|abil|ity
de|numer|able
de|numer|ably
de|nunci|ate
de|nunci|ates
de|nunci|at|ed
de|nunci|at|ing
de|nunci|a|tion +s
de|nunci|a|tive
de|nunci|ator +s
de|nunci|a|tory
Den|ver +s (city, US;
sandwich)
Den|ver boot +s
Den|ver|ite +s
deny
de|nies
de|nied
deny|ing
Denys (= Denis, saint)
deo|dar +s
de|odor|ant +s

de|odor|iz|a|tion
de|odor|ize
de|odor|iz|es
de|odor|ized
de|odor|iz|ing
de|odor|iz|er +s
Deo gra|tias
de|ontic
de|onto|logic|al
de|ontol|o|gist +s
de|ontol|ogy
Deo vol|ente
de|oxygen|ate
de|oxygen|ates
de|oxygen|at|ed
de|oxygen|at|ing
de|oxygen|at|ed
adjective
de|oxygen|a|tion
de|oxy|ribo|nucleic
dep +s
depan|neur +s
De|par|dieu, Gé|rard
(French actor)
de|part +s +ed +ing
de|part|ed adjective &
noun
de|part|ment +s
de|part|ment|al
de|part|ment|al|ism
de|part|ment|al|
iz|a|tion
de|part|ment|al|ize
de|part|ment|al|
iz|es
de|part|ment|al|ized
de|part|ment|al|
iz|ing
de|part|ment|al|ly
de|par|ture +s
de|pend +s +ed +ing
de|pend|abil|ity
de|pend|able
de|pend|ably
de|pend|ant +s noun
[☞ dependent
adjective]
de|pend|ence
de|pend|ency
de|pend|en|cies
de|pend|ent adjective
(for noun use
dependant)
de|pend|ent|ly
de|person|al|iz|a|tion
de|person|al|ize
de|person|al|iz|es
de|person|al|ized
de|person|al|iz|ing
de|pict +s +ed +ing
de|pict|er +s (use
depictor)
de|pic|tion +s

de|pict|ive
de|pict|or +s
dep|il|ate
dep|il|ates
dep|il|at|ed
dep|il|at|ing
dep|il|a|tion +s
de|pila|tory
de|pila|tor|ies
de Pisan, Chris|tine
(Italian-born French
writer)
de|plane
de|planes
de|planed
de|plan|ing
de|plete
de|pletes
de|plet|ed
de|plet|ing
de|plet|er +s
de|ple|tion +s
de|plor|able
de|plor|ably
de|plore
de|plores
de|plored
de|plor|ing
de|plor|ing|ly
de|ploy +s +ed +ing
de|ploy|ment +s
de|plume
de|plumes
de|plumed
de|plum|ing
de|polar|iz|a|tion +s
de|polar|ize
de|polar|iz|es
de|polar|ized
de|polar|iz|ing
de|polit|i|ciz|a|tion
de|polit|i|cize
de|polit|i|ciz|es
de|polit|i|cized
de|polit|i|ciz|ing
de|poly|mer|iz|a|tion
de|poly|mer|ize
de|poly|mer|iz|es
de|poly|mer|ized
de|poly|mer|iz|ing
de|pon|ent +s
de|popu|late
de|popu|lates
de|popu|lat|ed
de|popu|lat|ing
de|popu|la|tion +s
de|port +s +ed +ing
de|port|able
de|por|ta|tion +s
de|por|tee +s
de|port|ment +s

de|pose
de|pos|es
de|posed
de|pos|ing
de|posit
de|posits
de|posit|ed
de|posit|ing
de|posit|ary (trustee)
de|posit|aries
[☞ depository]
Depos|ition
(Christianity)
depos|ition +s (Law &
general use)
de|posit|or +s
de|posi|tory
(warehouse,
storehouse, etc.; for
trustee use
depositary)
de|posi|tor|ies
depot +s
dep|rav|a|tion +s
(perversion,
corruption)
[☞ deprivation]
de|prave
de|praves
de|praved
de|prav|ing
de|praved adjective
de|prav|ity
de|prav|ities
dep|re|cate (express
disapproval of,
censure; in 'self-
deprecating')
dep|re|cates
dep|re|cat|ed
dep|re|cat|ing
[☞ depreciate]
dep|re|cat|ing|ly
dep|re|ca|tion
(disapproval;
reproach; in 'self-
deprecation')
[☞ depreciation]
dep|re|ca|tive
dep|re|ca|tor +s
dep|re|ca|tory
(expressing
disapproval; in 'self-
deprecatory')
[☞ depreciatory]
de|pre|cia|ble
de|preci|ate (diminish
in value; disparage,
belittle)
de|preci|ates
de|preci|at|ed
de|preci|at|ing
[☞ deprecate]

de|preci|a|tion
(decrease in value;
belittlement)
[☞ deprecation]
de|preci|a|tory (that
depreciates;
disparaging)
[☞ deprecatory]
dep|re|da|tion +s
de|press
    de|press|es
    de|pressed
    de|press|ing
de|pres|sant +s
de|pressed adjective
de|press|ible
de|press|ing adjective
de|press|ing|ly
De|pres|sion (History)
de|pres|sion +s (in
    general use)
De|pres|sion glass
    De|pres|sion
    glass|es
de|pres|sive
de|pres|sor +s
de|pres|sur|iz|a|tion
de|pres|sur|ize
    de|pres|sur|iz|es
    de|pres|sur|ized
    de|pres|sur|iz|ing
dep|riv|a|tion +s
    (dispossession,
    denial; hardship)
[☞ depravation]
de|prive
    de|prives
    de|prived
    de|priv|ing
de|prived adjective
de pro|fun|dis
de|pro|gram
    de|pro|grams
    de|pro|grammed
    de|pro|gram|ming
depth +s
depth|less
depth per|cep|tion
dep|ur|ate
    dep|ur|ates
    dep|ur|at|ed
    dep|ur|at|ing
dep|ur|a|tion
dep|ur|ative
dep|ur|ator +s
depu|ta|tion +s
de|pute
    de|putes
    de|puted
    de|put|ing
depu|tiz|a|tion +s

depu|tize
    depu|tiz|es
    depu|tized
    depu|tiz|ing
dep|uty
    dep|uties
dep|uty chief +s
dep|uty min|is|ter +s
deputy|ship +s
De Quin|cey,
    Thom|as (English
    writer)
de|racin|ate
    de|racin|ates
    de|racin|at|ed
    de|racin|at|ing
de|racin|a|tion +s
de|rail +s +ed +ing
de|rail|leur +s
de|rail|ment +s
De|rain, André
    (French painter)
de|range
    de|ran|ges
    de|ranged
    de|ran|ging
de|ranged adjective
de|range|ment +s
de|ration +s +ed
    +ing
Der|bent (city, Russia)
Derby (city, England;
    horse race)
    Derbies
[☞ Darby]
Derby, Ed|ward
    George Geof|frey
    Smith Stan|ley, 14th
    Earl of (British prime
    minister)
[☞ Darby]
derby (any race; hat)
    der|bies
Derby|shire (county,
    England)
de|regis|ter +s +ed
    +ing
de|regu|late
    de|regu|lates
    de|regu|lat|ed
    de|regu|lat|ing
de|regu|la|tion
de|regu|la|tor +s
de|regu|la|tory
dere|lict +s
dere|lic|tion +s
de|ride
    de|rides
    de|rid|ed
    de|rid|ing
de|rid|er +s
de|rid|ing|ly
de ri|gueur

de|ris|ible
de|rision
de|ri|sive
de|ri|sive|ly
de|ri|sive|ness
de|ri|sory
de|riv|able
der|iv|a|tion +s
der|iv|a|tion|al
de|riv|a|tive +s
de|riv|a|tive|ly
de|rive
    de|rives
    de|rived
    de|riv|ing
derm|a|bra|sion +s
der|mal
derma|titis
derma|to|glyph|ic
derma|to|glyph|ic|
                    ally
derma|to|glyph|ics
derma|to|logic
derma|to|logic|al
derma|to|logic|al|ly
derma|tol|o|gist +s
derma|tol|ogy
der|mic
der|mis
der|nier cri
dero|gate
    dero|gates
    dero|gat|ed
    dero|gat|ing
dero|ga|tion +s
de|rog|a|tive
de|rog|a|tor|i|ly
de|rog|a|tory
der|rick +s
Der|rida, Jacques
    (French philosopher
    & critic)
Der|rid|ean +s
der|rière +s
derring-do (heroic
    courage)
[☞ daring]
der|rin|ger +s
der|ris
Derry (Londonderry)
der|vish
    der|vish|es
DES (diethylstilbestrol)
de Sade, Dona|tien
    Al|phonse
    Fran|çois, Comte
    ('Marquis de Sade',
    French writer)
de|salin|ate
    de|salin|ates
    de|salin|at|ed
    de|salin|at|ing
de|salin|a|tion +s

de|salin|ator +s
de|salin|iz|a|tion +s
de|salin|ize
    de|salin|iz|es
    de|salin|ized
    de|salin|iz|ing
de|salt +s +ed +ing
des|apare|cido +s
Des|Barres, Jo|seph
    Fred|erick Wal|let
    (English surveyor
    and colonial
    administrator in
    BNA)
de|scale
    de|scales
    de|scaled
    de|scal|ing
des|cant +s +ed +ing
Des|cartes, René
    (French philosopher
    & mathematician)
des|cend +s +ed +ing
des|cend|ant +s
des|cend|er +s
des|cend|ible
des|cent +s
    (downward
    movement etc.)
[☞ dissent, decent]
Des|champs, Yvon
    (Cdn comedian)
de|scram|ble
    de|scram|bles
    de|scram|bled
    de|scram|bling
de|scram|bler +s
de|scrib|able
de|scribe
    de|scribes
    de|scribed
    de|scrib|ing
de|scrib|er +s
de|scrip|tion +s
de|scrip|tive
de|scrip|tive|ly
de|scrip|tive|ness
de|scrip|tiv|ism
de|scrip|tiv|ist +s
de|scrip|tor +s
des|cry
    des|cries
    des|cried
    des|cry|ing
dese|crate
    dese|crates
    dese|crat|ed
    dese|crat|ing
dese|cra|tion +s
dese|cra|tor +s
de|seed +s +ed +ing
de|seed|er +s

de|seg|re|gate
de|seg|re|gates
de|seg|re|gat|ed
de|seg|re|gat|ing
de|seg|re|ga|tion
de|select +s +ed +ing
de|selec|tion +s
de|sensi|tiz|a|tion +s
de|sensi|tize
de|sensi|tiz|es
de|sensi|tized
de|sensi|tiz|ing
de|sensi|tiz|er +s
des|ert[1] +s (dry
barren land)
[☞ dessert]
de|sert[2] +s +ed +ing
(abandon; in 'just
deserts')
[☞ dessert]
des|ert boot +s
de|sert|ed adjective
de|sert|er +s
desert|ifi|ca|tion
(Geography)
[☞ decertification]
de|ser|tion +s
des|ert island +s
des|ert rat +s
de|serve
de|serves
de|served
de|serv|ing
de|served adjective
de|serv|ed|ly
de|serv|ed|ness
de|serv|ing adjective
de|serv|ing|ly
de|serv|ing|ness
desex
de|sex|es
de|sexed
de|sex|ing
de|sex|ual|ize
de|sex|ual|iz|es
de|sex|ual|ized
de|sex|ual|iz|ing
Des Gro|seil|liers,
Mé|dard Chouart
(French explorer)
dés|habil|lé
De Sica, Vit|torio
(Italian filmmaker)
desic|cant +s
desic|cate
desic|cates
desic|cat|ed
desic|cat|ing
desic|cat|ed adjective
desic|ca|tion
desic|ca|tive
desic|ca|tor +s
de|sid|era|tive +s

de|sid|er|atum
de|sid|er|ata
de|sign +s +ed +ing
desig|nate
desig|nates
desig|nat|ed
desig|nat|ing
desig|nat|ed adjective
desig|na|tion +s
desig|na|tor +s
de|signed adjective
de|sign|ed|ly
de|sign|er +s
de|sign|ing adjective
de|sir|abil|ity
de|sir|able
de|sir|able|ness
de|sir|ably
de|sire
de|sires
de|sired
de|sir|ing
de|sir|ous
de|sist +s +ed +ing
Des|jar|dins,
Al|phonse (Cdn
founder of caisse
populaire)
desk +s
desk-bound
de|skill +s +ed +ing
desk jock|ey +s
desk|top +s
des|man +s
des|mid +s
Des Moines (city, US)
Des|mou|lins, (Lucie
Sim|plice) Ca|mille
Be|noît (French
writer)
deso|late
deso|lates
deso|lat|ed
deso|lat|ing
deso|lat|ed adjective
deso|late|ly
deso|late|ness
deso|la|tion +s
deso|la|tor +s
de|sorb +s +ed +ing
de|sorp|tion
De Soto, Her|nan|do
(Spanish explorer)
de|spair +s +ed +ing
de|spair|ing adjective
de|spair|ing|ly
des|per|ado
des|per|adoes or
des|per|ados
des|per|ate
des|per|ate|ly
des|per|ate|ness
des|per|a|tion +s

de|spic|able
de|spic|ably
de|spise
de|spis|es
de|spised
de|spis|ing
de|spised adjective
de|spis|er +s
de|spite
de|spoil +s +ed +ing
de|spoil|er +s
de|spoil|ment +s
d'Espoir (bay,
Canada)
de|spoli|a|tion +s
de|spond +s +ed
+ing
de|spond|ence
de|spond|ency
de|spond|ent
de|spond|ent|ly
des|pot +s
des|pot|ic
des|pot|ic|ally
despot|ism
des Prés, Jos|quin
(= des Prez)
des Prez, Jos|quin
(Flemish composer)
des|qua|mate
des|qua|mates
des|qua|mat|ed
des|qua|mat|ing
des|qua|ma|tion
des|quama|tive
des res
plural des res
Des|ro|siers, Rob|ert
Guy (Cdn
choreographer)
Des|sa|lines, Jean
Jacques (Haitian
emperor)
Des|sau (city,
Germany)
des|sert +s (food)
[☞ desert, 'just
deserts']
des|sert spoon +s
dessert|spoon|ful +s
de|stabil|iz|a|tion +s
de|stabil|ize
de|stabil|iz|es
de|stabil|ized
de|stabil|iz|ing
de Staël, Ma|dame
(French writer)
de-Stalin|iz|a|tion
de Stijl
des|tin|a|tion +s
des|tine
des|tines

des|tined
des|tin|ing
des|tined adjective
des|tiny
des|tin|ies
des|ti|tute
des|ti|tu|tion
de|stream +s +ed
+ing
de|stream|ing noun
de-stress (relieve
stress)
de-stress|es
de-stressed
de-stress|ing
[☞ distress]
dest|rier +s
de|stroy +s +ed +ing
de|stroy|er +s
de|struct +s +ed +ing
de|struct|ibil|ity
de|struct|ible
de|struc|tion +s
de|struc|tive
de|struc|tive|ly
de|struc|tive|ness
de|sue|tude
de|sulphur|iz|a|tion
de|sulphur|ize
de|sulphur|iz|es
de|sulphur|ized
de|sulphur|iz|ing
des|ul|tor|i|ly
des|ul|tor|i|ness
des|ul|tory
de|tach
de|tach|es
de|tached
de|tach|ing
de|tach|able
de|tached adjective
de|tach|ed|ly
de|tach|ment +s
de|tail +s +ed +ing
de|tailed adjective
de|tail|ing noun
de|tain +s +ed +ing
de|tain|ee +s
de|tain|er +s
de|tain|ment
de|tan|gle
de|tan|gles
de|tan|gled
de|tan|gling
de|tan|gler +s
de|tect +s +ed +ing
de|tect|able
de|tect|ably
de|tec|tion +s
de|tec|tive +s
de|tec|tor +s

de|tent +s
(mechanical catch)
[☞ détente]
dé|tente +s (easing of
relations)
[☞ detent]
de|ten|tion +s
deter (discourage,
prevent)
de|ters
de|terred
de|ter|ring
[☞ debtor]
de|ter|gent +s
de|teri|or|ate
de|teri|or|ates
de|teri|or|at|ed
de|teri|or|at|ing
de|teri|or|a|tion +s
de|teri|ora|tive
deter|ment
de|ter|min|able
de|ter|min|acy
de|ter|min|ant +s
de|ter|min|ate
de|ter|min|ate|ly
de|ter|min|ate|ness
de|ter|min|a|tion +s
de|ter|mina|tive
de|ter|mina|tive|ly
de|ter|mine
de|ter|mines
de|ter|mined
de|ter|min|ing
de|ter|mined adjective
de|ter|min|ed|ly
de|ter|min|er +s
de|ter|min|ism
de|ter|min|ist +s
de|ter|min|is|tic
de|ter|min|is|tic|ally
de|ter|rence
de|ter|rent +s
de|test +s +ed +ing
de|test|able
de|test|ably
de|test|ation +s
de|test|er +s
de|thatch
de|thatch|es
de|thatched
de|thatch|ing
de|thatch|er +s
de|throne
de|thrones
de|throned
de|thron|ing
de|throned adjective
de|throne|ment +s
deton|ate
deton|ates
deton|at|ed
deton|at|ing

deton|a|tion +s
deton|a|tive
deton|ator +s
de|tour +s +ed +ing
detox
de|tox|es
de|toxed
de|tox|ing
de|toxi|cate
de|toxi|cates
de|toxi|cat|ed
de|toxi|cat|ing
de|toxi|ca|tion +s
de|toxi|fi|ca|tion +s
de|toxify
de|toxi|fies
de|toxi|fied
de|toxi|fy|ing
de|tract +s +ed +ing
de|trac|tion +s
de|tract|or +s
de|train +s +ed +ing
de|train|ment
de|tribal|iz|a|tion
de|tribal|ize
de|tribal|iz|es
de|tribal|ized
de|tribal|iz|ing
detri|ment +s
detri|ment|al
detri|ment|al|ly
de|trital
de|tritus
De|troit (city, US;
river, N America)
de trop
de|tumes|cence
de|tumes|cent
de|tune
de|tunes
de|tuned
de|tun|ing
Deu|ca|lion (Greek
Myth)
deuce +s (two etc.;
misfortune)
[☞ douce]
deuced
deuced|ly
deus ex mach|ina
deu|ter|agon|ist +s
deu|ter|ate
deu|ter|ates
deu|ter|at|ed
deu|ter|at|ing
deu|ter|at|ed adjective
deu|ter|a|tion +s
deu|ter|ium
deu|tero|canon|ical
deu|ter|on +s
Deu|ter|on|omy
(Bible)

Deutsche Mark +s
(= Deutschmark)
Deutsch|mark +s
deut|zia +s
deva +s (divine being)
[☞ diva]
de Val|era, Eamon
(Irish statesman)
de Va|llois, Dame
Nin|ette (English
dancer & ballet
director)
de|valu|a|tion +s
de|value
de|val|ues
de|val|ued
de|valu|ing
Deva|nag|ari
dev|as|tate
dev|as|tates
dev|as|tat|ed
dev|as|tat|ing
dev|as|tat|ing
adjective
dev|as|tat|ing|ly
dev|as|ta|tion +s
dev|as|ta|tor +s
de|vein +s +ed +ing
de|velop +s +ed +ing
de|velop|able
de|velop|er +s
de|velop|ment +s
de|velop|ment|al
de|velop|ment|al|ly
Dev|er|eux, Rob|ert
(2nd Earl of Essex)
Devi (Hinduism)
devi|ance +s
devi|ancy
devi|ant +s
devi|ate
devi|ates
devi|at|ed
devi|at|ing
devi|a|tion +s
devi|a|tion|al
devi|a|tion|ism
devi|a|tion|ist +s
de|vice +s
(contrivance;
scheme; design)
[☞ devise]
Devil (Satan)
devil (in general use)
dev|ils
dev|illed
devil|ling
devil|fish
plural devil|fish or
devil|fish|es
devil|ish
devil|ish|ly
devil|ish|ness

dev|illed adjective
devil-may-care
devil|ment +s
devil|ry
devil|ries
devil's ad|vo|cate +s
devil's bit +s
devil's claw +s
devil's club
devil's darn|ing
nee|dle +s
devil's food cake +s
Devil's Island (off
French Guiana)
devil's ivy
devil's paint|brush
devil's
paint|brush|es
devil's walk|ing
stick +s
devil|try (= devilry)
devil|tries
De|vine, Don|ald
Grant (Cdn
politician)
[☞ Divine]
de|vi|ous
de|vi|ous|ly
de|vi|ous|ness
de|vis|able (that may
be devised;
contrivable)
[☞ divisible]
de|vise (plan, invent;
Law)
de|vis|es
de|vised
de|vis|ing
[☞ device]
de|visee +s
de|vis|er +s (one who
plans or invents)
[☞ devisor, divisor]
de|vis|or +s (Law)
[☞ deviser, divisor]
de|vital|iz|a|tion
de|vital|ize
de|vital|iz|es
de|vital|ized
de|vital|iz|ing
de|vitri|fi|ca|tion
de|vitri|fy
de|vitri|fies
de|vitri|fied
de|vitri|fy|ing
de|void
de|voir +s
devo|lu|tion +s
devo|lu|tion|ary
devo|lu|tion|ism
devo|lu|tion|ist +s

de|volve
  de|volves
  de|volved
  de|volv|ing
de|volve|ment +s
Devon (county,
  England; island,
  Canada)
Devon|ian
Devon|shire
  (= Devon, England;
  cream)
Devon|shire, Vic|tor
  Chris|tian Wil|liam
  Cav|en|dish, 9th
  Duke of (governor
  general of Canada)
de|vote
  de|votes
  de|vot|ed
  de|vot|ing
de|vot|ed adjective
de|vot|ed|ly
de|vot|ed|ness
de|votee +s
de|vo|tion +s
de|vo|tion|al +s
de|vo|tion|al|ism
de|vour +s +ed +ing
de|vour|er +s
de|vour|ing|ly
de|vout
de|vout|ly
de|vout|ness
de Vries, Hugo Marie
  (Dutch botanist &
  geneticist)
dew +s +ed +ing
  (moisture)
  [☞ due]
dewan +s
Dewar, Sir James
  (Scottish physicist)
dewar +s (vacuum
  flask)
de|water +s +ed +ing
dew|berry
  dew|ber|ries
dew|claw +s
dew|drop +s
Dewey, John (US
  philosopher &
  educator)
  [☞ dewy]
Dewey Deci|mal
  Clas|si|fi|ca|tion
dew|i|er
dew|i|est
dew|i|ly
dew|i|ness
de Witt, Johan (Dutch
  politician)
dew|lap +s

DEW Line (Distant
  Early Warning)
de|worm +s +ed +ing
  (rid an animal of
  worms)
  [☞ dew worm]
de|worm|er +s
dew point +s
dew-pond +s
dew worm +s
  (earthworm)
dewy (wet with dew)
  dew|i|er
  dew|i|est
  [☞ Dewey]
dewy-eyed
dexa|metha|sone
Dexe|drine +s
  proprietary
dex|ter
dex|ter|ity
dex|ter|ous (adroit)
dex|ter|ous|ly
dex|ter|ous|ness
dex|tral +s
dex|tral|ity
dex|tral|ly
dex|tran +s
dextro|
  ampheta|mine +s
dextro|meth|or|phan
  hydro|bro|mide
dextro|rota|tion
dextro|rota|tory
dex|trorse
dex|trose (Chemistry)
  [☞ dextrous]
dex|trous
  (= dexterous:
  adroit)
  [☞ dextrose]
dex|trous|ly
  (= dexterously)
dex|trous|ness
  (= dexterousness)
DFC (Distinguished
  Flying Cross)
  DFCs
DFM (Distinguished
  Flying Medal)
  DFMs
DG (director general)
  DGs
DH (designated hitter)
  • noun
    DHs
  • verb
    DH's
    DH'd
    DH'ing
Dhaka (capital of
  Bangladesh)

dhal +s (lentil: use dal)
  [☞ Dahl, Dall
  sheep]
Dhan|bad (city, India)
dhan|sak
dhar|ma
dhar|na
Dhar|uk
Dhaula|giri
  (mountain, the
  Himalayas)
dhobi +s
Dho|far (province,
  Oman)
dho|lak +s
dhoti +s
dhow +s (ship)
  [☞ Dou, Tao]
dhur|na (use dharna)
dhur|ra +s (use durra)
dhur|rie +s
DI (Detective
  Inspector; drill
  instructor;
  designated import)
  DIs
dia|base +s
dia|betes
dia|betes in|sip|idus
dia|betes mel|li|tus
dia|bet|ic +s
diab|lerie
dia|bol|ic
dia|bol|ic|al
dia|bol|ic|al|ly
diab|ol|ism
diab|ol|ist +s
diab|ol|ize
  diab|ol|iz|es
  diab|ol|ized
  diab|ol|iz|ing
diab|olo +s
dia|chron|ic
dia|chron|ic|ally
di|achron|ism
di|achron|is|tic
di|achron|ous
di|achrony
di|ac|onal
di|ac|on|ate +s
dia|crit|ic +s
dia|crit|ic|al +s
dia|dem +s
Diad|ochi
  (Macedonian
  generals)
di|aer|esis
  di|aer|eses
dia|gen|esis
dia|gen|etic
Di|aghi|lev, Ser|gei
  Pav|lo|vich (Russian
  ballet impresario)

diag|nos|able
diag|nose
diag|nos|es
diag|nosed
diag|nos|ing
diag|no|sis
diag|no|ses
diag|nos|tic +s
diag|nos|tic|ally
diag|nos|ti|cian +s
diag|nos|tics
di|ag|on|al +s
di|ag|on|al|ly
dia|gram
dia|grams
dia|grammed
dia|gram|ming
dia|gram|mat|ic
dia|gram|mat|ic|ally
dia|kin|esis
di|akin|eses
dial (numbered face of
  a clock or telephone
  etc.; knob)
  dials
  dialed or dialled
  dial|ing or dial|ling
  [☞ diol]
dia|lect +s
dia|lect|al
dia|lect|ic +s
dia|lect|ic|al
dia|lect|ic|al|ly
dia|lect|ician
dia|lect|o|logic|al
dia|lect|ol|o|gist +s
dia|lect|ol|ogy
dial|er +s
dial|ler +s (use dialer)
dia|logic
dia|logic|al
dialo|gist +s
dia|logue
  dia|logues
  dia|logued
  dia|loguing
dial tone +s
dial up verb
  dials up
  dialed up
  or dialled up
  dial|ing up
  or dial|ling up
dial-up adjective
di|aly|sis
  di|aly|ses
dia|lyt|ic
dia|lyz|able
dia|lyze
  dia|lyz|es
  dia|lyzed
  dia|lyz|ing
dia|lyz|er +s

dia|mag|net|ic
dia|mag|net|ic|ally
dia|mag|net|ism
dia|manté
dia|man|tine
diam|eter +s
diam|etral
dia|met|ric
dia|met|ric|al
dia|met|ric|al|ly
dia|mine +s
dia|mond +s
dia|mond|back +s
dia|mond drill +s
  +ed +ing
Dia|mond Head
  (volcanic crater,
  Hawaii)
dia|mond|if|er|ous
dia|mond point +s
  (diamond-point
  when preceding a
  noun)
Diana (*Roman Myth*;
  English princess)
Dia|net|ics
dian|thus
  plural dian|thus or
  dian|thus|es
dia|pa|son +s
dia|pause
  dia|paus|es
  dia|paused
  dia|paus|ing
dia|per +s +ed +ing
  (absorbent cloth;
  Textiles; diamond
  pattern)
  [☞ diapir]
di|aph|an|ous
dia|phor|esis
dia|phor|et|ic +s
dia|phragm +s
dia|phrag|mat|ic
dia|pir +s (*Geology*)
  [☞ diaper]
dia|pir|ic
dia|pir|ic|ally
dia|pir|ism
di|arch|al
di|arch|ic
di|archy
  di|arch|ies
diar|ist +s
diar|is|tic
diar|rhea
diar|rheal
diar|rhet|ic (of
  diarrhea)
  [☞ diuretic,
  dioritic]
diary
  diar|ies

Dias, Bar|tolo|meu
  (Portuguese
  explorer)
  [☞ Díaz]
Di|as|pora *Judaism*
di|as|pora +s (*in
  general use*)
dias|poric
di|as|por|ist +s
dia|stase +s
dia|stas|ic
dia|stat|ic
dia|stole +s
dia|stol|ic
dia|thermy
diath|esis
dia|tom +s
dia|tom|aceous
  earth
dia|tom|ic
di|atom|ite +s
dia|ton|ic
dia|tribe +s
Díaz, Bar|tolo|meu
  (= Dias)
Díaz, Por|firio
  (Mexican president)
  [☞ Dias]
Díaz de Vivar,
  Rod|rigo (El Cid)
  [☞ Dias]
di|aze|pam +s
di|az|inon
diazo
diazo com|pound +s
di|basic
dib|ber +s
dib|ble +s
d'Iber|ville, Pierre Le
  Moyne (French-Cdn
  explorer)
dibs
dice
  • *plural of* die
  (numbered cube;
  Architecture)
  • *singular noun*
  (numbered cube)
  plural dice
  • *verb & noun* (cut food
  in cubes; gamble)
  dices
  diced
  dicing
  [☞ dais]
dicer +s
dicey
  dicier
  dici|est
di|cho|tomic
di|chot|om|ize
  di|chot|om|iz|es

di|chot|om|ized
di|chot|om|iz|ing
di|chot|om|ous
di|chot|omy
di|chot|om|ies
di|chro|ic
di|chro|ism
di|chro|matic
di|chro|ma|tism
dicier
dici|est
dick +s +ed +ing
  [☞ dik-dik]
Dick|ens, Charles
  John Huf|fam
  (English novelist)
dick|ens (in 'what the
  dickens' etc.)
Dick|ens|ian +s
Dick|ens|ian|ly
dick|er +s +ed +ing
Dick|ey, Rob|ert B.
  (Cdn politician)
dick|ey +s
  (automobile seat; *for*
  false shirt front *use*
  dickie)
  [☞ dicky, dickie]
dickey-bird +s (*use*
  dicky-bird)
dick|head +s
dick|ie +s (false shirt
  front; bow tie)
  [☞ dicky, dickey]
dickie-bow +s
Dick|in|son
dicky
  • *adjective* (unsound)
  dick|i|er
  dick|i|est
  • *noun* (automobile
  seat: *use* dickey)
  dick|ies
  [☞ dickie]
dicky-bird +s
dicot +s
di|coty|ledon +s
di|coty|ledon|ous
di|crot|ic
dicta
Dicta|phone +s
  proprietary
dic|tate
  dic|tates
  dic|tated
  dic|tat|ing
dic|ta|tion +s
dic|ta|tor +s
dic|ta|tor|ial
dic|ta|tor|ial|ly
dic|ta|tor|ship +s
dic|tion +s

dic|tion|ary
dic|tion|ar|ies
dic|tum
  dicta or dic|tums
dicty
did
di|dac|tic
di|dac|tic|ally
di|dac|ti|cism
did|dle
  did|dles
  did|dled
  did|dling
did|dler +s
did|dley (*use* diddly)
diddley-squat (*use
  diddly-squat*)
did|dly
diddly-squat
did|dums
Di|derot, Denis
  (French writer)
didger|idoo +s
didjer|idoo +s (*use
  didgeridoo*)
didn't
Dido (in the *Aeneid*)
dido
  didoes or didos
didst
Didy|ma (ancient
  sanctuary to Apollo)
di|dym|ium
die
  • *verb* (expire etc.)
  dies
  died
  dying
  • *noun* (numbered
  cube; *Architecture*)
  plural dice
  • *noun* (tool for
  stamping, engraving,
  etc.)
  plural dies
  [☞ dye]
die|back +s
die-cast
  die-casts
  die-cast
  die-casting
die-casting +s *noun*
Dief|en|baker (lake,
  Canada)
Dief|en|baker, John
  George (Cdn prime
  minister)
dief|fen|bachia +s
Diego Gar|cia (island,
  Indian Ocean)
die|hard +s
die-in +s
di|el|drin

di|elec|tric +s
di|elec|tric|ally
diem (in 'carpe diem' &
'per diem')
Dien Bien Phu (battle
site, Vietnam)
di|ene +s
die-off +s
Di|eppe (battle site,
France; town,
Canada)
Diesel, Ru|dolf
Chris|tian Karl
(German engineer)
diesel +s (engine etc.)
[☞ deasil]
diesel-electric +s
diesel|ing (use
dieselling)
diesel|iz|a|tion
diesel|ize
diesel|iz|es
diesel|ized
diesel|iz|ing
diesel|ling
Dies irae
die stamped
die stamp|ing
diet +s +ed +ing
diet|ary
diet|er +s
diet|etic
diet|etic|ally
diet|et|ics
di|ethyl|amide
di|ethyl ether
di|ethyl|stil|bes|trol
diet|ician +s (use
dietitian)
diet|itian +s
Diet|rich, Mar|lene
(German-born
entertainer)
diff
dif|fer +s +ed +ing
(be unlike; disagree)
[☞ defer]
dif|fer|ence (state of
being different, etc.)
dif|fer|en|ces
dif|fer|enced
dif|fer|en|cing
[☞ deference]
dif|fer|ent
dif|fer|en|tia
dif|fer|en|tiae
dif|fer|en|ti|able
dif|fer|en|tial (of
difference; Math;
gear)
[☞ deferential]
dif|fer|en|tial|ly
[☞ deferentially]

dif|fer|en|ti|ate
dif|fer|en|ti|ates
dif|fer|en|ti|at|ed
dif|fer|en|ti|at|ing
dif|fer|en|ti|at|ed
adjective
dif|fer|en|ti|a|tion +s
dif|fer|en|ti|ator +s
dif|fer|ent|ly
dif|fer|ent|ness
dif|fer|ing adjective
dif|fi|cult
dif|fi|cult|ly
dif|fi|cult|ness
dif|fi|culty
dif|fi|cul|ties
dif|fi|dence
dif|fi|dent
dif|fi|dent|ly
dif|fract +s +ed +ing
dif|frac|tion +s
dif|fract|ive
dif|fract|ive|ly
dif|fract|om|eter +s
dif|fuse (spread
widely)
dif|fus|es
dif|fused
dif|fus|ing
[☞ defuse]
dif|fused adjective
dif|fuse|ly
dif|fuse|ness
dif|fus|er +s
dif|fus|ible
dif|fu|sion +s
dif|fu|sion|ism
dif|fu|sion|ist +s
dif|fu|sive
dif|fus|or +s (use
diffuser)
dig
digs
dug
dig|ging
Digam|bara +s
di|gamma +s
Digby (town, Canada)
di|gest +s +ed +ing
di|gest|ant +s
di|gest|er +s
di|gest|ibil|ity
di|gest|ible
di|ges|tif +s noun
(drink etc. that aids
digestion; for cookie
use digestive)
[☞ digestive]
di|ges|tion +s
di|gest|ive +s
adjective & noun
(cookie etc. that aids

digestion; for drink
use digestif)
di|gest|ive|ly
Dig|ger +s (English
dissenter)
dig|ger +s
dig|gings
dight
digit +s
digit|al +s
digit|al audio tape
+s
digi|talin
digi|talis
digit|al|ize
digit|al|iz|es
digit|al|ized
digit|al|iz|ing
digit|al|ly
digit|al to ana|log
con|vert|er +s
digi|tate
digi|tate|ly
digi|ta|tion
digi|ti|grade +s
digit|iz|a|tion +s
digit|ize
digit|iz|es
digit|ized
digit|iz|ing
digit|iz|er +s
digni|fied adjective
digni|fied|ly
dig|nify
digni|fies
digni|fied
digni|fy|ing
digni|tary
digni|tar|ies
dig|nity
digni|ties
digox|in
di|graph +s
di|graph|ic
di|gress
di|gress|es
di|gressed
di|gress|ing
di|gress|er +s
di|gres|sion +s
di|gres|sive (tending
to digress)
[☞ degressive]
di|gres|sive|ly
di|gres|sive|ness
digs (lodgings)
di|hed|ral
di|hyd|ric
Dijon (city, France;
mustard)
dik-dik +s

dike (wall, ditch, etc.;
for lesbian use dyke)
dikes
diked
diking
dik|tat +s
di|lapi|date
di|lapi|dates
di|lapi|dat|ed
di|lapi|dat|ing
di|lapi|dat|ed
adjective
di|lapi|da|tion
di|lat|able
dila|ta|tion +s
dila|ta|tion|al
di|late
di|lates
di|lat|ed
di|lat|ing
di|la|tion +s
di|la|tor +s
dila|tor|i|ly
dila|tor|i|ness
dila|tory
dil|do +s
di|lem|ma +s
dil|et|tante
dil|et|tantes or
dil|et|tanti
dil|et|tant|ish
dil|et|tant|ism
Dili (city, Timor)
dili|gence +s
dili|gent
dili|gent|ly
dill +s
dill pickle +s
dill|weed
dilly
dil|lies
dil|li|er
dil|li|est
dilly|bag +s
dilly-dally
dilly-dallies
dilly-dallied
dilly-dallying
dilu|ent +s
di|lute
di|lutes
di|lut|ed
di|lut|ing
di|lut|ed adjective
di|lut|er +s
di|lu|tion +s
di|lu|vi|al
di|lu|vi|um
di|lu|via
dim
dim|mer
dim|mest

dims
dimmed
dim|ming
Di|Maggio, Jo|seph
  Paul ('Joe') (US
  baseball player)
dim-bulb +s
dime +s
dime bag +s
di|men|hy|drin|ate
dime novel +s
di|men|sion +s +ed
  +ing
di|men|sion|al
di|men|sion|al|ity
  di|men|sion|al|ities
di|men|sion|al|ly
di|men|sion|less
dimer +s
di|meric
di|mer|ous
dime store +s (dime-
  store *when preceding*
  a noun)
dim|eter +s (*Prosody*)
  [☞ Demeter]
dimin|ish
  dimin|ish|es
  dimin|ished
  dimin|ish|ing
dimin|ish|able
dimin|ished *adjective*
dimin|ish|ment +s
di|minu|endo +s
dim|in|u|tion +s
di|minu|tiv|al
di|minu|tive +s
di|minu|tive|ly
di|minu|tive|ness
dim|ity
  dimi|ties
dimly
dim|mer +s
dim|mer switch
  dim|mer switch|es
dim|mish
dim|ness
di|morph|ic
di|morph|ism
di|morph|ous
dim|ple
  dim|ples
  dim|pled
  dim|pling
dim|pled *adjective*
dim|ply
dim sum
  plural dim sum
dim-wit +s
dim-witted
din
  dins

dinned
din|ning
di|nar +s
Di|nar|ic Alps
  (mountains, Balkans)
din-din
din-dins (= din-din)
d'Indy, (Paul Marie
  Théo|dore) Vin|cent
  (French musician)
dine (eat)
  dines
  dined
  din|ing
  [☞ dyne]
din|er +s
di|nero
Din|esen, Isak
  (Danish writer)
din|ette +s
ding +s +ed +ing
ding-a-ling +s
Ding an sich
ding|bat +s
ding-dong +s
ding|er +s
din|ghy (boat)
  din|ghies
din|gi|er
din|gi|est
din|gi|ly
din|gi|ness
din|gle +s
dingo
  din|goes
din|gus
  din|gus|es
dingy (dirty, drab)
  din|gi|er
  din|gi|est
  [☞ dinghy]
din|ing *noun*
din|ing car +s
din|ing room +s
  (dining-room *when*
  preceding a noun)
dink +s +ed +ing
Dinka
  plural Dinka or
  Din|kas
din|kum
dinky
  dink|i|er
  dink|i|est
  dink|ies
din|ner +s
din|ner jack|et +s
dinner-jacketed
din|ner plate +s
dinner|time
dinner|ware
dino +s
dino|flagel|late +s

dino|saur +s
dino|saur|ian +s
dino|there +s
dint +s +ed +ing
dio|cesan +s
dio|cese +s
Dio|cle|tian (Roman
  emperor)
di|ode +s
di|oe|cious
Di|og|enes (Greek
  philosopher)
diol +s (*Chemistry*)
Dio|medes (*Greek
  Myth*)
Dion, Cé|line (Cdn
  singer)
  [☞ Dione, Dionne]
Dione (*Greek Myth*;
  moon of Saturn)
  [☞ Dion, Dionne]
Di|onne, Cé|cile,
  Yvonne, Émi|lie,
  An|nette, & Marie
  (Cdn quintuplets)
  [☞ Dion, Dione]
Di|onne, Mar|cel (Cdn
  hockey player)
  [☞ Dion, Dione]
Dio|nys|iac
Dio|nys|ian
  (= Dionysiac)
Dio|nys|ius, ('the
  Elder') (ruler of
  Syracuse)
Dio|nys|ius Ex|igu|us
  (Scythian
  chronologer)
Dio|nys|ius of
  Hali|car|nas|sus
  (Greek historian)
Dio|nys|us (*Greek
  Myth*)
  [☞ Dionysius]
di|op|ter +s (*use*
  dioptre)
di|optre +s
di|op|tric
di|op|trics
Dior, Chris|tian
  (French designer)
dio|rama +s
dio|ram|ic
dio|rite +s
dio|rit|ic (of diorite)
  [☞ diuretic,
  diarrhetic]
Dios|curi (*Greek Myth*)
di|ox|an (solvent)
  [☞ dioxin]
di|ox|ane (= dioxan)
di|ox|ide +s

di|ox|in +s (TCDD
  etc.)
  [☞ dioxan]
DIP (*Computing*)
  DIPs
dip
  dips
  dipped
  dip|ping
di|pep|tide +s
di|phen|hydra|mine
di|phos|phate +s
diph|ther|ia
diph|ther|ial
diph|ther|ic
diph|ther|it|ic
diph|ther|oid
diph|thong +s
diph|thong|al
diph|thong|iz|a|tion
diph|thong|ize
  diph|thong|iz|es
  diph|thong|ized
  diph|thong|iz|ing
diplo|coc|cus
  diplo|cocci
dip|lod|ocus
  dip|lod|ocus|es
dip|loid +s
dip|loidy
dip|lo|ma +s
dip|lo|macy
dip|lo|mat +s
  (member of the
  diplomatic corps)
dip|lo|mate +s
  (person holding a
  diploma)
dip|lo|mat|ic
dip|lo|mat|ic|ally
dip|lo|mat|ist +s
dip|lont +s
dip|lo|pia
dip|lo|tene +s
dip net +s
di|polar
di|pole +s
dip|per +s
dipper|ful +s
dip|pi|ness
dippy
  dip|pi|er
  dip|pi|est
dip|shit +s
dip|so +s
dip|so|mania
dip|so|maniac +s
dip|stick +s
DIP switch
  (*Computing*)
  DIP switch|es

dip switch
(*Automotive*)
dip switch|es
dipsy-doodle
dipsy-doodles
dipsy-doodled
dipsy-doodling
dip|teran +s
dip|ter|ous
dip|tych +s
**Dirac, Paul Ad|rian
Mau|rice** (English
physicist)
dire (grave; ominous;
urgent)
direr
dir|est
[☞ dyer]
dir|ect +s +ed +ing
direct-dial *verb &
adjective*
direct-dials
direct-dialed or
direct-dialled
direct-dialing or
direct-dialling
dir|ect dial|ing *noun*
dir|ect drive (direct-
drive *when preceding
a noun*)
dir|ec|tion +s
dir|ec|tion|al
dir|ec|tion|al|ity
dir|ec|tion|al|ly
dir|ec|tion|less
dir|ec|tive +s
dir|ect|ly
dir|ect|ness
Di|rec|toire
dir|ec|tor +s
dir|ec|tor|ate
dir|ec|tor gen|er|al
  dir|ec|tors gen|er|al
dir|ec|tor|ial
dir|ector's chair +s
dir|ec|tor|ship +s
Dir|ec|tory (*French
History*)
dir|ec|tory (*in general
use*)
  dir|ec|tor|ies
dir|ec|tory
  as|sist|ance
dir|ec|tress
dir|ec|trix
  dir|ec|tri|ces
dire|ful
dire|ful|ly
dire|ly
dire|ness
dirge +s
dirge|ful

dir|ham +s
(Moroccan currency)
[☞ Durham]
diri|gible
diri|gisme
diri|giste
dirk +s
dirndl +s
dirt
dirt bike +s
dirt cheap (dirt-
cheap *when
preceding a noun*)
dirt|i|ly
dirt|i|ness
dirt poor (dirt-poor
*when preceding a
noun*)
dirt road +s
dirty
dirt|i|er
dirt|i|est
dirt|ies
dirt|ied
dirty|ing
dirty thir|ties
dirty trick +s
dirty-trickster +s
dis
dis|ses
dissed
dis|sing
dis|abil|ity
dis|abil|ities
dis|able
dis|ables
dis|abled
dis|ab|ling
dis|abled *adjective*
dis|able|ment
dis|abuse
dis|abus|es
dis|abused
dis|abus|ing
di|sac|char|ide +s
dis|accord
dis|advan|tage
dis|advan|ta|ges
dis|advan|taged
dis|advan|ta|ging
dis|advan|taged
adjective
dis|advan|ta|geous
dis|advan|ta|geous|
  ly
dis|affect|ed
dis|affect|ed|ly
dis|affec|tion
dis|af|fili|ate
dis|af|fili|ates
dis|af|fili|ated
dis|af|fili|at|ing
dis|af|fili|a|tion

dis|affirm +s +ed
+ing
dis|affirm|a|tion
dis|aggre|gate
dis|aggre|gates
dis|aggre|gat|ed
dis|aggre|gat|ing
dis|aggre|ga|tion
dis|agree
dis|agrees
dis|agreed
dis|agree|ing
dis|agree|able
dis|agree|able|ness
dis|agree|ably
dis|agree|ment +s
dis|allow +s +ed
+ing
dis|allow|ance +s
dis|am|bigu|ate
dis|am|bigu|ates
dis|am|bigu|at|ed
dis|am|bigu|at|ing
dis|am|bigu|a|tion +s
dis|appear +s +ed
+ing
dis|appear|ance +s
dis|appoint +s +ed
+ing
dis|appoint|ed
adjective
dis|appoint|ed|ly
dis|appoint|ing
adjective
dis|appoint|ing|ly
dis|appoint|ment +s
dis|ap|pro|ba|tion
dis|ap|prov|al +s
dis|ap|prove
dis|ap|proves
dis|ap|proved
dis|ap|prov|ing
dis|ap|prov|ing
adjective
dis|ap|prov|ing|ly
dis|arm +s +ed +ing
dis|arma|ment +s
dis|arm|er +s
dis|arm|ing *adjective*
dis|arm|ing|ly
dis|arrange
dis|arran|ges
dis|arranged
dis|arran|ging
dis|arrange|ment +s
dis|array
dis|arti|cu|late
dis|arti|cu|lates
dis|arti|cu|lat|ed
dis|arti|cu|lat|ing
dis|arti|cu|la|tion +s

dis|assem|ble
dis|assem|bles
dis|assem|bled
dis|assem|bling
dis|assem|bler +s
dis|assem|bly
dis|associ|ate
dis|associ|ates
dis|associ|at|ed
dis|associ|at|ing
dis|associ|a|tion +s
dis|as|ter +s
dis|as|trous
dis|as|trous|ly
dis|avow +s +ed +ing
dis|avow|al +s
dis|band +s +ed +ing
dis|band|ment +s
dis|bar
dis|bars
dis|barred
dis|bar|ring
dis|bar|ment +s
dis|belief
dis|believe
dis|be|lieves
dis|be|lieved
dis|believ|ing
dis|believ|er +s
dis|believ|ing|ly
dis|bud
dis|buds
dis|budded
dis|bud|ding
dis|burden +s +ed
+ing
dis|bur|sal +s (act of
disbursing; money
paid out)
[☞ dispersal]
dis|burse (spend
money)
dis|burs|es
dis|bursed
dis|burs|ing
[☞ disperse]
dis|burse|ment +s
dis|burs|er +s (one
who disburses)
[☞ disperser]
disc +s
• *Disc* is preferred
for audio and video
recording terms
(*laser disc, Mini Disc,
disc jockey, disco*).
Use *disk* for
computer storage
devices other than
compact disc (*floppy
disk, optical disk,
diskette*), and for any
verb sense. In all
other cases except

for *disker* and *disk*
harrow use *disc* (*disc-shaped, disc brake, slipped disc*).
[☞ disk]
dis|calced
dis|card +s +ed +ing
dis|card|able
dis|car|nate
discar|na|tion
disc brake +s
dis|cern +s +ed +ing
dis|cern|er +s
dis|cern|ible
dis|cern|ibly
dis|cern|ing *adjective*
dis|cern|ing|ly
dis|cern|ment
dis|charge
  dis|char|ges
  dis|charged
  dis|char|ging
dis|charge|able
dis|char|ger +s
dis|ciple +s
dis|ciple|ship +s
disci|plin|able
disci|plin|ar|ian +s
disci|plin|ary
disci|pline
  disci|plines
  disci|plined
  disci|plin|ing
disc jock|ey +s
dis|claim +s +ed
  +ing
dis|claim|er +s
dis|close
  dis|clos|es
  dis|closed
  dis|clos|ing
dis|clos|er +s
dis|clos|ing *adjective*
dis|clo|sure +s
disc num|ber +s
disco
  • *noun*
  dis|cos
  • *verb*
  dis|coes
  dis|coed
  disco|ing
disc|ob|olus
  disc|ob|oli
disc|og|raph|er +s
disc|o|graph|ic|al
disc|og|raphy
  disc|og|raph|ies
disc|oid
dis|color +s +ed +ing
  (*use* discolour)
dis|color|a|tion +s

dis|colour +s +ed
  +ing
dis|colour|a|tion +s
  (*use* discoloration)
dis|com|bobu|late
dis|com|bobu|lates
dis|com|bobu|lat|ed
dis|com|bobu|lat|
           ing
dis|com|bobu|la|tion
dis|com|fit
  dis|com|fits
  dis|com|fit|ed
  dis|com|fit|ing
dis|com|fi|ture
  dis|com|fi|tures
  dis|com|fi|tured
  dis|com|fi|tur|ing
dis|com|fort +s +ed
  +ing
dis|com|mode
  dis|com|modes
  dis|com|mod|ed
  dis|com|mod|ing
dis|com|pose
  dis|com|pos|es
  dis|com|posed
  dis|com|pos|ing
dis|com|po|sure
dis|con|cert +s +ed
  +ing
dis|con|cert|ed|ly
dis|con|cert|ing
  adjective
dis|con|cert|ing|ly
dis|con|cer|tion
dis|con|cert|ment
dis|con|firm +s +ed
  +ing
dis|con|firm|a|tion
dis|con|form|ity
  dis|con|form|ities
dis|con|nect +s +ed
  +ing
dis|con|nect|ed
  adjective
dis|con|nect|ed|ly
dis|con|nect|ed|ness
dis|con|nec|tion +s
dis|con|so|late
dis|con|so|late|ly
dis|con|so|late|ness
dis|con|so|la|tion
dis|con|tent +s
dis|con|tent|ed
dis|con|tent|ed|ly
dis|con|tent|ed|ness
dis|con|tent|ment
dis|con|tinu|ance
dis|con|tinu|a|tion
dis|con|tinue
  dis|con|tinues

dis|con|tinued
dis|con|tinu|ing
dis|con|tinu|ity
  dis|con|tinu|ities
dis|con|tinu|ous
dis|con|tinu|ous|ly
dis|cord +s +ed +ing
dis|cord|ance +s
dis|cord|ancy
dis|cord|ant
dis|cord|ant|ly
disco|theque +s
dis|count +s +ed
  +ing
dis|count|able
dis|coun|ten|ance
  dis|coun|ten|an|ces
  dis|coun|ten|anced
  dis|coun|ten|an|cing
dis|count|er +s
dis|cour|age
  dis|cour|ages
  dis|cour|aged
  dis|cour|aging
dis|cour|age|ment +s
dis|cour|aging
  adjective
dis|cour|aging|ly
dis|course
  dis|cours|es
  dis|coursed
  dis|cours|ing
dis|cour|te|ous
dis|cour|te|ous|ly
dis|cour|te|ous|ness
dis|cour|tesy
  dis|cour|tes|ies
dis|cov|er +s +ed
  +ing
dis|cov|er|able
dis|cov|er|er +s
dis|cov|ery
  dis|cov|er|ies
Dis|cov|ery Day +s
dis|credit +s +ed
  +ing
dis|credit|able
dis|credit|ably
dis|credit|ed *adjective*
dis|creet +er +est
  (circumspect, tactful)
  [☞ discrete]
dis|creet|ly (tactfully)
  [☞ discretely]
dis|creet|ness (tact)
  [☞ discreteness]
dis|crep|ancy
  dis|crep|an|cies
dis|crep|ant
dis|crete (distinct)
  [☞ discreet]

dis|crete|ly
  (distinctly)
  [☞ discreetly]
dis|crete|ness
  (separateness)
  [☞ discreetness]
dis|cre|tion
dis|cre|tion|ary
dis|crimin|ant +s
dis|crimin|ate
  dis|crimin|ates
  dis|crimin|at|ed
  dis|crimin|at|ing
dis|crimin|ate|ly
dis|crimin|at|ing
  adjective
dis|crimin|at|ing|ly
dis|crimin|a|tion +s
dis|crimin|a|tive
dis|crimin|ator +s
dis|crimin|a|tory
dis|cur|sive
dis|cur|sive|ly
dis|cur|sive|ness
dis|cus (disc)
  dis|cus|es
  [☞ discuss]
dis|cuss (talk about;
  debate)
  dis|cuss|es
  dis|cussed
  dis|cuss|ing
  [☞ discus]
dis|cuss|able
dis|cuss|ant +s
dis|cuss|er +s
dis|cus|sion +s
dis|dain +s +ed +ing
dis|dain|ful
dis|dain|ful|ly
dis|ease +s
dis|eased
dis|econ|omy
  dis|econ|omies
dis|em|bark +s
dis|em|bark|a|tion +s
dis|em|bod|ied
  adjective
dis|em|bodi|ment +s
dis|em|body
  dis|em|bod|ies
  dis|em|bod|ied
  dis|em|body|ing
dis|em|bogue
  dis|em|bogues
  dis|em|bogued
  dis|em|boguing
dis|em|bowel
  dis|em|bowels
  dis|em|bow|elled
  dis|em|bowel|ling
dis|em|bow|elled
  adjective

dis|em|bowel|ment +s
dis|em|power +s +ed +ing
dis|em|powered *adjective*
dis|em|power|ment +s
dis|en|chant +s +ed +ing
dis|en|chant|ed *adjective*
dis|en|chant|ment +s
dis|en|cum|ber +s +ed +ing
dis|en|fran|chise
dis|en|fran|chis|es
dis|en|fran|chised
dis|en|fran|chis|ing
dis|en|fran|chised *adjective*
dis|en|fran|chise| ment +s
dis|en|gage
dis|en|gages
dis|en|gaged
dis|en|gaging
dis|en|gaged *adjective*
dis|en|gage|ment +s
dis|en|tangle
dis|en|tan|gles
dis|en|tan|gled
dis|en|tan|gling
dis|en|tangle|ment +s
dis|en|thral (*use* disenthrall)
dis|en|thrals
dis|en|thralled
dis|en|thral|ling
dis|en|thrall +s +ed +ing
dis|en|thral|ment +s
dis|en|title
dis|en|titles
dis|en|titled
dis|en|titling
dis|equi|lib|rium
dis|equi|lib|ria
dis|estab|lish
dis|estab|lish|es
dis|estab|lished
dis|estab|lish|ing
dis|estab|lish|ment +s
dis|esteem +s +ed +ing
dis|favor +s +ed +ing (*use* disfavour)
dis|fa|vour +s +ed +ing
dis|figur|a|tion +s

dis|fig|ure
dis|fig|ures
dis|fig|ured
dis|fig|ur|ing
dis|fig|ured *adjective*
dis|figure|ment +s
dis|fran|chise (= disenfranchise)
dis|fran|chis|es
dis|fran|chised
dis|fran|chis|ing
dis|fran|chised *adjective* (= disenfranchised)
dis|fran|chise|ment +s (= dis-enfranchisement)
dis|gorge
dis|gor|ges
dis|gorged
dis|gor|ging
dis|gorge|ment +s
dis|grace
dis|gra|ces
dis|graced
dis|gra|cing
dis|grace|ful
dis|grace|ful|ly
dis|grun|tled
dis|gruntle|ment +s
dis|guise
dis|guis|es
dis|guised
dis|guis|ing
dis|guised *adjective*
dis|gust +s +ed +ing
dis|gust|ed|ly
dis|gust|ing *adjective*
dis|gust|ing|ly
dis|gust|ing|ness
dish
dish|es
dished
dish|ing
dis|ha|bille (= *déshabillé*)
dis|har|moni|ous
dis|har|moni|ous|ly
dis|har|mon|ize
dis|har|mon|iz|es
dis|har|mon|ized
dis|har|mon|iz|ing
dis|har|mony
dis|har|mon|ies
dish|cloth +s
dis|heart|en +s +ed +ing
dis|heart|en|ing *adjective*
dis|heart|en|ing|ly
dis|heart|en|ment +s
dished *adjective*
di|shev|elled

di|shevel|ment +s
dish|ful +s
dish|i|er
dish|i|est
dish|like
dis|hon|est
dis|hon|est|ly
dis|hon|esty
dis|hon|est|ies
dis|hon|or +s +ed +ing (*use* dishonour)
dis|honor|able (*use* dishonourable)
dis|honor|able|ness (*use* dishonourableness)
dis|honor|ably (*use* dishonourably)
dis|hon|our +s +ed +ing
dis|honour|able
dis|honour|able|ness
dis|honour|ably
dish|pan +s
dish rack +s
dish|rag +s
dish soap +s
dish|towel +s
dish|wash|er +s
dish|wash|ing
dish|water
dishy
dish|i|er
dish|i|est
dis|illu|sion +s +ed +ing
dis|illu|sion|ment +s
dis|in|cen|tive +s
dis|inclin|a|tion +s
dis|in|cline
dis|in|clines
dis|in|clined
dis|in|clin|ing
dis|in|clined *adjective*
dis|in|fect +s +ed +ing
dis|infect|ant +s
dis|infec|tion +s
dis|in|fla|tion
dis|in|fla|tion|ary
dis|infor|ma|tion
dis|in|genu|ous
dis|in|genu|ous|ly
dis|in|genu|ous|ness
dis|in|herit +s +ed +ing
dis|in|herit|ance
dis|in|te|grate
dis|in|te|grates
dis|in|te|grat|ed
dis|in|te|grat|ing
dis|in|te|gra|tion +s

dis|in|te|gra|tor +s
dis|in|ter
dis|in|ters
dis|in|terred
dis|in|ter|ring
dis|in|ter|est
dis|in|ter|est|ed *adjective*
dis|in|ter|est|ed|ly
dis|in|ter|est|ed|ness
dis|in|ter|ment +s
dis|in|vest +s +ed +ing
dis|in|vest|ment +s
dis|join +s +ed +ing
dis|joint +s +ed +ing
dis|joint|ed *adjective*
dis|joint|ed|ly
dis|joint|ed|ness
dis|junct +s
dis|junc|tion +s
dis|junct|ive
dis|junct|ive|ly
dis|junc|ture +s
disk +s +ed +ing
• Use *disk* for all computer senses other than *compact disc* (e.g. *floppy disk*, *hard disk*, *optical disk*), for the sense 'harrow' (*disker, disk harrow*), and for any verb use. In all other senses *disc* is preferred (*disc brakes, disc-shaped, disc jockey, laser disc, slipped disc*).
[☞ disc]
disk drive +s
disk|er +s
disk|ette +s
disk har|row +s
disk jock|ey +s (*use* disc jockey)
disk|less
Disko (island off Greenland)
[☞ disco]
dis|lik|able
dis|like
dis|likes
dis|liked
dis|lik|ing
dis|like|able (*use* dislikable)
dis|lo|cate
dis|lo|cates
dis|locat|ed
dis|locat|ing
dis|loca|tion +s

dis|lodge
  dis|lodg|es
  dis|lodged
  dis|lodg|ing
dis|lodge|able
dis|lodge|ment +s
dis|loyal
dis|loyal|ist +s
dis|loyal|ly
dis|loyal|ty
  dis|loyal|ties
dis|mal
dis|mal|ly
dis|mal|ness
Dis|mal Swamp
  (swampland, US)
dis|man|tle
  dis|man|tles
  dis|man|tled
  dis|mant|ling
dis|mantle|ment +s
dis|mant|ler +s
dis|mast +s +ed +ing
dis|may +s +ed +ing
dis|may|ing *adjective*
dis|may|ing|ly
dis|mem|ber +s +ed
  +ing
dis|member|ment +s
dis|miss
  dis|miss|es
  dis|missed
  dis|miss|ing
dis|miss|al +s
dis|miss|ible
dis|mis|sive
dis|mis|sive|ly
dis|mis|sive|ness
dis|mount +s +ed
  +ing
Dis|ney, Wal|ter Elias
  ('Walt') (US
  animator)
Disney|esque
dis|obedi|ence +s
dis|obedi|ent
dis|obedi|ent|ly
dis|obey +s +ed +ing
dis|obey|er +s
dis|oblige
  dis|obliges
  dis|obliged
  dis|obli|ging
dis|obli|ging *adjective*
dis|or|der +s +ed
  +ing
dis|or|dered *adjective*
dis|or|der|li|ness
dis|or|der|ly
dis|or|gan|iz|a|tion
dis|or|gan|ize
  dis|or|gan|iz|es

dis|or|gan|ized
dis|or|gan|iz|ing
dis|or|gan|ized
  adjective
dis|ori|ent +s +ed
  +ing
dis|orien|tate
  dis|orien|tates
  dis|orien|tat|ed
  dis|orien|tat|ing
dis|orien|ta|tion
dis|own +s +ed +ing
dis|par|age
  dis|para|ges
  dis|par|aged
  dis|para|ging
dis|parage|ment +s
dis|para|ging
  adjective
dis|para|ging|ly
dis|par|ate
dis|par|ate|ly
dis|par|ate|ness
dis|par|ity
  dis|par|ities
dis|pas|sion
dis|pas|sion|ate
dis|pas|sion|ate|ly
dis|pas|sion|ate|ness
dis|patch
  dis|patch|es
  dis|patched
  dis|patch|ing
dis|patch|er +s
dis|pel
  dis|pels
  dis|pelled
  dis|pel|ling
dis|pel|ler +s
dis|pens|abil|ity
dis|pens|able
dis|pens|ary
  dis|pens|aries
dis|pen|sa|tion +s
dis|pen|sa|tion|al
dis|pense
  dis|pens|es
  dis|pensed
  dis|pens|ing
dis|pens|er +s
dis|per|sal +s (act of
  dispersing)
  [☞ disbursal]
dis|per|sant +s
dis|perse (scatter;
  distribute)
  dis|pers|es
  dis|persed
  dis|pers|ing
  [☞ disburse]
dis|pers|er +s (one
  who disperses)
  [☞ disburser]

dis|pers|ible
Dis|per|sion (*Judaism*)
dis|per|sion +s
  (*generally*)
dis|per|sive
dispir|it +s +ed +ing
dispir|it|ed *adjective*
dispir|it|ed|ly
dispir|it|ed|ness
dispir|it|ing *adjective*
dispir|it|ing|ly
dis|place
  dis|pla|ces
  dis|placed
  dis|pla|cing
dis|place|able
dis|place|ment +s
dis|pla|cer +s
dis|play +s +ed +ing
dis|play case +s
dis|play|er +s
dis|please
  dis|pleas|es
  dis|pleased
  dis|pleas|ing
dis|pleas|ing *adjective*
dis|pleas|ing|ly
dis|pleas|ure
dis|port +s +ed +ing
dis|pos|abil|ity
dis|pos|able +s
dis|pos|al +s
dis|pose
  dis|pos|es
  dis|posed
  dis|pos|ing
dis|posed *adjective*
dis|pos|er +s
dis|pos|ition +s
dis|pos|ition|al
dis|pos|sess
  dis|pos|sess|es
  dis|pos|sessed
  dis|pos|sess|ing
dis|pos|sessed
  adjective
dis|pos|ses|sion +s
dis|pos|ses|sor +s
dis|praise
  dis|prais|es
  dis|praised
  dis|prais|ing
dis|proof +s
dis|pro|por|tion +s
dis|pro|por|tion|al
dis|pro|por|tion|
        al|ity
dis|pro|por|tion|al|ly
dis|pro|por|tion|ate
dis|pro|por|tion|ate|
         ly
dis|pro|por|tion|ate|
         ness

dis|prov|able
dis|prove
  dis|proves
  dis|proved
  dis|prov|ing
Dis|pur (city, India)
dis|put|able
dis|put|ably
dis|put|ant +s
dis|pu|ta|tion +s
dis|pu|ta|tious
dis|pu|ta|tious|ly
dis|pu|ta|tious|ness
dis|pute
  dis|putes
  dis|put|ed
  dis|put|ing
dis|put|ed *adjective*
dis|put|er +s
dis|quali|fi|ca|tion +s
dis|qual|ify
  dis|quali|fies
  dis|quali|fied
  dis|quali|fy|ing
dis|quiet +s +ed +ing
dis|quiet|ing *adjective*
dis|quiet|ing|ly
dis|quiet|ude
dis|quisi|tion +s
dis|quisi|tion|al
Dis|raeli, Ben|ja|min
  (1st Earl of
  Beaconsfield, British
  prime minister)
dis|rate
  dis|rates
  dis|rat|ed
  dis|rat|ing
dis|regard +s +ed
  +ing
dis|regard|ful
dis|regard|ful|ly
dis|remem|ber +s
  +ed +ing
dis|repair
dis|reput|able
dis|reput|able|ness
dis|reput|ably
dis|repute
dis|re|spect +s +ed
  +ing
dis|re|spect|ful
dis|re|spect|ful|ly
dis|robe
  dis|robes
  dis|robed
  dis|rob|ing
dis|rupt +s +ed +ing
dis|rupt|er +s
dis|rup|tion +s
dis|rupt|ive
dis|rupt|ive|ly
dis|rupt|ive|ness

dis|rupt|or +s (use disrupter)
diss (use dis)
diss|es
dissed
diss|ing
dis|satis|fac|tion +s
dis|satis|fac|tory
dis|satis|fy
dis|satis|fies
dis|satis|fied
dis|satis|fy|ing
dis|sect +s +ed +ing
dis|sec|tion +s
dis|sect|or +s
dis|sem|blance
dis|sem|ble
dis|sem|bles
dis|sem|bled
dis|sem|bling
dis|sem|bler +s
dis|sem|bling|ly
dis|semin|ate
dis|semin|ates
dis|semin|ated
dis|semin|at|ing
dis|semin|ated
adjective
dis|semin|a|tion
dis|semin|ator +s
dis|sen|sion +s
dis|sent +s +ed +ing
(disagree; disagreement)
[☞ descent, decent]
Dis|sent|er +s
(Nonconformist)
dis|sent|er +s (in general use)
dis|sen|tient
dis|sent|ing adjective
dis|sent|ing|ly
dis|ser|ta|tion +s
dis|ser|ta|tion|al
dis|ser|vice +s
dis|sever +s +ed +ing
dis|sever|ance
dis|sever|ment
dis|si|dence
dis|si|dent +s
dis|sim|i|lar
dis|sim|i|lar|ity
dis|sim|i|lar|ities
dis|sim|i|lar|ly
dis|simi|late
(Phonetics)
dis|simi|lates
dis|simi|lat|ed
dis|simi|lat|ing
[☞ dissimulate]

dis|simi|la|tion +s
(Phonetics)
[☞ dissimulation]
dis|sim|ila|tory
dis|sim|ili|tude
dis|simu|late (feign, conceal; dissemble)
dis|simu|lates
dis|simu|lat|ed
dis|simu|lat|ing
[☞ dissimilate]
dis|simu|la|tion +s
(act of dissembling)
[☞ dissimilation]
dis|simu|la|tor +s
dis|si|pate
dis|si|pates
dis|si|pat|ed
dis|si|pat|ing
dis|si|pat|ed adjective
dis|si|pat|er +s (use dissipator)
dis|si|pa|tion +s
dis|si|pa|tive
dis|si|pa|tor +s
dis|soci|ate
dis|soci|ates
dis|soci|at|ed
dis|soci|at|ing
dis|soci|a|tion +s
dis|soci|ative
dis|solu|bil|ity
dis|sol|uble
dis|sol|ubly
dis|so|lute
dis|so|lute|ly
dis|so|lute|ness
dis|so|lu|tion +s
dis|solv|able
dis|solve
dis|solves
dis|solved
dis|solv|ing
dis|sol|vent +s
dis|son|ance +s
dis|son|ant +s
dis|son|ant|ly
dis|suade
dis|suades
dis|suad|ed
dis|suad|ing
dis|suad|er +s
dis|sua|sion
dis|sua|sive
dis|sua|sive|ly
dis|syllab|ic (use disyllabic)
dis|sylla|ble +s (use disyllable)
dis|sym|met|ric
dis|sym|met|ric|al
dis|sym|metry
dis|sym|met|ries

dis|taff +s
dis|tal
dis|tal|ly
dis|tance
dis|tan|ces
dis|tanced
dis|tan|cing
dis|tant
dis|tant|ly
dis|taste
dis|taste|ful
dis|taste|ful|ly
dis|taste|ful|ness
Di Stef|ano, Al|fredo
(Argentinian-born Spanish soccer player)
dis|tel|fink +s
dis|tem|per +s +ed +ing
dis|tem|pered adjective
dis|tend +s +ed +ing
dis|ten|si|bil|ity
dis|ten|sible
dis|ten|sion
dis|tich +s
dis|tich|ous
dis|tich|ous|ly
dis|til (use distill)
dis|tils
dis|tilled
dis|til|ling
dis|till +s +ed +ing
dis|til|late +s
dis|til|la|tion +s
dis|till|er +s
dis|til|lery
dis|til|ler|ies
dis|tinct
dis|tinc|tion +s
dis|tinct|ive
dis|tinct|ive|ly
dis|tinct|ive|ness
dis|tinct|ly
dis|tinct|ness
dis|tin|guish
dis|tin|guish|es
dis|tin|guished
dis|tin|guish|ing
dis|tin|guish|able
dis|tin|guished
dis|tort +s +ed +ing
dis|tort|ed adjective
dis|tort|ed|ly
dis|tort|ed|ness
dis|tor|tion +s
dis|tor|tion|al
dis|tor|tion|less
dis|tract +s +ed +ing
dis|tract|ed adjective
dis|tract|ed|ly

dis|tract|ibil|ity
dis|tract|ible
dis|trac|tion +s
dis|train +s +ed +ing
dis|train|ee +s
dis|train|er +s (use distrainor)
dis|train|ment +s
dis|train|or +s
dis|traint
dis|trait
dis|traught
dis|tress (trouble)
dis|tress|es
dis|tressed
dis|tress|ing
dis|tressed adjective
dis|tress|ful
dis|tress|ing adjective
dis|tress|ing|ly
dis|trib|ut|able
dis|tribu|tary
dis|tribu|tar|ies
dis|trib|ute
dis|trib|utes
dis|trib|ut|ed
dis|trib|ut|ing
dis|trib|ut|ed adjective
dis|tri|bu|tion +s
dis|tri|bu|tion|al
dis|tribu|tive
dis|tribu|tive|ly
dis|tribu|tor +s
dis|tribu|tor|ship +s
dis|trict +s +ed +ing
Dis|trict of
Col|um|bia (federal district, US)
dis|trust +s +ed +ing
dis|trust|er +s
dis|trust|ful
dis|trust|ful|ly
dis|turb +s +ed +ing
dis|turb|ance +s
dis|turbed adjective
dis|turb|er +s
dis|turb|ing adjective
dis|turb|ing|ly
di|sul|fide +s (use disulphide)
di|sul|phide +s
dis|union
dis|unit|ed
dis|unity
dis|use
dis|uses
dis|used
dis|us|ing
dis|util|ity
dis|util|ities
di|syllab|ic
di|sylla|ble +s

dit +s
ditch
  ditch|es
  ditched
  ditch|ing
ditch|digger +s
ditch|er +s
ditch water
di|theism
di|theist +s
dith|er +s +ed +ing
dith|ered *adjective*
dith|er|er +s
dith|er|ing *noun*
dith|ery
dithy|ramb +s
dithy|ram|bic
Diti|daht (= Nitinat)
  plural Ditidaht or
  Ditidahts
ditsy (*use* ditzy)
  dits|i|er
  dits|i|est
dit|tany
  dit|tan|ies
Ditto +s *proprietary*
  (offset printing press)
ditto
• *noun* (the same;
  duplicate)
  dit|tos
• *verb* (repeat)
  dit|toes
  dit|toed
  ditto|ing
ditto|graph|ic
dit|tog|raphy
  dit|tog|raph|ies
ditto marks
ditty
  dit|ties
ditty bag +s
ditty box
  ditty boxes
ditz
  ditz|es
ditzy
  ditz|i|er
  ditz|i|est
di|ur|esis
di|ur|et|ic +s
  (producing urine)
  [☞ diarrhetic,
  dioritic]
di|ur|nal
di|ur|nal|ly
diva +s (singer)
di|va|gate
  di|va|gates
  di|va|gat|ed
  di|va|gat|ing
di|va|ga|tion +s
di|valence

di|valen|cy
  (= divalence)
di|valent
divan +s
di|vari|cate
  di|vari|cates
  di|vari|cat|ed
  di|vari|cat|ing
di|vari|ca|tion +s
dive
  dives
  dived or dove
  dived
  div|ing
dive-bomb +s +ed
  +ing
dive-bomber +s
dive|master +s
diver +s
di|verge
  di|ver|ges
  di|verged
  di|ver|ging
di|ver|gence +s
di|ver|gency
  di|ver|gen|cies
di|ver|gent
di|ver|gent|ly
divers
• (more than one;
  sundry)
• (*plural of* diver)
di|verse (varied,
  mixed)
di|verse|ly
di|vers|ifi|ca|tion +s
di|vers|ify
  di|versi|fies
  di|versi|fied
  di|versi|fy|ing
di|ver|sion +s
di|ver|sion|al
di|ver|sion|ary
di|vers|ity
  di|vers|ities
di|vert +s +ed +ing
di|ver|ticu|lar
di|ver|ticu|litis
di|ver|ticu|losis
di|ver|ticu|lum
  di|ver|tic|ula
di|ver|ti|mento
  di|ver|ti|menti or
  di|ver|ti|men|tos
di|vert|ing *adjective*
di|vert|ing|ly
di|ver|tisse|ment +s
di|vest +s +ed +ing
di|vesti|ture +s
di|vest|ment +s
di|ves|ture +s
  (= divestiture)

div|ide
  div|ides
  div|id|ed
  div|id|ing
div|id|ed *adjective*
divi|dend +s
divi|dend yield +s
div|id|er +s
div|id|ing line +s
divi-divi (tree)
  divi-divis
  [☞ divvy]
div|in|a|tion +s
div|ina|tory
Div|ine (God;
  Providence)
  [☞ Devine]
div|ine (of God or a
  god; delightful;
  guess, predict; cleric)
  divin|er
  divin|est
  div|ines
  div|ined
  divin|ing
divine|ly
divine|ness
divin|er +s
div|ing *noun*
div|ing bell +s
div|ing board +s
div|ing suit +s
divin|ing rod +s
Divin|ity (God)
divin|ity (a god;
  godliness; theology;
  fudge)
  divin|ities
divin|iz|a|tion
divin|ize
  divin|iz|es
  divin|ized
  divin|iz|ing
div|is|ibil|ity
div|is|ible (that may
  be divided; Math)
  [☞ devisable]
div|ision +s
div|ision|al
div|ision|al|iz|a|tion
div|ision|al|ize
  div|ision|al|iz|es
  div|ision|al|ized
  div|ision|al|iz|ing
div|ision|al|ly
div|ision|ary
div|isive
div|isive|ly
div|isive|ness
div|isor +s (Math)
  [☞ devisor,
  deviser]

di|vorce
  di|vor|ces
  di|vorced
  di|vor|cing
di|vor|cee +s
div|ot +s
di|vulge
  di|vul|ges
  di|vulged
  di|vul|ging
di|vulge|ment +s
di|vul|gence +s
divvy (divide)
  div|vies
  div|vied
  divvy|ing
  [☞ divi-divi]
Di|wali (*Hinduism*)
diwan +s (*use* dewan)
Dixie (southern US)
Dixie cup +s
  proprietary
Dixie|land
Dixon En|trance
  (passage, N Pacific)
DIY (do-it-yourself)
Di|yar|ba|kir
  (province & its
  capital, Turkey)
DIY|er +s
diz|zi|ly
diz|zi|ness
dizzy
  diz|zi|er
  diz|zi|est
  diz|zies
  diz|zied
  dizzy|ing
dizzy|ing *adjective*
dizzy|ing|ly
DJ (disc jockey)
  DJs
  DJed
  DJing
Dja|kar|ta (capital of
  Indonesia)
djel|la|ba +s
djel|la|bah +s (*use*
  djellaba)
Djer|ba (island,
  Tunisia)
djib|ba +s (*use* jibba)
djib|bah +s (*use* jibba)
Dji|bou|ti (country &
  its capital, Africa)
Dji|bou|tian +s
Djilas, Milo|van
  (Yugoslav politician
  & writer)
djinn (= jinni: Islamic
  mythological spirit)
  plural djinn or

djinns
[☞ gin, Jin]
DL (disabled list)
DM (deputy minister)
DMs
DMA (direct memory access)
D-mark +s (Deutschmark)
DMT (dimethyltryptamine)
DMZ (demilitarized zone)
DMZs
DNA
DNAs
DND (Department of National Defence)
Dnie|per (river, Europe)
Dnies|ter (river, Europe)
Dni|pro|dzer|zhinsk (city, Ukraine)
Dni|pro|pe|trovsk (city, Ukraine)
do¹
• verb
does
did
done
doing
• noun
dos or do's
[☞ dew, due]
do² +s (Music)
[☞ doe, dough]
DOA (dead on arrival)
do|able
dob (implicate; betray)
dobs
dobbed
dob|bing
[☞ daub]
dob|bin +s
Dober|man +s
Dober|man pin|scher +s (= Doberman)
Dobos torte +s
Do|brich (city, Bulgaria)
do|bro +s
Do|bruja (region, Europe)
doc +s (doctor)
[☞ dock]
do|cent +s
do|cile
do|cile|ly
do|cil|ity
dock +s +ed +ing (for boats etc.; join in space; in a

courtroom; plant; cut, reduce; tail)
[☞ doc]
dock|age
dock|er +s
dock|et +s +ed +ing
dock|land +s
dock|side +s
dock-tailed
dock work|er +s
dock|yard +s
Doc Mar|tens proprietary
doc|tor +s +ed +ing
doc|tor|al
doc|tor|ate +s
doc|tor|ial
doc|tor|ly
Doc|tor Mar|tens proprietary
doctor|ship +s
doc|trin|aire +s
doc|trin|air|ism
doc|trin|al
doc|trin|al|ly
doc|trin|ar|ian +s
doc|trine +s
doc|trin|ism
doc|trin|ist +s
docu|drama +s
docu|drama|tist +s
docu|ment +s +ed +ing
docu|ment|able
docu|ment|al
docu|men|tar|ian +s
docu|men|tar|i|ly
docu|men|tar|ist +s
docu|men|tary
docu|men|tar|ies
docu|men|ta|tion +s
docu|ment|er +s
dod|der +s +ed +ing (totter; plant)
[☞ daughter]
dod|dered adjective
dod|der|er +s
dod|der|i|ness
dod|der|ing adjective
dod|dery
dod|dle +s
do|deca|gon +s
do|deca|hed|ral
do|deca|hed|ron
do|deca|hed|rons or do|deca|hedra
Do|deca|nese (islands, Greece)
do|deca|phon|ic
dodge (move quickly etc.)

dodg|es
dodged
dodg|ing
[☞ doge]
dodge ball
Dodge City (city, US)
dodg|em
dodg|er +s
Dodg|son, Charles Lut|widge (Lewis Carroll)
dodgy
dodg|i|er
dodg|i|est
dodo (bird; stupid person)
dodos or do|does
Do|doma (capital of Tanzania)
doe +s (female deer etc.)
[☞ do, doh, dough]
doe-eyed
Doen|itz, Karl (= Dönitz)
doer +s (one who acts or does)
[☞ dewar, dour]
does
• conjugated form of do
• plural of doe
doe|skin +s
doesn't
doest
doeth
doff +s +ed +ing
dog
dogs
dogged
dog|ging
do|gan +s offensive (Catholic)
[☞ Dogon]
dog-and-pony show +s
dog|bane +s
dog|berry
dog|ber|ries
dog bis|cuit +s
dog|cart +s
dog col|lar +s
dog daisy
dog dais|ies
dog days
doge +s (Venetian or Genoese chief magistrate)
[☞ dodge]
dog-eared
dog-eat-dog
dog|fight +s

dog|fish
plural dog|fish or dog|fish|es
dog|ged adjective
dog|ged|ly
dog|ged|ness
Dog|ger Bank (sandbank, North Sea)
dog|ger|el
dog|gie +s noun (= doggy)
[☞ doggy, dogie]
dog|gi|ness
dog|gish
doggo
dog|gone (darned)
[☞ Dogon]
doggy noun & adjective
dog|gies
doggy bag +s
dog hand|ler +s
dog-handling
dog|house +s
dogie +s (calf)
[☞ doggie]
dog|leg
dog|legs
dog|legged
dog|leg|ging
dog|legged adjective
dog|like
dog|ma +s
dog|mat|ic
dog|mat|ic|ally
dog|mat|ics
dogma|tism +s
dogma|tist +s
dogma|tize
dogma|tiz|es
dogma|tized
dogma|tiz|ing
dog meat
dog|nap
dog|naps
dog|napped
dog|nap|ping
dog|nap|per +s
dog|nap|ping noun
Dogon (African people & language)
plural Dogon or Do|gons
[☞ dogan, doggone]
do-good
do-gooder +s
do-goodery
do-goodism
dog-paddle
dog-paddles
dog-paddled
dog-paddling

Dogrib
  plural **Dogrib** or
  Dogribs
dog rose +s
dog sal|mon
  plural **dog sal|mon**
dogs|body
  dogs|bod|ies
dog|skin
dog|sled
  dog|sleds
  dog|sled|ded
  dog|sled|ding
dog|sled|ding *noun*
Dog Star
dog's tooth (violet; *for*
  check pattern *use*
  dog-tooth)
  dog's tooths or
  dog's teeth
  [☞ **dog-tooth**]
dog's tooth vio|let +s
dog tag +s
dog team +s
dog-tired
dog-tooth
  (*Architecture*; check
  pattern)
  dog-tooths or
  dog-teeth
  [☞ **dog's tooth**]
dog|trot +s
dog vio|let +s
dog|watch
  dog|watch|es
dog|wood +s
doh +s (*Music*: *use* do)
Doha (capital of
  Qatar)
doilied
doily
  doilies
do|ing +s *noun*
Dois|neau, Rob|ert
  (French
  photographer)
do-it-yourself
do-it-yourself|er +s
dojo +s
Dol|beau (town,
  Canada)
Dolby *proprietary*
dolce
dolce far niente
dolce vita
dol|drums
Dole, Rob|ert Jo|seph
  ('Bob') (US
  politician)
dole
  doles
  doled
  dol|ing

dole|ful
  dole|ful|ly
  dole|ful|ness
doler|ite +s
doli|cho|ceph|alic
doli|cho|ceph|al|ous
doll +s +ed +ing (toy
  etc.; dress up)
  [☞ **dal, Dahl**]
dol|lar +s
Dollard-des-
  Ormeaux
  (city, Canada)
Dol|lard des
  Or|meaux, Adam
  (French colonial
  commander)
dollar|iz|a|tion
dol|lar sign +s
Doll|fuss, Engel|bert
  (Austrian statesman)
doll|house +s
doll-like
dol|lop +s +ed +ing
doll's eyes
  (baneberry)
doll's house +s
dolly
  doll|lies
  doll|lied
  dolly|ing
  doll|li|er
  doll|li|est
dolly bird +s
dolly grip +s
Dolly Var|den
  • (fish)
  plural **Dolly Var|den**
  or **Dolly Var|dens**
  • (hat)
  plural **Dolly**
  Var|dens
dolma
  dol|mas or
  dol|ma|des
dol|man +s (clothing)
dol|men +s (tomb)
Dolo|mite +s
  (mountain range,
  Italy)
dolo|mite +s
dolo|mit|ic
dolor (*use* dolour)
dolor|ous
  dolor|ous|ly
dolour
dol|phin +s
dolphin|arium +s
dolt +s
dolt|ish
  dolt|ish|ly
  dolt|ish|ness
Dom

do|main +s (realm,
  estate, etc.; *Math*;
  Physics; *Computing*)
do|maine +s
  (vineyard)
dome
  domes
  domed
  dom|ing
domed *adjective*
dome-like
Dome of the Rock
Domes|day Book
  [☞ **doomsday**]
do|mes|tic +s
do|mes|tic|able
do|mes|tic|ally
do|mes|ti|cate
  do|mes|ti|cates
  do|mes|ti|cat|ed
  do|mes|ti|cat|ing
do|mes|ti|cat|ed
  adjective
do|mes|ti|ca|tion +s
do|mes|ti|city
  do|mes|ti|ci|ties
domi|cile
  domi|ciles
  domi|ciled
  domi|cil|ing
domi|ciled *adjective*
domi|cil|iary
dom|in|ance
dom|in|ant +s
  dom|in|ant|ly
dom|in|ate
  dom|in|ates
  dom|in|at|ed
  dom|in|at|ing
dom|in|at|ing
  adjective
dom|in|a|tion +s
dom|in|ator +s
dom|in|atrix
  dom|in|atri|ces or
  dom|in|atrix|es
dom|in|eer +s +ed
  +ing
dom|in|eer|ing
  adjective
dom|in|eer|ing|ly
Do|min|go, Plá|cido
  (Spanish-born tenor)
Dom|inic (saint)
Do|min|ica (island,
  West Indies)
do|min|ic|al
Do|min|ic|an +s
Do|min|ic|an
  Re|pub|lic
  (Caribbean country)
dom|inie +s
do|min|ion +s

Do|min|ion Day +s
Do|min|ion of
  Can|ada
Dom|ino, An|toine
  ('Fats') (US singer-
  songwriter)
dom|ino
  dom|inoes
dom|ino effect +s
Dom|itian (Roman
  emperor)
Don (rivers, Russia,
  Canada, Scotland &
  England)
don (senior member of
  a university or
  residence; high-
  ranking Mafia
  member; put on)
  dons
  donned
  don|ning
  [☞ **dawn**]
don|air +s
do|nate
  do|nates
  do|nat|ed
  do|nat|ing
Dona|tello (Italian
  sculptor)
do|na|tion +s
Donat|ism
Donat|ist +s
do|na|tor +s
done *adjective & past*
  participle of **do**
  (finished, ready,
  complete; tired;
  socially acceptable)
  [☞ **dun, Donne**]
donee +s (recipient of
  a gift)
  [☞ **donée**]
Don|egal (county,
  Ireland)
done|ness
doner kebab +s
  (spiced lamb, donair)
  [☞ **donor**]
Don|ets (basin,
  Ukraine; river,
  Europe)
Don|etsk (city,
  Ukraine)
dong +s +ed +ing
donga +s
don|gle +s
Dön|itz, Karl
  (German naval
  officer)
Doni|zetti,
  (Domen|ico)
  Gae|tano Maria
  (Italian composer)

don|jon +s (castle tower)
[☞ dungeon]
Don Juan +s (legendary Spanish nobleman; libertine)
Don Juan|ism
don|key +s
donkey|man
donkey|men
donkey's years
donk|ey work
donna +s (in 'prima donna')
Donna|cona (town, Canada; Iroquois chief)
Donne, John (English poet)
don|née +s (motif; basic fact)
[☞ donee]
Don|nelly, James, Johan|nah, Thom|as, John & Bridget (murder victims)
don|nish
don|nish|ly
don|nish|ness
donny|brook +s
donor +s (one who donates; atom, molecule)
[☞ doner kebab]
do-nothing +s
Don Quix|ote (fictional hero)
don|ship +s
don't
donut +s (in commercial use = doughnut)
doob +s
doob|ie +s
doo|dad +s
doo|dle
doo|dles
doo|dled
dood|ling
doodle|bug +s
dood|ler +s
dood|ling adjective
doodly-squat
doo-doo (excrement; trouble)
doof|us
doof|us|es
doo|hickey +s
Doo|little, Hilda (US writer)

doom +s +ed +ing (fate)
[☞ doum palm]
doom and gloom
doom-and-gloom (doom-and-gloom when preceding a noun)
doomed adjective
doom-laden
doom|say|er +s
doom|say|ing
dooms|day (day of judgment; time of destruction)
[☞ Domesday Book]
dooms|day clock
dooms|day cult +s
doom|ster +s
doomy
door +s (of a house or car etc.)
[☞ dour]
door|bell +s
door|case +s
do-or-die
doored adjective
door frame +s
door jamb +s
door|keep|er +s
door|knob +s
door knock|er +s
door|less
door|man
door|men
door|mat +s
door|nail +s
door|plate +s
door|post +s
door prize +s
door|sill +s
door|step +s
door|stop +s
door to door adverb
door-to-door adjective
door|way +s
door|yard +s
doo-wop
doo-wopper +s
dooz|er +s
dooz|ie +s (use doozy)
doozy
dooz|ies
dopa
dopa|mine
dopa|min|er|gic
dop|ant +s
dope
dopes
doped
dop|ing

dope fiend +s
doper +s
dope|ster +s
dopey
dop|i|er
dop|i|est
dop|i|ly
dop|i|ness
dop|ing noun
doppel|gänger +s
Dop|pler, Chris|tian (Austrian physicist)
Dop|pler +s (effect, shift, radar, etc.)
dopy (use dopey)
dop|i|er
dop|i|est
dor|ado +s
Dor|áti, Antal (Hungarian-born conductor)
Dor|ches|ter (towns, England & Canada)
Dor|ches|ter, 1st Daron (Guy Carleton)
Dor|dogne (department & river, France)
Dor|drecht (city, the Netherlands)
Doré (lake, Canada)
Doré, (Paul) Gus|tave (French illustrator)
doré
plural doré or dorés
Dor|ian +s (Hellenic people; Music)
[☞ Dorion]
Doric
Dor|ion (community, Canada)
[☞ Dorian]
Doris (region, ancient Greece)
dork +s
dorky
dork|i|er
dork|i|est
dorm +s
dor|mancy
dor|mant
dor|mer +s
dor|mie
dormi|tory
dormi|tor|ies
dor|mouse
dor|mice
dormy (use dormie)
do|ron|icum +s
dorp +s
dor|sal
dor|sal|ly

Dor|set (county, England; Aboriginal people)
plural Dor|set or Dor|sets
Dor|sey, Thom|as Fran|cis ('Tommy') (US bandleader)
dor|sum
dorsa
Dort (= Dordrecht, the Netherlands)
Dort|mund (city, Germany)
Dor|val (city, Canada)
dory
dor|ies
dory|man
dory|men
DOS (Computing)
[☞ doss]
dos|age +s
dose
doses
dosed
dos|ing
dosh
do-si-do +s +ed +ing
dos|im|eter +s
dosi|met|ric
dos|im|et|rist +s
dos|im|etry
Dos Pas|sos, John Roder|igo (US novelist)
doss (sleep; loaf; bed)
doss|es
dossed
doss|ing
[☞ DOS]
dos|sal
doss|er +s
doss-house +s
dos|si|er +s
dost
Dos|to|ev|skian
Dos|to|ev|sky, Fyodor Mikh|ail|ovich (Russian novelist)
Dos|toy|ev|skian (= Dostoevskian)
Dos|toy|ev|sky, Fyodor Mikh|ail|ovich (= Dostoevsky)
dot
dots
dotted
dot|ting
dot|age
dot|al
dot|ard +s

dote
  dotes
  doted
  dot|ing
doter +s
doth
dot|ing *adjective*
dot|ing|ly
dot ma|trix
dot ma|trix print|er +s
dot|ted *adjective*
dot|ter|el
  plural dot|ter|el or dot|ter|els
dot|ti|ly
dot|ti|ness
dot|tle +s
dot-to-dot
dotty
  dot|ti|er
  dot|ti|est
Dou, Ger|ard (Dutch painter)
  [☞ dhow, Tao]
Dou|ala (city, Cameroon)
Douay Bible
double
  doubles
  doubled
  doub|ling
Double-A
double-acting
double-action
double agent +s
double-barrelled
double bass
  double bass|es
double-bitted
double-blind
double-bogey +s +ed +ing
double boil|er +s
double-book +s +ed +ing
double-breast|ed
double-check +s +ed +ing
double chin +s
double-chinned
double-click +s +ed +ing
double clutch
  double clutch|es
  double clutched
  double clutch|ing
double-crested
double-cross
  double-crosses
  double-crossed
  double-crossing
double-crosser +s

double date
  double dates
  double dated
  double dat|ing
double-deal +s +ed +ing
double-dealer +s
double-dealing *noun & adjective*
double-deck
double-decked
double-decker +s
double-declutch
  double-declutch|es
  double-declutched
  double-declutch|ing
double dens|ity
double dig|ging
double-digit
double-dip
  double-dips
  double-dipped
  double-dipping
double-dipper +s
double-dipping *noun*
double door +s
double dutch
double-dyed
double eagle +s
double-edged
double en|tendre +s
double entry
  (double-entry *when preceding a noun*)
double-faced
double fault +s +ed +ing
double-figure
  adjective preceding a noun
double fig|ures *plural noun*
double-glazed
double glaz|ing
double-headed
double|head|er +s
double-hung
double in|dem|nity
double jeop|ardy
double-jointed
double-knit
double minor +s
double|ness
double oc|cu|pancy
double-paned
double-park +s +ed +ing
double play +s
double-quick
doub|ler +s
double-sided
double-sidedness
double space +s

double-spaced
double|speak
double stan|dard +s
double stop +s
double-stopping
doub|let +s
double take +s
double-talk +s +ed +ing
double-talking *adjective*
double-team +s +ed +ing
double-teaming *noun*
double|think
double time
  double times
  double timed
  double tim|ing
double-tonguing
double|tree +s
double wham|my
  double wham|mies
double-wide +s
double-wishbone
doub|loon +s
doub|lure +s
doub|ly
doubt +s +ed +ing (uncertainty; disbelieve)
  [☞ dout]
doubt|able
doubt|er +s
doubt|ful
doubt|ful|ly
doubt|ful|ness
doubt|ing|ly
doubt|ing Thom|as
  doubt|ing Thom|as|es
doubt|less
doubt|less|ly
douce (sober, gentle)
  [☞ deuce, Duce]
douche
  douches
  douched
  douch|ing
douch|ing *noun*
dough (flour & water mixture; money)
  [☞ doh, do, doe]
dough|boy +s
dough|i|er
dough|i|est
dough|i|ness
dough|nut +s
dought|i|ly
dought|i|ness
Dough|ty, Charles Mon|tagu (English travel writer)

doughty
  dought|i|er
  dought|i|est
doughy
  dough|i|er
  dough|i|est
Doug|las (capital of the Isle of Man; fir; pine; spruce; maple)
Doug|las, Lord Al|fred Bruce (English poet)
Doug|las, Sir James (governor of BC & Vancouver Island)
Doug|las, Thom|as Clem|ent ('Tommy') (Cdn politician)
Douglas-Home, Sir Alex (Baron Home of the Hirsel of Coldstream, British prime minister)
Doukh|obor +s
doum +s (tree)
  [☞ doom]
doum palm +s
dour (stern, gruff; sullen)
  [☞ dower]
dour|ly
dour|ness
Douro (river, Iberian peninsula)
dou|rou|couli +s
douse (soak; extinguish; suppress; *Nautical*)
  dous|es
  doused
  dous|ing
  [☞ dowse]
dout +s +ed +ing (extinguish)
  [☞ doubt]
dove +s
dove|cot +s (*use* dovecote)
dove|cote +s
dove|kie +s
dove|like
Dover (port, England; strait between England & France; city, US)
Dover sole
  plural Dover sole
dove|tail +s +ed +ing
dov|ish
dow|ager +s
dow|ager's hump +s
dow|di|ly
dow|di|ness

dow|dy
  dow|di|er
  dow|di|est
  dowd|ies
dowel wooden peg
  dow|els
  dow|elled
  dowel|ling
  [☞ Dowell]
Dow|ell, Sir An|thony
  (English dancer)
  [☞ dowel]
dow|elled adjective
dowel|ling noun
dower +s +ed +ing
  (widow's inheritance;
  talent; dowry)
  [☞ dour]
dower house +s
dower|less
dow|itch|er +s
Dow-Jones Aver|age
  proprietary
Dow|land, John
  (English lutenist)
Down (county,
  Northern Ireland)
down +s +ed +ing
down-and-dirty
down-and-out +s
down-and-outer +s
down-at-heel
  (= down-at-the-
  heels)
down-at-heels
  (= down-at-the-
  heels)
down-at-the-heels
down|beat +s
down|bound
down|cast +s
down|court
down|draft +s
down|er +s
down|fall +s
down|field
down-filled
down|grade
  down|grades
  down|grad|ed
  down|grad|ing
down|heart|ed
down|heart|ed|ly
down|heart|ed|ness
down|hill +s
down|hill|er +s
down|hole
down-home
down-homeness
down|i|er
down|i|est
down|i|ness
down in the mouth

down-island
down|land +s
down|light +s
down|link +s +ed
  +ing
down|load +s +ed
  +ing
down|load|able
down-market
down pay|ment +s
down|pipe +s
down|play +s +ed
  +ing
down|pour +s
down|range
down|rate
  down|rates
  down|rated
  down|rating
down|rig|ger +s
down|right
down|right|ness
down|river
Downs (region,
  England)
down|scale
  down|scales
  down|scaled
  down|scal|ing
down|shift +s +ed
  +ing
down|side +s
down|size
  down|siz|es
  down|sized
  down|siz|ing
down|siz|ing +s noun
down|slope +s
down|spout +s
Down's syn|drome
  or Down
  syn|drome
  • Although Down's
  syndrome is more
  common in general
  Cdn usage, it is the
  official policy of
  some groups to use
  the form Down
  syndrome.
down|stage
down|stairs
down|state
down|stat|er +s
down|stream
down street
down|stroke +s
down|swing +s
down tim|ber
down|time
down-to-earth
down|town +s
down|town|er +s

down|trend +s
down|trod|den
down|turn +s
down under (of or to
  Australia & New
  Zealand)
down|ward
down|ward|ly
down|wards
down|warp +s
down|wash
down|wind
downy
  down|i|er
  down|i|est
down|zone
  down|zones
  down|zoned
  down|zon|ing
dowry
  dow|ries
dowse (search for
  water etc.; for soak &
  extinguish use
  douse)
  dows|es
  dowsed
  dows|ing
  [☞ douse]
dows|er +s
dows|ing rod +s
Dow|son, Er|nest
  Chris|to|pher
  (English poet)
doxo|logic|al
dox|ol|ogy
  dox|ol|o|gies
doxo|rubi|cin
doxy
  dox|ies
doxy|cy|cline
doy|en +s (most
  prominent person)
doy|enne +s (most
  prominent female)
Doyle, Sir Ar|thur
  Conan (Scottish
  novelist)
D'Oyly Carte,
  Rich|ard (English
  impresario)
doze
  dozes
  dozed
  doz|ing
dozen
  plural dozen or
  doz|ens
doz|ens (ritual game)
doz|enth
doz|er +s
doz|i|ly
doz|i|ness

dozy
  doz|i|er
  doz|i|est
DP (displaced person)
  DPs
dpi (dots per inch)
drab
  drab|ber
  drab|best
  drabs
Drab|ble, Mar|garet
  (English writer)
drab|ble
  drab|bles
  drab|bled
  drab|bling
drab|ly
drab|ness
dra|caena +s
drachm +s
  (apothecaries'
  measure equal to
  3.89 grams; for
  ancient coin use
  drachma)
  [☞ dram]
drach|ma
  drach|mas or
  drach|mae
Draco (Athenian
  legislator;
  constellation)
dra|co|nian
dra|co|nian|ism
dra|con|ic
drae|ger|man
  drae|ger|men
draft (preliminary
  version; selection;
  military service;
  Banking; air current;
  beer; drink; water
  depth; pulling;
  Fishing)
  drafts
  draft|ed
  draft|ing
  [☞ draught]
draft|able
draft beer
draft board +s
  (Military)
  [☞ draughtboard]
draft card +s
draft dodg|er +s
draft dodg|ing
draf|tee +s
draft|er +s
draft horse +s
draft|i|er
draft|i|est
draft|i|ly
draft|i|ness
draft|ing noun

draft|ing table +s
drafts *plural of* draft
  [☞ draughts]
drafts|man
  drafts|men
drafts|man|ship
drafty
  draft|i|er
  draft|i|est
drag
  drags
  dragged
  drag|ging
drag and drop
dra|gée +s
drag end +s
drag|ger +s
dragger|man
  dragger|men
drag|gle
  drag|gles
  drag|gled
  drag|gling
draggy
  drag|gi|er
  drag|gi|est
drag|line +s
drag|net +s
drago|man
  drago|mans or
  drago|men
drag|on +s
drag|on boat +s
drag|on|et +s
dragon|fly
  dragon|flies
drag|on lady
  drag|on ladies
drag|on mouth +s
dragon|nade
  dragon|nades
  dragon|nad|ed
  dragon|nad|ing
dragon's blood +s
drag|on tree +s
drag|oon +s +ed +ing
drag queen +s
drag race +s
drag racer +s
drag racing
drag|ster +s
drag strip +s
drail +s
drain +s +ed +ing
drain|age +s
drain|board +s
drain|er +s
drain|ing board +s
drain|pipe +s
Draize test +s
Drake, Sir Fran|cis
  (English explorer)
drake +s

Drak|ens|berg
  (mountain range,
  Africa)
Drake Pas|sage
  (ocean passage
  between S America
  & Antarctica)
DRAM (*Computing*)
  DRAMs
dram +s (drink;
  avoirdupois measure
  equal to 1.77 grams;
  for apothecaries'
  measure equal to
  3.89 grams *use*
  drachm)
  [☞ drachm]
drama +s
dra|mat|ic
dra|mat|ic|ally
dra|mat|ics
dram|atis per|so|nae
drama|tist +s
drama|tiz|a|tion +s
drama|tize
  drama|tiz|es
  drama|tized
  drama|tiz|ing
drama|turg +s (*use*
  dramaturge)
drama|turge +s
drama|tur|gic
drama|tur|gic|al
drama|tur|gic|al|ly
drama|turgy
  drama|tur|gies
dram|edy
  dram|ed|ies
drank
drape
  drapes
  draped
  drap|ing
Dra|peau, Jean
  (Montreal mayor)
Dra|per, Henry (US
  astronomer)
Dra|per, Wil|liam
  Henry (Cdn
  politician & jurist)
drap|er +s
drap|ery
  drap|eries
dras|tic
dras|tic|ally
drat
  drats
  drat|ted
  drat|ting
drat|ted *adjective*
draught +s (*use* draft
  except in 'checkers'

senses of *draughts*
  and *draughtboard*)
  [☞ drought]
draught beer (*use*
  draft beer)
draught|board +s
  +ed +ing
  (checkerboard)
  [☞ draft board]
draught horse +s (*use*
  draft horse)
draughts *Brit.*
  (checkers)
  [☞ drafts]
draughts|man (*use*
  draftsman)
  draughtsmen
draughty (breezy: *use*
  drafty)
  draught|i|er
  draught|i|est
  [☞ droughty]
Dra|vid|ian +s
draw
  draws
  drew
  drawn
  draw|ing
draw back *verb*
  draws back
  drew back
  drawn back
  draw|ing back
draw|back +s *noun*
draw|bar +s
draw|bridge +s
draw|cord +s
draw|down +s
drawee +s
draw|er[1] +s (one who
  draws)
drawer[2] +s (sliding
  compartment)
draw|er|ful +s
drawers (pants)
draw|ing +s *noun*
draw|ing board +s
draw|ing card +s
draw|ing pin +s
drawing-room +s
draw|knife
  draw|knives
drawl +s +ed +ing
drawl|er +s
drawn *adjective*
drawn-out
drawn|work
draw play +s
draw|string +s
dray +s
dray horse +s
dray man
  dray men

Dray|ton, Mi|chael
  (English poet)
Dray|ton Val|ley
  (town, Canada)
dread +s +ed +ing
dread|ed *adjective*
dread|ful
dread|ful|ly
dread|ful|ness
dread|locked
dread|locks
dread|nought +s
dream
  dreams
  dreamed or dreamt
  dream|ing
dream|boat +s
dream catch|er +s
dream|er +s
dream|ful
dream|ful|ly
dream|i|er
dream|i|est
dream|i|ly
dream|i|ness
dream|land
dream|less
dream|less|ly
dream|like
dream|scape +s
dreamt
dream team +s
dream tick|et +s
dream|time
dream world +s
dreamy
  dream|i|er
  dream|i|est
drear
drear|i|ly
drear|i|ness
dreary
  drear|i|er
  drear|i|est
dreck
drecky
  dreck|i|er
  dreck|i|est
dredge
  dredg|es
  dredged
  dredg|ing
dredg|er +s
dree
  drees
  dreed
  dree|ing
dreg +s
dreggy
drei|del +s
dreidl +s (*use* dreidel)

Drei|ser, Theo|dore
Her|man Al|bert
(US novelist)
drench
drench|es
drenched
drench|ing
Dren|the (province,
the Netherlands)
Dres|den (city,
Germany)
Dres|den china
dress
dress|es
dressed
dress|ing
dres|sage
dress coat +s
dress code +s
dress|er +s
dress|er set +s
dress|i|er
dress|i|est
dress|i|ness
dress|ing +s noun
dress|ing case +s
dressing-down +s
noun
dress|ing gown +s
dress|ing room +s
dress|ing table +s
dress|maker +s
dress|making
dress up verb
dress|es up
dressed up
dress|ing up
dress-up noun
dressy
dress|i|er
dress|i|est
Drew, George
Alex|an|der (Cdn
politician)
drew
Drey|fus, Al|fred
(French army officer)
drib|ble
drib|bles
drib|bled
drib|bling
drib|bler +s
drib|blet +s (use
driblet)
drib|bly
drib|let +s
dribs and drabs
dried
drier +s (comparative
of dry; for a
machine or
substance that dries
use dryer)

dri|est
drift +s +ed +ing
drift|age
drift|er +s
drift ice
drift net +s
drift|wood
drill +s +ed +ing
drill|er +s
drill|ing noun
drill press
drill press|es
drill stem +s
drily (use dryly)
drink
drinks
drank
drunk
drink|ing
drink|abil|ity
drink|able
drink|er +s
drip
drips
dripped
drip|ping
drip-dry
drip-dries
drip-dried
drip-drying
drip-feed
drip-feeds
drip-fed
drip-feeding
drip fil|ter +s
drip|less
drip|pi|ly
drip|pi|ness
drip|ping adjective
drip|ping wet
drippy
drip|pi|er
drip|pi|est
driv|abil|ity (use
driveability)
driv|able (use
driveable)
drive
drives
drove
driv|en
driv|ing
drive|abil|ity
drive|able
drive by verb
drives by
drove by
driv|en by
driv|ing by
drive-by +s noun
drive in verb
drives in

drove in
driv|en in
driv|ing in
drive-in +s noun
driv|el
driv|els
driv|elled
drivel|ling
drive|line +s
drivel|ler +s
drivel|ling adjective
driv|en adjective
drive on verb
drives on
drove on
driv|en on
driv|ing on
drive-on adjective
driv|er +s
driv|er|less
driver's li|cence +s
driver's test +s
drive|shaft +s
drive shed +s
drive through verb
drives through
drove through
driv|en through
driv|ing through
drive-through +s
adjective & noun
drive-thru +s (in
commercial use
= drive-through)
drive-time
drive|train +s
drive|way +s
driv|ing adjective &
noun
driz|zle
driz|zles
driz|zled
driz|zling
driz|zly
Dr. Mar|tens
proprietary
DRO (deputy returning
officer)
DROs
Drogh|eda (port,
Ireland)
drogue +s
droid +s
droit +s
droit de sei|gneur
droke +s
droll +s
droll|ery
droll|eries
droll|ness
drolly
drom|ed|ary
drom|ed|aries

drone
drones
droned
dron|ing
dron|er +s
dron|go
dron|gos or
dron|goes
drool +s +ed +ing
droop +s +ed +ing
(sag)
[☞ drupe]
droop|i|ly
droop|i|ness
droop|ing adjective
droop|ing|ly
droopy
droop|i|er
droop|i|est
drop
drops
dropped
drop|ping
drop cloth +s
drop cook|le +s
drop-dead adverb &
adjective
drop down verb
drops down
dropped down
drop|ping down
drop-down adjective
drop-forge
drop-forges
drop-forged
drop-forging
drop-forged adjective
drop-forging noun
drop goal +s
drop in verb
drops in
dropped in
drop|ping in
drop-in +s adjective &
noun
drop kick +s noun
drop-kick verb
drop-kicks
drop-kicked
drop-kicking
drop-leaf
drop|let +s
drop off verb
drops off
dropped off
drop|ping off
drop-off +s
drop out verb
drops out
dropped out
drop|ping out
drop|out +s noun

drop pass
　drop pass|es
dropped *adjective*
drop|per +s
drop|pings
drop|seed
drop shot +s
drop|si|cal
drop|sy
　drop|sies
drop test +s +ed
　+ing
drop|top +s
drop|wort +s
drosh|ky
　drosh|kies
dro|soph|ila +s
dross
drossy
Drott|ning|holm
　(Swedish palace)
drought +s (dryness;
　dearth)
　[☞ draught]
droughty (dry)
　[☞ draughty]
drouth +s
　(= drought)
drouthy (= droughty)
Drouzh|ba (resort,
　Bulgaria)
drove
　droves
　droved
　drov|ing
drov|er +s
drove road +s
drov|ing *noun*
drown +s +ed +ing
drowse
　drows|es
　drowsed
　drows|ing
drows|i|ly
drows|i|ness
drowsy
　drows|i|er
　drows|i|est
drub
　drubs
　drubbed
　drub|bing
drub|bing +s *noun*
drudge
　drudg|es
　drudged
　drudg|ing
drudg|ery
drug
　drugs
　drugged
　drug|ging
drug ad|dict +s

drug|get +s
drug|gie +s (drug
　addict)
　[☞ druggy]
drug|gist +s
druggy (of drugs)
　drug|gi|er
　drug|gi|est
　[☞ druggie]
drug|less
drug|store +s
Druid +s
Druid|ic
Druid|ic|al
Druid|ism
drum
　• *noun* (*Music*; barrel;
　　eardrum;
　　Architecture; hill,
　　ridge)
　　plural drums
　• *noun* (fish)
　　plural drum or
　　drums
　• *verb*
　　drums
　　drummed
　　drum|ming
drum|beat +s
drum brake +s
drum dance +s
drum|fire
drum fish
　plural drum fish or
　drum fish|es
drum|head +s
Drum|hel|ler (city,
　Canada)
drum kit +s
drum|lin +s
drum ma|chine +s
drum|mer +s
Drum|mond,
　Wil|liam Henry
　(Cdn poet)
Drum|mond|ville
　(city, Canada)
drum roll +s
drum|stick +s
drunk +s +er +est
drunk|ard +s
drunk|en
drunk|en|ly
drunk|en|ness
drunk|ish
drunk tank +s
drup|aceous
drupe +s (fruit)
　[☞ droop]
drup|el +s
drupe|let +s
druse +s (*Mineralogy*)
　[☞ Druze]

drusy
druth|ers
Druz|ba
　(= Drouzhba,
　Bulgaria)
Druze +s (*Islam*)
　[☞ druse]
dry
　drier
　driest
　dries
　dried
　dry|ing
dry|able
dryad +s
dryas
　plural dryas
dry cell +s
dry clean +s +ed
　+ing
dry-cure
　dry-cures
　dry-cured
　dry-curing
dry-cured *adjective*
Dry|den (town,
　Canada)
Dry|den, John
　(English writer)
Dry|den, Ken|neth
　Wayne ('Ken') (Cdn
　hockey player &
　executive)
dry dock +s
dryer +s (machine or
　substance that dries)
　[☞ drier]
dry-eyed
dry fly *noun*
　dry flies
dry-fly *verb*
　dry-flies
　dry-flied
　dry-flying
dry goods
dry ice
dry|ish
dry land +s (land as
　opposed to sea)
dry|land +s (area with
　little rainfall; surface
　with no snow or ice)
dryly
dry-mount +s +ed
　+ing
dry-mounting *noun*
dry|ness
dry nurse +s
dry plate +s
dry|point +s

dry-roast +s +ed
　+ing
dry-roasted *adjective*
dry rot
dry-salt +s +ed +ing
dry-salter +s
dry-shod
dry sink +s
dry|stone
dry suit +s
dry|wall +s +ed +ing
dry|wall|er +s
dry|wall|ing *noun*
dry well +s
DSC (Distinguished
　Service Cross)
　DSCs
DSM (Distinguished
　Service Medal)
　DSMs
DSO (Distinguished
　Service Order)
　DSOs
DSP (digital signal
　processing; digital
　signal processor)
　DSPs
DTP (desktop
　publishing)
DT's (delirium
　tremens)
dual +s (twofold,
　double; *Grammar*)
　[☞ duel]
dual con|trol *adjective*
dual in-line
dual|ism +s
dual|ist +s (*Theology*;
　Philosophy)
　[☞ duellist]
dual|is|tic
dual|is|tic|ally
dual|ity
　dual|ities
dual|ize
　dual|iz|es
　dual|ized
　dual|iz|ing
dual|ly
dual-purpose
du|ath|lete +s
du|ath|lon +s
dub
　dubs
　dubbed
　dub|bing
Dubai (state & its
　capital, UAE)
du Barry, Com|tesse
　(French mistress of
　Louis XV)
Du|bawnt (lake &
　river, Canada)

dub|bin (waterproofing agent)
dub|bins
dub|bined
dubbin|ing
dub|bing +s *noun* (soundtrack)
Dub|ček, Alex|an|der (Czechoslovak statesman)
Dubé, Mar|cel (Cdn playwright)
Dubhe (star)
dubi|ety
dubi|eties
dubi|ous
dubi|ous|ly
dubi|ous|ness
dubi|ta|tion +s
Dub|lin (county & capital of Ireland)
Dub|lin|er +s
dub music
Du Bois, Wil|liam Ed|ward Burg|hardt (US activist)
dub poet|ry
Du|brov|nik (port, Croatia)
Du|buf|fet, Jean Phi|lippe Ar|thur (French artist)
ducal
duc|at +s
Duce (Mussolini) [☞ deuce, douce]
Du|champ, Mar|cel (French-born artist)
Du|chenne mus|cu|lar dys|trophy
duch|ess
duch|ess|es
du|chesse po|ta|toes
duchy (dukedom)
duch|ies [☞ Dutchie]
duck +s +ed +ing
duck|bill +s
duck-billed
duck-billed dino|saur +s
duck-billed platy|pus
duck-billed platy|pus|es
duck|board +s
duck boot +s
duck-dive
duck-dives
duck-dived
duck-diving

duck, duck, goose (game)
duck|er +s
ducking-stool +s
duck|ish
Duck Lake (town, Canada)
duck|ling +s
ducks and drakes
duck's ass (haircut)
duck's asses
duck|tail +s
duck|tailed
duck-walk +s +ed +ing
duck|weed +s
ducky
duck|ies
duct +s
duct|al (of a duct) [☞ ductile]
duct|ed
duc|tile (pliable, flexible) [☞ ductal]
duc|til|ity
duct|ing +s
duct|less
duct tape +s *noun*
duct-tape *verb*
duct-tapes
duct-taped
duct-taping
duct|work
dud +s
dude
dudes
duded
duding
Dudek, Louis (Cdn poet)
dude|ness
dude ranch
dude ranch|es
dud|ette +s
dud|ish
dudg|eon
Dud|ley, Rob|ert (Earl of Leicester, English courtier)
due +s (owed; ascribable; expected; directly) [☞ dew]
due date +s
duel (fight)
duels
duelled
duel|ling [☞ dual]
duel|ler +s

duel|list +s (participant in a duel) [☞ dualist]
duen|na +s
due pro|cess
duet +s +ed +ing
duet|tist +s
duff +s +ed +ing
duf|fel +s (*use* duffle)
duf|fel bag +s (*use* duffle bag)
duf|fel coat +s (*use* duffle coat)
duf|fer +s
Duf|fer|in (and Ava), 1st Mar|quess of (Frederick Temple Blackwood, governor general of Canada)
duf|fle +s
duf|fle bag +s
duf|fle coat +s
Du|fresne, Diane (Cdn entertainer)
dufus (= doofus)
dufus|es
Dufy, Raoul (French artist)
dug +s
du|gong *plural* du|gong or du|gongs
dug|out +s
duh
Du|ha|mel, Georges (French writer)
dui|ker +s
Duis|burg (city, Germany)
du jour (of the day; trendy) [☞ de jure]
Dukas, Paul Abra|ham (French composer)
duke
dukes
duked
duk|ing
duke|dom +s
Dul|bec|co, Ren|ato (US virologist)
dul|cet
dul|ci|mer +s
dull
dull|er
dull|est
dulls
dulled
dull|ing
dull|ard +s

dulled *adjective*
Dul|les, John Fos|ter (US diplomat)
dull|ish
dull|ness
dully (in a dull manner etc.) [☞ duly]
dul|ness (*use* dullness)
dulse
duly (in due manner etc.; properly) [☞ dually, dully]
Duma +s
Dumas, Alex|andre ('Dumas *père*', French writer)
Dumas, Alex|andre ('Dumas *fils*', French writer)
Du Maur|ier, Dame Daphne (English novelist)
Du Maur|ier, George Louis Pal|mel|la Bus|son (English illustrator & novelist)
dumb +er +est +s +ed +ing
dumb-ass
dumb|bell +s
dumb cane +s
dumb cluck +s
dumb|found +s +ed +ing
dumb|head +s
dumb|ly
dumb|ness
dumbo +s
dumb|struck
dumb wait|er +s
dum|dum +s (foolish person; bullet)
dum|found +s +ed +ing (*use* dumbfound)
Dum|fries (town, Scotland)
Dum|fries and Gal|lo|way (region, Scotland)
Dum|fries|shire (former county, Scotland)
dummy
dum|mies
dum|mied
dummy|ing
dummy run +s
Du|mont, Gab|riel (Cdn Metis leader)
dump +s +ed +ing

dump-and-chase
dump|er +s
dump|i|er
dump|i|est
dump|i|ness
dump|ing +s *noun*
dump|ing ground +s
dump|ling +s
dumps (low spirits)
Dump|ster +s
  proprietary
Dump|ster dive
Dump|ster dives
Dump|ster dived
Dump|ster div|ing
Dump|ster div|er +s
Dump|ster div|ing
  noun
dump truck +s
dumpy
  dump|i|er
  dump|i|est
dun (colour; debt
  collector; pester)
duns
dunned
dun|ning
  [☞ done, Donne]
Du|nant, Jean Henri
  (Swiss
  philanthropist)
Dun|bar, Wil|liam
  (Scottish poet)
Dun|bar|ton|shire
  (former county,
  Scotland)
Dun|can (city, Canada;
  Scottish king)
Dun|can, Isa|dora
  (US dancer)
dunce +s
dunce cap +s
dunce's cap +s
  (= dunce cap)
Dun|dalk (town,
  Ireland)
Dun|das (town &
  peninsula, Canada)
Dun|dee (city,
  Scotland)
dunder|head +s
dunder|head|ed
dune +s
dune buggy
  dune bug|gies
Dun|edin (cities, New
  Zealand & US)
dune grass
  dune grass|es
Dun|ferm|line (city,
  Scotland)
dung +s +ed +ing
dun|ga|ree +s

Dun|gen|ess crab +s
dun|geon +s +ed
  +ing (underground
  cell; imprison; *for*
  castle tower *use*
  donjon)
Dun|geons and
  Drag|ons
  proprietary
dung-heap +s
dung|hill +s
dunk +s +ed +ing
dunk|er +s
Dun|kirk (city, France)
dunk shot +s
dunk tank +s
Dun Lao|ghaire
  (town, Ireland)
dun|lin +s
Dun|lop, John Boyd
  (Scottish inventor)
dun|nage
Dun|net Head
  (headland, Scotland)
Dunne-Za
dun|ning let|ter +s
dun|ning no|tice +s
dunno
Dunn|ville (town,
  Canada)
Duns Sco|tus, John
  (Scottish theologian)
Dun|stan (saint)
duo +s
duo|deci|mal
duo|deci|mal|ly
duo|deci|mo +s
duo|denal
duo|den|um +s
duo|logue +s
duomo +s
du|op|ol|ist +s
du|op|o|lis|tic
du|op|oly
du|op|ol|ies
Duo-Tang +s
  proprietary
duo|tone +s
dup|able
Du|parc, (Marie
  Eu|gène) Henri
  (French composer)
dupe
  dupes
  duped
  dup|ing
dup|er +s
dup|ery
dup|ing *noun*
du|pion +s
duple

Du|ples|sis, Mau|rice
  Le Nob|let (Cdn
  politician)
du|plex
du|plex|es
du|plexed
du|plex|ing
du|plexed *adjective*
du|plex|ing *noun*
du|plic|able
dupli|cate
dupli|cates
dupli|cat|ed
dupli|cat|ing
dupli|ca|tion +s
dupli|ca|tive
dupli|ca|tor +s
du|pli|ci|tous
du|pli|city
du|pli|ci|ties
Dupré, Mar|cel
  (French musician)
du Pré, Jacque|line
  (English cellist)
Dupuy, Claude-
  Thomas (intendant
  of New France)
Du|quesne, Ange
Du|quesne de
  Menne|ville,
  Mar|quis (French
  governor general of
  New France)
dura +s
dur|abil|ity
dur|able +s
dur|able|ness
dur|ably
dura mater +s
du|ra|men
dur|ance
Du|ran|go (state & its
  capital, Mexico)
Du|rant, Wil|liam
  James ('Will') &
  Ariel (US historians)
  [☞ Durante]
Du|rante, James
  Fran|cis ('Jimmy')
  (US comedian)
  [☞ Durant]
Duras, Mar|guer|ite
  (French novelist &
  filmmaker)
dur|ation +s
dur|ation|al
dura|tive
Dur|ban (city, South
  Africa)
dur|bar +s
durch|kom|pon|iert
Dürer, Al|brecht
  (German artist)

dur|ess
Durga (*Hinduism*)
Dur|ham (county &
  city, England)
  [☞ durum, dirham]
Dur|ham, John
  George Lamb|ton,
  Earl of (British
  colonial
  administrator in
  BNA)
  [☞ dirham]
dur|ian +s
duri|crust +s
dur|ing
Durk|heim, Émile
  (French sociologist)
dur|mast +s
Dur|nan, Wil|liam
  Ar|nold ('Bill') (Cdn
  hockey player)
Du|ro|cher, Leo
  Er|nest (US baseball
  player)
dur|ra +s
Dur|rell, Law|rence
  George (English
  writer)
Dür|ren|matt,
  Fried|rich (Swiss
  writer)
durst
durum (wheat)
  [☞ Durham,
  dirham]
Duse, Eleo|nora
  (Italian actress)
Du|shan|be (capital of
  Tajikistan)
dusk +s
dusk|i|ly
dusk|i|ness
dusky
  dusk|i|er
  dusk|i|est
Düs|sel|dorf (city,
  Germany)
dust +s +ed +ing
dust|ball +s
dust-bath +s
dust|bin +s
dust bowl +s
dust bunny
  dust bun|nies
Dust|bust|er +s
  proprietary
dust cov|er +s
dust dev|il +s
dust|er +s
dust|er coat +s
dust|i|er
dust|i|est
dust|i|ly

dust|i|ness
dust|ing +s *noun*
dust jack|et +s
dust|less
dust|man
   dust|men
dust|pan +s
dust ruf|fle +s
dust sheet +s
dust storm +s
dust-up +s *noun*
dusty
   dust|i|er
   dust|i|est
dusty mil|ler +s
Dutch
Dutch apple cake +s
Dutch apple pie +s
Dutch elm dis|ease
Dutch Gui|ana
   (*former name for*
   Suriname,
   S America)
Dutch|ie +s
   (*doughnut*)
   [☞ duchy]
Dutch|man
   Dutch|men
Dutchman's
   breech|es
Dutchman's pipe +s
Dutch|woman
   Dutch|women
dut|eous
dut|eous|ly
dut|eous|ness
duti|able
duti|ful
duti|ful|ly
duti|ful|ness
Du|toit, Charles
   Édouard (Swiss
   conductor)
duty
   dut|ies
duty-free
du|um|vir +s
du|um|vir|ate +s
Du|va|lier, Fran|çois
   ('Papa Doc')
   (Haitian statesman)
Du|va|lier, Jean-
   Claude ('Baby Doc')
   (Haitian statesman)
du|vet +s
Du Vi|gneaud,
   Vin|cent (US
   biochemist)
dux|elles
duy|ker +s (*use*
   duiker)
DV

DVA (Department of
   Veterans Affairs)
D.V.M. (Doctor of
   Veterinary Medicine)
D.V.M.'s
Dvoř|ák, An|tonin
   Leo|pold (Czech
   composer)
dwale +s
dwarf
• *noun*
   dwarfs *or* dwarves
• *verb*
   dwarfs
   dwarfed
   dwarf|ing
dwarfed *adjective*
dwarf|ish
dwarf|ish|ness
dwarf|ism
dwarf-like
dweeb +s
dweeb|ish
dweeby
   dweeb|i|er
   dweeb|i|est
dwell
   dwells
   dwelt *or* dwelled
   dwell|ing
dwell|er +s
dwell|ing +s *noun*
dwell|ing place +s
dwin|dle
   dwin|dles
   dwin|dled
   dwin|dling
dwin|dling *adjective*
DX cod|ing
dyad +s
dy|ad|ic
Dyak (*use* Dayak)
   plural Dyak *or*
   Dyaks
dy|archy (*use*
   diarchy)
   dy|arch|ies
dyb|buk
   dyb|buk|im *or*
   dyb|buks
dye (colour; stain)
   dyes
   dyed
   dye|ing
   [☞ die]
dye|able
dyed-in-the-wool
dye|ing *conjugated*
   form of dye
   [☞ dying]
dyer +s (one who dyes
   cloth)
   [☞ dire]
dyer's broom

dyer's green|weed
dyer's oak +s
dye|stuff +s
Dyfed (county, Wales)
dying *adjective &*
   present participle of
   die
   [☞ dyeing]
dyke (lesbian; *for* wall,
   causeway, ditch,
   bathroom *or* igneous
   intrusion *use* dike)
   dykes
   dyked
   dyk|ing
dykey
Dylan, Bob (US
   singer-songwriter)
dy|nam|ic +s
dy|nam|ic|al
dy|nam|ic|al|ly
dy|nam|i|cist +s
dy|nam|ics
dyna|mism
dyna|mist +s
dyna|mite
   dyna|mites
   dyna|mit|ed
   dyna|mit|ing
dyna|mit|er +s
dy|namo +s
dyna|mom|eter +s
dy|nast +s
dy|nas|tic
dy|nas|tic|ally
dy|nasty
   dy|nas|ties
dyne +s (unit of force)
   [☞ dine]
Dysart, A. Al|li|son
   (Cdn politician)
dys|en|ter|ic
dys|en|tery
dys|func|tion +s
dys|func|tion|al
dys|lec|tic +s
   (= dyslexic)
dys|lexia
dys|lexic +s
dys|men|or|rhea
dys|men|or|rhoea
   (*use* dysmenorrhea)
dys|pep|sia
dys|pep|tic +s
dys|pha|sia
dys|pha|sic
dys|phor|ia
dys|pho|ric
dys|pla|sia
dys|plas|tic
dysp|nea
dysp|neic
dys|pro|sium

dys|to|cia
dys|ton|ia
dys|ton|ic
dys|to|pia +s
dys|to|pian +s
dys|troph|ic
dys|trophy
dys|uria
Dzaou|dzi (town,
   Mayotte)
Dzer|zhinsk (city,
   Russia)

E

E
• (letter; music note;
   mark; ecstasy)
   E's
• (emissivity; energy)
e
• (letter)
   e's
• (base of natural
   logarithms)
each
eager (keen)
   [☞ eagre]
eager|ly
eager|ness
eagle
   eagles
   eagled
   eag|ling
eagle eye +s
eagle-eyed
eagle owl +s
Eagle Pass (in
   Canada)
eag|let +s
Eagle|ton, Terry
   (English literary
   critic)
eagre +s (wave)
   [☞ eager]
Ea|kins, Thom|as (US
   painter)
ear +s
ear|ache +s
ear|bud +s
ear|drops
ear|drum +s
eared
ear|flap +s
ear|ful +s
Ear|hart, Amelia (US
   aviator)
ear|hole +s

earl +s (nobleman)
[☞ Earle, erl-king, URL]
earl|dom +s
Earle, David (Cdn choreographer)
ear|less
Earl Grey (Cdn governor general; British prime minister; tea)
ear|li|ness
Earl Mar|shal +s
ear|lobe +s
earl pala|tine
earls pala|tine
early
ear|li|er
ear|li|est
early bird +s (early-bird *when preceding a noun*)
ear|mark +s +ed +ing
ear|muff +s
earn +s +ed +ing (gain)
[☞ urn]
earned *adjective*
earned run aver|age +s
earn|er +s
earn|est
earn|est|ly
earn|est|ness
earn|ings
earnings-related
EARP (Environmental Assessment & Review Process)
Earp, Wyatt Berry Stapp (US frontiersman)
ear|phone +s
ear|piece +s
ear-piercing
ear|plug +s
ear|ring +s
ear|shot
ear-splitting
earth +s +ed +ing
earth|bound
earth clos|et +s
earth|en
earthen|ware +s
earth|i|er
earth|i|est
earth|i|ly
earth|i|ness
earth|li|ness
earth|ling +s
earth|ly
earth moth|er +s

earth|mov|er +s
earth|mov|ing
earth-nut +s
earth|quake +s
earth sci|ence +s
earth sci|en|tist +s
earth-shaking
earth-shatter|ing
earth-shatter|ing|ly
earth|shine
earth|star +s
earth tone +s
earth|ward
earth|wards
earth|work +s
earth|worm +s
earthy
earth|i|er
earth|i|est
ear|wax
ear|wig
ear|wigs
ear|wigged
ear|wig|ging
ease
eases
eased
eas|ing
easel +s
ease|ment +s
easer +s
eas|i|er
eas|i|est
eas|i|ly
eas|i|ness
East (particular region; *Bridge*)
east (compass point; direction)
East An|glia (region, England)
east|bound
East|bourne (town, England)
East Ender +s
Eas|ter +s
Eas|ter Bunny
Eas|ter Bun|nies
Eas|ter Island (in SE Pacific)
east|er|ly
east|er|lies
East|ern (of the Far or Middle East; of the Eastern Church)
east|ern (*in general use*)
East|ern bloc (countries formerly under Soviet domination)
east|ern|er +s
east|ern hemi|sphere

east|ern|most
East|ern rite +s
East|ern Town|ships (region, Canada)
East|er rising
Easter|tide
East India Com|pany
east|ing +s
East|main (river, Canada)
East|main Cree
plural East|main Cree or East|main Crees
East|man, George (US inventor)
east-northeast
east-southeast
east|ward
east|wardly
east|wards
East|wood, Clint (US actor & director)
easy
easi|er
easi|est
easy-care
easy chair +s
easy|going
easy lis|ten|ing (easy-listening *when preceding a noun*)
easy street
easy-to-use *adjective preceding a noun*
eat
eats
ate
eaten
eat|ing
eat|able +s
eater +s
eat|ery
eat|eries
eat|ing *adjective*
eat-in kitch|en +s
Eaton, Tim|othy (Cdn merchant)
eats
eau de co|logne
eaux de co|logne
eau de toi|lette
eaux de toi|lette
eau-de-vie
eaux-de-vie
eaves
eaves|drop
eaves|drops
eaves|dropped
eaves|drop|ping
eaves|drop|per +s
eaves|trough +s
eaves|trough|ing

ebb +s +ed +ing
Ebla (city, ancient Syria)
Ebola (river & district, Congo; virus)
ebon|ite
ebony
ebon|ies
Ebro (river, Spain)
ebul|li|ence
ebul|li|ency
ebul|li|ent
ebul|li|ent|ly
EBV (Epstein-Barr virus)
écarté
Ecce Homo
ec|cen|tric +s
ec|cen|tric|ally
ec|cen|tri|city
ec|cen|tri|ci|ties
Ec|cles, Sir John Carew (Australian physiologist)
Ec|cles, Wil|liam John (Cdn historian)
ec|cle|sial
Ec|clesi|as|tes (*Bible*)
ec|clesi|as|tic +s
ec|clesi|as|tic|al
ec|clesi|as|tic|al|ly
ec|clesi|as|ti|cism
Ec|clesi|as|ti|cus (*Apocrypha*)
ec|clesi|o|logic|al
ec|clesi|ol|o|gist +s
ec|clesi|ol|ogy
ec|crine
ec|dy|sis
ec|dy|ses
ECE (early childhood education; early childhood educator)
ECEs
ECG (electrocardiogram, electrocardiograph, etc.)
ECGs
ech|elon +s
eche|veria +s
ech|idna +s
echin|acea
ech|ino|derm +s
echi|noid +s
echi|nus
echi|nus|es
Echo (*Greek Myth*)
[☞ Eco]
echo (repetition; resound, imitate; *Computing*; *Bridge*)

echoes
echoed
echo|ing
[☞ eco]
echo|cardio|gram +s
echo|cardio|graph +s
echo|cardi|og|raph| er +s
echo|cardio|graph|ic
echo|cardi|og|raphy
echo cham|ber +s
echo|en|ceph|alo| gram +s
echo|en|cephal|og| raphy
echo|er +s
echo|ey
echo|gram +s
echo|graph +s
echo|ic
echo|ic|ally
echo|ism
echo|la|lia
echo|less
echo|locate
echo|lo|cates
echo|locat|ed
echo|locat|ing
echo|loca|tion
echo sound|er +s
echo-sounding
echo|virus
echo|virus|es
echt (genuine, typical)
Eck, Jo|hann (German theologian)
Eck|hart, Jo|han|nes ('Meis|ter') (German theologian)
eclair +s
eclamp|sia
eclamp|tic
éclat
eclec|tic +s
eclec|tic|ally
eclec|ti|cism
eclipse
eclips|es
eclipsed
eclips|ing
eclips|er +s
eclip|tic
ec|logue +s
eclo|sion +s
Eco, Um|ber|to (Italian novelist) [☞ Echo]
eco (ecology) [☞ echo]
eco|cid|al
eco|cide
eco-friend|ly

eco-label +s
eco-labelling
E. coli (= Escherichia coli)
eco|logic
eco|logic|al
eco|logic|al|ly
ecol|o|gist +s
ecol|ogy
ecol|o|gies
eco|museum +s
econo|box
econo|boxes
econo|met|ric
econo|met|ric|al
econo|met|ri|cian +s
econo|met|rics
econo|met|rist +s
eco|nom|ic
eco|nom|ic|al
eco|nom|ic|al|ly
eco|nom|ics
econo|mist +s
econo|mize
econo|miz|es
econo|mized
econo|miz|ing
econo|miz|er +s
econo|miz|ing noun
econ|omy
econ|omies
econ|omy size
economy-sized
eco|sphere +s
eco|system +s
eco|tage
eco-terror|ism
eco-terror|ist +s
eco|tonal
eco|tone +s
eco|tour +s
eco|tour|ism
eco|tour|ist +s
eco|type +s
eco|typ|ic
ecru +s
ec|stasy
ec|sta|sies
ec|stat|ic
ec|stat|ic|ally
ecto|blast +s
ecto|blas|tic
ecto|derm +s
ecto|derm|al
ecto|derm|ic
ecto|gen|esis
ecto|gen|etic
ecto|gen|etic|ally
ecto|morph +s
ecto|morph|ic
ecto|morphy
ecto|para|site +s

ecto|para|sit|ic
ec|top|ic
ecto|plasm
ecto|plas|mic
ECU (European Currency Unit) plural ECU or ECUs
Ecua|dor (country, S America)
Ecua|dor|ean +s
ecu|men|ical
ecu|men|ical|ly
ecu|men|ism
ec|zema
ec|zema|tous
ed
Edam (town, the Netherlands; cheese)
ed|aph|ic
Ed|berg, Stef|an (Swedish tennis player)
Edda +s
Eddaic
Eddic
Ed|ding|ton, Sir Ar|thur Stan|ley (English astronomer)
eddo
ed|does
Eddy, Ezra But|ler (US-born Cdn manufacturer)
Eddy, Mary Baker (US founder of Christian Science)
eddy
ed|dies
ed|died
eddy|ing
Eddy|stone Rocks (reef, off England)
edel|weiss plural edel|weiss
edema
ede|mas or ede|mata
ede|ma|tous
Eden +s
Eden, (Rob|ert) An|thony (1st Earl of Avon, British prime minister)
Eden|ic
edent|ate +s
edge
edges
edged
edg|ing
edged adjective
Edge|hill (battle site, England)
edge|less

edg|er +s
edge tool +s
edge|ways
edge|wise
Edge|worth, Maria (Anglo-Irish novelist)
edg|i|ly
edg|i|ness
edg|ing +s noun
edgy
edg|i|er
edg|i|est
edh +s (use eth)
ed|ibil|ity
ed|ible +s
edict +s
edict|al
edi|fi|ca|tion +s
edi|fice +s
edify
edi|fies
edi|fied
edi|fy|ing
edi|fy|ing adjective
edi|fy|ing|ly
Edin|burgh (capital of Scotland)
Edi|son, Thom|as Alva (US inventor)
edit +s +ed +ing
edit|able
edi|tion +s
edi|tio prin|ceps edi|tio|nes prin|ci|pes
edi|tor +s
edi|tor|ial +s
edi|tor|ial|ist +s
edi|tor|ial|ize
edi|tor|ial|iz|es
edi|tor|ial|ized
edi|tor|ial|iz|ing
edi|tor|ial|ly
editor-in-chief
editors-in-chief
editor|ship +s
Ed|mon|chuk (Edmonton)
Ed|mon|ton (city, Canada)
Ed|mon|ton|ian +s
Ed|mund (English kings)
Ed|mund Cam|pion (saint)
Ed|mund Iron|side (English king)
Ed|munds|ton (city, Canada)
EDP (electronic data processing)
Edson (town, Canada)

EDTA (ethylenediamine tetra-acetic acid)
educ|abil|ity
educ|able
edu|cat|able
edu|cate
  edu|cates
  edu|cat|ed
  edu|cat|ing
edu|cat|ed *adjective*
edu|ca|tion +s
edu|ca|tion|al
edu|ca|tion|al|ist +s
edu|ca|tion|al|ly
edu|ca|tion|ist +s
edu|ca|tive
edu|ca|tor +s
educe
  edu|ces
  educed
  edu|cing
educ|tion +s
edu|tain|ment
Ed|ward (British kings & princes; lake, Africa)
Ed|ward|ian +s
Ed|wards, Hen|ri|etta Lou|ise (Cdn women's rights activist)
Ed|wards, Jona|than (US theologian)
Ed|ward the Con|fes|sor (English king & saint)
EEG (electro-encephalogram, etc.)
  EEGs
eek *interjection*
  [☞ **eke**]
eel +s
Eelam (proposed Tamil homeland, Sri Lanka)
  [☞ **Elam**]
eel|grass
  eel|grass|es
eel-like
eel|pout
  plural **eel|pout** or **eel|pouts**
eel|worm +s
eely
e'en
eensy
eensy-weensy
e'er (ever)
  [☞ **ere, err**]

eerie (weird)
  eer|i|er
  eer|i|est
  [☞ **Erie, eyrie, aerie**]
  eer|i|ly
  eer|i|ness
EFA (essential fatty acid)
  EFAs
eff +s +ed +ing *euphemism*
ef|face
  ef|fa|ces
  ef|faced
  ef|fa|cing
ef|face|ment +s
ef|fect +s +ed +ing (result; bring about)
  [☞ **affect**]
ef|fect|ive +s (having an effect; efficient)
  [☞ **affective**]
ef|fect|ive|ly
ef|fect|ive|ness
ef|fec|tiv|ity (degree of being effective)
  ef|fec|tiv|ities
  [☞ **affectivity**]
ef|fect|or +s
ef|fec|tual
ef|fec|tual|ity
ef|fec|tual|ly
ef|fec|tual|ness
ef|fec|tu|ate
  ef|fec|tu|ates
  ef|fec|tu|at|ed
  ef|fec|tu|at|ing
ef|fec|tu|a|tion
ef|fem|in|acy
ef|fem|in|ate
ef|fem|in|ate|ly
ef|fen|di +s
ef|fer|ent
ef|fer|vesce
  ef|fer|ves|ces
  ef|fer|vesced
  ef|fer|ves|cing
ef|fer|ves|cence
ef|fer|ves|cent
ef|fete
ef|fete|ly
ef|fete|ness
ef|fi|ca|cious
ef|fi|ca|cious|ly
ef|fi|ca|cious|ness
ef|fi|cacy
  ef|fi|ca|cies
ef|fi|ciency
  ef|fi|cien|cies
ef|fi|cient
ef|fi|cient|ly

ef|figy
  ef|fi|gies
ef|fing *adjective*
ef|fleur|age
  ef|fleur|ages
  ef|fleur|aged
  ef|fleur|a|ging
ef|flor|esce
  ef|flor|es|ces
  ef|flor|esced
  ef|flor|es|cing
ef|flor|es|cence +s
ef|flor|es|cent
ef|flu|ence +s
ef|flu|ent +s
ef|flu|vium
  ef|flu|via
ef|flux
  ef|flux|es
ef|flux|ion +s
ef|fort +s
ef|fort|ful
ef|fort|ful|ly
ef|fort|less
ef|fort|less|ly
ef|fort|less|ness
ef|front|ery (audacity, insolence)
  ef|front|eries
  [☞ **affront**]
ef|ful|gence
ef|ful|gent
ef|ful|gent|ly
ef|fuse
  ef|fus|es
  ef|fused
  ef|fus|ing
ef|fu|sion +s
ef|fu|sive
ef|fu|sive|ly
ef|fu|sive|ness
EFT (electronic funds transfer)
  EFTs
eft +s
EFTA (European Free Trade Association)
EFTPOS (electronic funds transfer at point-of-sale)
e.g.
egad
egali|tar|ian +s
egali|tar|ian|ism
Egas Moniz, An|tónio (Cae|tano de Abreu Freire) (Portuguese neurologist)
Eg|bert (king of Wessex)
Eger (town, Hungary)
egg +s +ed +ing

egg and bacon (= eggs and bacon, plant)
egg beat|er +s
egg case +s
egg cell +s
egg cream +s
egg cup +s
egg drop soup +s
egg|head +s
egg|i|er
egg|i|est
egg|less
egg|nog +s
egg|plant +s
egg roll +s
eggs and bacon (plant)
eggs Ben|edict
egg|shell +s
egg tim|er +s
egg tooth
  egg teeth
egg white +s
eggy
  egg|i|er
  egg|i|est
egg yolk +s
eglan|tine +s
Eg|mont (volcano, New Zealand)
ego +s
ego|cen|tric
ego|cen|tric|ally
ego|cen|tric|ity
ego|cen|trism
ego-ideal +s
ego|ism
  • The senses of *egoism* and *egotism* overlap, but *egoism* alone is used in philosophy & psychology to mean 'self-interest'.
ego|ist +s
ego|is|tic
ego|is|tic|al
ego|is|tic|al|ly
ego|less
ego|mania
ego|maniac
ego|man|iacal
ego|tism
  • See Usage Note at *egoism*.
ego|tist +s
ego|tis|tic
ego|tis|tic|al
ego|tis|tic|al|ly
ego trip +s *noun*

ego-trip *verb*
  ego-trips
  ego-tripped
  ego-tripping
ego-tripper +s
Egoy|an, Atom (Cdn
  filmmaker)
egre|gious
egre|gious|ly
egre|gious|ness
egress
  egress|es
egret +s (bird)
  [☞ aigrette]
Egypt (country, Africa)
Egyp|tian +s
Egyp|tian|ism
Egypt|o|logic|al
Egypt|ol|o|gist +s
Egypt|ol|ogy
eh *interjection*
  [☞ aye]
Ehren|burg, Ilya
  Grig|ori|evich
  (Russian writer)
Ehr|lich, Paul
  (German
  bacteriologist)
EI (employment
  insurance)
Eich|mann, (Karl)
  Adolf (German Nazi
  administrator)
  [☞ Eijkman]
Eid (Muslim festival)
eider +s
eider|down +s
eider duck +s
eid|etic +s
eido|lon
  eido|lons or eido|la
Eif|fel, (Alex|andre)
  Gus|tave (French
  engineer)
Eigen, Man|fred
  (German chemist)
eigen|frequen|cy
  eigen|frequen|cies
eigen|func|tion +s
eigen|value +s
Eiger (mountain,
  Switzerland)
eight +s (number)
eight ball +s
eight|een +s
eight|een|mo +s
eight|eenth +s
eighteen-wheeler +s
eight|fold
eighth +s
eighth|ly
eighth note +s
eighth rest +s

800 num|ber +s
eight|i|eth +s
eight|some reel +s
eight-track +s
eighty
  eight|ies
eighty-eight
eighty-eighth +s
eighty-fifth +s
eighty-first +s
eighty-five
eighty-four
eighty-fourth +s
eighty-nine
eighty-ninth +s
eighty-one
eighty-second +s
eighty-seven
eighty-seventh +s
eighty-six
  eighty-sixes
  eighty-sixed
  eighty-sixing
eighty-sixth +s
eighty-third +s
eighty-three
eighty-two
Eijk|man, Chris|tiaan
  (Dutch physician)
Eilat (town, Israel)
Eind|hoven (city, the
  Netherlands)
  [☞ Einthoven]
ein|korn
Ein|stein, Al|bert
  (German physicist)
ein|stein|ium
Eint|hoven, Wil|lem
  (Dutch physiologist)
  [☞ Eindhoven]
Eire (Ireland)
  [☞ eyra]
eir|en|ic (*use* irenic)
Eisen|hower, Dwight
  David ('Ike') (US
  general & president)
Eisen|stadt (city,
  Austria)
  [☞ Eisenstaedt]
Eisen|staedt, Al|fred
  (German-born US
  photographer)
  [☞ Eisenstadt]
Eisen|stein, Ser|gei
  Mikh|ail|ovich
  (Soviet filmmaker)
eis|tedd|fod
  eis|tedd|fods or
  eis|tedd|fodau
eis|tedd|fod|ic
either
either-or

ejacu|late
  ejacu|lates
  ejacu|lat|ed
  ejacu|lat|ing
ejacu|la|tion +s
ejacu|la|tor +s
ejacu|la|tory
eject +s +ed +ing
ejecta
eject|able
ejec|tion +s
ejec|tion seat +s
eject|ment +s
eject|or +s
eject|or seat +s
Ekat|er|ino|dar
  (*former name of the*
  city of Krasnodar,
  Russia)
Ekat|er|ino|slav
  (*former name of*
  Dnipropetrovsk,
  Ukraine)
eke (in 'eke out')
  ekes
  eked
  eking
  [☞ eek]
EKG
  (electrocardiogram;
  electrocardiograph)
  EKGs
ekka +s
Ekman, Vagn
  Wall|frid (Swedish
  oceanographer)
el +s (elevated
  railway)
  [☞ ell]
elab|or|ate
  elab|or|ates
  elab|or|at|ed
  elab|or|at|ing
elab|or|ate|ly
elab|or|ate|ness
elab|or|a|tion +s
elae|agnus
  elae|agnus|es
Ela|gab|alus
  (= Heliogabalus,
  Roman emperor)
El Ala|mein (battle
  site, Egypt)
Elam (ancient Asian
  kingdom)
  [☞ Eelam]
Elam|ite +s
élan
eland +s
elapse
  elaps|es
  elapsed
  elaps|ing

elas|mo|branch +s
elas|mo|saur +s
elas|mo|saur|us
  (= elasmosaur)
elas|mo|saur|us|es
elas|tase
elas|tic +s
elas|tic|ally
elas|ti|cated
elas|ti|city
  elas|ti|ci|ties
elas|ti|cized
elas|tin +s
elas|to|mer +s
elas|to|mer|ic
Elat (= Eilat, Israel)
elate
  elates
  elated
  elat|ing
elat|ed *adjective*
elat|ed|ly
elat|ed|ness
elat|er +s
ela|tion (joy)
  [☞ illation]
E-layer
Elba (island, Italy)
  [☞ Elbe]
Elba|san (town,
  Albania)
Elbe (river, Europe)
  [☞ Elba]
El|bert (mountain, US)
Elbow (river, Canada)
elbow +s +ed +ing
elbow grease
elbow|ing *noun*
elbow pad +s
elbow room
El|brus (mountain,
  Russia)
El|burz (mountains,
  Iran)
Elche (town, Spain)
el cheapo +s
El Cid (Spanish
  soldier)
eld
elder +s
elder|berry
  elder|ber|ries
elder|care
elder|flower +s
Elder|hos|tel
  proprietary
Elder|hos|tel|er
  proprietary
elder|li|ness
elder|ly
elder|ship +s
eld|est

El Djem (town, Tunisia)
El Dor|ado (fabled Amazonian city)
El|dor|ado +s (any place of abundance or opportunity)
el|dritch
Elea|nor of Aqui|taine (queen of France & England)
Elea|nor of Cas|tile (queen of England)
ele|cam|pane +s
elect +s +ed +ing
elect|abil|ity
elect|able
elec|tion +s
Elec|tion Day (in the US)
elec|tion day (in general use)
elec|tion|eer +s +ed +ing
elec|tion|eer|ing noun
elect|ive +s
elect|ive|ly
elect|ive|ness
Elec|tor +s (German History)
elec|tor +s (voter; Electoral College member)
elec|tor|al
Elec|tor|al Col|lege (in the US)
elec|tor|al col|lege (in general use)
elec|tor|al|ly
elec|tor|ate +s
elec|tor|ship +s
Elec|tra (Greek Myth)
elec|tret +s
elec|tric +s
elec|tric|al
elec|tric|al|ly
elec|tric|al tape
elec|tric blue +s (electric-blue when preceding a noun)
elec|tri|cian +s
elec|tri|cian's tape (= electrical tape)
elec|tri|city
elec|tri|fi|ca|tion
elec|tri|fi|er +s
elec|tri|fy
elec|tri|fies
elec|tri|fied
elec|tri|fy|ing
elec|tro +s
elec|tro|acous|tic

elec|tro|cardio|gram +s
elec|tro|cardio|graph +s
elec|tro|cardio| graph|ic
elec|tro|cardio| graph|ic|ally
elec|tro|cardi| og|raphy
elec|tro|chem|ical
elec|tro|chem|ical|ly
elec|tro|chem|ist +s
elec|tro|chem|istry
elec|tro|con|vul|sive
elec|tro|cute
elec|tro|cutes
elec|tro|cut|ed
elec|tro|cut|ing
elec|tro|cu|tion +s
elec|trode +s
elec|tro|di|aly|sis
elec|tro|di|aly|ses
elec|tro|dy|nam|ic
elec|tro|dy|nam|ics
elec|tro|enceph|alo| gram +s
elec|tro|enceph|alo| graph +s
elec|tro|enceph|alo| graph|ic
elec|tro|enceph|alo| graph|ic|ally
elec|tro|enceph|al| og|raphy
elec|trol|o|gist +s
elec|tro|lumin|es| cence
elec|tro|lumin|es| cent
elec|troly|sis
elec|tro|lyte +s
elec|tro|lytic
elec|tro|lytic|al
elec|tro|lytic|al|ly
elec|tro|lyze
elec|tro|lyz|es
elec|tro|lyzed
elec|tro|lyz|ing
elec|tro|lyz|er +s
elec|tro|magnet +s
elec|tro|magnet|ic
elec|tro|magnet|ic| ally
elec|tro|magnet|ism
elec|tro|mechan|ical
elec|trom|eter +s
elec|trom|et|ric
elec|trom|etry
elec|tro|motive
elec|tro|myo|gram +s

elec|tro|myo|graph +s
elec|tro|myo|graph| ic
elec|tro|myo|graph| ic|ally
elec|tro|myog|raphy
elec|tron +s
elec|tro|nega|tive
elec|tro|nega|tiv|ity
elec|tron|ic
elec|tron|ic|ally
elec|tron|ics
elec|tron volt +s
elec|tro|phile +s
elec|tro|phil|ic
elec|tro|phor|esis
elec|tro|phor|et|ic
elec|tro|phor|et|ic| ally
elec|tro|phor|us
elec|tro|phori
elec|tro|physio| logic|al
elec|tro|physio| logic|al|ly
elec|tro|physi|ol|ogy
elec|tro|plate
elec|tro|plates
elec|tro|plat|ed
elec|tro|plat|ing
elec|tro|plat|er +s
elec|tro|pora|tion
elec|tro|posi|tive
elec|tro|scope +s
elec|tro|scop|ic
elec|tro|shock +s +ed +ing
elec|tro|stat|ic
elec|tro|stat|ic|ally
elec|tro|stat|ics
elec|tro|thera|peut|ic
elec|tro|thera|peut| ic|al
elec|tro|ther|apist +s
elec|tro|ther|apy
elec|tro|ther|mal
elec|tro|type
elec|tro|types
elec|tro|typed
elec|tro|typ|ing
elec|tro|typ|er +s
elec|tro|valence
elec|tro|valen|cy
elec|tro|valent
elec|tro|weak
elec|trum
elec|tu|ary
elec|tu|aries
ele|emosyn|ary
ele|gance
ele|gan|cy
ele|gant

ele|gant|ly
ele|giac +s
ele|giac|ally
ele|gist +s
ele|gize
ele|giz|es
ele|gized
ele|giz|ing
elegy
ele|gies
ele|ment +s
ele|men|tal
ele|men|tar|i|ly
ele|men|tar|i|ness
ele|men|tary
elen|chus
elen|chi
elenc|tic
ele|phant
plural ele|phants or ele|phant
ele|phant ear +s
ele|phant head
ele|phant|ia|sis
ele|phant|ine
ele|phant|oid
Ele|phant Pass (in Sri Lanka)
Eleu|sin|ian
ele|vate
ele|vates
ele|vat|ed
ele|vat|ing
ele|va|tion +s
ele|va|tion|al
ele|va|tor +s
ele|va|tory
elev|en +s
eleven|fold
eleven-plus
elev|ens|es
elev|enth +s
elf
elves
elf|in
elf|ish
elf-locks
Elgar, Sir Ed|ward Wil|liam (English composer)
Elgin, James Bruce, 8th Earl of (governor general of Canada)
[☞ Elgon]
Elgin, Thom|as Bruce, 7th Earl of (English art collector)
[☞ Elgon]
El Giza (= Giza, Egypt)

Elgon (volcano,
E Africa)
El Greco (Spanish
painter)
Eli (*Bible*)
[☞ Ely]
Elia (Charles Lamb)
elicit +s +ed +ing
(evoke, prompt)
[☞ illicit]
elicit|a|tion +s
elicit|or +s
elide
elides
elid|ed
elid|ing
eli|gi|bil|ity
eli|gible
eli|gibly
Eli|jah (Hebrew
prophet)
[☞ Elisha]
elim|in|able
elim|in|ate
elim|in|ates
elim|in|at|ed
elim|in|at|ing
elim|in|a|tion +s
elim|in|a|tive
elim|in|ator +s
Eliot (surname)
[☞ Elliot Lake]
Eliot, George (English
novelist)
Eliot, Thom|as
Stearns (US-born
English writer)
ELISA (enzyme-linked
immunosorbent
assay)
ELISAs
Elisa|beth|ville
(*former name for*
Lubumbashi,
Congo)
Eli|sha (disciple of
Elijah)
eli|sion +s
Ell|ista (city, Russia)
elite +s
elit|ism
elit|ist +s
elix|ir +s
Eliza|beth (English &
Romanian queens;
Russian empress;
saint)
Eliza|beth|an +s
Eliza|vet|pol (*former
name for* Gäncä,
Azerbaijan)
elk
plural elk or elks

elk|hound
Elk Island (national
park, Canada)
ell +s (L-shaped
object; measure of
length)
[☞ el]
Ellef Ring|nes (island,
Canada)
Elles|mere (island,
Canada; port,
England)
Ell|lice Islands (*former
name for* Tuvalu,
SW Pacific)
[☞ Ellis Island]
Ell|ling|ton, Ed|ward
Ken|nedy ('Duke')
(US musician)
Ell|liot Lake (city,
Canada)
[☞ Eliot]
ell|lipse +s
ell|lip|sis
ell|lip|ses
ell|lips|oid +s
ell|lips|oid|al
ell|lip|tic
ell|lip|tic|al
ell|lip|tic|al|ly
ell|lip|ti|city
Ellis (island, US)
[☞ Ellice Islands]
Ellis, Alex|an|der
John (English
philologist)
Ellis, (Henry)
Have|lock (English
physician & writer)
Ells|worth Land
(region, Antarctica)
elm +s
elm|wood
El|nath (star)
El Niño
elo|cu|tion
elo|cu|tion|ary
elo|cu|tion|ist +s
Elo|him (*Bible*)
Elo|hist
elon|gate
elon|gates
elon|gat|ed
elon|gat|ing
elon|gat|ed *adjective*
elon|ga|tion +s
elope
elopes
eloped
elop|ing
elope|ment +s
elop|er +s
elo|quence

elo|quent
elo|quent|ly
El Paso (city, US)
El Sal|va|dor (country,
Central America)
Elsan +s *proprietary*
else
else|where
Elsi|nore (port,
Denmark)
ELT (English
Language Teaching;
emergency locator
transmitter)
ELTs
eluant +s (*use* eluent)
Élu|ard, Paul (French
poet)
elu|ate +s
elu|ci|date
elu|ci|dates
elu|ci|dat|ed
elu|ci|dat|ing
elu|ci|da|tion +s
elu|ci|da|tive
elu|ci|da|tor +s
elu|ci|da|tory
elude (avoid, escape)
eludes
elud|ed
elud|ing
[☞ allude, elute]
elud|er +s
elu|ent +s
elu|sion (avoidance,
escape)
[☞ allusion,
elution, illusion]
elu|sive (tending or
seeking to elude)
[☞ allusive,
illusive]
elu|sive|ly (in an
elusive way)
[☞ allusively]
elu|sive|ness (elusive
nature)
[☞ allusiveness]
elute (*Chemistry*)
elutes
elut|ed
elut|ing
elu|tion (*Chemistry*)
[☞ elusion]
elu|tri|ate
elu|tri|ates
elu|tri|at|ed
elu|tri|at|ing
elu|tri|a|tion
elver +s
elves
elv|ish

Ely (city, England)
[☞ Eli]
Ely, Isle of (former
county, England)
[☞ Eli]
Elys|ian
Elys|ium (*Greek Myth*)
ely|tron
ely|tra
em +s (typesetting
measure)
'em (them)
ema|ci|ate
ema|ci|ates
ema|ci|at|ed
ema|ci|at|ing
ema|ci|at|ed *adjective*
ema|ci|a|tion
e-mail +s +ed +ing
ema|lan|geni *plural of*
lilangeni
eman|ate
eman|ates
eman|at|ed
eman|at|ing
eman|a|tion +s
eman|a|tive
eman|ci|pate
eman|ci|pates
eman|ci|pat|ed
eman|ci|pat|ing
eman|ci|pat|ed
adjective
eman|ci|pa|tion +s
Eman|ci|pa|tion
Proc|lam|a|tion
eman|ci|pa|tor +s
eman|ci|pa|tory
emas|cu|late
emas|cu|lates
emas|cu|lat|ed
emas|cu|lat|ing
emas|cu|la|tion +s
emas|cu|la|tor +s
emas|cu|la|tory
em|balm +s +ed +ing
em|balm|er +s
em|balm|ment +s
em|bank +s +ed +ing
em|bank|ment +s
em|bargo
em|bar|goes
em|bar|goed
em|bar|go|ing
em|bark +s +ed +ing
em|bark|a|tion +s
em|bar|ras de choix
[☞ embarrass]
*em|bar|ras de
ri|chesses*
[☞ embarrass]

em|bar|rass
em|bar|rass|es
em|bar|rassed
em|bar|rass|ing
[☞ *embarras de choix*, *embarras de richesses*]
em|bar|rassed *adjective*
em|bar|rassed|ly
em|bar|rass|ing *adjective*
em|bar|rass|ing|ly
em|bar|rass|ment +s
em|bar|rass|ment of rich|es
em|bassy
em|bas|sies
em|bat|tle
em|bat|tles
em|bat|tled
em|bat|tling
em|bat|tled *adjective*
em|bay +s +ed +ing
em|bay|ment +s
embed
em|beds
em|bed|ded
em|bed|ding
em|bed|ded|ness
em|bed|ment +s
em|bel|lish
em|bel|lish|es
em|bel|lished
em|bel|lish|ing
em|bel|lish|er +s
em|bel|lish|ment +s
em|ber +s
ember day +s
em|bez|zle
em|bez|zles
em|bez|zled
em|bez|zling
em|bez|zle|ment +s
em|bez|zler +s
em|bit|ter +s +ed +ing
em|bit|tered *adjective*
em|bit|ter|ment
em|bla|zon +s +ed +ing
em|blazon|ment +s
em|blem +s
em|blem|atic
em|blem|atic|al
em|blem|atic|al|ly
em|blem|a|tize
em|blem|a|tiz|es
em|blem|a|tized
em|blem|a|tiz|ing
em|ble|ments
em|bodi|ment +s

em|body
em|bod|ies
em|bod|ied
em|body|ing
em|bold|en +s +ed +ing
em|bol|ic
em|bol|ism +s
em|bol|us
em|boli
em|bon|point
em|boss
em|boss|es
em|bossed
em|boss|ing
em|bossed *adjective*
em|boss|er +s
em|boss|ing +s *noun*
em|boss|ment
em|bouch|ure +s
em|bour|geoise|ment +s
em|bowel
em|bowels
em|bow|elled
em|bowel|ling
em|bow|er +s +ed +ing
em|brace
em|bra|ces
em|braced
em|bra|cing
em|brace|able
em|bra|cer +s
em|bras|ure +s
em|bras|ured *adjective*
em|brit|tle
em|brit|tles
em|brit|tled
em|brit|tling
em|brittle|ment
em|bro|ca|tion +s
em|broid|er +s +ed +ing
em|broid|er|er +s
em|broid|ery
em|broid|eries
em|broil +s +ed +ing
em|broil|ment +s
em|bryo +s
embryo|gen|esis
embry|oid
embryo|logic
embryo|logic|al
embryo|logic|al|ly
embry|ol|o|gist +s
embry|ol|ogy
embry|on|al
embry|on|ic
embry|on|ic|ally

emcee
em|cees
em|ceed
em|cee|ing
em dash
em dash|es
emend +s +ed +ing
(remove errors from a text etc.)
[☞ amend]
emend|a|tion +s
em|er|ald +s
em|er|ald green +s
(emerald-green *when preceding a noun*)
em|er|ald|ine
emerge
emer|ges
emerged
emer|ging
emer|gence +s
emer|gency
emer|gen|cies
emer|gent
emeri|tus
emerse (*Botany*)
[☞ immerse]
emersed (*Botany*)
[☞ immersed]
emer|sion +s (act of emerging; reappearance of a celestial body after an eclipse etc.)
[☞ immersion]
Emer|son, Ralph Waldo (US philosopher & poet)
emery
emery board +s
emery cloth +s
Emesa (ancient city, Syria)
em|esis
em|etic +s
EMF (electromotive force; electromagnetic field)
EMFs
EMG (electromyogram, electromyograph, etc.)
EMGs
emic
emi|grant +s
emi|grate
emi|grates
emi|grat|ed
emi|grat|ing
emi|gra|tion +s
émi|gré +s

Emi Kous|si (volcano, Chad)
Emilia-Romagna (region, Italy)
emi|nence +s (distinction; important person; rounded projection; rising ground)
[☞ immanence, imminence]
émi|nence grise
émi|nences grises
emi|nent (distinguished, remarkable)
[☞ immanent, imminent]
emi|nent|ly (notably, exceptionally)
[☞ imminently]
emir +s (Muslim ruler)
[☞ emmer]
emir|ate +s
emis|sary
emis|sar|ies
emis|sion +s
emis|sive
emis|siv|ity
emit
emits
emit|ted
emit|ting
emit|ter +s
Em|man|uel (*Bible*)
Em|men|tal (cheese: *use* Emmenthal)
Em|men|tal|er (cheese: *use* Emmenthal)
Em|men|thal (cheese)
Em|men|thal|er (cheese: *use* Emmenthal)
emmer (wheat)
[☞ emir]
em|met +s
Emmy +s
emol|li|ence
emol|li|ent +s
emolu|ment +s
emote
emotes
emot|ed
emot|ing
emot|er +s
emoti|con +s
emo|tion +s
emo|tion|al
emo|tion|al|ism
emo|tion|al|ist +s
emo|tion|al|ity

emo|tion|al|ize
  emo|tion|al|iz|es
  emo|tion|al|ized
  emo|tion|al|iz|ing
emo|tion|al|ly
emotion|less
emo|tive
emo|tive|ly
emo|tive|ness
emo|tiv|ity
EMP (electromagnetic pulse)
  EMPs
em|pan|ada +s
em|panel
  em|panels
  em|pan|elled
  em|panel|ling
em|panel|ment +s
em|pa|thet|ic
em|pa|thet|ic|ally
em|path|ic
em|path|ic|ally
em|pa|thize
  em|pa|thiz|es
  em|pa|thized
  em|pa|thiz|ing
em|pathy
  em|pa|thies
Em|pedo|cles (Greek philosopher)
em|pen|nage +s
em|per|or +s
em|peror|ship +s
em|pha|sis
  em|pha|ses
em|pha|size
  em|pha|siz|es
  em|pha|sized
  em|pha|siz|ing
em|phat|ic
em|phat|ic|ally
em|phy|sema
em|phy|sema|tous
Em|pire +s (apple)
em|pire +s
em|pir|ic
em|pir|ic|al
em|pir|ic|al|ly
em|piri|cism
em|piri|cist +s
em|place
  em|pla|ces
  em|placed
  em|pla|cing
em|place|ment +s
em|plane
  em|planes
  em|planed
  em|plan|ing
em|ploy +s +ed +ing
em|ploy|abil|ity
em|ploy|able

em|ploy|ee +s
em|ploy|er +s
em|ploy|ment +s
em|por|ium
  em|poria or
  em|por|iums
em|pow|er +s +ed +ing
em|power|ment +s
emp|ress (female sovereign etc.)
  emp|ress|es
  [☞ impress]
emp|ti|ly
emp|ti|ness
empty
  emp|ti|er
  emp|ti|est
  emp|ties
  emp|tied
  empty|ing
empty-handed
empty-handed|ly
empty-headed
empty-headed|ness
empty nest|er +s
empty-net goal +s
empty-netter +s
Empty Quar|ter (= Rub' al Khali: desert, Arabian peninsula)
em|pur|ple
  em|pur|ples
  em|pur|pled
  em|purp|ling
em|py|ema
em|pyr|eal (of the heavens)
  [☞ imperial]
em|pyr|ean +s
emu +s
emu|late
  emu|lates
  emu|lat|ed
  emu|lat|ing
emu|la|tion +s
emu|la|tive
emu|la|tor +s
emu|lous
emu|lous|ly
emul|si|fi|able
emul|si|fi|ca|tion +s
emul|si|fi|er +s
emul|si|fy
  emul|si|fies
  emul|si|fied
  emul|si|fy|ing
emul|sion +s
emul|sion|ize
  emul|sion|iz|es
  emul|sion|ized
  emul|sion|iz|ing

emul|sive
en +s (typesetting measure)
en|able
  en|ables
  en|abled
  en|abling
en|abler +s
en|abling adjective
en|act +s +ed +ing
en|act|able
en|ac|tion +s
en|act|ive
en|act|ment +s
en|ac|tor +s
en|ac|tory
en|amel
  en|amels
  en|am|elled or en|am|eled
  en|amel|ling or en|amel|ing
en|amel|ler +s
enamel|ware
enamel|work
en|amor +s +ed +ing (use enamour)
en|am|our +s +ed +ing
en|antio|dro|mia
en|antio|mer +s
en|antio|mer|ic
en|antio|mer|ic|ally
en|antio|morph +s
en|antio|morph|ic
en|antio|morph|ism
en|antio|morph|ous
en|arth|ro|sis
  en|arth|ro|ses
en banc
en bloc
en|cae|nia +s
en|cage
  en|cages
  en|caged
  en|caging
en|camp +s +ed +ing
en|camp|ment +s
en|capsu|late
  en|capsu|lates
  en|capsu|lat|ed
  en|capsu|lat|ing
en|capsu|la|tion +s
en|capsu|la|tor +s
en|case
  en|cas|es
  en|cased
  en|cas|ing
en|case|ment +s
en|cash
  en|cash|es
  en|cashed
  en|cash|ing

en|cash|able
en|cash|ment +s
en|caus|tic +s
en|ceinte +s
En|cela|dus (Greek Myth; moon of Saturn)
en|ceph|alic
en|ceph|al|itic
en|ceph|al|itis
  en|ceph|al|it|ides
en|ceph|al|itis le|thar|gica
en|ceph|alo|gram +s
en|ceph|alo|graph +s
en|ceph|alo|myel|itis
en|ceph|alon
  en|ceph|alons or en|ceph|ala
en|ceph|alo|path|ic
en|ceph|al|op|athy
  en|ceph|al|op|athies
en|chain +s +ed +ing
en|chain|ment +s
en|chant +s +ed +ing
en|chant|ed adjective
en|chant|ed|ly
en|chant|er +s
en|chanter's night|shade +s
en|chant|ing adjective
en|chant|ing|ly
en|chant|ment +s
en|chant|ress
  en|chant|ress|es
en|chase
  en|chas|es
  en|chased
  en|chas|ing
en|chil|ada +s
en|chir|id|ion
  en|chir|id|ions or en|chir|idia
en|ci|pher +s +ed +ing
en|cipher|ment +s
en|cir|cle
  en|cir|cles
  en|cir|cled
  en|circ|ling
en|circle|ment +s
en|clasp +s +ed +ing
en|clave +s
en|clit|ic +s
en|clit|ic|ally
en|close
  en|clos|es
  en|closed
  en|clos|ing
en|closed adjective
en|clos|ure +s

en|code
en|codes
en|cod|ed
en|cod|ing
en|cod|er +s
en|comi|ast +s
en|comi|as|tic
en|comi|um
 en|comi|ums or
 en|comia
en|com|pass
 en|com|pass|es
 en|com|passed
 en|com|pass|ing
en|com|pass|ment +s
en|core +s
en|coun|ter +s +ed
 +ing
en|cour|age
 en|cour|ages
 en|cour|aged
 en|cour|aging
en|cour|age|ment +s
en|cour|ager +s
en|cour|aging
 adjective
en|cour|aging|ly
en|croach
 en|croach|es
 en|croached
 en|croach|ing
en|croach|er +s
en|croach|ment +s
en croûte
en|crust +s +ed +ing
en|crust|a|tion +s
en|crust|ment +s
en|crypt +s +ed +ing
en|cryp|tion +s
en|cul|tur|ate
 en|cul|tur|ates
 en|cul|tur|at|ed
 en|cul|tur|at|ing
en|cul|tur|a|tion
en|cum|ber +s +ed
 +ing
en|cumber|ment +s
en|cum|brance +s
en|cyc|lic|al +s
en|cyclo|paedia +s
 (*use* encyclopedia)
en|cyclo|paed|ic (*use*
 encyclopedic)
en|cyclo|paed|ism
 (*use* encyclopedism)
en|cyclo|paed|ist +s
 (*use* encyclopedist)
en|cyclo|pedia +s
en|cyclo|ped|ic
en|cyclo|ped|ism
En|cyclo|ped|ist +s
 (collaborator on the
 Encyclopédie)

en|cyclo|ped|ist +s
 (*in general use*)
en|cyst +s +ed +ing
 (become enclosed in
 a cyst)
en|cyst|a|tion
en|cyst|ed *adjective*
en|cyst|ment +s
end +s +ed +ing
en|danger
 en|dangers
 en|dan|gered
 en|danger|ing
en|dan|gered
 adjective
en|danger|ment
en|dear +s +ed +ing
en|dear|ing *adjective*
en|dear|ing|ly
en|dear|ment +s
en|deav|or +s +ed
 +ing (*use*
 endeavour)
en|deav|our +s +ed
 +ing
en|demic +s
en|dem|ic|ally
en|dem|icity
en|dem|ism +s
En|der|by Land (in
 Antarctica)
en|der|mic
en|der|mic|ally
En|ders, John
 Frank|lin (US
 virologist)
end-game +s
end|ing +s *noun*
en|dive +s
end|less
end|less|ly
end|less|ness
end line +s
end|most
end|note +s
endo|card|itic
endo|card|itis
endo|card|ium
 endo|card|ia
endo|carp +s
endo|carp|al
endo|carp|ic
endo|crine +s
endo|crino|logic|al
endo|crin|ol|o|gist +s
endo|crin|ol|ogy
endo|cyt|o|sis
endo|cyt|otic
endo|derm +s
endo|derm|al
endo|don|tics
endo|don|tist +s

endo|gamic
endog|am|ous
endog|amy
endo|gen|eity
en|dogen|ous
en|dogen|ous|ly
en|dogeny
endo|lymph
endo|lymph|at|ic
endo|met|rial
endo|metri|osis
endo|met|ri|tis
endo|met|rium
 endo|met|ria
endo|morph +s
endo|morph|ic
endo|morph|ism
endo|morphy
endo|para|site +s
endo|para|sit|ic
endo|phyte +s
endo|plasm
endo|plas|mic
end or|gan +s
en|dor|phin +s
en|dors|able
en|dors|a|tion +s
en|dorse
 en|dors|es
 en|dorsed
 en|dors|ing
en|dor|see +s
en|dorse|ment +s
en|dors|er +s
endo|scope +s
endo|scop|ic
endo|scopic|ally
endos|cop|ist +s
endos|copy
 endos|cop|ies
endo|skel|etal
endo|skel|eton +s
endo|sperm
endo|spore +s
endo|thel|ial
endo|thel|ium
 endo|thelia
endo|ther|mic
endo|thermy
endo|toxic
endo|toxin +s
en|dow +s +ed +ing
en|dowed *adjective*
en|dow|er +s
en|dow|ment +s
end|paper +s
end plate +s
end|play +s +ed +ing
end point +s
end run +s
end-stopped
end table +s

endue
 en|dues
 en|dued
 en|duing
en|dur|abil|ity
en|dur|able
en|dur|ance +s
en|dure
 en|dures
 en|dured
 en|dur|ing
en|dur|ing *adjective*
en|dur|ing|ly
en|duro +s
end use +s
end-user +s
end|ways
end|wise
En|dym|ion (*Greek
 Myth*)
end zone +s
enema +s
enemy
 en|emies
ener|get|ic
ener|get|ic|ally
ener|get|ics
ener|gize
 ener|giz|es
 ener|gized
 ener|giz|ing
ener|gized *adjective*
ener|giz|er +s
Ener|Guide
ener|gumen +s
en|ergy
 ener|gies
ener|vate (weaken)
 ener|vates
 ener|vat|ed
 ener|vat|ing
 [☞ innervate]
ener|vat|ing *adjective*
ener|va|tion
En|esco, Georges
 (Romanian
 composer)
Ene|wetak
 (= Eniwetok,
 N Pacific)
en fa|mille
en|fant ter|rible
 en|fants ter|ribles
en|fee|ble
 en|fee|bles
 en|fee|bled
 en|fee|bling
en|fee|bled *adjective*
en|feeble|ment +s
en fête
En|field +s (area,
 England; rifle)

en|fil|ade
  en|fil|ades
  en|fil|ad|ed
  en|fil|ad|ing
en|fold +s +ed +ing
  (wrap up; envelop;
  encompass)
  [☞ infold]
en|fold|ing *conjugated*
  form of enfold
  [☞ infolding]
en|force
  en|for|ces
  en|forced
  en|for|cing
en|force|abil|ity
en|force|able
en|for|ced|ly
en|force|ment +s
en|for|cer +s
en|fran|chise
  en|fran|chis|es
  en|fran|chised
  en|fran|chis|ing
en|fran|chise|ment
  +s
en|gage *verb*
  en|gages
  en|gaged
  en|gaging
  [☞ *engagé*]
en|ga|gé +s
  (committed; hired
  boatman)
  [☞ engage]
en|gaged *adjective*
en|gage|ment +s
en|gager +s
en|gaging *adjective*
en|gaging|ly
en|gaging|ness
Engel, Mar|ian (Cdn
  writer)
Engel|mann spruce
  plural Engel|mann
  spruce *or*
  Engel|mann
  spru|ces
En|gels, Fried|rich
  (German
  philosopher)
en|gen|der +s +ed
  +ing
en|gine
  en|gines
  en|gined
  en|gin|ing
en|gine block +s
en|gined *adjective*
en|gin|eer +s +ed
  +ing
en|gin|eer|ing *noun*
en|gine house +s
en|gine|less

en|gine room +s
Eng|land (country,
  UK)
Eng|lish
  Eng|lish|es
Eng|lish Break|fast
  (tea)
Eng|lish break|fast
  +s (meal)
Eng|lish Can|ad|ian
  +s *noun*
Eng|lish-Canadian
  adjective
Eng|lish Chan|nel
  (between England &
  France)
Eng|lish|man
  Eng|lish|men
Eng|lish|ness
Eng|lish|woman
  Eng|lish|women
en|gorge
  en|gor|ges
  en|gorged
  en|gor|ging
en|gorged *adjective*
en|gorge|ment +s
en|grain +s +ed +ing
  (*use* ingrain)
en|grained *adjective*
  (*use* ingrained)
en|grain|ed|ly (*use*
  ingrainedly)
en|gram +s
en|gram|mat|ic
en|grave
  en|graves
  en|graved
  en|grav|ing
en|graved *adjective*
en|grav|er +s
en|grav|ing +s *noun*
en|gross
  en|gross|es
  en|grossed
  en|gross|ing
en|grossed *adjective*
en|gross|ed|ly
en|gross|ing *adjective*
en|gross|ment
en|gulf +s +ed +ing
en|gulf|ment
en|hance
  en|han|ces
  en|hanced
  en|han|cing
en|hance|ment +s
en|han|cer +s
en|har|mon|ic
en|har|mon|ic|ally
en|igma +s
en|ig|mat|ic
en|ig|mat|ic|al

en|ig|mat|ic|al|ly
Eni|wetok (island,
  N Pacific)
en|jamb +s +ed +ing
en|jambed *adjective*
en|jambe|ment +s
  (*use* enjambment)
en|jamb|ment +s
en|join +s +ed +ing
en|join|ment
enjoy +s +ed +ing
en|joy|able
en|joy|able|ness
en|joy|ably
en|joy|er +s
en|joy|ment +s
en|keph|alin +s
en|kindle
  en|kin|dles
  en|kin|dled
  en|kind|ling
en|lace
  en|laces
  en|laced
  en|lacing
en|lace|ment
en|large
  en|lar|ges
  en|larged
  en|lar|ging
en|larged *adjective*
en|large|ment +s
en|lar|ger +s
en|light|en +s +ed
  +ing
en|light|ened
  adjective
en|light|en|er +s
en|light|en|ing
  adjective
En|light|en|ment
  (18th-c.
  philosophical
  movement)
en|light|en|ment
  (*in general use*;
  Buddhism)
en|list +s +ed +ing
en|list|ed *adjective*
en|list|er +s
en|list|ment
en|liven +s +ed +ing
en|liven|er +s
en|liven|ing *adjective*
en|liven|ment
en masse
en|mesh
  en|mesh|es
  en|meshed
  en|mesh|ing
en|mesh|ment +s
en|mity
  en|mi|ties

en|nead +s (group of
  nine)
  [☞ *the Aeneid*]
Ennis (town, Ireland)
en|noble
  en|nobles
  en|nobled
  en|nob|ling
en|noble|ment +s
en|nob|ling *adjective*
ennui (boredom,
  weariness)
  [☞ Anhui, Anouilh]
Enoch (*Bible*)
eno|logic|al (*use*
  oenological)
enol|o|gist +s (*use*
  oenologist)
enol|ogy (*use*
  oenology)
enor|mity
  enor|mi|ties
enor|mous
enor|mous|ly
enor|mous|ness
eno|sis
enough
en pas|sant
en|plane (= emplane)
  en|planes
  en|planed
  en|plan|ing
en|quire (*use* inquire)
  en|quires
  en|quired
  en|quir|ing
en|quir|er +s (*use*
  inquirer)
en|quir|ing *adjective*
  (*use* inquiring)
en|quir|ing|ly (*use*
  inquiringly)
en|quiry (*use* inquiry)
  en|quir|ies
en|rage
  en|rages
  en|raged
  en|raging
en|raged *adjective*
en|rage|ment
en rap|port
en|rap|ture
  en|rap|tures
  en|rap|tured
  en|rap|tur|ing
en|rich
  en|rich|es
  en|riched
  en|rich|ing
en|riched *adjective*
en|rich|ing *adjective*
en|rich|ment +s

en|robe
  en|robes
  en|robed
  en|rob|ing
en|rober +s
en|rol
  en|rols
  en|rolled
  en|rol|ling
en|roll +s +ed +ing
  (*use* enrol)
en|rol|lee +s
en|roll|ment +s (*use*
  enrolment)
en|rol|ment +s
en route
En|schede (city, the
  Netherlands)
en|sconce
  en|scon|ces
  en|sconced
  en|scon|cing
en|sem|ble +s
en|shrine
  en|shrines
  en|shrined
  en|shrin|ing
en|shrine|ment
en|shroud +s +ed
  +ing
en|sign +s
en|signcy
  en|sign|cies
en|sil|age
  en|sil|ages
  en|sil|aged
  en|sil|aging
en|sile
  en|siles
  en|siled
  en|sil|ing
en|slave
  en|slaves
  en|slaved
  en|slav|ing
en|slave|ment
en|slav|er +s
en|snare
  en|snares
  en|snared
  en|snar|ing
en|snare|ment
Ensor, James
  Syd|ney, Baron
  (Belgian artist)
ensue
  en|sues
  en|sued
  en|su|ing
en|su|ing *adjective*
en|suite +s
en|sure (make certain;
  secure; *for* issue or

obtain an insurance
  policy on *use* insure)
  en|sures
  en|sured
  en|sur|ing
en|tabla|ture +s
en|table|ment +s
en|tail +s +ed +ing
en|tail|ment +s
en|tan|gle
  en|tan|gles
  en|tan|gled
  en|tan|gling
en|tangle|ment +s
en|tasis
  en|tases
En|tebbe (town,
  Uganda)
en|tel|echy
  en|tel|echies
en|tente +s
En|tente Cor|di|ale
  (between Britain &
  France in 1904)
en|tente cor|di|ale
  (*in general use*)
  en|tentes cor|di|ales
en|ter +s +ed +ing
  (go into, enrol;
  record; submit)
  [☞ inter]
en|ter|er +s
en|ter|ic
enteric-coated
en|ter|itis
entero|bac|teria
  plural of
  enterobacterium
entero|bac|ter|ium
  entero|bac|teria
entero|col|itis
enter|os|tomy
  enter|os|to|mies
entero|virus
  entero|virus|es
Enter|phone +s
  proprietary
en|ter|prise +s
en|ter|pris|er +s
en|ter|pris|ing
  adjective
en|ter|pris|ing|ly
en|ter|tain +s +ed
  +ing
en|ter|tain|er +s
en|ter|tain|ing
  adjective
en|ter|tain|ing|ly
en|ter|tain|ment +s
en|thalpy
  en|thal|pies

en|thral (*use* enthrall)
  en|thrals
  en|thralled
  en|thral|ling
en|thrall +s +ed +ing
en|thrall|ing *adjective*
en|thrall|ment +s
en|thral|ment +s (*use*
  enthrallment)
en|throne
  en|thrones
  en|throned
  en|thron|ing
en|throne|ment +s
en|thuse
  en|thus|es
  en|thused
  en|thus|ing
en|thusi|asm +s
en|thusi|ast +s
en|thusi|as|tic
en|thusi|as|tic|ally
en|thy|meme +s
en|tice
  en|tices
  en|ticed
  en|ticing
en|tice|ment +s
en|ticer +s
en|ticing *adjective*
en|ticing|ly
en|tire +s
en|tire|ly
en|tire|ty
  en|tire|ties
en|ti|ta|tive
en|title
  en|titles
  en|titled
  en|titling
en|title|ment +s
en|tity
  en|ti|ties
en|tomb +s +ed +ing
en|tomb|ment +s
ento|mo|logic|al
ento|mol|o|gist +s
ento|mol|ogy
ento|moph|a|gous
ento|moph|il|ous
ento|para|site +s
ento|phyte +s (*use*
  endophyte)
en|tour|age +s
entr'acte +s
en|trails
en|train +s +ed +ing
en|train|ment +s
en|tram|mel
  en|tram|mels
  en|tram|melled
  or en|tram|meled

en|tram|mel|ling
  or en|tram|mel|ing
en|trance
  en|tran|ces
  en|tranced
  en|tran|cing
en|tranced *adjective*
en|trance|ment +s
en|trance|way +s
en|tran|cing *adjective*
en|tran|cing|ly
en|trant +s
en|trap
  en|traps
  en|trapped
  en|trap|ping
en|trap|ment +s
en|treat +s +ed +ing
en|treat|ing|ly
en|treaty
  en|treat|ies
entre|chat +s
entre|côte +s
Entre-Deux-Mers
  plural Entre-Deux-
  Mers
en|trée +s
entre|mets
  plural entre|mets
en|trench
  en|trench|es
  en|trenched
  en|trench|ing
en|trenched *adjective*
en|trench|ment +s
entre nous
entre|pôt +s
entre|pre|neur +s
entre|pre|neur|ial
entre|pre|neur|ial|
    ism
entre|pre|neur|ial|ly
entre|pre|neur|ism
entre|pre|neur|ship
entre|sol +s
en|trop|ic
en|trop|ic|ally
en|tropy
en|trust +s +ed +ing
en|trust|ment
entry
  en|tries
entry form +s
entry-level
Entry|phone +s
  proprietary
entry|way +s
en|twine
  en|twines
  en|twined
  en|twin|ing
en|twine|ment +s

enu|cle|ate
enu|cle|ates
enu|cle|at|ed
enu|cle|at|ing
enu|cle|a|tion +s
enum|er|able (that
may be enumerated)
[☞ innumerable]
enum|er|ate (specify
individually; count;
prepare a voters list)
enum|er|ates
enum|er|at|ed
enum|er|at|ing
[☞ innumerate]
enum|er|a|tion +s
enum|er|a|tive
enum|er|ator +s
enun|ci|ate
enun|ci|ates
enun|ci|at|ed
enun|ci|at|ing
enun|ci|a|tion
enun|ci|a|tive
enun|ci|ator +s
enure (Law take
effect: use inure)
en|ures
en|ured
en|ur|ing
[☞ inure]
en|ur|esis
en|ur|etic +s
en|vel|op +s +ed
+ing verb
en|vel|ope +s noun
en|vel|op|ment +s
en|ven|om +s +ed
+ing
envi|able
envi|ably
envi|er +s
envi|ous
envi|ous|ly
en|vir|on +s +ed +ing
en|viron|ment +s
en|viron|ment|al
en|viron|ment|al|ism
en|viron|ment|al|ist
+s
en|viron|ment|al|ly
en|viron|ment|al|ly
friend|ly adjective
(en|viron|mentally-friendly
when preceding a
noun)
en|vir|onment-
friend|ly
en|vir|ons
en|vis|age
en|vis|a|ges
en|vis|aged
en|vis|a|ging

en|visage|ment
en|vision +s +ed
+ing
en|voi +s (concluding
stanza or passage)
[☞ envoy]
en|voy +s (messenger,
representative; for
stanza or concluding
words use envoi)
envy
en|vies
en|vied
envy|ing
en|wrap
en|wraps
en|wrapped
en|wrap|ping
en|zo|otic +s
en|zym|atic
en|zym|atic|ally
en|zyme +s
en|zym|ic
en|zym|ol|ogy
Eocene
eolian (use aeolian)
eolith +s
eolith|ic
eon +s
Eos (Greek Myth)
eosin
eosin|o|phil +s
eosin|o|philia
eosin|o|phil|ic
epact +s
Epami|non|das
(Greek general)
ep|arch +s
ep|archy
ep|arch|ies
epaul|et +s (use
epaulette)
epaul|ette +s
épée +s
épée|ist +s
epeiro|gen|esis
epeiro|gen|ic
epeir|ogeny
epen|thesis
epen|theses
epen|thet|ic
ep|ergne +s
ep|exe|gesis
ep|exe|geses
ep|exe|get|ic
ep|exe|get|ic|al
ep|exe|get|ic|al|ly
ephah +s
eph|ebe +s
epheb|ic
ephed|ra +s
ephe|drine

ephem|era
• plural noun (short-
lived things)
singular
ephem|er|on
• singular noun (insect)
plural ephem|er|as
or ephem|erae
ephem|er|al
ephem|er|al|ity
ephem|er|al|ly
ephem|er|al|ness
ephem|er|is
ephem|er|ides
ephem|er|on
• (a short-lived thing)
plural ephem|era
• (insect: use
ephemera)
plural ephem|er|ons
Ephe|sians (New
Testament)
Eph|esus (ancient city,
Asia Minor)
eph|od +s
eph|or +s
ephor|ate +s
epi|blast +s
epic +s
epical
epical|ly
epi|car|di|al
epi|car|di|um
epi|car|dia
epi|carp +s
epi|ced|ian
epi|ced|ium
epi|cedia
epi|cene +s
epi|cen|tral
epi|centre +s
epi|con|tin|en|tal
epi|cotyl +s
Epic|tetus (Greek
philosopher)
epi|cure +s
Epi|cur|ean +s (of
Epicurus)
epi|cur|ean +s
(devoted to
enjoyment)
Epi|cur|ean|ism
epi|cur|ism
Epi|curus (Greek
philosopher)
epi|cycle +s
epi|cyc|lic
epi|cyc|loid +s
epi|cyc|loid|al
Epi|daur|us (ancient
city, Greece)
epi|dem|ic +s
epi|dem|ic|ally

epi|demi|o|logic
epi|demi|o|logic|al
epi|demi|o|logic|al|ly
epi|demi|ol|o|gist +s
epi|demi|ol|ogy
epi|der|mal
epi|der|mic
epi|der|mis
epi|derm|oid
epi|dia|scope +s
epi|didy|mis
epi|didy|mi|des
epi|dote +s
epi|dur|al +s
epi|gas|tric
epi|gas|tri|um
epi|gas|tria
epi|geal
epi|gene
epi|glot|tal
epi|glot|tic
epi|glot|tis
epi|glot|tis|es
epi|gone
epi|gones or
epi|goni
epi|gon|ic
epi|gram +s
epi|gram|mat|ic
epi|gram|mat|ic|ally
epi|gram|ma|tist +s
epi|gram|ma|tize
epi|gram|ma|tiz|es
epi|gram|ma|tized
epi|gram|ma|tiz|ing
epi|graph +s
epigraph|er +s
epi|graph|ic
epi|graph|ic|al
epi|graph|ic|al|ly
epigraph|ist +s
epi|graphy
epi|late
epi|lates
epi|lat|ed
epi|lat|ing
epi|la|tion +s
epi|lepsy
epi|lep|tic
epi|lim|nion
epi|lim|nia
epi|logue +s
epi|mer +s
epi|mer|ic
epi|mer|ism
epi|mer|ize
epi|mer|iz|es
epi|mer|ized
epi|mer|iz|ing
epi|nasty
epi|neph|rine
epi|phan|ic

epiph|an|ous
Epiph|any
(*Christianity*)
epiph|any
epiph|an|ies
epi|phenom|enal
epi|phenom|enon
epi|phenom|ena
epiphy|sis
epiphy|ses
epi|phyte +s
epi|phyt|ic
Epirus (region, Greece)
epis|co|pacy
epis|copa|cies
Epis|co|pal (of the Episcopal Church)
epis|co|pal (of or governed by bishops)
Epis|co|pal Church (the Anglican Church in the US & Scotland)
Epis|co|pal|ian +s (of the Episcopal Church)
epis|co|pal|ian +s (of an episcopal Church)
Epis|co|pal|ian|ism (beliefs etc. of the Episcopal Church)
epis|co|pal|ian|ism (beliefs etc. of an episcopal Church)
epis|co|pal|ism
epis|co|pal|ly
epis|co|pate +s
epi|sem|atic
episi|ot|omy
episi|ot|o|mies
epi|sode +s
epi|sod|ic
epi|sod|ic|ally
epi|stax|is
epi|stax|es
epi|stem|ic
epi|stem|ic|ally
epis|temo|logic|al
epis|temo|logic|al|ly
epis|tem|ol|o|gist +s
epis|tem|ol|ogy
epis|tem|ol|o|gies
epis|tle +s
epis|tol|ary
epis|tro|phe +s
epi|style +s
epi|taph +s
epi|tax|ial
epi|taxy
epi|thal|ami|al
epi|thal|amic

epi|thal|ami|um
epi|thal|amia
epi|thel|ial
epi|thel|ium
epi|thel|iums or
epi|thelia
epi|thet +s
epi|thet|ic
epi|thet|ic|al
epi|thet|ic|al|ly
epit|ome +s
epit|om|iz|a|tion +s
epit|om|ize
epit|om|iz|es
epit|om|ized
epit|om|iz|ing
epi|zo|on
epi|zoa
epi|zo|otic +s
epoch +s
epoch|al
epoch-making
epode +s
epo|nym +s
eponym|ous
eponym|ous|ly
EPOS (electronic point-of-sale)
ep|ox|ide +s
epoxy
epox|ies
epox|ied
epoxy|ing
EPROM (*Computing*)
ep|si|lon +s
Ep|som (town, England; salts)
Ep|stein, Brian (Beatles manager)
Ep|stein, Sir Jacob (US-born sculptor)
Epstein-Barr virus
epyl|lion
epyl|lia
equa|bil|ity
equable
equably
equal
equals
equalled
equal|ling
equal area pro|jec|tion +s
equal|i|tar|ian +s
equal|i|tar|ian|ism
equal|ity
equal|ities
equal|iz|a|tion +s
equal|ize
equal|iz|es
equal|ized
equal|iz|ing
equal|iz|er +s

equal|ly
equal sign +s
equals sign +s (= equal sign)
equa|nim|ity
equa|nim|ities
equani|mous
equat|able (that can be equated) [☞ equitable]
equate
equates
equat|ed
equat|ing
equa|tion +s
equa|tion|al
equa|tor +s
equa|tor|ial
Equa|tor|ial Guinea
Equa|tor|ial Guin|ean +s
equa|tor|ial|ly
equator|ward
equer|ry
equer|ries
eques|trian +s (of horses; horseback rider)
eques|tri|enne +s (female horseback rider)
equi|angu|lar
equi|dis|tance
equi|dis|tant
equi|dis|tant|ly
equi|lat|eral
equili|brate
equili|brates
equili|brat|ed
equili|brat|ing
equili|bra|tion
equili|bra|tor +s
equili|brist +s
equi|lib|rium
equi|lib|ria or equi|lib|riums
equine +s
equi|noc|tial
equi|nox
equi|nox|es
equip
equips
equipped
equip|ping
equip|age
equip|ment +s
equi|poise
equi|pois|es
equi|poised
equi|pois|ing
equi|poten|tial +s
equip|per +s
equi|prob|abil|ity

equi|prob|able
equit|able (fair; *Law*) [☞ equatable]
equit|able|ness
equit|ably
equi|ta|tion
equity
equi|ties
equiva|lence +s
equiva|lency
equiva|len|cies
equiva|lent +s
equiva|lent|ly
equivo|cal
equivo|cal|ity
equivo|cal|ly
equivo|cal|ness
equivo|cate
equivo|cates
equivo|cat|ed
equivo|cat|ing
equivo|ca|tion +s
equivo|ca|tor +s
equivo|ca|tory
ER (emergency room)
ERs
er (expressing hesitation) [☞ err]
ERA (earned run average; Equal Rights Amendment)
ERAs
era +s (epoch, period, age) [☞ eyra, Eire]
erad|ic|able
eradi|cant +s
eradi|cate
eradi|cates
eradi|cat|ed
eradi|cat|ing
eradi|ca|tion
eradi|ca|tor +s
eras|abil|ity
eras|able
erase
eras|es
erased
eras|ing
eras|er +s
Eras|mus, Desi|der|ius (Dutch scholar)
Eras|mus, Georges (Cdn politician)
Eras|tian +s
Eras|tian|ism
Eras|tus, Thom|as (Swiss theologian)
era|sure +s
Erato (*Roman Myth*)

Era|tos|thenes (Greek scholar)
er|bium
ere (before)
[☞ e'er, err, Eyre]
Ere|bus (mountain, Antarctica; *Greek Myth*)
Erech|theus (*Greek Myth*)
erect +s +ed +ing
erect|able
erect|ile
erec|tion +s
erect|ly
erect|ness
erect|or +s
Erect|or set +s
proprietary
ere|mite +s (recluse)
[☞ Ermite]
ere|mit|ic
ere|mit|ic|al
ere|mit|ism
ereth|ism
Er|furt (city, Germany)
erg
• (unit of energy)
plural ergs
• (sand dunes)
plural ergs or areg
erga|tive +s
erga|tiv|ity
ergo
er|gom|eter +s
ergo|nom|ic
ergo|nom|ic|ally
ergo|nom|ics
er|gono|mist +s
er|gos|terol
ergot +s
er|gota|mine
er|got|ism
erica +s
eri|ca|ceous
Erick|son, Ar|thur Charles (Cdn architect)
[☞ Ericsson]
Eric|son, Leif (= Leif Ericsson)
[☞ Erickson]
Erics|son, John (Swedish engineer)
[☞ Erickson]
Erics|son, Leif ('the Lucky') (Norse explorer)
[☞ Erickson]
Eric the Red (Norse explorer)
Eri|danus (constellation)

Erie (lake, N America; people, language)
plural Erie or Eries
[☞ eerie, aerie]
Eri|gena, John Sco|tus (Irish theologian)
erig|eron +s
Eriks|son, Leif (= Leif Ericsson)
[☞ Erickson]
Erin (Ireland)
[☞ Aaron, Aran, Arran]
Erinys (*Greek Myth*)
Erinyes
Eris (*Greek Myth*)
eris|tic +s
Eri|trea (independent state, Africa)
Eri|trean +s
Er|langer, Jo|seph (US physiologist)
erl-king +s (goblin, giant)
er|mine
plural er|mine or er|mines
er|mined
Er|mite (cheese)
[☞ eremite]
Ernst, Max (German artist)
erode
erodes
eroded
erod|ing
eroded *adjective*
erod|ible
er|ogen|ous
Eros (*Greek Myth*; *Astronomy*)
eros (love; libido; self-preservation)
ero|sion +s
ero|sion|al
ero|sive
erot|ic
erot|ica
erot|ic|ally
eroti|cism
eroti|ciz|a|tion
eroti|cize
eroti|ciz|es
eroti|cized
eroti|ciz|ing
eroti|cized *adjective*
eroto|gen|ic
erot|ogen|ous
eroto|mania
eroto|maniac +s
err +s +ed +ing (be mistaken)

[☞ ere, e'er, er, are]
er|rancy
er|rand +s
er|rant (erratic; itinerant; in 'knight errant')
[☞ arrant]
er|rant|ry
er|rat|ic +s
er|rat|ic|ally
er|ratum
er|rata
Er Rif (= Rif Mountains, Morocco)
er|ro|ne|ous
er|ro|ne|ous|ly
er|ro|ne|ous|ness
er|ror +s
error|less
er|satz
er|satz|es
Erse
erst
erst|while
eru|cic acid
eruc|ta|tion +s
eru|dite
eru|dite|ly
eru|di|tion
erupt +s +ed +ing (break out, burst forth; eject lava)
[☞ irrupt]
erup|tion +s (breakout; ejection of lava)
[☞ irruption]
erup|tive (tending to erupt)
[☞ irruptive]
ery|sip|elas
ery|thema
ery|themal
ery|them|at|ic
ery|thema|to|sus
ery|thema|tous
eryth|rism
eryth|ro|blast +s
eryth|ro|cyte +s
eryth|ro|cyt|ic
eryth|roid
eryth|ro|mycin +s
eryth|ro|poi|esis
eryth|ro|poi|etic
eryth|ro|poi|etin
Erz|ge|birge (mountains, Europe)
Erzu|rum (city, Turkey)
Esaki, Leo (Japanese physicist)

Esau (*Bible*)
Es|bjerg (port, Denmark)
es|ca|drille +s
es|cal|ate
escal|ates
escal|at|ed
escal|at|ing
es|cal|at|ing *adjective*
es|cal|a|tion +s
es|cal|ator +s
es|cal|lon|ia +s
es|cal|ope +s
es|cap|able
es|cap|ade +s
es|cape
es|capes
es|caped
es|cap|ing
es|capee +s
es|cape|ment +s
es|cap|er +s
es|cap|ism
es|cap|ist +s
es|cap|ol|o|gist +s
es|cap|ol|ogy
es|car|got +s
es|car|ole
es|carp|ment +s
es|char +s (scab)
[☞ Escher, esker]
es|chato|logic|al
es|chat|ol|o|gist +s
es|chat|ol|ogy
es|chat|ol|o|gies
es|cheat +s +ed +ing
Escher, Maur|its Cor|neille (Dutch artist)
[☞ eschar]
Esche|rich|ia coli
es|chew +s +ed +ing
es|chew|al +s
Es|cof|fier, (Georges) Au|guste (French chef)
es|cort +s +ed +ing
es|cri|toire +s
es|crow +s +ed +ing
es|cudo +s
es|cut|cheon +s
es|cut|cheoned
Es|dras (*Apocrypha*; *Vulgate*)
Esen|in, Ser|gey Alek|san|dro|vich (Russian poet)
Esfa|han (= Isfahan, Iran)
es|ker +s (ridge of sand or gravel)
[☞ eschar]

Es|kimo
plural Es|kimo or
Es|kimos
• In Canada, the
word Eskimo has
been superseded by
Inuit with reference
to the people and
Inuktitut with
reference to their
language.
Es|kimo dog +s
Es|kimo roll +s
ESL (English as a
second language)
ESN (electronic serial
number)
ESNs
esopha|geal
esopha|gus
esoph|agi or
esopha|gus|es
eso|ter|ic (intended
only for a select
group)
[☞ exoteric]
eso|ter|ica
eso|ter|ic|ally
eso|ter|icism
eso|ter|icist +s
ESP (extrasensory
perception)
es|pa|drille +s
es|pal|ier +s +ed
+ing
es|pal|iered adjective
Es|pan|ola (town,
Canada)
es|parto +s
es|pe|cial
es|pe|cial|ly
Es|per|an|tist +s
Es|per|anto
es|pial +s
es|pion|age
Es|pír|ito Santo
(state, Brazil)
es|plan|ade +s
Es|poir, Bay d' (inlet,
Canada)
es|poir +s
Es|po|sito, Phil|ip
An|thony ('Phil')
(Cdn hockey player)
es|pous|al +s
es|pouse
es|pous|es
es|poused
es|pous|ing
es|pous|er +s
es|presso +s
es|prit
es|prit de corps

espy
espies
espied
espy|ing
Es|qui|malt
(municipality,
Canada; people,
language)
plural Es|qui|malt or
Es|qui|malts
Es|qui|pu|las (town,
Guatemala)
es|quire +s
ess (the letter S)
esses
es|say +s +ed +ing
essay|ist +s
essay|is|tic
Essen (city, Germany)
[☞ Essene]
es|sence +s
Es|sene (Judaism)
[☞ Essen]
es|sen|tial +s
es|sen|tial|ism
es|sen|tial|ist +s
es|sen|ti|al|ity
es|sen|tial|iz|a|tion
es|sen|tial|ize
es|sen|tial|iz|es
es|sen|tial|ized
es|sen|tial|iz|ing
es|sen|tial|ly
es|sen|tial|ness
Esse|quibo (river,
Guyana)
Essex (county,
England; town,
Canada)
Essex, Rob|ert
Dev|er|eux, 2nd
Earl of (English
courtier)
est
es|tab|lish
es|tab|lish|es
es|tab|lished
es|tab|lish|ing
es|tab|lished adjective
es|tab|lis|her +s
es|tab|lish|ment +s
estab|lish|men|
tar|ian +s
estab|lish|men|
tar|ian|ism
es|tami|net +s
estan|cia +s
es|tate +s
Es|tates Gen|er|al
Este (Italian noble
family)
es|teem +s +ed +ing
es|teemed adjective

es|ter +s (Chemistry)
[☞ Esther]
es|ter|ase +s
es|teri|fi|ca|tion
es|ter|ify
es|teri|fies
es|teri|fied
es|teri|fy|ing
Es|te|van (city,
Canada)
Es|ther (Bible)
[☞ ester]
es|thete +s (use
aesthete)
es|thet|ic +s (use
aesthetic)
es|thet|ic|ally (use
aesthetically)
es|thet|ician +s (use
aesthetician)
es|theti|cism (use
aestheticism)
es|thet|ics (use
aesthetics)
Es|tienne, Henri,
Rob|ert & Henri
(members of French
printing family)
es|tim|able
es|tim|ably
es|ti|mate
es|ti|mates
es|ti|mat|ed
es|ti|mat|ing
es|ti|mat|ed adjective
es|ti|ma|tion +s
es|ti|ma|tive
es|ti|ma|tor +s
es|tival (use aestival)
es|tiv|ate (use
aestivate)
es|tiv|ates
es|tiv|at|ed
es|tiv|at|ing
es|tiv|a|tion (use
aestivation)
Es|tonia (country,
Europe)
Es|ton|ian +s
estop
es|tops
es|topped
es|top|ping
es|top|pel
esto|vers
es|tra|diol
es|trange
es|trang|es
es|tranged
es|trang|ing
es|tranged adjective
es|trange|ment +s
es|treat +s +ed +ing

Estre|ma|dura
(region, Portugal)
es|tro|gen +s
es|tro|gen|ic
es|tro|gen|ic|ally
es|trous adjective
es|trus noun
es|tu|ar|ine
es|tu|ary
es|tu|aries
esuri|ent
esuri|ent|ly
ETA (Basque
separatists;
estimated time of
arrival)
ETAs
eta +s (Greek letter)
éta|gère +s
et al.
eta|lon +s
et cet|era +s
etch
etch|es
etched
etch|ing
etch|ant +s
etch|er +s
etch|ing +s noun
eter|nal
eter|nal|ity
eter|nal|ize
eter|nal|iz|es
eter|nal|ized
eter|nal|iz|ing
eter|nal|ly
eter|nal|ness
eter|nity
eter|ni|ties
eter|nize
eter|niz|es
eter|nized
eter|niz|ing
Etes|ian
eth +s
etha|nal
(acetaldehyde)
[☞ ethanol]
eth|ane
eth|ane|diol
etha|nol (alcohol)
[☞ ethanal]
Ethel|bert (saint, king
of Kent)
Ethel|red (English
kings)
eth|ene
ether (anaesthetic &
solvent; sky;
substance
permeating space)
ether|eal
ether|eal|ity

ether|eal|ly
Eth|er|ege, Sir George (English dramatist)
ether|ic
ether|iz|a|tion
ether|ize
  ether|iz|es
  ether|ized
  ether|iz|ing
Ether|net
eth|ic +s
eth|ic|al
eth|ic|al|ity
eth|ic|al|ly
ethi|cist +s
eth|ics
ethi|nyl es|tra|diol
Ethi|opia (country, Africa)
Ethi|op|ian +s
Ethi|opic +s
eth|moid +s
eth|moid|al
eth|nic +s
eth|nic|al
eth|nic|ally
eth|ni|city
  eth|ni|ci|ties
ethno|archae|o|logic|al
ethno|archae|ol|o|gist +s
ethno|archae|ol|ogy
ethno|arche|o|logic|al (use ethnoarchaeological)
ethno|arche|ol|o|gist +s (use ethnoarchaeologist)
ethno|arche|ol|ogy (use ethnoarchaeology)
ethno|botan|ical
ethno|botan|ist +s
ethno|botany
ethno|centric
ethno|centric|ally
ethno|centri|city
ethno|centrism
ethno|cide +s
ethno|cultur|al
eth|nog|raph|er +s
ethno|graph|ic
ethno|graph|ic|al
ethno|graph|ic|al|ly
eth|nog|raphy
  eth|nog|raph|ies
ethno|histor|ian +s
ethno|histor|ic
ethno|histor|ic|al
ethno|histor|ic|al|ly

ethno|hist|ory
ethno|logic
ethno|logic|al
ethno|logic|al|ly
eth|nol|o|gist +s
eth|nol|ogy
ethno|method|o|logic|al
ethno|method|ol|o|gist +s
ethno|method|ol|ogy
ethno|music|o|logic|al
ethno|music|ol|o|gist +s
ethno|music|ol|ogy
etho|gram +s
etho|logic|al
etho|logic|al|ly
eth|ol|o|gist +s
eth|ol|ogy
ethos
  ethos|es
eth|oxy|ethane
ethyl
ethyl|ene
ethyl|ene gly|col
ethyl|en|ic
ethyne
etic
Étienne (= Estienne, French family of printers)
etio|late
  etio|lates
  etio|lat|ed
  etio|lat|ing
etio|lat|ed adjective
etio|la|tion +s
etio|logic
etio|logic|al
etio|logic|al|ly
eti|ol|ogy
eti|quette +s
Etna (volcano, Italy)
Etobi|coke (former city, Canada)
Eton col|lar +s
Eton|ian +s
Eton jack|et +s
Etosha Pan (saltwater depression, Namibia)
etrier +s
Etrog, Sorel (Romanian-born Cdn sculptor)
Etrog +s (Cdn film award)
Etru|ria (ancient state, Italy)
Etrus|can +s
étude +s
etui +s

etymo|logic|al
etymo|logic|al|ly
ety|mol|o|gist +s
ety|mol|o|gize
  ety|mol|o|giz|es
  ety|mol|o|gized
  ety|mol|o|giz|ing
ety|mol|ogy
  ety|mol|o|gies
ety|mon
  etyma
Etzel (Germanic Legend)
Eu|boea (island, Greece)
euca|lypt +s (= eucalyptus)
euca|lyp|tus
  euca|lyp|tus|es or euca|lyp|ti
eu|cary|ote +s (use eukaryote)
eu|cary|otic (use eukaryotic)
eucha|ris
  plural eucha|ris
Eucha|rist +s
Eucha|ris|tic
Eucha|ris|tic|al
Eucha|ris|tic|al|ly
eu|chre
  eu|chres
  eu|chred
  eu|chring
Euck|en, Ru|dolf Chris|toph (German philosopher)
Euclid (Greek mathematician)
Euclid|ean
Euclid|ian (use Euclidean)
eu|dae|mon|ic (use eudemonic)
eu|dae|mon|ism (use eudemonism)
eu|dae|mon|ist +s (use eudemonist)
eu|dae|mon|is|tic (use eudemonistic)
eu|demon|ic
eu|demon|ism
eu|demon|ist +s
eu|demon|is|tic
eudi|om|eter +s
eudio|met|ric
eudio|met|ric|al
eudi|om|etry
Eud|ist +s
Eu|gène, Prince (French-born Austrian general)
eu|gen|ic

eu|gen|ic|ally
eu|geni|cist +s
eu|gen|ics
Eu|gé|nie (empress of France)
eu|gen|ist +s
eu|glena
eu|kary|ote +s
eu|kary|otic
eula|chon
  plural eula|chon or eula|chons
Euler, Leon|hard (Swiss mathematician)
Euler, Ulf Svante von (Swedish physiologist)
Euler-Chelpin, Hans (Karl Aug|ust Simon) von (German-born Swedish biochemist)
eulo|gist +s
eulo|gis|tic
eulo|gis|tic|ally
eu|lo|gium
  eu|lo|gia or eu|lo|giums
eulo|gize
  eulo|giz|es
  eulo|gized
  eulo|giz|ing
eu|logy
  eulo|gies
Eu|meni|des (Greek Myth)
eun|uch +s (castrated man)
  [☞ Unix]
eu|ony|mus
  plural eu|ony|mus
eu|pep|tic
eu|phem|ism +s
eu|phem|is|tic
eu|phem|is|tic|ally
eu|phem|ize
  eu|phem|iz|es
  eu|phem|ized
  eu|phem|iz|ing
eu|phon|ic
eu|phoni|ous
eu|phoni|ous|ly
eu|phon|ium +s
eu|phon|ize
  eu|phon|iz|es
  eu|phon|ized
  eu|phon|iz|ing
eu|phony
  eu|phon|ies
eu|phor|bia +s
eu|phoria
eu|phori|ant +s

eu|phor|ic
eu|phor|ic|ally
Eu|phra|tes (river, Asia)
Eu|phro|syne (Greek Myth)
eu|phu|ism
eu|phu|ist +s
eu|phu|is|tic
eu|phu|is|tic|ally
Eur|asian +s
eur|eka +s
eu|rhyth|mic (use eurythmic)
eu|rhyth|mics (use eurythmics)
eu|rhyth|my (use eurythmy)
Eu|ripi|des (Greek dramatist)
Euro +s
Euro|bond +s
Euro-Canadian +s
Euro|cen|tric
Euro|cen|tri|city
Euro|cen|trism
Euro|cheque +s
Euro|com|mun|ism
Euro|com|mun|ist +s
Euro|crat +s
Euro|cur|rency
Euro|cur|ren|cies
Euro|dollar +s
Euro|market +s
Euro-MP
Euro-MPs
Eur|opa (Greek Myth; moon of Jupiter)
Eur|ope (continent)
Euro|pean +s
Euro|pean|ism
Euro|pean|ist +s
Euro|pean|iz|a|tion
Euro|pean|ize
Euro|pean|iz|es
Euro|pean|ized
Euro|pean|iz|ing
euro|pium
Euro|poort (port, the Netherlands)
Eurus (Greek Myth)
Eu|ry|ale (Greek Myth)
Eu|ry|dice (Greek Myth)
eu|ryth|mic
eu|ryth|mics
eu|ryth|my
Euse|bio (Portuguese soccer player)
Euse|bius of Caes|aria (bishop & historian)
Eus|tach|ian tube +s

eu|stasy
eu|stat|ic
eu|tec|tic +s
Eu|terpe (Greek & Roman Myth)
eutha|nasia +s
eutha|nize
eutha|niz|es
eutha|nized
eutha|niz|ing
eu|ther|ian +s
eu|troph|ic
eu|trophi|cate
eu|trophi|cates
eu|trophi|cat|ed
eu|trophi|cat|ing
eu|trophi|ca|tion
eu|tro|phy
EVA (extravehicular activity)
EVAs
evacu|ant +s
evacu|ate
evacu|ates
evacu|at|ed
evacu|at|ing
evacu|a|tion +s
evacu|a|tive
evacu|ator +s
evac|uee +s
evad|able
evade
evades
evad|ed
evad|ing
evad|er +s
evagin|ate
evagin|ates
evagin|at|ed
evagin|at|ing
evagin|a|tion +s
evalu|able
evalu|ate
evalu|ates
evalu|at|ed
evalu|at|ing
evalu|a|tion +s
evalu|a|tive
evalu|ator +s
evan|esce
evan|es|ces
evan|esced
evan|es|cing
evan|es|cence
evan|es|cent
evan|es|cent|ly
evan|gel +s
evan|gel|ic
evan|gel|ic|al
evan|gel|ic|al|ism
evan|gel|ic|al|ly
evan|gel|ism
evan|gel|ist +s

evan|gel|is|tic
evan|gel|iz|a|tion +s
evan|gel|ize
evan|gel|iz|es
evan|gel|ized
evan|gel|iz|ing
evan|gel|iz|er +s
Evans, Sir Ar|thur John (English archaeologist)
Evans, Gil (Cdn musician)
Evans, Her|bert Mc|Lean (US anatomist)
Evans, James (Cdn minister & linguist)
Evans, Mary Ann (George Eliot)
Evans, Walk|er (US photographer)
evap|or|able
evap|or|ate
evap|or|ates
evap|or|at|ed
evap|or|at|ing
evap|or|at|ed adjective
evap|or|a|tion +s
evap|or|a|tive
evap|or|ator +s
evap|or|ite +s
eva|sion +s
evas|ive
evas|ive|ly
evas|ive|ness
Eve (Bible)
eve +s
evec|tion +s
Evelyn, John (English writer)
even +er +est +s +ed +ing
even-handed
even-handed|ly
even-handed|ness
even|ing +s noun
even|ing wear
even|ly
even money (even-money when preceding a noun)
even|ness
evens
even|song +s
even-steven
even strength (even-strength when preceding a noun)
event +s
even-tempered
event|er +s
event|ful

event|ful|ly
event|ful|ness
even|tide
event|ing +s
event|less
even|tu|al
even|tu|al|ity
even|tu|al|ities
even|tu|al|ly
even|tu|ate
even|tu|ates
even|tu|at|ed
even|tu|at|ing
even|tu|a|tion
ever
ever|bear|ing
Ever|est (Himalayan mountain)
Ever|glades (marshland, US)
ever|green +s
ever|last|ing
ever|last|ing|ly
ever|last|ing|ness
ever|more
ever-present
evers|ible
ever|sion
Evert, Chris|tine Marie ('Chris') (US tennis player)
evert +s +ed +ing (turn an organ inside out)
every
every body (each body)
every|body (everyone, all)
every day (each day)
every|day (regular; usual; ordinary)
every|day|ness
Every|man
every one (each one)
every|one (everybody, all)
every place (each place)
every|place (everywhere)
every thing (each thing)
every|thing (all things)
every|where
Every|woman
evict +s +ed +ing
evic|tion +s
evict|or +s
evi|dence
evi|den|ces

evi|denced
evi|den|cing
evi|dent
evi|den|tial
evi|den|tial|ly
evi|den|tiary
evi|dent|ly
evil +s
evil|doer +s
evil|doing
evil eye +s
evil|ly
evil|ness
evil one
evince
  evin|ces
  evinced
  evin|cing
evin|cible
evin|cive
evis|cer|ate
  evis|cer|ates
  evis|cer|at|ed
  evis|cer|at|ing
evis|cer|a|tion
Evita (Eva Perón)
evo|ca|tion +s
evoc|a|tive
evoc|a|tive|ly
evoc|a|tive|ness
evoke
  evokes
  evoked
  evok|ing
evok|er +s
evo|lute +s
evo|lu|tion +s
evo|lu|tion|al
evo|lu|tion|al|ly
evo|lu|tion|ar|ily
evo|lu|tion|ary
evo|lu|tion|ism
evo|lu|tion|ist +s
evo|lu|tion|is|tic
evolv|able
evolve
  evolves
  evolved
  evolv|ing
evolve|ment
ev|zone +s
Ewe (people;
  language)
  plural Ewe
ewe +s (sheep)
  [☞ yew]
Ewen, (Wil|liam)
  Pater|son (Cdn
  painter)
ewe neck +s
ewe-necked
ewer +s

ex (former partner;
  exhibition; without)
  exes
ex|acer|bate
  ex|acer|bates
  ex|acer|bat|ed
  ex|acer|bat|ing
ex|acer|ba|tion +s
ex|act +s +ed +ing
ex|acta +s *US*
  (= exactor)
exact|able
exact|ing *adjective*
exact|ing|ly
exact|ing|ness
exac|tion +s
exact|itude
exact|ly
exact|ness
ex|acto (= X-acto)
exact|or +s
exact|or box
  exact|or boxes
ex|ag|ger|ate
  ex|ag|ger|ates
  ex|ag|ger|at|ed
  ex|ag|ger|at|ing
ex|ag|ger|at|ed
  adjective
ex|ag|ger|at|ed|ly
ex|ag|ger|at|ing|ly
ex|ag|ger|a|tion +s
ex|ag|ger|a|tive
ex|ag|ger|ator +s
exalt +s +ed +ing
  (praise; promote;
  ennoble)
  [☞ exult]
exal|ta|tion +s
  (praise; promotion;
  ennoblement;
  elation)
  [☞ exultation]
exalt|ed *adjective*
  (lofty, grand, noble;
  elated)
  [☞ exulted]
exalt|ed|ly
exalt|ed|ness
exam +s
exam|in|able
exam|in|a|tion +s
exam|in|a|tion|al
exam|ination-in-
  chief
  exam|inations-in-
  chief
exam|ine
  exam|ines
  exam|ined
  exam|in|ing
exam|inee +s
exam|in|er +s

ex|ample +s
ex ante
exan|thema
ex|arch +s
ex|arch|ate +s
ex|as|per|ate
  ex|as|per|ates
  ex|as|per|at|ed
  ex|as|per|at|ing
ex|as|per|at|ed
  adjective
ex|as|per|at|ed|ly
ex|as|per|at|ing
  adjective
ex|as|per|at|ing|ly
ex|as|per|a|tion
ex cath|edra
ex|cav|ate
  ex|cav|ates
  ex|cav|at|ed
  ex|cav|at|ing
ex|cav|a|tion +s
ex|cav|ator +s
ex|ceed +s +ed +ing
  (go beyond; surpass)
  [☞ accede]
ex|ceed|ing *adjective*
  & *adverb* (going
  beyond; surpassing)
  [☞ acceding]
ex|ceed|ing|ly
excel
  ex|cels
  ex|celled
  ex|cel|ling
ex|cel|lence +s
Ex|cel|lency
  Ex|cel|len|cies
ex|cel|lent
ex|cel|lent|ly
ex|cel|sior
ex|cept +s +ed +ing
  (exclude; not
  including; only)
  [☞ accept]
ex|cept|ed *adjective*
  (excluded)
  [☞ accepted]
ex|cept|ing *preposition*
  & *conjunction* (not
  including; only)
ex|cep|tion +s
ex|cep|tion|able
  (open to objection)
  [☞ exceptional]
ex|cep|tion|ably
ex|cep|tion|al
  (unusual;
  outstanding;
  disabled)
  [☞ exceptionable]
ex|cep|tion|al|ism
ex|cep|tion|al|ity

ex|cep|tion|al|ly
ex|cerpt +s +ed +ing
ex|cerpt|ible
ex|cerp|tion
ex|cess
  ex|cess|es
ex|ces|sive
ex|ces|sive|ly
ex|ces|sive|ness
ex|change
  ex|chan|ges
  ex|changed
  ex|chan|ging
ex|change|abil|ity
ex|change|able
ex|chan|ger +s
ex|change rate +s
Ex|change Rate
  Mech|an|ism
ex|chequer +s
ex|cimer +s
ex|cise
  ex|cis|es
  ex|cised
  ex|cis|ing
ex|cise|man
  ex|cise|men
ex|ci|sion +s
ex|cit|abil|ity
ex|cit|able
ex|cit|ably
ex|cit|ant +s
ex|cit|a|tion +s
ex|cit|a|tive
ex|cit|a|tory
ex|cite
  ex|cites
  ex|cit|ed
  ex|cit|ing
ex|cit|ed *adjective*
ex|cit|ed|ly
ex|cit|ed|ness
ex|cite|ment +s
ex|cit|er +s
ex|cit|ing *adjective*
ex|cit|ing|ly
ex|citon +s
ex|claim +s +ed +ing
ex|claim|er +s
ex|clam|a|tion +s
ex|clam|a|tory
ex|clave +s
ex|clo|sure +s
ex|clud|able
ex|clude
  ex|cludes
  ex|clud|ed
  ex|clud|ing
ex|clud|er +s
ex|clu|sion +s
ex|clu|sion|ary
ex|clu|sion|ism

ex|clu|sion|ist +s
ex|clu|sive
ex|clu|sive|ly
ex|clu|sive|ness
ex|clu|siv|ism
ex|clu|siv|ist +s
ex|clu|siv|ity
ex|cogi|tate
  ex|cogi|tates
  ex|cogi|tat|ed
  ex|cogi|tat|ing
ex|cogi|ta|tion +s
ex|com|muni|cate
  ex|com|muni|cates
  ex|com|muni|cat|ed
  ex|com|muni|
            cat|ing
ex|com|muni|ca|tion
  +s
ex|com|muni|ca|tive
ex|com|muni|ca|tor
  +s
ex|com|muni|ca|tory
ex-con +s
ex|cori|ate
  ex|cori|ates
  ex|cori|at|ed
  ex|cori|at|ing
ex|cori|a|tion
ex|cre|ment
ex|cre|ment|al
ex|cres|cence +s
ex|cres|cent
ex|cres|cen|tial
ex|creta
ex|crete
  ex|cretes
  ex|cret|ed
  ex|cret|ing
ex|cret|er +s
ex|cre|tion +s
ex|cre|tive
ex|cre|tory
ex|cruci|at|ing
ex|cruci|at|ing|ly
ex|cruci|a|tion
ex|cul|pate
  ex|cul|pates
  ex|cul|pat|ed
  ex|cul|pat|ing
ex|cul|pa|tion +s
ex|cul|pa|tory
ex|cur|sion +s
ex|cur|sion|ist +s
ex|cur|sus
  plural ex|cur|sus|es
  or ex|cur|sus
ex|cus|able
ex|cus|ably
ex|cusa|tory
ex|cuse
  ex|cus|es

ex|cused
ex|cus|ing
ex-directory
ex divi|dend
exec +s
exe|crable
exe|crably
exe|crate
  exe|crates
  exe|crat|ed
  exe|crat|ing
exe|cra|tion +s
exe|cra|tive
exe|cra|tory
exe|cut|able
exec|u|tant +s
exe|cute
  exe|cutes
  exe|cut|ed
  exe|cut|ing
exe|cu|tion +s
exe|cu|tion|ary
exe|cu|tion|er +s
exec|u|tive
exec|u|tive|ly
exec|u|tor +s
exec|u|tor|ial
exec|u|tor|ship
exec|u|tory
exec|u|trix
  exec|u|tri|ces or
  exec|u|trix|es
exe|gesis
  exe|geses
exe|gete +s
exe|get|ic
exe|get|ic|al
exem|plar +s
exem|plar|i|ly
exem|plar|i|ness
exem|plar|ity
exem|plary
exem|pli|fi|ca|tion +s
exem|pli|fy
  exem|pli|fies
  exem|pli|fied
  exem|pli|fy|ing
exem|plum
  exem|pla
ex|empt +s +ed +ing
exemp|tion +s
exe|quies
exer|cis|able
exer|cise (physical
  activity etc.)
  exer|cis|es
  exer|cised
  exer|cis|ing
  [☞ exorcise]
exer|cis|er +s
Exer|cycle +s
  proprietary
ex|ergue +s

ex|ert +s +ed +ing
  (use, apply, wield;
  strive)
  [☞ exsert]
exer|tion +s
Exe|ter (town,
  England)
exe|unt
ex|fil|trate
  ex|fil|trates
  ex|fil|trat|ed
  ex|fil|trat|ing
ex|fil|tra|tion
ex|foli|ate
  ex|foli|ates
  ex|foli|at|ed
  ex|foli|at|ing
ex|foli|a|tion +s
ex|foli|a|tive
ex gra|tia
ex|hal|able
ex|hal|a|tion +s
ex|hale
  ex|hales
  ex|haled
  ex|hal|ing
ex|haust +s +ed +ing
ex|haust|ed adjective
ex|haust|er +s
ex|haust|ibil|ity
ex|haust|ible
ex|haust|ing adjective
ex|haust|ing|ly
ex|haus|tion
ex|haust|ive
ex|haust|ive|ly
ex|haust|ive|ness
ex|haus|tiv|ity
ex|haust pipe +s
ex|hib|it +s +ed +ing
ex|hib|ition +s
ex|hib|ition|er +s
ex|hib|ition|ism
ex|hib|ition|ist +s
ex|hib|ition|is|tic
ex|hib|ition|is|tic|ally
ex|hib|itor +s
ex|hila|rate
  ex|hila|rates
  ex|hila|rat|ed
  ex|hila|rat|ing
ex|hila|rat|ed
  adjective
ex|hila|rat|ing
  adjective
ex|hila|rat|ing|ly
ex|hila|ra|tion +s
ex|hila|ra|tive
ex|hort +s +ed +ing
ex|hort|a|tion +s
ex|horta|tive
ex|horta|tory
ex|hort|er +s

ex|hum|a|tion +s
ex|hume
  ex|humes
  ex|humed
  ex|hum|ing
ex hy|poth|esi
exi|gence +s
exi|gency
  exi|gen|cies
exi|gent
exi|gu|ity
exigu|ous
exigu|ous|ly
exigu|ous|ness
exile
  ex|iles
  ex|iled
  exil|ing
exilic
exist +s +ed +ing
exist|ence +s
exist|ent +s
exis|ten|tial
exis|ten|tial|ism
exis|ten|tial|ist +s
exis|ten|tial|ly
exist|ing adjective
exit +s +ed +ing
ex lib|ris
  plural ex lib|ris
Ex|moor (area,
  England)
ex nihi|lo
exo|bio|logic|al
exo|biol|o|gist +s
exo|biol|ogy
Exo|cet +s proprietary
exo|crine
exo|cyt|o|sis
exo|cyt|otic
Exo|dus (Bible)
exo|dus
  exo|dus|es
ex of|fi|cio
exo|gam|ic
ex|og|am|ous
ex|og|amy
exo|gen|ous
exo|gen|ous|ly
exon +s
ex|on|er|ate
  ex|on|er|ates
  ex|on|er|at|ed
  ex|on|er|at|ing
ex|on|er|a|tion +s
ex|on|era|tive
ex|oph|thal|mic
ex|oph|thal|mos
ex|orbi|tance
ex|orbi|tant
ex|orbi|tant|ly

exor|cise (drive away evil influence)
  exor|cis|es
  exor|cised
  exor|cis|ing
  [☞ exercise]
exor|cism +s
exor|cist +s
exor|cize (drive away evil influence: *use* exorcise)
  exor|ciz|es
  exor|cized
  exor|ciz|ing
  [☞ exercise]
ex|or|dial
ex|or|dium
  ex|or|diums or
  ex|or|dia
exo|skel|etal
exo|skel|eton +s
exo|sphere +s
exo|spher|ic
exo|ter|ic (intended for all; popular)
  [☞ esoteric]
exo|ther|mal
exo|ther|mal|ly
exo|ther|mic
exo|ther|mic|ally
exot|ic +s
exot|ica
exot|ic|al|ly
exoti|cism
exotic|ness
exo|toxin +s
ex|pand +s +ed +ing
ex|pand|abil|ity
ex|pand|able
ex|pand|er +s
ex|pand|ing *adjective*
ex|panse +s
ex|pan|si|bil|ity
ex|pan|sible
ex|pan|sile
ex|pan|sion +s
ex|pan|sion|ary
ex|pan|sion|ism
ex|pan|sion|ist +s
ex|pan|sion|is|tic
ex|pan|sive
ex|pan|sive|ly
ex|pan|sive|ness
ex|pan|siv|ity
ex parte
ex|pat +s
ex|pati|ate
  ex|pati|ates
  ex|pati|at|ed
  ex|pati|at|ing
ex|pati|a|tion +s
ex|patia|tory

ex|patri|ate
  ex|patri|ates
  ex|patri|at|ed
  ex|patri|at|ing
ex|patri|a|tion +s
ex|pect +s +ed +ing
ex|pect|able
ex|pect|ably
ex|pect|ancy
  ex|pect|an|cies
ex|pect|ant +s
ex|pect|ant|ly
ex|pect|a|tion +s
ex|pec|tor|ant +s
ex|pec|tor|ate
  ex|pec|tor|ates
  ex|pec|tor|at|ed
  ex|pec|tor|at|ing
ex|pec|tor|a|tion +s
ex|pec|tor|ator +s
ex|pedi|ence
ex|pedi|ency
  ex|pedi|en|cies
ex|pedi|ent +s
ex|pedi|ent|ly
ex|ped|ite
  ex|ped|ites
  ex|ped|it|ed
  ex|ped|it|ing
ex|ped|it|er +s
ex|ped|ition +s
ex|ped|ition|ary
ex|ped|ition|er +s
ex|ped|ition|ist +s
ex|ped|itious
ex|ped|itious|ly
ex|ped|itious|ness
ex|ped|it|or +s
expel
  ex|pels
  ex|pelled
  ex|pel|ling
ex|pel|lable
ex|pel|lee +s
ex|pel|lent
ex|pel|ler +s
ex|pend +s +ed +ing
ex|pend|abil|ity
ex|pend|able
ex|pend|ably
ex|pendi|ture +s
ex|pense
  ex|pens|es
  ex|pensed
  ex|pens|ing
ex|pen|sive
ex|pen|sive|ly
ex|pen|sive|ness
ex|peri|ence
  ex|peri|en|ces
  ex|peri|enced
  ex|peri|en|cing
ex|peri|ence|able

ex|peri|enced *adjective*
ex|peri|en|cer +s
ex|peri|en|tial
ex|peri|en|tial|ism
ex|peri|en|tial|ist +s
ex|peri|en|tial|ly
ex|peri|ment +s +ed +ing
ex|peri|ment|al
ex|peri|ment|al|ism
ex|peri|ment|al|ist +s
ex|peri|ment|al|ly
ex|peri|men|ta|tion +s
ex|peri|ment|er +s
ex|pert +s
ex|per|tise *noun*
ex|pert|ize *verb*
  ex|pert|iz|es
  ex|pert|ized
  ex|pert|iz|ing
ex|pert|ly
ex|pert|ness
expi|ate
  expi|ates
  expi|ated
  expi|ating
expi|ation
expi|ator +s
ex|pia|tory
ex|pir|a|tion +s
ex|pira|tory
ex|pire
  ex|pires
  ex|pired
  ex|pir|ing
ex|piry
  ex|pir|ies
ex|plain +s +ed +ing
ex|plain|able
ex|plain|er +s
ex|plan|a|tion +s
ex|plana|tor|i|ly
ex|plana|tory
ex|plant +s
ex|plan|ta|tion +s
ex|plet|ive +s
ex|plic|able
ex|pli|cate
  ex|pli|cates
  ex|pli|cat|ed
  ex|pli|cat|ing
ex|pli|ca|tion +s
ex|pli|ca|tive
ex|pli|ca|tor +s
ex|pli|ca|tory
ex|plicit
ex|plicit|ly
ex|plicit|ness
ex|plod|able

ex|plode
  ex|plodes
  ex|plod|ed
  ex|plod|ing
ex|plod|ed *adjective*
ex|plod|er +s
ex|ploit +s +ed +ing
ex|ploit|abil|ity
ex|ploit|able
ex|ploit|a|tion +s
ex|ploit|a|tive
ex|ploit|er +s
ex|ploit|ive
Ex|ploits (river, Canada)
ex|plor|a|tion +s
ex|plor|a|tion|al
ex|plora|tive
ex|plora|tory
ex|plore
  ex|plores
  ex|plored
  ex|plor|ing
ex|plor|er +s
ex|plo|sion +s
ex|plo|sive +s
ex|plo|sive|ly
ex|plo|sive|ness
Expo +s
ex|po|nent +s
ex|po|nen|tial
ex|po|nen|tial|ly
ex|port +s +ed +ing
ex|port|abil|ity
ex|port|able
ex|port|a|tion +s
ex|port|er +s
ex|pose *verb*
  ex|pos|es
  ex|posed
  ex|pos|ing
ex|po|sé +s *noun*
ex|posed *adjective*
ex|pos|er +s
ex|pos|ition +s
ex|pos|ition|al
ex|posi|tive
ex|posi|tor +s
ex|posi|tory
ex post
ex post facto
ex|pos|tu|late
  ex|pos|tu|lates
  ex|pos|tu|lat|ed
  ex|pos|tu|lat|ing
ex|pos|tu|la|tion +s
ex|pos|tu|la|tory
ex|pos|ure +s
ex|pound +s +ed +ing
ex|pound|er +s

ex|press
  ex|press|es
  ex|pressed
  ex|press|ing
ex|pressed *adjective*
ex|press|er +s
ex|press|ible
ex|pres|sion +s
ex|pres|sion|al
ex|pres|sion|ism
ex|pres|sion|ist +s
ex|pres|sion|is|tic
ex|pres|sion|
        is|tic|ally
ex|pres|sion|less
ex|pres|sion|less|ly
ex|pres|sion|less|
         ness
ex|pres|sive
ex|pres|sive|ly
ex|pres|sive|ness
ex|pres|siv|ity
ex|press|ly
ex|pres|so +s
  (= espresso)
ex|press|way +s
ex|pro|pri|ate
  ex|pro|pri|ates
  ex|pro|pri|at|ed
  ex|pro|pri|at|ing
ex|pro|pri|a|tion +s
ex|pro|pri|ator +s
ex|pul|sion +s
ex|pul|sive
ex|punc|tion +s
ex|punge
  ex|pun|ges
  ex|punged
  ex|pun|ging
ex|pun|ger +s
ex|pur|gate
  ex|pur|gates
  ex|pur|gat|ed
  ex|pur|gat|ing
ex|pur|ga|tion +s
ex|pur|ga|tor +s
ex|purga|tor|ial
ex|purga|tory
ex|quis|ite +s
ex|quis|ite|ly
ex|quis|ite|ness
ex|san|guin|ate
  ex|san|guin|ates
  ex|san|guin|at|ed
  ex|san|guin|at|ing
ex|san|guin|a|tion +s
ex|sert +s +ed +ing
  (*Biology* put forth)
  [☞ exert]
ex-service
ex-service|man
  ex-service|men

ex-service|woman
  ex-service|women
ex|tant
ex|tem|por|an|eous
ex|tem|por|
        an|eous|ly
ex|tem|por|
       an|eous|ness
ex|tem|por|ar|i|ly
ex|tem|por|ar|i|ness
ex|tem|por|ary
ex|tem|pore
ex|tem|por|iz|a|tion
  +s
ex|tem|por|ize
  ex|tem|por|iz|es
  ex|tem|por|ized
  ex|tem|por|iz|ing
ex|tend +s +ed +ing
ex|tend|abil|ity
ex|tend|able
ex|tend|er +s
ex|tend|ibil|ity (*use*
  extendability)
ex|tend|ible (*use*
  extendable)
ex|ten|si|bil|ity
ex|ten|sible
ex|ten|sion +s
ex|ten|sion|al
ex|ten|sion|al|ly
ex|ten|sive
ex|ten|sive|ly
ex|ten|sive|ness
ex|ten|som|eter +s
ex|ten|sor +s
ex|tent +s
ex|tenu|ate
  ex|tenu|ates
  ex|tenu|at|ed
  ex|tenu|at|ing
ex|tenu|at|ing
  adjective
ex|tenu|at|ing|ly
ex|tenu|a|tion +s
ex|tenua|tory
ex|ter|ior +s
ex|ter|ior|ity
ex|ter|ior|ize
  ex|ter|ior|iz|es
  ex|ter|ior|ized
  ex|ter|ior|iz|ing
ex|ter|ior|ly
ex|ter|min|ate
  ex|ter|min|ates
  ex|ter|min|at|ed
  ex|ter|min|at|ing
ex|ter|min|a|tion +s
ex|ter|min|ator +s
ex|ter|mina|tory
ex|ter|nal +s
ex|ter|nal|ity
  ex|ter|nal|ities

ex|ter|nal|iz|a|tion +s
ex|ter|nal|ize
  ex|ter|nal|iz|es
  ex|ter|nal|ized
  ex|ter|nal|iz|ing
ex|ter|nal|ly
ex|tero|cep|tive
ex|tero|cep|tiv|ity
ex|tero|cep|tor +s
ex|terri|tor|ial
ex|terri|tor|ial|ity
ex|tinct
ex|tinc|tion +s
ex|tinct|ive
ex|tin|guish
  ex|tin|guish|es
  ex|tin|guished
  ex|tin|guish|ing
ex|tin|guish|able
ex|tin|guish|er +s
ex|tin|guish|ment
ex|tir|pate
  ex|tir|pates
  ex|tir|pat|ed
  ex|tir|pat|ing
ex|tir|pa|tion
ex|tir|pa|tor +s
extol
  ex|tols
  ex|tolled
  ex|tol|ling
ex|tol|ler +s
ex|tol|ment +s
ex|tort +s +ed +ing
ex|tort|er +s
ex|tor|tion +s
ex|tor|tion|ate
ex|tor|tion|ate|ly
ex|tor|tion|er +s
ex|tor|tion|ist +s
ex|tort|ive
ex|tra +s
extra-base hit +s
extra-billing
extra|cellu|lar
extra|cellu|lar|ly
extra|cor|por|eal
extra|cor|por|eal|ly
ex|tract +s +ed +ing
ex|tract|abil|ity
ex|tract|able
ex|trac|tion +s
ex|tract|ive +s
ex|tract|or +s
extra|curricu|lar
extra|curricu|lar|ly
extra|dit|able
extra|dite
  extra|dites
  extra|dit|ed
  extra|dit|ing
extra|di|tion

ex|tra|dos
  ex|tra|dos|es
extra|galac|tic
extra|judi|cial
extra|judi|cial|ly
extra|lin|guis|tic
extra|mari|tal
extra|mun|dane
extra|mural
extra|mural|ly
ex|tran|eous
ex|tran|eous|ly
ex|tran|eous|ness
extra|ordin|aire
extra|ordin|ar|i|ly
extra|ordin|ar|i|ness
extra|ordin|ary
ex|trapo|late
  ex|trapo|lates
  ex|trapo|lat|ed
  ex|trapo|lat|ing
ex|trapo|la|tion +s
ex|trapo|la|tive
ex|trapo|la|tor +s
extra|pyram|id|al
extra|sen|sory
extra|terres|trial +s
extra|terri|tor|ial
extra|terri|tor|ial|ity
ex|trava|gance +s
ex|trava|gant
ex|trava|gant|ly
ex|trava|ganza +s
ex|trava|sate
  ex|trava|sates
  ex|trava|sat|ed
  ex|trava|sat|ing
extra|va|sa|tion +s
extra|vascu|lar
extra|vehicu|lar
extra-virgin
Ex|trema|dura
  (region, Spain)
ex|treme
ex|treme|ly
ex|treme|ness
ex|trem|is (in '*in
  extremis*')
ex|trem|ism
ex|trem|ist +s
ex|trem|ity
  ex|trem|ities
ex|tric|able
ex|tri|cate
  ex|tri|cates
  ex|tri|cat|ed
  ex|tri|cat|ing
ex|tri|ca|tion
ex|trin|sic
ex|trin|sic|ally
extro|ver|sion
extro|vert +s

extro|vert|ed
ex|trude
  ex|trudes
  ex|trud|ed
  ex|trud|ing
ex|trud|ed *adjective*
ex|trud|er +s
ex|tru|sile
ex|tru|sion +s
ex|tru|sive
ex|uber|ance
ex|uber|ant
ex|uber|ant|ly
exu|date +s
exu|da|tion +s
exu|da|tive
exude
  ex|udes
  ex|uded
  ex|ud|ing
exult +s +ed +ing
  (rejoice; triumph;
  gloat)
  [☞ exalt]
exult|ancy
exult|ant
exult|ant|ly
exul|ta|tion +s
  (triumph; jubilation)
  [☞ exaltation]
exul|ting|ly
Exuma Cays (islands,
  the Bahamas)
ex|urb +s
ex|urban
ex|urban|ite +s
ex|urbia
ex|uviae
ex voto +s
eyas
  eyas|es
Eyck, Jan Van
  (Flemish painter)
eye (sight organ)
  eyes
  eyed
  eye|ing
  [☞ aye]
eye-appeal
eye|ball +s +ed +ing
eye|ball to eye|ball
  adverb
eyeball-to-eyeball
  adjective
eye bath +s
eye|blink +s
eye|bolt +s
eye|bright
eye|brow +s
eye-catcher +s
eye-catching
eye con|tact
eye|cup +s

eyed *adjective*
eye doc|tor +s
eye drop +s
eye|drop|per +s
eye|ful +s
eye|glass
  eye|glass|es
eye|hole +s
eye|lash
  eye|lash|es
eye|less
eye|let (small hole or
  ring; embroidered
  fabric; butterfly
  marking)
  eye|lets
  eye|leted
  eye|let|ing
  [☞ islet]
eye level (eye-level
  *when preceding a
  noun*)
eye|lid +s
eye lift +s
eye|like
eye|liner +s
eye mask +s
eye-opener +s
eye-opening
eye patch
  eye patch|es
eye|piece +s
eye-popper +s
eye-popping
eye-rhyme +s
eye|shade +s
eye|shadow +s
eye|shot
eye|sight
eye sock|et +s
eye|sore +s
eye-spot +s
eye-stalk +s
eye strain
Eye|tie +s *offensive*
eye tooth
  eye teeth
eye|wash
eye|wear
eye|wit|ness
  eye|wit|ness|es
  eye|wit|nessed
  eye|wit|ness|ing
eyra +s (wild cat)
  [☞ Eire]
Eyre (lake, Australia)
  [☞ Ayer, Ayers
  Rock]
Eyre, Ivan Ken|neth
  (Cdn painter)
  [☞ Ayer, Ayers
  Rock]

eyrie +s (nest, lofty
  position: *use* aerie)
Ezek|iel (*Bible*)
Ezra (*Bible*)

F

F
• (letter; note; mark)
  F's
• (Fahrenheit; farad;
  pencil softness; filial
  generation)
  [☞ eff]
F (faraday)
f
• (letter)
  f's
• (focal length; franc)
  [☞ eff]
f. (following page etc.)
  ff.
fa +s (*Music*)
fab
faba bean +s (*use*
  fava bean)
Fab|er|gé, Peter Carl
  (Russian jeweller)
Fa|bian +s
Fa|bian|ism
Fa|bian|ist +s
Fa|bius (Roman
  statesman)
fable
  fables
  fabled
  fab|ling
fabled *adjective*
fab|ler +s
fab|liau
  fab|li|aux
fab|ric +s (textile;
  framework)
  [☞ fabrique]
fab|ri|cate
  fab|ri|cates
  fab|ri|cat|ed
  fab|ri|cat|ing
fab|ri|ca|tion +s
fab|ri|ca|tor +s
fab|rique +s (vestry
  maintaining church
  property)
fabu|lism
fabu|list +s
fabu|lous
fabu|lous|ly
fabu|lous|ness

FAC (Firearms
  Acquisition
  Certificate)
  FACs
fa|cade +s
face
  faces
  faced
  fa|cing
face card +s
face cloth +s
face cord +s
face cream +s
faced *adjective*
face|less
face|less|ness
face|lift +s
face-lifted
face-lifting
face mask +s
face off *verb*
  faces off
  faced off
  fa|cing off
face|off +s *noun*
face pack +s
face paint +s
face paint|er +s
face paint|ing
face|plate +s
facer +s
face-saver +s
face-saving
facet +s
facet|ed
fa|cetiae
facet|ing
fa|cetious
fa|cetious|ly
fa|cetious|ness
face to face *adverb*
face-to-face *adjective*
face value +s
facia (dashboard,
  panel: *use* fascia)
  facias
  [☞ fascia, fieri
  facias]
fa|cial +s (beauty
  treatment; of the
  face; *for* of a fascia
  use fascial)
fa|cial|ly
fa|cies (*Pathology*;
  Geology)
  plural fa|cies
  [☞ fasces, fieri
  facias]
fa|cile
fa|cile|ly
fa|cile|ness

fa|cili|tate
fa|cili|tates
fa|cili|tat|ed
fa|cili|tat|ing
fa|cili|ta|tion
fa|cili|ta|tive
fa|cili|ta|tor +s
fa|cil|ity
fa|cili|ties
fa|cing +s *noun*
fac|simile
fac|similes
fac|similed
fac|simile|ing
fact +s
facta
fact-finder +s
fact-finding
fac|tion +s
fac|tion|al
fac|tion|al|ism
fac|tion|al|ly
fac|tious
fac|tious|ly
fac|tious|ness
fac|ti|tious
fac|ti|tious|ly
fac|ti|tious|ness
fac|ti|tive
fact|oid +s
Fac|tor, Max (US cosmetics manufacturer)
fac|tor +s +ed +ing
fac|tor|able
fac|tor|age
fac|tor eight (*use* factor VIII)
fac|tor VIII
fac|tor|ial
fac|tor|ial|ly
fac|tor|iz|a|tion
fac|tor|ize
fac|tor|iz|es
fac|tor|ized
fac|tor|iz|ing
fac|tory
fac|tor|ies
fac|totum +s
fac|tual
fac|tual|ity
fac|tual|ly
fac|tual|ness
fac|tum
fac|tums or facta
fac|ture
fac|ula
facu|lae
facu|lar
fac|ul|ta|tive
fac|ul|ta|tive|ly
fac|ulty
fac|ul|ties

fad +s
fad|dish
fad|dish|ly
fad|dish|ness
fad|dism
fad|dist +s
faddy
fade
fades
faded
fading
fade away *verb*
fades away
faded away
fading away
fade|away +s *noun*
fade in *verb*
fades in
faded in
fading in
fade-in +s *noun*
fade|less
fade out *verb*
fades out
faded out
fading out
fade-out +s *noun*
fader +s
fado +s
faecal (*use* fecal)
faeces (*use* feces)
Fa|enza (town, Italy)
faer|ie +s (fairyland; *for* imaginary being *use* fairy)
[☞ fairy]
Faer|oe +s (islands, N Atlantic)
[☞ faro, Faro, pharaoh]
Faero|ese
plural Faero|ese
faery (= faerie)
faer|ies
[☞ fairy]
Fa|fard, Jo|seph (Cdn sculptor)
faff +s +ed +ing
Faf|ner (= Fafnir)
Faf|nir (*Scandinavian Myth*)
fag
fags
fagged
fag|ging
fag-end +s
fag|got +s +ed +ing (*offensive* homosexual; bundle, bunch, stack; food)
fag|got|ing *noun*
fag|goty

faggy
fag|gi|er
fag|gi|est
fag hag +s
fag|ot +s (bundle, bunch, stack: *use* faggot)
[☞ faggot]
fah (*use* fa)
Fahd (king of Saudi Arabia)
Fahren|heit, Gab|riel Dan|iel (German physicist)
Fahren|heit (temperature scale)
fai|ence +s
fail +s +ed +ing (not succeed etc.)
[☞ faille]
failed *adjective*
fail|ing +s *noun, adjective, & preposition*
faille +s (fabric)
[☞ phial]
fail-safe
fail|ure +s
fain (willing; gladly)
[☞ fane, feign]
fai|né|ance
fai|né|ant +s
faint +er +est +s +ed +ing (indistinct; weak; remote; feeble; lose consciousness)
[☞ feint]
faint-hearted
faint-hearted|ly
faint-hearted|ness
faint|ly
faint|ness
fair +er +est +s +ed +ing (just; fine; clear; light-coloured; exhibition)
[☞ fare]
Fair|banks, Doug|las Elton (1883–1939, US filmmaker)
Fair|banks, Doug|las Jr. (b.1909, US filmmaker)
Fair|fax (of Cam|eron), Thom|as, 3rd Baron (English general)
fair|goer +s
fair|ground +s
fair-haired
fair|ing +s *noun* (streamlining

structure; gift)
[☞ faring]
fair|ish
Fair Isle (island, North Sea; knitwear)
fair|lead +s
fair|ly
fair-minded
fair-minded|ly
fair-minded|ness
fair|ness
fair play
fair-spoken
Fair|vale (village, Canada)
fair|way +s
fair-weather *adjective*
Fair|weather (mountain, BC–Alaska border)
fairy (imaginary being; *offensive* homosexual)
fair|ies
[☞ faerie, ferry]
fairy god|mother +s
fairy|land +s
fairy lights
fairy-like
fairy ring +s
fairy slip|per +s
fairy story
fairy stor|ies
fairy tale +s (fairy-tale *when preceding a noun*)
Fai|sal (king of Saudi Arabia)
Faisal|abad (city, Pakistan)
fait ac|com|pli
faits ac|com|plis
faith +s
faith|ful
faith|ful|ly
faith|ful|ness
faith heal|er +s
faith heal|ing +s
faith|less
faith|less|ly
faith|less|ness
faji|ta +s
fake
fakes
faked
fak|ing
fak|er +s
fak|ery
faker|ies
fa|kir +s
fa|la|fel +s

Fa|lange (Spanish
 political group)
 [☞ phalange]
Fa|lan|gism
Fa|lan|gist +s
Fa|lasha
 plural Fa|lasha or
 Fa|lashas
fal|cate
fal|chion +s
fal|ci|form
fal|con +s
fal|con|er +s
fal|con|et +s
fal|conry
fal|der|al +s (use
 folderol)
fald|stool +s
Falk|land +s (islands,
 S Atlantic)
Falk|ner, Wil|liam
 (= Faulkner)
fall
 falls
 fell
 fall|en
 fall|ing
Falla, Man|uel de
 (Spanish musician)
fal|la|cious
fal|la|cious|ly
fal|la|cious|ness
fal|lacy
 fal|la|cies
fall away verb
 falls away
 fell away
 fall|en away
 fall|ing away
fall|away +s noun
fall back verb
 falls back
 fell back
 fall|en back
 fall|ing back
fall|back +s noun
fall|en
fallen|ness
fall|er +s
fall|fish
 plural fall|fish
fall guy +s
fal|li|bil|ity
fal|li|ble
fal|li|bly
fall|ing +s noun
falling-out
 fallings-out
fall off verb
 falls off
 fell off
 fall|en off
 fall|ing off

fall-off +s noun
Fal|lo|pian tube +s
fall out verb
 falls out
 fell out
 fall|en out
 fall|ing out
fall|out +s noun
fall|low +s +ed +ing
fallow|ness
fall sup|per +s
false
 fals|er
 fals|est
false|hood
false|ly
false mem|ory
 syn|drome
false|ness
false Solomon's seal
 +s
fall|setto +s
false|work
fals|ies
falsi|fi|abil|ity
falsi|fi|able
falsi|fi|ca|tion +s
falsi|fi|er +s
fals|ify
 falsi|fies
 falsi|fied
 falsi|fy|ing
fals|ity
 fals|ities
Fal|staff|ian
Fal|ster (island,
 Denmark)
fal|ter +s +ed +ing
fal|ter|er +s
fal|ter|ing|ly
fame
famed
Fa|meuse +s (apple)
fam|il|ial
fam|il|iar +s
fam|ili|ar|ity
 fam|ili|ar|ities
famil|iar|iz|a|tion
famil|iar|ize
 famil|iar|iz|es
 famil|iar|ized
 famil|iar|iz|ing
fam|il|iar|ly
fam|ily
 fam|ilies
Fam|ily Com|pact
 (Cdn history)
fam|ily com|pact
 (any influential
 clique)
fam|ine +s

fam|ish
 fam|ish|es
 fam|ished
 fam|ish|ing
fam|ished adjective
fam|ous
fam|ous|ly
famous|ness
famu|lus
 fam|uli
fan
 fans
 fanned
 fan|ning
fan|atic +s
fan|atic|al
fan|atic|al|ly
fan|ati|cism
fan|ati|cize
 fan|ati|ciz|es
 fan|ati|cized
 fan|ati|ciz|ing
fan belt +s
fan|ci|able
fan|ci|er +s
fan|ci|est
fan|ci|ful
fan|ci|ful|ly
fan|ci|ful|ness
fan|ci|ly
fan|ci|ness
fan club +s
fancy
 fan|ci|er
 fan|ci|est
 fan|cies
 fan|cied
 fancy|ing
fancy dress
fancy-free
fancy man
 fancy men
fancy-pants
fancy woman
 fancy women
fancy-work
fan dance +s
fan dan|cer +s
fan|dangle +s
fan|dan|go
 fan|dan|goes or
 fan|dan|gos
fan|dom
fane +s (temple)
 [☞ fain, feign]
fan|fare +s
fan|faro|nade +s
fan|fold
fang +s
fanged
fang|less
fang-like
fan jet +s

fan|light +s
fan-like
fan mail
fan|ner +s
fanny
 fan|nies
Fanny Adams
fanny pack +s
fan|tail +s
fan|tailed
fan-tan
fan|ta|sia +s
fan|ta|sist +s
fan|ta|size
 fan|ta|siz|es
 fan|ta|sized
 fan|ta|siz|ing
fan|ta|siz|er +s
fan|tast +s
fan|tas|tic
fan|tas|tic|al
fan|tas|tic|al|ity
fan|tas|tic|al|ly
fan|tas|ti|cate
 fan|tas|ti|cates
 fan|tas|ti|cat|ed
 fan|tas|ti|cat|ing
fan|tas|ti|ca|tion +s
fan|tasy
 fan|ta|sies
 fan|ta|sied
 fan|tasy|ing
fantasy|land +s
Fante (use Fanti)
 plural Fante or
 Fan|tes
Fanti
 plural Fanti or
 Fan|tis
fan|zine +s
far
 fur|ther or far|ther
 fur|thest or far|thest
far|ad +s
fara|daic
Fara|day, Mi|chael
 (English scientist)
fara|day +s
Fara|day cage +s
Faraday's con|stant
 +s
far|ad|ic
far|an|dole +s
far|away adjective
farce +s
far|ceur +s
far|ci|cal
far|ci|cal|ity
far|ci|cal|ly
farcy (disease)
 [☞ Farsi]
fard|ed

fare (price; passenger; food; progress, turn out)
fares
fared
faring
[☞ fair]
Far East (E Asia)
Far East|ern
fare box
fare boxes
fare-thee-well +s
Fare|well (capes, Greenland & New Zealand)
fare|well +s
far|falle
far-fetched
far-flung
far gone
Fa|rid|abad (city, India)
far|ina +s
far|in|aceous
faring conjugated form of fare
[☞ fairing]
farl +s
farm +s +ed +ing
farm|able
farm club +s
farm|er +s
farmer's saus|age +s
farm gate +s
farm|hand +s
farm|house +s
farm|ing noun
farm|land +s
farm|stead +s
farm team +s
farm wife
farm wives
farm|yard +s
Farn|bor|ough (town, England)
Far|nese, Ales|san|dro (Pope Paul III)
Far|nese, Ales|san|dro, Duke of Parma (Italian statesman)
far|ness
Farn|ham (town, Canada)
Far North (of Canada)
Faro (port, Portugal)
[☞ Faeroe, pharaoh]
faro (card game)
[☞ Faeroe, pharaoh]

Faro|ese (= Faeroese)
plural Faro|ese
far-off
fa|rouche
fa|rouche|ly
Far|ouk (Egyptian king)
far-out
Far|quhar, George (Irish dramatist)
far|ra|gin|ous
far|rago
far|ragos or
far|ragoes
far-reaching
Far|rell, James Thom|as (US novelist)
far|rier +s
far|ri|ery
far|row +s +ed +ing
far|row|ing noun
far-seeing
Farsi (language)
[☞ farcy]
far-sighted
far-sighted|ly
far-sighted|ness
fart +s +ed +ing
far|ther
far|thest
far|thing +s
far|thin|gale +s
fart|lek
Far|uk (= Farouk, Egyptian king)
Far West (of Canada)
fas|ces (bundle of rods with axe blade)
[☞ facies]
fa|scia
• (Architecture; dashboard, panel)
fa|scias
• (Anatomy)
fa|sciae
[☞ fieri facias]
fa|scial (of a fascia)
[☞ facial]
fa|sci|ate
fa|sci|at|ed
fa|sci|a|tion
fas|cicle +s
fas|cicled
fas|cicu|lar
fas|cicu|late
fas|cicu|la|tion +s
fas|ci|cule +s
(= fascicle)
fas|cic|ulus
fas|cic|uli
fasci|itis

fas|cin|ate
fas|cin|ates
fas|cin|at|ed
fas|cin|at|ing
fas|cin|at|ed adjective
fas|cin|at|ing adjective
fas|cin|at|ing|ly
fas|cin|a|tion +s
fas|cin|ator +s
fas|cine +s
Fas|cism (specific Italian movement)
fas|cism (in general use)
Fas|cist +s (supporter of Italian Fascism)
fas|cist +s (in general use)
Fas|cis|tic (of Italian Fascism)
fas|cis|tic (in general use)
fash|ion +s +ed +ing
fash|ion|abil|ity
fash|ion|able
fash|ion|able|ness
fash|ion|ably
fash|ion|er +s
Fass|bin|der, Rai|ner Wer|ner (German filmmaker)
fast +er +est +s +ed +ing
fast|back +s
fast|ball +s
fast break +s (fast-break when preceding a noun)
fast-breeder +s
fas|ten +s +ed +ing
fas|ten|er +s
fas|ten|ing +s noun
fast food +s (fast-food when preceding a noun)
fast-forward +s +ed +ing
fas|tidi|ous
fas|tidi|ous|ly
fas|tidi|ous|ness
fas|tigi|ate
fast|ness
Fast|net (islet, Ireland)
fast pitch
fast talk noun
fast-talk +s +ed +ing verb
fast talk|er +s
fast-talking adjective
fast track noun (fast-track when preceding a noun)

fast-track +s +ed +ing verb
fast-tracker +s
fast-twitch
fat (obese; greasy; bituminous)
fat|ter
fat|test
fats
fat|ted
fat|ting
[☞ phat]
fatal
fatal|ism
fatal|ist +s
fatal|is|tic
fatal|is|tic|ally
fatal|ity
fatal|ities
fatal|ly
fat|back
fat cat +s (fat-cat when preceding a noun)
Fat City (Ottawa, Canada)
fate (destiny, doom etc.)
fates
fated
fat|ing
[☞ fete]
fated adjective
fate|ful
fate|ful|ly
fate|ful|ness
Fates (Greek Myth)
fat free (fat-free when preceding a noun)
fat|head +s
fat|head|ed
fat|headed|ness
fat hen (plant)
fath|er +s +ed +ing
father|hood
father-in-law
fathers-in-law
father|land +s
father|less
father|less|ness
father|like
father|li|ness
father|ly
Father of Con|fed|er|a|tion
Fath|ers of Con|fed|er|a|tion
Father's Day
fathom +s +ed +ing
fathom|able
fathom|less
fathom|less|ly

fat|ig|abil|ity
(= fatiguability)
fat|ig|able
(= fatiguable)
fa|ti|gua|bil|ity
fa|ti|guable
fa|tigue
fa|tigues
fa|tigued
fa|tiguing
fa|tigue|less
fatigue-party
fatigue-parties
Fat|iha
Fat|ihah (use Fatiha)
Fat|ima (daughter of
Muhammad; village,
Portugal)
Fat|imid +s
fat|less
fat|ling +s
fatly
fat|ness
fats
fatso +s
fat-soluble
fat|stock
fat|ten +s +ed +ing
fat|ten|er +s
fat|ten|ing adjective
fat|ti|ness
fat|tish
fatty
fat|ti|er
fat|ti|est
fat|ties
fatu|ity
fatu|ities
fatu|ous (silly)
[☞ ignis fatuus]
fatu|ous|ly
fatu|ous|ness
fatwa +s
fau|bourg +s
fau|ces
fau|cet +s
fau|cet|ry
fau|cial
Faulk|ner, Wil|liam
Cuth|bert (US
novelist)
fault +s +ed +ing
fault-finder +s
fault-finding
fault|i|er
fault|i|est
fault|i|ly
fault|i|ness
fault|less
fault|less|ly
fault|less|ness
fault line +s

fault plane +s
fault tol|er|ance
fault-tolerant
faulty
fault|i|er
fault|i|est
fault zone +s
faun +s (deity)
[☞ fawn, Fon]
fauna +s
faun|al
faun|ist +s
faun|is|tic
faun|is|tic|ally
Fau|nus (Roman Myth)
Fauré, Gab|riel
Ur|bain (French
composer)
Faust (German
necromancer)
Faust|ian
Faus|tus (= Faust)
faute de mieux
fau|teuil +s
Fauve +s
Fauv|ism
Fauv|ist +s
faux (imitation)
faux pas
plural faux pas
fava bean +s
fave +s
fa|vela +s
favor +s +ed +ing
(use favour)
favor|able (use
favourable)
favor|able|ness (use
favourableness)
favor|ably (use
favourably)
fa|vored adjective (use
favoured)
favor|er +s (use
favourer)
favor|ite +s (use
favourite)
favor|it|ism (use
favouritism)
fa|vour +s +ed +ing
fa|vour|able
fa|vour|able|ness
fa|vour|ably
fa|voured adjective
fa|vour|er +s
fa|vour|ite +s
fa|vour|it|ism
Fawkes, Guy (English
conspirator)
[☞ Fox, Foxe]
fawn +s +ed +ing
(young deer; behave

obsequiously)
[☞ faun, Fon]
fawn|ing adjective
fawn|ing|ly
fax
faxes
faxed
fax|ing
fay +s (fairy)
[☞ fey]
faze (disconcert)
fazes
fazed
faz|ing
[☞ phase]
fazed adjective
(disconcerted)
[☞ phased]
feal|ty
feal|ties
fear +s +ed +ing
fear|ful
fear|ful|ly
fear|ful|ness
fear|less
fear|less|ly
fear|less|ness
fear|some
fear|some|ly
fear|some|ness
feas|ibil|ity
feas|ible
feas|ibly
feast +s +ed +ing
feast day +s
feast|er +s
feat +s (achievement)
[☞ feet]
feath|er +s +ed +ing
feath|er bed +s noun
feather|bed verb
feather|beds
feather|bed|ded
feather|bed|ding
feather|bed|ding
noun
feather|brain +s
feather|brained
feath|ered adjective
feather-edge +s
feather-edged
feather|head +s
feather|headed
feather|i|ness
feather|ing noun
feather|less
feather|light
feath|er stitch noun
feath|er stitch|es
feather-stitch verb
feather-stitch|es
feather-stitched
feather-stitch|ing

feather|weight +s
feath|ery
fea|ture
fea|tures
fea|tured
fea|tur|ing
fea|tured adjective
feature-length
fea|ture|less
feb|ri|fugal
feb|ri|fuge +s
fe|brile
fe|bril|ity
Feb|ru|ary
Feb|ru|ar|ies
fecal
feces
Fech|ner, Gus|tav
Theo|dor (German
psychophysicist)
feck|less
feck|less|ly
feck|less|ness
fecu|lence
fecu|lent
fe|cund
fe|cund|abil|ity
fe|cund|ate
fe|cund|ates
fe|cund|at|ed
fe|cund|at|ing
fe|cund|a|tion
fe|cund|ity
Fed (Federal Reserve
Board or System)
fed
• past & past participle
of feed
• (FBI agent)
feds
[☞ Fed, feds]
fed|ay|ee
fed|ay|een
fed|er|al
fed|er|al|ism
fed|er|al|ist +s
fed|er|al|iz|a|tion
fed|er|al|ize
fed|er|al|iz|es
fed|er|al|ized
fed|er|al|iz|ing
fed|er|al|ly
fed|er|ate
fed|er|ates
fed|er|at|ed
fed|er|at|ing
fed|er|at|ed adjective
fed|er|a|tion +s
fed|er|a|tive
fe|dora +s
feds (the Cdn federal
government)
fed up

fee
fees
fee'd or feed
feeing
feeb +s
feeble
feebler
feeb|lest
feeble-minded
feeble-minded|ly
feeble-minded|ness
feeble|ness
feebly
feed
feeds
fed
feed|ing
feed|back +s
feed bag +s
feed dog +s
feed|er +s
feed|lot +s
feed|stock +s
feed|stuff +s
fee-for-service
feel
feels
felt
feel|ing
feel|er
feel-good
feel|ing +s noun &
adjective
feel|ing|ly
fee sim|ple
fees sim|ple
feet plural of foot
[☞ feat]
fee tail
fees tail
feign +s +ed +ing
(pretend; allege)
[☞ fain, fane]
feigned adjective
Fein|in|ger, Lyonel
Charles Ad|rian (US
painter)
feint +s +ed +ing
(fake; pretense)
[☞ faint]
Fei|sal (king of Saudi
Arabia: use Faisal)
feist|i|ly
feist|i|ness
feisty
feist|i|er
feist|i|est
fe|la|fel +s (use
falafel)
feld|spar +s
feld|spath|ic
feld|spath|oid +s

fe|lici|tate
fe|lici|tates
fe|lici|tat|ed
fe|lici|tat|ing
fe|lici|ta|tion +s
fe|lici|tous
fe|lici|tous|ly
fe|lici|tous|ness
fe|lici|ty
fe|lici|ties
fe|line +s
fe|lin|ity
Felix|stowe (town,
England)
fell +s +ed +ing
fel|la +s (fellow)
[☞ fellah]
fel|lah (Egyptian
peasant; for fellow
use fella)
fel|la|hin or
fel|la|heen
fel|late
fel|lates
fel|lat|ed
fel|lat|ing
fel|la|tio
fel|la|tor +s
fel|ler +s
feller-buncher +s
fell|field +s
Fel|lini, Fede|rico
(Italian filmmaker)
fel|loe +s (wheel rim)
[☞ fellow]
fel|low +s (man,
associate, etc.)
[☞ felloe]
fellow|ship +s
fellow-travel|ler +s
felly
fel|lies
fel|on +s
fe|loni|ous
fe|loni|ous|ly
fel|ony
fel|onies
fel|quiste +s
fel|sic
fel|spar +s
(= feldspar)
fel|spath|ic
(= feldspathic)
fel|spath|oid
(= feldspathoid)
felt +s +ed +ing
felt|ed adjective
felt|ing noun
felt pen +s
felt tip +s (felt-tip
when preceding a
noun)
felt-tipped

felty
fe|luc|ca +s
fell|wort +s
fe|male +s
female|ness
fem|in|ine +s
fem|in|ine|ly
fem|in|ine|ness
fem|in|in|ity
fem|in|in|ities
fem|in|ism +s
fem|in|ist +s
fem|in|iz|a|tion +s
fem|in|ize
fem|in|iz|es
fem|in|ized
fem|in|iz|ing
fem|in|ized adjective
femme +s
femme fa|tale
femmes fa|tales
fem|oral
femur
fe|murs or fem|ora
fen
• (marsh)
plural fens
• (Chinese currency)
plural fen
fence
fen|ces
fenced
fen|cing
fence|line +s
fence post +s
fen|cer +s
fence|row +s
fence-sitter +s
fence-sitting
fence|wire +s
fen|cible +s
fen|cing +s noun
fend +s +ed +ing
Fen|der, Leo (US
guitar maker)
fen|der +s
fender-bender +s
fender|less
Fé|ne|lon, Fran|çois
de Sali|gnac de La
Mothe (French
writer)
fen|es|tra
fen|es|trae
fen|es|tra oval|is
fen|es|tra ro|tun|da
fen|es|trate adjective
fen|es|trat|ed
fen|es|tra|tion +s
feng shui
Fe|ni|an +s
Fenian|ism
fen|land +s

fen|nec +s
fen|nel (food plant)
[☞ phenyl]
Fenno|scan|dia (land
mass, Europe)
fenny
feno|ter|ol
fenu|greek
feof|fee +s
feoff|ment +s
feof|for +s
feral
fer-de-lance +s
Fer|di|nand (Spanish,
Bohemian &
Hungarian kings;
Holy Roman
emperors)
Fer|gus (town,
Canada)
Fer|gus|on, George
How|ard (Cdn
politician)
feria +s
feri|al
Fer|land, Jean-Pierre
(Cdn singer-
songwriter)
Fer|lin|ghet|ti,
Law|rence
Mon|santo (US
writer)
Fer|man|agh (county,
Northern Ireland)
Fer|mat, Pierre de
(French
mathematician)
fer|mata +s
fer|ment +s +ed +ing
fer|ment|able
fer|men|ta|tion +s
fer|ment|a|tive
fer|ment|ed adjective
fer|ment|er +s
Fermi, En|rico
(Italian-born
physicist)
fer|mi +s
Fermi–Dirac
sta|tis|tics
fer|mi|on +s
fer|mi|um
fern +s
Fer|nan|do Póo
(former name for
Bioko, Equatorial
Guinea)
fern bar +s
fern|ery
fern|eries
Fer|nie (city, Canada)
ferny
fe|ro|cious

fe|ro|cious|ly
fe|ro|cious|ness
fe|roci|ty
fe|roci|ties
Fer|rara (city, Italy)
Fer|rari, Enzo (Italian car designer)
fer|rate +s
fer|ret +s +ed +ing
fer|ret|er +s
fer|rety
fer|ric
Fer|ris wheel +s
[☞ ferrous, pharos]
fer|rite +s
fer|rit|ic
fer|ri|tin +s
ferro|con|crete
ferro|elec|tric +s
ferro|elec|tri|city
ferro|mag|nes|ian
ferro|mag|net|ic
ferro|mag|net|ism
Fer|ron, Jacques (Cdn writer, founder of Rhinoceros Party)
fer|rous (containing iron)
[☞ Ferris wheel, pharos]
fer|rugin|ous
fer|rule +s (metal ring, cap or band; bushing)
[☞ ferule]
ferry (boat)
fer|ries
fer|ried
ferry|ing
[☞ fairy, faerie]
ferry boat +s
ferry|man
ferry|men
fer|tile
Fer|tile Cres|cent
fer|til|ity
fer|til|iz|able
fer|til|iz|a|tion +s
fer|til|ize
fer|til|iz|es
fer|til|ized
fer|til|iz|ing
fer|til|iz|er +s
fer|ula +s
fer|ule +s (flat piece of wood)
[☞ ferrule]
fer|vency
fer|vent
fer|vent|ly
fer|vid
fer|vid|ly
fer|vor (use fervour)

fer|vour
Fès (city, Morocco: use Fez)
fes|cue +s
fess (confess; Heraldry)
fess|es
fessed
fess|ing
fesse +s (Heraldry: use fess)
[☞ fess]
Fes|sen|den, Reg|in|ald Aub|rey (Cdn-born US inventor)
fess point +s
fest +s
fes|tal
fes|tal|ly
fes|ter +s +ed +ing
fes|ti|val +s
fes|tive
fes|tive|ly
fes|tive|ness
fes|tiv|ity
fes|tiv|ities
fes|toon +s +ed +ing
fes|toon|ery
Fest|schrift
Fest|schrift|en or Fest|schrifts
feta
fetal
fetch
fetch|es
fetched
fetch|ing
fetch|er +s
fetch|ing adjective
fetch|ing|ly
fete (festival; honour)
fetes
feted
fet|ing
[☞ fate, feat]
fête cham|pêtre
fêtes cham|pêtres
Fête na|tio|nale (du Qué|bec)
fetid
fetid|ly
fetid|ness
fet|ish
fet|ish|es
fetish|ism
fetish|ist +s
fetish|is|tic
fetish|iz|a|tion +s
fetish|ize
fetish|iz|es
fetish|ized
fetish|iz|ing

fet|lock +s
fetor +s (bad smell)
[☞ fetter]
fet|ter +s +ed +ing (shackle; restraint; bind)
fet|tle
fet|tles
fet|tled
fet|tling
fet|tler +s
fet|tuc|cine
fet|tu|cini (use fettuccine)
fetus
fetus|es
feud +s +ed +ing
feud|al
feud|al|ism
feud|al|ist +s
feud|al|is|tic
feud|al|iz|a|tion
feud|al|ize
feud|al|iz|es
feud|al|ized
feud|al|iz|ing
feu de joie
feux de joie
Feuer|bach, Lud|wig An|dreas (German philosopher)
Feuilles, Ri|vière aux (river, Canada)
feuil|le|té +s
feuil|le|ton +s
fe|ver +s
fever blis|ter +s
fe|vered
fever|few +s
fever|ish
fever|ish|ly
fever|ish|ness
fever|ous
fèves au lard
few +er +est (not many; some)
[☞ phew]
few|ness
fey +er +est (strange; affected; fated to die soon)
[☞ fay]
Fey|deau, Georges Léon Jules Marie (French dramatist)
feyly
fey|ness
Feyn|man, Rich|ard Phil|lips (US physicist)
Fez (city, Morocco)
fez (cap)
fez|zes

fi|acre +s
fi|an|cé +s male
fi|an|cée +s female
fian|chet|to
fian|chet|toes
fian|chet|toed
fian|chet|to|ing
Fi|an|na Fáil
fi|as|co +s
fiat +s
fib
fibs
fibbed
fib|bing
fib|ber +s
Fibo|nacci (Italian mathematician)
fibre +s
fibre|board +s
fibred adjective
fibre|fill
fibre|glass
fibre|less
fibre optic
fibre op|tics
fibri|form
fi|bril +s
fi|bril|lar
fi|bril|late
fi|bril|lates
fi|bril|lat|ed
fi|bril|lat|ing
fi|bril|la|tion +s
fib|rin
fib|rino|gen
fib|rin|oid
fib|rin|ous
fibro|blast +s
fi|broid +s
fi|bro|in
fi|broma
fi|bro|mas or fi|bro|mata
fibro|myal|gia
fi|bro|sis
fi|bro|ses
fibro|sit|ic
fibro|si|tis
fi|brot|ic
fi|brous
fi|brous|ly
fi|brous|ness
fib|ula
fibu|lae or fibu|las
fibu|lar
fiche
plural fiche or fiches
Fichte, Jo|hann Gott|lieb (German philosopher)
fichu +s
fickle
fickle|ness

fic|tile
fic|tion +s
fic|tion|al
fic|tion|al|ity
fic|tion|al|iz|a|tion +s
fic|tion|al|ize
  fic|tion|al|iz|es
  fic|tion|al|ized
  fic|tion|al|iz|ing
fic|tion|al|izer +s
fic|tion|al|ly
fic|tion|ist +s
fic|ti|tious
fic|ti|tious|ly
fic|ti|tious|ness
fic|tive
fic|tive|ness
ficus
  plural ficus
Ficus ben|ja|mina
  plural Ficus
  ben|ja|mina
fid +s
fid|dle
  fid|dles
  fid|dled
  fid|dling
fiddle|back +s
fiddle-de-dee
fiddle-faddle
  fiddle-faddles
  fiddle-faddled
  fiddle-faddling
fiddle|head +s
fid|dler +s
fiddle|sticks
fid|dling *noun &*
  adjective
fid|dly
  fid|dli|er
  fid|dli|est
Fidei Defen|sor
fide|ism
fide|ist +s
fide|is|tic
fi|del|ity
fidget
  fidgets
  fidget|ed
  fidget|ing
fidget|i|ness
fidgety
fi|du|cial
fi|du|ci|ary
  fi|du|ci|aries
fidus Acha|tes
fie *interjection*
  [☞ phi]
fief +s
fief|dom +s
field +s +ed +ing
field book +s

field dress
  field dress|es
  field dressed
  field dress|ing
field effect
  tran|sis|tor +s
field|er +s
fielder's choice
field|fare +s
field glass|es
field goal +s
field hand +s
field house +s
Field|ing, Henry
  (English novelist)
Field|ing, Wil|liam
  Ste|vens (Cdn
  politician)
field mouse
  field mice
Fields, W. C. (US
  comedian)
field|stone +s
field test +s +ed +ing
field test|er +s
field trip +s
field|work
field|work|er +s
fiend +s
fiend|ish
fiend|ish|ly
fiend|ish|ness
fiend|like
fierce
  fier|cer
  fier|cest
fierce|ly
fierce|ness
fieri fa|cias (*Law*)
fier|i|ly
fier|i|ness
fiery
  fier|i|er
  fier|i|est
Fies|ole, Gio|van|ni
  da (Fra Angelico)
fies|ta +s
Fife (former county,
  Scotland; in 'Red
  Fife')
  [☞ Phyfe]
Fife, Dun|can
  (= Phyfe)
fife
  fifes
  fifed
  fif|ing
fifer +s
fife rail +s
FIFO (first in, first out)
fif|teen +s
fif|teenth +s

Fifth (in 'take the Fifth'
  etc.)
fifth +s (*in general use*)
fifth-genera|tion
fifth|ly
fif|ti|eth +s
fifty
  fif|ties
fifty-eight +s
fifty-eighth +s
fifty-fifth +s
fifty-fifty
fifty-first +s
fifty-five +s
fifty|fold
fifty-four +s
fifty-fourth +s
fifty-nine +s
fifty-ninth +s
fifty-one +s
fifty-second +s
fifty-seven +s
fifty-seventh +s
fifty-six
  fifty-sixes
fifty-sixth +s
fifty-third +s
fifty-three +s
fifty-two +s
fig
  figs
  figged
  fig|ging
figgy duff +s
fight
  fights
  fought
  fight|ing
fight|er +s
fight|er bomb|er +s
fight|ing fit *adjective*
fight or flight (fight-
  or-flight *when
  preceding a noun*)
fig leaf
  fig leaves
fig|ment +s
Fig New|ton +s
  proprietary
fig|ur|al
fig|ur|a|tion +s
fig|ura|tive
fig|ura|tive|ly
fig|ura|tive|ness
fig|ure
  fig|ures
  fig|ured
  figur|ing
fig|ure eight +s
  (figure-eight *when
  preceding a noun*)
figure|head +s
figure|less

fig|ure skate +s
fig|ure skat|er +s
fig|ure skat|ing
figur|ine +s
fig|wort +s
Fiji (country, S Pacific)
Fiji|an +s
fila|gree +s (*use
  filigree*)
fila|greed (*use
  filigreed*)
fila|ment +s
fila|ment|ary
fila|ment|ed
fila|ment|ous
fil|aria
  fil|ariae
fil|ar|ial
fil|ar|iasis
  fil|ar|iases
fila|ture +s
fil|bert +s
filch
  filches
  filched
  filch|ing
filch|er +s
file (folder; document;
  Computing; line;
  smoothing tool)
  files
  filed
  fil|ing
  [☞ faille, phial]
filé (powdered
  sassafras)
  [☞ filet, fillet]
file name +s
filer +s
file serv|er +s
filet +s (net, lace; fillet
  of meat)
  [☞ fillet, filé]
filet mi|gnon
  filets mi|gnons
fil|ial
fili|al|ly
fili|ation +s
fili|beg +s
fili|bus|ter +s +ed
  +ing
fili|buster|er +s
fili|gree +s
fili|greed
fill|ing +s *noun*
Fili|pina +s (female
  native of the
  Philippines)
Fili|pino +s (native of
  the Philippines)
  [☞ Pilipino]
fill +s +ed +ing

fille de joie
  filles de joie
fill|er
- (person or thing that fills)
  plural fill|ers
- (Hungarian currency)
  plural fill|er
filles du roi
fil|let (meat; narrow strip, band or line; *Carpentry*; cut into strips; remove bones from)
  fil|lets
  fil|let|ed
  fil|let|ing
  [☞ filet, filet mignon, filé]
fil|let steak +s
fill in *verb*
  fills in
  filled in
  fill|ing in
fill-in +s *noun*
fill|ing +s *adjective & noun*
fil|lip (stimulus, excitement; snap; strike)
  fil|lips
  fil|liped
  fil|lip|ing
  [☞ Philip, Phillips]
fil|lis|ter +s
Fill|more, Mil|lard (US president)
fill up *verb*
  fills up
  filled up
  fill|ing up
fill-up +s *noun*
filly (young horse; girl)
  fil|lies
  [☞ Philly]
film +s +ed +ing
film|able
film|fest +s
film|goer +s
film|ic
film|i|er
film|i|est
film|i|ly
film|i|ness
film|maker +s
film|making
film noir
  films noirs
film|og|raphy
  film|og|raph|ies
Fil|mon, Gary (Cdn politician)
film strip +s

filmy
film|i|er
film|i|est
filo (pastry: *use* phyllo)
  [☞ Philo Judaeus]
Filo|fax *proprietary*
  Filo|faxes
filo|selle
fils (currency)
  plural fils
fils (the son, junior)
fil|ter +s +ed +ing (device for removing impurities)
  [☞ philtre]
filter|able
filter-feeder +s
filter-feeding
fil|ter tip +s
filter-tipped
filth
filth|i|ly
filth|i|ness
filthy
  filth|i|er
  filth|i|est
fil|trable (= filterable)
fil|trate
  fil|trates
  fil|trat|ed
  fil|trat|ing
fil|tra|tion
fim|bri|ate
fim|bri|at|ed
fin (projection on fish, aircraft, etc.; five-dollar bill)
  fins
  finned
  fin|ning
  [☞ Finn]
fin|able
fin|agle
  fin|agles
  fin|agled
  fin|agling
fin|agler +s
final +s *noun & adjective* (last, decisive; a final exam etc.)
  [☞ finale]
fi|nale +s *noun* (closing number in a performance etc.; conclusion)
  [☞ final]
final|ism
final|ist +s
final|is|tic

fi|nal|ity
  final|ities
final|iz|a|tion
final|ize
  final|iz|es
  final|ized
  final|iz|ing
final|ly *adverb* (at last)
  [☞ finale]
fi|nance
  fi|nan|ces
  fi|nanced
  fi|nan|cing
fi|nance|able
fi|nan|cial +s
fi|nan|cial|ly
fi|nan|cier +s
fi|nan|cing +s
fin|back +s
finch
  finch|es
find (discover etc.)
  finds
  found
  find|ing
  [☞ fined]
find|able
find|er +s
finder's fee +s
fin de si|ècle
find|ing +s *noun*
Find|ley, Tim|othy (Cdn writer)
fine
  finer
  fin|est
  fines
  fined
  fin|ing
fine|able (*use* finable)
fine art +s
fine cham|pagne
fined *past & past participle of* fine
fine-drawn
Fine Gael
fine-grain (*Photography*; consisting of small particles)
fine-grained (consisting of small particles)
fine|ly
fine|ness
fin|ery
fines herbes
fine-spun
fi|nesse
  fi|ness|es
  fi|nessed
  fi|ness|ing
fin|est

fine-tooth comb +s
fine-toothed comb
  +s (= fine-tooth comb)
fine-tune
  fine-tunes
  fine-tuned
  fine-tuning
fine tun|ing +s *noun*
Fingal's Cave (cave, Inner Hebrides)
fin|ger +s +ed +ing
finger|board +s
fin|ger bowl +s
finger-dry
  finger-dries
  finger-dried
  finger-drying
fin|gered *adjective*
fin|ger food +s
fin|ger hole +s
fin|ger|ing +s *noun*
finger|less
finger|ling +s
fin|ger man
  fin|ger men
finger|mark +s
finger|nail +s
fin|ger paint +s +ed +ing
finger|paint|er +s
finger|paint|ing +s *noun*
finger|pick +s +ed +ing
finger|pick|er +s
finger|play +s
fin|ger point|ing
finger|print +s +ed +ing
fin|ger pup|pet +s
finger-spell
  finger-spells
  finger-spelled or finger-spelt
  finger-spelling
fin|ger spel|ling *noun*
finger|tip +s
fin|ger weav|ing
finger-woven
fin|ial +s
fin|ical
fin|ick|ing
fin|icky
finis
fin|ish (end etc.)
  fin|ish|es
  fin|ished
  fin|ish|ing
  [☞ Finnish]
fin|ished *adjective*
fin|ish|er +s
fin|ish|ing *adjective*

fin|ish line +s
Finis|terre (cape, Spain)
fi|nite
finite|ly
finite|ness
finit|ism
fin|ito
fini|tude
fink +s +ed +ing
Fin|land (country & gulf, Europe)
Fin|land|iz|a|tion
Fin|land|ize
　Fin|land|iz|es
　Fin|land|ized
　Fin|land|iz|ing
fin|less
Finn +s (of Finland)
fin|nan had|die
finned adjective
Fin|nic
Fin|nish (of Finland)
　[☞ finish]
Finno-Ugrian +s
　(= Finno-Ugric)
Finno-Ugric +s
finny
fino +s
fin whale +s
fiord +s (use fjord)
　[☞ Grise Fiord]
fiori|tura
　fiori|ture
fip|ple +s
fir +s (tree)
　[☞ fur]
Fir|dausi (Persian poet)
Fir|dusi (Persian poet: use Firdausi)
fire
　fires
　fired
　firing
fire alarm +s
fire|arm +s
fire|back +s
fire|ball +s
fire|ball|er +s
fire|ball|ing
fire blight
fire|bomb +s +ed +ing
fire|box
　fire|boxes
fire|brand +s
fire|break +s
fire-breath|ing
fire|brick +s
fire brig|ade +s
fire|bug +s

fire|cherry
　fire|cher|ries
fire chief +s
fire|clay
fire con|trol
fire|crack|er +s
fire crew +s
fire|damp
fire de|part|ment +s
fire|dog +s
fire door +s
fire-drake +s
fire drill +s
fire-eater +s
fire en|gine +s
fire-engine red
fire es|cape +s
fire exit +s
fire ex|tin|guish|er +s
fire|fight +s
fire|fight|er +s
fire|fight|ing
fire|fly
　fire|flies
fire|guard +s
fire hall +s
fire|hose +s
fire|house +s
fire hy|drant +s
fire irons
fire|less
fire|light
fire|light|er +s
fire line +s
fire|lock +s
fire|man
　fire|men
fire mar|shal +s
fire-opal +s
fire|pit +s
fire|place +s
fire plug +s
fire|power
fire|proof
fire|proof|ing
firer +s
fire ran|ger +s
fire-resist|ance
fire-resist|ant
fire-retard|ant
fire ring +s
fire sale +s
fire screen +s
fire ship +s
fire|side +s
fire stairs
fire start|er +s
fire sta|tion +s
fire|storm +s
fire|thorn +s
fire tow|er +s

fire trap +s
fire truck +s
fire-wagon +s
fire-walking
fire|wall +s
fire war|den +s
fire-watcher +s
fire|water
fire|weed +s
fire|wood
fire|work +s
firing +s
firing line +s
firing pin +s
firing squad +s
fir|kin +s
firm +er +est +s +ed +ing
firma|ment +s
firma|ment|al
fir|man +s
firm|ly
firm|ness
firm|ware
firry (of a fir tree)
　[☞ furry]
first +s
first aid
first-aider +s
first base
first base|man
　first base|men
first-born +s
first class noun & adverb
first-class adjective
first-come, first-served
first-day cov|er +s
first-degree
first down +s
first|er +s
first-foot +s +ed +ing
first fruit +s
first-hand
first in, first out
First Lady (wife of US president)
　First Ladies
first lady (most prominent woman)
　first ladies
first|ling +s
first|ly
first mate +s
First Me|rid|ian
First Min|is|ter +s
first name +s
First Na|tion +s
first-nighter +s
First Peoples

first per|son (first-person when preceding a noun)
first-rate
first-rounder +s
first-run
first strike +s (first-strike when preceding a noun)
first-string +s
first-string|er +s
first team +s
first-time adjective preceding a noun
first-timer +s
First World
First World War
firth +s
fir tree +s
fisc +s
fis|cal +s
fis|cal|ly
Fisch|er (surname)
　[☞ Fisher]
Fisch|er, Emil Her|mann (German chemist)
Fisch|er, Hans (German chemist)
Fisch|er, Rob|ert James ('Bobby') (US chess player)
Fischer-Dieskau, Diet|rich (German singer)
Fish (Pisces)
fish
• noun:
　plural fish or fish|es
• verb
　fish|es
　fished
　fish|ing
fish|abil|ity
fish|able
fish and brewis
fish and chips
fish|boat +s
fish|bowl +s
fish|burger +s
fish cake +s
fish camp +s
fish eagle +s
Fish|er, Charles (Cdn politician)
　[☞ Fischer]
fish|er +s (person who fishes)
　[☞ fissure]
fisher|folk
fisher|man
　fisher|men
fisher|man knit +s

fisher|man's knit +s
(= fisherman knit)
fish|ery
fish|eries
Fish|es (Pisces)
fish eye +s (fish-eye
  when preceding a
  noun)
fish farm +s
fish farm|er +s
fish farm|ing
fish find|er +s
fish fin|ger +s
fish flake +s
fish fry
  fish fries
fish hawk +s
fish hook +s
fish house +s
fish hut +s
fish|i|er
fish|i|est
fish|i|ly
fish|i|ness
fish|ing noun
fish|ing boat +s
fish|ing camp +s
fish|ing hole +s
fish|ing line +s
fish|ing pole +s
fish|ing rod +s
fish|ing room +s
fish kill +s
fish knife
  fish knives
fish|like
fish meal
fish|monger +s
fish|net +s
fish|plate +s
fish pond +s
fish sauce
fish shed +s
fish slice +s
fish stick +s
fish store +s
fish|tail +s +ed +ing
fish tale +s
fish tank +s
fish|way +s
fish|wife
  fish|wives
fishy
  fish|i|er
  fish|i|est
fis|sile
fis|sil|ity
fis|sion +s +ed +ing
fis|sion|able
fis|sion bomb +s
fis|si|par|ity
fis|sip|ar|ous

fis|sip|ar|ous|ly
fis|sip|ar|ous|ness
fis|sure (crack)
fis|sures
fis|sured
fis|sur|ing
  [☞ fisher]
fist +s +ed +ing
fist|ed adjective
fist fight +s
fist fight|ing
fist-fuck +s +ed +ing
fist-fucker +s
fist-fucking noun
fist|ful +s
fist|ic
fisti|cuffs
fist|ing noun
fis|tula
  fis|tu|las or fis|tu|lae
fis|tu|lar
fis|tu|lous
fit
• adjective
  fit|ter
  fit|test
• verb (be of the right
  size & shape; be
  suitable or
  appropriate; make
  room for)
  fits
  fit|ted or fit
  fit|ting
• verb (furnish;
  prepare; measure a
  person for clothing)
  fits
  fit|ted
  fit|ting
• noun
  fits
fitch
  fitch|es
fit|ful
fit|ful|ly
fit|ful|ness
fitly
fit|ness
fit-out
fit|ted adjective
fit|ter +s
fit|ting +s noun &
  adjective
fit|ting|ly
fit|ting|ness
fit|ting room +s
Fit|ti|paldi, Emer|son
  (Brazilian race-car
  driver)
Fitz|ger|ald (surname)
  [☞ FitzGerald]

Fitz|ger|ald, Ed|ward
  (English poet)
Fitz|ger|ald, Ella (US
  singer)
Fitz|ger|ald, Fran|cis
  Scott Key (US
  novelist)
Fitz|Ger|ald
  (surname)
  [☞ Fitzgerald]
Fitz|Ger|ald, George
  Fran|cis (Irish
  physicist)
Fitz|Ger|ald, (Lionel)
  Le|Moine (Cdn
  artist)
Fitz|Ger|ald
  con|trac|tion +s
Fiume (= Rijeka,
  Croatia)
five +s
five-and-a-half +s
  (apartment)
five-and-dime +s
five-and-ten +s
five-a-side
five-finger
five|fold
five-hole
five hun|dred
five o'clock shad|ow
five-pin bowl|ing
fiver +s
fives
five-spice pow|der
five-star
five-year plan +s
fix
  fixes
  fixed
  fix|ing
fix|able
fix|ate
  fix|ates
  fix|at|ed
  fix|at|ing
fix|a|tion +s
fixa|tive +s
fixed-do
fixed focus (fixed-
  focus when preceding
  a noun)
fixed in|come +s
  (fixed-income when
  preceding a noun)
fixed link +s
fix|ed|ly
fix|ed|ness
fixed-wing
fixer +s
fixer-upper +s
fix|ing +s noun
fix-it +s

fix|ity
  fix|ities
fix|ture +s
fizz (effervesce;
  excitement)
fizz|es
fizzed
fizz|ing
  [☞ phiz]
fizz|i|ness
fiz|zle
  fiz|zles
  fiz|zled
  fiz|zling
fizzy
  fizz|i|er
  fizz|i|est
fjord +s (inlet)
  [☞ Grise Fiord]
flab
flab|ber|gast +s +ed
  +ing
flab|ber|gast|ed
  adjective
flab|bi|ly
flab|bi|ness
flabby
  flab|bi|er
  flab|bi|est
flac|cid
flac|cid|ity
flac|cid|ly
flack +s +ed +ing
  (publicist; promote;
  for anti-aircraft fire
  or adverse criticism
  use flak)
flack|ery
flag
  flags
  flagged
  flag|ging
flag-bearer +s
Flag Day (anniversary
  of a country's flag)
flag day +s Brit. (a tag
  day)
fla|gel|lant +s
fla|gel|lar
fla|gel|late (flog;
  having flagella)
  fla|gel|lates
  fla|gel|lat|ed
  fla|gel|lat|ing
  [☞ flageolet]
fla|gel|lat|ed adjective
fla|gel|la|tion +s
fla|gel|la|tor +s
fla|gel|la|tory
fla|gel|li|form
fla|gel|lum
  fla|gella

fla|geo|let +s (*Music*; kidney bean) [☞ flagellate]

flag|ger +s

flag|ging *adjective & noun*

fla|gi|tious

fla|gi|tious|ly

fla|gi|tious|ness

flag|man
flag|men

flag|on +s

flag|pole +s

fla|gran|cy

fla|grant

fla|grante de|licto

fla|grant|ly

flag|ship +s

Flag|stad, Kirs|ten (Norwegian soprano)

flag|staff +s

flag|stone +s

flag|stoned

flag-waver +s

flag-waving

Fla|her|ty, Rob|ert Jo|seph (US filmmaker)

flail +s +ed +ing

flair (aptitude; instinct; stylishness) [☞ flare]

flak (anti-aircraft fire; adverse criticism) [☞ flack]

flake
flakes
flaked
flak|ing

flak|ey (*use* flaky)
flak|i|er
flak|i|est

flak|i|ly

flak|i|ness

flak jack|et +s

flaky
flak|i|er
flak|i|est

flam|bé
flam|bés
flam|béed
flambé|ing

flam|beau
flam|beaux or
flam|beaus

Flam|bor|ough (town, Canada)

flam|boy|ance

flam|boy|ancy

flam|boy|ant

flam|boy|ant|ly

flame
flames
flamed
flam|ing

flame|less

flame|like

fla|men +s

fla|men|co +s

flame-out +s

flame-proof

flam|er +s

flame|stitch

flame-thrower +s

flame tree +s

flam|ing *adjective*

fla|mingo
fla|min|gos or
fla|min|goes

flam|mabil|ity

flam|mable

Flam|steed, John (English astronomer)

flamy

flan +s

Flan|ders (region, Europe)

flâ|neur +s

flange
flan|ges
flanged
flan|ging

flanged *adjective*

flange|less

flan|ger +s

flank +s +ed +ing

flank|er +s

flan|nel
flan|nels
flan|nelled or
flan|neled
flan|nel|ling or
flan|nel|ing

flan|nel|board +s

flan|nel|ette

flan|nel|graph +s

flannel-mouth +s

flannel-mouthed

flap
flaps
flapped
flap|ping

flap|doodle

flap|jack +s

flap|less

flap|per +s

flappy

flare (flame, light; outburst; widening)
flares
flared
flar|ing
[☞ flair]

flare out *verb*
flares out
flared out
flar|ing out

flare-out +s *noun*

flare up *verb*
flares up
flared up
flar|ing up

flare-up +s *noun*

flash
flash|es
flashed
flash|ing

flash back *verb*
flash|es back
flashed back
flash|ing back

flash|back +s *noun*

flash-board +s

flash|bulb +s

flash burn +s

flash card +s

flash cube +s

flash|er +s

flash fire +s

flash flood +s

flash-fry
flash-fries
flash-fried
flash-frying

flash gun +s

flash|i|er

flash|i|est

flash|i|ly

flash|i|ness

flash|ing +s *noun*

flash|lamp +s

flash|light +s

flash|over +s

flash|point +s

flashy
flash|i|er
flash|i|est

flask +s

flat
flat|ter
flat|test
flats
flat|ted
flat|ting

flat|bed +s

flat|boat +s

flat-bottomed

flat|bread +s

flat calm *adjective*

flat|car +s

flat-chested

flat|fish
plural flat|fish or
flat|fish|es

flat foot (flat arch of the foot)
flat feet

flat|foot (police officer)
flat|foots or flat|feet

flat-footed

flat-footed|ly

flat-footed|ness

flat-four +s

flat-head +s

flat-headed

flat|iron +s

flat|land +s

flat|land|er +s

flat|let +s

flat|line
flat|lines
flat|lined
flat|lin|ing

flat|lin|er +s

flat|ly

flat|mate +s

flat|ness

flat out (flat-out *when preceding the verb, adjective or noun it modifies*)

flat|pack +s +ed +ing

flat|packed *adjective*

flat race +s

flat|ten +s +ed +ing

flat|ten|er +s

flat|ter +s +ed +ing

flat|ter|er +s

flat|ter|ing *adjective*

flat|ter|ing|ly

flat|tery
flat|ter|ies

flat|tie +s

flat|tish

flat-top +s

flatu|lence

flatu|lency

flatu|lent

flatu|lent|ly

fla|tus

flat|ware

flat|water

flat|worm +s

Flau|bert, Gus|tave (French writer)

flaunt +s +ed +ing

flaunt|er +s

flaunty

flaut|ist +s (= flutist)

Fla|velle, Sir Jo|seph Wes|ley (Cdn philanthropist)

fla|ves|cent

Fla|vian +s (of Roman imperial dynasty)
fla|vin +s (yellow dye) [☞ flavine]
fla|vin ad|en|ine di|nucleo|tide
fla|vine +s (antiseptic; for yellow dye use flavin)
fla|vone +s
fla|von|oid +s
flavo|pro|tein +s
fla|vor +s +ed +ing (use flavour)
flavor|ful (use flavourful)
fla|vor|ing +s noun (use flavouring)
flavor|less (use flavourless)
flavor|ous
flavor|some (use flavoursome)
fla|vour +s +ed +ing
flavour|ful
fla|vour|ing +s noun
flavour|less
flavour|some
flaw +s +ed +ing
flawed adjective
flaw|less
flaw|less|ly
flaw|less|ness
flax
  flax|es
flax|en
flax|seed
flay +s +ed +ing
F-layer +s
flay|er +s
flea +s (insect) [☞ flee]
flea|bag +s
flea|bane +s
flea bite +s
flea-bitten
flea cir|cus
  flea cir|cus|es
flea col|lar +s
flea-flicker +s
flea mar|ket +s
flea|pit +s
flea|wort
flèche +s (Architecture)
fleck +s +ed +ing
flec|tion +s (use flexion)
flec|tion|al +s (use flexional)
flec|tion|less +s (use flexionless)
fled

fledge
  fledg|es
  fledged
  fledg|ing
fledged adjective
fledg|ling +s
flee (leave, escape)
  flees
  fled
  flee|ing
  [☞ flea]
fleece
  flee|ces
  fleeced
  flee|cing
fleece|able
fleeced adjective
flee|ci|ly
flee|ci|ness
fleecy
  flee|ci|er
  flee|ci|est
fleer +s +ed +ing
fleet +er +est +s +ed +ing
fleet-footed
fleet|ing adjective
fleet|ing|ly
fleet|ly
fleet|ness
Fleet Street
Flem|ing (surname; member of Flemish-speaking people) [☞ Flemming]
Flem|ing, Sir Alex|an|der (Scottish bacteriologist)
Flem|ing, Ian Lan|cas|ter (English spy novelist)
Flem|ing, Sir John Am|brose (English electrical engineer)
Flem|ing, Sir Sand|ford (Scottish-born Cdn civil engineer)
Flem|ish
  plural Flem|ish
Flem|ming, Hugh John (Cdn politician) [☞ Fleming]
flench (= flense)
  flench|es
  flenched
  flench|ing
flense
  flens|es
  flensed
  flens|ing
flens|er +s

flesh (skin, body, etc.)
  flesh|es
  fleshed
  flesh|ing
  [☞ flèche]
flesh and blood (flesh-and-blood when preceding a noun)
flesh col|our noun
flesh-coloured adjective
flesh-eating dis|ease
fleshed adjective
flesh fly
  flesh flies
flesh|i|er
flesh|i|est
flesh|i|ly
flesh|i|ness
flesh|less
flesh|ly
  flesh|li|er
  flesh|li|est
flesh|pot +s
flesh wound +s
fleshy
  flesh|i|er
  flesh|i|est
fletch
  fletch|es
  fletched
  fletch|ing
Fletch|er, John (English dramatist)
fletch|er +s
fletch|ing +s noun
fleur-de-lis (use fleur-de-lys)
  fleurs-de-lis
fleur-de-lys
  fleurs-de-lys
Fleuri|mont (town, Canada)
fleu|ron +s
Fleury, An|dré Her|cule de (French cardinal)
Flevo|land (province, the Netherlands)
flew past tense of fly [☞ flu, flue]
flews (lips of bloodhound etc.) [☞ flu, flue]
flex
  flex|es
  flexed
  flex|ing
flex|ibil|ity
flex|ible
flex|ibly
flex|ion +s

flex|ion|al
flex|ion|less
flexo|graph|ic
flex|og|raphy
flex|or +s
flex-time
flexu|os|ity
flexu|ous
flexu|ous|ly
flex|ur|al
flex|ure +s
flib|ber|ti|gib|bet +s
flick +s +ed +ing
flick|er +s +ed +ing
flick|ery
flick knife
  flick knives
fli|er +s noun (use flyer) [☞ flyer]
flight +s +ed +ing
flight bag +s
flight crew +s
flight deck +s
flight|i|er
flight|i|est
flight|i|ly
flight|i|ness
flight|less
flight lieu|ten|ant +s
flight line +s
flight of|fi|cer +s
flight path +s
flight plan +s
flight|seeing
flight ser|geant
flight test +s +ed +ing
flight test|ing noun
flighty
  flight|i|er
  flight|i|est
flim-flam
  flim-flams
  flim-flammed
  flim-flamming
flim-flammer +s
flim-flammery
  flim-flammer|ies
flim|si|ly
flim|si|ness
flim|sy
  flim|si|er
  flim|si|est
  flim|sies
flinch
  flinch|es
  flinched
  flinch|ing
flinch|er +s
flinch|ing|ly
Flin|ders (island, Australia)

flin|ders
Flin Flon (city, Canada)
fling
  flings
  flung
  fling|ing
fling|er +s
flint +s
flint corn
flint glass
flint|i|ly
flint|i|ness
flint|lock +s
Flint|shire (former county, Wales)
flinty
  flint|i|er
  flint|i|est
flip
  flips
  flipped
  flip|ping
flip chart +s
flip-flop
  flip-flops
  flip-flopped
  flip-flopping
flip|pancy
flip|pant
flip|pant|ly
flip|per +s
flip|per pie +s
flip|ping adjective & adverb
flip side +s
flip-top +s
flirt +s +ed +ing
flir|ta|tion +s
flir|ta|tious
flir|ta|tious|ly
flir|ta|tious|ness
flirty
  flirt|i|er
  flirt|i|est
flit
  flits
  flit|ted
  flit|ting
flitch
  flitch|es
flit|ter +s +ed +ing
fliv|ver +s
flix|weed
float +s +ed +ing
float|abil|ity
float|able
float|age
float|a|tion +s (use flotation)
float|base +s
float camp +s
float|er +s

Float|er coat +s
  proprietary
Float|er jack|et +s
  proprietary
float glass
float|house +s
float|ing adjective
float|ing|ly
float|ing point +s
  (floating-point when preceding a noun)
float plane +s
float tube +s
floaty
floc +s (mass of fine particles)
  [☞ flock]
floc|cu|late
  floc|cu|lates
  floc|cu|lat|ed
  floc|cu|lat|ing
floc|cu|la|tion +s
floc|cule +s
floc|cu|lence
floc|cu|lent
floc|cu|lus
  floc|culi
floc|cus
  floc|ci
flock +s +ed +ing
  (group of birds etc.; move in numbers; tufts of wool etc.; on wallpaper; for mass of fine particles use floc)
flocked adjective
flock|ing noun
flocky
Flod|den (battle site, England)
floe +s (floating sheet of ice)
  [☞ flow]
floe edge +s
flog
  flogs
  flogged
  flog|ging
flog|ger +s
flog|ging +s noun
Flood (Bible etc.)
flood +s +ed +ing
flood|gate +s
flood|ing noun
flood|light
  flood|lights
  flood|lit or flood|light|ed
  flood|light|ing
flood|lit adjective
flood plain +s
flood tide +s

flood water +s
flood|way +s
floor +s +ed +ing
floor|board +s
floor cloth +s
floor cov|er|ing +s
floor hock|ey
floor|ing +s
floor lamp +s
floor-length
floor|less
floor mod|el +s
floor plan +s
floor price +s
floor show +s
floor|walk|er +s
floo|zie +s
floozy (use floozie)
  floo|zies
flop
  flops
  flopped
  flop|ping
flop|house +s
flop|pi|ly
flop|pi|ness
floppy
  flop|pi|er
  flop|pi|est
  flop|pies
floppy disk +s
flop|tic|al proprietary
Flora (Roman Myth)
flora +s
flor|al +s
flor|al|ly
flor|eat
Flor|ence (city, Italy)
Flor|en|tine +s (of Florence; cookie)
flor|en|tine (served with spinach)
Flor|es (island, Indonesia)
flor|es|cence (a flowering)
  [☞ fluorescence]
flor|et +s
Flor|ey, How|ard Wal|ter, Baron (Australian pathologist)
Flor|ian|óp|olis (city, Brazil)
flori|at|ed
flori|bun|da +s
flori|cul|tur|al
flori|cul|ture
flori|cul|tur|ist +s
flor|id
Flor|ida (state, US)
Flor|ida Keys (islands, US)

flor|id|ity
flor|id|ly
flor|id|ness
flor|if|er|ous
flori|legium
  flori|legia or flori|legiums
flor|in +s
Flor|io, John (English scholar)
flor|ist +s
flor|is|tic
flor|is|tic|ally
flor|is|tics
flor|is|try
flor|uit
floss
  floss|es
  flossed
  floss|ing
floss|ing noun
flossy
  floss|i|er
  floss|i|est
flo|ta|tion +s
flo|tilla +s
flot|sam
flounce
  floun|ces
  flounced
  floun|cing
flounced adjective
flouncy
floun|der
- verb
  floun|ders
  floun|dered
  floun|der|ing
- noun (fish)
  plural floun|der or floun|ders
- noun (struggle, blunder)
  plural floun|ders
flour +s +ed +ing (grain meal)
  [☞ flower]
floured adjective (sprinkled with flour)
  [☞ flowered]
flour|ish
  flour|ish|es
  flour|ished
  flour|ish|ing
flour|ish|er +s
flour|ish|ing adjective
floury (like flour)
  flour|i|er
  flour|i|est
  [☞ flowery]
flout +s +ed +ing

flow +s +ed +ing
(move as water)
[☞ floe]
flow|able
flow|age
flow chart +s
flower +s +ed +ing
(*Botany*; blossom;
excellent thing)
[☞ flour]
flower|bea|rer +s
flower bed +s
flower box
flower boxes
flow|ered *adjective*
(with flowers)
[☞ floured]
flower|er +s
flower|et +s
flower girl +s
flower head +s
flower|i|ness
flower|ing *adjective*
(producing flowers)
[☞ flouring]
flower|less
flower|like
flower|pot +s
flow|ery (like or with
flowers; ornate)
[☞ floury]
flow|ing *adjective*
flow|ing|ly
flow|meter +s
flow|meter|ing
flown
flow|stone +s
flu +s (illness)
[☞ flue, flew,
flews]
flub
flubs
flubbed
flub|bing
fluc|tu|ant
fluc|tu|ate
fluc|tu|ates
fluc|tu|at|ed
fluc|tu|at|ing
fluc|tu|a|tion +s
flue +s (duct)
[☞ flu, flew, flews]
flue-cure
flue-cures
flue-cured
flue-curing
flue gas (flue-gas
*when preceding a
noun*)
flue gases
flu|ency
flu|en|cies
flu|ent

flu|ent|ly
flue pipe +s
fluff +s +ed +ing
fluff|ball +s
fluff|i|ly
fluff|i|ness
fluffy
fluff|i|er
fluff|i|est
flugel|horn +s
flugel|horn|ist +s
flu|id +s
flu|id|ic
flu|id|ics
flu|id|ity
fluid|iz|a|tion
fluid|ize
fluid|iz|es
fluid|ized
fluid|iz|ing
fluid|ized *adjective*
fluid|ly
fluid|ness
flu|id ounce +s
fluke
flukes
fluked
fluk|ing
fluk|ey (*use* fluky)
fluk|i|er
fluk|i|est
fluk|i|ly
fluk|i|ness
fluky
fluk|i|er
fluk|i|est
flu-like
flume +s
flum|mery
flum|mer|ies
flum|mox
flum|mox|es
flum|moxed
flum|mox|ing
flump +s +ed +ing
flung
flunk +s +ed +ing
flun|key +s (*use*
flunky)
flun|ky
flun|kies
flunky|ism
fluor|esce
fluor|es|ces
fluor|esced
fluor|es|cing
fluor|es|cein
fluor|es|cence
(emission of
radiation or light)
[☞ florescence]
fluor|es|cent +s

fluor|idate
fluor|id|ates
fluor|id|at|ed
fluor|id|at|ing
fluor|id|at|ed
adjective
fluor|id|a|tion
fluor|ide +s
fluor|in|ate
fluor|in|ates
fluor|in|at|ed
fluor|in|at|ing
fluor|in|at|ed
adjective
fluor|in|a|tion
fluor|ine
fluor|ite +s
fluoro|carbon +s
fluoro|scope
fluoro|scopes
fluoro|scoped
fluoro|scop|ing
fluoro|scop|ic
fluoro|scopic|ally
fluor|os|cop|ist +s
fluor|os|copy
fluor|os|cop|ies
fluor|osis
fluor|spar +s
fluox|etine
flur|ried *adjective*
flurry
flur|ries
flur|ried
flurry|ing
flush
flush|es
flushed
flush|ing
flush|able
flushed *adjective*
flush|er +s
flush|ing +s *noun*
Flush|ing
(= Vlissingen, the
Netherlands)
Flush|ing Meadow
(park, US)
flush|ness
flus|ter +s +ed +ing
flus|tered *adjective*
flute
flutes
flut|ed
flut|ing
flut|ed *adjective*
flute|like
flut|i|er
flut|i|est
flut|ing +s
flut|ist +s
flut|ter +s +ed +ing
flut|ter board +s

flut|ter|er +s
flut|ter|ing +s *noun*
flut|tery
fluty
flut|i|er
flut|i|est
flu|vial
flu|via|tile
flu|vio|gla|cial
flux
flux|es
fluxed
flux|ing
flux|gate +s
flux|ion +s
flux|ion|al
fly
• *verb* (move in or
through the air or
with speed; attack;
meet with success or
approval)
flies
flew
flown
fly|ing
• *verb* (*Baseball*)
flies
flied
fly|ing
• *noun* (insect; zipper;
tent covering;
flywheel; *Theatre*;
Baseball)
plural flies
• *noun* (carriage)
plural flys or flies
• *adjective*
flyer
fly|est
fly|able
fly aga|ric
fly ash
fly away *verb*
flies away
flew away
flown away
fly|ing away
fly-away *adjective*
preceding a noun
fly ball +s
fly-blow
fly-blown
fly boy +s
fly|bridge +s
fly by *verb*
flies by
flew by
flown by
fly|ing by
flyby +s *noun*
fly-by-night +s
fly-by-nighter +s
fly-by-wire

fly cast
  fly casts
  fly cast
  fly cast|ing
fly cast|er +s
fly cast|ing noun
fly|catch|er +s
fly-drive
  fly-drives
  fly-drove
  fly-driven
  fly-driving
fly-driver +s
flyer +s noun &
  comparative of fly
fly-fish
  fly-fishes
  fly-fished
  fly-fishing
fly fish|er +s
fly fish|er|man
  fly fish|er|men
fly-fishing noun
fly-half
  fly-halves
fly in verb
  flies in
  flew in
  flown in
  fly|ing in
fly-in +s noun &
  adjective
fly|ing noun &
  adjective
fly-leaf
  fly-leaves
fly|line +s
fly net +s
Flynn, Errol (US
  actor)
fly out verb
  • (depart; burst forth,
  gush)
  flies out
  flew out
  flown out
  fly|ing out
  • (Baseball)
  flies out
  flied out
  fly|ing out
fly-out adjective
  preceding a noun
fly|out +s noun
  (Baseball)
fly over verb
  flies over
  flew over
  flown over
  fly|ing over
fly|over +s noun
fly|paper +s

fly past verb
  flies past
  flew past
  flown past
  fly|ing past
fly|past +s noun
fly rod +s
fly rod|der +s
fly rod|ding
fly|sheet +s
fly|speck +s +ed
  +ing
fly|specked adjective
fly swat|ter +s
fly-tip
  fly-tips
  fly-tipped
  fly-tipping
fly-tipper +s
fly-tipping noun
fly|trap +s
fly|way +s
fly|weight +s
fly|wheel +s
f-number +s
FO (flying officer; field
  officer; forward
  observer)
  FOs
Fo, Dario (Italian
  playwright)
foal +s +ed +ing
foal|ing noun
foam +s +ed +ing
foam board +s
foam|flower +s
foam|ing adjective
foam|less
foam-like
foamy
  foam|i|er
  foam|i|est
fob
  fobs
  fobbed
  fob|bing
f.o.b. (free on board)
fo|cac|cia +s
focal
focal|iz|a|tion
focal|ize
  focal|iz|es
  focal|ized
  focal|iz|ing
Foch, Fer|di|nand
  (French general)
fo'c'sle +s
  (= forecastle)
focus
  • noun
  fo|cus|es or foci
  • verb
  fo|cus|es

fo|cused
  or fo|cussed
  fo|cus|ing
  or fo|cus|sing
focus|er +s
fod|der +s +ed +ing
foe (adversary)
  [☞ faux, Fo]
foehn +s (use föhn)
fog
  fogs
  fogged
  fog|ging
fog bank +s
fog|bound
fog-bow +s
fogey +s
fogey|dom
fogey|ish
fogey|ism
fogged adjective
fog|ger +s
Foggia (town, Italy)
fog|gi|ly
fog|gi|ness
fog|ging +s noun
foggy (obscured by
  fog)
  fog|gi|er
  fog|gi|est
fog|horn +s
fog lamp +s
fog|light +s
Fogo (island & town,
  Canada)
fogy (old-fashioned
  person: use fogey)
  fogies
  [☞ foggy]
fogy|dom (use
  fogeydom)
fogy|ish (use
  fogeyish)
fogy|ism (use
  fogeyism)
föhn +s
foi|ble +s
foie gras
foil +s +ed +ing
foist +s +ed +ing
Fo|kine, Michel
  (Russian
  choreographer)
Fok|ker, An|thony
  Her|man Ger|ard
  (Dutch aircraft
  designer)
fol|acin
fol|ate +s
fold +s +ed +ing
fold|able
fold|away adjective
fold-down adjective

fold|er +s
fol|der|ol +s
fold|ing adjective
fold-out +s noun &
  adjective
foley (Film sound
  effects)
  [☞ folly, folie à
  deux, folie de
  grandeur]
foli|aceous
foli|age +s
foli|aged
foli|ar
foli|ate
  foli|ates
  foli|at|ed
  foli|at|ing
foli|a|tion +s
folic acid
folie à deux
  fo|lies à deux
folie de gran|deur
  fo|lies de gran|deur
fo|lio +s
folk
  plural **folk** or **folks**
folk dance +s
folk dan|cer +s
folk dan|cing
Folke|stone (city,
  England)
folk fest +s
folk hero
  folk heroes
folk|ie +s (of folk
  music)
  [☞ folky]
folk|i|er
folk|i|est
folk|i|ness
folk|ish
folk|lore
folk|lor|ic
folk|lor|ist +s
folk|lor|is|tic
folk music
folk-rock
folk-rocker +s
folk|si|ness
folk|sing|er +s
folk|sing|ing
folk song +s
folksy
  folk|si|er
  folk|si|est
folk tale +s
folk|ways
folky (traditional; of
  folk culture)
  folk|i|er
  folk|i|est
  [☞ folkie]

fol|licle +s
fol|licu|lar
fol|licu|late
fol|licu|lat|ed
fol|low +s +ed +ing
fol|low|er +s
fol|low|ing +s noun & adjective
follow-my-leader Brit. (= follow-the-leader)
fol|low on verb
  fol|lows on
  fol|lowed on
  fol|low|ing on
follow-on adjective
fol|low spot +s
follow-the-leader
fol|low through verb
  fol|lows through
  fol|lowed through
  fol|low|ing through
follow-through +s noun
fol|low up verb
  fol|lows up
  fol|lowed up
  fol|low|ing up
follow-up +s noun
folly (foolishness; theatrical revue)
  fol|lies
  [☞ foley, folie à deux, folie de grandeur]
Fom|al|haut (star)
fo|ment +s +ed +ing
fo|men|ta|tion +s
fo|ment|er +s
Fon (people & language)
  plural Fon or Fons
  [☞ fawn, faun]
fond +er +est
Fonda, Henry Jaynes (US actor)
Fonda, Jane Sey|mour (US actress)
fon|dant +s
fon|dle
  fon|dles
  fon|dled
  fond|ling
fond|ler +s
fond|ly
fond|ness
fon|due +s
font +s
font|al
fon|ta|nelle +s

Fon|teyn, Dame Mar|got (English ballerina)
fon|tina
Fonyo, Ste|phen Charles ('Steve') (Cdn runner & activist)
Foo|chow (= Fuzhou, China)
food +s
food bank +s
food chain +s
food col|our|ing +s
food court +s
food|ery
  food|eries
food fair +s
food fish
  plural food fish or food fish|es
food grain +s
food group +s
foodie +s
food|land +s
food|less
food stamp +s
food|stuff +s
foo|fa|raw +s
fool +s +ed +ing
fool|ery
  fool|eries
fool|hard|i|ly
fool|hard|i|ness
fool|hardy
  fool|hard|i|er
  fool|hard|i|est
fool hen +s
fool|ish
fool|ish|ly
fool|ish|ness
fool|proof
fools|cap (paper)
fool's er|rand +s
fool's gold
fool's para|dise +s
fool's pars|ley +s
foot
• noun (twelve inches)
  plural feet or foot
• noun (all other senses but 'dregs')
  plural feet
• noun (dregs)
  plural foots
• verb
  foots
  foot|ed
  foot|ing
foot|age
foot-and-mouth dis|ease
foot|ball +s +ed +ing

foot|ball|er +s
foot|bath +s
foot|bed +s
foot|board +s
foot|bridge +s
foot-dragger +s
foot-dragging
foot|ed adjective
foot|er +s
foot|fall +s
foot-fault +s
foot|gear
foot guard +s
foot|hill +s
foot|hold +s
foot|ing +s noun
foo|tle
  foo|tles
  foo|tled
  foot|ling
foot|less
foot|lights
foot|ling adjective
foot|lock|er +s
foot|loose
foot|man
  foot|men
foot|mark +s
foot|note
  foot|notes
  foot|not|ed
  foot|not|ing
foot|pad +s
foot|path +s
foot|plate +s
foot-pound
  foot-pounds
foot-pound-second
foot|print +s
foot race +s
foot|rest +s
foot rot
Foot|sie (Stock Exchange)
foot|sie (in 'play footsie')
foot|slog
  foot|slogs
  foot|slogged
  foot|slog|ging
foot|slog|ger +s
foot sol|dier +s
foot|sore
foot|stalk +s
foot|step +s
foot|stool +s
foot|way +s
foot|wear
foot|well +s
foot|work
foo yong
fop +s

fop|pery
  fop|per|ies
fop|pish
fop|pish|ly
fop|pish|ness
for preposition & conjunction
  [☞ four, fore]
for|age (gather food)
  for|a|ges
  for|aged
  for|a|ging
for|age fish
  plural for|age fish or for|age fish|es
for|ager +s
fo|ra|men
  fo|ram|ina or fo|ra|mens
fo|ram|in|ate
fora|mini|fer +s
fora|mi|nif|er|an
  fora|mi|nif|era
fora|mi|nif|er|ous
tor|as|much
for|ay +s +ed +ing
forb +s
for|bad past tense of forbid (use forbade)
for|bade past tense of forbid
for|bear
• verb (abstain from)
  for|bears
  for|bore
  for|borne
  for|bear|ing
• noun (ancestor: use forebear)
  for|bears
for|bear|ance
Forbes (mountain, Canada)
for|bid
  for|bids
  for|bade
  for|bid|den
  for|bid|ding
for|bid|den adjective
for|bid|ding adjective
for|bid|ding|ly
for|bore
for|borne
for|bye
force
  for|ces
  forced
  for|cing
force|able (that may be forced)
  [☞ forcible]
forced adjective

force-feed
force-feeds
force-fed
force-feeding
force field +s
force|ful
force|ful|ly
force|ful|ness
force-land +s +ed
+ing
force ma|jeure
forces ma|jeures
force|meat +s
force out *verb*
for|ces out
forced out
for|cing out
force|out +s *noun*
force play +s
for|ceps
plural for|ceps
force pump +s
for|cer +s
For|ces (*Cdn Military*)
for|cible (involving
force)
[☞ forceable]
for|cibly
Ford, Ford Madox
(English novelist)
Ford, Ger|ald
Ru|dolph (US
president)
Ford, Glenn (Cdn-
born US actor)
Ford, Har|ri|son (US
actor)
Ford, Henry (US
industrialist)
Ford, John (English
dramatist)
Ford, John (US
filmmaker)
ford +s +ed +ing
ford|able
ford|less
fore +s (front etc.;
Golf)
[☞ for, four]
fore and aft *adverb*
fore-and-aft *adjective*
fore-and-aft rigged
fore|arm +s +ed +ing
fore|bear +s *noun*
(ancestor)
[☞ forbear]
fore|bode
fore|bodes
fore|bod|ed
fore|bod|ing
fore|bod|ing *noun &
adjective*
fore|bod|ing|ly

fore|brain +s
fore|cast
fore|casts
fore|cast or
fore|cast|ed
fore|cast|ing
fore|cast|er +s
fore|cast|ing *noun*
fore|castle +s
fore|check +s +ed
+ing
fore|check|er +s
fore|check|ing *noun*
fore|close
fore|clos|es
fore|closed
fore|clos|ing
fore|clos|ure +s
fore|court +s
fore|deck +s
for|edge +s (*Books:
use* fore-edge)
[☞ forage]
fore|doom +s +ed
+ing
fore-edge +s
fore|father +s
fore|finger +s
fore|foot
fore|feet
fore|front +s
fore|gather +s +ed
+ing
fore|go (precede in
place or time; *for*
abstain from, decline
use forgo)
fore|goes
fore|went
fore|gone
fore|go|ing
fore|goer +s
fore|go|ing *adjective*
(preceding)
fore|gone *adjective*
(preceding; in
'foregone
conclusion')
fore|ground +s +ed
+ing
fore|hand +s
fore|hand|ed
fore|head +s
for|eign
for|eign|er +s
foreign-going
foreign|ness
fore|judge
fore|judg|es
fore|judged
fore|judg|ing

fore|know
fore|knows
fore|knew
fore|known
fore|know|ing
fore|know|able
fore|know|ledge
fore|land +s
fore|leg +s
fore|limb +s
fore|lock +s
Fore|man, George
(US boxer)
[☞ Forman]
fore|man
fore|men
fore|mast +s
fore|most
fore|mother +s
fore|name +s
fore|noon +s
for|en|sic +s
for|en|sic|ally
fore|ordain +s +ed
+ing
fore|ordi|na|tion
fore|part +s
fore|paw +s
fore|peak +s
fore|person
fore|persons or
fore|people
fore|play
fore|quarters
fore|run
fore|runs
fore|ran
fore|run
fore|run|ning
fore|run|ner +s
fore|sail +s
fore|see
fore|sees
fore|saw
fore|seen
fore|see|ing
fore|see|abil|ity
fore|see|able
fore|see|ably
fore|seer +s
fore|shadow +s +ed
+ing
fore|shadow|ing +s
noun
fore|sheets
fore|shock +s
fore|shore +s
fore|short|en +s +ed
+ing
fore|short|en|ing +s
fore|show
fore|shows

fore|showed
fore|shown
fore|show|ing
fore|sight +s
fore|sight|ed
fore|sight|ed|ly
fore|sight|ed|ness
fore|sight|ful
fore|skin +s
for|est +s +ed +ing
fore|stall +s +ed +ing
fore|stall|er +s
fore|stal|ment +s
for|est|a|tion
fore|stay +s
For|est City (London,
Canada)
for|est|ed *adjective*
For|est|er, Cecil Scott
(English novelist)
[☞ Forrester,
Forster, Vorster]
for|est|er +s
fore|st fire +s
for|est green +s
(forest-green *when
preceding a noun*)
forest|land +s
for|est|ry
fore|taste +s
fore|tell
fore|tells
fore|told
fore|tell|ing
fore|tell|er +s
fore|thought
fore|token +s +ed
+ing
fore|told
fore|top +s
fore-topmast +s
fore-topsail +s
for|ever
for|ever|more
fore|warn +s +ed
+ing
fore|warn|er +s
fore|went *past tense of*
forego
[☞ forwent]
fore|wing +s
fore|woman
fore|women
fore|word +s
(preface)
[☞ forward]
fore|yard +s
For|far (town,
Scotland)
For|far|shire (*former
name for* Angus,
Scotland)
for|feit +s +ed +ing

for|feit|able
for|feit|er +s
for|feit|ure
for|fend +s +ed +ing
for|gather +s +ed
+ing (use
foregather)
for|gave
forge
for|ges
forged
for|ging
forge|able
for|ger +s
for|gery
for|ger|ies
for|get
for|gets
for|got
for|got|ten or for|got
for|get|ting
for|get|ful
for|get|ful|ly
for|get|ful|ness
forget-me-not +ε
for|get|table
for|get|ter +s
for|ging +s noun
for|giv|able
for|giv|ably
for|give
for|gives
for|gave
for|given
for|giv|ing
for|give|ness
for|giv|er +s
for|giv|ing adjective
for|giv|ing|ly
forgo (abstain from;
decline)
for|goes
for|went
for|gone
for|go|ing
[☞ forego]
for|go|ing conjugated
form of forgo
[☞ foregoing]
for|gone conjugated
form of forgo
[☞ foregone]
for|got
for|got|ten adjective
Foril|lon (national
park, Canada)
for|int +s
fork +s +ed +ing
fork|ball +s
forked adjective
fork|ful +s
fork|lift +s
fork-tender

for|lorn
for|lorn|ly
for|lorn|ness
form +s +ed +ing
(shape; document;
protocol; bench;
mould, frame; for
type locked in a
chase for printing use
forme)
form|able
for|mal +s
for|mal|de|hyde
for|ma|lin
for|mal|ism
for|mal|ist +s
for|mal|is|tic
for|mal|is|tic|ally
for|mal|ity
for|mal|ities
for|mal|iz|a|tion
for|mal|ize
for|mal|iz|es
for|mal|ized
for|mal|iz|ing
for|mal|ly
for|mal|ness
for|mal wear
For|man, Milos
(Czech-born
filmmaker)
[☞ Foreman]
for|mant +s
for|mat
for|mats
for|mat|ted
for|mat|ting
for|mate +s
for|ma|tion +s
for|ma|tion|al
form|a|tive +s
form|a|tive|ly
forme +s (type locked
in a chase for
printing)
[☞ form]
For|men|tera
(Mediterranean
island)
for|mer +s
for|mer|ly
form-fitting
For|mica proprietary
for|mic acid
for|mi|ca|tion
for|mid|able
for|mid|able|ness
for|mid|ably
form|less
form|less|ly
form|less|ness
For|mosa (former
name for Taiwan)

for|mu|la
for|mu|las or
for|mu|lae
for|mu|la|ic
for|mu|la|ic|ally
For|mu|la One
for|mu|lar|iz|a|tion
for|mu|lar|ize
for|mu|lar|iz|es
for|mu|lar|ized
for|mu|lar|iz|ing
for|mu|lary
for|mu|lar|ies
for|mu|late
for|mu|lates
for|mu|lat|ed
for|mu|lat|ing
for|mu|la|tion +s
for|mu|la|tor +s
for|mu|lism
for|mu|list +s
for|mu|lis|tic
for|mu|lize
for|mu|liz|es
for|mu|lized
for|mu|liz|ing
form|work +s
for|ni|cate
for|ni|cates
for|ni|cat|ed
for|ni|cat|ing
for|ni|ca|tion
for|ni|ca|tor +s
For|res|ter, Mau|reen
Kath|er|ine Stew|art
(Cdn contralto)
[☞ Forester,
Forster, Vorster]
for|sake
for|sakes
for|sook
for|sak|en
for|sak|ing
for|saken|ness
for|sak|er +s
For|sey, Eu|gene
All|fred (Cdn
politician)
for|sooth
For|ster, Ed|ward
Mor|gan (English
novelist)
[☞ Forester,
Forrester, Vorster]
for|swear
for|swears
for|swore
for|sworn
for|swear|ing
for|sythia +s
fort +s
Forta|leza (port,
Brazil)

Fort Am|herst
(historic site,
Canada)
Fort Anne (historic
site, Canada)
Fort Battle|ford
(historic site,
Canada)
Fort Beau|séjour
(historic site, New
Brunswick)
[☞ Beausejour]
Fort Cham|bly
(historic site,
Canada)
Fort-de-France
(capital of
Martinique)
forte +s (Music; strong
point)
forte|piano +s
(instrument)
forte-piano (Music
loud then soft)
Fort Erie (town,
Canada)
Fort Fran|ces (town,
Canada)
Fort Garry (former
name for Winnipeg,
Canada)
Fort George (historic
site, Canada)
Forth (river & firth,
Scotland)
forth (forward)
[☞ fourth]
forth|com|ing
forth|com|ing|ness
forth|right
forth|right|ly
forth|right|ness
forth|with
For|ties (part of the
North Sea)
for|ti|eth +s
for|ti|fi|able
for|ti|fi|ca|tion +s
for|ti|fi|er +s
for|ti|fy
for|ti|fies
for|ti|fied
for|ti|fy|ing
for|tis|simo
for|tis|simos or
for|tis|simi
for|ti|tude
Fort Knox (gold
depository, US)
Fort Lamy (former
name for
N'Djamena, Chad)

Fort Lang|ley (historic site, Canada)
Fort Mac|leod (town, Canada)
Fort Mal|den (historic site, Canada)
Fort Mc|Murray (*former name for* Wood Buffalo, Canada)
fort|night +s
fort|night|ly
fort|night|lies
Fort Prince of Wales (historic site, Canada)
Fort Qu'Appelle (town, Canada)
For|tran (*Computing*)
fort|ress
fort|ress|es
Fort Rodd Hill (historic site, Canada)
Fort St. James (historic site, Canada)
Fort St. John (city, Canada)
Fort Saint-Joseph (historic site, Canada)
Fort Sas|katch|ewan (city, Canada)
Fort Simp|son (village, Canada)
Fort Smith (town, Canada)
for|tuit|ous
for|tuit|ous|ly
for|tuit|ous|ness
for|tu|ity
for|tuit|ies
For|tuna (*Roman Myth*)
for|tun|ate
for|tun|ate|ly
For|tune (bay, Canada)
for|tune +s
For|tune 500
for|tune hunt|er +s
fortune-hunting
for|tune tell|er +s
fortune-telling
Fort Wil|liam (part of Thunder Bay, Canada)
Fort Worth (city, US)
forty
for|ties
forty-eight +s

forty-eighth +s
forty-fifth +s
forty-first +s
forty-five +s (record; gun; card game)
45 (record)
45s
.45 (gun)
.45s
forty|fold
forty-four +s
forty-fourth +s
forty|ish
forty-nine +s
forty-niner +s
forty-ninth +s
forty-ninth par|al|lel
forty-one +s
forty-ouncer +s
forty-pounder +s
forty-second +s
forty-seven +s
forty-seventh +s
forty-six
forty-sixes
forty-sixth +s
forty-third +s
forty-three +s
forty-two +s
forum +s
for|ward +s +ed +ing (to the front; attacking player; advance, promote) [☞ foreword]
for|ward|er +s
forward-looking
for|ward|ly
for|ward|ness
for|wards
forward-thinking
for|went *past tense of* forgo [☞ forewent]
Fo|sheim (peninsula, Canada)
fossa (shallow depression)
fos|sae [☞ fosse]
fosse +s (narrow trench) [☞ fossa]
Fosse Way (ancient road, England)
fos|sick +s +ed +ing
fos|sick|er +s
fos|sil +s
fos|sil fuel +s
fos|sil|if|er|ous
fos|sil|iz|a|tion

fos|sil|ize
fos|sil|iz|es
fos|sil|ized
fos|sil|iz|ing
fos|sor|ial
Fos|ter, Jodie (US actress)
Fos|ter, Ste|phen Col|lins (US composer)
Fos|ter, Wal|ter Ed|ward (Cdn politician)
fos|ter +s +ed +ing
fos|ter|age
fos|ter|er +s
fos|ter|ling +s
Fou|cault, Jean Ber|nard Léon (French physicist)
Fou|cault, Mi|chel Paul (French philosopher)
Fouc|quet, Nico|las (= Nicolas Fouquet) [☞ Jean Fouquet]
fouet|té +s
fought *conjugated form of* fight [☞ phot]
foul +er +est +s +ed +ing (offensive, dirty; illegal play; *Baseball*; tangle; spoil) [☞ fowl, Fowles]
foul|ard +s
foul|er *comparative of* foul [☞ fowler, Fowler]
foul|ing *conjugated form of* foul [☞ fowling]
foul line +s
foul|ly
foul-mouthed
foul|ness
foul up *verb*
fouls up
fouled up
foul|ing up
foul-up +s *noun*
found +s +ed +ing
foun|da|tion +s
foun|da|tion|al
found|er +s +ed +ing
found-in +s
found|ling +s
foun|dry
foun|dries
fount +s
foun|tain +s +ed +ing

foun|tained *adjective*
foun|tain|head +s
foun|tain pen +s
Fou|quet, Jean (French painter)
Fou|quet, Nico|las (French finance minister)
four +s (number) [☞ fore, for]
four-and-a-half +s (apartment)
four-by-four +s
4 × 4 (= four-by-four)
4 × 4s
Four Can|tons, Lake of the (= Lake Lucerne, Switzerland)
four|chette +s
four-colour
four-eyed
four-eyes *plural* four-eyes
four-flush
four-flushes
four-flushed
four-flushing
four-flusher +s
four|fold
4-H club
Four Hun|dred *US* (social elite)
Fou|rier, (Fran|çois Marie) Charles (French social reformer)
Fou|rier, (Jean Bap|tiste) Jo|seph (French mathematician)
Fou|rier|ism
four-in-hand +s
four-leaf clo|ver +s
four-letter word +s
four o'clock +s (plant)
four on the floor (gearshift)
four-part
four|pence
four|plex
four|plex|es
four-poster +s
four|score
four|some +s
four-square
four-star
four-stroke
four|teen +s
four|teenth +s
fourth +s (in number) [☞ forth, Forth]

fourth-genera|tion
fourth|ly
four-wheel
four-wheel drive
four-wheeler +s
fous|ty
fovea
  fo|veae
fo|veal
fo|veate
fowl (bird)
  plural fowl or fowls
  [☞ Fowles, foul]
fowl chol|era
Fow|ler, Henry
  Wat|son (English
  lexicographer)
Fow|ler, Fran|cis
  George (English
  lexicographer)
fowl|er +s (one who
  hunts fowl)
  [☞ fouler]
Fowles, John Rob|ert
  (English novelist)
fowl|ing noun
  (hunting of fowl)
  [☞ fouling]
fowl pest
Fox (people &
  language)
  plural Fox or Foxes
Fox (surname)
  [☞ Foxe, Fawkes]
Fox, Charles James
  (English reformer)
Fox, George (English
  founder of Quakers)
Fox, Ter|rance
  Stan|ley ('Terry')
  (Cdn runner &
  fundraiser)
fox
  foxes
  foxed
  fox|ing
fox|berry
  fox|ber|ries
Foxe (basin &
  peninsula, Canada)
Foxe, John (English
  clergyman & writer)
  [☞ Fox, Fawkes]
fox|fire
fox|glove +s
fox grape +s
fox|hole +s
fox|hound +s
fox|i|er
fox|i|est
fox|i|ly
fox|i|ness
fox|ing noun

fox|like
fox|tail +s
fox|trot
  fox|trots
  fox|trot|ted
  fox|trot|ting
foxy
  fox|i|er
  fox|i|est
foy|er +s
FR (Forest Region)
  FRs
Fra
frac|as
  plural frac|as
frac|tal +s
frac|tion +s
frac|tion|al
frac|tion|al|iz|a|tion
frac|tion|al|ize
  frac|tion|al|iz|es
  frac|tion|al|ized
  frac|tion|al|iz|ing
frac|tion|al|ly
frac|tion|ary
frac|tion|ate
  frac|tion|ates
  frac|tion|at|ed
  frac|tion|at|ing
frac|tion|a|tion +s
frac|tion|ator +s
frac|tion|ize
  frac|tion|iz|es
  frac|tion|ized
  frac|tion|iz|ing
frac|tious
frac|tious|ly
frac|tious|ness
frac|ture
  frac|tures
  frac|tured
  frac|tur|ing
frae|num (use
  frenum)
  frae|na
frag
  frags
  fragged
  frag|ging
fra|gile
fra|gile|ly
fra|gil|ity
  fra|gil|ities
frag|ment +s +ed
  +ing
frag|ment|al
frag|men|tar|i|ly
frag|men|tar|i|ness
frag|men|tary
frag|men|ta|tion +s
frag|ment|ize
  frag|ment|iz|es

frag|ment|ized
frag|ment|iz|ing
Fra|go|nard, Jean-
  Honoré (French
  painter)
fra|grance +s
fra|granced
fra|grant
fra|grant|ly
frail +er +est
frail|ly
frail|ness
frail|ty
  frail|ties
Frak|tur
fram|able (use
  frameable)
fram|besia (use
  framboesia)
fram|boesia
Frame, Janet
  Pat|er|son (New
  Zealand novelist)
frame
  framed
  framed
  fram|ing
frame|able
frame|less
fram|er +s
frame-up +s noun
frame|work +s
fram|ing +s noun
franc +s (currency)
  [☞ frank]
Franca, Celia (Cdn
  ballet director)
France (country,
  Europe)
France, Ana|tole
  (French writer)
Fran|ces (woman's
  name; in 'Fort
  Frances')
  [☞ Francis]
Fran|ces|ca, Piero
  della (Italian painter)
Franche-Comté
  (region, France)
fran|chise
  fran|chis|es
  fran|chised
  fran|chis|ing
fran|chis|ee +s
fran|chis|er +s (use
  franchisor)
fran|chis|or +s
Fran|cis (man's name;
  saints; king of
  France; Holy Roman
  & Austrian emperor)
  [☞ Frances, Fort
  Frances]

Fran|cis|can +s
Fran|cis of As|sisi
  (saint)
Fran|cis of Sales
  (saint)
Fran|cis Xavier
  (saint)
fran|cis|a|tion (use
  francization)
fran|cise (use
  francize)
  fran|cis|es
  fran|cised
  fran|cis|ing
fran|cium
fran|ciz|a|tion
fran|cize
  fran|ciz|es
  fran|cized
  fran|ciz|ing
Franck, César
  Au|guste (Belgian-
  born French
  musician)
  [☞ Frank]
Franck, James
  (German-born US
  physicist)
  [☞ Frank]
Fran|co, Fran|cis|co
  (Spanish general and
  statesman)
Fran|co +s
  (francophone)
fran|co|lin +s
Fran|conia (former
  duchy, Germany)
franco|phile +s
franco|philia
franco|phobe +s
franco|phobia
franco|phone +s
Franco|phonie
  (French nations)
franco|phonie
  (francophones in
  Canada)
fran|gi|bil|ity
fran|gible
fran|gi|pane +s
  (custard or cream;
  for tree or perfume
  use frangipani)
fran|gi|pani +s (tree;
  perfume)
  [☞ frangipane]
fran|glais
Frank (site of rock
  slide, Canada)
Frank, Anne (German
  diarist)
  [☞ Franck]
Frank +s (Germanic
  tribe)

frank +er +est +s
+ed +ing
(outspoken, open;
stamp; frankfurter)
[☞ franc]
frank|able
Frank|en|stein +s
Frank|en|stein|ian
Frank|en|thal|er,
Helen (US painter)
frank|er +s
Frank|fort (city, US)
[☞ Frankfurt]
Frank|furt (am Main)
(city, Germany)
[☞ Frankfort]
frank|furt|er +s
frank|in|cense
Frank|ish
Frank|lin (district &
mountains, Canada)
Frank|lin, Ar|etha
(US singer)
Frank|lin, Ben|ja|min
(US statesman &
scientist)
Frank|lin, Sir John
(English Arctic
explorer)
Frank|lin, Rosa|lind
Elsie (English
scientist)
Frank|lin, (Stel|la
Maria Sarah) Miles
(Australian novelist)
frank|lin +s
Franklin's gull +s
Frank|lin stove +s
frank|ly
frank|ness
frank|um
Fran|sas|kois
   plural Fran|sas|kois
fran|tic
fran|tic|ally
fran|tic|ness
Franz Fer|di|nand
(assassinated
archduke of Austria)
Franz Josef
(monarch of Austria
& Hungary)
Franz Josef Land
(islands, Arctic
Ocean)
frap
   fraps
   frapped
   frap|ping
frap|pé +s
fras|cati +s
Fraser (river, Canada)

Fraser (surname)
[☞ Frazer, Frazier]
Fraser, (John)
Mal|colm
(Australian prime
minister)
Fraser, Simon (US-
born Cdn explorer)
frass
frat +s
fra|ter|nal
fra|ter|nal|ism
fra|ter|nal|ly
fra|ter|nity
fra|ter|ni|ties
frater|niz|a|tion
frater|nize
frater|niz|es
frater|nized
frater|niz|ing
frat house +s
fratri|cid|al
fratri|cide +s
Frau (German woman)
Frauen
[☞ frow]
fraud +s
fraud|ster +s
fraudu|lence
fraudu|lent
fraudu|lent|ly
fraught
Fräu|lein +s
Fraun|hofer, Jo|seph
von (German
scientist)
Fraun|hofer line +s
fraxi|nella +s
fray +s +ed +ing
[☞ Frey]
Fray Ben|tos (city,
Uruguay)
Frazer, Sir James
George (Scottish
anthropologist)
[☞ Fraser, Frazier]
Frazier, Jo|seph
('Joe') (US boxer)
[☞ Frazer, Fraser]
fraz|il (ice)
[☞ frazzle]
fraz|zle (wear out;
shrivel up)
fraz|zles
fraz|zled
fraz|zling
[☞ frazil]
freak +s +ed +ing
(aberration; oddity;
fan; overreact)
[☞ phreak]
freak|i|er
freak|i|est

freak|i|ly
freak|i|ness
freak|ing adjective
(used as an
intensifier)
[☞ phreaking]
freak|ish
freak|ish|ly
freak|ish|ness
freak out verb
freaks out
freaked out
freak|ing out
freak-out +s noun
freak show +s
freaky
freak|i|er
freak|i|est
Fré|chette, Louis-
Honoré (Cdn poet)
[☞ freshet]
freckle
freckles
freckled
freck|ling
freckled adjective
freckle-faced
freck|ly
Fred|erick (Holy
Roman emperors,
kings of Prussia,
Germany, and
Denmark)
Fred|erick
Bar|ba|rossa (Holy
Roman emperor)
Fred|erick Wil|liam
(Elector of
Brandenburg; kings
of Prussia)
Fred|eric|ton (city,
Canada)
free
   freer
   freest
   frees
   freed
   free|ing
free-associ|ate
free-associ|ates
free-associ|at|ed
free-associ|at|ing
free|base
free|bas|es
free|based
free|bas|ing
free|bas|er +s
free|bie +s
free|board
free|boot +s +ed
+ing
free|boot|er +s
free|born

freed|man
(emancipated slave)
freed|men
[☞ Friedman]
free|dom +s
free fall +s noun
(free-fall when
preceding a noun)
free-fall verb
free-falls
free-fell
free-fallen
free-falling
free-fire zone +s
free-floating
free-for-all +s
free-form
free|hand adjective &
adverb
free-handed
free-handed|ly
free-handed|ness
free|hold +s
free|hold|er +s
free house +s
free lance +s
(medieval
mercenary)
[☞ freelance]
free|lance (self-
employed person,
etc.; for medieval
mercenary use free
lance)
free|lan|ces
free|lanced
free|lan|cing
free|lan|cer +s
free-liver +s
free-living
free|load +s +ed +ing
free|load|er +s
free|load|ing noun
free|ly
free|man
free|men
free mar|ket +s
free mar|ket|eer +s
free|mar|tin +s
Free|mason +s
Free|mason|ry (of
Freemasons)
free|mason|ry
(sympathy)
free|ness
free port +s
Free|post
freer
free-range
free|sia +s
free-spirit|ed
free-spoken
freest

free-standing
free|stone +s
free|style
free|styl|er +s
free-swimming
free|think|er +s
free|think|ing
free throw +s
Free|town (capital of
  Sierra Leone)
free trade
free trader +s
free|ware
free|way +s
free weight +s
free|wheel +s +ed
  +ing
free|wheel|er +s
free|wheel|ing
  adjective
free will noun
free-will adjective
freez|able
freeze (turn to ice;
  anaesthetize; Curling;
  stabilization of
  prices etc.)
  freez|es
  froze
  fro|zen
  freez|ing
  [☞ frieze]
freeze-dry
  freeze-dries
  freeze-dried
  freeze-drying
freeze-frame
  freeze-frames
  freeze-framed
  freeze-framing
freez|er +s
freez|er bag +s
freez|er burn +s
freeze-up +s noun
freez|ing noun &
  adjective
Frege, (Fried|rich
  Lud|wig) Gott|lob
  (German logician)
Frei|burg (im
  Breis|gau) (city,
  Germany)
freight +s +ed +ing
freight|age +s
freight car +s
freight|er +s
freight train +s
Fre|man|tle (city,
  Australia)
French
  French|es
  Frenched
  French|ing

French Can|ad|ian
  +s noun
French-Canadian
  adjective
French Congo (earlier
  name of French
  Equatorial Africa)
French Equa|tor|ial
  Af|ri|ca (former
  federation, Africa)
French French noun
French-French
  adjective
french-fried adjective
french fry noun
  french fries
french-fry verb
  french-fries
  french-fried
  french-frying
French Gui|ana
  (French department,
  S America)
French|ie +s (use
  Frenchy)
French|i|fied adjective
French|ify
  French|i|fies
  French|i|fied
  French|i|fy|ing
French im|mer|sion
French kiss
  French kiss|es
  French kissed
  French kiss|ing
French|man
  French|men
Frenchman's Butte
  (battle site, Canada)
French|ness
French pol|ish
  French pol|ish|es
  French pol|ished
  French pol|ish|ing
French Poly|nesia
  (French islands,
  S Pacific)
French Shore
  (regions, Canada)
French South|ern
  and Ant|arc|tic
  Ter|ri|tor|ies
  (French territory,
  Antarctica &
  S Indian Ocean)
French Sudan (former
  name for Mali,
  Africa)
French West Af|ri|ca
  (former federation,
  Africa)
French|woman
  French|women

Frenchy
  French|ies
Fre|neau, Phil|ip
  Morin (US writer)
fren|etic
fren|etic|ally
frenu|lum
  fren|ula
fre|num
  frena
fren|zied adjective
fren|zied|ly
frenzy
  fren|zies
  fren|zied
  frenzy|ing
Freon +s proprietary
fre|quency
  fre|quen|cies
fre|quent +s +ed
  +ing
fre|quen|ta|tion
fre|quen|ta|tive +s
fre|quent|er +s
fre|quent fli|er +ε
  (use frequent flyer)
fre|quent fly|er +s
fre|quent|ly
fres|co
  fres|coes
  fres|coed
  fresco|ing
fres|coed adjective
fres|co secco
fresh +er +est
fresh|en +s +ed +ing
fresh|en|er +s
fresh|er +s
fresh|et +s (rush or
  flood of water)
  [☞ Fréchette]
fresh-faced
Fresh|ie proprietary
fresh|ly
fresh|man
  fresh|men
fresh|ness
fresh wat|er +s noun
fresh|water adjective
fresh|water flea +s
Fres|nel, Au|gus|tin
  Jean (French
  physicist)
fres|nel +s (lens)
Fres|no (city, US)
fret
  frets
  fretted
  fret|ting
fret|board +s
fret|ful
fret|ful|ly
fret|ful|ness

fret|less
fret|saw +s
fret|ted adjective
fret|work +s
Freud, Anna
  (Austrian-born
  psychiatrist)
Freud, Lu|cian
  (German-born
  painter)
Freud, Sig|mund
  (Austrian
  psychotherapist)
Freud|ian +s
Freud|ian|ism
Frey (Scandinavian
  Myth)
  [☞ fray]
Freya (Scandinavian
  Myth: sister of Frey)
Freyr (= Frey)
fri|abil|ity
fri|able
fri|able|ness
friar +s (Christianity)
  [☞ fryer]
friar|ly
fri|ary
  friar|ies
fric|as|see
  fric|as|sees
  fric|as|seed
  fric|as|see|ing
frica|tive +s
fricot +s
fric|tion +s
fric|tion|al
fric|tion|less
Fri|day +s
fridge
  fridg|es
fridge-freezer +s
fried adjective
Frie|dan, Betty
  Naomi (US feminist)
Fried|man, Mil|ton
  (US economist)
Fried|rich, Cas|par
  David (German
  painter)
Friend +s (Quaker)
friend +s (in general
  use)
friend|ed adjective
friend|less
friend|li|ly
friend|li|ness
friend|ly
  friend|li|er
  friend|li|est
  friend|lies

Friend|ly Islands
(= Tonga: country,
S Pacific)
friend|ship +s
Frie|sian +s (of
Holsteins; for the
people & language of
Friesland use
Frisian)
Fries|land (province,
the Netherlands)
frieze +s (part of an
entablature;
decorative band;
Textiles)
frig
frigs
frigged
frig|ging
frig|ate +s
Frig|ga (Scandinavian
Myth)
frig|ging adjective
fright +s +ed +ing
fright|en +s +ed +ing
fright|en|er +s
fright|en|ing adjective
fright|en|ing|ly
fright|ful
fright|ful|ly
fright|ful|ness
fright wig +s
fri|gid
fri|gid|ity
frigid|ly
frigid|ness
fri|jo|les
frill +s +ed +ing
frilled adjective
frilled liz|ard +s
(= frill lizard)
frill|i|ness
frill liz|ard +s
frilly
frill|i|er
frill|i|est
frill|ies
fringe
frin|ges
fringed
frin|ging
fringed adjective
fringe|less
fringe|tree +s
frin|ging noun
fringy
frip|pery
frip|per|ies
Fris|bee +s
proprietary
Frisch, Karl von
(Austrian zoologist)

Frisch, Otto Rob|ert
(Austrian-born
physicist)
Frisch, Rag|nar
Anton Kit|til
(Norwegian
economist)
frisée
Frisia (ancient region,
NW Europe)
Fri|sian +s (islands off
NW Europe; people,
language)
frisk +s +ed +ing
frisk|er +s
frisk|i|ly
frisk|i|ness
frisky
frisk|i|er
frisk|i|est
fris|son +s
frit (mixture used to
make glass or
porcelain)
frits
frit|ted
frit|ting
[☞ fritz, frites]
frites (french fries)
frit fly
frit flies
frith +s
fri|til|lary
fri|til|lar|ies
frit|tata +s
frit|ter +s +ed +ing
frit to misto
fritz (in 'on the fritz')
[☞ frits]
Fri|ul|ian +s
Friuli-Venezia
Giu|lia (region, Italy)
friv|ol|ity
friv|ol|ities
frivo|lous
frivo|lous|ly
frivo|lous|ness
frizz
frizz|es
frizzed
frizz|ing
frizz|ies
frizz|i|ness
friz|zle
friz|zles
friz|zled
friz|zling
frizz|ly
frizzy
frizz|i|er
frizz|i|est
fro (in 'to and fro')
[☞ froe, frow]

Frö|bel, Fried|rich
(= Froebel)
Frö|bel|ian
(= Froebelian)
Frö|bel|ism
(= Froebelism)
Fro|bi|sher (bay,
Canada)
Fro|bi|sher, Sir
Mar|tin (English
explorer)
frock +s +ed +ing
frock coat +s
froe +s (cleaving tool)
[☞ fro)
Froe|bel, Fried|rich
Wil|helm Aug|ust
(German educator)
Froe|bel|ian
Froe|bel|ism
Frog +s offensive
(francophone,
French)
frog +s (amphibian
etc.)
frog|fish
plural frog|fish or
frog|fish|es
frogged
Frog|gie +s offensive
(= Froggy)
frog|ging +s
Frog|gy offensive
(francophone,
French)
Frog|gies
frog|gy (like a frog)
frog|hop|per +s
frog kick +s
frog|man
frog|men
frog|march
frog|march|es
frog|marched
frog|march|ing
frog|mouth +s
frog|spawn
froid|eur
fro|ing (in 'toing and
froing')
Frois|sart, Jean
(French historian)
frolic
frol|ics
frol|icked
frolick|ing
frol|ick|er +s
frolic|some
frolic|some|ly
frolic|some|ness
from preposition
[☞ Fromm, Frum]

fro|mage blanc
fro|mages blancs
fro|mage frais
fro|mages frais
Fromm, Erich
(German-born
psychoanalyst)
frond +s (Botany &
Zoology)
Fronde (French
History)
front +s +ed +ing
front|age +s
front|al +s
front|al|ly
front bench (front-
bench when
preceding a noun)
front bench|es
front-bencher +s
front|court +s
front|court|man
front|court|men
Front de
Li|bé|ra|tion du
Québec
front desk +s
front door +s
front-drive
front-driver +s
front|ed adjective
Fron|te|nac, Louis de
Buade, Comte de
(governor general of
New France)
front end +s (front-
end when preceding a
noun)
fron|tier +s
fron|tier|less
fron|tiers|man
fron|tiers|woman
fron|tiers|women
fron|tis|piece +s
front|less
front|let +s
front line +s (front-
line when preceding a
noun)
front-loader +s
front-loading
front man
front men
front of|fice +s
(front-office when
preceding a noun)
fron|ton +s
front page +s (front-
page when preceding
a noun)
front-pager +s

front|person
front|people
front-row *adjective*
  preceding a noun
front-runner +s
front-running
front|ward
front|wards
front-wheel drive
front|woman
front|women
frore
frosh
  plural frosh
Frost, Les|lie
  Mis|camp|bell (Cdn
  politician)
Frost, Rob|ert Lee
  (US poet)
frost +s +ed +ing
frost|bite
  frost|bites
  frost|bit
  frost|bit|ten
  frost|bit|ing
  frost|bit|ten *adjective*
frost|ed *adjective*
frost-free
frost heave +s
frost heav|ing
frost|i|ly
frost|i|ness
frost|ing +s *noun*
frost|less
frost line
frosty
  frost|i|er
  frost|i|est
froth +s +ed +ing
froth|i|ly
froth|i|ness
froth|ing *adjective &*
  noun
frothy
  froth|i|er
  froth|i|est
frot|tage
Froude, James
  An|thony (English
  historian)
frou-frou
frow +s (cleaving tool:
  use froe)
  [☞ fro, Frau]
fro|ward
fro|ward|ly
fro|ward|ness
frown +s +ed +ing
frown|er +s
frown|ing *adjective*
frown|ing|ly
frow|si|ness (*use*
  frowziness)

frowst
frow|sty
frow|sti|er
frow|sti|est
frowsy (*use* frowzy)
frow|si|er
frow|si|est
frow|zi|ness
frowzy
  frow|zi|er
  frow|zi|est
froze
fro|zen *adjective*
fro|zen|ly
fruc|tif|er|ous
fruc|ti|fi|ca|tion +s
fruc|ti|fy
  fruc|ti|fies
  fruc|ti|fied
  fruc|ti|fy|ing
fruc|tose
fruc|tu|ous
fru|gal
fru|gal|ity
fru|gal|ly
fru|gal|ness
fru|giv|or|ous
fruit
• *noun*
  plural fruit or fruits
• *verb*
  fruits
  fruit|ed
  fruit|ing
fruit|age
fruit|ar|ian +s
fruit|ar|ian|ism
fruit bat +s
fruit-body
  fruit-bodies
fruit|cake +s
fruit cup +s
fruit|ed *adjective*
fruit|er|er +s
fruit fly
  fruit flies
fruit|ful
fruit|ful|ly
fruit|ful|ness
fruit|i|er
fruit|i|est
fruit|i|ness
fruit|ing *adjective*
fruiting-body
  fruiting-bodies
fru|i|tion
fruit|less
fruit|less|ly
fruit|less|ness
fruit|let +s
fruit tree +s
fruit|wood

fruity
  fruit|i|er
  fruit|i|est
Frum, Bar|bara (Cdn
  journalist)
fru|menty
frump +s
frump|i|ly
frump|i|ness
frump|ish
frump|ish|ly
frumpy
  frump|i|er
  frump|i|est
Frunze (*former name*
  for Bishkek,
  Kyrgyzstan)
frus|trate
  frus|trates
  frus|trat|ed
  frus|trat|ing
frus|trat|ed *adjective*
frus|trat|ed|ly
frus|trat|er +s
frus|trat|ing *adjective*
frus|trat|ing|ly
frus|tra|tion +s
frus|tule +s
frus|tum
  frus|ta or frus|tums
fru|tes|cent
fru|ti|cose
Fry, Chris|to|pher
  Har|ris (English
  dramatist)
  [☞ Frye]
Fry, Eliza|beth
  (English activist)
  [☞ Frye]
fry
• *singular noun* (chip;
  fried dish)
  plural fries
• *plural noun* (young
  fish etc.; insignificant
  people)
• *verb*
  fries
  fried
  fry|ing
Frye, (Her|man)
  Nor|throp (Cdn
  literary critic)
  [☞ Fry]
fryer +s (one who
  fries; a thing for
  frying)
  [☞ friar]
fry|ing pan +s
fry pan +s
fry up *verb*
  fries up
  fried up
  fry|ing up

fry-up +s *noun*
f-stop +s
FTA (Free Trade
  Agreement)
FTP (file transfer
  protocol)
• *noun*
  FTPs
• *verb*
  FTP's
  FTP'd
  FTPing
Fuchs, (Emil) Klaus
  Jul|ius (German-
  born physicist)
fuchsia +s
fuch|sin
fuch|sine (= fuchsin)
fuck +s +ed +ing
fuck all
fuck|er +s
fuck|head +s
fuck|ing *adjective &*
  adverb
fuck up *verb*
  fucks up
  fucked up
  fuck|ing up
fuck-up +s *noun*
ful|coid
fucus
  fuci
fud|dle
  fud|dles
  fud|dled
  fud|dling
fud|dle dud|dle
fuddy-duddy
  fuddy-duddies
fudge
  fudg|es
  fudged
  fudg|ing
Fueh|rer +s (Hitler:
  use Führer)
fueh|rer +s (dictator:
  use führer)
  [☞ furor]
fuel
  fuels
  fuelled
  fuel|ling
fuel ef|fi|ciency
fuel-efficient
fuel-inject|ed
fuel injec|tion
fuel|wood
Fuen|tes, Car|los
  (Mexican writer)
fug
ful|ga|cious
ful|ga|cious|ly
ful|ga|cious|ness

fu|ga|city
fu|ga|ci|ties
fugal
fugal|ly
Fu|gard, Athol
Har|old Lan|ni|gan
(South African
dramatist)
Fug|ger (German
banking family)
fuggy
fug|gi|er
fug|gi|est
fugi|tive +s
fugi|tive|ly
fugle|man
fugle|men
fugue +s
fugued
fu|guist +s
Füh|rer +s (Hitler)
füh|rer +s (dictator)
[☞ furor]
Fu|jai|rah (state & its
capital, UAE)
Fuji (mountain, Japan)
Fu|jian (province,
China)
Fuji|yama (= Mount
Fuji, Japan)
Fu|kien (= Fujian:
province, China)
Fu|ku|oka (city,
Japan)
Fu|lani
plural Fu|lani or
Fu|lanis
Ful|bright, (James)
Wil|liam (US
senator)
ful|crum
ful|crums or ful|cra
ful|fil (use fulfill)
ful|fils
ful|filled
ful|fil|ling
ful|fill +s +ed +ing
ful|filled adjective
ful|fill|er +s
ful|fill|ing adjective
ful|fill|ment
ful|fil|ment (use
fulfillment)
Ful|ford, Rob|ert
Mar|shall Blount
(Cdn journalist)
ful|gent
ful|gur|a|tion +s
ful|gur|ite +s
fu|ligin|ous
full +er +est +s +ed
+ing
full|back +s

full blood (pure
descent)
[☞ full-blood]
full-blood +s (person
of full blood)
[☞ full blood]
full-blooded
full-blooded|ly
full-blooded|ness
full-blown
full-bodied
full bore
full-bottomed
full col|our (full-
colour when
preceding a noun)
full count +s (full-
count when preceding
a noun)
full-course adjective
full-court press
full deck
full dress (formal
clothes)
full-dress (thorough,
complete)
full dress uniform
Ful|ler, Rich|ard
Buck|min|ster (US
designer)
ful|ler +s +ed +ing
ful|ler|ene +s
fuller's earth
full-face
full-featured
full-figure (of entire
body; for large use
full-figured)
full-figured (large)
[☞ full-figure]
full-flavored (use full-
flavoured)
full-flavoured
full-fledged
full-frontal
full-grain
full-grown
full-length
full-mouthed
full|ness
full out adverb
full-out adjective
full page (full-page
when preceding a
noun)
full-scale
full-service
full-size +s
full-sized (use full-
size)
full-throat|ed
full time noun

full-time adjective &
adverb
full-timer +s
fully
fully-fashioned
fully-fledged (= full-
fledged)
ful|mar +s
ful|min|ant
ful|min|ate
ful|min|ates
ful|min|at|ed
ful|min|at|ing
ful|min|a|tion +s
ful|min|a|tory
ful|min|ic acid
ful|ness (use fullness)
ful|some
ful|some|ly
ful|some|ness
Ful|ton, Rob|ert (US
inventor)
ful|vous
fuma|role +s
fuma|rol|ic
fum|ble
fum|bles
fum|bled
fum|bling
fum|bler +s
fum|bling|ly
fume
fumes
fumed
fum|ing
[☞ Fiume]
fume|less
fu|met +s
fumier
fumi|est
fumi|gant +s
fumi|gate
fumi|gates
fumi|gat|ed
fumi|gat|ing
fumi|ga|tion +s
fumi|ga|tor +s
fuming|ly
fumi|tory
fumi|tor|ies
fumy
fumier
fumi|est
fun
funs
funned
fun|ning
Funa|futi (capital of
Tuvalu)
fu|nam|bu|list +s
Fun|chal (capital of
Madeira)

func|tion +s +ed
+ing
func|tion|al
func|tion|al|ism
func|tion|al|ist +s
func|tion|al|ity
func|tion|al|ly
func|tion|ary
func|tion|aries
func|tion|less
fund +s +ed +ing
fund|able
fun|da|ment +s
fun|da|men|tal +s
fun|da|men|tal|ism
fun|da|men|tal|ist +s
fun|da|men|tal|ity
fun|da|men|tal|ities
fun|da|men|tal|ly
fund|ed adjective
fund|er +s
fund|ing noun
fund|rais|er +s
fund|rais|ing
fun|dus
fundi
Fundy (bay & national
park, Canada)
fu|ner|al +s noun
fu|ner|ary
fu|ner|eal adjective
fu|ner|eal|ly
fun fair +s
fun fest +s
fun|gal
fungi
fun|gi|bil|ity
fun|gible
fun|gi|cid|al
fun|gi|cide +s
fun|gi|form
fun|gi|stat|ic
fun|giv|or|ous
fungo
fun|goes
fungo bat +s
fun|goid +s
fun|gous adjective
[☞ fungus]
fun|gus noun
fungi or fun|gus|es
[☞ fungous]
fun|house +s
fu|nicu|lar +s
Funk (island, Canada)
Funk, Casi|mir
(Polish-born US
biochemist)
funk +s +ed +ing
funk|i|ly
funk|i|ness

funky
funk|i|er
funk|i|est
fun|nel
fun|nels
fun|nelled
fun|nel|ling
funnel-like
fun|ni|ly
fun|ni|ness
funny
fun|ni|er
fun|ni|est
fun|nies
funny bone +s
funny busi|ness
funny farm +s
funny ha-ha
funny|man
funny|men
funny-peculiar
fun|ster +s
fur (animal hair etc.)
furs
furred
fur|ring
[☞ fir]
furan
fur|ball +s
fur-bearer +s
fur-bearing
fur|be|low +s
fur|be|lowed
fur|bish
fur|bish|es
fur|bished
fur|bish|ing
fur|bish|er +s
fur|cu|la +s
fur|cu|lar
fur|fur|aceous
Fur|ies (Greek Myth)
furi|ous
furi|ous|ly
furi|ous|ness
furl +s +ed +ing
furl|able
fur|less
fur|long +s
fur|lough +s +ed +ing
fur|mety
fur|nace +s
Fur|neaux (islands off Australia)
fur|nish
fur|nish|es
fur|nished
fur|nish|ing
fur|nished adjective
fur|nish|er +s
fur|nish|ings
fur|ni|ture

Fur|ni|vall, Fred|erick James (English philologist)
fur|or +s (uproar)
[☞ führer]
fur|ore +s (uproar: use furor)
[☞ führer]
furo|sem|ide
fur|piece +s
furred adjective
fur|ri|er +s
fur|ri|ery
fur|ri|est
fur|ri|ness
fur|row +s +ed +ing
furrow|less
fur|rowy
furry (covered with fur etc.)
fur|ri|er
fur|ri|est
[☞ firry]
fur seal +s
fur|ther +s +ed +ing
further|ance
fur|ther|er +s
further|more
further|most
fur|thest
fur|tive
fur|tive|ly
fur|tive|ness
fur-trading
fu|run|cle +s
fu|run|cu|lar
fu|run|cu|lo|sis
fu|run|cu|lous
Fury (Greek Myth)
Fur|ies
fury
fur|ies (rage)
[☞ furry]
Fury and Hecla Strait (passage, Cdn Arctic)
furze
furzy
fuse (blend by melting; Electricity; of explosives)
fuses
fused
fus|ing
fuse box
fuse boxes
fusee +s
fusel|age +s
fuse|less
Fu|seli, Henry (Swiss-born English painter)
[☞ fusilli]

fusel oil
[☞ fusil]
Fu|shun (city, China)
fusi|bil|ity
fus|ible
fusi|form
fu|sil +s (musket)
[☞ fusel oil]
fusil|eer +s (use fusilier)
fusil|ier +s
fusil|lade
fusil|lades
fusil|lad|ed
fusil|lad|ing
fu|sil|li (pasta)
[☞ Fuseli]
fu|sion +s
fusion|al
fuss
fuss|es
fussed
fuss|ing
fuss-budget +s
fuss|er +s
fuss|i|ly
fuss|i|ness
fuss|pot
fussy
fuss|i|er
fuss|i|est
fus|tian
fus|tic
fust|i|ly
fust|i|ness
fusty
fust|i|er
fust|i|est
fu|thorc
fu|tile
fu|tile|ly
fu|til|ity
fu|ton +s
fut|tock +s
fu|ture +s
future|less
fu|ture shock
futur|ism
futur|ist +s
futur|is|tic
futur|is|tic|ally
fu|tur|ity
fu|tur|ities
futur|ol|logic|al
futur|ol|o|gist +s
futur|ol|ogy
futz
futz|es
futzed
futz|ing
Fuxin (city, China)

fuze (of explosives: use fuse)
fuzes
fuzed
fuz|ing
[☞ fuse]
fuzee +s (use fusee)
Fu|zhou (city, China)
fuzz
fuzz|es
fuzzed
fuzz|ing
fuzz-box
fuzz-boxes
fuzz|i|ly
fuzz|i|ness
fuzzy
fuzz|i|er
fuzz|i|est
fyl|fot +s

G

G
• (letter; music note; thousand)
G's
• (gauss; gravitational constant; conductance)
[☞ gee]
g
• (letter)
g's
• (gram; gravity; acceleration due to gravity)
[☞ gee]
G7 (Group of Seven)
gab
gabs
gabbed
gab|bing
GABA (gamma-aminobutyric acid)
gab|ar|dine +s (twill-woven cloth; raincoat etc. made of this)
[☞ gaberdine]
gab|ble
gab|bles
gab|bled
gab|bling
gab|bler +s
gab|bro +s
gab|bro|ic
gab|broid

gabby
gab|bi|er
gab|bi|est
gab|er|dine +s (long
loose garment worn
in the Middle Ages;
for twill-woven cloth
or raincoat etc. made
of this *use*
gabardine)
Gabès (port, Tunisia)
gab|fest +s
ga|bion +s
ga|bion|age
Gable, Clark (US
actor)
gable +s
gabled *adjective*
gable end +s
Gabo, Naum
(Russian-born
sculptor)
Gabon (country,
Africa)
Gabon|ese
plural Gabon|ese
Gabor, Den|nis
(English engineer)
Gab|or|one (capital of
Botswana)
Gab|riel (*New
Testament*; *Islam*)
Gab|rieli, An|drea
(Italian composer)
Gab|rieli, Gio|van|ni
(Italian composer)
Gab|ri|ola (island,
Canada)
gach (*use* gatch)
gach|es
gached
gach|ing
gach|er +s (*use*
gatcher)
Gad (*Bible*)
gad
gads
gad|ded
gad|ding
gad|about +s
Gad|ar|ene
Gad|dafi, Mu'am|mer
Muham|mad al
(Libyan president)
gad|fly
gad|flies
gadg|et +s
gadg|et|eer +s
gadg|et|ry
gadg|ety
gad|oid +s
gado|lin|ite +s
gado|lin|ium

gad|roon +s
gad|rooned
Gads|den Pur|chase
(area, US)
gad|wall
plural gad|wall or
gad|walls
gad|zooks
Gaea (*Greek Myth*
= Gaia)
[☞ Gaya]
Gael +s (Gaelic Celt)
Gael|dom
Gael|ic (Celtic
language; of the
Celts)
Gael|tacht +s
gaff +s +ed +ing
(fishing implement;
spar; criticism,
abuse; in 'blow the
gaff')
[☞ gaffe]
gaffe +s (blunder)
[☞ gaff]
gaf|fer +s
Gafsa (town, Tunisia)
gag
gags
gagged
gag|ging
gaga
Ga|gar|in, Yuri
Alek|sey|evich
(Russian cosmonaut)
Gage, Thom|as
(English general &
colonial
administrator)
gage (pledge;
challenge;
greengage; nautical
position)
gages
gaged
gaging
[☞ gauge]
gag|gle
gag|gles
gag|gled
gag|gling
gag man
gag men
Ga|gnon, Clar|ence
(Cdn artist)
gag order +s
gag rule +s
gag|ster +s
Gaia (*Greek Myth*;
Earth)
[☞ Gaya]
Gaian +s
gai|ety

gai|jin
plural gai|jin
gail|lar|dia +s
gaily
gain +s +ed +ing
gain|able
gain|er +s
gain|ful
gain|ful|ly
gain|ful|ness
gain|say
gain|says
gain|said
gain|say|ing
gain|say|er +s
Gains|bor|ough,
Thom|as (English
painter)
Gai|seric
(= Genseric, Vandal
king)
gait +s (manner of
walking etc.)
[☞ gate]
gait|ed *adjective*
(having a specified
gait)
[☞ gated]
gait|er +s (leg
coverings)
[☞ gator]
gait|ered
Gaius (Roman jurist)
gal +s (girl; *Physics*)
[☞ gall]
gala +s (festive
occasion)
[☞ Galla]
gal|ac|tic
gal|ac|tose
gal|ago +s
Gala|had +s
(*Arthurian Legend*;
noble person)
gal|an|gal (rhizome of
ginger plant)
[☞ galingale]
gal|an|tine +s
Gal|apa|gos (islands,
west of Ecuador)
Gala|tea (*Greek Myth*:
sea nymph;
Pygmalion's statue)
[☞ Galatia]
Gal|ați (city, Romania)
Gal|atia (ancient
region, Asia Minor)
Gal|atian +s
Gal|atians (*New
Testament*)
Gal|axy (Milky Way)
gal|axy (*in general use*)
gal|axies

Galba, Ser|vius
Sul|pi|cius (Roman
emperor)
gal|ba|num
Gal|braith, John
Ken|neth (Cdn-born
US economist)
gale (wind; storm;
outburst; frolic; bog
myrtle)
gales
galed
galing
[☞ Gael]
galea
ga|leae or ga|leas
gale|ate
gale|at|ed
Galen (Greek
physician)
ga|lena +s
Gal|en|ic (of Galen)
gal|en|ic (made of
natural parts)
gal|en|ic|al +s
gal|ette +s
Gali|ano (island,
Canada)
Gal|ibi
plural Gal|ibi or
Gal|ibis
Gal|icia (regions,
Spain & E Europe)
Gal|ician +s
Gali|lean +s
Gali|lee (region,
ancient Palestine;
lake, Israel)
Gali|leo Gali|lei
(Italian astronomer)
gal|in|gale +s (sedge;
for rhizome of ginger
plant *use* galangal)
gall +s +ed +ing
(audacity; bitterness;
bile; gallbladder;
sore; annoy; insect
growth)
[☞ gal, Gaul, de
Gaulle]
Galla (people;
language)
plural Galla or
Gal|las
[☞ Galle, gala]
Gal|lant, Mavis
Les|lie (Cdn writer)
gal|lant +s +ed +ing
gal|lant|ly
gal|lant|ry
gal|lant|ries
gall|blad|der +s
Galle (port, Sri Lanka)
[☞ Galla]

gal|leon +s
gal|leria +s
gal|ler|ied
gal|lery
  gal|ler|ies
gal|ley +s
Gal|lia
  Nar|bon|en|sis
  (province,
  Transalpine Gaul)
gal|li|ard +s
Gal|lic (French;
  Gaulish)
  [☞ Gaelic]
Gal|lican +s
Gal|lican|ism
Gal|li|cism
Gal|li|cize
  Gal|li|ciz|es
  Gal|li|cized
  Gal|li|ciz|ing
galli|gas|kins
galli|maufry
  galli|mauf|ries
gal|lin|aceous
gal|ling adjective
gal|ling|ly
gal|li|nule +s
Gal|lip|oli (peninsula,
  Turkey)
gal|li|pot +s
gal|lium
gal|li|vant +s +ed
  +ing
gal|li|wasp +s
gal|lon +s
gal|lon|age +s
gal|loon +s
gal|lop +s +ed +ing
  (horse's pace; run
  with long strides)
  [☞ galop, Gallup,
  Gallup poll]
gal|lop|er +s
Gal|lo|way (area,
  Scotland)
gal|lo|way +s (cattle)
gal|lows
gall|stone +s
Gal|lup, George
  Hor|ace (US
  statistician)
  [☞ gallop, galop]
Gal|lup poll +s
gal|lus|es
gall wasp +s
Gal|lois, Éva|riste
  (French
  mathematician)
ga|loot +s
galop +s (dance)
  [☞ gallop, Gallup,
  Gallup poll]

ga|lore
ga|losh
  ga|losh|es
Gals|worthy, John
  (English writer)
Galt (community,
  Canada)
Galt, Sir Alex|an|der
  Til|loch (Cdn
  politician)
Gal|ton, Sir Fran|cis
  (English scientist)
ga|lumph +s +ed
  +ing
Gal|vani, Luigi
  (Italian anatomist)
gal|van|ic
gal|van|ic|ally
gal|van|ism
gal|van|iz|a|tion
gal|van|ize
  galv|an|iz|es
  gal|van|ized
  gal|van|iz|ing
gal|van|iz|er +s
gal|van|om|eter +s
gal|van|o|met|ric
Gal|ves|ton (city, US)
Gal|way (bay, county
  & town, Ireland)
gam
  gams
  gammed
  gam|ming
Gama, Vasco da
  (Portuguese
  explorer)
  [☞ gamma]
Gamay +s (hamlet,
  France; wine)
gam|bade +s
gam|bado
  gam|bad|os or
  gam|bad|oes
Gam|bia (country &
  river, Africa)
Gam|bian +s
Gam|bier (islands,
  S Pacific)
gam|bier
gam|bit +s
gam|ble (bet; take
  risks)
  gam|bles
  gam|bled
  gam|bling
  [☞ gambol]
gam|bler +s
gam|boge
gam|bol (frolic)
  gam|bols
  gam|bolled

gam|bol|ling
  [☞ gamble]
gam|brel +s
game
  games
  gamed
  gam|ing
  gamer
  gam|est
game bird +s
game|book +s
Game Boy +s
  proprietary
game-breaker
game-breaking
game|cock +s
game face +s
game fish
  plural game fish or
  game fish|es
game|fowl
  plural game|fowl or
  game|fowls
game|keeper +s
gam|elan +s
game|ly
game|ness
game plan +s
game point +s
gamer +s
  (enthusiastic
  participant;
  comparative of
  game)
  [☞ gammer]
game room +s
game show +s
games|man
  games|men
games|man|ship
game|some
game|some|ly
game|some|ness
game|ster +s
gamet|an|gium
  gamet|an|gia
gam|ete +s
gam|et|ic
gam|eto|cyte +s
gam|eto|gen|esis
gam|eto|phyte +s
gam|eto|phyt|ic
game-winner +s
gamey (use gamy)
  gam|i|er
  gam|i|est
gam|i|ly
gamin +s (street
  urchin)
  [☞ gammon]
gam|ine +s (female
  gamin; girl with
  boyish charm)

gam|i|ness
gamma +s (Greek
  letter; radiation;
  third; Astronomy)
  [☞ Gama]
gam|mer +s (old
  woman)
gam|mon +s +ed
  +ing (bacon;
  Backgammon; hoax,
  deceive)
  [☞ gamin]
gammy (lame)
  gam|mi|er
  gam|mi|est
Gamow, George
  (Russian-born
  physicist)
gamp +s
gamut +s
gamy (having strong
  scent; sensational;
  enthusiastic)
  gam|i|er
  gam|i|est
  [☞ gammy]
ga|nache
Gan|an|oque (town,
  Canada)
Gana|pati (Hinduism
  = Ganesha)
Gäncä (city,
  Azerbaijan)
Gance, Abel (French
  filmmaker)
Gand (= Ghent,
  Belgium)
Gan|der (town & river,
  Canada)
gan|der +s
Gan|der Bay boat +s
Gan|dhi (surname)
  [☞ gandy dancer]
Gan|dhi, In|dira
  Priya|dar|shini
  (Indian prime
  minister)
Gan|dhi, Ma|hat|ma
  (Indian spiritual
  leader)
Gan|dhi, Rajiv Ratna
  (Indian prime
  minister)
Gan|dhi|nagar (city,
  India)
gandy dan|cer +s
  (railway worker)
  [☞ Gandhi]
Ga|ne|sha (Hinduism)
gang +s +ed +ing
  (group; go)
  [☞ gangue]
gang agley

gang|bang +s +ed
+ing
gang|bang|er +s
gang-board +s
gang-boarded
gang|bust|er +s
gang|bust|ers
gang|er +s
Gan|ges (river, Asia)
gang|land
gan|gle
  gan|gles
  gan|gled
  gan|gling
gan|gliar (of ganglia)
gan|glier comparative
  of gangly
gan|gling adjective
gan|glion
  gan|glia or
  gan|glions
gan|gli|on|at|ed
gan|gli|on|ic
gan|gly
  gan|gli|er
  gan|gli|est
gang|plank +s
gang rape +s noun
gang-rape verb
  gang-rapes
  gang-raped
  gang-raping
gan|grene
  gan|grenes
  gan|grened
  gan|gren|ing
gan|gren|ous
gang|sta +s
gang|sta rap
gang|ster +s
gang|ster|ish
gang|ster|ism
Gang|tok (city, India)
gangue (earth)
  [☞ gang agley]
gang|way +s
gan|ja
gan|net +s
gan|net|ry
  gan|net|ries
gan|oid +s
Gansu (province,
  China)
gant|let +s
  (punishment, ordeal:
  use gauntlet)
gan|try
  gan|tries
Gany|mede (Greek
  Myth; moon of
  Jupiter)
gap +s

gape
  gapes
  gaped
  gaping
gaper +s
gape|worm +s
gaping|ly
gap|ped adjective
gappy
gap-toothed
gar +s
gar|age
  gar|ag|es
  gar|aged
  gar|ag|ing
garam ma|sala
Gara|mond, Claude
  (French type
  designer)
Ga|rant, Serge (Cdn
  musician)
garb +s +ed +ing
gar|bage
gar|bage bag +s
gar|bage can +s
garbage|man
  garbage|men
gar|bage mitt +s
gar|bage pail +s
gar|bage truck +s
gar|bagey
gar|ban|zo +s
gar|ble
  gar|bles
  gar|bled
  gar|bling
gar|bler +s
Garbo, Greta
  (Swedish-born US
  actress)
gar|board +s
gar|bol|o|gist +s
gar|bol|ogy
gar|bur|ator +s
Gar|cia, Jer|ome
  John ('Jerry') (US
  rock musician)
Gar|cía Lorca,
  Fede|rico (Spanish
  writer)
Gar|cía Már|quez,
  Gab|riel (Colombian
  novelist)
gar|çon
  gar|çons
Garda (Irish police;
  lake, Italy)
Gar|dai
gar|den +s +ed +ing
gar|dened adjective
gar|den|er +s
  [☞ Gardner]
gar|denia +s

gar|den|ing noun
garden-variety
Gard|ner, Ava
  La|vinia (US actress)
Gar|field, James
  Abram (US
  president)
gar|fish
  plural gar|fish
gar|ganey +s
gar|gan|tuan
gar|get
gar|gle
  gar|gles
  gar|gled
garg|ling
gar|goyle +s
gar|goyled adjective
gar|goyl|ish
Gari|baldi, Giu|seppe
  (Italian patriot)
gari|bal|di +s
gar|ish
gar|ish|ly
gar|ish|ness
Gar|land, Judy (US
  entertainer)
gar|land +s +ed +ing
gar|lic
gar|licky
gar|ment +s +ed
  +ing
gar|ment bag +s
gar|ment|ed adjective
Gar|neau, Marc (Cdn
  astronaut)
Gar|neau, François-
  Xavier (Cdn writer)
Gar|ner, Hugh (Cdn
  writer)
gar|ner +s +ed +ing
gar|net +s
gar|nish
  gar|nish|es
  gar|nished
  gar|nish|ing
gar|nish|ee
  gar|nish|ees
  gar|nish|eed
  gar|nish|ee|ing
gar|nish|ment +s
gar|ni|ture +s
Ga|ronne (river,
  France)
ga|rotte (use garrotte)
  ga|rottes
  ga|rot|ted
  ga|rot|ting
Ga|roua (city,
  Cameroon)
gar|pike
  plural gar|pike or
  gar|pikes

gar|ret +s
Gar|rick, David
  (English actor)
gar|ri|son +s +ed
  +ing
gar|rotte
  gar|rottes
  gar|rot|ted
  gar|rot|ting
gar|ru|lity
gar|ru|lous
gar|ru|lous|ly
gar|ru|lous|ness
Garry oak +s
  [☞ Gary]
Gar|ter (knighthood)
gar|ter +s +ed +ing
gar|ter belt +s
gar|ter snake +s
gar|ter stitch
  gar|ter stitch|es
garth +s
Ga|ruda
Gar|vey, Mar|cus
  Mo|siah (Jamaican
  political activist)
Gary (city, US)
  [☞ Garry oak, Fort
  Garry]
gas
  gases
  gassed
  gas|sing
gas|bag +s
gas bar +s
Gas|con, Jean (Cdn
  actor)
Gas|con +s (of
  Gascony)
Gas|cony (region,
  France)
gas-cooled
gas|eous
gas|eous|ness
gas field +s
gas fire +s
gas-fired
gas fire|place +s
gas fit|ter +s
gas guz|zler +s
gas-guzzling
gash
  gash|es
  gashed
  gash|ing
gasi|fi|ca|tion
gasi|fi|er +s
gas|ify
  gasi|fies
  gasi|fied
  gasi|fy|ing
Gas|kell, Mrs.
  Eliza|beth

Cleg|horn (English novelist)
gas|ket +s
gas|ket|ed
gas|kin +s
gas|light +s
gas|lit
gas|man
gas|men
gas mask +s
gas meter +s
gas|o|hol
gas oil
gas|o|line +s
gas|om|eter +s
gasp +s +ed +ing
Gaspé (town, peninsula & cape, Canada)
gas ped|al +s
gasp|er +s
gas|per|eau
gas|per|eaux
gas-permeable
Gas|pe|sian ǀ 3
gasp|ing|ly
gas plant +s
gas pump +s
gas ring +s
gassed *adjective*
Gas|sendi, Pierre (French astronomer)
Gas|ser, Her|bert Spen|cer (US physiologist)
gas|ser +s
gas|si|ness
gassy
gas|si|er
gas|si|est
Gast|ar|bei|ter
Gast|ar|bei|ters or Gast|ar|bei|ter
gast|haus
gast|haus|es
gas-tight
Gas|town (Vancouver neighbourhood)
gas|trec|tomy
gas|trec|to|mies
gas|tric
gas|trin
gas|tri|tis
gastro|enter|itis
gastro|enter|o|logic|al
gastro|enter|ol|o|gist +s
gastro|enter|ol|ogy
gastro|intes|tin|al
gas|tro|lith +s
gas|tro|nome +s
gas|tro|nom|ic

gas|tro|nom|ic|al
gas|tro|nom|ic|al|ly
gas|tron|omy
gas|tro|pod +s
gas|tropo|dous
gas|tro|scope +s
gas|tro|scop|ic
gas|trula
gas|tru|lae
gas|tru|la|tion
gas|works
gat +s (gun)
[☞ GATT]
gatch
gatch|es
gatched
gatch|ing
gatch|er +s
gate (hinged barrier etc.; dismissal; street; retain in prison)
gates
gated
gat|ing
[☞ gait]
ga|teau
ga|teaus or ga|teaux
gate|crash
gate|crash|es
gate|crashed
gate|crash|ing
gate|crash|er +s
gated *adjective* (having a wall or fence; enclosed)
[☞ gaited]
gate|fold +s
gate|house +s
gate|keep|er +s
gate|leg +s
gate|legged
gate|man
gate|men
gate money
gate|post +s
Gates, Hor|atio (US revolutionary general)
Gates, Wil|liam Henry ('Bill') (US computer entrepreneur)
Gates|head (city, England)
gate valve +s
gate|way +s
gath|er +s +ed +ing
gath|er|er +s
gath|er|ing +s *noun & adjective*
Gati|neau +s (city, river & hills, Canada)
Gat|ling +s

Gat|ling gun +s
ga|tor +s (alligator)
[☞ gaiter]
GATT (General Agreement on Tariffs and Trade)
Gat|wick (airport, England)
gauch (boast, boastful behaviour, show-off: use gatch)
gauch|es
gauched
gauch|ing
[☞ gotch, gauche]
gauche (tactless; socially awkward)
[☞ gauch, gouache]
gauche|ly
gauche|ness
gauch|er +s (show-off: use gatcher)
gauche|rie +s
gau|cho +s
gaud +s (gaudy thing)
[☞ god, Gawd]
Gau|daur, Jacob Gill, Jr. ('Jake') (Cdn football commissioner)
Gaudí, An|tonio (Spanish architect)
gaud|i|ly
gaud|i|ness
gaudy
gaud|i|er
gaud|i|est
gaud|ies
gauge (measure; thickness; graduated instrument; estimate; for nautical position use gage)
gauges
gauged
gauging
[☞ gage, gouge]
gauge|able
gauge pres|sure
gauge theory
Gau|guin, (Eu|gène Henri) Paul (French painter)
Gau|hati (city, India)
Gaul +s (ancient region, Europe; inhabitant of Gaul)
[☞ de Gaulle)
gau|leiter +s
Gaul|ish
Gaulle, Charles de (French general &

statesman)
[☞ Gaul]
Gaull|ism
Gaull|ist +s
gaunch
gaunch|es
Gaunt (*former name for* Ghent)
gaunt
gaunt|let +s
gaunt|let|ed
gaunt|ly
gaunt|ness
gaun|try (barrel stand: use gantry)
gaun|tries
gaur +s
Gauss, Karl Fried|rich (German mathematician)
gauss
plural gauss or gauss|es
Gauss|ian
dis|tri|bu|tion
Gau|tama (family name of Buddha)
Gau|tier, Théo|phile (French writer)
gauze +s
gauz|i|ly
gauz|i|ness
gauzy (like gauze)
gauz|i|er
gauz|i|est
[☞ Ghazi]
gave
gavel
gav|els
gav|elled
gav|el|ling
gavi|al +s
ga|votte +s
Gawd *interjection*
[☞ gaud]
gawk +s +ed +ing
gawk|er +s
gawk|i|ly
gawk|i|ness
gawk|ish
gawky
gawk|i|er
gawk|i|est
gaw|moge +s
gawp +s +ed +ing
gawp|er +s
Gay, John (English writer)
gay +er +est +s
Gaya (city, India)
[☞ Gaia]
ga|yal +s

gay-bash
  gay-bashes
  gay-bashed
  gay-bashing
gay-basher +s
gay bash|ing *noun*
Gaye, Mar|vin (US musician)
gay|feather +s
Gay-Lussac, Jo|seph Louis (French scientist)
gay|ness
gay|wings
  plural gay|wings
gaz|ania +s
Gaz|an|kulu (former homeland, South Africa)
Gaza Strip (territory, Middle East)
gaze
  gazes
  gazed
  gaz|ing
gaz|ebo
  gaz|ebos or gaz|eboes
gaz|elle +s
gaz|er +s
gaz|ette
  gaz|ettes
  gaz|et|ted
  gaz|et|ting
gaz|et|teer +s
Gaz|ian|tep (city, Turkey)
ga|zil|lion
  plural ga|zil|lion or ga|zil|lions
gaz|pa|cho +s
gaz|ump +s +ed +ing
gaz|ump|er +s
gaz|un|der +s +ed +ing
Gdańsk (city, Poland)
GDP (gross domestic product)
Gdynia (city, Poland)
Ge (*Greek Myth*)
gean +s (cherry)
  [☞ gene, jean, Jeans]
gear +s +ed +ing
gear|box
  gear|boxes
gear|ing *noun*
gear lever +s
gear|shift +s
gear|wheel +s
Geber (Arab chemist)
gecko
  geck|os or geck|oes

gee +s (*interjection*; dog command; one thousand dollars)
gee|gaw +s
gee-gee +s
geek +s
geeky
  geek|i|er
  geek|i|est
  [☞ Geikie]
Gee|long (city, Australia)
geese *plural of* goose
  [☞ geez]
gee whiz *interjection*
gee-whiz *adjective*
geez *interjection*
gee|zer +s (person)
  [☞ geyser]
ge|filte fish
Ge|hen|na
Gehrig, Henry Louis ('Lou') (US baseball player)
Geiger, Hans Jo|hann Will|helm (German physicist)
Geiger count|er +s
Geikie, Sir Archi|bald (Scottish geologist)
Geisel, Theo|dore Seuss (Dr. Seuss)
gei|sha
  plural gei|sha or gei|shas
Gejiu (city, China)
Geju (= Gejiu, China)
gel
  gels
  gelled
  gel|ling
  • *noun*
  • *verb* (apply gel to; *for* take definite form *or* harmonize use jell)
gel|ada
  plural gel|ada or gel|adas
gel|atin +s
gel|atine +s (*use* gelatin)
gel|atin|iz|a|tion
gel|atin|ize
  gel|atin|iz|es
  gel|atin|ized
  gel|atin|iz|ing
gel|atin|ous
gel|atin|ous|ly
gel|ation
gel|ato
  gel|ati
gel|coat +s
geld +s +ed +ing

Gel|der|land (province, the Netherlands)
geld|ing +s *noun*
gelid
gel|ig|nite
Gé|li|nas, Gra|tien (Cdn actor & director)
Gell-Mann, Mur|ray (US physicist)
gelly *Brit.* (gelignite)
  [☞ jelly]
Gel|sen|kir|chen (city, Germany)
gelt
gem
  gems
  gemmed
  gem|ming
Ge|mara (*Judaism*)
Gé|meaux
  plural Gé|meaux
Ge|mein|schaft
gemin|ate
  gemin|ates
  gemin|at|ed
  gemin|at|ing
gemin|ation
Gem|ini +s (constellation; *Zodiac*; award)
Gemi|nian +s
gem|like
gemma
  gem|mae
gem|ma|tion
gem|mule +s
gem|ol|o|gist +s
gem|ol|ogy
gems|bok
  plural gems|bok or gems|boks
gem|stone +s
gemüt|lich
gemüt|lich|keit
gen
  gens
  genned
  gen|ning
gen|darme +s
gen|darm|erie +s
gen|der +s
gender-bender +s
gender-bending
gen|dered
gen|der gap
gender|less
gender-neutral
gender-specif|ic
gene +s (*Biochemistry*)
  [☞ gean, jean, Jeans]

ge|nea|logic|al
ge|nea|logic|al|ly
ge|neal|o|gist +s
ge|neal|ogy
  ge|neal|o|gies
gene bank +s
gene pool +s
gen|era
gen|er|able
gen|er|al +s
gen|er|al ad|mis|sion (general-admission *when preceding a noun*)
gen|er|al|is|simo +s
gen|er|al|ist +s
gen|er|al|ity
  gen|er|al|ities
gen|er|al|iz|abil|ity
gen|er|al|iz|able
gen|er|al|iz|a|tion +s
gen|er|al|ize
  gen|er|al|iz|es
  gen|er|al|ized
  gen|er|al|iz|ing
gen|er|al|iz|er +s
gen|er|al|ly
gen|er|al|ness
general-purpose
gen|er|al|ship
gen|er|ate
  gen|er|ates
  gen|er|at|ed
  gen|er|at|ing
gen|er|a|tion +s
gen|er|a|tion|al
Gen|er|a|tion X
Gen|er|a|tion Xer +s
gen|er|a|tive
gen|er|ator +s
gen|er|ic +s
gen|er|ic|ally
gen|er|os|ity
  gen|er|os|ities
gen|er|ous
gen|er|ous|ly
gen|er|ous|ness
genes *plural of* gene
  [☞ jeans]
Gen|esis (*Bible*)
gen|esis (origin)
  gen|eses
gene-spliced
gene-splicing
Genet, Jean (French writer)
genet +s
gen|etic
gen|etic|al
gen|etic|al|ly
gen|eti|cist +s
gen|etics

Gen|eva (city & lake, Switzerland)
gen|eva +s (gin)
Gen|eva bands
Gen|eva gown +s
Gen|evan +s
Gen|ghis Khan (founder of the Mongol Empire)
gen|ial
geni|al|ity
gen|ial|ly
genic
Genie +s (award)
genie (spirit in a lamp or bottle; *for* spirit of Islamic mythology *use* jinni)
genies *or* genii
genii *plural of* genie & genius
gen|is|ta +s
gen|ital +s
gcn|ital|ia
geni|tiv|al
geni|tiv|al|ly
geni|tive
gen|ito|urin|ary
genius
• (person with exceptional talent or intellect)
 plural genius|es
• (tutelary spirit; character of a nation or age)
 plural genius|es *or* genii
genius loci
gen|lock +s
gen|lock|ing
Genoa (port, Italy; salami)
genoa +s (jib sail)
geno|cid|al
geno|cide +s
Geno|ese (of Genoa)
 plural Geno|ese
gen|oise +s (sponge cake)
gen|ome +s
genom|ic
geno|type +s
geno|typ|ic
genre +s
gens
 gen|tes
Gen|ser|ic (Vandal king)
Gent (= Ghent, Belgium)
gent +s
gen|ta|micin

gen|teel (refined; upper-class)
gen|teel|ism
gen|teel|ly
gen|teel|ness
gen|tes
gen|tian
Gen|tile +s (non-Jewish, non-Mormon, etc.)
gen|tile +s (of a tribe or nation; *Grammar*)
 [☞ genteel]
gen|til|ity
gen|tle
 gent|ler
 gent|lest
 gen|tles
 gen|tled
 gent|ling
gentle|folk
gentle|man
 gentle|men
gentle|man|li|ness
gentle|man|ly
gentle|man's
 agree|ment +s
gentle|men's
 agree|ment +s
 (= gentleman's agreement)
gentle|ness
gentle|woman
 gentle|women
gent|ly
gen|too +s
gen|tri|fi|ca|tion
gen|tri|fier +s
gen|tri|fy
 gen|tri|fies
 gen|tri|fied
 gen|tri|fy|ing
gen|try
genu|flect +s +ed +ing
genu|flec|tion +s
genu|flect|or +s
genu|ine
genu|ine|ly
genu|ine|ness
genus
 gen|era
Gen X
Gen-Xer +s
geo|cen|tric
geo|cen|tric|ally
geo|chem|ical
geo|chem|ist +s
geo|chem|istry
geo|chrono|logic|al
geo|chron|ol|o|gist +s
geo|chron|ol|ogy

geode +s
geo|des|ic
geod|esist +s
geod|esy
geo|det|ic
geod|ic
geo-econom|ics
Geof|frey of Mon|mouth (Welsh chronicler)
 [☞ Jeffrey]
geog|raph|er +s
geo|graph|ic
geo|graph|ic|al
geo|graph|ic|al|ly
geog|raphy
ge|oid +s
geo|logic
geo|logic|al
geo|logic|al|ly
geol|o|gist +s
geol|ogy
geo|mag|net|ic
geo|mag|net|ical|ly
geo|mag|net|ism
geo|mancy
geo|man|tic
geo|mat|ics
geom|eter +s
geo|met|ric +s
geo|met|ric|al
geo|met|ric|al|ly
geo|met|ri|cian +s
geom|etry
 geom|et|ries
geo|morph|ic
geo|morpho|logic|al
geo|morph|ol|o|gist +s
geo|morph|ol|ogy
ge|oph|agy
geo|physic|al
geo|physi|cist +s
geo|phys|ics
geo|polit|ical
geo|polit|ical|ly
geo|polit|ician +s
geo|pol|itics
Geor|die +s
George (British kings; saint)
George, Dan (Cdn actor)
George, Henry (US economist)
George|town (capital of Guyana; community, Canada)
 [☞ George Town]
George Town (port, Malaysia; capital of

the Cayman Islands)
 [☞ Georgetown]
geor|gette +s
Geor|gia (country, Europe; state, US; strait, Canada)
Geor|gian +s
Geor|gian Bay (in Canada)
geor|gic +s
Geor|gina (town, Canada)
geo|science +s
geo|scien|tist +s
geo|sphere +s
geo|station|ary
geo|stra|tegic
geo|stroph|ic
geo|syn|chron|ous
geo|tech|nic|al
geo|tex|tile +s
geo|ther|mal
geo|trop|ic
goo|trop|ism
Gera (city, Germany)
Ger|ald|ton (port, Australia)
gera|nium +s
ger|bera +s
ger|bil +s
ger|enuk +s
geri|at|ric +s
geria|tri|cian +s
geri|at|rics
Géri|cault, (Jean Louis André) Théo|dore (French painter)
Ger|itol *proprietary*
germ +s
Ger|man +s (of Germany)
ger|man (having the same parents or grandparents)
ger|man|der +s
ger|mane
ger|mane|ly
ger|mane|ness
Ger|man|ic (of Germans, Anglo-Saxons or Scandinavians; language)
ger|man|ic (of germanium)
Ger|man|icus Caesar (Roman general)
Ger|man|ist +s
ger|ma|nium
Ger|man|iz|a|tion

Ger|man|ize
Ger|man|iz|es
Ger|man|ized
Ger|man|iz|ing
Ger|man|iz|er +s
Ger|man shep|herd
+s
Ger|many (country,
Europe)
Ger|manys
germi|cid|al
germi|cide +s
ger|min|al
ger|min|al|ly
ger|min|ate
ger|min|ates
ger|min|at|ed
ger|min|at|ing
ger|min|a|tion
ger|min|a|tive
ger|min|ator +s
Ger|mis|ton (city,
South Africa)
germ line +s
germ|plasm
germy
Ger|on|imo (Apache
chief; interjection)
ger|on|toc|racy
ger|on|toc|ra|cies
ger|on|to|crat +s
ger|on|to|crat|ic
ger|on|to|logic|al
ger|on|tol|o|gist +s
ger|on|tol|ogy
gerry|man|der +s
+ed +ing
gerry|man|der|er +s
Gersh|win, George
(US songwriter)
Gersh|win, Ira (US
lyricist)
ger|und +s
ger|und|ive +s
Geryon (Greek Myth)
Gesamt|kunst|werk
Gesell|schaft
Gesell|schafts or
Gesell|schaften
Ges|ner, Abra|ham
(Cdn geologist &
inventor)
gesso
ges|soes
ges|soed
ge|stalt +s
ge|stalt|ism
ge|stalt|ist +s
Ge|stalt psych|ol|ogy
Ge|stapo
ges|tate
ges|tates

ges|tat|ed
ges|tat|ing
ges|ta|tion
ges|ta|tion|al
ges|ticu|late
ges|ticu|lates
ges|ticu|lat|ed
ges|ticu|lat|ing
ges|ticu|la|tion +s
ges|ticu|la|tive
ges|ticu|la|tor +s
ges|ticu|la|tory
ges|tur|al
ges|tur|al|ly
ges|ture
ges|tures
ges|tured
ges|tur|ing
ge|sund|heit
get
gets
got
got or got|ten
get|ting
get-at-able
get away verb
gets away
got away
got away
or got|ten away
get|ting away
get|away +s noun
get-go
Geth|sem|ane (New
Testament)
get out verb &
interjection
gets out
got out
got out
or got|ten out
get|ting out
get-out noun
get-rich-quick
get|table
get|ter +s +ed +ing
get to|geth|er verb
gets to|geth|er
got to|geth|er
got to|geth|er
or got|ten to|geth|er
get|ting to|geth|er
get-togeth|er +s noun
Getty, Don|ald Ross
(Cdn politician)
Getty, Jean Paul (US
industrialist)
Gettys|burg (battle
site, US)
get up verb
gets up
got up
got up or got|ten up
get|ting up

getup +s noun
get-up-and-go
Getz, Stan (US
saxophonist)
geum +s
gew|gaw +s
Ge|würz|tra|mi|ner
+s
gey|ser +s (hot spring;
water heater)
[☞ geezer]
GFCI (ground-fault
circuit interrupter)
GFCIs
GFI (ground-fault
interrupter)
GFIs
GG (Governor
General; Governor
General's Award)
GGs
Ghana (country,
Africa)
Ghan|aian +s
ghar|ial +s
ghast|li|ness
ghast|ly
ghast|li|er
ghast|li|est
ghat +s (steps to a
river; mountain pass)
Ghats (mountain
ranges, India)
ghaz|al +s
Ghazi +s (Islam)
Ghazi|abad (city,
India)
Ghaz|na|vid (Turkish
dynasty)
ghee (clarified butter)
Ghent (city, Belgium)
ghe|rao +s
gher|kin +s
(vegetable)
[☞ jerkin]
ghet|to
ghet|tos or
ghet|toes
ghet|to blast|er +s
ghetto|ize
ghetto|iz|es
ghetto|ized
ghetto|iz|ing
Ghi|bel|line +s
Ghi|ber|ti, Lor|enzo
(Italian sculptor)
ghil|lie +s (use gillie)
Ghir|lan|daio (Italian
painter)
ghost +s +ed +ing
ghost|bust|er +s
Ghost Dance
ghost|ing noun

ghost|like
ghost|li|ness
ghost|ly
ghost|li|er
ghost|li|est
ghost town +s
ghost-write
ghost-writes
ghost-wrote
ghost-written
ghost-writing
ghost|writer +s
ghoul +s
ghoul|ish
ghoul|ish|ly
ghoul|ish|ness
Ghul|ghu|leh (ancient
city, Afghanistan)
ghyll +s Brit. (= gill:
ravine, torrent)
GI (US soldier)
GIs
Gia|co|metti,
Al|ber|to (Swiss
artist)
giant +s
giant|ess
giant|ess|es
giant|ism
giant-killer +s
giant-like
Giant's Cause|way
(rock formation,
Ireland)
giaour +s
gi|ar|dia
gi|ar|dia|sis
Gib (Gibraltar)
gib +s (bolt, wedge,
pin)
[☞ jib]
gib|ber +s +ed +ing
(babble, chatter)
[☞ jibber]
gib|ber|el|lin +s
gib|ber|ing +s noun &
adjective
gib|ber|ish
gib|bet +s +ed +ing
Gib|bon, Ed|ward
(English historian)
gib|bon +s
Gib|bons, Or|lan|do
(English composer)
gib|bos|ity
gib|bous
Gibbs, Jo|siah
Wil|lard (US
chemist)
gibe (taunt: use jibe)
gibes
gibed

gibing
[☞ jibe; gybe]
gib|lets
Gibral|tar (headland
& strait,
E Mediterranean)
Gibral|tar|ian +s
Gib|ran, Kah|lil
(Lebanese-born US
writer & artist)
Gib|son (desert,
Australia)
Gib|son, Al|thea (US
tennis player)
Gib|son, Mel
Colum|cille Ger|ard
(US-born Australian
filmmaker)
Gib|son girl +s
GIC (guaranteed
investment
certificate)
GICs
gid|dap (= giddy-up)
gid|di|ly
gid|di|ness
giddy
gid|di|er
gid|di|est
gid|dies
gid|died
giddy|ing
giddy|ap (= giddy-
up)
giddy|ing adjective
giddy-up
Gide, André Paul
Guil|laume (French
writer)
Gid|eon +s (Bible;
memeber of Gideons
International)
Giel|gud, Sir (Ar|thur)
John (English actor
& director)
GIFT (gamete
intrafallopian
transfer)
gift +s +ed +ing
gift|ed adjective
gifted|ness
gift shop +s
gift|ware
gift wrap +s noun
gift-wrap verb
gift-wraps
gift-wrapped
gift-wrapping
Gifu (city, Japan)
gig
gigs
gigged
gig|ging
giga|byte +s

giga|flop +s
gi|gan|tesque
gi|gan|tic
gi|gan|tic|ally
gi|gan|tism
gig|gle
gig|gles
gig|gled
gig|gling
gig|gler +s
gig|gli|ness
gig|gly
gig|gli|er
gig|gli|est
GIGO (garbage in,
garbage out)
gig|olo +s
gi|got +s
gigue +s
Gijón (city, Spain)
Gila mon|ster +s
Gil|bert, Sir
Hum|phrey (English
explorer)
Gil|bert, Wil|liam
(English scientist)
Gil|bert, Sir Wil|liam
Schwenck (English
librettist)
Gil|bert and El|lice
Islands (former
British colony,
Pacific)
Gil|bert Islands
(islands, Kiribati)
gild (cover with gold;
for association use
guild)
gilds
gild|ed
gild|ing
gild|ed adjective
gild|er +s (one who
gilds)
[☞ guilder]
gild|ing noun
Gil|ead (in 'balm of
Gilead')
Gil|ga|mesh
(legendary Sumerian
king)
Gil|git (town, Pakistani
Kashmir)
gill +s +ed +ing (on
fish, mushrooms;
ravine, torrent; liquid
measure; young
woman)
gilled adjective
Gil|les|pie, John
Birks ('Dizzy') (US
musician)
gil|lie +s

gill net +s
gill|net|ter +s
gill net|ting
gilly|flower +s
Gil|man, Char|lotte
Anna Per|kins (US
writer)
gilt +s (gold-covered;
golden layer; sow)
[☞ guilt]
gilt-edged
gim|bal +s
gim|balled
gim|crack +s
gim|crack|ery
gim|let +s
gim|let eye +s
gimlet-eyed
gimme +s
gim|mick +s
gim|mickry
gim|micky
gimp +s +ed +ing
gimpy
gimp|i|er
gimp|i|est
gin (drink; Cards;
snare; in 'cotton gin')
gins
ginned
gin|ning
[☞ Jin, jinn, djinn]
gin-and-it
gin|ger +s +ed +ing
gin|ger ale +s
gin|ger beer +s
ginger|bread +s
gin|ger group +s
gin|ger|li|ness
gin|ger|ly
ginger|snap +s
gin|ger wine +s
gin|gery
ging|ham +s
gin|giva
gin|gi|vae
gin|gi|val
gin|gi|vitis
ging|ko (use ginkgo)
ging|kos or
ging|koes
gink +s
gink|go
gink|gos or
gink|goes
gin mill +s
gin|ner +s
gi|nor|mous
gin rummy
Gins|berg, Allen (US
poet)
gin|seng +s

Gior|gione (Italian
painter)
Giotto (di Bon|done)
(Italian painter)
Gio|van|ni de'
Med|ici (Pope Leo
X)
gippy tummy
gippy tum|mies
gipsy (use gypsy)
gip|sies
gir|affe +s
gir|an|dole +s
gira|sol +s
gira|sole +s (use
girasol)
Girau|doux,
(Hip|po|lyte) Jean
(French writer &
diplomat)
gird +s +ed +ing
gird|er +s
gir|dle
gir|dles
gir|dled
gird|ling
girl +s
girl Fri|day +s
girl|friend +s
Girl Guide +s
girl|hood
girl|ie +s
girl|ish
girl|ish|ly
girl|ish|ness
Girl Scout +s
girly (use girlie)
girl|ies
giro +s (credit
transfer)
[☞ gyro, guiro]
Gi|ronde (estuary,
France)
Gi|ron|din +s
Gi|ron|dist +s
girt adjective
girth +s +ed +ing
Gis|borne (city, New
Zealand)
Gis|card d'Estaing,
Va|léry (French
president)
Gish, Dor|othy (US
actress)
Gish, Lil|lian (US
actress)
Gis|sing, George
Rob|ert (English
novelist)
gist
git +s
gitch
Gitchi Mani|tou

gîte +s
Git|ksan
  plural Git|ksan or
  Git|ksans
git|tern +s
give
  gives
  gave
  given
  giv|ing
give-and-go
give-and-take
give away verb
  gives away
  gave away
  given away
  giv|ing away
give|away +s noun
give back verb
  gives back
  gave back
  given back
  giv|ing back
give|back +s noun
given +s
given|ness
giv|er +s
Giza (city, Egypt)
giz|mo +s
giz|zard +s
gla|bella
  gla|bel|lae
gla|bel|lar
gla|brous
glacé
Glace Bay (urban
  community, Nova
  Scotia)
gla|cial
gla|cial|ly
glaci|ated
glaci|ation +s
gla|cier +s (ice)
  [☞ glazier]
Gla|cier Bay
  Na|tion|al Park
  (park, US)
Gla|cier Na|tion|al
  Park (park, Canada)
glaci|o|logic|al
glaci|ol|o|gist +s
glaci|ol|ogy
gla|cis
  plural gla|cis
glad
  glad|der
  glad|dest
  glads
  glad|ded
  glad|ding
glad|den +s +ed +ing
glade +s
glad hand +s noun

glad-hand +s +ed
  +ing verb
glad-hander +s
gladi|ator +s
gladi|a|tor|ial
gladi|ola +s
  (= gladiolus)
gladi|olus
  gladi|oli or
  gladi|olus|es
glad|ly
glad|ness
glad rags
glad|some
Glad|stone, Wil|liam
  Ewart (British prime
  minister)
Glad|stone bag +s
Glago|lit|ic
glair (egg white;
  adhesive)
  [☞ glare]
glaire (egg white,
  adhesive: use glair)
  [☞ glare]
glair|eous
glairy (of egg white or
  adhesive)
  [☞ glary]
glaive +s
glam
glammy
glam|or +s (use
  glamour)
Gla|mor|gan (former
  county, Wales)
glam|or|iz|a|tion
glam|or|ize
  glam|or|iz|es
  glam|or|ized
  glam|or|iz|ing
glam|or|less (use
  glamourless)
glam|or|ous
glam|or|ous|ly
glam|our +s
glam|our|iz|a|tion
  (use glamorization)
glam|our|ize (use
  glamorize)
  glam|our|iz|es
  glam|our|ized
  glam|our|iz|ing
glam|our|less
glam|our|ous (use
  glamorous)
glam|our|ous|ly (use
  glamorously)
glamour|puss
  glamour|puss|es
glance
  glan|ces

glanced
  glan|cing
glan|cing|ly
gland +s
glan|dered
glan|der|ous
glan|ders
gland|ular
glans
  glan|des
glare (look; shine;
  smooth and glassy)
  glares
  glared
  glar|ing
  [☞ glair, glaire]
glare|less
glar|ing adjective
glar|ing|ly
glary (bright)
  [☞ glairy]
Glaser, Don|ald
  Ar|thur (US
  physicist)
Glas|gow (city,
  Scotland)
Glash|ow, Shel|don
  Lee (US physicist)
glas|nost
Glass, Phil|ip (US
  composer)
glass
  glass|es
  glassed
  glass|ing
glass-blower +s
glass-blowing
glassed adjective
glassed-in
glass fibre +s
glass|ful +s
glass|house +s
glass|ie +s noun (use
  glassy)
glass|i|er
glass|i|est
glass|i|ly
glass|ine
glass|i|ness
glass|less
glass|like
glass-maker +s
glass-making
glass|paper
glass|ware
glass wool
glass|works
glass|wort
glassy adjective &
  noun
  glass|i|er
  glass|i|est
  glass|less
  glass|ies

Glas|ton|bury (town,
  England)
Glas|we|gian +s
glatt ko|sher
Glau|ber's salt
Glau|ber's salts
  (= Glauber's salt)
glau|coma
glau|coma|tous
glau|cous
glau|cous gull +s
glaucous-winged
  gull +s
glaze
  glaz|es
  glazed
  glaz|ing
glaz|er (thing that
  glazes)
  [☞ glazier, Glaser]
glaz|ier +s (one who
  glazes windows)
  [☞ glazer, glacier,
  Glaser]
glaz|iery
glaz|ing noun
Glaz|unov,
  Alek|sandr
  Kon|stan|tin|ovich
  (Russian composer)
glazy
gleam +s +ed +ing
gleam|ing|ly
gleamy
glean +s +ed +ing
glean|er +s
glean|ings
glebe +s
glee
glee club +s
glee|ful
glee|ful|ly
glee|ful|ness
glee|some
gleet
Gleich|schal|tung
glen +s (valley)
  [☞ Glenn]
glen check +s
Glen|coe (massacre
  site, Scotland)
Glen|dower, Owen
  (Welsh chieftain)
Glen|eagles (valley &
  golf course,
  Scotland)
glen|garry
  glen|gar|ries
Glen More (= Great
  Glen, Scotland)
Glenn, John
  Her|schel, Jr. (US

astronaut &
politician)
glen|oid
glen plaid +s
Glen|rothes (town,
Scotland)
gley +s
glia +s
glial
glib
glib|ber
glib|best
glib|ly
glib|ness
glide
glides
glided
glid|ing
glider +s
glide|slope +s
glim +s
glim|mer +s +ed +ing
glim|mer|ing +s noun
& adjective
glim|mer|ing|ly
glimpse
glimps|es
glimpsed
glimps|ing
Glin|ka, Mikh|ail
Ivan|ovich (Russian
composer)
glint +s +ed +ing
gli|oma
gli|omas or
glio|mata
gli|osis
glis|sade
glis|sades
glis|sad|ed
glis|sad|ing
glis|sando
glis|sandi or
glis|san|dos
glis|sé +s
glis|ten +s +ed +ing
glis|ten|ing|ly
glis|ter +s +ed +ing
glitch
glitch|es
glit|ter +s +ed +ing
glit|ter|ati
glit|ter|ing|ly
Glit|ter|tind
(mountain, Norway)
glit|tery
glitz
glitz|i|ly
glitz|i|ness
glitzy
glitz|i|er
glitz|i|est
Gli|wice (city, Poland)

gloam|ing
gloat +s +ed +ing
gloat|er +s
gloat|ing|ly
glob +s
global
global|iz|a|tion
global|ize
global|iz|es
global|ized
global|iz|ing
global|ly
globe
globes
globed
glob|ing
globed adjective
globe|fish
plural globe|fish or
globe|fish|es
globe|flower +s
globe|like
globe|trot|ter +s
globe-trotting
glo|bi|ger|ina +s
glo|bin +s
glob|oid
glob|ose
globu|lar
globu|lar|ity
glob|ule +s
globu|lin +s
glock|en|spiel +s
glom
gloms
glommed
glom|ming
glom|eru|lar
glom|eru|lo|
          neph|ritis
glom|eru|lus
glom|eruli
gloom +s +ed +ing
(darkness; make or
be gloomy)
[☞ glume]
gloom and doom
(gloom-and-doom
when preceding a
noun)
gloom|i|ly
gloom|i|ness
gloomy
gloom|i|er
gloom|i|est
gloop
Gloos|cap (Aboriginal
Myth)
glop
glops
glopped
glop|ping
gloppy

Glor|ia +s (doxology)
glori|fi|ca|tion +s
glori|fied adjective
glori|fi|er +s
glori|fy
glori|fies
glori|fied
glori|fy|ing
glori|ole +s
glori|osa daisy
glori|osa dais|ies
glori|ous
glori|ous|ly
glori|ous|ness
Glori|ous Twelfth
glory
glor|ies
glor|ied
glory|ing
Glory Be +s
(doxology)
glory be interjection
glory-of-the-snow
+s
gloss
gloss|es
glossed
gloss|ing
glos|sal
glos|sar|ial
glos|sar|ist +s
glos|sary
glos|sar|ies
glos|sator +s
gloss|er +s
gloss|i|ly
gloss|i|ness
gloss|itis
glos|so|lalia
gloss|o|pharyn|geal
glossy
gloss|i|er
gloss|i|est
gloss|ies
glot|tal
glot|tic
glot|tis
glot|tises or
glot|tides
Glouces|ter (cities,
England & Canada)
Glouces|ter|shire
(county, England)
glove
gloves
gloved
glov|ing
glove|box
glove|boxes
glove com|part|ment
+s
gloved adjective
glove|less

glove|like
glov|er +s
glove side
glow +s +ed +ing
(shine; blush; radiate)
[☞ gloze]
glow|er +s +ed +ing
glower|ing|ly
glow|ing adjective
glow|ing|ly
glow-worm +s
glox|inia +s
gloze (extenuate,
excuse; comment;
fawn)
gloz|es
glozed
gloz|ing
gluca|gon
Gluck, Chris|toph
Willi|bald von
(German composer)
gluco|cor|ti|coid +s
glu|cose
gluco|side +s
gluco|sid|ic
glue
glues
glued
gluing or glue|ing
glue gun +s
glue-like
gluer +s
gluey
glu|i|er
glu|i|est
gluey|ness
glug
glugs
glugged
glug|ging
glum
glum|mer
glum|mest
glume +s (Botany)
[☞ gloom]
glum|ly
glum|ness
gluon +s
Glus|kap (Aboriginal
Myth: use Glooscap)
glut
gluts
glut|ted
glut|ting
gluta|mate +s
glu|tam|ic
gluta|mine
glutch
glutch|es
glutched
glutch|ing
glute +s

glu|teal
glu|ten
glu|teus
glu|tei
glu|teus max|imus
glu|tei max|imi
glu|tin|ous
glu|tin|ous|ly
glu|tin|ous|ness
glut|ton +s
glut|ton|ous
glut|ton|ous|ly
glut|tony
gly|cer|ide +s
gly|cer|ine
gly|cer|ol
gly|cine
glyco|gen +s
glyco|gen|ic
gly|col +s
gly|col|ic
glyco|lipid +s
gly|coly|sis
glyco|lytic
glyco|pro|tein +s
glyco|side +s
glyco|sid|ic
gly|cos|uria
gly|cos|uric
Glyn|dwr, Owen
 (= Glendower)
glyph +s
glyph|ic
gly|phos|ate
glyp|tic
glyp|to|dont +s
GM (general manager;
 George Medal)
GMs
G-man
 G-men
gnarled
gnarly
gnarl|i|er
gnarl|i|est
gnash
gnash|es
gnashed
gnash|ing
gnat +s
gnat|catch|er +s
gnaw +s +ed +ing
 (bite; corrode)
gnaw|ing adjective
gnaw|ing|ly
gneiss (Geology)
gneiss|es
 [☞ Neisse]
gneiss|ic
gneiss|oid
gneiss|ose
gnoc|chi

gnome +s (dwarf;
 financier; aphorism)
 [☞ Nome]
gnom|ic
gnom|ic|ally
gnom|ish
gno|mon +s (sundial;
 Geometry)
 [☞ nomen]
gno|mon|ic
gno|sis
Gnos|tic +s noun &
 adjective (of
 Gnosticism)
gnos|tic adjective (of
 esoteric knowledge)
Gnos|ti|cism
GNP (gross national
 product)
GNPs
gnu (antelope)
 plural gnus or gnu
 [☞ nu]
go
 goes
 went
 gone
 going
Goa (state, India)
goad +s +ed +ing
go-ahead noun &
 adjective
goal +s
goal|ball
goal|ie +s
goal|ie pad +s
goal|keep|er +s
goal|keep|ing
goal kick +s
goal-kicker +s
goal-kicking
goal|less
goal line +s
goal|mouth +s
goal pad +s
goal|post +s
goals-against
 aver|age
goal scor|er +s
goal-scoring
goal|tend|er +s
goal|tend|ing
Goan +s
Goa|nese
go|an|na +s
Goat (constellation;
 zodiac sign)
goat +s
goat-antelope +s
goa|tee +s (beard)
 [☞ goaty]
goa|teed
goat|herd +s

goat|ish
goat|like
goat's beard +s
goat|skin +s
goat|suck|er +s
goaty (like a goat)
goat|i|er
goat|i|est
 [☞ goatee]
gob
 gobs
 gobbed
 gob|bing
Göb|bels, Jo|seph
 (= Goebbels,
 German Nazi
 propagandist)
gob|bet +s
gob|ble
 gob|bles
 gob|bled
 gob|bling
gobble|de|gook
gobble|dy|gook (use
 gobbledegook)
gob|bler +s
Go|be|lin +s
 (tapestry)
 [☞ goblin]
go-between +s
Gobi (desert, Asia)
gob|let +s
gob|lin +s (dwarf-like
 creature)
 [☞ Gobelin]
gobo
 gobos or go|boes
gob|smacked
gob|smack|ing
gob|smack|ing|ly
gob|stop|per +s
goby (fish)
go|bies
 [☞ Gobi]
go-by (snub, slight)
go-cart +s
 (unpowered cart; for
 mini race car use go-
 kart)
God (supreme being)
god +s (deity; idol)
 [☞ gaud]
Go|dard, Jean-Luc
 (French filmmaker)
 [☞ Goddard]
Go|da|vari (river,
 India)
god|awful
God|bout, Jacques
 (Cdn writer &
 filmmaker)
god|child
 god|chil|dren

god|dam
 (= goddamn)
god|damm|it
god|damn
god|damned
god|damn|it
 (= goddammit)
God|dard, Rob|ert
 Hutch|ings (US
 physicist)
 [☞ Godard]
god|daugh|ter +s
god|dess
god|dess|es
Gode|froy de
 Bouil|lon (crusader)
Gödel, Kurt (Austrian-
 born US
 mathematician)
Gode|rich (town,
 Canada)
go|det +s
go-devil +s
god|father +s
God-fearing
God-forsak|en
 (= godforsaken)
god|for|saken
God-given
God|havn (town,
 Greenland)
god|head
god|hood
Go|diva, Lady
 (English
 noblewoman)
god|less
god|less|ness
god|like
god|li|ness
godly
god|mother +s
go|down +s
god|parent +s
God's acre +s
god|send +s
god|ship
Gods Lake (lake,
 Canada)
god|son +s
God|speed
Godt|håb (former
 name for Nuuk,
 Greenland)
Godu|nov, Boris
 Fyodor|ovich
 (Russian czar)
God|win, Wil|liam
 (English writer)
Godwin-Austen
 (= K2, mountain in
 Asia)
god|wit +s

Goeb|bels, (Paul)
Jo|seph (German
Nazi propagandist)
goer +s
Goer|ing, Her|mann
Wil|helm (= Göring)
goes
goest
goeth
Goethe, Jo|hann
Wolf|gang von
(German writer)
Goeth|ean +s
Goeth|ian +s (use
Goethean)
go|fer +s (person who
runs errands)
[☞ goffer, gopher]
gof|fer +s +ed +ing
(crimp; crimping
iron)
[☞ gofer, gopher]
Gog and Magog
(Bible)
go-getter +s
go-getting
gog|gle
gog|gles
gog|gled
gog|gling
goggle|box
goggle|boxes
goggle-eyed
gog|gly
Gogh, Vin|cent
Wil|lem Van (Dutch
painter)
go-go (dancer,
nightclub;
unrestrained;
speculative)
[☞ à gogo]
Gogol, Niko|lai
Vasili|evich
(Ukrainian-born
Russian writer)
Goi|ânia (city, Brazil)
Goiás (state, Brazil)
Goi|del +s
Goi|del|ic
go|ing +s noun
going away (going-
away when preceding
a noun)
going-over
goings-over
goings-on
goitre
goitred
goi|trous
go-kart +s (mini race
car)
[☞ go-cart]

Golan Heights (range
of hills, Israel–Syria
border)
Gol|con|da +s
gold +s
gold-beater +s
gold brick +s
Gold Coast (former
name for Ghana,
Africa; region,
Australia)
gold|crest +s
gold dig|ger +s
gold|en
Gold|en De|li|cious
plural Gold|en
De|li|cious
golden|eye +s
Gold|en Fleece (Greek
Myth)
Gold|en Gate
(channel, US)
Gold|en Hind (Francis
Drake's ship)
Gold|en Hinde
(mountain, Canada)
Gold|en Horde
Gold|en Horn (inlet,
Istanbul)
Gold|en Horse|shoe
(region, Canada)
gold|en|ly
golden|ness
golden|rod +s
Gold|en State
(California)
gold|eye
plural gold|eye or
gold|eyes
gold|field +s
gold-filled
gold|finch
gold|finch|es
gold|fish
plural gold|fish
Gold Glove +s
(Baseball)
Gold Glov|er +s
Gol|ding, Sir Wil|liam
Ger|ald (English
novelist)
gold leaf
Gold|man, Emma
(Lithuanian-born US
political activist)
Gold|mark, Peter
Carl (Hungarian-
born US inventor)
gold med|al +s (gold-
medal when
preceding a noun)
gold med|al|list +s
gold mine +s

gold min|er +s
gold min|ing
Gol|doni, Carlo
(Italian dramatist)
gold pan|ner +s
gold pan|ning
gold plate noun
gold-plate verb
gold-plates
gold-plated
gold-plating
gold-plated adjective
gold rush
gold rush|es
Gold|schmidt,
Vic|tor Mor|itz
(Swiss-born
Norwegian chemist)
gold seek|er +s
gold seek|ing
Gold|smith, Oli|ver
(Irish writer)
gold|smith +s
Gold Stick
gold thread +s
(thread)
gold|thread +s (plant)
gold-tone
Gold|wyn, Sam|uel
(Polish-born US
filmmaker)
go|lem +s
golf +s +ed +ing
golf bag +s
golf ball +s
golf cart +s
golf club +s
golf course +s
golf|er +s
golf shirt +s
Golgi, Cam|illo
(Italian histologist)
Golgi ap|par|at|us
plural Golgi
ap|par|at|us
Golgi body
Golgi bod|ies
Gol|go|tha
(Crucifixion site)
Gol|iath (Bible; beetle;
frog)
gol|li|wog +s
golly
gom|been
gom|been|ism
Gom|or|rah (Bible)
Gom|pers, Sam|uel
(English-born US
labour leader)
go|nad +s
go|nad|al
gonad|o|troph|ic (use
gonadotropic)

gonad|o|troph|in +s
(use gonadotropin)
gonad|o|trop|ic
gonad|o|trop|in +s
Gon|cha|rov, Ivan
(Russian novelist)
Gon|court, Ed|mond
de (French writer)
Gon|court, Jules de
(French writer)
gon|do|la +s
gon|do|lier +s
Gond|wana (ancient
continent)
Gond|wana|land
(= Gondwana)
gone
gon|er +s
gon|fa|lon +s
gon|fa|lon|ier +s
gong +s +ed +ing
goni|om|eter +s
gonio|met|ric
gonio|met|ric|al
goni|om|etry
gonna
gono|coc|cal
gono|coc|cus
gono|cocci
gon|or|rhea
gon|or|rhe|al
Gon|zaga, Aloy|sius
(saint)
gonzo
goo +s
goo|ber +s
goo|ber pea +s
good
• adjective & adverb
bet|ter
best
• noun
goods
Good Book (Bible)
good|bye +s
good cop/bad cop
good-for-nothing +s
Good Fri|day
good-hearted
Good Hope (cape,
South Africa)
good hu|mour
good-humoured
good-humoured|ly
good|ie +s (in 'goodie
bag'; for treat,
virtuous person or
interjection use
goody)
good|ie bag +s
good|ish
good|li|ness
good-looker +s

good-looking
good|ly
good|li|er
good|li|est
Good|man,
Ben|ja|min David
('Benny') (US
musician)
good-natured
good-natured|ly
good|ness
good night
goods
goods and ser|vi|ces
tax
good-tempered
good-tempered|ly
good-time *adjective*
good-timer +s
good|wife
good|wives
good|will
goody (treat; virtuous
person; interjection)
good|ies
[☞ goodie bag]
Good|year, Charles
(US inventor)
goody-goody
goody-goodies
goody two-shoes
plural goody two-
shoes
gooey
goo|i|er
goo|i|est
gooey|ness
goof +s +ed +ing
goof|ball +s
goofed *adjective*
goof|i|ly
goof|i|ness
goof-proof +s +ed
+ing
goof up *verb*
goofs up
goofed up
goof|ing up
goof-up +s *noun*
goofy
goof|i|er
goof|i|est
googlie-eyed
googly-eyed
(= googlie-eyed)
goo|gol +s
goo|gol|plex
goo|gol|plex|es
goo-goo
goo|i|er
goo|i|est

gook +s
• *Offensive* when
used of people.
goo|lie +s
gooly (*use* goolie)
goo|lies
goom|bah +s
goon +s
goon|ery
goony
goop
goop|i|ness
goopy
goop|i|er
goop|i|est
goose
• (bird)
plural geese
• (tailor's iron)
plural goos|es
• *verb*
goos|es
goosed
goos|ing
goose|berry
goose|ber|ries
goose|bump +s
goose egg +s
goose|flesh
goose|foot
goose|foots
goose grass
goose grass|es
goose|neck +s
goose pim|ple +s
goose step +s *noun*
goose-step *verb*
goose-steps
goose-stepped
goose-stepping
goose|tongue
go|pher +s (animal;
Computing)
[☞ gofer, goffer]
go|pher ball +s
Gor|ak|pur (city,
India)
gor|al +s
Gor|ba|chev, Mikh|ail
Serge|evich (Soviet
president)
gor|blimey
Gor|dian knot +s
Gor|di|mer, Na|dine
(South African
writer)
Gor|dium (ancient
city, Asia Minor)
Gor|don, Charles
George (British
general)

Gor|don, Charles
Wil|liam (Cdn
novelist)
Gor|don, Wal|ter
Lock|hart (Cdn
politician)
Gor|don riots
Gor|don set|ter +s
Gordy, Berry Jr. (US
record producer)
gore
gores
gored
gor|ing
Gör|eme (valley,
Turkey)
Gore-Tex *proprietary*
gorge
gor|ges
gorged
gor|ging
gor|geous
gor|geous|ly
gor|geous|ness
gor|ger +s
gor|get +s
Gor|gon +s (*Greek
Myth*)
gor|gon +s
(frightening or
repulsive person)
Gor|gon|ian (*Greek
Myth*)
gor|gon|ian +s (coral)
Gor|gon|zola +s
(village, Italy;
cheese)
gor|i|er
gor|i|est
gor|illa +s (ape;
agressive man)
[☞ guerrilla]
gor|i|ly
gor|i|ness
Gör|ing, Her|mann
Wil|helm (German
Nazi leader)
Gorky (*former name
for* Nizhni
Novgorod, Russia)
Gorky, Ar|shile
(Turkish-born
painter)
Gorky, Maxim
(Russian writer)
Gor|lov|ka (city,
Ukraine)
gorm|less
gorm|less|ly
gorm|less|ness
Gorno-Altaisk (city,
Russia)

go round *verb*
goes round
went round
gone round
going round
go-round +s *noun*
gorp
gorse +s
Gor|sedd
gorsy
gory
gor|i|er
gor|i|est
gosh
gos|hawk +s
gos|ling +s
go-slow +s *noun*
Gos|pel +s (*New
Testament*)
gos|pel +s (teaching
of Christ; truth;
reliable principle;
Music)
gos|pel|ler +s
Gos|pel side
gos|sa|mer +s
gos|sa|mery
gos|sip +s +ed +ing
gos|sip|er +s
gossip|monger +s
gos|sipy
gos|soon +s
got *conjugated form of*
get
[☞ ghat, Ghats]
gotch (underwear)
[☞ gauch]
gotcha +s
gotch|ies
Goth +s (Germanic
tribe)
goth (*Music*;
subculture & its
adherents)
Gotha (city, Germany)
[☞ Goethe]
Goth|am (village,
England; New York)
Goth|en|burg (port,
Sweden)
Goth|ic
Goth|ic|ally
Gothi|cism
Gothi|cize
Gothi|ciz|es
Gothi|cized
Gothi|ciz|ing
Got|land (island,
Sweden)
go-to guy +s
go-to-meeting
gotta
got|ten

Göt|ter|däm|mer|ung
Göt|tingen (town,
  Germany)
gou|ache +s (painting
  method)
  [☞ gauche]
Gouda +s (town, the
  Netherlands; cheese)
gouge (groove; chisel;
  swindle)
gou|ges
gouged
gou|ging
Gouin (reservoir,
  Canada)
Gouin, Sir Jean-
  Lomer (Cdn
  politician)
gou|lash
gou|lash|es
Gould, Glenn
  Her|bert (Cdn
  pianist)
Gould, Ste|phen Jay
  (US paleontologist)
Gou|nod, Charles
  Fran|çois (French
  composer)
gou|rami +s
gourd +s (fruit)
gourde +s (Haitian
  currency)
gourd|ful +s
gour|mand +s
gour|mand|ise
  (gluttony)
  [☞ gourmandize]
gour|mand|ism
gour|mand|ize (eat
  voraciously)
gour|mand|iz|es
gour|mand|ized
gour|mand|iz|ing
gour|mand|izer +s
gour|met +s
Gour|mont, Rémy de
  (French writer)
gout +s
goût de ter|roir
gout|i|ness
gout|weed
gouty
Gou|zen|ko, Igor
  Ser|gei|evich
  (Russian defector)
gov|ern +s +ed +ing
gov|ern|abil|ity
gov|ern|able
gov|ern|ance
gov|ern|ess
gov|ern|ess|es
gov|ern|essy
gov|ern|ment +s

gov|ern|ment|al
gov|ern|ment|al|ly
Gov|ern|ment House
gov|ernment-in-
  exile
gov|ernments-in-
  exile
gov|ern|or +s
gov|ern|or|ate +s
gov|ern|or gen|er|al
gov|ern|ors
gen|er|al
governor-general-in-
  council
gov|ernors-general-
  in-council
Gov|ernor Gen|eral's
  Award +s
governor-in-chief
gov|ernors-in-chief
governor-in-council
gov|ernors-in-
  council
gov|ern|or|ship +s
gowan +s
Gower, John (English
  poet)
gowk +s
gown +s +ed +ing
gowned adjective
goy
  goyim or goys
goy|ish
goy|ishe (use goyish)
GP (general
  practitioner)
GPs
GPA (grade point
  average)
GPAs
Graaf|ian
grab
  grabs
  grabbed
  grab|bing
grab bag +s
grab bar +s
grab|ber +s
grab|ble
  grab|bles
  grab|bled
  grab|bling
grabby
gra|ben
  plural gra|ben or
  gra|bens
grab rail +s
Grac|chi (Roman
  tribunes)
Grac|chus, Gaius
  Sem|pro|nius
  (Roman tribune)

Grac|chus, Ti|ber|ius
  Sem|pro|nius
  (Roman tribune)
Grace +s (Greek Myth;
  in 'Your Grace' etc.)
grace (in general use)
  graces
  graced
  gra|cing
grace|ful
grace|ful|ly
grace|ful|ness
grace|less
grace|less|ly
grace|less|ness
grace note +s
Gra|cias a Dios (cape,
  Central America)
gra|cile
gra|cil|ity
gra|cious
gra|cious|ly
gra|cious|ness
grackle +s
grad +s
grad|ate
  grad|ates
  grad|at|ed
  grad|at|ing
grada|tion +s
grada|tion|al
grada|tion|al|ly
grade
  grades
  graded
  grad|ing
grade point aver|age
  +s
grad|er +s
grade school +s
gra|di|ent +s
gra|din +s (use
  gradine)
gra|dine +s
grad|ual +s
grad|ual|ism
grad|ual|ist +s
grad|ual|is|tic
grad|ual|ly
grad|ual|ness
gradu|and +s
gradu|ate
  gradu|ates
  gradu|at|ed
  gradu|at|ing
gradu|at|ed adjective
gradu|a|tion +s
Grae|cism +s
Grae|cize
  Grae|ciz|es
  Grae|cized
  Grae|ciz|ing

Graf, Stef|fi (German
  tennis player)
graf|fiti
• singular noun & plural
  of graffito
• verb
  graf|fitis
  graf|fi|tied
  graf|fi|ting
graf|fi|tist +s
graf|fito
graf|fiti
graft +s +ed +ing
graft|er +s
Gra|ham (island,
  Canada)
  [☞ Grahame, Gram
  stain]
Gra|ham, Mar|tha
  (US dance teacher)
Gra|ham, Thom|as
  (Scottish chemist)
Gra|ham, Wil|liam
  Frank|lin ('Billy')
  (US preacher)
gra|ham (type of
  flour, cracker or
  wafer)
  [☞ gram]
Gra|hame, Ken|neth
  (Scottish writer)
  [☞ Graham, Gram
  stain]
Gra|ham Land (in
  Antarctica)
Grail
grain +s +ed +ing
grained adjective
grain|er +s
Grain|ger, (George)
  Percy Ald|ridge
  (Australian-born
  composer)
grain|i|ness
grain|less
grain side
grainy
  grain|i|er
  grain|i|est
gram +s (unit of mass;
  pulse plant or seed)
  [☞ graham]
grama +s (grass)
  [☞ gramma]
gram-atom +s
gram-equiva|lent +s
gram|in|aceous
gram|in|eous
gram|in|iv|or|ous
gram|ma +s
  (grandma)
  [☞ grama]
gram|mar +s

gram|mar|ian +s
gram|mar|less
gram|mat|ic|al
gram|mat|ic|al|ity
gram|mat|ic|al|ly
gram|mat|ic|al|ness
gram-molecule +s
Gram|my +s
  proprietary
Gram-negative
gram|o|phone +s
gram|o|phon|ic
gram|pa +s
Gram|pian +s
  (mountains, Scotland
  & Australia)
Gram-positive
gramps
gram|pus
  gram|pus|es
grampy
Gram|sci, An|tonio
  (Italian political
  theorist)
Gram's stain (use
  Gram stain)
Gram stain
gran +s
Gran|ada (cities,
  Spain & Nicaragua)
  [☞ Grenada]
grana|dilla +s (use
  grenadilla)
Gran|ados, En|ri|que
  (Spanish composer)
gran|ary
  gran|aries
Gran|by (city, Canada)
Gran Can|aria
  (Canary Island)
Gran Chaco (plain,
  S America)
grand
• adjective
  grand|er
  grand|est
• noun (piano)
  plural grands
• noun (thousand
  dollars)
  plural grand
gran|dad +s (use
  granddad)
gran|dad|dy (use
  granddaddy)
  gran|dad|dies
gran|dam +s
gran|dame +s (use
  grandam)
grand-aunt +s
Grand Banks
  (submarine plateau
  off Newfoundland)

Grand Centre (town,
  Canada)
grand|child
  grand|chil|dren
grand|dad +s
grand|daddy
  grand|dad|dies
grand|daugh|ter +s
Grande Comore
  (island off
  Madagascar)
grande dame
  grandes dames
gran|dee +s
Grande Prai|rie (city,
  Canada)
grand|eur
Grand Falls (town,
  Canada)
Grand Falls-Windsor
  (town, Canada)
grand|father +s +ed
  +ing
grand|father|ly
grand fi|nale
Grand Gui|gnol +s
gran|di|flora
grand|ilo|quence
grand|ilo|quent
grand|ilo|quent|ly
gran|di|ose
gran|di|ose|ly
gran|di|os|ity
grand jeté
  grands jetés
grand|kid +s
grand|ly
grand|ma +s
grand mal
grand|mama +s
Grand|ma Moses
  (Anna Mary
  Robertson Moses,
  US painter)
Grand Manan (island,
  Canada)
Grand Mar|nier +s
  proprietary
Grand Mas|ter +s (of
  knighthood,
  Freemasons etc.)
  [☞ grandmaster]
grand|master +s
  (Chess)
  [☞ Grand Master]
Grand-Mère (town,
  Canada)
Grand'Mère
  (= Grand-Mère,
  Canada)
grand|mother +s
grand|mother|ly
grand|nephew +s

grand|ness
grand|niece +s
grand|pa +s
grand|papa +s
grand|pappy
  grand|pap|pies
grand|par|ent +s
Grand Pré (historic
  site, Canada)
Grand Prix
  Grands Prix
grand sei|gneur
  grands sei|gneurs
grand|sire +s
grand slam +s
grand|son +s
grand|stand +s +ed
  +ing
grand|stand|er +s
grand-uncle +s
grange +s
gran|ita +s
gran|ite +s
granite|ware
gran|it|ic
gran|it|oid +s
grani|vore +s
gran|iv|or|ous
gran|nie +s (use
  granny)
granny
  gran|nies
Granny Smith +s
grano|dior|ite +s
gran|ola +s
Grant, Cary (English-
  born US actor)
Grant, Cuth|bert (Cdn
  Metis leader)
Grant, George
  Par|kin (Cdn social
  philosopher)
Grant, Ulys|ses
  Simp|son (US
  general & president)
grant +s +ed +ing
grant|able
grant|ed adjective
gran|tee +s
grant|er +s (in general
  use; for legal senses
  use grantor)
Granth (= Adi
  Granth)
Granth Sahib (= Adi
  Granth)
grant-in-aid
  grants-in-aid
grant|or +s (in legal
  use; for general senses
  use granter)
granu|lar
granu|lar|ity

granu|lar|ly
granu|late
  granu|lates
  granu|lat|ed
  granu|lat|ing
granu|la|tion +s
granu|la|tor +s
gran|ule +s
granu|lo|cyte +s
granu|lo|cyt|ic
granu|loma
  plural granu|loma or
  granu|lo|mata
granu|lo|ma|tous
Gran|ville (former
  name for Vancouver)
Granville-Barker,
  Har|ley (English
  drama critic)
grape +s
grape fern +s
grape|fruit
  plural grape|fruit or
  grape|fruits
grape|shot
grape sugar
grape|vine +s
grapey
graph +s +ed +ing
  [☞ Graf]
graph|eme +s
graph|em|ic
graph|em|ic|ally
graph|ic +s
graph|ic|al
graph|ic|al|ly
graphic|ness
graph|ics
graph|ite +s
graph|itic
graph|it|ize
  graph|it|iz|es
  graph|it|ized
  graph|it|iz|ing
graph|o|logic|al
graph|ol|o|gist +s
graph|ol|ogy
gra|ple +s (anchor)
  [☞ grapple]
grap|nel +s
grap|pa +s
Grap|pelli, Ste|phane
  (French musician)
grap|ple (wrestle,
  manage, grasp;
  grapnel)
grap|ples
grap|pled
grap|pling
  [☞ graple]
grap|pler +s
grap|to|lite +s
grapy (use grapey)

Gras|mere (village, England)
grasp +s +ed +ing
grasp|able
grasp|er +s
grasp|ing adjective
grasp|ing|ly
grasp|ing|ness
Grass, Gün|ter Wil|helm (German writer)
[☞ Grasse]
grass
  grass|es
  grassed
  grass|ing
grass|cloth +s
Grasse (town, France)
[☞ Grass]
grass|hop|per +s
grass|i|er
grass|i|est
grass|i|ness
grass|land +s
grass|less
grass|like
grass of Par|nas|sus
grass|roots
grass tree +s
grassy
  grass|i|er
  grass|i|est
grate (rub, scrape, shred; sound harshly; irritate; metal framework)
  grates
  grat|ed
  grat|ing
[☞ great]
grate|ful
grate|ful|ly
grate|ful|ness
grat|er +s (shredder)
[☞ greater]
Gra|tian (Roman emperor)
grati|fi|ca|tion +s
grati|fi|er +s
grat|ify
  grati|fies
  grati|fied
  grati|fy|ing
grati|fy|ing adjective
grati|fy|ing|ly
gra|tin +s
[☞ Grattan]
gra|ti|née +s
gra|ti|néed
grat|ing +s noun & adjective
grat|ing|ly
grat|is

grati|tude
Grat|tan, Henry (Irish statesman)
[☞ gratin]
gra|tuit|ous
gra|tuit|ous|ly
gra|tuit|ous|ness
gra|tu|ity
  gra|tuit|ies
grav|ad|lax (= gravlax)
gra|va|men
  gra|va|mina
grave
• noun, adjective & adverb
  graves
  grav|er
  grav|est
• verb (fix; engrave)
  graves
  graved
  grav|en or graved
  grav|ing
• verb (clean a ship's bottom)
  graves
  graved
  grav|ing
grave|dig|ger +s
grav|el
  grav|els
  grav|elled
  grav|el|ling
grav|el|ly (of gravel)
grave|ly (solemnly)
grave mark|er +s
grav|en
grave|ness
Graven|hurst (town, Canada)
Graven|stein +s
grav|er +s
Graves, Rob|ert Ranke (English writer)
Graves (wine)
  plural Graves
Graves' dis|ease
grave|side +s
grave|site +s
grave|stone +s
grave|yard +s
grav|id
grav|im|eter +s
gravi|met|ric
grav|im|etry
grav|ing dock +s
grav|itas
gravi|tate
  gravi|tates
  gravi|tat|ed
  gravi|tat|ing

gravi|ta|tion
gravi|ta|tion|al
gravi|ta|tion|al|ly
gravi|ton +s
grav|ity
  grav|ities
gravity-fed adjective
grav|ity feed noun
grav|lax
Grav|ol proprietary
  plural Grav|ol
grav|ure +s
gravy
  gra|vies
gravy boat +s
gravy train +s
Gray (surname)
[☞ Grey]
Gray, Asa (US botanist)
Gray, James Henry (Cdn historian)
Gray, John Ham|il|ton (premier of PEI)
Gray, John Ham|il|ton (premier of New Brunswick)
Gray, Thom|as (English poet)
gray +s +ed +ing +er +est (Physics; for colour use grey)
gray|beard +s (use greybeard)
gray|ling
  plural gray|ling or gray|lings
gray|wacke +s (use greywacke)
Graz (city, Austria)
graze
  graz|es
  grazed
  graz|ing
graz|er +s
gra|zier +s
gra|ziery
  gra|zier|ies
graz|ing +s noun
GRE (Graduate Record Examination)
  GREs
grease (lubricant)
  greas|es
  greased
  greas|ing
[☞ Gris]
grease|ball +s
grease gun +s
grease|less
grease mon|key +s
grease|paint +s

grease|proof
greas|er +s
grease trail +s
grease|wood +s
greas|i|ly
greas|i|ness
greasy
  greas|i|er
  greas|i|est
great +er +est +s (big, important, etc.)
[☞ grate]
great-aunt +s
Great Bear (Big Dipper; lake, Canada)
great|coat +s
Great Dane +s
Great|er (of a city)
great|er comparative of great
[☞ grater]
Great Glen (Scottish valley)
great-grand|child
  great-grand|chil|dren
great-grand|daugh|ter +s
great-grand|fath|er +s
great-grand|moth|er +s
great-grand|par|ent +s
great-grand|son +s
Great Grims|by (town, England)
great-hearted
great-hearted|ness
Great Lakes–St. Law|rence Low|lands (region, Canada)
great|ly
great-nephew +s
great|ness
great-niece +s
Great Rift Val|ley (in Africa)
great room +s
great-uncle +s
Great Zim|babwe
greave +s (shin armour)
[☞ grieve]
grebe +s
Gre|cian
Gre|cism +s (use Graecism)
Gre|cize (use Graecize)

Greciz|es
Gre|cized
Greciz|ing
Greco, El (Spanish painter)
Greco-Roman
Greece (country, Europe)
[☞ Gris, grease]
greed
greed|i|ly
greed|i|ness
greedy
greed|i|er
greed|i|est
Greek +s
Greek|ness
Gree|ley, Hor|ace (US journalist)
green +er +est +s +ed +ing
[☞ Greene]
Green|away, Cath|er|ine ('Kate') (English artist)
Green|away, Peter (English filmmaker)
green|back +s
green bean +s
green|belt +s
green|briar (use greenbrier)
green|brier
green card +s
green|chain +s
Greene, (Henry) Gra|ham (English novelist)
Greene, Lorne Hyman (Cdn actor)
Greene, Nancy (Cdn skier)
Greene, Rob|ert (English writer)
green|ery
green-eyed
green fee +s
green feed
green|field
Green|field Park (city, Canada)
green|finch
green|finch|es
green-fingered
green|fly
green|flies
green|gage +s
green|grocer +s
green|grocery
green|grocer|ies
green|heart +s
green|horn +s
green|house +s

green|ie +s (environmentalist)
[☞ greeny]
green|i|er
green|i|est
Green|ing +s (apple)
green|ing +s noun
green|ish
green|keep|er +s
Green|land (island off N America)
Green|land|er +s
green light +s noun
green-light +s +ed +ing verb
green|ling +s
green|ly
green|mail
green|mail|er +s
green|ness
Green|ock (town, Scotland)
Green Paper +s (report)
Green|peace
green room +s
green|sand
greens fee +s (= green fee)
greens|keep|er +s
green-stick frac|ture +s
green|stone +s
green|sward +s
green tea +s
green thumb +s
green-thumbed
green-thumber +s
green|wash
green|wash|es
green|washed
green|wash|ing
green|way +s
green|weed +s
Green|wich Mean Time
Green|wich Vil|lage (community, New York City)
green-winged teal +s
green|wood +s
greeny (greenish)
green|i|er
green|i|est
[☞ greenie]
Greer, Ger|maine (Australian feminist)
greet +s +ed +ing
greet|er +s
greet|ing +s noun
gre|gari|ous
gre|gari|ous|ly

gre|gari|ous|ness
Gre|gor|ian
Greg|ory (saints, popes)
Greg|ory, Lady Isa|bel|la Au|gus|ta (Irish dramatist)
Greg|ory of Nazi|an|zus (saint)
Greg|ory of Nyssa (saint)
Greg|ory of Tours (saint)
Greg|ory the Great (saint)
grem|lin +s
gremo|lata
Gre|nache
Gren|ada (country, W Indies)
[☞ Granada]
gren|ade +s
Gren|adi|an +s
grena|dier +s
grena|dilla +s
Grena|dine +s (islands, W Indies)
grena|dine +s
Gren|del
Gren|fell, Sir Wil|fred Thoma|son (Cdn medical missionary)
Gre|noble (city, France)
Gren|ville, George (British prime minister)
Gren|ville, Sir Rich|ard (English naval officer)
Gresh|am, Sir Thom|as (English financier)
Gresham's law
Gret|na Green (village, Scotland)
Gretz|ky, Wayne (Cdn hockey player)
Greuze, Jean-Baptiste (French painter)
grew past tense of grow
[☞ Groulx]
Grey (point, Canada; surname)
[☞ Gray]
Grey, Al|bert Henry George, 4th Earl (governor general of Canada)

Grey, Charles, 2nd Earl (English prime minister)
Grey, Lady Jane (queen of England)
Grey, Zane (US writer)
grey +er +est +s +ed +ing (colour)
[☞ gray]
grey|beard +s
Grey Cup +s
Grey Friar +s
grey goose
grey geese
grey|hound +s
grey|ish
grey jay +s
grey|lag +s
grey|ly
grey mul|let +s
grey|ness
Grey Nun +s
Grey Owl (English-born Cdn conservationist)
grey par|tridge +s
grey-scale +s
grey seal +s
grey squir|rel +s
grey|stone +s
grey|wacke +s
grey whale +s
grey wolf
grey wolves
grid +s
grid|ded
grid|dle
grid|dles
grid|dled
grid|dling
grid|dle cake +s
grid|iron +s
grid|lock +s
grid|locked
grid road +s
grief +s
Grieg, Ed|vard Hage|rup (Norwegian composer)
Grier|son, John (creator of the NFB)
griev|ance +s
grieve (suffer or cause grief)
grieves
grieved
griev|ing
[☞ greave]
griev|er +s
griev|ous
griev|ous|ly

griev|ous|ness
grif|fin +s (mythical creature)
[☞ griffon]
Grif|fith, Ar|thur (Irish president)
Grif|fith, David Wark (US filmmaker)
grif|fon +s (dog; vulture)
[☞ griffin]
grift +s +ed +ing
grifter +s
grig +s
grill +s +ed +ing (cooking apparatus; cook on a grill; interrogate; *for* latticed screen *or* metal grid on a car *use* grille)
gril|lage +s
grille +s (latticed screen; metal grid on a car)
[☞ grill]
grilled *adjective*
grill|er +s
grill|ing +s *noun*
grill room +s
grilse
  plural grilse
grim (severe; dreadful)
grim|mer
grim|mest
[☞ Grimm]
grim|ace
grim|aces
grim|aced
grim|acing
grim|acer +s
Gri|maldi (royal family of Monaco)
Gri|maldi, Fran|cesco Maria (Italian physicist & astronomer)
gri|mal|kin +s
grime
  grimes
  grimed
  grim|ing
grim|i|er
grim|i|est
grim|i|ly
grim|i|ness
grim|ly
Grimm, Jacob Lud|wig Carl (German folklorist)
Grimm, Wil|helm Carl (German folklorist)
grim|ness

Grim Reap|er
Grims|by (port, England; town, Canada)
grimy
  grim|i|er
  grim|i|est
grin
  grins
  grinned
  grin|ning
grinch
  grinch|es
grind
  grinds
  ground
  grind|ing
grind|er +s
grind|ing|ly
grind|stone +s
gringo +s
Grin|nell (peninsula, Canada)
grin|ner +s
grin|ning|ly
griot +s
grip (grasp, seize; control; stagehand; travelling bag)
  grips
  gripped
  grip|ping
[☞ grippe]
gripe (complain; *Nautical*)
  gripes
  griped
  grip|ing
[☞ grippe]
grip|er +s
gripe water
grip|ing|ly
grippe (flu)
[☞ gripe]
grip|per +s
grip|ping|ly
grip|py
  grip|pi|er
  grip|pi|est
Gris, Juan (Spanish painter)
gris|aille +s
Grise Fiord (fjord & hamlet, Canada)
griseo|ful|vin
gris|li|ness
gris|ly (ghastly; repulsive)
  gris|li|er
  gris|li|est
[☞ grizzly, gristly]
grist

gris|tle (cartilage)
[☞ grizzle]
grist|ly (containing gristle)
[☞ grisly, grizzly]
grist|mill +s
grist|mill|er +s
Grit +s (Liberal Party member or supporter)
grit (sand; coarseness; pluck; clench)
  grits
  gritted
  grit|ting
grits (grain, oats)
grit|ter +s
grit|ti|ly
grit|ti|ness
grit|ty
  grit|ti|er
  grit|ti|est
griz|zle (cry, complain; grey hair)
  griz|zles
  griz|zled
  griz|zling
[☞ gristle]
griz|zled *adjective*
griz|zler +s
griz|zly (bear; having grey hair; whining)
  griz|zlies
  griz|zli|er
  griz|zli|est
[☞ grisly, gristly]
groan +s +ed +ing
groan|er +s
groan|ing|ly
groat +s (coin; small sum)
[☞ Grote]
groats (grain)
gro|cer +s
gro|cery
  gro|cer|ies
gro|ceter|ia +s
Grod|no (= Hrodna, Belarus)
grog +s
grog|gi|ly
grog|gi|ness
grog|gy
  grog|gi|er
  grog|gi|est
grog|ram
groin +s +ed +ing (*Anatomy*; edge where vaults intersect)
[☞ groyne]
grom|met +s

Gro|myko, An|drei Andre|evich (Soviet statesman)
Gron|ing|en (city & province, the Netherlands)
groom +s +ed +ing
groom|er +s
grooms|man
  grooms|men
groove
  grooves
  grooved
  groov|ing
groov|i|ly
groov|i|ness
groovy
  groov|i|er
  groov|i|est
grope
  gropes
  groped
  grop|ing
grop|er +s
grop|ing|ly
Gro|pius, Wal|ter Adolph (German-born architect)
gros|beak +s
gro|schen +s
Gro|seil|liers, Mé|dard Chouart Des (French explorer)
gros|grain +s
Gros Morne (national park, Canada)
gros point
gross
  • *adjective*
  gross|er
  gross|est
  • *verb*
  gross|es
  grossed
  gross|ing
  • *noun*:
  plural gross
  [☞ gros point, Gros Morne, Gros Ventre, Grosz]
Grosse-Île (historic site, Canada)
Gross|glock|ner (mountain, Austria)
gross|ly
gross|ness
gross out *verb*
  gross|es out
  grossed out
  gross|ing out
gross-out +s *noun*

Gros Ventre
plural **Gros Ventre**
or **Gros Ventres**
Grosz, George
(German-born
painter)
Grote, George
(English historian)
[☞ **groat**]
gro|tesque +s
gro|tesque|ly
gro|tesque|ness
gro|tes|quer|ie +s
gro|tes|query (*use*
grotesquerie)
gro|tes|quer|ies
Gro|tius, Hugo (Dutch
jurist)
grot|ti|ness
grot|to
grot|toes or **grot|tos**
grot|toed
grotty
grot|ti|er
grot|ti|est
grouch
grouch|es
grouch|i|ly
grouch|i|ness
grouchy
grouch|i|er
grouch|i|est
Groulx, Lionel-
Adolphe (Cdn priest
& historian)
ground +s +ed +ing
ground|bait +s
ground ball +s
ground bass
ground bass|es
ground|break|ing +s
ground cover +s
ground crew +s
ground|ed *adjective*
ground|er +s
ground-fault cir|cuit
inter|rupt|er +s
ground|fish
plural **ground|fish** or
ground|fish|es
ground floor +s
(ground-floor *when*
preceding a noun)
ground|hog +s
Ground|hog Day +s
ground|ing +s *noun*
ground|less
ground|less|ly
ground|less|ness
ground level
(ground-level *when*
preceding a noun)
ground|ling +s

ground|nut +s
ground out *verb*
grounds out
ground|ed out
ground|ing out
ground|out +s *noun*
ground plan +s
ground rule +s
ground rule double
+s
ground|sel +s
ground|sheet +s
grounds|keep|er +s
grounds|man
grounds|men
ground|speed +s
ground|stroke +s
ground|swell +s
ground|water +s
ground|wood
ground|work
ground zero
group +s +ed +ing
group|age +s
group|er +s
group|ie +s
group|ing +s *noun*
group|think
group|ware
group work
grouse
• *noun* (game bird)
plural **grouse**
• *noun* (complaint)
plural **grous|es**
• *verb* (grumble,
complain)
grous|es
groused
grous|ing
grous|er +s
grout +s +ed +ing
grout|er +s
Grove, Fred|erick
Phil|ip (German-
born Cdn author)
grove +s
grov|el
grov|els
grov|elled
grov|el|ling
grov|el|ler +s
grov|el|ling *adjective*
grov|el|ling|ly
grovy
grow
grows
grew
grown
grow|ing
grow|able
grow|er +s
growl +s +ed +ing

growl|er +s
grow light
growl|ing|ly
growly
growl|i|er
growl|i|est
grown *adjective*
grown-up +s *adjective*
& *noun*
growth +s
groyne +s (jetty,
breakwater)
[☞ **groin**]
Groz|ny (city, Russia)
grub
grubs
grubbed
grub|bing
grub|ber +s
grub|bi|ly
grub|bi|ness
grub box
grub boxes
grubby
grub|bi|er
grub|bi|est
grub|stake
grub|stakes
grub|staked
grub|stak|ing
grub|sta|ker +s
Grub Street (writers)
grudge
grudg|es
grudged
grudg|ing
grudg|er +s
grudg|ing *adjective*
grudg|ing|ly
grudg|ing|ness
gruel
gruel|ling (*use*
gruelling)
gruel|ling|ly (*use*
gruellingly)
gruel|ling
gruel|ling|ly
grue|some
grue|some|ly
grue|some|ness
gruff +er +est
gruff|ly
gruff|ness
grum|ble
grum|bles
grum|bled
grum|bling
grum|bler +s
grum|bling +s
adjective & noun
grum|blingly
grum|bly
grump +s +ed +ing

grump|i|ly
grump|i|ness
grumpy
grump|i|er
grump|i|est
Grundy
Grun|dies
Grundy|ism
Grüne|wald, Mathias
(German painter)
grunge
grun|gi|ness
grungy
grun|gi|er
grun|gi|est
grun|ion
plural **grun|ion** or
grun|ions
grunt +s +ed +ing
grunt|er +s
Gru|yère (district,
Switzerland; cheese)
gryph|on +s (mythical
creature: *use* griffin)
[☞ **griffon**]
Gryt|viken
(settlement, South
Georgia)
GST (goods and
services tax)
G string +s (*Music*)
G-string +s (garment)
G-suit +s
GT +s (*Automotive*)
GTi (*Automotive*)
gua|ca|mole
Gua|da|la|jara (cities,
Mexico & Spain)
Gua|dal|canal (island,
Pacific)
Gua|dal|qui|vir (river,
Spain)
Gua|de|loupe (island
group, W Indies)
Gua|de|loup|ian +s
Gua|di|anax (river,
Spain & Portugal)
guai|ac +s
guai|ac|ol
guai|ac|um +s
guai|fen|esin
Guam (island, Pacific)
guan +s
gua|naco +s
Gua|na|juato (state &
its capital, Mexico)
Guang|dong
(province, China)
Guang|xi Zhuang
(region, China)
Guang|zhou (city,
China)
guan|ine

guano
• *noun*
guan|os
• *verb*
guan|oes
guan|oed
guano|ing
Guan|tán|amo (bay, Cuba)
guar
Guar|ani (people & language)
plural **Guar|ani** or **Guar|anis**
guar|ani (Paraguayan currency)
plural **guar|ani** or **guar|anis**
guar|an|tee (warranty; assurance; *for* a promise to pay another's debt *use* guaranty)
guar|an|tees
guar|an|teed
guar|an|tee|ing
guar|an|tor +s
guar|anty (promise to pay another's debt)
guar|an|ties
[☞ guarantee]
guard +s +ed +ing
guard|ant
guard|ed *adjective*
guard|ed|ly
guard|ed|ness
guard|house +s
guard|ian +s
guard|ian|ship
guard|rail +s
guard|room +s
guards|man
guards|men
Guar|neri, Giu|seppe ('del Gesù') (Italian violin maker)
Gua|te|mala (country, Central America)
Gua|te|mala City (capital of Guatemala)
Gua|te|mal|an +s
gua|va +s
Guaya|quil (city, Ecuador)
gub|bins
gu|ber|na|tor|ial
guck
gudg|eon
• (fish)
plural **gudg|eon**
• (hinge, pin, pivot)
plural **gudg|eons**

Gud|run (*Scandinavian Myth*)
guel|der rose +s
Guelph +s (city, Canada; medieval Italian faction)
gue|non +s
guer|don +s +ed +ing
Gue|ricke, Otto von (German engineer)
guer|il|la +s (soldier; activist: *use* guerrilla)
[☞ gorilla]
Guer|nica (town, Spain)
Guer|nica y Luno (= Guernica)
Guern|sey +s (island, English Channel; cow; lily)
Guer|rero (state, Mexico)
guer|ril|la +s (soldier; activist)
[☞ gorilla]
guess
guess|es
guessed
guess|ing
guess|able
guess|er +s
guess|ti|mate
guess|ti|mates
guess|ti|mat|ed
guess|ti|mat|ing
guess|work
guest +s +ed +ing
guest book +s
guest house +s
gues|ti|mate (*use* guesstimate)
gues|ti|mates
gues|ti|mat|ed
gues|ti|mat|ing
guest|ship
Gue|vara, Che (Argentinian revolutionary)
Guèvre|mont, Ger|maine (Cdn writer)
guff
guf|faw +s +ed +ing
Gug|gen|heim, Meyer (Swiss-born US industrialist)
GUI (graphical user interface)
GUIs
Gui|ana (region & highlands, S America; in

'French Guiana' & 'Dutch Guiana')
[☞ Guyana]
Gui|bord, Jo|seph (member of Institut canadien)
guid|able
guid|ance
Guide +s (*Scouting*)
guide
guides
guid|ed
guid|ing
guide|book +s
guide|line +s
guide|post +s
Guid|er +s (*Scouting*)
guid|er +s
guide|way +s
Guid|ing (*Scouting*)
Guido d'Arezzo (Italian music innovator)
gui|don +s
Gui|enne (= Guyenne, France)
guild +s (association)
[☞ gild]
guil|der +s (Dutch currency)
[☞ gilder]
Guild|ford (city, England)
guild|hall +s
guilds|man
guilds|men
guilds|woman
guilds|women
guile
guile|ful
guile|ful|ly
guile|less
guile|less|ly
guile|less|ness
Guilin (city, China)
Guillaume-Delisle (lake, Canada)
guil|le|mot +s
guil|loche +s
guil|lo|tine
guil|lo|tines
guil|lo|tined
guil|lo|tin|ing
guil|lo|tin|er +s
guilt +s (culpability etc.)
[☞ gilt]
guilt|i|er
guilt|i|est
guilt|i|ly
guilt|i|ness
guilt|less

guilt|less|ly
guilt|less|ness
guilt trip +s *noun*
guilt-trip *verb*
guilt-trips
guilt-tripped
guilt-tripping
guilty
guilt|i|er
guilt|i|est
Guinea (African country south of Guinea-Bissau; gulf, Atlantic)
guin|ea +s (currency)
Guinea-Bissau (African country north of Guinea)
guinea fowl
plural **guinea fowl** or **guinea fowls**
Guin|ean +s
guinea pig +s
guinea worm +s
Guin|evere (*Arthurian Legend*)
Guin|ness, Sir Alec (English actor)
guiro +s (musical instrument)
[☞ gyro, giro]
Guis|card, Rob|ert (Norman leader)
guise +s
gui|tar +s
guitar|ist +s
Gui|yang (city, China)
Gui|zhou (province, China)
Gui|zot, Fran|çois Pierre Guil|laume (French statesman)
Gu|ja|rat (state, India)
Gu|ja|rati +s
Guj|ran|wala (city, Pakistan)
Guj|rat (city, Pakistan)
gu|lag +s
Gul|barga (city, India)
gulch
gulch|es
gul|den
plural **gul|den** or **gul|dens**
gules
gulf +s
Gulf Stream
gulf|weed
gull +s +ed +ing
Gul|lah
plural **Gul|lah**
gul|lery
gul|ler|ies

gul|let +s
gul|ley +s *noun* (*use* gully)
gul|li|bil|ity
gul|lible
gul|libly
gull-wing
gully *noun & verb*
gul|lies
gul|lied
gully|ing
gulp +s +ed +ing
gulp|er +s
gulpy
gum
　gums
　gummed
　gum|ming
Gumbo (language)
gum|bo +s
gum|boil +s
gum|boot +s
gum|drop +s
gum line +s
gumma
　gum|mas *or*
　gum|mata
gum|ma|tous
gummi +s (jellylike candy)
　[☞ gummy]
gum|mi|ly
gum|mi|ness
gummy (of or like gum; sticky)
　gum|mi|er
　gum|mi|est
　[☞ gummi]
gump|tion
gum|shield +s
gum|shoe
　gum|shoes
　gum|shoed
　gum|shoe|ing
gum tree +s
gum|wood
gun
　guns
　gunned
　gun|ning
gun|boat +s
gun cot|ton
gun crew +s
gun deck +s
gun dog +s
gun|fight +s
gun|fight|er +s
gun|fire
gunge
　gun|ges
　gunged
　gun|ging
gung-ho

gungy
gunk +s +ed +ing
gunky
　gunk|i|er
　gunk|i|est
gun|less
gun|lock +s
gun|man
　gun|men
gun|metal
Gun|nar (*Scandinavian Myth*)
gunned *adjective*
gun|nel +s (fish; *for* ship edge *use* gunwale)
gun|ner +s
gun|nera +s
gun|nery
gunny
　gun|nies
gunny sack +s
gun|play
gun|point
gun|powder +s
gun|room +s
gun|run|ner +s
gun-running
gun|ship +s
gun|shot +s
gun-shy
gun|sight +s
gun|sling|er +s
gun|sling|ing
gun|smith +s
gun|smith|ing
gun|stock +s
Gun|ter, Ed|mund (English mathematician)
　[☞ Guntur]
Gun|ther (*Germanic Myth*)
Gun|tur (city, India)
　[☞ Gunter]
gun|wale +s (ship edge)
　[☞ gunnel]
Guo|min|dang (= Kuomintang)
guppy
　gup|pies
Gupta (Hindu dynasty)
Gup|tan
gurd|wara +s
gurdy
　gur|dies
gur|gle
　gur|gles
　gur|gled
　gurg|ling
gurg|ly

Gur|kha +s
gur|nard +s
gur|ney +s
gurry
guru +s
gush
　gush|es
　gushed
　gush|ing
gush|er +s
gush|i|ly
gush|i|ness
gush|ing *adjective*
gush|ing|ly
gushy
　gush|i|er
　gush|i|est
gus|set +s
gus|set|ed
gus|sied up (gussied-up *when preceding a noun*)
gussy
　gus|sies
　gus|sied
　gussy|ing
gust +s +ed +ing
gus|ta|tion
gus|ta|tive
gus|ta|tor|ial
gus|ta|tory
Gus|ta|vus (Swedish kings)
Gus|ta|vus Adol|phus (Swedish king)
gust|i|ly
gust|i|ness
gusto
gusty
　gust|i|er
　gust|i|est
gut
　guts
　gut|ted
　gut|ting
gut|bucket
Guten|berg, Jo|han|nes (German printer)
Guth|rie, Woody (US folksinger)
Guth|run (*use* Gudrun)
gut|less
gut|less|ly
gut|less|ness
gut-level
gut-shoot
　gut-shoots
　gut-shot
gut-shooting
gut-shooter +s

gut-shooting *noun*
gut-shot *adjective*
guts|i|ly
guts|i|ness
gutsy
　guts|i|er
　guts|i|est
gutta per|cha
gut|tate
gut|ted *adjective*
gut|ter +s +ed +ing
gut|ter|ing +s *noun*
gutter|snipe +s
gut|tur|al
gut|tur|al|ly
gutty
guv +s
Guy, John (governor of Newfoundland)
guy +s +ed +ing
Guy|ana (country, S America)
　[☞ French Guiana, Dutch Guiana, Guiana]
Guyan|ese
　plural Guyan|ese
Guy|enne (region, France)
Guy Fawkes' Night
guz|zle
　guz|zles
　guz|zled
　guz|zling
guz|zler +s
Gwa|lior (city, India)
Gwent (county, Wales)
Gwich'in
　plural Gwich'in
Gwyn, Elea|nor ('Nell') (English actress)
Gwyn|edd (county & former principality, Wales)
gybe (*Sailing*)
　gybes
　gybed
　gyb|ing
　[☞ gibe, jibe]
gym +s
gym|khana +s
gym|na|sium
　gym|na|siums *or*
　gym|na|sia
gym|nast +s
gym|nas|tic
gym|nas|tic|ally
gym|nas|tics
gym|noso|phist +s
gym|noso|phy
gymno|sperm +s
gymno|sperm|ous

gym shoe +s
gym|slip +s
gy|nae|ceum +s
(*Botany: use*
gynoecium)
gynae|co|logic (*use*
gynecologic)
gynae|co|logic|al (*use*
gynecological)
gynae|co|logic|al|ly
(*use*
gynecologically)
gynae|col|o|gist +s
(*use* gynecologist)
gynae|col|ogy (*use*
gynecology)
gynae|co|mas|tia (*use*
gynecomastia)
gy|nan|dro|morph +s
gy|nan|dro|morph|ic
gy|nan|dro|morph|
    ism
gy|nan|dro|morphy
gy|nan|drous
gyne|co|logic
gyne|co|logic|al
gyne|co|logic|al|ly
gyne|col|o|gist +s
gyne|col|ogy
gyne|co|mas|tia
gyno|cen|tric
gy|noe|cium (*Botany*)
gy|noe|cia
gyp
  gyps
  gypped
  gyp|ping
gypo +s (*use* gyppo)
gyp|po +s
gyppy tummy (*use*
  gippy tummy)
gyppy tum|mies
gyp|roc
gyp|rock (*use* gyproc)
gyp|seous
gyp|sif|er|ous
gyp|so|phila +s
gyp|sum
gypsum|board
gypsy
  gyp|sies
gypsy|ish
gyr|ate
  gyr|ates
  gyr|at|ed
  gyr|at|ing
gyr|a|tion +s
gyr|ator +s
gyra|tory
gyre
  gyres
  gyred
  gyr|ing

gyr|falcon +s
gyri
gyro +s (gyroscope,
  gyrocompass; pita
  sandwich)
  [☞ giro, guiro]
gyro|com|pass
gyro|com|pass|es
gyro|mag|net|ic
gyro|scope +s
gyro|scop|ic
gyro|scop|ic|ally
gyro|stabil|iz|er +s
gyrus
  gyri
Gyumri (city,
  Armenia)
Gzow|ski, Peter (Cdn
  broadcaster & writer)

H

H
• (letter; shape)
  H's
• (henry; magnetic
  field strength; heroin;
  pencil hardness)
h
• (letter)
  h's
• (Planck's constant)
ha *interjection*
Haa|kon (Norwegian
  king)
haar +s (fog)
Haar|lem (city, the
  Netherlands)
  [☞ Harlem]
Hab|ak|kuk (*Bible*)
haba|nera +s (dance)
haba|nero +s
  (pepper)
hab|eas cor|pus
haber|dash|er +s
haber|dash|ery
  haber|dash|eries
Haber|mas, Jür|gen
  (German social
  theorist)
ha|bili|ment +s
ha|bili|tate
  ha|bili|tates
  ha|bili|tat|ed
  ha|bili|tat|ing
ha|bili|ta|tion
hab|it +s
habit|abil|ity

habit|able
habit|able|ness
habit|ably
habi|tant +s
habi|tat +s
habi|ta|tion +s
habit-forming
ha|bitu|al
ha|bitu|al|ity
ha|bitu|al|ly
ha|bitu|al|ness
ha|bitu|ate
  ha|bitu|ates
  ha|bitu|at|ed
  ha|bitu|at|ing
ha|bitu|a|tion
habi|tué +s
Habs|burg
  (= Hapsburg,
  European dynasty)
há|ček +s
hach|ure
  hach|ures
  hach|ured
  hach|ur|ing
hach|ures
ha|cien|da +s
hack +s +ed +ing
hacka|more +s
hack|berry
  hack|ber|ries
hack|er +s
hack|ery
hack|ing *adjective*
hackle
  hackles
  hackled
  hack|ling
hack|ma|tack +s
hack|ney +s
hack|neyed
hack|saw +s
had
Hadar (star)
Ha|das|sah
had|dock
  plural had|dock
hade
  hades
  haded
  hading
Hadean
Hades (*Greek Myth*;
  New Testament)
Hadhra|maut (region,
  Yemen)
Had|ith
hadj (pilgrimage: *use*
  hajj)
had|ji +s (pilgrim: *use*
  hajji)
hadn't

Had|rian (Roman
  emperor)
Hadrian's Wall (in
  N England)
had|ron +s
had|ron|ic
hadro|saur +s
hadst
Haeck|el, Ernst
  Hein|rich (German
  biologist &
  philosopher)
haem +s (*use* heme)
haem|al (*use* hemal)
haemo|philia (*use*
  hemophilia)
haemo|phil|iac +s
  noun (*use*
  hemophiliac)
haemo|phil|ic
  adjective (*use*
  hemophilic)
haem|or|rhage (*use*
  hemorrhage)
haem|or|rhag|es
haem|or|rhaged
haem|or|rhag|ing
haem|or|rhag|ic (*use*
  hemorrhagic)
Hafiz, Shams al-Din
  Muham|mad
  (Persian poet)
hafiz
  plural hafiz or hafis
haf|ni|um
haft +s +ed +ing
Haf|tar|ah
Haf|tar|ot
hag +s
Hagar (*Bible*)
Hagen (city, Germany)
hag|fish
  plural hag|fish or
  hag|fish|es
Hag|gad|ah
  Hag|gad|ahs or
  Hag|gad|oth
Hag|gad|ic
Hag|gai (*Bible*)
Hag|gard, Sir (Henry)
  Rider (English
  novelist)
hag|gard
hag|gard|ly
hag|gard|ness
hag|gis
  hag|gis|es
hag|gish
hag|gle
  hag|gles
  hag|gled
  hag|gling
hag|gler +s

hag|gling *noun*
Hagia So|phia
(Byzantine edifice,
Istanbul)
Hagi|og|rapha
hagi|og|raph|er +s
hagio|graph|ic
hagio|graph|ic|al
hagi|og|raphy
hagi|og|raph|ies
hagi|ol|atry
hagi|ol|a|tries
hagio|logic|al
hagi|ol|o|gist +s
hagi|ol|ogy
hagi|ol|o|gies
hag|ridden
Hague, The (city, the
Netherlands)
[☞ Haig]
hah *interjection*
ha ha *interjection*
ha-ha +s (ditch)
Hahn, Otto (German
chemist)
[☞ Han]
Hah|ne|mann,
(Chris|tian
Fried|rich) Sam|uel
(German founder of
homeopathy)
hahn|ium
haick +s (Arab
garment: *use* haik)
[☞ hake]
Haida
plural Haida or
Hai|das
Haifa (port, Israel)
Haig, Doug|las (1st
Earl Haig of
Bemersyde, British
field marshal)
[☞ The Hague]
Haig-Brown,
Rod|er|ick (Cdn
writer &
conservationist)
haik +s (Arab
garment)
[☞ hake]
Hai|kou (capital of
Hainan)
[☞ haiku]
haiku (poem)
plural haiku
[☞ Haikou]
hail +s +ed +ing
(frozen rain; shower;
greet; come from)
[☞ hale]
hail|er +s
Haile Sel|as|sie
(Ethiopian emperor)

Hailey|bury (town,
Canada)
hail-fellow-well-met
hail-fellows-well-
met
Hail Mary +s
hail|stone +s
hail|storm +s
Hai|nan (island,
China)
Hai|naut (province,
Belgium)
Hai|phong (port,
Vietnam)
hair +s (on the head
etc.)
[☞ hare, Herr]
hair|ball +s
hair-brained (*use*
hare-brained)
hair-brained|ness
(*use* hare-
brainedness)
hair|breadth
hair|brush
hair|brush|es
hair care (hair-care
*when preceding a
noun*)
hair clip +s
hair|cloth
hair col|or +s (*use*
hair colour)
hair col|or|ing +s (*use*
hair colouring)
hair color|ist +s (*use*
hair colourist)
hair col|our +s
hair col|our|ing +s
hair col|our|ist +s
hair|cut +s
hair|cut|ter +s
hair|cut|ting
hair|do +s
hair|dress|er +s
hair|dress|ing
hair dry|er +s
haired
hair grass
hair grass|es
hair|grip +s
hair|i|er *comparative
of* hairy
[☞ harrier,
Harrier]
hair|i|est
hair|i|ness
hair|less
hair|like
hair|line +s
hair|net +s
hair|piece +s
hair|pin +s

hair-raising
hair's breadth
hair shirt +s (hair-
shirt *when preceding
a noun*)
hair|split|ter +s
hair|split|ting
hair|spray +s
hair|spring +s
hair|streak +s
hair|style +s
hair|styl|ing
hair|styl|ist +s
hair-trigger +s
hair|wing +s
hairy (hirsute; dicey,
harrowing)
hair|i|er
hair|i|est
[☞ harry]
Hais|la
plural Hais|la or
Hais|las
Haiti (Caribbean
country)
Hai|tian +s
Hai|tink, Ber|nard
Jo|hann Her|man
(Dutch conductor)
hajj (pilgrimage)
hajj|i +s (pilgrim)
hake (fish)
plural hake or hakes
[☞ haik]
haken|kreuz
haken|kreuze or
haken|kreuz|es
ha|kim +s
Hak|luyt, Rich|ard
(English geographer)
Hako|date (port,
Japan)
Ha|la|cha
Ha|la|chahs or
Ha|la|choth
Ha|la|chic
Ha|la|kah (*use*
Halacha)
Ha|la|kahs or
Ha|la|koth
Ha|la|kha (*use*
Halacha)
Ha|la|khahs or
Ha|la|khoth
Ha|la|khic (*use*
Halachic)
Ha|la|kic (*use*
Halachic)
halal (*Islam*)
halals
hal|lalled
halal|ling
[☞ *Hallel*]

hal|la|tion
hal|berd +s
hal|berd|ier +s
Hal|cion *proprietary*
(drug)
[☞ Halcyone,
halcyon]
hal|cyon +s (calm;
prosperous; bird)
[☞ Halcyone,
Halcion]
Hal|cyone (daughter
of Aeolus: *use*
Alcyone)
[☞ Halcion,
halcyon]
Hal|dane, John
Bur|don
San|der|son
(Scottish biologist)
Hal|dane, John Scott
(Scottish
physiologist)
Hal|di|mand (town,
Canada)
Hale, George El|lery
(US astronomer)
hale (healthy; drag)
hales
haled
haling
[☞ hail]
hale|ness
haler (currency)
plural haler or
hal|eru
Ha|lévy, (Jacques
Fran|çois)
Fro|men|tal (French
composer)
Haley, Wil|liam John
Clif|ton ('Bill') (US
singer-songwriter)
[☞ Halley, Halley's
comet]
half
halves
[☞ halve]
half a dozen
half-and-half
half-assed
half|back +s
half-baked
half bath +s
half|beak +s
half-blood +s
half-blooded
half board
half-boot +s
half-bottle +s
half-breed +s
half-brother +s
half-caste +s *offensive*

half-circle +s
half-cock
half-cocked
half course +s
half court +s (half-
   court *when preceding*
   a noun)
half-crown +s
half-cut
half day +s (half-day
   when preceding a
   noun)
half-dead
half dol|lar +s
half-dozen +s
half-drunk
half-duplex
half-hardy
half-hear
   half-hears
   half-heard
   half-hearing
half-hearted
half-hearted|ly
half-hearted|ness
half hitch
   half hitch|es
half-hour +s
half-hourly
half-integer +s
half-integral
half-life
   half-lives
half-light
half-litre +s
half-marathon +s
half-mast
half meas|ures
half moon +s
half-naked
half nel|son +s
half note +s
half pay
half|penny
   half|pen|nies or
   half|pence
half|penny|worth
half-pint +s
half-pipe +s
half sec|tion +s
half shell +s
half-sister +s
half size +s (half-size
   when preceding a
   noun)
half-slip +s
half-sole +s
half-sovereign +s
half-staff
half-starved
half-step +s
half-term +s

half-timber
half-timbered
half-timber|ing
half|time
half-title +s
half-ton +s
half|tone +s
half-track +s
half-truth +s
half-volley +s
half|way
half|way house +s
half|wit +s
half|wit|ted
half|wit|ted|ly
half|wit|ted|ness
half-yearly
Hali|bur|ton,
   Thom|as Chand|ler
   (Cdn author &
   politician)
hali|but
   plural hali|but
Hali|car|nas|sus
   (ancient Greek city)
hal|ide +s
Hali|fax (city, Canada)
Hali|fax, Ed|ward
   Fred|erick Lind|ley
   Wood, Earl of
   (British politician)
Hali|fax, George
   Mon|tagu Dunk,
   2nd Earl of (British
   statesman)
Hali|gon|ian +s
hali|otis
   plural hali|otis
hal|ite +s
hali|to|sis
Halko|mel|em
   plural Halko|mel|em
Hall (peninsula,
   Canada)
Hall, Charles Mar|tin
   (US chemist)
Hall, (Mar|guer|ite)
   Rad|clyffe (English
   writer)
hall +s (corridor; large
   room or building)
   [☞ haul]
hal|lal (*Islam: use*
   halal)
hall|lals
hall|lalled
hall|lal|ling
   [☞ *Hallel*]
Halle (city, Germany)
Hal|lel (*Judaism*)
   [☞ halal]
hal|le|lu|jah +s
   (= alleluia)

Hal|ler, Al|brecht von
   (Swiss physiologist)
   [☞ holler, hauler]
Hal|ley, Ed|mond or
   Ed|mund (English
   astronomer)
   [☞ Haley]
Halley's comet
hall|mark +s +ed
   +ing
Hall of Fame
   (building with
   memorials to famous
   people; people so
   memorialized)
   Halls of Fame
hall of fame (group of
   famous people in a
   particular sphere)
   halls of fame
Hall of Famer +s
hal|loo (*Fox Hunting;*
   in calling attention or
   expressing surprise)
   hal|loos
   hal|looed
   hal|loo|ing
hal|low +s +ed +ing
   (make holy; saint)
   [☞ halo]
hal|lowed *adjective*
Hal|low|een +s
hall|stand +s
Hall|statt
hal|lu|ces
hal|lu|cin|ant +s
hal|lu|cin|ate
   hal|lu|cin|ates
   hal|lu|cin|at|ed
   hal|lu|cin|at|ing
hal|lu|cin|a|tion +s
hal|lu|cin|ator +s
hal|lu|cina|tory
hal|lu|cino|gen +s
hal|lu|cino|gen|ic
hal|lux
   hal|lu|ces
hall|way +s
halm +s (*use* haulm)
Hal|ma|hera (island,
   Indonesia)
halo
• *noun* (light
   surrounding a
   person etc.)
   halos or ha|loes
• *verb* (surround with a
   halo)
   ha|loes
   ha|loed
   halo|ing
   [☞ hallow]
halo|gen +s
halo|gen|at|ed

halo|gen|a|tion
halo|gen|ic
ha|lon +s
halo|peri|dol
halo|phyte +s
halo|phyt|ic
halo|thane
Hals, Frans (Dutch
   painter)
halt +s +ed +ing
hal|ter +s
halter-break
   halter-breaks
   halter-broke
   halter-broken
   halter-breaking
hal|ter|es
hal|ter top +s
halt|ing *adjective*
halt|ing|ly
Hal|ton Hills (town,
   Canada)
hal|va +s (*use* halvah)
hal|vah +s
halve (divide into
   halves etc.)
   halves
   halved
   halv|ing
   [☞ have]
halves *plural of* half
hal|yard +s
Ham (*Bible*)
   [☞ Hamm]
ham
   hams
   hammed
   ham|ming
hama|dryad +s
hama|dryas
   hama|dryas|es
Hamal (star)
Hama|matsu (city,
   Japan)
hama|melis
   plural hama|melis
ham|an|tasch|en
ha|mar|tia
Hamas
ha|mat|sa +s
Ham|burg (city,
   Germany)
ham|burg +s
ham|burg|er +s
Ham|elin (= Hameln)
Ham|eln (town,
   Germany)
hames
ham-fisted
ham-fisted|ly
ham-fisted|ness
ham-handed
ham-handed|ly

ham-handed|ness
Ham|hung (city, North Korea)
Ham|il|car (Carthaginian general)
Ham|il|ton (city & inlet, Canada; cities, New Zealand, Bermuda, Scotland)
Ham|il|ton, Alex|an|der (US politician)
Ham|il|ton, Lady Emma (mistress of Lord Nelson)
Ham|il|ton, Sir Wil|liam Rowan (Irish mathematician & physicist)
Ham|il|ton|ian +s
Ham|ite +s
Ham|itic
Hamito-Semitic
ham|let +s
Hamm (city, Germany)
[☞ Ham]
Ham|mar|skjöld, Dag Hjal|mar Agné Carl (secretary-general of the UN)
ham|mer +s +ed +ing
hammer|beam +s
ham|mer drill +s
ham|mered adjective
ham|mer|er +s
Ham|mer|fest (town, Norway)
hammer|head +s
ham|mer|ing +s noun
hammer|less
hammer|lock +s
Ham|mer|stein, Oscar (US librettist)
hammer|toe +s
Ham|mett, (Sam|uel) Dash|iell (US novelist)
ham|mi|ly
ham|mi|ness
ham|mock +s (hanging bed; for forested ground rising above a marsh use hummock)
[☞ hummock]
Ham|mu|rabi (Babylonian king)
hammy
ham|mi|er
ham|mi|est
ham|per +s +ed +ing

Hamp|shire (county, England)
Hamp|stead (London suburb, England; town, Canada)
Hamp|ton (city, US)
Hamp|ton, Lionel (US musician)
Hamp|ton Roads (estuary, US)
ham|ster +s
ham|string
ham|strings
ham|strung
ham|string|ing
Ham|sun, Knut (Norwegian novelist)
ham|ulus
ham|uli
Han (Chinese dynasty; people & language, Canada)
plural Han
[☞ Hahn]
Han|cock, John (US politician)
hand +s +ed +ing
hand axe +s
hand|bag +s
hand|ball +s
hand|basket +s
hand|bell +s
hand|bill +s
hand|book +s
hand|brake +s
hand|car +s
hand|cart +s
hand-carve
hand-carves
hand-carved
hand-carving
hand-carved adjective
hand|clap +s
hand|craft +s +ed +ing
hand|craft|ed adjective
hand cream +s
hand|cuff +s +ed +ing
hand|ed adjective
hand|ed|ness
Han|del, George Fred|erick (German-born composer)
[☞ handle]
Han|del|ian
hand|ful +s
hand game +s
hand|glass
hand|glass|es
hand|grip +s
hand|gun +s

hand-held +s
hand|hold +s
handi|cap
handi|caps
handi|capped
handi|cap|ping
handi|capped adjective
handi|cap|per +s
handi|craft +s
hand|i|er
hand|i|est
hand|i|ly
hand|i|ness
hand|i|work +s
hand job +s
hand|ker|chief
hand|ker|chiefs or hand|ker|chieves
han|dle
han|dles
han|dled
hand|ling
[☞ Handel]
handle|abil|ity
handle|able
handle|bar +s
han|dled adjective
handle|less
hand|ler +s
hand|less
hand|line +s
hand|liner +s
hand|ling noun
hand|lining
hand|log|ger +s
hand|log|ging
hand|made (made by hand)
hand|maid +s (servant)
hand|maiden +s
hand-me-down +s
hand off verb
hands off
hand|ed off
hand|ing off
hand-off +s noun
hand out verb
hands out
hand|ed out
hand|ing out
hand|out +s noun
hand over verb
hands over
hand|ed over
hand|ing over
hand|over +s noun
hand-pick +s +ed +ing
hand-picked adjective

hand-print verb
hand-prints
hand-printed
hand-printing
hand|print +s noun
hand-printed adjective
hand pump +s
hand|rail +s
hand|saw +s
hand|sel
hand|sels
hand|selled or hand|seled
hand|sel|ling or hand|sel|ing
[☞ Hansel]
hand|set +s
hands-free
hand|shake +s
hand sig|nal +s
hands-off
hand|some (good-looking)
hand|som|er
hand|som|est
[☞ hansom]
hand|some|ly
hand|some|ness
hands-on
hand|spring +s
hand|stand +s
hand tool +s
hand|wash|ing +s
hand|work
hand|worked
hand|woven
hand-wringing
hand|writing
hand|writ|ten
Handy, Wil|liam Chris|to|pher (US musician)
handy
hand|i|er
hand|i|est
handy|man
handy|men
hang
• (suspend, dangle, hinge, linger, etc.)
hangs
hung
hang|ing
• (execute)
hangs
hanged
hang|ing
hang|ar +s (building housing aircraft)
[☞ hanger]
hangar|age
hang|ashore +s

Hang|chow
(= Hangzhou, China)
hang|dog
hang|er +s (object for hanging clothes; thing that hangs)
[☞ hangar]
hanger-on
hangers-on
hang-glide
hang-glides
hang-glided
hang-gliding
hang-glider +s
hang-gliding noun
hang|ing +s noun & adjective
hang|man
hang|men
hang|nail +s
hang out verb
hangs out
hung out
hang|ing out
hang|out +s noun
hang|over +s
Hang Seng index
hang tag +s
hang up verb
hangs up
hung up
hang|ing up
hang-up +s noun
Hang|zhou (city, China)
hank +s
han|ker +s +ed +ing
han|ker|er +s
han|ker|ing +s noun
han|kie +s (use hanky)
Hanks, Thom|as J. ('Tom') (US actor)
hanky
han|kies
hanky-panky
Han|lan, Ed|ward ('Ned') (Cdn athlete)
Han|ni|bal (Carthaginian general)
Hanoi (capital of Vietnam)
Han|over (city & former state, Germany; town, Canada; British royal house)
Han|over|ian +s
Hans (Arctic island)
Hansa
Han|sard

Hanse (use Hansa)
Han|se|atic League
Han|sel (in 'Hansel and Gretel')
han|sel (use handsel)
han|sels
han|selled or han|seled
han|sel|ling or han|sel|ing
Hansen's dis|ease
han|som +s (cab)
[☞ handsome]
hanta|virus
hanta|virus|es
Ha|nuk|kah
Hanu|man (Hinduism)
hanu|man +s (monkey)
Haora (= Howrah, India)
hap
haps
happed
hap|ping
hapax leg|om|en|on
hapax leg|om|ena
ha'penny
ha'pen|nies or ha'pence
hap|haz|ard
hap|haz|ard|ly
hap|haz|ard|ness
hap|less
hap|less|ly
hap|less|ness
hap|log|raphy
hap|loid +s
hap|lol|ogy
ha'p'orth (= halfpennyworth)
hap|pen +s +ed +ing
hap|pen|ing +s noun & adjective
happen|stance +s
hap|pi +s (coat)
hap|pi|ly
hap|pi|ness
happy (content; fortunate; pleasing)
hap|pi|er
hap|pi|est
[☞ happi]
happy face +s
happy-go-lucky
Happy Valley-Goose Bay (town, Canada)
Haps|burg (European dynasty)
hap|tic
har interjection
[☞ haar]
hara-kiri

har|angue
har|angues
har|angued
har|anguing
har|anguer +s
Har|ap|pa (ancient city, Asia)
Har|are (capital of Zimbabwe)
ha|rass (annoy, persecute)
ha|rass|es
ha|rassed
ha|rass|ing
[☞ Harris]
ha|rass|er +s
ha|rass|ing noun
ha|rass|ing|ly
ha|rass|ment
Har|bin (city, China)
har|bin|ger +s
har|bor +s +ed +ing (use harbour)
harbor|age (use harbourage)
harbor|less (use harbourless)
harbor|master +s (use harbourmaster)
har|bour +s +ed +ing
harbour|age
har|bour front (harbour|front when preceding a noun)
Har|bour Grace (town, Canada)
harbour|less
harbour|master +s
hard +er +est
hard and fast
hard-ass
hard-asses
hard-assed
hard|back +s
hard|ball +s
hard|bit|ten
hard|board
hard-boiled
hard bread
hard-cooked
hard copy (hard-copy when preceding a noun)
hard cop|ies
hard core +s (nucleus)
hard-core adjective (forming a nucleus; committed; explicit; relating to hard drugs)
hard|core (punk rock music)

hard|cover +s
hard disk +s
hard done by
hard-earned
Har|de|ca|nute (king of Denmark & England)
hard|en +s +ed +ing
hard|en|abil|ity
hard|en|able
hard|en|er +s
hard|en|ing +s noun
hard|hack +s
hard hat +s
hard-headed
hard-headed|ly
hard-headed|ness
hard-hearted
hard-hearted|ly
hard-hearted|ness
hard hit
hard-hitting
Har|di|ca|nute (= Hardecanute)
har|di|hood
har|di|ly
har|di|ness
Har|ding, War|ren Gama|liel (US president)
hard|ish
hard line +s (hard|line when preceding a noun)
hard-liner +s
hard luck (hard-luck when preceding a noun)
hard|ly
hard|ness
hard|ness|es
hard-nosed
hard of hear|ing
hard-on +s
hard|pack
hard|pan
hard pressed (hard-pressed when preceding a noun)
hard rock (Music)
[☞ hardrock miner, hardrock mining]
hard|rock min|er +s
hard|rock min|ing
hard|scrab|ble
hard-shell
hard-shelled (= hard-shell)
hard|ship +s
hard|tack
hard|top +s
Har|dwar (city, India)

hard|ware
hard-wearing
hard-wired
hard|wood +s
hard-working
Hardy, Oli|ver (US comedian)
Hardy, Thom|as (English writer)
hardy
har|di|er
har|di|est
hardy har har
Hare (Aboriginal people; language)
plural Hare or Hares
[☞ Herr]
hare (animal; run)
hares
hared
haring
[☞ hair]
hare|bell +s
hare-brained
hare-brained|ness
Hare|foot, Har|old (Harold I of England)
Hare Krish|na +s
hare|lip +s
hare|lipped
har|em +s (women of Muslim household; Zoology)
[☞ harum-scarum]
hare's-foot +s (clover)
hare|wood
Har|geisa (city, Somalia)
Har|geysa (= Hargeisa)
Har|greaves, James (English inventor)
har har interjection
[☞ haar]
hari|cot +s
Hari|jan +s
har|is|sa
hark +s +ed +ing
hark|en +s +ed +ing (use hearken)
Har|lem (New York neighbourhood)
[☞ Haarlem]
Har|le|quin (pantomime character)
har|le|quin +s (animal; duck; clown)
har|le|quin|ade
Har|ley Street (in London; medical specialists)

har|lot +s
har|lotry
Har|low (town, England)
Har|low, Jean (US actress)
harm +s +ed +ing
har|mat|tan +s
harm|ful
harm|ful|ly
harm|ful|ness
harm|less
harm|less|ly
harm|less|ness
har|mon|ic +s
har|mon|ica +s
har|mon|ic|ally
har|moni|ous
har|moni|ous|ly
har|moni|ous|ness
har|mon|ist +s
har|mon|is|tic
har|mon|ium +s
har|mon|iz|a|tion +s
har|mon|ize
har|mon|iz|es
har|mon|ized
har|mon|iz|ing
har|mon|iz|er +s
har|mony
har|mon|ies
Harms|worth, Al|fred Charles Wil|liam (1st Viscount Northcliffe)
har|ness
har|ness|es
har|nessed
har|ness|ing
har|ness|er +s
Haro (strait, North America)
[☞ harrow]
Har|old (English kings)
[☞ herald]
Haroun-al-Raschid (= Harūn ar-Rashīd)
harp +s +ed +ing
harp|er +s
Har|pers Ferry (battle site, US)
harp|ist +s
Har|poc|ra|tes (Greek Myth)
har|poon +s +ed +ing
har|poon|er
harp seal +s
harp|si|chord I s
harp|si|chord|ist +s
harpy (Greek & Roman Myth; greedy or

nagging person; eagle)
har|pies
har|que|bus
har|que|bus|es
Har|ri|cana (river, Canada)
har|ri|dan +s
Har|ri|er +s (jet)
har|ri|er +s (one who harries; hound; hawk; runner)
Har|ri|man, Wil|liam Aver|ell (US diplomat)
Har|ris (in the Outer Hebrides; tweed; surname)
[☞ harass]
Har|ris, Frank (Irish-born writer)
Har|ris, Joel Chand|ler (US writer)
Har|ris, Law|ren Stew|art (Cdn painter)
Har|ris, Mi|chael Deane ('Mike') (Cdn politician)
Har|ris, Roy Ells|worth (US composer)
Harris|burg (city, US)
Har|ri|son (lake, Canada)
Har|ri|son, Ben|ja|min (US president)
Har|ri|son, George (British singer-songwriter)
Har|ri|son, Sir Rex (English actor)
Har|ri|son, Wil|liam Henry (US president)
har|row +s +ed +ing (Agriculture; distress)
[☞ Haro]
har|row|er +s
har|row|ing adjective
har|row|ing|ly
har|rumph +s +ed +ing
harry (ravage; harass)
har|ries
har|ried
harry|ing
[☞ hairy]
harsh +er +est
harsh|en +s +ed +ing
harsh|ly
harsh|ness

Hart (surname)
[☞ Harte, heart]
Hart, Eve|lyn Anne (Cdn dancer)
Hart, John (Irish-born Cdn politician)
Hart, Lor|enz Mil|ton (US lyricist)
Hart, Moss (US playwright)
hart +s (male deer)
[☞ heart, Harte]
har|tal
Harte, (Fran|cis) Bret (US writer)
[☞ Hart, heart]
harte|beest
plural harte|beest or harte|beests
Hart|ford (city, US)
[☞ Hertford]
Hartle|pool (port, England)
harts|horn
hart's tongue +s
ha|rumph +s +ed +ing (use harrumph)
harum-scarum (reckless)
[☞ harem]
Harūn ar-Rashīd (caliph of Baghdad)
ha|rus|pex
ha|rus|pi|ces
ha|rus|picy
Har|vard (university, US; classification)
Har|vard, John (US cleric)
har|vest +s +ed +ing
har|vest|able
har|vest|er +s
har|vest|man
har|vest|men
Har|vey, Doug|las ('Doug') (Cdn hockey player)
Har|vey, Wil|liam (English physician)
Har|wich (port, England)
Hary|ana (state, India)
Harz (mountains, Germany)
has
has-been +s noun
Has|dru|bal (Carthaginian general)
hash
hash|es

hashed
hash|ing
hash browns
Hash|em|ite +s
ha|shish
hash mark +s
Hasid
  Hasid|im
Hasid|ic
Hasid|ism
Has|kal|ah
Has|mo|nean
hasn't
hasp +s +ed +ing
Has|selt (city,
  Belgium)
Has|sid (*use* Hasid)
  Has|sid|im
Has|sid|ic (*use*
  Hasidic)
Has|sid|ism (*use*
  Hasidism)
has|sle
  has|sles
  has|sled
  has|sling
has|sock +s
hast
hast|ate
haste
  hastes
  hast|ed
  hast|ing
hast|en +s +ed +ing
hasti|ly
hasti|ness
Hast|ings (battle site,
  England; community,
  Canada)
Hast|ings, War|ren
  (British colonial
  administrator)
hasti-note +s (*use*
  hasty note)
hasty
  hasti|er
  hasti|est
hasty note +s
hat
  hats
  hat|ted
  hat|ting
hat|band +s
hat box
  hat boxes
hatch
  hatch|es
  hatched
  hatch|ing
hatch|abil|ity
hatch|back +s
hatch|er +s

hatch|ery
  hatch|eries
hatch|et +s
hatchet-faced
hatchet|man
  hatchet|men
hatch|ing +s *noun*
hatch|ling +s
hatch|ment +s
hatch|way +s
hate
  hates
  hated
  hating
hate|able
hate|ful
hate|ful|ly
hate|ful|ness
hate mail
hate-monger +s
hate-monger|ing
hater +s (one who
  hates)
Hat|field, Rich|ard
  Ben|nett (Cdn
  politician)
hat|ful +s
hath
Hatha|way, Anne
  (wife of
  Shakespeare)
hatha yoga
Hath|or (*Egyptian
  Myth*)
hat|less
hat|pin +s
hatred +s
Hat|shep|sut
  (Egyptian queen)
hat stand +s
hat|ted *adjective*
hat|ter +s (one who
  makes hats)
hat trick +s
Hat|tu|sa (ancient city,
  Turkey)
hau|berk +s
Hau|den|au|sanee
  plural
  Hau|den|au|sanee
  or
  Hau|den|au|san|ees
haught|i|ly
haught|i|ness
haughty
  haught|i|er
  haught|i|est
haul +s +ed +ing
  (drag; amount towed
  or gained; distance)
  [☞ hall]
haul|age
haul|back +s

haul|er +s (one who
  hauls)
  [☞ holler, Haller]
haul|ing *noun*
haulm +s
haul out *verb*
  hauls out
  hauled out
  haul|ing out
haul|out +s *noun*
haunch
  haunch|es
haunt +s +ed +ing
haunt|ed *adjective*
haunt|er +s
haunt|ing +s *adjective
  & noun*
haunt|ing|ly
**Haupt|mann,
  Ger|hart** (German
  dramatist)
Hausa
  plural Hausa or
  Hau|sas
haus|frau +s
**Hauss|mann, Baron
  Georges-Eugène**
  (French urban
  planner)
  [☞ Housman,
  houseman]
haut|boy +s
haute (upper-class)
haute cou|ture
haute cui|sine
haute école
Haute-Norman|die
  (region, France)
hau|teur (haughtiness)
  [☞ auteur]
haut monde
haut-relief +s
Ha|vana +s (capital of
  Cuba; cigar)
ha|varti
have (possess etc.)
  has
  had
  hav|ing
  [☞ halve]
Havel, Vác|lav (Czech
  president)
ha|ven +s
have-not +s
haven't
ha|ver +s +ed +ing
haver|sack +s
haver|sine +s
havoc
  hav|ocs
  hav|ocked
  hav|ock|ing
haw +s +ed +ing

Ha|waii (state & its
  largest island, US)
Ha|wai|ian +s
haw haw
hawk +s +ed +ing
  (bird; hunt; sell;
  gossip; clear the
  throat; trowel)
  [☞ Hawke, hock]
**Hawke, Rob|ert
  James Lee**
  (Australian prime
  minister)
  [☞ hawk, hock]
hawk|er +s
Hawke's Bay (in New
  Zealand)
Hawkes|bury (town,
  Canada)
hawk-eyed
**Haw|king, Ste|phen
  Wil|liam** (English
  physicist)
**Haw|kins, Cole|man
  Ran|dolph** (US
  saxophonist)
Haw|kins, Sir John
  (English sailor)
hawk|ish
hawk|ish|ly
hawk|ish|ness
hawk-like
hawk moth +s
hawk-nosed
hawk owl +s
Hawks, How|ard (US
  filmmaker)
hawks|bill +s
**Hawks|moor,
  Nicho|las** (English
  architect)
hawk|weed +s
Haw|kyns, Sir John
  (= Sir John
  Hawkins)
**Haw|ley, San|ford
  Des|mond ('Sandy')**
  (Cdn jockey)
  [☞ Holly]
**Ha|worth, Sir Wal|ter
  Nor|man** (English
  chemist)
hawse +s
hawse hole +s
hawse pipe +s
haws|er +s
haw|thorn +s
**Haw|thorne,
  Na|than|iel** (US
  writer)
hay +s +ed +ing (dry
  grass; in 'hit the hay',

'make hay')
[☞ hey, heigh-ho]
hay|cock +s
Haydn, Franz
Jo|seph (Austrian
composer)
Hayek, Fried|rich
Aug|ust von
(Austrian-born
economist)
Hayes (river, Canada)
Hayes, Helen (US
actress)
hay fever
hay|field +s
hay fork +s
hay|ing noun
hay|lage +s
hay|loft +s
hay|maker +s
hay|making
hay|mow +s
hay|rack +s
hay rake +s
hay rick +s
hay|ride +s
Hay River (river &
town, Canada)
hay|seed +s
hay|stack +s
hay|wire +s
haz|ard +s +ed +ing
haz|ard|ous
haz|ard|ous|ly
haz|ard|ous|ness
haze
  hazes
  hazed
  haz|ing
ha|zel +s
hazel|nut +s
hazi|ly
hazi|ness
Haz|litt, Wil|liam
(English writer)
hazy
  hazi|er
  hazi|est
H-bomb +s
HCFC
(hydrochlorofluoro-
carbon)
HCFCs
hCG (human chorionic
gonadotropin)
hCGs
H.D. (Hilda Doolittle)
HDL (high-density
lipoprotein)
HDLs
he
Head, Sir Fran|cis
Bond (lieutenant-

governor of Upper
Canada)
head +s +ed +ing (of
a body etc.)
[☞ heed]
head|ache +s
head|achy
head|band +s
head|bang|er +s
head|bang|ing
head|board +s
head-butt +s +ed
  +ing
head case +s
head|cheese +s
head cold +s
head count +s
head|dress
  head|dress|es
head|ed adjective
head|er +s
head|first
head|frame +s
head game +s
head|gear
head|hunt +s +ed
  +ing
head|hunt|er +s
head|hunt|ing noun
head|i|er
head|i|est
head|i|ly
head|i|ness
head|ing +s noun
head|lamp +s
head|land +s
head|less (without a
head)
[☞ heedless]
head|light +s
head|line
  head|lines
  head|lined
  head|lining
head|liner +s
head|lock +s
head|long
head-man verb
  head-mans
  head-manned
  head-manning
head|man noun
  head|men
head|master +s
head|mis|tress
  head|mis|tress|es
head|most
head|note +s
head of state
  heads of state
head-on adjective &
adverb
head|phone +s

head|piece +s
head|pond +s
head|quar|ter +s +ed
  +ing verb
head|quar|ters noun
head|rest +s
head|room
head|sail +s
head scarf
  head scarves
head-scratch|ing
head|set +s
head|ship
head shop +s
head|shot +s
head-shrink|er +s
heads|man
  heads|men
head|space +s
head|spring +s
head|stall +s
head|stand +s
head start +s
head|stock +s
head|stone +s
head|stream +s
head|strong
head|strong|ly
head|strong|ness
heads up interjection
heads-up noun &
adjective
head|teach|er +s
head-to-head
head up verb
  heads up
  head|ed up
  head|ing up
head-up adjective
head wait|er +s
head|ward
head|water +s
head|way
head|wind +s
head|word +s
head|work
heady
  head|i|er
  head|i|est
heal +s +ed +ing
(cure; become
healthy again)
[☞ heel]
heal|able
heal-all +s
heal|er +s
heal|ing +s noun &
adjective
health
health care
health food
health|ful

health|ful|ly
health|ful|ness
health|i|ly
health|i|ness
healthy
  health|i|er
  health|i|est
Hea|ney, Seamus
Jus|tin (Irish poet)
heap +s +ed +ing
heaped adjective
heap|ing adjective
hear verb
  hears
  heard
  hear|ing
  [☞ here]
hear|able
heard conjugated form
of hear
Heard and
Mc|Don|ald
Islands (in Indian
Ocean)
hear|er +s
hear|ing +s noun
hear|ing aid +s
hear|ing ear dog +s
hark|en +s +ed +ing
Hearne, Sam|uel
(English explorer)
hear|say
hearse +s
Hearst (town, Canada)
Hearst, Sir Wil|liam
How|ard (Cdn
politician)
Hearst, Wil|liam
Ran|dolph (US
newspaper tycoon)
heart +s (Anatomy;
emotion; essence;
core; Cards)
[☞ hart, Harte]
heart|ache +s
heart at|tack +s
heart|beat +s
heart|break +s
heart|break|er +s
heart|break|ing
heart|break|ing|ly
heart|broken
heart|burn
heart|en +s +ed +ing
heart|en|ing adjective
heart|en|ing|ly
heart|felt
hearth +s
heart-healthy
hearth rug +s
hearth|stone +s
heart|i|er
heart|i|est

heart|i|ly
heart|i|ness
heart|land +s
heart|less
heart|less|ly
heart|less|ness
heart-lung ma|chine +s
heart rate +s
heart-rending
heart-rending|ly
heart-search|ing
hearts|ease +s
heart|sick
heart|sick|ness
heart-smart
heart|sore
heart-stopper +s
heart-stopping
heart|strings
heart|throb +s
heart to heart *adverb*
heart-to-heart +s
  noun & adjective
heart|warm|ing
heart|warm|ing|ly
heart|wood
heart|worm +s
hearty
  heart|i|er
  heart|i|est
  heart|ies
heat +s +ed +ing
heat|ed *adjective*
heat|ed|ly
heat|er +s
Heath, Sir Ed|ward Rich|ard George (British prime minister)
heath +s
hea|then
  plural hea|then or hea|thens
hea|then|dom
hea|then|ism
hea|ther +s
hea|thery
heath|land +s
Heath Rob|in|son
Heath|row (airport, England)
heathy
heat|ing *noun*
heat lamp +s
heat|less
heat|proof
heat pump +s
heat rash
  heat rash|es
heat-resist|ant
heat seek|er +s

heat-seeking
heat shield +s
heat sink +s
heat|stroke
heat-treat +s +ed +ing
heat treat|ment +s
heat wave +s
heave
• *verb* (lift; utter; throw; rise; vomit)
  heaves
  heaved
  heav|ing
• *verb* (in 'heave in sight' & 'heave to')
  heaves
  hove
  heav|ing
• *noun*
  heaves
heave-ho
heav|en +s
heav|en|li|ness
heav|en|ly
heaven-sent
heaven|ward
heaven|wards
heav|er +s
heav|i|er
heavier-than-air
heav|i|est
heav|i|ly
heav|i|ness
Heavi|side, Oli|ver (English scientist)
Heaviside–Kennelly layer (= Heaviside layer)
Heavi|side layer
heavy
  heav|i|er
  heav|i|est
  heav|ies
heavy-duty
heavy-footed
heavy-handed
heavy-handed|ly
heavy-handed|ness
heavy-hearted
heavy-set
heavy|weight +s
Heb|bel, Chris|tian Fried|rich (German writer)
heb|dom|adal
Hebe (*Greek Myth*; asteroid)
  [☞ heebie-jeebies]
Hebei (province, China)
Hé|bert, Anne (Cdn writer)

Hé|bert, Jacques (Cdn writer)
Hé|bert, Louis (French-Cdn colonist)
hebe|tude
Heb|raic
Heb|raic|ally
Heb|ra|ism +s
Heb|ra|ist +s
Heb|rais|tic
Heb|raize
  Heb|raiz|es
  Heb|ra|ized
  Heb|raiz|ing
Heb|rew +s
Heb|ri|dean +s
Heb|ri|des (islands off Scotland)
Heb|ron (city, West Bank)
Hec|ate (*Greek Myth*; strait, Canada)
heca|tomb +s
heck
heckle (harass; dress flax)
  heckles
  heckled
  heck|ling
  [☞ Haeckel]
heck|ler +s
heckuva
hec|tare +s
hec|tic
hec|tic|ally
hecto|gram +s
hecto|graph +s +ed +ing
hecto|litre +s
hecto|metre +s
Hec|tor (*Greek Myth*)
hec|tor +s +ed +ing (bully; domineer)
hec|tor|ing *adjective*
hec|tor|ing|ly
Hec|uba (*Greek Myth*)
he'd
hed|dle +s
he|der +s (*use* cheder)
hedge
  hedg|es
  hedged
  hedg|ing
hedge|hog +s
hedge-hop
  hedge-hops
  hedge-hopped
  hedge-hopping
hedge-hopper +s
hedge-hopping +s
  noun & adjective
hedg|er +s

hedge|row +s
he|don|ic
hedon|ism
hedon|ist +s
hedon|is|tic
he|dys|arum +s
heebie-jeebies
  [☞ Hebe]
heed +s +ed +ing (notice)
heed|ful
heed|ful|ly
heed|ful|ness
heed|less (careless)
heed|less|ly
heed|less|ness
hee-haw +s
hee hee
heel +s +ed +ing (part of foot etc.; shoe; conteptible person; dog command; part of ship; lean over)
  [☞ heal]
heel|ball
heel|less
heel|tap +s
Hefei (city, China)
heft +s +ed +ing
heft|i|ly
heft|i|ness
hefty
  heft|i|er
  heft|i|est
Hegel, Georg Wil|helm Fried|rich (German philosopher)
He|gel|ian +s
He|gel|ian|ism
hegem|onic
he|gem|ony
he|gem|onies
Hegi|ra (*Islam*)
hegi|ra +s (a general exodus)
heh heh
Hei|deg|ger, Mar|tin (German philosopher)
Hei|deg|ger|ian +s
Hei|del|berg (city, Germany)
heif|er +s
Hei|fetz, Ja|scha (Russian-born US violinist)
heigh-ho
height +s (highness)
  [☞ hight]
height|en +s +ed +ing

height|ened *adjective*
Heil|bronn (city, Germany)
Hei|long|jiang (province, China)
Heil|tsuk
plural Heil|tsuk or Heil|tsuks
Heim|lich (manoeuvre)
Heine, (Chris|tian Jo|hann) Hein|rich (German poet)
hein|ous
hein|ous|ly
hein|ous|ness
Heinz 57 (mongrel)
Heinz 57s
heir +s (inheritor)
heir ap|par|ent
heirs ap|par|ent
heir-at-law
heirs-at-law
heir|dom
heir|ess
heir|less (without an heir)
heir|loom
heir pre|sump|tive
heirs pre|sump|tive
heir|ship +s (status of an heir)
Hei|sen|berg, Wer|ner Karl (German physicist & philosopher)
heist +s +ed +ing
Hejaz (region, Saudi Arabia)
Heji|ra (*use* Hegira)
heji|ra +s (*use* hegira)
Hek|ate (*Greek Myth: use* Hecate)
[☞ Hecate]
Hekla (volcano, Iceland)
Hel (*Scandinavian Myth*: underworld abode or goddess)
[☞ hell, Helle]
Hela (= Hel)
[☞ Helle, HeLa]
HeLa (cell)
held
hel|den|tenor +s
Helen (daughter of Zeus)
[☞ Hellen, Hellene]
Hel|ena (city, US; saint)
he|len|ium +s
he|li|acal (*Astronomy*)
[☞ helical]

heli|an|the|mum +s
heli|an|thus
plural heli|an|thus
hel|ical (like a helix)
[☞ heliacal]
hel|ical|ly
heli|ces
heli|chry|sum +s
he|li|city
he|li|ci|ties
heli|coid +s
Heli|con (mountain, Greece)
heli|con +s
heli|cop|ter +s +ed +ing
Heli|go|land (island, North Sea)
heli-log
heli-logs
heli-logged
heli-logging
heli-logger +s
heli-logging +s
helio|cen|tric
helio|cen|tric|ally
He|lio|gaba|lus (Roman emperor)
helio|graph +s +ed +ing
helio|graph|ic
heli|og|raphy
heli|om|eter +s
Heli|op|olis (Egyptian city; ancient Greek name for Baalbek)
He|li|os (*Greek Myth*)
helio|stat +s
helio|stat|ic
helio|trope +s
helio|trop|ic
helio|trop|ism
heli|pad +s
heli|port +s
heli-skier +s
heli-skiing
heli|tack
he|li|um
helix
heli|ces
hell +s (abode of the dead; state of suffering or chaos)
[☞ Hel, Helle]
he'll
hell|acious
hell|acious|ly
Hel|lad|ic
hell-bent
hell|cat +s
hell|diver +s
Helle (*Greek Myth*)
[☞ Hel, Hela]

hel|le|bore +s
hel|le|bor|ine +s
Hel|len (legendary king & ancestor of the Hellenes)
[☞ Helen, Hellene]
Hel|lene +s (Greek)
[☞ Hellen, Helen]
Hel|len|ic
Hel|len|ism
Hel|len|ist +s
Hel|len|is|tic
Hel|len|iz|a|tion
Hel|len|ize
Hel|len|iz|es
Hel|len|ized
Hel|len|iz|ing
Hel|ler, Jo|seph (US novelist)
Hel|les|pont (*ancient name for* the Dardanelles)
hell|fire
hell|gram|mite +s
hell|hole +s
hell-hound +s
hell|lion +s
hell|ish
hell|ish|ly
hell|ish|ness
hell-like
Hell|man, Lil|lian Flor|ence (US dramatist)
hell|lo +s
hell|rais|er +s
hell|rais|ing
Hell's An|gel +s
hell's bells
Hells Can|yon (gorge, US)
hell's half acre
helluva
hell|ward
helm +s +ed +ing
Hel|mand (river, Afghanistan)
Helm|cken (waterfall, Canada)
hel|met +s
hel|met|ed
helmet|less
Helm|holtz, Her|mann Lud|wig Fer|di|nand von (German physiologist & physicist)
hel|minth +s
hel|minth|ia|sis
hel|minth|ic
hel|minth|oid
hel|minth|ol|ogy

Hel|mont, Jo|an|nes Bap|tis|ta van (Belgian chemist)
helms|man
helms|men
helms|man|ship
Hé|lo|ïse (lover of Abelard)
Hel|lot +s (serf in ancient Sparta)
hel|lot +s (*in general use*)
helot|ism
hel|otry
help +s +ed +ing
help|er +s
help|ful
help|ful|ly
help|ful|ness
help|ing +s *noun*
help|less
help|less|ly
help|less|ness
help|line +s
help|mate +s
help-wanted index
Hel|sing|borg (port, Sweden)
Hel|sinki (capital of Finland)
helter-skelter +s
helve +s
Hel|ve|tian +s
Hel|vet|ica *proprietary*
Hel|vé|tius, Claude Ad|rien (French philosopher)
hem
hems
hemmed
hem|ming
hem|ag|glu|tin|ate
hem|ag|glu|tin|ates
hem|ag|glu|tin|at|ed
hem|ag|glu|tin|at|ing
hem|ag|glu|tin|a|tion
hemal
he-man
he-men
he|mat|ic
hema|tin
hema|tite +s
hema|to|cele
hema|to|crit +s
hema|to|logic
hema|to|logic|al
hema|tol|o|gist +s
hema|tol|ogy
hema|toma +s
hema|toxy|lin
hema|turia
heme +s

hem|ero|cal|lis
plural
hem|ero|cal|lis
hemi|an|opia
(= hemianopsia)
hemi|an|op|sia
hemi|cellu|lose +s
hemi|chord|ate +s
hemi|cycle +s
hemi|demi|semi|
     quaver +s
hemi|hed|ral
Hem|ing|way, Er|nest
Mil|ler (US novelist)
hemi|ola +s
hemi|plegia
hemi|plegic +s
hem|ip|ter|ous
hemi|spher|al
hemi|sphere +s
hemi|spher|ic
hemi|spher|ic|al
hemi|stich +s
Hem|kund (lake,
India)
hem|line +s
hem|lock +s
hem|mer +s
hemo|coel +s
hemo|cya|nin
hemo|di|aly|sis
hemo|glo|bin
hemo|lymph
he|moly|sis
hemo|lytic
Hémon, Louis
(French-born Cdn
novelist)
hemo|philia
hemo|phil|iac +s
noun
hemo|phil|ic *adjective*
hem|or|rhage
hem|or|rhag|es
hem|or|rhaged
hem|or|rhag|ing
hem|or|rhag|ic
hem|or|rhoid +s
hem|or|rhoid|al
hemo|sta|sis
hemo|stat|ic
hemp +s
hemp|en
hem|stitch
hem|stitch|es
hem|stitched
hem|stitch|ing
hem|stitch|ing *noun*
hen +s
Henan (province,
China)

hen and chick|ens
(plant)
hens and chick|ens
hen|bane
hence
hence|forth
hence|forward
hench|man
hench|men
Hen|day, An|thony
(Cdn explorer)
Hen|der|son, Ar|thur
(British politician)
hen|dia|dys
Hen|drix, Jimi (US
guitarist)
hene|quen
henge +s
Hen|gist (Jutish
leader)
hen|house +s
Henie, Sonja
(Norwegian figure
skater)
Hen|ley +s
hen|na +s +ed +ing
hen|naed *adjective*
heno|theism
heno|theist +s
hen|peck +s +ed
+ing
hen|pecked *adjective*
Henry (Portuguese
prince; kings of
England, France &
Germany)
[☞ henry]
Henry, Jo|seph (US
physicist)
Henry, Mar|tha (Cdn
actress)
Henry, O. (US writer)
Henry, Pat|rick (US
statesman)
Henry, Wil|liam
Alex|an|der (Cdn
politician)
henry (unit of
inductance)
hen|ries or henrys
Hen|son, Jim (US
puppeteer)
Henze, Hans Wer|ner
(German composer)
hep (hepatitis; *for*
stylish, aware *or*
make stylish *use* hip)
hep|per
hep|pest
heps
hepped
hep|ping
[☞ hip]

hep|ar|in
hep|ar|in|iz|a|tion
hep|ar|in|ize
hep|ar|in|iz|es
hep|ar|in|ized
hep|ar|in|iz|ing
hep|ar|in|ized
adjective
hep|atic
hep|at|ica +s
hepa|titis
Hep|burn, Aud|rey
(US actress)
Hep|burn,
Kath|ar|ine (US
actress)
Hep|burn, Mitch|ell
Fred|erick (Cdn
politician)
hep|cat +s
Heph|aes|tus (*Greek
Myth*)
Hepple|white,
George (English
cabinetmaker)
hept|ad +s
hepta|gon +s
hept|ag|on|al
hepta|hed|ral
hepta|hed|ron
hepta|hed|rons or
hepta|hedra
hept|am|eter +s
hept|ane
hept|arch|ic
hept|arch|ic|al
hept|archy
hept|arch|ies
Hepta|teuch
hept|ath|lete +s
hept|ath|lon +s
hepta|valent
Hep|worth, Dame
(Joce|lyn) Bar|bara
(English sculptor)
her *pronoun*
[☞ Herr]
Hera (*Greek Myth*)
Hera|cles (*Greek name
for* Hercules)
Hera|cli|tus (Greek
philosopher)
Her|ac|lius (Byzantine
emperor)
Her|ak|lion (capital of
Crete)
her|ald +s +ed +ing
(messenger;
announce, usher in)
[☞ Harold]
her|ald|ic
her|ald|ic|ally
her|ald|ist +s

her|aldry
Herat (city,
Afghanistan)
herb +s
herb|aceous
herb|aceous|ness
herb|age
herb|al +s
herb|al|ism
herb|al|ist +s
herb|arium
herb|aria
herbed
Her|bert, George
(English poet)
herbi|cid|al
herbi|cide +s
herbi|vore +s
herb|iv|or|ous
herb Rob|ert
herby
herb|i|er
herb|i|est
Her|ce|go|vina
(= Herzegovina)
Her|ce|go|vin|ian +s
(= Herzegovinian)
Her|cu|lan|eum
(ancient Roman
town)
Her|cu|lean
Her|cu|les (*Greek &
Roman Myth*)
Her|cyn|ian
herd +s +ed +ing
(group; mob;
herdsman; tend or
drive animals)
[☞ heard]
Her|der, Jo|hann
Gott|fried von
(German writer)
herd|er +s
herd|ing *noun*
Herds|man
(constellation)
herds|man (*in general
use*)
herds|men
here (this place)
[☞ hear]
here|abouts
here|after
here|at
here|by
her|ed|it|able
her|ed|ita|ment +s
her|ed|i|tar|ily
her|ed|i|tar|i|ness
her|ed|i|tary
her|ed|ity

Here|ford +s (city,
England; cattle)
[☞ Hertford]
Here|ford|shire
(former county,
England)
[☞ Hertfordshire]
here|in
here|in|after
here|in|before
here|of
Her|ero
   plural Her|ero or
   Her|er|os
her|esi|arch +s
her|esy
   her|esies
her|et|ic +s
her|et|ic|al
her|et|ic|al|ly
here|to
here|to|fore
here|under
here|upon
here|with
herit|abil|ity
herit|able
herit|ably
herit|age +s
herky-jerky
herm +s
Her|man, Wood|row
   Charles ('Woody')
   (US musician)
herm|aphro|dite +s
herm|aphro|dite brig
   +s
herm|aphro|dit|ic
herm|aphro|dit|ic|al
herm|aphro|dit|ism
Herm|aphro|ditus
   (Greek Myth)
her|men|eut|ic
her|men|eut|ic|al
her|men|eut|ic|al|ly
her|men|eut|ics
Her|mes (Greek Myth)
Her|mes
   Tris|me|gis|tus
   (legendary
   alchemist)
her|met|ic
her|met|ic|al
her|met|ic|al|ly
her|meti|cism
her|met|ism
her|mit +s
her|mit|age +s
her|mit|ic
Her|mo|sillo (city,
   Mexico)
her|nia
   her|nias or her|niae

herni|at|ed
herni|at|ed disc +s
herni|ation
Her|ning (city,
   Denmark)
Hero (Greek Myth)
hero
   heroes
Herod (king of Judea)
Herod Agrip|pa
   (rulers of ancient
   Palestine)
Herod Anti|pas
   (tetrarch of Galilee &
   Peraea)
Her|od|ias (wife of
   Herod Antipas)
Her|od|otus (Greek
   historian)
hero|ic
hero|ic|ally
hero|in (drug)
hero|ine +s
   (courageous woman)
hero|ism
her|on +s (bird)
   [☞ Herren]
Heron of
   Alex|an|dria
   (= Hero of
   Alexandria)
   [☞ Herren]
her|onry
   her|on|ries
Hero of Alex|an|dria
   (Greek inventor)
Her|oph|ilus (Greek
   anatomist)
hero-worship
   hero-worships
   hero-worshipped
   hero-worship|ping
hero-worship|per +s
her|pes
her|pes sim|plex
herpes|virus
   herpes|virus|es
her|pes zos|ter
her|pet|ic
her|peto|logic|al
her|pet|ol|o|gist +s
her|pet|ol|ogy
Herr (German man)
   Her|ren
Her|ren plural of Herr
   [☞ heron]
Herren|volk
Her|rick, Rob|ert
   (English poet)
hcr|ring
   plural her|ring or
   her|rings
herring|bone +s

her|ring chok|er +s
her|ring roe
her|ring scull +s
Her|ri|ot, James
   (English veterinarian
   & writer)
hers
Her|schel (island,
   Canada)
Her|schel, Caro|line
   Lu|cre|tia (German-
   born astronomer)
Her|schel, Sir
   (Fred|erick)
   Wil|liam (German-
   born astronomer)
Her|schel, Sir John
   Fred|erick Wil|liam
   (British astronomer)
her|self
Hert|ford (town,
   England)
   [☞ Hartford,
   Hereford]
Hert|ford|shire
   (county, England)
   [☞ Herefordshire]
Hertz, Gus|tav
   Lud|wig (German
   physicist)
Hertz, Hein|rich
   Ru|dolf (German
   physicist)
hertz (unit of
   frequency)
   plural hertz
Hertz|ian
Her|ze|go|vina
   (region, Bosnia and
   Herzegovina)
Her|ze|go|vin|ian +s
Herzl, Theo|dor
   (Hungarian-born
   Zionist leader)
Her|zog, Wer|ner
   (German filmmaker)
he's
he/she
Hes|iod (Greek poet)
hesi|tance
hesi|tancy
hesi|tant
hesi|tant|ly
hesi|tate
   hesi|tates
   hesi|tat|ed
   hesi|tat|ing
hesi|tat|er +s
hesi|tat|ing|ly
hesi|ta|tion +s
hesi|ta|tive

Hes|peler
   (community,
   Canada)
Hes|per|ian
Hes|peri|des (Greek
   Myth)
hes|per|id|ium
   hes|per|idia
Hes|per|us
Hes|qui|aht
   plural Hes|qui|aht or
   Hes|qui|ahts
Hess, Vic|tor Franz
   Fran|cis (US
   physicist)
   [☞ Hesse]
Hess, (Wal|ther
   Rich|ard) Ru|dolf
   (German Nazi)
   [☞ Hesse]
Hesse (state,
   Germany)
   [☞ Hess]
Hesse, Her|mann
   (German-born Swiss
   writer)
   [☞ Hess]
Hes|sian +s (of
   Hesse; boot; fly)
hes|sian +s (burlap)
hest
Hes|tia (Greek Myth)
het +s
he|taera
   he|tae|ras or
   he|tae|rae
he|taira (use hetaera)
   he|tai|ras or
   he|tai|rai
het|ero +s
hetero|chro|mat|ic
hetero|clite +s
hetero|clit|ic
hetero|cyclic
hetero|dox
hetero|doxy
   hetero|dox|ies
hetero|dyne
   hetero|dynes
   hetero|dyned
   hetero|dyn|ing
heter|og|am|ous
heter|og|amy
hetero|gen|eity
hetero|gen|eous
hetero|gen|eous|ly
hetero|gen|eous|ness
hetero|gen|esis
hetero|gen|etic
heter|og|on|ous
heter|og|ony
hetero|graft +s
heter|ol|o|gous

heter|ol|ogy
heter|om|er|ous
hetero|morph|ic
hetero|morph|ism
hetero|morph|ous
heter|on|om|ous
heter|on|omy
hetero|phyl|lous
hetero|phyl|ly
hetero|polar
heter|op|ter|an +s
heter|op|ter|ous
hetero|sex|ism
hetero|sex|ist +s
hetero|sex|ual +s
hetero|sex|u|al|ity
hetero|sex|ual|ly
heter|o|sis
  heter|o|ses
hetero|taxy
hetero|trans|plant
hetero|troph|ic
hetero|zygote +s
hetero|zygous
het|man +s
het up
heu|chera +s
heur|is|tic +s
heur|is|tic|ally
he|vea +s
Hev|esy, George
  Charles de
  (Hungarian-born
  radiochemist)
hew (chop, cut)
  hews
  hewed
  hewn or hewed
  hew|ing
  [☞ hue, hue and
  cry, Hughes, Hugh
  Capet]
hew|er +s
Hew|itt, Fos|ter
  Wil|liam (Cdn
  broadcaster)
Hew|son, Paul (Bono)
hex
  hexes
  hexed
  hex|ing
hexa|chord +s
hex|ad +s
hexa|deci|mal
hexa|gon +s
hex|ag|on|al
hex|ag|on|al|ly
hexa|gram +s
hexa|hed|ral
hexa|hed|ron
  hexa|hed|rons or
  hexa|hedra
hex|am|eter +s

hexa|met|ric
hex|ane
hex|apla
hexa|pod +s
Hexa|teuch
hexa|valent
hex|ose +s
hey (interjection; in
  'what the hey')
  [☞ hay, heigh-ho]
hey|day +s
Heyer|dahl, Thor
  (Norwegian
  anthropologist)
Hez|bol|lah
Hez|ekiah (king of
  Judah)
HGH (human growth
  hormone)
H-hour
hi
• (greeting)
• (in commercial use
  = high)
  [☞ hie, jai alai]
hia|tal
hia|tus
  hia|tus|es
Hia|watha (Onondaga
  chief)
Hib
Hib|achi +s
hiber|nacu|lum
  hiber|nacu|la
hiber|nate
  hiber|nates
  hiber|nat|ed
  hiber|nat|ing
hiber|na|tion +s
hiber|na|tor +s
Hi|bern|ian +s
hi|bis|cus
  hi|bis|cus|es
hic interjection
  [☞ hick]
hic|cough +s +ed
  +ing (use hiccup)
hic|cup
  hic|cups
  hic|cuped or
  hic|cupped
  hic|cup|ing or
  hic|cup|ping
hic|cupy
hic jacet
hick +s (rural)
  [☞ hic]
hick|ey +s
Hick|ok, James
  But|ler ('Wild Bill')
  (US marshal)
hick|ory
  hick|or|ies

hicks|ville +s
hid
Hi|dal|go (state,
  Mexico)
hi|dal|go +s (Spanish
  gentleman)
hid|den adjective
hid|den|ly
hid|den|ness
hide
• verb (conceal)
  hides
  hid
  hid|den
  hid|ing
• verb (flog)
  hides
  hided
  hid|ing
• noun
  hides
  [☞ Hyde]
Hide-A-Bed +s
  proprietary
hide-and-go-seek
  (= hide-and-seek)
hide-and-seek
hide|away +s
hide|bound
hided adjective
hid|eos|ity
  hid|eos|ities
hid|eous
hid|eous|ly
hid|eous|ness
hide out verb
  hides out
  hid out
  hid|den out
  hid|ing out
hide|out +s noun
hider +s
hidey-hole +s
hid|ing +s noun
hid|ro|sis
hid|rot|ic
hidy-hole +s
  (= hidey-hole)
hie (go quickly)
  hies
  hied
  hie|ing or hying
  [☞ hi, high, jai alai]
hier|arch +s
hier|arch|al (of a
  hierarch)
hier|arch|ic
hier|arch|ic|al (of a
  hierarchy)
hier|arch|ism
hier|arch|ize
  hier|arch|izes

hier|arch|ized
hier|arch|iz|ing
hier|archy
  hier|arch|ies
hier|atic
hier|atic|ally
hier|oc|racy
  hier|oc|ra|cies
hiero|glyph +s
hiero|glyph|ic +s
hiero|glyph|ic|al
hiero|glyph|ic|al|ly
hier|ol|ogy
hiero|phant +s
hiero|phant|ic
hi-fi +s
hig|gle
  hig|gles
  hig|gled
  hig|gling
higgledy-piggledy
  higgledy-
  piggle|dies
high +er +est +s
  (lofty etc.)
  [☞ hi, hie, jai alai]
high achiev|er +s
high-achiev|ing
High Arc|tic
high|ball +s +ed +ing
high beam +s
high|bind|er +s
high-born
high|boy +s
high|brow +s
high|bush
  high|bush|es
high chair +s
High Church
High Church|man
  High Church|men
High Com|mis|sion
High
  Com|mis|sion|er +s
high-concept
high-cut
high-defini|tion
high-density
high-end
high|er comparative of
  high
higher-up +s noun
high|falu|tin
high-five
  high-fives
  high-fived
  high-fiving
high-fiving noun
high fli|er +s (use
  high flyer)
high-flown
high fly|er +s
high-flying

high-frequen|cy
adjective
High Ger|man
high-grade
high-grades
high-graded
high-grading
high-grading *noun*
high-handed
high-handed|ly
high-handed|ness
high hat +s *noun* (top hat; snobbish person; *for* cymbals *use* hi-hat)
high-hat *adjective & verb* (supercilious; treat snobbishly)
high-hats
high-hatted
high-hatting
[☞ hi-hat]
high-heeled
High Holi|days
high-impact
high|jinks (*use* hijinks)
high-kicking
High|land +s (of Scotland; in names of other mountainous places; cattle)
high|land +s (*in general use*)
High|land|er +s (of Scotland)
high|land|er +s (*in general use*)
high lead +s
high-level
high life (luxurious living)
high|life (African dance music)
high|light +s +ed +ing
high|light|er +s
high|ly
highly-strung
High Mass
High Mass|es
high-minded
high-minded|ly
high-minded|ness
High|ness (royalty)
High|ness|es
high|ness (state of being high)
high-octane
High Park (in Toronto)
[☞ Hyde Park]

high-pitched
high point +s
high-power *adjective*
high-powered
high pres|sure (high-pressure *when preceding a noun*)
high-profile
high-quality
high-ranking
high-rise +s
high-risk
High River (town, Canada)
high road +s
high rol|ler +s
high school +s (high-school *when preceding a noun*)
high sea +s
high-security
High|smith, Pa|tri|cia (US writer)
high-sounding
high-speed
high-spirit|ed
high-spirit|ed|ly
high-spirit|ed|ness
high-stakes
high-step
high-steps
high-stepped
high-stepping
high-stepper +s
high-stepping *adjective*
high stick +s *noun*
high-stick +s +ed +ing *verb*
high-sticking *noun*
high-strung
hight (called)
[☞ height]
high|tail +s +ed +ing
high tech *noun*
high-tech *adjective*
high tech|nol|ogy (high-technol|ogy *when preceding a noun*)
high-tensile
high ten|sion (high-tension *when preceding a noun*)
high-toned
high-top +s (shoe)
high volt|age +s (high-voltage *when preceding a noun*)
high water *noun*
high-water mark
high|way +s

highway|man
highway|men
high wire +s
hi-hat +s (cymbals)
[☞ high hat, high-hat]
hi|jab +s
hi|jack +s +ed +ing
hi|jack|er +s
Hijaz (= Hejaz, Saudi Arabia)
hi|jinks
hijra (*use* hegira)
hike (walk; increase; hoist)
hikes
hiked
hik|ing
[☞ haik]
hik|er +s
hik|ing *adjective*
Hila (Inuit deity)
hila *plural of* hilum
hil|ari|ous
hil|ari|ous|ly
hil|ari|ous|ness
hil|ar|ity
hil|ar|ities
Hil|ary (university term)
[☞ Hillary]
Hil|bert, David (German mathematician)
Hilda (saint)
Hilde|brand (Pope Gregory VII)
Hilde|gard of Bing|en (saint)
Hil|des|heim (city, Germany)
hill +s +ed +ing
Hil|lary, Sir Ed|mund Per|ci|val (New Zealand mountaineer)
[☞ Hilary]
hill|billy
hill|bil|lies
Hil|lel (Biblical scholar)
Hil|liard, Nicho|las (English painter)
hill|i|er
hill|i|est
hill|i|ness
hill|ock +s
hill|ocky
hill|side +s
hill|top +s
hilly
hill|i|er
hill|i|est

hilt +s +ed +ing
hilum
hila
Hil|ver|sum (town, the Netherlands)
him *pronoun*
[☞ hymn]
Hi|ma|chal Pra|desh (state, India)
Hima|lay|an
Hima|lay|as (mountains, Asia)
hi|mat|ion +s
Himm|ler, Hein|rich (German Nazi)
Hims (= Homs, Syria)
him|self
Hi|na|yana (*Buddhism*)
hind +s
hind|brain +s
Hin|de|mith, Paul (German composer)
Hin|den|burg (*German name for* Zabrze, Poland)
Hin|den|burg, Paul Lud|vig von Ben|eck|en|dorff und von (German field marshal & statesman)
Hin|den|burg Line
hin|der[1] +s +ed +ing (impede)
hind|er[2] (rear)
Hindi (language)
hind|most
hind|quar|ters
hin|drance +s
hind|sight
Hin|du +s (people)
Hindu|ism
Hindu|ize
Hindu|iz|es
Hindu|ized
Hindu|iz|ing
Hindu Kush (mountains, Pakistan & Afghanistan)
Hindu|stan (Indian subcontinent)
Hindu|stani
hind|wing +s
Hines, Earl ('Fatha Hines') (US bandleader)
[☞ Heinz 57]
hinge
hin|ges
hinged
hin|ging
hinged *adjective*

hinge|less
hinny
  hin|nies
Hin|shel|wood, Sir
  Cyril Nor|man
  (English chemist)
hint +s +ed +ing
hin|ter|land +s
Hin|ton (town,
  Canada)
hip (joint; *Architecture*;
  stylish, aware; rose
  fruit)
  hip|per
  hip|pest
  hips
  hipped
  hip|ping
  [☞ hep]
hip bone +s
hip boot +s
hip cat +s (*use*
  hepcat)
hip check +s *noun*
hip-check +s +ed
  +ing *verb*
hip flask +s
hip hop (hip-hop
  when preceding a
  noun)
hip-hopper +s
hip|hug|ger +s
hip-hugging
hip-length
hip|less
hiply
hip|ness
Hip|par|chus (Greek
  astronomer)
hip|pe|as|trum +s
hipped *adjective*
hip|pie +s (flower
  child)
  [☞ hippy]
hippie|dom
hip|po +s
hippo|cam|pal
hippo|cam|pus
  hippo|campi
hip pock|et +s
hip|po|cras
Hip|poc|ra|tes (Greek
  physician)
Hip|po|crat|ic
Hip|po|crene
hippo|drome +s
hippo|griff +s
hippo|gryph +s (*use*
  hippogriff)
Hip|poly|ta (queen of
  the Amazons)
Hip|poly|tus (son of
  Theseus)

Hip|pom|enes
  (husband of
  Atalanta)
hippo|pota|mus
  hippo|pota|mus|es
  or hippo|pot|ami
Hippo Re|gi|us
  (ancient Roman city)
hippy (having large
  hips; *for* flower child
  use hippie)
  hip|pi|er
  hip|pi|est
  hip|pies
hip roof +s
hip|ster +s
hip|ster|ism
hip waders
hir|able (*use* hireable)
hira|gana
hire (employ; rent)
  hires
  hired
  hir|ing
  [☞ higher]
hire|able
hire car +s
hire|ling +s
hir|er +s
hir|ing +s *noun*
Hiro|hito (emperor of
  Japan)
Hiro|shige, Ando
  (Japanese artist)
Hiro|shi|ma (city,
  Japan)
Hirsch, John
  Ste|phen (Cdn
  director)
hir|sute
hir|sute|ness
hir|sut|ism
his
His|pan|ic +s
His|pani|cize
  His|pani|ciz|es
  His|pani|cized
  His|pani|ciz|ing
His|pani|ola (island,
  Greater Antilles)
His|pan|ist +s
his|pid
Hiss, Alger (US public
  official)
hiss
  hiss|es
  hissed
  hiss|ing
  hiss|er +s
hissy
hissy fit +s
hist
his|ta|mine

his|ta|min|ic
his|ti|dine
histo|chem|ical
histo|chem|ical|ly
histo|chem|istry
histo|com|pat|ibil|ity
histo|gen|esis
histo|gen|etic
histo|gram +s
histo|logic
histo|logic|al
histo|logic|al|ly
his|tol|o|gist +s
his|tol|ogy
  his|tol|o|gies
his|toly|sis
histo|lytic
his|tone +s
histo|patho|logic
histo|patho|logic|al
histo|path|ol|o|gist
  +s
histo|path|ol|ogy
histo|plas|mo|sis
his|tor|ian +s
his|tori|ated
his|tor|ic
his|tor|ic|al
his|tor|ic|al|ly
his|tori|cism
his|tori|cist +s
his|tori|city
his|tori|ciz|a|tion +s
his|tori|cize
  his|tori|ciz|es
  his|tori|cized
  his|tori|ciz|ing
his|tori|cized
  adjective
his|tori|ciz|ing *noun &*
  adjective
his|tori|og|raph|er +s
his|torio|graph|ic
his|torio|graph|ic|al
his|tori|og|raphy
hist|ory
  hist|or|ies
his|tri|on|ic +s
his|tri|on|ic|ally
hit
  hits
  hit
  hit|ting
hit-and-miss
hit and roll +s
hit and run +s (hit-
  and-run *when*
  preceding a noun)
hit and stay +s
hit and stick +s

hitch
  hitch|es
  hitched
  hitch|ing
Hitch|cock, Sir
  Al|fred Jo|seph
  (English filmmaker)
Hitch|cock|ian
hitch|er +s
hitch|hike
  hitch|hikes
  hitch|hiked
  hitch|hik|ing
hitch|hik|er +s
hitch|hik|ing *noun*
hi-tech (*in commercial*
  use)
hither
hither|to
hither|ward
Hit|ler, Adolf (Nazi
  leader)
Hit|ler +s
  (overbearing person)
Hit|ler|ian
Hit|ler|ism
Hit|ler|ite +s
hit|less
hit list +s
hit|maker
hit man
  hit men
hit-or-miss
hit|table
hit|ter +s
Hit|tite +s
hit woman
  hit women
HIV (human
  immunodeficiency
  virus)
hive
  hives
  hived
  hiv|ing
hiya *interjection*
HLA (human
  leukocyte antigen)
  HLAs
h'm +s (= hmm)
HMD (head-mounted
  display)
  HMDs
hmm +s
HMO (health
  maintenance
  organization)
  HMOs
Hna|tyshyn, Ramon
  John ('Ray') (Cdn
  governor general)

ho +s (interjection;
  prostitute)
  [☞ hoe]
hoag|ie +s
hoagy (*use* hoagie)
  hoag|ies
hoar (grey-haired;
  hoarfrost)
  [☞ whore, hoer]
hoard +s +ed +ing
  (stash, store,
  stockpile)
  [☞ horde]
hoard|er +s
hoard|ing +s *noun*
hoar|frost
hoar|hound +s (*use*
  horehound)
hoar|i|er
hoar|i|est
hoar|i|ly
hoar|i|ness
hoarse (husky, raspy)
  hoars|er
  hoars|est
  [☞ horse]
hoarse|ly
hoars|en +s +ed +ing
  (make or become
  hoarse)
  [☞ whoreson]
hoarse|ness
hoary
  hoar|i|er
  hoar|i|est
ho|at|zin +s
hoax
  hoax|es
  hoaxed
  hoax|ing
hoax|er +s
hob +s
Ho|bart (city,
  Australia)
Hob|bema, Mein|dert
  (Dutch painter)
Hobbes, Thom|as
  (English philosopher)
Hobbes|ian +s
hob|bit +s
hob|ble
  hob|bles
  hob|bled
  hob|bling
hobble|bush
  hobble|bush|es
hobble|de|hoy +s
hob|ble skirt +s
hobby
  hob|bies
hobby horse +s
hobby|ist +s
hob|gob|lin +s

hob|nail +s
hob|nailed
hob|nob
  hob|nobs
  hob|nobbed
  hob|nob|bing
hob|nob|ber +s
hobo
  ho|boes or **hobos**
Hobson's choice
Ho|che|laga (former
  Iroquoian village)
Ho Chi Minh
  (president of North
  Vietnam)
Ho Chi Minh City
  (Saigon)
hock +s +ed +ing
  (joint, knuckle; wine;
  pawn)
  [☞ hawk, Hawke]
hock|ey
Hock|ney, David
  (English artist)
Hoc|quart, Gilles
  (intendant of New
  France)
hocus
  ho|cus|es
  ho|cussed
  ho|cus|sing
hocus-pocus
hod +s
Ho|dei|da (port,
  Yemen)
hodge|podge +s
Hodg|kin, Alan Lloyd
  (English physiologist)
**Hodg|kin, Dor|othy
  Crow|foot**
  (Egyptian-born
  chemist)
Hodgkin's dis|ease
hodo|graph +s
hoe (tool)
  hoes
  hoed
  hoe|ing
  [☞ ho]
hoe|cake +s
hoe|down +s
hoer +s (one using a
  hoe)
  [☞ hoar, whore]
Hofei (= Hefei, China)
Hoffa, James Rid|dle
  ('Jimmy') (US labour
  leader)
**Hoff|man, Dus|tin
  Lee** (US actor)
  [☞ Hofmann]
Hof|mann, Hans
  (German-born artist)
  [☞ Hoffman]

**Hof|manns|thal,
  Hugo von** (Austrian
  poet)
hog
  hogs
  hogged
  hog|ging
  [☞ Hogg]
**Hogan, (Wil|liam)
  Ben|ja|min** ('Ben')
  (US golfer)
Ho|garth, Wil|liam
  (English painter)
hog|back +s
Hogg, James (Scottish
  poet)
Hog|gar (mountains,
  Algeria)
hog|ger +s
hog|gery
  hog|ger|ies
hog|gish
hog|gish|ly
hog|gish|ness
hog|like
hog line +s
Hog|ma|nay +s
hog|nose snake +s
hog's back +s
  (= hogback)
hogs|head +s
hog-tie
  hog-ties
  hog-tied
  hog-tying
Hog|town (Toronto)
Hog|town|er +s
hog|wash
hog|weed +s
hog-wild
Hohen|stau|fen
  (German dynastic
  family)
Hohen|zol|lern
  (German dynastic
  family)
Hoh|hot (capital of
  Inner Mongolia)
Ho|ho|kam
  plural **Ho|ho|kam** or
  Ho|ho|kams
ho-hum
hoick +s +ed +ing
hoi pol|loi
hoi|sin
hoist +s +ed +ing
hoist|er +s
hoity-toity
Hokan
hoke
  hokes
  hoked
  hok|ing

hoked-up
hokey
  hoki|er
  hoki|est
hokey-cokey
hokey|ness
hokey-pokey
Hok|kai|do (island,
  Japan)
hokku
  plural **hokku**
hokum
**Ho|ku|sai,
  Kat|su|shika**
  (Japanese painter)
Hol|arc|tic
Hol|bein, Hans ('the
  Elder') (German
  painter)
Hol|bein, Hans ('the
  Young|er') (German
  painter)
hold
  holds
  held
  hold|ing
hold|able
hold|all
hold back *verb*
  holds back
  held back
  hold|ing back
hold|back +s *noun*
hold|er +s
hold fast *verb*
  holds fast
  held fast
  hold|ing fast
hold|fast +s *noun*
hold|ing +s *noun*
hold out *verb*
  holds out
  held out
  hold|ing out
hold|out +s *noun*
hold over *verb*
  holds over
  held over
  hold|ing over
hold-over +s *noun*
hold up *verb*
  holds up
  held up
  hold|ing up
hold|up +s *noun*
hole (empty space)
  holes
  holed
  hol|ing
  [☞ whole]
hole-and-corner
hole card +s

hole-in-one
  holes-in-one
holey (with holes)
  [☞ holy, wholly, Holi]
Holi (Hindu festival)
  [☞ holy, wholly]
Holi|day, Bil|lie (US singer)
holi|day +s +ed +ing
holi|day|er +s
holiday|maker +s
hol|i|er
holier-than-thou
hol|i|est
hol|i|ly
Hol|i|ness (title)
hol|i|ness
Hol|in|shed, Raph|ael (English chronicler)
hol|ism
hol|ist +s
hol|is|tic
hol|is|tic|ally
Hol|land (the Netherlands)
hol|land (linen)
hol|land|aise
Hol|land|er +s
Hol|lands (gin)
hol|ler +s +ed +ing (yell)
  [☞ Haller, hauler]
Hol|ler|ith, Her|man (US computer scientist)
hol|low +s +ed +ing
hollow-cheeked
hollow-eyed
hol|low|ly
hol|low|ness
hollow-point +s
hollow|ware
Holly, Buddy (US singer-songwriter)
  [☞ Hawley]
holly
  hol|lies
holly|hock +s
Holly|wood (Film)
holm +s (oak)
  [☞ hom, home]
Holmes, Ar|thur (English geophysicist)
Holmes, Oli|ver Wen|dell (1809–94; US writer)
Holmes, Oli|ver Wen|dell (1841–1935; US jurist)
Holmes, Sher|lock (fictional detective)

Holmes|ian
hol|mium
Holo|caust (Nazi mass murder of Jews)
holo|caust +s (large-scale destruction; sacrifice)
holo|caust|al
Holo|cene
holo|enzyme +s
Holo|fer|nes (Bible)
holo|gram +s
holo|graph +s
holo|graph|ic
holo|graph|ic|ally
hol|og|raphy
holo|hed|ral
holo|phyte +s
holo|phyt|ic
holo|thur|ian +s
holo|type +s
hols (holidays)
  [☞ Hals]
Holst, Gus|tav Theo|dore (English composer)
Hol|stein +s
Holstein-Friesian
hol|ster +s
holt +s
hol|ub|tsi
holus-bolus
holy (sacred etc.; as interjection)
  hol|i|er
  hol|i|est
  [☞ holey, Holi, wholly]
holy day +s (religious festival)
Holy|head (town, Wales)
holy moly
holy of hol|lies
Holy See (papacy)
holy|stone
  holy|stones
  holy|stoned
  holy|ston|ing
hom (plant; juice)
  [☞ holm, home]
homa
hom|age +s
hom|bre +s (man)
  [☞ ombre, ombré]
hom|burg +s (hat)
home (residence; be guided)
  homes
  homed
  hom|ing
  [☞ holm, hom]

home-baked
home base +s
home-based
home|body
  home|bod|ies
home|bound
home|boy +s
home|brew
home-brewed
home build|er +s
home|built
home|buy|er +s
home care
home carer +s
home|com|ing +s
home ec
home fires
home fry
  home fries
home|girl +s
home|grown
home ice (home-ice when preceding a noun)
Homel (city, Belarus)
home|land +s
home|less
home|less|ness
home|like
home|li|ness
home|ly
  home|li|er
  home|li|est
home|made
home|maker +s
home|making
home mov|ie +s
homeo|path +s
homeo|path|ic
homeo|path|ic|ally
hom|eop|ath|ist +s
hom|eop|athy
homeo|sta|sis
  homeo|sta|ses
homeo|stat|ic
homeo|therm +s
homeo|therm|al
homeo|therm|ic
homeo|thermy
home|owner +s
home owner|ship
home page +s
home plate
home port +s
Homer (Greek poet)
Homer, Wins|low (US painter)
homer +s +ed +ing
Ho|mer|ic
home|room +s
home run +s

homes plural & conjugated form of home
  [☞ Holmes]
home-school +s +ed +ing
home-school|er
home-school|ing noun
home|sick
home|sick|ness
home|site +s
home|spun +s
home|stand +s
home|stay +s
home|stead +s +ed +ing
home|stead|er +s
home stretch
  home stretch|es
home|style
home|town +s
home|ward
homeward-bound adjective preceding a noun
home|wards
home|work
home|work|er +s
home wreck|er +s
homey
  hom|i|er
  hom|i|est
homey|ness
homi|cid|al
homi|cide +s
hom|i|er
hom|i|est
homi|let|ic
homi|let|ic|al
hom|il|ist +s
hom|ily
  hom|ilies
hom|i|ness (use homeyness)
hom|ing adjective
hom|in|id +s
hom|in|oid +s
hom|iny
homme du nord
  hommes du nord
hom|mos (use hummus)
Homo (human genus)
homo +s
homo|cen|tric
homo|erot|ic
homo|eroti|cism
homo|erot|ism (= homoeroticism)
hom|og|am|ous
hom|og|amy
hom|ogen|ate +s

homo|gen|eity
homo|gen|eous (of
the same kind;
uniform)
[☞ homogenous]
homo|gen|eous|ly
homo|gen|eous|ness
homo|gen|etic
hom|ogen|iz|a|tion
hom|ogen|ize
hom|ogen|iz|es
hom|ogen|ized
hom|ogen|iz|ing
hom|ogen|ized
adjective
hom|ogen|iz|er +s
hom|ogen|ous
(Biology: having
common descent)
[☞ homogeneous]
hom|ogeny
homo|graft +s
homo|graph +s
homo|graph|ic
homo|log +s (use
homologue)
hom|olo|gate
hom|olo|gates
hom|olo|gat|ed
hom|olo|gat|ing
hom|olo|ga|tion
homo|logic|al
hom|olo|gize
hom|olo|giz|es
hom|olo|gized
hom|olo|giz|ing
hom|olo|gous
homo|logue +s
hom|ol|ogy
hom|olo|gies
homo|morph|ic
homo|morph|ic|ally
homo|morph|ism +s
homo|morph|ous
homo|morphy
homo|nym +s
homo|nym|ic
hom|onym|ous
homo|phobe +s
homo|phob|ia
homo|phob|ic
homo|phone +s
homo|phon|ic
homo|phon|ic|ally
hom|oph|on|ous
hom|oph|ony
hom|op|ter|an +s
hom|op|ter|ous
Homo sa|pi|ens
homo|sex|ual +s
homo|sex|u|al|ity
homo|sex|ual|ly
homo|zygos|ity

homo|zygote +s
homo|zygous
Homs (city, Syria)
hom|un|cu|lus
hom|un|cu|li
homy (use homey)
hom|i|er
hom|i|est
hon (honey,
sweetheart)
hon|cho
• noun
hon|chos
• verb
hon|choes
hon|choed
honcho|ing
Hon|dur|an +s
Hon|dur|as (country,
Central America)
hone
hones
honed
hon|ing
Hon|eck|er, Erich
(East German
statesman)
Hon|eg|ger, Ar|thur
(French composer)
hon|est
hon|est Injun
offensive
hon|est|ly
honest-to-God
honest-to-goodness
hon|esty
hon|est|ies
hon|ey +s
honey bag +s
honey|bee +s
honey buck|et +s
honey|bun +s
honey|bunch
honey|bunch|es
honey cake +s
honey|comb +s +ed
+ing
honey|combed
adjective
honey|dew +s
honey|eater +s
honeyed
honey|guide +s
honey-like
honey|moon +s +ed
+ing
honey|moon|er +s
honey sac +s
honey|suckle +s
honey-sweet
honey wag|on +s

Hong Kong (Special
Administrative
Region, China)
Hong Kong|er +s
Hon|gue|do (strait,
Canada)
Ho|ni|ara (capital of
the Solomon Islands)
hon|ied (use honeyed)
honk +s +ed +ing
honk|er +s
honk|ing adjective
honky offensive
hon|kies
honky-tonk +s
hon|nête homme
hon|nêtes hommes
Hono|lulu (city,
Hawaii)
hon|or +s +ed +ing
(use honour)
honor|able (use
honourable)
honor|able|ness (use
honourableness)
honor|ably (use
honourably)
honor|and +s
honor|ari|um
honor|ari|ums or
honor|aria
honor|ary
honor|ee +s (use
honouree)
honor|ific +s
honor|ific|ally
hon|or|is causa
Hon|our (title)
hon|our +s +ed +ing
Hon|our|able (title)
hon|our|able
hon|our|able|ness
hon|our|ably
hon|our|ary (use
honorary)
hon|our|ee +s
Hon|shu (island,
Japan)
hoo interjection
[☞ who]
Hooch, Pieter de
(Dutch painter)
hooch
hooch|es
Hood, Thom|as
(English poet)
hood +s +ed +ing
(covering, cover;
hoodlum)
'hood +s
(neighbourhood)
hood|ed adjective
hood|ie +s

Hood|less, Adel|aide
(Cdn social reformer)
hood|less
hood|like
hood|lum +s
hoo|doo +s +ed +ing
hood|wink +s +ed
+ing
hooey
hoof
• noun
hoofs or hooves
• verb
hoofs
hoofed
hoof|ing
hoof-and-mouth
dis|ease
hoofed adjective
hoof|er +s
hoof|print +s
Hoogh|ly (river, India)
hoo-ha +s
hoo-hah +s (= hoo-
ha)
hoo-haw +s (= hoo-
ha)
hook +s +ed +ing
[☞ Hooke]
hook|ah +s
hook and eye
hooks and eyes
hook-and-loop
Hooke, Rob|ert
(English scientist)
hooked adjective
Hook|er, Sir Jo|seph
Dal|ton (English
botanist)
Hook|er, Rich|ard
(English theologian)
hook|er +s
Hooke's law
hook|ey (in 'play
hookey': use hooky)
[☞ hooky]
hook|ing noun
hook|less
hook|let +s
hook|like
hook nose +s
hook-nosed
Hook of Hol|land
(port, the
Netherlands)
hook shot +s
hook|tend|er +s
hook up verb
hooks up
hooked up
hook|ing up
hook|up +s noun
hook|worm +s

hooky (in 'play
hooky'; like a hook;
catchy)
hook|i|er
hook|i|est
hoo|li|gan +s
hoo|li|gan|ism
hoop +s +ed +ing
(circular band;
Basketball; bind,
encircle)
[☞ whoop]
hoop|la
hoo|poe +s
hoops
hoop|ster +s
hoo|ray
Hoo|ray Henry
Hoo|ray Henrys or
Hoo|ray Hen|ries
hoose|gow +s
Hoo|sier +s
hoot +s +ed +ing
hootch (*use* hooch)
hootch|es
[☞ de Hooch]
hoot|en|anny
hoot|en|an|nies
hoot|er +s
hoots
Hoo|ver, Her|bert
Clark (US president)
Hoo|ver, John Edgar
(US FBI director)
Hoo|ver, Wil|liam
Henry (US
industrialist)
Hoo|ver +s
proprietary noun
(vacuum cleaner)
hoo|ver +s +ed +ing
verb (vacuum)
Hoo|ver|ville +s
hooves
hop
hops
hopped
hop|ping
Hope, An|thony
(English author)
Hope, Bob (US
comedian)
hope
hopes
hoped
hoping
hope|ful
hope|ful|ly
hope|ful|ness
Hopeh (= Hebei,
China)
hope|less
hope|less|ly

hope|less|ness
hoper +s
hop|head +s
hop horn|beam +s
Hopi
plural Hopi or Hopis
Hop|kins, Sir
An|thony Phil|ip
(Welsh actor)
Hop|kins, Sir
Fred|erick
Gow|land (English
biochemist)
Hop|kins, Ger|ard
Man|ley (English
poet)
Hop|kins, Johns (US
financier)
hop|lite +s
hopped up (hopped-
up *when preceding a
noun*)
Hop|per, Art (US
painter)
hop|per +s
hop|ping *noun &
adjective*
hop|ping mad
hop|ple
hop|ples
hop|pled
hop|pling
hop|sack
hop|sack|ing
hop|scotch
hop|scotch|es
hop|scotched
hop|scotch|ing
hora
Hor|ace (Roman poet)
[☞ Horus]
hor|ary
Hor|atian
horde +s (crowd,
pack)
[☞ hoard]
hore|hound +s
hor|izon +s
hor|izon|less
hori|zon|tal
hori|zon|tal|ity
hori|zon|tal|ly
hori|zon|tal|ness
hork +s +ed +ing
hor|mon|al
hor|mon|al|ly
hor|mone +s
Hor|muz (island &
strait, Middle East)
Horn (cape,
S America)
[☞ Horne]
horn +s +ed +ing

horn|beam +s
horn|bill +s
horn|blende +s
horn|book +s
Horn|by (island,
Canada)
Horne, Lena (US
performer)
[☞ Horn]
horned *adjective*
hor|net +s
hornet's nest +s
horn|fels
plural horn|fels or
horn|fels|es
horn|i|er
horn|i|est
horn|i|ness
horn|ist +s
horn|less
horn|like
Horn of Af|ri|ca
(peninsula, Africa)
horn|pipe +s
horn-rimmed
horn-rims
horn|swog|gle
horn|swog|gles
horn|swog|gled
horn|swog|gling
horn|swog|gler +s
horn|worm +s
horn|wort +s
horny
horn|i|er
horn|i|est
horo|loge +s
hor|ol|o|ger +s
horo|logic
horo|logic|al
hor|ol|o|gist +s
hor|ol|ogy
horo|scope +s
horo|scop|ic
hor|os|copy
Horo|witz, Vlad|i|mir
(Russian-born
pianist)
hor|ren|dous
hor|ren|dous|ly
hor|rible
hor|rible|ness
hor|ribly
hor|rid
hor|rid|ly
hor|rid|ness
hor|rif|ic
hor|rif|ic|ally
hor|ri|fi|ca|tion
hor|rify
hor|ri|fies

hor|ri|fied
hor|ri|fy|ing
hor|ri|fy|ing *adjective*
hor|ri|fy|ing|ly
hor|ri|pi|la|tion
hor|ror +s
horror-strick|en
horror-struck
Horsa (Jutish leader)
hors de com|bat
hors d'oeuvre
hors d'oeuvres
horse (animal; frame;
heroin; *Nautical*;
Mining; fool around)
hors|es
horsed
hors|ing
[☞ hoarse]
horse-and-buggy
horse|back
horse|bean +s
horse|box
horse|boxes
horse bun +s
horse-drawn
horse feath|ers
horse|flesh
horse|fly
horse|flies
horse|hair
horse|hide +s
horse laugh +s
horse|leech
horse|leech|es
horse|less
horse|like
horse mack|erel
plural
horse mack|erel or
horse mack|erels
horse|man
horse|men
horse|man|ship
horse|meat
Hor|sens (port,
Denmark)
horse opera
horse op|er|as
horse|play
horse|play|er +s
horse pond +s
horse|power
plural horse|power
horse race +s
horse racing
horse|radish
horse|radish|es
horse|shit
horse|shoe +s
Horse|shoe Falls
(part of Niagara
Falls)

horse|tail +s
horse-trade
  horse-trades
  horse-traded
  horse-trading
horse trad|er +s
horse-trading *noun*
horse|whip
  horse|whips
  horse|whipped
  horse|whip|ping
horse|woman
  horse|women
horsey *adjective*
  hors|i|er
  hors|i|est
  [☞ horsie]
hors|ie +s *noun*
  [☞ horsey]
hors|i|ly
hors|i|ness
horst +s
horsy *adjective (use*
  horsey)
  hors|i|er
  hors|i|est
  [☞ horsie]
hor|ta|tion +s
hor|ta|tive
hor|ta|tory
hor|ten|sia +s
horti|cul|tur|al
horti|cul|tur|al|ist +s
  (= horticulturist)
horti|cul|tur|al|ly
horti|cul|ture
horti|cul|tur|ist +s
Hor|ton (river,
  Canada)
Horus (*Egyptian Myth*)
  [☞ Horace]
ho|san|na +s
hose
  hoses
  hosed
  hos|ing
Hosea (*Bible*)
hose|pipe +s
hos|er +s
hos|ier +s
hos|iery
hos|pice +s
hos|pit|able
hos|pit|ably
hos|pi|tal +s
hos|pi|tal|ity
hos|pi|tal|iz|a|tion +s
hos|pi|tal|ize
  hos|pi|tal|iz|es
  hos|pit|al|ized
  hos|pit|al|iz|ing
hos|pi|tal|ler +s
Host +s (*Eucharist*)

host +s +ed +ing
  (person or thing that
  hosts; multitude;
  heavenly host)
hos|ta +s
hos|tage +s
hos|tage|ship
hos|tel +s (shelter,
  residence)
  [☞ hostile]
hos|tel|ler +s
hos|tel|ling
hos|telry
  hos|tel|ries
host|ess
  host|ess|es
hos|tile (antagonistic)
hos|tile|ly
hos|til|ity
  hos|til|ities
host|ler +s
hot
  hot|ter
  hot|test
  hots
  hot|ted
  hot|ting
hot air (hot-air *when*
  preceding a noun)
hot and sour soup +s
hot|bed +s
hot-blooded
hot but|ton +s (hot-
  button *when*
  preceding a noun)
hot|cake +s
hotch|potch
  hotch|potch|es
hot cross bun +s
hot dog +s *noun*
hot-dog *verb*
  hot-dogs
  hot-dogged
  hot-dogging
hot-dogger +s
ho|tel +s
Hotel-Dieu
ho|tel|ier +s
hot|foot +s +ed +ing
hot|head +s
hot|head|ed
hot|head|ed|ly
hot|head|ed|ness
hot|house +s
hot key +s +ed +ing
hot|line +s
hot|liner +s
hot|link +s +ed +ing
hotly
hot metal (hot metal
  when preceding a
  noun)
hot|ness

hot pants
hot pink +s (hot-pink
  when preceding a
  noun)
hot plate +s
hot|pot +s
hot-press
  hot-presses
  hot-pressed
  hot-pressing
hot rod +s *noun*
hot rod *verb*
  hot rods
  hot-rodded
  hot-rodding
hot rod|der +s
hot seat
hot shoe +s
hot|shot +s
hot spot +s
hot spring +s
Hot|spur (Sir Henry
  Percy)
hot|spur +s
hot stove *adjective*
hot-tempered
Hot|ten|tot
  plural Hot|ten|tot or
  Hot|ten|tots
hot|tish
hot tub +s
hot tub|ber +s
hot tub|bing
hot walk|er +s
hot water bot|tle +s
hot well +s
hot-wire
  hot-wires
  hot-wired
  hot-wiring
Houde, Camil|lien
  (Canadian politician)
Hou|dini, Harry (US
  escape artist)
Hou|don, Jean
  An|toine (French
  sculptor)
hound +s +ed +ing
hound|er +s
hound|ish
hound's tongue +s
hounds|tooth
houn|gan +s
hour +s (unit of time)
  [☞ our, Auer]
hour|glass
  hour|glass|es
houri +s (woman)
hour-long
hour|ly
House +s (legislature)

house
  hous|es
  housed
  hous|ing
house|boat +s
house|boat|ing
house|bound
house|boy +s
house|break
  house|breaks
  house|broke
  house|brok|en
  house|break|ing
house|break|er +s
house|break|ing *noun*
house|broken
  adjective
house call +s
house|carl +s
house|carle +s (*use*
  housecarl)
house church
  house church|es
house|clean +s +ed
  +ing
house|clean|ing *noun*
house|coat +s
house|dress
  house|dress|es
house fath|er +s
house|fly
  house|flies
house front +s
house|ful +s
house guest +s
house|hold +s
house|hold|er +s
house hunt|er +s
house hunt|ing
house|husband +s
house|keep|er +s
house|keep|ing
house league +s
house|leek +s
house|less
house lights
house|maid +s
house|man (intern;
  male servant)
  house|men
  [☞ Housman,
  Haussmann]
house mar|tin +s
house|master +s
house|mate +s
house|mis|tress
  house|mis|tress|es
house moth|er +s
House of As|sem|bly
House of Com|mons
House of Lords
House of
  Rep|resent|a|tives

house par|ent +s
house|plant +s
house-proud
house|room
house-sit
  house-sits
  house-sat
  house-sitting
house-sitter +s
house-sitting *noun*
Houses of
  Par|lia|ment
house-to-house
house|top +s
house trail|er +s
house-train +s +ed
  +ing
house-trained
  adjective
house|wares
house|warm|ing
house|wife
  house|wives
house|wife|ly
house|wifery
house|work
hous|ing +s *noun*
Hous|man, Al|fred
  Ed|ward (English
  poet)
  [☞ houseman,
  Haussmann]
Hous|ton (city, US)
  [☞ Huston]
HOV (high-occupancy
  vehicle)
  HOVs
Hove (town, England)
hove
hov|el +s
hov|er +s +ed +ing
hover|craft
  plural hover|craft
hover|er +s
hover|fly
  hover|flies
hover|port +s
how +s
  [☞ Howe]
How|ard, Cath|er|ine
  (wife of Henry VIII)
How|ard, Henry, 1st
  Earl of Sur|rey
  (English courtier &
  poet)
How|ard, John
  (English prison
  reformer)
How|ard, John
  Win|ston (Australian
  prime minister)
How|ard, Les|lie
  (English actor)

How|ard, Trev|or
Wal|lace (English
  actor)
how|beit
how|dah +s
how-de-do +s
how do you do
  (greeting)
how-do-you-do +s
  (awkward situation)
howdy
Howe, Cla|rence
  Deca|tur (Cdn
  engineer &
  politician)
Howe, Elias (US
  inventor)
Howe, Gor|don
  ('Gord|ie') (Cdn
  hockey player)
Howe, Jo|seph (Cdn
  politician)
Howe, Rich|ard (4th
  Viscount Howe,
  British admiral)
Howe, Wil|liam (5th
  Viscount Howe,
  British general)
howe'er
Howe Sound (inlet,
  Canada)
Howe Street (in
  Vancouver)
how|ever
how|itz|er +s
howl +s +ed +ing
How|land, Sir
  Wil|liam P. (US-born
  Cdn politician)
howl|er +s
howl|ing *adjective*
Howlin' Wolf (US
  singer-songwriter)
How|rah (city, India)
howsoe'er
how|so|ever
how-to +s
Hoxha, Enver
  (Albanian statesman)
hoy +s
hoya +s
hoy|den +s
hoy|den|ish
Hoyle, Sir Fred
  (English
  astrophysicist)
Hoyle (in 'according to
  Hoyle')
HPV (human
  papilloma virus)
HQ (headquarters)
  HQs

Hradec Krá|lové
  (town, Czech
  Republic)
Hrod|na (city, Belarus)
HRT (hormone
  replacement
  therapy)
Hsia-men (= Xiamen,
  China)
Hsian (= Xian, China)
HST (harmonized
  sales tax)
HTML (Hypertext
  Markup Language)
http (hypertext
  transfer protocol)
Hua Guo Feng
  (Chinese statesman)
Huai|nan (city, China)
Hual|laga (river, Peru)
Huam|bo (city,
  Angola)
Huás|car (Incan
  chieftain)
Huas|ca|rán
  (mountain, Peru)
hub +s
hub and spoke
  adjective
hubba hubba
Hub|bard +s
  (mountain, Yukon–
  Alaska border;
  squash)
Hub|ble, Edwin
  Pow|ell (US
  astronomer)
Hub|ble (constant;
  telescope)
hubble-bubble +s
hub|bub +s
hubby
  hub|bies
hub|cap +s
Hubei (province,
  China)
hub|less
Hubli (city, India)
hu|bris
hu|bris|tic
huck +s +ed +ing
hucka|back
huckle|berry
  huckle|ber|ries
huck|ster +s +ed
  +ing
huck|ster|ing *noun*
huck|ster|ish
huck|ster|ism
HUD (head-up display)
  HUDs
Hud|ders|field (town,
  England)

hud|dle
hud|dles
hud|dled
hud|dling
Hud|son (bay, strait, &
  town, Canada; river,
  US)
  [☞ Hudson Bay,
  Hudson's Bay]
Hud|son, Henry
  (English explorer)
Hud|son Bay (bay,
  Canada; *for* trading
  company, blanket,
  coat, *etc. use*
  Hudson's Bay)
Hud|son Bay
  Low|lands (region,
  Canada)
Hud|son Plat|form
  (region, Canada)
Hudson's Bay
  (trading company,
  blanket, coat, etc.)
  [☞ Hudson Bay]
Hudson's Bay
  blan|ket +s
Hudson's Bay
  blan|ket coat +s
Hudson's Bay coat
  +s
Hudson's Bay
  Com|pany
Hudson's Bay point
  blan|ket +s
Hué (city, Vietnam)
hue +s (colour)
  [☞ hew, Hughes,
  Hugh Capet]
hue and cry
hued (coloured etc.)
  [☞ hewed]
hue|less
huevos ran|cheros
huff +s +ed +ing
huff|i|ly
huff|i|ness
huff|ish
huffy
  huff|i|er
  huff|i|est
hug
  hugs
  hugged
  hug|ging
huge
  huger
  hugest
huge|ly
huge|ness
hug|gable
hug|ger +s
hugger-mugger

Hug|gins, Sir
Wil|liam (British
astronomer)
Hugh Capet (French
king)
Hughes, Ed|ward
James ('Ted')
(English poet)
Hughes, (James
Mer|cer) Langs|ton
(US writer)
Hughes, How|ard
Rob|ard (US
industrialist, aviator,
& filmmaker)
Hugli (= Hooghly)
Hugo, Vic|tor Marie
(French writer)
Hu|gue|not +s
huh
Huhe|hot (= Hohhot,
Inner Mongolia)
Hui|chol
plural Hui|chol or
Hui|chols
hula +s (dance; skirt)
[☞ Hula Hoop]
Hula Hoop +s
proprietary
hula-hula +s (= hula)
hulk +s +ed +ing
hulk|ing adjective
Hull (cities, Canada &
England)
Hull, Cor|dell (US
statesman)
Hull, Rob|ert Mar|vin
('Bobby') (Cdn
hockey player)
hull +s +ed +ing
hul|la|ba|loo +s
hum
hums
hummed
hum|ming
hu|man +s
hu|mane
hu|mane|ly
hu|mane|ness
human in|ter|est
(human-interest
when preceding a
noun)
human|ism
human|ist +s
human|is|tic
human|is|tic|ally
hu|mani|tar|ian +s
hu|mani|tar|ian|ism
hu|man|ity
hu|man|ities
human|iz|a|tion +s

human|ize
human|iz|es
human|ized
human|iz|ing
human|kind
human|ly
human|ness
human|oid +s
human rights
(human-rights when
preceding a noun)
Hum|ber (rivers,
Canada; estuary,
England)
Hum|ber|side
(county, England)
hum|ble
hum|bler
hum|blest
hum|bles
hum|bled
hum|bling
humble|bee +s
humble|ness
hum|bly
Hum|boldt (town,
Canada)
Hum|boldt,
Fried|rich Hein|rich
Alex|an|der, Baron
von (German
explorer & scientist)
Hum|boldt, (Karl)
Wil|helm, Baron
von (German
philologist)
hum|bug
hum|bugs
hum|bugged
hum|bug|ging
humbug|gery
hum|ding|er +s
hum|drum +s
hum|drum|ness
Hume, David
(Scottish
philosopher)
hu|mec|tant +s
hu|mer|al
hu|mer|us (bone)
hu|meri
[☞ humorous]
humic
humid
humi|dex
hu|midi|fi|ca|tion
hu|midi|fi|er +s
hu|mid|ify
hu|midi|fies
hu|midi|fied
hu|midi|fy|ing
hu|midi|stat +s

hu|mid|ity
hu|mid|ities
humid|ly
humi|dor +s
humi|fi|ca|tion
hum|ify
humi|fies
humi|fied
humi|fy|ing
hu|mili|ate
hu|mili|ates
hu|mili|at|ed
hu|mili|at|ing
hu|mili|at|ing
adjective
hu|mili|at|ing|ly
hu|mili|a|tion +s
hu|mili|ator +s
hu|mil|ity
hum|mable
hum|mer +s
humming|bird +s
hum|mock +s
(hillock; forested
ground rising above
marsh; ridge in
icefield)
[☞ hammock]
hum|mocky
hum|mus (chickpea
spread)
[☞ humus]
hu|mon|gous
hu|mor +s +ed +ing
(use humour)
humor|al
humor|esque +s
humor|ist +s
humor|is|tic
humor|less (use
humourless)
humor|less|ly (use
humourlessly)
humor|less|ness (use
humourlessness)
humor|ous (funny)
[☞ humerus]
humor|ous|ly
humor|ous|ness
hu|mour +s +ed +ing
humour|less
humour|less|ly
humour|less|ness
hump +s +ed +ing
hump|back +s
hump|backed
adjective
hump|back sal|mon
plural hump|back
sal|mon
hump|back whale +s
humped adjective

Hum|per|dinck,
En|gel|bert (German
composer)
humph +s +ed +ing
Hum|phrey, Hu|bert
Hor|atio (US
statesman)
hump|less
hump|ty dump|ty
hump|ty dump|ties
humpy
hump|i|er
hump|i|est
hump|ies
hu|mun|gous (use
humongous)
humus (soil
constituent)
[☞ hummus]
humusy
Hun +s (people)
[☞ hon]
Hunan (province,
China)
hunch
hunch|es
hunched
hunch|ing
hunch|back +s
hunch|backed
hun|dred
plural hun|dred or
hun|dreds
hundred|fold
hun|dredth +s
hundred|weight +s
Hun|dred Years War
hung adjective
Hun|gar|ian +s
Hun|gary (country,
Europe)
hun|ger +s +ed +ing
hung|over
hun|gri|ly
hun|gri|ness
hun|gry
hun|gri|er
hun|gri|est
hunk +s
hun|ker +s +ed +ing
hunky
hunk|i|er
hunk|i|est
hunk|ies
hunky-dory
Hun|len (waterfall,
Canada)
Hun|nish
Hunt, (James Henry)
Leigh (English
writer)

Hunt, (Will|liam) Hol|man (English painter)
hunt +s +ed +ing
hunt|able
hunt-and-peck
hunt|ed *adjective*
Hun|ter, John (Scottish anatomist)
hunt|er +s
hunter-gather|er +s
hunt|er green +s
hunt|er or|ange +s
hunter's moon
hunt|ing *noun*
Hun|ting|don|shire (former county, England)
Hun|ting|ton (city, West Virginia)
Hun|ting|ton Beach (city, California)
Hun|ting|ton's chorea
Hun|ting|ton's dis|ease (= Huntington's chorea)
hunt|ress
hunt|ress|es
hunts|man
hunts|men
Hunts|ville (city, US; town, Canada)
Hun|yadi, János (Hungarian general)
hur|dle (*Athletics*; obstruction; clear a hurdle; erect hurdles)
hur|dles
hur|dled
hurd|ling [☞ hurtle]
hurd|ler +s
hurdy-gurdy
hurdy-gurdies
hurl +s +ed +ing
hurl|er +s
hur|ley
hurl|ing *noun* (= hurley)
hurly-burly
Huron (lake, N America; people, language)
plural Huron or Hurons
Hur|onia (region, Canada)
hur|rah +s +ed +ing
hur|ray +s +ed +ing
hur|ri|cane +s
hur|ried *adjective*

hur|ried|ly
hur|ried|ness
hurry (rush)
hur|ries
hur|ried
hurry|ing [☞ houri]
hurry-scurry
hurst +s (hill; wood; sandbank) [☞ Hearst]
Hur|ston, Zora Neale (US novelist)
hurt
hurts
hurt
hurt|ing
hurt|ful
hurt|ful|ly
hurt|ful|ness
hurt|ing *adjective*
hur|tle (move rapidly)
hur|tles
hur|tled
hurt|ling [☞ hurdle]
Hus, Jan (= John Huss)
Hus|ain (= Hussein, Jordanian king)
Hus|ain, Sad|dam (= Saddam Hussein)
hus|band +s +ed +ing
hus|band|er +s
hus|band|hood
hus|band|less
hus|band|ly
hus|band|ry
hush
hush|es
hushed
hush|ing
hush|a|by
hush|a|bye (*use* hushaby)
hush-hush
hush puppy
hush pup|pies
husk +s +ed +ing
husk|i|ly
husk|i|ness
husky
husk|i|er
husk|i|est
husk|ies
Huss, John (Bohemian religious reformer)
hus|sar +s
Hus|sein (Jordanian king 1953–99)

Hus|sein, Ab|dul|lah ibn (Jordanian king 1946–51)
Hus|sein, Sad|dam (Iraqi president)
Hus|serl, Ed|mund Gus|tav Al|brecht (German philosopher)
Hus|site +s
Hus|sit|ism
hussy
hus|sies
hus|tings
hus|tle
hus|tles
hus|tled
hust|ling
hust|ler +s
Hus|ton, John (US-born Irish filmmaker) [☞ Houston]
hut (shelter)
huts
hut|ted
hut|ting [☞ Hutt, Lower Hutt]
hutch
hutch|es
Hutch|i|son, (Will|liam) Bruce (Cdn writer & journalist)
hut|like
hut|ment +s
Hutt, Will|liam Ian deWitt (Cdn actor)
Hut|ter|ite +s
Hut|ton, James (Scottish geologist)
Hutu
plural Hutu or Hutus
Hux|ley, Al|dous Leon|ard (English writer)
Hux|ley, Sir An|drew Field|ing (British physiologist)
Hux|ley, Sir Jul|ian (English biologist)
Hux|ley, Thom|as Henry (English biologist)
Hu Yao|bang (Chinese politician)
Huy|gens, Chris|tiaan (Dutch physicist & astronomer)
Huys|mans, Joris Karl (French novelist)
huz|zah +s

Hwange (town, Zimbabwe)
hwyl
hya|cinth +s
hya|cinth|ine
Hya|cin|thus (*Greek Myth*)
Hya|des (*Greek Myth*; star cluster)
hyal|in *noun*
hyal|ine *adjective*
hyal|ite +s
hyal|oid
hyal|uron|ic
hy|brid +s
hy|brid|ism
hy|brid|ist +s
hy|brid|ity
hy|brid|iz|able
hy|brid|iz|a|tion +s
hy|brid|ize
hy|brid|izes
hy|brid|ized
hy|brid|iz|ing
hy|brid|iz|er +s
hy|brid|oma
hy|brid|omas or hy|brid|omata
hyda|tid +s
hyda|tidi|form
Hyde, Doug|las (president of Eire)
Hyde, Ed|ward (Earl of Clarendon)
Hyde (in 'Jekyll and Hyde')
Hyde Park (in London) [☞ High Park]
Hy|dera|bad (cities, India & Pakistan)
Hydra (*Greek Myth*; constellation)
hy|dra +s (polyp; something hard to destroy)
hy|dran|gea +s
hy|drant +s
hy|drate
hy|drates
hy|drat|ed
hy|drat|ing
hy|drat|ed *adjective*
hy|dra|tion +s
hy|dra|tor +s
hy|draul|ic
hy|draul|ic|ally
hy|draul|ics
hy|dra|zine +s
hy|dride +s
hy|dri|od|ic
hy|dro +s
hydro|bro|mic

hydro|bro|mide
hydro|car|bon +s
hydro|cele +s
hydro|ceph|alic
hydro|ceph|al|us
hydro|chlor|ic
hydro|chlor|ide +s
hydro|corti|sone +s
hydro|cyan|ic
hydro|dynam|ic
hydro|dynam|ic|al
hydro|dynam|i|cist +s
hydro|dynam|ics
hydro|elec|tric
hydro|elec|tri|city
hydro|fluor|ic
hydro|foil +s
hy|dro|gen +s
hy|dro|gen|ase +s
hy|dro|gen|ate
hy|dro|gen|ates
hy|dro|gen|at|ed
hy|dro|gen|at|ing
hy|dro|gen|at|ed
adjective
hy|dro|gen|a|tion
hy|dro|gen|ous
hydro|geo|logic
hydro|geo|logic|al
hydro|geol|o|gist +s
hydro|geol|ogy
hy|drog|raph|er +s
hydro|graph|ic
hydro|graph|ic|al
hydro|graph|ic|al|ly
hy|drog|raphy
hy|droid +s
hydro|lase +s
hydro|logic
hydro|logic|al
hydro|logic|al|ly
hy|drol|o|gist +s
hy|drol|ogy
hy|droly|sis
hy|droly|ses
hydro|lytic
hydro|lyze
hydro|lyz|es
hydro|lyzed
hydro|lyz|ing
hydro|mag|net|ic
hydro|mech|an|ics
hy|drom|eter +s
hydro|met|ric
hy|drom|etry
hy|dron|ium ion +s
hydro|path|ic
hy|drop|ath|ist +s
hy|drop|athy
hydro|phil|ic
hydro|phobia

hydro|phob|ic
hydro|phob|icity
hydro|phone +s
hydro|phyte +s
hydro|plane
hydro|planes
hydro|planed
hydro|plan|ing
hydro pole +s
hydro|ponic
hydro|pon|ic|ally
hydro|pon|ics
hydro|quin|one
hydro|sphere
hydro|stat|ic
hydro|stat|ic|al
hydro|stat|ic|al|ly
hydro|stat|ics
hydro|ther|apist +s
hydro|ther|apy
hydro|ther|mal
hydro|ther|mal|ly
hydro|thor|ax
hydro|trop|ism
hy|drous
hy|drox|ide +s
hy|drox|on|ium ion +s
hy|droxyl +s
hydro|zoan +s
hyena +s
Hy|geia (Greek Myth)
hy|giene
hy|gien|ic
hy|gien|ic|ally
hy|gien|ics
hy|gien|ist +s
hy|grom|eter +s
hygro|met|ric
hy|grom|etry
hy|groph|il|ous
hygro|phyte +s
hygro|scope +s
hygro|scop|ic
hygro|scop|ic|ally
hygro|scop|icity
hying
hylo|morph|ism
hylo|zo|ism
Hymen (Greek Myth)
hy|men +s (Anatomy)
hy|men|al (of the hymen)
hy|men|eal (of marriage)
hy|men|ium
hy|menia
hy|men|op|ter|an +s
hy|men|op|ter|ous
hymn +s +ed +ing
(Music)
hym|nal +s

hym|nary
hym|nar|ies
hymn book +s
hym|nic
hym|nod|ist +s
hym|nody
hym|nod|ies
hym|nol|o|gist +s
hym|nol|ogy
hym|nol|o|gies
hy|oid +s
hyos|cine
hyos|cya|mine
hyp|aes|the|sia
(diminished sensitivity)
[☞ hyperaesthesia]
hyp|aes|thet|ic
(having hypaesthesia)
[☞ hyperaesthetic]
hyp|aeth|ral
hype
hypes
hyped
hyp|ing
hyped up (hyped-up
when preceding a noun)
hyper
hyper|active
hyper|active|ly
hyper|activ|ity
hyper|aemia (use hyperemia)
hyper|aemic (use hyperemic)
hyper|aes|the|sia
(excessive sensitivity)
[☞ hypaesthesia]
hyper|aes|thet|ic
(having hyperaesthesia)
[☞ hypaesthetic]
hyper|baric
hy|per|bola (curve)
hy|per|bolas or hy|per|bolae
hy|per|bole +s
(exaggeration)
hyper|bolic
hyper|bolic|al
hyper|bolic|al|ly
hy|per|bol|ism
hy|per|bol|ize
hy|per|bol|iz|es
hy|per|bol|ized
hy|per|bol|iz|ing
hy|per|bol|oid +s
hy|per|bol|oid|al
Hyper|bor|ean +s
noun (Greek Myth)

hyper|bor|ean +s
noun & adjective (of
the extreme north)
hyper|choles|terol|
aemia
(use hyper-
cholesterolemia)
hyper|choles|terol|
emia
hyper|con|scious
hyper|critic|al
(overcritical)
[☞ hypocritical]
hyper|critic|al|ly
(overcritically)
[☞ hypocritically]
hyper|cube +s
hyper|emia
hyper|emic
hyper|esthe|sia
(excessive
sensitivity: use
hyperaesthesia)
[☞ hypaesthesia]
hyper|esthet|ic
(having
hyperaesthesia: use
hyperaesthetic)
[☞ hypaesthetic]
hyper|extend +s +ed
+ing
hyper|exten|si|bil|ity
hyper|exten|sible
hyper|exten|sion +s
hyper|focal
hy|per|gamy
hy|per|gam|ies
hyper|gly|caemia
(excess of glucose:
use hyperglycemia)
[☞ hypoglycemia]
hyper|gly|caemic
(having
hyperglycemia: use
hyperglycemic)
[☞ hypoglycemic]
hyper|gly|cemia
(excess of glucose)
[☞ hypoglycemia]
hyper|gly|cemic
(having
hyperglycemia)
[☞ hypoglycemic]
hyper|golic
hy|peri|cum +s
hyper|infla|tion
Hy|peri|on (Greek
Myth; Astronomy)
[☞ hyperon]
hyper|kinet|ic
hyper|link +s +ed
+ing
hyper|market +s
hyper|media

hyper|metro|pia
hyper|metrop|ic
hy|per|on +s (particle)
[☞ Hyperion]
hyper|opia
hyper|opic
hyper|pla|sia
hyper|real
hyper|real|ism
hyper|real|ist +s
hyper|real|is|tic
hyper|real|ity
hyper|sensi|tive
hyper|sensi|tive|ness
hyper|sensi|tiv|ity
hyper|sonic
hyper|sonic|ally
hyper|space
hyper|spa|tial
hyper|sthene
hyper|ten|sion (high
  blood pressure)
[☞ hypotension]
hyper|ten|sive
  (having high blood
  pressure)
[☞ hypotensive]
hyper|text +s
Hyper|text Mark|up
  Lan|guage
hyper|text|ual
hyper|text|ual|ly
hyper|ther|mia (high
  body temperature)
[☞ hypothermia]
hyper|ther|mic
  (having high body
  temperature)
[☞ hypothermic]
hyper|thyroid +s (of
  hyperthyroidism)
[☞
  hypothyroidism]
hyper|thyroid|ism
  (excessive thyroid
  activity)
[☞
  hypothyroidism]
hyper|tonia
hyper|tonic
hyper|ton|icity
hyper|troph|ic
hy|per|troph|ied
hy|per|trophy
  hy|per|tro|phies
hyper|venti|late
  hyper|venti|lates
  hyper|venti|lat|ed
  hyper|venti|lat|ing
hyper|venti|la|tion
  (rapid breathing)
[☞
  hypoventilation]

hyp|esthe|sia
  (diminished
  sensitivity: use
  hypaesthesia)
[☞ hyperaesthesia]
hyp|esthet|ic (having
  hypaesthesia: use
  hypaesthetic)
[☞ hyperaesthetic]
hyp|eth|ral (use
  hypaethral)
hypha
  hy|phae
hy|phal
Hypha|sis (ancient
  Greek name for the
  Beas)
hy|phen +s +ed +ing
hy|phen|ate
  hy|phen|ates
  hy|phen|at|ed
  hy|phen|at|ing
hy|phen|at|ed
  adjective
hy|phen|a|tion +s
hypno|gen|esis
hyp|nol|o|gist +s
hyp|nol|ogy
hypno|paedia (use
  hypnopedia)
hypno|pedia
Hyp|nos (Greek Myth)
hyp|no|sis
hypno|ther|apist +s
hypno|ther|apy
hyp|not|ic +s
hyp|not|ic|ally
hypno|tism
hypno|tist +s
hypno|tiz|able
hypno|tize
  hypno|tiz|es
  hypno|tized
  hypno|tiz|ing
hypo +s
hypo|aller|gen|ic
hypo|blast +s
hypo|caust +s
hypo|chlor|ite +s
hypo|chlor|ous
hypo|chon|dria
hypo|chon|dri|ac +s
hypo|chon|dri|ac|al
hypo|cotyl +s
hyp|ocrisy
  hyp|ocri|sies
hypo|crite +s
hypo|critic|al (of
  hypocrisy)
[☞ hypercritical]
hypo|critic|al|ly (with
  hypocrisy)
[☞ hypercritically]

hypo|cyc|loid +s
hypo|cyc|loid|al
hypo|der|mic +s
hypo|der|mic|ally
hypo|gas|tric
hypo|gas|trium
  hypo|gas|tria
hypo|geal
hypo|gene
hypo|geum
  hypo|gea
hypo|gly|caemia
  (glucose deficiency:
  use hypoglycemia)
[☞ hyperglycemia]
hypo|gly|caemic
  (having
  hypoglycemia: use
  hypoglycemic)
[☞ hyperglycemic]
hypo|gly|cemia
  (glucose deficiency)
[☞ hyperglycemia]
hypo|gly|cemic
  (having
  hypoglycemia)
[☞ hyperglycemic]
hy|poid gear +s
hypo|lim|nion
  hypo|lim|nia
hypo|mania
hypo|manic +s
hypo|nas|tic
hypo|nasty
hypo|phys|eal
hypo|phys|ial (use
  hypophyseal)
hy|pophy|sis
  hy|pophy|ses
hy|pos|ta|sis
  hy|pos|ta|ses
hy|pos|ta|size
  hy|pos|ta|siz|es
  hy|pos|ta|sized
  hy|pos|ta|siz|ing
hypo|stat|ic
hypo|stat|ic|al
hy|pos|ta|tiz|a|tion
  +s
hy|pos|ta|tize
  hy|pos|ta|tiz|es
  hy|pos|ta|tized
  hy|pos|ta|tiz|ing
hypo|style
hypo|tac|tic
hypo|taxis
hypo|ten|sion (low
  blood pressure)
[☞ hypertension]
hypo|ten|sive (having
  hypotension)
[☞ hypertensive]
hy|pot|en|use +s

hypo|thal|amic
hypo|thal|amus
  hypo|thal|ami
hypo|ther|mia (low
  body temperature)
[☞ hyperthermia]
hypo|ther|mic
  (having
  hypothermia)
[☞ hyperthermic]
hy|poth|esis
  hy|poth|eses
hy|poth|esist +s
hy|poth|esize
  hy|poth|esiz|es
  hy|poth|esized
  hy|poth|esiz|ing
hy|poth|esiz|er +s
hypo|thet|ical +s
hypo|thet|ical|ly
hypo|thyroid (of
  hypothyroidism)
[☞
  hyperthyroidism]
hypo|thyroid|ism
  (subnormal thyroid
  activity)
[☞
  hyperthyroidism]
hypo|venti|la|tion
  (abnormally slow
  breathing)
[☞
  hyperventilation]
hypox|aemia (use
  hypoxemia)
hypox|aemic (use
  hypoxemic)
hypox|emia
hypox|emic
hy|poxia
hy|pox|ic
hypso|graph|ic
hypso|graph|ic|al
hyp|sog|raphy
hyp|som|eter +s
hypso|met|ric
hyrax
  hy|rax|es
hys|sop +s
hyster|ec|to|mize
  hyster|ec|to|miz|es
  hyster|ec|to|mized
  hyster|ec|to|miz|ing
hyster|ec|tomy
  hyster|ec|to|mies
hys|ter|esis
hys|teria +s
hys|ter|ic +s
hys|ter|ic|al
hys|ter|ic|al|ly
hys|ter|on pro|ter|on

I

I
- (letter)
I's
- (pronoun; ego; electric current)
i
- (letter)
i's
- (imaginary square root of minus one)
iamb +s
iam|bic +s
iam|bic|ally
iam|bus
    iam|bus|es or iambi
Iap|etus (Greek Myth; moon of Saturn)
Iaşi (city, Romania)
iatro|gen|esis
iatro|genic
Iba|dan (city, Nigeria)
Iban
    plural Iban
Ibar|ruri Gomez, Dol|ores ('La Pasionaria', Spanish Communist leader)
I-beam +s
Iberia (peninsula, Europe)
Iber|ian +s
Iber|ville (town, Canada)
Iber|ville, Pierre Le Moyne d' (French-Cdn explorer)
ibex
    ibex|es
ibid.
ibis
    ibis|es
Ibiza (island & its capital, Balearic Islands)
ibn Hus|sein, Ab|dul|lah (Jordanian king)
ibn-Khaldun (Arab historian)
ibn-Saud, Abdul-Aziz (king of Saudi Arabia)
Ibo
    plural Ibo or Ibos
Ibsen, Hen|rik Johan (Norwegian dramatist)
ibu|pro|fen

IC (integrated circuit)
    ICs
i/c (in charge)
Ica|rus (Greek Myth)
ICBM
    (intercontinental ballistic missile)
    ICBMs
ice
    ices
    iced
    icing
ice bag +s
ice|berg +s
ice|blink +s
ice-blue +s
ice|boat +s +ed +ing
ice|boat|er +s
ice|boat|ing noun
ice|bound
ice|box
    ice|boxes
ice|break|er +s
ice break|ing noun & adjective
ice bridge +s
ice buck|et +s
ice cap +s
ice-capped
ice chest +s
ice climb|er +s
ice climb|ing
ice-cold
ice cream +s
ice cream cone +s
ice cube +s
iced adjective
ice dance +s
ice dan|cer +s
ice dan|cing
iced tea +s
ice|fall +s
ice|field +s
ice-fish
    ice-fishes
    ice-fished
    ice-fishing
ice fish|er|man
    ice fish|er|men
ice fish|ing noun (ice-fishing when preceding a noun)
ice floe +s
ice fog
ice-free
ice house +s
ice jam +s
Ice|land (country, N Atlantic)
Ice|land|er +s
Ice|land|ic
ice lolly
    ice lol|lies

ice|maker +s
ice|man
    ice|men
ice milk
Iceni
ice-out +s
ice pack +s
ice pad +s
ice pan +s
ice pick +s
ice plant +s
ice rink +s
ice|scape +s
ice sheet +s
ice shelf
    ice shelves
ice skate +s noun
ice-skate verb
    ice-skates
    ice-skated
    ice-skating
ice-skater +s
ice-skating noun
ice tea +s (= iced tea)
ice time +s
ice wat|er +s
Ice|wine +s
    proprietary
ice|worm +s
I Ching
ich|neu|mon +s
ichor
ichor|ous
ich|thy|o|logic|al
ich|thy|ol|o|gist +s
ich|thy|ol|ogy
ich|thy|oph|a|gous
ich|thy|oph|agy
ich|thyo|saur +s
ich|thyo|saur|us
    ich|thyo|saur|us|es
ich|thy|o|sis
ich|thy|otic
icicle +s
icier
ici|est
icily
ici|ness
icing +s noun
ick
ick|i|ness
Ick|nield Way
icky
    ick|i|er
    ick|i|est
icon +s (devotional painting or statue; object of admiration; Computing; Linguistics)
icon|ic
icon|icity

icono|clasm +s
icono|clast +s
icono|clas|tic
icono|clas|tic|ally
icono|graph|er +s
icono|graph|ic
icono|graph|ic|al
icono|graph|ic|al|ly
icon|og|raphy
    icon|og|raph|ies
icon|ol|atry
icon|ol|ogy
icon|os|ta|sis
    icon|os|ta|ses
icosa|hed|ral
icosa|hed|ron
    icosa|hed|rons or icosa|hedra
ic|ter|ic
ic|ter|us
Ic|ti|nus (Greek architect)
ictus
    plural ictus or ic|tus|es
icy
    icier
    ici|est
ID (identification)
    IDs
Id (Muslim festival: use Eid)
I'd (I would; I had)
id +s (Psychology)
Ida (mountain, Crete; asteroid)
Idaho (state, US)
Ida|ho|an +s
Ida Red +s
idea +s
ideal +s
idea|less
ideal|ism +s
ideal|ist +s
ideal|is|tic
ideal|is|tic|ally
ideal|ity
    ideal|ities
ideal|iz|a|tion +s
ideal|ize
    ideal|iz|es
    ideal|ized
    ideal|iz|ing
ideal|iz|er +s
ideal|ly
ideate
    ideates
    ideat|ed
    ideat|ing
idea|tion +s
idea|tion|al
idea|tion|al|ly

idée fixe
  idées fixes
idée reçue
  idées reçues
idem
iden|ti|cal
iden|ti|cal|ly
iden|ti|fi|able
iden|ti|fi|ably
iden|ti|fi|ca|tion +s
iden|ti|fi|er +s
iden|tify
  iden|ti|fies
  iden|ti|fied
  iden|ti|fy|ing
Identi|kit *proprietary*
iden|tity
  iden|ti|ties
ideo|gram +s
ideo|graph +s
ideo|graph|ic
ideog|raphy
ideo|logic|al
ideo|logic|al|ly
ideol|o|gist +s
ideo|logue +s
ideol|ogy
  ideol|o|gies
ides
idiocy
  idio|cies
idio|lect +s
idio|lect|al
idio|lect|ic
idiom +s
idio|mat|ic
idio|mat|ic|ally
idio|path|ic
idiop|athy
  idiop|athies
idio|syn|crasy
  idio|syn|cra|sies
idio|syn|crat|ic
idio|syn|crat|ic|ally
idiot +s
idi|ot|ic
idi|ot|ic|ally
idiot-proof
idiot sa|vant
  idiot sa|vants or
  idiots sa|vants
idle (lazy; inactive; be idle; *Automotive*)
idler
idlest
idles
idled
idling
  [☞ idol, idyll]
idle|ness
idler +s
idly
Ido (language)

idol +s (object of worship)
  [☞ idle, idyll]
idol|ater +s
idol|atress
  idol|atress|es
idol|atrous
idol|atry
  idol|atries
idol|iz|a|tion
idol|ize
  idol|iz|es
  idol|ized
  idol|iz|ing
idol|iz|er +s
Idom|en|eus (*Greek Myth*)
idyl (blissful period; rural scene: *use* idyll)
  [☞ idle, idol]
idyll +s (blissful period; rural scene)
  [☞ idle, idol]
idyll|ic
idyll|lic|ally
idyll|list +s
idyll|lize
  idyll|liz|es
  idyll|lized
  idyll|liz|ing
i.e. (that is)
if +s *conjunction & noun*
  [☞ iff]
Ife (city, Nigeria)
iff (*Logic*; *Math*)
iffy
  if|fi|er
  if|fi|est
Ifni (former Spanish province, Morocco)
Ig +s (immunoglobulin)
Igbo (= Ibo)
  plural Igbo or Igbos
ig|loo +s
Ig|loo|lik (hamlet, Canada)
  [☞ Iglulik]
iglu +s (*use* igloo)
Ig|lu|lik (Inuit people, language)
  plural Ig|lu|lik
  [☞ Igloolik]
Ig|nati|eff, George (Russian-born Cdn diplomat)
Ig|na|tius of An|tioch (saint)
Ig|na|tius (of) Loy|ola (saint)
ig|ne|ous

ignis fatu|us
  ignes fatui
ignit|abil|ity
ignit|able
ig|nite
  ig|nites
  ignit|ed
  ignit|ing
ignit|er +s
ig|ni|tion +s
ig|ni|tron +s
ig|no|bil|ity
ig|noble
  ig|nob|ler
  ig|nob|lest
ig|nobly
ig|no|mini|ous
ig|no|mini|ous|ly
ig|no|mini|ous|ness
ig|no|miny
  ig|no|min|ies
ig|nor|able
ig|nor|amus
  ig|nor|amus|es
ig|nor|ance
ig|nor|ant
ig|nor|ant|ly
ig|nore
  ig|nores
  ig|nored
  ig|nor|ing
ig|nor|er +s
Igua|çu (river, Brazil)
igua|na +s
iguan|o|don +s
i.h.p. (indicated horsepower)
IJssel (river, the Netherlands)
IJssel|meer (lake, the Netherlands)
ikat +s
ike|bana
Ikh|na|ton (= Akhenaten, pharaoh)
ikon +s (devotional painting or statue: *use* icon)
  [☞ icon]
ilang-ilang +s (*use* ylang-ylang)
Il Duce (Mussolini)
ilea *plural of* ileum
  [☞ ilia]
ileac (of the ileum)
  [☞ iliac]
Île Bi|zard (island, Canada)
Île de Bona|ven|ture (island, Canada)
Île-de-France (region, France)

Île de Mont|réal (island, Canada)
Île des Soeurs (island, Canada)
Île d'Orléans (island, Canada)
ileitis
Île Jésus (island, Canada)
Île La|mèque (island, Canada)
ileos|tomy
  ileos|to|mies
Île Roy|ale (*former name for* Cape Breton Island)
Île Sainte-Hélène (island park, Canada)
Île Saint-Jean (*former name for* Prince Edward Island)
Îles de la Made|leine (islands, Canada)
Il|esha (city, Nigeria)
ileum (part of small intestine)
  ilea
  [☞ ilium]
ileus
ilex
  ilex|es
ilia *plural of* ilium
  [☞ ilea]
iliac (of the ilium)
  [☞ ileac]
Ilium (Troy)
  [☞ ilium]
ilium (pelvic bone)
  ilia
  [☞ ileum]
ilk
I'll (I shall; I will)
  [☞ isle]
ill +s
ill-advised
ill-advised|ly
ill-assort|ed
il|la|tion +s (deduction, conclusion)
  [☞ elation]
il|la|tive
il|la|tive|ly
ill-behaved
ill-bred
ill-conceived
ill-consid|ered
ill-defined
ill-disposed
ill ef|fect +s
il|legal +s
il|legal|ity
  il|legal|ities

il|legal|ly
il|legi|bil|ity
il|legi|ble
il|legi|bly
il|legit|im|acy
il|legit|im|ate +s
il|legit|im|ate|ly
ill-equipped
ill-fated
ill-favored (use ill-favoured)
ill-favoured
ill-fitting
ill-founded
ill-gotten
ill-humored (use ill-humoured)
ill-humoured
il|lib|er|al
il|lib|er|al|ity
il|lib|er|al|ities
il|lib|er|al|ly
il|licit (unlawful; secret)
[☞ elicit]
il|licit|ly
il|licit|ness
il|limit|abil|ity
il|limit|able
il|limit|ably
ill-informed
Il|li|nois (state, US)
il|liquid
il|liquid|ity
il|lit|er|acy (inability to read; ignorance)
[☞ aliteracy]
il|lit|er|ate +s (unable to read; ignorant)
[☞ aliterate, alliterate]
il|lit|er|ate|ly
il|lit|er|ate|ness
ill-judged
ill-mannered
ill-matched
ill-natured
ill-natured|ly
ill|ness
ill|ness|es
il|logic
il|logic|al
il|logic|al|ity
il|logic|al|ities
il|logic|al|ly
ill-omened
ill-prepared
ill-starred
ill-suited
ill-tempered
ill-timed
ill-treat +s +ed +ing

ill-treatment
il|lume
il|lumes
il|lumed
il|lum|ing
il|lumin|ance +s
il|lumin|ant +s
il|lumin|ate
il|lumin|ates
il|lumin|at|ed
il|lumin|at|ing
il|lumin|ati
il|lumin|at|ing adjective
il|lumin|at|ing|ly
il|lumin|a|tion +s
il|lumin|ator +s
il|lum|ine
il|lum|ines
il|lum|ined
il|lum|ing
il|lumin|ism
il|lumin|ist +s
ill-use
ill-uses
ill-used
ill-using
ill-used adjective
il|lu|sion (deception; false perception)
[☞ allusion, elusion]
il|lu|sion|al
il|lu|sion|ism
il|lu|sion|ist +s
il|lu|sion|is|tic
il|lu|sive (deceptive)
[☞ allusive, elusive]
il|lu|sor|i|ly
il|lu|sor|i|ness
il|lu|sory
illus|trate
illus|trates
illus|trat|ed
illus|trat|ing
illus|tra|tion +s
illus|tra|tion|al
illus|tra|tive
illus|tra|tive|ly
illus|tra|tor +s
il|lus|tri|ous
il|lus|tri|ous|ly
il|lus|tri|ous|ness
ill will
ill-wisher +s
Il|lyria (ancient region, Europe)
Il|lyr|ian +s
il|men|ite +s
Ilo|ilo (port, the Philippines)
Il|orin (city, Nigeria)

ILS (instrument landing system)
ILSs
I'm
image
im|ages
im|aged
im|aging
image|able
image|less
image-maker +s
image-making
im|ager +s
im|agery
im|age|ries
im|agin|able
im|agin|ably
im|agin|al
im|agin|ar|i|ly
im|agin|ary
im|agin|a|tion +s
im|agin|a|tive
im|agin|a|tive|ly
im|agin|a|tive|ness
im|agine
im|agines
im|agined
im|agin|ing
im|agin|er +s
im|agi|nes plural of imago
im|aging +s noun
im|agin|ings noun
im|agism
im|agist +s
im|agis|tic
im|agis|tic|ally
imago
im|agos or
im|agi|nes
imam +s
imam|ate +s
Imari
IMAX proprietary
im|bal|ance +s
im|be|cile +s
im|becile|ly
im|becil|ic
im|becil|ity
im|becil|ities
imbed (use embed)
im|beds
im|bed|ded
im|bed|ding
im|bibe
im|bibes
im|bibed
im|bib|ing
im|bib|er +s
im|bib|ition +s
im|bri|cate
im|bri|cates

im|bri|cat|ed
im|bri|cat|ing
im|bri|ca|tion +s
im|bro|glio +s
Im|bros (Turkish island)
im|brue
im|brues
im|brued
im|bru|ing
imbue
im|bues
im|bued
im|bu|ing
Im|ho|tep (Egyptian architect)
im|ide +s
im|ine +s
im|ip|ra|mine
imit|able
imi|tate
imi|tates
imi|tat|ed
imi|tat|ing
imi|ta|tion +s
imi|ta|tive
imi|ta|tiv|ely
imi|ta|tive|ness
imi|ta|tor +s
im|macu|lacy
im|macu|late
Im|macu|late
Con|cep|tion
im|macu|late|ly
im|macu|late|ness
im|man|ence (inherence; omnipresence)
[☞ imminence, eminence]
im|man|ency
im|man|ent (inherent; existing within the universe)
[☞ imminent, eminent]
im|man|ent|ism
im|man|ent|ist +s
Im|man|uel (Bible: use Emmanuel)
im|mater|ial
im|mater|ial|ism
im|mater|ial|ist +s
im|mater|ial|ity
im|mater|ial|ize
im|mater|ial|iz|es
im|mater|ial|ized
im|mater|ial|iz|ing
im|mater|ial|ly
im|mature
im|mature|ly
im|matur|ity
im|meas|ur|abil|ity

im|meas|ur|able
im|meas|ur|able|ness
im|meas|ur|ably
im|medi|acy
  im|medi|acies
im|medi|ate
im|medi|ate|ly
im|medi|ate|ness
im|medic|able
im|memor|ial
im|memor|ial|ly
im|mense
im|mense|ly
im|mense|ness
im|mens|ity
  im|mens|ities
im|merse (submerge, absorb in)
  im|mers|es
  im|mersed
  im|mers|ing
  [☞ emerse]
im|mersed (submerged; absorbed)
  [☞ emersed]
im|mer|sion +s (act of immersing; foreign language education; disappearance of celestial body during an eclipse etc.)
  [☞ emersion]
im|mi|grant +s
im|mi|grate
  im|mi|grates
  im|mi|grat|ed
  im|mi|grat|ing
im|mi|gra|tion +s
im|min|ence (impending nature)
  [☞ immanence, eminence]
im|min|ent (impending)
  [☞ immanent, eminent]
im|min|ent|ly (soon; soon to be)
  [☞ eminently]
im|mis|ci|bil|ity
im|mis|cible
im|mis|cibly
im|mitig|able
im|mitig|ably
im|mobile
im|mobil|ity
im|mobil|iz|a|tion
im|mobil|ize
  im|mobil|iz|es
  im|mobil|ized
  im|mobil|iz|ing
im|mobil|iz|er +s

im|mod|er|ate
im|mod|er|ate|ly
im|mod|er|ate|ness
im|mod|er|a|tion
im|modest
im|modest|ly
im|modesty
im|mol|ate
  im|mol|ates
  im|mol|at|ed
  im|mol|at|ing
im|mol|a|tion +s
im|mol|ator +s
im|moral
im|moral|ist +s
im|moral|ity
  im|moral|ities
im|moral|ly
im|mor|tal +s (not mortal)
  [☞ immortelle]
im|mor|tal|ity
im|mortal|iz|a|tion +s
im|mortal|ize
  im|mortal|iz|es
  im|mortal|ized
  im|mortal|iz|ing
im|mortal|ly
im|mor|telle +s (flower)
im|mov|abil|ity
im|mov|able
im|mov|able|ness
im|mov|ably
im|move|abil|ity (use immovability)
im|move|able (use immovable)
im|move|able|ness (use immovableness)
im|move|ably (use immovably)
im|mune
im|mun|ity
  im|mun|ities
im|mun|iz|a|tion +s
im|mun|ize
  im|mun|iz|es
  im|mun|ized
  im|mun|iz|ing
im|mun|iz|er +s
immuno|assay +s
immuno|chem|istry
immuno|com|pro|mised
immuno|defi|ciency
  im|muno|defi|cien|cies
immuno|defi|cient
immuno|fluor|es|cence

immuno|fluor|es|cent
immuno|genic
immuno|gen|icity
immuno|globu|lin +s
immuno|logic
immuno|logic|al
immuno|logic|al|ly
immun|ol|o|gist +s
immun|ol|ogy
  immun|ol|o|gies
immuno|sup|pres|sant +s
immuno|sup|pressed
immuno|sup|pres|sion
immuno|sup|pres|sive +s
immuno|thera|peut|ic
immuno|ther|apy
  immuno|ther|apies
im|mure
  im|mures
  im|mured
  im|mur|ing
im|mure|ment +s
im|mut|abil|ity
im|mut|able
im|mut|ably
imp +s
im|pact +s +ed +ing
im|pact|ed adjective
im|pac|tion
im|pair +s +ed +ing
im|paired adjective
im|pair|ment +s
im|pala
  plural im|pala
im|pale
  im|pales
  im|paled
  im|paling
im|pale|ment +s
im|paler +s
im|palp|abil|ity
im|palp|able
im|palp|ably
im|panel (use empanel)
  im|panels
  im|pan|elled
  im|panel|ling
im|part +s +ed +ing
im|par|ta|tion +s
im|par|tial
im|par|tial|ity
im|par|tial|ly
im|pass|abil|ity (of a road etc.)
  [☞ impassibility]

im|pass|able (that cannot be traversed)
  [☞ impassible]
im|pass|able|ness
im|pass|ably (to the point of impassability)
  [☞ impassibly]
im|passe +s
im|pas|si|bil|ity (impassivity)
  [☞ impassability]
im|pas|sible (impassive; not feeling pain or emotion)
  [☞ impassable]
im|pas|sibly (impassively)
  [☞ impassably]
im|pas|sion +s +ed +ing
im|pas|sioned adjective
im|pas|sive
im|pas|sive|ly
im|pas|sive|ness
im|pas|siv|ity
im|pasto
im|pa|tience (lack of patience)
  [☞ impatiens]
im|patiens (plant)
  [☞ impatience]
im|patient
im|patient|ly
im|peach
  im|peach|es
  im|peached
  im|peach|ing
im|peach|able
im|peach|ment +s
im|pec|ca|bil|ity
im|pec|cable
im|pec|cably
im|pecu|ni|os|ity
im|pecu|ni|ous
im|pecu|ni|ous|ly
im|pecu|ni|ous|ness
im|ped|ance +s
im|pede
  im|pedes
  im|peded
  im|ped|ing
im|pedi|ment +s
im|pedi|menta
im|pedi|ment|al
impel
  im|pels
  im|pelled
  im|pel|ling
im|pel|ler +s
im|pend +s +ed +ing

im|pend|ing *adjective*
im|pene|tra|bil|ity
im|pene|trable
im|pene|trable|ness
im|pene|trably
im|peni|tence
im|peni|tency
im|peni|tent
im|peni|tent|ly
im|pera|tive +s
im|pera|tive|ly
im|pera|tive|ness
im|pera|tor +s
im|pera|tor|ial
im|per|cep|ti|bil|ity
im|per|cep|tible
im|per|cep|tibly
im|per|cep|tive
im|per|cep|tive|ly
im|per|cep|tive|ness
im|per|cipi|ence
im|per|cipi|ent
im|per|fect +s
im|per|fec|tion +s
im|per|fec|tive +s
im|per|fect|ly
im|per|for|ate
im|per|ial +s (of an
   empire; non-metric;
   paper; beard)
   [☞ empyreal]
im|per|ial|ism
im|per|ial|ist +s
im|per|ial|is|tic
im|per|ial|is|tic|ally
im|per|ial|ize
   im|per|ial|iz|es
   im|per|ial|ized
   im|per|ial|iz|ing
im|per|ial|ly
Im|per|ial Order
   Daugh|ters of the
   Em|pire
im|peril
   im|perils
   im|per|illed
   im|peril|ling
im|peril|ment +s
im|peri|ous
im|peri|ous|ly
im|peri|ous|ness
im|perish|abil|ity
im|perish|able
im|perish|able|ness
im|perish|ably
im|per|ium +s
im|perma|nence
im|perma|nency
im|perma|nent
im|perma|nent|ly
im|perme|abil|ity
im|perme|able

im|permis|si|bil|ity
im|permis|sible
im|person|al
im|person|al|ity
im|person|al|ly
im|person|ate
   im|person|ates
   im|person|at|ed
   im|person|at|ing
im|person|a|tion +s
im|person|ator +s
im|pertin|ence
im|pertin|ent
im|pertin|ent|ly
im|per|turb|abil|ity
im|per|turb|able
im|per|turb|able|
          ness
im|per|turb|ably
im|pervi|ous
im|pervi|ous|ly
im|pervi|ous|ness
im|pe|ti|gin|ous
im|pe|tigo
im|petu|os|ity
im|petu|ous
im|petu|ous|ly
im|petu|ous|ness
im|petus
   im|petus|es
Im|phal (city, India)
impi +s
im|piety
   im|pieties
im|pinge
   im|pin|ges
   im|pinged
   im|pin|ging
im|pinge|ment +s
im|pin|ger +s
im|pious
im|pious|ly
im|pious|ness
imp|ish
imp|ish|ly
imp|ish|ness
im|plac|abil|ity
im|plac|able
im|plac|ably
im|plant +s +ed +ing
im|plant|a|tion +s
im|plaus|ibil|ity
   im|plaus|ibil|ities
im|plaus|ible
im|plaus|ibly
im|plead +s +ed +ing
im|ple|ment +s +ed
   +ing
im|ple|ment|able
im|ple|men|ta|tion
   +s
im|ple|ment|er +s

im|pli|cate
   im|pli|cates
   im|pli|cat|ed
   im|pli|cat|ing
im|pli|ca|tion +s
im|plica|tive
im|plica|tive|ly
im|plicit
im|plicit|ly
im|plicit|ness
im|plied *adjective*
im|plied|ly
im|plode
   im|plodes
   im|plod|ed
   im|plod|ing
im|plore
   im|plores
   im|plored
   im|plor|ing
im|plor|ing|ly
im|plo|sion +s
im|plo|sive
imply
   im|plies
   im|plied
   im|ply|ing
im|polite
im|polite|ly
im|polite|ness
im|polit|ic
im|polit|ic|ly
im|ponder|abil|ity
im|ponder|able
im|ponder|ably
im|port +s +ed +ing
im|port|able
im|port|ance
im|port|ant
im|port|ant|ly
im|port|a|tion +s
im|port|ed *adjective*
im|port|er +s
im|por|tun|ate
im|por|tun|ate|ly
im|por|tune
   im|por|tunes
   im|por|tuned
   im|por|tun|ing
im|por|tun|ity
   im|por|tun|ities
im|pose
   im|pos|es
   im|posed
   im|pos|ing
im|pos|ing *adjective*
im|pos|ing|ly
im|pos|ing|ness
im|pos|ition +s
im|pos|si|bil|ity
   im|pos|si|bil|ities
im|pos|sible
im|pos|sibly

im|post +s
im|pos|ter +s (one
   posing as another)
im|pos|tor +s (one
   posing as another:
   use imposter)
im|pos|ture +s
   (deception)
im|po|tence
im|po|tency
im|po|tent
im|po|tent|ly
im|pound +s +ed
   +ing
im|pound|able
im|pound|er +s
im|pound|ment +s
im|pover|ish
   im|pover|ish|es
   im|pover|ished
   im|pover|ish|ing
im|pover|ished
   adjective
im|pover|ish|ment +s
im|prac|tic|abil|ity
   im|prac|tic|abil|ities
im|prac|tic|able
im|prac|tic|able|ness
im|prac|tic|ably
im|prac|tical
im|practi|cal|ity
   im|practi|cal|ities
im|prac|tical|ly
im|pre|ca|tion +s
im|pre|ca|tory
im|precise
im|precise|ly
im|precise|ness
im|pre|ci|sion +s
im|preg|nabil|ity
im|preg|nable
im|preg|nably
im|preg|nate
   im|preg|nates
   im|preg|nat|ed
   im|preg|nat|ing
im|preg|na|tion +s
im|pres|ario +s
im|pre|scrip|tible
im|press (mark;
   impression; force
   into service)
   im|press|es
   im|pressed
   im|press|ing
im|press|ible
im|pres|sion +s
im|pres|sion|abil|ity
im|pres|sion|able
im|pres|sion|ably
im|pres|sion|al
Im|pres|sion|ism

Im|pres|sion|ist +s
(Impressionistic
artist)
im|pres|sion|ist +s
(impersonator)
Im|pres|sion|is|tic (of
Impressionism)
im|pres|sion|is|tic
(subjective)
im|pres|sion|
        is|tic|ally
im|pres|sive
im|pres|sive|ly
im|pres|sive|ness
im|press|ment +s
im|prest +s (loan)
  [☞ impressed]
im|pri|ma|tur +s
im|print +s +ed +ing
im|pris|on +s +ed
  +ing
im|prison|ment +s
im|pro +s
im|prob|abil|ity
  im|prob|abil|ities
im|prob|able
im|prob|ably
im|promp|tu +s
im|proper
im|proper|ly
im|pro|pri|ety
  im|pro|pri|eties
im|prov
im|prov|abil|ity
  im|prov|abil|ities
im|prov|able
im|prove
  im|proves
  im|proved
  im|prov|ing
im|proved adjective
im|prove|ment +s
Im|prove|ment
  Dis|trict +s
im|prov|er +s
im|provi|dence
im|provi|dent
im|provi|dent|ly
impro|vis|a|tion +s
impro|vis|a|tion|al
impro|visa|tor|ial
impro|visa|tor|ial|ly
impro|visa|tory
im|pro|vise
  im|pro|vis|es
  im|pro|vised
  im|pro|vis|ing
im|pro|vis|er +s
im|pru|dence +s
im|pru|dent
im|pru|dent|ly
im|pu|dence +s
im|pu|dent

im|pu|dent|ly
im|pugn +s +ed +ing
im|pugn|able
im|pugn|ment +s
im|pulse +s
im|pulse buy|er +s
im|pulse buy|ing
im|pul|sion +s
im|pul|sive
im|pul|sive|ly
im|pul|sive|ness
im|pul|siv|ity
im|pun|ity
  im|pun|ities
im|pure
im|pure|ly
im|pure|ness
im|pur|ity
  im|pur|ities
im|put|able
im|puta|tion +s
im|puta|tive
im|pute
  im|putes
  im|put|ed
  im|put|ing
in
  • preposition, adverb &
    adjective
  • noun (in 'have an in
    with someone' & 'the
    ins and outs')
  ins
  [☞ inn]
in|abil|ity
  in|abil|ities
in ab|sen|tia
in|access|ibil|ity
in|access|ible
in|access|ibly
in|accur|acy
  in|accur|acies
in|accur|ate
in|accur|ate|ly
in|action
in|acti|vate
  in|acti|vates
  in|acti|vat|ed
  in|acti|vat|ing
in|acti|va|tion +s
in|active
in|active|ly
in|activ|ity
in|ad|equa|cy
  in|ad|equa|cies
in|ad|equate
in|ad|equate|ly
in|admis|si|bil|ity
in|admis|sible
in|admis|sibly
in|adver|tence
in|adver|ten|cy
  in|adver|ten|cies

in|adver|tent
in|adver|tent|ly
in|advis|abil|ity
in|advis|able
in|alien|abil|ity
in|alien|able
in|alien|ably
in|alter|abil|ity
in|alter|able
in|alter|ably
in|amor|ata +s
  (female lover)
in|amor|ato +s (male
  lover)
inane
inane|ly
in|ani|mate
in|ani|mate|ly
in|ani|ma|tion
in|ani|tion
in|an|ity
  in|an|ities
in|appar|ent
in|appar|ent|ly
in|applic|abil|ity
in|applic|able
in|applic|ably
in|appos|ite
in|appos|ite|ly
in|appos|ite|ness
in|appre|cia|ble
in|appre|cia|bly
in|appre|ci|a|tion
in|appre|cia|tive
in|appro|pri|ate
in|appro|pri|ate|ly
in|appro|pri|ate|ness
inapt (inappropriate;
  for incompetent or
  absurd use inept)
in|apti|tude
  (inappropriateness;
  for incompetence use
  ineptitude)
in|apt|ly
  (inappropriately; for
  incompetently use
  ineptly)
in|arch
  in|arch|es
  in|arched
  in|arch|ing
in|argu|able
in|argu|ably
in|articu|lacy
in|articu|late
in|articu|late|ly
in|articu|late|ness
in|artis|tic
in|artis|tic|ally
in|as|much
in|atten|tion +s

in|atten|tive
in|atten|tive|ly
in|atten|tive|ness
in|audi|bil|ity
in|aud|ible
in|aud|ibly
in|aug|ur|al +s
in|aug|ur|ate
  in|aug|ur|ates
  in|aug|ur|at|ed
  in|aug|ur|at|ing
in|aug|ur|a|tion +s
in|aug|ur|ator +s
in|auspi|cious
in|auspi|cious|ly
in|auspi|cious|ness
in|authen|tic
in|authen|ti|city
in-basket +s
in be|tween
  preposition
in-between +s noun &
  adjective preceding a
  noun
in|between|er +s
in|board +s
in|born
in|bound +s +ed +ing
in|bounds adjective
  preceding a noun
in|bred adjective
in|breed
  in|breeds
  in|bred
  in|breed|ing
in|breed|ing adjective
in|built
Inca
  plural Inca or Incas
Inca|ic
in|calcul|abil|ity
in|calcul|able
in|calcul|ably
in cam|era
Incan
in|can|desce
  in|can|des|ces
  in|can|desced
  in|can|des|cing
in|can|des|cence
in|can|des|cent +s
in|can|des|cent|ly
in|cant +s +ed +ing
in|can|ta|tion +s
in|can|ta|tion|al
in|can|ta|tory
in|cap|abil|ity
  in|cap|abil|ities
in|cap|able
in|cap|ably
in|capa|ci|tant +s

in|capa|ci|tate
in|capa|ci|tates
in|capa|ci|tat|ed
in|capa|ci|tat|ing
in|capa|ci|tat|ed
adjective
in|capa|ci|ta|tion
in|capa|city
  in|capa|ci|ties
in|car|cer|ate
  in|car|cer|ates
  in|car|cer|at|ed
  in|car|cer|at|ing
in|car|cer|a|tion +s
in|car|cer|ator +s
in|car|na|dine
  in|car|na|dines
  in|car|na|dined
  in|car|na|din|ing
in|car|nate
  in|car|nates
  in|car|nat|ed
  in|car|nat|ing
In|car|na|tion
(*Christianity*)
in|car|na|tion +s (*in
general use*)
in|cau|tion
in|cau|tious
in|cau|tious|ly
in|cau|tious|ness
in|cendi|ar|ism
in|cendi|ary
  in|cendi|aries
in|cens|a|tion +s
in|cense
  in|cens|es
  in|censed
  in|cens|ing
in|cent +s +ed +ing
in|cen|tive +s
in|cen|tiv|ize
  in|cen|tiv|iz|es
  in|cen|tiv|ized
  in|cen|tiv|iz|ing
in|cept +s +ed +ing
in|cep|tion +s
in|cep|tive +s
in|cep|tor +s
in|certi|tude +s
in|ces|sancy
in|ces|sant
in|ces|sant|ly
in|ces|sant|ness
in|cest
in|ces|tu|ous
in|ces|tu|ous|ly
in|ces|tu|ous|ness
inch
  inch|es
  inched
  inch|ing

Inch|cape Rock (reef,
  North Sea)
inch|er +s
in|cho|ate
in|cho|ate|ly
in|cho|ate|ness
in|cho|ative
In|chon (port, South
  Korea)
inch|worm +s
in|ci|dence +s
in|ci|dent +s
in|ci|dent|al +s
in|ci|dent|al|ly
in|cin|er|ate
  in|cin|er|ates
  in|cin|er|at|ed
  in|cin|er|at|ing
in|cin|er|a|tion +s
in|cin|er|ator +s
in|cipi|ence
in|cipi|ency
in|cipi|ent
in|cipi|ent|ly
in|cise
  in|cis|es
  in|cised
  in|cis|ing
in|cised *adjective*
in|ci|sion +s
in|ci|sive
in|ci|sive|ly
in|ci|sive|ness
in|cis|or +s
in|cit|a|tion
in|cite (provoke)
  in|cites
  in|cit|ed
  in|cit|ing
  [☞ insight]
in|cite|ment +s
in|cit|er +s
in|civil|ity
  in|civil|ities
in|clem|en|cy
  in|clem|en|cies
in|clem|ent
in|clem|ent|ly
in|clin|a|tion +s
in|cline
  in|clines
  in|clined
  in|clin|ing
in|clined *adjective*
in|clin|er +s
in|clin|om|eter +s
in|clude
  in|cludes
  in|clud|ed
  in|clud|ing
in|clud|ed *adjective*
in|clud|ing *preposition*
in|clu|sion +s

in|clu|sive
in|clu|sive|ly
in|clu|sive|ness
in|clu|siv|ity
in|cog|nito +s
in|cog|ni|zance
in|cog|ni|zant
in|coher|ence
in|coher|ency
  in|coher|en|cies
in|coher|ent
in|coher|ent|ly
in|com|bust|ibil|ity
in|com|bust|ible
in|come +s
in|com|er +s
in|com|ing *adjective &
noun*
in|com|men|sur|
       abil|ity
in|com|men|sur|able
  +s
in|com|men|sur|ably
in|com|men|sur|ate
in|com|men|sur|ate|
       ly
in|com|men|sur|ate|
       ness
in|com|mode
  in|com|modes
  in|com|mod|ed
  in|com|mod|ing
in|com|modi|ous
in|com|modi|ous|ly
in|com|modi|ous|
       ness
in|com|munic|
       abil|ity
in|com|munic|able
in|com|munic|able|
       ness
in|com|munic|ably
in|com|muni|cado
in|com|muni|ca|tive
in|com|muni|ca|tive|
       ly
in|com|muni|ca|tive|
       ness
in|com|mut|able
in|com|mut|ably
in|compar|abil|ity
in|compar|able
in|compar|ably
in|compat|ibil|ity
  in|compat|ibil|ities
in|compat|ible
in|compat|ible|ness
in|compat|ibly
in|compe|tence
in|compe|tency
  in|compe|ten|cies
in|compe|tent +s
in|compe|tent|ly

in|com|plete
in|com|plete|ly
in|com|plete|ness
in|com|ple|tion +s
in|compre|hen|si|
       bil|ity
in|compre|hen|sible
in|compre|hen|sible|
       ness
in|compre|hen|sibly
in|compre|hen|sion
in|compress|ibil|ity
in|compress|ible
in|con|ceiv|abil|ity
in|con|ceiv|able
in|con|ceiv|able|ness
in|con|ceiv|ably
in|conclu|sive
in|conclu|sive|ly
in|conclu|sive|ness
in|condens|able
in|congru|ity
  in|congru|ities
in|congru|ous
in|congru|ous|ly
in|congru|ous|ness
in|connu
  • (fish)
    plural in|connu
  • (unknown person or
    thing)
    plural in|connus
in|con|secu|tive
in|con|secu|tive|ly
in|con|se|quence
in|con|se|quent
in|con|sequen|tial
in|con|sequen|tial|ity
  in|con|sequen|tial|
       ities
in|con|sequen|tial|ly
in|con|sequent|ly
in|con|sider|able
in|con|sider|ate
in|con|sider|ate|ly
in|con|sider|ate|ness
in|con|sider|a|tion
in|con|sis|tency
  in|con|sis|ten|cies
in|con|sis|tent
in|con|sis|tent|ly
in|consol|abil|ity
in|consol|able
in|consol|ably
in|con|son|ance
in|con|son|ant
in|con|son|ant|ly
in|con|spicu|ous
in|con|spicu|ous|ly
in|con|spicu|ous|
       ness

in|con|stancy
  in|con|stan|cies
in|con|stant
in|con|stant|ly
in|contest|abil|ity
in|contest|able
in|contest|ably
in|contin|ence
in|contin|ent
in|contin|ent|ly
in|contro|vert|ibil|ity
in|contro|vert|ible
in|contro|vert|ibly
in|conven|ience +s
in|conven|ient
in|conven|ient|ly
in|con|vert|ibil|ity
in|con|vert|ible
in|con|vert|ibly
in|coordin|a|tion
in|cor|por|ate
  in|cor|por|ates
  in|cor|por|at|ed
  in|cor|por|at|ing
in|cor|por|ated
  adjective
in|cor|por|a|tion +s
in|cor|por|ator +s
in|cor|por|eal
in|cor|por|eal|ity
in|cor|por|eal|ly
in|correct
in|correct|ly
in|correct|ness
in|corri|gi|bil|ity
in|corri|gible +s
in|corri|gible|ness
in|corri|gibly
in|corrupt|ibil|ity
in|corrupt|ible
in|corrupt|ibly
in|creas|able
in|crease
  in|creas|es
  in|creased
  in|creas|ing
in|creas|er +s
in|creas|ing|ly
in|cred|ibil|ity
in|cred|ible
in|cred|ibly
in|credu|lity
in|credu|lous
in|credu|lous|ly
in|credu|lous|ness
in|cre|ment +s
in|cre|men|tal
in|cre|men|tal|ism
in|cre|men|tal|ly
in|crim|in|ate
  in|crim|in|ates

in|crim|in|at|ed
in|crim|in|at|ing
in|crim|in|at|ing
  adjective
in|crim|in|a|tion +s
in|crim|in|a|tory
in|crust|a|tion +s (*use*
  encrustation*)
in|cu|bate
  in|cu|bates
  in|cu|bat|ed
  in|cu|bat|ing
in|cu|ba|tion +s
in|cu|ba|tion|al
in|cu|ba|tive
in|cu|ba|tor +s
in|cu|ba|tory
in|cu|bus
  in|cu|bus|es or
  in|cubi
in|cu|des
in|cul|cate
  in|cul|cates
  in|cul|cat|ed
  in|cul|cat|ing
in|cul|ca|tion +s
in|cul|ca|tor +s
in|cul|pate
  in|cul|pates
  in|cul|pat|ed
  in|cul|pat|ing
in|cul|pa|tion +s
in|cul|pa|tive
in|cul|pa|tory
in|cum|ben|cy
  in|cum|ben|cies
in|cum|bent +s
in|cun|able +s
in|cu|nabu|lum
  in|cu|nab|ula
incur
  in|curs
  in|curred
  in|cur|ring
in|cur|abil|ity
in|cur|able +s (that
  cannot be cured)
  [☞ incurrable]
in|cur|able|ness
in|cur|ably
in|curi|os|ity
in|curi|ous
in|curi|ous|ly
in|curi|ous|ness
in|cur|rable (that
  might be incurred)
  [☞ incurable]
in|cur|sion +s
in|curv|a|tion +s
in|curve
  in|curves
  in|curved
  in|curv|ing

in|curved *adjective*
incus (*Anatomy*)
  in|cu|des
in|cuse (stamp on a
  coin)
  in|cus|es
  in|cused
  in|cus|ing
in|debt|ed
in|debt|ed|ness
in|decen|cy
  in|decen|cies
in|decent
in|decent|ly
in|de|cipher|able
in|deci|sion
in|deci|sive
in|deci|sive|ly
in|deci|sive|ness
in|declin|able
in|decor|ous
in|decor|ous|ly
in|decor|ous|ness
in|decor|um
in|deed
in|defatig|abil|ity
in|defatig|able
in|defatig|ably
in|defeas|ibil|ity
in|defeas|ible
in|defeas|ibly
in|defect|ible
in|defens|ibil|ity
in|defens|ible
in|defens|ibly
in|defin|able
in|defin|ably
in|defin|ite
in|defin|ite|ly
in|defin|ite|ness
in|dehis|cence
in|dehis|cent
in|del|ibil|ity
in|del|ible
in|del|ibly
in|deli|cacy
  in|deli|ca|cies
in|deli|cate
in|deli|cate|ly
in|dem|ni|fi|ca|tion
  +s
in|dem|ni|fi|er +s
in|dem|nify
  in|dem|ni|fies
  in|dem|ni|fied
  in|dem|ni|fy|ing
in|dem|nity
  in|dem|ni|ties
in|demon|strable
ind|ene +s
in|dent +s +ed +ing
in|den|ta|tion +s

in|dent|er +s
in|den|tion +s
in|dent|or +s (*use*
  indenter)
in|den|ture
  in|den|tures
  in|den|tured
  in|den|tur|ing
in|den|tured *adjective*
in|den|ture|ship +s
in|dépen|dan|tiste +s
in|depend|ence
in|depend|ency
  in|depend|en|cies
in|depend|ent +s
in|depend|ent|ly
in-depth *adjective*
  preceding a noun
in|describ|abil|ity
in|describ|able
in|describ|ably
in|de|struct|ibil|ity
in|de|struct|ible
in|de|struct|ibly
in|deter|min|able
in|deter|min|ably
in|deter|min|acy
in|deter|min|ate
in|deter|min|ate|ly
in|deter|min|ate|ness
in|deter|min|a|tion
in|deter|min|ism
in|deter|min|ist +s
in|deter|min|is|tic
index
  in|dex|es or
  in|di|ces
in|dex|a|tion +s
in|dex|er +s
in|dex|ical
index-linked
index-linking
India (country, Asia)
In|di|an +s
In|di|ana (state, US)
In|di|an|an +s
In|dian|ap|olis (city,
  US)
Indic
indi|cate
  indi|cates
  indi|cat|ed
  indi|cat|ing
indi|ca|tion +s
in|dic|a|tive +s
in|dic|a|tive|ly
indi|ca|tor +s
in|di|ces
in|di|cia
in|dict +s +ed +ing
  (charge, accuse)
  [☞ indite]

in|dict|able
in|dict|ee +s
in|dict|er +s
in|dict|ment +s
in|die +s
(independent)
[☞ Indy]
In|dies (*Geography*)
in|dif|fer|ence +s
in|dif|fer|ent
in|dif|fer|ent|ism
in|dif|fer|ent|ist +s
in|dif|fer|ent|ly
indi|gence
indi|gene +s
in|digen|iz|a|tion +s
in|digen|ize
  in|digen|iz|es
  in|digen|ized
  in|digen|iz|ing
in|digen|ous
in|digen|ous|ly
in|digen|ous|ness
indi|gent
in|digest|ibil|ity
in|digest|ible
in|digest|ibly
in|diges|tion
in|digest|ive
Indi|girka (river, Russia)
in|dig|nant
in|dig|nant|ly
in|dig|na|tion
in|dig|nity
  in|dig|ni|ties
in|digo +s
indi|got|ic
in|direct
in|direc|tion
in|direct|ly
in|direct|ness
in|discern|ibil|ity
in|discern|ible
in|discern|ibly
in|disci|pline
in|disci|plined
in|dis|creet (revealing secrets; injudicious)
  [☞ indiscrete]
in|dis|creet|ly
in|dis|crete (not divided into distinct parts)
  [☞ indiscreet]
in|dis|cre|tion +s
in|dis|crim|in|ate
in|dis|crim|in|ate|ly
in|dis|crim|in|ate|ness
in|dis|crim|in|a|tion
in|dis|pens|abil|ity

in|dis|pens|able
in|dis|pens|able|ness
in|dis|pens|ably
in|dis|pose
  in|dis|pos|es
  in|dis|posed
  in|dis|pos|ing
in|dis|posed *adjective*
in|dis|pos|ition +s
in|disput|abil|ity
in|disput|able
in|disput|ably
in|dis|solu|bil|ity
in|dis|sol|uble
in|dis|sol|ubly
in|dis|tinct
in|dis|tinct|ive
in|dis|tinct|ive|ly
in|dis|tinct|ive|ness
in|dis|tinct|ly
in|dis|tinct|ness
in|dis|tin|guish|abil|ity
in|dis|tin|guish|able
in|dis|tin|guish|able|ness
in|dis|tin|guish|ably
in|dite (put into words)
  in|dites
  in|dit|ed
  in|dit|ing
  [☞ indict]
in|dium
in|di|vid|ual +s
in|di|vid|ual|ism
in|di|vid|ual|ist +s
in|di|vid|ual|is|tic
in|di|vid|ual|is|tic|ally
in|di|vidu|al|ity
  in|di|vidu|al|ities
in|di|vid|ual|iz|a|tion +s
in|di|vid|ual|ize
  in|di|vid|ual|iz|es
  in|di|vid|ual|ized
  in|di|vid|ual|iz|ing
in|di|vid|ual|ized *adjective*
in|di|vid|ual|ly
in|di|vidu|ate
  in|di|vidu|ates
  in|di|vidu|at|ed
  in|di|vidu|at|ing
in|di|vidu|a|tion +s
in|divis|ibil|ity
in|divis|ible
in|divis|ibly
Indo-Aryan +s
Indo-Canadian +s
Indo|china (region, Asia)

Indo|chinese
  plural Indo|chinese
in|docile
in|docil|ity
in|doc|trin|ate
  in|doc|trin|ates
  in|doc|trin|at|ed
  in|doc|trin|at|ing
in|doc|trin|a|tion +s
in|doc|trin|ator +s
Indo-European +s
Indo-Iranian
ind|ole +s
indole|acet|ic
in|dol|ence
in|dol|ent
in|dol|ent|ly
Ind|ol|o|gist +s
Ind|ol|ogy
in|domit|abil|ity
in|domit|able
in|domit|able|ness
in|domit|ably
Indo|nesia (country, Asia)
Indo|nes|ian +s
in|door
  [☞ Indore]
indoor-outdoor
in|doors
In|dore (city, India)
Indra (*Hinduism*)
in|draft +s
in|drawn
in|dri +s
in|dubit|able
in|dubit|ably
in|duce
  in|du|ces
  in|duced
  in|du|cing
in|duce|ment +s
in|du|cer +s
in|du|cible
in|duct +s +ed +ing
in|duct|ance +s
in|duc|tee +s
in|duc|tion +s
in|duct|ive
in|duct|ive|ly
in|duct|ive|ness
in|duct|or +s
in|dulge
  in|dul|ges
  in|dulged
  in|dul|ging
in|dul|gence +s
in|dul|gent
in|dul|gent|ly
in|dul|ger +s
in|duna +s

In|du|rain, Mi|guel (Spanish cyclist)
in|dur|ate
  in|dur|ates
  in|dur|at|ed
  in|dur|at|ing
in|dur|a|tion +s
in|dura|tive
Indus (river, Asia)
in|du|sial
in|du|sium
  in|du|sia
in|dus|trial +s
in|dus|trial|ism
in|dus|trial|ist +s
in|dus|trial|iz|a|tion
in|dus|trial|ize
  in|dus|trial|iz|es
  in|dus|trial|ized
  in|dus|trial|iz|ing
in|dus|trial|ly
in|dustrial-strength
in|dus|tri|ous
in|dus|tri|ous|ly
in|dus|tri|ous|ness
in|dus|try
  in|dus|tries
in|dwell
  in|dwells
  in|dwelt
  in|dwell|ing
in|dwell|er +s
Indy, (Paul Marie Théo|dore) Vin|cent d' (French musician)
Indy (*Motorsport*)
In|dies
  [☞ indie]
Indy|car +s
in|ebri|ate
  in|ebri|ates
  in|ebri|at|ed
  in|ebri|at|ing
in|ebri|at|ed *adjective*
in|ebri|a|tion +s
in|ebri|ety
in|edi|bil|ity
in|edible
in|educ|abil|ity
in|educ|able
in|effa|bil|ity
in|effable
in|effably
in|efface|abil|ity
in|efface|able
in|efface|ably
in|effect|ive
in|effect|ive|ly
in|effect|ive|ness
in|effec|tual
in|effec|tual|ity
  in|effec|tual|ities
in|effec|tual|ly

in|effec|tual|ness
in|effi|ca|cious
in|effi|ca|cious|ly
in|effi|ca|cious|ness
in|effi|cacy
  in|effi|ca|cies
in|effi|ciency
  in|effi|cien|cies
in|effi|cient
in|effi|cient|ly
in|egali|tar|ian
in|egali|tar|ian|ism
in|elas|tic
in|elas|tic|ally
in|elas|ti|city
in|ele|gance
in|elegant
in|elegant|ly
in|eligi|bil|ity
in|eli|gible
in|eli|gibly
in|eluct|abil|ity
in|eluct|able
in|eluct|ably
inept (incompetent, absurd; for inappropriate use inapt)
in|epti|tude +s (incompetence; for inappropriateness use inaptitude)
in|ept|ly (incompetently; for inappropriately use inaptly)
in|ept|ness
in|equal|ity
  in|equal|ities
in|equit|able
in|equit|ably
in|equity
  in|equi|ties
in|eradic|able
in|eradic|ably
in|err|ancy
in|err|ant (infallible)
  [☞ inherent]
in|errant|ist +s
inert
in|er|tia
in|er|tial
inert|ly
inert|ness
in|escap|abil|ity
in|escap|able
in|escap|ably
in|essen|tial +s
in|estim|able
in|estim|ably
in|evit|abil|ity
  in|evit|abil|ities

in|evit|able +s
in|evit|able|ness
in|evit|ably
in|exact
in|exact|i|tude +s
in|exact|ly
in|exact|ness
in|excus|able
in|excus|ably
in|exhaust|ibil|ity
in|exhaust|ible
in|exhaust|ibly
in|exor|abil|ity
in|exor|able
in|exor|ably
in|expedi|ency
in|expedi|ent
in|expen|sive
in|expen|sive|ly
in|expen|sive|ness
in|experi|ence
in|experi|enced
in|expert
in|expert|ly
in|expert|ness
in|expi|able
in|expi|ably
in|explic|abil|ity
in|explic|able
in|explic|ably
in|ex|plicit
in|ex|plicit|ness
in|express|ible
in|express|ibly
in|expres|sive
in|expres|sive|ly
in|expres|sive|ness
in|expun|gible
in ex|ten|so
in|extin|guish|able
in ex|tre|mis
in|extric|abil|ity
in|extric|able
in|extric|ably
in|falli|bil|ity
in|falli|ble
in|falli|bly
in|fam|ous
in|fam|ous|ly
in|famy
  in|fam|ies
in|fancy
  in|fan|cies
in|fant +s
in|fanta +s (monarch's daughter)
in|fante +s (monarch's son)
in|fanti|cid|al
in|fanti|cide +s
in|fant|ile
in|fant|il|ism

in|fant|il|ity
  in|fant|il|ities
in|fant|il|iz|a|tion
in|fant|il|ize
  in|fant|il|iz|es
  in|fant|il|ized
  in|fant|il|iz|ing
in|fan|try
  in|fan|tries
in|fantry|man
  in|fantry|men
in|farct +s
in|farct|ed
in|farc|tion +s
in|fatu|ate
  in|fatu|ates
  in|fatu|at|ed
  in|fatu|at|ing
in|fatu|at|ed adjective
in|fatu|a|tion +s
in|fauna
in|faun|al
in|feas|ibil|ity
in|feas|ible
in|fect +s +ed +ing
in|fec|tion +s
in|fec|tious
in|fec|tious|ly
in|fec|tious|ness
in|fect|ive
in|fect|ive|ness
in|fec|tiv|ity
in|fect|or +s
in|felici|tous
in|felici|tous|ly
in|felici|ty
  in|felici|ties
infer
  in|fers
  in|ferred
  in|fer|ring
in|fer|able
in|fer|ence +s
in|fer|en|tial
in|fer|en|tial|ly
in|fer|ior +s
in|fer|ior|ity
in|fer|ior|ly
in|fer|nal
in|fer|nal|ly
in|fer|no +s
in|fer|rable (use inferable)
in|fertile
in|fertil|ity
in|fest +s +ed +ing
in|fest|a|tion +s
in|fibu|late
  in|fibu|lates
  in|fibu|lat|ed
  in|fibu|lat|ing
in|fibu|la|tion +s
in|fidel +s

in|fidel|ity
  in|fidel|ities
in|field +s
in|field|er +s
in|fight|er +s
in|fight|ing
in|fill +s +ed +ing
in|fill|ing +s noun
in|fil|trate
  in|fil|trates
  in|fil|trat|ed
  in|fil|trat|ing
in|fil|tra|tion +s
in|fil|tra|tor +s
in|fin|ite
in|fin|ite|ly
in|fin|ite|ness
in|fini|tes|imal
in|fini|tes|imal|ly
in|fini|tival
in|fini|tival|ly
in|fini|tive +s
in|fini|tude +s
in|fin|ity
  in|fin|ities
in|firm
in|firm|ary
  in|firm|aries
in|firm|ity
  in|firm|ities
in|firm|ly
infix
  in|fix|es
  in|fixed
  in|fix|ing
in|fix|a|tion +s
in fla|grante de|licto
in|flame
  in|flames
  in|flamed
  in|flam|ing
in|flamed adjective
in|flam|er +s
in|flam|mabil|ity
in|flam|mable +s
in|flam|mable|ness
in|flam|mably
in|flam|ma|tion +s
in|flam|ma|tory
in|flat|able +s
in|flate
  in|flates
  in|flat|ed
  in|flat|ing
in|flat|ed adjective
in|flated|ly
in|flated|ness
in|flat|er +s (use inflator)
in|fla|tion +s
in|fla|tion-adjusted
in|fla|tion|ary
in|fla|tion|ism

in|fla|tion|ist +s
in|fla|tor +s
in|flect +s +ed +ing
in|flec|tion +s
in|flec|tion|al
in|flec|tion|al|ly
in|flec|tion|less
in|flect|ive
in|flex|ibil|ity
in|flex|ible
in|flex|ibly
in|flict +s +ed +ing
in|flict|able
in|flict|er +s (use inflictor)
in|flic|tion +s
in|flict|or +s
in|flight
in|flor|es|cence +s
in|flow +s
in|flow|ing
in|flu|ence
  in|flu|en|ces
  in|flu|enced
  in|flu|en|cing
in|flu|ence|able
in|flu|ence ped|dler +s
in|fluence-peddling
in|flu|en|cer +s
in|flu|ent +s
in|flu|en|tial +s
in|flu|en|tial|ly
in|flu|enza
in|flu|en|zal
in|flux
  in|flux|es
info
Info|bahn
info cen|tre +s
in|fold +s +ed +ing
(fold inwards)
[☞ enfold]
in|fold|ing +s noun
(inward fold)
[☞ enfolding]
info|mer|cial +s
in|form +s +ed +ing
in|formal
in|for|mal|ity
  in|for|mal|ities
in|formal|ly
in|form|ant +s
in|form|at|ics
in|for|ma|tion +s
in|for|ma|tion|al
in|for|ma|tion|al|ly
in|forma|tive
in|forma|tive|ly
in|forma|tive|ness
in|formed adjective
in|form|er +s

info|tain|ment
infra
infra|class
  infra|class|es
in|fract +s +ed +ing
in|frac|tion +s
in|fract|or +s
infra dig adjective
in|fran|gi|bil|ity
in|fran|gible
in|fran|gibly
infra|red
infra|sonic
infra|sonic|ally
infra|sound
infra|struc|tur|al
infra|struc|ture +s
in|fre|quen|cy
in|fre|quent
in|fre|quent|ly
in|fringe
  in|frin|ges
  in|fringed
  in|frin|ging
in|fringe|ment +s
in|frin|ger +s
in|fula
  in|fu|lae
in|fun|dibu|lar
in|furi|ate
  in|furi|ates
  in|furi|at|ed
  in|furi|at|ing
in|furi|at|ing adjective
in|furi|at|ing|ly
in|fuse
  in|fus|es
  in|fused
  in|fus|ing
in|fus|er +s
in|fus|ibil|ity
in|fus|ible
in|fusion +s
in|gather|ing +s
Inge, Wil|liam Ralph (English theologian)
In|gen|housz, Jan (Dutch scientist)
in|gen|ious (clever)
  [☞ ingenuous]
in|gen|ious|ly (cleverly)
  [☞ ingenuously]
in|gen|ious|ness (cleverness)
  [☞ ingenuousness]
in|genue +s
in|genu|ity (cleverness)
  in|genu|ities
in|genu|ous (candid; innocent)
  [☞ ingenious]

in|genu|ous|ly (candidly; innocently)
  [☞ ingeniously]
in|genu|ous|ness (candidness; innocence)
  [☞ ingeniousness]
Inger|soll (town, Canada)
in|gest +s +ed +ing
in|ges|tion +s
in|gest|ive
ingle|nook +s
in|glori|ous
in|glori|ous|ly
in|glori|ous|ness
in|going
in|got +s
in|grain +s +ed +ing
in|grained adjective
in|grain|ed|ly
in|grate +s
in|grati|ate
  in|grati|ates
  in|grati|at|ed
  in|grati|at|ing
in|grati|at|ing adjective
in|grati|at|ing|ly
in|grati|a|tion +s
in|grati|tude
in|gredi|ent +s
Ingres, Jean Au|guste Domi|nique (French painter)
in|gress
  in|gress|es
in|gres|sion +s
in-ground
in-group +s
in|grow|ing
in|grown
in|growth +s
in|guin|al
in|guin|al|ly
in|gurgi|tate
  in|gurgi|tates
  in|gurgi|tat|ed
  in|gurgi|tat|ing
in|gurgi|ta|tion +s
in|habit +s +ed +ing
in|habit|abil|ity
in|habit|able
in|habit|ant +s
in|habit|a|tion +s
in|habit|ed adjective
in|hal|ant +s
in|hal|ation +s
in|hale
  in|hales
  in|haled
  in|hal|ing

in|hal|er +s
in|har|moni|ous
in|har|moni|ous|ly
in|here
  in|heres
  in|hered
  in|her|ing
in|her|ence
in|her|ent (innate, essential)
  [☞ inerrant]
in|her|ent|ly
in|her|it +s +ed +ing
in|herit|abil|ity
in|herit|able
in|herit|ance +s
in|herit|or +s
in|heri|tress
  in|heri|tress|es
in|heri|trix
  plural in|heri|tri|ces
  or in|heri|trix|es
in|hesion
in|hib|it +s +ed +ing
in|hib|it|ed adjective
in|hib|ition +s
in|hib|it|ive
in|hib|it|or +s
in|hib|it|ory
in|homo|gen|eity
in|homo|gen|eous
in|hos|pit|able
in|hos|pit|able|ness
in|hos|pit|ably
in|hospi|tal|ity
in-house
in|human
in|humane
in|humane|ly
in|human|ity
  in|human|ities
in|human|ly
in|human|ness
in|hum|a|tion +s
in|hume
  in|humes
  in|humed
  in|hum|ing
in|imical
in|imical|ly
in|imit|abil|ity
in|imit|able
in|imit|ably
in|iqui|tous
in|iqui|tous|ly
in|iqui|tous|ness
in|iquity
  in|iqui|ties
in|itial
  in|itials
  in|itialled
  or in|itialed

in|itial|ling
or in|itial|ing
in|itial|ism +s
in|itial|iz|a|tion +s
in|itial|ize
in|itial|iz|es
in|itial|ized
in|itial|iz|ing
in|itial|ly
in|iti|ate
in|iti|ates
in|iti|at|ed
in|iti|at|ing
in|iti|a|tion +s
in|itia|tive +s
in|itia|tor +s
in|itia|tory
in|ject +s +ed +ing
in|ject|able
in|jec|tion +s
in|jection-moulded
in|jec|tion mould|ing
in|ject|or +s
in|jera
in-joke +s
in|judi|cious
in|judi|cious|ly
in|judi|cious|ness
in|junc|tion +s
in|junc|tive
in|jure
in|jures
in|jured
in|jur|ing
in|jured adjective
in|jur|er +s
in|juri|ous
in|juri|ous|ly
in|juri|ous|ness
in|jury
in|jur|ies
in|jus|tice +s
ink +s +ed +ing
In|ka|tha (Free|dom
Party)
ink blot test +s
ink cap +s
ink|er +s
ink|horn +s
ink|i|er
ink|i|est
ink|i|ness
ink-jet adjective
preceding a noun
ink|ling +s
ink pad +s
ink|stand +s
ink|well +s
inky
ink|i|er
ink|i|est
in|laid adjective
in|land

in|land|er +s
In|land Tlin|git
plural
In|land Tlin|git or
In|land Tlin|gits
in-law +s
inlay
in|lays
in|laid
in|lay|ing
in|lay|er +s
in|let +s
in|lier +s
in-line adjective
preceding a noun
in loco par|en|tis
inly
In|mar|sat
in|mate +s
in med|ias res
in me|mor|iam +s
in|most
inn +s (hotel; tavern)
[☞ in]
in|nards
in|nate
in|nate|ly
in|nate|ness
in|ner +s
inner city (inner-city
when preceding a
noun)
inner-direct|ed
Inner Heb|ri|des
(islands off Scotland)
inner|ly
Inner Mon|go|lia
(region, China)
inner|most
inner|ness
inner|spring
inner tube +s
in|nerv|ate (supply
with nerves)
in|nerv|ates
in|nerv|at|ed
in|nerv|at|ing
[☞ enervate]
in|nerv|a|tion +s
in|ning +s (Baseball)
in|nings (Cricket)
plural in|nings or
in|nings|es
Innis, Har|old Adams
(Cdn political
economist)
Innis|fail (town,
Alberta)
[☞ Innisfil]
Innis|fil (town,
Ontario)
[☞ Innisfail]
inn|keep|er +s

in|no|cence
In|no|cent (popes)
in|no|cent +s
in|no|cent|ly
in|nocu|ous
in|nocu|ous|ly
in|nocu|ous|ness
in|nomin|ate
in|nov|ate
in|nov|ates
in|nov|at|ed
in|nov|at|ing
in|nov|a|tion +s
in|nov|a|tion|al
in|nov|a|tive
in|nov|a|tive|ly
in|nov|a|tive|ness
in|nov|ator +s
in|nova|tory
Inns|bruck (city,
Austria)
inn-to-inn
Innu
plural Innu
in|nu|en|do
in|nu|en|does or
in|nu|en|dos
In|nu|itian Region
(uplands, Canada)
[☞ Inuit]
in|numer|abil|ity
in|numer|able
(countless)
[☞ enumerable]
in|numer|ably
in|numer|acy
in|numer|ate (not
possessing
mathematical ability)
[☞ enumerate]
in|observ|ance
in|ocula
in|ocu|lable
in|ocu|lant +s
in|ocu|late (vaccinate;
indoctrinate)
in|ocu|lates
in|ocu|lat|ed
in|ocu|lat|ing
[☞ inosculate]
in|ocu|la|tion +s (act
of inoculating)
[☞ inosculation]
in|ocu|la|tive
in|ocu|la|tor +s
in|ocu|lum
in|ocula
in|offen|sive
in|offen|sive|ly
in|offen|sive|ness
Inönü, Ismet (Turkish
prime minister)
in|oper|abil|ity

in|oper|able
in|oper|ably
in|opera|tive
in|opera|tive|ness
in|oppor|tune
in|oppor|tune|ly
in|oppor|tune|ness
in|ordin|ate
in|ordin|ate|ly
in|organ|ic +s
in|organ|ic|ally
in|oscu|late (join)
in|oscu|lates
in|oscu|lat|ed
in|oscu|lat|ing
[☞ inoculate]
in|oscu|la|tion +s (act
of inosculating)
[☞ inoculation]
in|osi|tol +s
in-patient +s
in pro|pria per|sona
input
in|puts
input or in|put|ted
in|put|ting
input/output
in|quest +s
in|quiet|ude
in|quill|ine +s
in|quire
in|quires
in|quired
in|quir|ing
in|quir|er +s
in|quir|ing adjective
in|quir|ing|ly
in|quiry
in|quir|ies
in|qui|si|tion +s
in|qui|si|tion|al
in|quisi|tive
in|quisi|tive|ly
in|quisi|tive|ness
in|quisi|tor +s
in|quisi|tor|ial
in|quisi|tor|ial|ly
in|quor|ate
in re
in|road +s
in|rush
in|rush|es
in|rush|ing
in|salu|bri|ous
in|salu|brity
in|sane
in|sane|ly
in|sani|tary
in|san|ity
in|san|ities
in|sati|abil|ity
in|sati|able

in|sati|able|ness
in|sati|ably
in|sati|ate
in|scape +s
in|scrib|able
in|scribe
  in|scribes
  in|scribed
  in|scrib|ing
in|scrib|er +s
in|scrip|tion +s
in|scrip|tion|al
in|scrip|tive
in|scrut|abil|ity
in|scrut|able
in|scrut|able|ness
in|scrut|ably
in|seam +s
in|sect +s
in|sec|tar|ium +s
in|secti|cid|al
in|secti|cide +s
in|sect|ile
in|secti|vore +s
in|sec|tiv|or|ous
in|secure
in|secure|ly
in|secur|ity
  in|secur|ities
in|semin|ate
  in|semin|ates
  in|semin|at|ed
  in|semin|at|ing
in|semin|a|tion +s
in|sens|ate
in|sens|ate|ly
in|sens|ibil|ity
  in|sens|ibil|ities
in|sens|ible
in|sens|ibly
in|sensi|tive
in|sensi|tive|ly
in|sensi|tiv|ity
  in|sensi|tiv|ities
in|sen|tience
in|sen|tient
in|separ|abil|ity
in|separ|able
in|separ|able|ness
in|separ|ably
in|sert +s +ed +ing
in|sert|able
in|sert|ed *adjective*
in|sert|er +s
in|ser|tion +s
in|ser|tion|al
in-service +s
inset
  in|sets
  inset *or* in|set|ted
  in|set|ting
in|set|ter +s

in|shal|lah
in|shore
in|side +s
in|side job
in|side out (inside-
  out *when preceding a*
  noun)
In|side Pas|sage (sea
  route, N America)
in|sid|er +s
in|sidi|ous
in|sidi|ous|ly
in|sidi|ous|ness
in|sight +s
  (perception)
  [☞ incite]
in|sight|ful
in|sight|ful|ly
in|sig|nia
• *plural noun* (badges
  etc.)
• *singular noun* (a
  badge etc.)
  in|sig|nias
in|sig|nifi|cance
in|sig|nifi|cancy
  in|sig|nifi|can|cies
in|sig|nifi|cant
in|sig|nifi|cant|ly
in|sin|cere
in|sin|cere|ly
in|sin|cer|ity
  in|sin|cer|ities
in|sinu|ate
  in|sinu|ates
  in|sinu|at|ed
  in|sinu|at|ing
in|sinu|at|ing
  adjective
in|sinu|at|ing|ly
in|sinu|a|tion +s
in|sinu|a|tive
in|sinu|ator +s
in|sinua|tory
in|sipid
in|sip|id|ity
in|sipid|ly
in|sipid|ness
in|sist +s +ed +ing
in|sist|ence +s
in|sist|ency
in|sist|ent
in|sist|ent|ly
in|sist|ing|ly
in situ
in|sobri|ety
in|so|far
in|sol|a|tion
  (exposure to the sun)
  [☞ insulation]
in|sole +s
in|sol|ence
in|sol|ent

in|sol|ent|ly
in|solu|bil|ity
in|solu|bil|ize
  in|solu|bil|iz|es
  in|solu|bil|ized
  in|solu|bil|iz|ing
in|sol|uble
in|sol|ubly
in|solv|able
in|sol|vency
  in|sol|ven|cies
in|sol|vent
in|som|nia
in|som|niac +s
in|so|much
in|souci|ance
in|souci|ant
in|souci|ant|ly
in|spect +s +ed +ing
in|spec|tion +s
in|spect|or +s
in|spect|or|ate +s
in|spect|or gen|er|al
  in|spect|ors
  gen|er|al
in|spec|tor|ial
in|spec|tor|ship +s
in|spir|a|tion +s
in|spir|a|tion|al
in|spir|a|tion|al|ly
in|spira|tory
in|spire
  in|spires
  in|spired
  in|spir|ing
in|spired *adjective*
in|spired|ly
in|spir|er +s
in|spir|ing *adjective*
in|spir|ing|ly
in|spirit +s +ed +ing
in|spirit|ing *adjective*
in|spirit|ing|ly
in|spis|sate
  in|spis|sates
  in|spis|sat|ed
  in|spis|sat|ing
in|spis|sa|tion +s
ins|pis|sa|tor +s
in|stabil|ity
  in|stabil|ities
in|stal (*use* install)
  in|stals
  in|stalled
  in|stal|ling
in|stall +s +ed +ing
in|stal|la|tion +s (act
  of installing; *Art*;
  establishment)
  [☞ instillation]
in|stall|er +s
in|stall|ment +s (*use*
  instalment)

in|stal|ment +s
in|stance
  in|stan|ces
  in|stanced
  in|stan|cing
in|stancy
in|stant +s
in|stan|tan|eity
in|stan|tan|eous
in|stan|tan|eous|ly
in|stan|tan|eous|ness
in|stan|ter
in|stan|tiate
  in|stan|tiates
  in|stan|tiat|ed
  in|stan|tiat|ing
in|stan|ti|a|tion +s
in|stant|ly
in|star +s
in|state
  in|states
  in|stat|ed
  in|stat|ing
in statu pu|pil|lari
in|staur|a|tion +s
in|staur|ator +s
in|stead
in|step +s
in|sti|gate
  in|sti|gates
  in|sti|gat|ed
  in|sti|gat|ing
in|sti|ga|tion +s
in|sti|ga|tor +s
in|stil (*use* instill)
  in|stils
  in|stilled
  in|stil|ling
in|still +s +ed +ing
in|stil|la|tion +s (act
  of instilling; thing
  instilled)
  [☞ installation]
in|still|ment +s
in|stinct +s
in|stinct|ive
in|stinct|ive|ly
in|stinc|tual
in|stinc|tual|ly
in|sti|tute
  in|sti|tutes
  in|sti|tut|ed
  in|sti|tut|ing
in|sti|tu|tion +s
in|sti|tu|tion|al
in|sti|tu|tion|al|ism
in|sti|tu|tion|al|iz|
  a|tion +s
in|sti|tu|tion|al|ize
  in|sti|tu|tion|al|iz|es
  in|sti|tu|tion|al|ized
  in|sti|tu|tion|al|iz|
    ing

in|sti|tu|tion|al|ized
  adjective
in|sti|tu|tion|al|ly
in-store *adjective*
  preceding a noun &
  adverb
in|struct +s +ed +ing
in|struc|tion +s
in|struc|tion|al
in|struct|ive
in|struct|ive|ly
in|struct|ive|ness
in|struct|or +s
in|struct|or|ship +s
in|struc|tress
  in|struc|tress|es
in|stru|ment +s +ed
  +ing
in|stru|men|tal +s
in|stru|men|tal|ism
in|stru|men|tal|ist +s
in|stru|men|tal|ity
  in|stru|men|tal|ities
in|stru|men|tal|ly
in|stru|men|ta|tion
  +s
in|sub|ordin|ate
in|sub|ordin|ate|ly
in|sub|ordin|a|tion
in|sub|stan|tial
in|sub|stan|tial|ity
in|sub|stan|tial|ly
in|suffer|able
in|suffer|able|ness
in|suffer|ably
in|suffi|cien|cy
  in|suffi|cien|cies
in|suffi|cient
in|suffi|cient|ly
in|suf|flate
in|suf|fla|tion +s
in|su|lar
in|su|lar|ism
in|su|lar|ity
in|su|lar|ly
in|su|late
  in|su|lates
  in|su|lat|ed
  in|su|lat|ing
in|su|la|tion +s
  (weatherproofing;
  isolation)
  [☞ insolation]
in|su|la|tive
in|su|la|tor +s
Insul|brick +s
in|su|lin +s
in|sult +s +ed +ing
in|sult|er +s
in|sult|ing *adjective*
in|sult|ing|ly
in|super|abil|ity

in|super|able
in|super|ably
in|sup|port|able
in|sup|port|able|ness
in|sup|port|ably
in|sur|abil|ity
in|sur|able
in|sur|ance +s
in|sure (issue or
  obtain an insurance
  policy on; *for* make
  certain *or* secure *use*
  ensure)
  in|sures
  in|sured
  in|sur|ing
in|sured *adjective &*
  noun
in|sur|er +s
in|sur|gence +s
in|sur|gen|cy
  in|sur|gen|cies
in|sur|gent +s
in|sur|mount|able
in|sur|mount|ably
in|sur|rec|tion +s
in|sur|rec|tion|ary
in|sur|rec|tion|ist +s
in|suscep|ti|bil|ity
in|suscep|tible
in|tact
in|tact|ness
in|tagli|at|ed
in|taglio
  • *noun*
  in|taglios
  • *verb*
  in|ta|glioes
  in|ta|glioed
  in|taglio|ing
in|take +s
in|tan|gibil|ity
in|tan|gible +s
in|tan|gibly
in|tar|sia +s
in|teger +s
in|te|gra|bil|ity
in|te|grable
in|te|gral +s
in|te|gral|ity
in|te|gral|ly
in|te|grand +s (*Math:*
  function to be
  integrated)
in|te|grant +s (thing
  that integrates)
in|te|grate
  in|te|grates
  in|te|grat|ed
  in|te|grat|ing
in|te|grat|ed *adjective*
in|te|gra|tion +s
in|te|gra|tion|ist +s

in|te|gra|tive
in|te|gra|tor +s
in|teg|rity
  in|teg|ri|ties
in|tegu|ment +s
in|tegu|ment|al
in|tegu|ment|ary
in|tel|lect +s
in|tel|lec|tion +s
in|tel|lect|ive
in|tel|lec|tual +s
in|tel|lec|tual|ism
in|tel|lec|tual|ist +s
in|tel|lec|tual|ity
in|tel|lec|tual|
    iz|a|tion +s
in|tel|lec|tual|ize
  in|tel|lec|tual|iz|es
  in|tel|lec|tual|ized
  in|tel|lec|tual|iz|ing
in|tel|lec|tual|ly
in|tel|li|gence +s
in|tel|li|gent
in|tel|li|gen|tial
in|tel|li|gent|ly
in|tel|li|gent|sia
in|tel|li|gi|bil|ity
in|tel|li|gible
in|tel|li|gibly
In|tel|sat
in|temper|ance
in|temper|ate
in|temper|ate|ly
in|temper|ate|ness
in|tend +s +ed +ing
in|tend|an|cy
  in|tend|an|cies
in|tend|ant +s
in|tend|ed +s *adjective*
  & noun
in|tend|ing *adjective*
in|tense
  in|tens|er
  in|tens|est
in|tense|ly
in|tense|ness
in|ten|si|fi|ca|tion +s
in|ten|si|fi|er +s
in|ten|si|fy
  in|ten|si|fies
  in|ten|si|fied
  in|ten|si|fy|ing
in|ten|sion +s (*Logic:*
  content of a
  concept)
  [☞ intention]
in|ten|sion|al (*Logic:*
  of attributes
  contained in a
  concept)
  [☞ intentional]

in|ten|sion|al|ity
  (state of being
  intensional)
  [☞ intentionality]
in|ten|sion|al|ly
  (*Logic:* by way of
  intension)
  [☞ intentionally]
in|ten|sity
  in|ten|si|ties
in|ten|sive +s
in|ten|sive|ly
in|ten|sive|ness
in|tent +s
in|ten|tion +s
  (purpose; *Logic:* a
  conception)
  [☞ intension]
in|ten|tion|al
  (deliberate; of the
  mind)
  [☞ intensional]
in|ten|tion|al|ity
  (state of being
  intentional)
  [☞ intensionality]
in|ten|tion|al|ly
  (deliberately)
  [☞ intensionally]
in|ten|tioned *adjective*
in|tent|ly
in|tent|ness
inter (bury)
  in|ters
  in|terred
  in|ter|ring
In|ter|ac *proprietary*
inter|act +s +ed +ing
inter|act|ant +s
inter|action +s
inter|action|al
inter|action|ism
inter|action|ist +s
inter|active
inter|active|ly
inter|activ|ity
inter alia
inter|atomic
inter|bank
inter|bed
  inter|beds
  inter|bed|ded
  inter|bed|ding
inter|breed
  inter|breeds
  inter|bred
  inter|breed|ing
in|ter|cal|ary
in|ter|cal|ate
  in|ter|cal|ates
  in|ter|cal|at|ed
  in|ter|cal|at|ing

in|ter|cal|at|ed
  adjective
in|ter|cal|a|tion +s
inter|cede
  inter|cedes
  inter|ced|ed
  inter|ced|ing
inter|ced|er +s
inter|cellu|lar
inter|cept +s +ed
  +ing
inter|cep|tion +s
inter|cep|tive
inter|cept|or +s
inter|ces|sion +s (act
  of interceding;
  prayer)
  [☞ intersession]
inter|cession|al
inter|ces|sor +s
inter|ces|sor|ial
inter|ces|sory
inter|change
  inter|chan|ges
  inter|changed
  inter|chan|ging
inter|change|abil|ity
inter|change|able
inter|change|able|
          ness
inter|change|ably
inter-church
inter|city
inter-class
inter|collegi|ate
inter|coloni|al
inter|com +s
inter|com|muni|cate
  inter|com|muni|
          cates
  inter|com|muni|
          cat|ed
  inter|com|muni|
          cat|ing
inter|com|muni|ca|
          tion
inter|com|muni|ca|
          tive
inter|com|mun|ion
  +s
inter|com|mun|ity
inter|con|nect +s +ed
  +ing
inter|connect|ed
  adjective
inter|connect|ed|
          ness
inter|connect|ing
  adjective
inter|connec|tion +s
inter|connec|tiv|ity
inter|contin|ent|al
inter|con|ver|sion +s

inter|con|vert +s +ed
  +ing
inter|convert|ible
inter|cool +s +ed
  +ing
inter|cool|er +s
inter|correl|ate
  inter|correl|ates
  inter|correl|at|ed
  inter|correl|at|ing
inter|correl|a|tion +s
inter|costal +s
inter|county
inter|course
inter|crop
  inter|crops
  inter|cropped
  inter|crop|ping
inter|crop|ping *noun*
inter|cross
  inter|cross|es
  inter|crossed
  inter|cross|ing
inter|crural
inter|cultur|al
inter|cultur|al|ism
inter|current
inter|cut
  inter|cuts
  inter|cut
  inter|cut|ting
inter-
  denomin|a|tion|al
inter|depart|ment|al
inter|depart|ment|al|
          ly
inter|depend +s +ed
  +ing
inter|depend|ence
inter|depend|ency
  inter|depend|en|
          cies
inter|depend|ent
inter|dict +s +ed
  +ing
inter|dic|tion +s
inter|dict|ory
inter|digit|al
inter|digi|tate
  inter|digi|tates
  inter|digi|tat|ed
  inter|digi|tat|ing
inter|disci|plin|ar|ity
inter|disci|plin|ary
in|ter|est +s +ed +ing
in|ter|est|ed *adjective*
in|ter|est|ed|ly
in|ter|est|ed|ness
in|ter|est|ing *adjective*
in|ter|est|ing|ly
in|ter|est|ing|ness
inter-ethnic

inter|face
  inter|faces
  inter|faced
  inter|facing
inter|facial
inter|facing +s *noun*
inter|faith
inter|fere
  inter|feres
  inter|fered
  inter|fer|ing
inter|fer|ence +s
inter|feren|tial
inter|fer|er +s
inter|fer|ing *adjective*
inter|fer|ing|ly
inter|fer|om|eter +s
inter|fero|met|ric
inter|fero|met|ric|
          ally
inter|fer|om|etry
inter|feron +s
inter|file
  inter|files
  inter|filed
  inter|filing
inter|fuse
  inter|fus|es
  inter|fused
  inter|fus|ing
inter|fusion +s
inter|galac|tic
inter|galac|tic|ally
inter|gener|a|tion|al
inter|glacial
inter|govern|ment|al
inter|govern|ment|al|
          ly
inter|grada|tion +s
inter|grade
  inter|grades
  inter|graded
  inter|grad|ing
inter-group
inter|growth
in|ter|im +s
In|ter|ior (of BC)
in|ter|ior +s (*in
  general use*)
in|ter|ior|ity
in|ter|ior|iz|a|tion +s
in|ter|ior|ize
  in|ter|ior|iz|es
  in|ter|ior|ized
  in|ter|ior|iz|ing
in|ter|ior|ly
inter|ject +s +ed
  +ing
inter|jec|tion +s
inter|jec|tion|al
inter|ject|or +s
inter|ject|ory

inter|lace
  inter|laces
  inter|laced
  inter|lacing
inter|lace|ment +s
Inter|lake (region,
  Canada)
Inter|laken (town,
  Switzerland)
inter|lan|guage +s
inter|lard +s +ed
  +ing
inter|leaf
  inter|leaves
inter|leave
  inter|leaves
  inter|leaved
  inter|leav|ing
inter|leukin +s
inter|library
inter|line
  inter|lines
  inter|lined
  inter|lining
inter|linear
inter|linea|tion +s
inter|lining +s *noun*
inter|link +s +ed
  +ing
inter|link|age +s
inter|linked *adjective*
inter|lock +s +ed
  +ing
inter|lock|er +s
inter|lock|ing
  adjective
inter|locu|tion +s
inter|locu|tor +s
inter|locu|tory
inter|lope
  inter|lopes
  inter|loped
  inter|lop|ing
inter|lop|er +s
inter|lude +s
inter|mar|riage +s
inter|marry
  inter|marries
  inter|married
  inter|marry|ing
inter|medi|acy
inter|medi|ary
  inter|medi|ar|ies
inter|medi|ate
  inter|medi|ates
  inter|medi|at|ed
  inter|medi|at|ing
inter|medi|ate|ly
inter|medi|ate|ness
inter|medi|a|tion +s
inter|medi|ator +s
in|ter|ment +s (burial)
  [☞ internment]

inter|mesh
inter|mesh|es
inter|meshed
inter|mesh|ing
inter|mezzo
inter|mezzi or
inter|mezzos
in|termin|able
in|termin|able|ness
in|termin|ably
inter|min|gle
inter|min|gles
inter|min|gled
inter|min|gling
inter-minister|ial
inter|mis|sion +s
inter|mit
inter|mits
inter|mit|ted
inter|mit|ting
inter|mit|tence
inter|mit|tency
inter|mit|tent
inter|mit|tent|ly
inter|mix
inter|mix|es
inter|mixed
inter|mix|ing
inter|mix|able
inter|mix|ture +s
inter|modal
inter|molecu|lar
inter|mon|tane
in|tern +s +ed +ing
  (recent medical
  graduate etc.)
in|ter|nal +s
in|ter|nal|ity
in|ter|nal|iz|a|tion +s
in|ter|nal|ize
in|ter|nal|iz|es
in|ter|nal|ized
in|ter|nal|iz|ing
in|ter|nal|ly
inter|nation|al +s
  [☞ Internationale]
Inter|nation|al Date
  Line
Inter|na|tio|nale
  (song)
inter|nation|al|ism
inter|nation|al|ist +s
inter|nation|al|ity
inter|nation|al|iz|
      a|tion
inter|nation|al|ize
inter|nation|al|iz|es
inter|nation|al|ized
inter|nation|al|iz|ing
inter|nation|al|ly
Inter|naut +s
inter|necine
in|tern|ee +s

In|ter|net proprietary
inter|net|work +s
inter|net|work|ing
in|tern|ist +s
in|tern|ment +s
  (confinement)
  [☞ interment]
inter|node +s
intern|ship
inter|nuclear
inter|nuncial
in|tero|cep|tive
inter-office
inter|oper|abil|ity
inter|oper|able
inter|oscu|late
inter|oscu|lates
inter|oscu|lat|ed
inter|oscu|lat|ing
inter|osseous
inter|pariet|al
inter|pariet|al|ly
in|ter|pel|late (in
  parliamentary
  proceedings)
in|ter|pel|lates
in|ter|pel|lat|ed
in|ter|pel|lat|ing
  [☞ interpolate]
in|ter|pel|la|tion +s
  (in parliamentary
  proceedings)
  [☞ interpolation]
in|ter|pel|la|tor +s (in
  parliamentary
  proceedings)
  [☞ interpolator]
inter|pene|trate
inter|pene|trates
inter|pene|trat|ed
inter|pene|trat|ing
inter|pene|tra|tion
  +s
inter|pene|tra|tive
inter|person|al
inter|person|al|ly
inter|phase
inter|planet|ary
inter|plant +s +ed
  +ing
inter|play
In|ter|pol
in|ter|pol|ate
  (interject, insert;
  estimate)
in|ter|pol|ates
in|ter|pol|at|ed
in|ter|pol|at|ing
  [☞ interpellate]
in|ter|pol|a|tion +s
  (an act of
  interpolating)
  [☞ interpellation]

in|ter|pola|tive
in|ter|pol|ator (one
  who interpolates)
  [☞ interpellator]
inter|pose
inter|pos|es
inter|posed
inter|pos|ing
inter|pos|ition +s
in|ter|pret +s +ed
  +ing
in|ter|pret|abil|ity
in|ter|pret|able
in|ter|pret|a|tion +s
in|ter|pret|a|tion|al
in|ter|pret|a|tive
in|ter|pret|er +s
in|ter|pret|ive
in|ter|pret|ive|ly
inter|prov|in|cial
inter|racial
inter|racial|ly
inter|reg|num
inter|reg|nums or
inter|regna
inter|relate
inter|relates
inter|relat|ed
inter|relat|ing
inter|relat|ed
  adjective
inter|related|ness
inter|rela|tion +s
inter|rela|tion|ship
  +s
in|terro|gate
in|terro|gates
in|terro|gat|ed
in|terro|gat|ing
in|terro|ga|tion +s
in|terro|ga|tion|al
in|ter|roga|tive +s
in|ter|roga|tive|ly
in|terro|ga|tor +s
in|ter|roga|tory
in|ter|roga|tor|ies
in|ter|rupt +s +ed
  +ing
in|ter|rupt|er +s
in|ter|rupt|ible
in|ter|rup|tion +s
in|ter|rupt|ive
in|ter|rupt|or +s (use
  interrupter)
in|ter|rupt|ory
inter|schol|as|tic
inter|sect +s +ed
  +ing
inter|sec|tion +s
inter|sec|tion|al
inter|ses|sion +s
  (university term or

  period between
  terms)
  [☞ intercession]
inter|sex
inter|sex|es
inter|sex|ual
inter|sex|u|al|ity
inter|space
inter|spaces
inter|spaced
inter|spacing
inter|species
inter|specif|ic
inter|sperse
inter|spers|es
inter|spersed
inter|spers|ing
inter|sper|sion +s
inter|stadi|al +s
inter|state +s
inter|stel|lar
in|ter|stice +s
inter|stitial
inter|stitial|ly
inter|subject|ive
inter|subject|ive|ly
inter|subjec|tiv|ity
inter|text|ual
inter|text|u|al|ity
inter|tidal
inter|track
inter-tribal
inter|twine
inter|twines
inter|twined
inter|twin|ing
inter|twine|ment +s
inter|twist +s +ed
  +ing
inter|val +s
inter|vale +s
inter|val|ic (use
  intervallic)
inter|val|lic
inter|vene
inter|venes
inter|vened
inter|ven|ing
inter|ven|er +s (use
  intervenor)
inter|ven|or +s
inter|ven|tion +s
inter|ven|tion|al
inter|ven|tion|ism
inter|ven|tion|ist +s
inter|ver|te|bral
inter|view +s +ed
  +ing
inter|view|ee +s
inter|view|er +s
inter|vocal|ic
inter|war

inter|weave
inter|weaves
inter|wove
inter|woven
inter|weav|ing
inter|work +s +ed
+ing
inter|woven *adjective*
in|tes|tacy
in|tes|ta|cies
in|tes|tate +s
in|tes|tin|al
in|tes|tine +s
inti
plural inti or intis
in|ti|fada
in|tim|acy
in|tim|acies
in|tim|ate
in|tim|ates
in|tim|at|ed
in|tim|at|ing
in|tim|ate|ly
in|tim|a|tion +s
in|timi|date
in|timi|dates
in|timi|dat|ed
in|timi|dat|ing
in|timi|dat|ing
adjective
in|timi|dat|ing|ly
in|timi|da|tion +s
in|timi|da|tor +s
in|tinc|tion
into
in|toler|able
in|toler|ably
in|toler|ance +s
in|toler|ant
in|toler|ant|ly
in|ton|ate
in|ton|ates
in|ton|at|ed
in|ton|at|ing
in|ton|a|tion +s
in|ton|a|tion|al
in|tone
in|tones
in|toned
in|ton|ing
in|ton|er +s
in toto
in|toxi|cant +s
in|toxi|cate
in|toxi|cates
in|toxi|cat|ed
in|toxi|cat|ing
in|toxi|cat|ing
adjective
in|toxi|cat|ing|ly
in|toxi|ca|tion +s
intra|cellu|lar
intra|cellu|lar|ly

intra|crani|al
in|tract|abil|ity
in|tract|able
in|tract|able|ness
in|tract|ably
intra|day
in|tra|dos
in|tra|dos|es
intra|molecu|lar
intra|mural
intra|mural|ly
intra|muscu|lar
intra|muscu|lar|ly
in|transi|gence
in|transi|gency
in|transi|gent +s
in|transi|gent|ly
in|transi|tive
in|transi|tive|ly
in|transi|tiv|ity
intra|psych|ic
intra|psych|ic|ally
intra|specif|ic
intra|uter|ine
intra|vascu|lar
intra|venous
intra|venous|es
intra|venous|ly
intra vires
in-tray +s
in|trep|id
in|trep|id|ity
in|trep|id|ly
in|tri|cacy
in|tri|ca|cies
in|tri|cate
in|tri|cate|ly
in|tri|gante +s
in|trigue
in|trigues
in|trigued
in|triguing
in|triguer +s
in|triguing *adjective*
in|triguing|ly
in|trin|sic
in|trin|sic|ally
in|tro +s
intro|duce
intro|du|ces
intro|duced
intro|du|cing
intro|du|cer +s
intro|du|cible
intro|duc|tion +s
intro|duc|tory
in|troit +s
intro|ject +s +ed
+ing
intro|jec|tion +s
intro|mis|sion +s

intro|mit
intro|mits
intro|mit|ted
intro|mit|ting
intro|mit|tent
in|tron +s
intro|spec|tion +s
intro|spec|tive
intro|spec|tive|ly
intro|spec|tive|ness
intro|ver|sion +s
intro|ver|sive
intro|vert +s +ed
+ing
intro|vert|ed *adjective*
intro|vert|ive
in|trude
in|trudes
in|trud|ed
in|trud|ing
in|trud|er +s
in|tru|sion +s
in|tru|sive
in|tru|sive|ly
in|tru|sive|ness
in|tub|ate
in|tub|ates
in|tub|at|ed
in|tub|at|ing
in|tub|a|tion +s
in|tuit +s +ed +ing
in|tuit|able
in|tui|tion +s
in|tui|tion|al
in|tui|tion|al|ism
in|tui|tion|ism
in|tui|tion|ist +s
in|tui|tive
in|tui|tive|ly
in|tui|tive|ness
in|tu|mesce
in|tu|mes|ces
in|tu|mesced
in|tu|mes|cing
in|tu|mes|cence +s
in|tu|mes|cent
in-turn +s (*Curling*)
[☞ intern]
intus|sus|cep|tion +s
Inuit
• *adjective*
• *plural noun* (people)
singular Inuk
• *singular noun*
(Inuktitut)
[☞ Innuitian
Region]
Inuit Ta|piri|sat of
Can|ada
Inuk
Inuit
Inuk|shuk +s
Inuk|ti|tut

in|un|date
in|un|dates
in|un|dat|ed
in|un|dat|ing
in|un|da|tion +s
In|upi|aq
In|upi|at
plural In|upi|at
inure (accustom to
something
unpleasant; *Law*:
take effect)
in|ures
in|ured
in|uring
inure|ment +s
in utero
Inu|via|luk|tun
Inu|vik (town,
Canada)
in vacuo
in|vade
in|vades
in|vad|ed
in|vad|ing
in|vad|er +s
in|vagin|ate
in|vagin|ates
in|vagin|at|ed
in|vagin|at|ing
in|vagin|a|tion +s
in|valid +s +ed +ing
in|vali|date
in|vali|dates
in|vali|dat|ed
in|vali|dat|ing
in|vali|da|tion
in|valid|ism
in|valid|ity
in|valid|ities
in|valid|ly
in|valu|able
in|valu|able|ness
in|valu|ably
in|vari|abil|ity
in|vari|able
in|vari|able|ness
in|vari|ably
in|vari|ance
in|vari|ant +s
in|va|sion +s
in|va|sive
in|vasive|ness
in|vec|tive +s
in|veigh +s +ed +ing
in|veigle
in|veigles
in|veigled
in|veig|ling
in|veigle|ment +s
in|vent +s +ed +ing
in|ven|tion +s
in|vent|ive

in|vent|ive|ly
in|vent|ive|ness
in|vent|or +s
in|ven|tory
  in|ven|tor|ies
  in|ven|tor|ied
  in|ven|tory|ing
Inver|car|gill (city, New Zealand)
Inver|ness (city, Scotland)
in|verse +s
in|verse|ly
in|ver|sion +s
in|ver|sive
in|vert +s +ed +ing
in|vert|ase
in|ver|te|brate +s
in|vert|ed adjective
in|vert|er +s
in|vert|ibil|ity
in|vert|ible
in|vest +s +ed +ing
in|vest|able
in|vest|ible (use investable)
in|ves|ti|gate
  in|ves|ti|gates
  in|ves|ti|gat|ed
  in|ves|ti|gat|ing
in|ves|ti|ga|tion +s
in|ves|ti|ga|tion|al
in|ves|ti|ga|tive
in|ves|ti|ga|tor +s
in|ves|ti|ga|tory
in|ves|ti|ture +s
in|vest|ment +s
in|vest|or +s
in|veter|acy
in|veter|ate
in|veter|ate|ly
in|vidi|ous
in|vidi|ous|ly
in|vidi|ous|ness
in|vigi|late
  in|vigi|lates
  in|vigi|lat|ed
  in|vigi|lat|ing
in|vigi|la|tion
in|vigi|la|tor +s
in|vig|or|ate
  in|vig|or|ates
  in|vig|or|at|ed
  in|vig|or|at|ing
  in|vig|or|at|ing adjective
in|vig|or|at|ing|ly
in|vig|or|a|tion
in|vig|or|a|tive
in|vig|or|ator +s
in|vinci|bil|ity
in|vin|cible
in|vin|cible|ness

in|vin|cibly
in|viol|abil|ity
in|viol|able
in|viol|ably
in|viol|acy
in|viol|ate
in|viol|ate|ly
in|viol|ate|ness
in|visi|bil|ity
in|vis|ible
in|vis|ible|ness
in|vis|ibly
in|vi|ta|tion +s
in|vi|ta|tion|al +s
in|vite
  in|vites
  in|vit|ed
  in|vit|ing
in|vit|ee +s
in|vit|er +s
in|vit|ing adjective
in|vit|ing|ly
in vitro
in vivo
in|voc|able
in|voca|tion +s
in|voca|tory
in|voice
  in|voi|ces
  in|voiced
  in|voi|cing
in|voke
  in|vokes
  in|voked
  in|vok|ing
in|vok|er +s
in|vo|luc|ral
in|vo|lucre +s
in|volun|tar|i|ly
in|volun|tar|i|ness
in|volun|tary
in|vol|ute +s
in|vol|uted
in|volu|tion +s
in|volu|tion|al
in|volve
  in|volves
  in|volved
  in|volv|ing
in|volved adjective
in|volve|ment +s
in|vul|ner|abil|ity
in|vul|ner|able
in|vul|ner|ably
in|ward
inward-looking
in|ward|ly
in|ward|ness
in|wards
in|weave
  in|weaves

in|wove
in|woven
in|weav|ing
in|wrap (use enwrap)
in|wraps
in|wrapped
in|wrap|ping
in|wrought
in-your-face adjective
  preceding a noun
I/O (input/output)
Io (Greek Myth; Astronomy)
iod|ate +s
iodic
iod|ide +s
iodin|ate
  iodin|ates
  iodin|at|ed
  iodin|at|ing
iodin|a|tion
iod|ine
iod|iz|a|tion
iod|ize
  iod|iz|es
  iod|ized
  iod|iz|ing
iodo|form
ion +s
Iona (island, Inner Hebrides)
[☞ Ionia]
Ion|esco, Eu|gène (Romanian-born dramatist)
ion ex|change (ion-exchange when preceding a noun)
ion ex|chan|ger +s
Ionia (ancient region, Asia Minor)
[☞ Iona]
Ion|ian +s
Ionic (Architecture; Ionian dialect)
ionic (of ions)
ion|ic|ally
ion|iz|able
ion|iz|a|tion
ion|ize
  ion|iz|es
  ion|ized
  ion|iz|ing
ion|iz|er +s
iono|phore +s
iono|sphere
iono|spher|ic
iota +s
IOU (debt)
  IOUs
Iowa (state & city, US)
Iowan +s

Ipati|eff, Vlad|i|mir Niko|lai|evich (Russian-born chemist)
ipe|cac +s
ipe|cacu|anha +s
Iphi|genia (Greek Myth)
IPO (initial public offering)
  IPOs
Ipoh (city, Malaysia)
ipo|moea +s
ipse dix|it +s
ipsi|lat|eral
ip|sis|sima verba
ipso facto
Ips|wich (town, England)
IQ (intelligence quotient)
  IQs
Iqal|uit (town, Canada)
Iqui|tos (city, Peru)
Iran (country, Middle East)
Iran|gate
Iran|ian +s
Iran-Iraq War
Iraq (country, Middle East)
Iraqi +s
iras|ci|bil|ity
iras|cible
iras|cibly
irate
irate|ly
irate|ness
IRBM (intermediate-range ballistic missile)
  IRBMs
IRC (International Reply Coupon; Internet Relay Chat)
  IRCs
ire
ire|ful
Ire|land (island, N Atlantic; country)
iren|ic
iren|ic|al (= irenic)
Irgun
Irian Jaya (province, Indonesia)
iri|da|ceous
iri|des|cence
iri|des|cent
iri|des|cent|ly
irid|ium
iri|dol|o|gist +s
iri|dol|ogy

Iris (*Greek Myth*)
iris (of the eye; plant)
iris|es
Irish
Irish|man
Irish|men
Irish|ness
Irish whis|key
Irish|woman
Irish|women
iritis
irk +s +ed +ing
irk|some
irk|some|ly
irk|some|ness
Ir|kutsk (city, Siberia)
iron +s +ed +ing
iron|bark +s
iron-bound
iron|clad +s
Iron Cur|tain
iron|er +s
Iron Gate (gorge,
Romania-Serbia
border)
iron|hand|ed
iron|ic
iron|ic|al
iron|ic|al|ly
iron|ing *noun*
iron|ist
iron|ize
iron|iz|es
iron|ized
iron|iz|ing
iron|less
iron-like
iron man (strong
man)
iron men
Iron|man (triathlon)
iron|master +s
iron|monger +s
iron|mongery
iron|monger|ies
iron-on
Irons, Jer|emy
(English actor)
iron|sides
iron|stone +s
iron|ware
iron|weed +s
iron|wood +s
iron|work
iron|work|er +s
iron|works
irony
iron|ies
Iro|quoi|an +s
Iro|quois
plural Iro|quois

Iro|quois Falls (town,
Canada)
ir|radi|ance
ir|radi|ant
ir|radi|ate
ir|radi|ates
ir|radi|at|ed
ir|radi|at|ing
ir|radi|a|tion
ir|radi|a|tive
ir|ration|al
ir|ration|al|ism
ir|ration|al|ist +s
ir|ration|al|ity
ir|ration|al|ities
ir|ration|al|ize
ir|ration|al|iz|es
ir|ration|al|ized
ir|ration|al|iz|ing
ir|ration|al|ly
Irra|waddy (river,
Burma)
ir|reclaim|able
ir|reclaim|ably
ir|recon|cil|abil|ity
ir|recon|cil|able
ir|recon|cil|able|ness
ir|recon|cil|ably
ir|recov|er|able
ir|recov|er|ably
ir|recus|able
ir|redeem|abil|ity
ir|redeem|able
ir|redeem|ably
ir|reden|tism
ir|reden|tist +s
ir|reduci|bil|ity
ir|redu|cible
ir|redu|cibly
ir|ref|rag|able
ir|ref|rag|ably
ir|refran|gible
ir|refut|abil|ity
ir|refut|able
ir|refut|ably
ir|regu|lar +s
ir|regu|lar|ity
ir|regu|lar|ities
ir|regu|lar|ly
ir|rela|tive
ir|rela|tive|ly
ir|rel|evance +s
ir|rel|evancy
ir|rel|evan|cies
ir|rel|evant
ir|rel|evant|ly
ir|reli|gion
ir|reli|gion|ist +s
ir|reli|gious
ir|reli|gious|ly
ir|reli|gious|ness
ir|remedi|able

ir|remedi|ably
ir|remis|sible
ir|remov|abil|ity
ir|remov|able
ir|remov|ably
ir|repar|abil|ity
ir|repar|able
ir|repar|able|ness
ir|repar|ably
ir|replace|able
ir|replace|ably
ir|repress|ibil|ity
ir|repress|ible
ir|repress|ible|ness
ir|repress|ibly
ir|re|proach|abil|ity
ir|re|proach|able
ir|re|proach|able|
ness
ir|re|proach|ably
ir|resist|ibil|ity
ir|resist|ible
ir|resist|ible|ness
ir|resist|ibly
ir|reso|lute
ir|reso|lute|ly
ir|reso|lute|ness
ir|reso|lu|tion
ir|resolv|abil|ity
ir|resolv|able
ir|respec|tive
ir|respec|tive|ly
ir|respon|sibil|ity
ir|respon|sible
ir|respon|sibly
ir|respon|sive
ir|respon|sive|ly
ir|respon|sive|ness
ir|retriev|abil|ity
ir|retriev|able
ir|retriev|ably
ir|rever|ence
ir|rever|ent
ir|rever|ent|ly
ir|revers|ibil|ity
ir|revers|ible
ir|revers|ibly
ir|revoc|abil|ity
ir|revoc|able
ir|revoc|ably
ir|rig|able
ir|rig|ate
ir|rig|ates
ir|rig|at|ed
ir|rig|at|ing
ir|rig|a|tion +s
ir|riga|tive
ir|rig|ator +s
irrit|abil|ity
irrit|able
irrit|ably
irri|tancy

irri|tant +s
irri|tate
irri|tates
irri|tat|ed
irri|tat|ing
irri|tat|ed|ly
irri|tat|ing *adjective*
irri|tat|ing|ly
irri|ta|tion +s
irri|ta|tive
irri|ta|tor +s
ir|rupt +s +ed +ing
(enter forcibly)
[☞ erupt]
ir|rup|tion +s (forcible
entrance; increase in
animal population)
[☞ eruption]
ir|rupt|ive (tending to
irrupt)
[☞ eruptive]
Ir|tysh (river, Asia)
Irv|ing, Sir Henry
(English actor)
Irv|ing, John
Wins|low (US
novelist)
Irv|ing, Ken|neth
Colin (Cdn
industrialist)
Irv|ing, Wash|ing|ton
(US writer)
is
Isaac (*Bible*)
Isa|bel|la I (Castilian
queen)
isa|gogic
isa|gogics
Isaiah (*Bible*)
isa|tin +s
ISBN (international
standard book
number)
ISBNs
is|chemia
is|chemic
Is|chia (island, Italy)
is|chi|al
is|chi|um
is|chia
ISDN (integrated
services digital
network)
ISDNs
Ise (city, Japan)
Ise|ler, Elmer Wal|ter
(Cdn choral
conductor)
isen|trop|ic
Is|eult (*Medieval
Legend*)
Isfa|han (city, Iran)

Isher|wood,
Chris|to|pher
Wil|liam Brad|shaw
(English writer)
Ishi|guro, Kazuo
(Japanese-born
English novelist)
Ish|mael (*Bible*)
Ish|mael|ite +s
Ish|tar (*Babylonian &*
Assyrian Myth)
Isi|dore of Se|ville
(saint)
isin|glass
Isis (*Egyptian Myth*)
Is|ken|de|run (city,
Turkey)
Islam
Is|lama|bad (capital
of Pakistan)
Is|lam|ic
Islam|ism
Islam|ist +s
Islam|iz|a|tion +s
Islam|ize
Islam|iz|es
Islam|ized
Islam|iz|ing
island +s +ed +ing
island|er +s
island-hop
island-hops
island-hopped
island-hopping
island-hopping *noun*
Islay (island, Scotland)
isle +s (island)
[☞ aisle, Île]
Isle of Man (in Irish
Sea)
Isle of Port|land
(peninsula, England)
Isle of Wight (off
S England)
islet +s (small island;
isolated tissue)
[☞ eyelet]
islets of
Lan|ger|hans
ism +s
Is|maili +s
Is|mail Pasha
(Egyptian statesman)
iso|bar +s
iso|bar|ic
iso|chro|mat|ic
iso|chron|ous
iso|chron|ous|ly
iso|clinal
iso|clin|ic
Isoc|ra|tes (Athenian
orator)
iso|cyan|ate +s

iso|dynam|ic
iso|elec|tric
iso|enzyme +s
iso|gloss
iso|gloss|es
iso|gon|ic
iso|hel +s
iso|hyet +s
iso|kin|etic
isol|able
iso|lat|able
iso|late
iso|lates
iso|lat|ed
iso|lat|ing
iso|lat|ed *adjective*
iso|lat|ing *adjective*
iso|la|tion +s
iso|la|tion|ism
iso|la|tion|ist +s
iso|la|tor +s
Is|olde (*Medieval*
Legend)
iso|leu|cine +s
iso|mer +s
iso|mer|ic
isom|er|ism
isom|er|iz|a|tion +s
isom|er|ize
isom|er|iz|es
isom|er|ized
isom|er|iz|ing
isom|er|ous
iso|met|ric|ally
iso|met|rics
isom|etry
iso|morph +s
iso|morph|ic
iso|morph|ism +s
iso|morph|ous
iso|ni|azid
iso|pleth +s
iso|pod +s
iso|propyl
isos|celes
isos|tasy
iso|stat|ic
iso|stat|ic|ally
iso|therm +s
iso|therm|al
iso|therm|al|ly
iso|ton|ic
iso|ton|ic|ally
iso|toni|city
iso|tope +s
iso|top|ic
iso|top|ic|ally
isot|opy
iso|trop|ic
iso|trop|ic|ally
isot|ropy

Ispa|han (= Isfahan,
Iran)
I spy
Is|rael (country &
former kingdom,
Middle East; the
Hebrew people)
Is|raeli +s
Is|rael|ite +s
Is|ra|fel (*Islam*)
Is|sa|char (*Bible*)
Issei
plural Issei
ISSN (international
standard serial
number)
ISSNs
issu|able
issu|ance +s
issu|ant
issue
issues
issued
issu|ing
issue|less
issu|er +s
Is|tan|bul (city,
Turkey)
isth|mian
Isth|mian games
isth|mus
isth|mus|es or
isthmi
istle +s
it
i.t.a. (initial teaching
alphabet)
Ital|ian +s
Ital|ian|ate
Ital|ic (of ancient
Italy)
ital|ic +s (*Typography*)
itali|ciz|a|tion +s
itali|cize
itali|ciz|es
itali|cized
itali|ciz|ing
Ital|iot +s
Italo-Canadian +s
Italy (country, Europe)
Ita|nagar (city, India)
Itar-Tass
itch
itch|es
itched
itch|ing
itch|i|ness
itchy
itch|i|er
itch|i|est
item +s
item|iz|a|tion +s

item|ize
item|iz|es
item|ized
item|iz|ing
item|iz|er +s
it|er|ate
it|er|ates
it|er|at|ed
it|er|at|ing
it|er|a|tion +s
it|era|tive
it|era|tive|ly
Ith|aca (island,
Greece)
ithy|phal|lic
itin|er|acy
(= itinerancy)
itin|er|ancy
itin|er|ant +s
itin|er|ary
itin|er|aries
itin|er|ate
itin|er|ates
itin|er|at|ed
itin|er|at|ing
itin|er|a|tion +s
Ito, Prince Hiro|bumi
(Japanese
statesman)
its (of or belonging to
it)
[☞ it's]
it's (it is; it has)
[☞ its]
it|self
itsy-bitsy
itty-bitty
Itur|bide, Agus|tín de
(Mexican
revolutionary)
IU (international unit)
IUs
IUD (intrauterine
device)
IUDs
IV (intravenous)
IVs
Ivan (grand dukes of
Muscovy; Russian
czar)
iver|mec|tin
Ives, Charles
Ed|ward (US
composer)
ivied
ivor|ied
Ivory, James (US
filmmaker)
ivory
ivor|ies
Ivory Coast (country,
Africa)

Iv|va|vik (park, Canada)
ivy (plant)
ivies
[☞ IV]
Iwo Jima (island, W Pacific)
ixia +s
Ixion (*Greek Myth*)
Izhevsk (city, Russia)
Izmir (city, Turkey)
Izmit (city, Turkey)
Iznik (city, Turkey)

J

J
• (letter)
　J's
• (joule)
j (letter)
　j's
jab
　jabs
　jabbed
　jab|bing
Jab|al|pur (city, India)
jab|ber +s +ed +ing
jab|ber|er +s
jab|ber|wocky
　jab|ber|wock|ies
Jabir ibn Hay|yan (Geber)
jab|iru +s
jabo|ran|di +s
ja|bot +s
jaca|mar +s
jaca|na +s
jaca|ran|da +s
ja|cinth +s
jack +s +ed +ing
　[☞ Jack pine, Jack tar]
jack|al +s
jack|a|napes
　plural jack|a|napes
Jack and Jill +s
jack|ass
　jack|ass|es
jack boat +s
jack|boot +s
jack|boot|ed
jack|daw +s
jack|et +s +ed +ing
jack|et|ed *adjective*
jacket|less
jack|fish
　plural jack|fish

Jack Frost
jack|fruit
　plural jack|fruit
jack|ham|mer +s +ed +ing
jack-in-office
　jacks-in-office
jack-in-the-box
　jack-in-the-boxes
jack-in-the-pulpit
jack|knife
• noun
　jack|knives
• verb
　jack|knifes
　jack|knifed
　jack|knif|ing
jack|light +s +ed +ing
jack|light|ing noun
jack of all trades
　jacks of all trades
jack-o'-lantern +s
Jack pine +s
jack plane +s
jack|pot +s
jack|rabbit +s
Jack Rus|sell +s (terrier)
jack|snipe +s
Jack|son (city, US)
Jack|son, Alex|an|der Young (Cdn painter)
Jack|son, An|drew (US president)
Jack|son, Don|ald (Cdn figure skater)
Jack|son, Glen|da (English actress)
Jack|son, Jesse Louis (US politician)
Jack|son, Ma|halia (US singer)
Jack|son, Mi|chael Joe (US singer-songwriter)
Jack|son, Thom|as Jona|than ('Stone|wall') (Confederate general)
Jack|son, Wil|liam Henry (Cdn-born labour leader)
Jack|son|ville (city, US)
jack|staff +s
jack|stone +s
jack|straw +s
Jack tar +s
Jack the Rip|per (English murderer)
Jacob (*Bible*)

Jaco|bean +s
Jac|obi, Derek George (English actor)
Ja|co|bi, Karl Gus|tav Jacob (German mathematician)
Jaco|bin +s
Jaco|bin|ic
Jaco|bin|ic|al
Jaco|bin|ism
Jaco|bite +s
Jaco|bit|ism
Ja|cobs, Jane (US-born Cdn urban theorist)
Jacob's lad|der +s
jaco|net +s
Jac|quard, Jo|seph Marie (French inventor)
jac|quard +s
jac|quard loom +s
Jacques-Cartier (mountain, Canada)
Jacques Car|tier Strait (channel, Canada)
jacti|ta|tion +s
Ja|cuzzi +s
　proprietary
jade +s
jaded
jaded|ly
jaded|ness
jade|ite +s
j'adoube
jae|ger +s (bird)
　[☞ Yeager]
Jaffa (city, Israel; orange)
Jaff|na (city & peninsula, Sri Lanka)
JAG (Judge Advocate General)
　JAGs
jag
　jags
　jagged
　jag|ging
jag|ged adjective
jag|ged|ly
jag|ged|ness
Jag|ger, Mi|chael Phil|ip ('Mick') (English singer-songwriter)
jaggy
　jag|gi|er
　jag|gi|est
jag|uar +s
jag|uar|undi +s
jai alai (sport)

jail +s +ed +ing
jail|bait
jail|bird +s
jail|break +s
jail|er +s
jail|house +s
jail|or +s (use jailer)
jail yard +s
Jain +s
Jain|ism
Jain|ist +s
Jai|pur (city, India)
Ja|karta (= Djakarta, Indonesia)
jake
Jal|ala|bad (city, Afghanistan)
Jal|an|dhar (= Jullundur, India)
Jalapa (En|ri|quez) (city, Mexico)
jala|peno +s
Jal|isco (state, Mexico)
jal|opy
　jal|op|ies
jal|ou|sie +s
jam (food; squeeze; *Music*; stoppage; predicament)
　jams
　jammed
　jam|ming
　[☞ jamb]
Ja|maica (Caribbean country)
Ja|mai|can +s
jamb +s (on a door frame)
jam|ba|laya +s
jam|bo|ree +s
jam|bust|er +s
James (kings of Scotland & England; saints)
James, Henry (US novelist)
James, Jesse Wood|son (US outlaw)
James, Dame Phyl|lis Dor|othy (English writer)
James, Thom|as (English explorer of Canada)
James, Wil|liam (US philosopher)
James Bay (in Canada)
Jame|son Raid
James|town (early British settlement,

US; capital of
  St. Helena)
jam|mer +s
jam|mies (pyjamas)
  [☞ **jammy**]
Jammu (town, India)
jammy (like jam)
  jam|mi|er
  jam|mi|est
  [☞ **jammies**]
Jam|nagar
jam-packed
jam-pail curl|ing
Jam|shed|pur (city,
  India)
Jam|shid (legendary
  Persian king)
Janá|ček, Leoš
  (Czech composer)
jan|gle
  jan|gles
  jan|gled
  jan|gling
jan|gly
janis|sary
  janis|sar|ies
jani|tor +s
jani|tor|ial
jani|zary (use
  janissary)
  jani|zar|ies
Jan Mayen (island,
  Arctic)
jan|ney +s +ed +ing
  (use janny)
jan|ney|ing noun (use
  jannying)
janny
  jan|nies
  jan|nied
  janny|ing
janny|ing noun
Jan|sen, Cor|nel|ius
  Otto (Flemish
  theologian)
Jan|sen|ism
Jan|sen|ist +s
Janu|ary
  Janu|aries
Janus (Roman Myth)
Jap +s offensive
Japan (country & sea,
  Asia)
japan
  ja|pans
  ja|panned
  japan|ning
Jap|an|ese
  plural **Jap|an|ese**
jape
  japes
  japed
  japing

japer
japery
  japer|ies
Ja|pheth (Bible)
japon|ica +s
**Jaques-Dalcroze,
  Émile** (Swiss
  composer)
jar
  jars
  jarred
  jar|ring
jardi|nière +s
jar|ful +s
jar|gon +s
jar|gon|is|tic
jar|gon|ize
  jar|gon|iz|es
  jar|gon|ized
  jar|gon|iz|ing
jar|goon +s
jarl +s
Jarls|berg proprietary
Jar|man, Derek
  (English artist &
  filmmaker)
jar|rah +s
jar|ring adjective
jar|ring|ly
Jar|row (town,
  England)
**Jaru|zel|ski,
  Woj|ciech Wit|old**
  (Polish prime
  minister)
Jas|min, Claude (Cdn
  writer)
jas|min +s (plant: use
  jasmine)
jas|mine +s (plant)
  [☞ **Jasmin**]
Jason (Greek Myth)
Jas|per (national park,
  Canada)
jas|per +s (stone)
**Jas|pers, Karl
  Theo|dor** (German
  philosopher)
jas|per|ware
Jassy (= Iaşi,
  Romania)
Jat +s
Jat|aka +s
jaun|dice
  jaun|dices
  jaun|diced
  jaun|di|cing
jaun|diced adjective
jaunt +s +ed +ing
jaunt|i|ly
jaunt|i|ness

jaunty
  jaunt|i|er
  jaunt|i|est
Jau|rès, Jean Léon
  (French journalist)
Java (island & sea,
  Indonesia)
java +s (coffee)
Java Man
Javan +s
Java|nese
  plural **Java|nese**
jav|elin +s
Javex proprietary
jaw +s +ed +ing
jaw|bone
  jaw|bones
  jaw|boned
  jaw|bon|ing
jaw|bon|ing noun
jaw|break|er +s
jaw|break|ing
jawed adjective
jaw|less
jaw|line +s
Jaws of Life
Jay, John (US jurist &
  diplomat)
jay +s
Jay|cee +s
jay|walk +s +ed +ing
jay|walk|er +s
jay|walk|ing noun
jazz
  jazz|es
  jazzed
  jazz|ing
jazz|bo +s
jazz|er +s
Jazz|er|cise
jazz|i|ly
jazz|i|ness
jazz|man
  jazz|men
jazzy
  jazz|i|er
  jazz|i|est
jeal|ous
jeal|ous|ly
jeal|ousy
  jeal|ous|ies
jean +s (denim)
  [☞ **gene**]
Jean Paul (German
  novelist)
  [☞ **John Paul**]
**Jeans, Sir James
  Hop|wood** (English
  astronomer)
jeans (denim pants)
  [☞ **genes**]
Jed|dah (= Jiddah,
  Saudi Arabia)

Jed|dore (lake,
  Canada)
Jeep +s proprietary
jeep|ers
jeer +s +ed +ing
jeer|ing|ly
jees|ly (= jeezly)
jeez interjection
jeez|ly
Jef|fer|son, Thom|as
  (US president)
Jef|fer|son City (city,
  US)
**Jef|frey, Fran|cis,
  Lord** (Scottish
  literary critic)
  [☞ **Geoffrey of
  Monmouth**]
jehad +s (use jihad)
Je|hosha|phat (Bible)
Je|ho|vah (Bible)
Je|ho|vah's Wit|ness
  **Je|ho|vah's
  Wit|ness|es**
Je|hov|ist +s
Jehu (Bible)
je|jun|al
je|june
je|june|ly
je|june|ness
je|junum +s
Jek|yll and Hyde
  (Jekyll-and-Hyde
  when preceding a
  noun)
jell +s +ed +ing verb
  (take definite form;
  harmonize)
  [☞ **gel**]
jel|la|ba +s (use
  djellaba)
**Jel|li|coe, John
  Rush|worth, 1st
  Earl** (English
  admiral)
jel|lied adjective
jelli|fi|ca|tion
jelli|fy
  jelli|fies
  jelli|fied
  jelli|fy|ing
Jell-O +s proprietary
jelly (gelatin-based
  foods)
  jel|lies
  jel|lied
  jelly|ing
  [☞ **gelly**]
jelly baby
  jelly babies
jelly bag +s
jelly bean +s

jelly|fish
plural jelly|fish or
jelly|fish|es
jelly|like
jelly roll +s
Jena (town, Germany)
je ne sais quoi
Jen|ghis Kahn
(= Genghis Khan)
Jen|kins's Ear
(Anglo-Spanish war)
Jen|ner, Ed|ward
(English physician)
Jen|ness, Dia|mond
(New Zealand-born
Cdn anthropologist)
jenny
jen|nies
**Jen|sen, Jo|han|nes
Vil|helm** (Danish
writer)
jeon (South Korean
currency)
plural jeon
[☞ jun]
jeop|ard|ize
jeop|ard|iz|es
jeop|ard|ized
jeop|ard|iz|ing
jeop|ardy
Jeph|thah (*Bible*)
Jerba (= Djerba,
Tunisia)
jer|boa +s
jere|miad +s
Jere|miah +s (*Bible*;
prophet of doom)
**Jerez (de la
Fron|tera)** (town,
Spain)
Jeri|cho (town,
Palestine)
jerk +s +ed +ing
jerk|er +s
jerk|i|ly
jer|kin +s (jacket)
jerk|i|ness
jerk|water
jerky
jerk|i|er
jerk|i|est
jero|boam +s
Jer|ome (saint)
**Jer|ome, Harry
Win|ston** (Cdn
athlete)
jerri|can +s (*use* jerry
can)
Jerry
Jer|ries
jerry-build
jerry-builds

jerry-built
jerry-building
jerry-built
jerry can +s
Jer|sey +s (Channel
Island; cattle)
jer|sey +s (*Textiles*;
garment)
Jer|sey City (city, US)
Jeru|sa|lem (city,
Middle East;
artichoke)
**Jes|per|sen, (Jens)
Otto Harry** (Danish
philologist)
jess
jess|es
jessed
jess|ing
jessa|mine +s
(= jasmine)
Jesse (*Bible*)
jest +s +ed +ing
jest|er +s
jest|ing|ly
Jesu (= Jesus)
Jes|uit +s
Jesu|it|ical
Jesu|it|ical|ly
Jesus (*New Testament*)
Jésus (island, Canada)
jet
jets
jetted
jet|ting
jet black +s (jet-
black *when preceding
a noun*)
jet boat +s
jet boat|er +s
jet boat|ing
jeté +s
jet lag
jet-lagged
jet|lin|er +s
jet-propelled
jet|sam
jet set (jet-set *when
preceding a noun*)
jet-setter +s
jet-setting
Jet Ski +s *proprietary
noun*
jet ski +s +ed +ing
verb
jet ski|er +s
jet ski|ing *noun*
jet stream +s
jet|ted *adjective*
jet|ti|son +s +ed +ing
jetty
jet|ties
Jet|way +s *proprietary*

jeu d'esprit
jeux d'esprit
jeun|esse dorée
**Jev|ons, Wil|liam
Stan|ley** (English
economist)
Jew +s
jewel (gem)
jew|els
jew|elled
jewel|ling
[☞ joule]
jewel box
jewel boxes
jewel case +s
jewel fish
plural jewel fish or
jewel fish|es
jew|elled *adjective*
jewel|ler +s
jewel|ler's rouge
jewel|lery
jewel-like
jewel|ry (*use*
jewellery)
jewel|weed +s
Jew|ess *offensive*
Jew|ess|es
Jew|ish
Jew|ish|ly
Jew|ish|ness
**Jewi|son, Nor|man
Fred|erick** (Cdn
filmmaker)
Jewry (Jewish people
or community)
Jew|ries
Jew's ear +s (plant)
Jew's harp +s
Jez|ebel +s (*Bible*;
immoral woman)
Jhan|si (city, India)
Jhe|lum (river, Asia)
Jiang Jie Shi
(= Chiang Kai-shek,
Chinese president)
Jiang|su (province,
China)
Jiang|xi (province,
China)
jib (sail; crane arm;
refuse to continue)
jibs
jibbed
jib|bing
[☞ gib]
jib|ba +s
jib|bah +s (*use* jibba)
jib|ber +s (one who
jibs)
[☞ gibber]
jib-boom +s

jibe (taunt; agree; *for
Nautical sense use*
gybe)
jibes
jibed
jib|ing
Jib|uti (= Djibouti,
Africa)
Jid|dah (port, Saudi
Arabia)
jiff +s
jiffy
jif|fies
jig
jigs
jigged
jig|ging
jig|ger +s
jiggery-pokery
jig|gle
jig|gles
jig|gled
jig|gling
jig|gly
Jiggs' din|ner +s
jig saw +s (tool)
jig|saw +s (puzzle)
jihad +s
Jilin (province & city,
China)
jill +s (young woman:
use gill)
[☞ gill]
jil|lion
plural jil|lion or
jil|lions
jill|ionth +s
jilt +s +ed +ing
Jim Crow
Jim Crow|ism
jim-dandy
jim-dandies
**Ji|mé|nez, Juan
Ramón** (Spanish
poet)
**Ji|mé|nez de
Cis|ner|os,
Fran|cis|co** (Spanish
statesman)
jim-jams
Jimmu (legendary
Japanese emperor)
jimmy
jim|mies
jim|mied
jimmy|ing
jimson +s
jim|son|weed +s
Jin (Chinese dynasties
AD 265–420 & 1115-
1234)
[☞ Qin, Chin, jinn,
djinn, gin]
Jinan (city, China)

jin|gle
  jin|gles
  jin|gled
  jin|gling
jin|gly
  jin|gli|er
  jin|gli|est
jingo +s
jingo|ism
jingo|ist +s
jingo|is|tic
jink +s +ed +ing
jink|er +s
jinn (= jinni: Islamic
  mythological spirit)
  plural jinn or jinns
  [☞ Jin, gin]
Jin|nah, Muham|mad
  Ali (founder of
  Pakistan)
jin|nee (Islamic
  mythological spirit:
  use jinni)
  jinn
jinni (Islamic
  mythological spirit)
  jinn
jinx
  jinx|es
  jinxed
  jinx|ing
jit|ney +s
jit|ter +s +ed +ing
jitter|bug
  jitter|bugs
  jitter|bugged
  jitter|bug|ging
jitter|bug|ger +s
jitter|i|ness
jit|tery
jiu-jitsu
jive
  jives
  jived
  jiv|ing
jiv|er +s
jizz
JK (junior
  kindergarten)
  JKs
jo (sweetheart)
  joes
  [☞ joe, Zhou]
Joa|chim (saint)
Joan ('Pope Joan',
  legendary figure)
Joan of Arc (French
  heroine)
João Pes|soa (city,
  Brazil)
Job (*Bible*)

job
  jobs
  jobbed
  job|bing
job|ber +s
job|bery
job|bie +s
job|bing *adjective*
job-hunt +s +ed +ing
job hunt|er +s
job-hunting *noun*
job|less
job|less|ness
job lot +s
Job's com|fort|er +s
job-share
  job-shares
  job-shared
  job-sharing
job-sharer +s
job-sharing *noun*
Job's tears
jobs|worth +s
Jo|burg
  (Johannesburg)
Jo|casta (*Greek Myth*)
Jock +s (Scotsman)
jock +s (jockstrap;
  athlete, sports fan;
  DJ; enthusiast;
  jockey)
jock|dom
jockey +s +ed +ing
jockey|ship
Jockey shorts
  proprietary
jock|ish
jock itch
jock|strap +s
joc|ose
joc|ose|ly
joc|os|ity
  joc|os|ities
jocu|lar
jocu|lar|ity
  jocu|lar|ities
jocu|lar|ly
joc|und
joc|und|ity
  joc|und|ities
joc|und|ly
Jodh|pur (city &
  former state, India)
jodh|purs (riding
  breeches)
joe +s (coffee; fellow)
  [☞ jo; Zhou]
Joe Bloggs
Joe Blow +s
joe-boy +s
joe job +s
Joel (*Bible*)

Joe-pie weed +s (*use*
  Joe-pye weed)
Joe Pub|lic
Joe-pye weed +s
Joe Six|pack
joey +s
Jof|fre, Jo|seph
  Jacques Cé|saire
  (French marshal)
jog
  jogs
  jogged
  jog|ging
jog|ger +s
jog|ging *noun*
jog|gle
  jog|gles
  jog|gled
  jog|gling
Jog|ja|karta
  (= Yogyakarta,
  Indonesia)
jog|trot
  jog|trots
  jog|trot|ted
  jog|trot|ting
Jogues, Isaac (saint)
Jo|han|nes|burg (city,
  South Africa)
John (saints; kings of
  England, Portugal &
  Poland; popes)
John, Au|gus|tus
  Edwin (Welsh
  painter)
John, Elton
  Her|cu|les (English
  singer-songwriter)
John, Gwen (Welsh
  painter)
john +s
John Birch|er +s
john|boat +s
John Bull
John Doe
John Dory
  John Dor|ies
John Han|cock +s
John Lack|land
  (English king)
john|ny
  john|nies
johnny|cake +s
John|ny Can|uck
johnny-come-lately
  johnny-come-
  latelies
Johnny-jump-up +s
johnny-one-note +s
Johnny-on-the-spot
John o'Groats
  (village, Scotland)

John Paul (popes)
  [☞ Jean Paul]
John Q. Pub|lic
Johns, Jas|per (US
  artist)
John So|bies|ki
  (Polish king)
John|son (surname)
  [☞ Jonson]
John|son, Al|bert
  (Cdn trapper &
  outlaw)
John|son, An|drew
  (US president)
John|son, Ben (Cdn
  sprinter)
John|son, Byron
  Inge|mar (Cdn
  politician)
John|son, Dan|iel
  (Cdn politician)
John|son, Earvin
  ('Magic') (US
  basketball player)
John|son, Jack (US
  boxer)
John|son, John
  Mer|cer (British-
  born Cdn politician)
John|son, Lyn|don
  Baines (US
  president)
John|son, Rob|ert
  (US guitarist &
  songwriter)
John|son, Sam|uel
  (English writer)
John|son|ian
Johns|ton, Fran|cis
  Hans ('Franz') (Cdn
  painter)
Johns|ton, Lynn (Cdn
  cartoonist)
Johns|tone (strait,
  Canada)
Johor (state, Malaysia)
Johor Ba|haru (city,
  Malaysia)
Jo|hore (= Johor,
  Malaysia)
joie de vivre
join +s +ed +ing
join|able
join|der
join|er +s
join|ery
joint +s +ed +ing
joint|ed *adjective*
joint|er +s
joint|less
joint|ly

joint stock (joint-
stock *when preceding
a noun*)
Join|ville, Jean de
(French historian)
joist +s
jo|joba +s
joke
  jokes
  joked
  jok|ing
jok|er +s
joke|ster +s
jokey
jok|i|ness
jok|ing|ly
jolie laide
  jo|lies laides
Jo|liet, Louis
(= Jolliet)
Jo|li|ette (city,
Canada)
[☞ Jolliet]
Joliot-Curie, Irène
(French nuclear
physicist)
Joliot-Curie, Jean-
Frédéric (French
nuclear physicist)
Jol|liet, Louis (Cdn
explorer)
[☞ Joliette]
jol|li|fi|ca|tion +s
jol|lify
  jol|li|fies
  jol|li|fied
  jol|li|fy|ing
jol|li|ness
jol|lity
  jol|li|ties
jolly
  jol|li|er
  jol|li|est
  jol|lies
  jol|lied
  jolly|ing
jolly boat +s
Jolly Jump|er +s
  proprietary
Jolly Rog|er +s
Jol|son, Al (US
entertainer)
jolt +s +ed +ing
jolty
  jolt|i|er
  jolt|i|est
Jo|nah +s (*Bible*;
bringer of bad luck)
Jona|than (*Bible*)
Jones, Inigo (English
architect)

Jones, John Paul
(Scottish-born US
admiral)
Jones, John Wal|ter
(Cdn politician)
Jones, (Ev|er|ett)
LeRoi (US writer)
Jones|es (in 'keep up
with the Joneses')
Jong, Erica Mann (US
writer)
jon|gleur +s
Jön|kö|ping (city,
Sweden)
Jon|quière (city,
Canada)
jon|quil +s
Jon|son, Ben|ja|min
('Ben') (English
writer)
[☞ Johnson]
Jop|lin, Janis Lyn (US
singer)
Jop|lin, Scott (US
composer)
Jor|dan (country &
river, Middle East)
Jor|dan, Mi|chael
Jef|frey (US
basketball player)
Jor|dan|ian +s
jor|um +s
Jo|seph (*Bible*; saint;
Holy Roman
emperor; lake,
Canada)
Jo|seph|ine
(= Joséphine de
Beauharnais, wife of
Napoleon)
Jo|seph of
Arima|thea (*New
Testament*)
Jo|seph|us, Flav|ius
(Jewish historian &
general)
josh
  josh|es
  joshed
  josh|ing
josh|er +s
josh|ing *noun*
josh|ing|ly
Joshua (*Bible*)
Joshua tree +s
Jo|siah (*Bible*)
Jo|sias (= Josiah)
Jos|quin (des Prez)
(Flemish composer)
joss
  joss|es

jos|tle
  jos|tles
  jos|tled
  jost|ling
jost|ler +s
jot
  jots
  jot|ted
  jot|ting
jot|ter +s
jot|ting +s *noun*
Jotun (*Scandinavian
Myth*)
Jotun|heim
(mountain range,
Norway;
Scandinavian Myth)
joual (variety of Cdn
French)
[☞ joule]
jouis|sance
Joule, James
Pres|cott (English
physicist)
joule +s (unit of
energy)
[☞ joual]
jounce
  joun|ces
  jounced
  joun|cing
joun|cing *noun*
jouncy
  joun|ci|er
  joun|ci|est
jour|nal +s
jour|nal|ese
jour|nal|ism
jour|nal|ist +s
jour|nal|is|tic
jour|nal|is|tic|ally
jour|nal|ize
  jour|nal|iz|es
  jour|nal|ized
  jour|nal|iz|ing
jour|ney +s +ed +ing
jour|ney|er +s
journey|man
  journey|men
jour|no +s
joust +s +ed +ing
joust|er +s
Jove (*Roman Myth*)
jov|ial
jovi|al|ity
jov|ial|ly
Jov|ian (Roman
emperor; of or like
Jupiter)
jowar
Jow|lett, Ben|ja|min
(English scholar)
jowl +s

jowled
jowly
joy +s +ed +ing
Joyce, James
Au|gus|tine
Aloy|sius (Irish
writer)
Joy|cean +s
joy|ful
joy|ful|ly
joy|ful|ness
joy|less
joy|less|ly
joy|ous
joy|ous|ly
joy|ous|ness
joy|ride
  joy|rides
  joy|rode
  joy|rid|den
  joy|rid|ing
joy|rid|er +s
joy|rid|ing *noun*
joy|stick +s
JP (Justice of the
Peace)
JPs
Juan Car|los (Spanish
king)
Juan de Fuca (strait,
N America)
Juan Fer|nan|dez
(Chilean islands)
Juá|rez, Ben|ito
Pablo (Mexican
president)
Juba (city, Sudan)
[☞ Jubba]
Jubal (*Bible*)
Jubba (river, Africa)
[☞ Juba]
ju|bi|lance
ju|bi|lant
ju|bi|lant|ly
Ju|bi|late +s (psalm)
ju|bi|late
  ju|bi|lates
  ju|bi|lat|ed
  ju|bi|lat|ing
ju|bi|la|tion
ju|bi|lee +s
Jub|ran, Kah|lil
(= Gibran)
Ju|daea (region,
ancient Palestine: *use*
Judea)
Ju|daean (*use*
Judean)
Judaeo-Christian
(*use* Judeo-
Christian)

Judah (Hebrew
  patriarch; tribe;
  kingdom)
Ju|da|ic
Ju|da|ica
Ju|da|ism
Ju|da|iz|a|tion +s
Ju|da|ize
  Ju|da|iz|es
  Ju|da|ized
  Ju|da|iz|ing
Ju|da|ized adjective
Ju|da|iz|er +s
Judas (apostles;
  traitor)
  Ju|das|es
judas (peephole)
  ju|das|es
Judas Is|car|iot
  (betrayer of Jesus)
Judas Mac|ca|baeus
  (leader of Jewish
  revolt)
Judas tree +s
jud|der +s +ed +ing
jud|dery
Jude (saint)
Judea (region, ancient
  Palestine)
Ju|dean
Judeo-Christian
judge
  judg|es
  judged
  judg|ing
Judge Ad|vo|cate
  Gen|er|al +s
judge|like
judge-made
judge|ment (use
  judgment)
judge|ment|al (use
  judgmental)
judge|ment|al|ly (use
  judgmentally)
Judge|ment Day (use
  Judgment Day)
Judg|es (Bible)
judge|ship +s
judg|ment +s
judg|ment|al
judg|ment|al|ly
Judg|ment Day
judi|care
judi|ca|ture +s
ju|di|cial
Ju|di|cial
  Com|mit|tee
Ju|di|cial
  Com|mit|tee of the
  Privy Coun|cil
ju|di|cial|ly

ju|di|ciary
  ju|di|ciar|ies
ju|di|cious
ju|di|cious|ly
ju|di|cious|ness
Ju|dith (Apocrypha)
judo
judo|ist +s
judo|ka
  plural judo|ka or
  judo|kas
Judy (wife of Punch)
  Ju|dies
judy (woman)
  ju|dies
jug
  jugs
  jugged
  jug|ging
jug-eared
jug|ful +s
jug|ger|naut +s
jug|gins
jug|gle
  jug|gles
  jug|gled
  jug|gling
jug|gler +s
jug|glery
jug|head +s
Jugo|slav +s (use
  Yugoslav)
Jugo|slav|ia (country,
  Europe: use
  Yugoslavia)
Jugo|slav|ian +s (use
  Yugoslavian)
jugu|lar +s
Ju|gur|tha (king of
  Numidia)
Ju|gur|thine
juice
  juices
  juiced
  juicing
juice bar +s
juice box
  juice boxes
juiced adjective
juice|less
juicer +s
juici|ly
juici|ness
juicy
  juici|er
  juici|est
ju-jitsu (use jiu-jitsu)
juju +s
ju|jube +s
ju-jutsu (use jiu-jitsu)
juke
  jukes

juked
juk|ing
juke|box
  juke|boxes
juke joint +s
juku
  plural juku or jukus
ju|lep +s
Jul|ian ('the Apostate',
  Roman emperor; of
  Julius Caesar;
  calendar; mountains)
  [☞ Julien, julienne]
Juli|ana (queen of the
  Netherlands)
Jul|ian Alps
  (mountains, Slovenia
  & Italy)
Ju|lien, Pau|line (Cdn
  entertainer)
  [☞ Julian]
juli|enne (Food)
  juli|ennes
  juli|enned
  juli|en|ning
juli|enned adjective
Juli|et (in 'Romeo and
  Juliet'; cap)
Jul|ius (pope)
Jul|ius Caesar
  (Roman general &
  statesman)
Jul|lun|dur (city,
  India)
July +s
jum|bie +s
jum|ble
  jum|bles
  jum|bled
  jum|bling
jum|bled adjective
Jumbo (mountain
  pass, Canada)
jum|bo +s
Jumna (river, India)
jump +s +ed +ing
jump|able
jump-cut
  jump-cuts
  jump-cut
  jump-cutting
jumped-up adjective
jump|er +s
jump|i|er
jump|i|est
jump|i|ly
jump|i|ness
jump|ing noun &
  adjective
jumping-off place
  +s
jumping-off point
  +s

jump jet +s
jump off verb
  jumps off
  jumped off
  jump|ing off
jump|off +s noun
jump rope
• noun
  jump ropes
• verb
  jumps rope
  jumped rope
  jump|ing rope
jump seat +s
jump|shot +s
jump-start +s +ed
  +ing
jump|suit +s
jumpy
  jump|i|er
  jump|i|est
jun (North Korean
  currency)
  plural jun
  [☞ jeon]
jun|co +s
junc|tion +s
junc|tion|al
junc|ture +s
June +s
Ju|neau (city, US)
  [☞ Juno]
June beetle +s
June|berry
  June|ber|ries
June bug +s
June grass
  June grass|es
Jung, Carl Gus|tav
  (Swiss psychologist)
Jung|frau (mountain,
  Switzerland)
Jung|ian +s
jun|gle +s
Jun|gle Gym +s
  proprietary
jungly
jun|ior +s
jun|ior|ity
juni|per +s
junk +s +ed +ing
Jun|ker +s (German
  aristocrat)
  [☞ younker]
junk|er +s
  (dilapidated vehicle)
junker|dom
Jun|kers, Hugo
  (German aircraft
  designer)
jun|ket +s +ed +ing
jun|ket|eer +s
jun|ket|eer|ing

jun|ket|ing +s *noun*
junk food (junk-food *when preceding a noun*)
junk heap +s
junk|ie +s (drug addict; aficionado) [☞ junky]
junk shop +s
junky (of or like junk; *for* aficionado *or* drug addict *use* junkie)
junk|i|er
junk|i|est
junk|ies
junk|yard +s
Juno +s (*Roman Myth*; asteroid; award) [☞ Juneau]
jun|ta +s
Ju|pi|ter (*Roman Myth*; planet)
Jura (mountain system, Europe; island, Inner Hebrides)
jural
Jur|as|sic
jur|at +s
jur|id|ical
jur|id|ical|ly
jur|ied *adjective*
juris|con|sult +s
juris|dic|tion +s
juris|dic|tion|al
juris|pru|dence
juris|pru|den|tial
jur|ist +s
jur|is|tic
jur|is|tic|al
jur|or +s
jury (*Law*)
jur|ies
[☞ Jewry]
jury|man
jury|men
jury-rig
jury-rigs
jury-rigged
jury-rigging
jury-rigged *adjective*
jury|woman
jury|women
Jus|sieu, An|toine Lau|rent de (French botanist)
jus|sive
just
jus|tice +s
justice|ship +s
jus|ti|ciable

jus|ti|ciary
jus|ti|ciar|ies
justi|fi|abil|ity
justi|fi|able
justi|fi|able|ness
justi|fi|ably
justi|fi|ca|tion +s
justi|fi|ca|tory
jus|ti|fied *adjective*
jus|ti|fi|er +s
jus|tify
jus|ti|fies
jus|ti|fied
jus|ti|fy|ing
Jus|tin (saint)
Jus|tin|ian (Byzantine emperor)
just-in-time *noun & adjective preceding a noun*
just|ly
just|ness
jut
juts
jut|ted
jut|ting
Jute +s (people)
jute +s (fibre; rope)
Jut|ish
Jut|land (peninsula & naval battle, Europe)
Jutra, Claude (Cdn filmmaker)
Ju|ven|al (Roman satirist)
ju|ven|al +s (young bird or racehorse) [☞ juvenile]
juven|es|cence
juven|es|cent
ju|ven|ile +s (young person, animal, etc.; immature; *Sports*)
ju|ven|ile dia|betes
juven|ile|ly
ju|venile-onset dia|betes (= juvenile diabetes)
juven|ilia
juven|il|ity
juxta|pose
juxta|pos|es
juxta|posed
juxta|pos|ing
juxta|pos|ition +s
juxta|pos|ition|al
Jyl|land (= Jutland)
Jy|väs|kylä (city, Finland)

K

K
• (letter; kilometre per hour; strikeout)
K's
• (kelvin; *Computing*; one thousand dollars etc.; kilometre distance)
k
• (letter)
k's
• (knot; constant)
K2 (mountain, Asia)
K-9 (police canine units)
ka +s (spirit) [☞ caw]
Kaaba (edifice, Mecca)
Kaba|lega (waterfall, Uganda)
Kab|bala (*Judaism*: *use* Kabbalah)
kab|bala (general mysticism: *use* cabbala)
Kab|balah (*Judaism*: *for general mystical sense use* cabbala)
Kab|bal|ism (*Judaism*)
kab|bal|ism (*in general use: use* cabbalism)
Kab|bal|ist +s (*Judaism*)
kab|bal|ist +s (*in general use: use* cabbalist)
Kab|bal|is|tic (*Judaism*)
kab|bal|is|tic (*in general use: use* cabbalistic)
Kabi|nett +s (wine)
kab|loo|na
plural kab|loo|na or kab|loo|nas or kab|loo|nat
ka|bob +s (*use* kebab)
ka|boodle +s (*use* caboodle)
ka|boom +s
ka|bu|ki
Kabul (capital of Afghanistan)
Kabwe (town, Zambia)
ka|chi|na +s

Kádár, János (Hungarian prime minister)
Kad|dish (Jewish prayer)
Kad|dish|im [☞ caddish]
kadi +s (judge: *use* qadi)
kaffee|klatsch
kaffee|klatsch|es
Kaf|fir +s (South African people, language; *offensive* black African) [☞ Kafir]
kaf|fi|yeh +s
Kafir +s (Afghan people) [☞ Kaffir]
Kafka, Franz (Czech novelist)
Kafka|esque
kaf|tan +s (*use* caftan)
ka|fuf|fle +s
Kago|shima (city, Japan)
ka|hu|na +s
Kai|feng (city, China)
Kai|gani
plural Kai|gani or Kai|ganis
Kain, Karen (Cdn dancer) [☞ Kane, Cain, Caine]
Kai|rouan (city, Tunisia)
kai|ser +s
Kai|sers|lau|tern (city, Germany)
kai|zen
kaka +s (parrot) [☞ caca]
Kaka|beka (waterfall, Canada)
kaka|po +s
kake|mono +s
kala azar
Kala|hari (desert, Africa)
kala|mata +s
kalan|choe +s
Ka|lash|nikov +s
kale +s
ka|leido|scope +s
ka|leido|scop|ic
ka|leido|scop|ic|ally
kal|ends (*use* calends)
Kal|goor|lie (town, Australia)

Kali (*Hinduism*)
[☞ **Cali**]
Kali|man|tan (region, Indonesia)
Ka|li|nin (*former name for* Tver, Russia)
Ka|li|nin, Mikh|ail Ivan|ovich (Soviet statesman)
Ka|li|nin|grad (city, Russia)
Kal|isz (city, Poland)
Kal|mar (city, Sweden)
kal|mia +s
Kal|muck (people; language)
plural **Kal|muck** or **Kal|mucks**
Kal|myk (= Kalmuck: people, language)
plural **Kal|myk** or **Kal|myks**
Kal|mykia *full name* **Kalmykia-Khalmg Tangch** (autonomous republic, Russia)
kal|ong +s
kalpa
Ka|luga (city, Russia)
Kal|yan (city, India)
Kama (*Hinduism*)
Kama Sutra
Kam|chat|ka (peninsula, Russia)
kame +s (glacial deposit)
Ka|men|skoe (*former name for* Dniprodzerzhinsk, Ukraine)
Kamensk-Uralsky (city, Russia)
Kamer|lingh Onnes, Heike (Dutch physicist)
kamik +s (boot)
kami|kaze +s
Ka|mila|roi
Kam|loops (city, Canada; trout)
Kam|pala (capital of Uganda)
kam|pong +s
Kam|pu|chea (*former name for* Cambodia)
Kam|pu|chean +s
kana +s
ka|naka +s
Kana|rese
plural **Kana|rese**
Ka|nata (city, Canada)

Kan|chen|junga (Himalayan mountain)
Kan|da|har (city, Afghanistan)
Kan|din|sky, Was|sily (Russian painter)
Kandy (city, Sri Lanka)
Kane, Paul (Irish-born Cdn painter)
[☞ **Kain, Cain, Caine**]
Kane Basin (in Canada)
Kan|gar (city, Malaysia)
kan|ga|roo +s
kan|ga|roo paw +s (plant)
Kang|chen|junga (= Mount Kanchenjunga)
Ka|Ngwane (former homeland, South Africa)
kanji
Kan|nada (language)
Kano (city, Nigeria)
Kan|pur (city, India)
Kan|san +s
Kan|sas (state, US)
Kan|sas City (cities, US)
Kansu (= Gansu, China)
Kant, Im|man|uel (German philosopher)
Kant|ian +s
Kant|ian|ism
Kanto (region, Japan)
Kao|hsiung (city, Taiwan)
kao|lin
kao|lin|ic
kaon +s
Kapa|chira (waterfall, Malawi)
kapell|meis|ter
plural
kapell|meis|ter
Ka|pitza, Pyotr Leonid|ovich (Russian physicist)
kapok +s
Kaposi's sar|coma
kapow
kappa +s (Greek letter)
[☞ **Capa**]
Kap|us|ka|sing (town & river, Canada)
kaput

Kara (Arctic sea)
kara|biner +s (*Mountaineering: use* carabiner)
[☞ **carabineer, carabinier, carabiniere**]
Ka|rachi (city, Pakistan)
Kara|futo (*Japanese name for* Sakhalin, Russia)
Kara|ite +s
Karaj (city, Iran)
Kara|jan, Her|bert von (Austrian conductor)
Kara|kor|am (mountain range, Asia)
[☞ **Karakorum**]
Kara|kor|um (ancient city, Mongolia)
[☞ **Karakoram**]
kara|kul +s (sheep)
[☞ **caracal, caracole**]
Kara Kum (desert, Asia)
Kara|man|lis, Kon|stan|tinos (Greek prime minister)
kara|oke (singing along with recorded music)
kar|at +s (measure of purity of gold)
[☞ **carat, caret**]
karate
karate chop +s *noun*
karate-chop *verb*
karate-chops
karate-chopped
karate-chopping
Kar|bala (city, Iraq)
Ka|relia (region, Europe)
Ka|rel|ian +s
Karen (state, Burma; people, language)
plural **Kar|ens** or **Karen**
[☞ **Charon**]
Ka|riba (dam & lake, Zambia–Zimbabwe border)
Karl (Charles XII of Sweden)
[☞ **Carl, Carle**]
Karl-Marx-Stadt (*former name for* Chemnitz, Germany)

Kar|loff, Boris (English-born US actor)
Kar|lovy Vary (town, Czech Republic)
Karls|bad (= Karlovy Vary)
Karls|ruhe (town, Germany)
karma
kar|mic
Kar|nak (monument site, Egypt)
[☞ **Carnac**]
Kar|nat|aka (state, India)
Karoo (plateau, South Africa)
[☞ **Carew**]
Kar|pov, Ana|toli Yev|geny|evich (Russian chess player)
Kar|roo (plateau, South Africa: *use* Karoo)
[☞ **Carew**]
Kars (city & province, Turkey)
Karsh, You|suf (Cdn photographer)
karst +s
karst|ic
kart +s (go-kart)
[☞ **cart**]
karyo|kin|esis
karyo|type +s
karyo|typic
karyo|typ|ing
kas|bah +s
kasha
Kash|mir (region, Asia)
[☞ **cashmere**]
Kash|miri +s
Kash|rut (= Kashruth)
Kash|ruth
Kaska
plural **Kaska** or **Kas|kas**
Kas|pa|rov, Gary (Azerbaijani chess player)
Kas|sel (city, Germany)
Kasur (city, Pakistan)
kata
kata|batic
kata|kana
Ka|tan|ga (*former name for* Shaba, Congo)

Kath|ak +s
Kathia|war
(peninsula, India)
Kath|man|du (capital
of Nepal)
kath|ode +s (use
cathode)
Kato|wice (city,
Poland)
kat|sura tree +s
Katte|gat (strait
between Sweden &
Denmark)
katy|did +s
Kauai (island, US)
Kauff|man,
An|geli|ca
(= Kauffmann)
[☞ Kaufman,
Koffman]
Kauff|mann, (Maria
Anna Cath|a|rina)
An|geli|ca (Swiss
painter)
[☞ Kaufman,
Koffman]
Kauf|man, George
Simon (US writer)
[☞ Kauffmann,
Koffman]
Kau|nas (city,
Lithuania)
Ka|un|da, Ken|neth
David (Zambian
president)
kauri +s (tree)
[☞ cowrie, cowry]
Kaus Aus|tral|is (star)
kava +s
Ka|válla (city, Greece)
Kav|eri (= Cauvery
River, India)
Ka|war|tha (lakes,
Canada)
Kawa|saki (city,
Japan)
Kaw|thoo|lay (former
name for Karen
State, Burma)
Kaw|thu|lei
(= Kawthoolay)
Kay (Arthurian Legend)
[☞ Kaye, cay]
kay|ak +s +ed +ing
kay|ak|er +s
kay|ak|ing noun
Kaye, Danny (US
actor)
[☞ Kay, cay]
kayo
• noun
kayos
• verb

kayoes
kayoed
kayo|ing
Kay|seri (city, Turkey)
Ka|zak +s (= Kazakh)
Ka|zakh +s
Kaz|akh|stan
(republic, Asia)
Kaz|ak|stan
(= Kazakhstan)
Kazan (city, Russia;
river, Canada)
Kazan, Elia (Turkish-
born director)
Kaz|an|tza|kis, Nikos
(Greek writer)
ka|zil|lion
plural ka|zil|lion or
ka|zil|lions
kazoo +s
kbyte +s
kea +s (parrot)
[☞ key]
Kean, Ed|mund
(English actor)
[☞ keen]
Keat|ing, Paul John
(Australian prime
minister)
Kea|ton, Jo|seph
Fran|cis ('Bus|ter')
(US filmmaker)
Keats, John (English
poet)
Keats|ian
ke|bab +s
Keble, John (English
churchman)
Keb|ne|kaise
(mountain, Sweden)
Kedah (state,
Malaysia)
kedge
kedg|es
kedged
kedg|ing
kedg|eree +s
keek +s +ed +ing
keel +s +ed +ing
[☞ Kiel]
keel|boat +s
keel|haul +s +ed
+ing
Kee|ling Islands
(= Cocos Islands)
keel|less
keel|son +s
keen +er +est +s +ed
+ing
[☞ Kean]
keen|er +s
keen|ly
keen|ness

keep
keeps
kept
keep|ing
keep|able
keep|er +s
keep-fit
keep|ing noun
keep|sake +s
kees|hond
kees|honds or
kees|hond|en
kees|ter +s (use
keister)
Kee|wa|tin (district,
Canada)
kef +s
kef|fi|yeh +s (use
kaffiyeh)
Kef|la|vik (village,
Iceland)
keg +s
Kegel ex|er|cise +s
keis|ter +s
Kei|tel, Wil|helm
Bode|win Jo|hann
Gus|tav (German
field marshal)
Kej|im|ku|jik
(national park,
Canada)
Kek|ulé von
Strad|onitz,
(Fried|rich) Aug|ust
(German chemist)
Ke|lan|tan (state,
Malaysia)
Kel|ler, Helen Adams
(US social reformer)
Kel|logg, Will Keith
(US entrepreneur)
Kellogg–Briand Pact
(= Kellogg Pact)
Kel|logg Pact
Kelly, Gene (US
dancer)
Kelly, Grace
Pa|tri|cia (US
actress)
Kelly, Petra Karin
(German political
leader)
kelly green +s
ke|loid +s
ke|loid|al
Ke|low|na (city,
Canada)
kelp +s
kel|pie +s
kcl|son +s (use
keelson)
Kelt +s (people: use
Celt)

kelt (fish)
plural kelt or kelts
[☞ celt]
Kel|vin, Wil|liam
Thom|son (Lord
Kelvin, Scottish
physicist)
kel|vin +s (unit of
temperature)
Kel|vin scale
Kemal, Mus|tafa
(Kemal Atatürk)
Keme|rovo (city,
Russia)
Kempe, Mar|gery
(English mystic)
Kem|pis, Thom|as à
(German theologian)
kempt
ken
kens
kenned or kent
ken|ning
Ken|dall, Ed|ward
Call|vin (US
biochemist)
kendo
Ken|drew, Sir John
Cowd|ery (English
biologist)
Ke|neal|ly, Thom|as
Mi|chael (Australian
novelist)
Ken|ne|be|ca|sis
(river, Canada)
Ken|nedy (mountain,
Canada)
Ken|nedy, Ed|ward
Moore ('Teddy') (US
politician)
Ken|nedy,
Jacque|line Lee
Bou|vier ('Jackie')
(US First Lady)
Ken|nedy, John
Fitz|ger|ald (US
president)
Ken|nedy, Rob|ert
Fran|cis (US
statesman)
ken|nel
ken|nels
ken|nelled
ken|nelling
Ken|nel|ly, Ar|thur
Edwin (English-born
engineer)
Ken|neth (Scottish
king)
ken|ning +s noun
keno
Ke|no|ju|ak (Cdn
artist)

Ken|ora (town, Canada)
ken|osis
ken|otic
Ken|sing|ton (district, London)
ken|speckle
Kent (county, England; peninsula, Canada)
Kent, Wil|liam (English architect & gardener)
kent conjugated form of ken
kente (cloth)
Kent|ish
kent|ledge
Ken|ton, Stan (US bandleader)
Ken|tuck|ian +s
Ken|tucky (state, US)
Kent|ville (town, Canada)
Kenya (country & mountain, Africa)
Ken|yan +s
Ken|yat|ta, Jomo (Kenyan statesman)
kepi +s
Kep|ler, Jo|han|nes (German astronomer)
Kep|ler|ian
kept
Ker|ala (state, India)
Kera|lite +s
kera|tin +s (fibrous protein)
[☞ carotene]
kera|tin|iz|a|tion
kera|tin|ize
kera|tin|iz|es
kera|tin|ized
kera|tin|iz|ing
kera|titis
kera|to|sis
kera|to|ses
kera|tot|ic
kera|tot|omy
kera|tot|omies
Kerch (city, Ukraine)
ker|chief +s
ker|chiefed
Ke|ren|sky, Alek|sandr Fyodor|ovich (Russian statesman)
kerf +s +ed +ing
ker|fuf|fle +s
Ker|gue|len (islands, Indian Ocean)
Kerk|rade (town, the Netherlands)

Ker|madec (islands, New Zealand)
ker|mes (oak; insect; dye)
plural ker|mes
ker|mis (fair; bazaar)
ker|mis|es
ker|mode +s
Kern, Jer|ome David (US songwriter)
kern +s +ed +ing (Printing; soldier; peasant)
kerne +s (soldier, peasant: use kern)
kerned adjective
ker|nel +s (of corn or a nut; seed; nucleus; Computing)
[☞ colonel]
kero|sene
Ker|ou|ac, Jack (US writer)
Kerry (county, Ireland)
[☞ Carey, Cary]
Kerry blue +s (dog)
ker|sey +s
ker|sey|mere +s
Kesey, Ken (US novelist)
Kes|sel|ring, Al|bert (German air force chief)
kes|trel +s
Kes|wick (towns, Canada & England)
keta
plural keta or ketas
ké|taine
keta|mine
ketch
ketch|es
ketch|up +s
ke|tone +s
ke|tonic
keton|uria
ke|to|sis
ke|tot|ic
Ket|ter|ing, Charles Frank|lin (US inventor)
ket|tle +s
kettle|drum +s
kettle|drum|mer +s
kettle|ful +s
ket|tle hole +s
Kev|lar proprietary
Kew Gar|dens (in England)
kew|pie +s (doll)
[☞ CUPE]

key +s +ed +ing (lock opener; on keyboard; Music; seed; Basketball; island; solution, explanation; essential)
[☞ quay, qui vive]
key|board +s +ed +ing
key|board|er +s
key|board|ist +s
key chain +s
key|er +s
key|frame +s
key grip +s
key|hole +s
Key Largo (island, US)
key|less
key lime +s
Keynes, John May|nard, 1st Baron (English economist)
Keynes|ian +s
Keynes|ian|ism
key|note +s
key|pad +s
key|press
key|press|es
key|punch
key|punch|es
key|punched
key|punch|ing
key|punch|er +s
key ring +s
key|stone +s
key|stroke +s
key|way +s
Key West (city, US)
key|word +s
Kha|bar|ovsk (city & territory, Russia)
Kha|cha|tur|ian, Aram Ilich (Russian composer)
khad|dar +s (= khadi)
khadi +s
khaki +s
Kha|lid (king of Saudi Arabia)
Khal|sa (Sikhism)
Kham|bat (= Gulf of Cambay, Arabian Sea)
kham|sin
khan +s (ruler, emperor; inn)
khan|ate +s
Kharg (island, Iran)
Khar|kiv (city, Ukraine)

Khar|toum (capital of Sudan)
khat +s (shrub)
Khay|litsa (township, South Africa)
Khay|yám (= Omar Khayyám)
Khe|dival
Khe|dive +s
Khe|div|ial
Kher|son (city, Ukraine)
Khmer +s
Khoi|khoi
plural Khoi|khoi
Khoi|san
Kho|meini, Ru|hol|lah (ayatollah)
Khon|su (Egyptian Myth)
Khor|ram|shahr (city, Iran)
khoum +s (Mauritanian currency)
[☞ coomb, cwm]
Khrush|chev, Ni|kita Ser|gey|evich (Soviet statesman)
Khufu (= Cheops, pharaoh)
[☞ Qufu]
Khul|na (city, Bangladesh)
Khun|je|rab (mountain pass, Himalayas)
Khy|ber (mountain pass, Hindu Kush)
kiang +s
kib|beh +s
kib|ble
kib|bles
kib|bled
kib|bling
kib|butz (collective)
kib|butz|im
[☞ kibitz]
kib|butz|nik +s
kibe +s
ki|bit|ka +s
kib|itz (joke; meddle)
kib|itz|es
kib|itzed
kib|itz|ing
[☞ kibbutz]
kib|itz|er +s
ki|bosh
ki|bosh|es
ki|boshed
ki|bosh|ing
kick +s +ed +ing

kick|able
kick ass *verb*
    kicks ass
    kicked ass
    kick|ing ass
kick-ass *adjective*
kick back *verb*
    kicks back
    kicked back
    kick|ing back
kick|back +s *noun*
kick|ball
kick-boxer +s
kick-boxing
kick butt *verb*
    kicks butt
    kicked butt
    kick|ing butt
kick-butt *adjective*
kick|er +s
kick|i|er
kick|i|est
kick|ing *adjective*
Kick|ing Horse Pass
    (mountain pass,
    Canada)
kick off *verb*
    kicks off
    kicked off
    kick|ing off
kick|off +s *noun*
kick|plate +s
kick-pleat +s
kick|shaw +s
kick|stand +s
kick-start +s +ed
    +ing
kick-starter +s
kick the can
kicky
    kick|i|er
    kick|i|est
Kid, Thom|as (= Kyd)
    [☞ Kidd]
kid
    kids
    kid|ded
    kid|ding
Kidd, Wil|liam
    ('Captain Kidd',
    Scottish pirate)
    [☞ Kyd]
kid|der +s
Kid|der|min|ster
    (town, England)
kid|die +s
kid|ding|ly
kiddo +s
kid|dush
kiddy (*use* kiddie)
    kid|dies
kid|lit

kid|nap
    kid|naps
    kid|napped
    kid|nap|ping
kid|nap|per +s
kid|nap|ping +s *noun*
kid|ney +s
kidney-shaped
kid|skin +s
kid|vid +s
Kiel (city & canal,
    Germany)
kiel|basa
Kielce (city, Poland)
Kier|ke|gaard, Søren
    Aabye (Danish
    philosopher)
Kier|ke|gaard|ian
kie|sel|guhr
Kies|low|ski,
    Krzysz|tof (Polish
    filmmaker)
Kiev (in 'chicken Kiev';
    for capital of Ukraine
    use Kyiv)
kif +s
Ki|gali (capital of
    Rwanda)
kike +s *offensive*
Ki|kongo
Ki|kuyu
    plural Ki|kuyu or
    Ki|kuyus
Kil|dare (county,
    Ireland)
kil|der|kin +s
kilim +s
Kili|man|jaro
    (mountain, Tanzania)
Kil|ken|ny (county &
    town, Ireland)
kill +s +ed +ing
Kil|lam, Izaak
    Wal|ton (Cdn
    financier)
Kil|lar|ney (town,
    Ireland)
kill|deer +s
kill|er +s
kil|lick +s
killi|fish
    plural killi|fish or
    killi|fish|es
kill|ing +s *noun*
kill|ing|ly
Kil|li|niq (island,
    Canada)
kill|joy +s
Kil|mar|nock (town,
    Scotland)
kiln +s
kilo +s
kilo|bit +s

kilo|byte +s
kilo|cal|orie +s
kilo|cycle +s
kilo|gram +s
kilo|hertz
    plural kilo|hertz
kilo|joule +s
kilo|litre +s
kilo|met|rage
kilo|metre +s
kilo|met|ric
kilo|pas|cal +s
kilo|ton +s
kilo|volt +s
kilo|watt +s
kilo|watt hour +s
kilt +s +ed +ing
kilt|ed *adjective*
kil|ter
kilt|ie +s
Kim|ber|ley +s (cities,
    Canada & South
    Africa; plateau,
    Australia)
kim|ber|lite +s
kim|chee
kim|chi (*use* kimchee)
Kim Il Sung (North
    Korean statesman)
ki|mo|no +s
ki|mo|noed
kin
kina
    plural kina
Kina|balu (mountain,
    Malaysia)
kin|aes|the|sia (*use*
    kinesthesia)
kin|aes|thet|ic (*use*
    kinesthetic)
kin|ase +s
Kin|bas|ket Lake
    (reservoir, Canada)
Kin|car|dine (town,
    Canada)
Kin|car|dine|shire
    (former county,
    Scotland)
Kin|chin|junga
    (= Mount
    Kanchenjunga)
kind +s +er +est
kinda
kin|der|gart|en +s
kin|der|gart|ner +s
Kin|ders|ley (town,
    Canada)
kind-hearted
kind-hearted|ly
kind-hearted|ness
kin|dle
    kin|dles

kin|dled
kin|dling
kin|dler +s
kind|li|ness
kin|dling +s *noun*
kind|ly
    kind|li|er
    kind|li|est
kind|ness
kin|dred
kine
kin|emat|ic
kin|emat|ic|ally
kin|emat|ics
kin|esics
kin|esi|ol|ogy
kin|esis
kin|es|the|sia
kin|es|thet|ic
kin|etic
kin|etic|ally
kin|et|ics
Kin|ette +s
kin|folk
King (mountain,
    Canada)
King, B. B. (US
    musician)
King, Bil|lie Jean (US
    tennis player)
King, George Edwin
    (Cdn politician)
King, Mar|tin Lu|ther
    (US civil-rights
    leader)
King, Wil|liam Lyon
    Mac|ken|zie (Cdn
    prime minister)
king +s +ed +ing
king|bird +s
King Charles
    span|iel +s
king|craft
king|cup +s
king|dom +s
kingdom come
king|fish
    plural king|fish or
    king|fish|es
king|fish|er +s
king|hood
king|less
king|let +s
king|like
king|li|ness
king|ly
king|maker +s
king|pin +s
king post +s
Kings (*Bible*)
king|ship
king-size

king-sized (= king-size)
Kings|ley, Ben
Krish|na Banji (English actor)
Kings|ton (cities, Jamaica & Canada)
Kings|ton-upon-Hull (= Hull, England)
Kings|town (capital of St. Vincent)
Kings|ville (town, Canada)
kink +s +ed +ing
kin|ka|jou +s
Kinki (region, Japan)
kink|i|ly
kink|i|ness
kinky
   kink|i|er
   kink|i|est
   [☞ Kinki, Japan]
kin|less
kin|ni|kin|nick
Kinross-shire (former county, Scotland)
Kin|sel|la, Wil|liam Pat|rick (Cdn writer)
Kin|sey, Al|fred Charles (US zoologist & sex researcher)
kins|folk
Kin|shasa (capital of Congo)
kin|ship
kins|man
   kins|men
kins|woman
   kins|women
Kin|tyre (peninsula, Scotland)
kiosk +s
Kiowa
   plural Kiowa or Kio|was
kip
• noun (nap; lodging; animal hide)
   plural kips
• noun (currency)
   plural kip or kips
• verb
   kips
   kipped
   kip|ping
Kip|ling, (Jo|seph) Rud|yard (English novelist)
kip|per +s +ed +ing
kir +s
Kirch|hoff, Gus|tav Rob|ert (German physicist)

Kirch|ner, Ernst Lud|wig (German painter)
Kir|ghiz (use Kyrgyz)
   plural Kir|ghiz
Kir|ghi|zia (= Kyrgyzstan)
Kiri|bati (country, SW Pacific)
Kirin (= Jilin, China)
Kiriti|mati (island, Kiribati)
Kirk (Church of Scotland)
   [☞ Kirke]
kirk +s (church)
Kirk|cud|bright|shire (former county, Scotland)
Kirke, Sir David (English adventurer)
   [☞ Kirk]
Kirk|land (city, Quebec)
Kirk|land Lake (city, Ontario)
Kir|kuk (city, Iraq)
Kirk|wall (town, Orkney Islands)
Kirov (= Vyatka, Russia; ballet company)
Ki|ro|va|bad (former name for Gäncä, Azerbaijan)
kir|pan +s
kirsch
   kirsch|es
kir|tle +s
Ki|ru|na (town, Sweden)
Ki|san|gani (city, Congo)
kis|met
kiss
   kiss|es
   kissed
   kiss|ing
kiss|able
kiss-and-cry
   kiss-and-cries
kiss and ride +s
kiss-and-tell adjective
kiss ass verb
   kiss|es ass
   kissed ass
   kiss|ing ass
kiss-ass noun
   kiss-ass-asses
kiss-curl +s
kiss|er +s

Kis|sin|ger, Henry Al|fred (US statesman)
kiss-off +s
kiss|o|gram +s
kissy
kissy-face +s
Ki|swa|hili
kit
   kits
   kit|ted
   kit|ting
Kita|kyu|shu (city, Japan)
kit bag +s
kitch|en +s
Kitch|en|er (city, Canada)
Kitch|en|er, (Hor|atio) Her|bert (1st Earl Kitche|ner of Khar|toum) (English statesman & field marshal)
kitchen|ette +s
kitchen-sink adjective preceding a noun
kitchen|ware +s
kite
   kites
   kited
   kit|ing
Kite|mark +s
kith
Kiti|mat (municipality, Canada)
kitsch
kitsch|i|ness
kitschy
   kitsch|i|er
   kitsch|i|est
Kit|se|las
   plural Kit|se|las
kit|ten +s +ed +ing
kit|ten|ish
kit|ten|ish|ly
kit|ten|ish|ness
Kit|ti|tian +s
kit|ti|wake +s
kit|ty
   kit|ties
kitty-corner
Kit|ty Hawk (town, US)
Kit|ty Lit|ter proprietary
Kit|wan|ga Fort (historic site, Canada)
Kitwe (city, Zambia)
Kitz|bühel (town, Austria)
kiva +s

Kivu (lake, Congo–Rwanda border)
Ki|wan|ian +s
Ki|wan|is
Kiwi +s (New Zealander)
kiwi +s (bird; fruit)
Klag|en|furt (city, Austria)
Klai|peda (city, Lithuania)
Klan (Ku Klux Klan)
   [☞ clan]
Klans|man (member of the Ku Klux Klan)
   Klans|men
   [☞ clansman]
Klans|woman (member of the Ku Klux Klan)
Klans|women
   [☞ clanswoman]
Klap|roth, Mar|tin Hein|rich (German chemist)
klax|on +s
Klee, Paul (Swiss painter)
   [☞ Clay]
Klee|nex proprietary
   Klee|nex|es
Klein (surname)
   [☞ Kline, Cline]
Klein, Abra|ham Moses (Cdn poet)
Klein, Cal|vin Rich|ard (US designer)
Klein, Mel|anie (English psychoanalyst)
Klein bot|tle +s
Kleist, (Bernd) Hein|rich Wil|helm von (German writer)
Klem|perer, Otto (German-born conductor)
klep|toc|racy
   klep|toc|ra|cies
klepto|crat
klepto|mania
klepto|maniac +s
Klerk, Fred|erik Wil|lem de (South African president)
Klerks|dorp (city, South Africa)
klez|mer +s
klick +s (kilometre)
   [☞ click]
klieg light +s

Klimt, Gus|tav
(Austrian artist)
Kline, Franz (US
painter)
[☞ **Klein, Cline**]
klip|sprin|ger +s
klis|ter +s
Klon|dike (river &
region, Canada)
Klon|diker +s
kloof +s
**Klop|stock,
Fried|rich Gott|lieb**
(German poet)
Klos|ters (resort,
Switzerland)
Klu|ane (lake &
national park,
Canada)
kludge +s
kludgy
klutz
klutz|es
klutzy
klutz|i|er
klutz|i|est
klys|tron +s
K-meson +s
knack +s
knack|er +s +ed +ing
knack|ered *adjective*
knack|wurst
knap (crest of a hill;
break stone)
knaps
knapped
knap|ping
[☞ **nap, nappe**]
knap|per +s
knap|sack +s
knap|weed +s
knar +s
knave +s (rogue;
Cards)
[☞ **nave**]
knav|ery
knav|eries
knav|ish
knav|ish|ly
knav|ish|ness
knawel +s
knead +s +ed +ing
(work dough or clay)
[☞ **need**]
knead|er +s
knee
knees
kneed
knee|ing
knee bend +s
knee|board +s +ed
+ing
knee|board|er +s

knee|board|ing *noun*
knee breech|es
knee|cap
knee|caps
knee|capped
knee|cap|ping
knee|cap|per +s
knee|cap|ping *noun*
knee-deep
knee-high +s
knee|hole +s
knee-jerk +s
knee joint +s
kneel
kneels
knelt or **kneeled**
kneel|ing
knee-length
kneel|er +s
knee pad +s
knee pants
knee-slapper +s
knee-slapping
knee sock +s
knees-up +s
knee-trembler +s
knee wall +s
knell +s +ed +ing
Knel|ler, Sir God|frey
(English painter)
knelt
Knes|set (Israeli
parliament)
knew *past tense of*
know
[☞ **new, gnu**]
Knicker|bock|er +s
(New Yorker)
knicker|bock|ers
(breeches)
knick|ers (pants;
underwear)
[☞ **nicker**]
knick-knack +s
knick-knackery
knife
• *noun*
knives
• *verb*
knifes
knifed
knif|ing
knife-edge +s
knife-grinder +s
knife|like
knife-pleat +s
knife-pleated
knife|point
knif|er +s
knife-thrower +s
knife-throwing
knif|ing +s *noun*
Knight (inlet, Canada)

knight +s +ed +ing
(titled man; military
attendant; *Chess*)
knight er|rant
knights er|rant
knight-errantry
knight|hood +s
knight|li|ness
knight|ly
(characteristic of a
knight)
[☞ **nightly**]
Knights|bridge
(district of London)
knish
knish|es
knit (make with yarn;
wrinkle one's brow)
knits
knit|ted or **knit**
knit|ting
[☞ **nit**]
knit|ter +s
knit|ting *noun*
knit|wear
knives
knob (handle; rounded
projection; hill;
candy)
knobs
knobbed
knob|bing
[☞ **nob**]
knob|bly
knob|by
knob|bi|er
knob|bi|est
knob|kerrie +s
knob-like
knock +s +ed +ing
(strike; criticize;
Automotive)
[☞ **nock, Nok**]
knock about *verb*
knocks about
knocked about
knock|ing about
knock|about +s
adjective & noun
knock back *verb*
knocks back
knocked back
knock|ing back
knock-back +s *noun*
knock down *verb*
knocks down
knocked down
knock|ing down
knock-down +s *noun*
& adjective
**knock-down,
drag-'em-out**
adjective

**knock-down,
drag-out**
adjective
knock|er +s
knocking-shop +s
knock-kneed
knock knees
knock-knock joke +s
knock off *verb*
knocks off
knocked off
knock|ing off
knock-off +s *noun*
knock on *verb*
knocks on
knocked on
knock|ing on
knock-on *noun &
adjective*
knock out *verb*
knocks out
knocked out
knock|ing out
knock|out +s *noun &
adjective*
knoll +s +ed +ing
knop +s
Knos|sos (ancient city,
Crete)
knot (tie; tree growth;
unit of speed;
nautical mile; bird)
knots
knot|ted
knot|ting
knot|grass
knot|grass|es
knot|head +s
knot|head|ed
knot|hole +s
knot|less
knot|ter +s
knot|ti|ly
knot|ti|ness (knotty
condition)
[☞ **naughtiness**]
knot|ting *noun*
knot|ty (having knots;
puzzling)
knot|ti|er
knot|ti|est
[☞ **naughty**]
knot|weed +s
knout +s +ed +ing
(scourge; flog)
[☞ **nowt**]
know
knows
knew
known
know|ing
[☞ **No, Nault**]
know|able
know-all +s

know|er +s
know-how *noun*
(expertise)
know|ing *noun &*
adjective
know|ing|ly
know|ing|ness
know-it-all +s
know|ledg|abil|ity
(*use*
knowledgeability)
know|ledg|able (*use*
knowledgeable)
know|ledg|able|ness
(*use*
knowledgeableness)
know|ledg|ably (*use*
knowledgeably)
know|ledge +s
know|ledge|abil|ity
know|ledge|able
know|ledge|able|
ness
know|ledge|ably
knowledge-based
known *adjective*
(publicly
acknowledged)
[☞ none]
Know-Nothing +s
(US political party)
know-nothing +s (*in*
general use)
know-nothing|ism
Knox, John (Scottish
Protestant reformer)
Knox|ville (city, US)
knuckle
knuckles
knuckled
knuck|ling
knuckle|ball +s
knuckle|ball|er +s
knuckle|bone +s
knuckle-duster +s
knuckle|head +s
knuckle|headed
knuck|ler +s
knuck|ly
knur +s
knurl +s +ed +ing
knurled *adjective*
knurr +s (*use* knur)
Knut (= Canute,
Danish king)
KO (knockout)
• *noun*
KOs
• *verb*
KO's
KO'd
KO'ing
koa +s

ko|ala +s (animal)
[☞ Kuala Lumpur,
Kuala Trengganu]
koan +s
kob +s (antelope)
Kobe (city, Japan)
ko|bold +s
Koch, (Hein|rich
Her|mann) Rob|ert
(German
bacteriologist)
Köchel num|ber +s
Ko|dály, Zol|tán
(Hungarian
composer)
Ko|di|ak +s
Koest|ler, Ar|thur
(English novelist)
Koff|man, Mor|ris
('Moe') (Cdn flutist)
[☞ Kaufman,
Kauffmann]
kofta +s
Ko|gawa, Joy
Nozo|mi (Cdn
writer)
Ko|hima (city, India)
Kohl, Hel|mut
(German chancellor)
kohl (makeup powder)
[☞ coal, cole]
kohl|rabi
kohl|rabies
koi (carp)
plural koi
Koil (former city,
India)
koine +s
ko|kanee
plural ko|kanee
Ko|kosch|ka, Oskar
(Austrian artist)
Kok|so|ak (river,
Canada)
Kola (peninsula,
Russia)
kola +s (tree: *use* cola)
kol|bas|sa
Kol|ha|pur (city, India)
ko|lin|sky
ko|lin|skies
kol|khoz
kol|khozes or
kol|khozy
Koll|witz, Käthe
(German artist)
Koly|ma (river,
Siberia)
koma|tik +s
kombu
Ko|mo|do (island,
Indonesia; lizard)
Kom|so|mol +s

Kom|so|molsk *full*
name Kom|somolsk-
on-Amur (city,
Russia)
Kongo (African
people; language)
plural Kongo or
Kon|gos
[☞ Congo]
Kö|nigs|berg
(= Kaliningrad,
Russia)
Konya (city, Turkey)
koo|doo +s (*use* kudu)
kook +s
kooka|burra +s
kook|i|ly
kook|i|ness
kooky
kook|i|er
kook|i|est
Kool-Aid +s
proprietary
Koo|ning, Wil|lem de
(US painter)
Koo|te|nai
• (US stretch of the
Kootenay River)
• (people, language:
use Kutenai)
plural Koo|te|nai
• The name
preferred by the
people themselves is
Ktunaxa Kinbasket.
[☞ Kootenay]
Koo|te|nay
• (river, lake & national
park, Canada)
• (people, language:
use Kutenai)
plural Koo|te|nay
• The name
preferred by the
people themselves is
Ktunaxa Kinbasket.
[☞ Kootenai]
ko|peck +s
ko|pek +s (*use*
kopeck)
kopje +s (hill)
kop|pie +s (hill: *use*
kopje)
kora +s
Koran +s
Ko|ran|ic
Korch|noi, Vik|tor
Lvo|vich (Russian
chess player)
Kor|do|fan (region,
Sudan)
Korea +s (peninsula &
countries, Asia)
[☞ chorea]

Ko|rean +s
korma
Kort|rijk (city,
Belgium)
kor|una +s (Czech &
Slovak currency)
Korup (national park,
Cameroon)
Kor|zyb|ski, Al|fred
Hab|dank Skar|bek
(US semanticist)
Kos (Greek island)
Kosci|usko
(mountain, Australia)
Kosci|usko,
Thad|deus (Polish
patriot)
ko|sher +s +ed +ing
Koš|ice (city, Slovakia)
Kos|ovar +s
Kos|ovo (Balkan
region)
Kos|suth, Lajos
(Hungarian
statesman)
Kos|tro|ma (city,
Russia)
Ko|sy|gin, Alek|sei
Niko|lay|evich
(Soviet statesman)
Kota (city, India)
Kota Ba|haru (city,
Malaysia)
Kota Kina|balu (city,
Malaysia)
Kotch|eff, Wil|liam
('Ted') (Cdn
filmmaker)
Kotka (city, Finland)
koto +s
Kou|chi|bou|guac
(national park,
Canada)
kou|miss
kou|prey +s
Kou|rou (town,
French Guiana)
Kow|loon (peninsula,
China)
kow|tow +s +ed +ing
Kra (isthmus,
Thailand)
[☞ craw]
kraal +s +ed +ing
(enclosure)
Krafft-Ebing,
Rich|ard, Baron von
(German physician)
kraft (wrapping paper)
Kragu|jevac (city,
Serbia)
krai +s (Russian
territory)

krait +s (snake)
Kraka|toa (island, Indonesia)
krak|en +s
Kras|no|dar (region & city, Russia)
Kras|no|yarsk (region & city, Russia)
Kraut +s offensive
kray +s (Russian territory: use krai)
Krebs, Sir Hans Adolf (English biochemist)
Kre|feld (town, Germany)
Kreis|ler, Fritz (Austrian-born violinist)
Krem|en|chuk (city, Ukraine)
Krem|lin (in Moscow)
krem|lin +s (in general use)
Krem|lin|ol|o|gist +s
Krem|lin|ol|ogy
krep|lach
Krieg|hoff, Cor|nel|ius David (Cdn painter)
krieg|spiel +s
Kriem|hild (Germanic Myth)
Kriem|hilde (Germanic Myth: use Kriemhild)
krill
 plural krill
krim|mer
kris (dagger)
 krises
Krish|na (river, India; Hinduism)
Krish|na|ism
Kriss Krin|gle (Santa Claus)
Kris|tall|nacht
Kris|ti|ania (former name for Oslo, Norway)
Kris|tian|sand (town, Norway)
Kroetsch, Rob|ert (Cdn writer)
krona
 • (Swedish currency)
 plural kro|nor
 • (Icelandic currency)
 plural kro|nur
 [☞ krone]
krone (Danish & Norwegian currency)
 kro|ner
 [☞ krona]

Kro|nos (Greek Myth: use Cronus)
Kron|stadt (German name for Braşov, Romania)
Kroo (people, language: use Kru)
 plural Kroo
 [☞ crew, cru]
kroon +s (Estonian currency)
 [☞ croon]
Kro|pot|kin, Peter (Russian anarchist)
Kru (people; language)
 plural Kru
 [☞ crew, cru]
Kru|ger, Ste|phan|us Jo|han|nes Paul|us (South African statesman)
kru|ger|rand +s
krumm|holz
 plural krumm|holz
Krupp, Al|fred (German arms manufacturer)
kryp|ton
Kryvy Rih (city, Ukraine)
Kshat|riya +s
Ktu|naxa Kin|bas|ket
 plural Ktu|naxa Kin|bas|ket
Kuala Lum|pur (capital of Malaysia)
Kuala Tereng|ganu (= Kuala Trengganu)
Kuala Treng|ganu (city, Malaysia)
Kuan|tan (city, Malaysia)
Kuan Yin (Buddhism)
ku|basa
Kub|lai Khan (Mongol emperor)
Kub|rick, Stan|ley (US filmmaker)
ku|chen
Ku|ching (city, Malaysia)
Ku|del|ka, James (Cdn choreographer)
kud|lik +s
kudos
kudu
 plural kudus or kudu
kudzu
Kuer|ti, Anton Emil (Cdn musician)
Kufic

kugel
Ku|gluk|tuk (hamlet, Canada)
Kui|by|shev (former name for Samara, Russia)
Ku Klux|er +s
Ku Klux Klan
Ku Klux Klans|man
 Ku Klux Klans|men
kukri +s
kulak +s
kulfi
Kul|tur
Kul|tur|kampf
Kum (= Qom, Iran)
 [☞ cum]
Kuma|moto (city, Japan)
Ku|masi (city, Ghana)
kumis (use koumiss)
ku|miss (use koumiss)
küm|mel
kum|quat +s
Kun, Béla (Hungarian statesman)
Kuna
 plural Kuna or Kunas
kun|da|lini
Kun|dera, Milan (Czech novelist)
Kung (people & language)
 plural Kung
 [☞ Küng]
Küng, Hans (Swiss theologian)
 [☞ Kung]
kung fu
K'ung Fu-tzu (Confucius)
Kun|lun Shan (mountains, China)
Kun|ming (city, China)
Kuo|min|tang
Kuo|pio (city, Finland)
kur|cha|tov|ium
Kurd +s (Muslim people)
Kurd|ish
Kurdi|stan (region, Asia)
Kure (city, Japan)
Kur|elek, Wil|liam (Cdn painter)
Kur|gan (city, Russia)
Ku|ril +s (islands, Russia: use Kurile)
Ku|rile +s (islands, Russia)

Kuro|sawa, Akira (Japanese filmmaker)
Kursk (city & battle site, Russia)
kur|ta +s
kurt|o|sis
Kuşa|dasi (town, Turkey)
Kush (in 'Hindu Kush'; for region of ancient Nubia or son of Ham use Cush)
Kuta|isi (city, Republic of Georgia)
Kutch (gulf & salt marsh, India)
Kutch|in (people, language)
 plural Kutch|in
 • The name preferred by the people themselves is Gwich'in.
Ku|te|nai (people, language)
 plural Ku|te|nai
 • The name preferred by the people themselves is Ktunaxa Kinbasket.
 [☞ Kootenai, Kootenay]
Ku|tu|zov, Mikh|ail Ilarion|ovich (Russian field marshal)
Kuujjua|aq (village, Canada)
Ku|wait (country, Middle East)
Ku|wait City (capital of Kuwait)
Ku|waiti +s
Kuz|bas Basin (= Kuznets Basin, Russia)
Kuz|nets, Simon Smith (US economist)
Kuz|nets Basin (region, Russia)
Kuz|netsk Basin (= Kuznets Basin, Russia)
kvass
kvell +s +ed +ing
kvetch
 kvetch|es
 kvetched
 kvetch|ing
kvetch|er +s
kvetch|ing noun

Kwa (people;
language)
plural Kwa
[☞ qua]
kwa|cha
plural kwa|cha
Kwa|giulth
plural Kwa|giulth
Kwa|ki|utl
plural Kwa|ki|utl
• The name
preferred by the
people themselves is
Kwagiulth.
Kwa|kwaka'wakw
plural
Kwa|kwaka'wakw
Kwa-kwa-la
(language)
Kwa|Nde|bele
(former homeland,
South Africa)
Kwang|chow
(= Guangzhou,
China)
Kwang|ju (city, South
Korea)
Kwang|si Chuang
(= Guangxi Zhuang,
China)
Kwang|tung
(= Guangdong,
China)
Kwan|za (festival)
kwan|za (Angolan
currency)
plural kwan|za or
kwan|zas
Kwan|zaa (festival:
use Kwanza)
kwa|shi|or|kor
Kwa|Zulu (former
homeland, South
Africa)
Kwei|chow
(= Guizhou, China)
Kwei|lin (= Guilin,
China)
Kwei|yang
(= Guiyang, China)
Kwe|sui (*former name
for* Hohhot, Inner
Mongolia)
KWIC (keyword in
context)
kyan|ite
kyat
plural kyat or kyats
Kyd, Thom|as
(English dramatist)
[☞ Kidd]
Kyiv (capital of
Ukraine)
kylin +s

kym|o|graph +s
kym|o|graph|ic
Kyoto (city, Japan)
ky|pho|sis
ky|pho|ses
ky|phot|ic
Kyr|gyz
plural Kyr|gyz
Kyr|gyz|stan
(country, Asia)
Kyrie +s
Kyrie elei|son +s
Kyu|shu (island,
Japan)
Kyzyl (city, Russia)
Kyzyl Kum (desert,
Asia)

L

L
• (letter; shape)
L's
• (litre; Lire;
Avogadro's constant)
[☞ el, ell]
l (letter)
l's
[☞ el, ell]
l. (poetry line)
ll.
la +s
laa|ger +s +ed +ing
(camp; entrenched
position)
[☞ lager]
Laa|youne
(= La'youn, Western
Sahara)
Lab +s (dog)
lab +s (laboratory)
La Baie (city, Canada)
Laba|no|ta|tion
la Barca, Pedro
Cal|de|rón de
(Spanish writer)
La Barre, Joseph-
Antoine Le Febvre
de (governor of New
France)
lab|a|rum +s
La|batt, John (1838–
1915; Cdn brewer)
La|batt, John Kin|der
(1803–66; Cdn
brewer)

La|batt, John
Sack|ville (1880–
1952; Cdn brewer)
lab coat +s
lab|da|num
label
labels
labelled
label|ling
label|ler +s
la|bel|lum
la|bel|la
label|mate +s
La|berge (lake,
Canada)
La|berge, Al|bert
(Cdn writer)
La|berge, Louis (Cdn
labour leader)
labia *plural of* labium
labi|al
labi|al|ize
labi|al|iz|es
labi|al|ized
labi|al|iz|ing
labi|al|ly
labia ma|jora
labia mi|nora
labi|ate +s
labile
la|bil|ity
labio|den|tal +s
labio|velar +s
labi|um
labia
labor +s +ed +ing
(*use* labour)
lab|ora|tory
lab|ora|tor|ies
la|bored *adjective* (*use*
laboured)
labor|er +s (*use*
labourer)
labor|ing|ly (*use*
labouringly)
labor-intensive (*use*
labour-intensive)
la|bor|i|ous
la|bor|i|ous|ly
la|bor|i|ous|ness
labor|ite +s (*use*
labourite)
labor-saving (*use*
labour-saving)
Labour (political
party)
labour +s +ed +ing
la|boured *adjective*
labour|er +s
labour|ing|ly
labour-intensive

Labour|ite +s
(supporter of Labour
Party)
labour|ite +s
(supporter of
organized labour)
labour-saving
labra
Lab|ra|dor +s (region,
highlands &
peninsula, Canada;
current & sea,
N Atlantic; dog; cod;
tea)
Lab|ra|dor City
(town, Canada)
Lab|ra|dor|ian +s
Lab|ra|dor Inuit
lab|ra|dor|ite +s
Lab|ra|dor re|triev|er
+s
Labrador-Ungava
(peninsula, Canada)
lab|ret +s
la|brum
labra
la|brus|ca +s
La Bru|yère, Jean de
(French moralist)
La|bu|an (island,
Malaysia)
la|bur|num +s
laby|rinth +s
laby|rinth|ian
laby|rinth|ine
lac +s (insect; resin;
for hundred
thousand *use* lakh)
[☞ lack]
Lacan, Jacques
Marie Émile (French
psychoanalyst)
La|can|ian +s
La|can|ian|ism
Lac-Brome (town,
Canada)
Lac|ca|dive (Indian
islands)
lac|co|lith +s
lace
laces
laced
lacing
lace cur|tain +s
laced *adjective*
La Ceiba (town,
Honduras)
lace|maker +s
lace|making
la|cer|ate
la|cer|ates
la|cer|at|ed
la|cer|at|ing

la|cer|at|ed *adjective*
la|cer|a|tion +s
la|cer|a|tive
la|cer|tian +s
lacer|til|ian +s
lacer|tine +s
lace up *verb*
laces up
laced up
lacing up
lace-up +s *noun*
lace|wing +s
lace|work
La|che|naie (town, Canada)
lach|es (*Law*)
Lach|es|is (*Greek Myth*)
La|chine (city, canal & rapids, Canada)
[☞ Lachenaie]
Lach|lan (river, Australia)
lach|rym|al (*use* lacrimal)
lach|rym|ator +s
lach|rym|a|tory
lach|rym|a|tor|ies
lach|rym|ose
lach|rym|ose|ly
La|chute (town, Canada)
laci|er
laci|est
laci|ly
laci|ness
lacing +s *noun*
la|cini|ate
la|cini|at|ed (= laciniate)
la|cini|a|tion +s
lack +s +ed +ing (be without; want)
[☞ lac]
lack|a|dais|ic|al
lack|a|dais|ic|ally
lack|a|dais|ic|al|ness
lack|ey +s +ed +ing
lack|ing *adjective*
lack|lustre
Lac la Ronge (lake, Canada)
La|clos, (Pierre Am|broise Fran|çois) Cho|der|los de (French novelist)
Lac-Mégantic (town, Canada)
La|combe (town, Canada)
La|combe, Al|bert (Cdn missionary)

La|co|nia (department & ancient region, Greece)
La|co|nian +s
la|con|ic
la|con|ic|ally
la|coni|cism
la|con|ism +s
La Cor|uña (= Corunna, Spain)
lac|quer +s +ed +ing
lac|quered *adjective*
lac|quer|er +s
lac|quer|ware
lac|rim|al
[☞ lachrymator, lachrymose]
lac|rim|a|tion +s
[☞ lachrymator, lachrymose]
la|crosse
Lac Seul (lake, Canada)
lac|tase +s
lac|tate
lac|tates
lac|tat|ed
lac|tat|ing
lac|tat|ing *adjective*
lac|ta|tion +s
lac|teal +s
lac|tes|cence +s
lac|tes|cent
lac|tic
lac|tif|er|ous
lacto|ba|cil|lus
lacto|ba|cil|li
lac|tom|eter +s
lac|tone +s
lacto-ovo-vegetar|ian +s
lacto|pro|tein +s
lac|tose
la|cu|na
la|cu|nae or la|cu|nas
la|cu|nal
la|cu|nar
la|cus|trine
lacy
laci|er
laci|est
lad +s
La|dakh (region, India)
lada|num (plant resin; *use* labdanum)
[☞ laudanum]
lad|der +s +ed +ing
lad|der|back +s
lad|die +s
lad|dish
lad|dish|ness

lade (*Transport*)
lades
laded
laden
lading
[☞ laid]
la-de-da (= la-di-da)
laden *adjective*
la-di-da
ladies
Ladies' Aid (society)
ladies' man
ladies' men
ladies' night +s
ladies' room +s
ladies' tress|es (= lady's tresses)
Ladin (Rhaeto-Romance dialect)
lading +s *noun*
La|di|no +s (Sephardic dialect; mestizo in Latin America)
[☞ Latino]
la|di|no +s (clover)
ladle
ladles
ladled
ladling
ladle|ful +s
Lado|ga (lake, Russia)
lady
ladies
Lady altar +s
lady|bird +s
Lady Boun|ti|ful +s
lady|bug +s
Lady chap|el +s
Lady Day +s
lady fern
lady|finger +s
lady friend +s
lady|hood
lady-in-waiting *plural* ladies-in-waiting
lady-killer +s
lady|like
lady love +s
lady|ness
lady's bed|straw +s
lady|ship +s
lady's maid +s
lady's man|tle +s
Lady|smith (towns, Canada & South Africa)
lady-smock +s
lady's slip|per +s
lady's smock +s (= lady-smock)
lady's tress|es

Laer|tes (*Greek Myth*)
laevo|ro|ta|tory (*use* levorotatory)
laevul|ose (*use* levulose)
La|fay|ette, Marie Jo|seph Paul Yves Roch Gil|bert du Mo|tier, Mar|quis de (French soldier)
l'affaire (controversy)
laff riot +s
La|fleur, Guy Da|mien (Cdn hockey player)
La|Fon|taine, Sir Louis-Hippo|lyte (Cdn politician)
La Fon|taine, Jean de (French poet)
lag
lags
lagged
lag|ging
lagan +s
lager +s (beer)
[☞ laager, lagger]
Lager|kvist, Pär Fabian (Swedish writer)
Lager|löf, Selma Ottil|iana Lovi|sa (Swedish novelist)
lager lout +s
lag|gard +s
lag|gard|ly
lag|gard|ness
lag|ger +s (one who lags)
[☞ lager, laager]
lag|ging +s *noun*
Lagi|mo|dière, Jean-Baptiste (Cdn fur trader)
Lagi|mo|dière, Marie-Anne (Cdn settler)
lago|morph +s
la|goon +s
la|goon|al
Lagos (city, Nigeria)
La Grande Ri|vière (river, Canada)
La|grange, Jo|seph Louis, Comte de (French mathematician)
La|gran|gian
lag time +s
La Guar|dia, Fio|rel|lo Henry (US politician)
lah +s (*use* la)

lahar +s
La|Have (river, Canada)
lah-di-dah (= la-di-da)
La|hore (city, Pakistan)
laic +s
laical
laical|ly
laicism
laiciz|a|tion +s
laicize
laiciz|es
lai|cized
laiciz|ing
laid *past & past participle of* lay
laid-back
lain *past participle of* lie
[☞ lane]
Laing, Ron|ald David (Scottish psychiatrist)
[☞ Lang, lang]
lair +s
lair|age +s
laird +s
laird|ship +s
laisser-faire (*use* laissez-faire)
laisser-passer +s (*use* laissez-passer)
laissez-faire
laissez-passer +s
laity
Laius (*Greek Myth*)
[☞ Lias]
La Jon|quière, Jacques-Pierre de Taf|fa|nel de La Jon|quière, Mar|quis de (governor of New France)
lake +s
lake boat +s
Lake Dis|trict (in England)
lake|fill
lake|front +s
Lake|head (Thunder Bay)
lake|head +s (shore farthest from a lake's outlet)
Lake|head|er +s
Lake|land (district, England; terrier)
lake|land +s (area with lakes)
lake|let +s

Lake Lou|ise (lake & resort, Canada)
Lake of the Woods (lake, Canada)
lak|er +s
lake|shore +s
lake|side
lake|view
lake|ward
lake|wards
lakh +s (hundred thousand)
La|ko|ta
plural La|ko|ta or La|ko|tas
Lak|shad|weep (islands, India)
Lak|shmi (*Hinduism*)
La-La Land (BC, California)
la-la land (dream world)
lala|pa|loo|za +s (*use* lollapalooza)
Lale|mant, Charles (French missionary)
Lale|mant, Jé|rôme (French missionary)
La|lique, René (French jeweller)
Lal|lan (= Lallans)
Lal|lans
lally|gag
lally|gags
lally|gagged
lally|gag|ging
La Lou|vière (city, Belgium)
lam (thrash; in 'on the lam')
lams
lammed
lam|ming
[☞ lamb]
lama +s (monk)
[☞ llama, Lammas Day]
Lama|ism
Lama|ist +s
La|marck, Jean Bap|tiste Pierre An|toine de Monet, Cheva|lier de (French naturalist)
la|marck|ian +s
La|marck|ism
La|Marsh, Julia Ver|lyn ('Judy') (Cdn politician)
Lamar|tine, Al|phonse Marie Louis de (French writer)

lama|sery
lama|ser|ies
La Mauri|cie (national park, Canada)
La|maze (method of childbirth)
Lamb, Charles (English essayist)
Lamb, Mary (English essayist)
Lamb, Wil|liam (Viscount Melbourne)
Lamb, Wil|lis Eu|gene, Jr. (US physicist)
lamb +s +ed +ing (young sheep)
[☞ lam]
lam|bada +s (dance)
lam|baste
lam|bastes
lam|bast|ed
lam|bast|ing
lamb|da +s (Greek letter)
lam|ben|cy
lam|bent
lam|bent|ly
lam|bert +s
Lam|beth (borough of London; conference)
lamb|kill +s
lamb|kin +s
lamb|like
Lam|bor|ghi|ni, Fer|ruc|cio (Italian car manufacturer)
lam|bre|quin +s
lamb's ears (plant)
plural lamb's ears
lamb|skin +s
lamb's let|tuce
lamb's quar|ters (plant)
lambs|wool +s
lame (disabled, limping; weak)
lamer
lam|est
lames
lamed
lam|ing
lamé +s (*Textiles*)
lame|brain +s
lame-brained
lame duck +s (lame-duck *when preceding a noun*)
la|mel|la
la|mel|lae
la|mel|lar
lam|el|late

lam|el|lat|ed
la|mel|li|branch +s
la|mel|li|corn +s
la|mel|li|form
lame|ly
lame|ness
la|ment +s +ed +ing
la|ment|able
la|ment|ably
lam|en|ta|tion +s
Lam|en|ta|tions (*Bible*)
la|ment|ed
la|ment|er +s
la|ment|ing|ly
La|mèque, Île (island, Canada)
lam|ina
lam|inae
lamin|ar
lamin|ate
lamin|ates
lamin|at|ed
lamin|at|ing
lamin|a|tion +s
lamin|ator +s
lamin|itis
lamin|ose
Lam|mas Day (English festival)
lam|mer|geier +s
lam|mer|geyer +s
(*use* lammergeier)
lamp +s +ed +ing
lamp|black
Lam|pe|dusa, Giu|seppe Tomasi de (Italian novelist)
lamp|less
lamp|light
lamp|light|er +s
lamp|lit
Lamp|man, Archi|bald (Cdn poet)
lam|poon +s +ed +ing
lam|poon|er +s
lam|poon|ery
lam|poon|ist +s
lamp|post +s
lam|prey +s
lamp|shade +s
lamp|shell +s
lamp|stand +s
LAN (local area network)
LANs
la|nai +s
Lan|ark|shire (former county, Scotland)
Lan|ca|shire (county, England)

Lan|cas|ter (city, England)

Lan|cas|ter, Bur|ton Ste|phen ('Burt') (US actor)

Lan|cas|ter, Ron|ald ('Ron') (Cdn football player & coach)

Lan|cas|ter Sound (in Canada)

Lan|cas|trian +s

lance
• noun (weapon; pipe) plural lan|ces
• noun (fish) plural lance or lan|ces
• verb (pierce with a lance or lancet; fling) lan|ces lanced lan|cing

lance|let +s (animal)

Lan|ce|lot (Arthurian Legend)

lan|ceo|late (lance-shaped)

lan|cer +s

lan|cet +s

lan|cet|ed

lanch (haul over land or ice) lanch|es lanched lanch|ing [☞ launch]

Lan|chow (= Lanzhou, China)

L'Ancienne-Lorette (city, Canada)

lan|cing conjugated form of lance [☞ Lansing]

Land, Edwin Her|bert (US inventor)

Land (German or Austrian state) Länd|er

land +s +ed +ing

Lan|dau, Lev David|ovitch (Soviet physicist)

lan|dau +s (carriage)

land bank +s

land base +s

land-based

land bridge +s

land claim +s

land|ed adjective

Länd|er plural of Land [☞ Landor]

land|er +s (spacecraft)

land|fall +s

land|fast

land|fill +s +ed +ing

land|form +s

land grant +s (land-grant when preceding a noun)

land|hold|er +s

land|hold|ing +s

land|ing +s noun

land|lady land|ladies

länd|ler plural länd|ler or länd|lers

land|less

land line +s

land|locked

land|loper +s

land|lord +s

land|lord|ism

land|lub|ber +s

land|mark +s

land mass land mass|es

land mine +s

land-office busi|ness land-office busi|ness|es

Lan|dor, Wal|ter Sav|age (English poet) [☞ Länder]

land|owner +s

land|owner|ship

land|own|ing

Lan|dow|ska, Wanda (Polish-born harpsichordist)

Land|race +s

Land|sat (island, Canada)

land|scape land|scapes land|scaped land|scap|ing

land|scap|er +s

land|scap|ing +s

land|scap|ist +s

Land|seer, Sir Edwin Henry (English painter)

Land's End (promontory, England)

land|slide +s

land|slip +s

lands|man lands|men

Land|stein|er, Karl (Austrian-born immunologist)

land|ward

land|wards

land|wash

lane +s (alley; road division; track; key) [☞ lain]

lane|way +s

Lang, Fritz (US filmmaker) [☞ Laing]

lang, k. d. born Kathy Dawn Lang (Cdn singer-songwriter) [☞ Laing]

Lan|ger|hans (Physiology)

Lan|ge|vin, André (Cdn writer)

Lan|ge|vin, Sir Hector-Louis (Cdn politician)

Lang|land, Wil|liam (English poet)

lang|lauf

Lang|ley (city, Canada)

Lang|ley, Sam|uel Pier|point (US aviation pioneer)

Lang|muir, Irv|ing (US chemist)

lan|gouste +s

lan|gous|tine +s

lang syne

Lang|ton, Ste|phen (Archbishop of Canterbury)

Lang|try, Lil|lie (English actress)

lan|guage +s

langue de chat langues de chat

Langue|doc (former province, France)

langue d'oc (dialect)

Languedoc-Roussil|lon (region, France)

langue d'oïl

lan|guid

lan|guid|ly

lan|guid|ness

lan|guish

lan|guish|es

lan|guished

lan|guish|ing

lan|guish|ing|ly

lan|guish|ment

lan|guor (lethargy; calm) [☞ langur]

lan|guor|ous

lan|guor|ous|ly

lan|gur +s (monkey) [☞ languor]

lank

lank|i|ly

lank|i|ness

lankly

lank|ness

lanky

lank|i|er

lank|i|est

lan|ner +s

lan|ner|et +s

lan|o|lin

Lans|downe, Henry Charles Keith Petty-Fitzmaurice, 5th Mar|quess of (governor general of Canada)

L'Anse aux Mea|dows (historic site, Canada)

Lan|sing (city, US) [☞ lancing]

lans|quenet +s

lan|tana +s

Lan|tau (island, Hong Kong)

lan|tern +s

lantern-jawed

lan|tha|nide +s

lan|tha|num

la|nu|go

lan|yard +s

Lan|za|rote (Canary island)

Lan|zhou (city, China)

Laoc|o|on (Greek Myth)

Lao|di|cean +s

Laoighis (= Laois, Ireland)

Laois (county, Ireland)

Laom|e|don (Greek Myth)

Laos (country, Asia)

Lao|tian +s

Lao-tzu (legendary founder of Taoism)

Laoze (= Lao-tzu)

lap laps lapped lap|ping [☞ Lapp]

La Palma (Canary island) [☞ Las Palmas]

laparo|scope +s

laparo|scop|ic

lapa|ros|copy lapa|ros|cop|ies

lapa|rot|omy lapa|rot|omies

La Paz (capital of Bolivia; city, Mexico)

lap|dog +s
lapel +s
la|pelled
lap|ful +s
lapi|dary
  lapi|dar|ies
lap|il|li
lapis laz|uli
La|pita (ancient
  Oceanic culture)
Lap|ith +s
La|place, Pierre
  Simon, Mar|quis de
  (French
  mathematician)
Lap|land (region,
  Europe)
Lap|land|er +s
La Plata (city,
  Argentina)
La Poca|tière (town,
  Canada)
La|pointe, Er|nest
  (Cdn politician)
La|porte, Pierre (FLQ
  victim)
Lapp +s
  (Scandinavian
  people)
  • The name
  preferred by the
  people themselves is
  Sami.
lapped *adjective*
lap|pet +s
lap|pet|ed
Lap|pish
lap pool +s
La Prai|rie (town,
  Canada)
lap robe +s
Lap|sang
lapse
  laps|es
  lapsed
  laps|ing
lapsed *adjective*
lapse rate +s
lap|strake +s
lap|sus lin|guae
  plural lap|sus
  lin|guae
Lap|tev (Arctic sea)
lap|top +s
lap|wing +s
Lara|mie (city, US)
lar|board +s
lar|cen|er +s
lar|cen|ist +s
lar|cen|ous
lar|cen|ous|ly
lar|ceny
  lar|cen|ies

larch
  larch|es
larch|wood
lard +s +ed +ing
lard-ass
  lard-asses
larder +s
Lard|ner, Ring|gold
  Wil|mer ('Ring') (US
  writer)
lar|don +s
lar|doon +s
  (= lardon)
lardy
  lard|i|er
  lard|i|est
lares (gods)
  [☞ lari]
large
  lar|ger
  lar|gest
  lar|ges
large cap +s (large-
  cap *when preceding a*
  noun)
large|ly
large-minded
large|mouth
  plural large|mouth
  or large|mouths
large|ness
large-print
large-scale
lar|gess (*use* largesse)
lar|gesse
large|tooth aspen +s
lar|ghet|to +s
larg|ish
largo +s
lari (Maldivian
  currency)
  plural laris or lari
  [☞ lares]
lar|iat +s
lar|i|gan +s (boot)
  [☞ larrikin]
La Rioja (region,
  Spain)
La|ris|sa (city, Greece)
lark +s +ed +ing
Lar|kin, Phil|ip
  Ar|thur (English
  writer)
lark|i|ness
lark|ish
lark|ish|ness
lark|spur
larky
larn +s +ed +ing
  (*jocular* = learn)
La Roche|fou|cauld,
  Fran|çois de

Mar|sil|lac, Duc de
  (French moralist)
La Ro|chelle (city,
  France)
La Rocque,
  Mar|guer|ite de
  (French-born Cdn
  heroine)
la Ronge (lake,
  Canada)
La|rousse, Pierre
  Atha|nase (French
  lexicographer)
lar|ri|gan +s (boot:
  use larigan)
lar|ri|kin +s
  (hooligan)
  [☞ larigan]
lar|rup
  lar|rups
  lar|ruped
  lar|rup|ing
larva
  lar|vae
lar|val
lar|vi|cid|al
lar|vi|cide +s
laryn|geal
laryn|gec|tomy
  laryn|gec|to|mies
laryn|git|ic
laryn|gitis
laryn|go|scope +s
laryn|got|omy
  laryn|got|omies
larynx
  la|ryn|ges
la|sa|gna +s
la|sa|gne +s (*use*
  lasagna)
La|Salle (city, Canada)
  [☞ La Salle,
  Lassalle]
La Salle, René-
  Robert Cave|lier,
  Sieur de (French
  explorer)
  [☞ Lassalle,
  LaSalle]
La Sarre (town,
  Canada)
las|car +s
las|civ|i|ous
las|civ|i|ous|ly
las|civ|i|ous|ness
lase (function as a
  laser)
  lases
  lased
  lasing
  [☞ laze, lace]
laser +s +ed +ing
  (light beam)
  [☞ lazar]

laser disc +s
lash
  lash|es
  lashed
  lash|ing
lash|er +s
lash|ing +s *noun*
lash|less
lash-up +s
Laski, Har|old
  Jo|seph (English
  political scientist)
Las|kin, Bora (Cdn
  judge)
Las Pal|mas (de Gran
  Ca|na|ria) (capital of
  the Canary Islands)
  [☞ La Palma]
La Spe|zia (city, Italy)
Las|queti (island,
  Canada)
lass
  lass|es
Lassa fever
  [☞ Lhasa]
Las|salle, Fer|di|nand
  (German politician)
  [☞ La Salle,
  LaSalle]
lassi (drink)
las|sie +s (young
  woman)
las|si|tude +s
las|so
  • *noun*
  las|sos or las|soes
  • *verb*
  las|soes
  las|soed
  las|so|ing
las|so|er +s
L'Assomp|tion (town,
  Canada)
last +s +ed +ing
last-ditch
last gasp (last-gasp
  when preceding a
  noun)
last|ing *adjective*
last|ing|ly
last|ing|ness
last|ly
last min|ute (last-
  minute *when*
  preceding a noun)
Last Moun|tain (lake,
  Canada)
Las Vegas (city, US)
lat +s
Lata|kia (city, Syria)
latch (fastener)
  latch|es

latched
latch|ing
[☞ laches]
latch|key +s
late
later
latest
late bloom|er +s
late-blooming
late|comer +s
la|teen
Late Latin
late|ly
late-model *adjective*
laten|cy
laten|cies
La Tène
late|ness
latent
latent|ly
lat|eral
lat|erals
lat|eralled
lat|eral|ling
lat|eral|ly
Lat|eran (site in Rome; councils; treaty; palace)
lat|erite +s
lat|erit|ic
La|ter|rière (town, Canada)
latex
latex|es or lati|ces
lath +s +ed +ing (thin strip)
lathe +s (woodworking machine)
lath|er +s +ed +ing
lath|ery
lathi +s
lati|ces *plural of* latex
[☞ lattices]
Lati|mer, Hugh (English clergyman)
Lat|in +s
Lat|ina +s
Lat|in|ate
Lat|in|ism +s
Lat|in|ist +s
Lat|in|iz|a|tion +s
Lat|in|ize
Lat|in|iz|es
Lat|in|ized
Lat|in|iz|ing
Lat|ino +s (Latin American in North America)
[☞ Ladino]
latish
la|tis|si|mus dorsi
la|tis|si|mi dorsi

lati|tude +s
lati|tud|inal
lati|tud|in|ally
lati|tudi|nar|ian +s
lati|tudi|nar|ian|ism
La|tium (ancient region, Italy)
lat|ke +s
La|to|na (*Roman Myth*)
La Tour, Charles de Saint-Étienne de (French colonizer)
La Tour, Françoise-Marie de Saint-Étienne de (Acadian heroine)
La Tour, Georges de (French painter)
la|trine +s
latte +s
lat|ten +s
lat|ter
latter-day
Latter-day Saint +s
lat|ter|ly
lat|tice
lat|ti|ces (interlaced structure)
[☞ latices]
lat|ticed
lat|tice|work +s
La Tuque (town, Canada)
Lat|via (country, Europe)
Lat|vian +s
Laud, Wil|liam (Archbishop of Canterbury)
laud +s +ed +ing (praise)
[☞ loud]
laud|abil|ity
laud|able
laud|ably
laud|a|num (drug)
[☞ ladanum]
laud|ation +s
laud|a|tory
Laud|er, Sir Harry Mac|Len|nan (Scottish entertainer)
lauds *noun*
laugh +s +ed +ing
[☞ laff riot]
laugh|able
laugh|ably
laugh|er +s
laugh|ing *noun & adjective*
laugh|ing|ly
laugh|ing|stock +s

laugh-line +s
laugh|ter
Laugh|ton, Charles (English-born US actor)
laugh track +s
launce (fish: *use* lance)
plural launce or laun|ces
[☞ lance]
Laun|ces|ton (city, Australia)
launch (set afloat; propel; begin; boat)
launch|es
launched
launch|ing
[☞ lanch]
launch|er +s
launch pad +s
laun|der +s +ed +ing
laun|der|er +s
laun|der|ette +s
laun|dress
laun|dress|es
laun|drette +s (*use* launderette)
laun|dro|mat +s
laun|dry
laun|dries
laundry|man
laundry|men
laundry|woman
laundry|women
Laur|asia (ancient continent)
Laure, Ca|role (Cdn entertainer)
laure|ate +s
laureate|ship +s
Laur|el, Stan (US comedian)
laur|el
laur|els
laur|elled
laur|el|ling
Lau|ren, Ralph (US designer)
[☞ Loren, loran]
Laur|ence, Mar|garet (Cdn writer)
[☞ Lawrence, Lorenz, Lorentz]
Lau|ren|deau, André (Cdn journalist & politician)
Lau|ren|tian +s (mountain range, geological region, plateau & shield, Canada)

Lau|ren|tides (Laurentian Mountains)
Lau|rier, Sir Wil|frid (Cdn prime minister)
laurus|ti|nus
laurus|ti|nus|es
Lau|sanne (town, Switzerland)
Lau|son, Jean de (French colonial administrator)
lav +s
lava +s
lav|abo +s
lav|age +s
Laval (city, Canada)
Laval, Fran|çois de (first bishop of Quebec)
Laval, Pierre (French statesman)
lava|lier +s (*use* lavaliere)
lava|liere +s
lava|like
La|val|lée, Ca|lixa (composer of 'O Canada')
laval|liere +s (*use* lavaliere)
lav|ation +s
lav|a|tor|ial
lav|a|tory
lav|a|tor|ies
lave
laves
laved
laving
lav|en|der +s
Laver, Rod|ney George ('Rod') (Australian tennis player)
laver +s
La Véren|drye, Pierre Gaul|tier de Va|rennes et de (Cdn fur trader)
lav|ish
lav|ish|es
lav|ished
lav|ish|ing
lav|ish|ly
lav|ish|ness
La|voi|sier, An|toine Lau|rent (French scientist)
Law, (An|drew) Bonar (British prime minister)
Law, John (Scottish financier)

Law (Pentateuch)
law +s
law-abiding
law-abiding|ness
law|break|er +s
law-breaking +s
law court +s
law|ful
law|ful|ly
law|ful|ness
law|giver +s
law|less
law|less|ly
law|less|ness
law|maker +s
law-making
law|man
  law|men
lawn +s +ed +ing
lawn bowl|er +s
lawn bowl|ing
lawn chair +s
lawn mow|er +s
lawny
Law|rence (surname; saint; in 'St. Lawrence River' etc.)
  [☞ **Laurence, Lorenz, Lorentz**]
Law|rence, Charles (British colonial administrator)
Law|rence, David Her|bert (English writer)
Law|rence, Er|nest Or|lan|do (US physicist)
Law|rence, Ger|trude (English actress)
Law|rence, Sir Thom|as (English painter)
Law|rence, Thom|as Ed|ward (Lawrence of Arabia)
law|ren|cium
law|suit +s
law|yer +s
law|yer|ly
lax +er +est
laxa|tive +s
lax|ity
lax|ly
Lax|ness, Hall|dór (Icelandic novelist)
lax|ness
lay
• (set; place on surface; produce egg; prepare; have sex with; position; not

professional, non-clerical; song)
lays
laid
lay|ing
• *past tense of* lie
  [☞ **lei, ley, Leh**]
lay|about +s
Laya|mon (English poet)
lay|away +s
lay-by +s
lay|er +s +ed +ing
lay|ered *adjective*
layer|ing +s *noun*
lay|ette +s
lay|man
  lay|men
lay off *verb*
  lays off
  laid off
  lay|ing off
lay|off +s *noun*
La'youn (capital of Western Sahara)
lay out *verb*
  lays out
  laid out
  lay|ing out
lay|out +s *noun*
lay|over +s
lay|person
  lay people or
  lay|persons
Lay|ton, Irv|ing Peter (Cdn writer)
lay up *verb*
  lays up
  laid up
  lay|ing up
lay|up +s *noun*
lay|woman
  lay|women
laz|ar +s (diseased person)
  [☞ **laser**]
laz|ar|et +s
laz|ar|ette +s (*use* lazaret)
laz|ar|et|to +s (= lazaret)
Laz|ar|ist +s
Laz|a|rus (*New Testament*)
laze (pass time lazily)
lazes
lazed
laz|ing
  [☞ **lase**]
laz|i|ly
laz|i|ness
Lazio (region, Italy)

lazy
laz|i|er
laz|i|est
lazy|bones
  plural **lazy|bones**
Lazy Su|san +s
LBO (leveraged buyout)
LBOs
LCD (liquid crystal display)
LCDs
LDC (less developed country)
LDCs
LDL (low-density lipoprotein)
LDLs
L-dopa
lea +s (meadow)
  [☞ **lee, ley, Leigh, Lie**]
leach *verb* (percolate; remove by percolation; slowly deprive of)
leach|es
leached
leach|ing
  [☞ **leech**]
leach|abil|ity
leach|able
leach|ate +s
Lea|cock, Ste|phen (Cdn writer)
lead[1] (direct; be in front of; spend; forefront; clue; leash; conductor; principal; *Curling*; open land)
leads
led
lead|ing
  [☞ **lied, Leeds**]
lead[2] +s +ed +ing (metal; blank space)
  [☞ **led**]
lead|able
Lead|belly (US guitarist)
leaded *adjective*
leaden
leaden|ly
leaden|ness
lead|er +s (forerunner; head; tape; plant shoot; *Fishing*; *Printing*)
  [☞ **lieder**]
leader|board +s
leader|less
leader|ship +s
lead foot
  lead feet

lead-footed
lead-free
lead head +s
lead head jig +s
lead-in +s
lead|ing +s *noun*
lead|ing edge
  (leading-edge *when preceding a noun*)
lead|less
lead off *verb*
  leads off
  led off
  lead|ing off
lead|off *adjective & noun*
lead time +s
lead|wort +s
Leaf +s (NHL team)
leaf
• *noun* (of a tree; of metal; paper)
  leaves
• *verb* (grow leaves; turn pages)
  leafs
  leafed
  leaf|ing
  [☞ **lief, Leif Ericsson**]
leaf|age
leaf blow|er +s
leaf|cut|ter +s
leaf-cutting
leafed
leaf green +s (leaf-green *when preceding a noun*)
leaf|hop|per +s
leaf|i|er
leaf|i|est
leaf|i|ness
leaf|less
leaf|let
  leaf|lets
  leaf|let|ed
  or **leaf|let|ted**
  leaf|let|ing
  or **leaf|let|ting**
leaf|like
leaf miner +s
leaf mold (*use* leaf mould)
leaf mould
leaf|roll
leafy
  leaf|i|er
  leaf|i|est
league
  leagues
  leagued
  leaguing
league-leading

leaguer +s
Leah (Bible)
leak +s +ed +ing
(hole through which
air or water escapes;
disclosure of
information)
[☞ leek]
leak|age +s
leak|er +s
Lea|key (surname)
[☞ leaky]
Lea|key, Louis
Sey|mour Bazett
(Kenyan
archaeologist)
Lea|key, Mary
Doug|las (English
archaeologist)
Lea|key, Rich|ard
Ers|kine Frere
(English
anthropologist)
leak|i|ness
leak-proof
leaky (having leaks)
leak|i|er
leak|i|est
[☞ Leakey]
Leam|ing|ton (town,
Canada)
Leam|ing|ton Spa
(town, England)
Lean, Sir David
(English filmmaker)
lean +s +ed +ing +er
+est (bend, slope;
thin, meagre)
[☞ lien]
lean-burn
Le|ander (Greek Myth)
lean|ing +s noun
lean|ly
lean|ness
lean-to +s
leap
leaps
leaped or leapt
leap|ing
leap|er +s
leap|frog
leap|frogs
leap|frogged
leap|frog|ging
leap year +s
Lear (Shakespearean
character)
[☞ leer, lehr]
Lear, Ed|ward
(English humorist)
Lear, Wil|liam
Pow|ell (US jet
manufacturer)

learn
learns
learned or learnt
learn|ing
learn|abil|ity
learn|able
learn|ed adjective
learn|ed|ly
learn|ed|ness
learn|er +s (one who
learns)
[☞ Lerner]
learn|ing noun
learn|ing dis|abled
learnt
Leary, Tim|othy
Fran|cis (US
educator & drug
pioneer)
[☞ leery]
leas|able
lease
leas|es
leased
leas|ing
lease|back +s
lease|hold +s
lease|hold|er +s
leas|er +s
leash (dog's lead;
restrain)
leash|es
leashed
leash|ing
[☞ Laois]
least
least|ways
least|wise
leath|er
leath|ers
leath|ered
leath|er|ing
leather|back +s
leather-bound
leather|ette
leather|i|ness
leather|leaf +s
leathern
leather|neck +s
leather|wear
leather|wood +s
leath|ery
leave
leaves
left
leav|ing
leaved adjective
(having leaves)
leaven +s +ed +ing
(ferment dough;
modify; influence)
[☞ levin]
leaven|ing noun

leav|er +s (one who
leaves)
[☞ lever]
leaves
leave-taking +s
leav|ings
Lea|vis, Frank
Ray|mond (English
literary critic)
Lea|vis|ite +s
Leba|nese
plural Leba|nese
Leba|non (country &
mountains, Middle
East)
Lebens|raum
Le|Blanc, Roméo
(Cdn governor
general)
[☞ Leblanc]
Le|blanc, Nico|las
(French chemist)
[☞ LeBlanc]
Le|bowa (former
homeland, South
Africa)
Le|brun, Al|bert
(French president)
Le|brun, Charles
(French artist)
Le Carré, John
(English novelist)
lech
lech|es
leched
lech|ing
lech|er +s
lech|er|ous
lech|er|ous|ly
lech|er|ous|ness
lech|ery
leci|thin +s
Le|clerc, Félix (Cdn
entertainer)
Le Cor|bu|sier
(French architect &
town planner)
lec|tern +s
lec|tin +s
lec|tion +s
lec|tion|ary
lec|tion|aries
lec|tor +s
lec|ture
lec|tures
lec|tured
lec|tur|ing
lec|tur|er +s
lec|ture|ship +s
LED (light-emitting
diode)
LEDs

led past & past
participle of lead[1]
[☞ lead[2]]
Leda (Greek Myth)
Led|better, Hud|die
Wil|liam (Leadbelly)
Leder|burg, Joshua
(US geneticist)
leder|hosen
ledge +s
ledged adjective
ledg|er +s
ledg|er line +s
ledger-tackle
ledgy
Leduc (city, Canada)
Leduc, Ozias (Cdn
painter)
Lee (surname)
[☞ Lie, Leigh]
Lee, Bruce (US actor)
Lee, Den|nis Bey|non
(Cdn writer)
Lee, James Mat|thew
(Cdn politician)
Lee, (Nelle) Har|per
(US novelist)
Lee, Rich|ard Henry
(US statesman)
Lee, Rob|ert Ed|ward
(US general)
Lee, Spike Shel|ton
Jack|son (US
filmmaker)
Lee, Tsung-Dao (US
physicist)
lee +s (shelter)
[☞ lea, ley]
lee|board +s
leech noun (aquatic
worm; healer;
sponger, parasite;
sail)
leech|es
[☞ leach]
leech|craft
Leeds (city, England)
leek +s (vegetable)
[☞ leak]
Lee Kuan Yew
(Singaporean prime
minister)
leer +s +ed +ing
(stare)
[☞ lehr, Lear]
leer|i|ness
leer|ing|ly
leery (wary; sly)
leer|i|er
leer|i|est
[☞ Leary]
lees (wine sediment;
dregs)

lee shore +s
lee side +s
Leeu|wen|hoek,
Anton van (Dutch
microscopist)
Lee|ward (Caribbean
islands)
lee|ward
lee|way
Le|febvre, Jean-
Pierre (Cdn
filmmaker)
left
left-centre
left field
left field|er +s
left-footed
left-hand
left-handed
left-handed|ly
left-handed|ness
left-hander +s
left|ie +s (use lefty)
left|ish
left|ism
left|ist +s
left-leaning
left|most
left-of-centre
left|over +s
left|ward
left|wards
left wing +s noun
left-wing adjective
left-winger +s
lefty
   left|ies
leg (limb) +s
   [☞ Legge]
leg|acy
   leg|acies
legal
legal|ese
legal|ism
legal|ist +s
legal|is|tic
legal|is|tic|ally
legal|ity
   legal|ities
legal|iz|a|tion
legal|ize
   legal|iz|es
   legal|ized
   legal|iz|ing
legal|ly
Le Gar|deur (town,
Canada)
Lé|ga|ré, Jo|seph
(Cdn painter)
leg|ate +s (papal
representative;
Roman History)
lega|tee +s

legate|ship +s
lega|tine
leg|a|tion +s (body of
deputies; diplomatic
minister's office)
   [☞ ligation]
le|gato +s
leg|ator +s
legend +s
legend|ar|i|ly
legend|ary
   (remarkable; of
   legends)
   [☞ legendry]
Le|gendre, Ad|rien
Marie (French
mathematician)
legend|ry (legends
collectively)
   [☞ legendary]
Léger (surname)
   [☞ ledger]
Léger, Fer|nand
(French painter)
Léger, Jules (Cdn
governor general)
Léger, Paul-Émile
(Cdn cardinal)
leger|de|main
leger line +s (use
ledger line)
Legge, Fran|cis
(governor of Nova
Scotia)
legged adjective
leg|ger +s
leg|gi|ness
leg|ging +s noun
leg|gy
   leg|gi|er
   leg|gi|est
   leg|gies
leg|hold +s
Leg|horn +s
   (= Livorno, Italy;
   fowl)
leg|horn +s (straw;
hat)
legi|bil|ity
legi|ble
legi|bly
le|gion +s
le|gion|ary
   le|gion|aries
le|gion|ella
le|gion|naire +s
le|gion|naires'
   dis|ease
leg iron +s
legis|late
   legis|lates
   legis|lat|ed
   legis|lat|ing

legis|la|tion +s
legis|la|tive
legis|la|tively
legis|la|tor +s
legis|la|ture +s
legit (legitimate)
   [☞ legate]
legit|im|acy
legit|im|ate
   legit|im|ates
   legit|im|at|ed
   legit|im|at|ing
legit|im|ate|ly
legit|im|at|ing
   adjective
legit|im|a|tion +s
legit|im|a|tiz|ation
   +s
legit|im|a|tize
   legit|im|a|tiz|es
   legit|im|a|tized
   legit|im|a|tiz|ing
legit|im|ism
legit|im|ist +s
legit|im|iz|a|tion +s
legit|im|ize
   legit|im|iz|es
   legit|im|ized
   legit|im|iz|ing
legit|im|iz|ing noun &
   adjective
leg|less
leg|man
   leg|men
Lego proprietary
leg of mut|ton (meat)
   legs of mut|ton
leg-of-mutton
   (sleeve; sail)
leg-over +s noun
leg rest +s
leg|room
leg trap +s
leg|ume +s
le|gum|in|ous
leg warm|er +s
leg|work
Leh (town, India)
   [☞ lei, ley, lay]
Lehár, Franz Fer|encz
(Hungarian
composer)
Le Havre (city,
France)
lehr +s (furnace)
lei
• (garland)
   leis
• (plural of leu)
   [☞ lay, ley, Leh]
Leib|nitz, Gott|fried
Will|helm
   (= Leibniz)

Leib|nitz|ian +s
   (= Leibnizian)
Leib|niz, Gott|fried
Will|helm (German
philosopher &
mathematician)
Leib|niz|ian +s
Leibo|vitz, Annie (US
photographer)
Leices|ter (city,
England; cheese)
   [☞ leister]
Leices|ter, Rob|ert
Dud|ley, Earl of
(English courtier)
Leices|ter|shire
(county, England)
Lei|den (city, the
Netherlands)
   [☞ Leyden jar]
Leif Erics|son ('the
Lucky', Norse
explorer)
   [☞ lief]
Leigh, Viv|ien
(English actress)
   [☞ Lee, Lie]
Lein|ster (province,
Ireland)
Leip|zig (city,
Germany)
leish|man|ia|sis
leis|ter +s +ed +ing
   (spear)
   [☞ Leicester]
lei|sure
lei|sured
lei|sure|li|ness
lei|sure|ly
lei|sure suit +s
lei|sure wear
leit|mo|tif +s
leit|mo|tiv +s (use
leitmotif)
Lei|trim (county,
Ireland)
Leix (= Laois, Ireland)
Le Jeune, Paul
(French missionary)
lek +s
Lek|will|tok
   plural Lek|will|tok
Le Lou|tre, Jean-
Louis (French priest)
Lely, Sir Peter (Dutch
painter)
LEM +s (lunar
excursion module)
Le|maître, Georges
Édouard (Belgian
astronomer)

lem|an +s (lover)
[☞ Le Mans, lemon, Lemmon]
Le Mans (town, France; *Motorsport*)
lem|ma
• (proposition; defined word)
lem|mas
• (heading; motto)
lem|ma|ta
lemme
lem|ming +s
lemming-like
Lem|mon, Jack (US actor)
[☞ lemon, leman]
Lem|nos (island, Greece)
lem|on +s (yellow fruit; colour; substandard car)
[☞ Lemmon, leman]
lem|on|ade +s
lemon grass
lemon grass|es
lemon-scented
lem|ony
lem|on yel|low (lemon-yellow *when preceding a noun*)
Le|Moyne (town, Canada)
[☞ Le Moyne]
Le Moyne, Charles Le Moyne de Lon|gueuil et de Châ|teau|guay (settler in New France)
[☞ LeMoyne]
Le Moyne, Pierre Le Moyne d'Iber|ville (French-Cdn explorer)
[☞ LeMoyne]
lem|pira +s
le|mur +s
Lena (river, Russia)
lend
lends
lent
lend|ing
lend|er +s
lend|ing *noun & adjective*
Lendl, Ivan (Czech tennis player)
Lend-Lease
length +3
length|en +s +ed +ing
length|en|er +s

length|en|ing *noun & adjective*
length|i|ly
length|i|ness
length|ways
length|wise
lengthy
length|i|er
length|i|est
leni|ence
leni|en|cy
leni|ent
leni|ent|ly
Lenin, Vlad|i|mir Ilich (Soviet statesman)
[☞ Lennon]
Lenin|akan (*former name for* Gyumri, Armenia)
Lenin|grad (*former name for* St. Petersburg, Russia)
Len|in|ism
Len|in|ist +s
le|ni|tion +s
leni|tive +s
leni|ty
leni|ties
Len|non, John (English musician)
[☞ Lenin]
Len|nox|ville (town, Canada)
leno +s
Le Nôtre, André (French gardener)
lens
lens|es
lensed
lens|ing
lens cap +s
lensed *adjective*
lens|ing +s *noun*
lens|less
lens|man
lens|men
Lent (*Christianity*)
lent *past & past participle of* lend
Lent|en
len|ti|cel +s
len|ticu|lar
len|til +s
lento
Lenya, Lotte (Austrian entertainer)
Leo +s (constellation; *Zodiac*; popes)
León (cities, Spain, Mexico & Nicaragua)
[☞ Lyon, leone]
Leon|ard, Sugar Ray (US boxer)

Leo|nar|do da Vinci (Italian artist & engineer)
Leon|ca|vallo, Rug|giero (Italian composer)
leone +s (Sierra Leonean currency)
Leo|nid +s
Leoni|das (Spartan king)
Leo|nine (of popes named Leo)
leo|nine +s (of or like a lion; *Prosody*)
leop|ard +s
leop|ard|ess
leop|ard|ess|es
leop|ard print +s (leopard-print *when preceding a noun*)
leop|ard's bane +s
leop|ard skin +s (leopard-skin *when preceding a noun*)
Leo|pold (Holy Roman emperor; Belgian kings)
Léo|pold|ville (*former name for* Kinshasa, Congo)
leo|tard +s (clothing)
[☞ Lyotard]
Le|page, Rob|ert (Cdn theatre & film director)
Le|pan|to (gulf & battle site, Ionian Sea)
lep|er +s
lepi|dop|ter|an +s
lepi|dop|ter|ist +s
lepi|dop|ter|ous
Lepi|dus, Mar|cus Aemil|lius (Roman statesman)
lep|re|chaun +s
lep|ro|sarium
lep|ro|saria
lep|ro|sy
lep|rous
lepta
Lep|tis Magna (ancient city, N Africa)
lep|ton
• (Greek monetary unit)
plural lepta
• (elementary particle)
plural lep|tons
lep|to|spir|o|sis
lep|to|tene

Ler|mon|tov, Mikh|ail Yuri|evich (Russian writer)
Ler|ner, Alan Jay (US lyricist)
[☞ learner]
Ler|wick (capital of the Shetland Islands)
Le|sage, Alain-René (French writer)
Le|sage, Jean (Cdn politician)
Les|bian +s (of Lesbos)
les|bian +s (homosexual)
les|bian|ism
Les|bos (island, Greece)
lèse-majesté
lese-majesty (= *lèse-majesté*)
le|sion +s
le|sioned
Le|so|tho (country, Africa)
less
les|see +s
les|see|ship +s
less|en +s +ed +ing (diminish)
[☞ lesson]
Les|seps, Fer|di|nand Marie, Vi|comte de (French diplomat)
less|er (not so great)
[☞ lessor]
lesser-known
Les|sing, Doris May (English writer)
Les|sing, Gott|hold Eph|raim (German writer)
les|son +s +ed +ing (teaching; instruction)
[☞ lessen]
les|sor +s (person who lets property by lease)
[☞ lesser]
lest
let
lets
let
let|ting
[☞ Lett, LETS]
let down *verb*
lets down
let down
let|ting down
let|down +s *noun*
leth|al
leth|al|ity

leth|al|ly
leth|ar|gic
leth|ar|gic|ally
leth|argy
Leth|bridge (city, Canada)
Lethe (mythical river; forgetfulness)
Lethe|an
Le|ticia (city, Colombia)
Leto (*Greek Myth*)
let off *verb*
lets off
let off
let|ting off
let-off +s *noun*
le tout
let out *verb*
lets out
let out
let|ting out
let-out +s *noun*
LETS (Local Exchange Trading System)
let's (let us)
[☞ LETS]
Lett +s (Latvian)
let|ter +s +ed +ing
let|ter box (mailbox)
let|ter boxes
letter|box (*Film*)
letter|box|es
letter|boxed
letter|box|ing
letter|boxed *adjective*
letter|box|ing *noun*
let|tered *adjective*
letter|form +s
letter|head +s
letter|ing +s *noun*
letter|man
letter|men
letter-perfect
letter|press
letter|press|es
letter-quality
let|ters of marque
let|ters pat|ent
Let|tish
let|tuce +s
let up *verb*
lets up
let up
let|ting up
let-up +s *noun*
leu (Romanian currency)
lei
[☞ lieu]
leu|cine +s
leuc|o|cyte +s (*use* leukocyte)

leuc|o|cyt|ic (*use* leukocytic)
leuc|o|cyt|o|sis (*use* leukocytosis)
leuc|o|cyt|o|ses
leuc|oma +s (*use* leukoma)
leuc|o|penia (*use* leukopenia)
leuc|or|rhea
leuc|or|rhoea (*use* leucorrhea)
leuc|o|sis (*use* leukosis)
leuc|ot|omy
leuc|ot|omies
leuk|emia +s
leuk|emic
leuk|o|cyte +s
leuk|o|cyt|ic
leuk|o|cyt|o|sis
leuk|o|cyt|o|ses
leuk|oma +s
leuk|o|penia
leuk|o|sis
leuk|o|tri|ene +s
Leu|ven (town, Belgium)
lev
leva
Le|vant (E Mediterranean)
Le|vant|er +s (of the Levant)
le|vant|er +s (wind)
Le|vant|ine +s
le|va|tor +s
levee +s (reception, assembly; embankment)
[☞ levy, Levi]
level
lev|els
lev|elled
level|ling
level-headed
level-headed|ly
level-headed|ness
Level|ler +s (17th-c. dissenter)
level|ler +s (*in general use*)
level|ly
level|ness
lever +s +ed +ing (handle; pry bar; lift)
[☞ leaver]
lever-action
lever|age
lever|ages
lever|aged
lever|aging
lever|aged *adjective*

lev|er|et +s
Lever|ku|sen (city, Germany)
Le Ver|rier, Ur|bain Jean Jo|seph (French astronomer)
Lé|vesque, René (Cdn politician)
Levi (*Bible*)
Levi, Carlo (Italian writer)
[☞ levee, levy]
Levi, Primo (Italian writer & chemist)
[☞ levee, levy]
levi|able
le|via|than +s
levi|gate
levi|gates
levi|gat|ed
levi|gat|ing
levi|ga|tion +s
lev|in +s (lightning)
[☞ leaven]
levir|ate
levir|at|ic
levir|at|ic|al
Lévis (city, Canada)
Lévis, François-Gaston de (French officer in New France)
Lévi-Strauss, Claude (French social anthropologist)
levi|tate
levi|tates
levi|tat|ed
levi|tat|ing
levi|ta|tion +s
levi|ta|tor +s
Le|vite +s
Le|vit|ical
Le|vit|icus (*Bible*)
lev|ity
levo|do|pa
levo|rota|tory
levu|lose
levy (collect taxes etc.; enlist troops; wage war; collection)
lev|ies
lev|ied
levy|ing
[☞ levee, Levi]
lewd (lecherous, obscene)
[☞ 'lude]
lewd|ly
lewd|ness
Lewes (town, England)
[☞ Lewis]

Lewis (island, Scotland; surname)
[☞ Lewes, Louis]
Lewis, Clive Sta|ples (British writer)
Lewis, David (Cdn politician)
Lewis, Fred|erick Carle|ton ('Carl') (US athlete)
Lewis, (Harry) Sin|clair (US novelist)
Lewis, Jerry Lee (US musician)
Lewis, Mat|thew Greg|ory (English writer)
Lewis, Meri|weth|er (US explorer)
Lewis, (Percy) Wynd|ham (English writer & artist)
lewis (lifting device)
lew|is|es
Lewis and Har|ris (= Lewis with Harris, Scotland)
Lewis gun +s
lewis|ite +s
Lewis with Har|ris (island, Scotland)
lex|eme +s
lex|ical
lex|ical|ly
lexi|cog|raph|er +s
lexi|co|graph|ic
lexi|co|graph|ical
lexi|co|graph|ical|ly
lexi|cog|raphy
lex|ico|logic|al
lex|ico|logic|ally
lexi|col|o|gist +s
lexi|col|ogy
lexi|con +s
Lex|ing|ton (battle site & city, US)
lexis
lex loci
lex tali|onis
ley +s (land sown with grass; line between prehistoric sites)
[☞ lay, lei, Leh, lea, lee]
Ley|den (= Leiden, the Netherlands)
Ley|den jar +s
ley line +s
Ley|rac, Mo|nique (Cdn performer)
Leyte (island, the Philippines)

lez|zie +s *offensive*
Lhasa +s (capital of Tibet; dog)
[☞ Lassa fever]
Lhasa Apso +s
lia|bil|ity
lia|bil|ities
li|able
li|aise
li|ais|es
li|aised
li|ais|ing
li|aison +s
li|ana +s
li|ane +s (*use* liana)
Liao (dynasty & river, China)
Liao|dong (peninsula, China)
Liao|ning (province, China)
liar +s (one who lies)
[☞ lyre]
Liard (river, Canada)
Lias (Jurassic strata)
[☞ Laius]
lias (blue limestone)
Lias|sic
li|at|ris
   plural li|at|ris
Lib +s (Liberal)
lib +s (liberal; liberation)
li|ba|tion +s
lib|ber +s
Libby, Wil|lard Frank (US chemist)
libel
li|bels
li|belled
li|bel|ling
li|bel|ler +s
li|bel|lous
li|bel|lous|ly
li|bel|ous (*use* libellous)
li|bel|ous|ly (*use* libellously)
Lib|erace (US pianist)
Lib|er|al +s (of the Liberal Party)
lib|er|al +s (*in general use*)
Liberal-Conserva|tive Party
Lib|eral|ism (principles of a Liberal Party)
lib|eral|ism (*in general use*)
lib|eral|ity
lib|eral|iz|a|tion +s

lib|eral|ize
lib|eral|iz|es
lib|eral|ized
lib|eral|iz|ing
lib|eral|iz|er +s
lib|eral|ly
lib|eral|ness
lib|er|ate
lib|er|ates
lib|er|at|ed
lib|er|at|ing
lib|er|at|ed *adjective*
lib|er|ation +s
lib|er|ation|ist +s
lib|er|ator +s
lib|er|atory
Li|beria (country, Africa)
Li|ber|ian +s
lib|er|tar|ian +s
lib|er|tar|ian|ism
lib|er|tin|age
lib|er|tine +s
lib|er|tin|ism
lib|er|ty
lib|er|ties
Lib|er|ty ship +s
li|bid|in|al
li|bid|in|al|ly
li|bid|in|ous
li|bid|in|ous|ly
li|bid|in|ous|ness
li|bi|do +s
Li Bo (= Li Po, Chinese poet)
Lib|ra +s (constellation; Zodiac)
Lib|ran +s
li|brar|ian +s
li|brar|ian|ship +s
li|brary
li|brar|ies
li|bra|tion +s
li|bret|tist +s
li|bret|to
li|bret|tos or li|bret|ti
Libre|ville (capital of Gabon)
Lib|rium *proprietary*
Libya (country, Africa)
Liby|an +s
lice *plural of* louse
li|cence +s *noun* (for verb use license)
li|cenced *adjective* (*use* licensed)
li|cence plate +s
li|cens|able
li|cense *verb*
li|cens|es

li|censed
li|cens|ing
[☞ licence *noun*]
li|censed *adjective*
li|cen|see +s
li|cen|sor +s
li|cen|sure
li|cen|tiate +s
li|cen|tious
li|cen|tious|ly
li|cen|tious|ness
li|chee +s (*use* lychee)
li|chen +s (plant organism; skin disease)
li|chened *adjective*
li|chen|ol|ogy
li|chen|ous
Lich|ten|stein, Roy (US artist)
[☞ Liechtenstein]
licit
licit|ly
lick +s +ed +ing
lick|er +s (one who licks)
[☞ liquor]
licker|ish (lecherous; covetous; fond of food)
[☞ licorice]
lickety-split
lick|ing +s *noun*
lick|spit|tle +s
lic|o|rice +s (plant extract; candy)
[☞ lickerish]
lic|tor +s
lid +s
lid|ded
lid|less
Lido (town, Italy)
lido +s (pool; beach)
lido|caine
Lido (di Mala|moc|co) (island reef, Adriatic)
Lie, Tryg|ve Halv|dan (UN secretary-general)
[☞ Lee, Leigh]
lie
• (be horizontal; rest flat; be situated; be admissible or sustainable; *Golf*; hiding place)
lies
lay
lain
lying
• (tell falsehoods; be

deceptive)
lies
lied
lying
[☞ lye]
Lieb|frau|milch +s
Liebig, Jus|tus von, Baron (German chemist & educator)
Lieb|knecht, Karl (German socialist leader)
Liech|ten|stein (Alpine principality)
[☞ Lichtenstein]
Liech|ten|stein|er +s
lied[1] (song)
lied|er
[☞ lead]
lied[2] *past & past participle of* lie
lied|er (songs)
lie down *verb*
lies down
lay down
lain down
lying down
lie-down +s *noun*
lief (gladly, willingly)
[☞ Leif Ericsson]
Liège (province & its capital, Belgium)
liege +s
lie in *verb*
lies in
lay in
lain in
lying in
lie-in +s *noun*
lien +s (right over another's property to protect a debt)
[☞ lean]
lieu (in 'lieu time', 'in lieu of')
lieu|ten|ancy
lieu|ten|an|cies
lieu|ten|ant +s
lieu|tenant-govern|or +s
LIF (life income fund)
LIFs
life
lives
life-and-death
life|belt +s
life|blood
life|boat +s
life|buoy +s
life cycle +s
life force +s
life form +s
life-giving

life|guard +s (at a pool etc.)
Life Guards (British regiment)
life jack|et +s
life|less
life|less|ly
life|less|ness
life|like
life|like|ness
life|line +s
life list +s
life|long
life-or-death
life pre|serv|er +s
lif|er +s
life raft +s
life|saver +s
life-saving
life-size (= life-sized)
life-sized
life|span +s
life|style +s
life-support
life's work
life-threaten|ing
life|time +s
life|way +s
Lif|fey (river, Ireland)
Lif|ford (town, Ireland)
lift +s +ed +ing
lift|able
lift|er +s
lift off verb
  lifts off
  lift|ed off
  lift|ing off
lift|off +s noun
lig
  ligs
  ligged
  lig|ging
liga|ment +s
liga|ment|al
liga|ment|ary
liga|ment|ous
lig|and +s
lig|ase
li|gate
  li|gates
  li|gat|ed
  li|gat|ing
li|ga|tion +s (surgical tie)
  [☞ legation]
liga|ture
  liga|tures
  liga|tured
  liga|tur|ing
li|ger +s (lion-tiger cross)
lig|ger +s (loafer)

light
• (ignite; illuminate; visible radiation; window; bright)
  lights
  lit
  lit or light|ed
  light|ing
  light|er
  light|est
• (find by chance; descend or land on; lay into; head out; of little weight)
  lights
  lit or light|ed
  light|ing
  light|er
  light|est
  [☞ lite]
light box
  light boxes
light bulb +s
light-emitting
light|en +s +ed +ing
light|en|er +s
light|en|ing
  conjugated form of lighten
  [☞ lightning]
light|er +s
light|er|age
lighter-than-air
  adjective preceding a noun
light|fast
light|fast|ness
light-fingered
Light|foot, Gor|don Mere|dith (Cdn singer-songwriter)
light-footed
light-footed|ly
light-handed
light-headed
light-headed|ly
light-headed|ness
light|heart|ed
light|heart|ed|ly
light|heart|ed|ness
light|house +s
light|ing noun
light|ish
light|keep|er +s
light|less
light|ly
light|ness
light|ning (electric discharge; quick)
  [☞ lightening]
light|ning bug +s
light|ning rod +s
light pen +s

light|proof
lights (lungs)
light|ship +s
light|some
light|some|ly
light|some|ness
light|speed
light|weight +s
light|wood +s
light-year +s
lig|neous
lig|ni|fi|ca|tion +s
lig|ni|fy
  lig|ni|fies
  lig|ni|fied
  lig|ni|fy|ing
lig|nin +s
lig|nite +s
lig|nit|ic
lig|no|caine
lig|num vitae
lig|roin
lig|ul|ate
lig|ule +s
Li|gu|ria (region, Italy)
Li|gu|rian +s (people, language; sea)
li|gus|trum +s
lik|abil|ity (use likeability)
lik|able (use likeable)
lik|able|ness (use likeableness)
lik|ably (use likeably)
like
  likes
  liked
  lik|ing
like|abil|ity
like|able
like|able|ness
like|ably
like|li|hood
like|li|ness
like|ly
  like|li|er
  like|li|est
like-minded
like-minded|ly
like-minded|ness
lik|en +s +ed +ing (compare)
  [☞ lichen]
like|ness
  like|ness|es
like|wise
lik|ing +s noun
Likud
li|kuta
  ma|kuta
li'l
lilac +s

lilan|geni
  ema|lan|geni
L'Île-Perrot (town, Canada)
lili|aceous
Lili|en|thal, Otto (German aviation pioneer)
Lil|ith (Jewish Myth)
Liliu|oka|lani, Lydia Kame|ke|ha (Hawaiian queen)
Lille (city, France)
Lil|li|put
Lil|li|pu|tian +s
Lil|loo|et (people, language; river, Canada)
  plural Lil|loo|et or Lil|loo|ets
Li|lon|gwe (capital of Malawi)
lilt +s +ed +ing
lilt|ing adjective
lily
  lil|ies
  [☞ Lyly]
lily-like
lily-livered
lily of the val|ley
  lil|ies of the val|ley
lily pad +s
lily-white
Lima (capital of Peru)
lima bean +s
Lim|as|sol (city, Cyprus)
limb +s +ed +ing (arm, leg, branch; component; Astronomy; Botany)
  [☞ limn]
limbed adjective
lim|ber +s +ed +ing
lim|ber|ness
lim|bic
limb|less
lim|bo +s
Lim|burg (provinces, Belgium & the Netherlands)
Lim|burg|er +s
lime
  limes
  limed
  liming
  [☞ Lyme disease, lyme grass]
lime grass (use lyme grass)
lime green +s (lime-green when preceding a noun)

lime|light
Lim|erick (county & town, Ireland)
lim|erick +s (verse)
lime|stone +s
lime|wash
lime|wash|es
lime water
Limey +s *offensive* (British)
[☞ limy]
limi|er
limi|est
lim|inal
limi|nal|ity
lim|it +s +ed +ing
lim|it|able
lim|it|a|tion +s
lim|it|a|tive
Lim|it|ed (after company names)
lim|it|ed *adjective*
lim|it|ed edi|tion +s (limited-edition *when preceding a noun*)
lim|it|ed|ness
lim|it|er +s
lim|it|ing *adjective*
lim|it|less
lim|it|less|ly
lim|it|less|ness
limn +s +ed +ing (draw, portray; illuminate; represent)
[☞ limb]
lim|ner +s
lim|no|logic|al
lim|nol|o|gist +s
lim|nol|o|gy
limo +s
Li|moges (city, France; porcelain)
Limón (city, Costa Rica)
limon|ite
Li|mou|sin +s (region, France; cattle)
[☞ limousine]
lim|ou|sine +s (car, bus)
[☞ Limousin]
limp +s +ed +ing
lim|pet +s
lim|pid
lim|pid|ity
lim|pid|ly
lim|pid|ness
limp|ing|ly
limp|kin +s
limp|ly
limp|ness

Lim|po|po (river, Africa)
limp-wristed
limy (of or like lime)
limi|er
limi|est
[☞ Limey]
linage +s (number of lines)
Lin Biao (Chinese statesman)
LINC (Language Instruction for Newcomers to Canada)
[☞ link]
linch|pin +s
Lin|coln (cities, US, England & Canada)
Lin|coln, Abra|ham (US president)
Lin|coln green (Lincoln-green *when preceding a noun*)
Lin|coln|shire (county, England)
linc|tus
linc|tus|es
Lind, James (Scottish physician)
Lind, Jenny (Swedish soprano)
lin|dane
Lind|bergh, Charles Au|gus|tus (US aviator)
Lin|de|mann, Fred|erick Alex|an|der (1st Viscount Cherwell, German-born physicist)
lin|den +s
Lin|dis|farne (island, England)
Lind|say (town, Canada)
[☞ linsey-woolsey]
Lind|say, (Nicho|las) Va|chel (US poet)
lindy
lin|dies
lin|died
lindy|ing
lindy hop
lindy hops
lindy hopped
lindy hop|ping
line
lines
lined
lining
lin|eage (ancestry)
[☞ linage]

lin|eal
lin|eal|ly
linea|ment +s
linear
Linear A
Linear B
linear|ity
linear|ities
linear|ize
linear|iz|es
linear|ized
linear|iz|ing
linear|ly
line art
linea|tion +s
line|back|er +s
line break +s
line-bred
line-breeding
line dance
line dan|ces
line danced
line dan|cing
line dan|cer +s
line dan|cing *noun*
line draw|ing
line drive +s
line-feed +s
Line Islands (in the Pacific)
line-item veto
line-item vetoes
line|man
line|men
line|mate +s
lin|en +s
lin|en|fold
line out *verb*
lines out
lined out
lining out
line-out +s *noun*
liner +s
liner|board
liner notes
line|score +s
lines|man
lines|men
line squall +s
line up *verb*
lines up
lined up
lining up
line|up +s *noun*
ling
plural ling
lin|ga +s
lin|gam +s
ling cod
plural ling cod
lin|ger +s +ed +ing
lin|ger|er +s
linge|rie

lin|ger|ing|ly
lingo
lin|gos or lin|goes
lingon|berry
lingon|ber|ries
lin|gua fran|ca +s
lin|gual
lin|gual|ly
lin|gui|form
lin|gui|ne
lin|gui|ni (*use* linguine)
lin|guist +s
lin|guis|tic
lin|guis|tic|ally
lin|guis|tics
lin|hay +s (*use* linny)
lini|er *comparative of* liny
[☞ linear]
lini|est
lini|ment +s
lining +s *noun*
link +s +ed +ing
[☞ LINC]
link|age +s
link|er +s
Lin|kö|ping (town, Sweden)
links (golf course)
[☞ lynx]
link up *verb*
links up
linked up
link|ing up
link-up +s *noun*
Lin|naean
Lin|naeus, Caro|lus (Swedish botanist)
Lin|nean (= Linnaean)
lin|net +s
lin|ney +s (*use* linny)
linny
lin|nies
lino +s
lino|cut +s
lino|cut|ting
Li|no|la *proprietary*
lino|leic acid
lino|len|ic acid
li|no|leum +s
li|no|leumed
Lino|type +s *proprietary*
Lin Piao (= Lin Biao, Chinese statesman)
lin|sang +s
lin|seed
linsey-woolsey +s (fabric)
[☞ Lindsay]
lin|stock +s

lint
lin|tel +s
lint|er +s
linty
liny
  lini|er
  lini|est
Linz (city, Austria)
Lion (constellation; Zodiac)
lion +s
lion|ess
  lion|ess|es
lion-hearted
lion|iz|a|tion +s
lion|ize
  lion|iz|es
  lion|ized
  lion|iz|ing
lion|iz|er +s
lion-like
Lions Club
Lions Gate Bridge (in Canada)
lion's share +s
lip
  lips
  lipped
  lip|ping
Lip|ari (islands, Italy)
lip|ase +s
lip balm +s
lip brush
  lip brush|es
Lip|chitz, Jacques (French sculptor)
Li|petsk (city, Russia)
lip gloss
  lip gloss|es
lip|id +s
lipid|o|sis
  lipid|o|ses
Lip|iz|zan|er +s (use Lippizaner)
lip|less
lip|like
lip|liner +s
Li Po (Chinese poet)
lip|oid
lipoid|o|sis (use lipidosis)
  lipoid|o|ses
lipo|pro|tein +s
lipo|some +s
lipo|suc|tion +s
lipped adjective
Lippi, Fil|ip|pi|no (Italian painter)
Lippi, Fra Filip|po (Italian painter)
Lip|pi|zan +s (use Lippizaner)
Lip|pi|zan|er +s

Lipp|mann, Gab|riel Jonas (French physicist)
lippy
  lip|pi|er
  lip|pi|est
  [☞ Lippi]
lip-read
  lip-reads
  lip-read
  lip-reading
lip-reader +s
lip-reading noun
lip-smacking
lip|stick +s
lip|sticked
lip-sync +s +ed +ing (use lip-synch)
lip-syncer +s (use lip-syncher)
lip-synch +s +ed +ing
lip-syncher +s
lip-synching noun
lip-syncing noun (use lip-synching)
li|quate
  li|quates
  li|quat|ed
  li|quat|ing
li|qua|tion
li|que|fa|cient +s
li|que|fac|tion +s
li|que|fac|tive
li|que|fi|able
li|que|fier +s
li|que|fy
  li|que|fies
  li|que|fied
  li|que|fy|ing
li|ques|cent
li|queur +s (flavoured spirit)
  [☞ liquor]
li|quid +s
li|quid|am|bar +s
li|quid|ate
  li|quid|ates
  li|quid|ated
  li|quid|at|ing
li|quid|a|tion +s
li|quid|ator +s
liquid-cooled
li|quid crys|tal
  dis|play +s
li|quid|ity
  li|quid|ities
li|quid|ize
  li|quid|iz|es
  li|quid|ized
  li|quid|iz|ing
li|quid|izer +s
li|quid|ly

li|quid|ness
li|quidy
li|qui|fi|able (use liquefiable)
li|qui|fier +s (use liquefier)
li|qui|fy (use liquefy)
  li|qui|fies
  li|qui|fied
  li|qui|fy|ing
li|quor +s +ed +ing (distilled spirit)
  [☞ licker, liqueur]
li|quor|ice +s (plant extract, candy: use licorice)
  [☞ lickerish]
li|quor|ish (lecherous, covetous, fond of food: use lickerish)
  [☞ licorice]
LIRA (locked-in retirement account)
  LIRAs
  [☞ Lyra]
lira (currency)
  lire
  [☞ Lyra]
Lis|bon (capital of Portugal)
li|sente
Lis|gar, Sir John Young, Baron (governor general of Canada)
lisle
Lis|mer, Ar|thur (Cdn painter)
lisp +s +ed +ing
lisp|er +s
lisp|ing adjective & noun
lisp|ing|ly
lis|som (use lissome)
lis|some
  lis|some|ly
  lis|some|ness
list +s +ed +ing
  [☞ Liszt]
list|able
list|ed adjective
lis|ten +s +ed +ing
  [☞ Liston]
lis|ten|abil|ity
lis|ten|able
lis|ten|er +s
lis|ten|er|ship +s
lis|ten|ing +s noun
Lis|ter, Jo|seph, 1st Baron (English surgeon)
list|er +s
lis|teria +s

lis|teri|osis
list|ing +s noun & adjective
list|less
list|lessly
list|less|ness
Lis|ton, Charles ('Sonny') (US boxer)
Lis|towel (town, Canada)
list|serv +s
Liszt, Franz (Hungarian composer)
lit
Li T'ai Po (= Li Po, Chinese poet)
lit|any
  lit|anies
litchi +s (use lychee)
lit crit
Lite +s proprietary (lite products)
lite +s (over-simplified; in commercial use: low-calorie or low-fat food or drink; courtesy light)
  [☞ light, lights]
lit|eracy
lit|eral +s (to the letter; misprint)
  [☞ littoral]
lit|eral|ism
lit|eral|ist +s
lit|eral|is|tic
lit|eral|ity
lit|eral|ize
  lit|eral|iz|es
  lit|eral|ized
  lit|eral|iz|ing
lit|eral|ly
literal-minded
lit|eral|ness
lit|er|ar|ily
lit|er|ar|i|ness
lit|er|ary
lit|er|ary crit|ic +s
literary-critical
lit|er|ate +s
lit|er|ate|ly
lit|er|ati
lit|er|atim
lit|er|a|ture +s (literary works)
  [☞ littérateur]
lith|arge
lithe
  lith|er
  lith|est
lithe|ly
lithe|ness

lithe|some
lith|ia
lith|ic
lithi|fi|ca|tion +s
lithi|fied *adjective*
lith|ify
　lithi|fies
　lithi|fied
　lithi|fy|ing
lith|ium
litho
● *noun*
　lithos
● *verb*
　lithoes
　lithoed
　litho|ing
litho|graph +s +ed
　+ing
lith|og|raph|er +s
litho|graph|ic
litho|graph|ic|ally
lith|og|raphy
　lith|og|raph|ies
litho|logic
litho|logic|al
litho|logic|ally
lith|ol|ogy
　lith|ol|o|gies
litho|phyte +s
litho|pone
litho|sphere
litho|spher|ic
lith|ot|om|ist +s
lith|ot|omy
　lith|ot|omies
litho|tripsy
　litho|trip|sies
litho|trip|ter +s
Lithu|ania (country,
　Europe)
Lithu|an|ian +s
lit|ig|able
liti|gant +s
liti|gate
　liti|gates
　liti|gated
　liti|gat|ing
liti|ga|tion +s
liti|ga|tor +s
liti|gious
liti|gious|ly
liti|gious|ness
lit|mus
li|to|tes
litre +s
lit|ter +s +ed +ing
lit|té|ra|teur +s
　(literary person)
　[☞ literature]
litter|bug +s
lit|ter|er +s
litter|mate +s

lit|tle
　lit|tler
　lit|tlest
Lit|tle Big|horn
　(battle site, US)
little-bitty
lit|tle known (little-
　known *when
　preceding a noun*)
little|leaf
little|neck +s
little|ness
Lit|tle Rock (city, US)
Lit|tle Rus|sian +s
　(Ukrainian)
lit|toral +s (shore)
　[☞ literal]
Lit|tré, (Maxi|mi|lien)
　Paul Émile (French
　lexicographer)
li|tur|gic|al
li|tur|gic|al|ly
li|tur|gics
lit|ur|gist +s
lit|urgy
　lit|ur|gies
Liu|chow (= Liuzhou)
Liu|zhou (city, China)
liv|abil|ity
liv|able
liv|able|ness
live
　lives
　lived
　liv|ing
live|abil|ity (*use
　livability*)
live|able (*use* livable)
live|able|ness (*use
　livableness*)
live-aboard +s *noun
　& adjective*
live action (live-
　action *when
　preceding a noun*)
lived-in *adjective*
live in *verb*
　lives in
　lived in
　liv|ing in
live-in +s *adjective &
　noun*
live|li|hood +s
liveli|ly
live|li|ness
live|long +s
live|ly
　live|li|er
　live|li|est
liven +s +ed +ing
live|ness

live out *verb*
　lives out
　lived out
　liv|ing out
live-out *adjective*
liv|er +s
liv|er|ied
liv|er|ish
liv|er|ish|ness
Liver|pool (city,
　England)
Liver|pud|lian +s
liver spots
liver|spotted
liver|wort +s (plant)
liver|wurst (sausage)
liv|ery
　liv|eries
livery|man
　livery|men
lives
Live|say, Dor|othy
　(Cdn writer)
live|stock
live trap +s *noun*
live-trap *verb*
　live-traps
　live-trapped
　live-trapping
live weight +s
live|well +s
live wire +s
live|yer +s (*use* livyer)
livid
livid|ity
livid|ly
livid|ness
liv|ing +s *noun &
　adjective*
liv|ing room +s
Living|stone (*former
　name for* Maramba,
　Zambia)
Living|stone, David
　(Scottish missionary
　& explorer)
Li|vo|nia (region,
　Europe)
Li|vo|nian +s
Li|vor|no (city, Italy)
livre +s
Livy (Roman
　historian)
liv|yer +s
lix|ivi|ate
　lix|ivi|ates
　lix|ivi|ated
　lix|ivi|ating
lix|ivi|ation
Liz|ard (promontory,
　England)
liz|ard +s

Ljub|lja|na (capital of
　Slovenia)
llama +s (animal)
　[☞ lama]
Llan|dud|no (town,
　Wales)
lla|nero +s
llano +s
Llew|elyn (prince of
　Wales)
Llosa, Jorge Mario
　Pedro Var|gas
　(Peruvian writer)
Lloyd, Gwen|eth (Cdn
　ballet director)
Lloyd, Har|old
　Clay|ton (US
　comedian)
Lloyd George, David
　(1st Earl Lloyd
　George of Dwyfor,
　English prime
　minister)
Lloyd|min|ster (city,
　Canada)
Lloyd's (underwriters)
Lloyd's Regis|ter
Lloyd Web|ber, Sir
　An|drew (English
　composer)
Llyw|elyn ap
　Gruf|fydd
　(= Llewelyn)
LM (lunar module)
　LMs
LNB (low noise
　blocker)
　LNBs
lo (interjection; *in
　commercial use*: not
　high)
　[☞ low, Loewe, Lot
　River]
Loach, Ken|neth
　('Ken') (English
　filmmaker)
loach
　plural loach *or*
　loach|es
load +s +ed +ing
　(burden; weight
　carried or borne;
　electric power)
　[☞ lode]
load|able
load-bearing
load cell +s
load|ed *adjective*
load|er +s
load|ing +s *noun*
load|master +s
load|star +s (*use*
　lodestar)

load|stone +s (*use* lodestone)
loaf
• *noun*
loaves
• *verb*
loafs
loafed
loaf|ing
Loaf|er +s *proprietary* (shoe)
loaf|er +s (idler)
loaf|ing *noun & adjective*
loam +s
loam|i|ness
loamy
loan +s +ed +ing (lend; something lent)
[☞ lone]
loan|able
loan|er +s (a thing lent; lender)
[☞ loner]
loan shark +s
loan|shark|ing
loan word +s
loath (reluctant)
loathe (detest)
loathes
loathed
loath|ing
loath|er +s
loath|ing *noun*
loath|some
loath|some|ly
loath|some|ness
loaves
lob
lobs
lobbed
lob|bing
Loba|chev|ski, Niko|lai Ivan|ovich (Russian mathematician)
lobar
lob|ate
lob|a|tion
lob|by
lob|bies
lob|bied
lob|by|ing
lob|by|ing *noun & adjective*
lob|by|ist +s
lobe +s (*Anatomy*)
[☞ Loeb]
lob|ec|tomy
lob|ec|to|mies
lobed *adjective*
lobe|less

lo|belia +s
Lo|bito (city, Angola)
Lobo +s
lob|ot|om|ize
lob|ot|om|izes
lob|ot|om|ized
lob|ot|om|iz|ing
lob|ot|om|ized *adjective*
lob|ot|omy
lob|ot|omies
lob|scouse
lob|ster +s +ed +ing
lob|ster|ing *noun*
lob|ster|man
lob|ster|men
lob|tail +s +ed +ing
lob|tail|ing *noun*
lob|ular
lob|ulate
lob|ule +s
lo|cal +s (of a particular area; resident)
[☞ locale]
local area net|work
lo|cale +s (scene, locality)
local|ism +s
local|ity
local|ities
local|iz|able
local|iz|a|tion +s
local|ize
local|iz|es
local|ized
local|iz|ing
local|ized *adjective*
local|iz|er +s
local|ly
local|ness
Lo|car|no (resort, Switzerland)
lo|cat|able
lo|cate
lo|cates
lo|cat|ed
lo|cat|ing
lo|ca|tion +s
lo|ca|tion|al
loca|tive +s
lo|ca|tor +s
loch +s (Scottish lake)
[☞ lough, lakh]
lochia +s
loch|ial
Loch Lo|mond (lake, Scotland)
Loch Morar (lake, Scotland)
Loch Ness (lake, Scotland)

loci
• *plural of* locus
• (engine)
locis
[☞ Loki]
loci clas|si|ci
locie +s (= loci: engine)
Lock, Édouard (Cdn choreographer)
[☞ Locke]
lock +s +ed +ing (security device; canal section; curl of hair; tuft)
[☞ loch, lough, lakh, lox]
lock|able
lock|down +s
Locke, John (English philosopher)
[☞ Lock]
Lock|ean
locked-in *adjective*
lock|er +s
Lock|er|bie (town, Scotland)
lock|er room +s (locker-room *when preceding a noun*)
lock|et +s
lock|jaw
lock|less
lock|nut +s
lock out *verb*
locks out
locked out
lock|ing out
lock|out +s *noun*
lock|smith +s
lock|smith|ing
lock|step *noun*
lock-step *adjective*
lock stitch
lock stitch|es
lock, stock, and bar|rel
lock up *verb*
locks up
locked up
lock|ing up
lock-up +s *noun*
Lock|yer, Sir Jo|seph Nor|man (English astronomer)
loco +s
loco|motion
loco|motive +s
loco|motor +s
loco|weed +s
locu|lar
locu|lus
locu|li

lo|cum +s
locum ten|ens
locum ten|en|tes
locus
loci
locus clas|si|cus
loci clas|si|ci
locus stan|di
lo|cust +s
lo|cu|tion +s
lo|cu|tion|ary
lode (vein of ore; rich source or supply)
[☞ load]
lo|den +s
lode|star +s
lode|stone +s
Lodge, David (John) (English writer)
Lodge, Sir Oli|ver Jo|seph (English physicist)
Lodge, Thom|as (English writer)
lodge (inn, house)
lodg|es
lodged
lodg|ing
[☞ loge]
lodge|ment +s
lodge|pole +s
lodg|er +s
lodg|ing +s *noun*
lodg|ment +s (*use* lodgement)
lodi|cule +s
lods et ventes
Łódź (city, Poland)
Loeb, Jacques (US biologist)
loess
loess|ial
Loewe, Fred|erick (US composer)
[☞ Low, Lot River]
Loewi, Otto (US pharmacologist & physiologist)
Lo|fo|ten (islands, Norway)
loft +s +ed +ing
loft|ed *adjective*
loft|i|ly
loft|i|ness
lofty
loft|i|er
loft|i|est
log
logs
logged
log|ging
Logan (mountain, Canada)

lo|gan +s
logan|berry
  logan|ber|ries
loga|rithm +s
loga|rith|mic
loga|rith|mic|ally
log|book +s
log boom +s
log drive +s
log driv|er +s
log dump +s
loge +s (theatre
  seating)
  [☞ lodge]
logged-off
logged-out
logged-over
log|ger +s (Forestry)
  [☞ lager, laager,
  lager lout]
log|ger|head +s
log|gia +s
log|ging noun
logic +s
logic|al
logic|al|ity
logic|al|ly
logi|cian +s
logi|er
logi|est
log in verb
  logs in
  logged in
  log|ging in
log-in +s noun
logis|tic
logis|tic|al
logis|tic|ally
logis|tics
log-jam +s
logo +s
logo|cen|tric
logo|cen|trism
logo|gram +s
log|om|achy
  log|om|ach|ies
log on verb
  logs on
  logged on
  log|ging on
log-on +s noun
log|or|rhea
Logos
logo|type +s
log-roll +s +ed +ing
log-roller +s
log-rolling noun
Lo|groño (town,
  Spain)
log|wood

logy
  logi|er
  logi|est
loin +s
loin|cloth +s
Loire (river, France)
loi|ter +s +ed +ing
loi|ter|er +s
Loki (Scandinavian
  Myth)
  [☞ loci]
loll +s +ed +ing
Lol|land (island,
  Denmark)
lol|la|pa|looza +s
Lol|lard +s
Lol|lard|ism
lol|li|pop +s
lol|lop +s +ed +ing
lolly
  lol|lies
lol|ly|gag (use
  lallygag)
  lol|ly|gags
  lol|ly|gagged
  lol|ly|gag|ging
Lomax, Alan (US
  ethnomusicologist)
Lom|bard, Peter
  (Italian theologian)
Lom|bard +s
Lom|bar|di, Vin|cent
  Thom|as ('Vince')
  (US football coach)
Lom|bard|ic
Lom|bar|do, Guy
  (Cdn bandleader)
Lom|bard Street
Lom|bar|dy (region,
  Italy; poplar)
Lom|bok (island,
  Indonesia)
Lom|bro|so, Cesare
  (Italian
  criminologist)
Lomé (capital of Togo)
lo|ment +s
lomen|ta|ceous
lo|men|tum +s
Lo|mond (loch,
  Scotland)
Lon|don (cities,
  England & Canada)
Lon|don, Jack (US
  novelist)
Lon|don|derry
  (county & city,
  Northern Ireland)
Lon|don|er +s
lone (solitary;
  uninhabited)
  [☞ loan]
lone|li|ness

lone|ly
  lone|li|er
  lone|li|est
loner +s (solitary
  person)
  [☞ loaner]
lone|some
lone|some|ly
lone|some|ness
Long, Craw|ford
  Wil|liam|son (US
  physician)
long +er +est +s +ed
  +ing
long ago adverb
long-ago adjective
long-awaited
Long Beach (city, US)
long|boat +s
long|bow +s
long car +s
long cart +s
long-case clock +s
long-chain adjective
long-dated
long-day
long-dead adjective
  preceding a noun
long dis|tance +s
  noun
long-distance
  adjective & adverb
long-drawn
long-drawn-out
longe (Horse Riding:
  use lunge)
  longes
  longed
  longe|ing
long|er +s
  (comparative of long;
  pole)
  [☞ longueur]
lon|ger|on +s
lon|gev|ity
lon|gev|ities
long-faced
Long|fel|low, Henry
  Wads|worth (US
  poet)
Long|ford (county &
  town, Ireland)
long gone (long-gone
  when preceding a
  noun)
long|hair +s
long|hand
long haul +s (long-
  haul when preceding
  a noun)
long-headed
long-headed|ness
long|horn +s

long|house +s
longi|corn +s
long|ing +s noun &
  adjective
long|ing|ly
Lon|gi|nus (ancient
  Greek scholar)
long|ish
Long Island (island,
  US)
longi|tude +s
longi|tud|in|al
longi|tud|in|ally
long john +s
long jump +s
long-jumper +s
long-lasting
long-legged
long-life adjective
long|line +s
long|liner +s
long|lining
long-lived
long-lost
long lot +s
Long March (Chinese
  History)
long march
  long march|es
long neck +s
long-playing
Long Point (spit,
  Canada)
long-range adjective
Long Range
  Moun|tains
  (mountain range,
  Canada)
long-run adjective
long-running
Long|shan
long ship +s
long|shore
long|shore|man
  long|shore|men
long shot +s
long-sighted
long-sighted|ly
long-sighted|ness
long-sleeved
long|spur +s
long-standing
long-suffer|ing
long-suffer|ing|ly
long-term adjective
long-time adjective
Lon|gueuil (city,
  Canada)
lon|gueur +s (tedious
  stretch)
long-waisted
long wave +s

long|ways
long-winded
long-winded|ly
long-winded|ness
long|wise
lo|ni|cera +s
loo +s (toilet)
[☞ lieu]
loo|fa +s (*use* loofah)
loo|fah +s
look +s +ed +ing
look-alike +s
look|er +s
looker-on
lookers-on
look-in +s *noun*
look|ing glass
look|ing glass|es
look|ism
look|ist +s
lookit
look-off +s *noun*
look out *verb*
looks out
looked out
look|ing out
look|out +s *noun*
look-see +s
looky
loom +s +ed +ing
loon +s
loon|ey tune +s *noun*
& *adjective* (*use*
loony-tune)
loon|ie +s (dollar)
[☞ loony]
loon|i|ness
loony (crazy; lunatic;
for dollar use loonie)
loon|i|er
loon|i|est
loon|ies
loony-tune +s
loop +s +ed +ing
(circular figure;
circuit; *Figure
Skating*; in 'out of the
loop', 'throw for a
loop')
[☞ loupe]
looped *adjective*
loop|er +s
loop|hole
loop|holes
loop|holed
loop|hol|ing
loop the loop *verb*
loops the loop
looped the loop
loop|ing the loop
loop-the-loop +s
noun

loopy
loop|i|er
loop|i|est
loose (not tight; free;
relaxed; inexact;
release; loosen;
shoot)
loos|er
loos|est
loos|es
loosed
loos|ing
[☞ lose]
loose-jointed
loose-leaf
loose-limbed
loose|ly
loos|en +s +ed +ing
loos|en|er +s
loose|ness
loose|strife +s
loosey-goosey
loot +s +ed +ing
(booty; plunder, rob)
[☞ lute]
loot|er +s
loot|ing +s
lop
lops
lopped
lop|ping
lope
lopes
loped
lop|ing
lop-eared
lop-ears
lo|phoph|or|ate +s
lopho|phore +s
Lop Nor (region,
China)
Lop Nur (= Lop Nor)
lop|o|lith +s
lop|per +s
lop|pet +s
loppy
lop|pi|er
lop|pi|est
lop|sided
lop|sided|ly
lop|sided|ness
lo|qua|cious
lo|qua|cious|ly
lo|qua|cious|ness
lo|quacity
lo|quat +s
lor *interjection*
[☞ lore, Laure]
loran (navigation
system)
[☞ Loren, Lauren]

Lorca, Fede|rico
Gar|cía (Spanish
poet)
Lord (God; title of
nobleman or peer)
lord +s +ed +ing
(nobleman; peer;
master; *Astrology*; in
'lord it over')
lord and lady (duck)
lords and ladies
Lord Howe (island,
SW Pacific)
lord|less
lord|like
lord|li|ness
lord|ly
lord|li|er
lord|li|est
lor|do|sis
lor|do|ses
lor|dot|ic
lord|ship +s
Lord's Prayer
Lordy *interjection*
lore (tradition;
Zoology)
[☞ lor, Laure,
Lorre]
Lore|lei +s
Loren, So|phia (Italian
actress)
[☞ Lauren, loran]
Lor|entz, Hen|drik
An|toon (Dutch
physicist)
[☞ Lorenz,
Lawrence,
Laurence]
Lorentz-FitzGer|ald
con|trac|tion +s
Lor|enz, Kon|rad
Zach|a|rias
(Austrian zoologist)
[☞ Lorentz,
Lawrence,
Laurence]
Lo|ren|zo de' Med|ici
(Florentine
statesman & arts
patron)
Lor|eto (town, Italy)
[☞ Loretto]
Lorette|ville (town,
Canada)
Lor|et|to (nuns)
[☞ Loreto]
lor|gnette +s
Lo|rient (town,
France)
lori|keet +s
loris
loris|es
lorn

Lorne, John Doug|las
Suth|er|land
Camp|bell,
Mar|quess of
(governor general of
Canada)
Lor|rain, Claude
(French painter)
Lor|raine (town,
Canada; region,
France; cross)
lor|raine (in 'quiche
lorraine')
Lorre, Peter (US
actor)
lorry (truck)
lor|ries
[☞ lory, Lorre]
Lor|tie, Louis (Cdn
pianist)
lory (parrot)
lor|ies
[☞ lorry, Lorre]
Los Ala|mos (nuclear
research site, US)
Los An|gel|es (city,
US)
lose (be deprived of;
misplace; be
defeated; elude)
loses
lost
losing
lose-lose
loser +s
losing *noun & adjective*
Lo Spa|gnol|etto
(José Ribera)
loss
loss|es
loss lead|er +s
loss-maker +s
loss-making
lost *adjective*
Lot (*Bible*; river,
France)
lot
lots
lotted
lot|ting
Lo|thair (Holy Roman
emperors)
Lo|thario +s
Lo|thian (region,
Scotland)
loti
ma|loti
lo|tion +s
loto +s *Quebec*
(lottery)
[☞ lotto]
lotsa
lotta

lot|tery
lot|ter|ies
lot|to +s (lottery;
game like bingo)
[☞ loto]
lotus
lotus|es
lotus-eater +s
Lotus Land (southern
BC)
lotus land +s (in
general use)
Lotus Sutra
Louang|phra|bang
(= Luang Prabang,
Laos)
louche
Lou|cheux
plural Lou|cheux
• The name
preferred by the
people themselves is
Gwich'in.
loud +er +est
(strongly audible,
noisy; gaudy)
loud|en +s +ed +ing
loud-hailer +s
loud|ly
loud|mouth +s
loud-mouthed
loud|ness
loud|speaker +s
Lou Geh|rig's
dis|ease
lough +s (Irish lake)
[☞ loch]
Lough|bor|ough
(town, England)
Lougheed, (Edgar)
Peter (Cdn
politician)
Louis (French kings)
Louis, Joe (US boxer)
[☞ Lewis]
louis
plural louis
Louis|bourg
(historical site,
Canada)
louis d'or
plural louis d'or
Lou|ise (lake &
waterfall, Canada)
Lou|ise|ville (town,
Canada)
[☞ Louisville]
Lou|isi|ana (state, US)
Lou|isi|anan +s
Lou|isi|an|ian +s
(= Louisianan)

Louis Napo|leon
(Napoleon III of
France)
Louis Phi|lippe
(French king)
Louis|ville (city, US)
[☞ Louiseville]
Lou Marsh Tro|phy
lounge
loun|ges
lounged
loun|ging
loun|ger +s
lounge|wear
loupe (magnifying
glass)
[☞ loop]
loup-garou
loups-garous
lour +s +ed +ing
(frown, menace: use
lower)
[☞ lower]
Lourdes (pilgrimage
site, France)
Lou|ren|ço Marques
(former name for
Maputo,
Mozambique)
louse
• (insect)
plural lice
• (person)
plural lous|es
louse|wort +s
lous|i|ly
lous|i|ness
lousy
lous|i|er
lous|i|est
lout +s
Louth (county,
Ireland)
lout|ish
lout|ish|ly
lout|ish|ness
Lou|vain (= Leuven,
Belgium)
lou|ver +s (use
louvre)
lou|vered (use
louvred)
louvre +s
louvred
lov|abil|ity
lov|able
lov|able|ness
lov|ably
lov|age
lovat +s
lovat green +s (lovat-
green when preceding
a noun)

love
loves
loved
lov|ing
love|abil|ity (use
lovability)
love|able (use
lovable)
love|able|ness (use
lovableness)
love|ably (use
lovably)
love-apple +s
love|bird +s
love bite +s
love child
love chil|dren
love|fest +s
love-hate
love-in +s
Love|lace, (Au|gus|ta)
Ada King,
Count|ess of
(English
mathematician)
Love|lace, Rich|ard
(English poet)
love|less
love|less|ly
love|less|ness
love life
love lives
loveli|ly
love|li|ness
Lov|ell, Sir (Al|fred
Charles) Ber|nard
(English astronomer)
love|lorn
love|ly
love|li|er
love|li|est
lovelies
love|making
lover +s
lovers' lane +s
love|seat +s
love|sick
love|sick|ness
love|struck
love|worthy
lovey +s (sweetheart;
affectionate)
[☞ luvvy]
lovey-dovey
lov|ing adjective &
noun
loving-kindness
loving|ly
loving|ness
Low, Sir David
Alex|an|der Cecil
(English cartoonist)

[☞ Loewe, Lot
River]
low +er +est +s +ed
+ing (not high; cattle
sound)
[☞ lo]
Low Arc|tic
low|ball +s +ed +ing
low-born
low|boy +s
low|brow +s
low|browed
low|brow|ism
low-budget
low|bush
low|bush|es
low-cal
low-calorie
Low Church
Low Coun|tries
(region, Europe)
low-cut
low-density
low|down
low-E
Low|ell, Amy
Law|rence (US poet)
Low|ell, James
Rus|sell (US writer)
Low|ell, Per|ci|val (US
astronomer)
Low|ell, Rob|ert
Traill Spence (US
poet)
low-emissiv|ity
low-end
lower +s +ed +ing
(comparative of low;
make or become
lower; frown,
menace)
Lower Arrow (lake,
Canada)
Lower Aus|tria (state,
Austria)
Lower Cal|i|for|nia
(= Baja California)
Lower Can|ada
(region, BNA)
lower case (lower-
case when preceding
a noun)
lower class (lower-
class when preceding
a noun)
lower class|es
Lower Fort Garry
(historic site,
Canada)
Lower Hutt (city, New
Zealand)
Lower Main|land
(region, Canada)

lower mid|dle class
(lower-middle-class
*when preceding a
noun*)
lower mid|dle
class|es
lower|most
Lower Sax|ony (state,
Germany)
Lowes|toft (town,
England)
Low Ger|man
low-grade
low-impact
low-income
low-inten|sity
low|ish
low-key
low-keyed
Low|land +s (of
Scotland)
low|land +s (*in
general use*)
Low|land|er +s (of
Scotland)
low|land|er +s (*in
general use*)
Low Latin
low-level
low-life +s
low-lifer +s
low|light +s
low|li|ness
lowly
low|li|er
low|li|est
low-lying
low main|ten|ance
adjective
low-minded
low-minded|ness
low|ness
low|pass
low-pitched
low post (low-post
*when preceding a
noun*)
low pres|sure *noun*
low-pressure
adjective
low pro|file +s (low-
profile *when
preceding a noun*)
low-rent
low-rental
low-rider +s
low-riding
low-rise +s
low-risk
Lowry, (Clar|ence)
Mal|colm (English
novelist)
low-slung

low-spirited
low-spirited|ness
low spirits
Low Sun|day +s
low-tech
low-technol|ogy
Low|ther, Pa|tri|cia
Lou|ise (Cdn poet)
low water (low-water
*when preceding a
noun*)
lox (smoked salmon;
liquid oxygen)
[☞ loch]
loyal
loyal|ism
Loyal|ist +s (United
Empire Loyalist; in
Northern Ireland)
loyal|ist +s (*in general
use*)
loyal|ly
Loyal|ty (islands,
SW Pacific)
loyal|ty
loyal|ties
Loy|ola, Ig|na|tius (of)
(saint)
loz|enge
loz|en|ges
LP (long-playing
record)
LPs
LPN (licensed practical
nurse)
LPNs
LRIF (locked-in
retirement fund)
LRIFs
LRT (transit)
LRTs
LSAT (Law School
Admission Test)
LSATs
LSD (drug)
l.s.d. (pounds, shillings
& pence)
LSI (large-scale
integration)
LSIs
Lua|laba (river, Africa)
Lu|an|da (capital of
Angola)
Luang Pra|bang (city,
Laos)
luau +s
Lu|ba|vitch *adjective*
Lu|ba|vitch|er +s
noun & adjective
lub|ber +s
lub|ber|ly
Lub|bock (city, US)
[☞ Lübeck]

lube
lubes
lubed
lub|ing
Lü|beck (city,
Germany)
[☞ Lubbock]
Lubi|con
plural Lubi|con or
Lubi|cons
Lu|bitsch, Ernst (US
filmmaker)
Lub|lin (city, Poland)
lu|bri|cant +s
lu|bri|cate
lu|bri|cates
lu|bri|cat|ed
lu|bri|cat|ing
lu|bri|ca|tion +s
lu|bri|ca|tive
lu|bri|ca|tor +s
lu|bri|cious
lu|bri|city
lu|bri|cous (*use*
lubricious)
Lubum|bashi (city,
Congo)
Luc, Frère (French
artist)
[☞ Luke]
Lucan (Roman poet)
Lu|ca|nia (mountain,
Canada)
Lucas, George (US
filmmaker)
Lucas van Ley|den
(Dutch artist)
Lucca (city, Italy)
lu|cen|cy
lu|cent
lu|cern (*use* lucerne)
Lu|cerne (lake &
resort, Switzerland)
lu|cerne
Lu|cian (Greek
satirist)
lucid
lu|cida (in 'camera
lucida')
lu|cid|ity
lu|cid|ly
lu|cid|ness
Lu|ci|fer (Satan;
morning star)
lu|ci|fer +s
lu|cif|er|ase
lu|cif|erin
Lu|cina (*Roman Myth*)
Lu|cite *proprietary*
luck +s +ed +ing
(fortune, chance)
[☞ lux, luxe]
luck|i|er

luck|i|est
luck|i|ly
luck|i|ness
luck|less
luck|less|ly
luck|less|ness
Luck|now (city, India)
lucky
luck|i|er
luck|i|est
lu|cra|tive
lu|cra|tive|ly
lu|cra|tive|ness
lucre
Lu|cre|tian
Lu|cre|tius (Roman
writer)
lucu|brate
lucu|brates
lucu|brat|ed
lucu|brat|ing
lucu|bra|tion +s
lucu|bra|tor +s
Lu|cul|lan
Lu|cul|lus, Lu|cius
Li|cin|ius (Roman
general)
lud (in 'my lud')
Luda (city, China)
Lud|dism
Lud|dite +s
'lude +s (Quaalude)
[☞ lewd]
Luden|dorff, Erich
(German general)
Ludhi|ana (city, India)
ludic
ludic|ally
ludi|crous
ludi|crous|ly
ludi|crous|ness
ludo
Lud|wig (Bavarian
kings)
Lud|wigs|hafen (city,
Germany)
luff +s +ed +ing
Luft|waffe
lug
lugs
lugged
lug|ging
Lu|gano (town,
Switzerland)
Lu|gansk (*Russian
name for* Luhansk,
Ukraine)
luge
luges
luged
luging

Luger +s *proprietary* (pistol)
[☞ **lugger**]
luger +s (one who luges)
[☞ **lugger**]
lug|gage +s
lug|ger +s (ship)
[☞ **Luger**]
Lu|go|si, Bela (US actor)
lug|sail +s
lu|gu|bri|ous
lu|gu|bri|ous|ly
lu|gu|bri|ous|ness
lug|worm +s
Lu|hansk (city, Ukraine)
Lu|kács, Georg (Hungarian philosopher & critic)
Luke (saint)
[☞ **Luc**]
luke|warm
luke|warm|ly
luke|warm|ness
lull +s +ed +ing
lul|la|by
  lul|la|bies
  lul|la|bied
  lul|la|by|ing
lull|ing *adjective*
lull|ing|ly
Lully, Jean-Baptiste (French composer)
Lully, Ray|mond (Spanish philosopher)
Lulu (island, Canada)
lulu +s
lum|bago
lum|bar (of the lower back)
lum|ber +s +ed +ing (move clumsily; *Forestry*)
lum|bered *adjective*
lum|ber|er +s
lum|ber|ing *noun & adjective*
lum|ber|ing|ly
lumber|jack +s
lumber|jacket +s
lumber|man
  lumber|men
lum|ber mill +s
lumber|yard +s
lumen
• (unit of luminous flux)
  plural **lu|mens**
• (cavity within tube or

cell)
  plural **lu|mina**
Lu|mière, Au|guste Marie Louis Nicho|las (French cinema pioneer)
Lu|mière, Louis Jean (French cinema pioneer)
lumin|aire +s
lumin|ance
lumin|ary
  lumin|aries
lumin|es|cence
lumin|es|cent
lumin|if|er|ous
lumin|os|ity
  lumin|os|ities
lumin|ous
lumin|ous|ly
lumin|ous|ness
lum|mox
  lum|mox|es
lump +s +ed +ing
lump|ec|tomy
  lump|ec|to|mies
lum|pen
lumpen|prole|tar|iat
lump|er +s
lump|fish
  lump|fish|es or
  lump|fish
lum|pia
lump|i|er
lump|i|est
lump|i|ly
lump|i|ness
lump|ish
lump|ish|ly
lump|ish|ness
lump|suck|er +s
lumpy
  lump|i|er
  lump|i|est
Lu|mum|ba, Pa|trice Hem|ery (Congolese statesman)
lun
Luna (*Roman Myth*)
lunacy
  luna|cies
luna moth +s
lunar
lun|ate +s
luna|tic
lun|a|tion +s
lunch
  lunch|es
  lunched
  lunch|ing
lunch box
  lunch boxes

lunch buck|et +s (lunch-bucket *when preceding a noun*)
lunch|eon +s
lunch|eon|ette +s
lunch|er +s
lunch kit +s
lunch pail +s (lunch-pail *when preceding a noun*)
lunch|room +s
lunch|time +s
Lund (city, Sweden)
Lundy's Lane (battle site, Canada)
Lunen|burg (town, Canada)
lun|ette +s
lung +s
lunge
• (thrust)
  lun|ges
  lunged
  lun|ging
• (*Horse Riding*)
  lun|ges
  lunged
  lunge|ing
• (muskellunge)
  plural **lunge** or
  lun|ges
lung|fish
  plural **lung|fish** or
  lung|fish|es
lung|ful +s
lun|gi +s
lung|less
lung|worm +s
lung|wort +s
luni|solar
lunk +s
lunk|er +s
lunk|head +s
lunk|head|ed
lun|ula
  lunu|lae
Luo|yang (city, China)
Luper|calia
lu|pin +s (flower: *use* lupine)
  [☞ **lupine**]
lu|pine +s (flower; of or like wolves)
lu|poid
lu|pous *adjective*
lupus *noun*
lupus ery|thema|to|sus
lupus vul|garis
lurch
  lurch|es
  lurched
  lurch|ing

lurch|er +s
lure
  lures
  lured
  luring
Lurex *proprietary*
lurid
lurid|ly
lurid|ness
lurk +s +ed +ing
lurk|er +s
Lu|saka (capital of Zambia)
lus|cious
lus|cious|ly
lus|cious|ness
lush
  lush|er
  lush|est
  lush|es
  lushed
  lush|ing
lush|ly
lush|ness
Lu|shun (port, China)
Lusi|tania (Roman province)
Lusi|tania (ship)
Lusi|tan|ian +s
lust +s +ed +ing
lust|ful
lust|ful|ly
lust|ful|ness
lust|i|er
lust|i|est
lust|i|ly
lust|i|ness
lus|tra
lus|tral
lus|trate
  lus|trates
  lus|trat|ed
  lus|trat|ing
lus|tra|tion +s
lustre
  lustres
  lustred
  lus|tring
lustre|less
lustre|ware
lus|trous
lus|trous|ly
lus|trous|ness
lus|trum
  lus|tra or **lus|trums**
lusty
  lust|i|er
  lust|i|est
lusus
lusus na|turae
lut|an|ist +s (*use* lutenist)

lute (instrument; clay; seal)
lutes
luted
lut|ing
[☞ loot]
lu|teal
lu|tein +s
lu|tein|iz|ing
lut|en|ist +s
lu|tetium
Lu|ther, Mar|tin (German theologian)
Lu|ther|an +s
Lu|ther|an|ism
lu|thier +s
Lu|thu|li, Al|bert John Mvum|bi (South African political leader)
Lu|tine Bell
lut|ing noun
Luton (town, England)
Lu|tu|li, Al|bert John Mvum|bi (= Luthuli)
Lutz
Lutz|es
luv|vie +s (sweetheart, actor: use luvvy)
[☞ lovey]
luvvy (sweetheart; actor)
luv|vies
[☞ lovey]
lux (unit of illumination)
plural lux
[☞ luxe]
luxe (luxury; deluxe)
[☞ lux]
Lux|em|bourg (country & its capital, Europe; province, Belgium)
[☞ Luxemburg]
Lux|em|bourg|er +s
Lux|em|burg, Rosa (German revolutionary)
[☞ Luxembourg]
Lux|em|burg|ish
Luxor (monument site, Egypt)
lux|uri|ance
lux|uri|ant
lux|uri|ant|ly
lux|uri|ate
lux|uri|ates
lux|uri|at|ed
lux|uri|at|ing
lux|uri|ous
lux|uri|ous|ly

lux|uri|ous|ness
lux|ury
lux|uries
Luzon (island, the Philippines)
Lviv (city, Ukraine)
Lvov (Russian name for Lviv, Ukraine)
lwei +s
Lyall|pur (former name for Faisalabad, Pakistan)
ly|can|thrope +s
ly|can|throp|ic
ly|can|thropy
lycée +s
Ly|ceum (of Aristotle)
ly|ceum +s (lecture hall etc.)
lychee +s
lych-gate +s
Lycia (ancient region, Asia Minor)
Ly|cian +s
lyco|pod +s
lyco|po|dium
Lycra proprietary
Ly|cur|gus (Spartan lawgiver)
Lyd|gate, John (English poet)
Lydia (ancient region, Asia Minor)
Lyd|ian +s
lye +s (alkaline substance; detergent)
[☞ lie]
Lyell, Sir Charles (Scottish geologist)
lying adjective
lying|ly
Lyly, John (English writer)
Lyme dis|ease
lyme grass
lymph
lymph|aden|op|athy
lymph|aden|op|athies
lymph|at|ic +s
lymph node +s
lymph|o|cyte +s
lymph|o|cyt|ic
lymph|oid
lymph|o|kine +s
lymph|oma
lymph|omas or lymph|o|mata
Lynch, John Mary ('Jack') (Irish prime minister)

lynch
lynch|es
lynched
lynch|ing
lynch|er +s
lynch|ing +s noun
lynch mob +s
lynch|pin +s (use linchpin)
Lynn, Dame Vera (English singer)
Lynx (constellation)
lynx (cat)
lynx|es or lynx
[☞ links]
lynx-eyed
Lyon (= Lyons, France)
[☞ León]
Lyons (city, France)
lyo|phil|ic
lyo|phil|iz|a|tion +s
lyo|phil|ize
lyo|phil|iz|es
lyo|phil|ized
lyo|phil|iz|ing
lyo|phob|ic
Lyo|tard, Jean-François (French philosopher)
[☞ leotard]
Lyra (constellation)
[☞ LIRA, lira]
lyr|ate
lyre +s (instrument)
lyre|bird +s
lyric +s
lyric|al
lyric|ally
lyri|cism
lyri|cist +s
lyr|ist +s
Lysan|der (Spartan general)
lyse
lyses
lysed
lys|ing
Lysen|ko, Tro|fim Denis|ovich (Soviet biologist)
ly|ser|gic
ly|ser|gic acid di|ethyl|amide
Ly|sima|chus (Macedonian general)
lysin +s (blood protein)
ly|sine (amino acid)
Ly|sip|pus (Greek sculptor)

lysis
lyses
Lysol proprietary
lyso|som|al
lyso|some +s
lyso|zyme +s
lyth|rum +s
lytic
Lyt|ton, 1st Baron (English writer)

M

M
• (letter; em)
M's
• (molar)
[☞ em]
m
• (letter)
m's
• (metre; mass)
[☞ em]
M-16
M-16s
M.A.
M.A.'s (Master of Arts)
ma +s (mother)
[☞ maw]
ma'am +s
ma-and-pa
Maas|tricht (city, the Netherlands)
Maat (Egyptian Myth)
Mac +s (guy; Scotsman; apple)
[☞ Mach]
mac +s (raincoat)
ma|cabre
mac|ad|am +s
maca|da|mia +s
mac|ad|am|iz|a|tion +s
mac|ad|am|ize
mac|ad|am|iz|es
mac|ad|am|ized
mac|ad|am|iz|ing
Mac|Alpin, Ken|neth (Scottish king)
Maca|nese
plural Maca|nese
Macao (Portuguese dependency)
Maca|pá (town, Brazil)
ma|caque +s

maca|roni
• (pasta)
• (dandy)
maca|ron|ies
maca|ron|ic +s
maca|roon +s
Mac|Arthur,
Doug|las (US
general)
[☞ McArthur]
Ma|cas|sar (oil; *for
strait or former name
for Ujung Pandang
use Makassar)
Macau (= Macao)
Mac|aulay (mountain,
Canada)
Mac|aulay, Dame
(Emilie) Rose
(English writer)
Mac|aulay, Thom|as
Bab|ing|ton, 1st
Baron (English
writer)
macaw +s
Mac|beth (Scottish
king)
Mac|Bride, Sean
(Irish statesman)
Mac|ca|baeus, Judas
(leader of Jewish
revolt)
Mac|ca|bean
Mac|ca|bee +s
Mac|Diar|mid, Hugh
(Scottish poet)
Mac|Don|ald
(surname)
[☞ Macdonald,
McDonald]
Mac|Don|ald, James
Ed|ward Her|vey
(Cdn painter)
Mac|Don|ald,
(James) Ram|say
(British prime
minister)
Mac|don|ald
(surname)
[☞ MacDonald,
McDonald]
Mac|don|ald,
An|drew Archi|bald
(Cdn politician)
Mac|don|ald, Angus
Lewis (Cdn
politician)
Mac|don|ald, Brian
(Cdn theatre
director)
Mac|don|ald, James
Wil|liam Gal|lo|way
('Jock') (Cdn artist)

Mac|don|ald, Sir
John Alex|an|der
(Cdn prime minister)
Mac|don|ald, John
Sand|field (Cdn
politician)
Mac|Don|nell
(mountain ranges,
Australia)
Mac|Don|nell, Miles
(Cdn soldier &
politician)
Mace *proprietary*
(disabling spray)
Maces
Maced
Ma|cing
mace +s (staff, club;
spice)
mace-bearer +s
macé|doine +s
Mace|don
(= Macedonia:
ancient country)
Mace|donia (ancient
country, Europe;
region, Greece;
Balkan republic)
Mace|don|ian +s
Maceió (city, Brazil)
macer|ate
macer|ates
macer|at|ed
macer|at|ing
macer|a|tion +s
macer|ator +s
Mac|gil|li|cuddy's
Reeks (hills, Ireland)
Mach, Ernst (Austrian
physicist)
[☞ match]
Mach (speed)
[☞ match]
mâche (lamb's lettuce)
ma|chete +s
Ma|chia|velli,
Nic|colò di
Ber|nar|do dei
(Florentine
statesman)
Ma|chia|vel|lian +s
ma|chia|vel|lian|ism
ma|chico|late
ma|chico|lates
ma|chico|lat|ed
ma|chico|lat|ing
ma|chico|lat|ed
adjective
ma|chico|la|tion +s
ma|chin|abil|ity
ma|chin|able
ma|chin|ate
ma|chin|ates

ma|chin|at|ed
ma|chin|at|ing
ma|chin|a|tion +s
ma|chin|ator +s
ma|chine
ma|chines
ma|chined
ma|chin|ing
ma|chine gun +s
noun (machine-gun
when *preceding a*
noun)
machine-gun *verb*
machine-guns
machine-gunned
machine-gunning
machine-gunner +s
machine-readable
ma|chin|ery
ma|chin|er|ies
ma|chine tool +s
machine-tooled
ma|chine wash
ma|chine wash|es
ma|chine washed
ma|chine wash|ing
ma|chine wash|able
ma|chin|ing *noun &*
adjective
ma|chin|ist +s
ma|chismo
Mach|meter +s
macho +s
Machu Pic|chu (Inca
town, Peru)
Ma|cias Nguema
(*former name for*
Bioko, Equatorial
Guinea)
mac|in|tosh (raincoat:
use mackintosh)
mac|in|tosh|es
[☞ Mackintosh,
McIntosh]
mack +s (raincoat: *use*
mac)
[☞ Mac, Mach]
Mac|kay (city,
Australia)
Mac|ken|zie (district,
municipality, river &
mountains, Canada)
Mac|ken|zie,
Alex|an|der (Cdn
prime minister)
Mac|ken|zie, Sir
Alex|an|der (Cdn
explorer)
Mac|ken|zie, Sir
Wil|liam (Cdn
railroad
entrepreneur)

Mac|ken|zie,
Wil|liam Lyon (Cdn
politician)
[☞ William Lyon
Mackenzie King]
Mac|ken|zie King
(island, Canada)
[☞ William Lyon
Mackenzie King]
Mac|kenzie-
Papineau
Bat|tal|ion
mack|erel
plural mack|erel or
mack|erels
Mack|i|naw (trout)
plural Mack|i|naw or
Mack|i|naws
mack|i|naw +s (cloth;
coat)
Mack|in|tosh,
Charles Ren|nie
(Scottish designer)
[☞ McIntosh]
mack|in|tosh
(raincoat)
mack|in|tosh|es
[☞ McIntosh]
macle +s
Mac|lean, Don|ald
Duart (English spy)
Mac|lean, John
Bayne (Cdn
publisher)
Mac|leish, Archi|bald
(US writer)
Mac|Len|nan, (John)
Hugh (Cdn novelist)
Mac|leod, James
Far|quhar|son (Cdn
police officer &
judge)
Mac|leod, John
James Rick|ard
(Scottish-born
physiologist)
Mac|Mil|lan
(surname)
[☞ Macmillan,
McMillan]
Mac|Mil|lan,
Alex|an|der Stir|ling
(Cdn politician)
Mac|Mil|lan, Sir
Er|nest Alex|an|der
Camp|bell (Cdn
conductor)
Mac|Mil|lan, Har|vey
Reg|in|ald (Cdn
businessman)
Mac|Mil|lan, Sir
Ken|neth (British
choreographer)

Mac|mil|lan,
(Mau|rice) Har|old
(1st Earl of Stockton,
English prime
minister)
[☞ MacMillan,
McMillan]
Mac|Neice,
(Fred|erick) Louis
(Irish poet)
Mac|phail, Agnes
Camp|bell (Cdn
politician)
Mac|pher|son, James
(Scottish poet)
[☞ McPherson]
Mac|qua|rie (river,
Australia)
mac|ramé
macro +s
macro|biot|ic +s
macro|carpa +s
macro|ceph|alic
macro|ceph|al|ous
macro|ceph|aly
macro|cosm +s
macro|cos|mic
macro|cos|mic|ally
macro|econom|ic
macro|econom|ics
macro|econo|mist +s
macro|evolu|tion +s
macro|evolu|tion|ary
macro|fossil +s
macro lens
  macro lens|es
macro|molecu|lar
macro|mol|ecule +s
mac|ron +s
macro|nutri|ent +s
macro|phage +s
macro|photog|raphy
macro|phyte +s
macro|pod +s
macro|scop|ic
macro|scop|ic|ally
mac|ula
  mac|ulae
mac|ula lutea
  mac|ulae lu|teae
macu|lar
macu|la|tion +s
MAD (mutual assured
destruction)
mad
  mad|der
  mad|dest
Mada|gas|can +s
Mada|gas|car
(country off Africa)
madam +s (form of
address for English-
speaking woman; in

'Madam Justice' etc.;
brothel keeper;
precocious girl)
[☞ **madame**]
Ma|dame (Island,
Canada)
ma|dame (form of
address for French-
speaking woman)
  mes|dames
[☞ **madam**]
Mada|was|ka (rivers,
Canada)
mad|cap +s
mad|den +s +ed +ing
mad|den|ing adjective
mad|den|ing|ly
mad|der +s
mad|ding adjective
made adjective & past
tense of make
[☞ **maid**]
made bea|ver
  plural made bea|ver
  or made bea|vers
made-for-televi|sion
made-for-TV
Ma|deira +s (islands
off Africa; river,
Brazil; wine; cake)
Ma|deir|an +s
Made|leine (islands,
Canada)
mad|el|eine +s
Made|lin|ot +s
ma|demoi|selle
  mes|demoi|selles or
  ma|demoi|selles
made-to-measure
made up (made-up
  when preceding a
  noun)
mad|house +s
Madhya Pra|desh
(state, India)
Madi|son (city, US)
Madi|son, James (US
president)
Madi|son Av|enue
(Advertising)
madly
mad|man
  mad|men
mad|ness
Ma|donna (Virgin
Mary; US singer)
ma|donna +s
(representation of
the Virgin Mary)
ma|donna lily
  ma|donna lil|ies

Ma|dras (city, India;
  former name for
  Tamil Nadu; curry)
ma|dras (cotton)
madre|pore +s
madre|por|ic
Ma|drid (capital of
Spain)
mad|rigal +s
mad|rigal|ian
mad|rigal|ist +s
ma|droña +s (use
  madroño)
ma|drone +s (use
  madroño)
ma|droño +s
Ma|dura (island,
Indonesia)
Madu|rai (city, India)
mad|woman
  mad|women
Mae|ce|nas, Gaius
Clin|ius (Roman
statesman & arts
patron)
[☞ **Mycenae**]
Mae|ce|nas (patron)
Mae|ce|nas|es
[☞ **Mycenae**]
mael|strom +s
mae|nad +s
mae|nad|ic
mae|nad|ism
maes|toso +s
maes|tro
  maes|tros or
  maes|tri
Maeter|linck, Count
Mau|rice (Belgian
writer)
Mae West +s
Mafe|king (town,
South Africa)
Mafia (criminal
organization in Italy
& US)
mafia +s (influential
clique)
mafic
Mafi|keng
(= Mafeking)
Mafi|oso (member of
the Mafia)
Mafi|osi
mafi|oso (member of
a mafia)
mafi|osi
mag +s
Mag|adha (ancient
kingdom, India)
Mag|adi (lake, Kenya)
maga|zine +s

Mag|dalen
• (= Mary
  Magdalene)
• (= Îles de la
  Madeleine, Canada)
mag|dalen +s
Mag|da|lena (river,
Colombia)
Mag|dalene, Mary
(saint)
Mag|dalen|ian
Mag|de|burg (city,
Germany)
mage +s
Magel|lan (strait,
S America)
Magel|lan,
Fer|di|nand
(Portuguese
explorer)
Magel|lan|ic
Magen David +s
ma|genta +s
Mag|giore (lake, Italy)
mag|got +s
mag|goty
Magh|reb
(= Maghrib)
Magh|rib (region,
Africa)
Magi (wise men)
magi plural of magus
ma|gian +s
magian|ism
magic
  magics
  magicked
  magick|ing
magic|al
magic|al|ly
ma|gi|cian +s
Magic Mark|er +s
  proprietary
Magi|not line
magis|ter|ial
magis|ter|ial|ly
magis|ter|ium
magis|tracy
  magis|tra|cies
magis|trate
Magis|trate's Court
magis|trate|ship
magis|tra|ture +s
Mag|le|mo|sian +s
mag|lev
magma
  mag|mata or
  mag|mas
mag|ma|tic
mag|ma|tic|ally
Magna Carta
Magna Charta
(= Magna Carta)

magna cum laude
Magna Grae|cia
(ancient Greek cities)
mag|na|nim|ity
mag|nani|mous
mag|nani|mous|ly
mag|nate +s
(business person)
[☞ magnet]
mag|ne|sia
mag|nes|ian
mag|nes|ite +s
mag|ne|sium
mag|net +s (thing that
attracts)
[☞ magnate]
mag|net|ic
mag|net|ic|ally
mag|net|ic disk +s
mag|net|ism
mag|net|ite +s
mag|net|iz|able
mag|net|iz|a|tion +s
mag|net|ize
mag|net|iz|es
mag|net|ized
mag|net|iz|ing
mag|net|iz|er +s
mag|neto +s
magneto-electric
magneto-electri|city
mag|neto|graph +s
mag|neto|hydro|
dynam|ic
mag|neto|hydro|
dynam|ics
mag|net|om|eter +s
mag|neto|met|ric
mag|net|om|etry
mag|neto|motive
mag|ne|ton +s
magneto-optic
magneto-optical
magneto-optics
mag|neto|sphere +s
mag|neto|spher|ic
mag|ne|tron +s
magni|fi|able
Mag|nifi|cat +s
magni|fi|ca|tion +s
mag|nifi|cence
mag|nifi|cent
mag|nifi|cent|ly
mag|nif|ico
mag|nif|icoes
magni|fi|er +s
mag|nify
magni|fies
magni|fied
magni|fy|ing
mag|nilo|quence
mag|nilo|quent

mag|nilo|quent|ly
Mag|nito|gorsk (city,
Russia)
mag|ni|tude +s
mag|no|lia +s
mag|nox
Mag|num +s (gun,
cartridge)
mag|num +s (wine
bottle)
mag|num opus
magna opera or
mag|num opus|es
Mag|nus|sen, Karen
Diane (Cdn figure
skater)
Magog (Bible; town,
Canada)
mag|pie +s
Ma|gritte, René
Fran|çois Ghis|lain
(Belgian painter)
ma|guey +s
Magus (wise man)
Magi
magus (Persian priest;
sorcerer)
magi
Mag|yar +s
Maha|bad (city, Iran)
Maha|bhar|ata
maha|raja +s
maha|rajah +s (use
maharaja)
maha|ra|nee +s
maha|rani +s (use
maharanee)
Maha|rash|tra (state,
India)
Maha|rash|trian +s
maha|rishi +s
ma|hatma +s
Maha|weli (river, Sri
Lanka)
Maha|yana
Mahdi +s (Islam)
Mahd|ism
Mahd|ist +s
Mah|fouz, Na|guib
(Egyptian novelist)
Ma|hi|can
(Algonquian people
of New York State)
plural Ma|hi|can or
Ma|hi|cans
[☞ Mohegan,
Mohican]
Mahi|lyow (city,
Belarus)
mahi mahi
plural mahi mahi
mah-jong

mah-jongg (use mah-
jong)
Mah|ler, Gus|tav
(Austrian composer)
ma|hog|any
ma|hog|an|ies
Mahón (port,
Minorca)
Ma|hone Bay (town &
inlet, Canada)
ma|ho|nia +s
Ma|hore (= Mayotte)
ma|hout +s
Mahov|lich, Fran|cis
Wil|liam ('Frank')
(Cdn hockey player)
Mah|ratta +s (use
Maratha)
Mah|ratti (use
Marathi)
Maia (Greek goddess;
Roman goddess)
[☞ Maya]
maid +s (servant;
young woman)
[☞ made]
mai|dan +s (open
space; parade
ground)
maid|en +s
(unmarried woman;
initial; soil; grown
from seed)
maiden|hair +s
Maiden|head (town,
England)
maiden|head +s
maiden|hood +s
maiden|ly
Maid Marian
maid|serv|ant +s
Maid|stone (town,
England)
mai|eut|ic
Mai|kop (city, Russia)
mail +s +ed +ing
(send letters or
messages; armour)
[☞ male]
mail|able
mail|bag +s
mail bomb +s +ed
+ing
mail|box
mail|boxes
mail drop +s
mailed adjective
Mail|er, Nor|man (US
writer)
mall|er +s (mail
dispatcher;
pamphlet)
[☞ malar]

mail-in +s
mail|ing +s noun
Mail|let, An|to|nine
(Cdn novelist)
Mail|lol, Aris|tide
(French artist)
mail|lot +s
mail|man
mail|men
mail merge
mail order +s noun
(mail-order when
preceding a noun)
mail-order +s +ed
+ing verb
mail|room +s
mail|shot +s
mail slot +s
maim +s +ed +ing
Mai|moni|des (Jewish
philosopher)
Main (river, Germany)
[☞ Maine, Mayne]
main +s (principal;
conduit, electricity;
ocean; in 'might and
main')
[☞ mane]
Maine (state, US)
[☞ Main, Mayne]
Main|er +s
main|frame +s
Main|land (islands,
Orkney & Shetland;
Cdn provinces
except
Newfoundland;
Lower Mainland)
main|land +s
main|land|er +s
main line +s (railway)
main|line
(established,
normative; vein;
inject drugs;
Forestry)
main|lines
main|lined
main|lin|ing
main|lin|er +s
main|ly
main|mast +s
main|sail +s
main|sheet +s
main|spring +s
main|stage +s
main|stay +s
main|stream +s +ed
+ing
main|stream|er +s
main|stream|ing
noun

main street +s
(principal street)
main|street +s +ed
+ing (campaign)
main|street|ing *noun*
main|tain +s +ed
+ing
main|tain|abil|ity
main|tain|able
main|tain|er +s
main|ten|ance +s
Main|te|non,
Mar|quise de
(mistress of Louis
XIV)
main|top +s
main|top|mast +s
main yard +s
Mainz (city, Germany)
maiol|ica (*use*
majolica)
Mair, Charles (Cdn
poet)
[☞ Mayer, Meir,
Mare]
mai|son de la
cul|ture
mai|sons de la
cul|ture
maison|ette +s
maison|nette +s (*use*
maisonette)
Maison|neuve, Paul
de Chome|dey de
(founder of
Montreal)
mai tai +s
Mait|land, Fred|eric
Wil|liam (English
historian)
maître d'
maître d's
maître d'hotel
maî|tres d'hotel
maize (corn)
ma|jes|tic
ma|jes|tic|ally
maj|esty
maj|es|ties
Maj|lis
majol|ica
Major, John (British
prime minister)
ma|jor +s +ed +ing
Ma|jor|ca (Balearic
island)
major-domo +s
major|ette +s
major gen|er|al +s
ma|jori|tar|ian +s
ma|jori|tar|ian|ism
ma|jor|ity
ma|jor|ities

major junior +s
major league +s *noun*
major-league
adjective
major-leaguer +s
major|ly
major|ship +s
maj|us|cu|lar
maj|us|cule +s
mak|able
Ma|kar|ios III
(Cypriot archbishop
& statesman)
Ma|kas|sar (strait
between Borneo &
Sulawesi; *former
name for* Ujung
Pandang, Indonesia)
[☞ Macassar oil]
make
makes
made
mak|ing
make-believe
make do *verb*
makes do
made do
mak|ing do
make-do *adjective*
make over *verb*
makes over
made over
mak|ing over
make-over +s *noun*
mak|er +s
make|shift +s
make up *verb*
makes up
made up
mak|ing up
make|up +s *noun*
make|weight +s
make-work
Mak|ga|dik|gadi
Pans (salt
depressions,
Botswana)
Makh|ach|ka|la (city,
Russia)
mak|ing +s *noun*
mako +s
ma|kuta
Mala|bar
Mall|abo (capital of
Equatorial Guinea)
mal|ab|sorp|tion +s
Ma|llac|ca
• (strait, SE Asia)
• (= Melaka,
Indonesian state &
its capital)
ma|llac|ca (cane)
[☞ Melaka]

Mal|achi (*Bible*)
mal|ach|ite +s
(mineral)
mala|co|logic|al
mala|col|o|gist +s
mala|col|ogy
mala|cos|tra|can +s
mal|adap|ta|tion +s
mal|adapt|ed
mal|adapt|ive
mal|adjust|ed
mal|adjust|ment +s
mal|admin|is|ter +s
+ed +ing
mal|admin|is|tra|tion
+s
mal|adroit
mal|adroit|ly
mal|adroit|ness
mal|ady (ailment)
mal|adies
[☞ milady]
Mal|aga (city, Spain;
wine)
Mala|gasy
Mala|gas|ies
mala|gueña
mal|aise
Mal|amud, Ber|nard
(US writer)
mala|mute +s
mala|pert +s
mala|prop +s
mala|prop|ism +s
mal|apro|pos
ma|llar +s (cheek
bone)
[☞ mailer]
Mäl|aren (lake,
Sweden)
mal|aria
mal|arial
mal|arian
mal|ari|ous
ma|llar|key
Mala|spina
(mountain, Canada)
mala|thion
Ma|lawi (country &
lake, Africa)
Ma|lawi|an +s
Ma|llay +s (people &
language;
archipelago &
peninsula, Asia)
Ma|llaya (former
country, Asia)
Ma|llay|alam
Ma|llay|an +s
Malayo-Polynes|ian
Ma|llay|sia (country,
Asia)
Ma|llay|sian +s

Mall|bec
Mal|colm (island,
Canada; Scottish
kings)
Mal|colm X (US
activist)
mal|con|tent +s
mal de mer
mal|dis|trib|ut|ed
mal|dis|tri|bu|tion +s
Mal|di|ves (country,
Indian Ocean)
Male (capital of the
Maldives)
male +s (sex)
[☞ mail]
Male|branche,
Nico|las (French
philosopher)
Mall|ecite
(= Maliseet)
plural Mall|ecite
[☞ malachite]
mal|edic|tion +s
mal|edic|tive
mal|edic|tory
mal|efac|tion +s
mal|efac|tor +s
mall|efic
mal|efi|cence
mal|efi|cent
Male|gaon (city,
India)
ma|lleic
mal|emute +s (*use*
malamute)
male|ness
Mal|en|kov, Georgi
Mak|si|mil|ian|ovich
(Soviet statesman)
Mal|evich, Kaz|i|mir
Sev|erin|ovich
(Russian artist)
ma|levo|lence
ma|levo|lent
ma|levo|lent|ly
mal|feas|ance
mal|feas|ant
mal|for|ma|tion +s
mal|formed
mal|func|tion +s +ed
+ing
Mali (country, Africa)
[☞ molly]
Mali|an +s
Mall|ibu (resort, US)
malic
malice
ma|li|cious
ma|li|cious|ly
ma|li|cious|ness

ma|lign +s +ed +ing
(injurious,
malevolent; slander)
[☞ Maligne,
moline]
ma|lig|nancy
ma|lig|nan|cies
ma|lig|nant
ma|lig|nant|ly
Ma|ligne (lake,
Canada)
[☞ malign, moline]
ma|lign|er +s
ma|lig|nity
ma|lig|ni|ties
ma|lign|ly
Ma|lines
(= Mechelen,
Belgium)
ma|lin|ger +s +ed
+ing
ma|lin|ger|er +s
Mali|now|ski,
Bron|is|ław Kas|par
(English
anthropologist)
Mali|seet
   plural Mali|seet
mall +s (stores;
sheltered walk;
game)
[☞ maul, moll,
Malle]
mal|lard
   plural mal|lards or
   mal|lard
Mal|lar|mé,
Sté|phane (French
poet)
Malle, Louis (French
filmmaker)
malle|abil|ity
mal|le|able
mal|le|ably
mal|lee +s
mal|leo|lus
   mal|leo|li
mal|let +s
mal|leus
   mal|lei
Mal|lor|ca
(= Majorca)
mal|low +s
Malmö (city, Sweden)
malm|sey +s
mal|nour|ished
mal|nour|ish|ment
mal|nutri|tion
mal|occlu|sion +s
mal|odor|ous
malo|lac|tic
Mal|ory, Sir Thom|as
(English writer)

Mal|peque +s (oyster)
Mal|peque Bay (inlet,
Canada)
Mal|pighi, Mar|cel|lo
(Italian microscopist)
Mal|pighi|an
Mal|pla|quet (battle
site, France)
mal|prac|tice +s
Mal|raux, André
Georges (French
writer)
malt +s +ed +ing
Malta (country,
Mediterranean)
malt|ed +s noun &
   adjective
Mal|tese
   plural Mal|tese
Mal|thus, Thom|as
Rob|ert (English
economist)
Mal|thu|sian
Mal|thu|sian|ism
malt|i|ness
malto|dex|trin
malt|ose
mal|treat +s +ed
+ing
mal|treat|er +s
mal|treat|ment +s
malty
   malt|i|er
   malt|i|est
Mal|va|sia
Mal|vern +s (hills,
England)
mal|ver|sa|tion
Mal|vi|nas
   (Argentinian name for
   the Falkland Islands)
mam +s
mama +s
mama's boy +s
mam|ba +s (snake)
mambo
• noun (dance; music)
   mam|bos
• verb (dance)
   mam|boes
   mam|boed
   mambo|ing
Mam|eluke +s
Mamet, David (US
dramatist)
mam|il|la
   mam|il|lae
mam|il|lary
mam|il|lat|ed
mamma
• (= mama: mother)
   plural mam|mas

• (breast)
   plural mam|mae
mam|mal +s
mam|mal|ian +s
mam|mal|o|gist +s
mam|mal|ogy
mam|mary
   mam|mar|ies
mam|mee +s (tree)
[☞ mammy]
mammi|form
mam|mil|la (use
   mamilla)
   plural mam|mil|lae
mam|mo|gram +s
mam|mog|raphy
Mam|mon
Mam|mon|ism
Mam|mon|ist +s
mam|moth +s
mammy (mother;
nanny)
   mam|mies
[☞ mammee]
Man (isle, Irish Sea)
[☞ Mann]
man
• noun
   men
• verb
   mans
   manned
   man|ning
mana (supernatural
power)
[☞ manna]
man|acle
   man|acles
   man|acled
   man|ac|ling
man|age
   man|ages
   man|aged
   man|aging
[☞ manège]
man|age|abil|ity
man|age|able
man|age|able|ness
man|age|ably
man|age|ment +s
man|ager +s
man|ager|ess
   man|ager|ess|es
man|ag|er|ial
man|ag|er|ial|ly
man|ager|ship +s
man|ag|ing adjective
Ma|na|gua (capital of
Nicaragua)
mana|kin +s (bird)
[☞ mannequin,
manikin]

Ma|nama (capital of
Bahrain)
ma|ñana +s
Ma|nas|seh (Bible)
man-at-arms
   men-at-arms
mana|tee +s
Ma|naus (city, Brazil)
Mana|watu (region &
river, New Zealand)
Mance, Jeanne
(colonist in New
France)
Man|ches|ter (city,
England)
man|chi|neel +s
Man|chu +s
Man|chu|ria (region,
China)
Man|chu|rian +s
Man|cini, En|rico
('Henry') (US
composer)
man|ciple +s
Man|cu|nian +s
Man|dae|an +s
man|dala +s
Man|da|lay (city,
Burma)
man|da|mus
Man|da|rin (language)
man|da|rin +s
(orange; collar; duck)
man|da|rin|ate +s
man|da|tary (one
who receives a
mandate)
   man|da|tar|ies
[☞ mandatory]
man|date
   man|dates
   man|dat|ed
   man|dat|ing
man|da|tor|ily
man|da|tory
(compulsory; for one
who receives a
mandate use
mandatary)
   man|da|tor|ies
man-day +s
Man|dela, Nel|son
Ro|lih|lahla (South
African president)
Man|del|shtam
(= Mandelstam)
Man|del|stam, Osip
Emily|evich
(Russian poet)
Man|de|ville,
Ber|nard de (English
writer)

Man|de|ville, Sir
  John (English
  nobleman)
man|dible +s
man|dibu|lar
man|dibu|late
man|do|lin +s
  (musical instrument;
  kitchen utensil)
man|do|line +s
  (kitchen utensil: *use*
  mandolin)
man|do|lin|ist +s
man|dor|la +s
man|drag|ora +s
man|drake +s
man|drel +s (shaft;
  cylindrical rod)
man|drill +s (baboon)
man|du|cate
  man|du|cates
  man|du|cat|ed
  man|du|cat|ing
man|du|ca|tion
man|du|ca|tory
mane +s (hair)
  [☞ main, Maine,
  Mayne]
man-eater +s
maned
manège (*Horse Riding*)
  [☞ manage]
mane|less
Manes (= Mani:
  Persian prophet)
  [☞ Mainz]
manes
Manet, Édouard
  (French painter)
  [☞ Monet]
man|eu|ver +s +ed
  +ing (*use*
  manoeuvre)
man|eu|ver|abil|ity
  (*use*
  manoeuvrability)
man|eu|ver|able (*use*
  manoeuvrable)
man|eu|ver|er +s (*use*
  manoeuvrer)
man Fri|day
  plural men Fri|day
  or man Fri|days
man|ful
man|ful|ly
man|ful|ness
man|ga|bey +s
man|ga|nese
man|gan|ic
man|gan|ous
mange
man|gel +s (beet)
  [☞ mangle]

mangel-wurzel +s
  (= mangel)
man|ger +s
mange-tout
  plural mange-tout
  or mange-touts
mangia-cake +s
mangi|er
mangi|est
mangi|ly
mangi|ness
man|gle (crush, ruin,
  disfigure; wringer)
  man|gles
  man|gled
  man|gling
  [☞ mangel]
man|gler +s
mango
  man|goes or
  man|gos
man|gold +s
  (= mangel)
mangold-wurzel +s
  (= mangel-wurzel)
man|gonel +s
man|go|steen +s
man|grove +s
mangy
  mangi|er
  mangi|est
man|handle
  man|han|dles
  man|han|dled
  man|hand|ling
Man|hat|tan (island,
  US)
man|hat|tan +s
Man|hat|tan|ite +s
man|hole +s
man|hood +s
man-hour +s
man|hunt +s
Mani (Persian
  prophet)
mania +s
ma|niac +s
man|iac|al
man|iac|al|ly
manic
Ma|nica|land
  (province,
  Zimbabwe)
man|ic|ally
manic-depres|sive
  +s
Mani|chae|an +s
Mani|chae|ism
Mani|chae|us
  (= Mani: Persian
  prophet)
Mani|che|an +s (*use*
  Manichaean)

Mani|chee +s
Mani|che|ism (*use*
  Manichaeism)
mani|cotti
Mani|cou|agan (river,
  Canada)
mani|cure
  mani|cures
  mani|cured
  mani|cur|ing
mani|cured *adjective*
mani|cur|ist +s
mani|fest +s +ed
  +ing
mani|fest|a|tion +s
mani|fest|a|tive
mani|fest|ly
mani|festo
  mani|festos or
  mani|fes|toes
mani|fold +s (various;
  thing with various
  parts)
  [☞ manyfold]
mani|fold|ly
mani|fold|ness
mani|kin +s (dwarf;
  lay figure;
  anatomical model)
  [☞ manakin,
  mannequin]
Man|ila (capital of the
  Philippines)
man|ila
man|illa (*use* manila)
man|ioc +s
man|iple +s
ma|nipu|la|bil|ity
ma|nipu|lable
ma|nipu|lat|able
ma|nipu|late
  ma|nipu|lates
  ma|nipu|lat|ed
  ma|nipu|lat|ing
ma|nipu|la|tion +s
ma|nipu|la|tive
ma|nipu|la|tive|ly
ma|nipu|la|tive|ness
ma|nipu|la|tor +s
ma|nipu|la|tory
Mani|pur (state, India)
Mani|puri +s
Mani|toba (province,
  lake & escarpment,
  Canada; maple)
Mani|toban +s
mani|tou +s
Mani|tou|lin (island,
  Canada)
Mani|waki (town,
  Canada)
man|kind

manky
  mank|i|er
  mank|i|est
man|less
man|like
man|li|ness
manly
  man|li|er
  man|li|est
man-made
Mann, Thom|as
  (German writer)
manna (food, benefit;
  laxative)
  [☞ mana]
manna-ash
  manna-ashes
Man|nar (island &
  town, Sri Lanka; gulf)
Mann Cup
manned *adjective*
man|ne|quin +s
  (model for displaying
  clothes)
  [☞ manakin,
  manikin]
man|ner +s (way;
  social habits; polite
  behaviour; style)
  [☞ manor]
man|nered *adjective*
Man|ner|ism (style of
  Italian art)
man|ner|ism +s
  (habit; excessive use
  of a style)
man|ner|ist +s
man|ner|is|tic
man|ner|is|tic|al
man|ner|is|tic|al|ly
man|ner|less
man|ner|li|ness
man|ner|ly
Mann|heim (city,
  Germany)
man|ni|kin +s (dwarf,
  lay figure,
  anatomical model:
  use manikin)
  [☞ manakin,
  mannequin]
Man|ning, Er|nest
  Charles (Cdn
  politician)
Man|ning, (Er|nest)
  Pres|ton (Cdn
  politician)
Man|ning, Oliv|ia
  Mary (English
  novelist)
man|nish
man|nish|ly
man|nish|ness

Mano (river, Africa)
mano-a-mano
man|oeu|ver +s +ed
+ing (use
manoeuvre)
man|oeu|ver|abil|ity
(use
manoeuvrability)
man|oeu|ver|able
(use manoeuvrable)
man|oeu|ver|er +s
(use manoeuvrer)
man|oeuv|rabil|ity
man|oeuv|rable
man|oeuvre
man|oeuv|res
man|oeuv|red
man|oeuv|ring
man|oeuv|rer +s
man-of-war
men-of-war
man|om|eter +s
mano|met|ric
man|om|etry
ma non trop|po
manor +s (house;
police jurisdiction)
[☞ manner]
manor|ial
man|power
man|qué
Man Ray (US artist)
Mans, Le (town &
motor-racing circuit,
France)
man|sard +s
man|sard|ed
Man|sart, Fran|çois
(French architect)
manse +s
Man|sel (island,
Canada)
Man|sell, Nigel
(English race-car
driver)
man|serv|ant
men|serv|ants
Mans|field,
Kath|er|ine (New
Zealand writer)
man|sion +s
man-size (= man-
sized)
man-sized
man|slaugh|ter +s
Man|son, Charles (US
cult leader)
Man|son, Sir Pat|rick
(Scottish physician)
man|sue|tude
Man|sur, Abu Ja'far
al- (Abbasid caliph)
manta +s

man-tailored
Man|tegna, An|drea
(Italian artist)
man|tel +s (of a
fireplace)
[☞ mantle]
man|tel|et +s
mantel|piece +s
mantel|shelf
mantel|shelves
man|tic
man|ti|core +s
man|tid +s
man|tilla +s
man|tis
plural man|tis or
man|tis|es
man|tissa +s
Man|tle, Mick|ey
Charles (US baseball
player)
man|tle (cloak; blush;
Zoology)
man|tles
man|tled
mant|ling
[☞ mantel]
mant|let +s (use
mantelet)
man|tra +s
man|trap +s
man|tua +s
Manu (Hindu Myth)
manu|al +s
manu|al|ly
manu|fac|tory
manu|fac|tor|ies
manu|fac|tur|abil|ity
manu|fac|tur|able
manu|fac|ture
manu|fac|tures
manu|fac|tured
manu|fac|tur|ing
manu|fac|tur|er +s
manu|mis|sion +s
manu|mit
manu|mits
manu|mit|ted
manu|mit|ting
ma|nure
ma|nures
ma|nured
ma|nur|ing
manu|script +s
Manu|tius, Aldus
(Italian printer)
Manx
many
many|fold (by many
times)
[☞ manifold]
many-sided
many-sided|ness

man|za|nilla +s
man|za|nita +s
Man|zoni,
Ales|san|dro (Italian
writer)
Mao|ism
Mao|ist +s
Maori
plural Maori or
Mao|ris
Mao Tse-tung
(= Mao Zedong)
Mao Ze|dong
(Chinese statesman)
map
maps
mapped
map|ping
maple +s
Maple Leaf +s (Cdn
flag; coin; NHL
team)
maple leaf (leaf of
the maple)
maple leaves
Maple Ridge
(municipality,
Canada)
maple syrup
map-maker +s
map-making
map|pable
map|per +s
map-reader +s
map-reading
Ma|puto (capital of
Mozambique)
ma|quette +s
ma|quila|dora +s
ma|quil|lage
Ma|quis
plural Ma|quis
mar
mars
marred
mar|ring
mara|bou +s (stork;
feather; jig)
mara|bout +s (hermit,
monk; shrine; for
stork, feather, or jig
use marabou)
ma|raca +s (rattle)
[☞ morocco]
Mara|caibo (city &
lake, Venezuela)
Mara|dona, Diego
Ar|man|do
(Argentinian soccer
player)
Ma|ram|ba (city,
Zambia)

Mara|nhão (state,
Brazil)
Mara|ñón (river, Peru)
mara|schi|no +s
mar|as|mic
mar|as|mus
Marat, Jean Paul
(French
revolutionary)
Ma|ra|tha +s
Ma|ra|thi
Mara|thon (town,
Canada)
mara|thon +s
mara|thon|er +s
ma|raud +s +ed +ing
ma|raud|er +s
Mar|bella (town,
Spain)
mar|ble
mar|bles
mar|bled
marb|ling
mar|bled adjective
marble|ize
marble|iz|es
marble|ized
marble|iz|ing
mar|bling +s noun
mar|bly
Mar|burg (city,
Germany; virus)
marc +s (grape
residue; brandy)
[☞ mark, marque]
marca|site +s
mar|cato
Mar|ceau, Mar|cel
(French mime artist)
mar|cel
mar|cels
mar|celled
mar|cel|ling
Mar|cel|lus, Mar|cus
Claud|ius (Roman
general)
mar|ces|cence +s
mar|ces|cent
March (month)
March|es
march
march|es
marched
march|ing
Mar|chand, Jean
(Cdn union leader &
politician)
march|er +s
March|es (regions,
Britain & Italy)
March hare +s
mar|chion|ess
mar|chion|ess|es

march|pane
march past +s noun
Mar|ci|ano, Rocky (US boxer)
Mar|coni, Gu|gliel|mo (Italian radio pioneer)
mar|coni +s
Marco Polo (Italian traveller)
Marcos, Fer|di|nand Edra|lin (president of the Philippines)
Mar|cus Aurel|ius (Roman emperor)
Mar|cuse, Her|bert (US philosopher)
Mar del Plata (town, Argentina)
Mardi Gras
Mar|duk (*Babylonian Myth*)
Mare, Wal|ter John de la (English writer)
[☞ Mair]
mare¹ +s (female horse)
mare² (sea; *Astronomy*)
maria or mares
[☞ Mari]
mare clau|sum
mare lib|erum
Ma|ren|go (battle site, Italy)
mare's nest +s
mare's tail +s
Mar|garet (queens of England & Navarre; English princess)
mar|gar|ine +s
Mar|ga|rita (island off Venezuela)
mar|ga|rita +s (cocktail)
[☞ marguerite]
mar|gay +s
marge +s
mar|gin +s +ed +ing
mar|gin|al +s
mar|gin|alia
mar|gin|al|ity
mar|gin|al|iz|a|tion +s
mar|gin|al|ize
　mar|gin|al|iz|es
　mar|gin|al|ized
　mar|gin|al|iz|ing
mar|gin|al|ly
mar|gin|ate
　mar|gin|ates
　mar|gin|at|ed
　mar|gin|at|ing

mar|gin|a|tion +s
mar|grav|ate +s
mar|grave +s
mar|grav|ine +s
Mar|grethe (Danish queens)
mar|guer|ite +s (daisy)
[☞ margarita]
Mari (ancient city, Syria)
[☞ mare²]
maria
mari|achi +s
Maria de' Med|ici (= Marie de Médicis)
Mar|ian
Mari|ana +s (islands & trench, W Pacific)
Maria Ther|esa (archduchess of Austria)
Mari|bor (city, Slovenia)
Marie (Romanian queen)
Marie An|toin|ette (French queen)
Marie Byrd Land (region, Antarctica)
Marie de l'Incarna|tion (writer & educator, New France)
Marie de Mé|di|cis (queen of France)
Marie Lou|ise (empress of France)
Marie-Victorin, Frère (Cdn botanist)
Marie|ville (town, Canada)
mari|gold +s
ma|ri|juana
ma|rim|ba +s
Marin, John (US painter)
mar|ina +s
mar|in|ade
• *noun*
　mar|in|ades
• *verb* (use marinate)
　mar|in|ades
　mar|in|ad|ed
　mar|in|ad|ing
mar|in|ara
mar|in|ate *verb*
　mar|in|ates
　mar|in|at|ed
　mar|in|at|ing
[☞ marinade]
mar|in|a|tion +s

mar|ine +s
mar|in|er +s
[☞ Marriner]
Mari|netti, Filip|po Tom|maso Emilio (Italian writer)
Mari|ol|atry
Mari|ol|ogy
mar|ion|ette +s
mari|posa lily
　mari|posa lil|ies
Mar|ist +s
mari|tal
mari|tal|ly
Mari|time +s (of NB, NS & PEI)
mari|time (of the sea)
Mari|time Com|mand
Mari|tim|er +s
Ma|ritsa (river, Europe)
Ma|riu|pol (city, Ukraine)
Mar|ius, Gaius (Roman general & politician)
Ma|ri|vaux, Pierre Car|let de Cham|blain de (French writer)
mar|jor|am +s
Mark (saint)
mark +s +ed +ing (sign etc.; currency)
[☞ marc, marque]
Mark An|tony (Roman general)
mark down *verb*
　marks down
　marked down
　mark|ing down
mark|down +s *noun*
marked *adjective*
mark|ed|ly
mark|ed|ness
mark|er +s (person or thing that marks)
[☞ markhor]
mar|ket +s +ed +ing
market|abil|ity
market|able
market-driven
mar|ket|eer +s
mar|ket|eer|ing
mar|ket|er +s
mar|ket|ing *noun*
market-maker +s
market|place +s
Mark|ham (town, Canada)
mark|hor +s (goat)
mark|ing +s *noun*

mark|ka
mark|kaa
Mar|kova, Dame Ali|cia (English dancer)
marks|man
　marks|men
marks|man|ship
mark up *verb*
　marks up
　marked up
　mark|ing up
mark|up +s *noun*
marl +s +ed +ing
Marl|bor|ough, 1st Duke of (English general)
marled *adjective*
Mar|ley, Rob|ert Nesta ('Bob') (Jamaican musician)
[☞ marly]
mar|lin (fish)
　plural mar|lin or mar|lins
mar|line +s (rope)
mar|line|spike +s (use marlinspike)
mar|lin|spike +s
Mar|lowe, Chris|to|pher (English writer)
marly (of or like marl)
[☞ Marley]
mar|mal|ade +s
Mar|mara (sea, Turkey)
[☞ Marmora]
Mar|mite *proprietary* (yeast extract)
mar|mite +s (cooking pot)
Mar|mora (town, Canada)
[☞ Marmara]
mar|mor|eal
mar|mor|eal|ly
mar|mo|set +s
mar|mot +s
Marne (river, France)
Maro|nite +s
Ma|roon +s (descendant of slaves)
ma|roon +s +ed +ing (colour; strand)
Mar|quand, John Phil|lips (US novelist)
marque +s (make of motor vehicle; in 'letters of marque')
[☞ mark, marc]

mar|quee +s (canopy;
sign; tent; famous)
[☞ marquis]
mar|quee val|ue +s
Mar|ques|as (islands,
S Pacific)
mar|quess (British
nobleman)
mar|quess|es
[☞ marquis,
marquise, Marquis,
Marquis wheat]
mar|quess|ate +s
(rank or domain of a
marquess)
[☞ marquisate]
mar|quet|erie (use
marquetry)
mar|quet|ry
Mar|quette, Jacques
(French missionary
& explorer)
Már|quez, Gab|riel
Gar|cía (Colombian
novelist)
Mar|quis, Don|ald
Rob|ert Perry
('Don') (US
humorist)
[☞ marquess]
mar|quis (Continental
nobleman)
mar|quises
[☞ marquee,
marquise,
marquess]
mar|quis|ate +s (rank
or domain of a
marquis)
[☞ marquessate]
mar|quise +s
(noblewoman)
[☞ marquis,
marquess]
Mar|quis wheat
Mar|ra|kech
(= Marrakesh)
Mar|ra|kesh (city,
Morocco)
mar|ram
mar|riage +s
mar|riage|abil|ity
mar|riage|able
mar|ried +s adjective
& noun
Mar|ri|ner, Sir
Nev|ille (English
conductor)
[☞ mariner]
mar|ron glacé
mar|rons gla|cés
mar|row +s
mar|row bone +s
marrow|fat

marrow|less
mar|rowy
marry (wed, unite,
combine; interjection)
mar|ries
mar|ried
marry|ing
[☞ merry, Mary]
Mars (Roman Myth;
planet)
Mar|sala +s
Mar|salis, Bran|ford
(US saxophone
player)
Mar|salis, Wyn|ton
(US trumpet player)
Mar|seil|laise
Mar|seille
(= Marseilles)
Mar|seilles (city,
France)
Marsh, Dame (Edith)
Ngaio (New Zealand
writer)
marsh
marsh|es
mar|shal (officer;
arrange; conduct)
mar|shals
mar|shal|led
mar|shal|ling
[☞ Marshall,
martial]
Mar|shall +s (islands,
NW Pacific)
[☞ marshal,
Martial]
Mar|shall, Don|ald Jr.
(victim of wrongful
conviction)
Mar|shall, George
Cat|lett (US
statesman)
Mar|shall, John (US
jurist)
Mar|shall, Lois
Cath|er|ine (Cdn
soprano)
Mar|shall, Thur|good
(US jurist)
mar|shal|ler +s
Mar|shall Plan
marshal|ship +s
marshed
marsh grass
marsh grass|es
marsh|i|ness
marsh|land +s
marsh mal|low +s
(plant)
[☞ marshmallow]
marsh|mal|low +s
(soft candy; soft-

willed person)
[☞ marsh mallow]
marshy
marsh|i|er
marsh|i|est
Mar|sil|ius of Padua
(Italian political
philosopher)
Mar|ston, John
(English playwright)
Mar|ston Moor
(battle site, England)
mar|sup|ial +s
Mar|sy|as (Greek
Myth)
mart +s
Mar|ta|ban (gulf,
Indian Ocean)
mar|ta|gon +s
Mar|tel, Charles
(Frankish ruler)
Mar|tel|lo tower +s
mar|ten +s (weasel-
like mammal; fur)
[☞ martin]
mar|tens|ite
mar|ten|sit|ic
Mar|tha (New
Testament)
Martha's Vine|yard
(island, US)
Mar|tial (Roman
epigrammatist)
[☞ Marshall]
mar|tial (of war;
warlike)
[☞ marshal]
mar|tial|ly
Mar|tian +s
Mar|tin (saint; popes)
Mar|tin, Ar|cher John
Por|ter (English
biochemist)
Mar|tin, Dean (US
entertainer)
Mar|tin, Paul Jo|seph
James (1903–92;
Cdn politician)
Mar|tin, Steve (US
comedian)
Mar|tin, Wil|liam
Mel|ville (Cdn
politician)
mar|tin +s (bird)
[☞ marten]
Mar|tin du Gard,
Roger (French
novelist)
Mar|ti|neau, Har|riet
(English writer)
mar|ti|net +s
mar|tin|gale +s

Mar|tini, Paul (Cdn
figure skater)
Mar|tini +s
Mar|ti|nique (island,
W Indies)
Mar|tin|mas
mart|let +s
mar|tyr +s +ed +ing
mar|tyr|dom +s
mar|tyr|ish
mar|tyr|o|logic|al
mar|tyr|ol|o|gist +s
mar|tyr|ol|ogy
mar|tyr|ol|o|gies
Mar|uts (Hinduism)
mar|vel
mar|vels
mar|velled
mar|vel|ling
Mar|vell, An|drew
(English poet)
mar|vel|ler +s
mar|vel|lous
mar|vel|lous|ly
mar|vel|lous|ness
marvy
marv|i|er
marv|i|est
Marx, Chico, Harpo,
Groucho, & Zeppo
(US comedians)
Marx, Karl Hein|rich
(German
philosopher)
Marx|ism
Marxism-Leninism
Marx|ist +s
Marxist-Leninist +s
Mary (New Testament
saints; queens of
England & Scotland)
[☞ marry, merry]
Mary Jane +s
Mary|land (state, US)
Mary Mag|da|len
(= Mary
Magdalene)
Mary Mag|da|lene
(saint)
Marys|town (town,
Canada)
Mary Stu|art (queen
of Scotland)
Mary Tudor (queen
of England)
mar|zi|pan
mar|zi|pans
mar|zi|panned
mar|zi|pan|ning
mas (masquerade)
[☞ mass]
masa

Ma|sac|cio (Italian
painter)
Ma|sada (ancient
fortress, Israel)
Masai
plural Masai or
Mas|ais
ma|sala +s
Mas|aryk, Jan
Gar|rigue
(Czechoslovak
statesman)
Mas|aryk, Tomáš
Gar|rigue
(Czechoslovak
president)
Mas|bate (island &
town, the
Philippines)
mas|cara +s
mas|car|aed
Mas|car|ene +s
(islands, Indian
Ocean)
mas|car|pone
mas|con +s
mas|cot +s
Mas|couche (town,
Canada)
mas|cu|line +s
mas|cu|lin|ist +s
mas|cu|lin|ity
mas|cu|lin|ize
mas|cu|lin|iz|es
mas|cu|lin|ized
mas|cu|lin|iz|ing
Mase|field, John
Ed|ward (English
writer)
maser +s (electronic
device)
[☞ mazer]
Ma|seru (capital of
Lesotho)
mash
mash|es
mashed
mash|ing
mash|er +s
Mash|had (city, Iran)
mash|ie +s
Ma|shona|land
(region, Zimbabwe)
mas|jid +s
mask +s +ed +ing
(face covering;
disguise)
[☞ masque]
masked adjective
masked ball +s
mask|er +s (person
who masks or wears

a mask)
[☞ masquer]
mask|ing adjective
mas|kin|onge
plural mas|kin|onge
or mas|kin|on|ges
maso|chism
maso|chist +s
maso|chis|tic
maso|chis|tic|ally
Mason, James
Nev|ille (English
actor)
Mason, John (English
colonial
administrator)
Mason +s
(Freemason; jar)
mason (builder) +s
+ed +ing
[☞ meson]
Mason and Dixon
Line (= Mason–
Dixon Line)
Mason–Dixon Line
Ma|son|ic
Ma|son|ite proprietary
Mason jar +s
Ma|son|ry
(Freemasonry)
ma|son|ry
Ma|sor|ah
Mas|or|ete +s
Mas|or|etic
masque +s
(entertainment)
[☞ mask]
mas|quer +s
(participant in a
masque)
[☞ masker]
mas|quer|ade
mas|quer|ades
mas|quer|ad|ed
mas|quer|ad|ing
mas|quer|ad|er +s
Mass (Eucharist)
Mass|es
[☞ mas]
mass (quantity of
matter, people, etc.)
mass|es
massed
mass|ing
[☞ mas]
Mas|sa|chu|setts
(state, US)
mas|sacre
mas|sacres
mas|sacred
mas|sac|ring
mas|sage
mas|sa|ges

mas|saged
mas|sa|ging
mas|sa|ger +s
mas|sa|sau|ga +s
(rattlesnake)
[☞ Mississauga]
Mas|sa|soit
(Wampanoag chief)
Mas|sawa (town,
Eritrea)
massed adjective
mass-energy
Mas|senet, Jules
Émile Fré|dé|ric
(French composer)
mas|seter +s
mas|seur +s
mas|seuse +s
Mas|sey, (Charles)
Vin|cent (Cdn
governor general)
Mas|sey, Dan|iel (Cdn
manufacturer)
Mas|sey, Hart
Almer|rin (Cdn
manufacturer &
philanthropist)
Mas|sey, Ray|mond
Hart (Cdn actor)
mas|si|cot
mas|sif +s
Mas|sif Cen|tral
(plateau, France)
Mas|sine, Léo|nide
Fedor|ovich (French
choreographer)
Mas|sin|ger, Phil|ip
(English dramatist)
mas|sive
mas|sive|ly
mas|sive|ness
mass|less
mass mar|ket +s
noun
mass-market +s +ed
+ing adjective & verb
mass-market|ed
adjective
Mas|so|rah (use
Masorah)
Mas|sor|ete (use
Masorete)
Mas|sor|et|ic (use
Masoretic)
mass-produce
mass-produces
mass-produced
mass-producing
mass-produced
adjective
mass pro|duc|tion
mast +s +ed +ing
mas|taba +s

mas|tec|tomy
mas|tec|to|mies
mast|ed adjective
mas|ter +s +ed +ing
master-at-arms
masters-at-arms
mas|ter|ful
mas|ter|ful|ly
mas|ter|ful|ness
mas|ter|less
mas|ter|li|ness
mas|ter|ly
master|mind +s +ed
+ing
master|piece +s
Mas|ters, Edgar Lee
(US writer)
master's degree +s
master|sing|er +s
master|work +s
mas|tery
mast|head +s +ed
+ing
mas|tic +s
mas|ti|cate
mas|ti|cates
mas|ti|cat|ed
mas|ti|cat|ing
mas|ti|ca|tion +s
mas|ti|ca|tor +s
mas|ti|ca|tory
mas|tiff +s
mas|titis
mas|to|don +s
mas|toid +s
mas|toid|itis
mas|tur|bate
mas|tur|bates
mas|tur|bat|ed
mas|tur|bat|ing
mas|tur|ba|tion
mas|tur|ba|tor +s
mas|tur|ba|tory
Ma|suria (region,
Poland)
Ma|sur|ian Lakes
(= Masuria)
mat (rug; pad; tangle;
picture border;
matrix)
mats
mat|ted
mat|ting
[☞ matte]
Mata|bele|land
(former province,
Southern Rhodesia)
mata|dor +s
Mata Hari (Dutch
dancer & secret
agent)
Ma|tane (town,
Canada)

Mata|pédia (river, Canada)
match (equal; contest; incendiary device)
match|es
matched
match|ing
match|board +s
match|book +s
match|box
match|boxes
match|ing *adjective*
match|less
match|less|ly
match|lock
match|make
match|makes
match|made
match|making
match|mak|er +s
match|making *noun & adjective*
match play
match|stick +s
match up *verb*
match|es up
matched up
match|ing up
match|up +s *noun*
match|wood
mate
mates
mated
mat|ing
maté (herbal tea)
mate|less
mate|lot +s (sailor)
mate|lote +s (stew)
mater +s (mother; in 'alma mater', 'dura mater', 'pia mater' & 'Stabat Mater')
mater|famil|ias
matres|famil|ias
ma|teri|al +s (matter, substance; physical; vital, relevant; *Law*) [☞ *matériel*]
ma|ter|ial|ism
ma|ter|ial|ist +s
ma|ter|ial|is|tic
ma|ter|ial|is|tic|ally
ma|ter|ial|ity
ma|ter|ial|iz|a|tion +s
ma|ter|ial|ize
mater|ial|iz|es
mater|ial|ized
mater|ial|iz|ing
ma|ter|ial|ly
ma|teria med|ica
ma|tér|iel (available resources)

mater|nal
mater|nal|ism
mater|nal|is|tic
mater|nal|ly
mater|nity
mate|ship
matey
mateys
mati|er
mati|est
matey|ness
math +s
math|emat|ical
math|emat|ical|ly
math|em|at|ician +s
math|emat|ics
Mathe|son, Alex|an|der Wal|lace (Cdn politician)
Mathie|son, John Alex|an|der (Cdn politician)
maths
mati|er
mati|est
Ma|tilda (English princess; swag; in 'waltz Matilda')
matin
mati|nee +s
mati|ness (*use* mateyness)
mat|ing +s *noun*
matins
Ma|tisse, Henri Emile Be|noît (French artist)
Mat|mata (town, Tunisia)
Mato Gros|so (state, W Brazil)
Mato Gros|so do Sul (state, SW Brazil)
matri|arch +s
matri|arch|al
matri|archy
matri|arch|ies
ma|tric
matri|ces
matri|cid|al
matri|cide +s
ma|tricu|late
ma|tricu|lates
ma|tricu|lat|ed
ma|tricu|lat|ing
ma|tricu|la|tion +s
matri|lin|eage
matri|lin|eal
matri|lin|eal|ly
matri|local
matri|local|ity
matri|mon|ial

matri|mon|ial|ly
matri|mony
matri|mon|ies
matri|oshka +s (*use* matryoshka)
mat|rix
matri|ces or mat|rix|es
ma|tron +s
ma|tron|hood +s
ma|tron|ly
matry|oshka +s
Mats|qui
plural Mats|qui
mat|su|take +s
Mat|su|yama (city, Japan)
Matta|gami (river, Canada)
matte +s (without gloss; smelting product; *Film*)
mat|ted *adjective*
mat|ter +s +ed +ing (substance; be of importance) [☞ mater]
Matter|horn (Alpine mountain)
mat|ter of fact +s *noun*
matter-of-fact *adjective*
matter-of-factly
matter-of-factness
Mat|thew (saint)
Mat|thew Paris (English chronicler)
Mat|thias (saint)
mat|ting *noun*
mat|tins (*use* matins)
mat|tock +s
mat|tress
mat|tress|es
mat|ur|a|tion
mat|ur|a|tion|al
ma|tur|a|tive
ma|ture
ma|tur|er
ma|tur|est
ma|ture|ly
ma|tur|ity
ma|tur|ities
matu|tinal
mat|zah +s (*use* matzo)
matzo
mat|zos or mat|zoth
mat|zoh +s (*use* matzo)
maud|lin

Maugham, Wil|liam Somer|set (English writer)
Maui (island, Hawaii)
maul +s +ed +ing (tear, mutilate; criticize; hammer, club; scrum) [☞ mall, moll]
maul|er +s [☞ Mahler]
maul|ing +s *noun*
Mau Mau *noun & adjective*: *plural* Mau Mau
mau-mau +s +ed +ing *verb*
Mauna Kea (volcano, Hawaii)
Mauna Loa (volcano, Hawaii)
maun|der +s +ed +ing
Maun|dy Thurs|day
Mau|pas|sant, (Henri René Al|bert) Guy de (French writer)
Maure|tania (former region, Africa) [☞ Mauritania]
Maure|tan|ian +s (of Mauretania) [☞ Mauritanian]
Maur|iac, Fran|çois (French writer)
Mau|rice (Dutch general) [☞ Morrice, Morris]
Mauri|tania (modern country, Africa) [☞ Mauretania]
Mauri|tan|ian +s (of Mauritania) [☞ Mauretanian]
Maur|itian +s
Maur|itius (country, Indian Ocean)
Mau|rois, André (French biographer)
Maury, Mat|thew Fon|taine (US oceanographer)
Mau|rya (Indian dynasty)
Mau|ryan
Mau|ser +s
proprietary
mau|so|leum +s
mausy (*use* mauzy)
maus|i|er
maus|i|est
mauve +s (colour)

mauzy
  mauz|i|er
  mauz|i|est
maven +s
mav|er|ick +s
mavis
  mavis|es
maw +s (stomach;
  mouth)
mawk|ish
mawk|ish|ly
mawk|ish|ness
max
  maxes
  maxed
  max|ing
maxi +s
max|illa
  max|il|lae
  max|il|lary
Maxim, Sir Hiram
  Ste|vens (English
  inventor)
max|im +s
max|ima
max|imal
max|imal|ist +s
max|imal|ly
Max|imil|ian
  (Mexican emperor;
  German king & Holy
  Roman emperor)
maxi|miz|a|tion +s
maxi|mize
  maxi|miz|es
  maxi|mized
  maxi|miz|ing
maxi|miz|er +s
max|imum
  max|imums or
  max|ima
maximum-security
maxi-pad +s
Max|well, (Ian)
  Rob|ert (English
  media entrepreneur)
Max|well, James
  Clerk (Scottish
  physicist)
max|well +s
May +s (month)
may
  • (plant)
  mays
  • (auxiliary verb)
  present **may**
  past **might**
Maya (people;
  language)
  plural **Maya** or
  Mayas
  [☞ **Maia**]

maya (Hinduism &
  Buddhism)
Mayan +s
may|apple +s
maybe +s
May Day +s (festival)
may|day +s (distress
  call)
May-December
Mayer, Louis Burt
  (US film executive)
  [☞ **Mair, Meir,**
  mayor]
may|est
may|flower +s
may|fly
  may|flies
may|hap
may|hem
may|ing noun
Mayne (island,
  Canada)
  [☞ **Main, Maine**]
mayn't
Mayo (county, Ireland)
Mayo, Charles
  Hor|ace (US
  surgeon)
mayo
mayon|naise +s
may|or +s (council
  official)
  [☞ **Mair, Mayer,**
  Meir]
mayor|al
mayor|alty
  mayor|al|ties
mayor|ship
May|otte (island,
  Indian Ocean)
may|pole +s
Mays, Wil|lie
  How|ard (US
  baseball player)
mayst
may|weed +s
maz|ard +s
Mazar-e-Sharif (city,
  Afghanistan)
Maza|rin, Jules
  (French statesman)
Maz|at|lán (resort,
  Mexico)
Maz|da|ism
maze +s (perplexing
  path, puzzle;
  complex
  arrangement)
  [☞ **maize, Mays**]
mazed adjective
mazel tov
mazer +s (bowl)
  [☞ **maser**]

ma|zuma
ma|zurka +s
mazy
  mazi|er
  mazi|est
maz|zard +s (use
  mazard)
Maz|zini, Giu|seppe
  (Italian nationalist
  leader)
M.B.A. (Master of
  Business
  Administration)
M.B.A.'s
Mba|bane (capital of
  Swaziland)
mba|qanga
MC (master of
  ceremonies)
MCs
MCd
MCing
Mc|Arthur (mountain,
  Canada)
  [☞ **MacArthur**]
Mc|Bride, Rich|ard
  (Cdn politician)
Mc|Cain, H.
  Har|ri|son (Cdn
  businessman)
Mc|Carthy, Jo|seph
  Ray|mond (US
  senator)
Mc|Carthy, Mary
  The|rese (US
  novelist)
Mc|Carthy|ism
Mc|Carthy|ite +s
Mc|Cart|ney, Sir
  (James) Paul
  (English singer-
  songwriter)
Mc|Clel|land, John
  Gor|don ('Jack')
  (Cdn publisher)
Mc|Clung, Nel|lie
  Leti|tia (Cdn
  suffragist)
Mc|Cor|mack, John
  (US tenor)
McCoy +s
Mc|Crae, John (Cdn
  medical officer &
  poet)
Mc|Cul|lers, Car|son
  Smith (US writer)
Mc|Cully, Jona|than
  (Cdn politician)
Mc|Don|ald (in 'Heard
  and McDonald
  Islands')
  [☞ **MacDonald,**
  Macdonald]

Mc|Doug|all,
  Wil|liam (Cdn
  politician)
Mc|Enroe, John
  Pat|rick (US tennis
  player)
Mc|Gar|rigle, Anna
  (Cdn singer-
  songwriter)
Mc|Gar|rigle, Kate
  (Cdn singer-
  songwriter)
McGee, Thom|as
  D'Arcy (Cdn
  politician)
Mc|Gill, James (Cdn
  businessman &
  philanthropist)
Mc|Intosh (apple)
  Mc|Intosh|es
  [☞ **Mackintosh**]
McJob +s
Mc|Kenna, Frank
  Jo|seph (Cdn
  politician)
Mc|Kin|ley (mountain,
  US)
Mc|Kin|ley, Wil|liam
  (US president)
Mc|Kin|ney, Louise
  (Cdn activist)
Mc|Kin|non,
  Cath|er|ine (Cdn
  entertainer)
Mc|Lach|lan, Sarah
  (Cdn singer-
  songwriter)
  [☞ **McLauchlan,**
  McLaughlin]
Mc|Laren, Nor|man
  (Cdn filmmaker)
Mc|Lauch|lan,
  Mur|ray Ed|ward
  (Cdn singer-
  songwriter)
  [☞ **McLachlan,**
  McLaughlin]
Mc|Laugh|lin,
  Aud|rey (Cdn
  politician)
  [☞ **McLauchlan,**
  McLachlan]
M'Clin|tock (channel,
  Canada)
Mc|Luhan, (Her|bert)
  Mar|shall (Cdn
  communications
  theorist)
Mc|Mahon, Fran|cis
  Mur|ray Pat|rick
  (Cdn industrialist)
Mc|Master, Wil|liam
  (Cdn businessman)

Mc|Millan, Edwin
Mat|ti|son (US
physicist)
[☞ MacMillan,
Macmillan]
Mc|Nair, John
Bab|bitt (Cdn
politician)
MCP (male chauvinist
pig)
MCPs
Mc|Pher|son, Aimee
Sem|ple (Cdn-born
evangelist)
[☞ Macpherson]
Mc|Tavish, Simon
(Cdn fur trader)
MD (doctor)
MDs
me
• *pronoun*
• *noun* (*Music*: use **mi**)
mea culpa +s
Mead, Mar|garet (US
anthropologist)
[☞ Meade, Mede,
meed]
mead +s (drink;
meadow)
[☞ meed, Meade,
Mede]
Meade, George
Gor|don (US
general)
[☞ Mead, Mede,
meed]
mead|ow +s
mead|ow grass
meadow|land +s
meadow|lark +s
mead|ow rue +s
meadow|sweet +s
mead|owy
Mea|ford (town,
Canada)
mea|ger (*use* meagre)
meager|ly (*use*
meagrely)
meager|ness (*use*
meagreness)
mea|gre
meagre|ly
meagre|ness
meal +s
meal|i|ness
meal|time +s
meal|worm +s
mealy
meal|i|er
meal|i|est
mealy bug +s
mealy-mouthed

mean (intend; unkind,
stingy; midway
point)
means
meant
mean|ing
mean|er
mean|est
[☞ mien, mesne]
me|and|er +s +ed
+ing
me|and|er|ing +s
noun & adjective
mean|ie +s
mean|ing +s *noun &*
adjective
mean|ing|ful
mean|ing|ful|ly
mean|ing|ful|ness
mean|ing|less
mean|ing|less|ly
mean|ing|less|ness
mean|ing|ly
mean|ly
mean|ness
means
mean-spirit|ed
mean-spirit|ed|ly
mean-spirit|ed|ness
means test +s *noun*
means-test +s +ed
+ing *verb*
meant
mean time (*Horology*)
mean|time
(intervening period;
meanwhile)
mean|while
meany (*use* meanie)
mean|ies
Meares (island,
Canada)
measles
meas|ly
meas|li|er
meas|li|est
meas|ur|abil|ity
meas|ur|able
meas|ur|ably
meas|ure
meas|ures
meas|ured
meas|ur|ing
meas|ured *adjective*
meas|ured|ly
meas|ure|less
meas|ure|less|ly
meas|ure|ment +s
meat +s (food;
substance)
[☞ meet, mete]
meat and po|ta|toes
(meat-and-potatoes

when preceding a
noun)
meat|ball +s
Meath (county,
Ireland)
meat|head +s
meat|hook +s
meat|i|er
meat|i|est
meat|i|ly
meat|i|ness
meat|less
meat loaf +s
meat pack|er +s
meat-packing
me|atus
plural me|atus or
me|atus|es
meaty
meat|i|er
meat|i|est
Mecca (pilgrimage
site, Saudi Arabia)
mec|ca +s (place that
attracts)
Mec|can +s
Mec|cano *proprietary*
mech|an|ic +s
mech|an|ic|al
mech|an|ic|al|ism
mech|an|ic|al|ly
mech|an|ic|al|ness
mech|an|ician +s
mech|an|ics
mech|an|ism +s
mech|an|ist +s
mech|an|is|tic
mech|an|is|tic|ally
mech|an|iz|a|tion +s
mech|an|ize
mech|an|iz|es
mech|an|ized
mech|an|iz|ing
mech|an|iz|er +s
mech|ano|recep|tion
mech|ano|recep|tive
mech|ano|recep|tor
+s
mecha|tron|ics
Me|che|len (city,
Belgium)
Mech|lin +s (lace)
me|choui +s
Meck|len|burg
(former state,
Germany)
Meck|lenburg-West
Pom|er|ania (state,
Germany)
meco|nium +s
Med (Mediterranean
Sea)
med +s

medal (award, trophy)
med|als
med|alled
med|al|ling
[☞ meddle, metal,
mettle]
med|alled *adjective*
med|al|lic
med|al|lion +s
med|al|list +s
Medan (city,
Indonesia)
Med|awar, Sir Peter
Brian (English
immunologist)
med|dle (interfere)
med|dles
med|dled
med|dling
[☞ medal, mettle,
metal]
med|dler +s (one who
meddles)
[☞ medlar]
meddle|some
(interfering)
[☞ mettlesome]
meddle|some|ly
meddle|some|ness
Mede +s (ancient
Persian)
[☞ Mead, Meade,
meed]
Medea (*Greek Myth*)
[☞ Media]
Me|del|lín (city,
Colombia)
med|evac
med|evacs
med|evaced
or med|evacked
med|evac|ing
or med|evack|ing
Media (ancient region,
Asia)
[☞ Medea]
media
• (*plural of* medium;
Communications)
• (*Anatomy*)
plural med|iae
med|ial
med|ial|ly
Med|ian (pertaining to
the Medes)
medi|an +s
medi|an|ly
medi|ant +s
medi|as|tin|al
medi|as|tin|um
medi|as|tina
medi|ate
medi|ates

medi|at|ed
medi|at|ing
medi|ate|ly
medi|a|tion +s
medi|ator +s
medi|atory
med|ic +s (doctor; *for* plant *use* medick)
med|ic|able
Medic|aid
med|ic|al +s
med|ic|al|iz|a|tion
med|ic|al|ize
  med|ic|al|iz|es
  med|ic|al|ized
  med|ic|al|iz|ing
med|ic|al|ly
med|ica|ment +s
Medi|care (in the US)
medi|care (in Canada)
medi|cate
  medi|cates
  medi|cat|ed
  medi|cat|ing
medi|ca|tion +s
medi|ca|tive
Medi|cean
Med|ici, Cath|er|ine de' (French queen)
Med|ici, Cos|imo de' (Florentine statesman)
Med|ici, Gio|van|ni de' (Pope Leo X)
Med|ici, Lor|enzo de' (Florentine statesman & arts patron)
Med|ici, Maria de' (= Marie de Médicis)
medi|cin|al +s
medi|cin|al|ly
medi|cine +s
Medi|cine Hat (city, Canada)
Medi|cine Line
Mé|di|cis, Marie de (queen of France)
med|ick +s (plant) [☞ medic]
med|ico +s
medi|ev|al
medi|ev|al|ism
medi|ev|al|ist +s
medi|ev|al|ize
  medi|ev|al|iz|es
  medi|ev|al|ized
  medi|ev|al|iz|ing
medi|ev|al|ly
Me|dina (city, Saudi Arabia)
me|dina +s

medi|ocre
medi|oc|rity
  medi|oc|ri|ties
medi|tate
  medi|tates
  medi|tat|ed
  medi|tat|ing
medi|ta|tion +s
medi|ta|tion|al
medi|ta|tive
medi|ta|tive|ly
medi|ta|tive|ness
medi|ta|tor +s
Medi|ter|ran|ean +s (sea; regional lands, people, etc.)
medi|um
• (middle degree; means of communication or conveyance; agency; environment; artistic material) *plural* **media** or medi|ums
• (medium-sized item; spiritualist) *plural* medi|ums
medium|ism
medium|is|tic
medium-range *adjective*
medium-security *adjective*
medium|ship
medium-sized
medi|vac (*use* medevac)
  medi|vacs
  medi|vaced or medi|vacked
  medi|vac|ing or medi|vack|ing
med|lar +s (tree & its fruit) [☞ meddler]
med|ley +s
Medoc
me|dul|la +s
me|dul|la ob|lon|gata *plural* me|dul|la ob|lon|ga|tas or me|dul|lae ob|lon|ga|tae
me|dul|lary
Me|dusa (*Greek Myth*)
me|dusa
  me|du|sae or me|du|sas
me|du|san
Meech Lake (lake, Canada; accord)

meed +s (reward) [☞ mead, Meade, Mede]
meek +er +est
meek|ly
meek|ness
Meel|paeg (lake, Canada)
meem|ies
meer|kat +s
meer|schaum +s
Mee|rut (city, India)
meet (encounter; satisfy; proper)
  meets
  met
  meet|ing [☞ meat, mete]
meet|ing +s *noun*
meet|ing house +s
meet|ly
meet|ness
meg +s
mega
mega|bit +s
mega|buck +s
mega|byte +s
mega|city
  mega|cities
mega|deal +s
mega|death +s
mega|dose +s
Me|gaera (*Greek Myth*)
mega|fauna
mega|flop +s
mega|hertz *plural* mega|hertz
mega|hit +s
mega|lith +s
mega|lith|ic
meg|alo|mania +s
meg|alo|maniac +s
meg|alo|man|iacal
meg|alo|man|ic
meg|alop|olis
  meg|alop|olis|es
meg|alo|pol|itan +s
meg|alo|saur +s
meg|alo|saur|us
  meg|alo|saur|us|es
mega-mall +s
mega-musical +s
Mé|gan|tic (hills, Canada)
mega|phone
  mega|phones
  mega|phoned
  mega|phon|ing
mega|phon|ic
mega|pod +s (*use* megapode)
mega|pode +s

mega|project +s
mega|ron +s
mega|spore +s
mega|star +s
mega|star|dom
mega|store +s
mega|ton +s
mega|ton|nage
mega|volt +s
mega|watt +s
Megha|laya (state, India)
Me|giddo (ancient city, Israel)
me|gilp +s
meg|ohm +s
me|grim +s
Me|hem|et Ali (pasha of Egypt; *use* Muhammad Ali)
Meigh|en, Ar|thur (Cdn prime minister)
Meiji
Meiji Tenno (emperor of Japan)
mei|o|sis (cell division; ironic understatement)
  mei|o|ses [☞ miosis]
mei|otic (of meiosis) [☞ miotic]
mei|otic|ally
Meir, Golda (Israeli stateswoman) [☞ Mair]
Meis|sen (city, Germany; porcelain)
meis|ter +s
Meister|singer *plural* Meister|singer
Meit|ner, Lise (Swedish physicist)
Me|kele (city, Ethiopia)
Mek|nès (city, Morocco)
Me|kong (river, Asia)
Me|laka (state & its capital, Indonesia) [☞ Malacca]
mel|amine +s
mel|an|cholia +s
mel|an|chol|ic +s
mel|an|chol|ic|ally
mel|an|choly
  mel|an|chol|ies
Me|lanch|thon, Phil|ipp (German theologian)
Mela|nesia (region, W Pacific)

Mela|nes|ian +s
mé|lange +s
mel|an|ic
mel|an|in +s
mel|an|ism
mel|an|oma +s
mel|an|o|sis
mel|an|o|ses
mel|an|otic
mela|to|nin
Melba, Dame Nel|lie
(Australian soprano)
Melba +s (toast;
apple)
Mel|bourne (city,
Australia)
Mel|bourne, Wil|liam
Lamb, 2nd
Vis|count (British
prime minister)
Mel|chior (one of the
Magi)
Mel|chior, Lau|ritz
Le|brecht Hom|mel
(US tenor)
Mel|chite +s
Mel|chiz|edek (Bible)
meld +s +ed +ing
Mele|ager (Greek
Myth)
melee +s
Mel|fort (city, Canada)
melic
Me|lilla (Spanish
enclave, Africa)
meli|lot +s
melior|ate
melior|ates
melior|at|ed
meliorat|ing
melior|a|tion +s
melior|a|tive
melior|ism
melior|ist +s
melior|is|tic
me|lis|ma
me|lis|mata or
me|lis|mas
me|lis|mat|ic
mel|lif|er|ous
mel|lif|lu|ence
mel|lif|lu|ent
mel|lif|lu|ous
mel|lif|lu|ous|ly
mel|lif|lu|ous|ness
mel|low +er +est +s
+ed +ing
mel|low|ly
mel|low|ness
Mel|mac proprietary
melo|deon +s
mel|od|ic
mel|od|ic|ally

melo|di|ous
melo|di|ous|ly
melo|di|ous|ness
melo|dist +s
melo|dize
melo|diz|es
melo|dized
melo|diz|ing
melo|diz|er +s
melo|drama +s
melo|dramat|ic
melo|dramat|ic|ally
melo|dramat|ics
melo|drama|tist +s
melo|drama|tize
melo|drama|tiz|es
melo|drama|tized
melo|drama|tiz|ing
mel|ody
mel|odies
melon +s
mel|ony
Melos (Greek island)
[☞ Miłosz]
Mel|pom|ene (Greek &
Roman Myth)
melt +s +ed +ing
melt|able
melt down verb
melts down
melt|ed down
melt|ing down
melt|down +s noun
melt|er +s
melt|ing adjective
melt|ing|ly
melt-in-the-mouth
melt-in-your-mouth
mel|ton
melt|water
Mel|ville (city, island,
lake & peninsula,
Canada)
Mel|ville, Her|man
(US writer)
mem|ber +s
mem|ber|less
mem|ber|ship +s
mem|brane +s
mem|bran|eous
(= membranous)
mem|bran|ous
meme +s
Memel (river, Europe;
German name for
Klaipeda, Lithuania)
me|mento
me|men|toes or
me|men|tos
me|mento mori
plural me|mento
mori

Mem|linc
(= Memling)
Mem|ling, Hans
(Flemish painter)
Mem|non (Greek
Myth)
memo +s
mem|oir +s
mem|oir|ist +s
mem|ora|bilia
mem|or|abil|ity
mem|or|able
mem|or|able|ness
mem|or|ably
memo|ran|dum
memo|randa or
memo|ran|dums
me|mor|ial +s
me|mor|ial|ist +s
me|mor|ial|iz|a|tion
+s
me|mor|ial|ize
me|mor|ial|iz|es
me|mor|ial|ized
me|mor|ial|iz|ing
me|mor|ial|iz|er +s
mem|or|iz|able
mem|or|iz|a|tion
mem|or|ize
mem|or|iz|es
mem|or|ized
mem|or|iz|ing
mem|or|iz|er +s
mem|or|iz|ing noun
mem|ory
mem|ories
Mem|phis (city, US;
ancient city, Egypt)
Mem|phré|ma|gog
(lake, Canada)
mem|sahib +s
men
men|ace
mena|ces
men|aced
mena|cing
mena|cer +s
mena|cing adjective
mena|cing|ly
mé|nage +s
mé|nage à trois
mé|nages à trois
men|ager|ie +s
Menai (strait, Wales)
Me|nan|der (Greek
dramatist)
mena|quin|one
men|arche
Men|cius (Chinese
philosopher)
Men|cken, Henry
Louis (US writer)
mend +s +ed +ing

mend|able
men|da|cious
men|da|cious|ly
men|da|city
men|da|ci|ties
Men|del, Gregor
Jo|hann (Moravian
monk & geneticist)
Men|de|leev, Dmitri
Ivan|ovich (Russian
chemist)
men|de|lev|ium
Men|del|ian +s
Men|del|ism
Men|dels|sohn, Felix
(German composer)
Men|dels|sohn,
Moses (German
philosopher)
Men|dels|sohn|ian
+s
mend|er +s
men|di|cancy
men|di|cant +s
men|di|city
mend|ing noun
Men|dip +s (hills,
England)
Men|doza (city,
Argentina)
Mene|laus (Greek
Myth)
Men|elik II (emperor
of Ethiopia)
Menes (pharaoh)
men|folk
Meng-tzu
(= Mencius, Chinese
philosopher)
Meng|zi (= Mencius,
Chinese philosopher)
men|haden
plural men|haden
men|hir +s
menial +s
menial|ly
Mé|nière's dis|ease
me|nin|geal
me|nin|ges
men|in|git|ic
men|in|gi|tis
me|nin|go|coc|cal
me|nin|go|coc|cus
me|nin|go|coc|ci
me|ninx
me|nin|ges
me|nis|coid
me|nis|cus
me|nisci
Men|non|ite +s
Men|non|it|ism
meno

men|ol|ogy
men|ol|o|gies
meno mosso
meno|paus|al
meno|pause
me|nor|ah +s
Me|norca
  (= Minorca, Balearic
  Islands)
men|or|rhagia
men|or|rhea
men|or|rhoea (*use*
  menorrhea)
Me|notti, Gian Carlo
  (US composer)
Menou d'Aul|nay,
  Charles de
  (governor of Acadia)
mensch
  mensch|en or
  mensch|es
men|ser|vants
men|ses
Men|she|vik +s
mens rea
men's room +s
men|stru|al
men|stru|ant +s
men|stru|ate
  men|stru|ates
  men|stru|at|ed
  men|stru|at|ing
men|stru|at|ing
  adjective
men|stru|a|tion +s
men|stru|ous
men|stru|um
  men|strua
men|sur|al
men|sur|a|tion +s
mens|wear
men|tal
men|tal|ism
men|tal|ist +s
men|tal|is|tic
men|tal|ity
  men|tal|ities
men|tal|ly
men|ta|tion
men|thol
men|thol|at|ed
men|tion +s +ed +ing
men|tion|able +s
men|tor +s +ed +ing
men|tor|ship +s
menu +s
menu-driven
Men|uhin, Sir Ye|hudi
  (English violinist)
Men|zies, Sir Rob|ert
  Gor|don (Australian
  prime minister)
meow +s +ed +ing

MEP +s (Member of
  the European
  Parliament)
me|peri|dine
Meph|isto|phe|lean
  (*use*
  Mephistophelian)
Meph|is|toph|eles
  (*German Legend*)
Meph|isto|phe|lian
meph|itic
meph|itis
  meph|itis|es
mer|bromin
mer|can|tile +s
mer|can|til|ism
mer|can|til|ist +s
mer|can|til|is|tic
mer|cap|tan +s
Mer|cator, Ger|ar|dus
  (Flemish
  cartographer)
mer|cen|ari|ness
mer|cen|ary
  mer|cen|ar|ies
mer|cer +s
mer|cer|ized
mer|cery
  mer|cer|ies
mer|chan|dise *noun &*
  verb
  mer|chan|dis|es
  mer|chan|dised
  mer|chan|dis|ing
mer|chan|dis|er +s
mer|chan|dize *verb*
  (*use* merchandise)
  mer|chan|diz|es
  mer|chan|dized
  mer|chan|diz|ing
  [☞ merchandise]
mer|chan|diz|er +s
  (*use* merchandiser)
Mer|chant, Is|mail
  (Indian filmmaker)
mer|chant +s
mer|chant|abil|ity
mer|chant|able
mer|chant|man
  mer|chant|men
Mer|cia (ancient
  kingdom, England)
  [☞ Murcia]
Mer|cian +s
Mer|cier (town,
  Canada)
Mer|cier, Hon|oré
  (Cdn politician)
merci|ful
merci|ful|ly
merci|ful|ness
merci|less
merci|less|ly

merci|less|ness
Mer|couri, Melina
  (Greek actress &
  politician)
Mer|credi, Ovide
  Wil|liam (Cdn
  Aboriginal leader)
Mer|cure, Pierre (Cdn
  composer)
Mer|cur|ial (of the
  planet Mercury)
mer|cur|ial +s (of the
  element mercury;
  volatile, lively)
mer|cur|ial|ity
mer|cur|ial|ly
mer|cur|ic
Mer|curo|chrome
  proprietary
mer|cur|ous
Mer|cury (*Roman
  Myth*; planet)
  [☞ Mercouri]
mer|cury
  mer|cur|ies
mercy
  mer|cies
  [☞ Mersey]
mere
  merest
  meres
  [☞ Meares]
Mere|dith, George
  (English writer)
mere|ly
mer|en|gue +s
  (dance)
  [☞ meringue]
mere|tri|cious
mere|tri|cious|ly
mere|tri|cious|ness
mer|gan|ser +s
merge
  mer|ges
  merged
  mer|ging
merged *adjective*
mer|gence
mer|ger +s
mer|ging +s *noun &*
  adjective
Mér|ida (cities, Spain
  & Mexico)
me|rid|ian +s
me|rid|ion|al +s
Méri|mée, Pros|per
  (French writer)
mer|ingue +s
  (dessert)
  [☞ merengue]
me|rino +s

Meri|oneth|shire
  (former county,
  Wales)
meri|stem
meri|stem|at|ic
merit +s +ed +ing
  [☞ Merritt]
merit|oc|racy
  merit|oc|ra|cies
merit|o|crat|ic
meri|tor|ious
meri|tor|ious|ly
meri|tor|ious|ness
merle +s
Mer|lin (*Arthurian
  Legend*)
mer|lin +s (falcon)
mer|lon +s (parapet)
Mer|lot +s
mer|maid +s
mer|maid's purse +s
Mer|man, Ethel (US
  singer)
mer|man
  mer|men
Meroe (ancient city on
  the Nile)
Mero|vin|gian +s
mer|ri|ly
mer|ri|ment
mer|ri|ness
Mer|ritt (city, Canada)
  [☞ merit]
merry (joyous)
  mer|ri|er
  mer|ri|est
  [☞ marry, Mary]
merry an|drew +s
merry-go-round +s
merry|maker +s
merry|making
merry widow +s
Mersa Ma|truh
  (town, Egypt)
Mer|sey (river,
  England)
  [☞ mercy]
Mer|sey|side (county,
  England)
Mer|sin (city, Turkey)
Mer|thyr Tyd|fil
  (town, Wales)
Mer|ton, Thom|as
  Fev|erel (US monk)
mesa +s
més|alli|ance +s
mes|cal +s
mes|ca|lin (*use*
  mescaline)
mes|ca|line
mes|clun +s
mes|dames
mes|demoi|selles

mes|em|bry|an|the|
    mum +s
mes|en|ceph|alon +s
mes|en|ter|ic
mes|en|ter|itis
mesen|tery
  mesen|ter|ies
mesh
  mesh|es
  meshed
  mesh|ing
Me|shach (Bible)
Me|shed
  (= Mashhad, Iran)
meshed adjective
mesh|ing +s noun &
  adjective
me|shuga
me|shug|ga (use
  meshuga)
me|shug|gah (use
  meshuga)
me|sial
me|sial|ly
mesic
Mes|mer, Franz
  Anton (Austrian
  physician)
mes|mer|ic
mes|mer|ic|ally
mes|mer|ism
mes|mer|ist +s
mes|mer|iz|a|tion
mes|mer|ize
  mes|mer|iz|es
  mes|mer|ized
  mes|mer|iz|ing
mes|mer|iz|er +s
mesne (intermediate)
  [☞ mean, mien]
Meso-America
  (Central America)
Meso-Americ|an +s
meso|blast +s
meso|derm +s
meso|derm|al
meso|lith|ic
meso|morph +s
meso|morph|ic
meson +s (Physics)
  [☞ mason]
meson|ic
meso|pause
meso|phyll +s
meso|phyte +s
Meso|po|tamia
  (ancient region, Asia)
Meso|po|ta|mian +s
meso|sphere
meso|spher|ic
meso|theli|oma +s
Meso|zoic
mes|quite +s

mess
  mess|es
  messed
  mess|ing
mes|sage
  mes|sa|ges
  mes|saged
  mes|sa|ging
mes|sa|ging noun
mes|sei|gneurs
mes|sen|ger +s
Mes|ser, Don|ald
  Charles Fred|erick
  (Cdn musician)
Mes|siaen, Oli|vier
  Eu|gène Pros|per
  Charles (French
  composer)
Mes|siah +s (Religion)
mes|siah +s (in
  general use)
Messiah|ship
Mes|si|anic (Religion)
mes|si|anic (in general
  use)
mes|si|an|ism
mess|i|er
mess|i|est
mes|sieurs
mess|i|ly
Mes|sina (city & strait,
  Italy)
mess|i|ness
mess|mate +s
mes|suage +s
mess up verb
  mess|es up
  messed up
  mess|ing up
mess-up +s noun
messy
  mess|i|er
  mess|i|est
mes|tiza +s female
mes|tizo +s female or
  male
met
meta|bol|ic
meta|bol|ic|ally
metab|ol|ism +s
metab|ol|ite +s
metab|ol|iz|able
metab|ol|ize
  metab|ol|iz|es
  metab|ol|ized
  metab|ol|iz|ing
meta|car|pal
meta|car|pus
  meta|carpi
meta|centre +s
meta|cen|tric

Meta|com|et
  (= Philip,
  Wampanoag chief)
meta|fic|tion +s
meta|fic|tion|al
meta|fic|tion|al|ity
meta|fic|tion|al|ly
meta|fic|tion|ist +s
meta|gen|esis
  meta|gen|eses
meta|gen|etic
Meta In|cog|nita
  (peninsula, Canada)
metal (hard shiny
  substance, etc.)
  met|als
  met|alled
  or met|aled
  met|al|ling
  or met|al|ing
  [☞ mettle, medal,
  meddle]
meta|lan|guage +s
met|alde|hyde
metal|head +s
meta|lin|guis|tic
meta|lin|guis|tics
me|tal|lic +s
me|tal|lic|ally
metal|li|city
  metal|li|ci|ties
metal|lif|er|ous
metal|liz|a|tion
metal|lize
  metal|liz|es
  metal|lized
  metal|liz|ing
me|tal|lo|graph|ic
me|tal|lo|graph|ic|
    ally
metal|log|raphy
metal|loid +s
metal|lur|gic
metal|lur|gic|al
metal|lur|gic|al|ly
metal|lur|gist +s
metal|lurgy
metal wood +s
metal|work
metal work|er +s
metal|work|ing
meta|mer +s
  (Chemistry)
meta|mere +s
  (Zoology)
meta|mer|ic
meta|mer|ism
meta|morph|ic
meta|morph|ism
meta|morph|ose
  meta|morph|os|es
  meta|morph|osed
  meta|morph|os|ing

meta|morph|o|sis
  meta|morph|o|ses
meta|phase +s
meta|phor +s
meta|phor|ic
meta|phor|ic|al
meta|phor|ic|al|ly
meta|phrase
  meta|phras|es
  meta|phrased
  meta|phras|ing
meta|phras|tic
meta|phys|ic +s
Meta|physic|al +s
  noun (poet)
meta|physic|al
  adjective
meta|physic|al|ly
meta|physi|cian +s
meta|phys|ics
meta|plasia +s
meta|plas|tic
meta|psych|o|logic|
    al
meta|psych|ol|ogy
meta|stabil|ity
meta|stable
me|tas|ta|sis
  me|tas|ta|ses
me|tas|ta|size
  me|tas|ta|siz|es
  me|tas|ta|sized
  me|tas|ta|siz|ing
meta|stat|ic
meta|tar|sal
meta|tar|sus
  meta|tarsi
me|tath|esis
  me|tath|eses
meta|thet|ic
meta|thet|ic|al
meta|zoan +s
Met|calf, Charles
  The|oph|ilus, 1st
  Baron (English
  colonial
  administrator)
Met|calf, John (Cdn
  writer)
Metch|ni|koff, Élie
  (Russian
  microbiologist)
mete (apportion, allot;
  measure; boundary,
  in 'metes and
  bounds')
  metes
  meted
  meting
  [☞ meat, meet]
metem|psych|o|sis
  metem|psych|o|ses
me|teor +s

Met|eora (region, Greece)
me|teor|ic
me|teor|ical|ly
me|teor|ite +s
me|teor|it|ic
me|teor|o|graph +s
me|teor|oid +s
me|teor|oid|al
me|teor|o|logic|al
me|teor|o|logic|al|ly
me|teor|ol|o|gist +s
me|teor|ol|ogy
me|ter +s +ed +ing (gauge; instrument or device for measuring; *for Prosody use* metre) [☞ metre]
meth
meth|adone
meth|am|pheta|mine +s
metha|nal (formaldehyde) [☞ methanol]
meth|ane
meth|ano|ic
meth|an|ol (methyl alcohol) [☞ methanal]
meth|aqua|lone
Methe|drine *proprietary*
me|thinks
  me|thought
me|thio|nine
meth|od +s
method-act +s +ed +ing *verb*
meth|od act|ing *noun*
meth|od ac|tor +s
mé|thode cham|pe|noise
meth|od|ic
meth|od|ic|al
meth|od|ic|al|ly
Meth|od|ism
Meth|od|ist +s (denomination)
meth|od|ist +s (*in general use*)
Me|tho|dius (saint)
meth|od|ize
  meth|od|iz|es
  meth|od|ized
  meth|od|iz|ing
meth|od|iz|er +s
meth|odo|logic|al
meth|od|o|logic|al|ly
meth|od|ol|o|gist +s
meth|od|ol|ogy
  meth|od|ol|o|gies

metho|trex|ate
me|thought
meths
Me|thu|selah +s (*Bible*; old person or thing)
me|thu|selah +s (wine bottle)
methyl +s
methyl|ate
  methyl|ates
  methyl|at|ed
  methyl|at|ing
methyl|at|ed *adjective*
methyl|a|tion
methyl|ene
methy|lic
met|ic +s
met|ic|al +s
me|ticu|lous
me|ticu|lous|ly
me|ticu|lous|ness
mé|tier +s
Metis
  plural Metis
Me|ton|ic cycle
meto|nym +s
meto|nym|ic
meto|nym|ic|al
meto|nym|ic|ally
me|tony|my
  me|tony|mies
me-too *adjective*
met|ope +s
metre +s (unit of length; *Prosody*) [☞ meter]
metre-kilogram-second
met|ric +s
met|ric|al
met|ric|al|ly
metri|cate
  metri|cates
  metri|cat|ed
  metri|cat|ing
metri|ca|tion +s
met|ric ton +s
met|ric tonne +s (= metric ton)
me|tritis
Metro (Toronto; Halifax-Dartmouth)
met|ro +s (metropolitan; subway)
metro|logic
metro|log|ic|al
met|rol|ogy
metro|nome +s
metro|nom|ic
metro|nom|ic|ally
metro|nym|ic +s

me|trop|olis
me|trop|olis|es
metro|pol|itan +s
metro|pol|itan|ism
me|tror|rha|gia
Met|ter|nich, Klem|ens (Austrian statesman)
met|tle +s (disposition; spirit; vigour) [☞ metal, meddle, medal]
mettle|some (spirited) [☞ meddlesome]
Metz (city, France)
Meulles, Jacques de (intendant of New France)
meu|nière
Meur|sault +s
Meuse (river, W Europe)
mew +s +ed +ing (cat cry; gull; hawk cage; confine) [☞ mu]
mewl +s +ed +ing (whimper) [☞ mule]
mews (buildings) [☞ muse]
Mexi|cali (city, Mexico)
Mex|ican +s
Mex|ico (country & gulf, N America)
Mex|ico City (capital of Mexico)
Meyer|beer, Gia|como (German composer)
Meyer|hof, Otto Fritz (US biochemist)
me|zer|eon +s
me|zu|zah
  me|zu|zahs or
  me|zu|zoth
Mézy, Au|gus|tin de Saf|fray de (French colonial administrator)
mezza|nine +s
mezza voce
mez|zo +s
mezzo-forte
Mezzo|gior|no (southern Italy)
mezzo-piano
mezzo-relievo +s
mezzo-soprano +s
mezzo|tint +s +ed +ing

MHA (Member of the House of Assembly)
MHAs
mho +s (unit of conductance) [☞ mow, *mot*, mo]
mi +s (*Music*) [☞ me]
Miami (city, US)
Miami|an +s
mi|asma
  mi|as|mas or
  mi|as|mata
mi|as|mal
mi|as|mat|ic
mi|as|mic
mic +s (microphone) [☞ mike, mick]
mica +s (mineral) [☞ Micah]
mi|ca|ceous
Micah (*Bible*) [☞ mica]
mica-schist +s
mice
mi|celle +s
Mi|chael (saint; Romanian king)
Michael|mas
Michel|angelo (Italian artist)
Mi|che|let, Jules (French historian)
Mi|chel|son, Al|bert Abra|ham (US physicist)
Mich|ener, (Dan|iel) Ro|land (Cdn governor general)
Mich|igan (state & lake, US)
Michi|gan|der +s
Mi|cho|acán (state, Mexico)
mick +s *offensive* (Irishman; Catholic)
mick|ey +s (liquor bottle; drink; in 'take the mickey')
Mick|ey Finn +s
Mick|ey Mouse *adjective*
mickey-taking
mickle +s
micky (in 'take the micky': *use* mickey)
Mic|mac (= Mi'kmaq) *plural* Mic|mac or Mic|macs
  • The spelling preferred by the

people themselves is
Mi'kmaq
micro +s
micro|analy|sis
  micro|analy|ses
micro|ana|lytic
mi|crobe +s
mi|crob|ial
mi|crob|ic
micro|bio|logic|al
micro|bio|logic|al|ly
micro|biol|o|gist +s
micro|biol|ogy
micro|brew +s +ed
  +ing
micro|brew|er +s
micro|brew|ery
  micro|brew|eries
micro|burst +s
micro|cas|sette +s
micro|ceph|alic
micro|ceph|aly
micro|chip
  micro|chips
  micro|chip|ped
  micro|chip|ping
micro|cir|cuit +s
micro|cir|cuit|ry
  micro|cir|cuit|ries
micro|cli|mate +s
micro|climat|ic
micro|climat|ic|ally
micro|code
  micro|codes
  micro|coded
  micro|cod|ing
micro|com|put|er +s
micro|cosm +s
micro|cos|mic
micro|cos|mic|ally
micro|dot +s
micro|econom|ic
micro|econom|ics
micro|elec|tron|ic
micro|elec|tron|ics
micro|environ|ment
  +s
micro|environ|ment|
  al
micro|evolu|tion
micro|evolu|tion|ary
micro|fibre +s
micro|fiche
  plural micro|fiche or
  micro|fiches
micro|film +s +ed
  +ing
micro|fine
micro|form +s
micro|gram +s
micro|graph +s
micro|grav|ity
  micro|grav|ities

micro|groove +s
micro|habi|tat +s
micro|instruc|tion +s
micro|lepi|dop|tera
micro|light +s
micro|lith +s
micro|lith|ic
micro|manage
  micro|man|ag|es
  micro|man|aged
  micro|man|ag|ing
micro|man|age|ment
micro|man|ag|er +s
mi|crom|eter +s
  (gauge for small
  measurements)
  [☞ micrometre]
micro|metre +s
  (millionth of a metre)
  [☞ micrometer]
mi|crom|etry
micro-mini +s
micro|mini|atur|iz|
  a|tion
mi|cron +s
Micro|nesia (region,
  W Pacific;
  association of island
  states)
Micro|nes|ian +s
micro|nutri|ent +s
micro-organ|ism +s
micro|phone +s
micro|phon|ic
micro|photo|graph
  +s
micro|photog|raphy
micro|proces|sor +s
micro|pro|gram +s
micro|proof
micro|pyle +s
micro|scope +s
micro|scop|ic
micro|scop|ic|al
micro|scop|ic|ally
mi|cro|scop|ist +s
mi|cros|copy
  mi|cros|cop|ies
micro|sec|ond +s
micro|som|al
micro|some +s
micro|sphere +s
micro|spore +s
micro|struc|tur|al
micro|struc|ture +s
micro|sur|geon +s
micro|sur|gery
micro|sur|gical
micro|switch
  micro|switch|es
micro|tome +s
micro|tonal

micro|tonal|ity
micro|tonal|ly
micro|tone +s
micro|tubule +s
micro|vil|lar
micro|vil|lous
  adjective
micro|vil|lus noun
  micro|villi
micro|wav|able (use
  microwaveable)
micro|wave
  micro|waves
  micro|waved
  micro|wav|ing
micro|wave|able
mic|tur|ate
  mic|tur|ates
  mic|tur|at|ed
  mic|tur|at|ing
mic|tur|ition
mid
mid-air
Midas (Greek Myth)
Mid-Atlantic Ridge
mid|brain +s
mid|day +s
mid|den +s
mid|dle +s
mid|dle age (time of
  life) (middle-age
  when preceding a
  noun)
middle-aged
Mid|dle Ages
  (History)
middle|brow +s
mid|dle C
middle class noun
  middle class|es
middle-class adjective
Mid|dle East (region
  of SW Asia &
  N Africa)
Mid|dle East|ern
Mid|dle Eng|lish
middle|game
middle-income
middle|man
  middle|men
middle-of-the-road
  adjective
middle-of-the-
  roader +s
middle-of-the-
  roadism
Mid|dles|brough
  (town, England)
Middle|sex (former
  county, England)
middle-sized
Middle|ton, Thom|as
  (English dramatist)

middle|weight +s
mid|dling +s
middy (midshipman;
  blouse)
mid|dies
  [☞ midi]
Mid|east
Mi|de|win
  (= Midewiwin)
Mi|de|wiwin
mid|field +s
mid|field|er +s
Mid|gard
  (Scandinavian Myth)
midge +s
midget +s
mid|gut +s
MIDI (musical
  instrument digital
  interface)
Midi (southern
  France)
midi +s (medium-
  length garment)
  [☞ middy]
Midi-Pyrénées
  (region, France)
mid-iron +s
Mid|land (town,
  Canada)
mid|land +s (interior
  of a country)
mid|land|er +s
Mid|lands (inland
  English counties)
mid-life
mid-line adjective
mid|line +s noun
Mid|lo|thian (former
  county, Scotland)
mid|night +s
mid|night blue
mid|ocean ridge +s
mid-off +s
mid-on +s
mid|point +s
mid-range
Mid|rash
  Mid|rash|im
Mid|rash|ic
mid|rib +s
mid|riff +s
mid-rise +s
mid|sec|tion +s
mid|ship +s
mid|ship|man
  mid|ship|men
mid|ships
mid|shore
mid-size +s adjective
  & noun
mid-sized adjective

mid|sole +s
midst
mid|stream
mid|sum|mer +s
Mid|sum|mer Day
Mid|summer's Day
(= Midsummer
Day)
mid-term +s
mid|town
Mid|way (Pacific
islands)
mid|way +s
mid-week
Mid|west (region, US)
Mid|west|ern
Mid|west|ern|er +s
mid|wife
mid|wives
mid|wif|ery
mid-winter +s
mien +s (look,
bearing)
[☞ mean, mesne]
Mies|ian
Mies van der Rohe,
Lud|wig (US
architect)
mife|pris|tone
miffed
MiG +s
mi|gawd
might (auxiliary verb;
strength)
[☞ mite]
might-have-been +s
might|i|ly
might|i|ness
mightn't
mighty
might|i|er
might|i|est
mignon|ette +s
mi|graine +s
mi|grain|ous
mi|grant +s
mi|grate
mi|grates
mi|grat|ed
mi|grat|ing
mi|gra|tion +s
mi|gra|tion|al
mi|gra|tor +s
mi|gra|tory
Mi|hail|ović,
Drago|ljub ('Draža')
(Chetnik leader)
mih|rab +s
mi|kado +s
mike (microphone;
microwave oven;
shirk work)

mikes
miked
mik|ing
[☞ mic]
Mi'kmaq
plural Mi'kmaq or
Mi'kmaqs
mikva +s (use
mikveh)
mik|vah +s (use
mikveh)
mik|veh +s
mil
• (million dollars)
plural mil
• (unit of diameter or
thickness)
plural mils
[☞ mill]
mi|lady
(noblewoman)
mi|ladies
Milan (city, Italy)
Milan|ese
plural Milan|ese
milch
milch cow +s
mild +er +est +s
mil|dew +s +ed +ing
mildew|cide +s
mil|dewed adjective
mil|dewy
mild|ish
mild|ly
mild-mannered
mild|ness
mile +s
mile|age +s
mile|post +s
miler +s
mile|stone +s
Mi|le|tus (ancient
Greek city)
mil|foil +s (plant)
[☞ mille feuille]
Mil|haud, Dar|ius
(French composer)
mili|ary
mi|lieu
mi|lieux or mi|lieus
mil|itan|cy
mil|itant +s
mil|itant|ism
mil|itant|ly
mil|itar|ia
mil|itar|i|ly
mil|itar|i|ness
mil|itar|ism
mil|itar|ist +s
mil|itar|is|tic
mil|itar|is|tic|ally
mil|itar|iz|a|tion

mil|itar|ize
mil|itar|iz|es
mil|itar|ized
mil|itar|iz|ing
mil|itary
mil|itar|ies
military-industri|al
com|plex
military-industri|al
com|plex|es
mil|itate
mil|itates
mil|itat|ed
mil|itat|ing
mil|itia +s
mil|itia|man
mil|itia|men
Milk (river,
N America)
milk +s +ed +ing
milk and water
(milk-and-water
when preceding a
noun)
milk|er +s
milk house +s
milk|i|er
milk|i|est
milk|i|ness
milk|maid +s
milk|man
milk|men
milk paint +s
milk run +s
milk|shake +s
milk|sop +s
milk vetch +s
milk vetch|es
milk|weed +s
milk-white
milk|wort +s
milky
milk|i|er
milk|i|est
Milky Way Gal|axy
Mill, James (Scottish
philosopher)
Mill, John Stu|art
(English philosopher)
mill +s +ed +ing
(building or
apparatus for
grinding or
processing; one
thousandth of a
dollar)
[☞ mil]
mill|able
Mil|lais, Sir John
Ever|ett (English
painter)
[☞ Millet, Millay]

Mil|lay, Edna Saint
Vin|cent (US poet)
[☞ Millet, Millais]
mill|board +s
mill dam +s
mille feuille +s (food)
[☞ milfoil]
mil|len|ar|ian +s
mil|len|ar|ian|ism
mil|len|ary (of a
millennium)
mil|len|aries
[☞ millinery]
mil|len|nial
mil|len|nial|ism
mil|len|nial|ist +s
mil|len|nium
mil|len|niums or
mil|len|nia
Mil|ler, (Alton) Glenn
(US bandleader)
Mil|ler, Ar|thur (US
dramatist)
Mil|ler, Henry
Val|en|tine (US
novelist)
mil|ler +s
Mil|let, Jean
Fran|çois (French
painter)
[☞ Millett, Millais,
Millay]
mil|let +s
Mil|lett, Kath|er|ine
Mur|ray ('Kate') (US
theorist)
[☞ Millet]
mill hand +s
Mill|haven
(penitentiary site,
Canada)
milli|am|meter +s
milli|amp +s
milli|am|pere +s
mil|liard +s
milli|bar +s
Milli|gan, Ter|ence
Alan ('Spike')
(British comedian)
[☞ Millikan]
milli|gram +s
Mil|li|kan, Rob|ert
An|drews (US
physicist)
[☞ Milligan]
milli|litre +s
milli|metre +s
mil|lin|er +s
mil|lin|ery (products
or trade of a milliner)
[☞ millenary]

mil|lion
plural mil|lion or
mil|lions
mil|lion|aire +s
mil|lion|air|ess
mil|lion|air|ess|es
mil|lion|fold
mil|lionth +s
milli|pede +s
milli|sec|ond +s
milli|volt +s
mill|pond +s
mill|race +s
mill rate +s
Mills, Sir John Lewis
  Er|nest Watts
  (English actor)
mill|stone +s
mill|stream +s
mill wheel +s
mill|work
mill work|er +s
mill|wright +s
Milne, Alan
  Alex|an|der (English
  writer)
Milne, David Brown
  (Cdn painter)
milo
mi|lord +s
Mi|łosz, Czes|law (US
  writer)
  [☞ Melos]
milpa +s
milque|toast +s
milt +s
milt|er +s
Mil|tia|des (Athenian
  general)
Mil|ton (town,
  Canada)
Mil|ton, John (English
  poet)
Mil|ton Keynes
  (town, England)
Mil|wau|kee (city, US)
Mil|wau|kee|an +s
Mimas (*Greek Myth*;
  Astronomy)
mime
  mimes
  mimed
  miming
mimeo
  mimeos
  mimeoed
  mimeo|ing
mimeo|graph +s +ed
  +ing
mimer +s
mi|mesis
mi|met|ic
mi|met|ic|ally

mimic
  mim|ics
  mim|icked
  mim|ick|ing
mim|ick|er +s
mim|ic|ry
  mim|ic|ries
Mimir (*Scandinavian
  Myth*)
Mi|mosa (star)
mi|mosa +s
mimu|lus
  mimu|luses
Min (language)
min +s (minute)
min|able
Mina|mata dis|ease
mina|ret +s
mina|ret|ed
Minas Basin (inlet,
  Canada)
Minas Ge|rais (state,
  Brazil)
mina|tory
mince
  min|ces
  minced
  min|cing
mince|meat
min|cer +s
Minch (Atlantic
  channel)
  Minch|es
min|cha
min|cing *adjective*
min|cing|ly
mind +s +ed +ing
mind-altering
Min|da|nao (island,
  the Philippines)
mind-bending
mind-blowing
mind-blowing|ly
mind-boggling
mind-boggling|ly
mind|ed *adjective*
mind|ed|ly
mind|ed|ness
mind|er +s
mind-expand|ing
mind|fuck +s +ed
  +ing
mind|fuck|er +s
mind|ful
mind|ful|ly
mind|ful|ness
mind game +s
mind|less
mind|less|ly
mind|less|ness
mind-numbing
mind-numbing|ly

Min|doro (island, the
  Philippines)
mind reader +s
mind reading
mind|scape +s
mind|set +s
mind's eye
mine
  mines
  mined
  min|ing
  [☞ Main]
mine|field +s
mine|lay|er +s
min|er +s (mine
  worker; burrowing
  insect)
  [☞ minor]
min|eral +s
min|eral|iz|a|tion
min|eral|ize
  min|eral|iz|es
  min|eral|ized
  min|eral|iz|ing
min|eral|ogic|al
min|eral|ogic|al|ly
min|eral|o|gist +s
min|eral|ogy
miner's let|tuce
Min|erva (*Roman
  Myth*)
mine shaft +s
min|es|trone +s
mine|sweep|er +s
mine|work|er +s
Ming +s (Chinese
  dynasty; porcelain)
Min|gan
Archi|pel|ago (park,
  Canada)
min|gi|ly
min|gle
  min|gles
  min|gled
  ming|ling
ming|ler +s
Min|gus, Charles
  ('Char|lie') (US
  musician)
mingy
  min|gi|er
  min|gi|est
mini +s
mini|ature +s
mini|atur|ist +s
mini|atur|iz|a|tion
mini|atur|ize
  mini|atur|iz|es
  mini|atur|ized
  mini|atur|iz|ing
mini-bar +s
mini-blind +s
mini-budget +s

mini|bus
  mini|bus|es
mini|cab +s
mini-cam +s
mini-camp +s
mini|com|put|er +s
Mini|coy (island
  group, Indian Ocean)
Mini Disc +s
  proprietary
mini|golf
mini|kin +s
min|im +s
min|ima
min|imal
min|imal|ism +s
min|imal|ist +s
min|imal|is|tic
mini-mall +s
min|imal|ly
mini-mart +s
mini|max
mini-mill +s
mini|miz|a|tion +s
mini|mize
  mini|miz|es
  mini|mized
  mini|miz|ing
mini|miz|er +s
min|imum
  min|imums or
  min|ima
minimum-security
  adjective
min|ing *noun*
min|ion +s (favourite;
  servant)
  [☞ minyan, filet
  mignon]
mini|pill +s
mini-putt
mini|series
  plural mini|series
mini|skirt +s
mini|skirt|ed
min|is|ter +s +ed
  +ing
min|is|ter|ial
min|is|ter|ial|ly
min|is|ter|ing
  adjective
Min|is|ter of the
  Crown
Min|is|ters of the
  Crown
Minister's Per|mit +s
min|is|trable
min|is|trant +s
min|is|tra|tion +s
min|istry
  min|is|tries
mini|van +s
mini|ver +s

mink (mammal; fur)
minks
[☞ **minx**]
minke +s (whale)
Min|kow|ski,
Her|mann (German mathematician)
Min|ne|ap|olis (city, US)
Min|nea|pol|itan +s
min|neo|la +s
minne|singer +s
Min|ne|sota (state, US)
Min|ne|so|tan +s
min|now +s
Miño (river, Iberia)
Min|oan +s
min|or +s +ed +ing (lesser; *Music*; *Sport*; young person; study)
[☞ **miner**]
Min|orca (Balearic island)
Min|or|can +s
Min|or|ite +s
min|or|ity
min|or|ities
minor-key *adjective*
minor league +s *noun*
minor-league *adjective*
minor-leaguer +s
Minos (*Greek Myth*)
Mino|taur (*Greek Myth*)
min|oxid|il
Minsk (capital of Belarus)
min|ster +s
min|strel +s
min|strel|sy
min|strel|sies
mint +s +ed +ing
mint|age +s
mint|ed *adjective*
mint green +s (mint-green *when preceding a noun*)
mint mark +s
Minto, Gil|bert John Mur|ray Kynyn|mond El|liot, 4th Earl of (governor general of Canada)
Minto Cup
Min|ton, Thom|as (English pottery manufacturer)
minty
mint|i|er
mint|i|est

minu|end +s
minu|et +s
minus
minus|es
min|us|cu|lar
min|us|cule +s
min|ute[1] (sixty seconds; record)
min|utes
min|ut|ed
min|ut|ing
mi|nute[2] (tiny)
mi|nut|est
mi|nute|ly
Minute|man
Minute|men
mi|nute|ness
minu|tia
minu|tiae
minx (girl)
minx|es
[☞ **minks**]
minx|ish
min|yan +s (*Judaism*)
[☞ **minion**]
Mio|cene +s
mio|sis (constriction of pupil)
mi|o|ses
[☞ **meiosis**]
mi|otic (of miosis)
[☞ **meiotic**]
MIPS (million instructions per second)
Mi|que|lon (French island)
Mira|beau, Hon|oré Gab|riel Ri|queti, Comte de (French revolutionary politician)
Mira|bel (town & airport, Canada)
mira|belle +s (plum; tree; liqueur)
mir|ab|ile dictu
mir|acle +s
mir|acu|lous
mir|acu|lous|ly
mir|acu|lous|ness
mira|dor +s
mir|age +s
Mira|michi (city & river, Canada)
Mir|anda
Mir|an|dize
Mir|an|diz|es
Mir|an|dized
Mir|an|diz|ing
mire
mires

mired
mir|ing
mire|poix
mirex
Mir|fak (star)
mir|id +s
mirin
mir|li|ton +s
Miró, Joan (Spanish painter)
mir|ror +s +ed +ing
mir|ror ball +s
mir|rored *adjective*
mir|ror im|age +s (mirror-image *when preceding a noun*)
mirth +s
mirth|ful
mirth|ful|ly
mirth|ful|ness
mirth|less
mirth|less|ly
mirth|less|ness
MIRV +s (missile)
Mir|vish, Edwin ('Hon|est Ed') (Cdn entrepreneur)
miry
Mir|zam (star)
mis|ad|dress
mis|ad|dress|es
mis|ad|dressed
mis|ad|dress|ing
mis|adven|ture +s
mis|align +s +ed +ing
mis|aligned *adjective*
mis|align|ment +s
mis|alli|ance +s
mis|allo|ca|tion +s
mis|ally
mis|allies
mis|allied
mis|ally|ing
mis|andry
mis|an|thrope +s
mis|an|throp|ic
mis|an|throp|ic|al
mis|an|throp|ic|al|ly
mis|an|throp|ist +s
mis|an|throp|ize
mis|an|throp|iz|es
mis|an|throp|ized
mis|an|throp|iz|ing
mis|an|thropy
mis|appli|ca|tion +s
mis|apply
mis|ap|plies
mis|ap|plied
mis|apply|ing
mis|ap|pre|hend +s +ed +ing

mis|ap|pre|hen|sion +s
mis|ap|pre|hen|sive
mis|ap|pro|pri|ate
mis|ap|pro|pri|ates
mis|ap|pro|pri|at|ed
mis|ap|pro|pri|at|ing
mis|ap|pro|pri|a|tion +s
mis|begot|ten
mis|behave
mis|be|haves
mis|be|haved
mis|behav|ing
mis|behav|iour +s
mis|cal|cu|late
mis|cal|cu|lates
mis|cal|cu|lat|ed
mis|cal|cu|lat|ing
mis|cal|cu|la|tion +s
mis|call +s +ed +ing
mis|car|ri|age +s
mis|carry
mis|car|ries
mis|car|ried
mis|carry|ing
mis|cast
mis|casts
mis|cast
mis|cast|ing
mis|ce|gen|a|tion
mis|cel|la|nea
mis|cel|lan|eous
mis|cel|lan|eous|ly
mis|cel|lan|eous|ness
mis|cel|lany
mis|cel|lan|ies
mis|chance +s
mis|chief +s
mischief-maker +s
mischief-making
mis|chiev|ous
mis|chiev|ous|ly
mis|chiev|ous|ness
misch metal
misci|bil|ity
mis|cible
mis|con|ceive
mis|con|ceives
mis|con|ceived
mis|con|ceiv|ing
mis|con|ceived *adjective*
mis|con|ceiv|er +s
mis|con|cep|tion +s
mis|con|duct +s +ed +ing
mis|con|struc|tion +s
mis|con|strue
mis|con|strues
mis|con|strued
mis|con|stru|ing

Mis|cou (island, Canada)
mis|count +s +ed +ing
mis|cre|ant +s
mis|cue
  mis|cues
  mis|cued
  mis|cue|ing
  or mis|cu|ing
mis|deal
  mis|deals
  mis|dealt
  mis|deal|ing
mis|deed +s
mis|demean|ant +s
mis|demean|or +s
  (use misdemeanour)
mis|demean|our +s
mis|de|scribe
  mis|de|scribes
  mis|de|scribed
  mis|de|scrib|ing
mis|de|scrip|tion +s
mis|diag|nose
  mis|diag|nos|es
  mis|diag|nosed
  mis|diag|nos|ing
mis|diag|no|sis
  mis|diag|no|ses
mis|dial
  mis|dials
  mis|dialed
  or mis|dialled
  mis|dial|ing
  or mis|dial|ling
mis|direct +s +ed +ing
mis|direct|ed adjective
mis|direc|tion +s
mis|doing +s
mis|doubt +s +ed +ing
mis|edu|cate
  mis|edu|cates
  mis|edu|cat|ed
  mis|edu|cat|ing
mis|edu|ca|tion +s
mise en scène
  mise en scènes or
  mises en scène
mis|em|ploy +s +ed +ing
mis|employ|ment +s
miser +s
mis|er|able
mis|er|able|ness
mis|er|ably
mi|seri|cord +s
miser|li|ness
miser|ly

mis|ery
  mis|eries
mis|feas|ance +s
mis|fire
  mis|fires
  mis|fired
  mis|firing
mis|fit +s
mis|for|tune +s
mis|giv|ing +s
mis|gov|ern +s +ed +ing
mis|govern|ment
mis|guid|ance
mis|guide
  mis|guides
  mis|guid|ed
  mis|guid|ing
mis|guid|ed adjective
mis|guid|ed|ly
mis|guid|ed|ness
mis|handle
  mis|han|dles
  mis|han|dled
  mis|hand|ling
mis|hap +s
mis|hear
  mis|hears
  mis|heard
  mis|hear|ing
Mish|ima, Yukio
  (Japanese writer)
mis-hit
  mis-hits
  mis-hit
  mis-hitting
mish|mash
  mish|mash|es
Mish|nah (Judaism)
Mish|naic
mis|iden|ti|fi|ca|tion +s
mis|iden|tify
  mis|iden|ti|fies
  mis|iden|ti|fied
  mis|iden|ti|fy|ing
mis|in|form +s +ed +ing
mis|infor|ma|tion
mis|in|formed adjective
mis|in|ter|pret +s +ed +ing
mis|in|ter|pret|a|tion +s
mis|in|ter|pret|er +s
mis|judge
  mis|judg|es
  mis|judged
  mis|judg|ing
mis|judge|ment +s
  (use misjudgment)
mis|judg|ment +s

Mis|kito (people & language)
  plural Mis|kito or Mis|ki|tos
  [☞ mosquito, Mosquito Coast]
Mis|kolc (city, Hungary)
mis|label
  mis|labels
  mis|labelled
  mis|label|ling
mis|lay
  mis|lays
  mis|laid
  mis|lay|ing
mis|lead
  mis|leads
  mis|led
  mis|lead|ing
mis|lead|er +s
mis|lead|ing adjective
mis|lead|ing|ly
mis|lead|ing|ness
mis|like
  mis|likes
  mis|liked
  mis|lik|ing
mis|man|age
  mis|man|ages
  mis|man|aged
  mis|man|ag|ing
mis|manage|ment +s
mis|match
  mis|match|es
  mis|matched
  mis|match|ing
mis|meas|ure
  mis|meas|ures
  mis|meas|ured
  mis|meas|ur|ing
mis|measure|ment +s
mis|name
  mis|names
  mis|named
  mis|nam|ing
mis|nomer +s
miso
mis|og|am|ist +s
mis|og|amy
mis|ogyn|ist +s
mis|ogyn|is|tic
mis|ogyn|ous
mis|ogyny
mis|per|ceive
  mis|per|ceives
  mis|per|ceived
  mis|per|ceiv|ing
mis|per|cep|tion +s
mis|pickel
mis|place
  mis|pla|ces

mis|placed
mis|pla|cing
mis|placed adjective
mis|place|ment +s
mis|play +s +ed +ing
mis|print +s +ed +ing
mis|pri|sion +s
mis|prize
  mis|priz|es
  mis|prized
  mis|priz|ing
mis|pro|nounce
  mis|pro|noun|ces
  mis|pro|nounced
  mis|pro|noun|cing
mis|pro|nun|ci|a|tion +s
mis|quo|ta|tion +s
mis|quote
  mis|quotes
  mis|quot|ed
  mis|quot|ing
mis|read
  mis|reads
  mis|read
  mis|read|ing
mis|read|ing +s noun
mis|remem|ber +s +ed +ing
mis|report +s +ed +ing
mis|repre|sent +s +ed +ing
mis|repre|sen|ta|tion +s
mis|repre|sent|a|tive
mis|rule
  mis|rules
  mis|ruled
  mis|rul|ing
miss
  miss|es
  missed
  miss|ing
miss|able
mis|sal +s
  (Catholicism)
  [☞ missile, mistle thrush]
mis|sal|ette +s
missed past & past participle of miss
  [☞ mist]
misses' (dress size)
  [☞ missus]
mis|shape
  mis|shapes
  mis|shaped
  mis|shap|ing
mis|shapen
mis|shapen|ly
mis|shapen|ness

mis|sile +s (projectile)
[☞ missal, mistle thrush]
mis|sil|eer +s
mis|sil|ery
mis|sing *adjective*
Mis|sion (municipality, Canada; furniture style)
mis|sion +s +ed +ing
mis|sion|ary
mis|sion|aries
mis|sion|iz|a|tion
mis|sion|ize
mis|sion|iz|es
mis|sion|ized
mis|sion|iz|ing
mis|sis (= missus: woman, wife)
mis|sis|es
[☞ misses']
Mis|sis|sauga (city, Canada; people, language)
plural Mis|sis|sauga or Mis|sis|sau|gas
[☞ massasauga]
Mis|sis|sip|pi (state & river, US; river, Canada)
Mis|sis|sip|pian +s
mis|sive +s
Misso|lon|ghi (city, Greece)
Mis|souri (river & state, US)
Mis|sour|ian +s
mis|speak
mis|speaks
mis|spoke
mis|spoken
mis|speak|ing
mis|spell
mis|spells
mis|spelled or mis|spelt
mis|spell|ing
mis|spelled *adjective*
mis|spell|ing +s *noun*
mis|spend
mis|spends
mis|spent
mis|spend|ing
mis|spent *adjective*
mis|state
mis|states
mis|stated
mis|stat|ing
mis|state|ment +s
mis|step +s
mis|sus (woman, wife)
mis|sus|es
[☞ misses']

missy
miss|ies
mist +s +ed +ing (vapour, fog)
[☞ missed]
mis|tak|able
mis|take
mis|takes
mis|took
mis|taken
mis|tak|ing
mis|taken *adjective*
mis|taken|ly
Mis|tas|sini (town & lake, Canada; Cree)
mis|ter[1] +s (man)
mist|er[2] +s (sprayer)
mist|i|er
mist|i|est
mist|i|ly
mis|time
mis|times
mis|timed
mis|tim|ing
mis|tim|ing *noun*
mist|i|ness
mis|title
mis|titles
mis|titled
mis|titling
mis|tle thrush
mis|tle thrush|es
mistle|toe +s
mist net
mist nets
mist net|ted
mist net|ting
mis|took
Mis|tral, Fré|dé|ric (French poet)
Mis|tral, Gab|ri|ela (Chilean poet)
mis|tral +s
mis|trans|late
mis|trans|lates
mis|trans|lat|ed
mis|trans|lat|ing
mis|trans|lat|ion +s
mis|treat +s +ed +ing
mis|treat|ment
mis|tress
mis|tress|es
mis|trial +s
mis|trust +s +ed +ing
mis|trust|ful
mis|trust|ful|ly
misty
mist|i|er
mist|i|est
misty-eyed

mis|type
mis|types
mis|typed
mis|typ|ing
mis|under|stand
mis|under|stands
mis|under|stood
mis|under|stand|ing
mis|under|stand|ing +s *noun*
mis|under|stood *adjective*
mis|usage +s
mis|use
mis|uses
mis|used
mis|using
mis|user +s
Mitch|ell, Joni (Cdn singer-songwriter)
Mitch|ell, Mar|garet (US novelist)
Mitch|ell, Peter (Cdn politician)
Mitch|ell, Wil|liam Or|mond (Cdn writer)
Mitch|um, Rob|ert (US actor)
mite (spider; small thing; *Sports*)
[☞ might]
Mith|ra|dates (= Mithridates)
Mith|ra|ic
Mith|ra|ism
Mith|ra|ist +s
Mith|ras (*Roman Myth*)
Mith|ri|dates (king of Pontus)
mitig|able
miti|gate
miti|gates
miti|gat|ed
miti|gat|ing
miti|gat|ing *adjective*
miti|ga|tion
miti|ga|tor +s
miti|ga|tory
Mitla (ancient city, Mexico)
mito|chon|drial
mito|chon|drion
mito|chon|dria
mito|gen
mito|genic
mi|to|sis
mi|to|ses
mi|tot|ic
mi|tot|ic|ally
mi|tral

mitre
mitres
mitred
mitring
mitre box
mitre boxes
mitred *adjective*
mitre|wort +s
Mit|siwa (= Massawa, Eritrea)
mitt +s
Mittel|eur|opa (central Europe)
Mittel|euro|pean +s
Mittel|land (canal, Germany)
mit|ten +s
mit|tened *adjective*
Mit|ter|rand, Fran|çois Mau|rice Marie (French president)
mitz|vah
mitz|voth or mitz|vahs
mix
mixes
mixed
mix|ing
mix|able
mix-and-match
mix-and-matches
mix down *verb*
mixes down
mixed down
mix|ing down
mix|down +s *noun*
mixed *adjective*
mixed blood +s *noun*
mixed-blood *adjective*
mixed farm +s (mixed-farm *when preceding a noun*)
mixed farm|ing
mixed grass (mixed-grass *when preceding a noun*)
mixed grass|es
mixed media (mixed-media *when preceding a noun*)
mixed-race
mixed-up *adjective*
mixed-use
mixer +s
Mix|master +s
• *proprietary* (food processor)
• (busy person)
Mix|tec
plural Mix|tec or Mix|tecs

mix|ture +s
mix up *verb*
  mixes up
  mixed up
  mix|ing up
mix-up +s *noun*
mizen +s (*use*
  mizzen)
mizen-mast +s (*use*
  mizzen-mast)
mizen-sail +s (*use*
  mizzen-sail)
Miz|oram (state,
  India)
miz|zen +s
mizzen-mast +s
mizzen-sail +s
miz|zle
  miz|zles
  miz|zled
  miz|zling
miz|zling *adjective*
miz|zly
MLA (Member of the
  Legislative
  Assembly)
  MLAs
Mma|batho (city,
  South Africa)
mmm *interjection*
MNA (Member of the
  National Assembly)
  MNAs
M'Naghten rules (*use*
  McNaughten rules)
mne|mon|ic +s
mne|mon|ic|ally
mne|mon|ics
mne|mon|ist +s
Mne|mo|syne (*Greek
  Myth*)
MO (modus operandi;
  medical officer;
  money order)
  MOs
mo +s (moment)
  [☞ mho, mow, *mot*]
moa +s
Moab|ite +s
moan +s +ed +ing
moan|er +s
moan|ful
moat +s +ed +ing
  (ditch)
  [☞ mote]
Mob (crime
  organization)
mob (crowd;
  populace)
  mobs
  mobbed
  mob|bing
mob|ber +s

mob|cap +s
Mo|bile (city, US)
mo|bile +s
mo|bil|ity
mo|bil|iz|able
mo|bil|iz|a|tion +s
mo|bil|ize
  mo|bil|iz|es
  mo|bil|ized
  mo|bil|iz|ing
mo|bil|iz|er +s
Mö|bius loop +s
Mö|bius strip +s
mob|oc|racy
  mob|oc|ra|cies
mob|ster +s
Mo|butu (Sese Seko)
  (president of Zaire)
Mo|butu Sese Seko
  (= Lake Albert,
  Africa)
moc|ca|sin +s
moc|ca|sined
mocha +s
mock +s +ed +ing
  (ridicule; sham, fake)
  [☞ Mach]
mock|able
mock|er +s
mock|ery
  mock|eries
mock-heroic
mock|ing *adjective*
mock|ing|bird +s
mock|ing|ly
mock or|ange +s
mock|tail +s
mocku|men|tary
  mocku|men|tar|ies
mock-up +s *noun*
mod +s
mod|acryl|ic +s
modal +s (of a mode)
  [☞ model]
mo|dal|ity
  mo|dal|ities
mo|dal|ly
mod cons
mode +s
model
  mod|els
  mod|elled or
  mod|eled
  mod|el|ling or
  mod|el|ing
mod|el|er +s (*use*
  modeller)
mod|el|ing *noun* (*use*
  modelling)
mod|el|ler +s
mod|el|ling *noun*
mo|dem +s
Mod|ena (city, Italy)

mod|er|ate
mod|er|ates
mod|er|at|ed
mod|er|at|ing
mod|er|ate|ly
mod|er|ate|ness
mod|er|a|tion +s
mod|er|at|ism
mod|er|ato +s
mod|er|ator +s
mod|er|ator|ial
mod|ern +s
modern-day
Mod|ern|ism (20th-c.
  artistic movement)
mod|ern|ism +s
  (religious movement;
  a modern quality or
  term)
mod|ern|ist +s
mod|ern|is|tic
mod|ern|is|tic|ally
mod|ern|ity
mod|ern|iz|a|tion +s
mod|ern|ize
  mod|ern|iz|es
  mod|ern|ized
  mod|ern|iz|ing
mod|ern|iz|er +s
mod|ern|ly
mod|ern|ness
mod|est
mod|est|ly
mod|esty
mod|icum
modi|fi|able
modi|fi|ca|tion +s
modi|fi|er +s
mod|ify
  modi|fies
  modi|fied
  modi|fy|ing
Modi|gliani,
  Ame|deo (Italian
  artist)
modil|lion +s
mod|ish
mod|ish|ly
mod|ish|ness
mod|iste +s
mod|ular
mod|ular|ity
mod|ular|iz|a|tion +s
modu|late
  modu|lates
  modu|lat|ed
  modu|lat|ing
modu|la|tion +s
modu|la|tor +s
modu|la|tory
mod|ule +s
mod|ulo

mod|ulus
  mod|uli
modus op|er|an|di
  modi op|er|an|di
modus vi|ven|di
  modi vi|ven|di
Moga|dishu (capital
  of Somalia)
mog|gie +s
Mogi|lev (*Russian
  name for* Mahilyow,
  Belarus)
Mo|gul +s (emperor of
  Delhi; *for* Mongolian
  or Muslim dynasty
  use Mughal)
mo|gul +s (important
  person; *Skiing*)
Mo|hács (town &
  battle site, Hungary)
mo|hair
Moham|med
  (= Muhammad,
  founder of Islam)
Moham|med II
  (Ottoman sultan of
  Turkey)
Moham|med Ali
  (= Muhammad Ali,
  pasha of Egypt)
  [☞ Muhammad
  Ali]
Moham|med|an +s
  offensive
Moham|merah
  (*former name for*
  Khorramshahr,
  Iran)
Mo|have Des|ert
  (= Mojave Desert)
Mo|hawk
• (people; language)
  plural Mo|hawk or
  Mo|hawks
• (*Figure Skating*)
  plural Mo|hawks
mo|hawk +s (haircut)
Mo|hegan
  (Algonquian people
  of Connecticut)
  plural Mo|hegan or
  Mo|heg|ans
  [☞ Mahican,
  Mohican]
mohel +s
Mohenjo-Daro
  (archaeological site,
  Pakistan)
Mo|hi|can (in *Last of
  the Mohicans*;
  haircut; *for*
  Algonquian people
  of New York State
  use Mahican; *for*

Algonquian people
of Connecticut *use*
Mohegan)
plural Mo|hi|can or
Mo|hi|cans
moho +s
Moholy-Nagy,
László (US artist)
Moho|rov|ičić
dis|con|tinu|ity
moi
moi|dore +s
moi|ety
moi|et|ies
moil +s +ed +ing
Moi|rai (*Greek Myth*)
moiré +s
Mois|san,
(Fer|di|nand
Fré|dé|ric) Henri
(French chemist)
moist +er +est
mois|ten +s +ed +ing
moist|ly
moist|ness
mois|ture +s
mois|ture|less
mois|tur|ize
mois|tur|iz|es
mois|tur|ized
mois|tur|iz|ing
mois|tur|iz|er +s
mois|tur|iz|ing
adjective
Mo|jave Des|ert (in
the US)
mojo +s
mok|sha
mol +s (SI unit: *use*
mole)
[☞ mole]
molal
molal|ity
molar +s
mo|lar|ity
mo|lar|ities
mo|las|ses
Mold (town, Wales)
mold +s +ed +ing
(*use* mould)
Mol|dau (= Vltava
River, Czech
Republic)
Mol|davia
• (= Moldova:
country, Europe)
• (former principality,
Europe)
mold|ed *adjective* (*use*
moulded)
mold|er[1] +s (person
who molds: *use*
moulder)

mol|der[2] +s +ed +ing
(rot: *use* moulder)
mold|ing +s noun (*use*
moulding)
Mol|dova (country,
Europe)
Mol|do|van +s
moldy (*use* mouldy)
mold|i|er
mold|i|est
mole[1] +s (animal; skin
blemish; pier; SI unit;
uterine tissue)
mole[2] (sauce)
mo|lecu|lar
mo|lecu|lar|ity
mo|lecu|lar|ly
mol|ec|ule
mol|ec|ules
mol|ec|uled
mol|ec|ul|ing
mole|hill +s
mole|skin +s
mo|lest +s +ed +ing
mo|lest|a|tion +s
mo|lest|er +s
Mo|lière (French
playwright)
Moli|nari, Guido (Cdn
painter)
mo|line (*Heraldry*)
[☞ malign,
Maligne]
Mo|lise (region, Italy)
moll +s (female
companion)
[☞ mall, maul]
mol|lie +s (fish: *use*
molly)
[☞ Mali]
mol|li|fi|ca|tion +s
mol|li|fi|er +s
mol|lify
mol|li|fies
mol|li|fied
mol|li|fy|ing
mol|lusc +s
mol|lusc|an
mol|lusc|oid
molly (fish)
mol|lies
[☞ Mali]
molly|cod|dle
molly|cod|dles
molly|cod|dled
molly|cod|dling
Mol|nár, Fer|enc
(Hungarian
playwright)
Mol|och (god)
mol|och +s (reptile)
Molo|tov (*former name
for* Perm, Russia)

Molo|tov,
Vya|che|slav
Mikh|ail|ovich
(Soviet statesman)
Molo|tov cock|tail +s
Mol|son, John (Cdn
brewer)
Mol|son, John Jr.
(Cdn brewer)
Mol|son mus|cle +s
mol|ten
molto
Mo|luc|ca +s (island
group, Indonesia)
moly
mol|ies
mo|lyb|date
mo|lyb|den|ite +s
mo|lyb|den|um
mom +s
[☞ Maugham]
mom-and-pop
adjective
Mom|basa (city,
Kenya)
mo|ment +s
mo|men|ta
mo|men|tar|i|ly
mo|men|tar|i|ness
mo|men|tary
mo|ment|ly
mo|men|tous
mo|men|tous|ly
mo|men|tous|ness
mo|men|tum
mo|men|ta
mom|ma +s
Momm|sen,
(Chris|tian
Mat|thias) Theo|dor
(German historian)
mommy
mom|mies
mommy track +s
mommy track|er +s
mommy track|ing
noun
Momus (*Greek Myth*)
Mon|aco (principality,
Europe)
mon|ad +s
mon|adel|phous
mon|ad|ic
mo|nad|nock +s
Mona|ghan (county &
town, Ireland)
Mona Lisa +s
mon|an|drous
mon|andry
mon|arch +s
mon|arch|al
mon|arch|ial
mon|arch|ic

mon|arch|ic|al
mon|arch|ic|al|ly
mon|arch|ism
mon|arch|ist +s
mon|archy
mon|arch|ies
Mona|shee
(mountains, Canada)
mon|as|tery
mon|as|ter|ies
mon|as|tic
mon|as|tic|ally
mon|as|ti|cism
mon|atom|ic
mon|aural
mon|aural|ly
mona|zite +s
Mön|chen|glad|bach
(city, Germany)
Monck, Charles
Stan|ley, 4th
Vis|count (governor
general of Canada)
[☞ Monk, Munch]
Monck, George (1st
Duke of Albemarle,
English general)
[☞ Monk, Munch]
Monck|ton, Rob|ert
(British officer in
BNA)
[☞ Moncton]
Monc|ton (city,
Canada)
[☞ Monckton]
mon|daine +s
Mon|dale, Wal|ter
Fred|erick (US
politician)
Mon|day +s
Monday-morning
quarter|back +s
mondo
Mon|dri|an, Piet
(Dutch painter)
Mone|gasque +s
Monet, Claude
(French painter)
[☞ Monnet,
Manet]
mon|et|ar|i|ly
mon|et|ar|ism
mon|et|ar|ist +s
mon|et|ary
mon|et|iz|a|tion
mon|et|ize
mon|et|iz|es
mon|et|ized
mon|et|iz|ing
money
mon|ies or mon|eys
money-back *adjective*
preceding a noun

money|bags
money|belt +s
money bill +s
money-changer +s
money-changing
moneyed
money-grubber +s
money-grubbing
money|lend|er +s
money|lend|ing
money|less
money-loser +s
money-losing
money-maker +s
money-making
money man
　money men
money-spinner +s
money's worth
money|wort +s
mon|ger +s
monger|ing
mon|go +s
Mon|gol +s (of
　Mongolia)
mon|gol +s offensive
　(person with Down's
　syndrome)
Mon|go|lia (country,
　Asia)
Mon|go|lian +s
mon|gol|ism offensive
Mon|gol|oid +s
　(division of
　humankind)
mon|gol|oid +s
　offensive (affected
　with Down's
　syndrome)
mon|goose +s
mon|grel +s
mon|grel|ism
mon|grel|iz|a|tion
mon|grel|ize
　mon|grel|iz|es
　mon|grel|ized
　mon|grel|iz|ing
'mongst
mon|ick|er +s (use
　moniker)
mon|ied adjective (use
　moneyed)
mon|ies
mon|ik|er +s
mo|nili|form
mon|ism +s
mon|ist +s
mon|is|tic
mon|ition +s
mon|itor +s +ed +ing
mon|itor|ial

mon|itor|ing noun &
　adjective
mon|itor|ship +s
mon|itory
　mon|itor|ies
Monk, George
　(= George Monck,
　English general)
　[☞ Monck, Munch]
Monk, Thelo|nious
　Sphere (US
　musician)
　[☞ Monck, Munch]
monk +s
mon|key +s +ed +ing
mon|key bars
mon|key flower +s
monkey|ish
monkey|shine +s
mon|key wrench
　noun
　mon|key wrench|es
monkey|wrench verb
　monkey|wrench|es
　monkey|wrenched
　monkey|wrench|ing
monkey|wrench|er
　+s
monkey|wrench|ing
　noun
monk|fish
　plural monk|fish
monk|ish
monk|ish|ly
monk|ish|ness
monks|hood +s
Mon|mouth|shire
　(former county,
　Wales)
Mon|net, Jean
　(French economist &
　politician)
　[☞ Monet]
mono +s
mono|acid
mono|amine +s
mono|basic
mono|bloc
mono|car|pic
mono|car|pous
mono|caus|al
Mon|ocer|os
　(constellation)
mono|chro|mat|ic
mono|
　chro|mat|ic|ally
mono|chroma|tism
mono|chrome +s
mono|chrom|ic
mon|ocle +s
mon|ocled
mono|clinal
mono|cline +s

mono|clin|ic
mono|clon|al
mono|coque +s
mono|cot +s
mono|coty|ledon +s
mono|coty|ledon|ous
mon|oc|racy
　mon|oc|ra|cies
mono|crat|ic
mono|crop +s
mono|crop|ping +s
mon|ocu|lar +s
mon|ocu|lar|ly
mono|cultur|al
mono|cul|ture +s
mono|cycle +s
mono|cyte +s
mono|cyt|ic
mon|od|ic
mon|od|ist +s
mono|drama +s
mon|ody
　mon|od|ies
mon|oe|cious
mono|fila|ment +s
mon|og|am|ist +s
mon|og|am|ous
mon|og|am|ous|ly
mon|og|amy
mono|gen|esis
mono|gen|etic
mono|geny
mono|glot +s
mono|gram +s
mono|gram|mat|ic
mono|grammed
mono|graph +s +ed
　+ing
mon|og|raph|er +s
mono|graph|ic
mono|hull +s
mono|hybrid +s
mono|kini +s
mono|layer +s
mono|lin|gual +s
mono|lin|gual|ism
mono|lith +s
mono|lith|ic
mono|lith|ic|ally
mono|logic
mono|logic|al
mon|ol|o|gist +s
mon|ol|o|gize
　mon|ol|o|giz|es
　mon|ol|o|gized
　mon|ol|o|giz|ing
mono|logue +s
mono|loguist +s
mono|mania
mono|maniac +s
mono|man|iacal
mono|mer +s

mono|mer|ic
mo|nom|ial +s
mono|molecu|lar
mono|morph|ic
mono|morph|ism +s
mono|morph|ous
mono|nuclear
mono|nucle|o|sis
mono|phon|ic
mono|phon|ic|ally
mon|oph|thong +s
mon|oph|thong|al
mono|phylet|ic
Mon|ophy|site +s
mono|plane +s
mono|pole +s
mon|op|ol|ist +s
mon|op|o|lis|tic
mon|op|o|lis|tic|ally
mon|op|ol|iz|a|tion
　+s
mon|op|ol|ize
　mon|op|ol|iz|es
　mon|op|ol|ized
　mon|op|ol|iz|ing
　mon|op|ol|iz|er +s
Mon|op|oly
　proprietary (game)
mon|op|oly
　mon|op|ol|ies
Mon|op|oly money
mono|rail +s
mono|sac|char|ide
　+s
mono|sodium
mono|sperm|ous
mono|syllab|ic
mono|syllab|ic|ally
mono|sylla|ble +s
mono|theism +s
mono|theist +s
mono|theis|tic
mono|theis|tic|ally
mono|tint +s
mono|tone +s
mono|ton|ic
mono|ton|ic|ally
mon|ot|on|ize
　mon|ot|on|iz|es
　mon|ot|on|ized
　mon|ot|on|iz|ing
mon|ot|on|ous
mon|ot|on|ous|ly
mon|ot|ony
　mon|ot|on|ies
mono|treme +s
Mono|type +s
　proprietary
　(machine)
mono|type +s
　(impression)
mono|typ|ic

mono|unsatur|at|ed
mono|valent
mon|ox|ide +s
mono|zygot|ic
Mon|roe, James (US president)
[☞ Munro]
Mon|roe, Mari|lyn (US entertainer)
[☞ Munro]
Mon|rovia (capital of Liberia)
Mons (town, Belgium)
mons
  mon|tes
mon|sei|gneur (French honourable title)
  mes|sei|gneurs
  [☞ monsignor]
mon|sieur (French conventional title)
  mes|sieurs
mon|signor (Catholic title)
  mon|signori or
  mon|signors
  [☞ monseigneur]
mon|soon +s
mon|soon|al
mons pubis
  mon|tes pubis
mon|ster +s
mon|stera +s
mon|strance +s
mon|stros|ity
  mon|stros|ities
mon|strous
mon|strous|ly
mon|strous|ness
mons Ven|eris
  mon|tes Ven|eris
mon|tage
  mon|tages
  mon|taged
  mon|ta|ging
Mon|ta|gnais
  plural Mon|ta|gnais
Mon|tagnais-Naskapi
  plural Mon|tagnais-Naskapi
Mon|tagu, Lady Mary Wort|ley (English writer)
Mon|taigne, Michel Ey|quem de (French essayist)
Mon|tale, Eu|genio (Italian writer)
Mon|tana (state, US)
Mon|tana, Joe (US football player)

Mon|tan|an +s
mon|tane
Mont Blanc (mountain, Europe)
mont|bre|tia +s
Mont|calm, Louis-Joseph de (Marquis de Montcalm, French army officer)
monte
Monte Albán (ancient city, Mexico)
Monte|bello (village, Canada)
Monte Carlo (resort, Monaco; Statistics)
Monte Cas|si|no (monastery, Italy)
Mon|tego Bay (city, Jamaica)
Monte|neg|rin +s
Monte|negro (Balkan republic)
Mon|terey (city, US, site of music festival)
  [☞ Monterrey]
Mon|terey Jack
Mon|ter|rey (city, Mexico)
  [☞ Monterey]
Mon|tes|quieu, Baron de la Brède et de (French political philosopher)
Mon|tes|sori, Maria (Italian educator)
Mon|teux, Pierre (US conductor)
Monte|verdi, Clau|dio (Italian composer)
Monte|video (capital of Uruguay)
Monte|zuma (Aztec emperors)
Monte|zuma's re|venge
Mont|fort, Simon de (Earl of Leicester, English soldier)
Mont|gol|fier, Jo|seph Michel (French balloonist)
Mont|gol|fier, Jacques Étienne (French balloonist)
Mont|gom|ery (city, US)
Mont|gom|ery, Ber|nard Law ('Monty') (1st Viscount Montgomery of

Alamein, British field marshal)
Mont|gom|ery, Lucy Maud (Cdn writer)
Mont|gom|ery|shire (former county, Wales)
month +s
month|ly
  month|lies
Mont Jacques-Cartier (mountain, Canada)
Mont-Joli (town, Canada)
Mont-Laurier (town, Canada)
Mont|magny (town, Canada)
Mont|magny, Charles Huault de (French colonial administrator)
Mont|martre (district, Paris)
Mont|moren|cy (waterfalls, Canada)
mont|moril|lon|ite +s
Mont|par|nasse (district, Paris)
Mont|pelier (city, US)
  [☞ Montpellier]
Mont|pel|lier (city, France)
  [☞ Montpelier]
Mont|ra|chet +s
Mont|real (city & island, Canada)
Mont|real|er +s
Montréal-Nord (city, Canada)
Montréal-Ouest (city, Canada)
Mon|treux (town, Switzerland)
Mon|trose, James Gra|ham, 1st Mar|quis of (Scottish general)
Monts, Pierre Du Gua de (French explorer)
Mont Sainte-Anne (mountain, Canada)
Mont Saint-Hilaire (mountain, Canada)
Mont-Saint-Hilaire (town, Canada)
Mont Saint-Michel (islet, France)
Monts Chic-Chocs (mountains, Canada)

Mont|ser|rat (island, W Indies)
Monts Notre-Dame (mountains, Canada)
Mont Trem|blant (mountain, Canada)
Mont-Tremblant (town, Canada)
monu|ment +s
monu|men|tal
monu|men|tal|ity
monu|men|tal|ize
  monu|men|tal|iz|es
  monu|men|tal|ized
  monu|men|tal|iz|ing
monu|men|tal|ly
moo +s +ed +ing (cattle sound)
  [☞ moue]
mooch
  mooch|es
  mooched
  mooch|ing
mooch|er +s
moo-cow +s
mood +s
Mood|ie, Su|san|na (Cdn writer)
  [☞ Moody]
mood|i|ly
mood|i|ness
mood swing +s
Moody, Dwight Lyman (US evangelist)
  [☞ Moodie]
moody
  mood|i|er
  mood|i|est
Moog +s proprietary
moo juice
moola (use moolah)
moo|lah
Moon, Sun Myung (Korean religious leader)
moon +s +ed +ing
moon|beam +s
moon boot +s
moon|calf
  moon|calves
moon-faced
moon|fish
  plural moon|fish or moon|fishes
moon|flower +s
Moon|ie +s (Unification Church member)
  [☞ moony]
moon|i|er
moon|i|est
moon|less

moon|light +s +ed +ing
moon|light|er +s
moon|lit *adjective*
moon|quake +s
moon|rise +s
moon|scape +s
moon|seed +s
moon|set +s
moon|shine +s
moon|shin|er +s
moon shot +s
moon|stone +s
moon|struck
moon|walk +s +ed +ing
moony (of the moon; listless, dreamy)
moon|i|er
moon|i|est
[☞ Moonie]
Moor +s (African people)
[☞ Moore, More]
moor +s +ed +ing (tie up a boat; upland)
[☞ mure]
moor|age +s
Moore (surname; township, Canada)
[☞ Moor, More, mure]
Moore, Archie (US boxer)
Moore, Brian (Cdn writer)
Moore, Dora Mavor (Cdn actress)
Moore, Dud|ley Stu|art John (English actor)
Moore, George Au|gus|tus (Irish novelist)
Moore, George Ed|ward (English philosopher)
Moore, Henry Spen|cer (English sculptor)
Moore, Mari|anne Craig (US poet)
Moore, Thom|as (Irish poet & musician)
Moores, Frank Duff (Cdn politician)
moor|hen +s
moor|ing +s *noun*
Moor|ish (of the Moors)

moor|ish (resembling moorland)
[☞ moreish]
moor|land +s
moory
Moose (river, Canada)
moose (animal)
plural moose
[☞ mousse]
moose|hair
moose|hide
Moose Jaw (city, Canada)
moose meat
moose milk
moose|wood
plural moose|wood or moose|woods
moo shu pork
Mooso|nee (community, Canada)
moot +s +ed +ing (insignificant; undecided; *Law*)
[☞ mute, Mut]
mop
mops
mopped
mop|ping
mope
mopes
moped
moping
mo|ped +s (motorcycle)
moper +s
mopey
mopi|er
mopi|est
mop|head +s
mop|head|ed
mopi|ly
mopi|ness
mop|pet +s
Mopti (city, Mali)
mopy (*use* mopey)
mopi|er
mopi|est
mo|quette +s
Mor|ada|bad (city, India)
mor|ain|al
mor|aine +s (glacial debris)
[☞ murrain]
mor|ain|ic
moral +s (ethical; virtuous; emotional; lesson)
[☞ morel]

mor|ale (mental attitude)
[☞ morel]
mor|al|ism
mor|al|ist +s
mor|al|is|tic
mor|al|is|tic|ally
mor|al|ity
mor|al|ities
mor|al|iz|a|tion +s
mor|al|ize
mor|al|iz|es
mor|al|ized
mor|al|iz|ing
mor|al|iz|er +s
mor|al|iz|ing|ly
mor|al|ly
Morar (loch, Scotland)
mo|rass
mo|rass|es
mora|tor|ium
mora|tor|iums or mora|toria
Mor|avia (region, Czech Republic)
Mor|avia, Al|ber|to (Italian writer)
Mor|avian +s
Mor|avian|town (battle site, Canada)
Mora|wetz, Oskar (Cdn composer)
Moray (former county, Scotland)
moray +s (eel)
[☞ mores]
Moray Firth (inlet, North Sea)
Moray|shire (= Moray)
mor|bid
mor|bid|ity
mor|bid|ly
mor|bid|ness
mor|dan|cy
mor|dant +s (caustic, corrosive)
[☞ mordent]
mor|dant|ly
Mor|den (town, Canada)
mor|dent +s (*Music*)
[☞ mordant]
Mor|dred (*Arthurian Legend*)
More, Han|nah (English writer)
[☞ Moore, Moor]
More, Sir Thom|as (English humanist scholar & Lord Chancellor)
[☞ Moore, Moor]

more (greater in quantity or degree)
[☞ moor]
Mo|reau, Jeanne (French actress)
More|cambe (bay, England)
more|ish (tasty)
[☞ moorish]
morel +s (edible fungus)
[☞ moral]
Mor|elia (city, Mexico)
mor|ello +s (cherry)
Mor|elos (state, Mexico)
Mor|enz, How|arth Wil|liam ('Howie') (Cdn hockey player)
more|over
mores (customs; in 'O tempora, O mores')
[☞ moray]
Mores|by (island, Canada)
Mor|esque
Mor|gan, Sir Henry (Welsh buccaneer)
Mor|gan, John Pier|pont (US financier)
Mor|gan, Thom|as Hunt (US zoologist)
Mor|gan +s (horse)
mor|gan|atic
mor|gan|atic|ally
Mor|gan le Fay (*Arthurian Legend*)
Mor|gen|taler, Henry (Cdn physician)
morgue +s
mori|bund
mori|bund|ity
Morin, Claude (Cdn politician)
Morin|ville (town, Canada)
mor|ish (tasty: *use* moreish)
[☞ moorish]
Mori|sot, Berthe Marie Pau|line (French painter)
Mori|yama, Ray|mond (Cdn architect)
Mor|ley, Ed|ward Wil|liams (US chemist)
Mor|ley, Thom|as (English organist & composer)

Mor|mon +s
Mor|mon|ism
morn +s (morning)
 [☞ mourn,
 Mourne]
Mor|nay, Phi|lippe
 de, Sei|gneur du
 Plessis-Marly (or
 Du|plessis-Mornay)
 (French Huguenot
 leader)
mor|nay
mor|ning +s (early
 part of the day)
 [☞ mourning]
morning-after pill +s
mor|ning coat +s
mor|ning glory
 mor|ning glor|ies
Moro +s
Mo|roc|can +s
Mo|roc|co (country,
 Africa)
mo|roc|co +s (leather)
 [☞ maraca]
moron +s
Mor|oni (capital of
 Comoros)
mor|on|ic
mor|on|ic|ally
mor|on|ism
mor|ose
mor|ose|ly
mor|ose|ness
Mor|peth (town,
 England)
morph +s +ed +ing
mor|pheme +s
mor|phem|ic
mor|phem|ic|ally
Mor|phe|us (Roman
 Myth)
mor|phia
mor|phine
mor|phing noun
morph|o|gen|esis
morph|o|gen|etic
morph|o|gen|ic
morph|o|logic
morph|o|logic|al
morph|o|logic|al|ly
mor|phol|o|gist +s
mor|phol|ogy
 mor|phol|o|gies
Mor|rice, James
 Wil|son (Cdn
 painter)
 [☞ Morris,
 Maurice]
Mor|ris, Ed|ward
 Pat|rick (1st Baron
 Morris, prime

minister of
 Newfoundland)
 [☞ Morrice,
 Maurice]
Mor|ris, Wil|liam
 (English designer)
 [☞ Maurice]
Mor|ris chair +s
mor|ris dance +s
mor|ris dan|cer +s
Mor|ri|son, James
 Doug|las ('Jim') (US
 singer-songwriter)
Mor|ri|son, Chloe
 An|thony ('Toni')
 (US novelist)
Mor|ri|son, George
 Ivan ('Van')
 (Northern Irish
 singer-songwriter)
mor|row +s
Morse, Sam|uel
 Fin|ley Breese (US
 inventor)
Morse code
mor|sel +s
mor|ta|della +s
mor|tal +s
mor|tal|ity
 mor|tal|ities
mor|tal|ly
mor|tar +s +ed +ing
mor|tar|board +s
mort|gage
 mort|gages
 mort|gaged
 mort|ga|ging
mort|gage|able
mort|ga|gee +s
mort|ga|ger +s (use
 mortgagor)
mort|ga|gor +s
mor|tice (use mortise)
 mor|ti|ces
 mor|ticed
 mor|ti|cing
mor|ti|cer +s (use
 mortiser)
mor|ti|cian +s
morti|fi|ca|tion
morti|fy
 morti|fies
 morti|fied
 morti|fy|ing
morti|fy|ing
morti|fy|ing|ly
Mor|ti|mer, John
 Clif|ford (English
 writer)
Mor|ti|mer, Roger de
 (8th Baron of
 Wig|more and 1st

Earl of March,
 English noble)
mor|tise
 mor|tis|es
 mor|tised
 mor|tis|ing
mor|tis|er +s
mort|main +s
Mor|ton, Jelly Roll
 (US musician)
mor|tu|ary
 mor|tu|aries
mor|ula
 mor|ulae
Mo|saic (of Moses)
mo|saic (arrangement
 of assorted pieces;
 virus)
 mo|saics
 mo|saicked
 mo|saick|ing
mo|sai|cist +s
mosa|saur +s
mosa|saur|us
 (= mosasaur)
 mosa|saur|us|es
Mos|cow (capital of
 Russia)
Mosel (river, Europe)
Mose|ley, Henry
 Gwyn Jef|freys
 (English physicist)
 [☞ Mosley]
Mo|selle (= Mosel
 River)
mo|selle +s
Moses (Bible)
Moses, Anna Mary
 Rob|ert|son
 ('Grandma Moses',
 US painter)
Moses, Edwin Cor|ley
 (US athlete)
Moses ben Mai|mon
 (Maimonides)
mosey +s +ed +ing
mosh (dance)
 moshes
 moshed
 mosh|ing
 [☞ mâche]
mo|shav
 mo|shav|im
mosh|er +s
mosh|ing +s
mosh pit +s
Mos|lem +s (use
 Muslim)
Mos|ley, Sir Os|wald
 Er|nald, 6th
 Bar|on|et (English
 fascist leader)
 [☞ Moseley]
mosque +s

mos|quito (insect)
 mos|qui|toes or
 mos|qui|tos
 [☞ Miskito]
Mos|quito Coast
 (coastal land,
 Nicaragua &
 Honduras)
 [☞ Miskito]
mosquito-netted
mos|quito net|ting
moss
 moss|es
 mossed
 moss|ing
Mos|sad
moss|back +s
moss|backed
moss berry
 moss ber|ries
moss|er +s
moss green +s
 (moss-green when
 preceding a noun)
moss-grown
moss|i|ness
moss|like
mossy
 moss|i|er
 moss|i|est
most
most|ly
Mosul (city, Iraq)
mot +s (witty saying)
 [☞ motte, mo]
mote +s (speck of
 dust)
 [☞ moat]
mo|tel (inn) +s
 [☞ mottle]
mo|tet +s
moth +s
moth|ball +s +ed
 +ing
moth-eaten
moth|er +s +ed +ing
mother|board +s
Moth|er Carey's
 chick|en +s
Moth|er Corp.
mother|fucker +s
mother|fuck|ing
Moth|er Goose
mother|hood
moth|er house +s
Moth|er Hub|bard +s
Moth|er|ing Sun|day
mother-in-law
 mothers-in-law
mother-in-law's
 tongue +s (plant)
mother|land +s
mother|less

mother|less|ness
mother|like
mother|li|ness
mother|lode +s
mother|ly
mother-naked
mother-of-pearl
mother's allow|ance
Mother's Day +s
moth|er ship +s
mother's ruin
Moth|er Ter|esa
  (Roman Catholic nun
  & missionary)
Moth|er Ther|esa
  (= Mother Teresa)
mother-to-be
  mothers-to-be
moth|er tongue +s
Mother|well, Rob|ert
  (US painter)
moth|proof +s +ed
  +ing
mothy
  moth|i|er
  moth|i|est
mo|tif +s
mo|tile
mo|til|ity
mo|tion +s +ed +ing
mo|tion|al
mo|tion|less
mo|tion|less|ly
mo|tiv|ate
  mo|tiv|ates
  mo|tiv|at|ed
  mo|tiv|at|ing
mo|tiv|a|tion +s
mo|tiv|a|tion|al
mo|tiv|a|tion|al|ly
mo|tiv|ator +s
mo|tive
  mo|tives
  mo|tived
  mo|tiv|ing
mo|tive|less
mo|tive|less|ly
mo|tive|less|ness
mo|tiv|ity
mot juste
  mots justes
mot|ley
  mot|li|er
  mot|li|est
mot|mot +s
moto|cross
moto|cross|er +s
mo|tor +s +ed +ing
motor|bike +s
motor|boat +s +ed
  +ing
motor|cade +s
motor car +s

motor|coach
  motor|coach|es
motor|cycle +s
motor|cyc|ling
motor|cyc|list +s
motor|home +s
motor|ist +s
motor|iz|a|tion
motor|ize
  motor|iz|es
  motor|ized
  motor|iz|ing
motor|man
  motor|men
motor|mouth +s
motor-mouthed
motor racing
motor|sail|er +s
motor scoot|er +s
motor|sport +s
motor|way +s
Mo|town (Detroit;
  Music)
motte +s (castle
  mound)
mot|tle (mark with
  spots or patches of
  colour)
  mot|tles
  mot|tled
  mot|tling
mot|tled adjective
mot|tling noun
motto
  mot|toes or mot|tos
MOU (memorandum
  of understanding)
  MOUs
moue +s (pout)
mouf|flon +s (use
  mouflon)
mouf|lon +s
mouil|lé
moul|jik +s (use
  muzhik)
mould +s +ed +ing
mould|able
mould|board +s
mould|ed adjective
mould|er[1] (person
  who moulds)
moul|der[2] +s +ed
  +ing (rot)
mould|i|ness
mould|ing +s noun
mouldy
  mould|i|er
  mould|i|est
Moul|mein (city,
  Burma)
moult +s +ed +ing
mound +s +ed +ing
mount +s +ed +ing

mount|able
moun|tain +s
moun|tain bike +s
moun|tain bik|er +s
moun|tain bik|ing
moun|tain|eer +s
moun|tain|eer|ing
moun|tain|ous
moun|tain|scape +s
moun|tain|side +s
moun|tain|top +s
moun|tainy
Mount|bat|ten, Louis
  Fran|cis Al|bert
  Vic|tor Nicho|las
  (1st Earl
  Mountbatten of
  Burma, British
  admiral)
moun|te|bank +s
moun|te|bank|ery
mount|ed +s adjective
  & noun
mount|er +s
Moun|tie +s
mount|ing +s noun
Mount Isa (city,
  Australia)
Mount Pearl (city,
  Canada)
Mount Revel|stoke
  (park, Canada)
Mount Royal
  (mountain & city,
  Canada)
mourn +s +ed +ing
  (show sorrow)
  [☞ morn, Mourne]
Mourne (mountains,
  Northern Ireland)
  [☞ mourn, morn]
mourn|er +s
mourn|ful
mourn|ful|ly
mourn|ful|ness
mourn|ing noun
  (expression of
  sorrow etc.)
  [☞ morning]
mourn|ing cloak +s
mourn|ing dove +s
mour|vèdre +s
Mou|sal|la (= Mount
  Musala, Bulgaria)
mouse
  • noun (rodent; feeble
    person)
    plural mice
  • noun (Computing)
    plural mice or
    mous|es
  • verb

mous|es
moused
mous|ing
[☞ mousse]
mouse|like
mouse pad +s
mous|er +s
mouse|trap
  mouse|traps
  mouse|trapped
  mouse|trap|ping
mousey (use mousy)
mous|i|er
mous|i|est
mous|i|ly
mous|i|ness
mous|saka +s
mousse (whipped
  food; hair foam)
  mouss|es
  moussed
  mouss|ing
  [☞ moose]
moussed adjective
mousse|line +s
Mous|sorg|sky,
  Mo|dest Petro|vich
  (= Mussorgsky,
  Russian composer)
mous|tache +s
mous|tached
mous|tach|io +s (use
  mustachio)
mous|tachi|oed (use
  mustachioed)
Mous|ter|ian
mousy
  mous|i|er
  mous|i|est
mouth +s +ed +ing
mouth-breath|er +s
mouthed adjective
mouth|er +s
mouth feel
mouth|ful +s
mouth|guard +s
mouth|i|er
mouth|i|est
mouth|less
mouth|part +s
mouth|piece +s
mouth-to-mouth
mouth|wash
  mouth|wash|es
mouth-watering
mouthy
  mouth|i|er
  mouth|i|est
mov|abil|ity
mov|able +s
movable-do
mov|able|ness
mov|ably

move
moves
moved
mov|ing
[☞ mauve]
move|able +s (use
  movable)
move|able|ness (use
  movableness)
move|ably (use
  movably)
move|ment +s
mov|er +s
mov|ie +s
movie|goer +s
movie-going
movie house +s
movie|land
movie|maker +s
movie|making
mov|ing adjective
mov|ing|ly
mow (cut down; pile;
  storage space)
mows
mowed
mowed or mown
mow|ing
[☞ mo, mho, mot]
Mowat, Farley (Cdn
  writer)
mow|er +s
moxa
moxi|bus|tion
moxie
Mo|zam|bi|can +s
Mo|zam|bique
  (country, Africa;
  channel, Indian
  Ocean)
Moz|art, (Jo|hann
  Chrys|os|tom)
  Wolf|gang
  Ama|deus (Austrian
  composer)
Moz|art|ean (use
  Mozartian)
Moz|art|ian
moz|za|rella
MP (Member of
  Parliament)
MPs
MPP (Member of
  Provincial
  Parliament)
MPPs
MPV (multi-purpose
  vehicle; minivan)
MPVs
MRI (magnetic
  resonance imaging)
MRIs

mRNA (messenger
  RNA)
Mr. Right
Mrs. Grun|dy
Mrs. Grun|dies
Mrs. Grundy|ism
MS-DOS proprietary
mu (letter)
[☞ mew]
Mu|bar|ak,
  (Muham|mad)
  Hosni Said
  (Egyptian statesman)
much
Mu|chin|ga
  (mountains, Zambia)
much|ly
much|ness
mucho
mucho di|nero
muci|lage +s
muci|la|gin|ous
muck +s +ed +ing
muck|a|muck +s
muck|er +s
muckety-muck +s
muck|i|er
muck|i|est
muck|i|ness
muckle +s
muck|rake
  muck|rakes
  muck|raked
  muck|rak|ing
muck|rak|er +s
muck|rak|ing noun
mucky
  muck|i|er
  muck|i|est
mucky-muck +s
muco|poly|
  sac|char|ide +s
mu|cosa
  mu|co|sae
mu|co|sal
mu|cos|ity
mu|cous adjective
  [☞ mucus]
mu|cous mem|brane
  +s
mucro
  mu|cro|nes
mu|cron|ate
mucus noun
  [☞ mucous]
mud +s
mud|bank +s
mud bath +s
mud brick +s
mud|cat +s
mud|di|er
mud|di|est
mud|di|ly

mud|di|ness
mud|dle
  mud|dles
  mud|dled
  mud|dling
muddle-headed
muddle-headed|ness
mud|dler +s
mud|dling|ly
muddy
  mud|di|er
  mud|di|est
  mud|dies
  mud|died
  muddy|ing
Mu|dé|jar
  Mu|dé|jar|es
mud|fish
  mud|fish or
  mud|fish|es
mud flap +s
mud flat +s
mud|flow +s
mud|guard +s
mud|hole +s
mud-lark +s +ed
  +ing
mud|pack +s
mud pie +s
mud puppy
  mud pup|pies
mud room +s
mud skip|per +s
mud|slide +s
mud|sling|er +s
mud|sling|ing
mud|stone +s
mud trout
  plural mud trout
mud-wrestle
  mud-wrestles
  mud-wrestled
  mud-wrestling
mud wrest|ler +s
mud wrest|ling noun
Muen|ster (cheese)
  [☞ Münster,
  Munster]
muesli
muez|zin +s
muff +s +ed +ing
muf|fin +s
muf|fle
  muf|fles
  muf|fled
  muf|fling
muf|fler +s
muf|ti +s
mug
  mugs
  mugged
  mug|ging

Mu|gabe, Rob|ert
  Gab|riel
  (Zimbabwean
  statesman)
mug|ful +s
mug|ger +s
mug|gi|ness
mug|ging +s noun
mug|gins
  plural mug|gins or
  mug|gins|es
muggy
  mug|gi|er
  mug|gi|est
Mu|ghal +s
  (Mongolian; Muslim
  dynasty)
  [☞ Mogul]
mugho pine +s
mugo pine +s (use
  mugho pine)
mug shot +s
mug-up +s
mug|wort +s
mug|wump +s
Muham|mad (founder
  of Islam)
Muham|mad II
  (= Mohammed II,
  Ottoman sultan)
Muham|mad Ali
  (pasha of Egypt; US
  boxer)
Mühl|hau|sen
  (German name for
  Mulhouse, France)
mu|ja|he|deen
mu|ja|he|din (use
  mujahedeen)
mu|ja|hi|deen (use
  mujahedeen)
mu|ja|hi|din (use
  mujahedeen)
Mu|kal|la (city,
  Yemen)
Muk|den (former name
  for Shenyang,
  China)
Mukh|er|jee, Bha|rati
  (Cdn writer)
muk|luk +s
mu|lat|to
  mu|lat|toes or
  mu|lat|tos
mul|berry
  mul|ber|ries
mulch
  mulch|es
  mulched
  mulch|ing
mulct +s +ed +ing

mule +s (animal;
plant; spinning
machine; shoe)
mule deer
  plural mule deer
mule skin|ner +s
mule|teer +s
muley +s
Mul|ha|cén
  (mountain, Spain)
Mül|heim (an der
  Ruhr) (city,
  Germany)
Mul|house (city,
  France)
mulie +s (*use* muley)
mul|ish
mul|ish|ly
mul|ish|ness
Mull (island, Inner
  Hebrides)
mull +s +ed +ing
mul|lah +s
mulled *adjective*
mul|lein +s
Mul|ler, Her|mann
  Jo|seph (US
  geneticist)
Mül|ler, (Fried|rich)
  Max (English
  philologist)
Mül|ler, Jo|hann
  (= Regiomontanus,
  German astronomer
  & mathematician)
Mül|ler, Jo|han|nes
  Peter (German
  anatomist)
Mül|ler, Paul
  Her|mann (Swiss
  chemist)
mul|ler +s
mul|let
  plural mul|let or
  mul|lets
mul|li|gan
mul|li|ga|tawny
Mul|li|ken, Rob|ert
  San|der|son (US
  chemist)
Mul|lin|gar (town,
  Ireland)
mul|lion +s
mul|lioned
Mul|ro|ney, (Mar|tin)
  Brian (Cdn prime
  minister)
Mul|tan (city,
  Pakistan)
multi|axial
multi-billion
multi|cellu|lar
multi|cellu|lar|ity

multi-channel
multi|col|or (*use*
  multicolour)
multi|col|ored (*use*
  multicoloured)
multi|col|our
multi|col|oured
multi|cult
multi|culti
multi|cul|tur|al
multi|cul|tur|al|ism
multi|cul|tur|al|ist +s
multi|cul|tur|al|ly
multi-dimension|al
multi-
  dimension|al|ity
multi|direc|tion|al
multi|disci|plin|ary
multi-ethnic
multi-faceted
multi|factor|ial
multi-family
multi|far|ious
multi|far|ious|ly
multi|fa|rious|ness
multi|fid
multi|flora +s
multi|focal
multi|form
multi|form|ity
multi-function
multi-function|al
multi-genera|tion|al
multi|grade
multi-grain
multi|hull +s
multi-lane
multi|lat|eral
multi|lat|eral|ism
multi|lat|eral|ist +s
multi|lat|eral|ly
multi-layer
multi-layered
multi-level
multi-levelled
multi|lin|gual
multi|lin|gual|ism
multi|media
multi|meter +s
multi-million
multi-million|aire +s
multi|nation|al +s
multi|nom|ial +s
multi-pack +s
mul|tip|ar|ous
multi|part|ite
multi-party
multi-party|ism
mul|tiple +s
multiple-choice
mul|tiple scler|osis

multi|plex
multi|plex|es
multi|plexed
multi|plex|ing
multi|plex|er +s
multi|plex|ing *noun &*
  adjective
multi|plex|or +s (*use*
  multiplexer)
multi|pli|able
multi|plic|able
multi|pli|cand +s
multi|pli|ca|tion +s
multi|plic|a|tive
multi|pli|city
multi|pli|ci|ties
multi|pli|er +s
multi|ply *verb &*
  adverb
multi|plies
multi|plied
multi|ply|ing
multi-point
multi|polar
multi|polar|ity
multi|pro|cess|ing
multi|pro|ces|sor +s
multi|pro|gram|ming
multi-purpose
multi|racial
multi|racial|ism
multi-sensory
multi-skilled
multi-skilling
multi-stage
multi-storey
multi-task +s +ed
  +ing
multi-tasking *noun &*
  adjective
multi-thread|ed
multi-thread|ing
multi-track +s +ed
  +ing
multi-tracked
  adjective
multi-tracking *noun*
multi|tude +s
multi|tud|in|ous
multi|tud|in|ous|ly
multi|tud|in|ous|ness
multi-use
multi-user
multi|valence
multi|valen|cy
multi|valent
multi|valve
multi|vari|ate
multi|vita|min +s
multi|vocal
multi-way
multi-year

mum
mums
mummed
mum|ming
Mum|bai (= Bombay,
  India)
mum|ble
mum|bles
mum|bled
mum|bling
mum|bler +s
mum|bling|ly
mumbo-jumbo +s
mu-meson +s
Mum|ford, Lewis (US
  sociologist)
mum|mer +s +ed
  +ing
mum|mer|ing *noun*
mum|mery
mum|mer|ies
mum|mi|chog +s
mum|mi|fi|ca|tion +s
mum|mi|fied *adjective*
mum|mi|fy
mum|mi|fies
mum|mi|fied
mum|mi|fy|ing
mum|ming +s *noun*
mummy
mum|mies
mumps
mumsy
mum|sies
Munch, Ed|vard
  (Norwegian painter)
munch
munch|es
munched
munch|ing
Munch|ausen's
  syn|drome
munch|er +s
munch|ies
munch|kin +s
munchy
mun|dane
mun|dane|ly
mun|dane|ness
mun|dan|ity
mun|dan|ities
mung bean +s
Mun|ich (city,
  Germany)
mu|ni|ci|pal
mu|ni|ci|pa|li|té
  ré|gio|nale de
  com|té
mu|ni|ci|pa|li|tés
  ré|gio|nales de
  com|té
mu|ni|ci|pal|ity
mu|ni|ci|pal|ities

mu|ni|ci|pal|iz|ation +s
mu|ni|ci|pal|ize
mu|ni|ci|pal|izes
mu|ni|ci|pal|ized
mu|ni|ci|pal|iz|ing
mu|ni|ci|pal|ly
muni|fi|cence
muni|fi|cent
muni|fi|cent|ly
mu|ni|ment +s
mu|ni|tion +s +ed +ing
Munro, Alice (Cdn writer)
[☞ Monroe]
Munro, Hec|tor Hugh (Saki)
[☞ Monroe]
Mun|see
plural Mun|see or Mun|sees
Mun|ster (province, Ireland)
[☞ Muenster, Münster]
Mün|ster (city, Germany)
[☞ Muenster, Munster]
munt|jac +s
munt|jak +s (*use* muntjac)
muon +s
muon|ic
mur|age +s
mural +s
mural|ist +s
Mura|saki Shi|kibu (Japanese writer)
Murat, Joa|chim (king of Naples)
MURB (multiple unit residential building)
MURBs
Mur|chi|son (rapids, Malawi; *former name for* Kabalega Falls, Uganda)
Mur|cia (region & city, Spain)
[☞ Mercia]
mur|der +s +ed +ing
murder|ball
mur|der|er +s
mur|der|ess
mur|der|ess|es
mur|der one
mur|der|ous
mur|der|ous|ly
mur|der|ous|ness

Mur|doch, Dame (Jean) Iris (English writer)
Mur|doch, (Keith) Ru|pert (US publisher & media entrepreneur)
mure (wall up)
mures
mured
mur|ing
[☞ murre, moor]
murex
mur|exes or mur|ices
muri|ate +s
muri|at|ic acid
Mur|illo, Bar|tolo|mé Este|ban (Spanish painter)
mur|ine
murk
murk|i|ly
murk|i|ness
murky
murk|i|er
murk|i|est
Mur|mansk (city, Russia)
mur|mur +s +ed +ing
mur|mur|er +s
mur|mur|ing *noun & adjective*
mur|mur|ous
Mur|nau, F. W. (German filmmaker)
Mur|phy, Emily (Cdn journalist & reformer)
Murphy's Law
mur|rain +s (disease)
[☞ moraine]
Mur|ray (river, Australia; surname)
[☞ murrey]
Mur|ray, (George) Gil|bert Aimé (English translator)
Mur|ray, Sir James Au|gus|tus Henry (Scottish lexicographer)
Mur|ray, (Morna) Anne (Cdn singer-songwriter)
murre +s (bird)
[☞ myrrh, mure]
murre|let +s
mur|rey +s (colour)
[☞ Murray, myrrh]
Mur|rum|bi|dgee (river, Australia)

mur|ther +s +ed +ing
[☞ Merthyr Tydfil]
Muru|roa (atoll, French Polynesia)
Mu|sala (mountain, Bulgaria)
Mus|ca|det +s
mus|ca|dine +s
mus|ca|rine
mus|ca|rin|ic
Mus|cat (capital of Oman)
mus|cat +s (wine; grape)
[☞ musket]
Mus|cat and Oman (*former name for* Oman)
mus|ca|tel +s
muscle (*Anatomy*; force)
muscles
muscled
musc|ling
[☞ mussel]
muscle-bound
muscled *adjective*
muscle-flexing
muscle|less
muscle|man (strong man; thug)
muscle|men
[☞ Mussulman]
muscle|wood
plural muscle|wood or muscle|woods
muscly
mus|co|vado
Mus|co|vite +s (of Moscow)
mus|co|vite +s (mica)
Mus|covy (former principality, Russia; duck)
mus|cu|lar
mus|cu|lar dys|trophy
mus|cu|lar|ity
mus|cu|lar|ly
mus|cu|la|ture +s
mus|cu|lo|skel|etal
Muse +s (*Greek & Roman Myth*)
[☞ mews]
muse (inspiration; ponder; murmur)
muses
mused
mus|ing
[☞ mews]
mu|seo|logic|al
mu|seol|o|gist +s
mu|seol|ogy

mu|sette +s
mu|seum +s
mush
mush|es
mushed
mush|ing
mush|er +s
mush|i|er
mush|i|est
mush|i|ly
mush|i|ness
mush|ing *noun*
mush|room +s +ed +ing
mush|room|ing *adjective & noun*
mush|roomy
mushy
mush|i|er
mush|i|est
music +s
[☞ musique concrète]
music|al +s (musical drama or movie)
musi|cale +s (concert)
musi|cal|ity
musi|cal|ize
music|al|iz|es
music|al|ized
music|al|iz|ing
music|al|ly
musi|cian +s
musi|cian|ly
musi|cian|ship
musico|logic|al
music|ol|o|gist +s
music|ol|ogy
mus|ing +s *noun*
mus|ing|ly
mu|sique con|crète
musk +s
musk deer
plural musk deer
mus|keg +s
mus|kel|lunge
plural mus|kel|lunge
mus|ket +s (gun)
[☞ muscat]
mus|ket|eer +s
mus|ket|ry
Mus|kie, Ed|mund Six|tus (US politician)
mus|kie (pike)
plural mus|kie or mus|kies
[☞ musky]
musk|i|ness
musk mal|low
musk|mel|on +s

Mus|ko|gean (language family)
Mus|ko|gee (people; specific Muskogean language)
plural Mus|ko|gee or Mus|ko|gees
Mus|koka (lake & region, Canada; chair)
musk|ox
plural musk|ox or musk|oxen
musk|rat +s
musk rose +s
musky (smelling of musk)
musk|i|er
musk|i|est
[☞ muskie]
Mus|lim +s
mus|lin
muso +s
mus|quash
mus|quash|es
muss
muss|es
mussed
muss|ing
mus|sel +s (mollusc)
[☞ muscle]
Mus|set, (Louis Charles) Al|fred de (French writer)
Mus|so|lini, Ben|ito Amil|care An|drea (Italian prime minister)
Mus|sorg|sky, Mo|dest Petro|vich (Russian composer)
Mus|sul|man (Muslim)
Mus|sul|mans or Mus|sel|men
[☞ muscleman]
mussy
must +s (*auxiliary verb*; grape juice; mustiness; frenzied state)
mus|tache +s (*use* moustache)
mus|tached (*use* moustached)
mus|tach|io +s
mus|tachi|oed
Mus|tafa Kemal (Kemal Atatürk)
mus|tang +s
mus|tard +s
mus|tardy
mus|tard yel|low +s (mustard-yellow

when preceding a noun)
mus|te|lid +s
mus|ter +s +ed +ing
musth (frenzied state: *use* must)
must-have +s
must|i|ly
must|i|ness
Mus|tique (Caribbean island)
mustn't
must-see +s
musty
must|i|er
must|i|est
Mut (*Egyptian Myth*)
[☞ mutt]
mut|abil|ity
mut|able
muta|gen +s
muta|gen|esis
muta|gen|ic
muta|gen|icity
muta|gen|ized
mu|tant +s
Mu|tare (town, Zimbabwe)
mu|tate
mu|tates
mu|tat|ed
mu|tat|ing
mu|tat|ed *adjective*
muta|tion +s
muta|tion|al
muta|tion|al|ly
mu|ta|tis mu|tan|dis
mute (silent; muffle; *Music*)
mutes
muted
mut|ing
[☞ moot]
muted *adjective*
mutely
mute|ness
muti|late
muti|lates
muti|lat|ed
muti|lat|ing
muti|la|tion +s
muti|la|tor +s
mu|tin|eer
mu|tin|ous
mu|tin|ous|ly
mu|tiny
mutin|ies
mutin|ied
mu|tiny|ing
mut|ism
Mutsu +s
Mut|su|hito (Meiji Tenno)

mutt +s (dog)
[☞ Mut]
mut|ter +s +ed +ing
mut|ter|er +s
mut|ter|ing|ly
mut|ton +s
mut|ton chop +s
mutton-head +s
mutton-headed
mut|tony
mu|tual (reciprocal; shared)
[☞ mutuel, mutule]
mu|tual|ism
mu|tual|ist +s
mu|tual|is|tic
mu|tual|ity
mu|tual|ly
mu|tuel +s (parimutuel)
[☞ mutule, mutual]
mu|tule +s (*Architecture*)
[☞ mutuel, mutual]
muu|muu +s
Muy|bridge, Ead|weard (US photographer)
Muzak *proprietary* (system for transmitting background music)
muzak (background music)
mu|zhik +s
Muz|tag (mountain, China)
muz|zi|er
muz|zi|est
muz|zi|ly
muz|zi|ness
muz|zle
muz|zles
muz|zled
muz|zling
muzzle|load|er +s
muzzle-loading
muz|zler +s
muzzy
muz|zi|er
muz|zi|est
MVP (most valuable player)
MVPs
my
my|al|gia +s
my|al|gic
My|an|mar (*official name of* Burma)
my|as|the|nia
my|as|the|nia gra|vis
my|as|then|ic
my|celi|al

my|celi|um
my|celia
My|ce|nae (ancient city, Greece)
[☞ Maecenas]
My|ce|nae|an +s
[☞ Maecenas]
myco|bac|ter|ial
myco|bac|ter|ium
myco|bac|teria
myco|logic|al
myco|logic|al|ly
my|col|o|gist +s
my|col|ogy
my|col|o|gies
myco|plasma
myco|plas|mas or myco|plas|mata
mycor|rhiza
mycor|rhi|zae or mycor|rhi|zas
mycor|rhi|zal
my|co|sis
my|co|ses
my|cot|ic
myco|toxin +s
my|dria|sis
my|el|in
my|el|in|ated
my|el|in|a|tion
my|el|itis
my|el|oid
my|el|oma
my|el|omas or my|elo|mata
Myko|lay|iv (city, Ukraine)
My|ko|nos (island, Greece)
Mylar
my|lo|don +s
My|men|singh (city, Bangladesh)
myna +s
mynah +s (*use* myna)
myo|car|di|al
myo|car|ditis
myo|car|di|um
myo|car|dia
myo|fib|ril +s
myo|genic
myo|glo|bin +s
my|ol|ogy
my|opia +s
my|op|ic
my|op|ic|ally
myo|sin
my|o|sis (constriction of pupil: *use* miosis)
[☞ meiosis]
myo|sote +s
myo|so|tis
myo|so|tis|es

my|otic (of myosis: *use* miotic) [☞ meiotic]
myo|tonia
myo|ton|ic
myr|iad +s
myr|ia|pod +s
myr|mi|don +s
my|roba|lan +s
Myron (Greek sculptor)
myrrh +s (resin; incense; sweet cicely) [☞ murre]
myr|rhic
myr|rhy (like myrrh) [☞ murrey]
myr|tle +s
my|self
Mysia (ancient region, Asia Minor)
Mys|ian +s
My|sore
• (city, India)
• (*former name for* Karnataka, India)
mys|teri|ous
mys|teri|ous|ly
mys|teri|ous|ness
mys|tery
   mys|ter|ies
mys|tic +s (mystical; mystical person) [☞ mystique]
mys|tic|al
mys|tic|al|ly
mysti|cism +s
mysti|fi|ca|tion +s
mys|tify
   mysti|fies
   mysti|fied
   mysti|fy|ing
mysti|fy|ing *adjective*
mysti|fy|ing|ly
mys|tique +s (air of mystery) [☞ mystic]
myth +s
myth|ic
myth|ic|al
myth|ic|al|ly
mythi|ciz|a|tion +s
mythi|cize
   mythi|ciz|es
   mythi|cized
   mythi|ciz|ing
myth|maker +s
myth|making
myth|og|raph|er +s
myth|og|raphy
mytho|logic
mytho|logic|al

mytho|logic|al|ly
myth|ol|o|gist +s
myth|olo|giz|a|tion +s
myth|ol|o|gize
   myth|ol|o|giz|es
   myth|ol|o|gized
   myth|ol|o|giz|ing
myth|ol|o|giz|er +s
myth|ol|ogy
   myth|ol|o|gies
mytho|mania
mytho|maniac
mytho|poeia
mytho|poeic
mytho|poet|ic
myth|os
myth|oi
Myti|lene (town, Greece)
myx|edema
myx|oma
   myx|omas or
   myx|omata
myxo|ma|to|sis
myxo|ma|tous
myxo|my|cete +s
myxo|virus
   myxo|virus|es

N

N

• (letter; en)
   N's
• (newton)
   [☞ en]
n (letter)
   n's
   [☞ en]
na
naan +s (bread: *use* nan) [☞ nan]
Naas (town, Ireland)
nab
   nabs
   nabbed
   nab|bing
Na|beul (town, Tunisia)
Nab|lus (town, West Bank)
na|bob +s
Nabo|kov, Vlad|i|mir Vlad|imor|ovich (Russian-born writer)
Nabo|kov|ian
Na|cala (city, Mozambique)
na|celle +s
nacho +s
nacre
na|cre|ous
nada
Nader, Ralph (US consumer advocate)
Nader|ite +s
na|dir +s
nae (not) [☞ nay]
nae|vus (*use* nevus)
   naevi
naff +s +ed +ing
naff|ing *adjective*
NAFTA
nag
   nags
   nagged
   nag|ging
naga +s
Naga|land (state, India)
Naga|saki (city, Japan)
nag|ger +s
nag|ging +s *noun & adjective*
nag|ging|ly
Nagorno-Karabakh (region, Azerbaijan)

Na|goya (city, Japan)
Nag|pur (city, India)
Nagy, Imre (Hungarian statesman)
nah
Naha (city, Japan)
Na|han|ni (park, Canada)
Na|huatl +s
Na|huat|lan
Nahum (*Bible*)
naiad
   nai|ads or nai|ades
naïf +s *adjective & noun*
nail +s +ed +ing
nail-biter +s
nail-biting
nail brush
   nail brush|es
nailed *adjective*
nail|er +s
nail|head +s
nail|less
nail punch
   nail punch|es
nail set +s
Nain (town, Canada)
nain|sook +s
Nai|paul, Sir Vidi|ad|har Suraj|pra|sad (Trinidadian writer)
naira
   plural naira
Nairn (= Nairnshire)
Nairn|shire (former county, Scotland)
Nai|ro|bi (capital of Kenya)
Nai|smith, James A. (Cdn inventor of basketball) [☞ Nasmyth]
naive *adjective* (innocent; credulous) [☞ nave]
naive|ly
naive|ness
naïv|eté +s
naiv|ety (= naïveté)
   naiv|eties
Najaf (city, Iraq)
naked *adjective*
naked|ly
naked|ness
Nakhi|che|van (*Russian name for* Naxçivan, Azerbaijan)
Na|kuru (city, Kenya)
Nal|chik (city, Russia)

Nam (Vietnam)
Nama
 plural **Nama** or
 Namas
Nam|an|gan (city,
 Uzbekistan)
Na|ma|qua|land
 (region, Africa)
namby-pamby
 namby-pambies
name
 names
 named
 nam|ing
name|able
name brand +s
name-calling
name day +s
name-drop
 name-drops
 name-dropped
 name-dropping
name-dropper +s
name-dropping *noun*
name|less
name|less|ly
name|less|ness
name|ly
name|plate +s
nam|er +s
name|sake +s
name tag +s
Namib (desert, Africa)
Na|mibia (country,
 Africa)
Na|mib|ian +s
nam pla
Namur (province & its
 capital, Belgium)
nan +s (grandmother;
 bread)
nana +s
Na|naimo (city,
 Canada)
 [☞ **Sne Nay Muxw**]
Na|naimo bar +s
Nanak (founder of
 Sikhism)
nance +s *offensive*
Nan|chang (city,
 China)
Nancy (city, France)
nancy *offensive*
 nan|cies
nancy boy +s
 offensive
Nandi
Nanga Par|bat
 (mountain, Pakistan)
Nan|jing (city, China)
nan|keen +s
Nan|king (= Nanjing,
 China; cherry tree)

Nan|ning (city, China)
nanny
 nan|nies
 nan|nied
 nanny|ing
nanny|berry
 nanny|ber|ries
nanny goat +s
nano|metre +s
nano|sec|ond +s
nano|techno|logic|al
nano|tech|nol|o|gist
 +s
nano|tech|nol|ogy
Nan|sen, Fridt|jof
 (Norwegian explorer
 & statesman)
Nantes (city, France)
Nan|ti|coke (city,
 Canada)
Nan|tuck|et (island,
 US)
Naoise (*Irish Myth*)
Naomi (*Bible*)
nap (sleep; fabric pile;
 baste; *Cards*;
 Gambling)
 naps
 napped
 nap|ping
 [☞ **knap, nappe**]
napa +s
na|palm +s +ed +ing
Napa|nee (town,
 Canada)
nape +s
nap|ery
Naph|ta|li
naph|tha
naph|tha|lene
naph|thal|ic
naph|thene +s
naph|then|ic
Na|pier (city, New
 Zealand)
**Na|pier, Sir Charles
 James** (English
 general)
Na|pier, John
 (Scottish
 mathematician)
Na|pier|ian
nap|kin +s
Na|ples (city, Italy)
nap|less
Napo|leon (French
 emperors)
napo|leon +s
Napo|leon|ic
nap|pa +s (*use* napa)
nappe +s (*Geology*)
 [☞ **nap, knap**]
napped *adjective*

nappy
 nap|pies
na|prox|en
Nara (city, Japan)
Na|ra|yan|ganj (city,
 Bangladesh)
Nar|bonne (city,
 France)
narc +s (narcotics
 officer)
 [☞ **nark**]
nar|cis|sism
nar|cis|sist +s
nar|cis|sis|tic
Nar|cis|sus (*Greek
 Myth*)
nar|cis|sus
 nar|cis|si or
 nar|cis|sus|es
narco|lepsy
narco|lep|tic +s
nar|co|sis
 nar|co|ses
narco|terror|ism
narco|terror|ist +s
nar|cot|ic +s
nar|cot|ic|ally
narco|tiz|a|tion +s
narco|tize
 narco|tiz|es
 narco|tized
 narco|tiz|ing
nard +s
nar|doo +s
Nares (strait, Arctic)
nares (nostrils)
nar|ghi|le +s
nar|gi|leh +s (*use*
 narghile)
nark +s +ed +ing
 (informer; decoy;
 annoying thing; *for*
 narcotics officer *use*
 narc)
narky
 nark|i|er
 nark|i|est
Nar|mada (river,
 India)
Nar|ra|gan|sett
nar|rat|able
nar|rate
 nar|rates
 nar|rat|ed
 nar|rat|ing
nar|ra|tion +s
nar|ra|tive +s
nar|ra|tive|ly
nar|ra|to|logic|al
nar|ra|tol|o|gist +s
nar|ra|tol|ogy
nar|ra|tor +s
nar|ra|tor|ial

nar|row +er +est +s
 +ed +ing
narrow|boat +s
narrow|cast
 narrow|casts
 narrow|cast or
 narrow|casted
 narrow|cast|ing
narrow|cast|er +s
narrow|cast|ing *noun*
nar|row gauge +s
 noun
narrow-gauge
 adjective
narrow|ish
narrow|ly
narrow-minded
narrow-minded|ly
narrow-minded|ness
narrow|ness
nar|thex
 nar|thex|es
Nar|vik (town,
 Norway)
nar|whal +s
nary (no; not a)
 [☞ **Neri, nares**]
NASA
nasal +s
na|sal|ity
nasal|iz|a|tion
nasal|ize
 nasal|iz|es
 nasal|ized
 nasal|iz|ing
nasal|ly
NASCAR
nas|cency
nas|cent
NASDAQ
nase|berry
 nase|ber|ries
Nase|by (battle site,
 England)
Nash (surname)
 [☞ **Nashe, gnash**]
**Nash, (Cyril)
 Knowl|ton** (Cdn
 journalist)
Nash, John (English
 town planner)
**Nash, (Fred|eric)
 Ogden** (US poet)
Nash, Thom|as
 (= Nashe)
Nashe, Thom|as
 (English writer)
 [☞ **Nash, gnash**]
Nash|ville (city, US)
Nasik (city, India)
Nas|kapi
 plural **Nas|kapi** or
 Nas|kapis

Na|smyth, James (Scottish inventor of steam hammer) [☞ Naismith]
naso|gas|tric
Nass (river, Canada)
Nas|sau (former duchy, Germany; capital of the Bahamas)
Nas|ser (lake, Egypt)
Nas|ser, Gamal Abdel (Egyptian statesman)
Nas|ser|ist +s
Nass-Gitksan
nas|ti|ly
nas|ti|ness
nas|tur|tium +s
nasty
nas|ti|er
nas|ti|est
nas|ties
Natal (city, Brazil; former province, South Africa)
natal
natal|ity
natal|ities
na|ta|tion
nata|tor|ium
nata|tor|iums or nata|tor|ia
natch
nates
Nathan (Bible)
nathe|less (= nathless)
nath|less
na|tion +s
na|tion|al
Na|tion|al Cap|ital Re|gion (in Canada)
na|tion|al|ism
na|tion|al|ist +s
na|tion|al|is|tic
na|tion|al|is|tic|ally
na|tion|al|ity
na|tion|al|ities
na|tion|al|iz|a|tion +s
na|tion|al|ize
na|tion|al|iz|es
na|tion|al|ized
na|tion|al|iz|ing
na|tion|al|ly
na|tion|hood +s
nation-state +s
na|tion|wide
na|tive +s
Na|tive Amer|ican +s
native-born
Na|tive Can|ad|ian +s
na|tive|ly

na|tive|ness
na|tiv|ism
na|tiv|ist +s
na|tiv|ity
na|tiv|ities
NATO (North Atlantic Treaty Organization)
Na|tron (lake, Tanzania)
na|tron
nat|ter +s +ed +ing
nat|ti|ly
nat|ti|ness
natty
nat|ti|er
nat|ti|est
nat|ural +s
natural-born
nat|ur|al|ism
nat|ur|al|ist +s
nat|ur|al|is|tic
nat|ur|al|is|tic|ally
nat|ur|al|iz|a|tion
nat|ur|al|ize
nat|ur|al|iz|es
nat|ur|al|ized
nat|ur|al|iz|ing
nat|ur|al|ized adjective
nat|ur|al|ly
nat|ur|al|ness
na|ture +s
na|tured
nature's call
na|tur|ism
na|tur|ist +s
nat|uro|path +s
nat|uro|path|ic
nat|ur|op|athy
Nauga|hyde proprietary
naught (nothing; worthless) [☞ nought]
naugh|ti|ly
naugh|ti|ness (naughty behaviour) [☞ knottiness]
naugh|ty (bad; indecent)
naugh|ti|er
naugh|ti|est
naugh|ti|ly [☞ knotty]
Nault, Fer|di|nand (Cdn ballet director)
naup|lius
naup|lii
Nauru (country, SW Pacific)
Nau|ru|an +s
nau|sea

nau|se|ate
nau|se|ates
nau|se|at|ed
nau|se|at|ing
nau|se|at|ed adjective
nau|se|at|ing adjective
nau|se|at|ing|ly
nau|seous
nau|seous|ly
nau|seous|ness
Nau|sicaa (Greek Myth)
nautch (dance)
nautch|es [☞ notch]
naut|ical
naut|ical|ly
naut|ilus
naut|ilus|es or naut|ili
nav +s
Nav|aho (use Navajo)
plural Nav|aho or Nav|ahos
nav|aid +s
Nav|ajo
plural Nav|ajo or Nav|ajos
naval (of the navy) [☞ navel]
Navan (town, Ireland)
Nava|nagar (former state, India)
nava|rin +s
Nava|rino (Greek bay & naval battle)
Na|varre (region, Spain)
nave +s (central part of a church; hub) [☞ knave]
navel +s (belly button) [☞ naval]
navel-gazing
navel or|ange +s
nav|icu|lar
nav|ig|abil|ity
nav|ig|able
navi|gate
navi|gates
navi|gat|ed
navi|gat|ing
navi|ga|tion +s
navi|ga|tion|al
navi|ga|tor +s
Nav|ra|ti|lova, Mar|tina (US tennis player)
navvy (labourer)
nav|vies
Navy (island, Canada)
navy (fleet; colour)
nav|ies

navy bean +s
navy blue +s
naw (no) [☞ gnaw]
nawab +s
Nax|çi|van (republic & its capital, Azerbaijan)
Naxos (Greek island)
nay +s (or rather; no) [☞ nae, Ney, neigh, né, née]
Naya|rit (state, Mexico)
nay|say|er +s
nay|say|ing
Naza|rene +s
Naza|reth (town, Israel)
Nazar|ite +s (use Nazirite)
Nazi +s
Nazi|dom
Nazi|fi|ca|tion
Nazi|fy
Nazi|fies
Nazi|fied
Nazi|fy|ing
Nazi|ism (use Nazism)
Nazir|ite +s
Naz|ism
NCM (non-commissioned member)
NCMs
NCO (non-commissioned officer)
NCOs
NDE (near-death experience)
NDEs
Nde|bele
plural Nde|bele or Nde|beles
N'Dja|mena (capital of Chad)
Ndola (city, Zambia)
NDP (New Democratic Party)
NDPer +s
né (born: used of a man) [☞ née]
Ne|an|der|thal +s (paleolithic human)
ne|an|der|thal +s (uncivilized or old-fashioned person)
neap +s (tide) [☞ neep]
Nea|pol|itan +s

near +er +est +s +ed
+ing
near|by
Ne|arc|tic
near-death
Near East (region of
SW Asia & N Africa)
Near East|ern
near|ish
near|ly
near|ness
Near North (region,
Canada)
near|shore
near|side
near|sight|ed
near|sight|ed|ly
near|sight|ed|ness
near-term adjective
neat +er +est +s
neat|en +s +ed +ing
Neath (town, Wales)
'neath
neat|ly
neat|ness
neat|nik +s
neat-o
neat's-foot oil
neb +s
Neb|bi|olo +s
neb|bish
neb|bish|es
neb|bishy
Neb|lina, Pico da
(mountain, Brazil)
Neb|raska (state, US)
Neb|ras|kan +s
Nebu|chad|nez|zar
(king of Babylon)
nebu|chad|nez|zar
+s
neb|ula
neb|ulae or neb|ulas
nebu|lar
nebu|lize
nebu|liz|es
nebu|lized
nebu|liz|ing
nebu|liz|er +s
nebu|los|ity
nebu|los|ities
nebu|lous
nebu|lous|ly
nebu|lous|ness
ne|ces|sar|ily
ne|ces|sary
ne|ces|sar|ies
ne|ces|si|tar|ian +s
ne|ces|si|tar|ian|ism
ne|ces|si|tate
ne|ces|si|tates

ne|ces|si|tat|ed
ne|ces|si|tat|ing
ne|ces|si|tous
ne|ces|sity
ne|ces|si|ties
Ne|chako (river &
reservoir, Canada)
Nech|tans|mere
(battle site, Scotland)
neck +s +ed +ing
Neck|ar (river,
Germany)
[☞ Necker]
neck|band +s
neck|cloth +s
necked adjective
Neck|er, Jacques
(director-general of
French finances)
[☞ Neckar]
neck|er +s
neck|er|chief +s
neck|lace
neck|laces
neck|laced
neck|lacing
neck|less
neck|let +s
neck|line +s
neck|tie +s
neck|wear
necro|bio|sis
necro|bio|ses
necro|biot|ic
necro|logic|al
necrol|o|gist +s
necrol|ogy
necrol|o|gies
necro|man|cer +s
necro|mancy
necro|man|tic
necro|phile +s
necro|philia
necro|phil|iac +s
necro|phil|ic
ne|croph|il|ism
necro|phobia
ne|crop|olis
ne|crop|olis|es
nec|ropsy
nec|rop|sies
ne|cro|sis
ne|cro|ses
ne|crot|ic
nec|ro|tize
nec|ro|tiz|es
nec|ro|tized
nec|ro|tiz|ing
fasci|itis
nec|tar +s

nec|tar|ean (of
nectar)
[☞ nectarine]
nec|tar|eous
nec|tar|ine +s (peach)
[☞ nectarean]
nec|tar|ous
nec|tary
nec|tar|ies
née (born: used of a
woman)
[☞ né]
need +s +ed +ing
(require)
[☞ knead]
need|ful
need|ful|ly
need|ful|ness
Need|ham, Jo|seph
(English scientific
historian)
need|i|er
need|i|est
need|i|ness
nee|dle
nee|dles
nee|dled
need|ling
needle|cord +s
needle|craft +s
nee|dled adjective
needle|fish
plural needle|fish or
needle|fish|es
nee|dle lace +s
needle-nose
needle|point +s +ed
+ing
need|ler +s
Nee|dles (English
rocks)
need|less
need|less|ly
need|less|ness
nee|dle stick +s
(needle-stick when
preceding a noun)
needle|woman
needle|women
needle|work
needle|work|er +s
need|ling noun
needn't
needs adverb
need-to-know
needy
need|i|er
need|i|est
Néel, Louis Eu|gène
Félix (French
physicist)
neem +s (tree)
[☞ Nîmes]

neep +s (turnip)
[☞ neap]
Nee|pa|wa (town,
Canada)
ne'er
ne'er-do-well +s
ne|fari|ous
ne|fari|ous|ly
ne|fari|ous|ness
Nefer|titi (Egyptian
queen)
neg +s
neg|late
neg|ates
neg|at|ed
neg|at|ing
neg|a|tion +s
nega|tive
nega|tives
nega|tived
nega|tiv|ing
nega|tive|ly
nega|tive|ness
nega|tiv|ism
nega|tiv|ist +s
nega|tiv|is|tic
nega|tiv|ity
neg|ator +s
Negev (region, Israel)
neg|lect +s +ed +ing
neg|lect|ed adjective
neg|lect|ful
neg|lect|ful|ly
neg|lect|ful|ness
neg|li|gee +s
neg|li|gence
neg|li|gent
neg|li|gent|ly
neg|li|gi|bil|ity
neg|li|gible
neg|li|gibly
Ne|gom|bo (town, Sri
Lanka)
ne|go|ti|abil|ity
ne|go|ti|able
ne|go|ti|ant +s
ne|go|ti|ate
ne|go|ti|ates
ne|go|ti|at|ed
ne|go|ti|at|ing
ne|go|ti|at|ed
adjective
ne|go|ti|at|ing noun
ne|go|ti|a|tion +s
ne|go|ti|ator +s
Ne|gress offensive
Ne|gress|es
Ne|gril|lo +s
Negri Sem|bi|lan
(state, Malaysia)
Ne|gri|to +s

Ne|gri|tude (pride in black or African culture) [☞ nigritude]
Negro
Ne|groes
• May cause offence.
Ne|groid +s
Ne|gros (island, the Philippines) [☞ Negroes]
Negus (Ethiopian title)
negus
negus|es
Nehe|miah (Bible)
Nehru, Jawa|har|lal (Indian statesman)
Nehru jack|et +s
Neh|ru|vian
neigh +s +ed +ing (whinny) [☞ nae]
neigh|bor +s +ed +ing (use neighbour)
neigh|bor|hood +s (use neighbourhood)
neigh|bor|ing adjective (use neighbouring)
neigh|bor|less (use neighbourless)
neigh|bor|li|ness (use neighbourliness)
neigh|bor|ly (use neighbourly)
neigh|bour +s +ed +ing
neigh|bour|hood +s
neigh|bour|ing adjective
neigh|bour|less
neigh|bour|li|ness
neigh|bour|ly
Neisse (rivers, Europe) [☞ gneiss]
nei|ther
Nejd (plateau, Saudi Arabia)
nek|ton
nek|ton|ic
Nel|li|gan, Émile (Cdn poet)
Nel|li|gan, Kate (Cdn actress)
Nel|lore (city, India)
nelly
nel|lies
Nel|son (city & river, Canada; city, New Zealand)

Nel|son, Hor|atio (English admiral)
Nel|son, Wil|lie (US singer-songwriter)
nel|son +s (Wrestling)
Nel|son|ian
ne|lum|bo +s
Neman (river, E Europe)
nem|atic +s
nem|ato|cyst +s
nema|tode +s
Nem|bu|tal proprietary
ne|mer|tean +s
ne|mer|tine +s (= nemertean)
nem|esia plural nem|esia or nem|esias
Nem|esis (Greek Myth)
nem|esis nem|eses
Ne|mu|nas (= Neman River, E Europe)
neo-classic
neo-classic|al
neo|clas|si|cism
neo|clas|si|cist +s
neo-colonial|ism
neo-colonial|ist +s
neo-con +s
neo-conserv|a|tism
neo-conserv|a|tive +s
neo|cor|tex
neo|corti|ces
neo|corti|cal
Neo-Darwin|ian +s
Neo-Darwin|ism
Neo-Darwin|ist +s
neo|dym|ium
neo-fascism
neo-fascist +s
neo-Georgian
neo-Gothic
neo-liberal +s
neo-liberal|ism
neo|lith|ic
neolo|gism +s
neolo|gist +s
neolo|gis|tic
neolo|gize neolo|giz|es neolo|gized neolo|giz|ing
neo|mycin
neon +s
neo|natal
neo|nate +s
neo|natol|o|gist +s
neo|natol|ogy

neo-Nazi +s
neo-Nazism
neo|phobia
neo|phob|ic
neo|phyte +s
neo|plasm +s
neo|plas|tic
Neo|platon|ic
Neo|platon|ism
Neo|platon|ist +s
neo|prene +s
Neop|tol|emus (Greek Myth)
neo-realism
neo-realist +s
neo|ten|ic
neo|ten|ous
neot|eny
neo|ter|ic
neo-tradition|al|ism
neo|trop|ical
Nepal (country, Asia)
Nepal|ese plural Nepal|ese
Nepali plural Nepali or Nep|alis
Ne|pean (city, Canada)
neph|el|om|eter +s
nephew +s
neph|rec|tomy neph|rec|to|mies
neph|rite +s
neph|rit|ic
neph|ritis
neph|ron +s
Ne|pisi|guit (river, Canada)
ne plus ultra
nepo|tism
nepo|tist +s
nepo|tis|tic
Nep|tune (Roman Myth; planet)
Nep|tun|ian
nep|tun|ium
nerd +s
nerd|i|ness
nerd|ish
nerdy
nerd|i|er
nerd|i|est
ner|eid +s (Greek Myth; worm)
Ner|eus (Greek Myth)
Neri, Phil|ip (saint) [☞ nary]
Nernst, Wal|ther Her|mann (German chemist)
Nero (Roman emperor)

ner|oli
Ne|ruda, Pablo (Chilean poet)
nerve
nerves
nerved
nerv|ing
nerve block +s
nerved adjective
nerve|less
nerve|less|ly
nerve|less|ness
nerve-racking
nerve-wracking (use nerve-racking)
Nervi, Pier Luigi (Italian engineer & architect)
nerv|i|er
nerv|i|est
nerv|i|ly
nerv|i|ness
nerv|ous
nerv|ous|ly
nerv|ous Nel|lie +s
nerv|ous|ness
nerv|ure +s
nervy
nerv|i|er
nerv|i|est
nes|cience
nes|cient
Ness (loch, Scotland)
ness
ness|es
nest +s +ed +ing
nest|able
nest box
nest boxes
nest|ed adjective
nest|er +s [☞ Nestor]
nes|tle
nes|tles
nes|tled
nest|ling
nest|like
nest|ling +s noun
nest|mate +s
Nes|tor (Greek Myth) [☞ nester]
Nes|tor|ian +s
Nes|tor|ian|ism
Nes|tor|ius (patriarch of Constantinople)
Net (Internet)
net
nets
net|ted
net|ting
Net|an|ya|hu, Ben|ja|min (Israeli statesman)

net|ball
net-cam +s
neth|er
Neth|er|land|er +s
Neth|er|land|ish
Neth|er|lands
(country, Europe)
Neth|er|lands
An|til|les (islands,
Caribbean)
nether|most
nether|world +s
net|iquette
net|mind|er +s
net|mind|ing
ne|tsu|ke
  plural ne|tsu|ke or
  ne|tsu|kes
Net surf +s +ed +ing
Net surf|er +s
Net surf|ing *noun*
net|ted *adjective*
net|ter +s
Net|til|ling (lake,
Canada)
net|ting +s *noun*
net|tle
  net|tles
  net|tled
  net|tling
net|work +s +ed
  +ing
net|worked *adjective*
net|work|er +s
net|work|ing +s *noun*
Neu|châ|tel (lake,
Switzerland)
neume +s
neur|al
neur|al|gia +s
neur|al|gic
neur|al|ly
neur|as|thenia
neur|as|then|ic
neur|itic
neur|itis
neuro|ana|tom|ical
neuro|anat|o|mist +s
neuro|anat|omy
neuro|bio|logic|al
neuro|biol|o|gist +s
neuro|biol|ogy
neuro|blas|toma
  neuro|blas|to|mas
  or
  neuro|blas|to|mata
neuro|chem|ical +s
neuro|chem|ist +s
neuro|chem|istry
neuro|genic
neur|og|lia
neur|og|lial

neuro|hor|mon|al
neuro|hor|mone +s
neuro|lep|tic +s
neuro|lin|guis|tic
neuro|lin|guis|tics
neuro|logic
neuro|logic|al
neuro|logic|al|ly
neur|ol|o|gist +s
neur|ol|ogy
neur|oma
  neur|omas or
  neuro|mata
neuro|muscu|lar
neur|on +s
neur|on|al
neuro|patho|logic|al
neuro|path|ol|o|gist
  +s
neuro|path|ol|ogy
neur|op|athy
  neur|op|athies
neuro|pep|tide +s
neuro|physio|logic|al
neuro|physi|ol|o|gist
  +s
neuro|physi|ol|ogy
neuro|psych|o|
           logic|al
neuro|psych|ol|o|gist
  +s
neuro|psych|ol|ogy
neur|op|ter|an +s
neur|op|ter|ous
neuro|sci|ence +s
neuro|scien|tist +s
neur|o|sis
  neur|o|ses
neuro|sur|geon +s
neuro|sur|gery
neuro|sur|gical
neur|otic +s
neur|otic|ally
neur|oti|cism
neur|ot|omy
  neur|ot|o|mies
neuro|toxic
neuro|tox|icity
neuro|toxin +s
neuro|trans|mis|sion
neuro|trans|mit|ter
  +s
Neu|sied|ler See
(lake, Europe)
neu|ter +s +ed +ing
neu|tered *adjective*
neu|ter|ing +s *noun*
Neu|tral (Aboriginal
people)
  plural Neu|tral or
  Neu|trals
neu|tral +s

neu|tral|ism
neu|tral|ist +s
neu|tral|ity
neu|tral|iz|a|tion +s
neu|tral|ize
  neu|tral|iz|es
  neu|tral|ized
  neu|tral|iz|ing
neu|tral|iz|er +s
neu|tral|ly
neu|tri|no +s
neu|tron +s
neutro|penia
neutro|phil +s
neutro|phil|ic
Neva (river, Russia)
Nev|ada +s (state, US;
lottery ticket)
Nev|ad|an +s
névé +s
never
never-ending
never|more
Never-Never
(Australian outback)
never-never
(instalment plan)
Never-Never
Coun|try (= Never-
Never Land,
Australia)
Never-Never Land
(region, Australia)
[☞ never-never
land]
never-never land +s
(imaginary place)
[☞ Never-Never
Land]
Ne|vers (city, France)
never|the|less
Nevis (island,
W Indies)
Nev|ski, Alex|an|der
(Russian saint)
nevus
nevi
new +er +est *adjective*
& *adverb*
[☞ knew, nu, gnu]
New Age
New Ager +s
New Agey
New|ark (city, US)
new|bie +s
new|born +s
New Brit|ain (island,
S Pacific)
New Bruns|wick
(province, Canada)
New Bruns|wick|er
  +s

New Cal|edon|ia
(island, S Pacific;
early name for BC
Interior)
new Can|ad|ian +s
New|castle (city,
Australia)
New|castle-under-
Lyme
(town, England)
New|castle-upon-
Tyne
(town, England)
New|comb, Simon
(Cdn-born US
astronomer)
New|comen,
Thom|as (English
engineer)
new|com|er +s
New Crit|ic +s
New Crit|ic|al
New Criti|cism
New Deal (*US History*)
New Delhi (capital of
India)
New Demo|crat +s
New Demo|crat|ic
Party
newel +s
Newf +s
new|fan|gled
Newf|ie +s
New For|est (region,
England)
new-found
New|found|land +s
(island, Canada; dog)
New|found|land|er
  +s
new-genera|tion
New Hamp|shire
(state, US)
New Hamp|shir|ite
  +s
new|ish
new jack swing
New Jer|sey (state,
US)
New Jer|sey|an +s
New Jer|sey|ite +s
(= New Jerseyan)
New Jeru|sa|lem
New Jour|nal|ism
New Jour|nal|ist +s
New King|dom
New|lands, John
Alex|an|der Reina
(English chemist)
New Left
New Left|ist +s
New Lis|keard (town,
Canada)

New Look (women's post-war clothing style)
new look +s (new image) (**new-look** *when preceding a noun*)
newly
newly|wed +s
New|man (surname) [☞ **von Neumann**]
New|man, Bar|nett (US painter)
New|man, John Henry (English theologian)
New|man, Paul (US filmmaker)
New|man, Peter Charles (Cdn writer)
New|mar|ket (towns, Canada & England)
new math
New Mex|ican +s
New Mex|ico (state, US)
New Or|leans (city, US)
New|port (towns, Wales & US)
New|port News (city, US)
New Right
New Right|ist +s
Newry (town, Northern Ireland)
news
news agency
news agen|cies
news|agent +s
news|boy +s
news|cast +s
news|cast|er +s
news flash
news flash|es
news|group +s
news|hawk +s
news|hound +s
news|i|er
news|i|est
news|less
news|letter +s
news|maga|zine +s
news|maker +s
news|making
news|man
news|men
news|monger +s
news|paper +s
news|paper|ing
news|paper|man
news|paper|men

news|paper|woman
news|paper|women
New|speak
news|print
news read|er +s
news|reel +s
news|room +s
news|stand +s
New Style (calendar)
new style +s (*in general use*; **new-style** *when preceding a noun*)
news|weekly
news|week|lies
news wire +s
news|woman
news|women
news|worthi|ness
news|worthy
newsy
news|i|er
news|i|est
news|ies
newt +s
New Tes|ta|ment
New|ton (mountain, Canada) [☞ **Newtown**]
New|ton, Sir Isaac (English physicist)
new|ton +s
New|ton|ian
New|town +s (apple) [☞ **Newton**]
New World (N & S America)
New Year's
New York (city & state, US)
New York City (in US)
New York|er +s
New York State (in US)
New Zea|land (country, S Pacific)
New Zea|land|er +s
next
next door (**next-door** *when preceding a noun*)
next-genera|tion
next of kin
next-to-last
nexus
nex|us|es
Ney, Michel (French marshal) [☞ **nay, neigh, nae, né, née**]
Ngali|ema (= Mount Stanley, Africa)

Ngami|land (region, Botswana)
Ng|bandi
NGO (non-governmental organization)
NGOs
Ngoro|ngoro (volcanic crater, Tanzania)
Nguni *plural* **Nguni**
NGV (natural gas vehicle)
NGVs
NHLer +s
Nhu|lun|buy (town, Australia)
nia|cin
Ni|ag|ara +s (river, peninsula & escarpment, N America; deluge)
Ni|ag|ara Falls (waterfall & cities, N America)
Niagara-on-the-Lake (town, Canada)
Nia|mey (capital of Niger)
nib
nibs
nibbed
nib|bing
nib|ble
nib|bles
nib|bled
nib|bling
nib|bler +s
nib|bly
nib|blies
Nibel|ung (*Germanic Myth*)
Nibel|ungs *or* Nibel|ung|en
Nibel|ung|en|lied
nib|let +s
nib|lick +s
nibs
NIC (newly industrialized country)
NICs
nicad
Ni|caea (ancient city & council site)
Ni|caean Creed (*use* Nicene Creed)
Nic|ar|agua (country & lake, Central America)
Nic|ar|a|guan +s
Nice (city, France) [☞ **niece**]

nice (pleasant, fine)
nicer
nicest
[☞ **gneiss, Neisse**]
nice-guy
nice|ly
Ni|cene Creed
nice|ness
nice-nice
nicety
nicet|ies
nicey-nice
nicey-nicey
niche
nich|es
niched
nich|ing
[☞ **Niš**]
niched *adjective*
Nich|iren
Nichol, Bar|rie Phil|lip ('bp') (Cdn poet) [☞ **nickel**]
Nicho|las (czars of Russia; saint) [☞ **Saint-Nicolas, Nicklaus**]
Nicho|las, Cyn|thia ('Cindy') (Cdn swimmer)
Nicho|las of Cusa (German cardinal)
Nichol|son, Jack (US actor) [☞ **Nicolson**]
Ni|chrome *proprietary*
Nicias (Athenian politician)
nick +s +ed +ing (cut; prison; dash; in 'the nick of time') [☞ **NIC**]
nick|el (element; coin)
nick|els
nick|elled
nick|el|ling
[☞ **Nichol**]
nick|el and dime *verb*
nickel-and-dimes
or nickels and dimes
nickel-and-dimed
or nickelled and dimed
nickel-and-diming
or nickelling and diming
nickel-and-dime *adjective*
Nick|el Belt (region, Canada)
Nick|el Cen|tre (town, Canada)
nick|el|ic

nickel|odeon +s
nick|el|ous
nick|er
- (one pound)
  plural **nick|er**
- (neigh)
  nick|ers
  nick|ered
  nick|er|ing
  [☞ **knickers**]
Nick|laus, Jack
Wil|liam (US golfer)
nick|name
  nick|names
  nick|named
  nick|nam|ing
Nico|bar (island group
off India)
ni|çoise
Nico|let (town,
Canada)
Nicol|son, Sir Har|old
George (English
diplomat & writer)
[☞ **Nicholson**]
Nico|sia (capital of
Cyprus)
nico|ti|ana
  plural nico|ti|ana
nico|tin|a|mide +s
nico|tine
nico|tin|ic
nic|ti|tate
  nic|ti|tates
  nic|ti|tat|ed
  nic|ti|tat|ing
nic|ti|ta|tion +s
nidi|fi|cate
  nidi|fi|cates
  nidi|fi|cat|ed
  nidi|fi|cat|ing
nidi|fi|ca|tion +s
nidi|fy
  nidi|fies
  nidi|fied
  nidi|fy|ing
nidus
  nidi
Nie|buhr, Bar|thold
Georg (German
historian)
Nie|buhr, Rein|hold
(US theologian)
niece +s (relative)
[☞ **Nice**]
ni|ello
  ni|elli or **ni|el|los**
ni|el|loed
Niel|sen, Carl Aug|ust
(Danish composer)
[☞ **Nilsson**]
Niel|sen +s (ratings)

Nie|meyer, (So|ares
Filho) Oscar
(Brazilian architect)
Nietz|sche, Fried|rich
Wil|helm (German
philosopher)
Nietz|sche|an +s
niff +s +ed +ing
niffy
  nif|fi|er
  nif|fi|est
Nifl|heim
(*Scandinavian Myth*)
nif|ti|ly
nif|ti|ness
nifty
  nif|ti|er
  nif|ti|est
Niger (country & river,
Africa)
Ni|geria (country,
Africa)
Ni|ger|ian +s
niger seed
nig|gard +s
nig|gard|li|ness
nig|gard|ly
nig|ger +s *offensive*
nig|gle
  nig|gles
  nig|gled
  nig|gling
nig|gling *adjective*
nig|gling|ly
nigh
night +s (darkness)
  [☞ **knight**]
night|cap +s
night|clothes
night|club +s
night|club|ber +s
night|club|bing
night crawl|er +s
night|dress
  night|dress|es
night|fall +s
night|gown +s
night|hawk +s
night|ie +s
(nightgown)
  [☞ **nighty-night**]
Night|in|gale,
Flor|ence (English
nurse)
night|in|gale +s
night|jar +s
night|less
night|life
night light +s
night-long
night|ly (at night;
every night)
  [☞ **knightly**]

night|mare +s
night|mar|ish
night|mar|ish|ly
night night
  interjection
night|shade +s
night|shirt +s
night side +s
night sight +s
night-soil
night|spot +s
night|stand +s
night|stick +s
night table +s
night|time +s
night vi|sion (night-
vision *when
preceding a noun*)
night|wear
nighty-night
  interjection
  [☞ **nightie**]
ni|gres|cence
ni|gres|cent
nig|ri|tude (blackness)
  [☞ **Negritude**]
nihil|ism
nihil|ist +s
nihil|is|tic
nihil ob|stat
Nii|gata (city, Japan)
Ni|jin|sky, Vas|lav
Fom|ich (Russian
dancer)
Nij|megen (town, the
Netherlands)
Nik|kei (*Stock
Exchange*)
Niko|laev (*Russian
name for* **Mykolayiv,**
Ukraine)
nil
nil des|per|an|dum
Nile (river, Africa)
Nile blue +s (Nile-
blue *when preceding
a noun*)
Nile green +s (Nile-
green *when preceding
a noun*)
nil|gai +s
Nil|giri (hills, India)
Nil|ot|ic
Nils|son, (Märta)
Bir|git (Swedish
soprano)
  [☞ **Nielsen**]
nim|ble
  nim|bler
  nim|blest
nimble|ness
nim|bly
nimbo|strat|us

nim|bus
  nim|bus|es or **nimbi**
nim|bused
NIMBY (not in my
backyard)
NIMBYs
Nîmes (city, France)
  [☞ **neem**]
niminy-piminy
Nim|itz, Ches|ter
Wil|liam (US
admiral)
Nim|rod (*Bible*)
nim|rod +s (hunter;
inept person)
Nim|rud
(Mesopotamian city)
Nin, Anaïs (US writer)
nin|com|poop +s
nin|com|poop|ery
nine +s
nine|bark +s
nine|fold
900 num|ber +s
nine|pin +s
niner +s
nine|teen +s
nine|teenth +s
nine-tenths
nine|ti|eth +s
nine-to-five
nine-to-fiver +s
nine|ty
  nine|ties
ninety-eight +s
ninety-eighth +s
ninety-fifth +s
ninety-first +s
ninety-five +s
ninety|fold
ninety-four +s
ninety-fourth +s
ninety-nine +s
ninety-ninth +s
ninety-one +s
ninety-second +s
ninety-seven +s
ninety-seventh +s
ninety-six
  ninety-sixes
ninety-sixth +s
ninety-third +s
ninety-three +s
ninety-two +s
Nin|eveh (city,
Assyria)
Ning|sia (= Ningxia)
Ning|xia (region,
China)
ninja +s
ninny
  nin|nies

ninth +s
ninth|ly
Niobe (*Greek Myth*)
nio|bic
nio|bium
nio|bous
Nip +s *offensive* (Japanese)
nip (pinch; sting; overtake; dash; hamburger; drink)
  nips
  nipped
  nip|ping
nipa +s
nip and tuck
  nips and tucks
Nip|igon (lake, Canada)
Nip|is|sing (lake, Canada)
nip|per +s
nip|pi|ly
nip|ping *adjective*
nip|ple +s
nip|ple|less
Nip|pon|ese
  plural **Nip|pon|ese**
nippy
  nip|pi|er
  nip|pi|est
Nirex (Nuclear Industry Radioactive Waste Executive)
nir|vana +s
nir|van|ic
Niš (city, Serbia)
  [☞ **niche**]
Nisei
  plural **Nisei**
Nisga'a
  plural **Nisga'a** or **Nisga'as**
Nish (= Niš, Serbia)
  [☞ **niche**]
Nish|ga (*use* Nisga'a)
  plural **Nish|ga** or **Nish|gas**
Nishnawbe-Aski
nisi
Nis|sen hut +s
nit +s (louse egg; idiot; warning)
  [☞ **knit**]
nite +s (*in commercial use* = night)
Ni|terói (city, Brazil)
Niti|nat
  plural **Niti|nat** or **Niti|nats**
nit|pick +s +ed +ing
nit|pick|er +s

nit|pick|ing *noun & adjective*
nit|picky
  nit|pick|i|er
  nit|pick|i|est
ni|trate
  ni|trates
  ni|trat|ed
  ni|trat|ing
ni|tra|tion
nitre
ni|tric
ni|tride
nitri|fi|able
nitri|fi|ca|tion +s
nitrify
  nitri|fies
  nitri|fied
  nitri|fy|ing
ni|trile
ni|trite +s
nitro
nitro|ben|zene
nitro|cellu|lose
nitro|gen
nitrogen-fixing
nitro|gen|ous
nitro|glycer|in (*use* nitroglycerine)
nitro|glycer|ine
nitro|sa|mine +s
ni|trous
nitty-gritty
nit|wit +s
Niue (island, S Pacific)
Niver|nais (former duchy, France)
nix (cancel, reject; nothing)
  nixes
  nixed
  nix|ing
  [☞ **Nyx**]
Nixon, Rich|ard Mil|hous (US president)
Nixon|ian +s
Nixon|ite +s
Nizhni Nov|go|rod (city, Russia)
Nizhni Tagil (city, Russia)
Nkru|mah, Kwame (Ghanaian prime minister)
NKVD (USSR secret police)
Nlaka'pamux
  plural **Nlaka'pamux**
No (Japanese drama)
  [☞ **Nault**]
no (negative)
  noes

no-account +s
Noah (*Bible*)
Noah's ark +s
nob +s (aristocrat; head)
  [☞ **knob**]
no-bake
no-ball +s +ed +ing
nob|ble (tamper with)
  nob|bles
  nob|bled
  nob|bling
  [☞ **noble**]
Nobel, Al|fred Bern|hard (Swedish chemist)
  [☞ **noble**]
Nobel|ist +s
nobel|ium
Nobel Prize +s
no|bil|iary
no|bil|ity
  no|bil|ities
noble (honourable; magnificent; aristocratic)
  nobler
  nob|lest
  nobles
  [☞ **Nobel, nobble**]
noble|man
  noble|men
noble|ness
no|blesse oblige
noble|woman
  noble|women
nobly
no|body
  no|bod|ies
no-brainer +s
nock +s +ed +ing (*Archery*)
  [☞ **knock, Nok**]
no confidence (no-confidence *when preceding a noun*)
noc|tam|bu|lism
noc|tam|bu|list +s
noc|tule +s
noc|turn +s (*Christianity*)
  [☞ **nocturne**]
noc|tur|nal
noc|tur|nal|ly
noc|turne +s (romantic musical composition; night scene)
  [☞ **nocturn**]
nod
  nods
  nod|ded
  nod|ding

nodal
nod|ding *adjective*
nod|ding|ly
nod|dle +s
noddy (simpleton; bird; bayman)
  nod|dies
  [☞ **nodi**]
node +s
nodi *plural of* nodus
  [☞ **noddy**]
nod|ical
nod|ose *adjective*
  [☞ **nodus**]
nod|os|ity
  nod|os|ities
nodu|lar
nodu|lat|ed
nodu|la|tion +s
nod|ule +s
nodu|lose
nodus *noun*
  nodi
  [☞ **nodose**]
Noel
noes *plural of* no
  [☞ **nose**]
Noe|ther, (Ama|lie) Emmy (German mathematician)
Noe|ther|ian
no|etic
no-fault
Nofre|tete (= Nefertiti, Egyptian queen)
no-frills
nog +s
nog|gin +s
nog|ging +s
no go *noun*
  no goes
no-go *adjective*
no-good +s
No|guchi, Hi|deyo (US bacteriologist)
Noh (Japanese drama: *use* No)
  [☞ **Nault**]
no-hit
no-hitter +s
no-hoper +s
nohow (in no way)
  [☞ **know-how**]
noil +s
noir +s
noir|ish
noise
  nois|es
  noised
  nois|ing
noise|less
noise|less|ly

noise|less|ness
noise|maker +s
noi|sette +s
nois|i|ly
nois|i|ness
noi|some
noi|some|ness
noisy
  nois|i|er
  nois|i|est
Nok (ancient Nigerian
  civilization)
  [☞ nock, knock]
no|lens vo|lens
nolle pro|se|qui
no-load
nolo con|ten|dere
no|mad +s
no|mad|ic
no|mad|ic|ally
nomad|ism
no man's land
nom|bril +s
nom de
  noms de
nom de guerre
  noms de guerre
nom de plume
  noms de plume
Nome (city, Alaska)
  [☞ gnome]
nom|en +s (name)
  [☞ gnomon]
nom|en|cla|tur|al
nom|en|cla|ture +s
  (system of names)
  [☞ *nomenklatura*]
nom|en|kla|tura (in
  the Soviet Union)
nom|in|al
nom|in|al|ism
nom|in|al|ist +s
nom|in|al|is|tic
nom|in|al|iz|a|tion +s
nom|in|al|ize
  nom|in|al|iz|es
  nom|in|al|ized
  nom|in|al|iz|ing
nom|in|al|ly
nom|in|ate
  nom|in|ates
  nom|in|at|ed
  nom|in|at|ing
nom|in|a|tion +s
nom|in|a|tive +s
nom|in|ator +s
nom|inee +s
nomo|gram +s
nomo|graph +s
nomo|graph|ic
nomo|graph|ic|ally
nom|og|raphy
nomo|thet|ic

non-Aborig|in|al +s
non-addict|ive
non|age +s
nona|gen|ar|ian +s
non-aggres|sion
non-aggres|sive
non-aggres|sive|ly
nona|gon +s
non-alcohol|ic +s
non-aligned
non-align|ment
non-allergen|ic
non-A, non-B
  hepa|titis
non-appear|ance +s
non|ary
  non|aries
non-attend|ance
non-believ|er +s
non-belliger|ency
non-belliger|ent +s
non-binding
non-
  biodegrad|abil|ity
non-biodegrad|able
non-biolog|ic|al
non-Canadian +s
non-capital
non-Catholic +s
nonce
non|cha|lance
non|cha|lant
non|cha|lant|ly
non-Christian +s
non-citizen +s
non-cleric|al
non-com +s
non-combat|ant +s
non-commer|cial
non-commis|sioned
non|com|mit|tal
non|com|mit|tal|ly
non-Commun|ist +s
  (with reference to a
  particular party)
non-commun|ist +s
  (*in general use*)
non-competi|tive
non-compli|ance
non-compli|ant
non com|pos
non com|pos men|tis
non-conduct|ing
non-conduct|ive
non-conduct|or +s
non-confidence
Non|con|form|ism
  (Nonconformist
  principles etc.)
non|con|form|ism (*in
  general use*)

Non|con|form|ist +s
  (Protestant outside
  established church)
non|con|form|ist +s
  (*in general use*)
Non|con|form|ity
  (Nonconformists or
  Nonconformist
  principles)
non|con|form|ity (*in
  general use*)
non-contribu|tory
non-contro|ver|sial
non-custod|ial
non-dairy
non-delivery
non-
  denomin|a|tion|al
non|de|script +s
non|de|script|ly
non|de|script|ness
non-destruc|tive
non-drinker +s
none (not any;
  canonical hour)
non|entity
  non|enti|ties
nones
non-essential +s
none|such (*use
  nonsuch*)
  none|such|es
no|net +s
none|the|less
non-Euclid|ean
non-European +s
non-event +s
non-exist|ence
non-exist|ent
non-fat
non|feas|ance +s
non-ferrous
non-fiction
non-fiction|al
non-flammable
non-flower|ing
non-fulfill|ment
non-function|al
non-govern|ment|al
non-human +s
non-import +s
non-infectious
non-interfer|ence
non-interven|tion
non-interven|tion|ist
  +s
non-invasive
non-issue +s
non-Jew ǀ3
non-Jewish
non|join|der
non-judgment|al

non|juring
non|juror +s
non-jury
non-linear
non-literary
non|logic|al
non|logic|al|ly
non-magnet|ic
non-member +s
non-member|ship
non-metal
non-metal|lic
non-metric
non-militant
non-military
non-moral
non-moral|ly
non-natural
non-negoti|able
non-nuclear
no-no +s
non-object|ive
non-observ|ance
no-nonsense
non-operation|al
non-organic
non|par|eil +s
non-partisan
non-party
non|pay|ment +s
non-penetra|tive
non-perform|ing
non-person +s
non-person|al
non-physic|al
non-physic|al|ly
non|plussed
non-poison|ous
non-politic|al
non-porous
non-prescrip|tion
non-product|ive
non-product|ive|ly
non-profes|sion|al
  +s
non-profit
non-prolif|er|a|tion
non-racial
non-react|ive
non-reader +s
non-refund|able
non-renew|able
non-residence
non-resident +s
non-residen|tial
non|resist|ance
non|resist|ant
non-restrict|ive
non-return|able
non-rigid
non-scientif|ic
non-scientist +s

non-sectar|ian
non|sense
non|sens|ical
non|sens|ical|ity
  non|sens|ical|ities
non|sens|ical|ly
non sequi|tur +s
non-sexist
non-sexual
non-sexual|ly
non-skid
non-slip
non-smoker +s
non-smoking
non-special|ist +s
non-specif|ic
non-standard
non-starter +s
non-status
non-steroid|al
non-stick
non-stop +s
non-subscrib|er +s
non|such
  non|such|es
non|suit +s
non-surgical
non-swimmer +s
non-tariff bar|rier +s
non-techni|cal
non-toxic
non-transfer|able
non-treaty
non-U
non-uniform
non-union
non-union|ized
non-use
non-user +s
non-verbal
non-verbal|ly
non-vintage
non-violence
non-violent
non-violent|ly
non-volatile
non-voter +s
non-voting
non-white +s
non-word +s
noo|dle
  noo|dles
  noo|dled
  nood|ling
noog|ie +s
nook +s
nook|ie
nooky (use nookie)
noon
noon|day
no one
noon hour +s

noon|tide
noon|time
noose
noos|es
noosed
noos|ing
Noot|ka (= Nuu-
  chah-nulth, people
  & language)
  plural Noot|ka
Noot|kan
Noot|ka Sound (inlet,
  Canada)
no|pal +s
nope
no place
nor (and not)
nor' (north)
NORAD (North
  American Aerospace
  Defence Command)
nor|adren|a|lin
nor|adren|a|line (use
  noradrenalin)
Nor-Am (North
  American)
Nor|dau, Max Simon
  (German writer)
Nor|den|skjöld, (Nils)
  Adolf Erik, Baron
  (Swedish explorer)
Nor|dic +s
nor|di|city
Nord|kyn
  (promontory,
  Norway)
Nord-Pas-de-Calais
  (region, France)
nor'easter +s
nor|epi|neph|rine
nor|ethin|drone
Nor|folk (city, US;
  county, England;
  island off Australia)
nori
Nori|ega, Man|uel
  An|tonio Mor|ena
  (Panamanian
  general)
norm +s
nor|mal +s
nor|malcy
  nor|mal|cies
nor|mal|ity
  nor|mal|ities
nor|mal|iz|a|tion
nor|mal|ize
  nor|mal|iz|es
  nor|mal|ized
  nor|mal|iz|ing
nor|mal|iz|er +s
nor|mally

Nor|man, Greg|ory
  John ('Greg')
  (Australian golfer)
Nor|man, Jes|sye (US
  soprano)
Nor|man +s (people,
  language;
  Architecture)
Nor|man|dy (former
  province, France)
Nor|man|ize
  Nor|man|iz|es
  Nor|man|ized
  Nor|man|iz|ing
nor|ma|tive
nor|ma|tive|ly
nor|ma|tive|ness
nor|ma|tiv|ity
normo|ten|sive +s
Norn
Norns (Scandinavian
  Myth)
Norr|kö|ping (city,
  Sweden)
Norse
Norse|man
  Norse|men
nor|ster|oid +s
North, Fred|erick,
  Lord (British prime
  minister)
North (particular
  region; Bridge)
north (compass point;
  direction)
North|amp|ton (town,
  England)
North|amp|ton|shire
  (county, England)
North|ants
  (= Northampton-
  shire)
North Battle|ford
  (city, Canada)
North Bay (city,
  Canada)
north|bound
north ca|noe +s
North Chan|nel (in
  Canada)
North|cliffe, 1st
  Vis|count (English
  newspaper
  proprietor)
North|east (particular
  region)
north|east (compass
  point; direction)
north|east|er +s
north|east|er|ly
north|east|er|lies
north|east|ern

North|east Pas|sage
  (seaway north of
  Europe & Asia)
north|east|ward
north|east|wards
north|er +s
north|erly
  north|er|lies
north|ern +s
North|ern Cir|cars
  (former region,
  India)
north|ern|er +s
north|ern
  hemi|sphere
north|ern lights
north|ern|most
north|ern|ness
North|ern Spy
  North|ern Spys or
  North|ern Spies
north|ing
north|land
north|lands
North|man
  North|men
north-northeast
north-northwest
north of 60
North Pen|der (island,
  Canada)
North Pole
  (northernmost point
  on earth)
north pole
  (northernmost
  celestial point; north
  magnetic pole)
North Rhine-
  Westphal|ia (state,
  Germany)
north-south
North Star (Polaris)
North Syd|ney (urban
  community, Nova
  Scotia)
North|um|ber|land
  (county, England;
  strait, Canada)
North|um|bria
  (region, England)
North|um|brian +s
north|ward
north|wards
North Warn|ing
  Sys|tem
North|west
  (particular region)
  [☞ North-West,
  North West]
north|west (compass
  point; direction)

North West Com|pany
North|west|er +s
(North West
Company employee)
north|west|er +s
(wind)
north|west|er|ly
north|west|er|lies
north|west|ern
[☞ North-Western
Territory]
**North-Western
Ter|ri|tory** (former
region, Canada:
united with Rupert's
Land in 1870 to form
the North-West
Territories)
**North-West Fron|tier
Prov|ince** (in
Pakistan)
**North West
Mount|ed Po|lice**
North|west Pas|sage
(seaway, Canada)
**North-West
Prov|ince** (in South
Africa)
**North|west
Re|bel|lion**
**North|west
Ter|ri|tor|ies**
(modern territory,
Canada)
**North-West
Ter|ri|tor|ies**
(former region,
Canada: formed in
1870 by the union of
the North-Western
Territory and
Rupert's Land)
**North|west
Ter|ri|tory** (former
region, US)
north|west|ward
north|west|wards
Nor|way (country,
Scandinavia)
Nor|we|gian +s
Nor'Wester +s
(= Northwester)
nor'wester +s (wind;
hat)
Nor|wich (city,
England)
nose
noses
nosed
nos|ing
nose|bag +s
nose|band +s
nose|bleed +s

nosed *adjective*
nose-dive
nose-dives
nose-dived
nose-diving
no-see-um +s
nose|gay +s
nose-piece +s
nose ring +s
nose tackle +s
nose-thumbing
nose wheel +s
nosey (*use* nosy)
nosi|er
nosi|est
Nosey Par|ker +s (*use*
Nosy Parker)
nosh
nosh|es
noshed
nosh|ing
nosh|er +s
no-show +s
nosh-up +s
nosi|er
nosi|est
nosi|ly
nosi|ness
nos|ing +s *noun*
nos|og|raphy
noso|logic|al
noso|logic|al|ly
nos|ol|o|gist +s
nos|ol|ogy
nos|tal|gia
nos|tal|gic
nos|tal|gic|ally
nos|tal|gist +s
nos|toc +s
Nos|tra|da|mus
(French astrologer)
nos|tril +s
nos|trum +s
nosy
nosi|er
nosi|est
Nosy Par|ker +s
not (expressing
negation)
[☞ knot, naught,
nought]
nota bene
nota|bil|ity
nota|bil|ities
nota|ble
nota|bly
no|tar|ial
no|tar|ial|ly
no|tar|ize
no|tar|izes
no|tar|ized
no|tar|iz|ing

no|tary
no|tar|ies
no|tary pub|lic
no|tar|ies pub|lic
no|tate
no|tates
no|tat|ed
no|tat|ing
no|tat|ed *adjective*
no|ta|tion +s
no|ta|tion|al
no|ta|tor +s
notch (nick, groove,
hole)
notch|es
notched
notch|ing
[☞ nautch]
notched *adjective*
notch|er +s
notchy
notch|i|er
notch|i|est
note
notes
noted
not|ing
note|book +s
noted *adjective*
note|less
note|let +s
note|pad +s
note|paper
note|worthi|ness
note|worthy
not-for-profit
noth|ing +s
noth|ing|ness
no|tice
noti|ces
no|ticed
noti|cing
no|tice|able
no|tice|ably
no|tice board +s
noti|fi|able
noti|fi|ca|tion +s
noti|fy
noti|fies
noti|fied
noti|fy|ing
no|tion +s
no|tion|al
no|tion|al|ly
noto|chord
no|tori|ety
no|tori|ous
no|tori|ous|ly
Notre Dame (bay,
Canada; university,
US)

Notre-Dame
(mountains, Canada;
cathedral, Paris)
no trump +s
Not|ta|wa|saga (bay,
Canada)
Not|ta|way (river,
Canada)
Not|ting|ham (town,
England)
Not|ting|ham|shire
(county, England)
Not|ting Hill (district
of London, England)
not|with|stand|ing
Nou|ad|hi|bou (town,
Mauritania)
Nou|ak|chott (capital
of Mauritania)
nou|gat +s
nought (the digit '0';
nothing; in 'noughts
and crosses')
[☞ naught]
Nou|méa (capital of
New Caledonia)
noun +s
nour|ish
nour|ish|es
nour|ished
nour|ish|ing
nour|ish|er +s
nour|ish|ing *adjective*
nour|ish|ing|ly
nour|ish|ment +s
nous
nou|veau
nou|veau riche
nou|veaux riches
nou|veau roman
nou|velle
nou|velle cui|sine
nou|velle vague
nova
novae or novas
Nova Lis|boa (*former
name for* Huambo,
Angola)
Nova Sco|tia
(province &
peninsula, Canada)
**Nova Sco|tia duck
toll|ing re|triev|er**
+s
Nova Sco|tian +s
Nov|aya Zem|lya
(islands off Russia)
novel +s
novel|ette +s
novel|et|tish
novel|ist +s
novel|is|tic
novel|iz|a|tion +s

novel|ize
  novel|iz|es
  novel|ized
  novel|iz|ing
novel|la +s
novel|ly
novel|ty
  novel|ties
Nov|em|ber +s
nov|ena +s
No|verre, Jean-
  Georges (French
  dance theorist)
Nov|go|rod (city,
  Russia)
nov|ice +s
Novi Sad (city, Serbia)
novi|ti|ate +s
Novo|caine
  proprietary
Novo|kuz|netsk (city,
  Russia)
Novo|si|birsk (city,
  Russia)
no vote +s
now
now|a|days
no way *adverb &*
  interjection
no|ways
Nowel (= Noel)
Nowell (= Noel)
no|where
no-win
no|wise
now|ness
nowt (nothing)
  [☞ knout]
nox|ious
nox|ious|ly
nox|ious|ness
noz|zle +s
NSAID (non-steroidal
  anti-inflammatory
  drug)
  NSAIDs
NSERC (Natural
  Sciences and
  Engineering
  Research Council)
NSF (not sufficient
  funds)
nth
nu +s (Greek letter)
  [☞ gnu]
nuance
  nuan|ces
  nu|anced
  nuan|cing
nu|anced *adjective*
nub
  nubs

nubbed
nub|bing
nub|bin +s
nub|ble +s
nub|bly
nubby
  nub|bi|er
  nub|bi|est
Nubia (ancient region
  of Egypt & Sudan)
Nu|bian +s
nu|bile
nu|bil|ity
nu|buck
nu|chal
nu|cle|ar
nuclear-free
nu|cle|ar power
nuclear-powered
nu|cle|ase +s
nu|cle|ate
  nu|cle|ates
  nu|cle|at|ed
  nu|cle|at|ing
nu|cle|a|tion
nu|clei
nu|cle|ic acid +s
nu|cle|olar
nu|cle|olus
  nu|cle|oli
nu|cle|on +s
nu|cle|on|ic
nu|cle|on|ics
nu|cleo|pro|tein +s
nu|cleo|side +s
nu|cleo|synth|esis
nu|cleo|syn|thet|ic
nu|cleo|tide +s
nu|cle|us
  nu|clei
nu|clide +s
nude +s
nudge
  nudg|es
  nudged
  nudg|ing
nudg|er +s
nudi|branch +s
nudi|bran|chi|ate +s
nud|ie +s
nud|ism
nud|ist +s
nud|ity
nud|nik +s
Nu|el|tin (lake,
  Canada)
Nuevo León (state,
  Mexico)
nuff
nug +s
nu|ga|tory
nug|get +s

nuis|ance +s
nuke (nuclear
  weapons etc.)
  nukes
  nuked
  nuk|ing
  [☞ Nuuk]
Nuku'alofa (capital of
  Tonga)
null +s +ed +ing
null|lah +s
Null|ar|bor (plain,
  Australia)
nul|li|fi|ca|tion +s
nul|li|fi|er +s
nul|li|fy
  nul|li|fies
  nul|li|fied
  nul|li|fy|ing
nul|lip|ara +s
nul|lip|ar|ous
nul|li|pore +s
nul|lity
  nul|li|ties
Numa Pom|pil|ius
  (legendary Roman
  king)
numb +s +ed +ing
  +er +est
num|bat +s
num|ber +s +ed +ing
num|bered *adjective*
num|ber|ing +s *noun*
  & adjective
number|less
Num|bers (*Bible*)
numb|ing *adjective*
numb|ing|ly
numb|les
numb|ly
numb|ness
numb|nuts
  plural numb|nuts
numb|skull +s
num|dah +s
numen
  nu|mina
num|er|able
num|er|acy
num|er|al +s
num|er|ate
num|er|a|tion +s
num|er|ator +s
num|er|ic
num|er|ic|al
num|er|ic|al|ly
num|ero|logic|al
num|er|ol|o|gist +s
num|er|ol|ogy
  num|er|ol|o|gies
num|ero uno
num|er|ous
num|er|ous|ly

num|er|ous|ness
Nu|midia (ancient
  kingdom, Africa)
Nu|mid|ian +s
nu|mina
nu|min|os|ity
nu|min|ous
nu|mis|mat|ic
nu|mis|mat|ic|ally
nu|mis|mat|ics
nu|mis|ma|tist +s
nummy
  num|mi|er
  num|mi|est
num|nah +s
num|skull +s (*use*
  numbskull)
nun +s (*Christianity*)
  [☞ none]
nuna|tak +s
Nuna|vut (territory,
  Canada)
nun-buoy +s
Nunc Di|mit|tis
nun|cha|ku +s
nun|chuk +s
nun|ci|a|ture +s
nun|cio +s
Nun|eaton (town,
  England)
Nunki (star)
nun|like
nun|nery
  nun|ner|ies
nun|nish
nunny-bag +s
Nuns' Island (= Île
  des Soeurs, Canada)
nuoc mam
nup|tial +s
Nur|em|berg (city,
  Germany)
Nur|eyev, Ru|dolf
  Hamet|ovich
  (Russian dancer)
nurse
  nurs|es
  nursed
  nurs|ing
nurse|maid +s
nurs|ery
  nurs|eries
nursery|man
  nursery|men
nurse's aide +s
nurs|ing *noun*
nurs|ling +s
nur|ture
  nur|tures
  nur|tured
  nur|tur|ing
nur|tur|er +s
Nut (*Egyptian Myth*)

nut
  nuts
  nut|ted
  nut|ting
nu|tant
nu|ta|tion
nut|bar +s
nut brown (nut-
  brown *when
  preceding a noun*)
nut|case +s
nut|crack|er +s
nut|gall +s
nut|hatch
  nut|hatch|es
nut|house +s
nut|let +s
nut|like
nut|meg +s
nu|tria +s
nutri|ent +s
nutri|ment +s
nutri|ment|al
nu|tri|tion
nu|tri|tion|al
nu|tri|tion|al|ly
nu|tri|tion|ist +s
nu|tri|tious
nu|tri|tious|ly
nu|tri|tious|ness
nutri|tive
nuts *adjective*
nuts and bolts *noun*
nuts-and-bolts
  adjective
nut|sedge +s
nut|shell +s
nut|so +s
nutsy
  nuts|i|er
  nuts|i|est
nut|ter +s
nut|ti|ly
nut|ti|ness
nutty
  nut|ti|er
  nut|ti|est
Nuu-chah-nulth
  plural
  Nuu-chah-nulth
Nuuk (capital of
  Greenland)
  [☞ nuke]
Nuxalk
  plural Nuxalk
nux vom|ica +s
nuz|zle
  nuz|zles
  nuz|zled
  nuz|zling
nyala
  plural nyala
Nyasa (lake, Africa)

Ny|asa|land (*former
  name for* Malawi)
nyc|tal|opia
nycti|trop|ic
Nye|rere, Jul|ius
  Kam|bar|age
  (Tanzanian
  statesman)
ny|lon +s
ny|loned
Nyman, Mi|chael
  (English composer)
nymph +s +ed +ing
nym|phae
nymph|al
nym|phal|id +s
nymph|ean
nymph|et +s
nym|pho +s
nym|pho|lepsy
nym|pho|lept +s
nym|pho|lep|tic
nym|pho|mania
nym|pho|maniac +s
nys|tag|mic
nys|tag|mus
ny|sta|tin
Nyun|gar
Nyx (*Greek Myth*)

O

o
• (letter; shape; zero;
  hug; in "X's and
  O's")
  O's
• (blood type;
  interjection; used
  before a name in
  direct address)
  [☞ oh, owe]
o (letter)
  o's
  [☞ oh, owe]
OAC (Ontario
  Academic Credit)
  OACs
oaf +s
oaf|ish
oaf|ish|ly
oaf|ish|ness
Oahu (island, Hawaii)
oak +s
Oak Bay (community
  & bay, Canada)
oaken
oak gall +s

oak|i|er
oak|i|est
oak|i|ness
Oak Island (island,
  Canada)
Oak|land (city, US)
Oak|ley, Annie (US
  sharpshooter)
oakum
Oak|ville (town,
  Canada)
oaky (of or like oaks)
  oak|i|er
  oak|i|est
  [☞ Okie]
oar +s (*Rowing*)
  [☞ ore, or]
oared
oar|fish
  plural oar|fish or
  oar|fish|es
oar|lock +s
oars|man
  oars|men
oars|man|ship
oars|woman
  oars|women
oasis
  oases
oast +s
oast|house +s
oat +s (cereal)
  [☞ haute, Oates]
oat|cake +s
oaten
Oates, Joyce Carol
  (US writer)
Oates, Titus (English
  conspirator)
oat grass
  oat grass|es
oath +s
oat|meal
oaty
  oat|i|er
  oat|i|est
Oaxa|ca (de Juá|rez)
  (city, Mexico)
Ob (river, Russia)
Oba|diah (*Bible*)
ob|bli|ga|to +s
ob|con|ic
ob|con|ic|al
ob|cor|date
ob|dur|acy
ob|dur|ate
ob|dur|ate|ly
ob|dur|ate|ness
obeah
obedi|ence +s
obedi|ent
obedi|ent|ly
obei|sance +s

obei|sant
ob|el|isk +s
ob|el|ize
  ob|el|iz|es
  ob|el|ized
  ob|el|iz|ing
ob|el|us
  obeli
Ober|am|mer|gau
  (village, Germany)
Ober|hau|sen (city,
  Germany)
Ober|on (*Folklore*;
  moon of Uranus)
obese
obes|ity
obey +s +ed +ing
obey|er +s
ob|fus|cate
  ob|fus|cates
  ob|fus|cat|ed
  ob|fus|cat|ing
ob|fus|ca|tion +s
ob|fus|ca|tory
OB/GYN +s
obi +s
obit +s
obi|ter dic|tum
  obi|ter dicta
obitu|ar|ist +s
obitu|ary
  obitu|aries
ob|ject +s +ed +ing
ob|jecti|fi|ca|tion +s
ob|ject|ify
  ob|jecti|fies
  ob|jecti|fied
  ob|jecti|fy|ing
ob|jec|tion +s
ob|jec|tion|able
ob|jec|tion|ably
ob|jec|tion|al
ob|jec|tiv|al
ob|ject|ive +s
ob|ject|ive|ly
ob|ject|ive|ness
ob|jec|tiv|ism
ob|jec|tiv|ist +s
ob|jec|tiv|is|tic
ob|jec|tiv|ity
ob|jec|tiv|iz|a|tion +s
ob|jec|tiv|ize
  ob|jec|tiv|iz|es
  ob|jec|tiv|ized
  ob|jec|tiv|iz|ing
ob|ject|or +s
object-orient|ed
objet +s
objet d'art
  objets d'art
ob|lan|ceo|late
ob|last +s
ob|late +s

ob|la|tion +s
ob|la|tion|al
ob|la|tory
obli|gate
  obli|gates
  obli|gat|ed
  obli|gat|ing
obli|ga|tion +s
obli|ga|tion|al
ob|li|ga|to +s (use obbligato)
ob|liga|tor|i|ly
ob|liga|tory
ob|lige
  ob|liges
  ob|liged
  ob|liging
ob|li|gee +s
ob|liger +s (person who obliges) [☞ obligor]
ob|liging adjective
ob|liging|ly
ob|liging|ness
ob|ligor +s (person legally bound to another) [☞ obliger]
ob|lique
  ob|liques
  ob|liqued
  ob|liquing
ob|lique|ly
ob|lique|ness
ob|liqui|ty
ob|liter|ate
  ob|liter|ates
  ob|liter|at|ed
  ob|liter|at|ing
ob|liter|a|tion +s
ob|liter|a|tive
ob|liter|ator +s
ob|liv|ion
ob|livi|ous
ob|livi|ous|ly
ob|livi|ous|ness
ob|long +s
ob|lo|quy
  ob|lo|quies
ob|nox|ious
ob|nox|ious|ly
ob|nox|ious|ness
oboe +s
oboe d'amore
  oboes d'amore
obo|ist +s
obol +s
Obote, (Apol|lo) Mil|ton (Ugandan prime minister)
ob|ovate
O'Brien, Edna (Irish writer)

O'Brien, Lu|cius Rich|ard (Cdn painter)
ob|scene
ob|scene|ly
ob|scen|ity
  ob|scen|ities
ob|scura (in 'camera obscura')
ob|scur|ant +s
ob|scur|ant|ism
ob|scur|ant|ist +s
ob|scur|a|tion +s
ob|scure
  ob|scures
  ob|scured
  ob|scur|ing
ob|scure|ly
ob|scur|ity
  ob|scur|ities
ob|sequi|al
ob|se|quies (funeral)
ob|sequi|ous (sycophantic)
ob|sequi|ous|ly
ob|sequi|ous|ness
ob|serv|able
ob|serv|ably
ob|serv|ance +s
ob|serv|ant
ob|serv|ant|ly
ob|ser|va|tion +s
ob|ser|va|tion|al
ob|ser|va|tion|al|ly
ob|serv|a|tory
  ob|serv|a|tor|ies
ob|serve
  ob|serves
  ob|served
  ob|serv|ing
ob|serv|er +s
ob|sess
  ob|sess|es
  ob|sessed
  ob|sess|ing
ob|sessed adjective
ob|ses|sion +s
ob|ses|sion|al
ob|ses|sion|al|ism
ob|ses|sion|al|ity
ob|ses|sion|al|ly
ob|ses|sive
ob|sessive-compul|sive
ob|ses|sive|ly
ob|ses|sive|ness
ob|sidian
ob|so|les|cence
ob|so|les|cent
ob|so|lete
ob|so|lete|ly
ob|so|lete|ness
ob|stacle +s

ob|stet|ric
ob|stet|ric|al
ob|stet|ric|al|ly
ob|stet|ri|cian +s
ob|stet|rics
ob|stin|acy
ob|stin|ate
ob|stin|ate|ly
ob|strep|er|ous
ob|strep|er|ous|ly
ob|strep|er|ous|ness
ob|struct +s +ed +ing
ob|struc|tion +s
ob|struc|tion|ism
ob|struc|tion|ist +s
ob|struct|ive
ob|struct|ive|ly
ob|struct|ive|ness
ob|struct|or +s
ob|tain +s +ed +ing
ob|tain|abil|ity
ob|tain|able
ob|tain|er +s
ob|tain|ment
ob|trude
  ob|trudes
  ob|trud|ed
  ob|trud|ing
ob|trud|er +s
ob|tru|sion +s
ob|tru|sive
ob|tru|sive|ly
ob|tru|sive|ness
ob|tund +s +ed +ing
ob|tuse
ob|tuse|ly
ob|tuse|ness
ob|verse +s
ob|verse|ly
ob|ver|sion +s
ob|vert +s +ed +ing
ob|vi|ate
  ob|vi|ates
  ob|vi|at|ed
  ob|vi|at|ing
ob|vi|a|tion
ob|vious
ob|vious|ly
ob|vious|ness
oca|rina +s
O'Casey, Sean (Irish dramatist)
Occam, Wil|liam of (English philosopher)
Occam's razor
oc|ca|sion +s +ed +ing
oc|ca|sion|al
oc|ca|sion|al|ly
Oc|ci|dent (N America & W Europe)

Oc|ci|dent|al +s noun
oc|ci|dent|al adjective
oc|ci|dent|al|ism
oc|ci|dent|al|ist +s
oc|ci|dent|al|ize
  oc|ci|dent|al|iz|es
  oc|ci|dent|al|ized
  oc|ci|dent|al|iz|ing
oc|ci|dent|al|ly
oc|cipi|tal
oc|ci|put +s
Oc|ci|tan
Oc|ci|tan|ian
oc|clude
  oc|cludes
  oc|clud|ed
  oc|clud|ing
oc|clud|ed adjective
oc|clu|sion +s
oc|clu|sive
oc|cult +s +ed +ing
oc|culta|tion +s
oc|cult|ism
oc|cult|ist +s
oc|cult|ly
oc|cu|pancy
  oc|cu|pan|cies
oc|cu|pant +s
oc|cu|pa|tion +s
oc|cu|pa|tion|al
oc|cu|pi|er +s
oc|cupy
  oc|cu|pies
  oc|cu|pied
  oc|cu|py|ing
occur (happen)
  oc|curs
  oc|curred
  oc|cur|ring
  [☞ ochre]
oc|cur|rence +s
ocean +s
ocean|arium
  ocean|ariums or ocean|aria
ocean|front +s
ocean-going
Oce|an|ia (Pacific islands)
Oce|an|ian +s
Ocean|ic (of Oceania)
ocean|ic (of the ocean)
Ocean|id (Greek Myth)
  Ocean|ids or Oce|ani|des
Ocean Island (= Banaba, Kiribati)
ocean|og|raph|er +s
ocean|o|graph|ic
ocean|og|raphy
ocean|side

Oce|a|nus (*Greek Myth*)
ocean|view
ocean|ward
ocel|lar
ocel|late
  (= ocellated)
  [☞ oscillate]
ocel|lat|ed (marked with ocelli)
  [☞ oscillated]
ocel|lus
  ocelli
oce|lot +s
och *interjection*
oche (*Darts*)
och|loc|racy
  och|loc|ra|cies
ochlo|crat +s
ochlo|crat|ic
ochre +s (clay & colour)
  [☞ ocker, okra]
och|re|ous
  (= ochrous)
och|rous
ocker +s (boorish Australian)
  [☞ ochre]
Ock|ham, Wil|liam of
  (= Occam)
o'clock
O'Con|nor, (Mary) Flan|nery (US writer)
O'Con|nor, Thom|as Power (Irish journalist & politician)
oco|til|lo +s
oct|ad +s
octa|gon +s
oct|ag|on|al
oct|ag|on|al|ly
octa|hed|ral
octa|hed|ron
  octa|hed|rons or octa|hed|ra
octal
oct|am|er|ous
oc|tane
oct|ant +s
octa|valent
oc|tave
Oc|tav|ian (Roman emperor)
oc|tavo +s
oc|ten|nial
oc|tet +s
Oc|to|ber +s (month)
  [☞ Oktoberfest]
Oc|to|brist +s

octo|cen|ten|ary
  octo|cen|ten|ar|ies
octo|deci|mo +s
octo|gen|ar|ian +s
octo|pod +s
octo|pus
  octo|pus|es or octo|pi
octo|roon +s
octo|syllab|ic
octo|sylla|ble +s
oc|troi +s
oc|tu|ple
  oc|tu|ples
  oc|tu|pled
  oc|tup|ling
ocu|lar +s (of the eyes)
  [☞ oscular]
ocu|lar|ly
ocu|late (having spots or eyes)
  [☞ osculate]
ocu|list +s
OD (overdose)
  ODs
  OD'd
  ODing
odal|isque +s
Odawa
  plural Odawa or Oda|was
odd +er +est
odd|ball +s
odd bod +s
Odd|fellow +s
odd|ity
  odd|ities
odd-job man
  odd-job men
odd jobs
oddly
odd|ment +s
odd|ness
odds
odds|maker +s
odds-on
ode +s
Oden|se (city, Denmark)
odeon
  odeons or odea
Oder (river, Europe)
  [☞ odour]
Odes|sa (city, Ukraine)
Odets, Clif|ford (US dramatist)
odeum (theatre)
  ode|ums or odea
  [☞ odium]
Odin (*Scandinavian Myth*)
odi|ous

odi|ous|ly
odi|ous|ness
odium (hatred, dislike)
  [☞ odeum]
Odo|acer (Germanic chieftain)
odom|eter +s
odom|etry
odont|oid
odon|to|logic|al
odon|tol|o|gist +s
odon|tol|ogy
odor +s (scent: *use* odour)
  [☞ Oder]
odor|if|er|ous
odor|if|er|ous|ly
odor|ous
odor|ous|ly
odour +s (scent)
  [☞ Oder]
odour|less
Odo|vacar
  (= Odoacer)
Odys|sean
Odys|seus (*Greek Myth*)
odys|sey +s
Oedi|pal
Oedi|pus (*Greek Myth*)
oeno|logic|al
oen|ol|o|gist +s
oen|ol|ogy
Oeno|ne (*Greek Myth*)
oeno|phile +s
oeno|phil|ic
oen|oph|il|ist +s
o'er
Oer|sted, Hans Chris|tian (Danish physicist)
oer|sted +s
oeuvre +s
of
ofay +s
off +s +ed +ing
Offa (Mercian king)
off-air
of|fal +s (entrails; refuse)
  [☞ awful]
Of|faly (county, Ireland)
off|beat +s
off-brand +s
off-Broad|way
off-camera
off-campus
off-centre
off chance
off-colour
off|cut +s

off-day +s
off-dry
off-duty
Of|fen|bach, Jacques (French composer)
of|fence +s
of|fence|less
of|fend +s +ed +ing
of|fend|er +s
of|fend|ing *adjective*
of|fense +s (*use* offence)
of|fen|sive +s
of|fen|sive|ly
of|fen|sive|ness
of|fer +s +ed +ing
of|feree +s
of|fer|er +s (*use* offeror)
of|fer|ing +s *noun*
of|fer|or +s
of|fer|tory
  of|fer|tor|ies
off-field
off-flavour +s
off-gas
  off-gases
  off-gassed
  off-gassing
off-gassing *noun*
off|hand
off|hand|ed
off|hand|ed|ly
off|hand|ed|ness
off-hour +s
off-ice
of|fice +s
  [☞ off-ice]
office-bearer +s
office-holder +s
office|mate +s
of|fi|cer +s +ed +ing
of|fi|cial +s
of|fi|cial|dom
of|fi|cial|ese
of|fi|cial|ism
of|fi|cial|ly
of|fi|ciant +s
of|fi|ci|ate
  of|fi|ci|ates
  of|fi|ci|at|ed
  of|fi|ci|at|ing
of|fi|ci|a|tion +s
of|fi|ci|ator +s
of|fi|cious
of|fi|cious|ly
of|fi|cious|ness
of|fing *noun*
off|ish
off-island
off-key
off-licence

off-line
off-load +s +ed +ing
off-peak
off-piste
off-price
off|print +s
off-putting
off-putting|ly
off-ramp +s
off-reserve
off-road
off-roader +s
off-roading
off-sale +s
off-screen
off-season +s
off|set
  off|sets
  off|set
  off|set|ting
off|shoot +s
off|shore
off|side +s
off-site
off-speed
off|spring
  plural off|spring
off|stage
off-street
off-the-rack
off-the-shelf *adjective*
  preceding a noun
off-the-shoulder
off-the-wall
off track (off-track
  when preceding a
  noun)
off-trail
off-white +s
off-world +s
off-worlder +s
off-year elec|tion +s
O'Flaher|ty, Liam
  (Irish writer)
oft
often +er +est
often|times
Oga|den (desert,
  Ethiopia)
ogam +s (*use* ogham)
Og|bo|mo|sho (city,
  Nigeria)
Ogden, Charles Kay
  (English linguist)
ogee +s
og|ham +s
Ogil|vie (mountains,
  Canada)
ogiv|al
ogive +s

ogle
  ogles
  ogled
  og|ling
og|ler +s
Ogle|thorpe, James
  Ed|ward (English
  colonial
  administrator)
Ogo|po|go
ogre +s
ogre|ish
ogress
  ogress|es
oh +s (*interjection*;
  zero)
  [☞ owe]
O. Henry (US writer)
O'Hig|gins,
  Ber|nar|do (Chilean
  revolutionary)
Ohio (state, US)
Ohio|an +s
OHIP
Ohm, Georg Simon
  (German physicist)
ohm +s (unit of
  resistance)
  [☞ om]
ohmic
ohm|meter +s
Ohm's law
oho
OHOSP
Ohrid (lake,
  SE Europe)
oi (= oy)
oidium
  oidia
oik +s
oil +s +ed +ing
oil-based
oil|bird +s
oil can +s
oil|cloth +s
oil|er +s
oil field +s
oil-fired
oil|i|er
oil|i|est
oil|i|ness
oil|man
  oil|men
oil pan +s
oil paper +s
oil patch
  oil patch|es
oil rig +s
oil rig|ger +s
oil sand +s
oil|seed +s
oil|skin +s
oil slick +s

oil|stone +s
oil well +s
oily
  oil|i|er
  oil|i|est
oink +s +ed +ing
oint|ment +s
Oire|ach|tas
Oirot-Tura (*former*
  name for Gorno-
  Altaisk, Russia)
Oisin (= Ossian,
  legendary Irish bard)
OJ (orange juice)
Ojib|wa
  plural Ojib|wa or
  Ojib|was
Ojib|way (*use*
  Ojibwa)
  plural Ojib|way or
  Ojib|ways
Ojib|we (*use* Ojibwa)
  plural Ojib|we or
  Ojib|wes
Oji-Cree
OK
• *noun*
  OKs
• *verb*
  OK's
  OK'd
  OK'ing
Oka (community,
  Canada; cheese)
Oka|nag|an (lake,
  valley & river,
  Canada; people &
  language)
  plural Oka|nag|an
okapi
  plural okapi or
  oka|pis
Okara (city, Pakistan)
Oka|van|go (river,
  Africa)
okay +s +ed +ing
  (= OK)
Oka|yama (city,
  Japan)
Okee|cho|bee (lake,
  US)
O'Keefe, Eu|gene
  (Cdn brewer)
  [☞ O'Keeffe]
O'Keeffe, Geor|gia
  (US painter)
  [☞ O'Keefe]
Oke|fen|okee (swamp,
  US)
okey-doke
okey-dokey
Okhotsk (sea,
  N Pacific)

Okie +s (native of
  Oklahoma)
  [☞ okey-doke,
  oaky]
Oki|nawa (region &
  island, Japan)
Okla|ho|ma (state,
  US)
Okla|ho|ma City (city,
  US)
Okla|ho|man +s
Oko|toks (town,
  Canada)
okra +s (plant, seed
  pod)
Ok|tober|fest
Olaf (kings of
  Norway; saint)
Öland (island,
  Sweden)
old
  older
  old|est
  [☞ auld lang syne]
old age
old-age home +s
old-age pen|sion +s
old-age pen|sion|er
  +s
old age se|cur|ity
old boy +s
old boy net|work +s
  (= old boys'
  network)
old boys' net|work
  +s
Old|castle, Sir John
  (English soldier)
olden
Ol|den|burg, Claes
  Thure (US sculptor)
Old Eng|lish
Old Eng|lish
  sheep|dog +s
olde worlde *jocular*
old-fashioned
old folks' home +s
Old Glory
old-growth *adjective*
Old|ham (town,
  England)
old|ie +s
old|ish
old-line *adjective*
old maid +s
old-maidish
Old|man (river,
  Canada)
old man's beard
old|ness
old people's home
  +s

Old Pre|tend|er (James Stuart, son of James II of England)
Olds (town, Canada)
Old Sarum (hill & historic site, England)
old|squaw +s
old|ster +s
old-stock
Old Style (calendar)
old style (*in general use*; old-style *when preceding a noun*)
Old Tes|ta|ment
old-time *adjective preceding a noun*
old-timer +s
old-timey
Ol|du|vai (gorge, Tanzania)
Old West
old wives' tale +s
old-woman|ish
Old World (Europe, Asia & Africa)
old-world (of old times)
ole|agin|ous
ole|an|der +s
ole|as|ter +s
ole|ate +s
olec|ra|non +s
ole|fin +s
ole|fine +s (*use* olefin)
oleic
oleo (*Aviation*; margarine) [☞ olio]
oleo|graph +s
oleo|graph|ic
ole|og|raphy
oleo|mar|gar|ine +s
oleo|res|in +s
Oles|tra *proprietary*
oleum
O lev|el +s
ol|fac|tion +s
ol|fac|tory
olib|anum
oli|garch +s
oli|garch|ic
oli|garch|ic|al
oli|garch|ic|al|ly
oli|garchy
oli|garch|ies
Oligo|cene
oligo|chaete +s
oligo|nucleo|tide +s
oli|gop|ol|ist +s
oli|gop|o|lis|tic

oli|gop|oly
oli|gop|ol|ies
oligo|sac|char|ide +s
oligo|troph|ic
oli|got|rophy
O-line +s
olio +s (mixed dish; hodgepodge) [☞ oleo]
Oli|phant, Betty (Cdn dance teacher)
oli|va|ceous
ol|ive +s
Oli|ver, John (Cdn politician)
Oli|ver, Jo|seph ('King Oliver', US musician)
Oliv|ier, Lau|rence Kerr (Baron Olivier of Brighton, English actor & director)
oliv|ine +s
olla po|dri|da +s
Olo|mouc (city, Czech Republic)
olo|ro|so +s
Ol|sztyn (city, Poland)
Olym|pia (plain, Greece; city, US)
Olym|pi|ad +s
Olym|pi|an +s
Olym|pic +s
Olympic-size (= Olympic-sized)
Olympic-sized
Olym|pus (*Greek Myth*; mountains, Greece & Cyprus)
om (mantra) [☞ ohm]
oma +s (grandmother) [☞ Omagh]
oma|dhaun +s
Omagh (town, Northern Ireland) [☞ oma]
Omaha (city, US; people & language) *plural* Omaha *or* Oma|has
Oman (country & gulf, Middle East)
Oma|ni +s
Omar Khay|yám (Persian poet & astronomer)
oma|sum
omasa
Omay|yad +s (*use* Umayyad)
ombre (card game) [☞ ombré, hombre]

ombré (shading) [☞ ombre, hombre]
om|buds|man
om|buds|men
om|buds|person +s
Om|dur|man (city, Sudan)
omega +s
omega-3 fatty acid
ome|let +s (*use* omelette)
ome|lette +s
omen +s +ed +ing
omened *adjective*
omen|tal
omen|tum
omen|ta
omer|ta
omi|cron +s
omin|ous
omin|ous|ly
omin|ous|ness
omis|sible
omis|sion +s
omis|sive
omit
omits
omit|ted
omit|ting
om|ma|tid|ium
om|ma|tidia
omni|bus
omni|buses
omni|compe|tence
omni|compe|tent
omni|direc|tion|al
omni|far|ious
OMNI|MAX *proprietary*
om|nipo|tence
om|nipo|tent
om|nipo|tent|ly
omni|pres|ence
omni|pres|ent
om|nis|cience
om|nis|cient
om|nis|cient|ly
omnium-gatherum
omni|vore +s
om|niv|or|ous
om|niv|or|ous|ly
om|niv|or|ous|ness
om|phal|os
Omsk (city, Russia)
on
on-again, off-again
on|ager +s
on-air
onan|ism
onan|ist +s
onan|is|tic

Ona|ping Falls (town, Canada)
Onas|sis, Aris|totle Soc|ra|tes (Greek shipping magnate)
Onas|sis, Jacque|line Lee Bou|vier Ken|nedy ('Jackie') (US First Lady)
on-base per|cent|age +s
on-board *adjective preceding a noun*
on-camera
once
once-in-a-lifetime
once-over +s
oncer +s
onco|gene +s
onco|gen|ic
onco|gen|icity
on|col|o|gist +s
onc|ol|ogy
on|com|ing
On|daatje, (Phil|ip) Mi|chael (Cdn writer)
on deck (on-deck *when preceding a noun*)
one +s
one-and-a-half +s (apartment)
one-armed ban|dit +s
one-dimension|al
one-dimension|al|ity
Onega (lake, Russia)
one-handed
one-horse
On|eida *plural* On|eida *or* On|eidas
O'Neill, Eu|gene Glad|stone (US playwright)
oneir|ic
onei|ro|mancy
one-liner +s
one-lunger +s
one-man
one|ness
one-night stand +s
one-off +s
one-on-one
one-piece
one-room
oner|ous
oner|ous|ly
oner|ous|ness
one|self
one-shot
one-sided

one-sidedly
one-sidedness
one-size-fits-all
one-step
one-stop
one-time
  one-times
  one-timed
  one-timing
one-timer +s
one-to-one
one-track mind
one-two
one-up
  one-ups
  one-upped
  one-upping
one-upmanship
one-way
one-woman
on|going
on|going|ness
on-ice
on|ion +s
onion dome +s
onion-domed
onion ring +s
On|ions, Charles
  Tal|but (English
  lexicographer)
onion skin
on|iony
Onley, Nor|man
  An|tony ('Toni')
  (Cdn painter)
  [☞ only]
on-line
on|look|er +s
on|look|ing
only
  [☞ Onley]
Ono, Yoko (US
  musician)
on-off
ono|mas|tic
ono|mas|tics
ono|mato|poeia
ono|mato|poeic
ono|mato|poeic|ally
Onon|daga
  plural Onon|daga or
  Onon|dagas
on-ramp +s
on-reserve
on|rush
  on|rush|es
on|rush|ing
on|screen
on-set (occurring on a
  production set)
onset +s (start; attack)
on|shore
on|side

on-site
on|slaught +s
on|stage
On|tar|ian +s
On|tario (province &
  lake, Canada)
on-the-job
on to (on as far as:
  travelled on to Regina;
  wise to: she's on to
  your tricks)
onto (to a position on:
  stepped onto the
  subway)
onto|gen|esis
onto|gen|etic
onto|gen|etic|ally
onto|gen|ic
onto|gen|ic|ally
onto|geny
onto|logic|al
onto|logic|al|ly
on|tol|o|gist +s
on|tol|ogy
onus
  onus|es
on|ward
on|wards
onyx
  onyx|es
oo|cyte +s
oo|dles
oog|am|ous
oog|amy
oo|gen|esis
ooh
  oohs
  oohed
  ooh|ing
ooh and ahh
  oohs and aahs
  oohed and aahed
  ooh|ing and aah|ing
Ook|pik +s
  proprietary
ooli|chan (use
  eulachon)
  plural ooli|chan or
  ooli|chans
oo|lite +s
oo|lit|ic
oo|log|ic|al
oolo|gist +s
ool|ogy
oo|long
oo|miak +s (use
  umiak)
oom|pah
oom|pah|pah
oomph
oophor|ec|tomy
  oophor|ec|to|mies
oops

oopsy daisy
Oort, Jan Hen|drik
  (Dutch astronomer)
ooze
  oozes
  oozed
  ooz|ing
  [☞ Ouse]
oozy (like ooze)
  [☞ Uzi]
op +s (operation;
  opportunity)
opa +s (grandfather)
  [☞ opah]
opaci|fi|ca|tion
opaci|fi|er +s
opaci|fy
  opaci|fies
  opaci|fied
  opaci|fy|ing
opa|city
  opaci|ties
opah +s (fish)
  [☞ opa]
opal +s
opal|esce
  opal|es|ces
  opal|es|ced
  opal|es|cing
opal|es|cence
opal|es|cent
opal|ine
opaque
  opaquer
  opaquest
  opaques
opaque|ly
opaque|ness
op art
op. cit.
OPEC (Organization of
  Petroleum Exporting
  Countries)
op-ed
open +s +ed +ing
open|able
open air (open-air
  when preceding a
  noun)
open-and-shut
open book noun
open-book adjective
open|cast
open con|cept
  adjective
open cus|tody (open-
  custody when
  preceding a noun)
open door noun &
  adjective
open-ended
open-endedness
open|er +s

open-eyed
open-face
open-faced
open-handed
open-handed|ly
open-handed|ness
open-heart
open-hearted
open-hearted|ness
open-hearth
open ice (open-ice
  when preceding a
  noun)
open|ing +s noun &
  adjective
open-line
open-liner +s
open|ly
open-minded
open-minded|ly
open-minded|ness
open-mouthed
open-necked
open|ness
open-plan
open-reel
open skies noun &
  adjective
open-toed
open|work
opera
  • singular noun:
    plural op|er|as
  • plural of opus
oper|abil|ity
oper|able
opera buffa
  opere buffe or
  opera buf|fas
opéra com|ique
  op|éras com|iques
oper|and +s
opera seria
  opere serie or
  opera serias
oper|ate
  oper|ates
  oper|at|ed
  oper|at|ing
oper|at|ic
oper|at|ic|ally
oper|at|ics
oper|ation +s
oper|ation|al
oper|ation|al|ly
oper|a|tive
oper|a|tive|ly
oper|a|tive|ness
oper|ator +s
oper|cu|lar
oper|cu|late

oper|cu|lum
  oper|cula
oper|etta +s
op|eron +s
ophi|cleide +s
ophid|ian +s
Ophir (Bible)
Ophiu|chus
  (constellation)
oph|thal|mia
oph|thal|mic
oph|thal|mo|logic|al
oph|thal|mol|o|gist
  +s
oph|thal|mol|ogy
oph|thal|mo|scope
  +s
oph|thal|mo|scop|ic
oph|thal|mos|copy
opi|ate
  opi|ates
  opi|at|ed
  opi|at|ing
opine
  opines
  opined
  opin|ing
opin|ion +s
opin|ion|at|ed
opi|oid +s
opium +s
opop|anax
  opop|anax|es
Opor|to (city,
  Portugal)
opos|sum +s
Op|pen|heimer,
  (Jul|ius) Rob|ert (US
  nuclear physicist)
op|pon|ency
op|pon|ent +s
op|por|tune
op|por|tune|ly
op|por|tune|ness
op|por|tun|ism
op|por|tun|ist +s
op|por|tun|is|tic
op|por|tun|is|tic|ally
op|por|tun|ity
  op|por|tun|ities
op|pos|able
op|pose
  op|pos|es
  op|posed
  op|pos|ing
op|pos|er +s
op|pos|ing adjective
op|pos|ite +s
op|pos|ite field
  (op|posite-field
  when preceding a
  noun)
op|pos|ite|ly

op|pos|ite|ness
op|pos|ition +s
op|pos|ition|al
op|pos|ition|al|ity
op|pos|ition|ist +s
op|press
  op|press|es
  op|pressed
  op|press|ing
op|pressed adjective
op|pres|sion +s
op|pres|sive
op|pres|sive|ly
op|pres|sive|ness
op|pres|sor +s
op|pro|bri|ous
op|pro|bri|ous|ly
op|pro|bri|um +s
op|pugn +s +ed +ing
op|pug|nance
op|pug|nancy
op|pug|nant
op|pug|na|tion
op|pugn|er +s
opsi|math +s
op|sim|athy
op|son|ic
op|son|in +s
op|son|iz|a|tion
op|son|ize
  op|son|iz|es
  op|son|ized
  op|son|iz|ing
ops room +s
opt +s +ed +ing
opt|a|tive +s
opt|a|tive|ly
opted-out adjective
  preceding a noun
op|tic +s
op|tic|al
op|tic|al disk +s
op|tic|al|ly
op|ti|cian +s
op|tics
op|tima
opti|mal
opti|mal|ity
opti|mal|ly
opti|mism
opti|mist +s
opti|mis|tic
opti|mis|tic|ally
opti|miz|a|tion +s
opti|mize
  opti|miz|es
  opti|mized
  opti|miz|ing
opti|miz|er +s
opti|mum
  op|tima or
  opti|mums

op|tion +s +ed +ing
op|tion|al
op|tion|al|ity
op|tion|al|ly
opto|elec|tron|ic +s
opto|met|ric
op|tomet|rist +s
op|tom|etry
opt out verb
  opts out
  opted out
  opt|ing out
opt-out +s noun &
  adjective
opu|lence
opu|lent
opu|lent|ly
opun|tia +s
opus
  opus|es or opera
opus|cule +s
opus|cu|lum
  opus|cula
Opus Dei
or (conjunction;
  Heraldry)
  [☞ ore, Orr, oar]
orach (use orache)
  orach|es
or|ache +s
or|acle +s (prophet)
  [☞ auricle]
or|acu|lar
or|acu|lar|ity
or|acu|lar|ly
oracy
Ora|dea (city,
  Romania)
oral +s (of the mouth)
  [☞ aural]
oral|ism
oral|ist
oral|ity
oral|ly (by means of
  the mouth)
  [☞ aurally]
Oran (city, Algeria)
or|ang +s (orangutan)
  [☞ orange]
Or|ange (town,
  France; river, South
  Africa; Dutch royal
  house; of
  Orangemen)
Or|ange, Wil|liam of
  (William III of
  England)
or|ange +s (fruit,
  colour)
  [☞ orang]
or|ange|ade +s
Orange|ism

Orange|man
  Orange|men
Orange|man's Day
or|ange peel (orange-
  peel when preceding
  a noun)
oran|gery
  oran|ger|ies
Orange|ville (town,
  Canada)
orange|wood
oran|gey
oran|gi|er
oran|gi|est
or|an|gu|tan +s
oran|gy (use orangey)
oran|gi|er
oran|gi|est
Or|anje|stad (capital
  of Aruba)
Ora|şul Stal|in (former
  name for Braşov,
  Romania)
orate
  orates
  orat|ed
  orat|ing
ora|tion +s
ora|tor +s
Ora|tor|ian +s
ora|tor|ical
ora|torio +s
ora|tory
  ora|tor|ies
ora|ture
orb +s +ed +ing
or|bicu|lar
or|bicu|lar|ity
or|bicu|lar|ly
Orbi|son, Roy Kel|ton
  (US singer-
  songwriter)
or|bit +s +ed +ing
or|bit|al +s
or|bit|er +s
orca +s
Or|cadi|an +s
or|chard +s
or|chard|ing
or|chard|ist +s
or|ches|tra +s
or|ches|tral
or|ches|tral|ly
or|ches|trate
  or|ches|trates
  or|ches|trat|ed
  or|ches|trat|ing
or|ches|tra|tion +s
or|ches|tra|tive
or|ches|tra|tor +s
or|chid +s
orchid|aceous
orchid|ist +s

or|chil +s
or|chil|la +s
or|chis
  or|chis|es
or|chi|tis
orcin
or|cin|ol
Orcus (*Roman Myth*)
Orczy, Baron|ess
  Em|mus|ca (English
  novelist)
or|dain +s +ed +ing
or|dain|er +s
or|dain|ment +s
or|deal +s
or|der +s +ed +ing
or|der|er +s
Order-in-Council
  Orders-in-Council
or|der|li|ness
or|der|ly
  or|der|lies
Order Paper +s
or|din|al +s
or|din|ance +s
  (decree; rite)
  [☞ ordnance]
or|din|and +s
or|din|ar|ily
or|din|ar|i|ness
or|din|ary
  or|din|aries
or|din|ate +s
or|din|a|tion +s
ord|nance (*Military*)
  [☞ ordinance]
Or|do|vi|cian
ord|ure +s
Or|dzho|ni|kidze
  (*former name for*
  Vladikavkaz,
  Russia)
Ore (mountains,
  Europe)
  [☞ Orr]
ore
• (*Mining*)
  plural ores
• (Scandinavian
  monetary unit)
  plural ore
  [☞ or, oar, aura]
ore|ad +s
ore body
  ore bod|ies
Öre|bro (city, Sweden)
orec|chiet|te
oreg|ano
Ore|gon (state, US)
Ore|gon|ian +s
Orel (city, Russia)
  [☞ oral, aural]

Oren|burg (city,
  Russia)
Ores|tes (*Greek Myth*)
Øre|sund (channel,
  Europe)
Orff, Carl (German
  composer)
org +s
or|gan +s
or|gan|dy
  or|gan|dies
or|gan|elle +s
or|gan|ic +s
or|gan|ic|ally
or|gani|cism
or|gani|cist +s
or|gan|ism +s
or|gan|ist +s
or|gan|iz|able
or|gan|iz|a|tion +s
or|gan|iz|a|tion|al
or|gan|iz|a|tion|al|ly
or|gan|ize
  or|gan|iz|es
  or|gan|ized
  or|gan|iz|ing
or|gan|ized *adjective*
or|gan|iz|er +s
organ of Corti
  or|gans of Corti
or|gano|gen|esis
or|gano|lep|tic
or|gano|metal|lic
or|ga|non +s
or|gano|
    phos|phor|ous
  adjective
or|gano|
    phos|phor|us
  noun
or|gan|um
  or|gana
or|gan|za +s
or|gasm +s +ed +ing
or|gas|mic
or|gas|mic|ally
or|gas|tic
or|gas|tic|ally
or|geat +s
orgi|as|tic
orgi|as|tic|ally
or|gu|lous
orgy
  or|gies
oribi
  plural oribi or ori|bis
oriel +s (window)
  [☞ oriole]
Ori|ent (E Asia)
ori|ent +s +ed +ing
  (establish position;
  pearl)

Ori|ent|al
• *adjective* (of E Asia)
• *offensive noun*
  (person of E Asian
  origin)
Ori|ent|als
ori|ent|al (eastern;
  pearl; rug; poppy)
Ori|ent|al|ism +s
  (idealized portrayal
  of the Orient)
ori|ent|al|ism (study
  of Oriental
  languages etc.)
ori|ent|al|ist +s
ori|ent|al|ize
  ori|ent|al|iz|es
  ori|ent|al|ized
  ori|ent|al|iz|ing
ori|ent|al|ly
orien|tate
  orien|tates
  orien|tat|ed
  orien|tat|ing
orien|ta|tion +s
orien|ta|tion|al
ori|ent|ed *adjective*
ori|en|teer +s +ed
  +ing
ori|en|teer|ing *noun*
ori|fice +s
ori|flamme +s
ori|gami
ori|ganum +s
Ori|gen (early
  Christian scholar)
ori|gin +s
ori|gin|al +s
ori|gin|al|ity
  ori|gin|al|ities
ori|gin|al|ly
ori|gin|ary
ori|gin|ate
  ori|gin|ates
  ori|gin|at|ed
  ori|gin|at|ing
ori|gin|a|tion +s
ori|gin|ator +s
Oril|lia (city, Canada)
ori|nasal
o-ring +s
Ori|noco (river,
  S America)
ori|ole +s (bird)
  [☞ oriel, aureole]
Orion (*Greek Myth*;
  Astronomy)
Orion's Belt
  (*Astronomy*)
ori|son +s
Oris|sa (state, India)
Oriya +s

Ork|ney +s (islands
  off Scotland)
Ork|ney|man
  Ork|ney|men
Or|lan|do (city, US)
orle +s
Or|lean|ist +s
Or|léans (city, France;
  island, Canada)
Orlon *proprietary*
or|lop +s
Orly (suburb of Paris)
Or|man|dy, Eu|gene
  (US conductor)
Or|mazd
  (*Zoroastrianism*
  = Ahura Mazda)
or|molu
Ormuz (= Hormuz,
  Iranian island)
Or|muzd
  (*Zoroastrianism*
  = Ahura Mazda)
orna|ment +s +ed
  +ing
orna|ment|al +s
orna|ment|al|ism
orna|ment|al|ly
orna|men|ta|tion +s
or|nate
or|nate|ly
or|nate|ness
or|neri|ness
or|nery
  or|neri|er
  or|neri|est
or|nith|ic
or|nith|is|chian +s
orni|tho|logic|al
orni|thol|o|gist +s
orni|thol|ogy
or|nitho|pod +s
or|nith|opter +s
oro|gen|esis
oro|gen|ic
or|ogeny
  or|ogen|ies
oro|graph|ic
oro|graph|ic|al
orog|raphy
Oro|moc|to (town,
  Canada)
Oron|tes (river, Asia)
oro|tund
oro|tund|ity
oro|tund|ly
Oroz|co, José
  Cle|mente (Mexican
  painter)
or|phan +s +ed +ing
or|phan|age +s
or|phaned *adjective*
or|phan|hood

Or|phean
Or|pheus (*Greek Myth*)
Or|phic
Or|phism
or|phrey +s
or|pi|ment
orpin +s (*use* orpine)
or|pine +s
Orr, Rob|ert Gor|don
('Bobby') (Cdn
hockey player)
[☞ Ore, oar, or]
or|rery
or|rer|ies
orris
or|ris|es
orris|root +s
Orser, Brian (Cdn
figure skater)
Orsk (city, Russia)
or|ta|nique +s
Or|tega (Saa|vedra),
Dan|iel (Nicaraguan
president)
Or|tega y Gas|set,
José (Spanish
philosopher)
ortho|chro|mat|ic
ortho|clase
ortho|don|tia
ortho|don|tic
ortho|don|tics
ortho|don|tist +s
Ortho|dox (of
Judaism or the
Eastern Church)
ortho|dox (correct,
approved;
conventional)
ortho|dox|ly
Ortho|doxy
(Orthodox Churches
or practice)
ortho|doxy (orthodox
doctrine;
correctness,
conventionality)
ortho|dox|ies
or|tho|epic
or|tho|epist +s
or|tho|epy
ortho|gen|esis
ortho|gen|etic
orth|og|onal
orth|og|onal|ity
orth|og|raph|er +s
ortho|graph|ic
ortho|graph|ic|al
ortho|graph|ic|al|ly
orth|og|raphy
orth|og|raph|ies
ortho|paed|ic
ortho|paed|ics

ortho|paed|ist +s
ortho|ped|ic (*use*
orthopaedic)
ortho|ped|ics (*use*
orthopaedics)
ortho|ped|ist +s (*use*
orthopaedist)
orth|op|ter|an +s
orth|op|ter|ous
orth|op|tic
orth|op|tics
orth|op|tist +s
ortho|rhom|bic
orth|ot|ic
orth|ot|ist +s
orto|lan +s
Orton, Joe (English
playwright)
Oruro (city, Bolivia)
Or|vi|eto (town, Italy)
Or|well, George
(English writer)
Or|well|ian
oryx
plural oryx or
oryxes
orzo
OS (operating system)
OSs
Osage
plural Osage or
Osa|ges
Osaka (city, Japan)
OSAP (Ontario
Student Assistance
Program)
Os|borne, John
James (English
playwright)
Oscan
Os|car +s
(Scandinavian kings;
Academy Award)
os|cil|late (swing;
vacillate)
os|cil|lates
os|cil|lat|ed
os|cil|lat|ing
[☞ ocellate]
os|cil|lat|ing *adjective*
os|cil|la|tion +s
os|cil|la|tor +s
os|cil|la|tory
os|cil|lo|gram +s
os|cil|lo|graph +s
os|cil|lo|graph|ic
os|cil|log|raphy
os|cil|lo|scope +s
os|cil|lo|scop|ic
os|cine
os|cin|ine (= oscine)
os|cula

os|cu|lar (of the
mouth)
[☞ ocular]
os|cu|late (*Math*; kiss)
os|cu|lates
os|cu|lated
os|cu|lat|ing
[☞ oculate]
os|cu|la|tion
os|cu|la|tory
os|cu|lum
os|cula
Osh (city, Kyrgyzstan)
Osh|awa (city,
Canada)
osier +s
Osi|jek (city, Croatia)
Os|iris (*Egyptian
Myth*)
Osler, Sir Wil|liam
(Cdn physician &
educator)
[☞ hostler]
Oslo (capital of
Norway)
Osman (founder of
the Ottoman
Dynasty)
Os|man|li +s
osmic
os|mium
osmo|regu|la|tion
os|mo|sis
os|mot|ic
os|mot|ic|ally
os|mund +s
os|mun|da +s
Osna|brück (city,
Germany)
os|prey +s
Ossa (mountains,
Greece & Tasmania)
os|sein +s (collagen)
os|seous
Os|se|tia (region, the
Caucasus)
Ossi +s (East German)
[☞ Aussie]
Os|sian (legendary
Irish warrior & bard)
[☞ ossein]
os|sicle +s
Os|sie (*for* East
German *use* Ossi; *for*
Australian *use*
Aussie)
Os|sietz|ky, Carl von
(German journalist)
os|si|fi|ca|tion
os|sify
os|si|fies
os|si|fied
os|si|fy|ing

osso bucco
osso buco (*use* osso
bucco)
os|suary
os|suar|ies
oste|itis
Os|tend (city,
Belgium)
os|ten|sible
os|ten|sibly
os|ten|ta|tion
os|ten|ta|tious
os|ten|ta|tious|ly
osteo|arth|ritis
osteo|blast +s
osteo|blas|tic
osteo|clast +s
osteo|clas|tic
osteo|gen|esis
osteo|gen|etic
osteo|logic|al
osteo|logic|al|ly
oste|ol|o|gist +s
oste|ol|ogy
osteo|mal|acia
osteo|mal|acic
osteo|myel|itis
osteo|path +s
osteo|path|ic
oste|op|athy
osteo|por|osis
osteo|por|otic
osteo|sar|coma +s
Ostia (ancient city,
Italy)
os|tin|ato
os|tin|atos or
os|tin|ati
os|tium
ostia
Ost|mark +s
os|tomy
os|to|mies
Ost|polit|ik
os|tra|cism
os|tra|cize
os|tra|ciz|es
os|tra|cized
os|tra|ciz|ing
Os|trava (city, Czech
Republic)
os|trich
os|trich|es
os|trich|like
Os|tro|goth +s
Os|tro|goth|ic
Ost|wald, (Fried|rich)
Wil|helm (German
chemist)
Os|wald, Lee Har|vey
(suspected J.F.K.
assassin)
Os|wego tea

OT (overtime; offensive tackle; occupational therapist; Old Testament)
OTs
Otago (region, New Zealand)
other +s
other-direct|ed
other-direct|ed|ness
other|ness
other|where
other|wise
other world +s
other|world|li|ness
other|world|ly
Oth|man (= Osman, founder of the Ottoman Dynasty)
Otho (= Otto, German king & Holy Roman emperor)
Otho, Mar|cus Sal|vius (Roman emperor)
otic
oti|ose
oti|ose|ness
ot|itis
ot|itis media
oto|laryn|go|logic|al
oto|laryn|gol|o|gist +s
oto|laryn|gol|ogy
oto|lith
oto|lith|ic
oto|logic|al
otol|o|gist +s
otol|ogy
O'Toole, Peter Seamus (British actor)
oto|rhino| laryn|gol|o|gist +s
oto|rhino| laryn|gol|ogy
oto|scope +s
oto|scop|ic
Ot|ran|to (strait, Mediterranean)
ot|tava rima +s
Ot|tawa (Cdn capital & river; *for* Aboriginal people *use* Odawa)
plural **Ot|tawa** or **Ot|tawas**
Ot|ta|wan +s
Otter, Sir Wil|liam Dil|lon (Cdn soldier)
ot|ter +s

Otter|burn Park (town, Canada)
Otto (German king & Holy Roman emperor)
Otto, Niko|laus Aug|ust (German engineer)
otto (essential oil)
[☞ **auto**]
Otto|man +s (Turkish empire & dynasty; Turk)
otto|man +s (furniture; fabric)
Oua|ga|dou|gou (capital of Burkina Faso)
oua|na|niche
plural **oua|na|niche**
oubli|ette +s
ouch
Ouden|arde (battle site, Flanders)
Oudh (region, India)
ought (*auxiliary verb* used to express obligation etc.; nought)
[☞ **aught**]
oughtn't
ou|giya +s (*use* ouguiya)
ou|guiya +s
Ouiat|chou|ane (waterfall, Canada)
Ouida (English novelist)
Ouija board +s
proprietary
Oulu (city, Finland)
ounce +s
oun|cer +s
our *possessive adjective*
[☞ **hour, Auer**]
Our Fath|er (God)
Our Lady (the Virgin Mary)
Our Lady's bed|straw +s
Our Lord (God, Jesus Christ)
ours
our|self
our|selves
Ouse (rivers, England)
ousel +s (*use* ouzel)
oust +s +ed +ing
oust|ed *adjective*
oust|er +s
out +s +ed +ing (not in etc.)
[☞ **owt**]

outa (= outta)
out|age +s
out-and-out
Outa|ouais (region, Canada)
Ou|tardes, Ri|vière aux (river, Canada)
out|back +s
out|back|er +s
out|bid
 out|bids
 out|bid
 out|bid|ding
out|board +s
out|bound
out|break +s
out|breed
 out|breeds
 out|bred
 out|breed|ing
out|build|ing +s
out|burst +s
out|cast +s (rejected person; tramp)
out|caste (person without caste)
 out|castes
 out|cast|ed
 out|cast|ing
out|class
 out|class|es
 out|classed
 out|class|ing
out|come +s
out|crop
 out|crops
 out|cropped
 out|crop|ping
out|crop|ping +s
noun
out|cross
 out|cross|es
 out|crossed
 out|cross|ing
out|cry
 out|cries
out|dated
out|dis|tance
 out|dis|tan|ces
 out|dis|tanced
 out|dis|tan|cing
outdo
 out|does
 out|did
 out|done
 out|doing
out|door +s
out|doors|man
 out|doors|men
out|doors|woman
 out|doors|women
out|doorsy
out|er +s

Outer Heb|ri|des (islands off Scotland)
Outer Mon|go|lia (*former name for* Mongolia)
outer|most
outer|wear
out|face
 out|faces
 out|faced
 out|facing
out|fall +s
out|field +s
out|field|er +s
out|fight
 out|fights
 out|fought
 out|fight|ing
out|fit
 out|fits
 out|fit|ted
 out|fit|ting
out|fit|ter +s
out|flank +s +ed +ing
out|flow +s
out|fly
 out|flies
 out|flew
 out|flown
 out|fly|ing
out|fox
 out|fox|es
 out|foxed
 out|fox|ing
out|gas
 out|gas|es
 out|gassed
 out|gas|sing
out|gener|al
 out|gener|als
 out|gener|alled
 out|gener|al|ling
outgo
 out|goes
 out|went
 out|gone
 out|going
out|going +s *noun &*
adjective
out|gross
 out|gross|es
 out|grossed
 out|gross|ing
out|group +s
out|grow
 out|grows
 out|grew
 out|grown
 out|grow|ing
out|growth +s
out|guess
 out|guess|es

out|guessed
out|guess|ing
out|gun
  out|guns
  out|gunned
  out|gun|ning
out|harbour +s
out|house +s
out|ing +s *noun*
out|jump +s +ed
  +ing
out|land|er +s
out|land|ish
out|land|ish|ly
out|land|ish|ness
out|last +s +ed +ing
out|law +s +ed +ing
out|lawry
out|lay +s
out|let +s
out|lier +s
out|line
  out|lines
  out|lined
  out|lining
out|live
  out|lives
  out|lived
  out|liv|ing
out|look +s
out|lying
out|man|eu|ver +s
  +ed +ing (*use*
  outmanoeuvre)
out|man|oeu|ver +s
  +ed +ing (*use*
  outmanoeuvre)
out|man|oeuvre
  out|man|oeuv|res
  out|man|oeuv|red
  out|man|oeuv|ring
out|match
  out|match|es
  out|matched
  out|match|ing
out-migration +s
out|moded
out|most
out|num|ber +s +ed
  +ing
out-of-body
out-of-court
out of date (out-of-
  date *when preceding*
  a noun)
out-of-pocket
out of print
out-of-province
out-of-sight
out-of-the-way
out-of-town
out-of-towner +s
out-of-work

out|pace
  out|paces
  out|paced
  out|pacing
out|patient +s
out|per|form +s +ed
  +ing
out|per|form|ance +s
out|place|ment +s
out|play +s +ed +ing
out|point +s +ed
  +ing
out|poll +s +ed +ing
out|port +s
out|port|er +s
out|post +s
out|pour|ing +s
out|put
  out|puts
  out|put
  or out|put|ted
  out|put|ting
out|rage
  out|rages
  out|raged
  out|raging
out|raged *adjective*
out|ra|geous
out|ra|geous|ly
out|ra|geous|ness
out|ran
out|rank +s +ed +ing
outré
out|reach
  out|reach|es
  out|reached
  out|reach|ing
Outre|mont (city,
  Canada)
out|ride
  out|rides
  out|rode
  out|rid|den
  out|rid|ing
out|rid|er +s
out|rid|ing *noun*
out|rig|ger +s
out|right
out|right|ness
outro +s
out|rode
out|run
  out|runs
  out|ran
  out|run
  out|run|ning
out|score
  out|scores
  out|scored
  out|scor|ing
out|sell
  out|sells

out|sold
out|sell|ing
out|set
out|shine
  out|shines
  out|shone
  out|shin|ing
out|shoot
  out|shoots
  out|shot
  out|shoot|ing
out|side +s
out|sider +s
out|size +s
out|sized
out|skirts
out|smart +s +ed
  +ing
out|sold
out|sole +s
out|source
  out|sources
  out|sourced
  out|sourcing
out|sourcing *noun*
out|spend
  out|spends
  out|spent
  out|spend|ing
out|spoken
out|spoken|ly
out|spoken|ness
out|spread
  out|spreads
  out|spread
  out|spread|ing
out|stand|ing
out|stand|ing|ly
out|station +s
out|stay +s +ed +ing
out|step
  out|steps
  out|stepped
  out|step|ping
out|stretch
  out|stretch|es
  out|stretched
  out|stretch|ing
out|stretched
  adjective
out|strip
  out|strips
  out|stripped
  out|strip|ping
outta
out|take +s
out-talk +s +ed +ing
out-think
  out-thinks
  out-thought
  out-thinking

out-thrust
  out-thrusts
  out-thrust
  out-thrust|ing
out to lunch
out-turn +s
out|vote
  out|votes
  out|vot|ed
  out|vot|ing
out|ward +s
out|ward|ly
out|ward|ness
out|wards
out|wash
  out|wash|es
out|wear
  out|wears
  out|wore
  out|worn
  out|wear|ing
out|weigh +s +ed
  +ing
out|went
out|wit
  out|wits
  out|wit|ted
  out|wit|ting
out|with
out|wore
out|work +s +ed
  +ing
out|work|er +s
out|worn
ouzel +s
ouzo +s
ova
oval
Oval Of|fice
Ovam|bo
  plural Ovam|bo or
  Ovam|bos
Ovam|bo|land
  (region, Namibia)
ovar|ian
ovari|ec|tomy
  ovari|ec|to|mies
ovary
  ovar|ies
ovate
ova|tion +s
ova|tion|al
oven +s
oven|bird +s
oven|proof
oven-ready
oven|ware
over
over|abun|dance +s
over|abun|dant
over|abun|dant|ly

over|achieve
  over|achieves
  over|achieved
  over|achiev|ing
over|achieve|ment
  +s
over|achiev|er +s
over|act +s +ed +ing
over|active
over|activ|ity
over|age +s (surplus)
over-age (too old)
over|all +s
over|alled
over-ambition
over-ambitious
over-ambitious|ly
over-anxiety
over-anxious
over-anxious|ly
over|arch
  over|arch|es
  over|arched
  over|arch|ing
over|arch|ing
  adjective
over|arm
over|ate *past tense of*
  overeat
  [☞ overrate]
over|awe
  over|awes
  over|awed
  over|awing
over|bal|ance
  over|bal|an|ces
  over|bal|anced
  over|bal|an|cing
over|bear
  over|bears
  over|bore
  over|borne
  over|bear|ing
over|bear|ing
  adjective
over|bear|ing|ly
over|bear|ing|ness
over|bid
  over|bids
  over|bid
  over|bid|ding
over|bid|der +s
over|bite +s
over|blouse +s
over|blown
over|board
over|book +s +ed
  +ing
over|boot +s
over|bore
over|borne
over|bought

over|build
  over|builds
  over|built
  over|build|ing
over|build|ing *noun*
over|bur|den +s +ed
  +ing
over|burden|some
over|busy
over|buy
  over|buys
  over|bought
  over|buy|ing
over|call +s +ed +ing
over|came
over|capa|city
over|capit|al|ize
  over|capit|al|iz|es
  over|capit|al|ized
  over|capit|al|iz|ing
over|cast
  over|casts
  over|cast
  over|cast|ing
over|caution
over|cautious
over|cautious|ly
over|cautious|ness
over|charge
  over|char|ges
  over|charged
  over|char|ging
over|check +s
over|cloud +s +ed
  +ing
over|coat +s
over|come
  over|comes
  over|came
  over|come
  over|coming
over|commit
  over|commits
  over|commit|ted
  over|commit|ting
over|commit|ment
over|compen|sate
  over|compen|sates
  over|compen|sat|ed
  over|compen|sat|
    ing
over|compen|sa|tion
over|compen|sa|tory
over|confi|dence
over|confi|dent
over|confi|dent|ly
over|cook +s +ed
  +ing
over|cooked *adjective*
over|critic|al
over|critic|al|ly
over|crowd +s +ed
  +ing

over|crowd|ed
  adjective
over|crowd|ing *noun*
over|cut
  over|cuts
  over|cut
  over|cut|ting
over|cut|ting *noun*
over|deter|min|a|tion
  +s
over|deter|mine
  over|deter|mines
  over|deter|mined
  over|deter|min|ing
over|devel|op
  over|devel|ops
  over|devel|oped
  over|devel|op|ing
over|devel|op|ment
over|do (do to excess)
  over|does
  over|did
  over|done
  over|doing
  [☞ overdue]
over|done *adjective*
over|dosage
over|dose
  over|doses
  over|dosed
  over|dos|ing
over|draft +s
over|dramat|ic
over|drama|tize
  over|drama|tiz|es
  over|drama|tized
  over|drama|tiz|ing
over|draw
  over|draws
  over|drew
  over|drawn
  over|drawing
over|draw|er +s
over|drawn *adjective*
over|dress
  over|dress|es
  over|dressed
  over|dress|ing
over|dressed *adjective*
over|drink
  over|drinks
  over|drank
  over|drunk
  over|drink|ing
over|drive
over|dub
  over|dubs
  over|dubbed
  over|dub|bing
over|due (not yet paid,
  returned, delivered,
  etc.)
  [☞ overdo]
over|eager

over|eager|ly
over|eager|ness
over easy
over|eat
  over|eats
  over|ate
  over|eaten
  over|eat|ing
over|eat|er +s
over|eat|ing *noun*
over-educate
  over-educates
  over-educat|ed
  over-educat|ing
over-educat|ed
  adjective
over-elabor|ate
over-elabor|ate|ly
over-emotion|al
over-emotion|al|ly
over|empha|sis
over|empha|size
  over|empha|siz|es
  over|empha|sized
  over|empha|siz|ing
over|enthusi|asm
over|enthusi|as|tic
over|enthusi|as|tic|
    ally
over|esti|mate
  over|esti|mates
  over|esti|mat|ed
  over|esti|mat|ing
over|esti|ma|tion +s
over|excite
  over|excites
  over|excit|ed
  over|excit|ing
over|excit|ed
  adjective
over|excite|ment
over-exercise
  over-exercis|es
  over-exercised
  over-exercis|ing
over|exert +s +ed
  +ing
over|exer|tion
over|expand +s +ed
  +ing
over|expan|sion
over|expose
  over|expos|es
  over|exposed
  over|expos|ing
over|expo|sure +s
over|extend +s +ed
  +ing
over|extend|ed
  adjective
over|exten|sion +s
over|famil|iar
over|famili|ar|ity

over|feed
over|feeds
over|fed
over|feed|ing
over|fill +s +ed +ing
over|fine
over|fish
over|fish|es
over|fished
over|fish|ing
over|fish|ing noun
over|flight +s
over|flow +s +ed
+ing
over|fly
over|flies
over|flew
over|flown
over|fly|ing
over|fond
over|fond|ly
over|fond|ness
over|fulfil (use
overfulfill)
over|fulfils
over|ful|filled
over|fulfil|ling
over|fulfill +s +ed
+ing
over|fulfill|ment
over|fulfil|ment (use
overfulfillment)
over|full
over|gener|al|iz|
a|tion +s
over|gener|al|ize
over|gener|al|iz|es
over|gener|al|ized
over|gener|al|iz|ing
over|gener|ous
over|gener|ous|ly
over|glaze +s
over-govern +s +ed
+ing
over-governed
adjective
over-govern|ment
over|graze
over|graz|es
over|grazed
over|graz|ing
over|grazed adjective
over|graz|ing noun
over|ground
over|grow
over|grows
over|grew
over|grown
over|grow|ing
over|grown adjective
over|growth +s
over|hand

over|hang
over|hangs
over|hung
over|hang|ing
over|hang|ing
adjective
over|harvest +s +ed
+ing
over|harvest|ing
noun
over|hasti|ly
over|hasty
over|haul +s +ed
+ing
over|head +s
over|hear
over|hears
over|heard
over|hear|ing
over|heat +s +ed
+ing
over|heat|ed adjective
over|heat|ing noun
over|hype
over|hypes
over|hyped
over|hyp|ing
over|hyped adjective
Over|ijssel (province,
the Netherlands)
over|indulge
over|indul|ges
over|indulged
over|indul|ging
over|indul|gence +s
over|indul|gent
over|inflat|ed
over|issue
over|issues
over|issued
over|issu|ing
over|joyed
over|kill
over|laden
over|laid past & past
participle of overlay
over|lain past
participle of overlie
over|land
Over|land|er +s
over|lap
over|laps
over|lapped
over|lap|ping
over|lap|ping noun &
adjective
over-large
over|lay
• verb & noun (place
over; cover;
transparency;
Computing)

over|lays
over|laid
over|laying
• past tense of overlie
over|leaf
over|leap
over|leaps
over|leaped
or over|leapt
over|leaping
over-lever|age
over-lever|ages
over-lever|aged
over-lever|aging
over-lever|aged
adjective
over|lie (lie on top of)
over|lies
over|lay
over|lain
over|lying
over|load +s +ed
+ing
over|long
over|look +s +ed
+ing
over|look|er +s
over|lord +s
over|lord|ship +s
over|ly (excessively)
[☞ overlie]
over|lying adjective
over|man
• verb
over|mans
over|manned
over|man|ning
• noun
over|men
over|man|ning noun
over|mantel +s
over-many
over|master +s +ed
+ing
over|master|ing
adjective
over|match
over|match|es
over|matched
over|match|ing
over|mighty
over|much
over|night +s +ed
+ing
over|night|er +s
over-optimism
over-optimis|tic
over|pack +s +ed
+ing
over|pack|aged
over|pack|aging
over|paid adjective

over|paint +s +ed
+ing
over-particu|lar
over|pass
over|pass|es
over|pay
over|pays
over|paid
over|pay|ing
over|pay|ment +s
over|play +s +ed
+ing
over|plus
over|plus|es
over|popu|lat|ed
over|popu|la|tion
over|power +s +ed
+ing
over|power|ing
adjective
over|power|ing|ly
over-prescribe
over-prescribes
over-prescribed
over-prescrib|ing
over-prescrip|tion
over|price
over|prices
over|priced
over|pricing
over|priced adjective
over|print +s +ed
+ing
over|produce
over|produ|ces
over|produced
over|produ|cing
over|produc|tion +s
over|proof
over|protect|ed
adjective
over|protect|ive
over|quali|fied
over|ran
over|rate (esteem too
highly)
over|rates
over|rat|ed
over|rat|ing
[☞ overate]
over|rat|ed adjective
over|reach
over|reach|es
over|reached
over|reach|ing
over|reach|er +s
over|reach|ing noun &
adjective
over|react +s +ed
+ing
over|reac|tion +s

over|refine
  over|refines
  over|refined
  over|refin|ing
over|refine|ment
over|reli|ance
over|repre|sent +s
  +ed +ing
over|ride
  over|rides
  over|rode
  over|rid|den
  over|rid|ing
over|rid|ing *adjective*
over|ripe
over|ripe|ness
over-rotate
  over-rotates
  over-rotated
  over-rotating
over-rotation +s
over|ruff +s +ed
  +ing
over|rule
  over|rules
  over|ruled
  over|rul|ing
over|run
  over|runs
  over|ran
  over|run
  over|run|ning
over|sam|pling
over|saw
over-scrupu|lous
over|sea (foreign)
over|seas
over|see (supervise)
  over|sees
  over|saw
  over|seen
  over|see|ing
over|seer +s
over|sell
  over|sells
  over|sold
  over|sell|ing
over-sensitive
over-sensitive|ness
over|sensitiv|ity
over|set
  over|sets
  over|set
  over|set|ting
over|sew
  over|sews
  over|sewed
  over|sewn
  or over|sewed
  over|sew|ing
over|sexed
over|shadow +s +ed
  +ing
over|shirt +s

over|shoe +s
over|shoot
  over|shoots
  over|shot
  over|shoot|ing
over|shot *adjective*
over|side
over|sight +s
over|simpli|fi|ca|tion
  +s
over|simpli|fied
  adjective
over|simpli|fy
  over|simpli|fies
  over|simpli|fied
  over|simpli|fy|ing
over|size
over|sized
over|skate
  over|skates
  over|skated
  over|skat|ing
over|skirt +s
over|sleep
  over|sleeps
  over|slept
  over|sleep|ing
over|sold
over-solici|tous
over|soul
over|special|iz|a|tion
over|special|ize
  over|special|iz|es
  over|special|ized
  over|special|iz|ing
over|spend
  over|spends
  over|spent
  over|spend|ing
over|spend|er +s
over|spend|ing *noun*
over|spill +s
over|spread
  over|spreads
  over|spread
  over|spread|ing
over|staff +s +ed
  +ing
over|state
  over|states
  over|stat|ed
  over|stat|ing
over|state|ment +s
over|stay +s +ed
  +ing
over|steer +s +ed
  +ing
over|step
  over|steps
  over|stepped
  over|step|ping
over|stimu|late
  over|stimu|lates

  over|stimu|lat|ed
  over|stimu|lat|ing
over|stimu|la|tion
over|stock +s +ed
  +ing
over|storey +s
over|story (*use*
  overstorey)
  over|stories
over|strain +s +ed
  +ing
over|stress
  over|stress|es
  over|stressed
  over|stress|ing
over|stretch
  over|stretch|es
  over|stretched
  over|stretch|ing
over|stretched
  adjective
over|stuff +s +ed
  +ing
over|stuffed *adjective*
over|sub|scribe
  over|sub|scribes
  over|sub|scribed
  over|sub|scrib|ing
over|sub|scribed
  adjective
over|subtle
over|supply
  over|supplies
  over|supplied
  over|supply|ing
overt
over|take
  over|takes
  over|took
  over|tak|en
  over|tak|ing
over|task +s +ed
  +ing
over|tax
  over|tax|es
  over|taxed
  over|tax|ing
over-the-counter
over-the-top
over|throw
  over|throws
  over|threw
  over|thrown
  over|throw|ing
over|thrust +s
over|time +s
over|tire
  over|tires
  over|tired
  over|tiring
over|tired *adjective*
overt|ly
overt|ness
over|tone +s

over|took
over|top
  over|tops
  over|topped
  over|top|ping
over|train +s +ed
  +ing
over|trick +s
over|trump +s +ed
  +ing
over|ture +s
over|turn +s +ed
  +ing
over|use
  over|uses
  over|used
  over|using
over|value
  over|values
  over|valued
  over|valu|ing
over|view +s
over|water +s +ed
  +ing
over|ween|ing
over|ween|ing|ly
over|ween|ing|ness
over|weight +s +ed
  +ing
over|whelm +s +ed
  +ing
over|whelm|ing
  adjective
over|whelm|ing|ly
over|whelm|ing|ness
over|wind
  over|winds
  over|wound
  over|wind|ing
over|winter +s +ed
  +ing
over|work +s +ed
  +ing
over|worked *adjective*
over|write
  over|writes
  over|wrote
  over|writ|ten
  over|writ|ing
over|writ|ing *noun*
over|writ|ten
  adjective
over|wrought
over|zeal|ous
Ovid (Roman poet)
ovi|duct +s
ovi|duct|al
Oviedo (city, Spain)
ovi|form
ovine
ovi|par|ity
ovip|ar|ous
ovip|ar|ous|ly

ovi|posit
  ovi|posits
  ovi|posit|ed
  ovi|posit|ing
ovi|pos|ition
ovi|posit|or +s
ovoid +s
ovolo
  ovoli
ovo|tes|tis
  ovo|tes|tes
ovo|vivi|par|ity
ovo|vi|vip|ar|ous
ovu|lar
ovu|late
  ovu|lates
  ovu|lat|ed
  ovu|lat|ing
ovu|la|tion +s
ovu|la|tory
ovule +s
ovum
  ova
owe (be in debt)
  owes
  owed
  owing
Owen, Sir Rich|ard
  (English
  paleontologist)
Owen, Rob|ert (Welsh
  social reformer)
Owen, Wil|fred
  (English poet)
Owens, Jesse (US
  athlete)
Owen Sound (city &
  inlet, Canada)
owing adjective
owl +s
owl|ery
  owl|er|ies
owlet +s
owl|ish
owl|ish|ly
owl|ish|ness
owl-like
owly
own +s +ed +ing
owned adjective
owner +s
owner|less
owner|ship +s
own goal +s
owt (anything)
  [☞ out]
ox
  oxen
ox|al|ate +s
ox|al|ic
ox|al|is
  ox|al|is|es
ox|blood

ox|bow +s
Ox|bridge
ox cart +s
oxen plural of ox
  [☞ auxin]
Oxen|stier|na, Count
  Axel Gus|tafs|son
  (Swedish statesman)
Oxen|stjer|na, Count
  Axel Gus|tafs|son
  (= Oxenstierna)
oxer +s
ox-eye +s
ox-eyed
ox-eye daisy
  ox-eye dais|ies
Ox|ford (city &
  university, England;
  shirt)
ox|ford +s (shoe;
  cloth)
Ox|ford blue +s
  (Oxford-blue when
  preceding a noun)
Ox|ford|shire (county,
  England)
ox-hide +s
oxi|dant +s
oxi|dase +s
oxi|da|tion +s
oxi|da|tion|al
oxi|da|tive
ox|ide +s
oxi|diz|able
oxi|diz|a|tion +s
oxi|dize
  oxi|diz|es
  oxi|dized
  oxi|diz|ing
oxi|dized adjective
oxi|diz|er +s
ox|lip +s
Ox|on|ian +s
ox|peck|er +s
ox|tail +s
ox|ter +s
ox-tongue +s
Oxus (former name for
  Amu Darya River)
oxy|acetyl|ene
oxy|acid +s
oxy|gen
oxy|gen|ate
  oxy|gen|ates
  oxy|gen|at|ed
  oxy|gen|at|ing
oxy|gen|a|tion +s
oxy|gen|ator +s
oxy|gen|ic
oxy|gen|ous
oxy|hemo|glo|bin
oxy|mor|on +s
oxy|mor|on|ic

oxy|mor|on|ic|ally
oxy|tetra|cy|cline
oxy|to|cin +s
oxy|tone +s
oxy|trope +s
oy
oya|mel
oyer and ter|mi|ner
oyes (use oyez)
oyez
oys|ter +s +ed +ing
oyster|catch|er +s
oys|ter|ing noun
oyster|man
  oyster|men
oys|ter white +s
  (oyster-white when
  preceding a noun)
oy vey
Oz
Ozark +s (mountains,
  US)
Ozawa, Seiji
  (Japanese
  conductor)
ozo|cer|ite +s
ozo|ker|ite +s (use
  ozocerite)
ozone
ozone-friend|ly
ozon|ic
ozon|iz|a|tion +s
ozon|ize
  ozon|iz|es
  ozon|ized
  ozon|iz|ing
ozon|iz|er +s
Oz|zie +s (= Aussie:
  Australian)
  [☞ Ossi]

P

P
• (letter)
  P's
• (poise; proton)
  [☞ pee, pea]
p
• (letter)
  p's
• (penny, pence)
  [☞ pee, pea]
p. (page)
  pp.
PA (public address
  system)
  PAs

pa +s (father)
  [☞ pah, The Pas,
  pas]
paan (chewing leaf)
  [☞ pan, panne,
  pawn]
pa'anga +s
Paarl (town, South
  Africa)
PABA (para-
  aminobenzoic acid)
Pab|lum proprietary
  (cereal for infants)
pab|lum (insipid
  entertainment etc.)
pab|ulum
  (nourishment for the
  mind; insipid
  entertainment etc.)
PAC (political action
  committee)
  PACs
paca +s
pace (step etc.)
  paces
  paced
  pa|cing
pace (with due
  deference to)
pace car +s
pace|maker +s
pa|cer +s
pace|set|ter +s
pace-setting +s
pacey (use pacy)
  paci|er
  paci|est
pa|cha +s (Turkish
  title: use pasha)
  [☞ pasha]
Pach|el|bel, Jo|hann
  (German composer)
pa|chin|ko
pa|chi|si (ancient
  game)
  [☞ Parcheesi]
Pa|chu|ca (de Soto)
  (city, Mexico)
pachy|derm +s
pachy|der|ma|tous
pachy|san|dra +s
pachy|tene
paci|er
paci|est
Pa|cif|ic (ocean; in
  names of flora &
  fauna)
pa|cif|ic (tranquil)
pa|cif|ic|ally
paci|fi|ca|tion +s
paci|fi|ca|tory
paci|fi|er +s
paci|fism

paci|fist +s
paci|fis|tic
paci|fy
  paci|fies
  paci|fied
  paci|fy|ing
pa|cing +s *noun*
Pa|cino, Al (US actor)
pack +s +ed +ing
pack|able
pack|age
  pack|ages
  pack|aged
  pack|aging
pack|ager +s
pack|aging +s *noun*
packed *adjective*
pack|er +s
pack|et +s
packet|ize
  packet|iz|es
  packet|ized
  packet|iz|ing
packet-switched
pack|et switch|ing
pack horse +s
pack|ing
pack|ing house +s
pack rat +s
pack|sack +s
pack|saddle +s
pack train +s
pack trip +s
pact +s
pacy
  paci|er
  paci|est
pad
  pads
  pad|ded
  pad|ding
Pa|dang (city, Indonesia)
pad|ded *adjective*
pad|ding +s *noun*
pad|dle
  pad|dles
  pad|dled
  pad|dling
paddle|ball
paddle|boat +s
pad|dle boat|ing
pad|dler +s
paddle|wheel +s
paddle|wheel|er +s
pad|dling *noun & adjective*
pad|dock +s +ed +ing
Paddy *offensive* (Irishman)
Pad|dies
[☞ patty, Patti]

paddy (rice field; rice; rage)
  pad|dies
  [☞ patty]
paddy field +s
paddy wag|on +s
pade|mel|on +s
Pade|rew|ski, Ig|nacy Jan (Polish musician and statesman)
pad|lock +s +ed +ing
Padma (river, Bangladesh)
pa|douk +s
padre +s
pa|drone +s
pad Thai
Padua (city, Italy)
paean +s (song of praise)
  [☞ paeon, peon, pion]
pael|la +s
paeon +s (metrical foot)
  [☞ paean, peon, pion]
Pa|ga|lu (*former name for* Annobón, Equatorial Guinea)
Pagan (town, Burma)
  [☞ Peigan]
pa|gan +s (heathen)
Paga|nini, Nic|co|lò (Italian musician)
pagan|ism
Page, Pa|tri|cia Kath|leen ('P.K.') (Cdn writer)
  [☞ Paige]
page
  pages
  paged
  paging
pa|geant +s
pa|geant|ry
  pa|geant|ries
page|boy +s
pager +s
Paget, Sir James, 1st Bar|on|et (English pathologist)
page-turner +s
page-turning
pagin|al
pagin|ate
  pagin|ates
  pagin|at|ed
  pagin|at|ing
pagin|a|tion +s
paging *noun*
Pag|lia, Ca|mille Anna (US critic)

Pa|gnol, Mar|cel (French filmmaker)
pa|goda +s
PAH (polycyclic aromatic hydrocarbon)
  PAHs
pah *interjection*
  [☞ pa, pas]
Pa|hang (state, Malaysia)
Pah|lavi, Muham|mad Reza (1919–80; shah of Iran)
Pah|lavi, Reza (1878–1944; shah of Iran)
Pah|lavi (Persian writing system & language)
pa|hoe|hoe
paid (*past & past participle of* pay *in all senses except* smear a ship with tar; *adjective*)
  [☞ payed]
paid-up *adjective preceding a noun*
Paige, Leroy Rob|ert ('Satch|el') (US baseball player)
  [☞ Page]
pail +s (bucket)
  [☞ pale]
pail|ful +s
Pai|lin (town, Cambodia)
pail|lasse +s (*use* palliasse)
pail|lette +s
pain +s +ed +ing (hurt; effort)
  [☞ pane, Paine, Paine Towers]
Paine, Thom|as (English-born political writer)
pained *adjective* (expressing pain)
  [☞ paned]
Paine Tow|ers (peaks, Chile)
pain|ful
pain|ful|ly
pain|ful|ness
pain|kill|er +s
pain|kill|ing
pain|less
pain|less|ly
pain|less|ness
pains|tak|ing
pains|tak|ing|ly

pains|tak|ing|ness
paint +s +ed +ing
paint|able
paint|ball
paint|ball|er +s
paint|box
  paint|boxes
paint|brush
  paint|brush|es
paint-by-number
paint|ed *adjective*
paint|er +s
paint|er|li|ness
paint|er|ly
paint|ing +s *noun*
paint shop +s
paint stick +s
paint strip|per +s
paint|work
painty
  paint|i|er
  paint|i|est
pair
• (set of two; in 'au pair')
  plural pairs or pair
• (join in two)
  pairs
  paired
  pair|ing
  [☞ pare, pear, père]
pair bond +s +ed +ing
pair bond|ing *noun*
paired *adjective*
  [☞ pared-down]
pair|ing +s (set of two)
  [☞ paring]
pairs skat|er +s
pairs skat|ing
pair|wise
paisa
  paise
Pais|ley (town, Scotland)
Pais|ley, Ian Rich|ard Kyle (Northern Irish politician)
pais|ley +s
pa|ja|ma +s (*use* pyjama)
pak +s (package: *in commercial use*)
pa|keha
  plural pa|keha or pa|kehas
Paki +s *offensive*
Pak|istan (country, Asia)
Pak|istani +s
pa|kora +s

Pakse (town, Laos)
Pakxe (= Pakse, Laos)
pal (friend)
pals
palled
pal|ling
[☞ pall]
pal|ace +s (building)
[☞ Pallas]
pala|cin|ke
(= palacsinta)
plural pala|cin|ke
pala|csin|ta
plural pala|csin|ta
pal|adin +s
pal|ais
plural pal|ais
pal|an|keen +s (*use*
palanquin)
pal|an|quin +s
pal|at|abil|ity
pal|at|able
pal|at|able|ness
pal|at|ably
pal|at|al +s
pal|at|al|iz|a|tion +s
pal|at|al|ize
pal|at|al|iz|es
pal|at|al|ized
pal|at|al|iz|ing
pal|at|al|ly
pal|ate +s (roof of
mouth; taste)
[☞ palette, pallet]
pa|la|tial
pa|la|tial|ly
pal|at|in|ate +s
pal|at|ine +s
Palau (island group,
Pacific)
pa|lav|er +s +ed +ing
Pa|law|an (island, the
Philippines)
pa|laz|zo +s
Pale (former English
territory, Ireland &
France)
pale (lacking colour;
weak; stake;
boundary; district;
'beyond the pale';
Heraldry)
paler
palest
pales
paled
paling
[☞ pail]
palea
pa|leae
Pale|arc|tic
pale|face +s
pale|ly

Pa|lem|bang (city,
Indonesia)
pale|ness
Pa|len|que (ancient
Mayan city, Mexico)
paleo|anthro|po|
logic|al
paleo|anthro|pol|o|
gist +s
paleo|anthro|pol|ogy
paleo|botan|ic|al
paleo|botan|ist +s
paleo|botany
Paleo|cene
paleo|clima|tol|o|gist
+s
paleo|clima|tol|ogy
paleo|eco|logic|al
paleo|ecolo|gist +s
paleo|ecol|ogy
paleo|geog|raph|er
+s
paleo|geog|raphy
paleog|raph|er +s
paleo|graph|ic
paleo|graph|ic|al
paleo|graph|ic|al|ly
paleog|raphy
paleo|lith|ic
paleo|magnet|ic
paleo|magnet|ism
paleon|to|logic|al
paleon|tol|o|gist +s
paleon|tol|ogy
Paleo|zoic
Pa|ler|mo (city, Italy)
Pal|es|tine (territory,
Middle East)
Pal|es|tin|ian +s
pa|les|tra +s
Pal|es|trina,
Gio|van|ni Pier|luigi
da (Italian
composer)
pal|ette +s (board for
mixing paint; range
of colours, tones)
[☞ palate, pallet]
pal|ette knife
(*Painting*; blunt
kitchen knife)
pal|ette knives
[☞ pallet]
Paley, Wil|liam
(English theologian)
pal|frey +s
Pal|grave, Fran|cis
Tur|ner (English
writer)
Pali (language)
[☞ pally]
pali|mony
pal|imp|sest +s

pal|imp|ses|tic
pal|in|drome +s
pal|in|drom|ic
pal|in|drom|ist +s
pal|ing +s *noun*
pal|in|gen|esis
pal|in|gen|etic
pal|in|ode +s
pali|sade +s
Pali|sades (cliffs, US)
pal|ish
Palk (strait between
Sri Lanka & India)
pall +s +ed +ing
(coffin covering;
shoulder band;
Heraldry; become
uninteresting)
[☞ pal, pawl, pol]
pal|la|dia
Pal|la|dian
Pal|la|dian|ism
Pal|la|dio, An|drea
(Italian architect)
pal|la|dium
pal|la|dia
Pal|las (*Greek Myth*;
Astronomy)
[☞ palace]
pall|bear|er +s
pal|let +s (mattress,
bed; transporting
platform, skid;
sculptor's blade;
projection; *for* board
for mixing paint *or*
range of colours,
tones, etc. *use*
palette)
[☞ palate, palette
knife]
pal|let|ize
pal|let|iz|es
pal|let|ized
pal|let|iz|ing
pal|lia
pal|li|asse +s
pal|li|ate
pal|li|ates
pal|li|at|ed
pal|li|at|ing
pal|li|a|tion
pal|li|a|tive
pal|li|a|tive|ly
pal|li|a|tor +s
pal|lid
pal|lid|ity
pal|lid|ly
pal|lid|ness
Pal|liser, Hugh
(English naval
officer)

Pal|liser, John (Irish
sportsman &
explorer)
pal|lium
pal|liums or pal|lia
pall-mall (game)
[☞ pell-mell]
pal|lor
pally (friendly)
pal|li|er
pal|li|est
[☞ Pali]
palm +s +ed +ing
(tree, leaf; hand;
pass; conceal)
[☞ pom]
pal|ma|ceous
**Palma (de
Mal|lor|ca)** (capital
of the Balearic
Islands)
[☞ Palme]
pal|mar (of the palm
of the hand)
Pal|mas (town, Brazil)
pal|mate
pal|mat|ed
pal|mate|ly
pal|ma|tion +s
Palm Beach (town,
US)
palm|corder +s
**Palme, (Sven) Olof
Jo|a|chim** (Swedish
prime minister)
[☞ Palma]
palmed *adjective*
Palme d'Or
Palmes d'Or
**Palmer, Ar|nold
Dan|iel** (US golfer)
Palmer, Ed|ward
(Cdn politician)
palmer +s (pilgrim;
monk; fly)
[☞ palmar]
**Palmer|ston, Henry
John Tem|ple, 3rd
Vis|count** (English
prime minister)
Palmer|ston North
(city, New Zealand)
pal|mette +s
pal|metto +s
palm|ful +s
pal|mier[1] +s (pastry)
palm|i|er[2] +s
comparative of
palmy
palm|i|est
palm|ist +s
palm|is|try
palmi|tate +s

pal|mit|ic
palm read|er +s
Palm Springs (resort, US)
Palm Sun|day
palm|top +s
palm wine +s
palmy (of palms; prosperous)
palm|i|er
palm|i|est
[☞ pommy]
Pal|myra (ancient city, Syria)
pal|myra +s
Palo Alto (city, US)
Palo|mar (mountain, US)
palo|mino +s
pa|loo|ka +s
palo|verde +s
palp +s
palp|abil|ity
palp|able
palp|ably
palp|al
pal|pate
pal|pates
pal|pat|ed
pal|pat|ing
pal|pa|tion
pal|pe|bral
pal|pi|tant
pal|pi|tate
pal|pi|tates
pal|pi|tat|ed
pal|pi|tat|ing
pal|pi|ta|tion +s
pal|pus
palpi
palsa +s
pals|grave +s
pal|sied adjective
palsy
pal|sies
pal|sied
palsy|ing
palsy-walsy
palsy-walsier
palsy-walsiest
pal|ter +s +ed +ing
pal|ter|er +s
pal|tri|ness
pal|try
pal|tri|er
pal|tri|est
paly|no|logic|al
paly|nol|o|gist +s
paly|nol|ogy
Pamir +s (mountains, Asia)
pampa +s

pam|pas grass
pam|pas grass|es
pam|per +s +ed +ing
pam|pered adjective
pam|per|ing noun
pamph|let +s +ed +ing
pamph|let|eer +s +ed +ing
pamph|let|eer|ing noun
Pam|phyl|ia (ancient region, Asia Minor)
Pam|phyl|ian +s
Pam|plona (city, Spain)
Pan (Greek Myth)
pan (cooking vessel; basin; gunlock; face; criticize; punch; search for gold; swing camera; for chewing leaf use paan)
pans
panned
pan|ning
[☞ panne]
pana|cea +s
pana|cean
pa|nache +s
Pa|naji (city, India)
Pan|ama (country & canal, Central America)
Pan|ama City (capital of Panama)
pan|ama hat +s
Pan|ama|nian +s
pan and scan (pan-and-scan when preceding a noun)
pana|tela +s
pana|tel|la +s (use panatela)
Panay (island, the Philippines)
pan-broil +s +ed +ing
pan|cake
pan|cakes
pan|caked
pan|cak|ing
pan|cetta
pan|chayat +s
Pan|chen lama +s
pan|chro|mat|ic
pan|creas
pancre|as|es
pan|creat|ic
pan|crea|tin
pan|crea|titis
panda +s

pan|dan +s
pan|danus
pan|danus|es
Pan|darus (Greek Myth)
pan|dect +s
pan|dem|ic +s
pan|de|mon|ium
pan|der +s +ed +ing
pan|der|er +s
pan|der|ing noun
P & H (postage & handling)
Pan|dit, Vijaya Lak|shmi (Indian politician)
pan|dit +s (Hindu learned in Sanskrit & Indian philosophy: use pundit)
[☞ pundit]
pan|dit|ry (use punditry)
P & L (profits & loss)
Pan|dora (Greek Myth)
Pan|dora's box
pane +s (glass; stamps)
[☞ pain, Paine, Paine Towers]
paned adjective (with glass)
[☞ pained]
pa|neer +s
pan|egyr|ic +s
pan|egyric|al
pan|egyr|ist +s
pan|egyr|ize
pan|egyr|iz|es
pan|egyr|ized
pan|egyr|iz|ing
panel
pan|els
pan|elled
pan|el|ling
pan|el|ling +s noun
pan|el|list +s
pan|et|tone
pan|et|toni
[☞ Panneton]
pan|fish
plural pan|fish
pan|fish|ing
pan-fried adjective
pan-fry
pan-fries
pan-fried
pan-fry|ing
pan|ful +s
pang +s
panga +s
Pan|gaea (continent)
Pan|glos|sian

Pang|nir|tung (hamlet, Canada; hat)
pan|go|lin +s
pan|gram +s
pan|handle
pan|han|dles
pan|han|dled
pan|hand|ling
pan|hand|ler +s
panic
pan|ics
pan|icked
pan|ick|ing
pan|icky
pan|icle +s
pan|icled
panic-strick|en
panic-struck
pan|ino
pan|ini
pan|jan|drum +s
Pan|jim (= Panaji, India)
Pank|hurst, Chris|ta|bel (English suffragist)
Pank|hurst, Em|me|line (English suffragist)
Pank|hurst, (Es|telle) Syl|via (English suffragist)
pan|leuc|o|penia (use panleukopenia)
pan|leuk|o|penia
pan|like
Pan|mun|jom (village, Korea)
panne (velvet)
[☞ paan]
Panne|ton, Phil|lipe (Cdn writer)
[☞ panettone]
pan|nier +s
Pan|non|ia (ancient country, Europe)
pan|op|lied
pan|oply
pan|op|lies
pan|op|tic
pan|orama +s
pan|oram|ic
pan|oram|ic|ally
pan pipe +s
pan|sexual
pan|sexual|ity
pansy
pan|sies
pant +s +ed +ing
pan|ta|lets
pan|ta|lettes (use pantalets)

Pan|ta|loon (Italian character)
pan|ta|loons
Panta|nal (region, Brazil)
pan|tech|nicon +s
Pan|tel|le|ria (Italian island)
pan|the|ism
pan|the|ist +s
pan|the|is|tic
pan|the|is|tic|al
pan|the|is|tic|al|ly
Pan|the|on (in Rome)
pan|the|on +s (in general use)
Pan|ther (waterfall, Canada)
pan|ther +s
pant|ies
pan|tile +s
pan|tiled
pant|ing|ly
panto +s
panto|graph +s
panto|graph|ic
panto|mime
panto|mimes
panto|mimed
panto|mim|ing
panto|mim|ic
panto|then|ic
pan|try
pan|tries
pants
pant|suit +s
panty
pant|ies
panty|hose
panty|waist
pan|zer +s
pan|zerot|to
pan|zerot|ti
pap +s
papa +s (father)
[☞ pawpaw, poppa]
pap|acy
pap|acies
Papa|dop|oul|os, George (Greek prime minister)
papa|dum +s (use pappadum)
Pap|ago
plural Pap|ago or Pap|agos
pa|pain
papal
papal|ly
Papal States (in Italy)
Pap|an|dreou, An|dreas George

(Greek prime minister)
pap|ar|azzo
pap|ar|azzi
papaw +s (tree, fruit: use pawpaw)
pa|paya +s
Pape|ete (capital of French Polynesia)
Papen, Franz von (German Chancellor)
paper +s +ed +ing (writing or printing material; wallpaper)
[☞ papier mâché]
paper|back +s
paper|bark +s
paper|board +s
paper boy +s
paper chase +s
paper clip +s noun
paper-clip verb
paper-clips
paper-clipped
paper-clipping
paper|er +s
paper girl +s
paper|hang|er +s
paper|less
paper|maker +s
paper|making
paper mill +s
paper-pusher +s
paper-pushing
paper-thin
paper tow|el +s
paper|weight +s
paper|work
paper|work|er +s
papery
Paph|la|gonia (ancient region, Asia Minor)
Paph|la|gon|ian +s
papier mâché (paper mixed with glue)
pa|pil|ion|aceous
pap|il|la
pap|il|lae
pap|il|lary
pap|il|late
pap|il|loma
pap|il|lomas or pap|il|lo|mata
pap|il|lon
pap|il|lose
Pap|ineau, Louis-Joseph (Cdn politician)
Papineau-Couture, Jean (Cdn composer & instructor)
pap|ism

pap|ist +s
pap|is|try
pa|poose +s (child)
[☞ pappus, pappose]
pap|pa|dum +s
pap|par|delle
pap|pose adjective (of plant hairs)
[☞ papoose, pappus]
Pap|pus (Greek mathematician)
pap|pus noun (plant hairs)
pappi
[☞ papoose, pappose]
pappy
pap|pies
pap|pier
pap|pi|est
pap|rika +s
pap|rikas (plural of paprika; for stew use paprikash)
pap|ri|kash
Pap smear +s
Papua (region, Papua New Guinea)
Pap|uan +s
Papua New Guinea (country, Oceania)
Papua New Guin|ean +s
pap|ula (= papule)
papu|lae or papu|las
papu|lar
pap|ule +s
papu|lose
papyr|o|logic|al
papyr|ol|o|gist +s
papyr|ol|ogy
pa|pyr|us
pa|pyri
par (average; equality; Golf; face value)
pars
parred
par|ring
[☞ parr]
Pará (state, Brazil)
para +s
para|bio|sis
para|bio|ses
para|biot|ic
par|able +s
para|bola +s
para|bol|ic
para|bol|ic|ally
para|bol|oid +s
para|bol|oid|al

Para|cel +s (islands, China Sea)
Para|cel|sian
Para|cel|sus (Swiss physician)
para|ceta|mol +s
para|chute
para|chutes
para|chut|ed
para|chut|ing
para|chut|ist +s
Para|clete
pa|rade
pa|rades
pa|rad|ed
pa|rad|ing
pa|rad|er +s
para|di|chloro|ben| zene
para|did|dle
para|did|dles
para|did|dled
para|did|dling
para|digm +s
para|dig|mat|ic
para|dig|mat|ic|ally
para|dis|aical (= paradisiacal)
para|disal
para|dise
para|dis|iacal
para|dis|ical
para|dox
para|dox|es
para|dox|ical
para|dox|ical|ly
par|af|fin +s
para|glide
para|glides
para|glid|ed
para|glid|ing
para|glid|er +s
para|glid|ing noun
para|goge +s
para|gogic
para|gon +s
para|graph +s +ed +ing
para|graph|ic
Para|guay (country, S America)
Para|guay|an +s
Para|íba (state, Brazil)
para|keet +s
para|lan|guage
par|alde|hyde
para|legal +s
para|lei|pom|ena (use paralipomena)
para|leip|sis (use paralipsis)
para|leip|sis|es
para|li|pom|ena

para|lip|sis
  para|lip|sis|es
par|al|lac|tic
par|al|lax
  par|al|lax|es
par|al|lel +s +ed +ing
parallel|epi|ped +s
par|al|lel|ism +s
par|al|lelo|gram +s
par|alo|gism +s
par|alo|gist +s
par|alo|gize
  par|alo|giz|es
  par|alo|gized
  par|alo|giz|ing
Para|lym|pi|an +s
Para|lym|pic +s
para|lys|a|tion +s
  (*use* paralyzation)
para|lyse (*use*
  paralyze)
  para|lys|es
  para|lysed
  para|lys|ing
para|lys|ing|ly (*use*
  paralyzingly)
par|aly|sis
  par|aly|ses
para|lytic +s
para|lytic|ally
para|lyz|a|tion +s
para|lyze
  para|lyz|es
  para|lyzed
  para|lyz|ing
para|lyz|ing|ly
para|magnet|ic
para|magnet|ism +s
Para|mar|ibo (capital
  of Suriname)
para|meci|um
  para|mecia or
  para|meci|ums
para|med|ic +s
para|medic|al
par|am|eter +s
param|eter|iz|a|tion
  +s
param|eter|ize
  param|eter|iz|es
  param|eter|ized
  param|eter|iz|ing
para|met|ric
param|et|riz|a|tion
  +s (*use*
  parameterization)
param|et|rize (*use*
  parameterize)
  param|et|riz|es
  param|et|rized
  param|et|riz|ing
para|mil|itary
  para|mil|itar|ies

par|amo +s
para|mount
para|mount|cy
para|mount|ly
par|amour +s
Paraná (city,
  Argentina; state,
  Brazil; river,
  S America)
  [☞ piranha]
par|ang +s
para|noia +s
para|noiac +s *noun &*
  adjective
para|noiac|ally
para|noic *adjective*
para|noid +s
para|normal
para|pente +s
para|pet +s
par|aph +s
para|pher|nalia
para|phras|able
para|phrase
  para|phras|es
  para|phrased
  para|phras|ing
para|phras|tic
para|plegia
para|plegic +s
para|profes|sion|al
  +s
para|psycho|logic|al
para|psych|ol|o|gist
  +s
para|psych|ol|ogy
para|quat
para|sail +s +ed +ing
para|sail|ing *noun*
para|selene
  para|sel|enae
para|site +s
para|sit|ic
para|sit|ic|al
para|sit|ic|ally
para|siti|cide +s
para|sit|ism
para|sit|iz|a|tion
para|sit|ize
  para|sit|iz|es
  para|sit|ized
  para|sit|iz|ing
para|sit|oid +s
para|sit|o|logic|al
para|sit|ol|o|gist +s
para|sit|ol|ogy
para|sol +s
para|statal +s
para|sympa|thet|ic
para|synth|esis
para|syn|thet|ic
para|tac|tic

para|tac|tic|ally
para|taxis
pa|ratha +s
para|thion
para|thyroid +s
para|troop +s
para|troop|er +s
para|typhoid
para|vane +s
par|boil +s +ed +ing
par|buckle
  par|buckles
  par|buckled
  par|buck|ling
Par|cae (*Roman Myth*)
par|cel
  par|cels
  par|celled
  par|cel|ling
parch
  parch|es
  parched
  parch|ing
parched *adjective*
Par|chee|si *proprietary*
  (board game)
  [☞ pachisi]
parch|ment +s
pard +s
pard|ner +s (partner)
  [☞ pardoner]
par|don +s +ed +ing
par|don|able
par|don|ably
par|don|er +s
  (distributor of
  pardons)
  [☞ pardner]
pare (trim, cut off)
  pares
  pared
  paring
  [☞ pair, pear, *père*]
pared-down
pare|gor|ic +s
par|en|chyma
par|en|chym|al
par|en|chyma|tous
par|ens pat|riae
Pa|rent, Simon-
  Napoleon (Cdn
  politician)
par|ent +s +ed +ing
par|ent|age +s
par|ent|al
par|ent|al|ly
par|en|ter|al
par|en|ter|al|ly
par|en|the|sis
  par|en|the|ses
par|en|the|size
  par|en|the|siz|es

par|en|the|sized
par|en|the|siz|ing
par|en|thet|ic
par|en|thet|ic|al
par|en|thet|ic|al|ly
parent|hood
par|ent|ing *noun*
parent-in-law
  parents-in-law
parent-teacher
  as|so|ci|a|tion +s
parer +s
par|esis
  par|eses
par|es|the|sia
  par|es|the|siae
par|etic
Par|eto, Vil|fredo
  Fred|erico Damaso
  (Italian economist)
par|eve
par ex|cel|lence
par|fait +s
par|fleche +s
parge
  par|ges
  parged
  par|ging
parget
  par|gets
  par|get|ed
  par|get|ing
par|ging *noun*
par|heli|acal
par|helic
par|heli|on (sun dog)
  par|helia
  [☞ perihelion]
pa|riah +s
pa|ri|et|al
pari|mutu|el +s
paring +s (pared
  portion; act of
  cutting; in 'paring
  knife')
  [☞ pairing]
pari passu
Paris (capital of
  France; town,
  Canada; *Greek Myth*)
Paris, Mat|thew
  (English chronicler)
par|ish (ecclesiastical
  & administrative
  district)
  par|ish|es
  [☞ perish]
pa|rish|ion|er +s
par|ish pump
  (parish-pump *when*
  preceding a noun)
Paris|ian +s (person
  or thing of Paris)

Paris|ienne +s
(woman of Paris)
par|ity
  par|ities
Pari|zeau, Jacques
(Cdn politician)
Park, Mungo (Scottish
explorer)
Park, Nick (English
animator)
park +s +ed +ing
par|ka +s
park|ade +s
park-and-ride
park belt +s
Park Chung Hee
(South Korean
statesman)
Par|ker, Charles
Chris|to|pher
('Char|lie') (US
saxophonist)
Par|ker, Dor|othy
Roths|child (US
humorist)
Par|ker, Mat|thew
(Archbishop of
Canterbury)
Par|ker House roll +s
park|ette +s (small
park)
park|i|er
park|i|est
par|kin
park|ing *noun*
Par|kin|son, Cyril
North|cote (English
historian)
par|kin|son|ian +s
Par|kin|son|ism
Par|kinson's dis|ease
Par|kinson's law
park|land +s
park-like
Parks|ville (city,
Canada)
park|way +s
parky
  park|i|er
  park|i|est
par|lance
par|lay +s +ed +ing
(exploit
circumstances;
Gambling)
  [☞ **parley**]
Parl|by, Mary Irene
(Cdn labour leader)
par|ley +s +ed +ing
(informal truce)
  [☞ **parlay**]
par|lia|ment +s

par|lia|men|tar|ian
+s
par|lia|ment|ary
Par|lia|ment Hill (in
Ottawa)
parlor +s (*use*
parlour)
par|lour +s
parlour|maid +s
par|lous
par|lous|ly
par|lous|ness
Parma (city, Italy)
Par|meni|des (Greek
philosopher)
Par|me|san
parmi|giana (made
with Parmesan
cheese)
  [☞ **parmigiano**]
Parmi|gian|ino
(Italian painter)
Parmi|giano
(= Parmigianino,
Italian painter)
parmi|giano
(Parmesan cheese)
  [☞ **parmigiana**]
Par|nas|sian +s
Par|nas|sus
(mountain, Greece)
Par|nell, Charles
Stew|art (Irish
nationalist)
Par|nell|ite +s
pa|ro|chi|al
pa|ro|chi|al|ism +s
pa|ro|chi|al|ity
pa|ro|chi|al|ly
par|od|ic
par|od|ic|ally
par|od|ist +s
par|od|is|tic
par|ody
  par|od|ies
  par|od|ied
  par|ody|ing
par|ol +s (made by
word of mouth;
declaration)
  [☞ **parole**]
par|ole (release of a
prisoner; individual's
linguistic behaviour)
  par|oles
  par|oled
  par|ol|ing
  [☞ **parol**]
par|olee +s
par|ono|masia +s
paro|nym +s
par|onym|ous
Paros (Greek island)

par|otid +s
par|ot|itis
Par|ou|sia
par|ox|ysm +s
par|oxys|mal
par|oxy|tone +s
par|quet (flooring)
  par|quets
  par|queted
  par|quet|ing
  [☞ **parkette**]
par|quet|ry
Parr, Cath|er|ine (wife
of Henry VIII)
Parr, John (British
colonial
administrator)
parr (young salmon)
  plural **parr** or **parrs**
  [☞ **par**]
parri|cid|al
parri|cide +s
par|rot +s +ed +ing
parrot|fish
  plural **parrot|fish** or
  parrot|fishes
Parry (sound, channel
& islands, Canada)
  [☞ **Perry**]
Parry, Sir Wil|liam
Ed|ward (English
explorer)
  [☞ **Perry**]
parry (ward off; deal
with)
  par|ries
  par|ried
  parry|ing
  [☞ **perry, pari**
  passu]
Parry Sound (town,
Canada)
parse
  pars|es
  parsed
  pars|ing
par|sec +s
Par|see +s (*use* Parsi)
pars|er +s
Par|si +s
parsi|moni|ous
parsi|moni|ous|ly
parsi|moni|ous|ness
parsi|mony
pars|ley
pars|leyed
pars|nip +s
par|son +s
par|son|age +s
par|son|ical
Par|sons, Sir Charles
Al|ger|non (English
engineer)

Par|sons, Tal|cott (US
sociologist)
part +s +ed +ing
par|take
  par|takes
  par|took
  par|taken
  par|tak|ing
par|taker +s
part|er +s (thing
divided into parts)
par|terre +s (garden;
ground floor)
par|theno|gen|esis
par|theno|gen|etic
par|theno|gen|etic|
               ally
Par|the|non (temple,
Athens)
Par|thia (ancient
Asian kingdom)
Par|thian +s
par|tial +s
par|tial|ity
par|tial|ly
par|tial|ness
Par|tici|pac|tion
(organization)
par|tici|pac|tion
(exercise)
par|tici|pant +s
par|tici|pate
  par|tici|pates
  par|tici|pat|ed
  par|tici|pat|ing
  par|tici|pa|tion
  par|tici|pa|tive
par|tici|pa|tor +s
par|tici|pa|tory
par|ti|cip|ial *adjective*
par|ti|cip|ial|ly
par|ti|ciple +s *noun*
par|ticle +s
par|ticle|board +s
parti-colored (*use*
parti-coloured)
parti-coloured
par|ticu|lar +s
par|ticu|lar|ism
par|ticu|lar|ist +s
par|ticu|lar|is|tic
par|ticu|lar|ity
  par|ticu|lar|ities
par|ticu|lar|iz|a|tion
+s
par|ticu|lar|ize
  par|ticu|lar|iz|es
  par|ticu|lar|ized
  par|ticu|lar|iz|ing
par|ticu|lar|ly
par|ticu|late +s
part|ier +s
part|ing +s *noun*

parti pris
Parti Qué|bé|cois
Parti Rouge
par|ti|san +s
par|ti|san|ship
par|tita
  par|titas or par|tite
par|tite
par|ti|tion +s
par|ti|tioned
par|ti|tion|er +s
par|ti|tion|ist +s
par|ti|tive +s
par|ti|tive|ly
part|ly
part|ner +s +ed +ing
part|ner|ing *noun*
part|ner|less
part|ner|ship +s
par|took
part owner +s
Par|tridge (island,
  Canada)
par|tridge
  plural par|tridge or
  par|tridges
par|tridge|berry
  par|tridge|ber|ries
part-skim
part-song +s
part-time
part-timer +s
par|turi|ent
par|tur|ition +s
part|way
party
  par|ties
  par|tied
  party|ing
  [☞ parti-coloured,
  parti pris, Parti
  Québécois, Parti
  Rouge]
party|er +s (*use*
  partier)
party-goer +s
party|ing +s
party-poop +s
party-pooper +s
party-pooping
par|ure +s
Par|vati (*Hinduism*)
parve (*use* pareve)
par|venu +s
par|vis
  par|vis|es
par|vise +s (*use*
  parvis)
parvo|virus
  parvo|virus|es
Pas, The (town,
  Canada)

pas (dance step)
  plural pas
Pasa|dena (city, US)
Pas|cal, Blaise
  (French
  mathematician &
  philosopher)
Pas|cal (*Computing*)
pas|cal +s (unit of
  pressure)
pas|chal (of Easter or
  Passover)
pas de chat
  plural pas de chat
pas de deux
  plural pas de deux
pas de quatre
  plural pas de quatre
pas de trois
  plural pas de trois
pa|sha +s (Turkish
  title; powerful
  person)
pash|ka (dessert: *use*
  paska)
  [☞ paska]
pashm
Pash|to
Pasi|phaë (*Greek
  Myth*)
paska (bread; dessert)
pas|kha (dessert: *use*
  paska)
  [☞ paska]
paso doble +s
Paso|lini, Pier Paolo
  (Italian filmmaker)
pasque flower +s
pas|quin|ade +s
pass
  pass|es
  passed
  pass|ing
pass|able (adequate;
  unobstructed)
  [☞ passible]
pass|able|ness
pass|ably
pas|sa|caglia +s
pas|sage
  pas|sages
  pas|saged
  pas|sa|ging
pas|sage|way +s
pas|sage|work
Pas|sama|quoddy
  (people, language;
  bay, Canada)
  plural
  Pas|sama|quoddy
pas|sant
pass|band +s
pass|book +s

pass card +s
Pas|schen|daele
  (battle site, Belgium)
passé
passed *past & past
  participle of* pass
  [☞ past]
passed ball +s
passed pawn +s
pas|sel +s
passe|ment|erie +s
pas|sen|ger +s
pas|senger-mile +s
passe-partout +s
pass|er +s
passer|by
  passers|by
pas|ser|ine +s
pas|si|bil|ity
pas|sible (capable of
  suffering)
  [☞ passable]
pas|sim
pass|ing +s *noun &
  adjective*
pass|ing|ly
Pas|sion (*Christianity*)
pas|sion +s
  (enthusiasm)
pas|sion|al +s
pas|sion|ate
pas|sion|ate|ly
pas|sion|ate|ness
pas|sion fruit
  plural pas|sion fruit
  or pas|sion fruits
pas|sion|less
Pas|sion|tide
pas|siv|ate
  pas|siv|ates
  pas|siv|at|ed
  pas|siv|at|ing
pas|siv|a|tion
pas|sive
passive-aggres|sive
pas|sive|ly
pas|sive|ness
pas|siv|ity
pass-key +s
Pas|sos, John
  Roder|igo Dos (US
  novelist)
Pass|over +s
pass|port +s
pass rush
pass rush|er +s
pass-rushing
pass-through +s
pass time *verb*
  passes time
  passed time
  pass|ing time
  [☞ pastime]

pass|word +s
Passy, Fré|dé|ric
  (French economist)
past +s (gone by;
  former time; beyond;
  Grammar)
  [☞ passed]
pasta +s
paste
  pastes
  pasted
  past|ing
paste|board +s
pas|tel
pastel|ist +s (*use*
  pastellist)
pastel|list +s
pas|tern +s
Pas|ter|nak, Boris
  Leonid|ovich
  (Russian writer)
paste-up +s
Pas|teur, Louis
  (French
  bacteriologist)
pas|teur|iz|a|tion
pas|teur|ize
  pas|teur|iz|es
  pas|teur|ized
  pas|teur|iz|ing
pas|teur|iz|er
pas|tic|cio +s
pas|tiche
  pas|tich|es
  pas|tiched
  pas|tich|ing
pas|ti|cheur +s
pasti|er
pasti|est
pas|tille +s
pas|ti|ly
pas|time +s *noun*
  (hobby etc.)
pas|ti|ness
past|ing +s *noun*
pas|tis
  plural pas|tis
past|ness
pas|tor +s +ed +ing
  (minister; starling)
  [☞ Pasteur]
pas|tor|al +s (play or
  poem; of herds; of a
  pastor; used for
  pasture)
  [☞ pastorale]
pas|tor|ale (musical
  play or composition)
  pas|tor|ales or
  pas|tor|ali
pas|tor|al|ism
pas|tor|al|ist +s
pas|tor|al|ly

pas|tor|ate +s
pas|tor|ship +s
pas|trami
pas|try
  pas|tries
pas|tur|age +s
pas|ture (land; graze)
  pas|tures
  pas|tured
  pas|tur|ing
  [☞ Pasteur]
pasty
  pasti|er
  pasti|est
  past|ies
PA system +s
pat (slap gently;
  stroke; dab;
  thoroughly known;
  apt; facile; in 'stand
  pat', 'down pat')
  pats
  pat|ted
  pat|ting
  [☞ pâte]
pata|gium
  pata|gia
Pata|gonia (region,
  S America)
Pata|gon|ian +s
Pa|tali|putra (former
  name for Patna,
  India)
patch
  patch|es
  patched
  patch|ing
patch cord +s
patch|er +s
patch|i|ly
patch|i|ness
patch|ouli
patch|work +s +ed
  +ing
patchy
  patch|i|er
  patch|i|est
pat-down +s
pate +s (head)
pâte +s (paste for
  making porcelain)
pâté +s (food)
pâté de foie gras
  pâtés de foie gras
pa|tel|la
  pa|tel|las or
  pa|tel|lae
pa|tel|lar
pa|tel|late
paten +s (shallow
  dish; circular plate)
  [☞ patten, Patton,
  Paton]
pat|en|cy

pat|ent +s +ed +ing
pat|ent|abil|ity
pat|ent|able
pat|en|tee +s
pat|ent leath|er +s
  (patent-leather when
  preceding a noun)
pat|ent|ly
pat|ent|or +s
Pater, Wal|ter
  Hor|atio (English
  essayist)
pater +s
pater|famil|ias
  patres|famil|ias
pa|ter|nal
pa|ter|nal|ism
pa|ter|nal|ist +s
pa|ter|nal|is|tic
pa|ter|nal|is|tic|ally
pa|ter|nal|ly
pa|ter|nity
pater|noster +s
path +s
Pa|than +s
path-breaker +s
path-breaking
Pathé, Charles
  (French film pioneer)
pa|thet|ic
pa|thet|ic|ally
Path|find|er +s
  (Scouting)
path|find|er +s
  (trailblazer; aircraft
  pilot)
path|less
patho|gen +s
patho|gen|esis
patho|gen|etic
patho|gen|ic
patho|gen|icity
path|ogeny
patho|logic
patho|logic|al
patho|logic|al|ly
path|ol|o|gist +s
path|ol|ogy
  path|ol|o|gies
pa|thos
path|way +s
pa|tience
pa|tient +s
pa|tient|ly
pa|tina +s
pat|in|ated
pat|in|a|tion +s
pat|io +s
pa|tis|ser|ie +s
patly
Pat|mos (island,
  Greece)

Patna (city, India)
pat|ness
pa|tois
  plural pa|tois
Paton, Alan Stew|art
  (South African writer
  & politician)
  [☞ Patton]
pa|toot +s
pa|toot|ie +s
Pat|ras (city, Greece)
patri|arch +s
patri|arch|al
patri|arch|al|ist +s
patri|arch|al|ly
patri|arch|ate +s
patri|arch|ism +s
patri|archy
  patri|arch|ies
patri|ate
  patri|ates
  patri|at|ed
  patri|at|ing
patri|a|tion +s
pa|tri|cian +s
pa|trici|ate
  pa|trici|ates
  pa|trici|at|ed
  pa|trici|at|ing
patri|cid|al
patri|cide +s
Pat|rick (saint)
patri|lin|eal
patri|lin|eal|ly
patri|local
patri|local|ity
patri|mon|ial
patri|mony
  patri|mon|ies
Pa|tri|ot +s (missile)
  [☞ Patriote]
pa|tri|ot +s
Pa|triote +s
  (supporter of
  Papineau)
  [☞ Patriot]
patri|ot|ic
patri|ot|ic|ally
pa|triot|ism
pa|tris|tic +s
Pa|troc|lus (Greek
  Myth)
pa|trol
  pa|trols
  pa|trolled
  pa|trol|ling
pa|trol|ler +s
patrol|man
  patrol|men
pa|tron +s
pa|tron|age
pa|tron|al

pa|tron|ess
  pa|tron|ess|es
pa|tron|iz|a|tion
pa|tron|ize
  pa|tron|iz|es
  pa|tron|ized
  pa|tron|iz|ing
pa|tron|iz|er +s
pa|tron|iz|ing
  adjective
pa|tron|iz|ing|ly
patro|nym|ic +s
pa|troon +s
patsy
  pat|sies
Pat|taya (resort,
  Thailand)
pat|ten +s (shoe)
  [☞ paten, Patton,
  Paton, patent
  leather]
pat|ter +s +ed +ing
pat|tern +s +ed +ing
pat|tern|ing +s noun
pat|tern|less
Pat|ter|son, Wal|ter
  (British colonial
  administrator)
Pat|ter|son, Wil|liam
  John (Cdn politician)
Patti, Adel|ina
  (Spanish-born Italian
  singer)
  [☞ patty, Paddy]
pat|tie +s (small cake,
  candy, pie etc.: use
  patty)
  [☞ paddy]
Pat|ti|son, James
  Allan (Cdn
  businessman)
Pat|ton, George
  Smith (US general)
  [☞ Paton, paten,
  patten, patent
  leather]
Pat|tul|lo, Thom|as
  Duf|fer|in (Cdn
  politician)
patty (small cake,
  candy, pie etc.)
  pat|ties
  [☞ Patti, paddy]
patty cake (game)
patty|pan +s
patu|lous
paua +s
pau|city
  pauci|ties
Paul (saint; popes;
  emperor of Russia;
  king of Greece)
  [☞ pawl, pol, pall]

Paul, Les (US guitarist & inventor)
Paula Red +s
Pauli, Wolf|gang (Austrian physicist)
[☞ **Pawley**]
Pauli ex|clu|sion prin|ci|ple
Paul|ine
Paul|ing, Linus Carl (US chemist)
Paul|ist +s
pau|low|nia +s
paunch
  paunch|es
paunch|i|ness
paunchy
  paunch|i|er
  paunch|i|est
pau|per +s (poor person)
  [☞ **popper**]
pau|per|dom
pau|per|ism
pau|per|iz|a|tion
pau|per|ize
  pau|per|iz|es
  pau|per|ized
  pau|per|iz|ing
pau|piette +s
Pau|san|ias (ancient Greek geographer)
pause
  paus|es
  paused
  paus|ing
pav|an +s (= pavane)
pa|vane +s
Pa|va|rotti, Lu|ciano (Italian tenor)
pave
  paves
  paved
  pav|ing
pavé +s
pave|ment +s
pav|er +s
pa|vil|ion +s +ed +ing
pa|vil|ioned adjective
pav|ing +s noun
pav|ior +s
pav|iour +s (use pavior)
Pav|lov, Ivan Petro|vich (Russian physiologist)
Pav|lova, Anna Pav|lov|na (Russian dancer)
pav|lova +s
Pav|lov|ian
Pavo (constellation)

pavo|nine
paw +s +ed +ing (animal foot)
  [☞ **pa, pas, The Pas**]
pawk|i|ly
pawk|i|ness
pawky
  pawk|i|er
  pawk|i|est
pawl +s (lever)
  [☞ **pall, pol**]
Paw|ley, How|ard Rus|sell (Cdn politician)
  [☞ **Pauli**]
pawn +s +ed +ing (Chess; deposit as security)
  [☞ **paan**]
pawn|brok|er +s
pawn|brok|ing
Paw|nee
  plural **Paw|nee** or **Paw|nees**
pawn|shop +s
paw|paw +s (tree; fruit)
  [☞ **papa, poppa**]
pax
pay
  • (give payment etc.)
  pays
  paid
  pay|ing
  • (smear a ship with tar)
  pays
  payed
  pay|ing
  [☞ **Pei**]
pay|able +s
pay-as-you-earn
pay-as-you-go
pay back verb
  pays back
  paid back
  pay|ing back
pay|back +s noun
pay|cheque +s
pay|day +s
pay dirt
pay down verb
  pays down
  paid down
  pay|ing down
pay|down +s noun
payed (past & past participle of **pay** only in sense smear a ship with tar)
  [☞ **paid**]
pay|ee +s (person paid)

[☞ **Pays Basque, Pays de la Loire**]
pay|er +s
Pay|ette, Lise (Cdn broadcaster & politician)
pay|load +s
pay|master +s
pay|ment +s
pay|nim +s
pay off verb
  pays off
  paid off
  pay|ing off
pay|off +s noun
pay|ola +s
pay out verb
  pays out
  paid out
  pay|ing out
pay|out +s noun
pay-per-view
pay phone +s
pay|roll +s
Pays Basque (region, Spain & France)
Pays de la Loire (region, France)
pay slip +s
pay stub +s
pay-TV
Paz, Oc|tavio (Mexican writer)
PC (personal computer; Progressive Conservative)
PCs
PCB (toxic compound)
PCBs
PDA (personal digital assistant)
PDAs
PD day +s (professional development day)
pea +s (plant & its seed)
  [☞ **p, pee, pease pudding**]
Pea|body, George (US financier & philanthropist)
pea brain +s
pea-brained
peace (tranquility; absence of war etc.)
  [☞ **piece**]
peace|able
peace|able|ness
peace|ably
peace bond +s
Peace Corps

peace|ful
peace|ful|ly
peace|ful|ness
peace|keep|er +s
peace|keep|ing
peace|maker +s
peace|making
peace|nik +s
Peace River (town & river, Canada)
peace|time
peach
  peach|es
  peached
  peach|ing
peach|es and cream (peaches-and-cream when preceding a noun)
pea|chick +s
peach|i|ness
peach Mel|ba +s
peachy
  peach|i|er
  peach|i|est
peachy-keen
pea|coat +s
Pea|cock, Thom|as Love (English writer)
Pea|cock (star)
pea|cock +s
pea|cock blue (peacock-blue when preceding a noun)
pea|fowl
  plural **pea|fowl**
pea green (pea-green when preceding a noun)
pea|hen +s
pea jack|et +s
peak +s +ed +ing (point projecting upward; mountain etc.; highest; waste away, look sickly)
  [☞ **peek, pique, Peke, Pik Pobedy**]
Peak Dis|trict (plateau, England)
peaked[1] adjective (having a peak)
peak|ed[2] adjective (sickly, pale)
peak|i|ness
peaky
  peak|i|er
  peak|i|est
peal +s +ed +ing (sound)
  [☞ **peel, Peale**]

Peale, Nor|man
Vin|cent (US
evangelist)
[☞ Peel, peal]
pea|meal bacon
pea|nut +s
pea|nut but|ter
pea|nutty
pear +s (fruit)
[☞ pair, pare, *père*]
Pearl (river, China)
pearl +s +ed +ing
(gem; colour; in
names of flora &
fauna)
[☞ purl]
pearled *adjective*
pearl|er +s
pearl|es|cence +s
pearl|es|cent
Pearl Har|bor (naval
base, Hawaii)
pearl|i|ness
pearl|ized
pearl|ware
pearly
   pearl|i|er
   pearl|i|est
Pearly Gates
Pears, Sir Peter
(English tenor)
**Pearse, Pat|rick
Henry** (Irish
nationalist & poet)
[☞ Pierce, Peirce]
**Pear|son, John
An|drew** (Cdn
architect)
Pear|son, Karl
(English
mathematician)
**Pear|son, Les|ter
Bowles ('Mike')**
(Cdn prime minister)
Peary, Rob|ert Edwin
(US explorer)
[☞ peri]
Peary cari|bou
   plural Peary
   cari|bou
Peary Land (region,
Greenland)
peas|ant +s
peas|ant|ry
Peas|ants' Re|volt
peas|anty
pease (= pea)
   plural pease
pease pud|ding +s
pea|shoot|er +s
pea soup +s (soup;
fog; *offensive* French
Canadian; pea-soup

*when preceding a
noun)*
pea-souper +s (fog;
offensive French
Canadian)
peat +s (decomposed
vegetable matter)
[☞ Pete]
peat bog +s
peat|land +s
peat moss
   peat moss|es
peaty
peau de soie (fabric)
pea|vey +s
pea vine +s
peavy (*use* peavey)
   pea|vies
peb|ble
   peb|bles
   peb|bled
   peb|bling
peb|bled *adjective*
pebble-dash
pebble-dashed
peb|bly
pec +s (pectoral
muscle)
[☞ peck]
pe|can +s (nut;
hickory)
[☞ pekan]
pec|ca|dillo
   pec|ca|dil|loes or
   pec|ca|dil|los
pec|can|cy
pec|cant (sinning)
[☞ piquant,
picante]
pec|cary
   pec|car|ies
Pe|chen|ga (region,
Russia)
Pe|chora (river,
Russia)
**Peck, (El|dred)
Greg|ory** (US actor)
peck +s +ed +ing
(strike with beak etc.;
kiss; measure of
capacity)
[☞ pec]
peck|er +s
pecker|head +s
pecker|wood +s
**Peck|ford, (Al|fred)
Brian** (Cdn
politician)
peck|ish
pec|or|ino +s
Pécs (city, Hungary)
pec|ten (comblike
structure; mollusc)

pec|tens or
pec|tines
[☞ pectin]
pec|tic
pec|tin +s
(polysaccharide used
in jams etc.)
[☞ pecten]
pec|tin|ate
pec|tor|al +s
pecu|late
   pecu|lates
   pecu|lat|ed
   pecu|lat|ing
pecu|la|tion
pecu|la|tor +s
pe|cu|liar +s
pe|cu|li|ar|ity
   pe|cu|li|ar|ities
pe|cu|liar|ly
pe|cu|ni|ar|ily
pe|cu|ni|ary
peda|gogic
peda|gogic|al
peda|gogic|ally
peda|go|gics
peda|gogue +s
peda|gogy
   peda|go|gies
pedal (foot-operated
lever; operate using
pedals; of the foot)
ped|als
ped|alled
ped|al|ling
[☞ peddle]
pedal boat +s
ped|al|er +s (one who
works the pedals on
a bike etc.: *use*
pedaller)
[☞ peddler]
ped|al|ler +s (one
who works the
pedals on a bike etc.)
[☞ peddler]
ped|alo +s
pedal-pusher +s
ped|ant +s
ped|an|tic
ped|an|tic|ally
ped|ant|ry
   ped|ant|ries
ped|ate
ped|dle (sell; promote)
   ped|dles
   ped|dled
   ped|dling
[☞ pedal]
ped|dler +s (one who
sells)
[☞ pedaller]
ped|er|ast +s

ped|er|asty
ped|es|tal +s
ped|es|trian +s
ped|es|trian|iz|a|tion
ped|es|trian|ize
   ped|es|trian|iz|es
   ped|es|trian|ized
   ped|es|trian|iz|ing
pedi|at|ric
pedia|tri|cian +s
pedi|at|rics
pedi|cab +s
pedi|cel +s (stalk
bearing a flower;
eye-stalk)
[☞ pedicle]
pedi|cel|late
ped|icle +s (stalk
supporting a tumour;
tissue, graft)
[☞ pedicel]
pe|dicu|lar
pe|dicu|lat|ed
pe|dicu|lo|sis
pe|dicu|lous
pedi|cure
pedi|cures
pedi|cured
pedi|cur|ing
pedi|gree +s
pedi|greed
pedi|ment +s
pedi|men|tal
pedi|ment|ed
ped|lar +s (one who
sells: *use* peddler)
[☞ pedaller]
pedo|logic|al
ped|ol|o|gist +s
ped|ol|ogy
ped|om|eter +s
pedo|phile +s
pedo|philia
pedo|phil|iac
Pedro (emperors of
Brazil)
Pedro Ximen|ez
ped|uncle +s
ped|un|cu|lar
ped|un|cu|late
ped|un|cu|lat|ed
ped|way +s
pee (urinate; urine)
   pees
   peed
   pee|ing
[☞ p, pea]
Peebles|shire (former
county, Scotland)
peed off
peek +s +ed +ing
(peep, look)

[☞ peak, pique, Peke]
peek|a|boo
Peel (river, Canada)
  [☞ Peale]
Peel, Paul (Cdn painter)
  [☞ Peale]
Peel, Sir Rob|ert (British prime minister)
  [☞ Peale]
peel +s +ed +ing (strip outer layer; covering, skin, rind; speed; *Curling*; shovel; tower)
  [☞ peal]
peel|er +s
peel|ing +s *noun*
peen +s +ed +ing
Peene|munde (rocket testing site, Germany)
peep +s +ed +ing
  [☞ Pepys]
pee-pee +s
peep|er +s
peep|hole +s
peep|ing Tom +s
peeps *conjugated form of* peep
  [☞ Pepys]
peep show +s
peep-toe
peep-toed
pee|pul +s (bo tree)
  [☞ people]
peer +s +ed +ing (gaze; noble; equal)
  [☞ pier, pier glass, Pierre]
peer|age +s
peer|ess (female peer)
  peer|ess|es
  [☞ Pyrrhus]
peer|less
peer re|view
peer-reviewed
peer re|view|er +s
peeve
  peeves
  peeved
  peev|ing
peeved *adjective*
peev|ish
peev|ish|ly
peev|ish|ness
pee|wee +s (*Sport*; very small)
  [☞ pewee]
pee|wit +s
Peg (Winnipeg)

peg
  pegs
  pegged
  peg|ging
Pega|sus (*Greek Myth*; *Astronomy*)
peg|board +s
pegged *adjective*
Peggys Cove (village, Canada)
peg leg +s
peg-legged
peg|ma|tite +s
peg|ma|tit|ic
Pegu (city, Burma)
Peguis (Cdn Saulteaux chief; people)
  plural Peguis
Pei, Ieoh Ming (US architect)
Pei|gan (people & language)
  plural Pei|gan or Pei|gans
  [☞ Pagan]
pei|gnoir +s
Peirce, Charles San|ders (US philosopher)
  [☞ Pierce, Pearse, Pears]
Pei|sis|tra|tus (= Pisistratus, Athenian tyrant)
pe|jor|a|tion
pe|jor|a|tive +s
pe|jor|a|tive|ly
pekan +s (animal)
  [☞ pecan]
Peke +s (Pekingese dog)
  [☞ peak, peek, pique]
Pe|kin|ese (*use* Pekingese)
  plural Pe|kin|ese
Pe|king (= Beijing, China)
Pe|king|ese
  plural Pe|king|ese
pekoe +s (tea)
  [☞ picot, Pico]
pel|age +s
Pela|gian +s
Pela|gian|ism
pela|gic
Pela|gius (British monk)
pel|ar|gon|ium +s
Pelé (Brazilian soccer player)
  [☞ Pelée]

pele +s (tower: *use* peel)
  [☞ peal, Peale]
Pelée (mountain, Martinique)
  [☞ Pelé]
Pelee (island & point, Canada)
  [☞ Pelly]
Pel|eus (*Greek Myth*)
pelf
Pel|ham +s (town, Canada; horse's bit)
peli|can +s
Pel|ion (mountain, Greece)
pel|isse +s (cloak)
pel|ite +s (rock)
  [☞ polite]
pel|it|ic
pel|lagra
pel|lag|rous
Pel|latt, Sir Henry Mill (Cdn entrepreneur)
pel|let +s +ed +ing
Pel|le|tier, Gé|rard (Cdn journalist & politician)
Pel|le|tier, Pierre-Joseph (French chemist)
Pel|le|tier, Wil|fred (Cdn Odawa philosopher)
Pel|le|tier, Wil|frid (Cdn conductor & music director)
pel|let|iz|a|tion
pel|let|ize
  pel|let|iz|es
  pel|let|ized
  pel|let|iz|ing
pel|let|iz|ing *noun*
pel|licle +s
pel|licu|lar
pel|li|tory
  pel|li|tor|ies
pell-mell +s (recklessly; confusion)
  [☞ pall-mall]
pel|lu|cid
pel|lu|cid|ity
pel|lu|cid|ly
Pelly (river, Canada)
  [☞ Pelee]
Pelly Bay (bay & hamlet, Canada)
  [☞ Pelee]
pel|met +s
Pelo|pon|nese (peninsula, Greece)

Pelo|pon|nes|ian +s
Pelo|pon|nes|us (= the Peloponnese)
Pe|lops (*Greek Myth*)
pe|lorus
  pe|lorus|es
pe|lota +s
pelt +s +ed +ing
pelt|ry
  pelt|ries
pel|vic
pel|vis
  pel|vis|es or pel|ves
Pemba (city, Mozambique; island off Tanzania)
Pem|broke (cities, Canada & Wales)
Pem|broke|shire (former county, Wales)
pem|mican
pem|phig|oid
pem|phig|us
pen
  pens
  penned
  pen|ning
  [☞ Penn]
penal
penal|iz|a|tion
penal|ize
  penal|iz|es
  penal|ized
  penal|iz|ing
penal|ly
pen|al|ty
  pen|al|ties
pen|al|ty box
  pen|al|ty boxes
pen|al|ty kill|er +s
pen|al|ty kill|ing
pen|ance +s
pen and ink (pen-and-ink *when preceding a noun*)
Pen|ang
  • (island & state, Malaysia)
  • (= George Town, Malaysian city)
pe|na|tes
pen-based
pence
pen|chant +s
pen|cil
  pen|cils
  pen|cilled
  pen|cil|ling
pen|cilled *adjective*
pen|cil line +s (pencil-line *when preceding a noun*)

pencil-pusher +s
pencil-pushing
pencil-thin
pen|dant +s *noun*
  [☞ pendent]
pen|den|cy
pen|dent *adjective*
  [☞ pendant]
pen|den|tive +s
pend|ing
pen|dragon
pen|du|lous
pen|du|lously
pen|du|lum +s
Pe|nel|ope (*Greek Myth*)
pene|plain +s
pene|plane +s (*use peneplain*)
Pene|tang
  (= Penetanguishene)
Pene|tan|gui|shene
  (town, Canada)
pene|tra|bil|ity
pene|trable
pene|tra|lia
pene|trant
pene|trate
  pene|trates
  pene|trat|ed
  pene|trat|ing
pene|trat|ing *adjective*
pene|trat|ing|ly
pene|tra|tion +s
pene|tra|tive
pene|tra|tor +s
Pen|field, Wil|der Graves (Cdn neurosurgeon)
pen|friend +s
pen|guin +s
peni|cil|late
peni|cil|lin +s
penile
pen|in|sula +s
pen|in|su|lar
penis
  penis|es
peni|tence
peni|tent +s
peni|ten|tial
peni|ten|tial|ly
peni|ten|tiary
  peni|ten|tiar|ies
peni|tent|ly
pen|knife
  pen|knives
pen|light +s
pen|man
  pen|men
penman|ship

Penn, Wil|liam
  (founder of Pennsylvania)
pen name +s
pen|nant +s
penne (pasta)
penni (Finnish currency)
  pen|niä
penni|less
penni|less|ly
penni|less|ness
Pen|nine +s (chain of hills, England)
pen|non
Penn|syl|va|nia +s (state, US)
Penn|syl|va|nian +s
penny
• (individual coin)
  plural pen|nies
• (*Brit.* sum of money)
  plural pence
  [☞ penni, penne]
penny ante *noun*
penny-ante *adjective*
Penny Black +s
penny|cress
  penny|cress|es
penny dread|ful +s
  (penny-dreadful *when preceding a noun*)
penny-pincher +s
penny-pinching
penny|royal +s
penny|weight +s
penny|whistle +s
penny-wise
penny|wort +s
penny|worth
Pen|ob|scot
  plural Pen|ob|scot or Pen|ob|scots
peno|logic|al
penol|o|gist +s
penol|ogy
pen pal +s
pen-pusher +s
pen-pushing
pen|sée +s
pen|sile
pen|sion +s +ed +ing (payment)
pen|sion +s (boarding house)
pen|sion|abil|ity
pen|sion|able
pen|sion|er +s
pen|sion|less
pen|sive
pen|sive|ly
pen|sive|ness

pen|ste|mon +s
pen|stock +s
pent
penta|chloro|phenol
pent|acle +s
pent|ad +s
penta|dac|tyl
Penta|gon (US military leadership)
penta|gon +s
pent|ag|on|al
penta|gram +s
penta|hed|ral
penta|hed|ron
  penta|hed|rons or penta|hedra
pent|am|er|ous
pent|am|eter +s
pent|amid|ine
pent|ane
pent|angle +s
Penta|teuch
Penta|teuch|al
pent|ath|lete +s
pent|ath|lon +s
penta|ton|ic
penta|valent
Pente|cost
Pente|cost|al +s
Pente|costal|ism +s
Pente|costal|ist +s
Pen|the|si|lea (*Greek Myth*)
pent|house +s
Pen|tic|ton (city, Canada)
penti|mento
  penti|menti
Pent|land Firth (channel north of Scotland)
pento|barbi|tal
pento|barbi|tone
pent|ose +s
Pento|thal *proprietary*
pent|ste|mon +s (*use* penstemon)
pent up (pent-up *when preceding a noun*)
pentyl
pen|ult +s
pen|ul|tim|ate +s
pen|umbra
  pen|um|brae or pen|um|bras
pen|um|bral
pen|uri|ous
pen|uri|ous|ly
pen|uri|ous|ness
pen|ury
  pen|ur|ies

Penza (city, Russia)
Pen|zance (town, England)
Pen|zias, Arno Allan (US astrophysicist)
peon +s (drudge; labourer; attendant)
  [☞ paean, paeon, pion]
peon|age
peony
  peon|ies
people (persons)
  peoples
  peopled
  peop|ling
  [☞ peepul]
people|hood
people me|ter +s
people mov|er +s
people-watch
  people-watches
  people-watched
  people-watch|ing
people-watch|er +s
people-watch|ing *noun*
Peoria (city, US)
pep
  peps
  pepped
  pep|ping
Pepin (the Short) (Frankish king)
pep|lum +s
pepo +s
pep|per +s +ed +ing
pepper|corn +s
pep|per grass
  pep|per grass|es
pep|per|i|ness
pep|per mill +s
pepper|mint +s
pepper|minty
pep|per|oni
pep|per pot +s
pep|per root +s
pep|pery
pep|pi|ly
pep|pi|ness
peppy
  pep|pi|er
  pep|pi|est
pep|sin
pep|tic
pep|tide +s
pep|tone +s
Pepys, Sam|uel (English diarist)
Pé|quiste +s
per *preposition*
  [☞ purr]
per|adven|ture +s

Perak (state, Malaysia)
per|ambu|late
  per|ambu|lates
  per|ambu|lat|ed
  per|ambu|lat|ing
per|ambu|la|tion +s
per|ambu|la|tor +s
per|ambu|la|tory
per annum
perc
  (perchloroethylene)
  [☞ **perk**]
per|cale
per cap|ita
Percé (town & rock, Canada)
per|ceiv|able
per|ceive
  per|ceives
  per|ceived
  per|ceiv|ing
per|ceiv|er +s
per cent *adverb* (in every hundred: *forty per cent*)
  [☞ **percent**]
per|cent +s *noun* (percentage, percentage point: *an increasing percent of the population*; *a quarter of a percent*)
  [☞ **per cent**]
per|cent|age +s
per|cent|ile +s
per|cept +s
per|cep|ti|bil|ity
per|cep|tible
per|cep|tibly
per|cep|tion +s
per|cep|tion|al
per|cep|tive
per|cep|tive|ly
per|cep|tive|ness
per|cep|tiv|ity
per|cep|tual
per|cep|tual|ly
perch
  • (high resting place; measure of length)
  perch|es
  perched
  perch|ing
  • (fish)
  plural **perch** or perch|es
per|chance
perch|er +s
Per|che|ron +s
per|chlor|ate +s
per|chlor|ic
per|chloro|ethyl|ene
per|cipi|ence

per|cipi|ent +s
per|cipi|ent|ly
per|co|late
  per|co|lates
  per|co|lat|ed
  per|co|lat|ing
per|co|la|tion +s
per|co|la|tor +s
per con|tra
per|cuss
  per|cuss|es
  per|cussed
  per|cuss|ing
per|cus|sion +s
per|cus|sion|ist +s
per|cus|sive
per|cus|sive|ly
per|cus|sive|ness
per|cuta|neous
Percy, Sir Henry ('Harry Hotspur', English soldier)
Percy, Thom|as (English antiquarian)
per diem
per|di|tion
per|dur|abil|ity
per|dur|able
per|dur|ably
père +s (father)
  [☞ **pair, pare, pear**]
Père David's deer
  plural **Père David's deer**
pere|grin|ate
  pere|grin|ates
  pere|grin|at|ed
  pere|grin|at|ing
pere|grin|a|tion +s
pere|grin|ator +s
pere|grine +s
Perel|man, Sid|ney Jo|seph (US writer)
  [☞ **Perlman**]
per|emp|tor|i|ly
per|emp|tor|i|ness
per|emp|tory
per|en|nial +s
per|en|ni|al|ity
per|en|nial|ly
Peres, Shi|mon (Israeli prime minister)
  [☞ **Pérez Galdós, Pérez de Cuéllar**]
pere|stroi|ka
Pérez de Cuél|lar, Ja|vier (UN secretary-general)
  [☞ **Peres**]
Pérez Gal|dós, Ben|ito (Spanish

novelist)
  [☞ **Peres**]
per|fect +s +ed +ing
per|fecta +s
perfect-bound
per|fect|er +s
per|fect|ibil|ity
per|fect|ible
per|fec|tion +s
per|fec|tion|ism
per|fec|tion|ist +s
per|fec|tion|is|tic
per|fec|tive +s
per|fect|ly
per|fect|ness
per|fecto +s
per|fer|vid
per|fer|vid|ly
per|fer|vid|ness
per|fidi|ous
per|fidi|ous|ly
per|fidy
per|foli|ate
per|for|ate
  per|for|ates
  per|for|at|ed
  per|for|at|ing
per|for|at|ed *adjective*
per|for|a|tion +s
per|fora|tive
per|for|ator +s
per|force
per|form +s +ed +ing
per|form|able
per|form|ance +s
per|forma|tive
per|form|er +s
per|form|ing *adjective*
per|fume
  per|fumes
  per|fumed
  per|fum|ing
per|fumed *adjective*
per|fum|er +s
per|fum|ery
  per|fum|eries
per|fumy
per|func|tor|i|ly
per|func|tor|i|ness
per|func|tory
per|fuse
  per|fus|es
  per|fused
  per|fus|ing
per|fu|sion +s
per|fu|sive
Per|ga|mene +s
Per|ga|mum (ancient city, Asia Minor)
per|go|la +s

Per|go|lesi, Gio|van|ni Bat|tis|ta (Italian composer)
per|haps
peri +s (fairy; graceful thing)
peri|anth +s
Péri|bon|ka (river, Canada)
peri|car|di|al
peri|car|ditis
peri|car|di|um
  peri|car|dia
peri|carp +s
peri|chon|drium
  peri|chon|dria
Peri|clean
Peri|cles (Athenian statesman)
peri|cope +s
peri|dot +s
peri|dot|ite +s
peri|dot|itic
peri|gean
peri|gee +s
peri|glacial
Péri|gord (area, France)
peri|gyn|ous
peri|heli|on (orbital point closest to sun)
  peri|helia
  [☞ **parhelion**]
peril
  per|ils
  per|illed
  per|il|ling
peri|il|ous
peri|il|ous|ly
peri|il|ous|ness
peri|lune +s
peri|lymph
peri|im|eter +s
peri|met|ric
peri|natal
peri|natal|ly
peri|neal
peri|neum
  peri|neums or peri|nea
per|iod +s
per|iod|ate +s
peri|od|ic[1] (intermittent)
per|iod|ic[2] (acid)
peri|od|ic|al
peri|od|ic|al|ly
period|icity
period|iz|a|tion +s
peri|odon|tal
peri|odon|tics
peri|odon|tist +s
peri|odon|tol|ogy

peri|os|teal
peri|os|teum
  peri|os|tea
peri|os|titis
peri|pa|tet|ic
peri|pa|tet|ic|ally
peri|pa|teti|cism
peri|pet|eia +s
per|iph|eral
per|iph|eral|ly
per|iph|ery
  per|iph|eries
peri|phras|is
  peri|phras|es
peri|phras|tic
peri|phras|tic|ally
per|ip|ter|al
peri|scope +s
peri|scop|ic
peri|scop|ic|ally
per|ish (die)
  per|ish|es
  per|ished
  per|ish|ing
  [☞ parish]
per|ish|abil|ity
per|ish|able +s
per|ish|able|ness
per|ish|er +s
per|ish|ing adjective
per|ish|ing|ly
peri|sperm +s
per|isso|dac|tyl +s
peri|stal|sis
peri|stal|tic
peri|stal|tic|ally
peri|stome +s
peri|style +s
peri|ton|eal
peri|ton|eum
  peri|ton|eums or
  peri|tonea
peri|ton|itis
peri|vascu|lar
peri|wig +s
peri|winkle +s
per|jure (lie under
  oath)
  per|jures
  per|jured
  per|jur|ing
  [☞ purger]
per|jured adjective
per|jur|er +s
per|juri|ous
per|jury
  per|jur|ies
perk +s +ed +ing
  (raise quickly; in
  'perk up'; perquisite;
  percolate,
  percolator)
  [☞ perc]

perk|i|ly
Per|kin, Sir Wil|liam
  Henry (English
  chemist)
perk|i|ness
perky
  perk|i|er
  perk|i|est
Per|lis (state,
  Malaysia)
perl|ite
Perl|man, It|zhak
  (Israeli-born
  violinist)
  [☞ Perelman]
Perm (city, Russia)
perm +s +ed +ing
perma|cul|tur|al
perma|cul|ture
perma|cul|tur|ist +s
perma|frost +s
perma|nence
perma|nency
perma|nent +s
perma|nent|ly
perma|nent press
  (per|manent-press
  when preceding a
  noun)
per|man|gan|ate +s
per|man|gan|ic
per|mea|bil|ity
per|me|able
per|me|ance
per|me|ant
per|me|ate
  per|me|ates
  per|me|at|ed
  per|me|at|ing
per|me|a|tion
per|meth|rin
Per|mian
per mil
per mill (use per mil)
per|mis|si|bil|ity
per|mis|sible
per|mis|sibly
per|mis|sion +s
per|mis|sive
per|mis|sive|ly
per|mis|sive|ness
per|mit
  per|mits
  per|mit|ted
  per|mit|ting
per|mit|tee +s
per|mit|ter +s
per|mit|tiv|ity
per|mu|tate
  per|mu|tates
  per|mu|tat|ed
  per|mu|tat|ing
per|mu|ta|tion +s

per|mu|ta|tion|al
per|mute
  per|mutes
  per|mut|ed
  per|mut|ing
Per|nam|buco
  • (state, Brazil)
  • (former name for
  Recife, Brazil)
per|ni|cious
per|ni|cious|ly
per|ni|cious|ness
per|nick|ety
Per|nod +s proprietary
per|ogy
  per|ogies
Perón (surname)
  [☞ perron]
Perón, (Maria) Eva
  Duarte de ('Evita',
  Argentinian
  politician)
Perón, Juan
  Do|min|go
  (Argentinian
  president)
Perón, Maria Es|trela
  ('Isa|bel')
  (Argentinian
  president)
pero|neal
Peron|ism
Peron|ist +s
per|or|ate
  per|or|ates
  per|or|at|ed
  per|or|at|ing
per|or|a|tion +s
per|oxi|dase +s
per|ox|ide
  per|ox|ides
  per|ox|id|ed
  per|ox|id|ing
perp +s
Per|pen|dicu|lar
  (Architecture)
per|pen|dicu|lar +s
  (in general use)
per|pen|dicu|lar|ity
per|pen|dicu|lar|ly
perpe|trate
  perpe|trates
  perpe|trat|ed
  perpe|trat|ing
perpe|tra|tion
perpe|tra|tor +s
per|pet|ual
per|petu|al|ly
per|petu|ate
  per|petu|ates
  per|petu|at|ed
  per|petu|at|ing
per|petu|a|tion

per|petu|ator +s
perpe|tu|ity
  perpe|tu|ities
Per|pignan (city,
  France)
per|plex
  per|plex|es
  per|plexed
  per|plex|ing
per|plexed adjective
per|plex|ing adjective
per|plex|ing|ly
per|plex|ity
  per|plex|ities
per|quis|ite +s
Per|rault, Charles
  (French writer)
Per|rier +s proprietary
Per|rin, Jean
  Bap|tiste (French
  chemist)
per|ron +s (staircase)
  [☞ Perón]
Perry, Mat|thew
  Cal|braith (US naval
  officer who opened
  trade with Japan)
  [☞ Parry]
Perry, Oli|ver
  Haz|ard (US naval
  officer, War of 1812)
  [☞ Parry]
perry (pear drink)
  per|ries
  [☞ parry, pari
  passu]
Perse, Saint-John
  (French poet)
  [☞ purse]
per se
per|se|cute
  per|se|cutes
  per|se|cut|ed
  per|se|cut|ing
per|se|cu|tion +s
per|se|cu|tor +s
per|se|cu|tory
Per|seid +s (meteor
  shower)
Per|seph|one (Greek
  Myth)
Per|sep|olis (city,
  ancient Persia)
Per|seus (Greek Myth;
  Astronomy)
perse|ver|ance
per|sev|er|ate
  per|sev|er|ates
  per|sev|er|at|ed
  per|sev|er|at|ing
per|sev|er|a|tion +s
perse|vere
  perse|veres

perse|vered
perse|ver|ing
Per|shing, John
Jo|seph ('Black
Jack') (US general)
Per|shing +s
Per|sia
• (ancient kingdom,
Asia)
• (*former name for*
Iran)
Per|sian +s
persi|flage
per|sim|mon +s
per|sist +s +ed +ing
per|sis|tence
per|sis|tency
per|sis|tent
per|sis|tent|ly
per|snick|ety
per|son +s
per|sona
  per|sonas or
  per|sonae
per|son|able
per|son|able|ness
per|son|ably
per|son|age +s
per|sona grata
  per|sonae gratae
per|son|al +s (private;
  in person;
  disparaging; of the
  body; *Grammar*;
  personal ad)
  [☞ personnel]
per|son|al|ism
per|son|al|ist +s
per|son|al|ity
  per|son|al|ities
per|son|al|iz|a|tion
per|son|al|ize
  per|son|al|iz|es
  per|son|al|ized
  per|son|al|iz|ing
per|son|al|ly
per|son|al|ty
  per|son|al|ties
per|sona non grata
  per|sonae non gratae
per|son|ate
  per|son|ates
  per|son|at|ed
  per|son|at|ing
per|son|a|tion +s
per|son|ator +s
per|son|hood
per|soni|fi|ca|tion +s
per|soni|fi|er +s
per|soni|fy
  per|soni|fies
  per|soni|fied
  per|soni|fy|ing

per|son|nel
  (employees)
  [☞ personal]
person-to-person
per|spec|tiv|al
per|spec|tive +s
per|spec|tive|ly
Per|spex *proprietary*
per|spi|ca|cious
per|spi|ca|cious|ly
per|spi|ca|cious|ness
per|spi|ca|city
per|spi|cu|ity
per|spicu|ous
per|spicu|ous|ly
per|spicu|ous|ness
per|spir|a|tion
per|spir|a|tory
per|spire
  per|spires
  per|spired
  per|spir|ing
per|suad|abil|ity
per|suad|able
per|suade
  per|suades
  per|suad|ed
  per|suad|ing
per|suad|er +s
per|sua|sible
per|sua|sion +s
per|sua|sive
per|sua|sive|ly
per|sua|sive|ness
pert +er +est
per|tain +s +ed +ing
Perth (city, Australia;
  towns, Scotland &
  Canada)
Perth|shire (former
  county, Scotland)
per|tin|a|cious
per|tin|a|cious|ly
per|tin|a|cious|ness
per|tina|city
per|tin|ence
per|tin|ent
per|tin|ent|ly
pert|ly
pert|ness
per|turb +s +ed +ing
per|turb|able
per|turb|a|tion +s
per|turb|ative
per|turb|ing|ly
per|tus|sis
Peru (country,
  S America)
Peru|gia (city, Italy)
Peru|gino, Il (Italian
  painter)
per|uke +s

per|usal +s
per|use
  per|us|es
  per|used
  per|us|ing
per|us|er +s
Per|utz, Max
  Fer|di|nand (English
  biochemist)
Peru|vian +s
Per|uzzi, Bal|das|sare
  Tomas|so (Italian
  architect)
perv +s
per|vade
  per|vades
  per|vad|ed
  per|vad|ing
per|va|sion
per|va|sive
per|va|sive|ly
per|va|sive|ness
per|verse
per|verse|ly
per|verse|ness
per|ver|sion +s
per|vers|ity
  per|vers|ities
per|ver|sive
per|vert +s +ed +ing
per|vert|ed *adjective*
per|vert|ed|ly
per|vert|er +s
per|vious
per|vious|ness
pervy
  perv|i|er
  perv|i|est
Pe|sach
pes|eta +s
pe|sewa +s
Pe|sha|war (city,
  Pakistan)
Pe|shitta
pesk|i|ly
pesk|i|ness
pesky
  pesk|i|er
  pesk|i|est
peso +s
pes|sary
  pes|sar|ies
pes|sim|ism
pes|sim|ist +s
pes|sim|is|tic
pes|sim|is|tic|ally
pest +s
Pesta|lozzi, Jo|hann
  Hein|rich (Swiss
  education reformer)
pes|ter +s +ed +ing
pest|house +s
pesti|cid|al

pesti|cide +s
pest|ifer|ous
pesti|lence +s
pesti|lent
pesti|len|tial
pesti|len|tial|ly
pesti|lent|ly
pestle
  pes|tles
  pes|tled
  pest|ling
pesto
pet
  pets
  pet|ted
  pet|ting
Pé|tain, (Henri)
  Phi|lippe Omer
  (French general &
  statesman)
petal +s
pet|alled
petal-like
petal|oid
pé|tanque
pe|tard +s
pet|asus
  pet|asus|es
Peta|wawa (river,
  Canada)
Pete (in "for Pete's
  sake")
  [☞ peat]
pe|techia
  pe|tech|iae
pe|tech|ial
Peter (*Bible*; Russian
  czar)
peter +s +ed +ing
Peter|bor|ough (cities,
  England & Canada)
Peter|head +s
Peter|loo
Peter Pan +s
Peter Prin|ciple
Peters, Ar|thur (Cdn
  politician)
Peters, Fred|erick
  (Cdn politician)
peter|sham +s
Peter|son, Oscar
  Em|man|uel (Cdn
  pianist)
Peter's pence
Peter the Her|mit
  (French monk)
pethi|dine
peti|olar
peti|o|late
peti|ole +s
Pe|tipa, Mar|ius
  Ivan|ovich (French
  dancer)

petit bour|geois
  pet|its bour|geois
Petit|co|di|ac (river, Canada)
pe|tite +s (small; dainty)
pet|ite bour|geoi|sie
petit four
  pet|its fours
pe|ti|tion +s +ed +ing
pe|ti|tion|er +s
pe|ti|tio prin|cipii
petit mal (petit-mal *when preceding a noun*)
petit point +s (embroidery; stitch)
pet|its pois (small peas)
Pet|öfi, Sán|dor (Hungarian revolutionary poet)
Petra (ancient city, Jordan)
Pe|trarch (Italian poet)
Pe|trarch|an
pet|rel +s (bird)
  [☞ petrol]
Petri dish
  Petri dish|es
Pet|rie, Sir (Wil|liam Mat|thew) Flin|ders (English archaeologist)
petri|fac|tion +s
petri|fied *adjective*
pet|ri|fy
  petri|fies
  petri|fied
  petri|fy|ing
petro|chem|ical +s
petro|chem|istry
petro|dollar +s
petro|glyph +s
Petro|grad (*former name for* St. Petersburg, Russia)
pet|rog|raph|er +s
petro|graph|ic
petro|graph|ic|al
petro|graph|ic|al|ly
pet|rog|raphy
pet|rol +s (gasoline)
  [☞ petrel]
pet|rol|atum
pet|rol bomb +s *noun*
petrol-bomb +s +ed +ing *verb*
pet|rol|eum
Pet|rolia (town, Canada)
petro|logic

petro|logic|al
pet|rol|o|gist +s
pet|rol|ogy
Pe|tron|ius, Gaius (Roman writer)
Petro|pav|lovsk (city, Kazakhstan)
Petro|pavlovsk-Kamchat|sky (city, Russia)
pet|rous
Petro|za|vodsk (city, Kazakhstan)
Pet|sa|mo (*former name for* Pechenga, Russia)
petti|coat +s
petti|coat|ed
pet|ti|er
pet|ti|est
petti|fog
  petti|fogs
  petti|fogged
  petti|fog|ging
petti|fog|ger +s
petti|fog|gery
petti|fog|ging *noun*
petti|fog|ging|ly
pet|ti|ly
pet|ti|ness
pet|tish
pet|tish|ly
pet|tish|ness
petty (unimportant, trivial; contemptible; *Law* of lesser importance)
  pet|ti|er
  pet|ti|est
  [☞ petit bourgeois, petit four, petit mal, petit point, petits pois]
petty bour|geois (*use* petit bourgeois)
  plural petty bour|geois
petty bour|geoi|sie (*use* petite bourgeoisie)
petty cash
petty of|fi|cer +s
petu|lance +s
petu|lant
petu|lant|ly
Petun
  plural Petun
pe|tu|nia +s
Pevs|ner, An|toine (French artist)
pew +s (church bench or compartment)
  [☞ più]

pe|wee +s (bird)
  [☞ peewee]
pe|wit +s (*use* peewit)
pew|less
pew|ter
pew|ter|er +s
pewter|smith +s
pew|tery
pey|ote +s
pey|ot|ism
PFD (personal flotation device)
  PFDs
pfen|nig +s
pH (acidity or alkalinity)
Phae|dra (*Greek Myth*)
Phae|drus, Gaius Jul|ius (Roman fabulist)
Phae|thon (*Greek Myth*)
phae|ton +s
phage +s
phago|cyte +s
phago|cyt|ic
phago|cyt|ize
  phago|cyt|iz|es
  phago|cyt|ized
  phago|cyt|iz|ing
phago|cyt|ose
  phago|cyt|os|es
  phago|cyt|osed
  phago|cyt|os|ing
phago|cyt|o|sis
phal|ange +s (= phalanx: bone)
  [☞ Falange]
pha|lan|geal
pha|lan|ger +s
phal|anx
  phal|anx|es or phal|an|ges
phala|rope +s
phal|lic
phal|lic|ally
phal|li|cism
phallo|cen|tric
phallo|cen|tri|city
phallo|cen|trism +s
phal|lus
  phal|lus|es or phal|li
phan|ero|gam +s
phan|ero|gam|ic
phan|er|og|am|ous
Phan|ero|zoic
phan|tasm +s
phan|tas|ma|goria +s
phan|tas|ma|gor|ic
phan|tas|ma|gor|ic|al
phan|tas|mal
phan|tas|mic

phan|tast +s (*use* fantast)
phan|tasy (*use* fantasy)
  phan|ta|sies
phan|tom +s
phar|aoh +s (Egyptian ruler)
  [☞ faro, Faro, Faeroe, pharos]
phara|onic
Phari|saic
Phari|saic|al
Phari|saism
Phari|see +s
Phari|see|ism (*use* Pharisaism)
pharma|care
phar|ma|ceut|ical +s
phar|ma|ceut|ical|ly
phar|ma|cist +s
phar|ma|cog|nosy
phar|ma|co|kin|etic
phar|ma|co|kin|etic|ally
phar|ma|co|kin|et|ics
phar|ma|co|logic
phar|ma|co|logic|al
phar|ma|co|logic|al|ly
phar|ma|col|o|gist +s
phar|ma|col|ogy
phar|ma|co|poeia +s
phar|ma|co|poeial
phar|macy
  phar|ma|cies
phar|os (lighthouse)
  phar|os|es
  [☞ pharaoh]
pharyn|geal
pharyn|gitis
pharynx
  pha|ryn|ges
phase (stage, period; *Chemistry*; conduct in stages)
  phas|es
  phased
  phas|ing
  [☞ faze]
phase in *verb*
  phas|es in
  phased in
  phas|ing in
phase-in +s *noun & adjective*
phase out *verb*
  phas|es out
  phased out
  phas|ing out
phase-out +s *noun & adjective*
phas|er +s

phas|ic
phat (excellent, cool)
  phat|ter
  phat|test
phat|ic
Ph.D.
  Ph.D.'s
pheas|ant +s
pheas|ant|ry
  pheas|ant|ries
phen|cycli|dine
pheno|barbi|tal
pheno|barbi|tone
pheno|cryst +s
phe|nol +s (Chemistry)
  [☞ phenyl]
phe|nol|ic +s
phenol|phthal|ein
phe|nom +s
phe|nom|ena
phe|nom|en|al
phe|nom|en|al|ism
phe|nom|en|al|ist +s
phe|nom|en|al|is|tic
phe|nom|en|al|ize
  phe|nom|en|al|iz|es
  phe|nom|en|al|ized
  phe|nom|en|al|iz|ing
phe|nom|en|al|ly
phe|nom|eno|logic|al
phe|nom|eno|logic|
      al|ly
phe|nom|en|ol|o|gist
  +s
phe|nom|en|ol|ogy
phe|nom|en|on
  phe|nom|ena
pheno|thia|zine +s
pheno|type +s
pheno|typ|ic
pheno|typ|ic|ally
phenyl (Chemistry)
  [☞ fennel, phenol]
phenyl|alan|ine
phenyl|keton|uria
pheny|toin
phero|mon|al
phero|mone +s
phew interjection
  [☞ few]
phi +s (Greek letter)
  [☞ fie]
phial +s (bottle)
  [☞ faille]
Phi Beta Kap|pa +s
Phid|ias (ancient
  Athenian sculptor)
Phila|del|phia (city,
  US)
phila|del|phus
  phila|del|phus|es
phi|lan|der +s +ed
  +ing

phi|lan|der|er +s
phil|an|thrope +s
phil|an|throp|ic
phil|an|throp|ic|ally
phil|an|throp|ist +s
phil|an|thropy
  phil|an|throp|ies
phila|tel|ic
phila|tel|ic|ally
phil|atel|ist +s
phil|ately
Phil|by, Har|old
  Ad|rian Rus|sell
  ('Kim') (English spy)
Phi|le|mon (New
  Testament; Greek
  Myth)
phil|harmon|ic +s
Phil|ip (Spanish,
  Macedonian &
  French kings; Duke
  of Edinburgh;
  Wampanoag chief;
  saints)
  [☞ Philipps,
  Phillips, fillip]
Phil|ip Au|gus|tus
  (Philip II of France)
Phil|ip of Va|lois
  (Philip VI of France)
Phil|ippi (city, ancient
  Macedonia)
Phil|ip|pi|ans (New
  Testament)
phil|ip|pic +s
Phil|ip|pine adjective
  (of the Philippines)
  [☞ Filipina,
  Filipino, Pilipino]
Phil|ip|pines (country,
  SE Asia)
  [☞ Filipina,
  Filipino, Pilipino]
Phil|ip|pop|olis
  (ancient name for
  Plovdiv, Bulgaria)
Phil|ipps, Rich|ard
  (British colonial
  administrator)
  [☞ Phillips, fillip]
Phil|ip the Fair (Philip
  IV of France)
Phil|ip the
  Hand|some (Philip I
  of Spain)
Phil|is|tine +s
  (ancient people)
phil|is|tine +s
  (uncultured person)
phil|is|tin|ism
Phil|lips (screwdriver)
  [☞ Philipps, fillip]
Philly (Philadelphia)
  [☞ filly]

philo|den|dron
  philo|den|drons or
  philo|den|dra
Philo Ju|daeus
  (Jewish philosopher)
  [☞ phyllo]
philo|logic|al
philo|logic|al|ly
phil|ol|o|gist +s
phil|ol|o|gize
  phil|ol|o|giz|es
  phil|ol|o|gized
  phil|ol|o|giz|ing
phil|ol|ogy
Philo|mel (Greek
  Myth)
Philo|mela (Greek
  Myth: use Philomel)
philo|pro|geni|tive
philo|sophe +s
phil|oso|pher +s
philo|soph|ic
philo|soph|ic|al
philo|soph|ic|al|ly
phil|oso|phize
  phil|oso|phiz|es
  phil|oso|phized
  phil|oso|phiz|ing
phil|oso|phiz|er +s
phil|oso|phy
  phil|oso|phies
phil|tre +s (love
  potion)
  [☞ filter]
phi|mo|sis
phi|mot|ic
Phin|ti|as (legendary
  friend of Damon)
Phiz (English
  illustrator)
  [☞ fizz]
phiz (face)
  [☞ fizz]
phizz (face: use phiz)
  [☞ fizz]
phleb|itic
phleb|itis
phleb|ot|o|mist +s
phleb|ot|o|mize
  phleb|ot|o|miz|es
  phleb|ot|o|mized
  phleb|ot|o|miz|ing
phleb|ot|omy
  phleb|ot|o|mies
phlegm (Physiology;
  coolness, apathy;
  bodily humour)
phleg|mat|ic
phleg|mat|ic|ally
phlegmy
phloem +s (Botany)
phlo|gis|ton
phlox
  phlox|es

Phnom Penh (capital
  of Cambodia)
pho|bia +s
phob|ic
Phoe|be (daughter of
  Uranus & Gaia;
  moon of Saturn)
phoe|be +s
Phoe|bus (Apollo)
Phoe|ni|cia (ancient
  country,
  E Mediterranean
  coast)
Phoe|ni|cian +s
Phoe|nix (city, US;
  island group,
  Kiribati)
phoe|nix
  phoe|nix|es
phon|ate
  phon|ates
  phon|at|ed
  phon|at|ing
phon|a|tion
phona|tory
phone
  phones
  phoned
  phon|ing
phone book +s
phone booth +s
phone card +s
phone in verb
  phones in
  phoned in
  phon|ing in
phone-in +s noun
phon|eme +s
phon|emic
phon|em|ics
phone phreak +s
phon|er +s
phon|etic
phon|etic|ally
phon|et|ician +s
phon|et|ics
phoney (use phony)
  phon|i|er
  phon|i|est
  phon|eys
phon|ic
phon|ic|ally
phon|ics
phon|i|er
phon|i|est
phon|i|ly
phon|i|ness
phono
phono|gram +s
phono|graph +s
phono|graph|ic
phon|og|raphy
phono|logic|al

phono|logic|al|ly
phon|ol|o|gist +s
phon|ol|ogy
phon|on +s
phony
  phon|i|er
  phon|i|est
  phon|ies
phony-baloney
phooey
phor|esy
phor|etic
phos|gene
phos|phat|ase +s
phos|phate +s
phos|phat|ic
phos|phene +s
  (sensation in eye)
  [☞ phosphine]
phos|phide +s
phos|phine +s (gas)
  [☞ phosphene]
phos|phin|ic
phos|phite +s
phos|pho|lipid +s
phos|pho|pro|tein +s
phos|phor +s
phos|phor|esce
  phos|phor|es|ces
  phos|phor|esced
  phos|phor|es|cing
phos|phor|es|cence
  +s
phos|phor|es|cent
phos|phor|es|cent|ly
phos|phor|ic
phos|phor|ite
phos|phor|ous
  adjective
  [☞ phosphorus,
  phosphoresce]
phos|phor|us noun
  [☞ phosphorous,
  phosphoresce]
phos|phoryl|ate
  phos|phoryl|ates
  phos|phoryl|at|ed
  phos|phoryl|at|ing
phos|phoryl|a|tion
  +s
phot +s (unit of
  illumination)
phot|ic
photo +s
photo-aging
photo|biol|ogy
photo|call +s
Photo CD +s
  proprietary
photo|cell +s
photo|chem|ical
photo|chem|ical|ly
photo|chem|istry

photo|chrom|ic
photo|col|lage +s
photo|compos|ition
photo|copi|able
photo|cop|ied
  adjective
photo|copi|er +s
photo|copy
  photo|cop|ies
  photo|cop|ied
  photo|copy|ing
photo|degrad|able
photo|diode +s
photo|dynam|ic
photo|elec|tric
photo|elec|tri|city
photo|elec|tron +s
photo|emis|sion
photo es|say +s
photo fin|ish
  photo fin|ish|es
photo|finish|er +s
photo|finish|ing
pho|tog +s
photo|gen|ic
photo|gen|ic|ally
photo|gram
photo|gram|met|ric
photo|gram|met|rist
  +s
photo|gram|metry
photo|graph +s +ed
  +ing
photo|graph|able
pho|tog|raph|er +s
photo|graph|ic
photo|graph|ic|ally
pho|tog|raphy
photo|grav|ure +s
photo ID
photo|jour|nal|ism
photo|jour|nal|ist +s
photo|jour|nal|is|tic
photo|lith|og|raph|er
  +s
photo|litho|graph|ic
photo|lith|og|raphy
pho|toly|sis
photo|lytic
pho|tom|eter +s
photo|met|ric
pho|tom|etry
photo|micro|graph
  +s
photo|microg|raphy
photo|mon|tage +s
photo|multi|plier +s
pho|ton +s
pho|ton|ic
pho|ton|ics
photo-offset
photo op +s

photo|period +s
photo|period|ic
photo|period|ism
photo|phobia
photo|phob|ic
photo-realism
photo-realist +s
photo-realis|tic
photo|recep|tor +s
photo-
  reconnais|sance
photo|sensi|tive
photo|sensi|tiv|ity
photo|sphere +s
photo|spher|ic
Photo|stat +s
  proprietary noun
photo|stat verb
  photo|stats
  photo|stat|ted
  photo|stat|ting
photo|stat|ic
photo|syn|the|sis
photo|syn|the|size
  photo|syn|the|siz|es
  photo|syn|the|sized
  photo|syn|the|siz|
             ing
photo|syn|thet|ic
photo|syn|thet|ic|
             ally
photo|sys|tem +s
photo|tran|sis|tor +s
photo|troph|ic
  (= phototropic)
photo|trop|ic
photo|trop|ism
photo|vol|taic
photo|vol|taics
phras|al
phras|al|ly
phrase
  phras|es
  phrased
  phras|ing
phrase book +s
phrase|o|gram +s
phrase|o|logic|al
phrase|ol|ogy
  phrase|ol|o|gies
phras|ing +s noun
phreak +s +ed +ing
  (one who makes
  fraudulent use of a
  telephone)
phreak|ing +s
  (telephone fraud)
phre|atic
phren|ic
phren|o|logic|al
phren|ol|o|gist +s
phren|ol|ogy

Phry|gia (ancient
  region, Asia Minor)
Phry|gian +s
phthal|ate +s
phthal|ic
phthis|ic
phthis|ic|al
phthis|is
Phu|ket (island &
  resort, Thailand)
phut
Phutha|dit|jhaba
  (town, South Africa)
phyco|logic|al
phy|col|o|gist +s
phy|col|ogy
phyco|my|cete +s
Phyfe, Dun|can (US
  furniture designer)
phyla
phy|lac|tery
  phy|lac|ter|ies
phy|let|ic
phy|let|ic|ally
phyl|lo (pastry)
  [☞ Philo Judaeus]
phyl|lode +s
phyllo|quin|one
phyllo|tac|tic
phyllo|taxis
phyl|lox|era
phylo|gen|esis
phylo|gen|etic
phylo|gen|etic|ally
phy|logeny
  phy|logen|ies
phy|lum
  phyla
phys. ed.
physic
  phys|ics
  phys|icked
  phys|ick|ing
phys|ic|al +s
phys|ic|al|ism
phys|ic|al|ist +s
phys|ic|al|is|tic
phys|ic|al|ity
phys|ic|al|ly
phys|ic|al|ness
phys|ician +s
physi|cist +s
phys|ico|chem|ical
phys|ics
physio +s
physi|oc|racy
  physi|oc|ra|cies
physio|crat +s
physio|crat|ic
physio|gnom|ic
physio|gnom|ic|al
physio|gnom|ic|al|ly

physi|ognom|ist +s
physi|ognomy
  physi|ognom|ies
physi|og|raph|er +s
physio|graph|ic
physio|graph|ic|al
physi|og|raphy
physio|logic
physio|logic|al
physio|logic|al|ly
physi|ol|o|gist +s
physi|ol|ogy
  physi|ol|o|gies
physio|ther|apist +s
physio|ther|apy
phy|sique +s
phyto|chem|ical
phyto|chem|ist +s
phyto|chem|istry
phyto|chrome
phyto|gen|esis
phy|togeny
phyto|geog|raph|er +s
phyto|geo|graph|ic
phyto|geog|raphy
phyto|patho|logic|al
phyto|path|ol|o|gist +s
phyto|path|ol|ogy
phy|toph|a|gous
phyto|plank|ton
phy|tot|omy
phyto|toxic
phyto|tox|icity
phyto|toxin +s
PI (private
  investigator)
  PIs
pi +s (Greek letter;
  ratio of
  circumference to
  diameter)
pi|acu|lar
Piaf, Edith (French
  singer)
pi|affe
  pi|affes
  pi|affed
  pi|af|fing
Pia|get, Jean (Swiss
  psychologist)
Pia|get|ian *adjective*
pia mater +s
piani
pian|ism
pian|is|simo
  pian|is|simos or
  pian|is|simi
pian|ist +s
pian|is|tic
pian|is|tic|ally

piano
• (instrument)
  plural pianos
• (soft passage)
  plural pianos or
  piani
piano-accordion +s
piano|forte +s
Pian|ola +s
  proprietary
piano|less
piano no|bile
  piani no|bili
pias|sava +s
pi|astre +s
Piauí (state, Brazil)
piaz|za +s
pi|broch +s
pic (picture)
  pix or pics
  [☞ pick]
pica +s (type size;
  abnormal craving)
  [☞ pika]
pica|dor +s
pi|can|te (spicy, hot)
  [☞ piquant,
  peccant]
Pi|card, Jean (French
  astronomer)
  [☞ Piccard]
Pic|ardy (region,
  France)
picar|esque
picar|oon +s
Pi|cas|so, Pablo
  Ruiz y (Spanish
  painter)
pic|ay|une +s
Pic|ca|dilly (street,
  London)
pic|ca|lilli +s
pic|ca|ninny *offensive*
  (= pickaninny)
  pic|ca|nin|nies
Pic|card, Au|guste
  (Belgian physicist)
  [☞ Picard]
Pic|card, Jean Felix
  (US aeronautical
  engineer)
  [☞ Picard]
pic|colo +s
pick +s +ed +ing
  (select, choice;
  probe; pluck; pointed
  tool; plectrum)
  [☞ pic]
picka|ninny *offensive*
  picka|nin|nies
pick|axe +s
pick|er +s

pick|er|el
  plural pick|er|el or
  pick|er|els
pick|erel|weed +s
Pick|er|ing (town,
  Canada)
Pick|er|ing, Ed|ward
  Charles (US
  astronomer)
Pick|er|ing, Wil|liam
  Hay|ward (US
  engineer)
Pick|er|ing, Wil|liam
  Henry (US
  astronomer)
pick|et +s +ed +ing
  (protest group; stake)
  [☞ piquet]
pick|et|er +s
pick|et fence +s
  (picket-fence *when*
  preceding a noun)
pick|et line +s
Pick|ford, Mary (Cdn-
  born US actress)
pick|i|er
pick|i|est
pick|i|ness
pick|ings
pickle
  pickles
  pickled
  pick|ling
pickled *adjective*
pick|ler +s
pick|lock +s
pick-me-up +s
pick off *verb*
  picks off
  picked off
  pick|ing off
pick|off +s *noun*
pick|pocket +s +ed
  +ing
pick|pocket|ing +s
pick up *verb*
  picks up
  picked up
  pick|ing up
pick|up +s *noun &*
  adjective
pick-up sticks
Pick|wick|ian
picky
  pick|i|er
  pick|i|est
pick-your-own
pic|nic (outdoor meal)
  pic|nics
  pic|nicked
  pic|nick|ing
  [☞ pyknic]
pic|nick|er +s

pic|nicky
Pico da Neb|lina
  (mountain, Brazil)
Pico della
  Miran|dola,
  Gio|van|ni, Count
  (Italian philosopher)
Pico de Ori|zaba
  (= Citlaltépetl,
  Mexico)
picot +s (loop in lace
  or embroidery)
  [☞ pekoe]
pic|ric
Pict +s
Pict|ish
picto|gram +s
picto|graph +s
picto|graph|ic
pic|tog|raphy
pic|tor|ial +s
pic|tor|ial|ly
Pic|tou (town,
  Canada)
pic|ture
  pic|tures
  pic|tured
  pic|tur|ing
pic|ture book +s
  (picture-book *when*
  preceding a noun)
picture-perfect
pic|ture post|card +s
  (picture-postcard
  when preceding a
  noun)
pic|tur|esque
pic|tur|esque|ly
pic|tur|esque|ness
picture-writing
pid|dle
  pid|dles
  pid|dled
  pid|dling
pid|dler +s
pid|dling *adjective*
pid|dly
pid|dock +s
pid|gin +s (language)
  [☞ pigeon]
pidgin|iz|a|tion +s
pidgin|ize
  pidgin|iz|es
  pidgin|ized
  pidgin|iz|ing
pie +s (food; magpie;
  former Indian
  currency; in 'pie in
  the sky', 'easy as
  pie')
  [☞ pi]
pie|bald +s

piece (portion; item, article; firearm; join)
pieces
pieced
piecing
[☞ peace]
pièce de ré|sis|tance
pièces de ré|sis|tance
piece|meal
piece rate +s
piece|work
piece|work|er +s
pie chart +s
pie crust +s
pie|crust table +s
pied
pied-à-terre
pieds-à-terre
Pied|mont (region, Italy)
pied|mont +s
Pied|mont|ese
plural Pied|mont|ese
pie-dog +s (use pye-dog)
Pied Piper +s
pie-eyed
pie-faced
Pie|gan (use Peigan)
plural Pie|gan or Pie|gans
pie pan +s
pie plate +s
pier +s (dock; Architecture)
[☞ peer, Pierre]
Pierce, Frank|lin (US president)
[☞ Peirce, Pearse, Pears]
pierce
pier|ces
pierced
pier|cing
pierced adjective
pier|cer +s
pier|cing adjective
pier|cing|ly
pier glass
pier glass|es
Piero della Fran|cesca (Italian painter)
Pierre (city, US)
Pierre|fonds (city, Canada)
Pier|rot +s
pie-shaped
Pietà +s
Pieter|maritz|burg (city, South Africa)
piet|ism

piet|ist +s
piet|is|tic
piet|is|tic|al
piety
piet|ies
piezo|elec|tric
piezo|elec|tric|ally
piezo|elec|tri|city
piez|om|eter +s
pif|fle
pif|fles
pif|fled
pif|fling
pif|fler +s
pif|fling adjective
pig
pigs
pigged
pig|ging
Pi|geon (river, Canada)
pi|geon +s (bird; simpleton; concern)
[☞ pidgin]
pi|geon breast +s
pigeon-breast|ed
pi|geon chest +s
pigeon-chested
pigeon|hole
pigeon|holes
pigeon|holed
pigeon|hol|ing
pi|geon|ry
pi|geon|ries
pigeon-toed
pig|gery
pig|ger|ies
pig|gish
pig|gish|ness
piggy
pig|gies
pig|gi|er
pig|gi|est
piggy|back +s +ed +ing
piggy bank +s
pig|head|ed
pig|headed|ly
pig|headed|ness
pig-ignorant
pig in a blan|ket
pigs in a blan|ket
pig|let +s
pig|like
pig|ment +s +ed +ing
pig|men|tary
pig|men|ta|tion +s
pig|men|tosa
pigmy (use pygmy)
pig|mies
pig|nut +s

pig out verb
pigs out
pigged out
pig|ging out
pig-out +s noun
pig|pen +s
pig|skin +s
pig|stick|er +s
pig|sty
pig|sties
pig|tail +s
pig|tailed
pig|weed +s
pika +s (animal)
[☞ pica]
pike
• (fish)
   plural pike
• (weapon; peak; tollgate; road; Diving)
   pikes
   piked
   pik|ing
pike-perch
   plural pike-perch or pike-perches
pik|er +s
pike|staff +s
Pik Po|bedy (mountain, Kyrgyzstan)
pi|laf +s
pi|las|ter +s
pi|las|tered
Pi|late, Pon|tius (New Testament)
[☞ pilot]
pi|lau +s
pil|chard +s
pile
piles
piled
pil|ing
pil|eate
pil|eat|ed
pile|driv|er +s
pile|less
piles
pile up verb
piles up
piled up
pil|ing up
pile|up +s noun
pi|leus
pilei
pil|fer +s +ed +ing
pil|fer|age
pil|fer|er +s
pil|grim +s
pil|grim|age +s
pil|ing +s noun

Pili|pino (Philippine language)
[☞ Filipino, Filipina, Philippine]
pill +s +ed +ing
pil|lage
pil|lages
pil|laged
pil|la|ging
pil|la|ger +s
pil|lar +s
pil|lared
pillar|less
pill|box
pill|boxes
pil|lion +s
pil|lock +s
pil|lory
pil|lor|ies
pil|lor|ied
pil|lory|ing
pil|low +s +ed +ing
pillow|case +s
pil|low slip +s
pil|low talk +s
pil|lowy
pill-popper +s
pill-popping
pil|lu|lar (use pilular)
pil|lule +s (use pilule)
pil|lu|lous (use pilulous)
pil|ose (hairy)
pil|os|ity
pi|lot +s +ed +ing
[☞ Pilate]
pilot|age
pilot fish
   plural pilot fish
pilot|house +s
pilot|less
pil|ous (hairy: use pilose)
Pil|sen (city, Czech Republic)
Pil|sen|er +s (use Pilsner)
Pils|ner +s
Pil|sud|ski, Josef (Klem|ens) (Polish statesman)
Pilt|down man
pilu|lar
pil|ule +s
pilu|lous
pi|men|to +s
pi me|son +s
pi|mien|to +s
(– pimento)
pimp +s +ed +ing
pim|per|nel +s
pimp|ing noun
pim|ple +s

pim|pled *adjective*
pim|ply
PIN (personal
  identification
  number)
  PINs
pin
  pins
  pinned
  pin|ning
pina co|lada +s
pina|fore +s
Pin|ang (= Penang,
  Malaysia)
pi|nata +s
Pina|tubo (volcano,
  the Philippines)
pin|ball
pince-nez
  plural pince-nez
pin|cer +s
pinch
  pinch|es
  pinched
  pinch|ing
pinch|beck +s
pinched *adjective*
pinch|er +s (one who
  pinches)
  [☞ Doberman
  pinscher]
pin cherry
  pin cher|ries
pinch hit +s *noun*
pinch-hit *verb*
  pinch-hits
  pinch-hit
  pinch-hitting
pinch-hitter +s
pinch|penny
  pinch|pen|nies
pinch-run
  pinch-runs
  pinch-ran
  pinch-running
pinch-runner +s
Pinck|ney, Charles
  Cotes|worth (US
  diplomat)
Pin|court (town,
  Canada)
pin|curl +s
pin|cushion +s
Pin|dar (Greek poet)
Pin|dar|ic
Pin|dus (mountain
  range, Greece)
pine
  pines
  pined
  pining
pin|eal
pine|apple +s

pine cone +s
pine mar|ten +s
pine nut +s
Pine Pass (mountain
  pass, Canada)
Pi|nero, Sir Ar|thur
  Wing (English
  playwright)
pin|ery
  pin|er|ies
pine|sap +s
pine tar
pin|etum
  pin|eta
pine|wood +s
piney
pin|feather +s
ping +s +ed +ing
ping|er +s
pin|go +s
ping-pong
pin|guid
pin|head +s
pin|head|ed
pin|headed|ness
pin-high
pin|hole +s
pin|ion +s +ed +ing
  (wing; bind wings or
  arms; cogwheel)
  [☞ piñon, Pinyin]
pink +s +ed +ing +er
  +est
pink-collar
Pink|er|ton, Allan (US
  detective)
pink eye
pink|ie +s (*use* pinky)
pink|ing *adjective*
pink|ish
pink|ly
pink|ness
pinko
  pink|os *or* pink|oes
pink slip +s *noun*
pink-slip *verb*
  pink-slips
  pink-slipped
  pink-slipping
pinky
  pink|ies
pin|less
pinna
  pin|nae *or* pin|nas
pin|nace +s
pin|na|cle
  (culmination, peak)
  pin|na|cles
  pin|nac|led
  pin|nac|ling
  [☞ pinochle]
pin|nate
pin|nate|ly

pin|na|tion
pinni|ped +s
pin|nu|lar
pin|nule +s
pinny
  pin|nies
Pino|chet, Au|gus|to
  (Chilean general &
  statesman)
pi|nochle +s (card
  game)
  [☞ pinnacle]
pi|nole
pi|ñon +s (pine & its
  seed)
Pi|not +s
Pinot Blanc +s
Pinot Noir +s
pin|point +s +ed
  +ing
pin|prick +s
Pin|sent, Gor|don
  Ed|ward (Cdn actor
  & writer)
pin|stripe +s
pin|striped
pint +s
pinta +s
pin|tail +s
Pin|ten|dre
  (municipality,
  Canada)
Pin|ter, Har|old
  (English playwright)
Pin|ter|esque
pin|tle +s
pin|to +s
pint-size (= pint-
  sized)
pint-sized
pin|tuck +s
pin|tucked
pin|tuck|ing
pin up *verb*
  pins up
  pinned up
  pin|ning up
pin-up +s *noun*
pin|wale
pin|wheel +s +ed
  +ing
pin|worm +s
piny (*use* piney)
Pin|yin (system for
  transliterating
  Chinese)
  [☞ piñon, pinion]
pin|yon +s (pine & its
  seed: *use* piñon)
  [☞ pinion, Pinyin]
Pin|zón, Mar|tín
  Alon|zo (Spanish
  navigator)

Pin|zón, Vi|cente
  Yáñez (Spanish
  navigator)
pio|let +s
pion +s (pi meson)
  [☞ peon, paeon,
  paean]
pi|on|eer +s
pi|on|eer|ing
pi|on|ic
pious (devout;
  sanctimonious)
  [☞ Pius]
pious|ly
pious|ness
Pioz|zi, Hes|ter
  Lynch (English
  writer & friend of
  Samuel Johnson)
pip
  pips
  pipped
  pip|ping
pi|pal +s (bo tree: *use*
  peepul)
  [☞ people]
pipe
  pipes
  piped
  piping
pipe bomb +s
pipe|clay +s +ed
  +ing
pipe clean|er +s
pipe dream +s
pipe|fish
  plural pipe|fish *or*
  pipe|fish|es
pipe|fit|ter +s
pipe|fit|ting
pipe|ful +s
pipe|less
pipe|line
  pipe|lines
  pipe|lined
  pipe|lin|ing
pipe|lin|ing *noun*
piper +s
pi|peri|dine
pipe|stem +s
pipe-stone
pip|ette (tube)
  pip|ettes
  pip|et|ted
  pip|et|ting
  [☞ pipit]
pipe|work +s
pip|ing +s *noun &*
  adjective
pip|ing hot
pipis|trelle +s
pip|it +s (bird)
  [☞ pipette]

pip|kin +s
pip|pin +s
pip|sis|sewa +s
pip|squeak +s
pipy
pi|quan|cy
pi|quant (pungent;
  stimulating)
  [☞ peccant,
  picante]
pi|quant|ly
pique (arouse, wound;
  enmity)
  piques
  piqued
  pi|quing
  [☞ peak, peek,
  Peke]
piqué (*Textiles, Dance*)
pi|quet (*Cards*)
pir|acy
  pira|cies
Pi|raeus (port,
  Athens)
Piran|del|lian
Piran|dello, Luigi
  (Italian playwright)
Pira|nesi, Gio|van|ni
  Bat|tis|ta or
  Giam|bat|tista
  (Italian engraver)
Pira|nesi|an
pi|ranha +s (fish)
pir|ate
  pir|ates
  pir|at|ed
  pir|at|ing
pir|at|ed *adjective*
pir|at|ic
pir|at|ic|al
pir|at|ic|al|ly
piri piri
pi|rogue +s
pi|roshki
  plural pi|roshki or
  pi|rosh|kis
pirou|ette
  pirou|ettes
  pirou|et|ted
  pirou|et|ting
Pisa (city, Italy)
pis aller
Pisan, Chris|tine de
  (French writer)
Pisan +s (of Pisa)
Pi|sano, An|drea
  (Italian sculptor)
Pi|sano, Gio|van|ni
  (Italian sculptor)
Pi|sano, Nic|ola
  (Italian sculptor)
Pi|sano, Nino (Italian
  sculptor)

pis|ca|tor|ial
pis|ca|tor|ial|ly
pis|ca|tory
Pis|cean +s
Pis|ces (constellation;
  Zodiac)
pisci|cul|tur|al
pisci|cul|ture
pisci|cul|tur|ist +s
pis|cina (basin)
  pis|cinae or
  pis|cinas
pis|cine (of fish)
Piscis Aus|tri|nus
  (constellation)
pisciv|or|ous
pish
Pish|pek (= Bishkek,
  Kyrgyzstan)
Pi|sidia (ancient
  region, Asia Minor)
Pi|sid|ian +s
pisi|form +s
Pi|sis|tra|tus
  (Athenian tyrant)
pis|mire +s
piss
  piss|es
  pissed
  piss|ing
piss|ant +s
Pis|sarro, Ca|mille
  (French painter)
pissed *adjective*
pissed off
piss|er +s
piss|oir +s
piss-poor
piss-pot +s
piss-up +s
pissy
  piss|i|er
  piss|i|est
pis|ta|chio +s
pis|ta|chio green +s
  (pis|tachio-green
  *when preceding a
  noun*)
piste +s
pis|til +s (*Botany*)
  [☞ pistol]
pis|til|late
pis|tol (gun)
  pis|tols
  pis|tolled
  pis|tol|ling
  [☞ pistil]
pis|tole +s (coin)
pistol-grip +s
pistol-whip
  pistol-whips
  pistol-whipped
  pistol-whipping

pis|ton +s
pis|ton en|gine +s
piston-engined
pis|tou
pit
  pits
  pit|ted
  pit|ting
  [☞ Pitt]
pita +s (bread)
  [☞ pitta]
pit-a-pat
pit bull +s (terrier)
pit-bull (fierce,
  aggressive)
Pit|cairn (islands,
  S Pacific)
pitch
  pitch|es
  pitched
  pitch|ing
pitch-black
pitch|blende +s
pitch-dark
pitched *adjective*
pitch|er +s
pitcher|ful +s
pitch|fork +s +ed
  +ing
pitch|man
  pitch|men
pitch out *verb*
  pitch|es out
  pitched out
  pitch|ing out
pitch|out +s *noun*
pitchy
  pitch|i|er
  pitch|i|est
pit|eous
pit|eous|ly
pit|eous|ness
pit|fall +s
pith
pit|head +s
Pithe|can|thro|pus
pith|i|ly
pith|i|ness
pithos
  pithoi
pithy
  pith|i|er
  pith|i|est
piti|able
piti|able|ness
piti|ably
piti|ful
piti|ful|ly
piti|ful|ness
piti|less
piti|less|ly
piti|less|ness
pit-lamping

Pit|man, Sir Isaac
  (English shorthand
  inventor)
pit|man
  • (miner)
    plural pit|men
  • (connecting rod)
    plural pit|mans
piton +s
Pi|tons (mountains,
  St. Lucia)
Pitot tube +s
pit prop +s
pit socks
pit stop +s
Pitt (SW Pacific island)
Pitt, Wil|liam ('the
  Elder'), 1st Earl of
  Chat|ham (English
  secretary of state)
Pitt, Wil|liam ('the
  Young|er') (English
  prime minister)
pitta +s (bird)
  [☞ pita]
pit|tance +s
pit|ted *adjective*
pitter-patter
Pitt Mead|ows
  (municipality,
  Canada)
Pitts|burgh (city, US)
Pitts|burgh|er +s
pi|tu|itary
  pi|tu|itar|ies
pit viper +s
pity
  pities
  pitied
  pity|ing
pity|ing *adjective*
pity|ing|ly
pityr|ia|sis
  pityr|ia|ses
più (*Music* more)
  [☞ pew]
più mosso
Pius (popes)
  [☞ pious]
pivot +s +ed +ing
pivot|al
pix (pictures, movies;
  for container, chest
  use pyx)
pixel +s
pixel|ate (display as
  or divide into pixels)
  pixel|ates
  pixel|at|ed
  pixel|at|ing
  [☞ pixilated]

pixel|a|tion +s (image divided into pixels) [☞ **pixillation**]
pixie +s
pixie|ish
pix|il|at|ed (crazy) [☞ **pixelated**]
pix|il|a|tion (film technique in which actors appear animated: *use* **pixillation**) [☞ **pixelation**]
pix|il|lat|ed (crazy: *use* **pixilated**) [☞ **pixelated**]
pix|il|la|tion (film technique in which actors appear animated) [☞ **pixelation**]
pixy (*use* **pixie**)
  pix|ies
Pizan, Chris|tine de (= **Pisan**)
Pi|zarro, Fran|cis|co (Spanish conquistador)
pi|zazz (*use* **pizzazz**)
piz|za +s
piz|zazz
piz|zeria +s
pizzi|cato
  pizzi|catos or
  pizzi|cati
piz|zle +s
PJs (pyjamas)
PK (preacher's kid)
  PKs
plac|abil|ity
plac|able (easily placated) [☞ **placeable**]
plac|ably
plac|ard +s
pla|cate (pacify)
  pla|cates
  pla|cat|ed
  pla|cat|ing
  pla|cated *past & past participle of* **placate** [☞ **plicated**]
pla|cat|ing|ly
pla|ca|tion +s (appeasement) [☞ **plication**]
pla|ca|tor +s
pla|ca|tory
place (position; situate)
  places
  placed
  pla|cing [☞ **plaice**]

place|able (able to be placed)
pla|cebo +s
place kick +s *noun*
place-kick +s +ed +ing *verb*
place-kicker +s
place|less
place|man
  place|men
place|mat +s
place|ment +s
place name +s
pla|centa
  pla|cen|tas or
  pla|cen|tae
pla|cen|tal
Pla|cen|tia (bay, Canada)
pla|cer +s
pla|cid
pla|cid|ity
pla|cid|ly
pla|cid|ness
pla|cing +s *noun*
plack|et +s
plac|oid
pla|gal
plage +s (bright region on sun) [☞ **plague**]
pla|giar|ism
pla|giar|ist +s
pla|giar|is|tic
pla|giar|ize
  pla|giar|iz|es
  pla|giar|ized
  pla|giar|iz|ing
pla|giar|iz|er +s
pla|gio|clase +s
plague (disease; afflict, harass)
  plagues
  plagued
  plaguing [☞ **plage**]
plaice (fish)
  plural **plaice** or
  plai|ces
plaid +s
plain +er +est +s +ed +ing (clear; ordinary; simple; prairie; mourn) [☞ **plane**]
plain|chant +s
plain clothes (**plain|clothes** *when preceding a noun*)
plain Jane +s *noun*
plain-Jane *adjective*
plain|ly
plain|ness

Plains (region, N America)
plains bison
  plural **plains bison**
plains buf|falo
  plural **plains buf|falo** or
  plains buf|fa|loes
Plains Cree
  plural **Plains Cree** or
  Plains Crees
Plains In|di|an +s
plains|man
  plains|men
Plains of Abra|ham (battle site, Canada)
plain|song +s
plain-spoken
plaint +s
plain|tiff +s (person bringing legal action against another)
plain|tive (mournful)
plain|tive|ly
plain|tive|ness
plain-vanilla
plait +s +ed +ing (braid) [☞ **plate**]
Pla|mon|don, Luc (Cdn songwriter)
plan
  plans
  planned
  plan|ning
pla|nar (of or like a plane) [☞ **planer**]
pla|nar|ian +s
Plan B
plan|chet +s (metal disc)
plan|chette +s (writing board)
Planck, Max Karl Ernst Lud|wig (German physicist)
Planck con|stant (= **Planck's constant**)
Planck's con|stant
plane (flat surface; airplane; level; smoothening tool; tree)
  planes
  planed
  plan|ing [☞ **plain**]
plane|load +s
plane-polar|iz|a|tion
plane-polar|ized

plan|er (tool) [☞ **planar**]
plan|et +s
plan|et|ar|ium
  plan|et|ar|iums or
  plan|et|aria
plan|et|ary
plan|et|es|imal +s
plan|et|oid +s
plan|et|ol|ogy
plane tree +s
planet|wide
plan|form +s
plan|gency
plan|gent
plan|gent|ly
plan|im|eter +s
plani|met|ric
plani|met|ric|al
plani|met|ric|al|ly
plan|im|etry
plan|ish
  plan|ish|es
  plan|ished
  plan|ish|ing
plan|ish|er +s
plani|sphere +s
plani|spher|ic
plank +s +ed +ing (lumber etc.) [☞ **Planck**]
planked *adjective*
plank house +s
plank|ing *noun*
plank|ton
plank|ton|ic
planned *adjective*
plan|ner +s
plan|ning *noun*
plano|concave
plano|convex
plant +s +ed +ing
plant|able
Plan|ta|genet +s (English royal house)
plan|tain +s
plan|tar +s (of the side of the foot)
plan|ta|tion +s
plant|er +s (thing that plants)
planter's punch
  planter's punch|es
planti|grade +s
plant|ing +s *noun*
plant|let +s
plant|like
plants|man
  plants|men
plaque +s

plash
plash|es
plashed
plash|ing
plash|ing *adjective*
plashy
plash|i|er
plash|i|est
plasm +s (= plasma)
plas|ma +s
plas|mat|ic
plas|mic
plas|mid +s
plas|min
plas|mino|gen
plasmo|desma
plasmo|des|mata
plas|mo|dial
plas|mo|dium
plas|modia
plas|moly|sis
Plas|sey (battle site, India)
plas|ter +s +ed +ing
plaster|board +s
plas|tered *adjective*
plas|ter|er +s
plaster|work +s
plas|tery
plas|tic +s
plas|tic|ally
Plas|ti|cine *proprietary*
plas|ti|city
plas|ti|ciz|a|tion
plas|ti|cize
plas|ti|ciz|es
plas|ti|cized
plas|ti|ciz|ing
plas|ti|ciz|er +s
plas|ticky
plas|tid +s
plas|tral
plas|tron +s
plat
plats
plat|ted
plat|ting
Pla|taea (battle site, ancient Greece)
plat du jour
plats du jour
Plate (river, S America)
plate (dish; thin flat object, etc.; cover with thin layer)
plates
plat|ed
plat|ing
[☞ plait]
pla|teau
• *noun*

pla|teaus or
pla|teaux
• *verb*
pla|teaus
pla|teaued
pla|teau|ing
plate|ful +s
plate glass
plate|less
plate|let +s
plat|en +s
plat|er +s
plate rail +s
plat|form +s
Plath, Syl|via (US poet)
plat|ing +s *noun*
pla|tin|ic
plat|in|iz|a|tion +s
plat|in|ize
plat|in|iz|es
plat|in|ized
plat|in|iz|ing
plat|in|oid +s
plat|in|um +s
plat|in|um blond +s
plati|tude +s
plati|tud|in|ize
plati|tud|in|iz|es
plati|tud|in|ized
plati|tud|in|iz|ing
plati|tud|in|ous
Plato (Greek philosopher)
Pla|ton|ic (of Plato; ideal; in 'Platonic solid' & 'Platonic body')
[☞ Plutonic]
pla|ton|ic (not sexual)
[☞ plutonic]
Pla|ton|ic|ally
Pla|ton|ism
Pla|ton|ist +s
pla|toon +s +ed +ing
Platt|deutsch
plat|ter +s
Platts|burgh (battle site, US)
platy|hel|minth +s
platy|pus
platy|pus|es
platyr|rhine +s
plau|dit +s
plaus|ibil|ity
plaus|ible
plaus|ibly
Plau|tus, Titus Mac|cius (Roman dramatist)
play +s +ed +ing
playa +s
play|abil|ity

play|able
play-act +s +ed +ing
play-acting *noun*
play-action +s
play-actor +s
play back *verb*
plays back
played back
play|ing back
play|back +s *noun*
play|bill +s
play|book +s
play|boy +s
play-by-play +s
play|dough +s
play down *verb*
plays down
played down
play|ing down
play|down +s *noun*
Play|er, Gary Jim (South African golfer)
play|er +s
Play|fair, John (Scottish geologist)
play|ful
play|ful|ly
play|ful|ness
play|goer +s
play|ground +s
play|group +s
play|house +s
play|let +s
play|list +s +ed +ing
play|maker +s
play|making
play|mate +s
play off *verb*
plays off
played off
play|ing off
play|off +s *noun*
play|pen +s
play|room +s
play|school +s
play|set +s
play|suit +s
play|thing +s
play|time +s
play|wright +s
[☞ playwriting]
play|writing
[☞ playwright]
plaza +s
plea +s
plea bar|gain +s +ed +ing
pleach
pleach|es
pleached
pleach|ing
plead +s +ed +ing

plead|able
plead|er +s
plead|ing +s *noun*
plead|ing|ly
pleas|ance +s
pleas|ant
pleas|ant|ly
pleas|ant|ness
pleas|antry
pleas|ant|ries
please
pleas|es
pleased
pleas|ing
pleased *adjective*
pleas|ing *adjective*
pleas|ing|ly
pleas|ur|able
pleas|ur|able|ness
pleas|ur|ably
pleas|ure
pleas|ures
pleas|ured
pleas|ur|ing
pleas|ure dome +s
pleat +s +ed +ing
pleat|ed *adjective*
pleat|ing *noun*
pleb +s (plebeian)
plebe +s (military cadet)
ple|be|ian +s
ple|be|ian|ism
pleb|is|cit|ary
pleb|is|cite +s
plec|trum
plec|trums or
plec|tra
pledge
pledg|es
pledged
pledg|ing
pledge|able
pledg|ee +s
pledg|er +s (*in general use*)
pledg|or +s (*Law*)
Pleia|des (*Greek Myth*; *Astronomy*)
plein-air
pleio|trop|ic
pleio|trop|ism
plei|ot|ropy
Pleis|to|cene
Plekh|anov, Georgy Valen|tin|ovich (Russian revolutionary)
plen|ary
plen|aries
pleni|poten|tiary
pleni|poten|tiar|ies
pleni|tude +s

plen|teous
plen|teous|ly
plen|teous|ness
plen|ti|ful
plen|ti|ful|ly
plen|ti|ful|ness
plenty
plen|um +s
pleo|chro|ic
pleo|chro|ism
pleo|morph|ic
pleo|morph|ism
pleo|nasm +s
pleo|nas|tic
pleo|nas|tic|ally
ple|sio|saur +s
Ples|sis|ville (town, Canada)
ples|sor +s
pleth|ora +s
pleth|or|ic
pleth|or|ic|ally
pleura
• (lung membrane)
   plural pleurae
• *plural of* pleuron
pleur|al (of pleurae or pleura)
   [☞ plural]
pleur|isy
pleur|it|ic
pleur|on (side of an arthropod's body)
   plural pleura
   [☞ pleura]
pleuro|pneu|monia
Plev|en (town, Bulgaria)
plew +s
plexi|form
Plexi|glas *proprietary*
plex|or +s
plex|us
   plural plex|us or plex|us|es
pli|abil|ity
pli|able
pli|able|ness
pli|ably
pli|ancy
pli|ant
pli|ant|ly
pli|cate (folded)
   [☞ placate]
pli|cat|ed (folded)
   [☞ placated]
pli|ca|tion +s (fold)
   [☞ placation]
plié +s
pliers
plight +s +ed +ing
Plim|soll (mark, line)

plim|soll +s (shoe)
plink +s +ed +ing
plinky
plinth +s
Pliny ('the Elder') (Roman historian)
Pliny ('the Young|er') (Roman senator & writer)
Plio|cene
plissé
plod
   plods
   plod|ded
   plod|ding
plod|der +s
plod|ding *adjective*
plod|ding|ly
ploidy
   ploi|dies
Ploi|eşti (city, Romania)
plonk +s +ed +ing (set down; thud; wine)
   [☞ Planck]
plop
   plops
   plopped
   plop|ping
plo|sion +s
plo|sive +s
plot
   plots
   plot|ted
   plot|ting
Plo|tinus (Roman philosopher)
plot|less
plot|less|ness
plot line +s
plot|ter +s
Plough (the Big Dipper)
plough +s +ed +ing (*use* plow *except in* ploughman & ploughshare)
plough|able (*use* plowable)
ploughed *adjective* (*use* plowed)
plough|er +s (*use* plower)
plough|man
   plough|men
   [☞ *Piers Plowman*]
plough|man's lunch
   plough|man's lunch|es
plough|share +s
Plov|div (city, Bulgaria)

plover +s
plow +s +ed +ing
plow|able
plowed *adjective*
plow|er +s
plow|man (*use* ploughman *except in* Piers Plowman)
   plow|men
plow|share +s (*use* ploughshare)
ploy +s (scheme)
ploye +s (pancake)
pluck +s +ed +ing
pluck|er +s
pluck|i|ly
pluck|i|ness
plucky
   pluck|i|er
   pluck|i|est
plug
   plugs
   plugged
   plug|ging
plug and play (plug-and-play *when preceding a noun*)
plugged *adjective*
plugged-in
plug|ger +s
plug|hole +s
plug-in +s
plug-ugly
   plug-uglies
plum +s (fruit; colour; coveted)
   [☞ plumb]
plum|age
plum|aged
plumb +s +ed +ing (lead weight; vertical; exactly, downright; measure depth; explore)
   [☞ plum]
plum|bago +s
plumb bob +s
plum|be|ous
plumb|er +s (one who fits & repairs plumbing)
   [☞ Plummer]
plumber's friend +s
plumber's help|er +s
plumber's snake +s
plum|bic
plumb|ing
plum|bism
plumb line +s
plum|bous
plum cake +s
plum-coloured
plum duff +s

plume
   plumes
   plumed
   plum|ing
plumed *adjective*
plume|less
plume|like
plum|i|er *comparative of* plumy
   [☞ plummier]
plum|i|est *superlative of* plumy
   [☞ plummiest]
Plum|mer, (Ar|thur) Chris|to|pher Orme (Cdn actor)
   [☞ plumber]
plum|met +s +ed +ing
plummy (like plums; having a deep voice)
   plum|mi|er
   plum|mi|est
plum|ose
plump +er +est +s +ed +ing
plump|ish
plump|ly
plump|ness
plumpy
plum|ule +s
plumy (adorned with plumes)
   plum|i|er
   plum|i|est
   [☞ plummy]
plun|der +s +ed +ing
plun|der|er +s
plunge
   plun|ges
   plunged
   plun|ging
plun|ger +s
plunk +s +ed +ing
plu|perfect
plur|al +s (more than one; *Grammar*)
   [☞ pleural]
plur|al|ism
plur|al|ist +s
plur|al|is|tic
plur|al|is|tic|ally
plur|al|ity
   plur|al|ities
plur|al|iz|a|tion +s
plur|al|ize
   plur|al|iz|es
   plur|al|ized
   plur|al|iz|ing
plur|al|ly
plus
   plus|es

Plus-15
Plus-15s
plus ça change
plus-fours
plush +er +est
plush|ly
plush|ness
plushy
plush|i|er
plush|i|est
plus-minus
plus-minuses
Plu|tarch (Greek
biographer)
Pluto (*Greek Myth*;
Astronomy)
plu|toc|racy
plu|toc|ra|cies
pluto|crat +s
pluto|crat|ic
pluto|crat|ic|ally
pluton +s
Plu|to|nian (of Pluto;
infernal)
Plu|to|nian (*Geology*)
Plu|ton|ic (of the god
Pluto; infernal)
[☞ Platonic]
plu|ton|ic (*Geology*)
[☞ platonic]
plu|to|nium
plu|vial +s
plu|vi|ous
ply
plies
plied
ply|ing
Ply|mouth (city,
England; town, US;
capital of
Montserrat)
Ply|mouth Breth|ren
Ply|mouth Rock +s
(historical site, US;
chicken)
ply|wood +s
PM (Prime Minister;
post-mortem;
Provost Marshal)
PMs
pneu|mat|ic
pneu|mat|ic|ally
pneu|mat|ics
pneu|mato|logic|al
pneu|ma|tol|ogy
pneu|mato|phore +s
pneumo|coc|cal
pneumo|coc|cus
pneumo|coc|ci
pneumo|coni|osis
pneumo|coni|oses

pneumo|cys|tis
car|inii
pneu|monia
pneumo|gas|tric
pneumo|mon|ec|tomy
pneu|mon|ec|to|
mies
pneu|monia +s
pneu|mon|ic
pneu|mon|itis
pneumo|thor|ax
Po (river, Italy)
[☞ Poe]
po +s (chamber pot)
[☞ peau de soie]
poach
poach|es
poached
poach|ing
poach|er +s
Poca|hon|tas
(Powhatan princess)
pock +s +ed +ing
(pustule; scar)
[☞ pox]
pocked *adjective*
pock|et +s +ed +ing
pocket|able
pock|et book +s
(paperback)
pocket|book +s
(purse; financial
resources; notebook)
pocket|ful +s
pock|et knife
pock|et knives
pocket|less
pocket-size
(= pocket-sized)
pocket-sized
pock|et veto
pock|et vetoes
pock|et vetoed
pock|et veto|ing
pock|mark +s
pock|marked
pocks *plural of* pock
[☞ pox]
pocky
poco
PO'd (pissed off)
pod
pods
pod|ded
pod|ding
pod|agra
pod|ag|ral
pod|ag|ric
pod|ag|rous
Pod|bor|ski, Steve
(Cdn downhill skier)
pod|ded *adjective*
podgi|ness

Pod|gor|ica (capital of
Montenegro)
podgy
podgi|er
podgi|est
podi|at|ric
podi|at|rist +s
podi|atry
po|dium
po|diums or podia
Pod|olsk (city, Russia)
pod|sol +s (*use*
podzol)
pod|sol|ic (*use*
podzolic)
pod|sol|ize (*use*
podzolize)
pod|sol|iz|es
pod|sol|ized
pod|sol|iz|ing
pod|zol +s
pod|zol|ic
pod|zol|ize
pod|zol|iz|es
pod|zol|ized
pod|zol|iz|ing
Poe, Edgar Allan (US
writer)
[☞ Po, Po Hai,
peau de soie]
poem +s (verse etc.)
[☞ pome]
poesy (poetry)
[☞ posey, posy]
poet +s
poet|aster +s
poet|ess
poet|ess|es
poet|ic
poet|ic|al
poet|ic|al|ly
poeti|cize
poeti|ciz|es
poeti|cized
poeti|ciz|ing
poet|ics
poet|ize
poet|iz|es
poet|ized
poet|iz|ing
Poet Laure|ate
Poet Laure|ates or
Poets Laure|ate
poet|ry
poet|ries
Poets' Cor|ner (in
Westminster Abbey)
po-faced
pogey (welfare or
unemployment
benefits)
[☞ pogy]

Pogo +s *proprietary*
(hot dog)
pogo +s (toy; dance)
pogo|nia +s
Pogo stick +s
proprietary (hot dog)
pogo stick +s *noun*
(toy)
pogo-stick +s +ed
+ing *verb* (jump on a
pogo stick; dance)
po|grom +s
pogy (fish; *for* welfare
benefits *use* pogey)
pogies
Po Hai (= Bo Hai,
China)
poi
poign|ance
poign|ancy
poign|ant
poign|ant|ly
poi|kilo|therm +s
poi|kilo|therm|al
poi|kilo|therm|ic
poilu +s
Poin|caré, Jules-
Henri (French
mathematician)
poin|ci|ana +s
poin|settia +s
point +s +ed +ing (*in
all but Dance senses*)
[☞ pointe]
point-and-click
point-and-shoot +s
point-blank
point blan|ket +s
point-counter|point
pointe (*Dance*)
Pointe-à-Pitre (town,
Guadeloupe)
Pointe-Claire (city,
Canada)
point|ed *adjective*
point|ed|ly
point|ed|ness
Poin|telle *proprietary*
Pointe-Noire (city,
Republic of the
Congo)
point|er +s
pointe shoe +s
pointe work
point form (point-
form *when preceding
a noun*)
Point Grey (peninsula,
Canada)
point guard +s
point|i|er
point|i|est
poin|til|lism

poin|til|list +s
poin|til|lis|tic
point|ing *noun*
point|less
point|less|ly
point|less|ness
point man
  point men
point-of-purchase
point-of-sale
Point Pelee (national
  park, Canada)
point spread +s
point-to-point +s
pointy
  point|i|er
  point|i|est
pointy head +s
pointy-headed
pois (in 'petits pois')
poise (composure;
  equilibrium; balance;
  viscosity)
  pois|es
  poised
  pois|ing
poised *adjective*
poi|sha
  plural poi|sha
poi|son +s +ed +ing
  [☞ Poisson]
poi|son|er +s
poi|son|ing +s *noun*
poi|son|ous
poi|son|ous|ly
poison-pen let|ter +s
Pois|son, Siméon-
  Denis (French
  mathematical
  physicist)
Pois|son
  dis|tri|bu|tion
Poi|tier, Sid|ney (US
  actor)
Poi|tiers (city, France)
Poi|tou (former
  province, France)
Poitou-Charentes
  (region, France)
poke
  pokes
  poked
  pok|ing
poke check +s *noun*
poke-check +s +ed
  +ing *verb*
poke-checking *noun*
pok|er +s
poker face +s
poker-faced
poke|weed +s
pok|ey +s (prison)
  [☞ poky]

pok|i|ly
pok|i|ness
poky (cramped; slow)
  pok|i|er
  pok|i|est
  [☞ pokey]
pol +s (politician)
  [☞ pall, pawl, Paul]
po|lack +s *offensive*
  (Polish person)
  [☞ pollack,
  pollock]
Po|land (country,
  Europe)
Po|lan|ski, Roman
  (French filmmaker)
Po|lanyi, John
  Charles (Cdn
  chemist)
polar
Polar Fleece
  proprietary
polar|im|eter +s
po|lari|met|ric
polar|im|etry
Po|lar|is (star; missile)
po|lari|scope +s
po|lari|scop|ic
po|lar|ity
  po|lar|ities
polar|iz|able
polar|iz|a|tion +s
polar|ize
  polar|iz|es
  polar|ized
  polar|iz|ing
polar|iz|er +s
po|laro|graph|ic
polar|og|raphy
Po|lar|oid +s
  proprietary
pol|der +s
Pole +s (Polish
  person)
Pole, Reg|in|ald
  (English clergyman)
pole (post; extremity
  of axis of rotation;
  Magnetism; each of
  two opposite points;
  in 'pole position')
  poles
  poled
  pol|ing
  [☞ poll]
pole|axe
  pole|axes
  pole|axed
  pole|axing
pole barn +s
pole bean +s
pole|cat +s
po|lem|ic +s

po|lem|ic|al
po|lem|ic|al|ly
po|lemi|cist +s
po|lemi|cize
  po|lemi|ciz|es
  po|lemi|cized
  po|lemi|ciz|ing
po|len|ta
pole pos|ition +s
pole star +s
pole vault *noun*
pole-vault +s +ed
  +ing *verb*
pole vault|er +s
pole|ward
pole|wards
po|lice (law
  enforcement agency;
  control, regulate)
  po|li|ces
  po|liced
  po|li|cing
  [☞ pelisse, polis]
police|man
  police|men
police|woman
  police|women
pol|icy (plan, program;
  sagacity; insurance
  contract)
  poli|cies
  [☞ pollices]
policy|hold|er +s
policy-maker +s
policy-making
polio
polio|myel|itis
polio|virus
  polio|virus|es
polis (city state)
  plural po|leis
  [☞ police]
poli-sci
Po|lish (of Poland;
  language)
pol|ish (shine; refine)
  pol|ish|es
  pol|ished
  pol|ish|ing
pol|ish|er +s
polit|buro +s
po|lite (courteous)
  po|lit|er
  po|lit|est
po|lite|ly
po|lite|ness
po|li|tesse
Po|li|tian (Italian
  writer)
pol|itic
  pol|itics
  pol|it|icked
  pol|itick|ing

pol|it|ic|al
pol|it|ic|al|ly (in a
  political way)
  [☞ politicly]
pol|it|ic|al|ly correct
pol|it|ician +s
pol|iti|ciz|a|tion +s
pol|iti|cize
  pol|iti|ciz|es
  pol|iti|cized
  pol|iti|ciz|ing
pol|itick|ing *noun*
pol|it|ic|ly
  (judiciously;
  prudently)
  [☞ politically]
pol|it|ico +s
pol|itics
pol|ity
  pol|ities
Polk, James Knox (US
  president)
polka
  pol|kas
  pol|kaed or polka'd
  polka|ing
polka dot +s *noun*
polka-dot *adjective*
polka-dotted
poll +s +ed +ing
  (vote, survey; head;
  cut the top of; check
  the status of)
  [☞ pole]
pol|lack (fish: use
  pollock)
  plural pol|lack
  [☞ polack]
pol|lard +s +ed +ing
poll cap|tain +s
pol|len +s
pol|lex (thumb)
  pol|li|ces
  [☞ Pollux]
pol|li|ces *plural of*
  pollex
  [☞ policies]
pol|lin|ate
  pol|lin|ates
  pol|lin|at|ed
  pol|lin|at|ing
pol|lin|a|tion +s
pol|lin|ator +s
poll|ing *noun &*
  adjective
pol|lin|if|er|ous
polli|wog +s (use
  pollywog)
Pol|lock, (Paul)
  Jack|son (US
  painter)

poll|lock (fish)
plural poll|lock
[☞ polack]
poll|ster +s
poll tax
poll taxes
pol|lut|ant +s
pol|lute
pol|lutes
pol|lut|ed
pol|lut|ing
pol|lut|ed adjective
pol|lut|er +s
pol|lu|tion +s
Pol|lux (Greek Myth;
star)
[☞ pollex]
Polly|anna +s
Polly|anna|ish
Polly|anna|ism
polly|wog +s
Polo, Marco (Italian
traveller)
polo +s
polo|naise +s
polo neck +s
polo|nium
Pol Pot (Cambodian
leader)
Pol|tava (city,
Ukraine)
pol|ter|geist +s
Pol|tor|atsk (former
name for Ashgabat,
Turkmenistan)
pol|troon +s
pol|troon|ery
poly +s
poly|amide +s
poly|an|drous
poly|andry
poly|an|thus
poly|an|thus|es
poly|bag
poly|bags
poly|bagged
poly|bag|ging
Po|lybi|us (Greek
historian)
poly|carbon|ate +s
Poly|carp (saint)
poly|chaet|an
poly|chaete +s
poly|chaet|ous
poly|chlor|in|ated
bi|phenyl +s
poly|chro|mat|ic
poly|chro|ma|tism
poly|chrome +s
poly|chromed
poly|chrom|ic
poly|chrom|ous
poly|chromy

Poly|clei|tus
(= Polyclitus)
poly|clin|ic +s
Poly|cli|tus (Greek
sculptor)
poly|cotton +s
poly|crystal|line
poly|cyclic
poly|dac|tyl
Poly|deu|ces (Greek
Myth)
poly|ester +s
poly|ethene
poly|ethyl|ene
poly|gamic
po|lygam|ist +s
po|lygam|ous
po|lygam|ous|ly
po|lygamy
poly|gene +s
poly|gen|esis
poly|gen|etic
poly|genic
po|lygen|ism
po|lygen|ist +s
po|lygeny
poly|glot +s
poly|glot|ism
poly|glot|tism (use
polyglotism)
poly|gon +s
po|lygon|al
po|lygon|um +s
poly|graph +s
poly|graph|er +s
po|lygyn|ous
po|lygyny
poly|hed|ral
poly|hed|ron
poly|hed|rons or
poly|hedra
poly|his|tor +s
Poly|hym|nia (Greek
& Roman Myth)
poly|math +s
poly|math|ic
po|lym|athy
poly|mer +s
poly|mer|ase +s
poly|meric
poly|mer|ism
poly|mer|iz|a|tion +s
poly|mer|ize
poly|mer|iz|es
poly|mer|ized
poly|mer|iz|ing
po|lymer|ous
poly|morph|ic
poly|morph|ism
poly|morph|ous
Poly|nesia (region,
Pacific Ocean)

Poly|nes|ian +s
poly|neur|itic
poly|neur|itis
Poly|nices (Greek
Myth)
poly|nom|ial +s
poly|nucleo|tide +s
po|lynya +s
polyp +s
polyp|ary
polyp|aries
poly|pep|tide +s
poly|phase
poly|phasic
Poly|phe|mus (Greek
Myth)
po|lyph|on|al
poly|phone +s
poly|phon|ic
poly|phon|ic|ally
po|lyph|on|ous
po|lyph|ony
po|lyph|on|ies
poly|phos|phate +s
poly|phylet|ic
poly|ploid +s
poly|ploidy
poly|pod
poly|pody
poly|pod|ies
polyp|oid
polyp|ous
poly|propyl|ene +s
poly|rhythm +s
poly|rhyth|mic
poly|sac|char|ide +s
poly|sem|ic
poly|sem|ous
poly|semy
poly|sty|rene
poly|syllab|ic
poly|syllab|ic|ally
poly|sylla|ble +s
poly|tech|nic +s
poly|tetra|fluoro|
ethyl|ene
poly|theism
poly|theist +s
poly|theis|tic +s
poly|thene
poly|tonal
poly|tonal|ity
poly|unsat|ur|ate +s
poly|unsat|ur|ated
poly|ureth|ane +s
poly|valence
poly|valent
poly|vinyl
poly|zoan +s
pom +s (dog; offensive
Briton)
[☞ palm]

Poma proprietary
pom|ace
pom|ade
pom|ades
pom|ad|ed
pom|ad|ing
pom|an|der +s
pome +s (fruit)
[☞ poem]
pom|egran|ate +s
pom|elo +s
Pom|er|ania (region,
Europe)
Pom|er|an|ian +s
pom|fret (fish)
plural pom|fret or
pom|frets
[☞ pommes frites]
pom|mel noun (knob;
saddle part; for verb
use pummel)
pom|mels
pom|melled
pom|mel|ling
pom|mel horse +s
pommes frites
(potatoes)
pom|mie +s offensive
(= pommy)
[☞ palmy]
pommy offensive
(British person)
pom|mies
[☞ palmy]
Pomo (people)
plural Pomo or
Pomos
po-mo (postmodern)
pomo|logic|al
pom|ol|o|gist +s
pom|ol|ogy
pomp
Pom|pa|dour,
Ma|dame de
(French arts patron
& mistress of Louis
XV)
pom|pa|dour +s
pom|pa|doured
pom|pano +s
Pom|pei|an
Pom|peii (ancient city,
Italy)
Pom|pey (Roman
general)
Pom|pi|dou, Georges
Jean Ray|mond
(French statesman)
pom|pom +s
(ornament; plant)
pom-pom +s (gun)
pom|pommed

pom|pon +s
(= pompom)
[☞ pom-pom]
pom|poned
(= pompommed)
pom|pos|ity
pom|pos|ities
pom|pous
pom|pous|ly
pom|pous|ness
'pon (upon)
[☞ pawn]
ponce
pon|ces
ponced
pon|cing
Ponce de León, Juan
(Spanish explorer)
pon|cey
pon|ci|er
pon|ci|est
pon|cho +s
pon|choed
poncy (use poncey)
pon|ci|er
pon|ci|est
pond +s +ed +ing
pon|der +s +ed +ing
pon|der|abil|ity
pon|der|able
pon|der|osa +s
pon|der|ous
pon|der|ous|ly
pon|der|ous|ness
Pondi|cherry (city &
territory, India)
pond|weed +s
pone +s
pong +s +ed +ing
pon|gal
pon|gee (Textiles)
[☞ pongy]
pon|gid +s
pon|go +s
pongy (smelly)
pon|gi|er
pon|gi|est
[☞ pongee]
poniard +s
pönnu|kö|kur +s
Pon|oka (town,
Canada)
pons
pontes
pons asin|orum
pon|tes asin|orum
pons Var|olii
pon|tes Var|olii
Ponte, Lor|enzo Da
(Italian writer)
Pon|tiac (Odawa
chief)

Ponti|anak (city,
Indonesia)
ponti|fex
pon|tifi|ces
Ponti|fex Maxi|mus
pon|tiff +s
pon|tif|ical +s
pon|tif|ical|ly
pon|tifi|cate
pon|tifi|cates
pon|tifi|cat|ed
pon|tifi|cat|ing
pon|tifi|ca|tion +s
pon|tifi|ces
Pon|tine Marsh|es (in
Italy)
Pon|tius Pi|late
(Roman procurator
of Judea)
pon|toon +s +ed +ing
pon|tooned adjective
Pon|top|pi|dan,
Hen|rik (Danish
writer)
Pon|tus (ancient
region, Asia Minor)
pony
pon|ies
pon|ied
pony|ing
pony|tail +s
pony|tailed
Ponzi
poo +s +ed +ing
(excrement;
defecate; for
interjection use pooh)
poo|bah +s (use
pooh-bah)
pooch
pooch|es
poo|dle +s
poof +s (interjection;
derogatory:
effeminate man,
homosexual)
[☞ pouf, pouffe]
poof|ter +s
poofy
poof|i|er
poof|i|est
pooh (interjection; for
excrement use poo)
[☞ poo]
pooh-bah +s
pooh-pooh +s +ed
+ing (dismiss)
[☞ poo-poo]
pooja +s (use puja)
pool +s +ed +ing
(accumulation of
liquid; billiards;
common supply;

joint venture;
Gambling)
[☞ pul, pule]
Poole (town, England)
pool hall +s
pool|room +s
pool|side
Poona (city, India)
poon|tang
poop +s +ed +ing
pooped adjective
poop|er scoop|er +s
poo-poo +s +ed +ing
(excrement;
defecate)
[☞ pooh-pooh]
poopy
poor +er +est (not
rich, etc.)
[☞ pore, pour]
poor-boy
Poor Clare +s
poor|house +s
poor|ly
poor-mouth +s +ed
+ing
poor|ness
pop
pops
popped
pop|ping
pop|corn
Pope, Alex|an|der
(English poet)
Pope, James
Col|ledge (Cdn
politician)
Pope, Wil|liam Henry
(Cdn politician)
pope +s
pope|dom
Pope Joan (legendary
pope)
pope|less
Pope|mobile
popery offensive
(Catholicism)
[☞ potpourri]
pope's nose +s
pop-eyed
pop fly
pop flies
pop|gun +s
popin|jay +s
popish offensive
popish|ly offensive
pop|lar +s
pop|lin +s
pop|lit|eal +s
Popo|caté|petl
(volcano, Mexico)

pop out verb
pops out
popped out
pop|ping out
pop-out adjective
pop|out +s noun
pop|over +s
poppa +s (father,
grandfather)
[☞ papa, pawpaw]
poppa|dum +s (use
pappadum)
Pop|per, Sir Karl
Rai|mund (English
philosopher)
pop|per +s (thing that
pops; muscle
relaxant)
[☞ pauper]
pop|pet +s
pop|pied
pop|ple
pop|ples
pop|pled
pop|pling
pop|ply
pop-psych
pop-psychol|ogy
poppy
pop|pies
pop|pi|er
pop|pi|est
poppy|cock
poppy seed +s
(poppy-seed when
preceding a noun)
Pop|sicle +s
proprietary
pop|sie +s (use popsy)
pop|ster +s
popsy
pop|sies
pop-top +s
popu|lace (the
masses)
popu|lar
popu|lar|ism +s
popu|lar|ity
popu|lar|iz|a|tion +s
popu|lar|ize
popu|lar|iz|es
popu|lar|ized
popu|lar|iz|ing
popu|lar|iz|er +s
popu|lar|ly
popu|late
popu|lates
popu|lat|ed
popu|lat|ing
popu|la|tion +s
popu|lism
popu|list +s
popu|lis|tic

popu|lous (densely populated)
[☞ **populace**]
popu|lous|ly
popu|lous|ness
pop up *verb*
　pops up
　popped up
　pop|ping up
pop-up +s *noun &*
　adjective
por|beagle +s
por|cel|ain +s
por|cel|lan|eous
por|cel|lan|ous
porch
　porch|es
　[☞ **Porsche**]
porched
porch|less
por|cine (piglike)
por|cini (mushroom)
　plural **por|cini**
Por|cu|pine (river,
　N America)
por|cu|pine +s
pore (tiny opening in
　skin etc.; in 'pore
　over': study,
　contemplate)
　pores
　pored
　por|ing
　[☞ **pour, poor**]
porgy
　por|gies
Pori (city, Finland)
Po River (in Italy)
pork
pork bar|rel (pork-
　barrel *when*
　preceding a noun)
pork-barrel|ler +s
pork-barrel|ling
pork|er +s
pork pie +s (pork|pie
　when preceding a
　noun)
porky
　pork|i|er
　pork|i|est
　pork|ies
porky-pie +s
porn
porno
por|nog|raph|er +s
porno|graph|ic
porno|graph|ic|ally
por|nog|raphy
por|os|ity
por|ous
por|ous|ly
por|ous|ness

por|phyria
por|phyr|in +s
por|phy|rit|ic
por|phyry
　por|phyr|ies
por|poise +s
por|ridge +s
por|ridgy
por|rin|ger +s
Porsche, Fer|di|nand
　(Austrian car
　designer)
port +s +ed +ing
　(harbour; wine; left;
　window, opening;
　carry a rifle;
　Computing)
　[☞ **Porte, porte**
　cochère]
port|abil|ity
port|able +s
port|ably
por|tage
　por|tages
　por|taged
　por|ta|ging
Por|tage la Prai|rie
　(city, Canada)
por|tal +s (doorway;
　vein)
　[☞ **porthole**]
Port Al|ber|ni (city,
　Canada)
porta|men|to
　porta|men|ti
porta-potty
　porta-potties
Port Ar|thur
　(community, Canada;
　former name for
　Lushun, China)
porta|tive
Port au Choix
　(historic site,
　Canada)
Port au Port
　(peninsula, Canada)
Port-au-Prince
　(capital of Haiti)
Port Blair (city, South
　Andaman Island)
Port Col|borne (city,
　Canada)
Port Co|quit|lam
　(city, Canada)
port|cul|lis
　port|cul|lis|es
port|cul|lised
port de bras
Porte (Ottoman court)
porte co|chère +s
Port Elgin (town,
　Canada)

Port Eliza|beth (city,
　South Africa)
por|tend +s +ed +ing
por|tent +s
por|ten|tous
por|ten|tous|ly
por|ten|tous|ness
Por|ter, Cole Al|bert
　(US songwriter)
Por|ter, Sir George
　(Baron Porter of
　Ludenham, English
　chemist)
Por|ter, Kath|er|ine
　Anne (US writer)
Por|ter, Rod|ney
　Rob|ert (English
　biochemist)
Por|ter, Wil|liam
　Sid|ney (O. Henry)
por|ter +s
porter|age +s
porter|house +s
Port Étienne (*former*
　name for
　Nouadhibou,
　Mauritania)
port|folio +s
Port-Gentil (city,
　Gabon)
Port Har|court (city,
　Nigeria)
Port Hardy
　(municipality,
　Canada)
port|hole +s (window
　on a ship; opening
　for a gun)
　[☞ **portal**]
Port Hope (town,
　Canada)
por|tico
　por|ti|coes or
　por|ti|cos
por|ti|coed
por|*ti|ère* +s
por|tion +s +ed +ing
por|tion|less
Port|land (cities, US;
　peninsula, England;
　cement)
Port|laoighise
　(= Portlaoise)
Port|laoise (town,
　Ireland)
port|li|ness
Port Louis (capital of
　Mauritius)
port|ly
　port|li|er
　port|li|est

Port Mahon
　(= Mahón, capital of
　Minorca)
port|man|teau
　port|man|teaus or
　port|man|teaux
Port Moody (city,
　Canada)
Port Mores|by
　(capital of Papua
　New Guinea)
Porto (= Oporto,
　Portugal)
　[☞ **Puerto**]
Pôrto Alegre (city,
　Brazil)
porto|bello +s
Port of Spain (capital
　of Trinidad and
　Tobago)
por|to|lan +s
por|to|lano +s
Porto Novo (capital of
　Benin)
Pôrto Velho (town,
　Brazil)
Port Pe|trovsk (*former*
　name for
　Makhachkala,
　Russia)
por|trait +s
por|trait|ist +s
por|trait|ure +s
por|tray +s +ed +ing
por|tray|able
por|tray|al +s
por|tray|er +s
Port-Royal (*former*
　name for **Annapolis**
　Royal, Canada)
Port Said (city, Egypt)
Port Salut (cheese)
port|side (of a ship)
　[☞ **Port Said**]
Ports|mouth (naval
　base, England)
Port Stan|ley (town,
　Falkland Islands)
Port Sudan (city,
　Sudan)
Por|tu|gal (country,
　Europe)
Por|tu|guese
　plural **Por|tu|guese**
por|tu|laca +s
pose
　poses
　posed
　pos|ing
pose|able
Po|sei|don (*Greek*
　Myth)

Posen (= Poznań, Poland)
poser +s (puzzling question; one who poses)
pos|eur +s (one who behaves affectedly)
posey (affected, pretentious)
[☞ posy, poesy]
posh +er +est
posh|ness
pos|it +s +ed +ing (postulate)
[☞ posset]
pos|ition +s +ed +ing
pos|ition|al
pos|ition|al|ly
pos|ition|er +s
posi|tive +s
posi|tive|ly
posi|tive|ness
posi|tiv|ism
posi|tiv|ist +s
posi|tiv|is|tic
posi|tiv|ity
posi|tron +s
poso|logic|al
po|sol|ogy
pos|se +s (gang)
pos|sess
pos|sess|es
pos|sessed
pos|sess|ing
pos|ses|sion +s
pos|ses|sive +s
pos|ses|sive|ly
pos|ses|sive|ness
pos|ses|sor +s
pos|ses|sory
pos|set +s (drink)
[☞ posit]
pos|si|bil|ity
pos|si|bil|ities
pos|sible +s
pos|sibly
pos|sum +s
post +s +ed +ing
post|age
post|al
post|al|ly
post-and-beam
post|bag +s
post|box
post|boxes
post|card +s
post-chaise +s
post-classic|al
post|code +s
post-coital
post-coital|ly
post-coloni|al

post-coloni|al|ism
post-coloni|al|ist +s
post-Confed|er|a|tion
post-consum|er
post|date
post|dates
post|dat|ed
post|dat|ing
post-doc +s
post-doctor|al
post|ed *adjective*
post-emergence
post-emergent
post|er +s +ed +ing
post|er boy +s
post|er child
post|er chil|dren
poste res|tante
post|er girl +s
pos|ter|ior +s
pos|ter|ior|ity
pos|ter|ior|ly
pos|ter|ity
pos|tern +s
post|er paint +s
post-feminism
post-feminist +s
post|fix
post|fix|es
post|fixed
post|fix|ing
post|glacial +s
post-grad +s
post-graduate +s
post-haste
post hoc
post|hole +s
post|hu|mous
post|hu|mous|ly
post-hypnot|ic
sug|ges|tion +s
post|ie +s
pos|til|ion +s
pos|til|lion +s (*use* postilion)
Post-Impres|sion|ism
Post-Impres|sion|ist +s
post-industri|al
post-industri|al|ism
post|ing +s *noun*
Post-it +s *proprietary*
Post-it Note +s
proprietary
post|lude +s
post|man
post|men
post|mark +s +ed +ing
post|master +s

post|master gen|er|al
post|masters gen|er|al
post-menopaus|al
post-menopaus|al|ly
post-menopause
post-millen|nial
post-millen|nial|ism
post-millen|nial|ist +s
post|mis|tress
post|mis|tress|es
post|mod|ern
post|modern|ism
post|modern|ist +s
post|modern|ity
post-mortem +s
post|natal
post|natal|ly
post-nuptial
post of|fice +s
post of|fice box
post of|fice boxes
post-op
post-operative
post-operative|ly
post|paid
post|partum
post|pon|able
post|pone
post|pones
post|poned
post|pon|ing
post|pone|ment +s
post|pon|er +s
post pos|ition (*Horse Racing*)
post|pos|ition +s (*Grammar*)
post|pos|ition|al
post|posi|tive +s
post|posi|tive|ly
post-prandi|al
post-produc|tion
post-punk
post|script +s
post-season +s
post-second|ary
post-structur|al
post-structur|al|ism
post-structur|al|ist +s
post-tax
post-traumat|ic
pos|tu|lancy
pos|tu|lant +s
pos|tu|late
pos|tu|lates
pos|tu|lat|ed
pos|tu|lat|ing
pos|tu|la|tion +s
pos|tu|la|tor +s

pos|tur|al
pos|ture
pos|tures
pos|tured
pos|tur|ing
pos|tur|er +s
post-war
post|woman
post|women
posy (flower bunch; ring inscription)
po|sies
[☞ posey, poesy, posse]
pot
pots
pot|ted
pot|ting
pot|abil|ity
pot|able +s
pot|age +s (thick soup)
pot|ash
po|tas|sic
po|tas|sium
po|tassium-argon dat|ing
po|ta|tion +s
po|ta|to
po|ta|toes
pot-au-feu
plural pot-au-feu
pot-bellied
pot-belly
pot-bellies
pot|boil|er +s
pot-bound
po|teen +s
Po|tem|kin, Grig|ori Alek|san|dro|vich (Russian officer & statesman)
Po|tem|kin (Russian battleship)
po|tence
po|tency
po|ten|cies
po|tent
po|ten|tate +s
po|ten|tial +s
po|ten|ti|al|ity
po|ten|ti|al|ities
pot|en|tial|ly
po|tenti|ate
po|tenti|ates
po|tenti|at|ed
po|tenti|at|ing
po|tenti|a|tion +s
po|ten|til|la +s
po|ten|ti|om|eter +s
po|ten|tio|met|ric
po|tent|ly
Po|tenza (town, Italy)

pot|ful +s
pot|head +s
poth|er +s +ed +ing
pot-herb +s
pot hold|er +s
pot|hole +s
pot|holed
pot|holer +s
pot|holing
pot-hook +s
pot-hunter +s
po|tion +s
pot|latch
  pot|latch|es
pot|latch|ing
pot light +s
pot light|ing
pot|luck +s
Po|to|mac (river, US)
Poto|sí (city, Bolivia)
pot pie +s
pot plant +s
pot|pour|ri +s (dried flowers; mixture)
Pots|dam (city, Germany)
pot|sherd +s
pot|shot +s
pot|tage +s (soup, stew)
pot|ted adjective
Pot|ter, (Helen) Bea|trix (English writer)
Pot|ter, Paul|us (Dutch artist)
pot|ter +s +ed +ing
Pot|ter|ies (district, England)
potter's field +s
potter's wheel +s
pot|tery
  pot|ter|ies
pot|ti|ness
pot|to +s
potty
  pot|ties
  pot|ti|er
  pot|ti|est
potty train +s +ed +ing
pouch
  pouch|es
  pouched
  pouch|ing
pouched adjective
pouchy
pouf +s (clothing appendage; for cushion use pouffe; for derogatory sense use poof)
[☞ poof]

poufed
pouffe +s (cushion)
  [☞ pouf, poof]
poul|ard +s
Pou|lenc, Fran|cis Jean Mar|cel (French composer)
poult +s
poult|er|er +s
poul|tice
  poul|ti|ces
  poul|ticed
  poul|ti|cing
poult|ry
pounce
  poun|ces
  pounced
  poun|cing
poun|cer +s
pouncet-box
  pouncet-boxes
Pound, Ezra Wes|ton Loo|mis (US poet)
pound +s +ed +ing
pound|age +s
pound|al +s
pound cake +s
pound|er +s
Pound|ian +s
pound|ing +s noun
pound ster|ling
  pounds ster|ling
pour +s +ed +ing (flow, dispense liquid etc.)
  [☞ pore, poor]
pour|able
pour|er +s
Pous|sin, Nico|las (French painter)
pout
  • (sulk)
  pouts
  pout|ed
  pout|ing
  • (eelpout)
  plural pout or pouts
pout|er +s
pou|tine +s
pout|ing|ly
pouty
  pout|i|er
  pout|i|est
pov|erty
poverty-strick|en
Po|vung|ni|tuk (river, Canada)
POW (prisoner of war)
  POWs
pow interjection
pow|der +s +ed +ing

pow|der blue +s (powder-blue when preceding a noun)
pow|dered adjective
pow|der keg +s
powder|man
  powder|men
powder-puff +s
pow|dery
Pow|ell, Cecil Frank (English physicist)
Pow|ell, (John) Enoch (English politician)
Pow|ell, Mi|chael La|tham (English filmmaker)
Pow|ell River (municipality, Canada)
pow|er +s +ed +ing
power-assist|ed
power|boat +s
power-broker +s
power-broking
pow|ered adjective
power|ful
power|ful|ly
power|ful|ness
power|house +s
power|less
power|less|ly
power|less|ness
power|lift|er +s
power|lift|ing
power line +s
power plant +s
power play +s (power-play when preceding a noun)
power-sharing
power tool +s
power|train +s
Pow|ha|tan (Algonquian chief; people)
  plural Pow|ha|tan or Pow|ha|tans
pow|wow +s +ed +ing
Powys (county, Wales; former Welsh kingdom)
Powys, John Cow|per (Welsh writer)
Powys, Llew|elyn (Welsh writer)
Powys, Theo|dore Fran|cis (Welsh writer)
pox (disease characterized by pocks)
  [☞ pocks]

poxy
  pox|i|er
  pox|i|est
Poz|nań (city, Poland)
prac|tic|abil|ity
prac|tic|able
prac|tic|able|ness
prac|tic|ably
prac|tical
practi|cal|ity
  practi|cal|ities
prac|tical|ly
prac|tical|ness
prac|tice (noun; for verb use practise)
  prac|ti|ces
  prac|ticed
  prac|ti|cing
prac|ticed adjective (use practised)
prac|ti|cer +s (use practiser)
prac|ti|cian +s
prac|ti|cing adjective (use practising)
prac|ti|cum +s
prac|tise (verb; for noun use practice)
  prac|tis|es
  prac|tised
  prac|tis|ing
prac|tised adjective
prac|tis|er +s
prac|tis|ing adjective
prac|ti|tion|er +s
prae|cipe +s
prae|mu|nire +s
prae|nomen +s
prae|sid|ium +s (use presidium)
prae|tor +s
prae|tor|ial
prae|tor|ian +s
prae|tor|ship +s
prag|mat|ic
prag|mat|ic|ally
prag|mat|ics
prag|ma|tism
prag|ma|tist +s
prag|ma|tis|tic
Prague (capital of the Czech Republic)
prahu +s
Praia (capital of the Cape Verde Islands)
Prai|rie +s (Cdn region)
prai|rie +s (in general use & names of flora & fauna)
praise
  prais|es

praised
prais|ing
praise|ful
prais|er +s
praise|worthi|ly
praise|worthi|ness
praise|worthy
Prak|rit
pra|line +s
prall|trill|er +s
pram +s
prana
prance
  pran|ces
  pranced
  pran|cing
pran|cer +s
pran|di|al
Prandtl, Lud|wig
  (German physicist)
prang +s +ed +ing
prank +s
prank|ish
prank|ish|ly
prank|ish|ness
prank|ster +s
prank|ster|ism
praseo|dym|ium
prat +s
  [☞ Pratt]
prate
  prates
  prated
  prat|ing
prat|er +s
prat|fall +s
prat|ie +s
prat|in|cole +s
prat|ing *adjective*
pra|tique +s
Prato (city, Italy)
Pratt, Edwin John
  (Cdn poet)
Pratt, (John)
  Chris|to|pher (Cdn
  painter)
Pratt, Mary (Cdn
  painter)
prat|tle
  prat|tles
  prat|tled
  prat|tling
prat|tler +s
prat|tling *adjective*
prau +s (*use* prahu)
prawn +s +ed +ing
prax|is
  prax|es
Prax|it|eles (Athenian
  sculptor)
pray +s +ed +ing (say
  prayers)
  [☞ prey]

pray|er +s
  (invocation,
  supplication; one
  who prays)
  [☞ preyer]
pray|er book +s
prayer|ful
prayer|ful|ly
prayer|ful|ness
prayer|less
pray|ing man|tis
  plural
  pray|ing man|tis or
  pray|ing man|tis|es
preach
  preach|es
  preached
  preach|ing
preach|able
preach|er +s
preach|er|ly
preach|i|ness
preach|ment +s
preachy
  preach|i|er
  preach|i|est
pre|adoles|cence
pre|adoles|cent +s
Preak|ness
pre|amble +s
pre|amp +s
pre|ampli|fied
pre|ampli|fi|er +s
pre-arrange
  pre-arranges
  pre-arranged
  pre-arranging
pre-arranged
  adjective
pre-arrange|ment +s
pre|atom|ic
preb|end +s
preb|end|al
preb|end|ary
  preb|end|aries
preb|end|ary|ship +s
pre-board +s +ed
  +ing
pre-boarding *noun*
pre-book +s +ed
  +ing
pre-bookable
  adjective
Pre|cam|brian
pre|cancer|ous
pre|car|ious
pre|car|ious|ly
pre|car|ious|ness
pre|cast
pre|caution +s
pre|caution|ary

pre|cede (come or go
  before)
  pre|cedes
  pre|ced|ed
  pre|ced|ing
  [☞ proceed]
pre|ced|ence
pre|ced|ent +s
  (previous case,
  model)
pre|ced|ent|ed
  adjective
pre|ced|ent|ly
pre|cen|tor +s (one
  who leads a choir or
  congregation)
pre|cen|tor|ship +s
pre|cept +s
pre|cep|tive
pre|cep|tor +s
pre|cep|tor|ial
pre|cep|tor|ship +s
pre|cess (*Astronomy*)
  pre|cess|es
  pre|cessed
  pre|cess|ing
  [☞ process]
pre|ces|sion +s
  (*Astronomy*)
  [☞ procession]
pre|ces|sion|al
  (*Astronomy*)
  [☞ processional]
pre-Christian
pre|cinct +s
pre|ci|os|ity
pre|cious
pre|cious|ly
pre|cious|ness
pre|cip
preci|pice +s
pre|cipit|abil|ity
pre|cipit|able
pre|cipi|tance
pre|cipi|tancy
pre|cipi|tant +s
pre|cipi|tate
  pre|cipi|tates
  pre|cipi|tat|ed
  pre|cipi|tat|ing
pre|cipi|tate|ly
pre|cipi|tate|ness
pre|cipi|ta|tion +s
pre|cipi|ta|tor +s
pre|cipi|tous
pre|cipi|tous|ly
pre|cipi|tous|ness
pré|cis
  • *noun* (summary,
  abstract)
  plural pré|cis
  • *verb* (summarize)

pré|cises
pré|cised
pré|cis|ing
pre|cise (exact)
pre|cise|ly
pre|cise|ness
pre|ci|sion
pre|ci|sion|ism
pre|ci|sion|ist +s
pre|classic|al
pre|clinic|al
pre|clude
  pre|cludes
  pre|clud|ed
  pre|clud|ing
pre|clu|sion
pre|clu|sive
pre|co|cial
pre|co|cious
pre|co|cious|ly
pre|co|cious|ness
pre|co|city
pre|cog|ni|tion
pre|cog|ni|tive
pre|coit|al
pre|coit|al|ly
pre-colonial
pre-Columbian
pre|con|ceive
  pre|con|ceives
  pre|con|ceived
  pre|con|ceiv|ing
pre|con|cep|tion +s
pre|con|di|tion +s
  +ed +ing
pre-Confeder|a|tion
pre|con|iz|a|tion
pre|con|ize
  pre|con|iz|es
  pre|con|ized
  pre|con|iz|ing
pre|con|scious
pre|con|scious|ness
pre-contact
pre|cook +s +ed +ing
pre|cool +s +ed +ing
pre|cor|dial
pre|cur|sor +s
pre|cur|sory
pre|cut
  pre|cuts
  pre|cut
  pre|cut|ting
pred|aceous
  (= predacious)
pred|aceous|ness
  (= predaciousness)
pred|acious
pred|acious|ness
pred|acity
pre|date
  pre|dates

pre|dat|ed
pre|dat|ing
pred|a|tion +s
pred|a|tor +s
pred|a|tor|i|ly
pred|a|tor|i|ness
pred|a|tory
pre-dawn
pre|decease
  pre|deceas|es
  pre|deceased
  pre|deceas|ing
pre|deces|sor +s
pre-decimal
pre|della +s
pre|des|tin|ar|ian +s
pre|des|tin|ate
  pre|des|tin|ates
  pre|des|tin|at|ed
  pre|des|tin|at|ing
pre|des|tin|a|tion
pre|des|tine
  pre|des|tines
  pre|des|tined
  pre|des|tin|ing
pre|deter|min|able
pre|deter|min|ate
pre|deter|min|a|tion
pre|deter|mine
  pre|deter|mines
  pre|deter|mined
  pre|deter|min|ing
pre|dica|ment +s
predi|cant +s
predi|cate
  predi|cates
  predi|cat|ed
  predi|cat|ing
predi|ca|tion +s
predi|ca|tive
predi|ca|tive|ly
pre|dict +s +ed +ing
pre|dict|abil|ity
pre|dict|able
pre|dict|ably
pre|dic|tion +s
pre|dict|ive
pre|dict|ive|ly
pre|dict|or +s
pre|digest +s +ed
  +ing
pre|diges|tion
pre|dilec|tion +s
pre|dis|pose
  pre|dis|pos|es
  pre|dis|posed
  pre|dis|pos|ing
pre|dis|pos|ition +s
pred|ni|sone
pre|domin|ance
pre|domin|ant
pre|domin|ant|ly

pre|domin|ate
  pre|domin|ates
  pre|domin|at|ed
  pre|domin|at|ing
pre|domin|ate|ly
  (= predominantly)
pre|dynas|tic
pre-echo
  pre-echoes
pre-eclamp|sia
pre-eclamp|tic
pre-embryo +s
pre-embryon|ic
pree|mie +s
pre-eminence
pre-eminent
pre-eminent|ly
pre-empt +s +ed
  +ing
pre-emption +s
pre-emptive
pre-emptive|ly
pre-emptor +s
pre-emptory
preen +s +ed +ing
preen|er +s
pre-exist +s +ed
  +ing
pre-exist|ence
pre-exist|ent
pre|fab +s
pre|fabri|cate
  pre|fabri|cates
  pre|fabri|cat|ed
  pre|fabri|cat|ing
pre|fabri|ca|tion +s
pref|ace
  pref|aces
  pref|aced
  pref|acing
prefa|tor|ial
prefa|tory
pre|fect
pre|fect|oral
pre|fec|tor|ial
pre|fec|tur|al
pre|fec|ture +s
pre|fer
  pre|fers
  pre|ferred
  pre|fer|ring
pref|er|abil|ity
pref|er|able
pref|er|ably
pref|er|ence +s
pref|er|en|tial
pref|er|en|tial|ly
pre|fer|ment +s
pre|ferred adjective
pre|figur|a|tion +s
pre|figur|a|tive

pre|fig|ure
  pre|fig|ures
  pre|fig|ured
  pre|figur|ing
pre|figure|ment +s
pre|fix
  pre|fix|es
  pre|fixed
  pre|fix|ing
pre-flight
pre|form +s +ed +ing
pre|form|a|tion
pre|forma|tive +s
pre|front|al
pre-game
preg|gers
pre|glacial
preg|nancy
  preg|nan|cies
preg|nant
preg|nant|ly
pre-hearing +s
pre|heat +s +ed +ing
pre|hen|sile
pre|hen|sil|ity
pre|hen|sion
pre-Hispan|ic
pre|histor|ian +s
pre|histor|ic
pre|histor|ic|ally
pre|hist|ory
  pre|hist|or|ies
pre|human +s
pre-ignition
pre-industri|al
pre|judge
  pre|judg|es
  pre|judged
  pre|judg|ing
pre|judg|ment +s
pre|judi|ca|tion
preju|dice
  preju|di|ces
  preju|diced
  preju|di|cing
preju|diced adjective
preju|di|cial
preju|di|cial|ly
prel|acy
  prel|acies
pre-lapsar|ian
prel|ate +s
prel|at|ic|al
pre-law
pre|lim +s
pre|lim|in|ar|i|ly
pre|lim|in|ary
  pre|lim|in|aries
pre|lin|guis|tic
pre|liter|ate
pre|load +s +ed +ing
pre|load|ed adjective

pre|lude
  pre|ludes
  pre|lud|ed
  pre|lud|ing
pre|lud|ial
pre|mari|tal
pre-match
pre|mature
pre|mature|ly
pre|matur|ity
pre|maxil|lary
pre-med +s
pre|medi|ca|tion
pre|medi|tate
  pre|medi|tates
  pre|medi|tat|ed
  pre|medi|tat|ing
pre|medi|tat|ed
  adjective
pre|medi|ta|tion
pre|medi|ta|tive
pre|meno|paus|al
pre|men|stru|al
pre|mier +s (first
  minister; first)
  [☞ premiere]
pre|mier dan|seur
  (leading male
  dancer)
  pre|miers dan|seurs
pre|miere (first show;
  show or be
  presented first; for
  first or first minister
  use premier)
  pre|mieres
  pre|miered
  pre|mier|ing
pre|mière dan|seuse
  (leading female
  dancer)
  pre|mières
  dan|seuses
premier|ship +s
pre|millen|nial
pre|millen|nial|ism
pre|millen|nial|ist +s
Prem|in|ger, Otto
  Lud|wig (US
  filmmaker)
prem|ise (proposition,
  basis; state by way of
  introduction)
  prem|is|es
  prem|ised
  prem|is|ing
  [☞ premises]
prem|is|es (buildings,
  grounds, etc.)
prem|iss (proposition,
  basis: use premise)
  prem|iss|es
  [☞ premise,
  premises]

pre|mium +s
pre|mix
  pre|mix|es
  pre|mixed
  pre|mix|ing
pre|mixed *adjective*
pre|molar +s
pre|mon|ition +s
pre|moni|tor|i|ly
pre|moni|tory
pre|natal
pre|natal|ly
pre|nuptial
pre|occu|pa|tion +s
pre|occu|pied
  adjective
pre|occupy
  pre|occu|pies
  pre|occu|pied
  pre|occu|py|ing
pre-op
pre|opera|tive
pre|opera|tive|ly
pre|ordain +s +ed
  +ing
pre|ordained
  adjective
pre-owned
prep
  preps
  prepped
  prep|ping
pre|pack +s +ed +ing
pre|pack|age
  pre|pack|ages
  pre|pack|aged
  pre|pack|aging
pre|pack|aged
  adjective
pre|packed *adjective*
pre|paid
prep|ar|a|tion +s
pre|para|tive +s
pre|para|tive|ly
prep|ara|tor|i|ly
prep|ara|tory
pre|pare
  pre|pares
  pre|pared
  pre|par|ing
pre|pared|ness
pre|par|er +s
pre|pay
  pre|pays
  pre|paid
  pre|pay|ing
pre|pay|able
pre|pay|ment +s
pre|pense (deliberate,
  intentional)
  [☞ propensity]

pre|plan
  pre|plans
  pre|planned
  pre|plan|ning
pre|pon|der|ance
pre|pon|der|ant
pre|pon|der|ant|ly
pre|pon|der|ate
  pre|pon|der|ates
  pre|pon|der|at|ed
  pre|pon|der|at|ing
pre|pon|der|ate|ly
pre|pose (*Linguistics*)
  pre|pos|es
  pre|posed
  pre|pos|ing
  [☞ propose]
prep|os|ition +s
  (*Grammar*)
  [☞ proposition]
prep|os|ition|al (of or
  like a preposition)
  [☞ propositional]
prep|os|ition|al|ly
pre|posi|tive +s
pre|pos|sess
  pre|pos|sess|es
  pre|pos|sessed
  pre|pos|sess|ing
pre|pos|sess|ing
  adjective
pre|pos|ses|sion +s
pre|pos|ter|ous
pre|pos|ter|ous|ly
pre|pos|ter|ous|ness
pre|potence
pre|potency
pre|potent
prep|pie (*use* preppy)
  prep|pies
  prep|pi|er
  prep|pi|est
preppy
  prep|pies
  prep|pi|er
  prep|pi|est
pre|prandi|al
pre|print +s +ed +ing
pre|print|ed *adjective*
pre|pro|cess
  pre|pro|cess|es
  pre|pro|cessed
  pre|pro|cess|ing
pre|pro|ces|sor +s
pre-produc|tion
pre-program
  pre-programs
  pre-programmed
  pre-program|ming
prep school +s
pre|puber|tal
pre|pubes|cent +s
pre|publi|ca|tion

pre|puce +s
pre|putial
pre-qualify
  pre-qualifies
  pre-qualified
  pre-qualify|ing
pre|quel +s
Pre-Raphael|ite +s
  (of the Pre-
  Raphaelite
  Brotherhood)
pre-Raphael|ite
  (reminiscent of Pre-
  Raphaelite art)
Pre-Raphael|it|ism
pre-record +s +ed
  +ing
pre-record|ed
  adjective
pre-release +s
pre|requi|site +s
pre|roga|tive +s
  (privilege, right)
  [☞ prorogue,
  prorogation]
pres|age
  pres|ages
  pres|aged
  pres|aging
pre|sage|ful
pres|ager +s
pres|by|opia
pres|by|opic
pres|by|ter +s
pres|byt|er|al
pres|byt|er|ate +s
pres|by|ter|ial
Pres|by|ter|ian +s
Pres|by|ter|ian|ism
pres|by|tery
  pres|by|ter|ies
pre|school +s
pre|school|er +s
pre|science
pre|scient
pre|scient|ly
pre|scind +s +ed
  +ing
Pres|cott (town,
  Canada)
Pres|cott, Rob|ert
  (British colonial
  administrator)
Pres|cott, Wil|liam
  Hick|ling (US
  historian)
pre-screen +s +ed
  +ing
pre|scribe
  (recommend;
  authorize medication
  etc.; assert

  authoritatively)
  pre|scribes
  pre|scribed
  pre|scrib|ing
  [☞ proscribe]
pre|scrib|er +s
pre|script +s
pre|scrip|tion +s
  (*Medicine*; act of
  prescribing;
  authoritative ancient
  custom or right)
  [☞ proscription]
pre|script|ive
  (prescribing,
  prescribed)
  [☞ proscriptive]
pre|script|ive|ly
pre|script|ive|ness
pre|scrip|tiv|ism
pre|scrip|tiv|ist +s
pre-season +s
pre-select +s +ed
  +ing
pre-selection +s
pres|ence +s
pres|ent[1] +s *noun &*
  adjective
pre|sent[2] +s +ed +ing
  verb
pre|sent|abil|ity
pre|sent|able
pre|sent|able|ness
pre|sent|ably
pres|en|ta|tion +s
pres|en|ta|tion|al
pres|en|ta|tion|al|ly
present-day
pre|sent|er +s (one
  who makes a
  presentation)
  [☞ precentor]
pre|senti|ment +s
pres|ent|ism
pres|ent|ist +s
pres|ent|ly
pre|sent|ment +s
pres|ent|ness
pres|erv|able
pres|er|va|tion +s
pres|er|va|tion|ist +s
pres|erv|a|tive +s
pre|serve
  pre|serves
  pre|served
  pre|serv|ing
pre|serv|er +s
pre-set *verb &*
  adjective
  pre-sets
  pre-set
  pre-setting
pre|set +s *noun*

pre-settle|ment
pre-shrink
  pre-shrinks
  pre-shrank
  or pre-shrunk
  pre-shrunk
  pre-shrink|ing
  pre-shrunk *adjective*
pre|side
  pre|sides
  pre|sid|ed
  pre|sid|ing
pres|iden|cy
  pres|iden|cies
pres|ident +s (head of
  state, company etc.)
  [☞ precedent]
president-elect
  pres|idents-elect
presi|den|tial
presi|den|tial|ly
pre|sid|ium +s
Pres|ley, Elvis Aron
  (US singer)
pre|soak +s +ed +ing
pre|socrat|ic +s
press
  press|es
  pressed
  press|ing
press|back
press|board +s
press box
  press boxes
press-button +s
press|er +s
press gang +s *noun*
press-gang +s +ed
  +ing *verb*
press|ing +s *adjective*
  & *noun*
press|ing|ly
press|man
  press|men
press room +s
press run +s
press-up +s
pres|sure
  pres|sures
  pres|sured
  pres|sur|ing
pressure-cook +s
  +ed +ing
pres|sure cook|er +s
pressure-treat +s
  +ed +ing
pressure-treated
  adjective
pres|sur|iz|a|tion
pres|sur|ize
  pres|sur|iz|es

pres|sur|ized
pres|sur|iz|ing
pres|sur|ized *adjective*
Pres|ter John
  (legendary king)
presti|digi|ta|tion
presti|digi|ta|tor +s
pres|tige
pres|tige|ful
pres|ti|gious
pres|ti|gious|ly
pres|ti|gious|ness
pres|tis|simo +s
presto +s
presto chango
Pres|ton (city,
  England; community,
  Canada)
Pres|ton|pans (battle
  site, Scotland)
pre-stressed
Prest|wick (town,
  Scotland)
pre|sum|able
pre|sum|ably
pre|sume
  pre|sumes
  pre|sumed
  pre|sum|ing
pre|sum|ed|ly
pre|sump|tion +s
pre|sump|tive
pre|sump|tive|ly
pre|sump|tu|ous
pre|sump|tu|ous|ly
pre|sump|tu|ous|
                ness
pre|sup|pose
  pre|sup|poses
  pre|sup|posed
  pre|sup|pos|ing
pre|sup|pos|ition +s
pre|synap|tic
prêt-à-porter
pre-tax
pre|teen +s
pre|tence +s (*use*
  pretense)
pre|tend +s +ed +ing
pre|tend|ed *adjective*
pre|tend|er +s
pre|tense +s
pre|ten|sion +s
pre|ten|tious
pre|ten|tious|ly
pre|ten|tious|ness
pret|erit +s (*use*
  preterite)
pret|er|ite +s
pre|term
preter|natur|al
preter|natur|al|ism
preter|natur|al|ly

pre|test +s +ed +ing
  (preliminary test)
  [☞ protest]
pre|text +s
Pre|toria
  (administrative
  capital of South
  Africa)
Pretoria-
  Witwatersrand-
        Vereeniging
  (province, South
  Africa)
Pre|tor|ius, An|dries
  Wil|helm|us
  Jaco|bus (Afrikaner
  soldier)
Pre|tor|ius,
  Mar|thin|us Wes|sel
  (Afrikaner soldier &
  statesman)
pre-treat +s +ed
  +ing
pre-treatment +s
pre|trial +s
pretti|fi|ca|tion +s
pretti|fi|er +s
pretti|fy
  pretti|fies
  pretti|fied
  pretti|fy|ing
pret|ti|ly
pret|ti|ness
pretty
  pret|ti|er
  pret|ti|est
  pret|ties
  pret|tied
  pretty|ing
pretty boy +s (pretty-
  boy *when preceding a*
  noun)
pret|zel
  pret|zels
  pret|zelled
  pret|zel|ling
pret|zelled *adjective*
pre|vail +s +ed +ing
pre|vail|ing *adjective*
pre|vail|ing|ly
preva|lence
preva|lent
preva|lent|ly
pre|vari|cate
  pre|vari|cates
  pre|vari|cat|ed
  pre|vari|cat|ing
pre|vari|ca|tion +s
pre|vari|ca|tor +s
pre|veni|ent
  (preceding)
  [☞ provenience]
pre|vent +s +ed +ing
pre|vent|abil|ity

pre|vent|able
pre|venta|tive
pre|venta|tive|ly
pre|vent|er +s
pre|ven|tion +s
pre|vent|ive
pre|vent|ive|ly
pre|view +s +ed +ing
Pre|vin, André
  George (US
  conductor)
pre|vi|ous
pre|vi|ous|ly
pre|vi|ous|ness
pre|vise
  pre|vis|es
  pre|vised
  pre|vis|ing
pre|vision +s
  (foresight)
  [☞ provision]
pre|vision|al
  (pertaining to
  foresight)
  [☞ provisional]
Prev|ost, Sir George
  (governor-in-chief of
  BNA)
Pré|vost, André (Cdn
  composer &
  educator)
Pré|vost d'Exiles,
  Antoine-François,
  Abbé (French
  novelist)
pre-war
pre|wash
  pre|wash|es
  pre|washed
  pre|wash|ing
pre-wire
  pre-wires
  pre-wired
  pre-wiring
prex
  prex|es
prexy
  prex|ies
prey +s +ed +ing
  (victim; hunt;
  victimize; oppress)
  [☞ pray]
prey|er +s (one who
  hunts or takes
  advantage)
  [☞ prayer]
Prez, Jos|quin des
  (Flemish composer)
prez
  prez|zes
prez|zie +s
Priam (*Greek Myth*)
pri|ap|ic
pri|ap|ism

Pria|pus (*Greek Myth*)
Pri|bi|lof (islands off
  Alaska)
Price, (Mary)
  Leon|tyne (US
  singer)
Price, Vin|cent (US
  actor)
price
  prices
  priced
  pricing
priced *adjective*
price-earnings ratio
price-fixing
price goul|ging
price|less
price|less|ly
price|less|ness
price list +s
pricer +s
price-sensitive
price tag +s
pricey
  prici|er
  prici|est
prici|ness
prick +s +ed +ing
prick|er +s
prick|et +s
prickle
  prickles
  prickled
  prick|ling
prick|li|ness
prick|ly
  prick|li|er
  prick|li|est
pricy (*use* pricey)
  prici|er
  prici|est
Pride, Sir Thom|as
  (instigator of Pride's
  Purge)
pride
  prides
  prided
  prid|ing
pride|ful
pride|ful|ly
prie-dieu
  prie-dieux
priest +s +ed +ing
priest|craft
priest|ess
  priest|ess|es
priest hole +s
  (= priest's hole)
priest|hood
Priest|ley, John
  Boyn|ton (English
  writer)
  [☞ priestly]

Priest|ley, Jo|seph
  (English scientist)
  [☞ priestly]
priest|like
priest|li|ness
priest|ly
  [☞ Priestley]
priest's hole +s
prig +s
prig|gery
prig|gish
prig|gish|ly
prig|gish|ness
Pri|go|gine, Ilya
  (Belgian chemist)
prim
  prim|mer
  prim|mest
  prims
  primmed
  prim|ming
prima bal|ler|ina +s
pri|macy
  pri|ma|cies
prima donna +s
prima donna-ish
pri|maeval (*use*
  primeval)
pri|maeval|ly (*use*
  primevally)
prima facie
pri|mal
pri|mar|i|ly
pri|mary
  pri|mar|ies
pri|mate +s
pri|matial
prima|to|logic|al
prima|tol|o|gist +s
prima|tol|ogy
prima|vera +s
prime
  primes
  primed
  prim|ing
prime min|is|ter +s
prime min|is|ter|ial
prime min|is|ter|ship
  +s
Prime Min|is|ter's
  Of|fice
prime|ness
prim|er +s (textbook;
  paint; igniting cap;
  Biochemistry)
prime time (prime-
  time *when preceding
  a noun*)
pri|meval
pri|meval|ly
primi|grav|ida
  primi|grav|idae
prim|ing +s *noun*

pri|mip|ara
  pri|mip|aras or
  pri|mip|arae
primi|par|ity
pri|mip|ar|ous
primi|tive +s
primi|tive|ly
primi|tive|ness
primi|tiv|ism
primi|tiv|ist +s
prim|ly
prim|mer *comparative
  of* prim
  [☞ primer]
prim|ness
primo +s
Primo de Ri|vera,
  José An|tonio
  (Spanish politician)
Primo de Ri|vera,
  Mi|guel (Spanish
  general)
primo|geni|tary
primo|geni|tor +s
  (ancestor)
primo|geni|ture
  (rights belonging to
  the first-born child)
pri|mor|dial
pri|mor|di|al|ity
pri|mor|di|al|ly
pri|mor|dium
  primor|dia
Pri|mor|sky Krai
  (territory, Russia)
primp +s +ed +ing
Prim|rose (lake,
  Canada)
prim|rose +s
prim|rose yel|low +s
  (primrose-yellow
  *when preceding a
  noun*)
prim|ula +s
prim|um mo|bile +s
Pri|mus *proprietary*
  Pri|mus|es
pri|mus inter pares
prince +s
Prince Al|bert (city,
  peninsula & national
  park, Canada)
Prince Charles
  (island, Canada)
Prince Charm|ing +s
prince|dom +s
Prince Ed|ward
  Island (province &
  national park,
  Canada)
Prince George (city,
  Canada)
prince|like

prince|li|ness
prince|ling +s
prince|ly
  prince|li|er
  prince|li|est
Prince of Wales
  (island & strait,
  Canada; *former name
  for* Penang,
  Malaysia)
Prince of Wales'
  Fort (= Fort Prince
  of Wales, Canada)
Prince Pat|rick
  (island, Canada)
Prince Ru|pert (city,
  Canada)
Prince Rupert's
  Land (= Rupert's
  Land, Canada)
prince's feath|er +s
prin|cess
  prin|cess|es
prin|ci|pal +s
  adjective & noun
  (main; leading figure;
  school head; capital;
  person acted for by
  another; rafter)
  [☞ principle]
prin|ci|pal|ity
  prin|ci|pal|ities
prin|ci|pal|ly
prin|ci|pal|ship +s
prin|ci|pate
prin|ci|ple +s *noun*
  (fundamental truth;
  law; moral guidline;
  chemical
  constituent)
  [☞ principal]
prin|ci|pled
prink +s +ed +ing
print +s +ed +ing
print|abil|ity
print|able
print|ed *adjective*
print|er +s
printer's dev|il +s
print|ery
  print|eries
print|head +s
print|ing +s *noun*
print|maker +s
print|making
print out *verb*
  prints out
  print|ed out
  print|ing out
print|out +s *noun*
print run +s
print shop +s
pri|on +s

Prior, Mat|thew
(English poet)
pri|or +s
prior|ate +s
prior|ess
  prior|ess|es
pri|ori|tiz|a|tion +s
pri|ori|tize
  pri|ori|tiz|es
  pri|ori|tized
  pri|ori|tiz|ing
pri|or|ity
  pri|or|ities
prior|ship +s
pri|ory
  pri|or|ies
Pri|pet (= Pripyat
  River)
Pri|pyat (river,
  E Europe)
Pris|cian (Byzantine
  grammarian)
prise (pry, remove;
  leverage)
  pris|es
  prised
  pris|ing
  [☞ prize]
prism +s
pris|mat|ic
pris|mat|ic|ally
pris|moid +s
pris|moid|al
pris|on
  pris|ons
  pris|oned
  pris|on|ing
pris|on|er +s
pris|oner's base
pris|si|ly
pris|si|ness
prissy
  pris|si|er
  pris|si|est
Priš|tina (city,
  Kosovo)
pris|tine
Prit|chett, Sir Vic|tor
  Saw|don (English
  writer)
pri|thee
pri|vacy
  pri|va|cies
pri|vate +s
pri|va|teer +s
pri|va|teer|ing
pri|vate|ly
pri|vate member's
  bill
• When discussing
  several bills
  introduced by

several members,
use the plural form
private members'
bills; when
discussing several
bills introduced by
one member, use
private member's
bills.
pri|va|tion +s
priv|a|tive
pri|va|tiz|a|tion +s
pri|va|tize
  pri|va|tiz|es
  pri|va|tized
  pri|va|tiz|ing
priv|et +s
priv|il|ege
  priv|il|eges
  priv|il|eged
  priv|il|eging
priv|il|eged adjective
priv|i|ly
priv|ity
  priv|ities
privy
  priv|ies
Privy Coun|cil +s
privy coun|cil|lor +s
Privy Coun|cil
  Of|fice
privy coun|sel|lor +s
  (use privy
  councillor)
prix fixe +s
prize (award; value
  highly; captured ship
  etc.; for pry, remove
  or leverage use
  prise)
  priz|es
  prized
  priz|ing
prize|fight +s
prize|fight|er +s
prize|fight|ing
prize-giving +s
prize money
prize|win|ner +s
prize|win|ning
PRO (public relations
  officer)
  PROs
pro +s
proa +s (= prahu)
pro|active
pro|active|ly
pro-am +s
prob +s
prob|abil|is|tic
prob|abil|ity
  prob|abil|ities

prob|able +s (likely)
  [☞ probeable]
prob|ably
pro|band +s
pro|bate
  pro|bates
  pro|bat|ed
  pro|bat|ing
pro|ba|tion
pro|ba|tion|al
pro|ba|tion|ary
pro|ba|tion|er +s
pro|ba|tion|er|ship
  +s
pro|ba|tive
probe
  probes
  probed
  prob|ing
probe|able (that may
  be probed)
  [☞ probable]
prob|er +s
prob|ing|ly
pro|bity
prob|lem +s
prob|lem|atic
prob|lem|atic|al
prob|lem|atic|al|ly
prob|lem|a|tiz|a|tion
  +s
prob|lem|a|tize
  prob|lem|a|tiz|es
  prob|lem|a|tized
  prob|lem|a|tiz|ing
pro bono
pro|bos|cid|ean +s
pro|bos|cid|ian +s
  (use proboscidean)
pro|bos|cis
  pro|bos|cis|es or
  pro|bos|ces
pro|caine
pro|cary|ote +s (use
  prokaryote)
pro|ced|ur|al
pro|ced|ur|al|ly
pro|ced|ure +s
pro|ceed +s +ed +ing
  (move forwards;
  continue)
  [☞ precede]
pro|ceed|ing +s noun
pro|ceeds
pro|cess (course of
  action; processed;
  appendage; operate
  on; develop; walk in
  a procession)
  pro|cess|es
  pro|cessed
  pro|cess|ing
pro|cess|able

pro|ces|sion +s
  (ceremonial march;
  emanation)
  [☞ precession]
pro|ces|sion|al (of a
  procession)
  [☞ precessional]
pro|ces|sion|ist +s
pro|ces|sor +s
procès-verbal
  procès-verbaux
pro-choice
pro|claim +s +ed
  +ing
pro|claim|er +s
proc|lam|a|tion +s
pro|clit|ic +s
pro|cliv|ity
  pro|cliv|ities
Pro|clus (Greek
  philosopher)
pro|consul +s
pro|consul|ar
Pro|co|pius
  (Byzantine historian)
pro|cras|tin|ate
  pro|cras|tin|ates
  pro|cras|tin|at|ed
  pro|cras|tin|at|ing
pro|cras|tin|a|tion +s
pro|cras|tin|ator +s
pro|cre|ant
pro|cre|ate
  pro|cre|ates
  pro|cre|at|ed
  pro|cre|at|ing
pro|cre|ation
pro|cre|ative
pro|cre|ator +s
Pro|crus|tean
Pro|crus|tes (Greek
  Myth)
procto|logic|al
proc|tol|o|gist +s
proc|tol|ogy
proc|tor +s +ed +ing
proc|tor|ial
proctor|ship +s
procto|scope +s
procto|scop|ic
proc|tos|copy
  proc|tos|cop|ies
pro|cum|bent
pro|cur|able
pro|cur|al +s
proc|ur|a|tion +s
proc|ur|ator +s
proc|ura|tor|ial
proc|ur|ator|ship
pro|cure
  pro|cures
  pro|cured
  pro|cur|ing

pro|cure|ment +s
pro|cur|er +s
pro|cur|ess
  pro|cur|ess|es
Pro|cyon (star)
prod
  prods
  prod|ded
  prod|ding
prod|der +s
prodi|gal +s
prodi|gal|ity
prodi|gal|ly
pro|di|gious
pro|di|gious|ly
pro|di|gious|ness
prod|igy
  prodi|gies
pro|drom|al
pro|drome +s
pro|drom|ic
prod|uce¹ *noun*
pro|duce² *verb*
  pro|du|ces
  pro|duced
  pro|du|cing
pro|du|cer +s
pro|du|ci|bil|ity
pro|du|cible
prod|uct +s
pro|duc|tion +s
pro|duc|tion|al
pro|duct|ive
pro|duct|ive|ly
pro|duct|ive|ness
pro|duc|tiv|ity
  pro|duc|tiv|ities
pro|em +s
prof +s
pro-family
prof|an|a|tion +s
pro|fane
  pro|fanes
  pro|faned
  pro|fan|ing
pro|fane|ly
pro|fan|er +s
pro|fan|ity
  pro|fan|ities
pro|fess
  pro|fess|es
  pro|fessed
  pro|fess|ing
pro|fessed *adjective*
pro|fess|ed|ly
pro|fes|sion +s
pro|fes|sion|al +s
pro|fes|sion|al|ism
pro|fes|sion|al|
     iz|a|tion +s
pro|fes|sion|al|ize
  pro|fes|sion|al|iz|es

pro|fes|sion|al|ized
  pro|fes|sion|al|iz|ing
pro|fes|sion|al|ly
pro|fes|sor +s
pro|fes|sor|ate
pro|fes|sor|ial
pro|fes|sor|ial|ly
pro|fes|sor|iate
pro|fes|sor|ship +s
prof|fer +s +ed +ing
pro|fi|cien|cy
  pro|fi|cien|cies
pro|fi|cient
pro|fi|cient|ly
pro|file
  pro|files
  pro|filed
  pro|fil|ing
pro|fil|er +s
pro|fil|ist +s
prof|it +s +ed +ing
  (gain; benefit)
  [☞ prophet]
prof|it|abil|ity
prof|it|able
prof|it|able|ness
prof|it|ably
profi|teer +s +ed
  +ing
pro|fit|er|ole +s
profit|less
profit-sharing
profit-taking
prof|li|gacy
prof|li|gate +s
prof|li|gate|ly
pro forma
pro|found +er +est
pro|found|ly
pro|found|ness
pro|fund|ity
  pro|fund|ities
pro|fuse
pro|fuse|ly
pro|fuse|ness
pro|fu|sion +s
prog (food)
  [☞ Prague]
pro|geni|tive
pro|geni|tor +s
pro|geni|tor|ial
pro|geny
  pro|gen|ies
pro|ges|ter|one
pro|ges|tin +s
pro|ges|to|gen +s
pro|glot|tid +s
pro|glot|tis
  pro|glot|tides
prog|nath|ic
prog|nath|ism
prog|nath|ous

prog|no|sis
  prog|no|ses
prog|nos|tic
prog|nos|tic|ally
prog|nos|ti|cate
  prog|nos|ti|cates
  prog|nos|ti|cat|ed
  prog|nos|ti|cat|ing
prog|nos|ti|ca|tion +s
prog|nos|ti|ca|tive
prog|nos|ti|ca|tor +s
pro|gram
  pro|grams
  pro|grammed
  pro|gram|ming
pro|gram|mabil|ity
pro|gram|mable
pro|gram|mat|ic
pro|gram|mat|ic|ally
pro|gramme (*use*
  program)
  pro|grammes
  pro|grammed
  pro|gram|ming
pro|gram|mer +s
pro|gram|ming *noun*
progress
  pro|gress|es
  pro|gressed
  pro|gress|ing
pro|gres|sion +s
pro|gres|sion|al
pro|gres|sive
Pro|gres|sive
  Con|serv|a|tive +s
pro|gres|sive|ly
pro|gres|sive|ness
pro|gres|siv|ism
pro|gres|siv|ist +s
prog rock (prog-rock
  when preceding a
  noun)
pro|hibit +s +ed +ing
Pro|hibi|tion (legal
  ban on alcohol sales
  & production)
pro|hibi|tion +s (*in*
  general use)
pro|hibi|tion|ary
pro|hibi|tion|ism
pro|hibi|tion|ist +s
pro|hibi|tive
pro|hibi|tive|ly
pro|hibi|tive|ness
pro|hibi|tor +s
pro|hibi|tory
pro|ject +s +ed +ing
pro|ject|ile +s
pro|jec|tion +s
pro|jec|tion|ist +s
pro|ject|ive
pro|ject|ive|ly
pro|ject|or +s

pro|kary|ote +s
pro|kary|ot|ic
Pro|kof|iev, Ser|gei
  Serge|evich (Russian
  composer)
Pro|kop|evsk (city,
  Russia)
pro|lac|tin
pro|lapse
  pro|laps|es
  pro|lapsed
  pro|laps|ing
pro|late
pro|late|ly
prole +s
pro|leg +s
pro|legom|en|on
  pro|legom|ena
pro|legom|en|ous
pro|lep|sis
  pro|lep|ses
pro|lep|tic
pro|le|tar|ian +s
pro|le|tar|ian|ism
pro|le|tar|ian|
     iz|a|tion
pro|le|tar|ian|ize
  pro|le|tar|ian|iz|es
  pro|le|tar|ian|ized
  pro|le|tar|ian|iz|ing
pro|le|tar|iat
pro-life
pro-lifer +s
pro|lif|er|ate
  pro|lif|er|ates
  pro|lif|er|at|ed
  pro|lif|er|at|ing
pro|lif|er|a|tion +s
pro|lif|er|a|tive
pro|lif|er|ator +s
pro|lif|er|ous
pro|lif|ic
pro|lif|ic|acy
pro|lif|ic|al|ly
pro|lif|ic|ness
pro|line +s
pro|lix
pro|lix|ity
pro|lix|ly
pro|locu|tor +s
PRO|LOG (*Computing*)
pro|logue
  pro|logues
  pro|logued
  pro|loguing
pro|long +s +ed +ing
pro|long|a|tion +s
pro|longed *adjective*
pro|long|er +s
pro|lu|sion +s
pro|lu|sory
prom +s

prom|en|ade
  prom|en|ades
  prom|en|ad|ed
  prom|en|ad|ing
prom|en|ad|er +s
pro|metha|zine
Pro|me|thean
Pro|me|theus (*Greek Myth*)
pro|me|thium
prom|in|ence +s
prom|in|ent
prom|in|ent|ly
pro|mis|cu|ity
pro|mis|cu|ous
pro|mis|cu|ous|ly
pro|mis|cu|ous|ness
prom|ise
  prom|ises
  prom|ised
  prom|is|ing
Prom|ised Land (*Bible*)
prom|ised land +s (*in general use*)
prom|isee +s
prom|iser +s (*in general use*)
  [☞ promisor]
prom|is|ing *adjective*
prom|is|ing|ly
prom|isor (*Law*)
  [☞ promiser]
prom|is|sory
promo +s
prom|on|tory
  prom|on|tor|ies
pro|mot|abil|ity
pro|mot|able
pro|mote
  pro|motes
  pro|mot|ed
  pro|mot|ing
pro|mot|er +s
pro|mo|tion +s
pro|mo|tion|al
pro|mo|tive
prompt +s +ed +ing
prompt-book +s
prompt|er
prompt|ing +s *noun*
prompt|i|tude
prompt|ly
prompt|ness
prom|ul|gate
  prom|ul|gates
  prom|ul|gat|ed
  prom|ul|gat|ing
prom|ul|ga|tion +s
prom|ul|ga|tor +s
pro|mulge
  pro|mul|ges

pro|mulged
pro|mul|ging
pro|nate
  pro|nates
  pro|nat|ed
  pro|nat|ing
pro|na|tion
pro|na|tor +s
prone
prone|ly
prone|ness
prong +s +ed +ing
pronged *adjective*
prong|horn +s
pro|nom|inal
pro|nom|inal| iz|a|tion
pro|nom|inal|ize
  pro|nom|inal|iz|es
  pro|nom|inal|ized
  pro|nom|inal|iz|ing
pro|nom|inal|ly
pro|noun +s
pro|nounce
  pro|noun|ces
  pro|nounced
  pro|noun|cing
pro|nounce|abil|ity
pro|nounce|able
pro|nounced *adjective*
pro|noun|ced|ly
pro|nounce|ment +s
pro|noun|cer +s
pronto
pro|nun|cia|mento +s
pro|nun|ci|a|tion +s
pro-nuncio +s
proof +s +ed +ing
proof line +s
proof|read
  proof|reads
  proof|read
  proof|read|ing
proof|read|er +s
proof|read|ing *noun*
prop
  props
  propped
  prop|ping
pro|pae|deut|ic +s
pro|pae|deut|ic|al
propa|ganda
propa|gand|ism
propa|gand|ist +s
propa|gand|is|tic
propa|gand| is|tic|ally
propa|gand|ize
  propa|gand|iz|es
  propa|gand|ized
  propa|gand|iz|ing

propa|gate
  propa|gates
  propa|gat|ed
  propa|gat|ing
propa|ga|tion +s
propa|ga|tive
propa|ga|tor +s
pro|pane
pro|pan|one
pro|pel (drive, thrust; urge)
  pro|pels
  pro|pelled
  pro|pel|ling
  [☞ propyl]
pro|pel|lant +s (*noun*; for adjective use propellent)
pro|pel|lent *adjective*
pro|pel|ler +s
pro|peller-head +s
pro|pene
pro|pen|sity (inclination, tendency)
  pro|pen|si|ties
  [☞ prepense]
prop|er +s
prop|er|ly
prop|er|ness
prop|er|tied
Pro|per|tius, Sex|tus (Roman poet)
prop|erty
  prop|er|ties
prop|erty|less
pro|phase
proph|ecy *noun*
  proph|ecies
  [☞ prophesy]
proph|esi|er +s
proph|esy *verb*
  proph|esies
  proph|esied
  proph|esy|ing
  [☞ prophecy]
Proph|et (Muhammad; Joseph Smith)
proph|et +s (foreteller)
  [☞ profit]
prophet|ess
  prophet|ess|es
prophet|hood
proph|et|ic
proph|et|ic|al
proph|et|ic|al|ly
prophet|ism
pro|phyl|ac|tic +s
pro|phyl|ac|tic|ally
pro|phyl|ax|is
  pro|phyl|ax|es

pro|pin|quity
pro|pi|on|ate +s
pro|pi|on|ic
pro|piti|ate
  pro|piti|ates
  pro|piti|at|ed
  pro|piti|at|ing
pro|piti|a|tion
pro|piti|a|tor +s
pro|piti|a|tor|ily
pro|piti|a|tory
pro|pi|tious
pro|pi|tious|ly
pro|pi|tious|ness
prop-jet +s
prop|olis
pro|pon|ent +s
Pro|pon|tis (ancient name for the Sea of Marmara)
pro|por|tion +s +ed +ing
pro|por|tion|al
pro|por|tion|al|ity
  pro|por|tion|al|ities
pro|por|tion|al|ly
pro|por|tion|ate
pro|por|tion|ate|ly
pro|por|tioned *adjective*
pro|pos|al +s
pro|pose (put forward for consideration; offer to wed)
  pro|pos|es
  pro|posed
  pro|pos|ing
  [☞ prepose]
pro|posed *adjective*
pro|pos|er +s
prop|os|ition +s +ed +ing (proposal, offer; statement)
  [☞ preposition]
prop|os|ition|al (of or like a proposition)
  [☞ prepositional]
pro|pound +s +ed +ing
pro|pound|er +s
pro|pran|ol|ol
pro|pri|etary
pro|pri|etor +s
pro|pri|etor|ial
pro|pri|etor|ial|ly
pro|pri|etor|ship +s
pro|pri|etress
  pro|pri|etress|es
pro|pri|ety
  pro|pri|eties
pro|prio|cep|tion
pro|prio|cep|tive
pro|prio|cep|tor +s

prop|to|sis
  prop|to|ses
pro|pul|sion
pro|pul|sive
pro|pyl +s (*Chemistry*)
pro|py|laeum
  pro|py|laea
pro|pyl|ene
pro|pyne
pro rata
pro-rate
  pro-rates
  pro-rated
  pro-rating
  pro-rated *adjective*
pro-ration
pro|roga|tion +s
  (*Parliamentary*)
  [☞ prerogative]
pro|rogue
  (*Parliamentary*)
  pro|rogues
  pro|rogued
  pro|roguing
  [☞ prerogative]
pro|saic
pro|saic|ally
pro|scen|ium
  pro|scen|iums or
  pro|scenia
pro|sciut|to +s
pro|scribe (denounce,
  prohibit; banish)
  pro|scribes
  pro|scribed
  pro|scrib|ing
  [☞ prescribe]
pro|scrip|tion +s (act
  of proscribing)
  [☞ prescription]
pro|scrip|tive
  (proscribing)
  [☞ prescriptive]
prose
  proses
  prosed
  pros|ing
pro|sect|or +s
pros|ecut|able
pros|ecute
  pros|ecutes
  pros|ecut|ed
  pros|ecut|ing
pros|ecu|tion +s
pros|ecu|tor +s
pros|ecu|tor|ial
pros|elyte +s
pros|elyt|ism
pros|elyt|iz|a|tion
pros|elyt|ize
  pros|elyt|iz|es
  pros|elyt|ized
  pros|elyt|iz|ing

pros|elyt|iz|er +s
pros|en|chyma
pros|en|chym|al
pros|en|chyma|tous
Pros|er|pina
  (= Proserpine)
Pros|er|pine (*Roman
  Myth*)
pros|i|er
pros|i|est
pros|ify
  prosi|fies
  prosi|fied
  prosi|fy|ing
pros|i|ly
pro|sim|ian +s
pros|i|ness
pro|sit
pros|od|ic
pros|od|ic|ally
pros|od|ist +s
pros|ody
proso|pog|raph|er +s
proso|po|graph|ic
proso|po|graph|ic|al
proso|pog|raphy
  proso|pog|raph|ies
proso|po|peia (*use
  prosopopoeia*)
proso|po|poeia
pros|pect +s +ed
  +ing
pros|pect|ing *noun*
pro|spect|ive
pro|spect|ive|ly
pro|spect|or +s
pro|spec|tus
  pro|spec|tus|es
pros|per +s +ed +ing
pros|per|ity
pros|per|ous
pros|per|ous|ly
Prost, Alain (French
  race-car driver)
pros|ta|glan|din +s
pros|tate +s
pros|ta|tec|tomy
  pros|ta|tec|to|mies
pros|tat|ic
pros|thesis
  pros|theses
pros|thet|ic
pros|thet|ics
pros|ti|tute
  pros|ti|tutes
  pros|ti|tut|ed
  pros|ti|tut|ing
pros|ti|tu|tion +s
pros|trate
  pros|trates
  pros|trat|ed
  pros|trat|ing
pros|tra|tion +s

pro|style +s
prosy
  pros|i|er
  pros|i|est
pro|tac|tin|ium
pro|tag|on|ist +s
Pro|tag|or|as (Greek
  philosopher)
prot|amine +s
prot|asis
  prot|ases
pro|tat|ic
pro|tea +s (shrub)
  [☞ protei]
pro|tean
pro|te|ase +s
pro|tect +s +ed +ing
pro|tect|ant +s
pro|tect|ed *adjective*
pro|tec|tion +s
pro|tec|tion|ism
pro|tec|tion|ist +s
pro|tect|ive
pro|tect|ive|ly
pro|tect|ive|ness
pro|tect|or +s
pro|tect|or|ate +s
pro|tec|tress
  pro|tec|tress|es
pro|te|ge +s
pro|tei *plural of*
  proteus
  [☞ protea]
pro|tein +s
pro|tein|aceous
pro|tein|oid +s
pro tem
pro tem|pore
pro|te|oly|sis
  pro|te|oly|ses
pro|teo|lytic
Pro|tero|zoic
pro|test +s +ed +ing
  (dissent etc.)
  [☞ pretest]
Prot|est|ant +s
  (*Christianity*)
prot|est|ant +s
  (protesting person)
Prot|est|ant|ism
pro|tes|ta|tion +s
pro|test|er +s
pro|test|ing|ly
pro|test|or +s (*use
  protester*)
Pro|teus (*Greek Myth*;
  Astronomy)
pro|teus (bacterium)
  pro|tei or
  pro|teus|es
pro|tha|la|mion (*use
  prothalamium*)
  pro|tha|la|mia

pro|tha|la|mium
  pro|tha|la|mia
pro|thal|lium
  pro|thal|lia
pro|thal|lus
  pro|thalli
proth|esis
  proth|eses
pro|thet|ic
pro|tho|no|tary
  pro|tho|no|tar|ies
pro|tist
pro|tist|ol|ogy
pro|tium
proto|col +s
proto|lan|guage +s
pro|ton +s
pro|ton|ic
proto|plasm
proto|plas|mic
proto|plast +s
proto|plas|tic
proto|star +s
proto|ther|ian +s
proto|typ|al
proto|type
  proto|types
  proto|typed
  proto|typ|ing
proto|typ|ic
proto|typ|ic|al
proto|typ|ic|al|ly
proto|zoal
proto|zoan +s *noun &
  adjective*
proto|zoic
proto|zoon *noun (use
  protozoan*)
  proto|zoa
pro|tract +s +ed +ing
pro|tract|ed *adjective*
pro|tract|ed|ly
pro|tract|ed|ness
pro|tract|ile
pro|trac|tion +s
pro|tract|or +s
pro|trude
  pro|trudes
  pro|trud|ed
  pro|trud|ing
pro|tru|sible
pro|tru|sile
pro|tru|sion +s
pro|tru|sive
pro|tuber|ance +s
pro|tuber|ant
proud +er +est (full of
  pride)
  [☞ prowed]
Prou|dhon, Pierre
  Jo|seph (French
  writer)
proud|ly

Proust, Jo|seph Louis (French chemist)
Proust, Mar|cel (French writer)
Proust|ian
Prout, Wil|liam (English chemist)
prov|able
prov|ably
prove
  proves
  proved
  prov|en or proved
  prov|ing
prov|en *adjective*
prov|en|ance +s
Pro|ven|çal +s (of Provence; language; *Cooking*)
pro|ven|çale (*Cooking*: use Provençal)
  [☞ Provençal]
Pro|vence (former province, France)
Provence-Alpes-Côte d'Azur (region, France)
Pro|ven|cher, Joseph-Norbert (Cdn prelate)
prov|en|der
pro|ven|ience +s (origin)
  [☞ prevenient]
prov|erb +s
pro|verb|ial
pro|verb|ial|ly
pro|vide
  pro|vides
  pro|vid|ed
  pro|vid|ing
pro|vid|ed *conjunction*
Provi|dence (city, US; God)
provi|dence (protective care; foresight)
provi|dent
provi|den|tial
provi|den|tial|ly
provi|dent|ly
pro|vid|er +s
pro|vid|ing *conjunction*
Pro|vimi *proprietary*
prov|ince +s
prov|ince|hood
province-wide
prov|in|cial
prov|in|cial|ism
prov|in|cial|ist +s
prov|in|ci|al|ity

prov|in|cial|iz|a|tion
prov|in|cial|ize
  prov|in|cial|iz|es
  prov|in|cial|ized
  prov|in|cial|iz|ing
prov|in|cial|ly
pro|vi|sion +s +ed +ing (supply)
  [☞ prevision]
Pro|vi|sion|al +s (of the IRA)
  [☞ previsional]
pro|vi|sion|al (temporary)
  [☞ previsional]
pro|vi|sion|al|ity
pro|vi|sion|al|ly
pro|vi|sion|er +s
pro|vi|sion|ing *noun*
pro|vi|sion|less
pro|viso +s
pro|vi|sor|i|ly
pro|vis|ory
pro|vita|min +s
Pro|vo +s (member of Provisional IRA)
  [☞ provost]
pro|voca|teur +s
pro|vo|ca|tion +s
pro|voca|tive
pro|voca|tive|ly
pro|voca|tive|ness
pro|vok|able
pro|voke
  pro|vokes
  pro|voked
  pro|vok|ing
pro|vok|ing *adjective*
pro|vok|ing|ly
pro|vo|lone +s
pro|vost +s (officer, official)
  [☞ Provo]
provost|ship +s
prow +s
prowed (having a prow)
prow|ess
prowl +s +ed +ing
prowl|er +s
prox|emics
prox|im|al
prox|im|al|ly
prox|im|ate
prox|im|ate|ly
prox|im|ity
prox|imo
proxy
  prox|ies
Pro|zac +s *proprietary*
prude +s
pru|dence
pru|dent

pru|den|tial
pru|den|tial|ly
pru|dent|ly
prud|ery
  prud|eries
Prud|hoe (bay, Alaska)
prud|ish
prud|ish|ly
prud|ish|ness
pru|in|ose
prune
  prunes
  pruned
  prun|ing
pru|nel|la +s
prun|er +s
prun|ey
pruri|ence
pruri|ency
pruri|ent
pruri|ent|ly
pruri|gin|ous
prur|igo
prur|it|ic
prur|itus
Prus|sia (former German kingdom)
Prus|sian +s
prus|sic
Prut (river, Europe)
Pruth (= Prut River)
pry
  pries
  pried
  pry|ing
pry bar +s
pry|ing *adjective*
pry|ing|ly
Prynne, Wil|liam (English pamphleteer)
psalm +s (sacred song)
  [☞ Somme]
psalm|ic
psalm|ist +s
psalm|ody
Psal|ter +s (Book of Psalms)
psal|ter|ium
  psal|ter|ia
psal|tery (*Music*)
  psal|ter|ies
pseph|ol|o|gist +s
pseph|ol|ogy
pseud +s (pretentious person)
Pseud|epig|rapha (Jewish writings)
pseud|epig|rapha (spurious writings generally)
pseud|epi|graph|ic

pseu|do +s
pseudo|carp +s
pseudo|ephe|drine
pseudo|morph +s
pseudo|morph|ic
pseudo|morph|ism
pseudo|morph|ous
pseudo|nym +s
pseudo|nym|ity
pseud|onym|ous
pseud|onym|ous|ly
pseudo|pod +s
pseudo|po|dium
  pseudo|podia
pseudo-science +s
pseudo-scientif|ic
pshaw
psi +s (twenty-third Greek letter; parapsychological phenomena)
  [☞ xi]
psilo|cybin
psit|ta|cine +s
psit|ta|co|sis
psoas
  psoai or psoae
psor|ia|sis
psori|at|ic
psst
PST (provincial sales tax)
psych +s +ed +ing (psychology; prepare or affect mentally)
Psy|che (*Greek Myth*)
psy|che +s (soul; spirit; mind)
  [☞ psych]
psyche|delia
psyche|delic +s
psyche|delic|ally
psychi|at|ric
psychi|at|ric|al
psychi|at|ric|al|ly
psych|ia|trist +s
psych|iatry
psych|ic +s
psych|ic|al
psych|ic|al|ly
psy|cho +s
psycho|active
psycho|ana|lyse (use psychoanalyze)
  psycho|ana|lys|es
  psycho|ana|lysed
  psycho|ana|lys|ing
psycho|analy|sis
psycho|ana|lyst +s
psycho|ana|lyt|ic
psycho|ana|lyt|ic|al
psycho|ana|lyt|ic|ally

psycho|ana|lyze
  psycho|ana|lyz|es
  psycho|ana|lyzed
  psycho|ana|lyz|ing
psycho|babble
psycho|biog|raph|er
  +s
psycho|
     bio|graph|ical
psycho|biog|raphy
  psycho|
     biog|raph|ies
psycho|bio|logic|al
psycho|biol|o|gist +s
psycho|biol|ogy
psycho|drama +s
psycho|dynam|ic
psycho|
     dynam|ic|ally
psycho|dynam|ics
psycho|gen|esis
psycho|gen|ic
psycho|graph|ic
psycho|graph|ics
psycho|histor|ian +s
psycho|histor|ic
psycho|histor|ic|al
psycho|hist|ory
psycho|kin|esis
psycho|kinet|ic
psycho|lin|guist +s
psycho|lin|guis|tic
psycho|lin|guis|tics
psych|o|logic|al
psych|o|logic|al|ly
psych|ol|o|gist +s
psych|ol|o|gize
  psych|ol|o|giz|es
  psych|ol|o|gized
  psych|ol|o|giz|ing
psych|ol|ogy
  psych|ol|o|gies
psycho|metric
psycho|metric|ally
psycho|metrics
psych|om|etrist +s
psych|om|etry
psycho|motor
psycho|neuro|sis
  psycho|neuro|ses
psycho|neurot|ic
psycho|path +s
psycho|path|ic
psycho|path|ic|ally
psycho|
     patho|logic|al
psycho|path|ol|o|gist
  +s
psycho|path|ol|ogy
  psycho|
     path|ol|o|gies
psycho|pathy

psycho|
  pharma|co|logic|al
psycho|
  pharma|col|o|gist
    +s
psycho|
  pharma|col|ogy
psycho|physic|al
psycho|physi|cist +s
psycho|phys|ics
psycho|
    physio|logic|al
psycho|physi|ol|ogy
  psycho|
    physi|ol|o|gies
psycho|pomp +s
psycho|sex|ual
psycho|sex|ual|ly
psych|o|sis
  psych|o|ses
psycho|social
psycho|social|ly
psycho|somat|ic
psycho|somat|ic|ally
psycho|surgery
psycho|surgi|cal
psycho|thera|peut|ic
psycho|ther|apist +s
psycho|ther|apy
  psycho|ther|apies
psy|chot|ic +s
psy|chot|ic|ally
psycho|trop|ic
psy|chrom|eter +s
psy|chrom|et|ic
psyl|lium +s (plantain
  or its seeds)
  [☞ cilium]
Ptah (*Egyptian Myth*)
ptar|migan
  plural ptar|migan or
  ptar|migans
pteri|do|logic|al
pteri|dol|o|gist +s
pteri|dol|ogy
pteri|do|phyte +s
ptero|dac|tyl +s
ptero|pod +s
ptero|saur +s
Ptol|em|aic
Ptol|emy (Greek
  astronomer &
  geographer)
Ptol|emy I (king of
  Egypt)
pto|maine +s
ptoo|ey
pto|sis
ptot|ic
ptya|lin
pub +s
pub|bing *noun*

pub-crawl +s +ed
  +ing
pu|ber|tal
pu|ber|ty
pubes
pu|bes|cence
pu|bes|cent
pubic
pubis
  pubes
pub|lic +s
pub|lic ac|cess
  (public-access *when*
  preceding a noun)
pub|li|can +s
pub|li|ca|tion +s
pub|li|cist +s
pub|li|cis|tic
pub|li|city
pub|li|cize
  pub|li|ciz|es
  pub|li|cized
  pub|li|ciz|ing
pub|lic key +s
  (public-key *when*
  preceding a noun)
pub|lic|ly
pub|lic spir|it
public-spirited
public-spirited|ly
public-spirited|ness
pub|lish
  pub|lish|es
  pub|lished
  pub|lish|ing
pub|lish|able
pub|lished *adjective*
pub|lish|er +s
pub|lish|ing *noun*
Puc|cini, Gia|como
  (Italian composer)
puce
Puck (mischievous
  sprite)
puck +s
pucka (*use* pukka)
puck|er +s +ed +ing
puck|ery
puck|hand|ler +s
puck-handling
puck|ish
puck|ish|ly
puck|ster +s
pud +s
pud|ding +s
pud|dingy
pud|dle
  pud|dles
  pud|dled
  pud|dling
puddle-jumper +s
pud|dler +s
pud|dly

pu|den|dal
pu|den|dum
  pu|den|da
pudge
pudgi|ly
pudgi|ness
pudgy
  pudgi|er
  pudgi|est
Pueb|la (state & its
  capital, Mexico)
Pueb|la de Zara|goza
  (= city of Puebla,
  Mexico)
Pueb|lo (people)
  plural Pueb|lo or
  Pueb|los
pueb|lo +s (village)
puer|ile
puer|ile|ly
puer|il|ity
  puer|il|ities
puer|per|al
Puer|to Cor|tés (city,
  Honduras)
Puer|to Limón
  (= Limón, Costa
  Rica)
Puer|to Plata (resort,
  Dominican Republic)
Puer|to Rican +s
Puer|to Rico
  (Caribbean island)
Puer|to Val|lar|ta
  (resort, Mexico)
puff +s +ed +ing
puff|ball +s
puffed up (puffed-up
  when preceding a
  noun)
puff|er +s
puffer|fish
  plural puffer|fish or
  puffer|fish|es
puff|ery
puff|i|ly
puf|fin +s
puff|i|ness
puffy
  puff|i|er
  puff|i|est
pug
  pugs
  pugged
  pug|ging
Puget Sound (inlet,
  US)
pug|garee +s
  (= puggree)
pug|ging *noun*
pug|gree +s
pugil|ism
pugil|ist +s

pugil|is|tic
pugil|is|tic|ally
Pugin, Au|gus|tus
  Welby North|more
  (English architect)
Puglia (= Apulia,
  Italy)
pug mill +s
pug|na|cious
pug|na|cious|ly
pug|na|cious|ness
pug|na|city
pug-nose +s
pug-nosed
pug|ree +s (use
  puggree)
Pug|wash (village,
  Canada)
puh-lease (= puh-
  leeze)
puh-leeze
puisne (judge ranking
  below chief justice)
puis|sance +s
puis|sant
puis|sant|ly
puja +s
Puka|skwa (national
  park, Canada)
puke
  pukes
  puked
  puk|ing
pukey
pukka
puk|kah (use pukka)
pul (Afghan currency)
  puls or puli
  [☞ pule]
pula +s (Botswanan
  currency)
pul|chri|tude
pul|chri|tud|in|ous
pule (cry, whimper)
  pules
  puled
  pul|ing
  [☞ pul]
Pul|itz|er, Jo|seph
  (US)
Pul|itz|er Prize +s
pulk +s
pulka +s (= pulk)
pull +s +ed +ing
pull back verb
  pulls back
  pulled back
  pull|ing back
pull|back +s noun
pull down verb
  pulls down
  pulled down
  pull|ing down

pull-down adjective
pull|er +s
pull|let +s
pull|ley +s +ed +ing
Pull|man +s
pull off verb
  pulls off
  pulled off
  pull|ing off
pull-off +s noun &
  adjective
pull on verb
  pulls on
  pulled on
  pull|ing on
pull-on +s noun &
  adjective
pull out verb
  pulls out
  pulled out
  pull|ing out
pull|out +s noun &
  adjective
pull over verb
  pulls over
  pulled over
  pull|ing over
pull|over +s noun
pull-type
pul|lu|late
  pul|lu|lates
  pul|lu|lat|ed
  pul|lu|lat|ing
pul|lu|la|tion
pull up verb
  pulls up
  pulled up
  pull|ing up
pull-up +s noun
pul|mon|ary
pul|mon|ate
pul|mon|ic
pulp +s +ed +ing
pulp cut|ter +s
pulp|er +s
pulp|i|ness
pulp|ing noun
pul|pit +s
pulp|wood
pulpy
  pulp|i|er
  pulp|i|est
pul|que
pul|sar +s
pul|sate
  pul|sates
  pul|sat|ed
  pul|sat|ing
pul|sa|tile
pul|sa|til|la +s
pul|sa|tion +s
pul|sa|tor +s
pul|sa|tory

pulse
  puls|es
  pulsed
  puls|ing
pulse|less
Pulu (Tiglath-pileser
  III, king of Assyria)
pul|ver|iz|a|tion +s
pul|ver|ize
  pul|ver|iz|es
  pul|ver|ized
  pul|ver|iz|ing
pul|ver|iz|er +s
puma +s
pum|ice
  pumi|ces
  pumi|iced
  pumi|cing
pu|mi|ceous
pum|mel verb (thump,
  beat; trounce;
  criticize)
  pum|mels
  pum|melled
  pum|mel|ling
  [☞ pommel]
pump +s +ed +ing
pump-action
pumped adjective
pump|er +s
pum|per|nick|el +s
pump fake +s noun
pump-fake verb
  pump-fakes
  pump-faked
  pump-faking
pump|handle
  pump|han|dles
  pump|han|dled
  pump|hand|ling
pump|house +s
pump|jack +s
pump|kin +s
pump|kin seed +s
  (seed of pumpkin)
pumpkin|seed (fish)
  plural pumpkin|seed
  or pumpkin|seeds
pump out verb
  pumps out
  pumped out
  pump|ing out
pump-out +s noun
pump-priming
pump room +s
pun
  puns
  punned
  pun|ning
Punch (puppet
  character; horse)
  Punch|es

punch
  punch|es
  punched
  punch|ing
punch bowl +s
punch-drunk
punched adjective
pun|cheon +s
punch|er +s
punch|i|er
punch|i|est
punch|i|ly
Pun|chin|ello +s
punch|i|ness
punch|less
punch|line +s
punch out verb
  punch|es out
  punched out
  punch|ing out
punch|out +s noun
punch up verb
  punch|es up
  punched up
  punch|ing up
punch-up +s noun
punchy
  punch|i|er
  punch|i|est
punc|tate
punc|ta|tion +s
punc|tilio +s
punc|tili|ous
punc|tili|ous|ly
punc|tili|ous|ness
punc|tual
punc|tu|al|ity
punc|tual|ly
punc|tu|ate
  punc|tu|ates
  punc|tu|at|ed
  punc|tu|at|ing
punc|tu|at|ed
  adjective
punc|tu|a|tion +s
punc|ture
  punc|tures
  punc|tured
  punc|tur|ing
pun|dit +s (Hindu
  learned in Sanskrit &
  Indian philosophy;
  expert)
  [☞ Pandit]
pun|ditry
Pune (= Poona, India)
pun|gency
  pun|gen|cies
pun|gent
pun|gent|ly
Punic
puni|er
puni|est

puni|ly
puni|ness
pun|ish
  pun|ish|es
  pun|ished
  pun|ish|ing
pun|ish|able
pun|ish|er +s
pun|ish|ing *adjective*
pun|ish|ing|ly
pun|ish|ment +s
puni|tive
puni|tive|ly
Pun|jab (province, Pakistan; state, India)
Pun|jabi +s
punk +s
pun|kah +s
punk|er +s
punk|ish
punky
pun|net +s
pun|ning *noun & adjective*
pun|ning|ly
pun|ster +s
punt +s +ed +ing
Punta Arenas (city, Chile)
punt|er +s
puny (undersized; feeble)
  puni|er
  puni|est
  [☞ puisne]
pup
  pups
  pupped
  pup|ping
pupa
  pupae
pupal (of pupae)
  [☞ pupil]
pu|pate
  pu|pates
  pu|pat|ed
  pu|pat|ing
pu|pa|tion
pu|pil +s (student; in eyes)
  [☞ pupal]
pupil|age (*use* pupillage)
pupil|ar (*use* pupillar)
pupil|lage
pupil|lar
pupil|lary
pup|pet +s
pup|pet|eer +s
pup|pet|eer|ing
pup|petry
Pup|pis (constellation)

puppy
  pup|pies
puppy|hood
puppy|ish
puppy love
pup tent +s
Pu|rana (*Hinduism*)
Pu|ran|ic
Pur|beck
pur|blind
pur|blind|ness
Pur|cell (mountain range, Canada)
Pur|cell, Ed|ward Mills (US physicist)
Pur|cell, Henry (English composer)
pur|chas|able
pur|chase
  pur|chas|es
  pur|chased
  pur|chas|ing
pur|chas|er +s
pur|dah
Purdy, Al|fred Wel|ling|ton (Cdn writer)
pure
  purer
  pur|est
pure|bred +s
purée
  pur|ées
  pur|éed
  purée|ing
pure laine +s
pure|ly
pure|ness
pur|fle
  pur|fles
  pur|fled
  purf|ling
purf|ling *noun*
pur|ga|tion
pur|ga|tive +s
pur|ga|tor|ial
pur|ga|tory
  pur|ga|tor|ies
purge
  pur|ges
  purged
  pur|ging
pur|ger +s (that which purges)
  [☞ perjure]
puri +s
puri|fi|ca|tion +s
puri|fi|ca|tory
puri|fi|er +s
pur|ify
  puri|fies
  puri|fied
  puri|fy|ing

Purim (*Judaism*)
pur|ine +s
pur|ism
pur|ist +s
pur|is|tic
Puri|tan +s (*Christianity*)
puri|tan +s (*in general use*)
puri|tan|ical
puri|tan|ical|ly
Puri|tan|ism (*Christianity*)
puri|tan|ism (*in general use*)
pur|ity
  pur|ities
purl +s +ed +ing (stitch; ornamental border; swirl & babble)
  [☞ pearl]
purl|er +s
pur|lieu
  pur|lieus
pur|lin +s
pur|loin +s +ed +ing
pur|loin|er +s
pur|ple
  purp|ler
  purp|lest
  purp|les
  purp|led
  purp|ling
purple|ness
purp|lish
purp|ly
pur|port +s +ed +ing
pur|port|ed|ly
pur|pose
  pur|pos|es
  pur|posed
  pur|pos|ing
purpose-built
purpose-designed
pur|pose|ful
pur|pose|ful|ly
pur|pose|ful|ness
pur|pose|less
pur|pose|less|ly
pur|pose|less|ness
pur|pose|ly
purpose-made
pur|pos|ive
pur|pos|ive|ly
pur|pos|ive|ness
pur|pura
pur|pur|ic
purr +s +ed +ing (cat sound)
  [☞ per]

purse
  purs|es
  pursed
  purs|ing
  [☞ Perse]
purs|er +s
purse seine +s
purse sein|er +s
purse sein|ing
purse strings
purs|lane +s
pur|su|able
pur|su|ance
pur|su|ant
pur|su|ant|ly
pur|sue
  pur|sues
  pur|sued
  pur|su|ing
pur|su|er +s
pur|suit +s
puru|lence
puru|lency
puru|lent
puru|lent|ly
pur|vey +s +ed +ing
pur|vey|or +s
pur|view +s
pus (liquid matter)
  [☞ puss]
Pusan (city, South Korea)
Pusey, Ed|ward Bou|verie (English theologian)
push
  push|es
  pushed
  push|ing
push-bike +s
push broom +s
push but|ton +s *noun*
push-button *adjective*
push|cart +s
push|chair +s
push|er +s
push|i|er
push|i|est
push|i|ly
push|i|ness
push|ing *adjective*
push|ing|ly
Push|kin, Alek|sandr Serge|evich (Russian writer)
push|over +s
push-pin +s
push-pull
push|rod +s
push-start +s +ed +ing
Push|tu (= Pashto)

push up *verb*
push|es up
pushed up
push|ing up
push-up +s *noun &*
adjective
pushy
push|i|er
push|i|est
pusil|lan|im|ity
pusil|lan|im|ous
pusil|lan|im|ous|ly
puss (cat; girl; face)
puss|es
[☞ pus]
pussy
puss|ies
pussy|cat +s
pussy|foot +s +ed
+ing
pussy|foot|er +s
pussy|toes
pussy-whip
pussy-whips
pussy-whipped
pussy-whipping
pussy wil|low +s
pus|tu|lar
pus|tu|late
pus|tu|lates
pus|tu|lat|ed
pus|tu|lat|ing
pus|tu|la|tion +s
pus|tule +s
pus|tu|lous
put (place)
puts
put
put|ting
[☞ putt]
pul|ta|tive
pul|ta|tive|ly
put down *verb*
puts down
put down
put|ting down
put-down +s *noun*
put in *verb*
puts in
put in
put|ting in
put-in +s *noun*
Put|nam, Is|rael (US
general)
[☞ Puttnam]
Put|nam, Rufus (US
soldier)
[☞ Puttnam]
put on *verb*
puts on
put on
put|ting on
put-on +s *noun*

put out *verb &*
adjective
puts out
put out
put|ting out
put-out +s *noun*
put-put (*use* putt-
putt)
put-puts
put-putted
put-putting
pu|tre|fa|cient
pu|tre|fac|tion
pu|tre|fac|tive
pu|tre|fy
pu|tre|fies
pu|tre|fied
pu|tre|fy|ing
pu|tres|cence
pu|tres|cent
pu|trid
pu|trid|ity
pu|trid|ly
pu|trid|ness
putsch
putsch|es
putsch|ist +s
putt (*Golf*)
putts
putt|ed
putt|ing
put|tee +s (leg
wrapping)
[☞ putty]
put|ter[1] +s +ed +ing
(in 'putter around'
etc.)
putt|er[2] +s (*Golf*)
put|ter|er +s
Putt|nam, Sir David
Ter|ence (English
filmmaker)
[☞ Putnam]
putto
putti
putt-putt +s +ed
+ing
putty (compound for
glazing, patching,
sealing etc.)
put|ties
put|tied
putty|ing
[☞ puttee]
put up *verb*
puts up
put up
put|ting up
put-up *adjective*
putz
putz|es
putzed
putz|ing

Puvis de
Cha|vannes, Pierre
Cé|cile (French
painter)
puz|zle
puz|zles
puz|zled
puz|zling
puz|zled *adjective*
puzzle|ment +s
puz|zler +s
puz|zling *adjective*
puz|zling|ly
PWA (person with
AIDS)
PWAs
PWC (personal
watercraft)
PWCs
PWR (pressurized
water reactor)
PWRs
PX (post exchange)
PXs
pya +s
pye-dog +s
py|el|itis
pyelo|neph|ritis
py|emia
py|emic
pyg|maean
Pyg|ma|lion
(legendary sculptor;
king of Tyre)
pyg|mean (*use*
pygmaean)
pygmy
pyg|mies
py|jama +s
pyk|nic +s (stocky)
[☞ picnic]
py|lon +s
pyl|or|ic
pyl|or|us
pyl|ori
Pym, John (English
parliamentarian)
Pyn|chon, Thom|as
(US writer)
Pyong|yang (capital
of North Korea)
pyor|rhea
pyra|can|tha +s
pyra|mid +s +ed
+ing
pyr|am|idal
pyr|am|idal|ly
pyra|mid|ic
pyra|mid|ic|al
pyra|mid|ic|al|ly
Pyra|mus (legendary
lover of Thisbe)
pyre +s

Pyr|en|ean
Pyr|en|ees
(mountains, Europe)
pyr|eth|rin +s
pyr|eth|roid +s
pyr|eth|rum +s
py|ret|ic
Pyrex *proprietary*
pyr|ex|ia
pyr|ex|ial
pyr|ex|ic
pyr|id|ine
pyr|id|ox|ine
pyr|imi|dine +s
pyr|ite +s (iron
disulphide; fool's
gold)
py|rit|es (any of
various sulphides,
esp. pyrite)
pyr|it|ic
pyr|it|ize
pyr|it|iz|es
pyr|it|ized
pyr|it|iz|ing
pyr|it|ous
pyro +s
pyro|clas|tic
pyro|elec|tric
pyro|elec|tri|city
pyro|gal|lic
pyro|gal|lol
pyro|gen|ic
pyr|og|raph|er +s
pyr|og|raphy
pyrohy
pyrola +s
pyro|lyse (*use*
pyrolyze)
pyro|lys|es
pyro|lysed
pyro|lys|ing
pyr|oly|sis
pyro|lytic
pyro|lyze
pyro|lyz|es
pyro|lyzed
pyro|lyz|ing
pyro|mania
pyro|maniac +s
pyro|man|iacal
pyr|om|eter +s
pyro|met|ric
pyro|met|ric|ally
pyr|om|etry
pyr|ope +s
pyro|phor|ic
pyr|osis
pyro|tech|nic
pyro|tech|nic|al
pyro|tech|ni|cian +s
pyro|tech|nics

pyro|tech|nist +s
pyro|techny
pyr|ox|ene
pyr|oxy|lin
Pyr|rha (*Greek Myth*)
pyr|rhic +s
Pyr|rho (Greek
philosopher)
Pyr|rhon|ism
Pyr|rhon|ist +s
Pyr|rhus (king of
Epirus)
pyru|vate +s
pyru|vic
pys|anka
pys|anky
Py|thag|oras (Greek
philosopher)
Py|thag|or|ean +s
Pyth|ia (priestess of
Apollo)
Pyth|ian
Pyth|ias (legendary
friend of Damon)
Py|thon (*Greek Myth*)
py|thon +s
py|thon|ess
py|thon|ess|es
py|thon|ic
py|uria
pyx (container, chest)
pyx|es
[☞ pix]
pyx|id|ium
pyx|idia
pyxis
pyx|ides

Q

Q
• (letter)
Q's
• (*Biblical Studies*)
[☞ cue, queue,
Kew Gardens]
q (letter)
q's
[☞ cue, queue,
Kew Gardens]
Qabis (= Gabès,
Tunisia)
Qad|dafi, Mu'ammer
(= Gaddafi)
qadi +s (judge)
Qaf|sah (= Gafsa,
Tunisia)

Qal|lun|aaq
Qal|lun|aat
Q & A (question &
answer)
Q & As
Qara|ghan|dy (city,
Kazakhstan)
Qatar (sheikdom,
Middle East)
[☞ catarrh]
Qa|tari +s
Qat|tara
De|pres|sion
(region, Africa)
QB (quarterback;
Queen's Bench)
QBs
Q.C. (Queen's
Counsel)
Q.C.'s
Q fever
qi (vital life source)
[☞ chi]
Qian Long (Chinese
emperor)
qibla
Qin (Chinese dynasty
221–206 BC)
[☞ Qing, Jin]
Qing (Chinese dynasty
1644–1912)
[☞ Qin, Jin, ching]
Qing|dao (city, China)
Qing|hai (province,
China)
Qiqi|har (city, China)
qiv|iut
Qom (city, Iran)
Q-ship +s
QSO (quasi-stellar
object)
QSOs
q.t. (in 'on the q.t.')
Q-tip +s *proprietary*
qua (in the capacity of)
[☞ Kwa]
Quaa|lude +s
proprietary
quack +s +ed +ing
(duck sound;
unqualified doctor)
[☞ CWAC]
quack|ery
quack grass
quack|ish
quad +s (quadrangle,
quadruplet,
quadruple jump, etc.;
chairlift; blank type)
[☞ *quod erat
demonstrandum*]
Quad|ra (island,
Canada)

quad|ra|gen|ar|ian
+s
Quad|ra|ges|ima
quad|ran|gle +s
quad|ran|gu|lar
quad|rant +s
quad|rant|al
quad|ra|phon|ic
quad|ra|phon|ic|ally
quad|ra|phon|ics
quad|raph|ony
quad|rat +s (area for
ecological study)
quad|rate (square or
rectangular object;
bone, muscle;
conform)
quad|rates
quad|rat|ed
quad|rat|ing
quad|rat|ic +s
quad|ra|ture +s
quad|ren|nial
quad|ren|nial|ly
quad|ren|nium
quad|ren|niums or
quad|ren|nia
quad|ric +s
quad|ri|ceps
plural quad|ri|ceps
quad|ri|fid
quad|ri|lat|eral +s
quad|rille +s
quad|ril|lion
plural quad|ril|lion
or quad|ril|lions
quad|ri|part|ite
quad|ri|plegia
quad|ri|plegic +s
quad|ri|valent
quad|riv|ium
quad|rivia
quad|roon +s
quad|ro|phon|ic (*use*
quadraphonic)
quad|ro|phon|ic|ally
(*use*
quadraphonically*)
quad|ro|phon|ics (*use*
quadraphonics)
quad|ru|man|ous
quad|ru|ped +s
quad|ru|pedal
quad|ruple
quad|ruples
quad|rupled
quad|rup|ling
quad|rup|let +s
quad|ru|plex
quad|ru|plex|es
quad|rup|li|cate
quad|rup|li|cates

quad|rup|li|cat|ed
quad|rup|li|cat|ing
quad|rup|li|ca|tion
+s
quad|rup|ly
quaes|tor +s
quaes|tor|ial
quaes|tor|ship +s
quaff (drink)
[☞ coif]
quaff|able
quaff|er +s (one who
quaffs)
[☞ coiffeur]
quag +s
quag|ga +s
quag|gy
quag|mire +s
qua|haug +s (*use*
quahog)
qua|hog +s
quaich +s (cup)
Quai d'Orsay (street,
Paris)
quail
• *noun*:
plural quail or quails
• *verb*
quails
quailed
quail|ing
[☞ Quayle]
quaint +er +est
quaint|ly
quaint|ness
quake (tremble;
earthquake)
quakes
quaked
quak|ing
[☞ quaich]
Quak|er +s
Quaker|ish
Quaker|ism
quaky
quaki|er
quaki|est
quali|fi|able
quali|fi|ca|tion +s
quali|fi|ca|tory
quali|fied *adjective*
quali|fi|er +s
quali|fy
quali|fies
quali|fied
quali|fy|ing
quali|fy|ing *adjective*
quali|ta|tive
quali|ta|tive|ly
qual|ity
qual|ities
qualm +s
qualm|ish

quan|dary
  quan|dar|ies
quan|go +s
quan|ta
quan|tal
quan|tal|ly
quan|ti|fi|able
quan|ti|fi|ca|tion +s
quan|ti|fi|er +s
quan|tify
  quan|ti|fies
  quan|ti|fied
  quan|ti|fy|ing
quan|ti|tate
  quan|ti|tates
  quan|ti|tat|ed
  quan|ti|tat|ing
quan|ti|ta|tive
quan|ti|ta|tive|ly
quan|ti|tive
quan|ti|tive|ly
quan|tity
  quan|ti|ties
quan|tiz|a|tion
quan|tize
  quan|tiz|es
  quan|tized
  quan|tiz|ing
quan|tum
  quan|ta
quantum-
  mechan|ic|al
quan|tum
  mech|an|ics
Qu'Appelle (river,
  Canada)
quar|an|tine
  quar|an|tines
  quar|an|tined
  quar|an|tin|ing
quark +s
Quarles, Fran|cis
  (English poet)
quar|rel
  quar|rels
  quar|relled
  quar|rel|ling
quar|rel|ler +s
quar|rel|some
quar|rel|some|ness
quar|ri|er +s
quarry
  quar|ries
  quar|ried
  quarry|ing
quarry|man
  quarry|men
quart +s
quar|tan
quar|ter +s +ed +ing
quar|ter|age +s
quarter|back +s +ed
  +ing

quarter|deck +s
quarter-final +s
quar|ter horse +s
quarter-hour +s
quar|ter|ing +s noun
quar|ter|ly
  quar|ter|lies
quarter|master +s
quarter-miler +s
quar|tern +s
quarter-round
quarter|saw
  quarter|saws
  quarter|sawed
  quarter|sawn or
  quarter|sawed
  quarter|saw|ing
quarter|staff +s
quarter-tone +s
quar|tet +s
quar|tic
quar|tier +s (district)
  [☞ Cartier]
quar|tile +s
quar|to +s
quartz
  quartz|es
quartz|ite +s
qua|sar +s
quash
  quash|es
  quashed
  quash|ing
quasi
Quasi|modo,
  Sal|va|tore (Italian
  poet)
quas|sia +s
quater|cen|ten|ary
  quater|cen|ten|aries
Qua|ter|nary
  (Geology)
qua|ter|nary
  qua|ter|nar|ies
qua|ter|nion +s
quat|rain +s
quatre|foil +s
quattro|cento
qua|ver +s +ed +ing
qua|ver|ing|ly
qua|very
quay +s (dock)
  [☞ key]
Quayle, James
  Dan|forth ('Dan')
  (US politician)
  [☞ quail]
quay|side +s
queas|i|ly
queas|i|ness
queasy
  queas|i|er
  queas|i|est

Que|bec (province,
  Canada)
Que|bec City (city,
  Canada)
Que|bec|er +s
Que|beck|er +s (use
  Quebecer)
Qué|bé|cois (of
  Quebec)
  plural Qué|bé|cois
Qué|bé|coise +s
  (female of Quebec)
Que|chua
  plural Que|chua or
  Que|chuas
Que|chu|an
Queen, El|lery
  (pseudonym of two
  US writers)
queen +s +ed +ing
Queen Anne
  (furniture,
  architecture)
Queen Anne's lace
  +s
Queen Anne's War
Queen Char|lotte +s
  (islands, sound &
  strait, Canada)
queen|cup +s
queen|dom +s
Queen Eliza|beth
  (islands, Canada)
Queen Eliza|beth
  Fore|land
  (promontory,
  Canada)
queen|less
queen|like
queen|li|ness
queen|ly
  queen|li|er
  queen|li|est
Queen Mab
Queen Mary
  (mountain, Canada)
Queen Maud (gulf,
  Canada; land,
  Antarctica)
queen mother +s
queen of the prai|rie
  +s
Queens (borough, US)
Queen's (university,
  Canada; former name
  for Laois, Ireland)
Queens|berry Rules
queen's cup +s
queen|ship +s
queen-size (= queen-
  sized)
queen-sized

Queens|land (state,
  Australia)
Queens|land|er +s
Queen's Park
Queen's Plate
Queens|ton Heights
  (battle site, Canada)
queer +s +ed +ing
queer|ly
queer|ness
quell +s +ed +ing
quell|er +s
quench
  quench|es
  quenched
  quench|ing
quench|er +s
que|nelle +s
Que|ré|taro (state &
  its capital, Mexico)
quern +s
queru|lous
queru|lous|ly
queru|lous|ness
query
  quer|ies
  quer|ied
  query|ing
que|sa|dil|la +s
Ques|nay, Fran|çois
  (French economist)
Ques|nel (city,
  Canada)
quest +s +ed +ing
quest|er +s
ques|tion +s +ed
  +ing
ques|tion|able
ques|tion|ably
ques|tion|er +s
ques|tion|ing +s noun
ques|tion|ing|ly
ques|tion mark +s
ques|tion|naire +s
ques|tion per|iod +s
Quet|ta (city, Pakistan)
quet|zal +s
Quet|zal|có|atl
  (Toltec & Aztec god)
queue (lineup;
  Computing; pigtail)
  queues
  queued
  queuing or
  queue|ing
  [☞ cue, Kew
  Gardens]
queue-jump +s +ed
  +ing
queue jump|er +s
Que|zon City (city,
  the Philippines)

Que|zon y Mol|ina, Man|uel Luis (Philippine statesman)

Qufu (birthplace of Confucius) [☞ Khufu]

quib|ble
quib|bles
quib|bled
quib|bling
quib|bler +s
quib|bling adjective
quib|bling|ly

quiche +s

quiche lor|raine +s

Qui|chua (= Quechua) plural Qui|chua or Qui|chu|as

Qui|chu|an (= Quechuan)

quick +er +est +s (fast; flesh below nails; in 'cut to the quick') [☞ KWIC]

quick bread +s

quick|en +s +ed +ing

quick-fire

quick|ie +s

quick|lime +s

quick|ly

quick march
quick march|es

quick|ness

quick|sand +s

quick|silver

quick|step
quick|steps
quick|stepped
quick|step|ping

quick-witted

quick-witted|ness

quid
• (pound sterling) plural quid
• (lump of chewing tobacco) plural quids

quid|dity
quid|di|ties

quid pro quo

qui|es|cence

qui|es|cent

quiet +er +est +s +ed +ing

quiet|en +s +ed +ing

quiet|ism

quiet|ist +s

quiet|is|tic

quiet|ly

quiet|ness

quiet|ude

qui|etus
qui|etus|es

quiff +s

quiffed

Quil|ico, Louis (Cdn baritone)

quill +s +ed +ing

Quiller-Couch, Sir Ar|thur Thom|as (English writer)

quill|ing noun

quill|work

quill|worked

quill|wort +s

quilt +s +ed +ing

quilt|ed adjective

quilt|er +s

quilt|ing +s noun

quina|crine

quin|ary

quin|az|ol|ine +s

quince +s

quin|cen|ten|ary
quin|cen|ten|aries

quin|cen|ten|nial +s

Quin|cey, Thom|as De (English writer) [☞ Quincy Adams, quinsy, quinzhee]

quin|cun|cial

quin|cunx
quin|cunx|es

Quin|cy Adams (mountain, Canada) [☞ Quincey, quinsy, quinzhee]

quin|el|la +s

quin|ine

quinoa +s

quin|ol|ine +s

quin|one +s

quin|qua|gen|ar|ian +s

Quin|qua|ges|ima

quin|quen|nial

quin|quen|nial|ly

quin|quen|nium
quin|quen|niums or quin|quen|nia

quin|que|reme +s

quin|que|valent

quin|sy (throat inflammation)
quin|sies [☞ Quincey, Quincy Adams, quinzhee]

quint +s

quin|ta +s

quin|tal +s (weight)

Quin|tana Roo (state, Mexico)

quin|tes|sence

quint|es|sen|tial

quint|es|sen|tial|ly

quin|tet +s

quin|tile +s (Statistics) [☞ quintal]

Quin|til|ian (Roman rhetorician)

quin|til|lion
plural quin|til|lion or quin|til|lions

quin|til|lionth +s

quin|tuple
quin|tuples
quin|tupled
quin|tup|ling

quin|tup|let +s

quin|tup|li|cate
quin|tup|li|cates
quin|tup|li|cat|ed
quin|tup|li|cat|ing

quin|zhee +s (snow shelter) [☞ quinsy, Quincey, Quincy Adams]

quin|zie +s (snow shelter: use quinzhee) [☞ quinsy, Quincey, Quincy Adams]

quip
quips
quipped
quip|ping

quip|ster +s

quipu +s

quire +s (paper) [☞ choir]

quirk +s

quirk|i|ly

quirk|i|ness

quirk|ish

quirky
quirk|i|er
quirk|i|est

quirt +s +ed +ing

quis|ling +s

Quis|pam|sis (town, Canada)

quit
• (give up; resign; cease; behave)
quits
quit
quit|ting
• (leave)
quits
quit or quitted
quit|ting

quitch
quitch|es

quitch grass

quite

Quito (capital of Ecuador)

quits

quit|tance +s

quit|ter +s

quiv|er +s +ed +ing

quiver|ful +s

quiver|ing|ly

quiv|ery

qui vive (in 'on the qui vive')

quix|ot|ic

quix|ot|ic|ally

quix|ot|ism +s

quiz
quiz|zes
quizzed
quiz|zing

quiz|master +s

quiz|zer +s

quiz|zic|al

quiz|zic|al|ity

quiz|zic|al|ly

qul|liq +s

Qum (= Qom, Iran)

Qum|ran (discovery site of Dead Sea scrolls)

quod erat dem|on|stran|dum [☞ quad]

quod|libet +s

quod|libet|ar|ian +s

quoin +s +ed +ing (cornerstone; external angle; wedge)

quoin|ing +s noun

quoit +s +ed +ing

quon|dam

Quon|set +s proprietary

quor|um +s

quota +s

quot|abil|ity

quot|able

quo|ta|tion +s

quote
quotes
quot|ed
quot|ing

quoth

quo|tid|ian +s

quo|tient +s

Quran +s (= Koran)

Qwa|qwa (former homeland, South Africa)

QWER|TY

R

R
• (letter)
R's
• (R-value; Réaumur;
roentgen; rand;
electrical resistance;
organic radical)
r (letter)
r's
Ra (*Egyptian Myth*)
[☞ rah]
Raan|es (peninsula,
Canada)
Rabat (capital of
Morocco)
Ra|baul (town, Papua
New Guinea)
rab|bet (*Carpentry*)
rab|bets
rab|bet|ed
rab|bet|ing
[☞ rabbit]
rabbi +s (Jewish
religious leader)
[☞ Rabi]
rab|bin|ate +s
rab|bin|ic
rab|bin|ic|al
rab|bin|ic|al|ly
rab|bit (animal;
chatter)
rab|bits
rab|bit|ed
rab|bit|ing
[☞ rabbet]
rabbit|brush
rabbit|bush
(= rabbitbrush)
rab|bit punch *noun*
rab|bit punch|es
rabbit-punch *verb*
rabbit-punches
rabbit-punched
rabbit-punching
rab|bity
rab|ble +s
rabble-rouser +s
rabble-rousing
Rabe|lais, Fran|çois
(French satirist)
Rabe|lais|ian +s
Rabi, Isidor Isaac (US
physicist)
[☞ rabbi]
rabid
rabid|ity
rabid|ly
rabid|ness
ra|bies

Rabin, Yit|zhak
(Israeli prime
minister)
rac|coon +s
Race (cape, Canada)
race
races
raced
ra|cing
race car +s (race-car
*when preceding a
noun*)
race|course +s
race|goer +s
race|horse +s
race|mate +s
ra|ceme +s
ra|cem|ic
racem|iz|a|tion
racem|ize
racem|iz|es
racem|ized
racem|iz|ing
racem|ose
racer +s
race|track +s
race|way +s
Rachel (*Bible*)
ra|chid|ial
ra|chis
ra|chis|es or
ra|chi|des
rach|it|ic
rach|itis
Rach|man|inov,
Ser|gei Vasil|evich
(Russian composer)
ra|cial
racial|ism
racial|ist +s
racial|ly
raci|er
raci|est
raci|ly
Ra|cine, Jean
Bap|tiste (French
dramatist)
raci|ness
ra|cing *noun &
adjective*
ra|cism
ra|cist +s
rack +s +ed +ing
(framework; injure,
torture; lamb;
Billiards; antlers;
draw off wine etc.;
clouds; be driven by
wind; horse's gait; in
'rack up', 'rack one's
brains', 'rack and
ruin')
[☞ wrack]

rack-and-pinion
rack|et +s +ed +ing
(noise; scheme;
business; *for* bat
used in tennis etc. *or*
snowshoe *use*
racquet)
racket|ball +s (*use*
racquetball)
rack|et|eer +s
rack|et|eer|ing
rack|ety
rack rate +s
rack-rent +s +ed
+ing
ra|clette +s
racon|teur +s
ra|coon +s (*use*
raccoon)
rac|quet +s (bat used
in tennis etc.;
snowshoe)
[☞ racket]
rac|quet|ball +s
racy
raci|er
raci|est
rad +s
RADA (Royal
Academy of
Dramatic Art)
radar +s
Rad|cliffe, Ann
(English novelist)
rad|dle
rad|dles
rad|dled
rad|dling
rad|dled *adjective*
Radha (*Hinduism*)
ra|dial +s
ra|dial arm saw +s
ra|di|al|ly
ra|dian +s
radi|ance
radi|ant +s
radi|ant|ly
radi|ate
radi|ates
radi|at|ed
radi|at|ing
radi|a|tion +s
radi|a|tion|al
radi|a|tive
radi|ator +s
rad|ical +s (of the
root; fundamental;
revolutionary;
Chemistry; Chinese
character)
[☞ radicle]
rad|ical chic
rad|ical|ism

rad|ical|iz|a|tion
rad|ical|ize
rad|ical|iz|es
rad|ical|ized
rad|ical|iz|ing
rad|ical|ly
rad|ical|ness
ra|dic|chio +s
rad|ices
rad|icle +s (plant
embryo rootlet;
nerve or vein
subdivision)
[☞ radical]
rad|icu|lar
radii
radio
• *noun*
ra|dios
• *verb*
ra|dioes
ra|dioed
radio|ing
radio|active
radio|active|ly
radio|activ|ity
radio as|tron|omy
radio|bio|logic|al
radio|biol|o|gist +s
radio|biol|ogy
radio|carbon +s
radio|chem|ical
radio|chem|ist +s
radio|chem|istry
radio collar +s *noun*
radio-collar +s +ed
+ing *verb*
radio-controlled
radio|element +s
radio|genic
radio|gram +s
radio|graph +s +ed
+ing
radi|og|raph|er +s
radio|graph|ic
radio|graph|ic|ally
radi|og|raphy
radio|iso|tope +s
radio|iso|top|ic
radio|lar|ian +s
radio|logic
radio|logic|al
radi|ol|o|gist +s
radi|ol|ogy
radi|om|eter +s
radio|met|ric
radi|om|etry
radio|nu|clide +s
radio-opacity
(= radiopacity)
radio-opaque
(= radiopaque)
radi|opa|city

radi|opaque
radio phone +s
radio|phon|ic
radio|scop|ic
radi|os|copy
  radi|os|cop|ies
radio|sonde +s
radio-telegram +s
radio-telegraph +s
radio-telegraphy
radio tele|phone +s
radio tele|phon|ic
radio teleph|ony
radio tele|scope +s
radio|thera|peut|ic
radio|ther|apist +s
radio|ther|apy
rad|ish
  rad|ish|es
Radis|son, Pierre-
  Esprit (French-born
  fur trader)
ra|dium
ra|dius
  radii or ra|dius|es
radix
  rad|ices
Rad|nor|shire (former
  county, Wales)
Radom (city, Poland)
ra|dome +s
radon
rad|ula
  rad|ulae
radu|lar
Rae|burn, Sir Henry
  (Scottish painter)
Rae-Edzo (hamlet,
  Canada)
raf|fia +s
raff|ish
raff|ish|ly
raff|ish|ness
raf|fle
  raf|fles
  raf|fled
  raf|fling
Raf|fles, Sir
  (Thom|as)
  Stam|ford (English
  colonial
  administrator)
Raf|san|jani, Ali
  Akbar Hash|emi
  (Iranian statesman &
  religious leader)
raft +s +ed +ing
raft|er +s (one who
  travels by raft)
raf|ter +s (beam)
raf|tered
raft|ing noun

rafts|man
  rafts|men
rag (torn cloth etc.;
  inferior newspaper;
  scold, torment;
  entertainment;
  ragtime tune; in 'rag
  on' & 'rag the puck')
rags
ragged
rag|ging
  [☞ ragg]
raga +s
  (improvisational
  Indian music)
  [☞ ragga]
raga|muf|fin +s (child
  in ragged clothing;
  for fan etc. of ragga
  music use
  raggamuffin)
rag-and-bone
rag|bag +s
rag doll +s
rage
  rages
  raged
  raging
rage|ful
rager +s
ragg (wool, yarn)
  [☞ rag]
ragga (popular music
  based on reggae &
  hip hop)
  [☞ raga]
ragga|muf|fin +s (of
  ragga music)
  [☞ ragamuffin]
rag|ged adjective
rag|ged|ly
rag|ged|ness
rag|gedy
raggedy-ass
raggedy-assed
raggedy-jacket +s
rag|ging noun
raggle-taggle
raging adjective
rag|lan +s
Rag|na|rök
  (Scandinavian Myth)
ra|gout +s
rag|pick|er +s
rag-rolled
rag roll|ing
rag rug +s
rags-to-riches
rag|tag
rag|tail
rag|time
rag|top +s

Ra|gusa (former name
  for Dubrovnik,
  Croatia)
rag|weed +s
rag|worm +s
rag|wort +s
rah (cheer)
  [☞ Ra, raw]
rah-rah
rai (Music)
  [☞ rye, wry, Ray,
  Reye's syndrome]
raid +s +ed +ing
  (attack)
  [☞ rayed]
raid|er +s
rail +s +ed +ing
  (handrail etc.; rant;
  bird)
  [☞ rale]
rail|bird
rail|er +s
rail fence +s
rail gun +s
rail|head +s
rail|ing +s noun &
  adjective
rail|lery
  rail|ler|ies
rail|man
  rail|men
rail|road +s +ed +ing
rail|road|er +s
rail|way +s
rail|way|man
  rail|way|men
rail yard +s
rail|ment +s
rain +s +ed +ing
  (falling water etc.)
  [☞ reign, rein]
rain|bow +s
rain|bowed
rain check +s
rain cloud +s
rain|coat +s
rain date +s
rain|drop +s
rain|fall +s
rain for|est +s
rain gauge +s
Rai|nier (mountain,
  US)
Rai|nier III (prince of
  Monaco)
rain|i|er
rain|i|est
rain|i|ly
rain|i|ness
rain|less (without
  rain)
  [☞ reinless]
rain|maker +s

rain|making
rain out verb
  rains out
  rained out
  rain|ing out
rain|out +s noun
rain|proof
rain shad|ow +s
rain|storm +s
rain-swept
rain|water
rain|wear
Rainy (lake & river,
  Canada)
  [☞ Reni]
rainy
  rain|i|er
  rain|i|est
Rai|pur (city, India)
rais|able
raise (lift, bring up)
  rais|es
  raised
  rais|ing
  [☞ raze]
rais|er +s (that which
  raises)
  [☞ razor]
rai|sin +s (dried
  grape)
rai|siny
rai|son d'être
  rai|sons d'être
raita
Raj
raja +s
raj|ah +s (use raja)
Ra|jas|than (state,
  India)
Ra|jas|thani +s
raja yoga
Raj|kot (city, India)
Raj|put +s
Raj|pu|tana (ancient
  region, India)
Raj|shahi (city, India)
rake
  rakes
  raked
  rak|ing
raked adjective
rake-off
rak|er +s
raki +s
rak|ish
rakish|ly
rakish|ness
raku
rale (rattling sound in
  lungs)
  [☞ rail]

Ralegh, Sir Wal|ter
(= Sir Walter
Raleigh)
Ra|leigh (city, US)
[☞ **rally**]
Ra|leigh, Sir Wal|ter
(English explorer &
courtier)
[☞ **rally**]
ral|len|tando
ral|len|tan|dos or
ral|len|tandi
ral|li|er +s
rally
ral|lies
ral|lied
rally|ing
[☞ **Raleigh**]
RAM (*Computing*)
Ram (constellation;
Zodiac)
ram
rams
rammed
ram|ming
Rama (*Hinduism*)
Rama|dan (*Islam*)
Raman, Sir
Chan|dra|sekh|ara
Ven|kata (Indian
physicist)
[☞ **ramen**]
Raman ef|fect
Ra|ma|nu|jan,
Srini|vasa
Aai|yan|gar (Indian
mathematician)
ram|ble
ram|bles
ram|bled
ramb|ling
ramb|ler +s
ramb|ling +s *noun*
ramb|ling|ly
Ram|bo +s
(aggressive man)
[☞ **Rimbaud**]
Rambo|esque
Rambo|ism
ram|bunc|tious
ram|bunc|tious|ly
ram|bunc|tious|ness
ram|bu|tan +s
Ra|meau, Jean-
Philippe (French
musician)
ram|ekin +s
ramen (noodles)
[☞ **Raman**]
Ram|eses (= Ramses)
Rame|zay, Claude de
(French colonial
administrator)
[☞ **Ramsay**]

ram|ie +s (plant; fibre)
[☞ **rammy**]
rami|fi|ca|tion +s
rami|fy
rami|fies
rami|fied
rami|fy|ing
Ra|mil|lies (battle site,
Belgium)
ra|min +s (tree, wood)
[☞ **ramen, Raman**]
ram|jet +s
ram|mer +s
rammy (fight)
ram|mies
[☞ **ramie**]
Ramón y Cajal,
San|ti|ago (Spanish
physician)
ra|mose
ramp +s +ed +ing
ram|page
ram|pages
ram|paged
ram|pa|ging
ram|pa|geous
ram|pa|ger +s
ram|pancy
ram|pant
ram|pant|ly
ram|part +s +ed +ing
ram|pion +s
ram-raid +s +ed +ing
ram-raider +s
ram-raiding +s *noun*
ram|rod
ram|rods
ram|rod|ded
ram|rod|ding
Ram|say (surname)
[☞ **Ramezay**]
Ram|say, Allan
(Scottish writer)
Ram|say, James
An|drew Broun (1st
Marquis of
Dalhousie, British
colonial
administrator)
Ram|say, Sir Wil|liam
(Scottish chemist)
Ram|ses (kings of
Egypt)
ram|shackle
ram's-horn snail +s
ram|sons
ran *conjugated form of*
run
[☞ **Rann of Kutch**]
ranch
ranch|es
ranched
ranch|ing

ranch|er +s
ranch|ero +s
ranch hand +s
ranch house +s
Ran|chi (city, India)
ranch|ing *noun*
ranch|land +s
ranch-style
ran|cid
ran|cid|ity
ran|cid|ness
ran|cor|ous
ran|cor|ous|ly
ran|cour +s
(spitefulness)
[☞ **ranker**]
Rand
(= Witwatersrand,
South Africa)
Rand, Ayn (US writer)
rand +s
R & B
R & D
Ran|ders (city,
Denmark)
Rand for|mu|la
ran|di|er
ran|di|est
ran|di|ly
ran|di|ness
Ran|dolph, Ed|mund
Jen|nings (US
politician)
Ran|dolph, John (US
politician)
Ran|dom (island,
Canada)
ran|dom
ran|dom|iz|a|tion
ran|dom|ize
ran|dom|iz|es
ran|dom|ized
ran|dom|iz|ing
ran|dom|ly
ran|dom|ness
R and R
Rand|stad
(conurbation, the
Netherlands)
randy
ran|di|er
ran|di|est
ran|ee +s (raja's
widow, Hindu queen:
use rani)
rang +s (*conjugated
form of* ring; lot)
ran|ga|tira +s
range
ranges
ranged
ran|ging
range|find|er +s

range|land +s
ran|ger +s
Ran|goon (capital of
Burma)
rangy
ran|gi|er
ran|gi|est
rani +s (raja's widow;
Hindu queen)
Ran|jit Singh (Sikh
ruler)
rank +s +ed +ing +er
+est
rank and file (rank-
and-file *when
preceding a noun*)
rank-and-filer +s
rank|er (soldier)
[☞ **rancour**]
rank|ing +s *noun &
adjective*
Ran|kin Inlet (inlet &
hamlet, Canada)
ran|kle
ran|kles
ran|kled
rank|ling
rank|ly
rank|ness
Rann of Kutch (salt
marsh, India)
ran|sack +s +ed +ing
ran|sack|er +s
Ran|som, John
Crowe (US poet &
critic)
ran|som +s +ed +ing
rant +s +ed +ing
Rant|er +s (member
of English sect)
rant|er +s
rant|ing|ly
ra|nun|cul|aceous
ra|nun|cul|us
ra|nun|cul|us|es or
ra|nun|culi
rap (knock; criticize;
charge; talk; *Music*)
raps
rapped
rap|ping
[☞ **wrap**]
ra|pa|cious
ra|pa|cious|ly
ra|pa|cious|ness
ra|pa|city
rape
rapes
raped
rap|ing
rape|seed
rape-shield

Raph|ael (Italian painter; *Bible*)
rap|id +s
rapid-fire
rapid|ity
rapid|ly
rapid|ness
ra|pier +s
rap|ine +s
ra|pini
rap|ist +s
rap|pel
(*Mountaineering*)
rap|pels
rap|pelled
rap|pel|ling
[☞ repel]
rap|per +s (rap musician)
[☞ wrapper]
rap|port +s (relationship)
rap|por|teur +s (one who prepares reports for a governing body)
rap|proche|ment +s
rap|scal|lion +s
rap sheet +s
rapt
rapt|ly
rapt|ness
rap|tor +s
rap|tor|ial
rap|ture +s
rap|tur|ous
rap|tur|ous|ly
rara avis
rarae aves
rare
rarer
rar|est
rare|bit
rare earth +s (rare-earth *when preceding a noun*)
rar|efac|tion +s
rar|efied *adjective*
rar|efy
rar|efies
rar|efied
rar|efy|ing
rare|ly
rare|ness
rari|fac|tion +s (*use* rarefaction)
rari|fied (*use* rarefied)
rar|ify (*use* rarefy)
rari|fies
rari|fied
rari|fy|ing
rar|ing *adjective*

rar|ity
rar|ities
Raro|tonga (S Pacific island)
Raro|ton|gan +s
Ras al Khai|mah (state & its capital, UAE)
ras|cal +s
ras|cal|ity
ras|cal|ities
ras|cal|ly
rash
rash|es
rash|er +s
rash|ly
rash|ness
Rask, Rasm|us Chris|tian (Danish philologist)
Ras|min|sky, Louis (Cdn banker)
Ras|mus|sen, Knud Johan Vic|tor (Danish anthropologist)
rasp +s +ed +ing
rasp|berry
rasp|ber|ries
rasp|ing|ly
Ras|pu|tin, Grig|ori Efimo|vich (Russian monk)
raspy
rasp|i|er
rasp|i|est
ras|sle
ras|sles
ras|sled
ras|sling
[☞ razzle-dazzle]
ras|sler +s
Ras|ta +s
Rasta|far|ian +s
Rasta|far|ian|ism
ras|ter +s
ras|ter|iz|a|tion +s
ras|ter|ize
ras|ter|iz|es
ras|ter|ized
ras|ter|iz|ing
ras|ter|iz|er +s
Ras|tya|pino (*former name for* Dzerzhinsk, Russia)
rat
rats
ratted
rat|ting
rat|abil|ity (*use* rateability)
rat|able (*use* rateable)
rat|ably (*use* rateably)

rata|fia +s
rata|plan +s
rat-a-tat-tat
rata|touille +s
rat|bag +s
ratch|et +s +ed +ing
rate
rates
rated
rat|ing
rate|abil|ity
rate|able
rate|ably
rate|pay|er +s
rater +s
rat fink +s
rathe
rath|er
rat|hole +s
raths|keller +s
rati|fi|able
rati|fi|ca|tion +s
rati|fier +s
rat|ify
rati|fies
rati|fied
rati|fy|ing
rat|ing +s *noun*
ratio +s
rati|ocin|ate
rati|ocin|ates
rati|ocin|at|ed
rati|ocin|at|ing
rati|ocin|a|tion
rati|ocin|a|tive
rati|ocin|ator +s
ra|tion +s +ed +ing
ration|al *adjective*
[☞ rationale]
ration|ale +s *noun*
[☞ rational]
ration|al|ism
ration|al|ist +s
ration|al|is|tic
ration|al|is|tic|ally
ration|al|ity
ration|al|iz|a|tion +s
ration|al|ize
ration|al|iz|es
ration|al|ized
ration|al|iz|ing
ration|al|iz|er +s
ration|al|ly
rat|ite +s
rat|line +s
ra|toon +s +ed +ing
rat pack +s
rat race +s
rat's nest +s
rat's tail +s (= rat-tail; rat's-tail *when preceding a noun*)
rat-tail +s

rat-tailed
rat|tan +s
rat-tat-tat
rat|ter +s
rat|ti|er
rat|ti|est
Ratti|gan, Sir Ter|ence Mer|vyn (English dramatist)
rat|ti|ly
rat|ti|ness
rat|tle
rat|tles
rat|tled
rat|tling
rat|tler +s
rattle|snake +s
rattle|trap
rat|tling *adjective & adverb*
rat|tling|ly
rat|tly
ratty
rat|ti|er
rat|ti|est
rau|cous
rau|cous|ly
rau|cous|ness
Rau|dot, Antoine-Denis (intendant of New France)
raunch
raunch|i|ly
raunch|i|ness
raunchy
raunch|i|er
raunch|i|est
[☞ Ranchi]
Rau|schen|berg, Rob|ert (US artist)
rav|age
rav|ages
rav|aged
rav|aging
rav|ager +s
rave
raves
raved
rav|ing
Ravel, (Mau|rice) Jo|seph (French composer)
ravel
rav|els
rav|elled
rav|el|ling
rav|elin +s
rav|el|ling +s *noun*
raven +s +ed +ing (crow; to devour, hunt or plunder)
[☞ ravin]
Rav|enna (city, Italy)

rav|en|ous
rav|en|ous|ly
rav|en|ous|ness
raver +s
rave-up +s
Ravi (river, Asia)
ravin +s (robbery;
  capture of prey)
  [☞ raven]
rav|ine +s
rav|ined
rav|ing +s noun,
  adjective & adverb
rav|ing|ly
ravi|oli
rav|ish
  rav|ish|es
  rav|ished
  rav|ish|ing
rav|ish|er +s
rav|ish|ing adjective
rav|ish|ing|ly
rav|ish|ment
raw +er +est +s
  (uncooked, not
  processed,
  inexperienced, etc.)
  [☞ rah, Ra]
Rawal|pindi (city,
  Pakistan)
raw-boned
raw|hide +s
rawly
  [☞ Raleigh]
raw|ness
Ray (cape, Canada)
  [☞ Re, Reye]
Ray, John (English
  naturalist)
  [☞ Re]
Ray, Man (US artist)
  [☞ Re]
Ray, Sat|ya|jit (Indian
  filmmaker)
  [☞ rai, rye, wry,
  Reye's syndrome]
ray +s +ed +ing (light
  beam; radiation; fish;
  for Music sense use re)
  [☞ in re]
rayed adjective
  (having rays)
ray gun +s
Ray|leigh, John
  Wil|liam Strutt, 3rd
  Baron (English
  physicist)
ray|less
ray|let +s
Raynaud's (disease,
  phenomenon,
  syndrome)
  [☞ Renault]

rayon +s
Rayside-Balfour
  (town, Canada)
ray-traced
ray tracing
raze (destroy; erase)
  razes
  razed
  raz|ing
  [☞ raise]
Ra|zil|ly, Isaac de
  (French colonial
  administrator)
razor +s +ed +ing
  (shaving instrument)
  [☞ raiser]
razor|back +s
razor|bill +s
razor-billed
razor blade +s
razor-edged
razor's edge
razor-sharp
razz
  razz|es
  razzed
  razz|ing
razza|ma|tazz
  (= razzmatazz)
raz|zle
razzle-dazzle
razz|ma|tazz
RBI (run batted in)
  plural RBI or RBIs
RCMP (Royal Cdn
  Mounted Police)
  RCMPs
RDA (recommended
  daily allowance)
  RDAs
RDI (recommended
  daily intake)
  RDIs
rDNA (recombinant
  DNA)
Re (= Ra, Egyptian
  sun god)
re (regarding; Music)
re (in 'in re')
re|absorb +s +ed
  +ing
re|absorp|tion
reach
  reach|es
  reached
  reach|ing
reach|able
reach|er +s
re|acquaint +s +ed
  +ing
re|acquaint|ance

re|acquire
  re|acquires
  re|acquired
  re|acquir|ing
re|acqui|si|tion
react +s +ed +ing
  (respond)
re-act +s +ed +ing
  (act a role again)
re|act|ance
re|act|ant
re|ac|tion +s
re|ac|tion|ary
  re|ac|tion|aries
re|acti|vate
  re|acti|vates
  re|acti|vat|ed
  re|acti|vat|ing
re|acti|va|tion +s
re|act|ive
re|ac|tiv|ity
  re|ac|tiv|ities
re|act|or +s
Read, Ken|neth John
  ('Ken') (Cdn skier)
  [☞ Reade, Reed,
  Reid]
read verb, noun &
  adjective (interpret
  writing etc.; writing;
  interpretation;
  educated by reading)
  reads
  read
  read|ing
  [☞ reed, red, rede,
  redd]
read|abil|ity
read|able
re-address
  re-address|es
  re-addressed
  re-address|ing
Reade, Charles
  (English writer)
  [☞ Read, Reed,
  Reid, rede]
read|er +s
reader-friend|ly
read|er|ly
reader-response
reader|ship +s
read|i|ly
read|i|ness
Read|ing (town,
  England)
  [☞ Redding]
read|ing +s
  (interpreting writing
  etc.)
  [☞ reeding]
re|adjust +s +ed +ing
re|adjust|ment +s
re|admis|sion +s

re|admit
  re|admits
  re|admit|ted
  re|admit|ting
read-only mem|ory
re|adopt +s +ed +ing
re|adop|tion +s
read|out +s
read/write
ready (prepared etc.)
  read|i|er
  read|i|est
  read|ies
  read|ied
  ready|ing
  [☞ reddy]
ready-made +s
ready-mix noun &
  adjective
ready-mixed
  adjective
ready-to-wear +s
re|affirm +s +ed +ing
re|affirm|a|tion +s
Rea|gan, Ron|ald
  Will|son (US
  president)
  [☞ Regan]
Rea|gan|esque
Rea|gan|ism
Rea|gan|ite +s
Rea|gan|om|ics
re|agent +s
real[1] +er +est
  (authentic; actually
  existing; in 'real
  estate')
  [☞ reel]
real[2] +s (currency)
real es|tate
re|algar
re|align +s +ed +ing
re|align|ment +s
real|ism
real|ist +s
real|is|tic
real|is|tic|ally
re|al|ity
  re|al|ities
real|iz|abil|ity
real|iz|able
real|iz|a|tion +s
real|ize
  real|iz|es
  real|ized
  real|iz|ing
real|iz|er +s
real life (real-life
  when preceding a
  noun)
re|allo|cate
  re|allo|cates

re|allo|cat|ed
re|allo|cat|ing
re|allo|ca|tion +s
real|ly
realm +s
real|ness
real|politik
real|politik|er +s
real time (real-time
  when preceding a
  noun)
Real|tor +s
  proprietary (member
  company of the
  Canadian Real Estate
  Association)
real|tor +s (*in general
  use*: real estate
  agent)
real|ty
real world +s *noun*
real-world *adjective*
ream +s +ed +ing
  (large quantity of
  paper etc.; widen a
  hole; extract juice; in
  'ream out':
  reprimand)
  [☞ Reims]
ream|er +s
re|analy|sis
  re|analy|ses
re|analyze
  re|analyz|es
  re|analyzed
  re|analyz|ing
re|animate
  re|animates
  re|animat|ed
  re|animat|ing
re|anima|tion +s
reap +s +ed +ing
reap|er +s
re|appear +s +ed
  +ing
re|appear|ance +s
re|appli|ca|tion +s
re|apply
  re|applies
  re|applied
  re|apply|ing
re|appoint +s +ed
  +ing
re|appoint|ment +s
re|appor|tion +s +ed
  +ing
re|appor|tion|ment
  +s
re|apprais|al +s
re|appraise
  re|apprais|es
  re|appraised
  re|apprais|ing
rear +s +ed +ing

rear end +s *noun*
  (rear-end *when
  preceding a noun*)
rear-end +s +ed +ing
  verb
rear-ender +s
rear|er +s
rear|guard +s
rear|ing *noun*
re|arm +s +ed +ing
re|arma|ment +s
rear|most
re|arrange
  re|arran|ges
  re|arranged
  re|arran|ging
re|arrange|ment +s
re|arran|ging *noun*
re|arrest +s +ed +ing
rear sight +s
rear-view +s
rear|ward
rear|wards
rear-wheel drive
rea|son +s +ed +ing
rea|son|able
rea|son|able|ness
rea|son|ably
rea|soned *adjective*
rea|son|er +s
rea|son|ing +s *noun*
re|assem|ble
  re|assem|bles
  re|assem|bled
  re|assem|bling
re|assem|bly
re|assert +s +ed +ing
re|asser|tion +s
re|assess
  re|assess|es
  re|assessed
  re|assess|ing
re|assess|ment +s
re|assign +s +ed
  +ing
re|assign|ment +s
re|assur|ance +s
re|assure
  re|assures
  re|assured
  re|assur|ing
re|assur|ing *adjective*
re|assur|ing|ly
re|attach
  re|attach|es
  re|attached
  re|attach|ing
re|attach|ment +s
re|attain +s +ed +ing
re|attain|ment +s
Réau|mur, René
  An|toine Fer|chault

de (French
  naturalist)
Réau|mur (denoting
  temperature)
reave (deprive of;
  carry off; plunder)
  reaves
  reft
  reav|ing
  [☞ reeve]
re|awak|en +s +ed
  +ing
re|awak|en|ing +s
  noun
Reb
re|bar +s
re|barba|tive
re|bat|able
re|bate
  re|bates
  re|bat|ed
  re|bat|ing
reb|be +s
reb|betz|in +s
re|bec +s
Reb|ecca (*Bible*)
  [☞ Rebekah]
re|beck +s (*use* rebec)
Reb|ekah +s
  (Oddfellow; *for
  Biblical name use*
  Rebecca)
reb|el[1] +s *noun*
rebel[2] *verb*
  re|bels
  re|belled
  re|bell|ing
re|bel|lion +s
re|bel|lious
re|bel|lious|ly
re|bel|lious|ness
re|bind
  re|binds
  re|bound
  re|bind|ing
re|birth +s
re|birth|ing
re|boot +s +ed +ing
re|bore
  re|bores
  re|bored
  re|bor|ing
re|born
re|bound +s +ed
  +ing
re|bound|er +s
re|bound|ing *noun*
re|bozo +s
re|broad|cast
  re|broad|casts
  re|broad|cast
  or re|broad|cast|ed

re|broad|cast
re|broad|cast|ing
re|buff +s +ed +ing
re|build
  re|builds
  re|built
  re|build|ing
re|buke
  re|bukes
  re|buked
  re|buk|ing
re|buk|er +s
re|buk|ing|ly
re|burial +s
re|bury
  re|buries
  re|buried
  re|bury|ing
re|bus
  re|bus|es
re|but
  re|buts
  re|but|ted
  re|but|ting
re|but|table
re|but|tal +s
re|but|ter +s
rec (recreational)
  [☞ wreck, reck]
re|calci|trance
re|calci|trant +s
re|calci|trant|ly
re|calcu|late
  re|calcu|lates
  re|calcu|lat|ed
  re|calcu|lat|ing
re|calcu|la|tion +s
re|cal|esce
  re|cal|esces
  re|cal|esced
  re|cal|es|cing
re|cal|es|cence
re|cal|es|cent
re|call +s +ed +ing
re|call|able
re|cant +s +ed +ing
re|can|ta|tion +s
re|cant|er +s
re|cap
  re|caps
  re|capped
  re|cap|ping
re|capit|al|iz|a|tion
  +s
re|capit|al|ize
  re|capit|al|iz|es
  re|capit|al|ized
  re|capit|al|iz|ing
re|capitu|late
  re|capitu|lates
  re|capitu|lat|ed
  re|capitu|lat|ing
re|capitu|la|tion +s

re|cap|ture
  re|cap|tures
  re|cap|tured
  re|cap|tur|ing
re|cast
  re|casts
  re|cast
  re|cast|ing
recce (reconnoitre)
  recces
  recced
  recce|ing
re|cede (go or shrink back)
  re|cedes
  re|ced|ed
  re|ced|ing
  [☞ reseed]
re|ceipt +s +ed +ing (act of receiving; bill)
  [☞ reseat]
re|ceipt|ed adjective
re|ceiv|able +s
re|ceive
  re|ceives
  re|ceived
  re|ceiv|ing
re|ceived adjective
re|ceiv|er +s
re|ceiv|er gen|er|al
  re|ceiv|ers gen|er|al
re|ceiv|er|ship +s
re|ceiv|ing adjective
re|cen|sion +s
Re|cent (Holocene)
re|cent
re|cent|ly
re|cent|ness
re|cep|tacle +s
re|cep|tion +s
re|cep|tion|ist +s
re|cep|tive
re|cep|tive|ness
re|cep|tiv|ity
re|cep|tor +s
re|cess
  re|cess|es
  re|cessed
  re|cess|ing
re|cessed adjective
re|ces|sion +s (economic decline; withdrawal)
  [☞ rescission]
re|ces|sion|al +s
re|ces|sion|ary
re|cession-proof
re|ces|sive +s
re|ces|sive|ness
re|charge
  re|char|ges
  re|charged
  re|char|ging

re|charge|able +s
re|char|ger +s
ré|chauf|fé +s
re|check +s +ed +ing
re|cher|ché
re|chris|ten +s +ed +ing
re|cid|iv|ism
re|cid|iv|ist +s
Re|cife (city, Brazil)
re|ci|pe +s
re|cipi|ency
re|cipi|ent +s
re|cipro|cal +s
re|cipro|cal|ity
  re|cipro|cal|ities
re|cipro|cal|ly
re|cipro|cate
  re|cipro|cates
  re|cipro|cat|ed
  re|cipro|cat|ing
re|cipro|cat|ing adjective
re|cipro|ca|tion +s
re|cipro|ca|tor +s
reci|proci|ty
  reci|proci|ties
re|circu|late
  re|circu|lates
  re|circu|lat|ed
  re|circu|lat|ing
re|circu|la|tion +s
re|cital +s
re|cital|ist +s
reci|ta|tion +s
reci|ta|tive +s
re|cite
  re|cites
  re|cit|ed
  re|cit|ing
re|cit|er +s
reck +s +ed +ing (heed; be important)
  [☞ wreck, rec]
reck|less
reck|less|ly
reck|less|ness
reck|on +s +ed +ing (calculate; expect)
  [☞ recon]
reck|on|able
reck|on|ing +s noun
re|claim +s +ed +ing
re|claim|able
re|claimed adjective
re|claim|er +s
rec|lam|a|tion +s
re|classi|fi|ca|tion +s
re|classi|fy
  re|classi|fies
  re|classi|fied
  re|classi|fy|ing

re|cline
  re|clines
  re|clined
  re|clin|ing
re|clin|er +s
re|clin|ing adjective
re|clothe
  re|clothes
  re|clothed
  re|cloth|ing
re|cluse +s
re|clu|sion
re|clu|sive
re|code
  re|codes
  re|cod|ed
  re|cod|ing
re|cogni|sance +s (use recognizance)
rec|og|ni|tion +s
rec|og|niz|abil|ity
rec|og|niz|able
rec|og|niz|ably
re|cogni|zance +s
rec|og|nize
  rec|og|niz|es
  rec|og|nized
  rec|og|niz|ing
rec|og|niz|er +s
re|coil +s +ed +ing
re|coil|less
re|col|lect +s +ed +ing (remember)
re-collect +s +ed +ing (collect again; recover)
re|col|lec|tion +s
re|col|lec|tive
Récol|let +s
re|col|on|iz|a|tion +s
re|col|on|ize
  re|col|on|iz|es
  re|col|on|ized
  re|col|on|iz|ing
re|com|bin|ant +s
re|com|bin|a|tion +s
re|com|bine
  re|com|bines
  re|com|bined
  re|com|bin|ing
re|com|mence
  re|com|men|ces
  re|com|menced
  re|com|men|cing
re|com|mence|ment +s
rec|om|mend +s +ed +ing
rec|om|mend|able
rec|om|men|da|tion +s
rec|om|mend|er +s

re|com|mis|sion +s +ed +ing
re|com|mit
  re|com|mits
  re|com|mit|ted
  re|com|mit|ting
re|com|mit|ment
re|com|mit|tal +s
re|com|pense
  re|com|pens|es
  re|com|pensed
  re|com|pens|ing
re|com|pose
  re|com|pos|es
  re|com|posed
  re|com|pos|ing
re|com|pos|ition
re|com|pu|ta|tion +s
re|com|pute
  re|com|putes
  re|com|put|ed
  re|com|put|ing
recon (reconnaissance)
  [☞ reckon]
re|con|cep|tual|iz|a|tion +s
re|con|cep|tual|ize
  re|con|cep|tual|iz|es
  re|con|cep|tual|ized
  re|con|cep|tual|iz|ing
rec|on|cil|abil|ity
rec|on|cil|able
rec|on|cile
  rec|on|ciles
  rec|on|ciled
  rec|on|cil|ing
rec|on|cile|ment +s
rec|on|ciler +s
rec|on|cili|a|tion +s
rec|on|cili|a|tory
rec|on|dite
rec|on|dite|ly
rec|on|dite|ness
re|con|di|tion +s +ed +ing
re|con|fig|ur|a|tion +s
re|con|fig|ure
  re|con|fig|ures
  re|con|fig|ured
  re|con|fig|ur|ing
re|con|firm +s +ed +ing
re|con|firm|a|tion
re|con|nais|sance +s
re|con|nect +s +ed +ing
re|con|nec|tion +s
rec|on|noiter +s +ed +ing (use reconnoitre)

rec|on|noitre
  rec|on|noi|tres
  rec|on|noi|tred
  rec|on|noi|tring
re|con|quer +s +ed
  +ing
re|con|quest
re|con|se|crate
  re|con|se|crates
  re|con|se|crat|ed
  re|con|se|crat|ing
re|con|se|cra|tion +s
re|con|sider +s +ed
  +ing
re|con|sider|a|tion
re|con|sti|tute
  re|con|sti|tutes
  re|con|sti|tut|ed
  re|con|sti|tut|ing
re|con|sti|tu|tion +s
re|con|struct +s +ed
  +ing
re|con|struct|able
re|con|struct|ible (use
  reconstructable)
Re|con|struc|tion (US
  History)
re|con|struc|tion +s
  (in general use)
re|con|struct|ive
re|con|struct|or +s
re|con|text|ual|iz|
      a|tion
re|con|text|ualize
  re|con|text|ual|iz|es
  re|con|text|ual|ized
  re|con|text|ual|iz|
      ing
re|con|vene
  re|con|venes
  re|con|vened
  re|con|ven|ing
re|con|ver|sion
re|con|vert +s +ed
  +ing
rec|ord[1] +s noun
re|cord[2] +s +ed +ing
  verb
re|cord|abil|ity
re|cord|able
re|cord-breaking
re|cord|er +s
re|corder|ship +s
rec|ord hold|er +s
re|cord|ing +s noun
re|cord|ist +s
re|count +s +ed +ing
re|coup +s +ed +ing
  [☞ recuperate]
re|coup|able
re|coup|ment
re|course

re|cover +s +ed +ing
  (regain; return to
  health)
re-cover +s +ed +ing
  (cover again;
  reupholster)
re|cover|abil|ity
re|cover|able
re|cover|er +s
re|cover|ing adjective
  (convalescent)
re|cov|ery
  re|cov|eries
rec|re|ancy
rec|re|ant +s
rec|re|ant|ly
re|create
  re|cre|ates
  re|creat|ed
  re|creat|ing
rec|rea|tion[1] +s
  (entertainment etc.)
re|crea|tion[2] +s
  (creation of
  something again)
rec|rea|tion|al
rec|rea|tion|al|ly
rec|rea|tion|ist +s
rec|reat|ive
re|crim|in|al|iz|a|tion
re|crim|in|al|ize
  re|crim|in|al|iz|es
  re|crim|in|al|ized
  re|crim|in|al|iz|ing
re|crim|in|ate
re|crim|in|a|tion +s
re|crim|in|a|tive
re|crim|in|a|tory
rec room +s
re|cross
  re|cross|es
  re|crossed
  re|cross|ing
re|cru|desce
  re|cru|des|ces
  re|cru|desced
  re|cru|des|cing
re|cru|des|cence +s
re|cru|des|cent
re|cruit +s +ed +ing
re|cruit|able
re|cruit|er +s
re|cruit|ment
re|crys|tal|liz|a|tion
re|crys|tal|lize
  re|crys|tal|liz|es
  re|crys|tal|lized
  re|crys|tal|liz|ing
recta plural of rectum
rec|tal
rec|tal|ly
rect|angle +s
rect|angu|lar

rect|angu|lar|ity
rect|angu|lar|ly
recti plural of rectus
rec|ti|fi|able
rec|ti|fi|ca|tion +s
rec|ti|fi|er +s
rect|ify
  recti|fies
  recti|fied
  recti|fy|ing
rec|ti|lin|eal
rec|ti|linear
rec|ti|linear|ity
rec|ti|linear|ly
rec|ti|tude
recto +s
rec|tor +s
rec|tor|ate +s
rec|tor|ial
rec|tor|ship +s
rec|tory
  rec|tor|ies
rec|trix
  rec|tri|ces
rec|tum
  rec|tums or recta
rec|tus
  recti
re|cum|bency
re|cum|bent
re|cum|bent|ly
re|cu|per|ate
  re|cu|per|ates
  re|cu|per|at|ed
  re|cu|per|at|ing
  [☞ recoup]
re|cu|per|a|tion
re|cu|per|a|tive
re|cu|per|ator +s
recur
  re|curs
  re|curred
  re|cur|ring
re|cur|rence +s
re|cur|rent
re|cur|rent|ly
re|cur|ring adjective
re|cur|sion +s
re|cur|sive
re|cur|sive|ly
re|cur|vate
re|curve
  re|curves
  re|curved
  re|curv|ing
re|cus|al
recu|sancy
recu|sant +s
re|cuse
  re|cus|es
  re|cused
  re|cus|ing

re|cut
  re|cuts
  re|cut
  re|cut|ting
re|cycla|bil|ity
re|cyc|lable +s
re|cycle
  re|cycles
  re|cycled
  re|cyc|ling
re|cyc|ler +s
re|cyc|ling noun
Red +s (rivers,
  N America & Asia;
  lake & bay, Canada;
  sea between Asia &
  Africa; Communist)
red (colour)
  red|der
  red|dest
  reds
  [☞ read, redd]
re|dact +s +ed +ing
re|dac|tion +s
re|dac|tion|al
re|dact|or +s
redan +s (fortification)
  [☞ redden]
red-backed
red-bait +s +ed +ing
red-baiter +s
red-baiting +s
Red Baron (Baron von
  Richthofen)
Red Bay (inlet &
  community, Canada)
red-berry
  red-berries
red-blooded
red-blooded|ness
red|breast +s
red-breast|ed
red-brick
red|bud +s
red|cap +s
red card +s noun
red-card +s +ed +ing
  verb
Red Cham|ber
red|coat +s
red|currant +s
redd (clear up;
  compose; riverbed
  hollow)
  redds
  redd
  redd|ing
  [☞ read, red]
Red Deer (city & river,
  Canada)
red deer
  plural red deer

Red De|li|cious
plural **Red
De|li|cious**
red|den +s +ed +ing
(turn red)
Red|ding, Otis (US
singer-songwriter)
[☞ **Reading**]
red|dish
Red|ditch (town,
England)
red|dle
reddy (reddish)
[☞ **ready**]
rede (counsel;
interpret a riddle or
dream)
redes
reded
reding
[☞ **read, reed,
Reid, Reade**]
re|decor|ate
re|decor|ates
re|decor|at|ed
re|decor|at|ing
re|decor|a|tion
re|dedi|cate
re|dedi|cates
re|dedi|cat|ed
re|dedi|cat|ing
re|dedi|ca|tion +s
re|deem +s +ed +ing
re|deem|able
re|deem|er +s
re|define
re|defines
re|defined
re|defin|ing
re|defin|i|tion +s
re|demp|tion +s
re|demp|tive
Re|demp|tor|ist +s
Red En|sign +s
re|deploy +s +ed
+ing
re|deploy|ment +s
re|design +s +ed
+ing
re|deter|min|a|tion
+s
re|deter|mine
re|deter|mines
re|deter|mined
re|deter|min|ing
re|devel|op +s +ed
+ing
re|devel|op|er +s
re|devel|op|ment +s
red-eye +s
red-eyed
red-faced
Red Fife

red|fish
plural **red|fish** or
red|fish|es
red flag
red flags
red flag|ged
red flag|ging
**Red|ford, (Charles)
Rob|ert** (US
filmmaker)
Red|grave, Lynn
(English actress)
**Red|grave, Sir
Mi|chael
Scuda|more** (English
actor)
Red|grave, Van|essa
(English actress)
red gum +s
red-handed
red|head +s
red-headed
red hot +s *noun*
red-hot *adjective*
re|dial
re|dials
re|dialed
or **re|dialled**
re|dial|ing
or **re|dial|ling**
redid
Red In|di|an +s
offensive
Red In|di|an Lake (in
Canada)
redin|gote +s
re|direct +s +ed +ing
re|direc|tion +s
re|dis|cov|er +s +ed
+ing
re|dis|cov|ery
re|dis|cov|er|ies
re|dis|so|lu|tion
re|dis|solve
re|dis|solves
re|dis|solved
re|dis|solv|ing
re|dis|trib|ute
re|dis|trib|utes
re|dis|trib|ut|ed
re|dis|trib|ut|ing
re|dis|tri|bu|tion +s
re|dis|tri|bu|tion|ist
+s
re|dis|tribu|tive
re|dis|trict +s +ed
+ing
re|div|ide
re|div|ides
re|div|id|ed
re|div|id|ing
re|div|ision
redi|vivus

Red Lake (lake &
town, Canada)
red-letter
red light +s (**red-light**
*when preceding a
noun*)
red line *noun*
red|line *verb*
red|lines
red|lined
red|lin|ing
redly
**Red|mond, John
Ed|ward** (Irish
politician)
red|neck +s
red-necked
red|ness
redo
• *verb*
redoes
redid
redone
redo|ing
• *noun*
redos
red|ol|ence
red|ol|ent
red|ol|ent|ly
Redon, Odi|lon
(French painter)
re|double
re|doubles
re|doubled
re|doub|ling
re|doubt +s
re|doubt|able
re|doubt|ably
re|dound +s +ed
+ing
redox (reduction &
oxidation)
[☞ **redux**]
red|poll +s
re|draft +s +ed +ing
re|draw
re|draws
re|drew
re|drawn
re|draw|ing
re-dress (dress again)
re-dresses
re-dressed
re-dressing
re|dress (rectify;
compensation)
re|dress|es
re|dressed
re|dress|ing
re|dress|able
re|dress|al +s
re|dress|er +s
re|dress|or +s (*use*
redresser)

Red River (rivers,
N America & Asia)
Red Rome Beauty
Red Rome Beaut|ies
red|root +s
Red Rover
Red Sea (between
Asia & Africa)
red shift +s
red-shifted
red|shirt +s +ed +ing
red|skin +s *offensive*
red|start +s
red-tailed
red-throated
Red Tory
Red Tor|ies
Red Tory|ism
re|duce
re|duces
re|duced
re|ducing
re|duced *adjective*
re|ducer +s
re|duci|bil|ity
re|du|cible
re|duct|ase
*re|duc|tio ad
ab|sur|dum*
re|duc|tion +s
re|duc|tion|ism
re|duc|tion|ist +s
re|duc|tion|is|tic
re|duc|tive
re|duc|tive|ly
re|duc|tive|ness
re|dun|dancy
re|dun|dan|cies
re|dun|dant
re|dun|dant|ly
re|dupli|cate
re|dupli|cates
re|dupli|cat|ed
re|dupli|cat|ing
re|dupli|ca|tion +s
re|dupli|ca|tive
redux (restored)
[☞ **redox**]
red|water
red|wing +s
red-winged
red|wood +s
red worm +s
ree|bok +s
re-echo
re-echoes
re-echoed
re-echoing
Reed, Lou (US
musician)
[☞ **Read, Reade,
Reid**]

Reed, Wal|ter (US
physician)
[☞ Read, Reade,
Reid]
reed +s +ed +ing
(plant; *Music*;
Weaving; moulding)
[☞ read, rede]
reed bed +s
reed|buck +s
reed|ed *adjective*
(*Music*)
[☞ reded]
reed|i|er
reed|i|est
reed|i|ness
reed|ing +s
(moulding)
[☞ reading, reding]
re-edit
re-edits
re-edited
re-editing
re-edition +s
reed|man
reed|men
re-educate
re-educates
re-educat|ed
re-educat|ing
re-education
reedy
reed|i|er
reed|i|est
reef +s +ed +ing
reef|er +s (marijuana
cigarette; jacket;
refrigerated vehicle)
[☞ refer]
reef|point +s
reefy
reek +s +ed +ing
(stink)
[☞ wreak]
reeky (stinky)
reek|i|er
reek|i|est
reel +s +ed +ing
(winding device,
spool; dance, music;
wind; stagger)
[☞ real]
re-elect +s +ed +ing
re-election +s
reel|er +s (person or
thing that reels)
[☞ realer]
re-eligible
reel-to-reel
re-emerge
re-emerges
re-emerged
re-emerging
re-emergence

re-emphasis
re-emphases
re-emphasize
re-emphasiz|es
re-emphasized
re-emphasiz|ing
re-employ +s +ed
+ing
re-employ|ment
re-enact +s +ed +ing
re-enactment +s
re-engineer +s +ed
+ing
re-engineer|ing *noun*
re-enlist +s +ed +ing
re-enlist|er +s
re-enter +s +ed +ing
re-entrance +s
re-entrant +s
re-entry
re-entries
re-equip
re-equips
re-equipped
re-equipping
re-equipment
re-erect +s +ed +ing
re-establish
re-establish|es
re-established
re-establish|ing
re-establish|ment
re-evaluate
re-evaluates
re-evaluat|ed
re-evaluat|ing
re-evalua|tion +s
reeve (town leader,
magistrate, official;
thread, fasten; bird)
reeves
rove or reeved
reev|ing
[☞ reave, reive]
reeve|ship +s
re-examin|a|tion +s
re-examine
re-examines
re-examined
re-examin|ing
re-export +s +ed
+ing
ref
refs
reffed
ref|fing
re|face
re|faces
re|faced
re|facing
re|fash|ion +s +ed
+ing
re|fec|tory
re|fec|tor|ies

refer *verb*
re|fers
re|ferred
re|fer|ring
[☞ reefer]
re|fer|able
ref|eree
ref|erees
ref|ereed
ref|eree|ing
ref|ereed *adjective*
ref|eree|ing *noun*
ref|er|ence
ref|er|en|ces
ref|er|enced
ref|er|en|cing
ref|er|en|dum
ref|er|en|dums or
ref|er|en|da
ref|er|ent +s
ref|er|en|tial
ref|er|en|ti|al|ity
re|fer|ral +s
re|ferred *adjective*
ref|fing +s
re|fill +s +ed +ing
re|fill|able
re|finance
re|finan|ces
re|financed
re|finan|cing
re|finan|cing *noun*
re|fine
re|fines
re|fined
re|fin|ing
re|fined *adjective*
re|fine|ment +s
re|fin|er +s
re|fin|ery
re|fin|eries
re|fin|ing *noun*
re|finish
re|finish|es
re|fin|ished
re|finish|ing
refit
re|fits
re|fitted
re|fit|ting
re|fit|ting *noun*
re|flag
re|flags
re|flagged
re|flag|ging
re|flate
re|flates
re|flat|ed
re|flat|ing
re|fla|tion +s
re|flect +s +ed +ing
re|flect|ance
re|flect|ing *adjective*

re|flec|tion +s
re|flect|ive
re|flect|ive|ly
re|flect|ive|ness
re|flec|tiv|ity
re|flec|tiv|ities
re|flect|or +s
re|flex
re|flex|es
re|flexed *adjective*
re|flex|ibil|ity
re|flex|ible
re|flex|ive
re|flex|ive|ly
re|flex|ive|ness
re|flex|iv|ity
re|flex|ly
re|flex|ol|o|gist +s
re|flex|ol|ogy
re|float +s +ed +ing
re|flux
re|flux|es
re|focus
re|focus
re|fo|cused
or re|fo|cussed
re|focus|ing
or re|focus|sing
re|forest +s +ed +ing
re|forest|a|tion
re|forge
re|forges
re|forged
re|forging
Re|form (of the
Reform Party;
Judaism)
re|form +s +ed +ing
(*in general use*:
change; improve)
[☞ re-form]
re-form +s +ed +ing
(form anew)
[☞ reform]
re|form|able
re|format
re|formats
re|format|ted
re|format|ting
Ref|or|ma|tion
(*Christianity*)
ref|or|ma|tion +s (*in
general use*: change,
improvement)
[☞ re-formation]
re-formation +s (act
or process of
forming anew)
[☞ reformation]
Ref|or|ma|tion|al
re|forma|tory
re|forma|tor|ies

Re|formed *adjective*
(*Christianity*)
re|formed *adjective* (*in general use*)
Re|form|er +s
(member of the Reform Party)
re|form|er +s (*in general use*)
re|form|ism
re|form|ist +s
re|formu|late
re|formu|lates
re|formu|lat|ed
re|formu|lat|ing
re|formu|lat|ed *adjective*
re|formu|la|tion +s
re|fract +s +ed +ing
re|fract|ed *adjective*
re|frac|tion +s
re|fract|ive
re|frac|tiv|ity
re|frac|tom|eter +s
re|fract|or +s
re|frac|tor|i|ly
re|frac|tor|i|ness
re|frac|tory
re|frac|tor|ies
re|frain +s +ed +ing
re|freeze
re|freez|es
re|froze
re|frozen
re|freez|ing
re|fresh
re|fresh|es
re|freshed
re|fresh|ing
re|freshed *adjective*
re|fresh|er +s
re|fresh|ing *adjective*
re|fresh|ing|ly
re|fresh|ment +s
re|fried beans
re|friger|ant +s
re|friger|ate
re|friger|ates
re|friger|at|ed
re|friger|at|ing
re|friger|at|ed *adjective*
re|friger|a|tion
re|friger|ator +s
re|froze
re|frozen
reft
re|fuel
re|fuels
re|fuelled
re|fuel|ling
ref|uge +s
refu|gee +s

re|fu|gium
re|fu|gia
re|ful|gent
re|fund +s +ed +ing
re|fund|able
re|fund|ing *noun*
re|fur|bish
re|fur|bish|es
re|fur|bished
re|fur|bish|ing
re|fur|bished *adjective*
re|fur|bish|ing *noun*
re|fur|bish|ment +s
re|furn|ish
re|furn|ish|es
re|furn|ished
re|furn|ish|ing
re|fus|al +s
re|fuse¹ *verb*
re|fus|es
re|fused
re|fus|ing
ref|use² *noun*
re|fuse|nik +s
re|fut|abil|ity
re|fut|able
re|fut|al +s
refu|ta|tion +s
re|fute
re|futes
re|fut|ed
re|fut|ing
reg +s
re|gain +s +ed +ing
regal (royal)
[☞ regale]
re|gale (entertain; feast; liquor ration)
re|gales
re|galed
re|gal|ing
[☞ regal]
re|galia
regal|ity
regal|ities
regal|ly
Regan, Ger|ald
Au|gus|tine (Cdn politician)
[☞ Reagan]
re|gard +s +ed +ing
re|gard|ing *preposition*
re|gard|less
re|gard|less|ness
re|gath|er +s +ed +ing
re|gat|ta +s
Re|gency (of specific periods)
re|gency (*in general use*)
re|gen|cies

re|gener|ate
re|gener|ates
re|gener|at|ed
re|gener|at|ing
re|gener|a|tion +s
re|gener|a|tive
re|gener|ator +s
re|gent +s
reg|gae
Reg|gio di Ca|lab|ria
(city, Italy)
regi|cide
re|gie +s
re|gild +s +ed +ing
re|gime +s
regi|men +s
regi|ment +s
regi|ment|al
regi|men|ta|tion
regi|ment|ed
Re|gina (city, Canada)
Re|gina (reigning queen)
Re|gin|an +s
Regio|mon|tanus
(German astronomer)
re|gion +s
re|gion|al +s
region|al|ism +s
region|al|ist +s
region|al|iz|a|tion +s
region|al|ize
region|al|iz|es
region|al|ized
region|al|iz|ing
re|gion|al|ly
re|gis|seur +s
regis|ter +s +ed +ing
regis|ter|able
regis|tered *adjective*
regis|trable
(= registerable)
regis|trant +s
regis|trar +s
Regis|trar Gen|er|al
Regis|trars
Gen|er|al
regis|trar|ship +s
regis|tra|tion +s
regis|tra|tion|al
regis|try
regis|tries
Re|gi|us pro|fes|sor +s
reg|nal
reg|nant
rego|lith +s
re|grade
re|grades
re|grad|ed
re|grad|ing

re|gress
re|gress|es
re|gressed
re|gress|ing
re|gres|sion +s
re|gres|sive
re|gres|sive|ly
re|gres|sive|ness
re|gres|siv|ity
re|gret
re|grets
re|gret|ted
re|gret|ting
re|gret|ful
re|gret|ful|ly
re|gret|ful|ness
re|gret|table
re|gret|tably
re|group +s +ed +ing
re|group|ment +s
re|grow
re|grows
re|grew
re|grown
re|grow|ing
re|growth +s
regu|lar +s
regu|lar|ity
regu|lar|ities
regu|lar|iz|a|tion +s
regu|lar|ize
regu|lar|iz|es
regu|lar|ized
regu|lar|iz|ing
regu|lar|ly
regu|lar sea|son
(regular-season *when preceding a noun*)
regu|late
regu|lates
regu|lat|ed
regu|lat|ing
regu|la|tion +s
regu|la|tive
regu|la|tor +s
regu|la|tory
Regu|lus, Mar|cus
Atil|ius (Roman general)
Regu|lus (star)
re|gur|gi|tate
re|gur|gi|tates
re|gur|gi|tat|ed
re|gur|gi|tat|ing
re|gur|gi|ta|tion
rehab
re|habs
re|habbed
re|hab|bing
re|habili|tate
re|habili|tates

re|habili|tat|ed
re|habili|tat|ing
re|habili|ta|tion
re|habili|ta|tive
re|hash
  re|hash|es
  re|hashed
  re|hash|ing
re|hear
  re|hears
  re|heard
  re|hear|ing
re|hears|able
re|hears|al +s
re|hearse
  re|hears|es
  re|hearsed
  re|hears|ing
re|heat +s +ed +ing
re|heat|er +s
re|heel +s +ed +ing
reho|boam +s
re|house
  re|hous|es
  re|housed
  re|hous|ing
re|hy|drat|able
re|hy|drate
  re|hy|drates
  re|hy|drat|ed
  re|hy|drat|ing
re|hy|dra|tion
Reich, Steve (US composer)
Reich, Wil|helm (Austrian psychologist)
Reich +s (German nation)
Reich|ian
Reichs|tag
Reid (surname)
  [☞ Read, Reade, Reed, rede]
Reid, (Daphne) Kate (Cdn actress)
Reid, George Agnew (Cdn painter)
Reid, Thom|as (Scottish philosopher)
Reid, Wil|liam Ron|ald (Cdn sculptor)
reifi|ca|tion +s
reify
  re|ifies
  re|ified
  reify|ing
reign +s +ed +ing (rule, prevail)
  [☞ rein, rain]

reign|ing *adjective* (ruling)
  [☞ reining, raining]
re|ignite
  re|ignites
  re|ignit|ed
  re|ignit|ing
re|igni|tion
Reign of Ter|ror (*French History*)
reign of ter|ror (*in general use*)
  reigns of ter|ror
reiki
re|im|burs|able
re|im|burse
  re|im|burs|es
  re|im|bursed
  re|im|burs|ing
re|im|burse|ment +s
re|im|port +s +ed +ing
re|im|port|a|tion +s
re|impose
  re|impos|es
  re|im|posed
  re|impos|ing
re|impos|ition
Reims (city, France)
rein +s +ed +ing (horse strap; control)
  [☞ reign, rain]
re|incar|nate
  re|incar|nates
  re|incar|nat|ed
  re|incar|nat|ing
re|incar|na|tion +s
re|incor|por|ate
  re|incor|por|ates
  re|incor|por|at|ed
  re|incor|por|at|ing
re|incor|por|a|tion
Rein|deer (lake, Canada)
rein|deer
  plural rein|deer
re|infect +s +ed +ing
re|infec|tion
re|inforce
  re|infor|ces
  re|inforced
  re|infor|cing
re|inforce|ment +s
re|infor|cer +s
Rein|hardt, Django (Belgian guitarist)
Rein|hardt, Max (Austrian theatre director)
re|injure
  re|injures
  re|injured
  re|injur|ing

re|injury
  re|injur|ies
rein|less (without reins)
  [☞ rainless]
re|insert +s +ed +ing
re|inser|tion +s
re|install +s +ed +ing
re|instal|la|tion +s
re|instate
  re|instates
  re|instat|ed
  re|instat|ing
re|instate|ment +s
re|insti|tute
  re|insti|tutes
  re|insti|tut|ed
  re|insti|tut|ing
re|insur|ance
re|insure
  re|insures
  re|insured
  re|insur|ing
re|insur|er +s
re|inte|grate
  re|inte|grates
  re|inte|grat|ed
  re|inte|grat|ing
re|inte|gra|tion +s
re|inter
  re|inters
  re|interred
  re|inter|ring
re|inter|ment +s
re|inter|pret +s +ed +ing
re|inter|pret|a|tion +s
re|intro|duce
  re|intro|du|ces
  re|intro|duced
  re|intro|du|cing
re|intro|duc|tion +s
re|invent +s +ed +ing
re|inven|tion +s
re|invest +s +ed +ing
re|invest|ment +s
re|invig|or|ate
  re|invig|or|ates
  re|invig|or|at|ed
  re|invig|or|at|ing
re|invig|or|a|tion
re|issue
  re|issues
  re|issued
  re|issu|ing
re|iter|ate
  re|iter|ates
  re|iter|at|ed
  re|iter|at|ing
re|iter|a|tion +s
re|iter|a|tive

Reit|man, Ivan (Cdn filmmaker)
reive (plunder)
  reives
  reived
  reiv|ing
  [☞ reeve]
reiv|er +s
re|ject +s +ed +ing
re|ject|able
re|jec|tion +s
re|jec|tion|ist +s
re|ject|ive
re|ject|or +s
rejig
  re|jigs
  re|jigged
  re|jig|ging
re|jig|ger +s +ed +ing
re|joice
  re|joices
  re|joiced
  re|joi|cing
re|joi|cer +s
re|joi|cing *noun*
re|join +s +ed +ing
re|join|der +s
re|juven|ate
  re|juven|ates
  re|juven|at|ed
  re|juven|at|ing
re|juven|a|tion +s
re|juven|ator +s
re|juven|esce
  re|juven|es|ces
  re|juven|esced
  re|juven|es|cing
re|juven|es|cence
re|juven|es|cent
re|key +s +ed +ing (key again)
  [☞ recce, reeky]
re|kin|dle
  re|kin|dles
  re|kin|dled
  re|kind|ling
re|label
  re|labels
  re|labelled
  re|label|ling
re-laid *past & past participle of* **re-lay**
  [☞ relayed]
re|lapse
  re|laps|es
  re|lapsed
  re|laps|ing
re|laps|er +s
re|lat|able
re|late
  re|lates
  re|lat|ed
  re|lat|ing
re|lat|ed *adjective*

re|lat|ed|ness
re|la|tion +s
re|la|tion|al
re|la|tion|al|ly
re|la|tion|ship +s
rela|tive +s
rela|tive|ly
rela|tiv|ism
rela|tiv|ist +s
rela|tiv|is|tic
rela|tiv|is|tic|al|ly
rela|tiv|ity
rela|tiv|iz|a|tion
rela|tiv|ize
　rela|tiv|iz|es
　rela|tiv|ized
　rela|tiv|iz|ing
re|launch
　re|launch|es
　re|launched
　re|launch|ing
relax
　re|lax|es
　re|laxed
　re|lax|ing
re|lax|ant +s
re|lax|a|tion +s
re|laxed *adjective*
re|laxed-fit
re|lax|ed|ly
re|lax|ed|ness
re|lax|er +s
re|lax|ing *adjective*
re|lay +s +ed +ing
　(pass on; shift; race)
re-lay (lay again)
　re-lays
　re-laid
　re-laying
re|learn
　re|learns
　re|learned
　or re|learnt
　re|learn|ing
re|leas|able
re|lease
　re|leas|es
　re|leased
　re|leas|ing
re|leas|ee +s
re|leas|er +s (*in
　general use*)
re|leas|or +s (*Law*)
rel|egate
　rel|egates
　rel|egat|ed
　rel|egat|ing
rel|ega|tion
re|lent +s +ed +ing
re|lent|less
re|lent|less|ly
re|lent|less|ness
rel|evance

rel|evancy
rel|evant
rel|evant|ly
re|li|abil|ity
re|li|able
re|li|able|ness
re|li|ably
re|li|ance
re|li|ant
rel|ic +s (ancient
　object or custom;
　human remains)
rel|ict +s (surviving
　species or geological
　structure; widow)
re|lief +s
re|liev|able
re|lieve
　re|lieves
　re|lieved
　re|liev|ing
re|lieved *adjective*
re|liev|ed|ly
re|liev|er +s
re|lievo +s
re|light
　re|lights
　re|lit
　re|lit or re|light|ed
　re|light|ing
re|li|gion +s
re|li|gion|ist +s
re|li|gion|less
re|li|giose (excessively
　religious)
re|li|gi|os|ity
re|li|gious
　plural re|li|gious
re|li|gious|ly
re|li|gious|ness
re|line
　re|lines
　re|lined
　re|lin|ing
re|lin|quish
　re|lin|quish|es
　re|lin|quished
　re|lin|quish|ing
re|lin|quish|ment
reli|quary
　reli|quar|ies
rel|ish
　rel|ish|es
　rel|ished
　rel|ish|ing
rel|ish|able
re|live
　re|lives
　re|lived
　re|liv|ing
rel|leno +s
re|load +s +ed +ing
re|locat|able

re|locate
　re|lo|cates
　re|locat|ed
　re|locat|ing
re|loca|tion +s
re|luc|tance
re|luc|tant
re|luc|tant|ly
rely
　relies
　relied
　rely|ing
REM (rapid eye
　movement)
　REMs
rem (unit of radiation)
　plural rem or rems
re|main +s +ed +ing
re|main|der +s
re|main|dered
　adjective
re|mains
re|make
　re|makes
　re|made
　re|making
re|mand +s +ed +ing
rem|an|ence
rem|an|ent *adjective*
　(residual; of
　magnetism)
　[☞ remnant]
re|mark +s +ed +ing
　[☞ Remarque]
re|mark|able
re|mark|ably
Re|marque, Erich
　Maria (German
　novelist)
re|mar|riage +s
re|marry
　re|mar|ries
　re|mar|ried
　re|marry|ing
re|mas|ter +s +ed
　+ing
re|mas|tered *adjective*
re|master|ing +s
　noun
re|match
　re|match|es
Rem|brandt
　(Har|mensz van
　Rijn) (Dutch painter)
re|meas|ure
　re|meas|ures
　re|meas|ured
　re|measur|ing
re|measure|ment +s
re|medi|able
re|med|ial

rem|edy
　rem|edies
　rem|edied
　rem|edy|ing
re|mem|ber +s +ed
　+ing
re|mem|ber|er +s
re|mem|brance +s
re|mind +s +ed +ing
re|mind|er +s
re|mind|ful
rem|in|isce
　rem|in|is|ces
　rem|in|isced
　rem|in|is|cing
rem|in|is|cence +s
rem|in|is|cent
rem|in|is|cen|tial
rem|in|is|cent|ly
re|mise
　re|mis|es
　re|mised
　re|mis|ing
re|miss
re|mis|sible
re|mis|sion +s
re|mis|sive
re|miss|ness
remit
　re|mits
　re|mit|ted
　re|mit|ting
re|mit|table
re|mit|tal +s
re|mit|tance +s
re|mit|tee +s
re|mit|tent
re|mit|ter +s
re|mix
　re|mix|es
　re|mixed
　re|mix|ing
re|mix|er +s
rem|nant +s (small
　remaining quantity;
　leftover)
　[☞ remanent]
re|model
　re|models
　re|modelled
　re|model|ling
re|model|ler +s
re|mold +s +ed +ing
　(*use* remould)
re|mon|strance +s
re|mon|strant
rem|on|strate
　rem|on|strates
　rem|on|strat|ed
　rem|on|strat|ing
rem|on|stra|tion +s
re|mon|stra|tive
rem|on|stra|tor +s

re|mon|tant
rem|ora +s
re|morse
re|morse|ful
re|morse|fully
re|morse|less
re|morse|less|ly
re|morse|less|ness
re|mort|gage
  re|mort|gages
  re|mort|gaged
  re|mort|gaging
re|mote
  re|mot|er
  re|mot|est
  re|motes
re|mote con|trol +s
remote-controlled
re|mote|ly
re|mote|ness
re|mou|lade
re|mould +s +ed
  +ing
re|mount +s +ed
  +ing
re|mov|abil|ity
re|mov|able
re|mov|al +s
re|move
  re|moves
  re|moved
  re|mov|ing
re|moved *adjective*
re|mov|er +s
re|muner|ate
  re|muner|ates
  re|muner|at|ed
  re|muner|at|ing
re|muner|a|tion +s
re|muner|a|tive
Remus (*Roman Myth*)
Ren|ais|sance
  (*European History*)
ren|ais|sance +s
  (rebirth)
renal
re|name
  re|names
  re|named
  re|nam|ing
Renan, Jo|seph
  Er|nest (French
  historian)
re|nas|cence +s
  (rebirth, renaissance)
  [☞ Renaissance]
re|nas|cent
Re|nault, Louis
  (French car
  engineer)
  [☞ Raynaud]

Re|nault, Mary
  (British-born
  novelist)
rend
  rends
  rent
  rend|ing
Ren|dell, Ruth
  Bar|bara (English
  writer)
ren|der +s +ed +ing
ren|der|er +s
ren|der|ing +s *noun*
ren|dez|vous
  • *noun*:
    plural ren|dez|vous
  • *verb*
    ren|dez|vouses
    ren|dez|voused
    ren|dez|vous|ing
ren|di|tion +s
rene|gade
  rene|gades
  rene|gad|ed
  rene|gad|ing
re|nege
  re|neges
  re|neged
  re|neg|ing
re|neg|er +s
re|negoti|able
re|negoti|ate
  re|negoti|ates
  re|negoti|at|ed
  re|negoti|at|ing
re|negoti|a|tion +s
re|new +s +ed +ing
re|new|abil|ity
re|new|able
re|new|al +s
re|new|er +s
Ren|frew (town,
  Canada)
Ren|frew|shire
  (former county,
  Scotland)
Reni, Guido (Italian
  painter)
reni|form
renin
Rennes (city, France)
  [☞ Wren]
ren|net +s
ren|nin +s
Reno (city, US)
reno +s (renovation)
  [☞ Renault]
Re|noir, Jean (French
  filmmaker)
Re|noir, (Pierre)
  Au|guste (French
  painter)

re|nomin|ate
  re|nomin|ates
  re|nomin|at|ed
  re|nomin|at|ing
re|nomin|a|tion +s
re|nounce
  re|noun|ces
  re|nounced
  re|noun|cing
re|nounce|ment +s
re|noun|cer +s
reno|vate
  reno|vates
  reno|vat|ed
  reno|vat|ing
reno|va|tion +s
reno|va|tor +s
re|nown
re|nowned
rent +s +ed +ing
  (tenant's payment
  etc.; tear; *past & past
  participle of* rend)
  [☞ *rente*]
rent|abil|ity
rent|able
rent|al +s
rent con|trol +s
rent-controlled
rente +s (rental
  payment during
  seigneurial era)
  [☞ *rent*]
rent|er +s
rent-free
ren|tier +s
re|num|ber +s +ed
  +ing
re|nunci|ant +s
re|nunci|a|tion +s
re|nunci|a|tory
re|occu|pa|tion
re|occupy
  re|occu|pies
  re|occu|pied
  re|occu|py|ing
re|occur
  re|occurs
  re|occurred
  re|occur|ring
re|occur|rence +s
re|offend +s +ed
  +ing
re-offer +s +ed +ing
re|open +s +ed +ing
re|open|ing +s *noun*
re|order +s +ed +ing
re|organ|iz|a|tion +s
re|organ|ize
  re|organ|iz|es
  re|organ|ized
  re|organ|iz|ing
re|organ|iz|er +s

re|orient +s +ed +ing
re|orien|tate
  re|orien|tates
  re|orien|tat|ed
  re|orien|tat|ing
re|orien|ta|tion +s
rep +s (representative;
  repertory; fabric;
  reputation;
  repetition)
re|pack +s +ed +ing
re|pack|age
  re|pack|ages
  re|pack|aged
  re|pack|aging
re|pack|aging *noun*
re|paid
re|paint +s +ed +ing
re|pair +s +ed +ing
re|pair|able
re|pair|er +s
repair|man
  repair|men
re|pand
re|paper +s +ed +ing
rep|ar|able
rep|ar|a|tion +s
rep|ara|tive
re|par|tee +s
re|par|ti|tion +s +ed
  +ing
re|pass
  re|pass|es
  re|passed
  re|pass|ing
re|past +s
re|patri|ate
  re|patri|ates
  re|patri|at|ed
  re|patri|at|ing
re|patri|a|tion +s
re|pave
  re|paves
  re|paved
  re|pav|ing
re|pay
  re|pays
  re|paid
  re|pay|ing
re|pay|able
re|pay|ment +s
Rep by Pop
re|peal +s +ed +ing
re|peal|able
re|peat +s +ed +ing
re|peat|abil|ity
re|peat|able
re|peat|ed *adjective*
re|peat|ed|ly
re|peat|er +s
re|pech|age +s

repel (repulse; force
  back)
  re|pels
  re|pelled
  re|pel|ling
  [☞ rappel]
re|pel|lant +s *noun*
  (*use* repellent)
re|pel|lency
re|pel|lent +s *adjective*
  & *noun*
re|pel|lent|ly
re|pel|ler +s
re|pent +s +ed +ing
re|pent|ance
re|pent|ant
re|pent|er +s
Re|pen|tigny (city,
  Canada)
re|percus|sion +s
re|percus|sive
rep|er|toire +s
rep|er|tory
  rep|er|tor|ies
ré|pé|ti|teur +s
rep|eti|tion +s
rep|eti|tious
rep|eti|tious|ly
rep|eti|tious|ness
repeti|tive
repeti|tive|ly
repeti|tive|ness
re|phrase
  re|phras|es
  re|phrased
  re|phras|ing
re|pine
  re|pines
  re|pined
  re|pin|ing
re|place
  re|places
  re|placed
  re|placing
re|place|able
re|place|ment +s
re|placer +s
re|plan
  re|plans
  re|planned
  re|plan|ning
re|plant +s +ed +ing
re|play +s +ed +ing
re|plen|ish
  re|plen|ish|es
  re|plen|ished
  re|plen|ish|ing
re|plen|ish|er +s
re|plen|ish|ment
re|plete
re|pletion +s
re|plev|in +s

re|plevy
  re|plev|ies
  re|plev|ied
  re|plevy|ing
rep|lica +s
rep|lic|abil|ity
rep|lic|able
rep|li|cate
  rep|li|cates
  rep|li|cat|ed
  rep|li|cat|ing
rep|li|ca|tion +s
rep|li|ca|tive
rep|li|ca|tor +s
re|pli|er +s
reply
  re|plied
  re|plies
  re|ply|ing
repo +s
re|point +s +ed +ing
re|popu|late
  re|popu|lates
  re|popu|lat|ed
  re|popu|lat|ing
re|popu|la|tion
re|port +s +ed +ing
  (announce, describe;
  accuse; present
  oneself to)
  [☞ rapport]
re|port|able
rep|or|tage +s
re|port|ed|ly
re|por|ter +s
  (journalist;
  stenographer)
  [☞ rapporteur]
re|por|tor|ial
re|por|tor|ial|ly
re|pos|al +s
re|pose
  re|pos|es
  re|posed
  re|pos|ing
re|pose|ful
re|pose|ful|ly
re|pose|ful|ness
re|pos|ition +s +ed
  +ing
re|posi|tory
  re|posi|tor|ies
re|pos|sess
  re|pos|sess|es
  re|pos|sessed
  re|pos|sess|ing
re|pos|ses|sion +s
re|pos|ses|sor +s
repot
  re|pots
  re|pot|ted
  re|pot|ting
re|pous|sé +s

repp (fabric: *use* rep)
  [☞ rep]
rep|re|hend +s +ed
  +ing
rep|re|hen|si|bil|ity
rep|re|hen|sible
rep|re|hen|sibly
rep|re|hen|sion +s
rep|re|sent +s +ed
  +ing
rep|re|sent|abil|ity
rep|re|sent|able
rep|resen|ta|tion +s
rep|resen|ta|tion|al
**rep|resen|ta|tion|al|
        ism**
**rep|resen|ta|tion|al|
        ist** +s
Rep|re|sent|a|tive +s
  (member of US
  House of
  Representatives)
rep|re|sent|a|tive +s
  (*in general use*)
rep|re|sent|a|tive|ly
**rep|re|sent|a|tive|
        ness**
re|press
  re|press|es
  re|pressed
  re|press|ing
re|pressed *adjective*
re|press|er +s (*use*
  repressor)
re|press|ible
re|pres|sion +s
re|pres|sive
re|pres|sive|ly
re|pres|sive|ness
re|press|or +s
re|prieve
  re|prieves
  re|prieved
  re|priev|ing
repri|mand +s +ed
  +ing
re|print +s +ed +ing
re|print|er +s
re|pris|al +s
re|prise
  re|pris|es
  re|prised
  re|pris|ing
re|pro +s
re|proach
  re|proach|es
  re|proached
  re|proach|ing
re|proach|able
rc|proach|er +s
re|proach|ful
re|proach|ful|ly
re|proach|ful|ness

re|proach|ing|ly
repro|bate
  repro|bates
  repro|bat|ed
  repro|bat|ing
repro|ba|tion
re|pro|cess
  re|pro|cess|es
  re|pro|cessed
  re|pro|cess|ing
re|pro|cess|ing *noun*
re|pro|duce
  re|pro|du|ces
  re|pro|duced
  re|pro|du|cing
re|pro|du|cer +s
re|pro|du|ci|bil|ity
re|pro|du|cible
re|pro|du|cibly
re|pro|duc|tion +s
re|pro|duct|ive
re|pro|duct|ive|ly
re|pro|duct|ive|ness
re|pro|gram
  re|pro|grams
  re|pro|grammed
  re|pro|gram|ming
re|pro|gram|mable
re|pro|gramme (*use*
  reprogram)
  re|pro|grammes
  re|pro|grammed
  re|pro|gram|ming
repro|graph|ic
rep|rog|raphy
re|proof +s
re|prov|able
re|prove
  re|proves
  re|proved
  re|prov|ing
re|prov|er +s
re|prov|ing *adjective*
re|prov|ing|ly
rep|tile +s
rep|til|ian +s
re|pub|lic +s
Re|pub|lic|an +s
  (supporter of US
  party; advocate of
  united Ireland)
re|pub|lic|an +s (*in
  general use*)
re|pub|lic|an|ism
re|pub|li|ca|tion
re|pub|lish
  re|pub|lish|es
  re|pub|lished
  re|pub|lish|ing
re|pudi|ate
  re|pudi|ates
  re|pudi|at|ed
  re|pudi|at|ing

re|pudi|a|tion +s
re|pudi|ator +s
re|pug|nance
re|pug|nant
re|pug|nant|ly
re|pulse
  re|puls|es
  re|pulsed
  re|puls|ing
re|pul|sion +s
re|pul|sive
re|pul|sive|ly
re|pul|sive|ness
re|pur|chase
  re|pur|chas|es
  re|pur|chased
  re|pur|chas|ing
rep|ut|able
rep|ut|ably
repu|ta|tion +s
re|pute
re|put|ed
re|put|ed|ly
re|quest +s +ed +ing
re|quest|er +s
Requi|em +s (Catholic Mass)
requi|em +s (music; memorial; shark)
re|quire
  re|quires
  re|quired
  re|quir|ing
re|quire|ment +s
re|quir|er +s
requi|site +s
requi|site|ly
requi|si|tion +s
requi|si|tion|er +s
requi|si|tion|ist +s
re|quit|al +s
re|quite
  re|quites
  re|quit|ed
  re|quit|ing
reran
re|read
  re|reads
  re|read
  re|read|ing
re|read|able
re|read|ing +s noun
re-record +s +ed +ing
re-record|ing +s noun
rere|dos
  rere|dos|es
re-release
  re-releas|es
  re-released
  re-releas|ing
re-ride +s
re-roof +s +ed +ing

re|route
  re|routes
  re|rout|ed
  re|rout|ing
rerun
  re|runs
  reran
  rerun
  re|run|ning
res (residence; resolution; for reserve use rez)
  reses
re|salable (use resaleable)
re|sale +s
re|sale|able
re|sched|ule
  re|sched|ules
  re|sched|uled
  re|sched|ul|ing
re|scind +s +ed +ing
re|scind|able
re|scis|sion +s (cancellation)
re|script +s
res|cu|able
res|cue
  res|cues
  res|cued
  res|cu|ing
res|cuee +s
res|cu|er +s
re|seal +s +ed +ing
re|seal|able
re|search
  re|search|es
  re|searched
  re|search|ing
re|search|able
re|search|er +s
re|seat +s +ed +ing (seat again)
  [☞ receipt]
re|sect +s +ed +ing
re|sec|tion +s
re|sec|tion|al
re|seda +s
re|seed +s +ed +ing (seed again)
  [☞ recede]
re|sell
  re|sells
  re|sold
  re|sell|ing
re|sell|er +s
re|sem|blance +s
re|sem|blant
re|sem|ble
  re|sem|bles
  re|sem|bled
  re|sem|bling
re|sent +s +ed +ing

re|sent|ful
re|sent|ful|ly
re|sent|ful|ness
re|sent|ment +s
res|erp|ine
re|serv|able
res|er|va|tion +s
re|serve
  re|serves
  re|served
  re|serv|ing
re|served adjective
re|serv|ed|ly
re|serv|ed|ness
re|serv|er +s
re|serv|ist +s
res|er|voir +s
Ré|ser|voir Gouin (in Canada)
reset
  re|sets
  reset
  re|set|ting
re|set|table
re|set|tle
  re|set|tles
  re|set|tled
  re|set|tling
re|settle|ment +s
re|shape
  re|shapes
  re|shaped
  re|shap|ing
re|shoot
  re|shoots
  re|shot
  re|shoot|ing
re|shuffle
  re|shuf|fles
  re|shuf|fled
  re|shuf|fling
res|ide
  res|ides
  resid|ed
  resid|ing
resi|dence +s
resi|dency
  resi|den|cies
resi|dent +s
resi|den|tial
resi|den|tial|ly
resi|den|tiary
  resi|den|tiar|ies
resi|dent|ship +s
re|sidua
re|sid|ual +s
re|sid|ual|ly
re|sid|uary
resi|due +s
re|sidu|um
  re|sidua
re|sign +s +ed +ing (give up, quit)

re-sign +s +ed +ing (sign again)
re|sig|na|tion +s
re|signed adjective (reconciled)
  [☞ re-signed]
re|sign|ed|ly
re|sign|ed|ness
re|sign|er +s
resile
  re|siles
  re|siled
  resil|ing
re|sili|ence
re|sili|ency
re|sili|ent
re|sili|ent|ly
resin +s +ed +ing
res|in|ate (treat or treated with resin)
  res|in|ates
  res|in|at|ed
  res|in|at|ing
  [☞ resonate]
res|in|oid +s
res|in|ous
re|sist +s +ed +ing
re|sist|ance +s
re|sist|ant
resist|er +s (one who resists)
  [☞ resistor]
re|sist|ibil|ity
re|sist|ible
re|sist|ive
re|sis|tiv|ity
re|sist|less
re|sist|less|ly
re|sis|tor +s (electrical device)
  [☞ resister]
re|siz|able
re|size
  re|sizes
  re|sized
  re|siz|ing
re-skill +s +ed +ing
re|sold
re|sol|uble (that can be resolved or analyzed)
re-soluble (that can be dissolved again)
Reso|lute (settlement, Canada)
reso|lute
reso|lute|ly
reso|lute|ness
reso|lu|tion +s
re|solv|abil|ity
re|solv|able

re|solve
  re|solves
  re|solved
  re|solv|ing
re|solved *adjective*
re|solv|ed|ly
re|solv|ed|ness
re|solv|er +s
res|on|ance +s
res|on|ant
res|on|ant|ly
res|on|ate (resound)
  res|on|ates
  res|on|at|ed
  res|on|at|ing
  [☞ resinate]
res|on|ator +s
re|sorb +s +ed +ing
re|sorb|ence
re|sorb|ent
re|sor|cin|ol
re|sorp|tion
re|sorp|tive
re|sort +s +ed +ing
re|sort|er +s
re|sound +s +ed +ing
re|sound|ing *adjective*
re|sound|ing|ly
re|source
  re|sour|ces
  re|sourced
  re|sour|cing
re|source|ful
re|source|ful|ly
re|source|ful|ness
re|source|less
re|source|less|ness
re|sour|cing *noun*
RESP (Registered
  Educational Savings
  Plan)
  RESPs
re|spect +s +ed +ing
re|spect|abil|ity
re|spect|able
re|spect|ably
re|spect|ed *adjective*
re|spect|er +s
re|spect|ful
re|spect|ful|ly
re|spect|ful|ness
re|spect|ing
  preposition
re|spect|ive
re|spect|ive|ly
re|spell
  re|spells
  re|spelled
  or re|spelt
  re|spell|ing
Res|pighi, Otto|rino
  (Italian composer)
re|spir|able

res|pir|a|tion +s
res|pir|ator +s
res|pira|tory
re|spire
  re|spires
  re|spired
  re|spir|ing
res|pite
  res|pites
  res|pit|ed
  res|pit|ing
re|splen|dence
re|splen|dency
re|splen|dent
re|splen|dent|ly
re|spond +s +ed +ing
re|spond|ent +s
re|spond|er +s
re|sponse +s
re|spon|sibil|ity
  re|spon|sibil|ities
re|spon|sible
re|spon|sible|ness
re|spon|sibly
re|spon|sive
re|spon|sive|ly
re|spon|sive|ness
re|spon|sor|ial
re|spon|sory
  re|spon|sor|ies
re|spray +s +ed +ing
rest +s +ed +ing
  (repose; pause;
  remainder)
  [☞ wrest]
re|stage
  re|stages
  re|staged
  re|staging
re|start +s +ed +ing
re|state
  re|states
  re|stat|ed
  re|stat|ing
re|state|ment +s
res|tau|rant +s
res|tau|ran|teur +s
  (= restaurateur)
res|tau|ra|teur +s
rest|ed *adjective*
rest|ful
Res|ti|gouche (river &
  battle site, Canada;
  salmon)
resti|tu|tion +s
resti|tu|tive
rest|ive
rest|ive|ness
rest|less
rest|less|ly
rest|less|ness
re|stock +s +ed +ing
re|stor|able

Res|tor|a|tion (*English
  History*)
res|tor|a|tion +s (*in
  general use*)
res|tor|a|tion|ism
res|tor|a|tion|ist +s
re|stor|a|tive +s
re|store
  re|stores
  re|stored
  re|stor|ing
re|stored *adjective*
re|stor|er +s
re|strain +s +ed +ing
re|strained *adjective*
re|strain|ed|ly
re|strain|er +s
re|straint +s
re|strict +s +ed +ing
re|strict|ed *adjective*
re|stric|tion +s
re|strict|ive
re|strict|ive|ly
re|strict|ive|ness
re|string
  re|strings
  re|strung
  re|string|ing
rest|room +s
re|struc|ture
  re|struc|tures
  re|struc|tured
  re|struc|tur|ing
re|struc|tur|ing *noun*
re|style
  re|styles
  re|styled
  re|styl|ing
re|sub|mit
  re|sub|mits
  re|sub|mit|ted
  re|sub|mit|ting
re|sult +s +ed +ing
re|sult|ant +s
re|sume (begin again;
  for summary of work
  experience etc. *use*
  resumé)
  re|sumes
  re|sumed
  re|sum|ing
re|su|mé +s
  (summary of work
  experience etc.)
re|sump|tion +s
re|sump|tive
re|sup|ply
  re|sup|plies
  re|sup|plied
  re|sup|ply|ing
re|sur|face
  re|surfa|ces

re|sur|faced
re|surfa|cing
re|sur|gence +s
re|sur|gent
resur|rect +s +ed
  +ing
Resur|rec|tion
  (*Christianity*)
resur|rec|tion +s (*in
  general use*)
re-survey +s +ed
  +ing
re|susci|tate
  re|susci|tates
  re|susci|tat|ed
  re|susci|tat|ing
re|susci|ta|tion +s
re|susci|ta|tive
re|susci|ta|tor +s
ret
  rets
  ret|ted
  ret|ting
re|table +s
re|tab|lo +s
re|tail +s +ed +ing
re|tail|er +s
re|tail|ing *noun*
re|tain +s +ed +ing
re|tain|er +s
re|take
  re|takes
  re|took
  re|taken
  re|tak|ing
re|tali|ate
  re|tali|ates
  re|tali|at|ed
  re|tali|at|ing
re|tali|a|tion +s
re|talia|tory
re|tard +s +ed +ing
  (delay, slow; *offensive*
  developmentally
  handicapped)
  [☞ ritard]
re|tard|ance
re|tard|ancy
re|tard|ant +s
re|tard|ate +s
re|tar|da|tion +s
re|tarda|tory
re|tard|ed *adjective*
re|tard|er +s
retch (gag, vomit)
  retch|es
  retched
  retch|ing
  [☞ wretch]
retch|ing *noun*
rete
  retia

re|tell
  re|tells
  re|told
  re|tell|ing
re|tell|er +s
re|tell|ing +s *noun*
re|ten|tion +s
re|ten|tive
re|ten|tive|ness
re|think
  re|thinks
  re|thought
  re|think|ing
retia
reti|cence
reti|cent
ret|icle +s
re|ticu|la
re|ticu|lar
re|ticu|late
  re|ticu|lates
  re|ticu|lat|ed
  re|ticu|lat|ing
re|ticu|la|tion +s
reti|cule +s
re|ticu|lo|cyte +s
re|ticu|lo|endo|
           thel|ial
re|ticu|lum
  re|ticu|la
retie
  re|ties
  re|tied
  re|tying
Retin-A *proprietary*
ret|ina +s
ret|in|al
retin|itis
retin|itis
  pig|men|tosa
retino|blas|toma
  retino|blas|to|mas
  or
  retino|blas|to|mata
ret|in|ol
retin|op|athy
  retin|op|athies
reti|nue +s
re|tire
  re|tires
  re|tired
  re|tir|ing
re|tired *adjective*
re|tir|ee +s
re|tire|ment +s
re|tir|ing *adjective*
re|title
  re|titles
  re|titled
  re|titling
re|told
re|took
re|tool +s +ed +ing

re|tort +s +ed +ing
re|touch
  re|touch|es
  re|touched
  re|touch|ing
re|touch|er +s
re|touch|ing *noun*
re|trace
  re|traces
  re|traced
  re|tracing
re|tract +s +ed +ing
re|tract|able
re|tract|ile
re|trac|tion +s
re|tract|ive
re|tract|or +s
re|train +s +ed +ing
re|train|ing *noun*
re|trans|mis|sion +s
re|trans|mit
  re|trans|mits
  re|trans|mit|ted
  re|trans|mit|ting
re|tread +s +ed +ing
re|treat +s +ed +ing
re|treat|ant +s
re|trench
  re|trench|es
  re|trenched
  re|trench|ing
re|trench|ment +s
re|trial +s
retri|bu|tion +s
re|tribu|tive
re|triev|able
re|triev|al +s
re|trieve
  re|trieves
  re|trieved
  re|triev|ing
re|triev|er +s
ret|ro +s
retro|active
retro|active|ly
retro|activ|ity
retro|fit
  retro|fits
  retro|fit|ted
  retro|fit|ting
retro|flex
retro|flexed
retro|flex|ion
retro|grade
  retro|grades
  retro|graded
  retro|grad|ing
retro|gress
  retro|gress|es
  retro|gressed
  retro|gress|ing
retro|gres|sion +s
retro|gres|sive

retro|rocket +s
re|trorse
re|trorse|ly
retro|spect +s
retro|spec|tion +s
retro|spect|ive +s
retro|spect|ive|ly
retro|ster|nal
retro|ver|sion +s
retro|vert|ed
retro|viral
retro|virus
  retro|virus|es
retry
  re|tries
  re|tried
  re|try|ing
ret|sina +s
re|tune
  re|tunes
  re|tuned
  re|tun|ing
re|turn +s +ed +ing
re|turn|able
re|turned *adjective*
re|turn|ee +s
re|turn|er +s
re|tuse
re|tying
re|type
  re|types
  re|typed
  re|typ|ing
Reu|ben +s (*Bible*;
  sandwich)
  [☞ Rubens]
Reuch|lin, Johann
  (German humanist)
re|unifi|ca|tion
re|unify
  re|uni|fies
  re|uni|fied
  re|unify|ing
Ré|union (island,
  Indian Ocean)
re|union +s
re|unite
  re|unites
  re|united
  re|uniting
re|uphol|ster +s +ed
  +ing
re|uphol|stery
re|usable
reuse
  re|uses
  re|used
  re|using
re|used *adjective*
Reu|ter, Paul Jul|ius,
  Baron von (German
  news pioneer)

rev
  revs
  revved
  rev|ving
re|vaccin|ate
  re|vaccin|ates
  re|vaccin|at|ed
  re|vaccin|at|ing
re|vaccin|a|tion +s
re|valu|a|tion +s
re|value
  re|values
  re|valued
  re|valu|ing
re|vamp +s +ed +ing
re|vanch|ism
re|vanch|ist +s
RevCan
re|veal +s +ed +ing
re|veal|er +s
re|veal|ing *adjective*
re|veal|ing|ly
re|veget|ate
  re|veget|ates
  re|veget|at|ed
  re|veget|at|ing
re|vegeta|tion
rev|eil|le +s (wake-up
  call)
ré|veil|lon +s
revel
  rev|els
  rev|elled
  rev|el|ling
Rev|el|a|tion (*New
  Testament*)
rev|el|a|tion +s (*in
  general use*)
rev|el|a|tory
rev|el|ler +s
rev|elry
  rev|el|ries
Revel|stoke (city,
  Canada)
rev|en|ant +s
re|venge
  re|ven|ges
  re|venged
  re|ven|ging
re|venge|ful
re|ven|ger +s
rev|enue +s
rev|enu|er +s
re|verb +s
re|ver|ber|ant
re|ver|ber|ant|ly
re|ver|ber|ate
  re|ver|ber|ates
  re|ver|ber|at|ed
  re|ver|ber|at|ing
re|ver|ber|a|tion +s
re|ver|ber|a|tive
re|ver|ber|ator +s

re|ver|ber|a|tory
Re|vere, Paul (US patriot)
re|vere (venerate)
  re|veres
  re|vered
  re|ver|ing
  [☞ revers]
rev|er|ence +s
rev|er|end +s (deserving reverence)
rev|er|ent (feeling or showing reverence)
rev|er|en|tial
rev|er|en|tial|ly
rev|er|ent|ly
rev|erie +s
re|vers (turned-back edge of a garment) plural re|vers
  [☞ reverse]
re|ver|sal +s
re|verse (opposite; turn the other way around)
  re|vers|es
  re|versed
  re|vers|ing
  [☞ revers]
re|verse|ly
re|vers|er +s
re|vers|ibil|ity
re|vers|ible
re|vers|ibly
re|ver|sion +s
re|ver|sion|al
re|ver|sion|ary
re|vert +s +ed +ing
re|vert|er +s
re|vert|ible
revet (fortify a wall)
  re|vets
  revet|ted
  revet|ting
  [☞ rivet]
revet|ment +s
re|view +s +ed +ing (study; revision; critique; journal)
  [☞ revue]
re|view|able
re|view|er
re|vile
  re|viles
  re|viled
  re|vil|ing
re|vile|ment +s
re|vil|er +s
re|vil|ing noun
re|vis|able

re|vise
  re|vis|es
  re|vised
  re|vis|ing
re|vis|er +s
re|vision +s
re|vision|ary
re|vision|ism
re|vision|ist +s
re|visit +s +ed +ing
re|vis|ory
re|vital|iz|a|tion +s
re|vital|ize
  re|vital|iz|es
  re|vital|ized
  re|vital|iz|ing
re|viv|able
re|vival +s
re|vival|ism
re|vival|ist +s
re|vival|is|tic
re|vive
  re|vives
  re|vived
  re|viv|ing
re|vivi|fi|ca|tion
re|vivi|fy
  re|vivi|fies
  re|vivi|fied
  re|vivi|fy|ing
re|voc|able
revo|ca|tion +s
revo|ca|tory
re|voke
  re|vokes
  re|voked
  re|vok|ing
re|vok|er +s
re|volt +s +ed +ing
re|volt|ing adjective
re|volt|ing|ly
revo|lute
revo|lu|tion +s
Revo|lu|tion|ary (of the American or French Revolutions etc.)
  Revo|lu|tion|aries
revo|lu|tion|ary (in general use)
  revo|lu|tion|aries
revo|lu|tion|ist +s
revo|lu|tion|ize
  revo|lu|tion|iz|es
  revo|lu|tion|ized
  revo|lu|tion|iz|ing
Ré|vo|lu|tion tran|quille
re|volve
  re|volves
  re|volved
  re|volv|ing
re|volv|er +s

re|volv|ing door +s (re|volving-door when preceding a noun)
re|vue +s (Theatre)
re|vul|sion +s
re|ward +s +ed +ing
re|ward|ing adjective
re|ward|ing|ly
re|ward|less
re|wash
  re|wash|es
  re|washed
  re|wash|ing
re|weigh +s +ed +ing
re|wind
  re|winds
  re|wound
  re|wind|ing
re|wind|er +s
re|wir|able
re|wire
  re|wires
  re|wired
  re|wir|ing
re|word +s +ed +ing
re|work +s +ed +ing
re|work|ing +s noun
re|wrap
  re|wraps
  re|wrapped
  re|wrap|ping
re|write
  re|writes
  re|wrote
  re|writ|ten
  re|writ|ing
Rex (reigning king)
Reye's syn|drome
Rey|kja|vik (capital of Iceland)
Rey|nolds, Sir Joshua (English painter)
Rey|nolds num|ber +s
rez (reserve, reservation)
  rez|zes
  [☞ res]
re|zone
  re|zones
  re|zoned
  re|zon|ing
Rh (rhesus: in 'Rh factor', 'Rh-positive' etc.)
Rhada|man|thine
Rhada|man|thus (Greek Myth)
Rhaeto-Romance
Rhaeto-Romanic
rhap|sode +s
rhap|sod|ic

rhap|sod|ical
rhap|sod|ical|ly
rhap|sod|ist +s
rhap|sod|ize
  rhap|sod|iz|es
  rhap|sod|ized
  rhap|sod|iz|ing
rhap|sody
  rhap|sod|ies
rhat|any
  rhat|an|ies
Rhea (Greek Myth)
rhea +s
Rhee, Syng|man (Korean statesman)
Rheims (= Reims, France)
Rhen|ish
rhe|nium
rheo|logic|al
rhe|ol|o|gist +s
rhe|ol|ogy
rheo|stat +s
rheo|stat|ic
rhe|sus
rhe|tor +s
rhet|or|ic +s
rhet|or|ic|al
rhet|or|ic|al|ly
rhet|or|ician +s
rheum +s (discharge)
rheum|at|ic
rheum|at|ic|ally
rheum|at|icky
rheuma|tism
rheuma|toid
rheum|ato|logic|al
rheuma|tol|o|gist +s
rheuma|tol|ogy
rheumy (full of rheum)
rhinal
Rhine (river, Europe)
Rhine|land (region, Germany)
Rhineland-Palatin|ate (state, Germany)
rhine|stone +s
rhin|itis
Rhino +s (Rhinoceros Party member)
rhino
  plural rhinos or rhino
Rhin|ocer|os (Rhinoceros Party member)
  plural Rhin|ocer|os or Rhin|ocer|os|es
rhin|ocer|os
  plural rhin|ocer|os or rhin|ocer|os|es

rhino|plas|tic
rhino|plasty
  rhino|plas|ties
rhi|zo|bium
  rhi|zo|bia
rhi|zoid +s
rhi|zoid|al
rhi|zoma|tous
rhi|zome +s
rhizo|pod +s
Rh-negative
rho +s (Greek letter)
rhoda|mine +s
Rhode Island (state, US)
Rhode Island|er +s
Rhode Island Green|ing +s
Rhode Island Red +s
Rhodes (Greek island & its capital)
Rhodes, Cecil John (South African statesman)
Rhodes, Edgar Nel|son (Cdn politician)
Rho|desia (*in former names for* Zambia & Zimbabwe)
Rho|desian +s
Rhodes Schol|ar +s
Rhodes Schol|ar|ship +s
rho|dium
rhodo|chros|ite +s
rhodo|den|dron +s
Rhod|ope (Balkan mountains)
rho|dop|sin
rho|dora +s
rhomb +s (rhombus)
rhombi
rhom|bic
rhombo|hed|ral
rhombo|hed|ron
  rhombo|hed|rons or rhombo|hed|ra
rhom|boid +s
rhom|boid|al
rhom|boid|eus
  rhom|boid|ei
rhom|bus
  rhom|bus|es or rhombi
Rhon|dda (district, Wales)
Rhone (river, Europe)
  [☞ roan]
Rhône-Alpes (region, France)

RHOSP (Registered Home Ownership Savings Plan)
  RHOSPs
rhotic
Rh-positive
rhu|barb +s
Rhum (island, Inner Hebrides)
  [☞ rheum, rum]
rhumb +s (compass point; rhumb line)
rhum|ba (*use* rumba)
  rhum|bas
  rhum|baed or rhumba'd
  rhumba|ing
rhyme (*Prosody*)
  rhymes
  rhymed
  rhym|ing
  [☞ rime]
rhym|er +s
rhyme|ster +s
rhyo|lite +s
rhyo|lit|ic
Rhys, Jean (English writer)
rhythm +s
rhythm and blues (rhythm-and-blues *when preceding a noun*)
rhyth|mic
rhyth|mic|al
rhyth|mic|al|ly
rhyth|mi|city
rhythm|less
rial +s (Iranian & Omani currency)
  [☞ riyal, rile, Ryle]
Ri|alto (Venetian island)
rib
  ribs
  ribbed
  rib|bing
rib|ald
rib|ald|ry
rib|and +s
ribbed *adjective*
Rib|ben|trop, Joa|chim von (German Nazi statesman)
rib|bing +s *noun*
rib|bit
rib|bon +s
rib|boned
ribbon|fish
  plural ribbon|fish or ribbon|fish|es
rib cage +s

Ri|bera, José (or Ju|sepe) de (Spanish painter)
rib-eye +s
rib-knit +s
rib|less
rib|lets
ribo|flavin
ribo|nucle|ic
rib|ose
ribo|som|al
ribo|some +s
rib-tickler +s
rib-tickling
Ri|car|do, David (English economist)
Rice, Elmer (US writer)
Rice, Sir Tim|othy Miles Bin|don (English lyricist)
rice +s
rice cake +s
ricer +s
ri|cer|car +s
ric|er|care +s (= ricercar)
rice-root +s
Rich, Ad|ri|enne Ce|cile (US writer)
Rich, Ber|nard ('Buddy') (US drummer)
rich +er +est
Rich|ard (kings of England)
Ri|chard, Henri ('Pock|et Rock|et') (Cdn hockey player)
Ri|chard, (Jo|seph Henri) Mau|rice ('Rock|et') (Cdn hockey player)
Rich|ards, Ivor Arm|strong (English critic)
Rich|ard|son, John (Cdn soldier & writer)
Rich|ard|son, Sir Ralph David (English actor)
Rich|ard|son, Sam|uel (English novelist)
Rich|ardson's ground squir|rel +s
Riche|lieu (river, Canada)
Riche|lieu, Ar|mand Jean du Ples|sis (French statesman)
rich|en +s +ed +ing

rich|es
Rich|ler, Mor|de|cai (Cdn writer)
rich|ly
Rich|mond (cities, Canada & US; borough of London)
Rich|mond and Len|nox, Charles Len|nox, 4th Duke of (governor-in-chief of BNA)
Rich|mond Hill (city, Canada)
Richmond-upon-Thames (= Richmond, England)
rich|ness
Rich|ter, Bur|ton (US physicist)
Rich|ter, Jo|hann Paul Fried|rich (= Jean Paul)
Rich|ter scale
Richt|hof|en, Baron Man|fred von (Red Baron)
ricin
rick +s +ed +ing
rick|et|i|ness
rick|ets
rick|ett|sia
  rick|ett|siae or rick|ett|sias
rick|ett|sial
rick|ety
rick|ey +s
rick|rack +s
rick|sha +s (*use* rickshaw)
rick|shaw +s
rico|chet +s +ed +ing
ri|cotta
ric|rac +s (*use* rickrack)
ric|tal
ric|tus
  ric|tus|es
rid
  rids
  rid
  rid|ding
rid|able (*use* rideable)
rid|dance
rid|ded *archaic past & past participle of* rid
rid|den *adjective*
rid|dle
  rid|dles
  rid|dled
  rid|dling
rid|dler +s

rid|dling *adjective*
rid|dling|ly
RIDE (random spot check program)
ride
  rides
  rode
  rid|den
  rid|ing
ride|able
Ri|deau (river, canal & falls, Canada)
Ri|deau Hall
ride off *verb*
  rides off
  rode off
  rid|den off
  rid|ing off
ride-off +s *noun*
ride on *verb*
  rides on
  rode on
  rid|den on
  rid|ing on
ride-on *adjective*
  preceding a noun
rider +s
rider|less
rider|ship
ridge
  ridges
  ridged
  ridg|ing
ridged *adjective &*
  conjugated form of
  ridge
  [☞ rigid]
ridge|pole +s
ridge|top +s
Ridge|way (battle site, Canada)
ridge|way +s
ridgy
  ridg|i|er
  ridg|i|est
ridi|cule
  ridi|cules
  ridi|culed
  ridi|cul|ing
ri|dicu|lous
ri|dicu|lous|ly
ri|dicu|lous|ness
rid|ing +s *noun*
Rid|ing Moun|tain (escarpment & national park, Canada)
Rid|ley, Nicho|las (English bishop)
Rief|en|stahl, Leni (German filmmaker)
Riel, Louis (Metis leader)

Rie|mann, (Georg Fried|rich) Bern|hard (German mathematician)
Rie|mann|ian
Ri|en|zi, Cola di (Italian popular leader)
Ri|en|zo, Cola di (= Rienzi)
Ries|ling +s
Rif (mountains, Morocco)
  [☞ riff, RRIF]
ri|fam|pi|cin
ri|fam|pin
rife
rife|ness
riff +s +ed +ing (musical phrase)
  [☞ Rif, RRIF]
rif|fle
  rif|fles
  rif|fled
  rif|fling
riff-raff
rifle
  rifles
  rifled
  rif|ling
rifle|man
  rifle|men
rif|ling *noun*
rift +s +ed +ing
Rift Val|ley (in Great Rift Valley, Africa)
rift val|ley +s
rig
  rigs
  rigged
  rig|ging
Riga (capital of Latvia)
  [☞ Ryga]
riga|ma|role +s (= rigmarole)
riga|toni
Rigel (star)
rigged *adjective*
rigged out *adjective*
rig|ger +s (person involved in rigs or rigging; Forestry; Rowing; ship)
  [☞ rigor, rigour, de rigueur]
rig|ging +s *noun*
Right (in 'Right Honourable' & 'Right Reverend')
  [☞ Wright]
right +s +ed +ing +er +est (just; correct; opposite of left; angle; fair claim;

restore; immediately; quite)
  [☞ rite, wright, write]
right|able (that can be righted)
right angle +s
right-angled
right-centre (Baseball)
right|eous
right|eous|ly
right|eous|ness
right|er +s (comparative of right; in 'animal righter' etc.)
  [☞ writer]
right field
right field|er +s
right-footed
right|ful
right|ful|ly
right|ful|ness
right hand +s *noun*
right-hand *adjective*
right-handed
right-handed|ly
right-handed|ness
right-hander +s
Right Hon|our|able
right|ish
right|ism
right|ist +s
right|less (without rights)
  [☞ riteless]
right|less|ness
right|ly
right-minded
right|most
right|ness
righto
right-of-centre
right-of-way
  rights-of-way
Right Rev|er|end
right|sizing
right-thinking
right-to-life
right-to-lifer +s
right|ward
right|wards
right wing +s *noun*
right-wing *adjective*
right wing|er +s
righty
  right|ies
rigid (inflexible)
rigid|ify
  rigid|ifies
  rigid|ified
  rigid|ify|ing

rigid|ity
  rigid|ities
rigid|ly
rigid|ness
rig|ma|role +s
rig|or +s (feeling of cold; rigidity; in 'rigor mortis'; for severity, exactitude, strictness, austerity use rigour)
  [☞ rigger, de rigueur]
rigor mor|tis
rigor|ous
rigor|ous|ly
rigor|ous|ness
rig|our +s (severity, exactitude, strictness, austerity)
  [☞ rigor, rigger, de rigueur]
rig out *verb*
  rigs out
  rigged out
  rig|ging out
rig-out +s *noun*
Rig-Veda (Hinduism)
Rij|eka (city, Croatia)
rijst|tafel
Rila (mountains, Bulgaria)
rile (irritate, stir up)
  riles
  riled
  riling
  [☞ rial, riyal, Ryle]
Rilke, Rai|ner Maria (Austrian poet)
rill +s (stream; channel; for cleft on moon's surface use rille)
rille +s (cleft on moon's surface)
  [☞ rill]
ril|lettes
rim
  rims
  rimmed
  rim|ming
Rim|baud, (Jean Nicho|las) Ar|thur (French poet)
rime (frost; archaic variant of rhyme)
  rimes
  rimed
  riming
  [☞ rhyme]
rim|fire
Rim|ini (city, Italy)
Rim|mon (deity)

Ri|mou|ski (city, Canada)
rim|rock +s
Rimsky-Korsakov, Niko|lai Andre|evich (Russian composer)
rimy
  rimi|er
  rimi|est
rind +s +ed +ing
rind|ed *adjective*
rin|der|pest
rind|less
ring
• (circle etc.)
  rings
  ringed
  ring|ing
• (sound)
  rings
  rang
  rung
  ring|ing
  [☞ wring]
ring|bark +s +ed +ing
ring bear|er +s
ring-billed
ring|bolt +s
ringed *adjective*
ring|er +s (imposter; substitute; thing that rings)
  [☞ wringer]
Ringer's solu|tion
ring|ette
ring|ing *adjective* (that rings)
  [☞ wringing]
ring|ing|ly
ring|lead|er +s
ring|less
ring|let +s
ring|let|ed
ring|lety
ring|master +s
ring|neck +s
ring-necked
ring-pull +s
ring road +s
ring|side
ring|sider +s
ring|tail +s
ring-tailed
ring toss
ring|worm +s
rink +s
rink rat +s
rink|side
rinky-dink
rins|able

rinse
  rins|es
  rinsed
  rins|ing
rins|er +s
Rio (= the city of Rio de Janeiro, Brazil)
Rio Bran|co (city, Brazil)
Rio de Ja|neiro (state & its capital, Brazil)
Rio de Oro (arid region, Africa)
Rio Gran|de (river, N America)
Rio Gran|de do Norte (state, Brazil)
Rio Gran|de do Sul (state, Brazil)
Ri|oja +s
Rio Muni (area, Equatorial Guinea)
Rio Negro (river, S America)
Rio|pelle, Jean-Paul (Cdn artist)
riot +s +ed +ing (violent disturbance)
  [☞ ryot]
riot|er +s
riot|ous
riot|ous|ly
riot|ous|ness
rip
  rips
  ripped
  rip|ping
ri|par|ian
rip cord +s
ripe
  riper
  rip|est
ripe|ly
rip|en +s +ed +ing
ripe|ness
Rip|ley, George (US social reformer)
  [☞ ripply]
rip off *verb*
  rips off
  ripped off
  rip|ping off
rip-off +s *noun*
ri|poste
  ri|postes
  ri|post|ed
  ri|post|ing
ripped *adjective*
rip|per +s
rip|ping *adjective*
rip|ping|ly

rip|ple
  rip|ples
  rip|pled
  rip|pling
rip|plet +s
rip|ply (having ripples)
  [☞ Ripley]
rip-rap
  rip-raps
  rip-rapped
  rip-rapping
rip-roaring
rip-roaring|ly
rip|saw +s
rip|snort|er +s
rip-snorting
rip-snorting|ly
rip|stop
rip|tide +s
Rip Van Win|kle
RISC (*Computing*)
  RISCs
  [☞ risk]
rise
  rises
  rose
  risen
  ris|ing
  [☞ Reye's syndrome]
ris|er +s
rishi +s
risi|bil|ity
ris|ible
ris|ibly
ris|ing +s *noun & adjective*
risk +s +ed +ing (chance of loss; expose to risk)
  [☞ RISC]
risk-averse
risk|i|ly
risk|i|ness
risky
  risk|i|er
  risk|i|est
Ri|sor|gi|mento
ris|otto +s
ris|qué
ris|sole +s
rit. (ritardando)
  [☞ writ]
Rit|alin *proprietary*
ri|tard +s (*Music*)
  [☞ retard]
rit|ar|dando
  rit|ar|dan|dos or
  rit|ar|dandi
Ritch|ie, John W. (Cdn politician)
rite +s (religious observance, ritual)

  [☞ right, write, wright]
rite|less (without a rite)
rit|or|nello
  rit|or|nel|los or
  rit|or|nelli
rit|ual +s
rit|ual|ism
rit|ual|ist +s
rit|ual|is|tic
rit|ual|is|tic|ally
rit|ual|iz|a|tion +s
rit|ual|ize
  rit|ual|iz|es
  rit|ual|ized
  rit|ual|iz|ing
rit|ual|ly
ritz
ritz|i|ly
ritz|i|ness
ritzy
  ritz|i|er
  ritz|i|est
rival
  ri|vals
  ri|valled
  rival|ling
ri|val|rous
ri|valry
  rival|ries
rive
  rives
  rived
  riven
  riv|ing
riv|er +s
Ri|vera, Diego (Mexican painter)
river|bank +s
river|bed +s
river|boat +s
river drive +s *noun*
river-drive *verb*
  river-drives
  river-drove
  river-driven
  river-driving
river driv|er +s
river|front +s
river|ine
river|less
river lot +s
river|man
  river|men
River|side (city, US)
river|side
River|view (town, Canada)
riv|et +s +ed +ing (nail, bolt; join)
  [☞ revet]
rivet|er +s

rivet|ing *adjective*
Rivi|era (Mediterranean coastal region)
Ri|vière aux Feuilles (river, Canada)
Ri|vière aux Ou|tardes (river, Canada)
Ri|vière-du-Loup (town, Canada)
Rivne (city, Ukraine)
rivu|let +s
Riy|adh (capital of Saudi Arabia)
riyal +s (Saudi, Qatari & Yemeni currency) [☞ **rial**, **Ryle**]
Rizal, José (Philippine nationalist)
Riz|zio, David (secretary to Mary, Queen of Scots)
RN (registered nurse)
RNs
RNA (ribonucleic acid; registered nursing assistant)
RNAs
roach
• (cockroach; cigarette butt; *Nautical*) *plural* **roach|es**
• (fish) *plural* **roach** or **roach|es**
roach clip +s
road +s (street) [☞ **rode**, **Rhodes Scholar**, **Rhode Island**]
road apple +s
road|bed +s
road|block +s
road cut +s
road|eo +s (driving or cycling competition) [☞ **rodeo**]
road gang +s
road hock|ey
road hog +s
road|hold|ing
road|house +s
road|ie +s
road|kill +s
road-killed
road|less
road map +s
road|run|ner +s
road salt
road show +s
road|side +s
road sign +s

road|stead +s
road|ster +s
road test +s *noun*
road-test +s +ed +ing *verb*
Road Town (capital of the British Virgin Islands)
road trip +s *noun*
road-trip *verb*
road-trips
road-tripped
road-tripping
road|way +s
road-weary
road|work +s
road|worthi|ness
road|worthy
roam +s +ed +ing
roam|er +s
roan +s [☞ **Rhone**]
roar +s +ed +ing
roar|er +s
roar|ing *adjective*
roar|ing|ly
Roar|ing Twen|ties
roast +s +ed +ing
roast|er +s
roast|ing +s *adjective & noun*
rob
robs
robbed
rob|bing
Ro|barts, John Par|men|ter (Cdn politician)
Robbe-Grillet, Alain (French novelist)
rob|ber +s
rob|bery
rob|ber|ies
Rob|bia, An|drea della (Italian ceramicist)
Rob|bia, Luca della (Italian ceramicist)
Rob|bins, Jer|ome (US choreographer) [☞ **robin**]
robe
robes
robed
robing
Rob|ert (kings of Scotland)
Rob|erts, Sir Charles George Doug|las (Cdn writer)
Rob|ert|son +s *proprietary* (screwdriver etc.)

Rob|ert the Bruce (Robert I of Scotland)
Rober|val (town, Canada)
Rober|val, Jean-François de La Rocque, Sieur de (French colonial explorer)
Robe|son, Paul Bus|till (US entertainer & activist) [☞ **Robson**]
Robes|pierre, Maxi|mi|lien Fran|çois Marie Isi|dore de (French revolutionary)
Robi|chaud, Louis Jo|seph (Cdn politician)
rob|in +s [☞ **Robbins**]
Robin Hood +s (legendary outlaw)
rob|inia +s
robin's egg blue +s (**robin's-egg-blue** *when preceding a noun*)
Rob|in|son, Ed|ward G. (US actor)
Rob|in|son, Edwin Ar|ling|ton (US poet)
Rob|in|son, Jack Roos|evelt ('Jackie') (US baseball player)
Rob|in|son, Mary (Irish president)
Rob|in|son, Sugar Ray (US boxer)
Rob|in|son, Wil|liam ('Smokey') (US singer-songwriter)
Rob|lin, Duf|fer|in ('Duff') (Cdn politician)
Rob|lin, Sir Rod|mond Palen (Cdn politician)
robor|ant +s
ro|bot +s
ro|bot|ic
ro|bot|ic|ally
ro|bot|icist +s
ro|bot|ics
ro|bot|iz|a|tion
ro|bot|ize
ro|bot|iz|es
ro|bot|ized
ro|bot|iz|ing

Rob Roy (Scottish outlaw)
Rob|son (mountain, Canada) [☞ **Robeson**]
ro|bust +er +est
ro|busta +s
ro|bust|ly
ro|bust|ness
ROC (Canada outside Quebec)
roc +s (bird)
ro|caille +s
roc|am|bole +s
roche mou|ton|née
roches mou|ton|nées
Ro|cher Percé (prominent offshore rock, Canada)
Ro|ches|ter (city, US; town, England)
Ro|ches|ter, John Wil|mot, 2nd Earl of (English poet)
roch|et +s
Rock (Newfoundland; Gibraltar) [☞ **ROC**]
rock +s +ed +ing (*Geology*; *Music*; sway, shake) [☞ **roc**]
rock|a|billy
Rock|all (N Atlantic islet)
rock and roll +s +ed +ing (= **rock 'n' roll**; **rock-and-roll** *when preceding a noun*)
rock and roll|er +s (= **rock 'n' roller**)
rock bed +s
rock bot|tom *noun*
rock-bottom *adjective*
rock-bound
rock|burst +s
Rock|cliffe (Park) (neighbourhood, Canada)
rock climb +s +ed +ing
rock climb|er +s
rock climb|ing *noun*
Rock Cor|nish game hen +s
rock cress
rock cut +s
rock dove +s
Rocke|fel|ler, John Davi|son (US industrialist)

Rocke|fel|ler, John
Davi|son Jr. (US
philanthropist)
Rocke|fel|ler, Nel|son
Ald|rich (US vice-
president)
rock|er +s
rock|ery
rock|eries
rock|et +s +ed +ing
(missile; engine;
plant)
[☞ roquet]
rocket|eer +s
rock|et|ry
rock|et ship +s
rock|fall +s
rock|fish
plural rock|fish or
rock|fish|es
Rock For|est (town,
Canada)
Rock|hamp|ton (city,
Australia)
rock-hard
rock|hop|per +s
rock|hound +s
rock|hound|ing
rock|i|er
Rock|ies (= Rocky
Mountains,
N America)
rock|i|est
rock|i|ly
rock|i|ness
Rock|ing|ham,
Charles Watson-
Wentworth, 2nd
Mar|quess of
(British prime
minister)
Rock|land (town,
Canada)
rock|like
rock|ling
plural rock|ling or
rock|lings
Rock|ne, Knute
Ken|neth (US
football coach)
rock 'n' roll +s +ed
+ing
rock 'n' roll|er +s
rock pool +s
rock-ribbed
rock rose +s
rock salt
rock slide +s
rock-solid
rock-steady adjective
rock|steady noun
rocku|men|tary
rocku|men|tar|ies

rock|weed +s
Rock|well, Nor|man
(US artist)
rock|wool
rocky
rock|i|er
rock|i|est
Rocky Moun|tain +s
(mountain system,
N America; goat;
spotted fever)
Rocky Moun|tain
House (town,
Canada)
ro|coco
rod +s
[☞ Fort Rodd Hill]
Rod|den|berry,
Eu|gene Wes|ley
('Gene') (Star Trek
creator)
rode +s (past tense of
ride; rope)
[☞ road, Rhode
Island]
ro|dent +s
ro|den|tial
ro|den|ti|cide +s
rodent-like
rodeo (competition for
cattle roping &
wrestling etc.)
ro|de|os
ro|de|oed
rodeo|ing
[☞ roadeo]
Rodg|ers, Rich|ard
Charles (US
composer)
[☞ Rogers]
Rodin, (René
Fran|çois) Au|guste
(French sculptor)
rod|less
rod-like
rod|man
rod|men
Rod|ney, George
Brydg|es, 1st Baron
(English admiral)
rod|ney +s
rodo|mon|tade
Roe, Sir (Edwin)
Al|liott Ver|don
(English aircraft
designer)
[☞ Rowe]
roe
• (fish eggs or milt)
plural roes
• (deer)
plural roe or roes
[☞ row, rho]

roe|buck
plural roe|buck or
roe|bucks
roe-deer
plural roe-deer
Roent|gen, Wil|helm
Kon|rad (German
physicist)
roent|gen +s
roent|geno|graph|ic
roent|geno|
graph|ic|ally
roent|gen|og|raphy
roent|gen|ol|ogy
roent|gen rays
Roese|lare (town,
Belgium)
Roeth|ke, Theo|dore
(US poet)
ro|ga|tion +s
ro|ga|tion|al
roger +s +ed +ing
Rogers (mountain
pass, Canada;
surname)
[☞ Rodgers]
Rogers, Al|bert
Bow|man (US-born
railway surveyor)
Rogers, Gin|ger (US
actress)
Rogers, Sir Rich|ard
George (English
architect)
Rogers, Stan (Cdn
singer-songwriter)
Rogers, Wil|liam
Penn Adair ('Will')
(US humorist)
Roget, Peter Mark
(English philologist)
rogue
rogues
rogued
roguing
roguery
roguer|ies
rogues' gal|lery
rogues' gal|ler|ies
roguish
roguish|ly
roguish|ness
'roid +s
'roid rage
roil +s +ed +ing
(agitate)
[☞ royal]
roily (turbidly,
agitatedly)
[☞ royally]
rois|ter +s +ed +ing
rois|ter|er +s

rois|ter|ing adjective &
noun
rois|ter|ous
Ro|land (hero of
Chanson de Roland)
[☞ Rolland]
role +s (part played in
a film etc.)
[☞ roll]
role play noun
role-play +s +ed
+ing verb
role play|er +s
role-playing
Rolf (= Rollo, Norse
chieftain)
roll +s +ed +ing (turn
over; display film
credits; sound; rob;
list; food)
[☞ role]
roll|able
Rol|land, Ro|main
(French writer)
[☞ Roland]
roll|away +s
roll back verb
rolls back
rolled back
roll|ing back
roll|back +s noun
roll bar +s
roll cage +s
roll call +s
rolled adjective
roll|er +s
roller|ball +s
Roller|blade +s
proprietary noun
roller|blade verb
roller|blades
roller|blad|ed
roller|blad|ing
roller|blad|er +s
roller|coast +s +ed
+ing
roll|er coast|er +s
noun
roller-coaster +s +ed
+ing adjective & verb
Roll|er Derby
proprietary
Roll|er Der|bies
roll|er skate
roll|er skates
roll|er skat|ed
roll|er skat|ing
roll|er skat|er +s
rol|lick +s +ed +ing
rol|lick|ing adjective
roll|ie +s
[☞ roly-poly]
roll|mop +s

roll-neck +s
Rollo (Norse chieftain)
roll on *verb*
  rolls on
  rolled on
  roll|ing on
roll-on +s *adjective &*
  noun
roll-on roll-off
roll out *verb*
  rolls out
  rolled out
  roll|ing out
roll|out +s *noun*
roll over *verb*
  rolls over
  rolled over
  roll|ing over
roll|over +s *noun*
Rolls, Charles
  Stew|art (English car
  manufacturer)
roll|top
roll up *verb*
  rolls up
  rolled up
  roll|ing up
roll-up +s *adjective &*
  noun
roll-your-own +s
Rolo|dex *proprietary*
  Rolo|dex|es
roly-poly
  roly-polies
ROM (read-only
  memory)
  ROMs
  [☞ rhomb]
Rom (gypsy)
  Roma
  [☞ rhomb]
Roma +s (tomato)
  [☞ Rama]
ro|maine
Ro|mains, Jules
  (French writer)
romaji
Rom|an +s (of Rome;
  alphabet)
roman (typeface)
roman à clef
  romans à clef
Roman Cath|olic +s
Ro|mance (languages)
ro|mance (love affair;
  excitement; *Music*;
  Literature; woo)
  ro|man|ces
  ro|manced
  ro|man|cing
ro|man|cer +s
Roman|esque

roman-fleuve
  romans-fleuves
Ro|ma|nia (country,
  Europe)
Ro|ma|nian +s
Ro|man|ic
Roman|ism
Roman|ist +s
roman|iz|a|tion
roman|ize
  roman|iz|es
  roman|ized
  roman|iz|ing
Ro|mano
Roma|nov (Russian
  dynasty)
Roma|now, Roy John
  (Cdn politician)
Rom|ans (*Bible*)
Ro|mansh
ro|man|tic +s
ro|man|tic|ally
Ro|man|ti|cism
  (artistic movement
  beginning in the late
  19th c.)
ro|man|ti|cism (any
  romantic tendency in
  art etc.)
ro|man|ti|cist +s
ro|man|ti|ciz|a|tion
  +s
ro|man|ti|cize
  ro|man|ti|ciz|es
  ro|man|ti|cized
  ro|man|ti|ciz|ing
Rom|any
  Rom|an|ies
Rome (capital of Italy;
  Roman Empire)
  [☞ roam]
Rome Beauty
  Rome Beaut|ies
Romeo +s
Rom|ish
romp +s +ed +ing
romp|er +s
rompy
  romp|i|er
  romp|i|est
Rom|ulus (*Roman
  Myth*)
Ron|ces|valles (battle
  site, Spain)
Ron|ce|vaux
  (= Roncesvalles)
ron|deau (*Prosody*)
  ron|deaux
  [☞ rondo]
ron|del +s
rondo +s (*Music*)
  [☞ rondeau]

Ron|dônia (state,
  Brazil)
Ronga
  plural Ronga or
  Ron|gas
ronin
  plural ronin
Ron|sard, Pierre de
  (French poet)
Rönt|gen, Wil|helm
  Kon|rad
  (= Roentgen)
rönt|gen +s (*use*
  roentgen)
rönt|geno|graph|ic
  (*use*
  roentgenographic)
rönt|geno|
      graph|ic|ally
  (*use*
  roentgenographically)
rönt|gen|og|raphy
  (*use*
  roentgenography)
rönt|gen|ol|ogy (*use*
  roentgenology)
roo +s (kangaroo)
  [☞ rue, roux]
rood +s (crucifix;
  quarter of an acre)
  [☞ rude]
roof +s +ed +ing
roofed *adjective*
roof|er +s
roof gar|den +s
roof|ing +s *noun*
roof|less
roof|line +s
roof rack +s
roof|top +s
roof|tree +s
rook +s +ed +ing
rook|ery
  rook|eries
rook|ie +s
room +s +ed +ing
  (space; enclosed part
  of building; lodge)
  [☞ rheum]
room|er +s
room|ette +s
room|ful +s
room|ie +s *noun*
  (roommate)
  [☞ roomy,
  rheumy]
room|i|ness
room|ing house +s
room|mate +s
roomy *adjective*
  (spacious)
  room|i|er
  room|i|est

  [☞ roomie,
  rheumy]
Roon|ey, Mick|ey (US
  actor)
Roos|evelt, (Anna)
  Elea|nor (US
  humanitarian &
  diplomat)
Roos|evelt, Frank|lin
  Del|ano (US
  president)
Roos|evelt,
  Theo|dore (US
  president)
Roos|evelt|ian +s
roost +s +ed +ing
roost|er +s
roost|er tail +s
Root (mountain,
  Canada–Alaska
  border)
root +s +ed +ing
  (part of plant; origin;
  Math; fix; rummage;
  cheer)
  [☞ route]
root ball +s
root beer +s
root can|al +s
root|ed *adjective*
root|ed|ness
root|er +s
  (rummaging animal;
  fan)
  [☞ router]
rootin' tootin'
roo|tle
  roo|tles
  roo|tled
  root|ling
root|less
root|less|ness
root|let +s
root|like
root-mean-square
  +s
root|si|ness
root|stock +s
root|sy
  root|si|er
  root|si|est
rooty
rope
  ropes
  roped
  rop|ing
rope-a-dope
rope burn +s
rope dan|cer +s
rope lad|der +s
rope|like
roper +s
rope-walker +s

ropey (*use* ropy)
  ropi|er
  ropi|est
rop|ing +s *noun*
ropy
  ropi|er
  ropi|est
Roque|fort *proprietary*
ro|quet +s +ed +ing
  (*Croquet*)
  [☞ rocket]
Ror|aima (mountain,
  S America; state,
  Brazil)
ror|qual +s
Ror|schach
  (*Psychology*)
ros|aceous
Ros|ario (city,
  Argentina)
ros|ary
  ros|aries
Ros|com|mon (county
  & town, Ireland)
rose +s
rosé +s
ros|eate
Ros|eau (capital of
  Dominica)
  [☞ Rosseau]
rose|bay +s
Rose|bery, 5th Earl of
  (British prime
  minister)
rose|bowl +s
rose-breasted
rose|bud +s
rose bush
  rose bush|es
rose chaf|er +s
rose-coloured
Rose|dale
  (neighbourhood,
  Canada)
rose|fish
  plural rose|fish or
  rose|fish|es
rose|hip +s
rose|like
rose|maling
rose|mary
Rose|mère (town,
  Canada)
Rosen|berg, Al|fred
  (German Nazi)
Rosen|berg, Jul|ius &
  Ethel (US spies)
ros|eola
ros|eo|lar
ros|eo|lous
rose pink *noun*
rose-pink *adjective*
rose red *noun*

rose-red *adjective*
rose|root +s
rose-tinted
Ros|etta stone +s
ros|ette +s
rose|water
rose|wood +s
Rosh Cho|desh
  (*Judaism*)
Rosh Hash|anah
  (*Judaism*)
roshi +s
Rosi|cru|cian +s
ros|i|er
ros|i|est
ros|i|ly
ros|in +s +ed +ing
ros|i|ness
ros|iny
Ros|kilde (city,
  Denmark)
Ross (dependency,
  sea, ice shelf,
  Antarctica; rifle)
  [☞ Ross's gull]
Ross, Diana (US
  singer)
Ross, Sir George
  Wil|liam (Cdn
  politician)
Ross, (James)
  Sin|clair (Cdn writer)
Ross, Sir James Clark
  (English explorer)
Ross, Sir John
  (English explorer)
Ross, Sir Ron|ald
  (English physician)
Ross and Crom|arty
  (former county,
  Scotland)
Ros|seau (lake,
  Canada)
  [☞ Roseau]
Ros|sel|lini, Ro|ber|to
  (Italian filmmaker)
Ros|setti, Chris|tina
  Geor|gina (English
  poet)
Ros|setti, Dante
  Gab|riel (English
  painter & poet)
Ros|si|gnol (lake,
  Canada)
Ros|sini, Gioac|chino
  An|tonio (Italian
  composer)
Ross|lare (port,
  Ireland)
Ross's gull +s
Ros|tand, Ed|mond
  (French writer)
ros|ter +s +ed +ing

rösti
Ros|tock (city,
  Germany)
Ros|tov (= Rostov-
  on-Don, Russia)
Rostov-on-Don (city,
  Russia)
ros|tra
ros|tral
ros|tral|ly
ros|trate
Ros|trop|ovich,
  Msti|slav
  Leo|pold|ovich (US
  musician)
ros|trum
  ros|tra or ros|trums
rosy
  ros|i|er
  ros|i|est
rot (decay; disease;
  nonsense)
  rots
  rot|ted
  rot|ting
  [☞ wrought]
Rota (*Catholicism*)
rota +s (roster)
Ro|tar|ian +s
Ro|tary (club)
ro|tary
  ro|tar|ies
rotary-dial
ro|tat|able
ro|tate
  ro|tates
  ro|tat|ed
  ro|tat|ing
ro|ta|tion +s
ro|ta|tion|al
ro|ta|tion|al|ly
ro|ta|tor +s
ro|ta|tory
rota|virus
  rota|virus|es
rote (routine; in 'by
  rote')
  [☞ wrote]
rote|none
rot|gut
Roth, Phil|ip Mil|ton
  (US writer)
  [☞ wroth]
Roth|er|ham (city,
  England)
Roth|ko, Mark (US
  painter)
Roths|child, Meyer
  Am|schel (German
  financier)
roti +s
roti|fer +s
ro|tini

ro|tis|serie
  ro|tis|ser|ies
  ro|tis|ser|ied
  ro|tis|serie|ing
roto|grav|ure +s
rotor +s
Roto-Rooter +s
  proprietary
Roto|rua (city, New
  Zealand)
roto|till +s +ed +ing
Roto|till|er +s
rot|ten +er +est
rot|ten|ness
rot|ten|stone
rot|ter +s
Rot|ter|dam (city, the
  Netherlands)
rot|ting *adjective*
Rott|weil|er +s
ro|tund
ro|tun|da +s
ro|tund|ity
Rou|ault, Georges
  Henri (French artist)
roué +s
Rouen (city, France)
rouge (red colouring;
  Football; polishing
  agent; colour)
  rouges
  rouged
  rou|ging
rouge +s (*Quebec
  Politics*)
rouge-et-noir
Rou|get de Lisle,
  Claude Jo|seph
  (composer of 'La
  Marseillaise')
rough +er +est +s
  +ed +ing (coarse;
  rugged; harsh;
  approximate)
  [☞ ruff]
rough|age +s
rough-and-tumble
rough|cast
rough cut +s *noun*
rough-cut *adjective*
rough|en +s +ed +ing
rough-hew
  rough-hews
  rough-hewed
  rough-hewn
  rough-hewing
rough-hewn *adjective*
rough|house
  rough|hous|es
  rough|housed
  rough|hous|ing
rough|hous|ing *noun*

rough in *verb*
  roughs in
  roughed in
  rough|ing in
rough-in +s *noun*
rough|ing *noun*
rough-legged
rough|ly (in a rough
  manner)
  [☞ **ruffly**]
rough|neck +s +ed
  +ing
rough|ness
rough|out +s
rough ride +s
Rough Rider +s
  (Ottawa CFL team)
Rough|rider +s
  (Saskatchewan CFL
  team)
rough|rider +s
rough|shod
roughy
  rough|ies
rou|ille
rou|lade +s
rou|leau
  rou|leaux *or*
  rou|leaus
rou|lette +s
  rou|let|ted
Rou|melia
  (= Rumelia, former
  Ottoman territory)
round +s +ed +ing
  +er +est
round|about +s
round|ed *adjective*
round|ed|ly
round|ed|ness
round|el +s
round|elay +s
round|er +s
Round|head +s
round|house +s
round|ish
round|ly
round|ness
round rob|in +s
  (round-robin *when
  preceding a noun*)
round-shouldered
rounds|man
  rounds|men
round table +s
  (round-table *when
  preceding a noun*)
round-the-clock
round trip +s (round-
  trip *when preceding a
  noun*)
round-tripper +s

round up *verb*
  rounds up
  round|ed up
  round|ing up
round|up +s *noun*
round|wood
round|worm +s
roup
roupy
rous|able
rouse
  rous|es
  roused
  rous|ing
rous|er +s
rous|ing *adjective*
rous|ing|ly
Rousse (= Ruse,
  Bulgaria)
**Rous|seau, Henri
  Julien** ('le
  Doua|nier') (French
  painter)
**Rous|seau, Jean-
  Jacques** (French
  philosopher)
**Rous|seau, (Pierre
  Étienne) Théo|dore**
  (French painter)
Rous|seau|ian
Rous|seau|ist +s
Rous|sil|lon (former
  province, France)
roust +s +ed +ing
roust|about +s
rout +s +ed +ing
  (defeat, retreat;
  rummage; cut a
  groove)
  [☞ **route**]
route (path, course)
  routes
  rout|ed
  rout|ing
  [☞ **root, rout**]
route march
  route march|es
  route marched
  route march|ing
rout|er +s (tool used
  for cutting grooves;
  Computing)
  [☞ **rooter**]
rou|tine +s
rou|tine|ly
rou|tin|iz|a|tion
rou|tin|ize
  rou|tin|iz|es
  rou|tin|ized
  rou|tin|iz|ing
roux (sauce thickener)
  plural **roux**
  [☞ **rue**]

Rouyn-Noranda (city,
  Canada)
Ro|van|iemi (town,
  Finland)
rove
  roves
  roved
  rov|ing
Rov|er +s (*Scouting*)
rov|er +s
rov|ing *adjective*
Rovno (= Rivne,
  Ukraine)
row +s +ed +ing
  (column, tier; propel
  with oars; dispute)
  [☞ **Rowe, roe, rho**]
rowan +s
rowan|berry
  rowan|ber|ries
rowan tree +s
row|boat +s
row|di|ly
row|di|ness
rowdy
  row|di|er
  row|di|est
  row|dies
row|dy|ism
Rowe, Nicho|las
  (English dramatist)
  [☞ **Roe**]
rowel
  row|els
  row|elled
  row|el|ling
row|er +s
row house +s
**Row|land|son,
  Thom|as** (English
  artist)
row|lock +s
Rown|tree (family of
  English
  entrepreneurs &
  philanthropists)
**Roxas (y Acuña),
  Man|uel** (Philippine
  statesman)
Rox|boro (town,
  Canada)
Rox|burgh|shire
  (former county,
  Scotland)
Roy, Gab|ri|elle (Cdn
  novelist)
Royal (mountain,
  Canada)
roy|al +s (regal)
  [☞ **roil**]
Roy|ale, Île (*former
  name for* **Cape
  Breton Island,**
  Canada)

royal|ism
royal|ist +s
royal|ly (regally)
  [☞ **roily**]
roy|al|ty
  roy|al|ties
royal 'we'
**Royce, Sir
  (Fred|erick) Henry**
  (English engine
  designer)
Royce, Jo|siah (US
  philosopher)
roz|zer +s
RPG (report program
  generator; rocket-
  propelled grenade;
  role-playing game)
  RPGs
rpm (revolutions per
  minute)
  rpms
RPN (registered
  practical nurse)
  RPNs
RRIF (Registered
  Retirement Income
  Fund)
  RRIFs
RRSP (Registered
  Retirement Savings
  Plan)
  RRSPs
RSI (repetitive strain
  injury)
  RSIs
RSP (Retirement
  Savings Plan)
  RSPs
RSVP (reply)
• *noun*
  RSVPs
• *verb*
  RSVP's
  RSVP'd
  RSVP'ing
RU-486
rub
  rubs
  rubbed
  rub|bing
Rub' al Khali (desert,
  Arabian peninsula)
ru|bato
  ru|ba|tos *or* ru|bati
rub|ber +s
rubber-chicken
rubber-faced
rubber|i|ness
rubber|ize
  rubber|iz|es
  rubber|ized
  rubber|iz|ing

rubber|neck +s +ed
  +ing
rubber|neck|er +s
rub|ber stamp +s
  noun
rubber-stamp +s +ed
  +ing *verb*
rub|bery
rub|bing +s *noun*
rub|bish
  rub|bish|es
  rub|bished
  rub|bish|ing
rub|bishy
rub|ble +s (debris)
rub|bly
rubby (alcoholic)
  rub|bies
rub down *verb*
  rubs down
  rubbed down
  rub|bing down
rub-down +s *noun*
rube +s
Rube Gold|berg
  adjective
ru|bella
ru|bel|lite +s
Ru|bens, Sir Peter
  Paul (Flemish
  painter)
  [☞ Reuben]
ru|beo|la
Ru|bi|con (stream,
  Italy)
ru|bi|cund
ru|bi|cund|ity
ru|bid|ium
Rubik's cube +s
  proprietary
Rub|in|stein, Anton
  Grigor|evich
  (Russian composer)
Rub|in|stein, Artur
  (US pianist)
ru|ble +s (currency)
  [☞ rubble]
ru|bric +s
ru|bric|al
rubri|cate
  rubri|cates
  rubri|cat|ed
  rubri|cat|ing
rubri|ca|tion +s
rubri|ca|tor +s
ruby (red gem)
  ru|bies
  ru|bied
  ruby|ing
  [☞ rubby]
ruby-throat|ed
ruche +s (frill)
ruched

ruch|ing
ruck +s +ed +ing
ruckle
  ruckles
  ruckled
  ruck|ling
ruck|sack +s
ruck|us
  ruck|us|es
ruc|tion +s
rud|beck|ia +s
rudd
  plural rudd
rud|der +s +ed +ing
rud|der|less
rud|di|ly
rud|di|ness
rud|dle
  rud|dles
  rud|dled
  rud|dling
ruddy
  rud|di|er
  rud|di|est
rude (impolite; abrupt)
  ruder
  rud|est
  [☞ rood]
rude|ly
rude|ness
ruder|al +s
rudi|ment +s
rudi|men|tar|i|ly
rudi|men|tar|i|ness
rudi|ment|ary
rud|ish
Ru|dolf (*former name
  for* Lake Turkana,
  Kenya)
Ru|dolf (crown prince
  of Austria; German
  king)
Rudra (*Hinduism*)
rue (regret; pity;
  shrub)
  rues
  rued
  rue|ing or ruing
  [☞ roo, roux]
rue|ful
rue|ful|ly
rue|ful|ness
ruff +s +ed +ing
  (neck frill; fringe;
  bird; fish; trump;
  dog's bark)
  [☞ rough]
ruffe +s (fish: *use* ruff)
  [☞ ruff, rough]
ruffed *adjective*
ruf|fian +s
ruf|fian|ism
ruf|fian|ly

ruf|fle
  ruf|fles
  ruf|fled
  ruf|fling
ruf|fly (having ruffles)
  [☞ roughly]
rufi|yaa
  plural rufi|yaa
ruf|ous
rug +s
Rugby (town,
  England)
rugby
rug|ged
rug|ged|iz|a|tion
rug|ged|ized
rug|ged|ly
rug|ged|ness
rug|ger
ru|gosa +s
ru|gose
ru|gose|ly
ru|gos|ity
rug rat +s
Ruhr (region,
  Germany)
ruin +s +ed +ing
  (wreck; remains;
  downfall)
  [☞ rune]
ruin|a|tion
ruin|ous
ruin|ous|ly
ruin|ous|ness
Ruis|dael, Jacob van
  (Dutch painter)
Rule, Jane Vance
  (US-born Cdn writer)
rule
  rules
  ruled
  rul|ing
rule book +s
rule|less
rul|er +s
ruler|ship +s
rul|ing +s *noun &
  adjective*
Rum (= Rhum, Inner
  Hebrides)
rum (alcohol; odd;
  difficult)
  rums
  rum|mer
  rum|mest
  [☞ rhumb]
Ru|ma|nia
  (= Romania)
Ru|ma|nian +s
  (= Romanian)
rumba
  rum|bas

rum|baed
  or rumba'd
  rumba|ing
rum baba +s
rum|ble
  rum|bles
  rum|bled
  rum|bling
rum|bler +s
rum|ble seat +s
rum|ble strip +s
rum|bling +s *noun*
rum|bus|tious
rum|bus|tious|ly
rum|bus|tious|ness
Ru|melia (former
  Ottoman territory,
  Europe)
rumen
  ru|mens or ru|mina
ru|min|ant +s
ru|min|ate
  ru|min|ates
  ru|min|at|ed
  ru|min|at|ing
ru|min|a|tion +s
ru|mina|tive
ru|mina|tive|ly
rumly
rum|mage
  rum|ma|ges
  rum|maged
  rum|ma|ging
rum|ma|ger +s
rummy
  rum|mies
  rum|mi|er
  rum|mi|est
rum|ness
ru|mor +s +ed +ing
  (*use* rumour)
ru|mored *adjective*
  (*use* rumoured)
ru|mor mon|ger +s
  (*use* rumour
  monger)
ru|mor mon|ger|ing
  (*use* rumour
  mongering)
ru|mour +s +ed +ing
ru|moured *adjective*
ru|mour mon|ger +s
ru|mour mon|ger|ing
rump +s
rum|ple
  rum|ples
  rum|pled
  rum|pling
rum|pled *adjective*
rump|less
rum|ply
rum|pus
  rum|pus|es

rum|pus room +s
rum-runner +s
rum-running
run
  runs
  ran
  run
  run|ning
run|about +s
run-and-shoot
run around *verb*
  runs around
  ran around
  run around
  run|ning around
run|around +s *noun*
run away *verb*
  runs away
  ran away
  run away
  run|ning away
run|away +s *noun &*
  adjective
run|cible spoon +s
Run|cie, Rob|ert
  Alex|an|der
  Ken|nedy, Baron
  (Archbishop of
  Canterbury)
run|cin|ate
Run|dle (mountain,
  Canada)
run down *verb*
  runs down
  ran down
  run down
  run|ning down
run|down +s *noun &*
  adjective
Rund|stedt, Karl
  Ru|dolf Gerd von
  (German field
  marshal)
rune +s (letter; secret;
  poem)
rung +s (ladder step;
  level; *past participle*
  of ring)
  [☞ wrung]
runged
rung|less
runic
run-in +s
run|nable
run|nel +s
run|ner +s
runner-up
  runners-up
run|ning +s *noun &*
  adjective
run|ning board +s
run|ning shoe +s

runny
run|ni|er
run|ni|est
Runny|mede (site of
  Magna Carta
  signing)
run off *verb*
  runs off
  ran off
  run off
  run|ning off
run|off +s *noun*
run-of-the-mill
runt +s
run-through +s
runt|ish
runty
run up *verb*
  runs up
  ran up
  run up
  run|ning up
run-up +s *noun*
run|way +s
Run|yon, Al|fred
  Damon (US writer)
Runyon|esque
ru|pee +s
Ru|pert (river,
  Canada)
Ru|pert, Prince
  (English general &
  governor of HBC)
Ru|pert's Land
  (historic region,
  Canada)
ru|piah
  plural ru|piah or
  ru|piahs
rup|tur|able
rup|ture
  rup|tures
  rup|tured
  rup|tur|ing
rural
rur|al|ism
rur|al|ist +s
rur|al|ity
rur|al|iz|a|tion
rur|al|ize
  rur|al|iz|es
  rur|al|ized
  rur|al|iz|ing
rur|al|ly
Rurik +s (Russian
  dynasty)
Ruri|tan|ian
Ruse (city, Bulgaria)
ruse +s
rush (hurry; charge;
  plant)
  rush|es

rushed
rush|ing
[☞ ruche]
Rush|die, (Ahmed)
  Sal|man (Indian-
  born English writer)
rush|er +s
rush hour +s
rush|ing|ly
rush|light +s
rush|like
Rush|more (sculpted
  mountain, US)
rushy
Rusk, (David) Dean
  (US statesman)
rusk +s
Rus|kin, John
  (English critic)
Rus|sell (surname)
  [☞ rustle]
Rus|sell, Ber|trand
  Ar|thur Wil|liam
  (English philosopher)
Rus|sell, George
  Wil|liam (Irish poet)
Rus|sell, Henry
  Nor|ris (US
  astronomer)
Rus|sell, John (British
  prime minister)
Rus|sell, Ken (English
  filmmaker)
rus|set +s
rus|sety
Rus|sia (country,
  Eurasia)
Rus|sian +s
Rus|sian|iz|a|tion
Rus|sian|ize
  Rus|sian|iz|es
  Rus|sian|ized
  Rus|sian|iz|ing
Russian|ness
Rus|si|fi|ca|tion
Rus|sify
  Rus|si|fies
  Rus|si|fied
  Rus|si|fy|ing
Rus|ski +s *offensive*
Rus|sky *offensive*
  (= Russki)
  Rus|skies
Russo-Japanese
Russo|phile +s
Russo|phobe +s
Russo|phobia
Russo-Turkish
rust +s +ed +ing
rust belt +s
rust|bucket +s
rus|tic +s
rus|tic|ally

rus|ti|cate
  rus|ti|cates
  rus|ti|cat|ed
  rus|ti|cat|ing
rus|ti|ca|tion +s
rus|ti|city
rust|i|er
rust|i|est
rust|i|ly
rust|i|ness
rus|tle
  rus|tles
  rus|tled
  rust|ling
  [☞ Russell]
rust|ler +s
rust|less
rust|proof +s +ed
  +ing
rusty
  rust|i|er
  rust|i|est
rut
  ruts
  rutted
  rut|ting
ruta|baga +s
Ruth (*Bible*)
Ruth, George
  Her|man ('Babe')
  (US baseball player)
Ru|the|nia (region,
  Europe)
Ru|the|nian +s
ru|the|nium
Ruth|er|ford,
  Alex|an|der
  Cam|eron (Cdn
  politician)
Ruth|er|ford, Sir
  Er|nest (1st Baron
  Rutherford of
  Nelson, English
  physicist)
ruth|er|ford|ium
Ruth|ian
ruth|less
ruth|less|ly
ruth|less|ness
ru|tile +s
rut|tish
rutty
Ruwen|zori
  (mountain range,
  Africa)
Ruys|dael, Jacob van
  (= Jacob van
  Ruisdael, Dutch
  painter)
RV (recreational
  vehicle)
  RVs
R-value +s

Rwan|da (country, Africa)
Rwan|dan +s
Ryan, Claude (Cdn politician)
Rya|zan (city, Russia)
Ryb|insk (city, Russia)
rye +s (plant; whisky; bread)
 [☞ **rai, wry, Ray,** Reye's syndrome]
rye|grass
 rye|grass|es
Ryer|son, Adol|phus Eg|er|ton (Cdn educator)
rye whisky
 rye whis|kies
Ryga, George (Cdn writer)
 [☞ **Riga**]
Ryle, Gil|bert (English philosopher)
Ryle, Sir Mar|tin (English astronomer)
ryo|kan +s
ryot +s (Indian peasant)
 [☞ **riot**]
Rysy (mountain, Slovakia)
Ryu|kyu (islands, W Pacific)
Ryur|ik (= Rurik, Russian dynasty)

S

S
• (letter; shape)
 S's
• (siemens)
 [☞ **ess**]
s
• (letter)
 s's
• (second; shilling)
 [☞ **ess**]
Saale (river, Germany)
Saan|ich (municipality & peninsula, Canada; people & language)
 plural Saan|ich
Saar (river, Europe; region, Germany)
Saar|brück|en (city, Germany)
Saar|in|en, Eero (US architect)

Saar|land (state, Germany)
Saba (island, Netherlands Antilles)
saba|dil|la +s
Sabah (state, Malaysia)
Saba|tier, Paul (French chemist)
sab|ayon +s
Sab|ba|tar|ian +s
Sab|ba|tar|ian|ism
Sab|bath +s
sab|bat|ical +s
sab|bat|ical|ly
sab|icu +s
Sabin, Al|bert Bruce (US microbiologist)
Sabin (vaccine)
Sab|ine +s (ancient people; peninsula, Canada)
Sab|ine's gull +s
Sable (cape & island, Canada)
sable +s
sabled *adjective*
sable|fish
 plural sable|fish
sably
sabot +s
sabo|tage
 sabo|tages
 sabo|taged
 sabo|ta|ging
saboted
sabo|teur +s
sab|ra +s
Sab|ra|ta (= Sabratha)
Sab|ra|tha (Phoenician city, N Africa)
sabre +s
sabre-rattling
sabre saw +s
sabre-toothed
Sac (people: *use* Sauk)
 plural Sac or Sacs
 [☞ **Sachs**]
sac +s (plant or animal cavity; membrane around a cyst etc.)
 [☞ **sack**]
sac|cade +s
sac|cad|ic
sac|char|ide +s
sac|char|in (sugar substitute)
sac|char|ine +s (sweet; excessively sentimental thing)
sac|char|ose +s

Sacco, Nic|ola (Italian-born anarchist)
sac|cu|lar
sac|cule +s
sacer|dot|al
sacer|dot|al|ism
sacer|dot|al|ist +s
sacer|dot|al|ly
sa|chem +s
Sacher|torte +s
sa|chet +s (scented packet; bag)
 [☞ **sashay**]
Sachs, Hans (German writer)
Sachs, Nelly Leonie (German writer)
sack +s +ed +ing (bag; bed; dismissal; dress; *Football*; plunder; wine)
 [☞ **sac**]
sack|but +s
sack|cloth
sack|ful +s
sack|ing +s *noun*
sack|like
Sack|ville (town, Canada)
Sack|ville, Thom|as (1st Earl of Dorset, English dramatist)
Sackville-West, Vic|toria Mary ('Vita') (English writer)
sacra
sac|ral
sac|ral|iz|a|tion
sac|ral|ize
 sac|ral|iz|es
 sac|ral|ized
 sac|ral|iz|ing
sac|ra|ment +s
sac|ra|men|tal
sac|ra|men|tal|ism
sac|ra|men|tal|ist +s
sac|ra|men|tal|ity
sac|ra|men|tal|ly
Sac|ra|mento (city & river, US)
sac|rar|ium
 sac|rar|ia
sacred
sacred|ly
sacred|ness
sac|ri|fice
 sac|ri|fi|ces
 sac|ri|ficed
 sac|ri|fi|cing
sac|ri|fi|cial
sac|ri|fi|cial|ly

sac|ri|lege +s
sac|ri|le|gious
sac|ri|le|gious|ly
sac|ris|tan +s
sac|ris|ty
 sac|ris|ties
sac|ro|iliac
sacro|sanct
sacro|sanct|ity
sac|rum
 sacra
sad
 sad|der
 sad|dest
sad-ass
Sadat, (Muham|mad) Anwar al- (Egyptian president)
Sad|dam Hus|sein (Iraqi president)
sad|den +s +ed +ing
sad|dhu +s (*use* sadhu)
sad|dish
sad|dle
 sad|dles
 sad|dled
 sad|dling
saddle|back +s
saddle|backed
saddle|bag +s
saddle-bow +s
sad|dle cloth +s
sad|dle horn +s
sad|dle horse +s
saddle|less
sad|dler +s
 [☞ **Sadler's Wells**]
sad|dlery
 sad|dler|ies
sad|dle shoe +s
sad|dle soap
sad|dle sore +s *noun*
saddle-sore *adjective*
sad|dle stitch *noun*
 sad|dle stitch|es
saddle-stitch *verb*
 saddle-stitches
 saddle-stitched
 saddle-stitch|ing
saddle-stitched *adjective*
saddle-stitch|ing *noun*
sad|dle tree +s
Sad|du|cean
Sad|du|cee +s
Sade, Dona|tien Al|phonse Fran|çois, Comte de ('Marquis de Sade', French writer)
sadhu +s

sad|ism
sad|ist +s
sad|is|tic
sad|is|tic|ally
Sad|ler|miut
  plural Sad|ler|miut
  or Sad|ler|miuts
Sad|ler's Wells
  (theatre, England)
sadly
sad|ness
sado-masochism
sado-masochist +s
sado-masochis|tic
sad sack +s (sad-sack
  when preceding a
  noun)
Safa|qis (= Sfax,
  Tunisia)
sa|fari +s
Safa|vid +s
Saf|die, Moshe (Cdn
  architect)
safe
  safer
  safest
  safes
safe|cracker +s
safe|guard +s
safe house +s
safe|keep|ing
safe|light +s
safe|ly
safe|ness
safe|ty
  safe|ties
safe|ty de|posit box
  safe|ty de|posit
  boxes
safe|ty pin +s noun
safety-pin verb
  safety-pins
  safety-pinned
  safety-pinning
saf|flower +s
saf|fron +s
saf|froned
saf|frony
saf|ra|nin (use
  safranine)
saf|ra|nine
sag
  sags
  sagged
  sag|ging
saga +s
sag|acious
sag|acious|ly
sag|acity
saga|more +s
Sagan, Carl Ed|ward
  (US astronomer)

Sagan, Fran|çoise
  (French writer)
sage +s
sage|brush
sage green +s (sage-
  green when preceding
  a noun)
sage|hood
sage|ly
sage|ness
sag|gar +s (Pottery)
  [☞ sagger]
sag|ger +s (something
  that sags; for Pottery
  sense use saggar)
saggy (that sags)
  sag|gi|er
  sag|gi|est
sagit|tal
Sagit|tar|ian +s
Sagit|tar|ius
  (constellation;
  Zodiac)
sagit|tate
sago +s
sa|guaro +s
Sa|gue|nay (river,
  Canada)
Sa|guia el Hamra
  (river & region,
  Western Sahara)
sagy (like sage)
  [☞ saggy]
Saha, Megh|nad
  (Indian physicist)
Sa|hara (desert,
  Africa)
Sa|haran
Sahel (region, Africa)
Sahel|ian
sahib +s
Sahtu Dene
  plural Sahtu Dene
sa|huaro +s (use
  saguaro)
Said, Ed|ward W. (US
  critic)
said adjective
saiga +s
Sai|gon (city, Vietnam)
sail +s +ed +ing
  (Nautical)
  [☞ sale]
sail|able (that can be
  sailed)
  [☞ saleable]
sail|board +s
sail|board|er +s
sail|board|ing
sail|boat +s
sail|cloth +s
sailed adjective

sail|er +s (sailing
  vessel)
  [☞ sailor]
sail|fish
  plural sail|fish or
  sail|fish|es
sail|less
sail|maker +s
sail|making
sail|or +s (person who
  sails)
  [☞ sailer]
sail|or|ly
sail|past +s
sail|plane +s
sain|foin
saint +s +ed +ing
St. Al|bert (city,
  Canada)
St. An|drews (towns,
  Scotland & Canada)
St. An|drew's (feast
  day; cross)
St. An|thony cross
  St. An|thony
  cross|es
St. An|thony's cross
  (use St. Anthony
  cross)
  St. An|thony's
  cross|es
St. An|thony's fire
Saint-Antoine (town,
  Canada)
St. Bar|tholo|mew's
  Day
Saint-Basile-le-
  Grand
  (town, Canada)
St. Ber|nard +s
  (Alpine pass; dog)
Saint-Bruno-de-
  Montarville
  (city, Canada)
St. Cath|ar|ines (city,
  Ontario)
  [☞ St. Catherine,
  Sainte-Catherine]
Saint-Charles (battle
  site, Canada)
St. Chris|to|pher and
  Nevis,
  Fed|er|a|tion of
  (= St. Kitts and
  Nevis)
St. Clair (river & lake,
  N America)
Saint-Constant
  (town, Canada)
St. Croix (US Virgin
  Island; river,
  N America)
St. David's Day

Saint-Denis (capital
  of Réunion; city,
  France; village,
  Canada)
Sainte-Adèle (resort,
  Canada)
Sainte-Agathe-des-
  Monts
  (town, Canada)
Sainte-Anne
  (mountain, Canada)
Sainte-Anne-de-
  Beaupré
  (town, Canada)
Sainte-Anne-de-
  Bellevue
  (canal, Canada)
Sainte-Anne-des-
  Monts
  (town, Canada)
Sainte-Anne-des-
  Plaines
  (town, Canada)
Sainte-Beuve,
  Charles Au|gus|tin
  (French critic)
Sainte-Catherine
  (town, Quebec)
  [☞ St. Catharines]
saint|ed adjective
Sainte-Foy (city &
  battle site, Canada)
Sainte-Hélène
  (island, Canada)
  [☞ St. Helens]
Sainte-Julie (city,
  Canada)
St. Elias (mountain
  range & peak,
  N America)
St. Elmo's fire
Sainte-Marie (town,
  Canada)
Sainte-Marie, Buffy
  (Cdn singer-
  songwriter)
Sainte-Marie-
  Among-the-
  Hurons
  (historic site,
  Canada)
Saint-Émile (town,
  Canada)
Saint-Émilion +s
  (town, France; wine)
Sainte-Thérèse (city,
  Canada)
Saint-Étienne (city,
  France)
Saint-Eustache (city,
  Canada)
Saint-Exupéry,
  An|toine Marie

Roger de (French novelist & aviator)

Saint-Félicien (town, Canada)

St. Fran|cis (lake, Canada)

Saint-François
- (river, Canada)
- (= Lake St. Francis)

Saint-Georges (city, Canada)

St. George's (capital of Grenada; channel between Wales & Ireland; feast day; cross)

St. Got|thard (Alpine pass)

St. Hel|ena (S Atlantic island)

St. Helen|ian +s

St. Hel|ens (volcano, US; town, England) [☞ Sainte-Hélène]

St. Hel|ier (capital of Jersey, Channel Islands)

Saint-Hilaire (mountain, Canada) [☞ Mont-Saint-Hilaire]

saint|hood

Saint-Hubert (city, Canada)

Saint-Hyacinthe (city, Canada)

St. James (fort, Canada; street in Montreal)

Saint-Jean (lake, Canada)

Saint-Jean, Île (former name for Prince Edward Island)

Saint-Jean-Baptiste Day (= Fête nationale)

Saint-Jean-Chrysos|tome (town, Canada)

Saint-Jean-Port-Joli (municipality, Canada)

Saint-Jean-sur-Richelieu (city, Canada)

Saint-Jérôme (city, Canada)

Saint John (city & river, New Brunswick)

St. John (US Virgin Island; fort, Canada)

St. John Am|bu|lance

St. John's (capital of Newfoundland; capital of Antigua and Barbuda)

St. John's Island (former name for Prince Edward Island)

St. John's wort

St. Jo|seph (island & fort, Canada)

Saint-Just, Louis An|toine Léon de (French revolutionary leader)

St. Kitts
- (island, W Indies)
- (nickname for St. Catharines)

St. Kitts and Nevis (country, W Indies)

Saint-Lambert (city, Canada)

Saint Lau|rent, Yves Ma|thieu (French designer)

St. Lau|rent, Louis Ste|phen (Cdn prime minister)

Saint-Laurent (city, Canada)

St. Law|rence (river, seaway & gulf, N America)

St. Law|rence Is|lands (national park, Canada)

Saint-Lazare (municipality, Canada)

Saint-Léonard (city, Canada)

saint|li|er

saint|li|est

saint|like

saint|li|ness

St. Louis (city, US)

Saint-Louis (lake, Canada)

Saint-Louis-de-France (town, Canada)

Saint-Louis-du-Ha! Ha! (municipality, Canada)

Saint-Luc (town, Canada)

St. Lucia (country, W Indies)

St. Lu|cian +s

saint|ly

saint|li|er

saint|li|est

Saint-Malo (town, France)

St. Mar|garets (bay, Canada)

St. Mar|tin (island, Caribbean) [☞ San Martín]

St. Martin's sum|mer

St. Marys (river, Nova Scotia; town, Ontario)

St. Mary's (river, Ontario & Michigan; bay & university, Canada)

Saint-Maurice (river, Canada)

Saint-Michel, Mont (islet, France)

St. Mor|itz (resort, Switzerland)

Saint-Nazaire (town, France)

St. Nicho|las (Santa Claus)

Saint-Nicolas (municipality, Canada)

Saint-Ours (canal, Canada)

St. Pat|rick's Day

St. Paul (city, US; town, Canada)

saint|paul|ia +s

St. Peters|burg (cities, Russia & US)

Saint-Pierre (town & lake, Canada)

Saint-Pierre and Mi|que|llon (French possession, N America)

St. Pöl|ten (city, Austria)

Saint-Rédemp|teur (town, Canada)

Saint-Rémi (town, Canada)

Saint-Romuald (town, Canada)

Saint-Saëns, (Charles) Ca|mille (French composer)

saint's day saints' days

Saint-Simon, Claude-Henri de Rouv|roy, Comte de (French philosopher)

Saint-Simon, Louis de Rouv|roy, Duc de (French writer)

St. So|phia (Byzantine edifice, Istanbul)

St. Ste|phen (town, Canada)

St. Thom|as (city, Canada; US Virgin Island)

Saint-Timothée (municipality, Canada)

Saint-Tropez (resort, France)

St. Val|en|tine's Day

St. Vin|cent (cape, Portugal)

St. Vin|cent and the Grena|dines (country, W Indies)

St. Vitus's dance

Sai|pan (island, Northern Marianas)

saith

Sakai (city, Japan)

sake +s (purpose; benefit; Japanese drink) [☞ saki]

saker +s

Sakh|alin (island off Russia)

Sakh|arov, An|drei Dmitri|evich (Russian nuclear physicist)

Saki (Scottish writer)

saki +s (monkey; for Japanese drink use sake)

Sakta +s

Sakti (Hinduism) [☞ Shakhty]

Sakt|ism

sa|laam +s +ed +ing ('peace'; salute; compliment) [☞ Salam]

Sala|berry, Charles-Michel d'Irum|berry de (Cdn soldier)

Salaberry-de-Valley|field (city, Canada)

salable (that may be sold: use saleable) [☞ sailable]

sal|acious

sal|acious|ly

sal|acious|ness

sal|acity

sal|ad +s

Sala|din (sultan of
  Egypt & Syria)
salal +s
Salam, Abdus
  (Pakistani physicist)
  [☞ Salem, salaam]
Sala|man|ca (city,
  Spain)
sala|man|der +s
sala|man|drine
sa|lami +s
Sala|mis (Greek
  island)
sal am|mo|niac
Sal|ang (mountain
  pass, Afghanistan)
sall|ar|ied adjective
sal|ary
  sall|ar|ies
  sall|ar|ied
  sall|ary|ing
salary|man
  salary|men
Sala|zar, An|tonio de
  Oli|veira
  (Portuguese prime
  minister)
sal|buta|mol
Sal|chow +s
sale +s (exchange of
  goods for money)
  [☞ sail]
sale|abil|ity
sale|able (that may be
  sold)
  [☞ sailable]
Salem (cities, Oregon,
  Massachusetts &
  India)
salep
Sal|erno (city, Italy)
sale|room +s
Sal|esian +s (religious
  society member)
  [☞ Silesian]
sales|lady
  sales|ladies
sales|man
  sales|men
sales|man|ship
sales|person
  sales|people or
  sales|persons
sales|room +s
sales|woman
  sales|women
Sal|ford (city,
  England)
Salian +s
Salic
sal|icin
sa|li|cion|al +s
sa|li|cyl|ate +s

sali|cyl|ic
sali|ence
sali|ency
sali|ent +s
sali|ent|ly
Sali|eri, An|tonio
  (Italian composer)
sal|ifer|ous
sal|ina +s
sa|line +s
Sal|in|ger, Jer|ome
  David (US writer)
sal|in|ity
  sal|in|ities
sal|in|iz|a|tion
salin|om|eter +s
Salis|bury
  • (city, England)
  • (former name for
    Harare, Zimbabwe)
Salis|bury, Rob|ert
  Ar|thur Tal|bot
  Gascoigne-Cecil,
  3rd Mar|quess of
  (British prime
  minister)
Sal|ish (people & their
  Salishan language)
  plural Sal|ish
  • The name
    preferred by the
    people themselves is
    Sne Nay Muxw.
Sal|ish|an (language
  group)
sal|iva +s
sali|vary
sali|vate
  sali|vates
  sali|vat|ed
  sali|vat|ing
sali|va|tion
Salk, Jonas Ed|ward
  (US microbiologist)
sal|let +s
sal|low +er +est +s
  +ed +ing
sal|low|ish
sal|low|ness
sal|lowy
Sal|lust (Roman
  historian)
Sally (Salvation Army)
sally (set out; charge;
  banter)
  sal|lies
  sal|lied
  sally|ing
Sally Ann
Sally Lunn +s
sally port +s

sal|ma|gundi +s (dish
  of meat and
  anchovies; mixture)
  [☞ Solomon
  Gundy]
sal|ma|nazar +s
sal|mi +s
sal|mon
  plural sal|mon or
  sal|mons
Sal|mon Arm
  (municipality,
  Canada)
salmon|berry
  salmon|ber|ries
salmon-coloured
sal|mon|ella
  sal|mon|el|lae or
  sal|mon|el|las
sal|mon|el|lo|sis
sal|mon|id +s
sal|mon|oid +s
sal|mon pink noun
salmon-pink adjective
Sal|ome (New
  Testament)
sal|on +s
Sal|on|ika
  (= Thessaloníki,
  Greece)
sal|oon +s
salop|ettes
Sal|op|ian +s
sal|pi|con
sal|pi|glos|sis
sal|pin|gec|tomy
  sal|pin|gec|to|mies
sal|pin|gitis
sal|sa +s
salsa verde
sal|sify
  sal|si|fies
SALT (Strategic Arms
  Limitation Talks or
  Treaty)
salt +s +ed +ing
salt and pep|per
  adjective
sal|ta|tion +s
sal|ta|tion|ism
sal|ta|tion|ist +s
sal|ta|tor|ial
sal|ta|tory
salt|box
  salt|boxes
salt|bush
  salt|bush|es
salt|cellar +s
salt|chuck +s
Sal|teaux
  (= Saulteaux)
  plural Sal|teaux
salt|ed adjective

salt|er +s (truck for
  scattering salt; one
  who treats fish with
  salt)
  [☞ Psalter]
salt|ery (factory for
  processing fish)
  salt|er|ies
  [☞ psaltery]
salt fish
salt-glaze
salt-glazed
salt|ie +s (ship)
  [☞ salty]
salt|i|er
salt|i|est
sal|ti|grade +s
Sal|tillo (city, Mexico)
sal|tim|boc|ca
salt|ine +s
salt|i|ness
salt|ing +s noun
sal|tire +s
Salt Lake City (city,
  US)
salt lick +s
salt marsh
  salt marsh|es
salt mine +s
salt|ness
salt pan +s
salt|petre
salt pond +s
salt pork
salt shak|er +s
Salt|spring (island,
  Canada)
salt water noun
salt|water adjective
  preceding a noun
salt|wort +s
salty (containing salt;
  racy, vulgar;
  characteristic of
  sailors)
  salt|i|er
  salt|i|est
  [☞ saltie]
sa|lu|bri|ous
sa|lu|bri|ous|ly
sa|lu|bri|ous|ness
sa|lu|brity
Sa|luki +s
salu|tary
salu|ta|tion +s
sa|lu|ta|tory
sa|lute
  sa|lutes
  sa|lut|ed
  sa|lut|ing
Sa|lu|tin, Rick (Cdn
  writer)
salv|able

Sal|va|dor (city, Brazil)
Sal|va|dor|an +s
Sal|va|dor|ean +s (= Salvadoran)
sal|vage (recover; rescue)
  sal|va|ges
  sal|vaged
  sal|va|ging
  [☞ **selvage**]
sal|vage|able
sal|va|ger +s
sal|va|tion (redemption)
  [☞ **solvation**]
Sal|va|tion Army
Sal|va|tion|ism (principles of the Salvation Army)
sal|va|tion|ism
Sal|va|tion|ist +s (member of the Salvation Army)
sal|va|tion|ist +s
salve
  salves
  salved
  salv|ing
sal|ver +s (tray)
  [☞ **salvor**]
Salve Re|gina
sal|via +s
salv|ific
salvo
  sal|voes or **sal|vos**
sal vol|at|ile
sal|vor +s (salvager)
  [☞ **salver**]
Sal|ween (river, Asia)
Salz|burg (city, Austria)
Salz|git|ter (city, Germany)
Salz|kam|mer|gut (region, Austria)
SAM (surface-to-air missile)
  SAMs
sam|adhi
Samar (island, the Philippines)
Sam|ara (city, Russia)
  [☞ **Samarra**]
sam|ara +s
Sam|aria (ancient region & city, Palestine)
Sama|rin|da (city, Indonesia)
Sam|ar|itan +s
Sam|ar|itan|ism
sam|ar|ium

Sam|ar|kand (city, Uzbekistan)
Sam|ar|qand (= Samarkand)
Sam|arra (city, Iraq)
  [☞ **Samara**]
Sama-Veda
samba
  sam|bas
  sam|baed or **samba'd**
  samba|ing
sam|bal +s
Sam Browne +s
sam|buca +s
same
same-day
same|ness
same-sex
samey
  sami|er
  sami|est
samey|ness
sam|fu +s
Samhain +s
Sam Hill
Sami
Sami|an +s
Sam|iel +s
sami|er
sami|est
sami|sen +s
sam|ite +s
sam|iz|dat
Sam|nite +s
Samoa (island group, Polynesia)
Samo|an +s
Samos (island, Greece)
sam|osa +s (food)
  [☞ **Somoza**]
samo|var +s
Samo|yed +s
Samo|yed|ic
samp
sam|pan +s
sam|phire +s
sam|ple
  sam|ples
  sam|pled
  sam|pling
sam|pler +s
sam|pling +s *noun*
sam|sara
sam|skara
Sam|son
Sam|uel (*Bible*)
samu|rai
  plural **samu|rai**
San (people & language group)
  plural **San**

san +s
San'a (capital of Yemen)
Sanaa (= San'a)
San An|dreas fault
San An|ton|ian +s
San An|tonio (city, US)
sana|tor|ium
  sana|tor|iums or **sana|toria**
San Car|los de Bari|loche (resort, Argentina)
San|cerre +s
sanc|ta
sanc|ti|fi|ca|tion +s
sanc|ti|fy
  sanc|ti|fies
  sanc|ti|fied
  sanc|ti|fy|ing
sanc|ti|moni|ous
sanc|ti|moni|ous|ly
sanc|ti|moni|ous|ness
sanc|ti|mony
sanc|tion +s +ed +ing
sanc|tity
  sanc|ti|ties
sanc|tu|ary
  sanc|tu|ar|ies
sanc|tum
  sanc|tums or **sanc|ta**
sanc|tum
  sanc|tor|um
  sanc|ta sanc|tor|um or **sanc|tum**
  sanc|tor|ums
Sanc|tus
  Sanc|tus|es
Sand, George (French novelist)
sand +s +ed +ing
san|dal +s
sandal|foot
san|dalled
sandal|wood +s
Sandal|wood Island (= Sumba, Indonesia)
san|da|rac
san|da|rach (*use* sandarac)
sand|bag
  sand|bags
  sand|bagged
  sand|bag|ging
sand|bag|ger +s
sand|bank +s
sand|bar +s

sand|blast +s +ed +ing
sand|blast|er +s
sand|box
  sand|boxes
Sand|burg, Carl (US writer)
sand|castle +s
sand|cherry
  sand|cher|ries
sand dab +s
sand eel +s
sand|er +s
sand|er|ling +s
sand|fly
  sand|flies
sand|glass
  sand|glass|es
sand|grouse
  plural **sand|grouse**
san|dhi (*Grammar*)
sand|hill +s
sand|hog +s
sand hop|per +s
San Diego (city, US)
sand|i|er
sand|i|est
sand|i|ness
San|di|nis|ta +s
S&L (savings and loan)
  S&Ls
sand|lot +s
sand|lot|ter +s
S&M (sado-masochism)
sand|man
  sand|men
sand paint|ed
sand paint|er +s
sand paint|ing +s
sand|paper +s +ed +ing
sand|papery
sand|piper +s
sand|pit +s
sand|stone +s
sand|storm +s
sand-table +s
sand trap +s
sand-wash
  sand-washes
  sand-washed
  sand-washing
sand-washed *adjective*
sand wedge +s
sand|wich
  sand|wich|es
  sand|wiched
  sand|wich|ing
Sand|wich Islands (*former name for* Hawaii)

sand|wort +s
sandy (of or like sand)
sand|i|er
sand|i|est
[☞ sandhi]
sandy|ish
sane (of sound mind;
reasonable)
saner
sanest
[☞ seine]
sane|ly
sane|ness
San|for|ized
proprietary
San Fran|cis|can +s
San Fran|cis|co (city,
US)
sang
san|gar +s
Sang|er, Fred|erick
(English biochemist)
Sang|er, Mar|garet
Hig|gins (US birth
control campaigner)
sang-froid
sangha +s (Buddhism)
[☞ Sogne]
san|giov|ese
Sango
san|gria +s
san|guin|ary
san|guine +s
san|guine|ly
San|hed|rin
sani|tar|ian +s
sani|tar|i|ly
sani|tar|ium
(= sanatorium)
sani|tar|iums or
sani|taria
sani|tary
sani|ta|tion
sani|tiz|a|tion
sani|tize
sani|tiz|es
sani|tized
sani|tiz|ing
sani|tiz|er +s
sani|tor|ium
(= sanatorium)
sani|tor|iums or
sani|toria
san|ity
San Jose (city, US)
[☞ San José]
San José (capital of
Costa Rica)
[☞ San Jose]
San Juan (capital of
Puerto Rico)
sank

San Luis Pot|osí
(state & its capital,
Mexico)
San Mar|ino (country,
Europe)
San Mar|tín, José de
(Argentinian soldier)
[☞ St. Martin, Sint
Maarten]
san|nyasi
plural san|nyasi
san|nyas|in
(= sannyasi)
plural san|nyas|in
San Pedro Sula (city,
Honduras)
sans
San Sal|va|dor
(capital of
El Salvador)
sans-culotte +s
sans-culott|ism
San Sebas|tián (city,
Spain)
San|sei
plural San|sei
san|sev|eria +s
san|se|vi|eria +s (use
sanseveria)
San|skrit
San|skrit|ic
San|skrit|ist +s
San|so|vino, Jac|opo
(Italian sculptor &
architect)
sans ser|if +s
Santa +s
Santa Ana (city, US;
city & volcano,
El Salvador)
[☞ Santayana]
Santa Anna, An|tonio
López de (Mexican
president)
[☞ Santayana]
Santa Bar|bara (city,
US)
Santa Cata|rina
(state, Brazil)
Santa Claus
Santa Claus|es
Santa Cruz (city,
Bolivia)
Santa Cruz (de
Tene|rife) (city,
Canary Islands)
Santa Fe (cities,
Argentina & US)
Santa Fean +s
Santa Mon|ica (city,
US)
Santa Mon|ican +s

San|tan|der (city,
Spain)
Santa Rosa +s
Santa So|phia
(Byzantine edifice,
Istanbul)
Santa|yana, George
(US philosopher)
San|tee
plural San|tee or
San|tees
Sante|ria
san|tero +s
San|ti|ago (capital of
Chile)
San|ti|ago de
Com|po|stela (city,
Spain)
San|ti|ago de Cuba
(city, Cuba)
Santo Do|min|go
(capital of the
Dominican Republic)
san|to|lina +s
san|ton|ica +s
san|tonin
San|tor|ini (= Thera,
Greece)
San|tos (city, Brazil)
san|yasi (use
sannyasi)
plural san|yasi
São Fran|cis|co (river,
Brazil)
São Luís (city, Brazil)
Saône (river, France)
São Paulo (state & its
capital, Brazil)
São Tomé and
Prin|cipe (country,
Gulf of Guinea)
sap
saps
sapped
sap|ping
sapan|wood (use
sappanwood)
sa|pele +s
sap|ful
sapid
sapid|ity
sapi|ence
sapi|ent
sapi|en|tial
sapi|ent|ly
Sapir, Ed|ward (US
linguist &
anthropologist)
sap|less
sap|ling +s
sapo|dilla +s
sap|on|aceous
sap|oni|fi|able

sap|oni|fi|ca|tion
sap|on|ify
sap|oni|fies
sap|oni|fied
sap|oni|fy|ing
sap|onin +s
sap|pan|wood
sap|per +s
Sap|phic adjective (of
Sappho; lesbian)
sap|phics noun (verse)
sap|phire +s
sap|phire blue +s
(sapphire-blue when
preceding a noun)
sap|phir|ine
Sap|pho (Greek poet)
sap|pi|ly
sap|pi|ness
Sap|poro (city, Japan)
sappy
sap|pi|er
sap|pi|est
sapro|genic
sapro|phyte +s
sapro|phyt|ic
sap|suck|er +s
sap|wood
SAR (search and
rescue)
[☞ Saar]
sara|band +s
sara|bande +s (use
saraband)
Sara|cen
Sara|cen|ic
Sara|gossa (city,
Spain)
Sarah (Bible)
[☞ Serra Peaks]
Sara|jevan +s
Sara|jevo (capital of
Bosnia and
Herzegovina)
sar|angi +s
Sar|ansk (city, Russia)
Saran Wrap
proprietary
sar|ape +s (use
serape)
Sara|toga (battle site,
US)
Sara|tov (city, Russia)
Sara|wak (state,
Malaysia)
sar|casm +s
sar|cas|tic
sar|cas|tic|ally
Sar|cee
plural Sar|cee or
Sar|cees

sar|coma
  sar|co|mas or
  sar|co|mata
sar|coma|to|sis
sar|coma|tous
sar|coph|agus
  sar|coph|agi
sar|co|plasm
sar|cous
sard +s
Sar|da|napa|lus
  (Assyrian king)
sar|dine +s
Sar|dinia
  (Mediterranean
  island; former
  kingdom, Europe)
Sar|din|ian +s
Sar|dis (ancient city,
  Asia Minor)
sar|don|ic
sar|don|ic|ally
sar|doni|cism
sard|onyx
saree +s (use sari)
Sar|gasso (W Atlantic
  sea)
sar|gasso
  sar|gas|sos or
  sar|gas|soes
sar|gas|sum
  (= sargasso)
  sar|gassa
sarge (= sergeant)
Sar|gent, Sir (Henry)
  Mal|colm Watts
  (English conductor)
  [☞ sergeant]
Sar|gent, John
  Sing|er (US painter)
  [☞ sergeant]
Sar|godha (city,
  Pakistan)
Sar|gon (founder of
  Akkad; Assyrian
  king)
sari +s
sarin
Sark (Channel island)
sark|i|ly
sark|i|ness
sarky
  sark|i|er
  sark|i|est
Sar|ma|tia (ancient
  region, Europe)
Sar|ma|tian +s
sar|men|tose
sar|men|tous (use
  sarmentose)
Sar|nia (city, Canada)
sar|nie +s
sarod +s

sar|ong +s
Sar|on|ic (gulf,
  Greece)
saros
Sar|pedon (Greek
  Myth)
Sarre (= Saar,
  Germany)
sarsa|pa|rilla +s
sar|sen +s
SAR Tech +s
Sarto, An|drea del
  (Italian painter)
sar|tor|ial
sar|tor|ial|ly
sar|tor|ius
  sar|torii
Sartre, Jean-Paul
  (French
  existentialist)
Sar|trean +s
Sar|trian +s (use
  Sartrean)
Sarum (Christianity; in
  'Old Sarum')
  [☞ Ceram]
sash
  sash|es
sa|shay +s +ed +ing
  (saunter)
  [☞ sachet]
sashed adjective
sa|shi|mi
Sas|ka|bush
  (Saskatoon)
Sas|katch|ewan
  (province & river,
  Canada)
Sas|katch|ewan|ian
  +s
Sas|ka|toon (city,
  Canada)
sas|ka|toon +s
sas|quatch
  plural sas|quatch or
  sas|quatch|es
sass
  sass|es
  sassed
  sass|ing
sas|saby
  sas|sa|bies
sas|sa|fras
  sas|sa|fras|es
Sas|san|ian +s
Sas|san|id +s
Sas|sen|ach +s
  offensive
sas|si|ly
sas|si|ness
Sas|soon, Sieg|fried
  Lor|raine (English
  writer)

sassy
  sas|si|er
  sas|si|est
sas|trugi
SAT proprietary
  (Scholastic Aptitude
  Test)
  SATs
sat
Satan (the Devil)
sat|ang
  plural sat|angs or
  sat|ang
satan|ic
satan|ic|ally
Satan|ism
Satan|ist +s
satay +s
satch|el +s
sate
  sates
  sated
  sating
saté +s (use satay)
sateen
sat|el|lite +s
Sati (wife of Siva)
  [☞ Satie]
sati +s (widow's self-
  immolation: use
  suttee)
sati|able
sati|ate
  sati|ates
  sati|at|ed
  sati|at|ing
sati|ation
Satie, Erik Al|fred
  Les|lie (French
  composer)
sa|ti|ety
sat|in +s +ed +ing
satin|wood +s
sat|iny
sat|ire +s (parody)
sa|tir|ic
sa|tir|ic|al
sa|tir|ic|al|ly
sat|ir|ist +s
sat|ir|iz|a|tion +s
sat|ir|ize
  sat|ir|iz|es
  sat|ir|ized
  sat|ir|iz|ing
satis|fac|tion +s
satis|fac|tor|i|ly
satis|fac|tor|i|ness
satis|fac|tory
satis|fi|able
satis|fy
  satis|fies
  satis|fied
  satis|fy|ing

satis|fy|ing adjective
satis|fy|ing|ly
Sato Eisaku
  (Japanese prime
  minister)
sa|tori
sat|rap +s
sat|rapy
  sat|rap|ies
Sat|suma (former
  province, Japan)
sat|suma +s
sat|ur|able
sat|ur|ant +s
sat|ur|ate
  sat|ur|ates
  sat|ur|at|ed
  sat|ur|at|ing
sat|ur|at|ed adjective
sat|ur|a|tion +s
Sat|ur|day +s
Sat|urn (Roman Myth;
  planet)
Sat|urna (island,
  Canada)
Sat|ur|na|lia (Roman
  festival)
sat|ur|na|lia (orgy)
  plural sat|ur|na|lia
  or sat|ur|na|lias
sat|ur|na|lian
Sat|urn|ian
sat|urni|id +s
sat|ur|nine
sat|ur|nine|ly
sat|ya|graha +s
satyr +s (woodland
  creature; lecher;
  butterfly)
  [☞ satire]
satyr|ia|sis
sa|tyrid +s
sauce
  sauces
  sauced
  sau|cing
sauce|boat +s
sauced adjective
sauce|less
sauce|pan +s
sau|cer +s
sauce tar|tare
  (= tartar sauce)
sau|ci|ly
sau|ci|ness
saucy
  sau|ci|er
  sau|ci|est
Saud (ibn
  Abdul-Aziz) (Saudi
  Arabian king)

Saudi +s (of Saudi
  Arabia)
  [☞ **Soddy**]
Saudi Ara|bia
  (country, Asia)
Saudi Ara|bian +s
sauer|braten +s
sauer|kraut
sau|ger
  plural **sau|ger** or
  sau|gers
Sauk
  plural **Sauk** or **Sauks**
Saul (*Bible*)
Saul of Tar|sus
  (St. Paul)
Saul|teaux
  plural **Saul|teaux**
Sault Ste. Marie (city,
  Canada; town, US)
  [☞ **the Soo**]
sauna +s (steam bath)
  [☞ **sangha, San'a,**
  Sogne]
Saun|ders, Sir
  Charles Ed|ward
  (Marquis wheat
  developer)
saun|ter +s +ed +ing
saun|ter|er +s
saur|ian
saur|is|chian +s
sauro|pod +s
saury (fish)
  saur|ies
  [☞ **sori**]
saus|age +s
Saus|sure,
  Fer|di|nand de
  (Swiss linguist)
Saus|sur|ean +s
sauté
  sau|tés
  sau|téed
  sauté|ing
Sau|ternes (district,
  France; wine)
  plural **Sau|ternes**
Sauvé, Jeanne
  Ma|thilde (Cdn
  governor general)
Sau|vi|gnon +s
Sau|vi|gnon Blanc +s
sav|able
sav|age
  sav|ages
  sav|aged
  sav|aging
sav|age|ly
sav|age|ness
sav|agery
  sav|age|ries

Savai'i (SW Pacific
  island)
sa|van|na +s (*use*
  savannah)
Sa|van|nah (city, US)
sa|van|nah +s
sa|van|nah spar|row
  +s
Sav|an|na|ket
  (= Savannakhet)
Sav|an|na|khet (town,
  Laos)
sav|ant +s
Sav|ard, Félix-
  Antoine (Cdn
  educator & writer)
sa|vate
save
  saves
  saved
  sav|ing
save|able (*use*
  savable)
sav|eloy +s
saver +s (person or
  thing that saves)
  [☞ **savour**]
Sav|ery, Thom|as
  (English engineer)
  [☞ **savoury,**
  savory]
savin +s
sav|ine +s (*use* **savin**)
sav|ing +s *noun*
sav|ior +s (*use*
  saviour)
sav|iour +s
sav|oir faire
Sav|ona|rola,
  Gi|ro|la|mo
  (Dominican
  preacher)
Sav|on|linna (town,
  Finland)
savor +s +ed +ing
  (enjoy, characteristic
  taste: *use* **savour**)
  [☞ **saver**]
savor|i|ly (*use*
  savourily)
savor|i|ness (*use*
  savouriness)
savor|less (*use*
  savourless)
savory (herb; *for* tasty,
  not sweet *or* pleasant
  use **savoury**)
  savor|ies
  [☞ **Savery**]
sav|our +s +ed +ing
  (enjoy; characteristic
  taste etc.)
  [☞ **saver**]
sav|our|i|ly

sav|our|i|ness
sav|our|less
sav|oury (tasty; not
  sweet; pleasant)
  sav|our|ies
  [☞ **savory, Savery**]
Savoy +s (region,
  France; cabbage)
Savoy|ard +s
Savu (sea, Indian
  Ocean)
savvy
  sav|vi|er
  sav|vi|est
  sav|vies
  sav|vied
  savvy|ing
saw
  saws
  sawed
  sawn or **sawed**
  saw|ing
saw|bill +s
saw blade +s
saw|bones
  plural **saw|bones**
saw|buck +s
Saw|chuk, Ter|rence
  Gor|don ('Terry')
  (Cdn hockey player)
saw|dust
sawed *past & past*
  participle of **saw**
  [☞ **sod**]
sawed-off
saw|fish
  plural **saw|fish** or
  saw|fish|es
saw|fly
  saw|flies
saw|grass
saw|horse +s
saw|like
saw|log +s
saw|mill +s
saw|mill|er +s
saw|mill|ing
sawn
sawn-off
saw off *verb*
  saws off
  sawed off
  saw|ing off
saw-off +s *noun*
saw pit +s
saw|tooth
saw|toothed
saw-whet owl +s
saw|yer +s
sax
  saxes
saxa|tile
Saxe-Coburg-Gotha

sax|horn +s
sax|ico|line
sax|ico|lous
saxi|frage +s
sax|ist +s
sax|man
  sax|men
Saxo Gram|mat|icus
  (Danish historian)
Sax|on +s
Saxon|ism
Sax|ony (state &
  region, Germany)
sax|ony
  sax|on|ies
Saxony-Anhalt (state,
  Germany)
saxo|phone +s
saxo|phon|ic
saxo|phon|ist +s
say (utter etc.)
  says
  said
  say|ing
  [☞ **sei**]
say|able
say|er +s
Say|ers, Dor|othy
  Leigh (English
  writer)
say|ing +s *noun*
sayo|nara
say-so
say|yid +s
scab
  scabs
  scabbed
  scab|bing
scab|bard +s
scabbed *adjective*
scab|bi|ness
scabby
  scab|bi|er
  scab|bi|est
sca|bies (skin disease)
sca|bi|ous (plant;
  affected with
  scabies)
  plural **sca|bi|ous**
scab|like
scab|rous
scab|rous|ly
scab|rous|ness
scad +s
Scaf|ell Pike
  (mountain, England)
scaf|fold +s +ed +ing
scaf|fold|er
scaf|fold|ing +s *noun*
scag +s (*use* **skag**)
sca|glio|la
scal|abil|ity
scal|able

scalar +s (*Math*)
  [☞ **scaler**]
scala|wag +s
scald +s +ed +ing
  (burn; *for* bard *use*
  skald)
scald|ing *adjective*
scale
  scales
  scaled
  scal|ing
scaled *adjective*
scale|less
sca|lene +s
scaler +s (*Forestry*)
  [☞ **scalar**]
Scales (*Zodiac*)
scali|er
scali|est
Scali|ger, Jo|seph
  Jus|tus (French
  scholar)
Scali|ger, Jul|ius
  Caesar (French
  scholar)
scali|ness
scal|la|wag +s (*use*
  scalawag)
scal|lion +s
scal|lop +s +ed +ing
scal|lop|er +s
scal|lop|ing *noun*
scal|lo|pini (*use*
  scaloppine)
scal|ly|wag +s (*use*
  scalawag)
scal|op|pine
scalp +s +ed +ing
scal|pel +s
scalp|er +s
scalp|less
scaly
  scali|er
  scali|est
scam
  scams
  scammed
  scam|ming
scam|mer +s
scamp +s +ed +ing
scam|per +s +ed
  +ing
scam|pi
scamp|ish
scan
  scans
  scanned
  scan|ning
scan|dal +s
scan|dal|ize
  scan|dal|iz|es
  scan|dal|ized
  scan|dal|iz|ing

scandal|monger +s
scan|dal|ous
scan|dal|ous|ly
scan|dal|ous|ness
Scan|di|navia (region,
  Europe)
Scan|di|nav|ian +s
scan|dium
scan|nable
scan|ner +s
scan|sion
scant +s +ed +ing
scant|i|ly
scant|i|ness
scant|ling *noun*
scant|ly
scant|ness
scanty
  scant|i|er
  scant|i|est
Scapa Flow (strait,
  Orkney Islands)
scape +s
scape|goat +s +ed
  +ing
scape|goat|er +s
scape|goat|ing *noun*
scape|grace +s
scaph|oid +s
scap|ula
  scapu|lae *or*
  scapu|las
scapu|lar +s
scapu|lary
  scapu|lar|ies
scar
  scars
  scarred
  scar|ring
scar|ab +s
scara|bae|id +s
Scar|bor|ough
  (former city, Canada)
scarce
  scar|cer
  scar|cest
scarce|ly
scarce|ness
scar|city
  scar|ci|ties
scare
  scares
  scared
  scaring
scare|crow +s
scared *adjective*
  (afraid)
  [☞ **scarred**]
scaredy-cat +s
scare|monger +s
scare|monger|ing
scarer +s

scarf
• (garment, cloth)
  scarves *or* scarfs
• (join, joint; eat
  greedily)
  scarfs
  scarfed
  scarf|ing
scarfed *adjective*
scarf|pin +s
scari|er
scari|est
scari|fi|ca|tion +s
scari|fier +s
scari|fy
  scari|fies
  scari|fied
  scari|fy|ing
scari|ly
scari|ness
scari|ous
scar|lat|ina
Scar|latti, (Giu|seppe)
  Domen|ico (Italian
  composer)
Scar|latti, (Pietro)
  Ales|san|dro
  Gas|pare (Italian
  composer)
scar|less
scar|let +s
scarp +s +ed +ing
scar|per +s +ed +ing
scarred *adjective*
  (marked with scars)
  [☞ **scared**]
Scar|ron, Paul
  (French writer)
scarves
scary (frightening)
  scari|er
  scari|est
  [☞ **skerry**]
scat (leave; jazz; feces)
  scats
  scat|ted
  scat|ting
  [☞ **skat**]
scat|back +s
scathe
  scathes
  scathed
  scath|ing
scath|ing *adjective*
scath|ing|ly
scato|logic|al
scat|ol|ogy
scat|ter +s +ed +ing
scatter|brain +s
scatter|brained
scat|tered *adjective*
scat|ter|er +s
scatter|gram +s

scatter|gun +s
scat|ter|ing +s *noun*
scat|ter plot +s
scatter|shot
scat|ti|ly
scat|ti|ness
scatty
  scat|ti|er
  scat|ti|est
scaup +s
scav|enge
  scav|en|ges
  scav|enged
  scav|en|ging
scav|en|ger +s
scena +s
scen|ar|io +s
scen|ar|ist +s
scend +s +ed +ing
  (wave impulse;
  plunge)
scene +s (place;
  incident; part of a
  drama)
  [☞ **seen**]
scen|ery (natural or
  artificial
  surroundings)
  [☞ **senary**]
scene|ster +s
scen|ic +s
scen|ic|ally
scen|og|raph|er +s
sceno|graph|ic
scen|og|raphy
scent +s +ed +ing
  (smell)
  [☞ **sent, cent**]
scent|ed *adjective*
scent|less
scep|tic +s (doubter:
  use skeptic)
  [☞ **septic**]
scep|tic|al (*use*
  skeptical)
scep|tic|al|ly (*use*
  skeptically)
scep|ti|cism (*use*
  skepticism)
scep|tre +s
scep|tred
schaden|freude
Schafer, (Ray|mond)
  Mur|ray (Cdn
  composer)
sched|ul|ar *adjective*
  [☞ **scheduler**]
sched|ule
  sched|ules
  sched|uled
  sched|ul|ing
sched|ul|er +s *noun*
  [☞ **schedular**]

sched|ul|ing *noun*
Scheele, Carl
  Wil|helm (Swedish
  chemist)
scheel|ite +s
schef|flera +s
Sche|hera|zade
  (*Arabian Nights*
  narrator)
Scheldt (river, Europe)
Schel|ling, Fried|rich
  Wil|helm Jo|seph
  von (German
  philosopher)
schema
  schem|ata or
  schem|as
schem|at|ic +s
schem|at|ic|ally
schema|tism +s
schema|tiz|a|tion +s
schema|tize
  schema|tiz|es
  schema|tized
  schema|tiz|ing
scheme
  schemes
  schemed
  schem|ing
schem|er +s
schem|ing +s *noun*
schem|ing|ly
sche|mozzle +s (*use*
  shemozzle)
scherz|ando
  scherz|andos or
  scherz|andi
scherzo +s
Schia|pa|relli, Elsa
  (French designer)
Schia|pa|relli,
  Gio|van|ni Vir|ginio
  (Italian astronomer)
Schil|ler, (Jo|hann
  Chris|toph)
  Fried|rich von
  (German writer)
schil|ling +s (Austrian
  currency)
  [☞ shilling]
Schind|ler, Oskar
  (German rescuer of
  Jews)
schip|perke +s
schism +s
schis|mat|ic
schis|mat|ic|al
schis|mat|ic|al|ly
schist +s
schis|tose
schis|tos|ity
schis|to|some +s
schis|to|som|ia|sis

schiz|an|thus
  schiz|an|thus|es
schizo +s *offensive*
schizo|carp +s
schizo|carp|ic
schizo|carp|ous
schiz|oid +s
schizo|phre|nia
schizo|phren|ic +s
Schle|gel, Aug|ust
  Wil|helm von
  (German scholar &
  translator)
Schle|gel, Fried|rich
  von (German
  philosopher)
Schleier|macher,
  Fried|rich Ernst
  Dan|iel (German
  theologian)
schle|miel +s
schlep
  schleps
  schlepped
  schlep|ping
schlepp +s +ed +ing
  (*use* schlep)
schlep|per +s
schleppy
  schlep|pi|er
  schlep|pi|est
Schles|wig (former
  Danish duchy)
Schleswig-Holstein
  (state, Germany)
Schlick, Mor|itz
  (German
  philosopher)
Schlie|mann,
  Hein|rich (German
  archaeologist)
schlier|en +s
schlock
schlocky
  schlock|i|er
  schlock|i|est
schlub +s
schlub|by
schlump +s
schmaltz
schmaltzy
  schmaltz|i|er
  schmaltz|i|est
schmatte +s (*use*
  shmatte)
schmear
Schmidt, Hel|mut
  Hein|rich
  Wal|de|mar
  (German Chancellor)
schmo
  schmoes

schmooze
  schmooz|es
  schmoozed
  schmooz|ing
schmooz|er +s
schmoozy
  schmooz|i|er
  schmooz|i|est
schmuck +s +ed +ing
  (objectionable
  person; hit, flatten)
schmucky
  schmuck|i|er
  schmuck|i|est
Schna|bel, Artur
  (Austrian-born
  pianist)
schnapps
  plural schnapps
schnau|zer +s
schnit|zel +s
Schnitz|ler, Ar|thur
  (Austrian writer)
schnor|rer +s
schnoz (*use* schnozz)
  schnoz|zes
schnozz
  schnozz|es
schnoz|zle +s
schnozz|ola +s
Schoen|berg, Ar|nold
  Franz Wal|ter (US
  composer)
schol|ar +s
schol|ar|li|ness
schol|ar|ly
schol|ar|ship +s
scho|las|tic +s
scho|las|tic|ally
scho|las|ti|cism
scho|li|ast +s
scho|li|as|tic
scho|li|um
  scho|lia
school +s +ed +ing
school age (school-
  age *when preceding a*
  noun)
school-aged
school board +s
school|boy +s
school bus
  school buses
school|child
  school|children
school|er +s
school|girl +s
school|house +s
school|ing *noun*
school leaver +s
school-leaving
school|man
  school|men

school|marm +s
school|marm|ish
school|marm|ism
school|master +s
school|master|ing
school|master|ly
school|mate +s
school|mis|tress
  school|mis|tress|es
school|room +s
school|teacher +s
school teach|ing
school work
school|yard +s
school year +s
schoon|er +s
Schop|en|hauer,
  Ar|thur (German
  philosopher)
schorl +s
schot|tische +s
  (polka)
Schrey|er, Ed|ward
  Rich|ard (Cdn
  governor general)
Schröd|inger, Erwin
  (Austrian physicist)
schtick +s (*use* shtick)
Schu|bert, Franz
  Peter (Austrian
  composer)
Schu|bert|ian
Schulz, Charles (US
  cartoonist)
Schu|mann, Clara
  Jo|seph|ine
  (German pianist)
Schu|mann, Rob|ert
  Alex|an|der
  (German composer)
schuss
  schuss|es
  schussed
  schuss|ing
schwa +s
Schwann, Theo|dor
  Am|brose Hu|bert
  (German
  physiologist)
Schwarz|eneg|ger,
  Ar|nold (US actor)
Schwarz|kopf,
  Nor|man (US
  general)
Schweit|zer, Al|bert
  (German medical
  missionary)
Schwer|in (city,
  Germany)
Schwyz (city,
  Switzerland)
sci|at|ic
sci|at|ica

sci|ence +s
sci|en|tif|ic
sci|en|tif|ic|ally
sci|en|tism +s
sci|en|tist +s
sci|en|tis|tic
Sci|en|tol|o|gist +s
Sci|en|tol|ogy
  proprietary
sci-fi
scili|cet
scilla +s (plant)
  [☞ Scylla]
Scil|lo|nian
Scilly (islands off
  England)
  Scil|lies
scim|itar +s
scin|tig|raphy
scin|til|la +s
scin|til|lant
scin|til|late
  scin|til|lates
  scin|til|lat|ed
  scin|til|lat|ing
scin|til|lat|ing
  adjective
scin|til|lat|ing|ly
scin|til|la|tion +s
sciol|ism
sciol|ist +s
sciol|is|tic
scion +s (plant shoot;
  descendant)
Scipio Aemil|ianus
  (Roman general)
Scipio Af|ri|canus
  (Roman general)
sci|rocco +s (*use*
  sirocco)
scir|rhoid
scir|rhos|ity
scir|rhous *adjective* (of
  a scirrhus or scirrhi)
scir|rhus *noun*
  (carcinoma)
  scir|rhi
scis|sile
scis|sion +s
scis|sor +s +ed +ing
scis|sor kick +s *noun*
scissor-kick +s +ed
  +ing *verb*
scis|sors
sclera +s
scler|al
scler|en|chyma
scler|ite +s
sclero|derma
sclero|phyll +s
sclero|pro|tein +s
scler|osed

scler|os|ing
scler|o|sis
  scler|o|ses
sclero|ther|apy
scler|otic +s
sclero|titis
scler|ous
Sco|bie, Ste|phen
  (Cdn writer)
scoff +s +ed +ing
scoff|er +s
scoff|law +s
scold +s +ed +ing
scold|er +s
scold|ing +s *noun*
scold|ing|ly
sco|lex
  sco|le|ces or
  sco|li|ces
scoli|o|sis
  scoli|o|ses
scoli|otic
scom|brid +s
scom|broid +s
sconce +s
Scone (ancient
  Scottish settlement)
scone +s
scoop +s +ed +ing
scoop|able
scoop|er +s
scoop|ful +s
scoop neck +s
  (scoop-neck *when*
  preceding a noun)
scoop-necked
scoot +s +ed +ing
scoot|er +s
scope
  scopes
  scoped
  scop|ing
scoped *adjective*
Scopes Trial
sco|pola|mine
scop|ula
  scop|ulae
scor|bu|tic
scor|bu|tic|ally
scorch
  scorch|es
  scorched
  scorch|ing
scorched earth
scorch|er +s
scorch|ing *adjective*
scorch|ing|ly
score
  • (*in all senses except*
  set of twenty)
  scores
  scored

scor|ing
  • (set of twenty)
  plural score or scores
score|board +s
score|card +s
score|keep|er +s
score|keep|ing
score|less
scor|er +s
score|sheet +s
scoria
  scor|iae
scori|aceous
scor|ing *noun*
scorn +s +ed +ing
scorn|er +s
scorn|ful
scorn|ful|ly
scorn|ful|ness
Scor|pian +s *noun &*
  adjective (person
  born under the sign
  of Scorpio)
  [☞ Scorpion]
Scor|pio +s
  • (zodiacal sign or
  person born under it)
  • (= Scorpius:
  constellation)
scor|pi|oid +s
Scor|pion *noun* (the
  constellation
  Scorpius; the
  zodiacal sign
  Scorpio)
  [☞ Scorpian]
scor|pion +s
scor|pion fish
  plural scor|pion fish
  or scor|pion fish|es
scor|pion fly
  scor|pion flies
Scor|pius
  (constellation)
Scor|sese, Mar|tin
  (US filmmaker)
scor|zon|era +s
Scot +s (of Scotland)
  [☞ Scott, Scots]
scot +s (tax)
  [☞ Scott]
Scotch (Scottish;
  Scots; whisky)
  Scotch|es
scotch (frustrate;
  wound; line, slash;
  wheel block; hold
  back)
  scotch|es
  scotched
  scotch|ing
Scotch bon|net +s
Scotch broom +s

Scotch broth
Scotch egg +s
Scotch|gard
  proprietary
Scotch|gard|ed
  proprietary
Scotch-Irish
Scotch|man
  Scotch|men
Scotch mist
Scotch pie +s
Scotch pine +s
Scotch snap +s
Scotch Tape +s
  proprietary noun
Scotch-tape
  proprietary verb
  Scotch-tapes
  Scotch-taped
  Scotch-taping
Scotch ter|rier +s
Scotch this|tle +s
Scotch whisky
  Scotch whis|kies
Scotch|woman
  Scotch|women
sco|ter
  plural sco|ter or
  sco|ters
scot-free
sco|tia +s
Scot|land (country,
  Great Britain)
Scot|land Yard
scot|oma
  scot|o|mata
Scots (Scottish;
  dialect)
  [☞ Scott]
Scots|man
  Scots|men
Scots|woman
  Scots|women
Scott (surname; cape,
  Canada)
  [☞ Scot, scot-free]
Scott, Bar|bara Ann
  (Cdn skater)
Scott, Dun|can
  Camp|bell (Cdn
  writer)
Scott, Fran|cis
  Reg|in|ald ('F.R.')
  (Cdn social reformer)
Scott, Rid|ley (English
  filmmaker)
Scott, Rob|ert Fal|con
  (English explorer)
Scott, Thom|as
  (executed by Metis)
Scott, Sir Wal|ter
  (Scottish writer)
Scot|ti|cism +s

Scot|tie +s
Scot|tish (of Scotland)
   [☞ schottische]
Scot|tish|ness
scoun|drel +s
scoun|drel|ism
scoun|drel|ly
scour +s +ed +ing
scour|er +s
scourge
   scour|ges
   scourged
   scour|ging
scour|ger +s
scour|ing adjective
Scouse +s (of
   Liverpool)
scouse (lobscouse)
Scous|er +s
Scout +s (Scouting)
scout +s +ed +ing
Scout|er +s (Scouting)
scout|er +s
Scout|ing noun
   (activity of Boy
   Scouts)
scout|ing noun
scout|master +s
scout's hon|our
scow +s
scowl +s +ed +ing
scowl|er +s
Scrab|ble proprietary
   (game)
scrab|ble (grope,
   scramble)
   scrab|bles
   scrab|bled
   scrab|bling
scrag
   scrags
   scragged
   scrag|ging
scrag|gi|ly
scrag|gi|ness
scrag|gly
scraggy
   scrag|gi|er
   scrag|gi|est
scram
   scrams
   scrammed
   scram|ming
scram|ble
   scram|bles
   scram|bled
   scram|bling
scram|bler +s
scran
Scran|ton (city, US)
scrap
   scraps

scrapped
scrap|ping
scrap|book +s
scrape
   scrapes
   scraped
   scrap|ing
scrap|er +s
scrap heap +s
scrap|ie
scrap|ing +s noun
scrap|per +s
scrap|pi|ly
scrap|pi|ness
scrap|ple
scrap|py
   scrap|pi|er
   scrap|pi|est
scrap|yard +s
scratch
   scratch|es
   scratched
   scratch|ing
scratch-and-sniff
scratch-and-win +s
scratch|board +s
scratch|er +s
scratch|i|ly
scratch|i|ness
scratch pad +s
scratch|proof
scratchy
   scratch|i|er
   scratch|i|est
scrav|el
   scrav|els
   scrav|elled
   or scrav|eled
   scrav|el|ling
   or scrav|el|ing
scrawb +s +ed +ing
   (use scrob)
scrawl +s +ed +ing
scrawly
scrawn|i|ness
scrawny
   scrawn|i|er
   scrawn|i|est
scream +s +ed +ing
scream|er +s
scream|ing|ly
scream|ing
   meem|ies
scree +s
screech
   screech|es
   screeched
   screech|ing
screech|er +s
screech in verb
   screech|es in
   screeched in
   screech|ing in

screech-in +s noun
screechy
   screech|i|er
   screech|i|est
screed +s
screen +s +ed +ing
screen|able
screen door +s
screened shot +s
screen|er +s
screen|ing +s noun
screen|play +s
screen print +s noun
screen-print +s +ed
   +ing verb
screen-printed
   adjective
screen print|ing noun
screen saver +s
screen shot +s
screen test +s
screen|writ|er +s
screen|writ|ing
screw +s +ed +ing
screw|able
screw|ball +s
screw|ball|er +s
screw cap +s
screw|driv|er +s +ed
   +ing
screwed adjective
screw|er +s
screw|i|er
screw|i|est
screw|i|ness
screw pine +s
screw plate +s
screw-top +s
screw up verb
   screws up
   screwed up
   screw|ing up
screw-up +s noun
screwy
   screw|i|er
   screw|i|est
Scri|abin, Alek|sandr
   Nikola|evich
   (Russian composer)
scribal (of scribes)
scrib|ble (write
   messily)
   scrib|bles
   scrib|bled
   scrib|bling
scrib|bler +s
scrib|blings noun
scrib|bly
Scribe, (Au|gus|tin)
   Eu|gène (French
   dramatist)

scribe
scribes
scribed
scrib|ing
scrib|er +s
scrim +s
scrim|mage
   scrim|ma|ges
   scrim|maged
   scrim|ma|ging
scrim|ma|ger +s
scrimp +s +ed +ing
scrimp|er +s
scrimpy
   scrimp|i|er
   scrimp|i|est
scrim|shan|der +s
scrim|shaw +s +ed
   +ing
scrip +s
script +s +ed +ing
script|ed adjective
script|ing adjective
scrip|tor|ial
scrip|tor|ium
   scrip|toria or
   scrip|tor|iums
scrip|tur|al
scrip|tur|al|ly
Scrip|ture +s (Bible)
scrip|ture +s (in
   general use)
script|writer +s
script|writing
scritch
   scritch|es
scritch|ing
scriv|ener +s
scrob
   scrobs
   scrobbed
   scrob|bing
scro|bicu|late
scrod +s
scrof|ula
scrofu|lous
scroll +s +ed +ing
scroll bar +s
scrolled adjective
scroll saw +s
scroll|work
Scrooge +s
scro|tal
scro|tum
   scrota or scro|tums
scrounge
   scroun|ges
   scrounged
   scroun|ging
scroun|ger +s
scrub
   scrubs

scrubbed
scrub|bing
scrub|bable
scrub|ber +s
scrub brush
scrub brush|es
scrub|by
scrub|bi|er
scrub|bi|est
scrub|land +s
scrub|woman
scrub|women
scruff +s +ed +ing
scruff|i|ly
scruff|i|ness
scruffy
scruff|i|er
scruff|i|est
scrum
scrums
scrummed
scrum|ming
scrum|mage
scrum|ma|ges
scrum|maged
scrum|ma|ging
scrum|ma|ger +s
scrum|my
scrum|mi|er
scrum|mi|est
scrum|ple
scrum|ples
scrum|pled
scrump|ling
scrump|tious
scrump|tious|ly
scrump|tious|ness
scrumpy
scrump|ies
scrunch
scrunch|es
scrunched
scrunch|ing
scrunch-dry
scrunch-dries
scrunch-dried
scrunch-drying
scrun|cheon +s
scrunch|ie +s (use
scrunchy)
scrun|chin +s (use
scruncheon)
scrun|chion +s (use
scruncheon)
scrunchy
scrunch|ies
scru|ple
scru|ples
scru|pled
scrup|ling
scru|pu|los|ity
scru|pu|lous
scru|pu|lous|ly
scru|pu|lous|ness

scru|tin|eer +s
scru|tin|ize
scru|tin|iz|es
scru|tin|ized
scru|tin|iz|ing
scru|tin|iz|er +s
scru|tiny
scru|tin|ies
scry
scries
scried
scry|ing
scry|er +s
SCSI (Small Computer
Systems Interface)
SCSIs
scu|ba +s
scuba dive
scuba dives
scuba dived
scuba div|ing
scuba div|er +s
scuba div|ing noun
Scud +s (missile)
scud
scuds
scud|ded
scud|ding
scuff +s +ed +ing
scuffed adjective
scuf|fle
scuf|fles
scuf|fled
scuf|fling
scuf|fler +s
scull +s +ed +ing
(Rowing; caplin
migration)
[☞ skull]
scull|er +s
scul|lery
scul|ler|ies
scul|lion +s
scul|pin +s
sculpt +s +ed +ing
sculpt|ing noun
sculp|tor +s
sculp|tress
sculp|tress|es
sculp|tur|al
sculp|tur|al|ly
sculp|ture
sculp|tures
sculp|tured
sculp|tur|ing
sculp|tured adjective
scum
scums
scummed
scum|ming
scum|bag +s
scum|ball +s

scum|ble
scum|bles
scum|bled
scum|bling
scum-bucket +s
scum|my
scum|mi|er
scum|mi|est
scun|cheon +s
scun|ner +s +ed +ing
Scun|thorpe (town,
England)
scup
plural scup
scup|per +s +ed +ing
scurf
scurfy
scurf|i|er
scurf|i|est
scur|ril|ity
scur|ril|ities
scur|ri|lous
scur|ri|lous|ly
scur|ri|lous|ness
scurry
scur|ries
scur|ried
scur|ry|ing
S-curve +s
scur|vi|ly
scur|vy
scur|vi|er
scur|vi|est
scut +s
scuta
scut|age
Scu|tari (= Shkodër,
Albania)
scutch
scutch|es
scutched
scutch|ing
scutch|eon +s
scutch|er +s
scute +s
scu|tel|lum
scu|tel|la
scut|ter +s +ed +ing
scut|tle
scut|tles
scut|tled
scut|tling
scuttle|butt +s
scu|tum
scuta
scut|work
scuzz
scuzz|es
scuzz|bag +s
scuzz|ball +s
scuz|zi|ness

scuz|zy (squalid,
sleazy)
scuz|zi|er
scuz|zi|est
[☞ SCSI]
Scylla (Greek Myth; in
'Scylla and
Charybdis')
[☞ scilla]
scy|pho|zoan +s
scythe
scythes
scythed
scyth|ing
Scythia (ancient
region, Asia &
SE Europe)
Scyth|ian +s
sea +s (body of water)
[☞ see, si]
sea|bag +s
sea bass
plural sea bass or
sea bass|es
sea|bed +s
sea|bird +s
sea|board +s
sea|boot +s
Sea|borg, Glenn
Theo|dore (US
chemist)
sea|borne
sea-chest +s
sea|coast +s
sea|cock +s
sea cow +s
sea dog +s
Sea-Doo +s
proprietary
sea fan +s
sea|far|er +s
sea|far|ing
sea floor +s
sea|foam +s
sea|foam green +s
(seafoam-green
when preceding a
noun)
sea|food +s
sea|front +s
sea|girt
sea-going
Sea|gram, Jo|seph
Emm (Cdn distiller)
sea grape +s
sea|grass
sea|grass|es
sea green +s (sea-
green when preceding
a noun)
sea|gull +s
sea hare +s
sea horse +s

Sea Is|land cot|ton
sea|kale
sea kayak +s +ed +ing
sea kayak|er +s
sea kayak|ing noun
sea|kind|li|ness
sea|kind|ly
seal +s +ed +ing
seal|able
sea lane +s
seal|ant +s
sealed-beam
seal|er +s
sea level +s
seal flip|per pie +s
sea|lift +s
sea lily
  sea lil|ies
seal|ing noun
  (canning; fastening;
  seal hunting)
  [☞ ceiling]
sea lion +s
seal oil +s (seal-oil
  when preceding a
  noun)
seal|point +s
seal|skin +s
Sealy|ham ter|rier +s
sea lyme grass
seam +s +ed +ing
  (junction; join)
  [☞ seem]
sea|man (sailor)
  sea|men
  [☞ semen,
  siemens]
sea|man|ship
sea|mark +s
seamed adjective
  [☞ seemed]
seam|er +s
sea mile +s
seam|less
seam|less|ly
seam|less|ness
sea|mount +s
sea mouse
  sea mice
seam|stress
  seam|stress|es
seamy
  seam|i|er
  seam|i|est
Seanad (upper House
  in Irish Parliament)
se|ance +s
sea pen +s
Sea Peoples
sea pie +s
sea pink +s
sea|plane +s

sea|port +s
sea|quake +s
sear +s +ed +ing
  (scorch; gun part; for
  withered use sere)
  [☞ cere, seer, sere,
  Cyr]
search
  search|es
  searched
  search|ing
search|able
search and re|place
  (search-and-replace
  when preceding a
  noun)
search and res|cue
  noun & adjective
search|er +s
search|ing adjective
search|ing|ly
search|light +s
search|master +s
sear|ing adjective
sear|ing|ly
Searle, Ron|ald
  Wil|liam Ford|ham
  (English artist)
sea salt +s
sea|scape +s
sea|shell +s
sea|shore +s
sea|sick
sea|sick|ness
sea|side +s
sea snake +s
sea|son +s +ed +ing
  (time period; spice)
  [☞ seisin]
sea|son|able
sea|son|ably
sea|son|al
sea|son|al|ity
sea|son|al|ly
sea|son|ing +s noun
sea|son|less
sea|son's tick|et +s
  (= season ticket)
sea|son tick|et +s
  (season-ticket when
  preceding a noun)
sea stack +s
sea star +s
seat +s +ed +ing
seat belt +s
seat|ed adjective
seat|ing noun
seat|less
seat|mate +s
SEATO (Southeast
  Asia Treaty
  Organization)
seat-of-the-pants

sea trout
  plural sea trout or
  sea trouts
seat sale +s
Se|attle (city, US)
Seattle|ite +s
sea|wall +s
sea|ward
sea|wards
sea|way +s
sea|weed +s
sea|weedy
sea|worth|i|ness
sea|worthy
sea-wrack +s
seb|aceous
Se|bas|tian (saint)
Se|bas|to|pol (naval
  base, Ukraine)
seb|or|rhea
seb|or|rhe|ic
sebum
sec +s
se|cant +s
seca|teurs
secco +s
se|cede
  se|cedes
  se|ced|ed
  se|ced|ing
se|ced|er +s
se|ces|sion +s
se|ces|sion|al
se|ces|sion|ism
se|ces|sion|ist +s
Se|chelt (peninsula &
  municipality,
  Canada; people,
  language)
  plural Se|chelt
se|clude
  se|cludes
  se|clud|ed
  se|clud|ing
se|clud|ed adjective
se|clu|sion +s
seco|barbi|tal
Seco|nal proprietary
sec|ond[1] +s +ed +ing
  (next after first; time;
  endorse)
  [☞ secund]
se|cond[2] +s +ed +ing
  (transfer)
  [☞ secund]
sec|ond|ar|i|ly
sec|ond|ar|i|ness
sec|ond|ary
  sec|ond|ar|ies
sec|ond base
sec|ond base|man
  sec|ond base|men
second-best

sec|ond class noun
second-class adjective
  & adverb
Sec|ond Com|ing (of
  Christ)
sec|ond com|ing (in
  general use)
second-degree
se|cond|ee +s
se|cond|er +s
sec|ond gen|er|a|tion
  noun
second-genera|tion
  adjective
second-growth
second-guess
  second-guesses
  second-guessed
  second-guessing
sec|ond hand +s
  noun
second-hand adjective
  & adverb
second-in-command
second-last
sec|ond|ly
  (furthermore)
  [☞ secundly]
se|cond|ment +s
se|condo
se|condi
second-rate
second-ratedness
sec|ond rater +s
second-run
sec|ond stor|ey
  (second-storey when
  preceding a noun)
second-strike
sec|ond string +s
  noun
second-string
  adjective
sec|ond string|er +s
sec|ond team noun
second-team
  adjective
Sec|ond World War
Se|cord, Laura (Cdn
  hero)
se|crecy
se|cret +s noun &
  adjective
  [☞ secrete]
se|cret|a|gogue +s
sec|re|taire +s
sec|re|tar|ial
sec|re|tar|iat +s
sec|re|tary (office
  employee; official;
  desk)
sec|re|tar|ies
  [☞ secretory]

secretary-general +s
sec|re|tary|ship +s
se|crete *verb*
  se|cretes
  se|cre|ted
  se|cret|ing
  [☞ secret]
se|cre|tin
se|cre|tion +s
se|cret|ive
se|cret|ive|ly
se|cret|ive|ness
se|cret|ly
se|cre|tory
  (concerned with
  secretion)
  [☞ secretary]
Sec|State
sect +s (religious
  group)
  [☞ sekt]
sect|ar|ian +s
sect|ar|ian|ism
sect|ary
  sect|ar|ies
sec|tion +s +ed +ing
sec|tion|al +s
sec|tion|al|ism
sec|tion|al|ist +s
sec|tion|al|ize
  sec|tion|al|iz|es
  sec|tion|al|ized
  sec|tion|al|iz|ing
sec|tion|al|ly
sec|tor +s
sec|tor|al
sec|tor|ial
  (= sectoral)
secu|lar
secu|lar|ism
secu|lar|ist +s
secu|lar|ity
secu|lar|iz|a|tion
secu|lar|ize
  secu|lar|iz|es
  secu|lar|ized
  secu|lar|iz|ing
secu|lar|ly
se|cund (*Botany*
  arranged on one
  side)
  [☞ second]
se|cund|ly (*Botany*)
  [☞ secondly]
secur|able
se|cure
  se|cures
  se|cured
  secur|ing
  secur|er
  secur|est
secure|ly

Se|curi|tate (former
  Romanian security
  force)
se|curi|tiz|a|tion
se|curi|tize
  se|curi|tiz|es
  se|curi|tized
  se|curi|tiz|ing
se|cur|ity
  se|cur|ities
Se|cur|ity Coun|cil
Secwepemc
  (= Shuswap)
  plural Secwepemc
Sedan (battle site,
  France)
sedan +s
sed|ate
  sed|ates
  sed|at|ed
  sed|at|ing
sed|ate|ly
sed|ate|ness
sed|ation
seda|tive +s
sed|en|tar|i|ly
sed|en|tar|i|ness
sed|en|tary
Seder +s
sed|er|unt +s
sedge +s
Sedge|moor (battle
  site, England)
Sedg|wick, Adam
  (English geologist)
sedgy
sed|ile (chancel seat)
  sed|ilia
  [☞ cedilla]
sedi|ment +s
sedi|ment|ary
sedi|ment|a|tion
sedi|ment|o|logic|al
sedi|ment|olo|gist +s
sedi|ment|ol|ogy
se|di|tion
se|di|tious
se|di|tious|ly
Sedna (*Inuit
  Mythology*)
se|duce
  se|du|ces
  se|duced
  se|du|cing
se|duced *adjective*
se|du|cer +s
se|du|cible
se|duc|tion +s
se|duc|tive
se|duc|tive|ly
se|duc|tive|ness
se|duc|tress
  se|duc|tress|es

se|du|lity
sedu|lous
sedu|lous|ly
sedu|lous|ness
se|dum +s
see (view etc.; diocese)
  sees
  saw
  seen
  see|ing
  [☞ sea, si]
see|able
seed +s +ed +ing
  (*Botany*; *Sports*;
  Chemistry)
  [☞ cede]
seed|bed +s
seed|cake +s
seed coat +s
seed corn
seed-eater +s
seed-eating
seed|er +s
seed|i|er
seed|i|est
seed|i|ly
seed|i|ness
seed|less
seed|ling +s
seed pearl +s
seed pod +s
seeds|man
  seeds|men
seed|time
seedy (pertaining to
  seed; dilapidated,
  shabby, disreputable)
  seed|i|er
  seed|i|est
  [☞ cedi]
See|ger, Pete (US
  singer-songwriter)
see|ing *conjunction &
  noun*
See|ing Eye dog +s
  proprietary
seek (search for)
  seeks
  sought
  seek|ing
  [☞ Sikh, seekh
  kebab]
seek|er +s
seekh ke|bab +s
seek|ing *conjugated
  form of* seek
  [☞ Siking]
seem (appear to be)
  seems
  seemed
  seem|ing
  [☞ seam]

seem|ing *adjective &
  noun*
seem|ing|ly
seem|li|ness
seem|ly
  seem|li|er
  seem|li|est
seen *past participle of*
  see
  [☞ scene]
seep +s +ed +ing
seep|age +s
seer +s (one who sees;
  prophet)
  [☞ sere, sear, cere,
  Cyr]
seer|sucker +s
see-saw +s +ed +ing
seethe
  seethes
  seethed
  seeth|ing
seeth|ing|ly
see-through
Se|fer|is, George
  (Greek writer)
seg|ment +s +ed
  +ing
seg|ment|al
seg|ment|al|ly
seg|ment|ary
seg|ment|a|tion +s
sego +s
Sego|via (city, Spain)
Sego|via, An|drés
  (Spanish guitarist)
seg|re|gate
  seg|re|gates
  seg|re|gat|ed
  seg|re|gat|ing
seg|re|ga|tion +s
seg|re|ga|tion|al
seg|re|ga|tion|ist +s
seg|re|ga|tive
segue
  segues
  segued
  segue|ing or
  seguing
Sehn|sucht +s
sei +s (whale)
  [☞ say]
sei|cento
seiche +s
Sei|fert, Jaro|slav
  (Czech writer)
sei|gneur +s (feudal
  lord; landholder)
sei|gneur|ial
sei|gneury
  sei|gneur|ies
sei|gnior|age +s

sei|gnor|age +s (*use* seigniorage)
Seine (river, France)
seine (fishing net)
seines
seined
sein|ing
[☞ sane]
sein|er +s
sein|ing *noun*
seisin +s (possession of land by freehold)
seis|mic
seis|mic|al
seis|mic|al|ly
seis|mi|city
seis|mo|gram +s
seis|mo|graph +s
seis|mo|graph|ic
seis|mo|graph|ic|al
seis|mo|logic|al
seis|mo|logic|al|ly
seis|molo|gist +s
seis|mol|ogy
seiz|able
seize
seiz|es
seized
seiz|ing
seiz|er +s
seizin +s (*use* seisin)
seiz|ing +s *noun*
seiz|ure +s
se|jant
Sek|ani
  plural Sek|ani or Sek|anis
Sekh|met (*Egyptian Myth*)
sekt +s (wine)
[☞ sect]
selach|ian +s
selah
Se|lang|or (state, Malaysia)
Sel|craig, Alex|an|der (= Alexander Selkirk, marooned Scottish sailor)
sel|dom
se|lect +s +ed +ing
se|lect|able
se|lec|tion +s
se|lec|tion|al
se|lec|tion|al|ly
se|lect|ive
se|lect|ive|ly
se|lect|ive|ness
se|lec|tiv|ity
  se|lec|tiv|ities
se|lect|ness
se|lect|or +s

selen|ate +s (*Chemistry*)
[☞ selenite]
Sel|ene (*Greek Myth*)
sel|en|ic
sel|en|ious
selen|ite +s (*Mineralogy*)
[☞ selenate]
selen|itic
sel|en|ium
selen|og|raph|er +s
sel|eno|graph|ic
selen|og|raphy
selen|olo|gist +s
selen|ol|ogy
Seles, Mon|ica (tennis player)
Seleu|cid +s
self
• (individual)
  selves
• (flower)
  selfs
self-abasement +s
self-abasing
self-abnega|tion +s
self-absorbed
self-absorp|tion +s
self-abuse +s
self-accusa|tion +s
self-accusa|tory
self-acting
self-action +s
self-activity
self-actual|iz|a|tion +s
self-actual|ize
  self-actual|iz|es
  self-actual|ized
  self-actual|iz|ing
self-addressed
self-adhesive
self-adjust|ing
self-admira|tion
self-advance|ment +s
self-advertise|ment
self-advertis|ing
self-affirm|a|tion +s
self-aggrand|ize|ment
self-aggrand|iz|ing
self-analys|ing (*use* self-analyzing)
self-analysis
  self-analyses
self-analyz|ing
self-appoint|ed
self-approv|al +s
self-assert|ing
self-assertion +s
self-assert|ive

self-assert|ive|ness
self-assess|ment +s
self-assurance +s
self-assured
self-assured|ly
self-aware
self-awareness
self-basting
self-betray|al +s
self-catering
self-censor|ship +s
self-centered (*use* self-centred)
self-centred
self-centred|ly
self-centred|ness
self-cleaning
self-closing
self-collect|ed
self-conceit +s
self-conceit|ed
self-confessed
self-confidence
self-confident
self-confident|ly
self-congratu|la|tion +s
self-congratu|la|tory
self-conscious
self-conscious|ly
self-conscious|ness
self-consist|ency
self-consist|ent
self-consti|tut|ed
self-contained
self-contain|ment
self-contempt
self-contemp|tu|ous
self-content
self-content|ed
self-contra|dict|ing
self-contra|dic|tion +s
self-contra|dict|ory
self-control
self-controlled
self-correct|ing
self-created
self-creation
self-critical
self-criticism +s
self-deceit
self-deceiv|er +s
self-deceiv|ing
self-deception +s
self-deceptive
self-defeat|ing
self-defence
self-defensive
self-deluded
self-delusion +s
self-denial

self-denying
self-depend|ence
self-depend|ent
self-deprecat|ing
self-deprecat|ing|ly
self-depreca|tion +s
self-depreca|tory
self-depreci|a|tion +s
self-deprecia|tory
self-destroy|ing
self-destruct +s +ed +ing
self-destruc|tion
self-destruct|ive
self-destruct|ive|ly
self-determin|a|tion
self-determined
self-determin|ing
self-develop|ment
self-direct|ed
self-disci|pline
self-disci|plined
self-discov|ery
  self-discov|eries
self-disgust
self-doubt +s
self-doubting
self-educat|ed
self-education
self-efface|ment +s
self-effacing
self-effacing|ly
self-elected
self-employed
self-employ|ment
self-empower|ing
self-empower|ment
self-esteem +s
self-evidence
self-evident
self-evident|ly
self-examin|a|tion +s
self-exile
self-exiled
self-explan|a|tory
self-expres|sion +s
self-expres|sive
self-feeder +s
self-feeding
self-fertile
self-fertil|ity
self-fertil|iz|a|tion +s
self-fertil|ized
self-fertil|iz|ing
self-finance
  self-finances
  self-financed
  self-financing
self-financing
  adjective

self-flagel|la|tion +s
self-flatter|ing
self-flattery
self-forget|ful
self-forget|ful|ness
self-fulfill|ing
self-fulfill|ment
self-fulfil|ment (use
  self-fulfillment)
self-generat|ed
self-generat|ing
self-glorifi|ca|tion +s
self-glorify|ing
self-governed
self-govern|ing
self-govern|ment
self-guided
self-hate
self-hater +s
self-hatred
self-heal +s (plant)
self-help
self|hood
self-image +s
self-immola|tion
self-importance
self-important
self-important|ly
self-imposed
self-improve|ment
  +s
self-improv|ing
self-incrimin|a|ting
self-incrimin|a|tion
  +s
self-induced
self-inductance
self-induction
self-induct|ive
self-indulgence +s
self-indulgent
self-indulgently
self-inflicted
self-insurance
self-insure
  self-insures
  self-insured
  self-insuring
self-interest +s
self-interest|ed
self-involved
self-involve|ment
self|ish
self|ish|ly
self|ish|ness
self-justifi|ca|tion +s
self-justify|ing
self-knowledge
self|less
self|less|ly
self|less|ness
self-loader +s

self-loading
self-loathing
self-locking
self-love
self-made
self-mastery
self-medicate
  self-medicates
  self-medicat|ed
  self-medicat|ing
self-medica|tion
self-mockery
self-mocking
self-motivat|ed
self-motiva|tion +s
self-murder +s
self-murder|er +s
self-mutila|tion +s
self-neglect
self|ness
self-parodic
self-parody
  self-parodies
self-parody|ing
self-perpetu|at|ing
self-perpetu|a|tion
self-pity
self-pitying
self-pitying|ly
self-pollin|at|ed
self-pollin|at|ing
self-pollin|a|tion
self-portrait +s
self-possessed
self-posses|sion
self-praise
self-preser|va|tion
self-preserv|ing
self-proclaimed
self-propagat|ing
self-propaga|tion
self-propelled
self-propel|ling
self-protec|tion +s
self-protect|ive
self-raising
self-realiz|a|tion
self-referen|tial
self-referen|tial|ity
self-regard
self-regard|ing
self-regulat|ing
self-regula|tion
self-regula|tory
self-reliance
self-reliant
self-reliant|ly
self-renewal +s
self-reproach
  self-reproach|es
self-reproach|ful
self-respect

self-respect|ing
self-restrained
self-restraint
self-reveal|ing
self-revela|tion +s
self-righteous
self-righteous|ly
self-righteous|ness
self-righting
self-rising
self-rule
self-sacri|fice
self-sacri|fi|cing
self|same
self-satisfac|tion
self-satisfied
self-satisfy|ing
self-sealing
self-seed +s +ed +ing
self-seeder +s
self-seeding adjective
self-seeker +s
self-seeking
self-select|ed
self-select|ing
self-selection
self-serve +s
self-service
self-serving
self-sow
  self-sows
  self-sowed
  self-sown
  or self-sowed
  self-sowing
self-sown
self-starter +s
self-sterile
self-steril|ity
self-styled
self-sufficien|cy
self-sufficient
self-sufficient|ly
self-sugges|tion
self-support
self-support|ing
self-surren|der
self-sustained
self-sustain|ing
self-tanner +s
self-tanning
self-tapping
self-taught
self-torture
self-understand|ing
self-will
self-willed
self-winding
self-worth
Sel|juk (Turkish
  dynasty)
Sel|juk|ian +s

Sel|kirk (mountains,
  Canada)
Sel|kirk, Alex|an|der
  (Scottish sailor)
Sel|kirk, Thom|as
  Doug|las, 5th Earl
  of (Red River
  colonizer)
Sel|kirk set|tler +s
Sel|kirk|shire (former
  county, Scotland)
sell (exchange for
  money)
  sells
  sold
  sell|ing
  [☞ cel, cell, Szell]
sell|able
Sella|field (nuclear
  installation, England)
sell-by date +s
sell|er +s (a person or
  product that sells)
  [☞ cellar]
Sel|lers, Peter
  (English comic actor)
seller's mar|ket
sell off verb
  sells off
  sold off
  sell|ing off
sell-off +s noun
Sello|tape +s
  proprietary
sello|tape verb
  sello|tapes
  sello|taped
  sello|tap|ing
sell out verb
  sells out
  sold out
  sell|ing out
sell|out +s noun
selt|zer +s
sel|vage (Textiles;
  Geology; lock)
sel|vedge +s (Textiles,
  Geology, lock: use
  selvage)
selves
Sel|wyn (mountains,
  Canada)
Selye, Hans Hugo
  Bruno (Cdn
  physician)
Selz|nick, David
  Oli|ver (US
  filmmaker)
SEM (scanning
  electron microscope)
  SEMs
seman|tic
seman|tic|ally
seman|ti|cist +s

seman|tics
sema|phore
  sema|phores
  sema|phored
  sema|phor|ing
sema|phor|ic
sema|phor|ic|ally
Se|mar|ang (city, Indonesia)
sem|blable +s
sem|blance +s
semé (Heraldry)
semée (Heraldry: use semé)
Semei (city, Kazakhstan)
Sem|ele (Greek Myth)
sem|eme +s
semen (reproductive fluid)
  [☞ seaman, siemens]
se|mes|ter +s
se|mes|tered
se|mes|ter|ing
Semey (= Semei, Kazakhstan)
semi +s (semi-detached home; semifinal; semi-trailer)
  [☞ semé, Semei]
semi-annual
semi-annual|ly
semi|aqua|tic
semi-arid
semi-auto +s
semi-automat|ic +s
semi-autono|mous
semi-basement +s
semi|breve +s
semi|circle +s
semi|circu|lar
semi|colon +s
semi|conduct|ing
semi|conduct|or +s
semi-conscious
semi-conscious|ly
semi-conscious|ness
semi|cylin|der +s
semi|cylin|drical
semi-desert +s
semi-detached +s
semi|diameter +s
semi-documen|tary
  semi-documen|taries
semi-double
semi|final +s
semi|final|ist +s
semi-finished
semi-fitted
semi|fluid +s

semi-formal +s
semi|gloss
  semi|gloss|es
semi-independ|ent
semi-invalid +s
semi-liquid +s
Sé|mil|lon +s
semi-lunar
semi-monthly
sem|inal (of semen; original)
  [☞ Seminole]
sem|in|al|ly
sem|in|ar +s
sem|in|ar|ian +s
sem|in|ar|ist +s
sem|in|ary
  sem|in|ar|ies
sem|in|ifer|ous
Sem|in|ole +s (people; language)
  [☞ seminal]
semi-official
semi-official|ly
semio|logic|al
semi|ol|o|gist +s
semi|ol|ogy
semi-opaque
semi|ot|ic
semi|ot|ic|al
semi|ot|ic|al|ly
semi|ot|ician +s
semi|ot|ics
Semi|pa|la|tinsk (former name for Semei, Kazakhstan)
semi-palmat|ed
semi-permanent
semi-permanent|ly
semi-permeabil|ity
semi-permeable
semi-precious
semi-private
semi-pro +s
semi-profes|sion|al +s
semi-profes|sion|al|ly
semi|quaver +s
Se|mira|mis (Greek Myth)
semi-retired
semi-retire|ment
semi-rigid
semi-skilled
semi-soft
semi-solid
semi-submer|sible +s
semi-sweet
semi-synthet|ic
Sem|ite +s

Sem|itic
Sem|it|ism
Sem|it|ist +s
semi|tonal
semi|tone +s
semi-trailer +s
semi-transpar|ent
semi-tropic|al
semi-tropics
semi-vowel +s
semi-weekly
Sem|mel|weis, Ignaz Phil|ipp (Austro–Hungarian obstetrician)
semo|lina
sem|per|vivum +s
sem|pi|ter|nal
sem|pi|ter|nal|ly
sem|plice
sem|pre
Sem|tex
sen|ary (of six)
  [☞ scenery]
Sen|ate +s (upper chamber of Parliament, Congress, etc.)
  [☞ Sennett]
sen|ate +s (university governing body; Roman History)
  [☞ sennet]
sen|ator +s
sen|ator|ial
sen|ator|ship +s
send (cause to go)
  sends
  sent
  send|ing
  [☞ scend]
send|able
Sen|dai (city, Japan)
Sen|dak, Mau|rice Ber|nard (US artist)
sen|dal
send|er +s
Sen|dero Lumin|oso
send off verb
  sends off
  sent off
  send|ing off
send-off +s noun
send up verb
  sends up
  sent up
  send|ing up
send-up +s noun
Sen|eca, Lu|cius An|naeus ('the Young|er') (Roman statesman & dramatist)

Sen|eca, Mar|cus (or Lu|cius) An|naeus ('the Elder') (Roman rhetorician)
Sen|eca (people; language; snakeroot)
  plural Sen|eca or Sen|ecas
Sene|felder, (Johan Nepo|muk Franz) Aloys (German writer)
Sen|egal (country, Africa)
Sen|egal|ese
  plural Sen|egal|ese
Sene|gam|bia (region, West Africa)
Sene|gam|bian
sen|esce
  sen|es|ces
  sen|esced
  sen|es|cing
sen|es|cence
sen|es|cent
sene|schal +s
senhor (Portuguese or Brazilian man)
  senhors or senhores
  [☞ señor, signor]
senhora +s (Portuguese woman; Brazilian married woman)
  [☞ señora, signora]
senhor|ita +s (Brazilian unmarried woman)
  [☞ señorita]
se|nile +s
sen|il|ity
sen|ior +s (of superior age, rank, etc.)
  [☞ señor, senhor, signor, seigneur]
sen|ior|ity
sen|iti
  plural sen|iti
Senna, Ayr|ton (Brazilian racing driver)
senna
Sen|nach|erib (Assyrian king)
sen|net +s (trumpet call)
  [☞ senate]
Sen|nett, Mack (Cdn-born filmmaker)
  [☞ Senate]
sen|night +s
se|ñor (Spanish-speaking man)

se|ñores
[☞ senhor, signor]
se|ñora +s (Spanish-speaking married woman)
[☞ senhora, signora]
señor|ita +s (Spanish-speaking unmarried woman)
[☞ senhorita]
sens|ate
sen|sa|tion +s
sen|sa|tion|al
sen|sa|tion|al|ism
sen|sa|tion|al|ist +s
sen|sa|tion|al|is|tic
sen|sa|tion|al|ize
sen|sa|tion|al|iz|es
sen|sa|tion|al|ized
sen|sa|tion|al|iz|ing
sen|sa|tion|al|ly
sense (faculty of sensation; judgment; meaning)
senses
sensed
sens|ing
[☞ cense, cens]
sense|less
sense|less|ly
sense|less|ness
sens|ibil|ity
sens|ibil|ities
sens|ible
sens|ible|ness
sens|ibly
sensi|tive +s
sensi|tive|ly
sensi|tive|ness
sensi|tiv|ity
sensi|tiv|ities
sensi|tiz|a|tion
sensi|tize
sensi|tiz|es
sensi|tized
sensi|tiz|ing
sensi|tiz|er +s
sensi|tom|eter +s
sensor +s (device that responds to light, heat, motion, etc.)
[☞ censor, censer, censure]
sen|sor|ial
sen|sor|ial|ly
sen|sor|ily
sen|sor|ium
sen|soria or sen|sor|iums
sen|sory
sen|su|al
sen|su|al|ism

sen|su|al|ist +s
sen|su|al|ity
sen|su|al|ize
sen|su|al|iz|es
sen|su|al|ized
sen|su|al|iz|ing
sen|su|al|ly
sen|su|ous
sen|su|ous|ly
sen|su|ous|ness
sent +s (past & past participle of send; Estonian monetary unit)
[☞ scent; cent]
sente (monetary unit of Lesotho)
li|sente
sen|tence
sen|ten|ces
sen|tenced
sen|ten|cing
sen|ten|cing +s noun
sen|ten|tial
sen|ten|tious
sen|ten|tious|ly
sen|ten|tious|ness
sen|tience
sen|tiency
sen|tient
sen|tient|ly
senti|ment +s
senti|ment|al
senti|ment|al|ism
senti|ment|al|ist +s
senti|men|tal|ity
senti|men|tal|ities
senti|ment|al|iz|a|tion
senti|ment|al|ize
senti|ment|al|iz|es
senti|ment|al|ized
senti|ment|al|iz|ing
senti|ment|al|ly
sen|ti|nel
sen|ti|nels
sen|ti|nelled
sen|ti|nel|ling
sen|try
sen|tries
Se|nus|si
plural Se|nus|si
Seoul (capital of South Korea)
[☞ Seul]
sepal +s
sep|ar|abil|ity
sep|ar|able
sep|ar|able|ness
sep|ar|ably
sep|ar|ate
sep|ar|ates

sep|ar|at|ed
sep|ar|at|ing
sep|ar|ate|ly
sep|ar|ate|ness
sep|ar|a|tion +s
sep|ara|tism +s
sep|ara|tist +s
sep|ara|tive
sep|ar|ator +s
Seph|ar|di
Seph|ar|dim
Seph|ar|dic
sep|ia +s
se|poy +s
sep|puku
sep|sis
sep|ses
sept +s
septa
sep|tal
sep|tate
sep|ta|tion
Sep|tem|ber +s
sep|ten|arius
sep|ten|arii
sep|ten|ary
sep|ten|ar|ies
sep|ten|nial
sep|tet +s
sep|tic +s (in 'septic tank', 'septic system' etc.)
sep|tic|ally
septi|cemia
septi|cemic
sep|ti|city
Sept-Îles (city, Canada)
sep|til|lion
plural sep|til|lion or sep|til|lions
sep|toria
sep|tua|gen|ar|ian +s
Sep|tua|ges|ima
Sep|tua|gint
sep|tum
septa
se|pul|chral
se|pul|chral|ly
sep|ul|chre +s
sep|ul|ture +s
se|qua|cious
se|qua|cious|ly
se|qua|city
se|quel +s
se|quela
se|quelae
se|quence
se|quen|ces
se|quenced
se|quen|cing
se|quen|cer +s
se|quent

se|quen|tial
se|quen|tial|ity
se|quen|tial|ly
se|quent|ly
se|ques|ter +s +ed +ing
se|ques|trable
se|ques|tral
se|ques|trate
se|ques|trates
se|ques|trat|ed
se|ques|trat|ing
se|ques|tra|tion
se|ques|tra|tor +s
se|ques|trum
se|ques|tra
se|quin +s
se|quined
se|quinned (use sequined)
se|quoia +s
sera plural of serum
[☞ Serra, Sarah, Syrah]
serac +s
sera|glio +s
serai +s
Seram (= Ceram Sea)
[☞ serum, Sarum]
ser|ape +s
ser|aph (Bible; heavenly being)
ser|aph|im or ser|aphs
[☞ serif]
ser|aph|ic
ser|aph|ic|ally
Sera|pis (Egyptian Myth)
Serb +s
Serbia (Balkan republic)
Serb|ian +s
Serbo-Croat
Serbo-Croatian
sere +s (withered; sequence of ecological communities; for gun part use sear)
[☞ cere, sear, seer, Cyr]
Ser|em|ban (city, Malaysia)
ser|en|ade
ser|en|ades
ser|en|ad|ed
ser|en|ad|ing
ser|en|ad|er +s
ser|en|ata +s
ser|en|dip|it|ous
ser|en|dip|it|ous|ly

ser|en|dip|ity
  ser|en|dip|ities
se|rene (tranquil; calm)
  se|ren|er
  se|ren|est
  [☞ serine]
se|rene|ly
se|rene|ness
Ser|en|geti (plain, Tanzania)
se|ren|ity
serf +s (feudal labourer)
  [☞ surf]
serf|dom
serf|hood
serge +s (fabric)
  [☞ surge]
ser|geancy
  ser|gean|cies
ser|geant +s
  [☞ Sargent]
sergeant-at-arms
  sergeants-at-arms
sergeant|ship +s
ser|ger +s
Ser|gipe (state, Brazil)
ser|ial +s (forming a series; habitual; periodical)
  [☞ cereal, surreal]
seri|al|ism (Music)
  [☞ surrealism]
seri|al|ist +s (Music)
  [☞ surrealist]
seri|al|ity (sequentiality)
  [☞ surreality]
seri|al|iz|a|tion +s
seri|al|ize
  serial|iz|es
  serial|ized
  serial|iz|ing
seri|al|ly (sequentially)
  [☞ surreally]
seri|ate
  seri|ates
  seri|at|ed
  seri|at|ing
seri|atim
seri|a|tion +s
seri|ceous
seri|cul|tur|al
seri|cul|ture
seri|cul|tur|ist +s
seri|ema +s
ser|ies (set or sequence of things)
  plural ser|ies
  [☞ Ceres, cerise]

ser|if +s (Printing)
  [☞ seraph]
ser|ifed
seri|graph +s
ser|ig|raph|er +s
ser|ig|raphy
ser|ine (amino acid)
  [☞ serene]
ser|inga +s (rubber tree; for mock orange or lilac use syringa)
serio-comic
serio-comical|ly
ser|ious (solemn; earnest; significant)
  [☞ Sirius]
ser|ious|ly
ser|ious|ness
ser|mon +s
ser|mon|ette +s
ser|mon|ic
ser|mon|ize
  ser|mon|iz|es
  ser|mon|ized
  ser|mon|iz|ing
ser|mon|iz|er +s
sero|con|ver|sion +s
sero|con|vert +s +ed +ing
sero|logic
sero|logic|al
sero|logic|al|ly
ser|ol|o|gist +s
ser|ol|ogy
sero|nega|tive
sero|nega|tiv|ity
sero|posi|tive
sero|posi|tiv|ity
ser|osa +s
ser|os|al
ser|os|ity
sero|tonin
ser|ous (of or like serum; watery)
  [☞ cirrus, scirrhus, scirrhous]
Ser|pens (constellation)
ser|pent +s
ser|pen|tine
  ser|pen|tines
  ser|pen|tined
  ser|pen|tin|ing
ser|pigin|ous
ser|ran|id +s
Serra Peaks (in Canada)
  [☞ Sarah]
ser|rate
  ser|rates
  ser|rat|ed
  ser|rat|ing

ser|rat|ed adjective
ser|ra|tion +s
ser|ried
ser|ru|late
ser|ru|la|tion +s
Ser|tor|ius, Quin|tus (Roman soldier)
serum (fluid)
  sera or ser|ums
  [☞ Ceram, Sarum]
ser|val +s
ser|vant +s
servant|hood
servant|less
serve
  serves
  served
  serv|ing
serv|er +s
Ser|ve|tus, Mi|chael (Spanish theologian)
Ser|vice, Rob|ert Wil|liam (Cdn writer)
ser|vice
  ser|vi|ces
  ser|viced
  ser|vi|cing
ser|vice|abil|ity
ser|vice|able
ser|vice|able|ness
ser|vice|ably
service|berry
  service|ber|ries
ser|viced adjective
service|man
  service|men
service|woman
  service|women
ser|vi|ette +s
ser|vile
ser|vile|ly
ser|vil|ity
serv|ing +s noun
ser|vi|tor +s
ser|vi|tude +s
ser|vo +s
servo-mechan|ism +s
servo-motor +s
sesa|me +s
sesa|moid +s
Se|sotho
ses|qui|cen|ten|ary
  ses|qui|cen|ten|aries
ses|qui|cen|ten|nial
ses|sile
ses|sion +s (meeting; term; governing body)
  [☞ cession]
ses|sion|al

Ses|sions, Roger Hunt|ing|ton (US composer)
ses|terce +s
ses|ter|tius
  ses|ter|tii
ses|tet +s
ses|tina +s
Set (= Seth, Egyptian god)
set
  sets
  set
  set|ting
seta
  setae
se|ta|ceous
set aside verb
  sets aside
  set aside
  set|ting aside
set-aside +s noun
set back verb
  sets back
  set back
  set|ting back
set|back +s noun
Seth (Egyptian Myth)
se|tif|er|ous
se|tiger|ous
set off verb
  sets off
  set off
  set|ting off
set-off +s noun
Seton, Er|nest Thomp|son (N American naturalist)
se|tose
Se|tswa|na (language; plural of Tswana)
sett +s (badger's burrow, paving stone: use set)
set|tee +s
set|ter +s
set|ting +s noun
set|tle
  set|tles
  set|tled
  set|tling
settle|able
set|tled adjective
settle|ment +s
set|tler +s (one who settles in a new place)
  [☞ settlor]
set|tler's ef|fects
set|tlor (one who creates a trust)
  [☞ settler]

set to *verb*
  sets to
  set to
  set|ting to
set-to +s *noun*
Setú|bal (town,
  Portugal)
set up *verb*
  sets up
  set up
  set|ting up
set-up +s *noun &*
  adjective
Seul (lake, Canada)
  [☞ Seoul]
Seurat, Georges
  Pierre (French
  painter)
Seuss, Dr. (US writer
  & illustrator)
Se|vas|to|pol
  (= Sebastopol,
  Ukraine)
sev|en +s
seven|fold
seven-minute icing
Seven Oaks (battle
  site, Canada)
seven|teen +s
seven|teenth +s
sev|enth +s
Seventh-day
  Ad|vent|ist +s
seventh|ly
seven|ti|eth
seven|ty
  sev|enties
seventy-eight +s
  (record)
78 (record)
  78s
seventy-eighth +s
seventy-fifth +s
seventy-first +s
seventy-five +s
seventy|fold
seventy-four +s
seventy-fourth +s
seventy-nine +s
seventy-ninth +s
seventy-one +s
seventy-second +s
seventy-seven +s
seventy-seventh +s
seventy-six
  seventy-sixes
seventy-sixth +s
seventy-third +s
seventy-three +s
seventy-two +s
Seven Years War
sev|er +s +ed +ing
sev|er|able +s

sev|er|al
sev|er|ally
sev|er|al|ty
sev|er|ance +s
se|vere
  se|verer
  se|ver|est
se|vere|ly
se|ver|ity
Sev|ern (rivers,
  Canada & Britain)
Se|ver|naya Zem|lya
  (islands off Russia)
Sev|ero|dvinsk (city,
  Russia)
Se|verus, Sep|tim|ius
  (Roman emperor)
se|viche (*use* ceviche)
Sévi|gné, Mar|quise
  de (French letter
  writer)
Se|ville (city, Spain;
  orange)
Sèvres (suburb of
  Paris; porcelain)
sew (stitch)
  sews
  sewed
  sewn or sewed
  sew|ing
  [☞ sow]
sew|age +s
Sew|ard, Wil|liam
  Henry (US
  politician)
sew|er +s (gutter,
  conduit; one who
  sews)
  [☞ sower, suer]
sewer|age +s
sew|ing *noun*
  (needlework)
  [☞ sowing]
sewn *past participle of*
  sew
  [☞ sown, sone,
  Saône]
sex
  sexes
  sexed
  sex|ing
sexa|gen|ar|ian +s
Sexa|ges|ima
sexa|ges|imal +s
sexa|ges|imal|ly
sex|cen|ten|ary
  sex|cen|ten|aries
sexed *adjective*
sex|en|nial
sex|er +s
sex|i|er
sex|i|est
sex|i|ly

sex|i|ness
sex|ism
sex|ist +s
sex|less
sex|less|ly
sex|less|ness
sex-linked
sex|ologic|al
sex|ol|o|gist +s
sex|ol|ogy
sex|part|ite
sex|pert +s
sex|ploit|a|tion
sex|pot +s
sex-starved
sext +s
sex|tant +s
sex|tet +s
sex|til|lion
  plural sex|til|lion or
  sex|til|lions
sex|til|lionth +s
sex|ton +s
sex|tuple
  sex|tuples
  sex|tupled
  sex|tup|ling
sex|tup|let +s
sex|tup|ly
sex|ual
sex|u|al|ity
sex|ual|iz|a|tion
sex|ual|ize
  sex|ual|iz|es
  sex|ual|ized
  sex|ual|iz|ing
sex|ual|ly
sexy
  sex|i|er
  sex|i|est
Sey|chelles (country,
  Indian Ocean)
Sey|chel|lois
  plural Sey|chel|lois
Sey|mour, Fred|erick
  (governor of BC)
Sey|mour, Jane (wife
  of Henry VIII)
Sey|mour, Lynn
  (Cdn-born dancer)
sez
Sfax (city, Tunisia)
Sfor|za, Carlo, Count
  (Italian diplomat)
Sfor|za, Fran|cesco
  (Italian condottiere)
Sfor|za, Lodo|vico
  (Italian condottiere)
sfor|zan|do
  sfor|zan|dos or
  sfor|zan|di

sfor|za|to
  sfor|za|tos or
  sfor|za|ti
sfu|mato
sgraf|fito
  sgraf|fiti
Shaan|xi (province,
  China: capital, Xian)
  [☞ Shanxi]
Shaba (region, Congo)
Shab|bat
Shab|bes (*use*
  Shabbos)
shab|bi|ly
shab|bi|ness
Shab|bos
shabby
  shab|bi|er
  shab|bi|est
shabby|ish
shabu-shabu
shack +s +ed +ing
shackle
  shackles
  shackled
  shack|ling
shack|town +s
shacky
shad
  plural shad or shads
shad|berry
  shad|ber|ries
shad|blow +s
Shad|bolt, Jack
  Leon|ard (Cdn artist)
shad|bush
  shad|bush|es
shad|dock +s
shade
  shades
  shaded
  shad|ing
shade|less
shad|fly
  shad|flies
shad|i|er
shad|i|est
shad|i|ly
shad|i|ness
shad|ing +s *noun*
sha|doof +s
shad|ow +s +ed +ing
shad|ow box *noun*
  shad|ow boxes
shadow|box *verb*
  shadow|box|es
  shadow|boxed
  shadow|box|ing
shad|ow box|ing
  noun
shadow|er
shadow|graph +s
shadow|i|ness

shadow|less
shad|owy
Shad|rach (*Bible*)
shady
  shad|i|er
  shad|i|est
shaft +s +ed +ing
Shaftes|bury,
  An|thony Ash|ley
  Coop|er, 1st Earl of
  (English statesman)
Shaftes|bury,
  An|thony Ash|ley
  Coop|er, 7th Earl of
  (English social
  reformer)
shaft|ing +s *noun*
shag
  shags
  shagged
  shag|ging
shaga|nap|pi +s
shag|bark
shagged
shag|ger +s
shag|gi|ly
shag|gi|ness
shaggy
  shag|gi|er
  shag|gi|est
shaggy-dog
shaggy|mane +s
shag|reen
Shah, Karim Al-
  Hussain (Aga Khan)
  [☞ Shaw]
shah +s (monarch of
  Iran)
Shah Alam (city,
  Malaysia)
shah|dom +s
Shah Jahan (emperor
  of India)
Shahn, Ben (US
  painter)
  [☞ Shan]
shaikh +s (*use* sheik)
shak|able (*use*
  shakeable)
shake (agitate; drink;
  shingle)
  shakes
  shook
  shak|en
  shak|ing
  [☞ sheik]
shake|able
shake down *verb*
  shakes down
  shook down
  shak|en down
  shak|ing down
shake|down +s *noun*

shake out *verb*
  shakes out
  shook out
  shak|en out
  shak|ing out
shake-out +s *noun*
Shak|er +s (religious
  sect)
shak|er +s (*in general
  use*)
Shaker|ism
shak|er knit
  (shaker-knit *when
  preceding a noun*)
Shake|speare,
  Wil|liam (English
  dramatist)
Shake|spear|ean
Shake|spear|ean|ism
Shake|spear|ian (*use*
  Shakespearean)
Shake|spear|ian|ism
  (*use*
  Shakespeareanism)
shake up *verb*
  shakes up
  shook up
  shak|en up
  shak|ing up
shake|up +s *noun*
Shakhty (city, Russia)
  [☞ Sakti]
shak|i|ly
shak|i|ness
shako +s
Shak|ti (*Hinduism*: *use*
  Sakti)
  [☞ Shakhty]
shaku|hachi +s
shaky
  shak|i|er
  shak|i|est
shale +s
shaley
shall
  present shall
  past should
shal|lop +s
shal|lot +s (onion)
  [☞ Shalott]
shal|low +er +est +s
  +ed +ing
shal|low|ly
shal|low|ness
sha|lom
Sha|lott (in 'The Lady
  of Shalott')
  [☞ shallot]
shalt
shaly (= shaley)
sham
  shams

shammed
sham|ming
sha|man +s
sha|man|ic
sha|man|ism
sha|man|is|tic
sha|man|is|tic|ally
shama|teur +s
shama|teur|ism
sham|ble
  sham|bles
  sham|bled
  sham|bling
sham|bles
sham|bol|ic
shame
  shames
  shamed
  sham|ing
shame|faced
shame|faced|ly
shame|faced|ness
shame|ful
shame|ful|ly
shame|ful|ness
shame|less
shame|less|ly
shame|less|ness
Sha|mir, Yit|zhak
  (Israeli statesman)
sham|mer +s
shammy (= chamois:
  leather)
  sham|mies
  [☞ chamois]
sham|poo
  sham|poos
  sham|pooed
  sham|poo|ing
sham|poo|er +s
sham|rock +s
shamus
  shamus|es
Shan (Thai people,
  language)
  plural Shan or Shans
  [☞ Shahn]
Shan|dong (province,
  China)
shan|dy
  shan|dies
Shang (Chinese
  dynasty)
Shang|hai (city,
  China)
shang|hai
  shang|hais
  shang|haied
  shang|hai|ing
Shang|hai|nese
  plural
  Shang|hai|nese
Shan|go

Shangri-La
shank +s +ed +ing
Shan|kar, Ravi
  (Indian musician)
Shan|kar, Uday
  (Indian dancer)
shanked *adjective*
Shan|non (river &
  airport, Ireland)
Shan|non, Claude
  El|wood (US
  engineer)
Shan|si (= Shanxi,
  China)
  [☞ Shensi]
shan't
Shan|tou (city, China)
Shan|tung
  (= Shandong,
  China)
shan|tung +s
shanty (shack, cabin,
  camp; song)
  shan|ties
shanty|man
  shanty|men
shanty|town +s
Shan|xi (province,
  China: capital,
  Taiyuan)
  [☞ Shaanxi]
shap|able
shape
  shapes
  shaped
  shap|ing
shape|able (*use*
  shapable)
shaped *adjective*
shape|less
shape|less|ly
shape|less|ness
shape|li|ness
shape|ly (well
  proportioned)
  shape|li|er
  shape|li|est
  [☞ Shapley]
shap|er +s
shape-shifter +s
shape-shifting
Shap|ley, Har|low
  (US astronomer)
  [☞ shapely]
shar|able (*use*
  shareable)
shard +s
share
  shares
  shared
  shar|ing
share|able

share|crop
 share|crops
 share|cropped
 share|crop|ping
share|crop|per +s
share|hold|er +s
share|hold|ing
sharer +s
share|ware
sha|riah (Islam)
 [☞ Sharjah]
sha|rif +s (descendant of Muhammad; Muslim leader)
 [☞ sheriff]
Shar|jah (state & its capital, UAE)
 [☞ shariah]
shark +s
shark|skin +s
Shar|on (region, Israel)
 [☞ Charon]
sharp +er +est +s +ed +ing
sharp-edged
Shar-Pei +s
sharp|en +s +ed +ing
sharp|en|er +s
sharp|er +s
Sharpe|ville (township, South Africa)
sharp-featured
sharp|ie +s
sharp|ish
sharp|ly
sharp|ness
sharp-shin +s
sharp-shinned
sharp|shoot|er +s
sharp|shoot|ing
sharp-tailed
sharp-tongued
sharp-witted
sharp-witted|ly
sharp-witted|ness
shash|lik +s
shas|ta +s
Shas|tra +s
shat
Shatt al-Arab (river, Asia)
shat|ter +s +ed +ing
shat|ter|er +s
shat|ter|ing noun
shat|ter|ing|ly
shatter|proof
Shaula (star)
shave
 shaves
 shaved

shav|en
shav|ing
shave|ling +s
shav|er +s
Sha|vian +s
shav|ing +s noun
Sha|vuot
Sha|vuoth (use Shavuot)
Shaw (surname)
 [☞ Shah]
Shaw, Artie (US bandleader)
Shaw, George Ber|nard (Irish writer)
Shaw, Wal|ter Rus|sell (Cdn politician)
sha|war|ma +s
Sha|wini|gan (city, Canada)
Sha|winigan-Sud (town, Canada)
shawl +s
shawled
shawm +s
Shaw|nee
 plural Shaw|nee or Shaw|nees
Shays, Dan|iel (US rebel leader)
sha|zam
Shcher|ba|kov (former name for Rybinsk, Russia)
shchi +s
she pronoun
 [☞ shea]
s/he
shea +s (tree)
 [☞ Shia]
sheaf
• noun (bundle)
 sheaves
• verb (bundle into sheaves)
 sheafs
 sheafed
 sheaf|ing
 [☞ sheave]
shear (clip; remove by cutting; strain; cutter)
 shears
 sheared
 shorn or sheared
 shear|ing
 [☞ sheer]
sheared past & past participle of shear
 [☞ shirred]
shear|er +s

shear|ing conjugated form of shear
 [☞ shirring]
shear|ling +s
shear|water +s
sheath +s noun
sheathe verb
 sheathes
 sheathed
 sheath|ing
sheath|ing +s noun
sheath|less
sheave (pulley wheel; bundle into sheaves)
 sheaves
 sheaved
 sheav|ing
 [☞ sheaf]
sheaves plural of sheaf & sheave
Sheba (ancient country)
she|bang
she|been +s
She|bib, Don|ald (Cdn filmmaker)
shed
 sheds
 shed
 shed|ding
she'd (she had, she would)
shed|der +s
she-devil +s
sheen +s +ed +ing
sheeny
• adjective
 sheen|i|er
 sheen|i|est
• offensive noun
 sheen|ies
sheep
 plural sheep
sheep|dog +s
sheep|fold +s
sheep herd|er +s
sheep|ish
sheep|ish|ly
sheep|ish|ness
sheep|like
sheep|man
 sheep|men
sheep's eyes
sheep's fes|cue
sheep|shank +s
sheep|skin +s
sheep|walk +s
sheer +er +est +s +ed +ing (complete; steep; diaphanous; fabric; swerve; deviation; slope)
 [☞ shear]

sheer|legs
sheer|ly
sheer|ness
sheesh
sheet +s +ed +ing
sheet|ing +s noun
sheet metal +s
Sheet|rock proprietary
Shef|field (city, England)
she/he
sheik +s (Arab or Muslim leader)
sheik|dom +s
sheikh +s (use sheik)
sheikh|dom +s (use sheikdom)
sheila +s (girl)
 [☞ Scheele]
shek|el +s
Shel|burne (town, Canada)
shell|drake +s
shell|duck +s
shelf
 shelves
shelf|ful +s
shelf life
 shelf lives
shelf-like
shell +s +ed +ing
she'll
shell|lac
 shell|lacs
 shell|lacked
 shell|lack|ing
shell|lack|ing +s noun
shell|back +s
shelled adjective
Shel|ley, Mary Woll|stone|craft (English novelist)
 [☞ shelly]
Shel|ley, Percy Bysshe (English poet)
 [☞ shelly]
shell|fire
shell|fish
 plural shell|fish or shell|fish|es
shell game +s
shell hole +s
shell-less
shell-like
shell pink +s noun
shell-pink adjective
shell shock
shell-shocked
shell suit +s
shell|work

shelly (of or like shells)
[☞ Shelley]
Shel|ta
shel|ter +s +ed +ing
shel|ter belt +s
shel|tered *adjective*
shel|ter|er +s
shelter|less
shelter|wood
shel|tie +s
shelty (*use* sheltie)
shel|ties
shelve
shelves
shelved
shelv|ing
shelved *adjective*
shelv|er +s
shelves
shelv|ing +s *noun*
Shem (*Bible*)
Shema (*Judaism*)
she|moz|zle +s
Shen|an|doah (river, US)
she|nani|gan +s
Shen|si (= Shaanxi, China)
[☞ Shansi]
Shen|yang (city, China)
Shen|zhen (city, China)
Sheol
Shep|ard, Alan
Bart|lett, Jr. (US astronaut)
shep|herd +s +ed +ing
shep|herd|ess
shep|herd|ess|es
shepherd's crook +s
shepherd's pie +s
shepherd's purse +s
Shera|ton, Thom|as (English furniture maker)
[☞ Sheridan]
Shera|ton (furniture style)
sher|bet +s
Sher|brooke (city, Canada)
Sher|brooke, Sir John Coape (British colonial administrator)
sherd +s
she|reef +s (*use* sharif)
[☞ sheriff]

Sheri|dan, Phil|ip Henry (US cavalry officer)
[☞ Sheraton]
Sheri|dan, Rich|ard Brins|ley (Irish dramatist)
[☞ Sheraton]
sher|if +s (descendant of Muhammad, Muslim leader: *use* sharif)
[☞ sheriff]
sher|iff +s (court official; officer)
[☞ sharif]
sheriff|dom
Sher|lock +s
Sher|lock Holmes
Sher|man, Wil|liam Tecum|seh (US general)
Sher|pa
plural Sher|pa or Sher|pas
sher|ried
Sher|ring|ton, Sir Charles Scott (English physiologist)
sherry
sher|ries
's-Hertogen|bosch (city, the Netherlands)
Sher|wood, Rob|ert Emmet (US dramatist)
she's
Shet|land +s (islands, Scotland; wool, pony, sheepdog)
Shet|land|er +s
Shev|ard|nadze, Ed|uard Am|vrosi|evich (Georgian statesman)
Shev|chenko, Taras Hryhor|ovych (Ukrainian poet)
shew|bread
Shia (*Islam*)
plural Shia or Shias
Shi'a (*use* Shia)
plural Shi'a or Shi'as
Shiah (*use* Shia)
plural Shiah or Shi|ahs
shi|atsu
shib|bo|leth +s
shied
shield +s +ed +ing
shield|less

Shields, Carol (Cdn writer)
shiel|ing +s
shier (*comparative of* shy: *use* shyer)
[☞ shire, Shire]
shiest (*use* shyest)
shift +s +ed +ing
shift|able
shift|er +s
shift|i|er
shift|i|est
shift|i|ly
shift|i|ness
shift|ing
shift|less
shift|less|ly
shift|less|ness
shift-on-the-fly
shift work
shift worker +s
shifty
shift|i|er
shift|i|est
shi|gel|la
shi|gel|lae or
shi|gel|las
shig|el|lo|sis
shig|el|lo|ses
Shih Tzu +s
Shi|ism
shii|ta|ke +s
Shi|ite +s
Shi|jia|zhuang (city, China)
Shi|ko|ku (island, Japan)
shik|sa +s *offensive*
shik|se +s *offensive* (= shiksa)
shill +s +ed +ing
shil|le|lagh +s
shil|ling +s (Kenyan, Tanzanian, Ugandan, Somalian & former British currency)
[☞ schilling]
Shil|long (city, India)
shilly-shally
shilly-shallies
shilly-shallied
shilly-shally|ing
shilly-shally|er +s
shilly-shally|ing *noun*
shim
shims
shimmed
shim|ming
shim|mer +s +ed +ing
shim|mer|ing *adjective*

shim|mer|ing|ly
shim|mery
shim|my
shim|mies
shim|mied
shimmy|ing
shin (part of leg; climb)
shins
shinned
shin|ning
[☞ Sinn Fein]
shin|dig +s
shin|dy
shin|dies
shine
• (cast or emit light; glow, gleam; excel)
shines
shone or shined
shin|ing
• (polish)
shines
shined
shin|ing
[☞ sinh]
shin|er +s
shin|gle
shin|gles
shin|gled
shin|gling
shin|gled *adjective*
shin|gles
shin|gly
shin guard +s
shin|i|er
shin|i|est
shin|i|ly
shin|i|ness
shin|ing *adjective*
shin|ing|ly
shin|leaf
shin|leafs or
shin|leaves
shin|ny (hockey; climb)
shin|nies
shin|nied
shinny|ing
shin pad +s
shin|plaster +s
shin splints
Shin|to
Shin|to|ism
Shin|to|ist +s
shin|ty
shin|ties
shiny (bright)
shin|i|er
shin|i|est
[☞ shinny]
ship
ships

shipped
ship|ping
ship|board
ship-broker +s
ship|build|er +s
ship|build|ing
ship|lap
ship|less
ship|load +s
ship|master +s (ship's
  captain)
ship|mate +s
ship|ment +s
ship-money
ship|own|er +s
ship|pable
ship|per +s
ship|ping *noun*
ship-rigged
ship's arti|cles
ship's bis|cuit +s
ship's boat +s
ship's com|pany
ship|shape
ship's mas|ter +s
  (official presiding
  over signing of ship's
  articles etc.)
  [☞ shipmaster]
ship's pa|pers
ship-to-shore
ship|worm +s
ship|wreck +s +ed
  +ing
ship|wright
ship|yard +s
Shi|raz (city, Iran)
shi|raz
  shi|raz|es
Shire +s (horse)
shire +s (county)
shirk +s +ed +ing
  (avoid work)
  [☞ SSHRC]
shirk|er +s
Shir|ley Tem|ple +s
shirred (gathered with
  rows of stitches;
  baked)
shir|ring +s (multiple
  rows of stitching)
shirt +s
shirt-dress
  shirt-dresses
shirt|ed
shirt front +s
shirt|i|er
shirt|i|est
shirt|ing
shirt|less
shirt sleeve +s (shirt-
  sleeve *when
  preceding a noun*)

shirt-sleeved
shirt-tail +s
shirt|waist +s
shirt|waist|er +s
shirty
  shirt|i|er
  shirt|i|est
shish ke|bab +s
shit
  shits
  shat or shit
  or shit|ted
  shit|ting
shit|bag +s
shit|box
  shit|boxes
shit-faced
shit|head +s
shit|head|ed
shit|house +s
shit|less
shit list +s
shit|load +s
shit-scared
shit|ter +s
shit|ty
  shit|ti|er
  shit|ti|est
shiur
  shiur|im
shiv +s
Shiva (Hindu god)
shiva (*Judaism*; in 'sit
  shiva')
shivah (*Judaism*: use
  shiva)
Shiva|ism
Shiva|ite +s
shiv|a|ree +s (noisy
  gathering; serenade)
shiv|er +s +ed +ing
shiv|er|ing|ly
shiv|ery (cold,
  shivering)
  [☞ shivaree]
Shizu|oka (city,
  Japan)
Shko|dër (city,
  Albania)
shle|miel +s (*use
  schlemiel*)
shlep (*use schlep*)
  shleps
  shlepped
  shlep|ping
shlock (*use schlock*)
shlub +s (*use schlub*)
shlump +s (*use
  schlump*)
shmaltz (*use
  schmaltz*)
shmat|te +s

shmooze (*use
  schmooze*)
  shmooz|es
  shmoozed
  shmooz|ing
shmuck +s
  (objectionable
  person: *use*
  schmuck)
  [☞ schmuck]
shnor|rer +s (*use
  schnorrer*)
shoal +s +ed +ing
shock +s +ed +ing
shock|able
shock-absorb|ing
shock cord +s
shock-corded
shocked *adjective*
shock|er +s
shock|ing *adjective*
shock|ing|ly
shock|ing|ness
shock|ing pink +s
  (shocking-pink *when
  preceding a noun*)
shock jock +s
Shock|ley, Wil|liam
  Brad|ford (US
  physicist)
shock|proof
shock re|sist|ant
  (shock-resist|ant
  *when preceding a
  noun*)
shock wave +s
shod *adjective*
shod|di|ly
shod|di|ness
shoddy
  shod|di|er
  shod|di|est
  shod|dies
shoe (footwear etc.)
  shoes
  shod or shoed
  shoe|ing
  [☞ shoo, choux]
shoe|bill +s
shoe|box
  shoe|boxes
shoed *adjective*
shoe|horn +s
shoe|lace +s
shoe|less
Shoe|maker, Wil|liam
  Lee ('Wil|lie') (US
  jockey)
shoe|maker +s
shoe|making
shoe|pac +s (*use
  shoepack*)
shoe|pack

shoer +s
shoe|shine +s
shoe|string +s
shoe|tree +s
sho|far (horn)
  sho|fars or sho|froth
  [☞ chauffeur]
sho|gun +s
sho|gun|ate +s
shoji
  plural shoji
Sho|la|pur (city, India)
Sholo|khov, Mikh|ail
  Alek|san|dro|vich
  (Soviet novelist)
Sho|na +s
shone *past & past
  participle of* shine
  [☞ Shan, Shahn]
shoo (drive away)
  shoos
  shooed
  shoo|ing
  [☞ choux, shoe]
shoo|fly
shoo-in +s
shook +s *adjective &
  noun*
shoot (discharge a
  projectile, etc.; new
  plant growth)
  shoots
  shot
  shoot|ing
  [☞ chute, Shute]
shoot|abil|ity
shoot|able
shoot-around +s
shoot-'em-up +s
shoot|er +s
shoot|ing +s *noun &
  adjective*
shoot|ist +s (one who
  shoots)
  [☞ chutist]
shoot|out +s
shop
  shops
  shopped
  shop|ping
shop|ahol|ic +s
shop floor +s (shop-
  floor *when preceding
  a noun*)
shop|front +s
shop|girl +s
shop|keep|er +s
shop|keep|ing
shop|less
shop|lift +s +ed +ing
shop|lift|er +s
shop|lift|ing +s

shoppe +s (*in commercial use* = shop)
shop|per +s
shop|ping *noun*
shop|py
shop-soiled
shop talk
shop work|er +s
shop|worn
shore
  shores
  shored
  shor|ing
shore|bird +s
shore|fast
shore|front +s
shore|less
shore|line +s
shore lunch
  shore lunch|es
shore|side +s
shore|ward
shore|wards
shor|ing +s *noun*
shorn *adjective*
short +er +est +s +ed +ing
short-acting
short|age +s
short|all +s
short|bread +s
short|cake +s
short chain +s (short-chain *when preceding a noun*)
short|change
  short|changes
  short|changed
  short|changing
short-circuit +s +ed +ing
short|com|ing +s
short|cover|ing
short|cut
  short|cuts
  short|cut
  short|cut|ting
short-eared
short|en +s +ed +ing
short|en|ing +s *noun*
short|fall +s
short fuse +s
short-fused
short|grass
  short|grass|es
short|hair +s
short|haired
short|hand
short-handed
short-haul
short hop +s *noun*

short-hop *verb*
  short-hops
  short-hopped
  short-hopping
Short|horn +s
shortie +s (clothing) [☞ shorty]
short|ish
short list +s *noun*
short|list +s +ed +ing *verb*
short-lived
short loin +s
short|ly
short|ness
short order +s (short-order *when preceding a noun*)
short-range
short rib +s
shorts
short-sheet +s +ed +ing
short-sighted
short-sighted|ly
short-sighted|ness
short-sleeved
short-staffed
short|stop +s
short temper +s
short-tempered
short term (short-term *when preceding a noun*)
short-termism
short-termist +s
short time (short-time *when preceding a noun*)
short-track
short-waisted
short-wave +s
short-winded
shorty (short person; *for* clothing *use* shortie)
  short|ies
Sho|sho|ne
  plural Sho|sho|ne or Sho|sho|nes
Shosta|ko|vich, Dmitri Dmitri|evich (Russian composer)
shot +s
shot-blast +s +ed +ing
shot-blasting *noun*
shot clock +s
shot|crete
shot glass
  shot glass|es

shot|gun
  shot|guns
  shot|gunned
  shot|gun|ning
shot|gun|ner +s
shot|gun|ning *noun*
shot|maker +s
shot|making *noun*
shot put
shot put|ter +s
should
shoul|der +s +ed +ing
shoul|der bag +s
shoul|der blade +s
shoul|dered *adjective*
shoulder-high
shoulder-length
shoul|der pad +s
shouldn't
shout +s +ed +ing
shout|er +s
shove
  shoves
  shoved
  shov|ing
shov|el
  shov|els
  shov|elled
  shov|el|ling
shov|el|er +s (*use* shoveller)
shovel|ful +s
shovel|head +s
shov|el|ler +s
show
  shows
  showed
  shown or showed
  show|ing
show band +s
show|biz
show|bizzy
show|boat +s +ed +ing
show|boat|er +s
show|boat|ing *noun*
show busi|ness
show-card +s
show|case
  show|cas|es
  show|cased
  show|cas|ing
show-cause hear|ing +s
show|down +s
shower +s +ed +ing
shower head +s
shower|less
shower|proof
showery
show|girl +s
show|goer +s

show|ground +s
show home +s
show house +s
show|i|er
show|i|est
show|i|ly
show|i|ness
show|ing +s *noun*
show|man
  show|men
show|man|ship
shown
show off *verb*
  shows off
  showed off
  shown off
  or showed off
  show|ing off
show-off +s *noun*
show-offish
show-offish|ly
show-offy
show|piece +s
show|place +s
show ring +s
show|room +s
show|stop|per +s
show-stopping
show|time +s
show tune +s
showy
  show|i|er
  show|i|est
shrank
shrap|nel +s
shred
  shreds
  shred|ded
  shred|ding
shred|der +s
Shreve|port (city, US)
shrew +s
shrewd
shrewd|ly
shrewd|ness
shrew|ish
shrew|ish|ly
shrew|ish|ness
Shrews|bury (town, England)
shriek +s +ed +ing
shriek|er +s
shrift +s
shrike +s
shrill +er +est +s +ed +ing
shrill|ness
shrilly
  shrill|i|er
  shrill|i|est
shrimp
  plural shrimp or shrimps

shrimp|er +s
shrimp-like
shrine
  shrines
  shrined
  shrin|ing
Shrin|er +s
shrink
  shrinks
  shrank *or* shrunk
  shrunk
  shrink|ing
shrink|able
shrink|age +s
shrink|er +s
shrink wrap +s *noun*
shrink-wrap *verb*
  shrink-wraps
  shrink-wrapped
  shrink-wrapping
shrink-wrapped
  adjective
shrive
  shrives
  shrove
  shriv|en
  shriv|ing
shriv|el
  shriv|els
  shriv|elled
  shriv|el|ling
shroom +s
Shrop|shire (county, England)
shroud +s +ed +ing
shrove
Shrove|tide
Shrove Tues|day
shrub +s
shrub|bery
  shrub|ber|ies
shrub|by
  shrub|bi|er
  shrub|bi|est
shrug
  shrugs
  shrugged
  shrug|ging
shrunk
shrunk|en
shtetl
  shtetls *or* shtet|lach
shtick +s
Shu|ben|aca|die (river, Canada)
shuck +s +ed +ing
shuck|er +s
shucks
shud|der +s +ed +ing
shud|der|ing|ly
shud|dery

shuf|fle
  shuf|fles
  shuf|fled
  shuf|fling
shuffle|board
shuf|fler +s
shul +s
Shu|men (city, Bulgaria)
shun
  shuns
  shunned
  shun|ning
shunt +s +ed +ing
shunt|er +s
shush
  shush|es
  shushed
  shush|ing
Shus|ter, Frank (Cdn comedian)
Shus|ter, Joe (Cdn creator of Superman)
Shus|wap (people & language; lake, Canada)
  plural Shus|wap *or* Shus|waps
shut
  shuts
  shut
  shut|ting
shut down *verb*
  shuts down
  shut down
  shut|ting down
shut|down +s *noun*
Shute, Nevil (English novelist)
shut-eye
shut in *verb*
  shuts in
  shut in
  shut|ting in
shut-in +s *noun*
shut off *verb*
  shuts off
  shut off
  shut|ting off
shut-off +s *noun &*
  adjective
shut out *verb*
  shuts out
  shut out
  shut|ting out
shut|out +s *noun*
shut|ter +s +ed +ing
shutter|bug +s
shutter|less
shut|tle
  shut|tles
  shut|tled
  shut|tling

shuttle|cock +s
shy
  shyer *or* shier
  shy|est *or* shiest
  shies
  shied
  shy|ing
Shy|lock +s
  derogatory
shyly
shy|ness
shy|ster +s
si (musical note)
Sia|chen (glacier, India)
Sial|kot (city, Pakistan)
Siam (*former name for* Thailand)
sia|mang +s
Siam|ese
  plural Siam|ese
Sian (= Xian, China)
sib +s
Sibel|ius, Jean (Finnish composer)
Si|ber|ia (region, Russia)
Si|ber|ian +s
sibi|lance
sibi|lancy
sibi|lant +s
sibi|late
  sibi|lates
  sibi|lat|ed
  sibi|lat|ing
sibi|la|tion +s
Sibiu (city, Romania)
Sib|ley (peninsula, Canada)
Sib|ley, Dame An|toin|ette (English dancer)
sib|ling +s
sib|ship +s
sibyl +s
sibyl|line
sic (accurately reported)
  [☞ sic, sick]
sic (attack; send to attack)
  sics
  sicced
  sic|cing
  [☞ sic, sick]
sic bo
sic|ca|tive +s
sice +s (*use* syce)
Si|chuan (province, China)
  [☞ Szechuan]
Sicil|ian +s (of Sicily)
  [☞ caecilian]

Sicily (Italian island)
  [☞ cicely, Sisley]
sick +s +ed +ing +er +est (ill etc.; *for* attack *use* sic)
  [☞ sic]
sick bay +s
sick|bed +s
sick|en +s +ed +ing
sick|en|er +s
sick|en|ing *adjective*
sick|en|ing|ly
sick|ie +s
sick|ish
sick|ish|ly
sickle +s
sickle bar +s
sickle cell +s (sickle-cell *when preceding a noun*)
sick|li|ness
sick|ly
  sick|li|er
  sick|li|est
sick|ness
  sick|ness|es
sicko +s
sick|room +s
sicky (*use* sickie)
  sick|ies
Sid|dhar|tha Gau|tama (Buddha)
Sid|dons, Sarah (English actress)
side
  sides
  sided
  siding
  [☞ Port Said]
side arm +s (weapon)
side|arm +s +ed +ing (throw, pitch)
side|arm|er +s
side|band +s
side|bar +s
side|board +s
side|burns
side|car +s
side|chair +s
side cut|ters
side-cutting
sided *adjective*
sided|ly
sided|ness
side door +s (side-door *when preceding a noun*)
side-dress
  side-dresses
  side-dressed
  side-dressing
side ef|fect +s
side|hill +s

side im|pact +s (side-
impact *when
preceding a noun*)
side|kick +s
side|less
side|light +s
side|light|ing
side|line +s
side|lock +s
side|long
side|man (musician)
side|men
[☞ sidesman]
side|meat
side plate +s
si|dereal
side ribs
sid|er|ite +s
sid|er|itic
side road +s
sid|ero|phore +s
sid|ero|stat +s
side|saddle +s
side-scan
side|show +s
side|slip
side|slips
side|slipped
side|slip|ping
sides|man (church
usher)
sides|men
[☞ sideman]
sides|person +s
side|split +s
side-splitter +s
side-splitting
side|step
side|steps
side|stepped
side|step|ping
side|step|per +s
side street +s
side stroke
side-swipe
side-swipes
side-swiped
side-swiping
side table +s
side|track +s +ed
+ing
side trip +s
side-valve +s
side view +s (side-
view *when preceding
a noun*)
side|walk +s
side|walk|less
side wall +s
side|ward
side|wards
side|ways
side|wheel|er +s

side|whis|ker +s
Side|wind|er +s
(missile)
side|wind|er +s
(snake; punch)
side|wise
Sidi bel Abbès (town,
Algeria)
siding +s *noun*
sidle
sidles
sidled
sidling
Sid|ney (town, BC)
[☞ North Sydney,
Sydney]
Sid|ney, Sir Phil|lip
(English poet)
Sidon (city, Lebanon)
Si|don|ian
Sidra (Mediterranean
gulf)
SIDS (sudden infant
death syndrome)
Sie|ben|ge|birge
(hills, Germany)
siege +s
Sieg|fried (*Germanic
Myth*)
Sieg|fried Line
Sie|mens, Sir
(Charles) Wil|liam
(German-born
English engineer)
Sie|mens, (Ernst)
Wer|ner von
(German engineer)
Sie|mens, Karl
Wil|helm (= Sir
Charles William
Siemens)
sie|mens (unit of
conductance)
plural sie|mens
Siena (city, Italy)
[☞ sienna]
Sien|ese
plural Sien|ese
Sien|kie|wicz,
Hen|ryk Adam
Alex|an|der Pius
(Polish writer)
si|en|na +s (earth;
pigment)
[☞ Siena]
Si|er|ra +s (= Sierra
Nevada, US)
si|er|ra +s
Si|er|ra Leone
(country, Africa)
Si|er|ra Leon|ean +s
Si|er|ra Madre +s
(mountain system,
Mexico)

Si|er|ra Madre del
Sur (mountain
range, Mexico)
Si|er|ra Nev|ada
(mountain ranges,
Spain & US)
si|esta +s
sieur +s
sieve
sieves
sieved
siev|ing
sie|vert
sift +s +ed +ing
sift|er +s
sift|ings
Sif|ton, Ar|thur Lewis
(Cdn politician)
Sif|ton, Sir Clif|ford
(Cdn politician)
SIG (special interest
group)
SIGs
sig +s (*Computing*
signature)
[☞ cig]
sigh +s +ed +ing
(long audible breath)
[☞ psi, xi]
sight +s +ed +ing
(vision; viewing
device; observe)
[☞ site, cite]
sight|ed *adjective*
sight|ed|ness
sight|er +s
sight|ing +s *noun*
sight|less
sight|less|ly
sight|less|ness
sight|line +s
sight-read
sight-reads
sight-read
sight-reading
sight-reader +s
sight-reading *noun*
sight|see
sight|sees
sight|saw
sight|see|ing
sight|see|ing *noun*
sight|seer +s
sight-sing
sight-sings
sight-sang
sight-sung
sight-singing
sight-singing *noun*
sight un|seen
sigil +s
SIGINT (signals
intelligence)

Sig|is|mund (Holy
Roman emperor)
sig|lum
sigla
sig|ma +s
sig|moid +s
sig|moid|al
sig|moid|o|scope
sig|moid|o|scop|ic
sig|moid|o|
scop|ic|ally
sig|moid|os|copy
sig|moid|os|cop|ies
sign +s +ed +ing
(signal etc.)
[☞ sine, syne, sin]
sign|able
Signac, Paul (French
painter)
sign|age
sig|nal
sig|nals
sig|nalled
sig|nal|ling
sig|nal box
sig|nal boxes
Sig|nal Hill (historic
site, Canada)
sig|nal|ler +s
sig|nal|ly
sig|nal|man
sig|nal|men
signal-to-noise
sig|na|tory
sig|na|tor|ies
sig|na|ture +s
sign|board +s
sign|ee +s
sig|net +s (seal)
[☞ cygnet]
sig|nifi|cance +s
sig|nifi|cant
sig|nifi|cant|ly
sig|nifi|ca|tion +s
sig|ni|fied +s *noun*
sig|ni|fier
sig|ni|fy
sig|ni|fies
sig|ni|fied
sig|ni|fying
sign|ing +s *noun*
sign off *verb*
signs off
signed off
sign|ing off
sign-off +s *noun*
sign on *verb*
signs on
signed on
sign|ing on
sign-on +s *noun*

si|gnor (Italian man)
si|gnori
[☞ **señor, senhor**]
si|gnora (married
Italian woman)
si|gnoras or si|gnore
[☞ **señor, senhora**]
si|gnore
• (= signor: Italian
man)
plural si|gnori
• (*plural of* signora)
si|gnor|ina
si|gnor|inas or
si|gnor|ine
sign|post +s
Sig|urd (*Norse Legend*)
**Siha|nouk, Prince
Noro|dom**
(Cambodian ruler)
sika +s
Sikh +s (adherent of
Sikhism)
[☞ **seekh kebab**]
Sikh|ism
Siking (*former name
for* **Xian**, China)
Sik|kim (state, India)
Sik|kim|ese
plural Sik|kim|ese
**Si|kor|sky, Igor
Ivan|ovich** (Russian-
born aircraft
designer)
Sik|sika
plural Sik|sika or
Sik|sikas
silage
si|lence
si|len|ces
si|lenced
si|len|cing
si|lenced *adjective*
si|len|cer +s
si|lent +s
si|lent|ly
Si|len|us (woodland
deity & teacher of
Dionysus)
si|len|us (any of
various woodland
deities)
si|leni
Si|lesia (region,
Europe)
Si|lesian +s (of
Silesia)
[☞ **Salesian**]
sil|hou|ette
sil|hou|ettes
sil|hou|et|ted
sil|hou|et|ting
sili|ca
sili|cate +s

si|li|ceous
si|li|cic
si|li|ci|fi|ca|tion
si|li|ci|fy
si|li|ci|fies
si|li|ci|fied
si|li|ci|fy|ing
si|li|cious (*use*
siliceous)
sili|con (element used
in electronics &
glass)
[☞ **silicone**]
sili|con car|bide
sili|con chip +s
sili|cone (compound
used in caulking,
adhesives,
waterproofing
agents, rubber, etc.)
sili|cones
[☞ **silicon**]
sili|cone im|plant +s
Sili|con Val|ley
(industrial region,
US)
**Sili|con Val|ley
North** (industrial
region, Canada)
sili|con waf|er +s
sili|co|sis
sili|co|ses
sili|cot|ic
sili|qua
sili|quae
si|lique +s (= siliqua)
sili|quose
sili|quous
silk +s +ed +ing
silk-cotton tree +s
silk|en
silk|i|er
silk|i|est
silk|i|ly
silk|i|ness
silk-like
silk|screen +s +ed
+ing
silk stock|ing +s
(silk-stocking *when
preceding a noun*)
silk|worm +s
silky
silk|i|er
silk|i|est
sill +s
**Sil|lan|pää, Frans
Eemil** (Finnish
writer)
Sil|lery (town,
Canada)
silli|ly
sil|li|man|ite +s

sil|li|ness
Sills, Bev|er|ley (US
soprano)
silly
sil|li|er
sil|li|est
sil|lies
[☞ **Scilly**]
silly-billy
silly-billies
Silly Putty *proprietary*
silo +s
Si|lone, Ig|nazio
(Italian novelist)
silt +s +ed +ing
silt|a|tion
silt|stone +s
silty
silt|i|er
silt|i|est
Si|lur|ian
silva (*use* sylva)
sil|vae or sil|vas
sil|van (*use* sylvan)
Sil|van|us (*Roman
Myth*)
sil|ver +s +ed +ing
silver|back +s
silver|berry
silver|ber|ries
silver|fish
plural silver|fish or
silver|fish|es
silver-gilt
silver-grey +s
Sil|ver|heels, Jay
(Cdn-born actor)
sil|ver|i|ness
sil|ver|ing *noun*
sil|vern
sil|ver plate
silver-plated
silver|point +s
silver|side +s (fish;
beef)
silver|sides (fish
= silverside)
plural silver|sides
silver|smith +s
silver|smith|ing
silver|tip +s
silver-tongue +s
silver-tongued
silver|ware
silver|weed +s
sil|very
silvi|cul|tur|al
silvi|cul|ture
silvi|cul|tur|ist +s
sim +s
Sim|birsk (city,
Russia)
sim|cha

Sim|chas Torah
Sim|chat Torah
(= Simchas Torah)
Sim|coe (lake,
Canada)
Sim|coe, John Graves
(lieutenant-governor
of Upper Canada)
**Sime|non, Georges
Jo|seph Chris|tian**
(French novelist)
Sim|eon (*Bible*)
[☞ **simian**]
Sim|eon Styl|ites
(saint)
sim|eth|i|cone
Sim|fer|o|pol
Sim|hath Torah
(= Simchas Torah)
sim|ian +s (of apes)
[☞ **Simeon**]
sim|i|lar
sim|i|lar|ity
sim|i|lar|ities
sim|i|lar|ly
sim|ile +s
sim|ili|tude +s
Simil|ka|meen (river,
Canada)
Simla (city, India)
Sim|men|tal +s
sim|mer +s +ed +ing
sim|nel cake +s
sim|oleon +s
Simon (saint)
[☞ **Symons**]
Simon, (Mar|vin) Neil
(US playwright)
Simon, Paul (US
singer-songwriter)
sim|oni|ac
sim|oni|acal
Sim|oni|des (Greek
poet)
simon-pure
si|mony
sim|oom +s
sim|oon +s
(= simoom)
simp +s
sim|pat|ico
sim|per +s +ed +ing
sim|per|ing|ly
sim|ple
sim|pler
sim|plest
sim|ples
simple-minded
simple-minded|ly
simple-minded|ness
simple|ness
Sim|ple Simon +s
simple|ton +s

sim|plex
  sim|plex|es
sim|pli|city
  sim|pli|ci|ties
sim|pli|fi|ca|tion +s
sim|pli|fy
  sim|pli|fies
  sim|pli|fied
  sim|pli|fy|ing
sim|plis|tic
sim|plis|tic|ally
Sim|plon (mountain pass, Switzerland)
sim|ply
Simp|son (peninsula, Canada; desert, Australia)
Simp|son, Sir George (HBC governor)
Simp|son, Sir James Young (Scottish surgeon)
Simp|son, Oren|thal James ('O.J.') (US celebrity)
Simp|son, Wal|lis (wife of Edward VIII)
simu|la|crum
  simu|lacra
simu|late
  simu|lates
  simu|lat|ed
  simu|lat|ing
simu|lat|ed adjective
simu|la|tion +s
simu|la|tive
simu|la|tor +s
simul|cast
  simul|casts
  simul|cast
  simul|cast|ing
simul|cast|ing noun
simul|tan|eity
  simul|tan|eit|ies
simul|tan|eous
simul|tan|eous|ly
simul|tan|eous|ness
SIN (social insurance number)
  SINs
sin[1] (transgression)
  sins
  sinned
  sin|ning
sin[2] (sine)
Sinai (peninsula, Egypt)
Sina|itic
Sina|loa (state, Mexico)
Sin|atra, Fran|cis Al|bert ('Frank') (US entertainer)

sin bin +s
since
sin|cere
  sin|cer|er
  sin|cer|est
sin|cere|ly
sin|cere|ness
sin|cer|ity
  sin|cer|it|ies
sin|cipi|tal
sin|ci|put +s
Sin|clair, Upton Beall (US novelist)
Sind (province, Pakistan)
Sindhi +s
sine +s (trigonometric function)
  [☞ sign, syne]
sine|cure +s
sine|cur|ism
sine|cur|ist +s
sine die
sine qua non
sinew +s +ed +ing
sinew|less
sinewy
sin|fonia +s
sin|foni|etta +s
sin|ful
sin|ful|ly
sin|ful|ness
sing
  sings
  sang
  sung
  sing|ing
  [☞ Singh, singe]
sing|able
sing|along +s
Singa|pore (country, Asia)
Singa|por|ean +s
singe
  singes
  singed
  singe|ing
Sing|er, Isaac Bash|evis (US writer)
Sing|er, Isaac Mer|rit (US inventor)
sing|er +s
singer-songwriter +s
Singh (Sikh surname; warrior title)
Sing|hal|ese (use Sinhalese)
  plural Sing|hal|ese
sing|ing +s noun & adjective

sin|gle
  sin|gles
  sin|gled
  sin|gling
single-acting
single-blind
single-breast|ed
single-digit
single|foot +s +ed +ing
single-handed
single-handed|ly
single|hood
single-issue
single-lens re|flex
  single-lens re|flex|es
single-minded
single-minded|ly
single-minded|ness
single|ness
single par|ent (single-parent when preceding a noun)
sin|gles bar +s
single-seater +s
single-sex
single-spaced
sing|let +s
single|ton +s
sin|gle tree +s
single-use adjective preceding a noun
single-user +s adjective preceding a noun
sin|gly
Sing Sing (prison, US)
sing|song +s
sing|songy
sin|gu|lar +s
sin|gu|lar|ity
  sin|gu|lar|ities
sin|gu|lar|iz|a|tion +s
sin|gu|lar|ize
  sin|gu|lar|iz|es
  sin|gu|lar|ized
  sin|gu|lar|iz|ing
sin|gu|lar|ly
sinh (hyperbolic sine)
Sin|hal|ese
  plural Sin|hal|ese
Sining (= Xining, China)
sin|is|ter
sin|is|ter|ly
sin|is|ter|ness
sin|is|tral
sin|is|tral|ity
sin|is|tral|ly
sin|is|trorse

sink
  sinks
  sank or sunk
  sunk
  sink|ing
  [☞ Cinque Ports, sync]
sink|able
sink|age
sink|er +s
sinker|ball +s
sinker|ball|er +s
sink|ful +s
sink|hole +s
Sin|kiang (= Xinjiang, China)
sin|less
sin|less|ly
sin|less|ness
sin|ner +s
Sinn Fein
Sinn Fein|er +s
sino-atrial
Sino-Japanese
sino|logic|al
sin|ol|o|gist +s
sino|logue +s
sin|ol|ogy
Sino-Tibetan
sin|se|milla
sin|se|mil|lan
sin|ter +s +ed +ing
sin|tered adjective
Sint Maar|ten (Dutch name for St. Martin) [☞ San Martín]
Sin|tra (town, Portugal)
sinu|ate
Sin|uiju (city, North Korea)
sinu|os|ity
  sinu|os|ities
sinu|ous
sinu|ous|ly
sinu|ous|ness
sinus
  sinus|es
sinus|itis
sinus|oid +s
sinus|oid|al
sinus|oid|al|ly
Sion Religion (= Zion) [☞ scion]
Siou|an
Sioux (people & language)
  plural Sioux
sip
  sips
  sipped
  sip|ping
si|phon +s +ed +ing

si|phon|age
si|phon|al
si|phon|ic
si|phono|phore +s
sip|pable
sip|per +s
sip|pet +s
Si|quei|ros, David
  Al|faro (Mexican
  painter)
sir +s
Sir|ach (*Apocrypha*)
sir|dar +s
Sir|dar|yo (river, Asia)
sire
  sires
  sired
  siring
siree
siren +s
siren|ian +s
Sir|ius (star)
  [☞ serious]
sir|loin +s
si|rocco +s
sir|rah +s (form of
  address)
  [☞ Syrah]
sir|ree (*use* siree)
Sirte (= Gulf of Sidra)
sis
sisal +s
sis-boom-bah
sis|kin +s
Sis|ley, Al|fred
  (French painter)
  [☞ cicely, Sicily]
Sis|mondi, Jean
  Charles Léo|nard
  Si|monde de (Swiss
  historian)
sis|si|fied
sis|si|ness
sissy
  sis|sies
  sis|si|er
  sis|si|est
sissy|ish
sis|ter +s
sis|ter ger|man
  sis|ters ger|man
sister|hood +s
sister-in-law
  sisters-in-law
sister|less
sister|li|ness
sister|ly
sis|ter uter|ine
  sis|ters uter|ine
Sis|tine (of popes
  called Sixtus; of the
  Sistine Chapel)

[☞ cystine,
  cysteine]
sis|trum
  sis|tra
Sisy|phean
Sisy|phus (*Greek
  Myth*)
sit
  sits
  sat
  sit|ting
Sita (*Hinduism*)
sitar +s
sitar|ist +s
sit|com +s
sit down *verb*
  sits down
  sat down
  sit|ting down
sit-down +s *noun &
  adjective*
site (location; locate)
  sites
  sited
  siting
  [☞ sight, cite]
site-specif|ic
sit in *verb*
  sits in
  sat in
  sit|ting in
sit-in +s *noun*
Sitka +s
sit|rep +s
sits *conjugated form of*
  sit
  [☞ sitz bath]
Sit|tang (river, Burma)
Sit|ter, Wil|lem de
  (Dutch
  mathematician)
sit|ter +s
sit|ting +s *noun &
  adjective*
Sit|ting Bull (Sioux
  chief)
situ
situ|ate
  situ|ates
  situ|at|ed
  situ|at|ing
situ|a|tion +s
situ|a|tion|al
situ|a|tion|al|ly
situ|a|tion|ism
situ|a|tion|ist +s
sit up *verb*
  sits up
  sat up
  sit|ting up
sit-up +s *noun*
sit-upon +s *noun*

Sit|well, Dame Edith
  Lou|isa (English
  writer)
sitz bath +s
SIU (special
  investigations unit)
  SIUs
Siva (= Shiva, Hindu
  god)
  [☞ shiva]
Si|walik Hills
  (Himalayan foothills)
Si|wash
  Si|wash|es
six
  sixes
six|er +s
six-figure
six|fold
six-gun +s
six-pack +s
six|pence +s
six|penny
six-shooter +s
six-string +s
six|teen +s
six|teenth +s
sixth +s
sixth form +s
sixth-former +s
sixth|ly
six|ti|eth +s
Sixty (60th parallel)
sixty
  six|ties
sixty-eight +s
sixty-eighth +s
sixty-fifth +s
sixty-first +s
sixty-five +s
sixty|fold
sixty-four +s
sixty-fourth +s
sixty-nine +s
sixty-ninth +s
sixty-one +s
sixty-second +s
sixty-seven +s
sixty-seventh +s
sixty-six
  sixty-sixes
sixty-sixth +s
sixty-third +s
sixty-three +s
sixty-two +s
siz|able
siz|ably
sizar +s (student)
  [☞ sizer]
sizar|ship +s

size
  sizes
  sized
  siz|ing
size|able (*use* sizable)
size|ably (*use* sizably)
sized *adjective*
sizer +s (one who
  sizes)
  [☞ sizar]
siz|zle
  siz|zles
  siz|zled
  siz|zling
siz|zler +s
siz|zling *adjective &
  adverb*
sjam|bok +s +ed
  +ing
ska
skag
Skag|er|rak (strait
  between Norway &
  Denmark)
skald +s (bard)
  [☞ scald]
skald|ic
Skan|da (*Hinduism*)
skank +s +ed +ing
skat (*Cards*)
  [☞ scat]
skate
• (bladed or wheeled
  footwear; crook)
  skates
  skated
  skat|ing
• (fish)
  plural skate *or*
  skates
skate-a-thon +s
skate|board +s +ed
  +ing
skate|board|er +s
skate|board|ing *noun*
skate guard +s
skate lace +s
skat|er +s
skat|ing *noun*
skean +s (dagger)
  [☞ skein]
skean-dhu +s
sked
  skeds
  sked|ded
  sked|ding
ske|dad|dle
  ske|dad|dles
  ske|dad|dled
  ske|dad|dling
Skeena (river &
  mountains, Canada)
skeet

skeet|er +s
skeg +s
skein +s (yarn; tangle; flock)
[☞ skean]
skel|etal
skel|etal|ly
skel|eton +s
Skel|eton Coast (of Namibia)
skel|eton|ic
skel|eton|ize
skel|eton|iz|es
skel|eton|ized
skel|eton|iz|ing
Skel|ton, John (English poet)
skep
skep|tic +s
skep|tic|al
skep|tic|ally
skep|ti|cism
skerry (reef)
sker|ries
sketch
sketch|es
sketched
sketch|ing
sketch|book
sketch|er +s
sketch map +s
sketch pad +s
sketch|i|ly
sketch|i|ness
sketchy
sketch|i|er
sketch|i|est
skew +s +ed +ing
skew|back +s
skew|bald +s
skew|er +s +ed +ing
skew|ness
skew-whiff
ski
skis
skied
ski|ing
ski|able
Ski|athos (Greek island)
ski-bob
ski-bobs
ski-bobbed
ski-bobbing
ski-bobber +s
skid
skids
skid|ded
skid|ding
skid|der
skid|ding noun

skid|doo +s +ed +ing
(leave: use skidoo)
[☞ skidoo]
Ski-Doo +s
proprietary noun
ski|doo +s +ed +ing
verb (snowmobile; leave)
ski|doo|er +s
ski|doo|ing noun
skid road +s
skid road|er +s
skid row
skid|way +s
ski|er +s
skiff +s
skif|fle
ski|ing noun
ski|jor|er +s
ski|jor|ing
ski jump +s
ski jump|er +s
ski jump|ing
skil|ful
skil|ful|ly
skil|ful|ness
ski lift +s
skill +s
skilled adjective
skil|less (use skill-less)
skil|let +s
skill|ful (use skilful)
skill|ful|ly (use skilfully)
skill|ful|ness (use skilfulness)
skill-less
skim
skims
skimmed
skim|ming
skim|mer +s
skim|mia +s
skimp +s +ed +ing
skimp|i|ly
skimp|i|ness
skimpy
skimp|i|er
skimp|i|est
skin
skins
skinned
skin|ning
skin care (skin-care when preceding a noun)
skin deep
skin div|er +s
skin div|ing
skin-flick +s
skin|flint +s
skin|ful +s

skin game +s (swindle)
[☞ skins game]
skin|head +s
skink +s
skin|less
skin-like
skinned adjective
Skin|ner, Bur|rhus Fred|eric (US psychologist)
skin|ner +s
Skin|ner|ian
skin|ni|ness
skin|ny
skin|ni|er
skin|ni|est
skin|nies
skin|ny dip +s noun
skinny-dip verb
skinny-dips
skinny-dipped
skinny-dipping
skin|ny dip|per +s
skinny-dipping noun
skins game +s (Golf)
[☞ skin game]
skint
skin-tight
skip
skips
skipped
skip|ping
skip|jack
• (tuna)
plural skip|jack or skip|jacks
• (boat)
plural skip|jacks
ski plane +s
skip|per +s +ed +ing
skip rock +s
skirl +s +ed +ing
skir|mish
skir|mish|es
skir|mished
skir|mish|ing
skir|mish|er +s
skirr +s +ed +ing
skirt +s +ed +ing
skirt|ed adjective
skirt|ing +s noun
skit +s
skit|ter +s +ed +ing
skit|tery
skit|tish
skit|tish|ly
skit|tish|ness
skit|tle +s
skive
skives
skived
skiv|ing

skiv|er +s
skivvy
skiv|vies
skiv|vied
skivvy|ing
skoal (use skol)
skol
skoo|kum
Skopje (capital of the republic of Macedonia)
skor|dalia
skort +s
Skry|abin, Alek|sandr Nikola|evich (= Scriabin)
skua +s
skul|dug|gery
skulk +s +ed +ing
skulk|er +s
skull +s (skeleton head)
[☞ scull]
skull|dug|gery (use skulduggery)
skull|cap +s
skulled
skunk +s +ed +ing
skunky
skunk|i|er
skunk|i|est
sky
skies
skied
sky|ing
[☞ Skye]
sky blue +s (sky-blue when preceding a noun)
sky|box
sky|boxes
sky-clad
sky|dive
sky|dives
sky|dived
sky|div|ing
sky|div|er +s
sky|div|ing
Skye (Scottish island; terrier)
skyey
sky-high
sky|hook +s
sky|jack +s +ed +ing
sky|jack|er +s
sky|jack|ing +s noun
sky|lark +s +ed +ing
sky|less
sky|light +s
sky|light|ed
sky|line +s
sky|lit

sky|rock|et +s +ed +ing
sky|sail +s
sky|scape +s
sky|scrap|er +s
sky|walk
sky|ward
sky|wards
sky|watch|er +s
sky|way +s
sky|writ|er +s
sky|writ|ing
slab
  slabs
  slabbed
  slab|bing
slack +er +est +s +ed +ing
slack|en +s +ed +ing
slack|er +s
slack|ly
slack|ness
slacks
slack suit +s
slag
  slags
  slagged
  slag|ging
Slag|gard (mountain, Canada)
slag|gy
  slag|gi|er
  slag|gi|est
slag heap +s
slain
slainte
slake
  slakes
  slaked
  slak|ing
slaked *adjective*
slal|om +s +ed +ing
slalom|er +s
slam
  slams
  slammed
  slam|ming
slam-bang
slam-dance
  slam-dances
  slam-danced
  slam-dancing
slam-dancer +s
slam-dancing
slam dunk +s *noun*
slam-dunk +s +ed +ing *verb*
slam|mer +s
slan|der +s +ed +ing
slan|der|er +s
slan|der|ous
slan|der|ous|ly
slang +s +ed +ing

slang|i|ly
slang|i|ness
slang|ing match
  slang|ing match|es
slangy
  slang|i|er
  slang|i|est
slant +s +ed +ing
slant-eyed
slant|wise
slanty
slap
  slaps
  slapped
  slap|ping
slap bang
slap|dash
slap-happy
slap|shot +s
slap|stick
slap-up
slash
  slash|es
  slashed
  slash|ing
slash-and-burn
slash|er
slash|ing *noun*
slat +s
slate
  slates
  slated
  slat|ing
slate blue (slate-blue *when preceding a noun*)
slate-coloured
slate grey (slate-grey *when preceding a noun*)
slater +s
slath|er +s +ed +ing
slat|ing *noun*
slat|ted
slat|tern +s
slat|tern|li|ness
slat|tern|ly
slaty
slaugh|ter +s +ed +ing
slaugh|ter|er +s
slaugh|ter|house +s
slaugh|ter|ous
Slav +s
Slave (river, Canada)
slave
  slaves
  slaved
  slav|ing
slave-driver +s
slave|hold|er +s
slave|hold|ing

Slave Lake (town, Canada)
slav|er +s +ed +ing
slav|ery
slave ship +s
Slav|ey
  plural Slav|ey or Slav|eys
Slav|ic
slav|ish
slav|ish|ly
Slav|ist +s
Slav|onic
Slavo|phile +s
slaw +s
slay (kill)
  slays
  slew
  slain
  slay|ing
  [☞ sleigh]
slay|er +s
slay|ing +s *noun*
SLBM (submarine-launched ballistic missile)
  SLBMs
SLCM (sea-launched cruise missile)
  SLCMs
sleaze
  sleaz|es
  sleazed
  sleaz|ing
sleaze|bag +s
sleaze|ball +s
sleaz|i|ly
sleaz|i|ness
sleaz|oid +s
sleazy
  sleaz|i|er
  sleaz|i|est
sled
  sleds
  sled|ded
  sled|ding
sled|der +s
sled|ding *noun*
sled dog +s
sledge
  sledges
  sledged
  sledg|ing
sledge|ham|mer +s
sleek +er +est
sleek|ly
sleek|ness
sleep
  sleeps
  slept
  sleep|ing
sleep|er +s
sleep|er seat +s

sleep|i|er
sleep|i|est
sleep|i|ly
sleep|i|ness
sleep|less
sleep|less|ly
sleep|less|ness
sleep over *verb*
  sleeps over
  slept over
  sleep|ing over
sleep|over +s *noun*
sleep set +s
sleep|shirt +s
sleep|walk +s +ed +ing
sleep|walk|er +s
sleep|wear
sleepy
  sleep|i|er
  sleep|i|est
sleepy|head +s
sleet
sleety
sleeve +s
sleeved
slee|veen +s
sleeve|less
sleeve notes
sleev|ing
sleigh +s +ed +ing (sled)
  [☞ slay]
sleigh bed +s
sleigh bell +s
sleigh|ing *noun*
sleight +s (deceptive trick, dexterity, cunning; in 'sleight of hand')
  [☞ slight]
slen|der +er +est
slen|der|ize
  slen|der|iz|es
  slen|der|ized
  slen|der|iz|ing
slen|der|ly
slen|der|ness
slept
sleuth +s +ed +ing
slew +s +ed +ing (swing around; skid; large quantity or number; *past tense of* slay; *for* mire, marsh, estuary *use* slough)
slice
  slices
  sliced
  slicing
slice|able
sliced *adjective*

slice of life *noun*
  slices of life
slice-of-life *adjective*
slicer +s
slick +er +est +s +ed +ing
slick|er +s
slick|ly
slick|ness
slide
  slides
  slid
  slid|ing
slid|er +s
slide rule +s
slide show +s
slight +s +ed +ing
  (inconsiderable;
  slender; insult)
  [☞ sleight]
slight|ing|ly
slight|ly
slight|ness
Sligo (county & town,
  Ireland)
slim
  slim|mer
  slim|mest
  slims
  slimmed
  slim|ming
slime
  slimes
  slimed
  slim|ing
slime|ball +s
slim|i|er
slim|i|est
slim|i|ly
slim|i|ness
slim|line
slim|ly
slim|mer +s
slim|ming *noun*
slim|ness
slimy
  slim|i|er
  slim|i|est
sling
  slings
  slung
  sling|ing
sling|back +s
sling|er +s
sling|shot +s
slink
  • (move sneakily or
  alluringly)
  slinks
  slunk
  slink|ing
  • (produce young

  prematurely)
  slinks
  slinked
  slink|ing
slink|i|ly
slink|i|ness
slinky
  slink|i|er
  slink|i|est
slip
  slips
  slipped
  slip|ping
slip|case +s
slip|cased
slip|cover +s
slip|form +s +ed
  +ing
slip-joint pliers
slip-knot +s
slip-on +s *noun &
  adjective*
slip|page +s
slipped *adjective*
slip|per +s
slip|pered
slip|per|i|ness
slipper|wort +s
slip|pery
  slip|per|i|er
  slip|per|i|est
slip|pi|ness
slip|py
  slip|pi|er
  slip|pi|est
slip-ring +s
slip-road +s
slip|shod
slip|stitch
  slip|stitch|es
  slip|stitched
  slip|stitch|ing
slip|stream +s
slip up *verb*
  slips up
  slipped up
  slip|ping up
slip-up +s *noun*
slip|way +s
slit
  slits
  slit
  slit|ting
slit-eyed
slither +s +ed +ing
slith|ery
slit-like
slit|ted *adjective*
slit|ter +s
slitty
  slit|ti|er
  slit|ti|est
Sliven (city, Bulgaria)

sliver +s +ed +ing
sliv|ered *adjective*
slivo|vitz
Sloan, John French
  (US painter)
  [☞ Sloane]
Sloane, Sir Hans
  (British naturalist)
Sloane +s (= Sloane
  Ranger)
Sloane Ran|ger +s
Sloaney (= Sloany)
Sloany
slob +s
slob|ber +s +ed +ing
slob|bery
slob|bish
slobby
sloe +s (blackthorn)
  [☞ slow]
sloe-eyed
sloe gin +s
slog
  slogs
  slogged
  slog|ging
slo|gan +s
slo|ganed
slogan|eer +s +ed
  +ing
slogan|eer|ing *noun*
slogan|ize
  slogan|iz|es
  slogan|ized
  slogan|iz|ing
slogan|iz|ing *noun*
slog|ger +s
slo-mo (slow motion)
sloop +s
sloop-rigged
slop
  slops
  slopped
  slop|ping
slope
  slopes
  sloped
  slop|ing
sloped *adjective*
slope|side
slo-pitch
slop|pi|ly
slop|pi|ness
sloppy
  slop|pi|er
  slop|pi|est
slosh
  slosh|es
  sloshed
  slosh|ing
sloshed *adjective*
sloshy

slot
  slots
  slot|ted
  slot|ting
slot|back +s
sloth +s
sloth|ful
sloth|ful|ly
sloth|ful|ness
slot|ted *adjective*
slouch
  slouch|es
  slouched
  slouch|ing
slouchy
  slouch|i|er
  slouch|i|est
Slough (town,
  England)
slough[1] (marsh, pond,
  estuary)
  [☞ slew]
slough[2] +s +ed +ing
  (shed; discarded skin
  etc.)
slough grass
  slough grass|es
slough of des|pond
sloughy
Slo|vak +s
Slo|vakia (country,
  Europe)
Slo|vak|ian +s
slov|en +s (untidy
  person; wagon)
Slo|vene +s (of
  Slovenia)
Slo|venia (country,
  Europe)
Slo|ven|ian +s
slov|en|li|ness
slov|en|ly
slow +er +est +s +ed
  +ing (not fast)
  [☞ sloe, sloe gin,
  slo-mo, slo-pitch]
slow burn (slow-burn
  when preceding a
  noun)
slow-burning
slow|coach
  slow|coach|es
slow dance
  slow dan|ces
  slow danced
  slow dan|cing
slow down *verb*
  slows down
  slowed down
  slow|ing down
slow|down +s *noun*
slow-footed
slow|ish

slow|ly
slow mo|tion (slow-
   motion *when*
   preceding a noun)
slow|ness
slow-pitch (*use* slo-
   pitch)
slow|poke +s
slow-release
slow-twitch
slow-wave
slow-witted
slow-witted|ness
slow-worm +s
SLR (single-lens reflex)
   SLRs
slub
   slubs
   slubbed
   slub|bing
sludge
   sludg|es
sludgy
   sludg|i|er
   sludg|i|est
slue (swing around,
   skid: *use* slew)
   slues
   slued
   slu|ing
   [☞ slew, slough]
sluff +s +ed +ing
   (shed, discard skin
   etc.: *use* slough)
   [☞ slough]
slug
   slugs
   slugged
   slug|ging
slug|a|bed +s
slug|fest +s
slug|gard +s
slug|gard|li|ness
slug|gard|ly
slug|ger +s
slug|gish
slug|gish|ly
slug|gish|ness
sluice
   sluices
   sluiced
   sluicing
sluice box
   sluice boxes
sluice gate +s
sluice|way +s
slum
   slums
   slummed
   slum|ming
slum|ber +s +ed +ing
slum|ber|er +s
slum|ber|ous

slum|brous
   (= slumberous)
slum|gul|lion +s
slum|lord +s
slum|mi|ness
slummy
   slum|mi|er
   slum|mi|est
slump +s +ed +ing
slumped *adjective*
slung
slunk
slur
   slurs
   slurred
   slur|ring
slurp +s +ed +ing
Slurpee +s *proprietary*
   (flavoured ice)
slurpy (wet, slurping)
   slurp|i|er
   slurp|i|est
slurry
   slur|ries
slush
   slush|es
   slushed
   slush|ing
slush|i|ness
slush pile +s
slushy
   slush|i|er
   slush|i|est
   slush|ies
slut +s
slut|tish
slut|tish|ness
sly +er +est
sly|boots
   plural sly|boots
slyly
sly|ness
slype +s
S/M (= S&M)
smack +s +ed +ing
smack dab
smack|er
smack|eroo +s
small +er +est +s
small-bore
small cap +s (small-
   cap *when preceding a
   noun*)
small game (small-
   game *when preceding
   a noun*)
small|hold|er +s
small hold|ing +s
small|ish
small-minded
small-minded|ly
small-minded|ness

small|mouth
   plural small|mouth
   or small|mouths
small|ness
small|pox
small-scale
small-sword +s
small talk *noun*
small-talk +s +ed
   +ing *verb*
small-time
small-timer +s
small-town
small-towner +s
Small|wood
   (reservoir, Canada)
Small|wood, Jo|seph
   Rob|erts ('Joey')
   (Cdn politician)
smalt
smarm +s +ed +ing
smarm|i|ly
smarm|i|ness
smarmy
   smarm|i|er
   smarm|i|est
Smart, Eliza|beth
   (Cdn writer)
smart +er +est +s
   +ed +ing
smart alec +s (*use*
   smart aleck)
smart al|eck +s
smart-alecky
smart-ass *adjective*
smart|ass *noun*
   smart|asses
smart-assed
smart card +s
smart|en +s +ed +ing
smart|ing|ly
smart|ish
smart|ly
smart money (smart-
   money *when
   preceding a noun*)
smart-mouth +s +ed
   +ing
smart|ness
smart|weed +s
smarty
   smart|ies
smarty-pants
   plural smarty-pants
smash
   smash|es
   smashed
   smash|ing
smash-and-grab +s
smashed *adjective*
smash|er +s
smash|ing *adjective*
smash|ing|ly

smash-mouth
smash up *verb*
   smash|es up
   smashed up
   smash|ing up
smash-up +s *noun*
smat|ter|er +s
smat|ter|ing
smear +s +ed +ing
smear|er +s
smeary
smec|tic +s
smeg|ma
smell +s +ed +ing
smell|er +s
smell|i|ness
smelly
   smell|i|er
   smell|i|est
smelt
• (fish)
   plural smelt or
   smelts
• (*Mining*)
   smelts
   smelt|ed
   smelt|ing
• (= smelled)
smelt|er +s
smelt|ery
   smelt|eries
Smersh
Smet|ana, Bed|řich
   (Czech composer)
smew +s
smidge
   smidg|es
smidg|en +s
smidg|eon +s (*use*
   smidgen)
smidg|in +s (*use*
   smidgen)
smi|lax
   smi|lax|es
smile
   smiles
   smiled
   smil|ing
smile|less
smil|er +s
smil|ey +s
smil|ing *adjective*
smil|ing|ly
smirch
   smirch|es
   smirched
   smirch|ing
smirk +s +ed +ing
smirk|er +s
smirk|ing|ly
smirky
   smirk|i|er
   smirk|i|est

smit
smite
smites
smote
smit|ten
smit|ing
smit|er +s
Smith, Adam
(Scottish economist)
Smith, Ar|thur James
Mar|shall (Cdn poet
& critic)
Smith, Bes|sie (US
singer)
Smith, David Ro|land
(US sculptor)
Smith, Don|ald
Alex|an|der, 1st
Baron Strath|cona
and Mount Royal
(Cdn fur trader &
financier)
Smith, Gold|win (Cdn
journalist)
Smith, Ian Doug|las
(Rhodesian prime
minister)
Smith, John (colonial
explorer)
Smith, Jo|seph (US
Mormon leader)
Smith, Lois (Cdn
dancer)
Smith, Dame
Mar|garet Nat|alie
('Maggie') (English
actress)
Smith, Syd|ney
(English churchman
& essayist)
Smith, Wil|liam
(English geologist)
smith +s
smith|er|eens
Smith|ers (town,
Canada)
smith|ery
smith|eries
Smith|field (district of
London, England)
smith|ing
Smiths Falls (town,
Canada)
Smith|son, James
(English scientist)
Smith|son|ian
In|sti|tu|tion
smithy
smith|ies
smit|ten adjective
smock +s +ed +ing
smocked adjective
smock|ing noun
smog

smoggy
smog|gi|er
smog|gi|est
smog|less
smok|able
smoke
smokes
smoked
smok|ing
smoke|able (use
smokable)
smoke and mirrors
(smoke-and-
mirrors when
preceding a noun)
smoke-dried adjective
smoke-dry
smoke-dries
smoke-dried
smoke-drying
smoke-free
smoke|house +s
smoke jump +s +ed
+ing
smoke jump|er +s
smoke|less
smok|er +s
smoker's cough +s
smoke|screen +s
smoke shop +s
smoke|stack +s
smokey (police; for of
or like smoke use
smoky)
smok|eys or
smok|ies
smok|i|er
smok|i|est
[☞ smokie]
smok|ie +s (hot dog)
[☞ smokey,
smoky]
smok|i|ly
smok|i|ness
smok|ing noun &
adjective
smoko +s
smoky (of or like
smoke)
smok|i|er
smok|i|est
[☞ smokey,
smokie]
smol|der +s +ed +ing
(use smoulder)
smol|der|ing adjective
(use smouldering)
smol|der|ing|ly (use
smoulderingly)
Smo|lensk (city,
Russia)
Smol|lett, To|bias
George (Scottish
novelist)

smolt
    plural smolts or
    smolt
smooch
smooch|es
smooched
smooch|ing
smooch|er +s
smoochy
smooch|i|er
smooch|i|est
smoosh (squash)
smoosh|es
smooshed
smoosh|ing
smooth +er +est +s
+ed +ing adjective,
verb, noun & adverb
smooth|able
smooth|bore +s
smoothe verb (use
smooth)
smoothes
smoothed
smooth|ing
smooth|en +s +ed
+ing
smooth|er +s
smooth-faced
smooth|ie +s (smooth
person; drink)
smooth|ish
smooth|ly
smooth|ness
smooth talk noun
smooth-talk +s +ed
+ing verb
smooth talk|er +s
smooth-talking
adjective
smooth-tongued
smoothy (drink: use
smoothie)
smooth|ies
[☞ smoothie]
s'more +s
smorg +s
smor|gas|bord +s
smote
smoth|er +s +ed +ing
smoth|ery
smoul|der +s +ed
+ing
smoul|der|ing
smoul|der|ing|ly
smudge
smudg|es
smudged
smudg|ing
smudge|less
smudg|i|ly
smudg|i|ness

smudgy
smudg|i|er
smudg|i|est
smug
smug|ger
smug|gest
smug|gle
smug|gles
smug|gled
smug|gling
smug|gler +s
smug|gling noun
smug|ly
smug|ness
smush (squash)
smush|es
smushed
smush|ing
smut
smuts
smut|ted
smut|ting
Smuts, Jan
Chris|tiaan (South
African prime
minister)
smut|ti|ly
smut|ti|ness
smutty
smut|ti|er
smut|ti|est
Smyr|na (ancient city,
Asia Minor)
Smythe,
Con|stan|tine
Falk|land Cary
('Conn') (Cdn
hockey
entrepreneur)
snack +s +ed +ing
snack bar +s
snack|er +s
snacky
snaf|fle
snaf|fles
snaf|fled
snaf|fling
snafu +s +ed +ing
snag
snags
snagged
snag|ging
snagged adjective
snag|ger +s
snag|gle|tooth
snag|gle|teeth
snaggle-toothed
snaggy
snail +s
snail-like
snail mail
snail's pace

snake
  snakes
  snaked
  snak|ing
snake|bark
snake|bite +s
snake-bitten
snake dance +s *noun*
snake-dance *verb*
  snake-dances
  snake-danced
  snake-dancing
snake|like
snake oil +s (snake-oil *when preceding a noun*)
snake|pit +s
snake-rail fence +s
snake|root +s
snake's head +s (plant)
snake|skin
snakey (*use* snaky)
  snak|i|er
  snak|i|est
snak|i|ly
snak|i|ness
snak|ish
snaky
  snak|i|er
  snak|i|est
snap
  snaps
  snapped
  snap|ping
snap bean +s
snap-brim +s
snap-brimmed
snap|dragon +s
snap|pable
snap|per +s
snap|pi|ly
snap|pi|ness
snap|ping *adjective*
snap|ping|ly
snap|pish
snap|pish|ly
snap|pish|ness
snappy
  snap|pi|er
  snap|pi|est
snap shot +s (*Hockey*)
snap|shot +s (*Photography*)
snare
  snares
  snared
  snar|ing
snare drum +s
snar|er +s
snarf +s +ed +ing

snarky
  snark|i|er
  snark|i|est
snarl +s +ed +ing
snarl|er +s
snarl|ing|ly
snarl-up +s
snarly
  snarl|i|er
  snarl|i|est
snatch
  snatch|es
  snatched
  snatch|ing
snatch|er +s
snatchy
snaz|zi|ly
snaz|zi|ness
snaz|zy
  snaz|zi|er
  snaz|zi|est
Snead, Sam (US golfer)
sneak
  sneaks
  snuck *or* sneaked
  sneak|ing
sneak|er +s
sneak|ered
sneak|i|ly
sneak|i|ness
sneak|ing *adjective*
sneak|ing|ly
sneaky
  sneak|i|er
  sneak|i|est
sneer +s +ed +ing
sneer|er +s
sneer|ing *adjective*
sneer|ing|ly
sneeze
  sneez|es
  sneezed
  sneez|ing
sneez|er +s
sneeze|weed +s
sneeze|wort +s
sneezy
snell +s +ed +ing
Snell's law
Sne Nay Muxw (people & language) *plural* Sne Nay Muxw
snick +s +ed +ing
snick|er +s +ed +ing
snick|er|ing|ly
snide
snide|ly
snide|ness
sniff +s +ed +ing
sniff|er +s
sniff|i|er

sniff|i|est
sniff|i|ly
sniff|i|ness
sniff|ing|ly
snif|fle
  snif|fles
  snif|fled
  snif|fling
snif|fler +s
snif|fly
sniffy
  sniff|i|er
  sniff|i|est
snif|ter +s
snig|ger +s +ed +ing
snig|ger|er +s
snig|ger|ing|ly
snip
  snips
  snipped
  snip|ping
snipe
  • (bird)
    plural snipe *or* snipes
  • (act of sniping)
    plural snipes
  • *verb*
    snipes
    sniped
    sniping
snipe eel +s
snipe fish
  plural snipe fish *or* snipe fish|es
sniper +s
sniping *noun*
snip|pet +s
snip|pety
snip|pi|ly
snip|pi|ness
snip|ping +s *noun*
snip|py
  snip|pi|er
  snip|pi|est
snit +s
snitch
  snitch|es
  snitched
  snitch|ing
snivel
  sniv|els
  sniv|elled
  sniv|el|ling
sniv|el|ler +s
sniv|el|ling *adjective*
sniv|el|ling|ly
snob +s
snob|bery
  snob|ber|ies
snob|bish
snob|bish|ly
snob|bish|ness

snob|bism
snob|by
  snob|bi|er
  snob|bi|est
SNOBOL (programming language)
sno-cone +s (= snow cone)
snog
  snogs
  snogged
  snog|ging
snog|ger +s
snood +s
snook
  • (gesture)
    plural snooks
  • (fish)
    plural snook *or* snooks
snook|er +s +ed +ing
snoop +s +ed +ing
snoop|er +s
snoopy
snoose (tobacco)
snoot +s
snoot|ful +s
snoot|i|ly
snoot|i|ness
snooty
  snoot|i|er
  snoot|i|est
snooze (sleep)
  snooz|es
  snoozed
  snooz|ing
snooz|er +s
snoozy
  snooz|i|er
  snooz|i|est
snore
  snores
  snored
  snor|ing
snor|er +s
snor|kel
  snor|kels
  snor|kelled *or* snor|keled
  snor|kel|ling *or* snor|kel|ing
snor|kel|ler +s
Snor|ri Stur|lu|son (Icelandic historian)
snort +s +ed +ing
snort|er +s
snot +s
snot-nosed
snot|ti|ly
snot|ti|ness

snot|ty
  snot|ti|er
  snot|ti|est
snout +s
snout|ed
snout|like
snouty
Snow, Charles Percy
  (English novelist)
Snow, Clar|ence
  Eu|gene ('Hank')
  (Cdn singer-
  songwriter)
Snow, Mi|chael
  James Aleck (Cdn
  artist)
snow +s +ed +ing
Snow Apple +s
snow|ball +s +ed
  +ing
  [☞ SNOBOL]
snow|bank +s
snow|belt +s
snow|berry
  snow|ber|ries
snow|bird +s
snow-blind
snow-blinded
snow blind|ness
snow blow|er +s
snow|board +s
snow|board|er +s
snow|board|ing
snow boot +s
snow|bound
snow|cap +s
snow-capped
snow cone +s
Snow|don (mountain,
  Wales)
Snow|donia (region,
  Wales)
snow|drift +s
snow|drop +s
snow|fall +s
snow fence +s
snow fen|cing
snow|field +s
snow|flake +s
snow|flea +s
snow flur|ry
  snow flur|ries
snow glass|es
snow gog|gles
snow goose
  snow geese
snow house +s
snow|i|ly
snow|i|ness
snow-in-summer
snow job +s

snow knife
  snow knives
snow|less
snow|like
snow line +s
snow ma|chine +s
snow-making
snow|man
  snow|men
snow|melt
snow|mobile +s
snow|mobil|er +s
snow|mobil|ing
snow|pack +s
snow-packed
snow pea +s
snow|plough +s +ed
  +ing (use
  snowplow)
snow|plow +s +ed
  +ing
snow|scape +s
snow|shed +s
snow|shoe
  snow|shoes
  snow|shoed
  snow|shoe|ing
snow|shoer +s
snow shov|el +s
snow|snake +s
snow|storm +s
snow|suit +s
snow|throw|er +s
snow tire +s
snow-white adjective
snowy
  snow|i|er
  snow|i|est
snub
  snubs
  snubbed
  snub|bing
snub|ber +s
snub|bing|ly
snub nose +s
snub-nosed
snuck
snuff +s +ed +ing
snuff box
  snuff boxes
snuf|fer +s
snuf|fle
  snuf|fles
  snuf|fled
  snuf|fling
snuf|fler +s
snuf|fly
snug
  snug|ger
  snug|gest
snug|gery
  snug|ger|ies

snug|gle
  snug|gles
  snug|gled
  snug|gling
snug|gly adjective
  (cosy; inviting
  snuggling)
  snug|gli|er
  snug|gli|est
  [☞ snugly]
Snug|li +s proprietary
  (baby pouch)
snug|ly adverb (in a
  snug manner;
  securely;
  comfortably)
  [☞ snuggly]
snug|ness
snye +s
so (adverb &
  conjunction; Music)
  [☞ sew, sow]
soak +s +ed +ing
  (wet)
  [☞ soke]
soak|age
soaked adjective
soak|er +s
soak|ing +s noun &
  adjective
so-and-so
  so-and-sos
soap +s +ed +ing
soap|bark +s
soap|berry
  soap|ber|ries
soap|box
  soap|box|es
soap|less
soap|stone +s
soap|suds
soap|wort +s
soapy
  soap|i|er
  soap|i|est
soar +s +ed +ing (fly
  etc.)
  [☞ sore]
soar|er +s
soar|ing adjective
soar|ing|ly
Soave +s (wine)
  [☞ suave]
SOB (son of a bitch)
  SOBs
sob
  sobs
  sobbed
  sob|bing
soba
sob|bing|ly
so|ber +er +est +s
  +ed +ing

sober|ing|ly
sober|ly
sober-sided
sober sides
So|bies|ki, John
  (John III, Polish king)
so|bri|ety
so|bri|quet +s
sob sis|ter +s
soc (sociology)
  [☞ sock, Sauk]
soca
soc|age
so-called
SOCAN (Society of
  Composers, Authors
  and Music Publishers
  of Canada)
soc|cage (use socage)
soc|cer
Sochi (city, Russia)
so|cia|bil|ity
so|cia|ble
so|cia|ble|ness
so|cia|bly
so|cial +s
so|cial climb|ing
  noun (social-
  climbing when
  preceding a noun)
So|cial Cred|it
  (political party)
so|cial cred|it
  (economic theory)
So|cial Cred|it|er +s
so|cial Dar|win|ism
so|cial Dar|win|ist +s
so|cial in|sur|ance
  num|ber +s
so|cial|ism
so|cial|ist +s
so|cial|is|tic
so|cial|is|tic|ally
so|cial|ite +s
so|cial|ity
so|cial|iz|a|tion
so|cial|ize
  so|cial|iz|es
  so|cial|ized
  so|cial|iz|ing
so|cial|ized adjective
so|cial|ly
so|cial work
so|cial work|er +s
so|ciet|al
so|ciet|al|ly
so|ci|ety
  so|ci|eties
So|ci|ety Islands (in
  French Polynesia)
So|cin|ian +s
So|cin|ian|ism

So|ci|nus, Faus|tus
(Italian theologian)
So|ci|nus, Lael|ius
(Italian theologian)
socio|bio|logic|al
socio|bio|logic|ally
socio|biol|o|gist +s
socio|biol|ogy
socio-cultur|al
socio-cultur|ally
socio-econom|ic
socio-econom|ic|ally
socio|lin|guist +s
socio|lin|guis|tic
socio|lin|guis|tic|ally
socio|lin|guis|tics
socio|logic|al
socio|logic|ally
soci|ol|o|gist +s
soci|ol|ogy
socio|metric
socio|metric|ally
soci|om|et|rist +s
soci|om|etry
socio|path +s
socio|path|ic
soci|op|athy
socio-political
sock
• (footwear)
socks or
in commercial use
sox
• (punch)
socks
socked
sock|ing
[☞ Sauk]
socked in *adjective*
sock|et
sock|ets
sock|et|ed
sock|et|ing
sock|ette +s (short
sock)
sock|et wrench
sock|et wrench|es
sock|eye (salmon)
plural sock|eye
[☞ Sakai]
socko
socle +s
So|cotra (island,
Arabian Sea)
Soc|ra|tes (Greek
philosopher)
So|crat|ic +s
So|crat|ic|ally
So|cred +s
sod (turf; person)
sods
sod|ded

sod|ding
[☞ sawed, Sade]
soda +s
so|dal|ity
so|dal|ities
soda pop +s
sod|bust|er +s
sod|den +s +ed +ing
sod|den|ly
sod|den|ness
sod|die +s
sod|ding *adjective*
Soddy, Fred|erick
(English physicist)
[☞ Saudi]
soddy (*use* soddie)
sod|dies
sodic
so|dium
Sodom +s (*Bible;*
corrupt place)
sod|om|ite
sod|om|ize
sod|om|iz|es
sod|om|ized
sod|om|iz|ing
sod|omy
Sod's Law
sod-turning +s
Soeurs (island,
Canada)
so|ever
sofa +s
sofa bed +s
sof|fit +s
Sofia (capital of
Bulgaria)
[☞ Hagia Sophia]
soft +er +est +s
sof|ta +s
soft|ball +s
soft-boiled
soft-centred
soft-core
soft|cover +s
soft drink +s
soft|en +s +ed +ing
soft|en|er
soft-focus *adjective*
soft goods
soft-headed
soft-headed|ness
soft-hearted
soft-hearted|ness
soft|ie +s
soft|ish
soft-land +s +ed
+ing
soft land|ing +s *noun*
soft|ly
softly-softly
soft|ness

soft-paste
soft pedal +s *noun*
soft-pedal *verb*
soft-pedals
soft-pedalled
soft-pedalling
soft porn (soft-porn
when preceding a
noun)
soft sell +s *noun*
soft-sell *verb*
soft-sells
soft-sold
soft-selling
soft-shoe (tap dance)
soft-shoes
soft-shoed
soft-shoeing
soft-side
soft-skinned
soft soap +s *noun*
soft-soap +s +ed
+ing *verb*
soft-spoken
soft tis|sue +s (soft-
tissue *when*
preceding a noun)
soft-top +s
soft|ware +s
soft|wood +s
softy (*use* softie)
soft|ies
sog|gi|ly
sog|gi|ness
soggy
sog|gi|er
sog|gi|est
Sogne (fjord, Norway)
soh +s (*Music: use* so)
soi-disant
soi|gné *male*
soi|gnée *female*
soil +s +ed +ing
soil|less
soiree +s
soixante-neuf
so|journ +s +ed +ing
so|journ|er +s
soke (*British Law*)
[☞ soak]
Sol (*Roman Myth*)
[☞ Saul, Seoul]
sol
• (*Music; Chemistry;*
coin of New France)
plural sols
• (monetary unit of
Peru)
plural soles
[☞ sole, soul]
sola
• (stage direction for

female: alone; *for*
male use solus)
• (plant)
solas
sol|ace (comfort)
sol|aces
sol|aced
sol|acing
so|la|na|ceous
sol|ar +s (of the sun;
room)
[☞ Soleure]
sol|ar|ium
sol|ar|iums or
sol|aria
sol|ar|iz|a|tion
sol|ar|ize
sol|ar|iz|es
sol|ar|ized
sol|ar|iz|ing
solar plex|us
plural solar plex|us
or solar plex|us|es
solar power
solar-powered
so|la|tium
so|la|tia
sold *adjective &*
conjugated form of
sell
[☞ soled]
solder +s +ed +ing
(fuse metals, wires,
etc.)
solder|able
solder|er +s
solder|ing iron +s
solder|less
sol|dier +s +ed +ing
sol|dier|ly
sol|diery
sol|dier|ies
sold-out *adjective*
preceding a noun
sole
• *adjective* (lone)
• *noun* (fish)
plural sole or soles
• *noun & verb*
(underside of foot or
shoe etc.)
soles
soled
sol|ing
[☞ soul, Seoul, sol]
sol|ecism +s
sol|ecist +s
sol|ecis|tic
soled *adjective &*
conjugated form of
sole
[☞ sold]
sole|ly (only)
[☞ soli]

sol|emn
sol|em|ness
so|lem|nity
  sol|lem|ni|ties
sol|em|niz|a|tion +s
sol|em|nize
  sol|em|niz|es
  sol|em|nized
  sol|em|niz|ing
sol|emn|ly
sol|en|oid +s
sol|en|oidal
So|lent (channel,
  England)
sole plate +s
So|leure
  (= Solothurn,
  Switzerland)
sol-fa +s +ed +ing
sol|feg|gio
  sol|feg|gi
soli *plural of* solo
  [☞ solely]
so|licit +s +ed +ing
so|licit|a|tion
so|lici|tor +s
so|licitor-client
  priv|ilege
so|lici|tor gen|er|al
  so|lici|tors gen|eral
so|lici|tous
so|lici|tous|ly
so|lici|tous|ness
so|lici|tude
sol|id +s
Soli|dar|ity (Polish
  trade union
  movement)
soli|dar|ity
  soli|dar|ities
solid col|our +s
solid-coloured
sol|idi
so|lid|ifi|ca|tion
so|lid|ifi|er
so|lid|ify
  so|lid|ifies
  so|lid|ified
  so|lid|ify|ing
so|lid|ity
  so|lid|ities
sol|id|ly
sol|id|ness
solid state *noun &*
  adjective
sol|idus
  sol|idi
soli|fluc|tion
so|lilo|quist +s
so|lilo|quize
  so|lilo|quiz|es
  so|lilo|quized
  so|lilo|quiz|ing

so|lilo|quy
  so|lilo|quies
Soli|man
  (= Suleiman, sultan
  of the Ottoman
  Empire)
  [☞ Solomon]
sol|ip|sism
sol|ip|sist +s
sol|ip|sis|tic
sol|ip|sis|tic|ally
soli|taire +s
soli|tar|i|ly
soli|tar|i|ness
soli|tary
  soli|tar|ies
soli|tude +s
sol|miz|a|tion
solo
• (*Music*)
  plural solos or soli
• (unaccompanied
  flight etc.; *Cards*;
  Dance)
  plural solos
• *verb*
  soloes
  soloed
  solo|ing
solo|ist +s
Solo|mon +s (king of
  Israel; wise person;
  SW Pacific islands)
Solo|mon Grun|dy
  (= Solomon Gundy)
  Solo|mon Grun|dies
  [☞ salmagundi]
Solo|mon Gundy
  (herring dish)
  Solo|mon Gun|dies
  [☞ salmagundi]
Solo|monic
Solo|mon's seal +s
So|lon +s (Athenian
  statesman;
  lawmaker)
Solo|thurn (canton &
  its capital,
  Switzerland)
sol|stice +s
sol|sti|tial
Solti, Sir Georg
  (British conductor)
solu|bil|ity
solu|bil|iz|a|tion
solu|bil|ize
  solu|bil|iz|es
  solu|bil|ized
  solu|bil|iz|ing
sol|uble
solus (stage direction
  for male: alone; *for*
  female use sola)
  [☞ solace]

sol|ute +s
solu|tion
Solu|trean +s
solv|abil|ity
solv|able
sol|vate
  sol|vates
  sol|vat|ed
  sol|vat|ing
sol|va|tion (chemical
  association between
  solute & solvent)
solve
  solves
  solved
  solv|ing
sol|vency
sol|vent +s
solv|er +s
Sol|way Firth (inlet,
  Irish Sea)
Soly|man
  (= Suleiman, sultan
  of the Ottoman
  Empire)
  [☞ Solomon]
Sol|zhe|nit|syn,
  Alek|sandr
  Isa|evich (Russian
  novelist)
soma +s
So|mali
  plural So|mali or
  So|malis
So|mal|ia
So|mal|ian
So|mali|land (in
  'British Somaliland',
  'French Somaliland')
So|mali Pen|in|sula
  (= Horn of Africa)
som|at|ic
som|at|ic|ally
som|at|ol|ogy
som|ato|troph|in
  (= somatotropin)
som|ato|trop|in
som|ato|type +s
sombre
sombre|ly
sombre|ness
som|brero +s
some (unspecified
  amount)
  [☞ sum, Somme]
some|body
  some|bod|ies
some|day
some|how
some|one +s
some|place

Som|ers, Harry
  Stew|art (Cdn
  composer)
som|er|sault +s +ed
  +ing
Som|er|set (island,
  Canada; county,
  England)
Som|er|ville, Mary
  (English scientist)
some|thing +s
some|time
some|times
some|way
some|ways
some|what
some|when
some|where
some|wheres
som|ite +s
som|itic
Somme (river & battle
  site, France)
som|me|lier +s
som|nam|bu|lant
som|nam|bu|lantly
som|nam|bu|late
  som|nam|bu|lates
  som|nam|bu|lated
  som|nam|bu|lat|ing
som|nam|bu|lism
som|nam|bu|list +s
som|nam|bu|lis|tic
som|nam|bu|lis|tic|
    ally
som|nif|er|ous
som|no|lence
som|no|lency
som|no|lent
som|no|lent|ly
Som|oza (surname)
  [☞ samosa]
Som|oza (De|bayle),
  Ana|sta|sio
  (Nicaraguan
  president 1967–72 &
  1974–79)
Som|oza (De|bayle),
  Luis (Nicaraguan
  president)
Som|oza (Gar|cía),
  Ana|sta|sio
  (Nicaraguan
  president 1937–47 &
  1951–6)
son +s (male
  offspring)
  [☞ sun]
son|ant +s
so|nar +s
so|nata +s
sona|tina +s
sonde +s

Sond|heim, Ste|phen Joshua (US songwriter)
sone +s (unit of loudness)
[☞ **Saône, sown, sewn**]
son et lu|mière
Song (= Sung, Chinese dynasty)
song +s
song|bird +s
song|book +s
song|ful
Song Hong (= Red River, Asia)
song-like
song|smith +s
song|ster +s
song|stress
song|stress|es
song|writ|er +s
song|writ|ing
son|ic
son|ic|ally
son-in-law
sons-in-law
son|less
son|net +s
son|net|eer +s
son|net|eer|ing
sonny (form of address)
son|nies
sono|buoy +s
son of a bitch
sons of bitch|es
sonofabitching
son of a gun
sono|gram +s
sono|graph +s
sonog|raph|er +s
sono|graph|ic
sono|graph|ic|ally
sonog|raphy
So|nora (state, Mexico)
So|nor|an
so|nor|ity
so|nor|ities
so|nor|ous
so|nor|ous|ly
so|nor|ous|ness
son|ship
son|sie (*use* sonsy)
son|si|er
son|si|est
sonsy
son|si|er
son|si|est
Son|tag, Susan (US writer)

Soo (Sault Ste. Marie, Canada)
[☞ **Sue, sou, Sioux, xu**]
sook +s (wimp, sissy)
[☞ **souk**]
sooky baby
sooky babies
soon +er +est
soon|ish
soo|pol|lalie +s
soot +s +ed +ing (fire residue)
sooth (truth)
[☞ **soothe**]
soothe (calm, relieve)
soothes
soothed
sooth|ing
[☞ **sooth**]
sooth|er +s
sooth|ing *adjective*
sooth|ing|ly
sooth|say|er +s
sooth|say|ing
soot|i|ness
sooty
soot|i|er
soot|i|est
sop
sops
sopped
sop|ping
sopal|lil|lie +s (*use* soopollalie)
So|phia (= Sofia, Bulgaria)
soph|ism +s
soph|ist +s
so|phis|tic
so|phis|tical
so|phis|tic|ally
so|phis|ti|cate
so|phis|ti|cates
so|phis|ti|cat|ed
so|phis|ti|cat|ing
so|phis|ti|cat|ed *adjective*
so|phis|ti|cat|ed|ly
so|phis|ti|ca|tion +s
soph|istry
soph|is|tries
Soph|o|cles (Greek dramatist)
soph|o|more +s
soph|o|moric
Sophy
So|phies
sopo|rific +s
sopo|rific|ally
sop|pi|ly
sop|pi|ness
sop|ping *adjective*

sop|ping wet
soppy
sop|pi|er
sop|pi|est
sop|ra|nino +s
sop|rano
sop|ranos or
sop|rani
sora
plural sora or soras
sor|bet +s
sorb|itol
sor|cer|er +s
sor|cer|ess
sor|cer|ess|es
sor|cer|ous
sor|cery
sor|cer|ies
sor|did
sor|did|ly
sor|did|ness
sor|dino
sor|dini
sore +s (painful; angry; wound)
[☞ **soar**]
sore|head +s
Sorel (city, Canada)
[☞ **sorrel**]
Sorel, Georges Eu|gène (French philosopher)
[☞ **sorrel**]
sore|ly
sore|ness
sor|ghum +s
sori *plural of* sorus
Sor|opti|mist +s
soror|al
soror|ity
soror|ities
so|ro|sis (fruit)
so|ro|ses
[☞ **cirrhosis**]
sorp|tion
sor|rel +s (plant, tree; colour; animal)
[☞ **Sorel**]
Sor|ren|to (town, Italy)
sor|ri|er
sor|ri|est
sor|ri|ly
sor|ri|ness
sor|row +s +ed +ing
sor|row|ful
sor|row|fully
sor|row|ful|ness
sor|row|ing *adjective*
sorry (remorseful, regretful)
sor|ri|er

sor|ri|est
[☞ **saury, sori**]
sort +s +ed +ing
sorta
sort|able
sort|er +s
sor|tie
sor|ties
sor|tied
sor|tie|ing
sor|ti|lege +s
sort|ing *noun*
sorus
sori
SOS
SOSs
Sos|now|iec (city, Poland)
so-so
sos|tenu|to +s
sot +s (drunkard)
[☞ **sought**]
so|teri|o|logic|al
so|teri|ol|ogy
Sothic
Sotho
plural Sotho or
So|thos
so|tol +s
sot|tish
sotto voce
sou +s (former French coin)
[☞ **sue, xu, Soo, Sault Ste. Marie**]
Sou|bi|rous, Marie Ber|narde (St. Bernadette)
sou|brette +s
sou|bri|quet +s (*use* sobriquet)
sou|chong +s
souf|fle +s (murmur)
[☞ **soufflé**]
souf|flé +s (*Cooking*)
[☞ **souffle**]
souf|fléd *adjective*
Sou|frière (volcanoes, Guadeloupe & St. Vincent)
sough +s +ed +ing (rushing or murmuring sound)
sought *past & past participle of* seek
[☞ **sot**]
sought-after
souk +s (bazaar)
[☞ **sook**]
sou|kous
soul +s (spirit; *Music*; animating element)
[☞ **sole, Seoul, sol**]

soul-destroy|ing
soul|ful
soul|ful|ly
soul|ful|ness
soul kiss *noun*
soul kiss|es
soul-kiss *verb*
soul-kisses
soul-kissed
soul-kissing
soul|less (having no soul)
[☞ solus, solace]
soul|less|ly
soul|less|ness
soul|mate +s
soul-search|ing +s
soul-stirring
sound +s +ed +ing +er +est
sound-alike +s
sound-and-light *adjective preceding a noun*
sound bite +s
sound|board +s
sound box
sound boxes
sound card +s
sound check +s
sound|er +s
sound hole +s
sound|ing +s *noun & adjective*
sound|less
sound|lessly
sound|less|ness
sound|ly
sound|man
sound|men
sound|ness
sound post +s
sound|proof +s +ed +ing
sound|proof|ing *noun*
sound|scape +s
sound stage +s
sound sys|tem +s
sound|track +s
sound wave +s
soup +s +ed +ing
soup-and-fish
soup|çon +s
soup du jour
soups du jour
souped-up *adjective*
soup|i|ness
soup|like
soup spoon +s
soupy
soup|i|er
soup|i|est
sour +s +ed +ing

source
sources
sourced
sourcing
source|book +s
source|less
sourcing *noun*
sour|dough +s
Souris (river, towns, Canada)
sour|ish
sour|ly
sour|ness
sour|puss
sour|puss|es
sour|sop +s
sour|wood +s
Sousa, John Phil|lip (US composer)
[☞ Sousse, Susa]
sousa|phone +s
sousa|phon|ist +s
sous-chef +s
souse (soak)
souses
soused
sous|ing
[☞ Dr. Seuss, Sousse]
soused *adjective*
sous|er +s
Sousse (city, Tunisia)
[☞ souse, Sousa, Susa, Dr. Seuss]
sou|tache +s
sou|tane +s
South (particular region; *Bridge*)
south (compass point; direction)
South|amp|ton (city, England; island, Canada)
South|amp|ton, Henry Wriothes|ley, 3rd Earl of (patron of Shakespeare)
south|bound
South|down +s
South|east (particular region)
south|east (compass point; direction)
south|easter +s
south|easter|ly
south|easter|lies
south|east|ern
south|east|ern|er +s
south|east|ern|most
south|east|ward
south|east|wards
Southend-on-Sea (town, England)

south|erly
south|er|lies
South|ern (of the US South)
south|ern (in general use)
south|ern|er +s
southern-fried
south|ern hemi|sphere
South|ern In|dian Lake (in Canada)
south|ern lights
south|ern|most
south|ern wood +s (shrub)
Southey, Rob|ert (English poet)
south|ing +s *noun*
South Na|han|ni (river, Canada)
south of 60
south|paw +s
South Pen|der (island, Canada)
South Pole (southernmost point on earth)
south pole (southernmost celestial point; south magnetic pole)
South|port (town, England)
south-southeast
south-southwest
south|ward
south|wards
South|west (particular region)
south|west (in general use)
South West Af|ri|ca (former name for Namibia)
south|wester +s
south|wester|ly
south|wester|lies
south|west|ern
south|west|ern|er +s
south|west|ern|most
South|west Mira|mi|chi (river, Canada)
south|west|ward
south|west|wards
Sou|tine, Chaim (French painter)
sou|ven|ir +s
souv|laki +s
sou'west|er +s
sover|eign +s
sover|eign|ist +s

sover|eign|ly
sover|eign|tist +s (= sovereignist)
sover|eign|ty
sover|eign|ties
sover|eignty-associ|a|tion
Soviet +s (of the Soviet Union)
soviet +s (council)
Soviet|ism
Soviet|iz|a|tion
Soviet|ize
Soviet|iz|es
Soviet|ized
Soviet|iz|ing
Soviet|ol|o|gist +s
Soviet Union (former country)
sow (plant a field with seed; cover; female pig etc.; iron; thistle)
sows
sowed
sown or sowed
[☞ sew, sough]
sow|belly
sow|bug +s
sower +s (one who sows seed)
[☞ sewer]
So|wetan +s
So|weto (urban area, South Africa)
sow|ing *noun* (planting)
[☞ sewing]
sown *past participle of* sow
[☞ sone, sewn, Saône]
sow this|tle +s
sox (in commercial use)
soy
soya
soya bean +s (= soybean)
soya bur|ger +s
soya milk (= soy milk)
soya sauce (= soy sauce)
soy|bean +s
soy|bean meal (= soymeal)
soy|burger +s (= soya burger)
Soy|inka, Wole (Nigerian writer)
soy|meal
soy milk
soy sauce
soz|zled

Spa (town, Belgium)
spa +s
Spaak, Paul Henri
(Belgian statesman)
[☞ Spock]
space
spaces
spaced
spa|cing
space age (space-age
when preceding a
noun)
space bar +s
space|craft
plural space|craft
spaced *adjective*
space flight +s
space|lab +s
space|man
space|men
space|port +s
space probe +s
spacer +s
space-saving
space|ship +s
space|suit +s
space-time
space|walk +s
space|walk|er +s
space|walk|ing
spacey
spaci|er
spaci|est
spa|cial (*use* spatial)
spa|cing +s *noun*
spa|cious
spa|cious|ly
spa|cious|ness
Spackle *proprietary*
noun
spackle *verb*
spackles
spackled
spack|ling
spack|ling *adjective*
spacy (*use* spacey)
spaci|er
spaci|est
spade (shovel; *Cards*)
spades
spad|ed
spad|ing
[☞ spayed]
spade|fish
plural spade|fish or
spade|fish|es
spade|foot +s
spade|ful +s
spade|work
spa|di|ceous
spadix
spadi|ces

spae (foretell)
spaes
spaed
spae|ing
[☞ Spey, spay]
spaetzle
spa|ghetti
spa|ghetti|like
spa|ghet|tini
spa|ghetti strap +s
(spa|ghetti-strap
when preceding a
noun)
Spa|gnol|etto, Lo
(José Ribera)
spahi +s
Spain (country,
Europe)
spake (*archaic past*
tense of speak)
spall +s +ed +ing
Spal|lan|zani,
Laz|zaro (Italian
physiologist)
spall|ing +s
Spal|lum|cheen
(municipality,
Canada)
spal|peen +s
Spam *proprietary*
(canned meat)
spam (*Computing*)
spams
spammed
spam|ming
spam|mer +s
spam|ming *noun*
span
spans
spanned
span|ning
spana|ko|pita
span|dex
span|dexed
span|drel +s
spang
span|gle
span|gles
span|gled
span|gling
span|gled *adjective*
Spang|lish
span|gly
Span|iard +s
Span|iard's Bay
(town & inlet,
Canada)
span|iel +s
Span|ish (people,
language; river,
Canada)
Spanish-American
War

Span|ish Main
(S American coast)
Span|ish|ness
Span|ish Town (town,
Jamaica)
spank +s +ed +ing
spank|er +s
spank|ing +s *noun,*
adverb & adjective
span|ner +s
span|worm +s
spar
spars
sparred
spar|ring
spare
spares
spared
spar|ing
spare|ly
spare|ness
spare|ribs
sparge
spar|ges
sparged
spar|ging
spar|ger +s
spar|ing *adjective*
(frugal)
[☞ sparring]
spar|ing|ly
spar|ing|ness
Spark, Dame Mur|iel
Sarah (Scottish
novelist)
Spark +s (*Scouting*)
spark +s
spark-gap +s
spark|ish
spar|kle
spar|kles
spar|kled
spark|ling
spark|ler +s
spark|less
spark|ling *adjective*
spark|ling|ly
spark|ly
spark plug +s
(*Automotive*)
spark|plug +s
(person)
sparky
spark|i|er
spark|i|est
spar|ling
plural spar|ling or
spar|lings
spar|ring *noun*
(fighting)
spar|row +s
spar|row hawk +s
spar|ry

sparse
spars|er
spars|est
sparse|ly
sparse|ness
spars|ity
Spar|ta (city, Greece)
Spar|ta|cist +s
Spar|ta|cus (leader of
slave revolt against
Rome)
Spar|tan +s (of or like
Sparta; apple)
spar|tan (stark,
austere)
spar|tina +s
spar tree +s
spasm +s +ed +ing
spas|mod|ic
spas|mod|ic|ally
Spas|sky, Boris
Vasily|evich
(Russian chess
player)
spas|tic
spas|tic|ally
spas|ticity
spat
spats
spat|ted
spat|ting
spatch|cock +s +ed
+ing
spate +s
spath|aceous
spathe +s
spa|tial
spa|tial|ity
spa|tial|ize
spa|tial|iz|es
spa|tial|ized
spa|tial|iz|ing
spa|tial|ly
spatio|temp|oral
spatio|temp|or|ally
Spät|lese
Spät|leses or
Spät|lesen
spat|ter +s +ed +ing
spat|ter|dash
spat|ter|dash|es
spat|ter|dock +s
spat|ula +s
spatu|late
spav|in +s
spav|ined
spawn +s +ed +ing
spawn|er +s
spay (sterilize)
[☞ Spey, spae]
spayed *adjective*
(sterilized)

spaz
  spaz|zes
  spazzed
  spaz|zing
speak (talk etc.)
  speaks
  spoke
  spok|en
  speak|ing
  [☞ Speke]
speak|able
speak|easy
  speak|eas|ies
speak|er +s
speak|er|phone +s
speak|er|ship
speak|ing noun &
  adjective
Spear (cape, Canada)
  [☞ Speer]
spear +s +ed +ing
spear car|ri|er +s
spear|fish|ing
spear grass
  spear grass|es
spear|gun +s
spear|head +s +ed
  +ing
spear|ing noun
spear|man
  spear|men
spear|mint
spear point +s
spear|wort +s
spec (specification;
  speculation; in 'on
  spec')
  specs
  spec'd
  spec'ing
  [☞ speck]
spec'd adjective (built
  to specifications)
  [☞ specked]
spe|cial +s
spe|cial|ism
spe|cial|ist +s
spe|cial|ity
  (= specialty)
  spe|cial|ities
spe|cial|iz|a|tion +s
spe|cial|ize
  spe|cial|iz|es
  spe|cial|ized
  spe|cial|iz|ing
spe|cial|ized adjective
spe|cial|ly
spe|cial needs
  (special-needs when
  preceding a noun)
spe|cial|ness
Spe|cial Olym|pics

spe|cialty
  spe|cial|ties
speci|ate
  speci|ates
  speci|at|ed
  speci|at|ing
speci|ation
spe|cie (coins)
spe|cies (category,
  kind; Catholicism;
  Law)
  plural spe|cies
species|ism
species|ist +s
speci|fi|able
spe|cif|ic
spe|cif|ic|ally
speci|fi|ca|tion +s
speci|fi|city
  speci|fi|ci|ties
spe|cif|ic|ness
speci|fi|er
speci|fy
  speci|fies
  speci|fied
  speci|fy|ing
speci|men +s
speci|os|ity
spe|cious
spe|cious|ly
spe|cious|ness
speck +s +ed +ing
  (small spot)
  [☞ spec, specs]
specked adjective
  (dotted with specks)
  [☞ spec'd]
speckle
  speckles
  speckled
  speck|ling
specky
specs (eyeglasses;
  specifications)
spec sheet +s
spec|tacle +s
spec|tacled
spec|tacles
spec|tacu|lar
spec|tacu|lar|ly
spec|tate
  spec|tates
  spec|tat|ed
  spec|tat|ing
spec|ta|tor +s
spec|ta|tor|ial
spec|ta|tor|ship
Spec|tor, Phil (US
  record producer)
  [☞ spectre]
spec|tra
spec|tral
spec|tral|ly

spectre +s (ghost)
  [☞ Spector]
spec|tro|gram +s
spec|tro|graph +s
spec|tro|graph|ic
spec|tro|
      graph|ic|ally
spec|trog|raphy
spec|tro|helio|graph
  +s
spec|tro|helio|scope
  +s
spec|trom|eter +s
spec|tro|met|ric
spec|trom|etry
spec|tro|
      pho|tom|eter +s
spec|tro|
      photo|met|ric
spec|tro|
      pho|tom|etry
spec|tro|scope +s
spec|tro|scop|ic
spec|tro|scop|ical
spec|tros|cop|ist +s
spec|tros|copy
  spec|tros|cop|ies
spec|trum
  spec|tra or
  spec|trums
specu|la
specu|lar
specu|late
  specu|lates
  specu|lat|ed
  specu|lat|ing
specu|la|tion +s
specu|la|tive
specu|la|tive|ly
specu|la|tive|ness
specu|la|tor +s
specu|lum
  specu|la or
  specu|lums
sped
speech
  speech|es
Speech from the
  Throne
  Speech|es from the
  Throne
speech|ifi|ca|tion +s
speech|ifi|er +s
speech|ify
  speech|ifies
  speech|ified
  speech|ify|ing
speech-language
speech|less
speech|less|ly
speech|less|ness
speech-reading
speech|writ|er +s

speech writ|ing
speed
  speeds
  sped or speed|ed
  speed|ing
speed bag +s
speed|ball +s
speed|boat +s
speed|boat|er +s
speed|boat|ing
speed bump +s
speed-dial +s
speed-dialing
speed|er +s
speed freak +s
speed|i|er
speed|i|est
speed|i|ly
speed|i|ness
speed|ing noun &
  adjective
speed metal
speedo +s
speed|om|eter +s
speed-read
  speed-reads
  speed-read
  speed-reading
speed-reader +s
speed skat|er +s
speed skat|ing
speed|ster +s
speed up verb
  speeds up
  sped up
  or speeded up
  speed|ing up
speed-up +s noun
speed|way +s
speed|well +s
speedy
  speed|i|er
  speed|i|est
Speer, Albert (Nazi
  architect)
  [☞ Cape Spear]
speiss (metallic
  compound)
Speke, John
  Han|ning (English
  explorer)
  [☞ speak]
spele|o|logic|al
spele|ol|o|gist +s
spele|ol|ogy
spell
  • noun
    spells
  • (use letters etc.;
    indicate)
    spells
    spelled or spelt

spell|ing
• (relieve)
spells
spelled
spell|ing
spell|able
spell|bind
spell|binds
spell|bound
spell|bind|ing
spell|bind|er +s
spell|bind|ing
adjective
spell|bind|ing|ly
spell|bound adjective
spell-check +s +ed
+ing
spell check|er +s
spell|er +s
spell|ing noun
spelt
spe|lunk|er +s
spe|lunk|ing
Spen|cer, Lady Diana
Fran|ces (Princess of
Wales)
[☞ Spenser]
Spen|cer, Her|bert
(English sociologist)
[☞ Spenser]
spen|cer +s
spend
spends
spent
spend|ing
spend|able
Spen|der, Sir
Ste|phen (English
poet)
spend|er +s
spend|thrift +s
Spen|gler, Os|wald
(German
philosopher)
Spen|ser, Ed|mund
(English poet)
[☞ Spencer]
Spen|ser|ian
spent adjective
sperm
plural sperm or
sperms
sperm|a|ceti
sperm|ary
sperm|aries
sperm|at|ic
sperm|a|tid +s
sperm|at|o|cyte +s
sperm|at|o|gen|esis
sperm|at|o|gon|ium
sperm|at|o|gonia
sperm|at|o|phore +s
sperm|at|o|phyte +s

sperm|at|o|zoal
sperm|at|o|zoan
adjective
[☞ spermatozoon]
sperm|at|o|zoid +s
sperm|at|o|zoon
noun
sperm|at|o|zoa
[☞ spermatozoan]
sperm|i|cid|al
sperm|i|cid|ally
sperm|i|cide +s
spew +s +ed +ing
spew|er +s
Spey (river, Scotland)
[☞ spay, spae]
SPF (sun protection
factor)
SPFs
sphag|num +s
sphal|er|ite +s
spher|al
sphen|oid +s
sphen|oid|al
spher|al
sphere
spheres
sphered
spher|ing
spher|ic
spher|ical
spher|ical|ly
spher|icity
spher|oid +s
spher|oid|al
spher|oid|icity
spher|ular
spher|ule +s
spher|ul|ite +s
spher|ul|itic
sphinc|ter +s
sphinc|teral
sphinc|teric
sphin|gid +s
Sphinx (Greek Myth;
famous Egyptian
statue)
sphinx (type of
Egyptian figure;
mysterious person)
sphinx|es
sphyg|mo|graph +s
sphyg|mo|graph|ic
sphyg|mog|raphy
sphyg|mo|ma|nom|
eter +s
sphyg|mo|mano|
metric
spic +s offensive
Spica (star)
spica +s (bandage;
spikelike form)
spic and span
spic|ate

spic|ated
spic|cato
spice (flavouring etc.)
spices
spiced
spi|cing
[☞ speiss]
spice|bush
spice|bush|es
Spice Islands (former
name for Molucca
Islands)
spi|ci|er
spi|ci|est
spi|ci|ly
spi|ci|ness
spick-and-span (use
spic and span)
spicu|lar
spicu|late
spic|ule +s
spicy
spi|ci|er
spi|ci|est
spi|der +s +ed +ing
spi|der flower +s
spider|ish
spider|man
spider|men
spi|der mite +s
spider|web +s
spider|wort +s
spi|dery
spiel +s +ed +ing
Spiel|berg, Ste|ven
(US filmmaker)
spiel|er +s
spiff +s +ed +ing
spif|fi|ly
spif|fing adjective
spif|fy
spif|fi|er
spif|fi|est
spig|ot +s
spike
spikes
spiked
spik|ing
spike|let +s
spike|nard +s
spik|i|ly
spik|i|ness
spiky
spik|i|er
spik|i|est
spile +s
spill
spills
spilled or spilt
spill|ing
spill|age +s
Spil|lane, Mick|ey
(US writer)

spill|er +s
spill|li|kin +s
spill|over +s
spill|way +s
spilt
spin
spins
spun
spin|ning
spina bif|ida
spin|ach
spin|achy
spin|al +s (of the
spine; epidural)
spin|al|ly
spin|arama +s
spin|cast|er +s
spin|dle
spin|dles
spin|dled
spind|ling
spindle-shanked
spindle|shanks
plural
spindle|shanks
spindle-shaped
spin|dle tree +s
spind|ly
spind|li|er
spind|li|est
spin|drift +s
spine +s
spine-chiller +s
spine-chilling
spined
spi|nel +s
(Mineralogy)
[☞ spinal]
spine|less
spine|less|ly
spine|less|ness
spin|et +s
spine tin|gler +s
spine-tingling
spin|i|er
spin|i|est
spini|fex
spini|fexes
spin|i|ness
spin|na|ker +s
spin|ner +s
spin|ner|bait +s
spin|ner|et +s
spin|ney +s (thicket)
[☞ spinny]
spin|ning noun
spin|ning wheel +s
spinny (crazy)
spin|ni|er
spin|ni|est
[☞ spinney]
spin|off +s
spin|ose

spin|ous (= spinose)
Spi|noza, Bar|uch de
(Dutch philosopher)
Spi|noz|ism
Spi|noz|ist +s
Spi|noz|is|tic
spin|ster +s
spin|ster|hood
spin|ster|ish
spin|thari|scope +s
spin|to +s
spin|ule +s
spin|u|lose
spin|u|lous
spiny (having spines;
thorny)
spin|i|er
spin|i|est
[☞ spinny,
spinney]
spir|acle +s
spir|acu|lar
spi|raea +s (use
spirea)
spir|al
spir|als
spir|alled
or spir|aled
spiral|ling
or spiral|ing
spiral-bound
spiral|ing (use
spiralling) adjective
spiral|ling adjective
spiral|ly
spir|ant +s
spire
spires
spired
spir|ing
spi|rea +s
spir|il|lum
spir|il|la
spir|it
spir|its
spirit|ed
spirit|ing
spirit|ed adjective
spirit|ed|ly
spirit|ed|ness
spirit|less
spirit|less|ly
spirit|less|ness
spirit|ual +s
spirit|ual|ism +s
spirit|ual|ist +s
spirit|ual|is|tic
spirit|u|al|ity
spirit|u|al|ities
spirit|u|al|iz|a|tion
spirit|u|al|ize
spirit|u|al|iz|es

spirit|u|al|ized
spirit|u|al|iz|ing
spirit|u|al|ly
spirit|ual|ness
spirit|u|ous
spirit|u|ous|ness
spiro|chete +s
spiro|gyra +s
spi|rom|eter +s
spi|rom|etry
spiru|lina +s
spiry
spit
• (saliva; rain; eject)
spits
spat or spit
spit|ting
• (skewer)
spits
spit|ted
spit|ting
[☞ spitz]
spit and polish (spit-
and-polish when
preceding a noun)
spit|ball +s +ed +ing
spit|ball|er +s
spitch|cock +s +ed
+ing
spit curl +s
spite
spites
spited
spit|ing
spite|ful
spite|ful|ly
spite|ful|ness
Spit|fire +s (plane)
spit|fire +s (person)
spit-roast +s +ed
+ing
spits (sunflower seeds)
[☞ spitz]
Spits|berg|en
(Norwegian island)
spit|ter +s
spit|tle
spit|toon +s
spit|ty
Spitz, Mark An|drew
(US swimmer)
spitz (dog)
spitz|es
[☞ spits]
spiv +s
spiv|vish
spiv|vy
splake +s
splanch|nic
splash
splash|es
splashed
splash|ing

splash|back +s
splash|board +s
splash down verb
splash|es down
splashed down
splash|ing down
splash|down +s noun
splash|guard +s
splashy
splash|i|er
splash|i|est
splat
splats
splat|ted
splat|ting
splat|ter +s +ed +ing
splat|ter|punk
splay +s +ed +ing
splay foot
splay feet
splay-footed
spleen
spleen|ful
spleen|wort +s
spleeny
spleen|i|er
spleen|i|est
splen|dent
splen|did
splen|did|ly
splen|did|ness
splen|dif|er|ous
splen|dif|er|ous|ly
splen|dif|er|ous|ness
splen|dor +s (use
splendour)
splen|dour +s
splen|ec|tomy
splen|ec|to|mies
splen|etic
splen|etic|ally
splen|ial
splen|ic
splen|ius
splenii
spleno|meg|aly
spleno|meg|alies
splice
spli|ces
spliced
spli|cing
spliced adjective
spli|cer +s
spliff +s
spline
splines
splined
splin|ing
splint +s +ed +ing
splin|ter +s +ed +ing
splin|tery
Split (cape, Canada;
city, Croatia)

split
splits
split
split|ting
split-finger +s
adjective & noun
split-fingered
adjective (= split-
finger)
split-level +s
split pea +s
split-rail
split-screen +s
split sec|ond +s
(split-second when
preceding a noun)
split|ter +s
split|ting adjective
split up verb
splits up
split up
split|ting up
split-up +s noun
splodge
splodg|es
splodged
splodg|ing
splodgy
splodg|i|er
splodg|i|est
splosh
splosh|es
sploshed
splosh|ing
splotch
splotch|es
splotched
splotch|ing
splotchy
splotch|i|er
splotch|i|est
splurge
splur|ges
splurged
splur|ging
splut|ter +s +ed +ing
splut|ter|er +s
Spock, Ben|ja|min
Mc|Lane (US
pediatrician)
[☞ Spaak]
spoil +s +ed +ing
spoil|age +s
spoiled past & past
participle of spoil
spoil|er +s
spoils|man
spoils|men
spoil|sport +s
spoilt Brit. (= spoiled)
Spo|kane (city, US)
spoke
spokes

spoked
spok|ing
spoked *adjective*
spok|en *adjective*
spoke|shave +s
spokes|man
  spokes|men
spokes|person
  spokes|persons or
  spokes|people
spokes|woman
  spokes|women
Spo|leto (town, Italy)
spoli|a|tion
spoli|ator +s
spolia|tory
spon|daic
spon|dee +s
spon|dyl|itic
spon|dyl|itis
sponge
  spon|ges
  sponged
  spon|ging
sponge|able
sponge cake +s
sponge|like
sponge puck +s
spon|ger +s
spon|gi|form
spon|gi|ly
spon|gi|ness
spongy
  spon|gi|er
  spon|gi|est
spon|sion +s
spon|son +s
spon|sor +s +ed +ing
spon|sor|ial
spon|sor|ship
spon|tan|eity
spon|tan|eous
spon|tan|eous|ly
spon|tan|eous|ness
spoof +s +ed +ing
spoof|er +s
spoof|ery
spook +s +ed +ing
spook|i|ly
spook|i|ness
spooky
  spook|i|er
  spook|i|est
spool +s +ed +ing
spool|er
spool|ing *noun*
spoon +s +ed +ing
spoon bait +s
spoon|bill +s
spoon bread +s
spoon|er +s
spoon|er|ism +s

spoon-feed
  spoon-feeds
  spoon-fed
  spoon-feeding
spoon|ful +s
spoon|i|ly
spoon|i|ness
spoony
  spoon|i|er
  spoon|i|est
  spoon|ies
spoor +s +ed +ing
  (track, scent)
  [☞ spore]
spoor|er
Spora|des (Greek
  island groups)
spor|adic
spor|adic|ally
spor|an|gial
spor|an|gium
  spor|an|gia
spore +s (plant
  reproductive cell)
  [☞ spoor]
sporo|cyst +s
sporo|gen|esis
spor|ogony
sporo|phore +s
sporo|phyte +s
sporo|phyt|ic
sporo|zo|ite +s
spor|ran +s
sport +s +ed +ing
sport|coat +s
sport|er +s
sport fish
  plural sport fish or
  sport fish|es
sport fish|er|man
  sport fish|er|men
sport fish|ery
  sport fish|eries
sport fish|ing
sport|i|er
sport|i|est
sport|i|ly
sport|i|ness
sport|ing *adjective*
sport|ing|ly
sport|ive
sport|ive|ly
sport|ive|ness
sports car +s
sports|cast +s
sports|cast|er +s
sports coat +s
  (= sportcoat)
sport shirt +s
  (= sports shirt)
sports jack|et +s
sports|man
  sports|men

sports|man|like
sports|man|ly
sports|man|ship
sports|person
  sports|persons or
  sports|people
sports|plex
  sports|plex|es
sports shirt +s
sports|wear
sports|woman
  sports|women
sports|writ|er +s
sport ute +s
sport-utility
  sport-utilities
sporty
  sport|i|er
  sport|i|est
spor|u|late
  spor|u|lates
  spor|u|lat|ed
  spor|u|lat|ing
spor|u|la|tion
spor|ule
spot
  spots
  spot|ted
  spot|ting
spot check +s *noun*
spot-check +s +ed
  +ing *verb*
spot|less
spot|less|ly
spot|less|ness
spot|light
  spot|lights
  spot|light|ed
  or spot|lit
  spot|light|ing
spot-on
spot|ted *adjective*
spot|ter +s
spot|ti|ly
spot|ti|ness
spot|ting *noun*
spot|ty
  spot|ti|er
  spot|ti|est
spot weld +s +ed
  +ing
spot weld|er +s
spous|al
spouse +s
Spouse's Al|low|ance
spout +s +ed +ing
spout|er +s
sprad|dle
  sprad|dles
  sprad|dled
  sprad|dling
sprag +s
sprain +s +ed +ing

sprang
sprat +s
Sprat|ly (islands,
  South China Sea)
sprawl +s +ed +ing
sprawl|ing *adjective*
sprawl|ing|ly
spray +s +ed +ing
spray can +s
spray-dry
  spray-dries
  spray-dried
  spray-drying
spray dry|er +s
spray|er
spray gun +s
spray on *verb*
  sprays on
  sprayed on
  spray|ing on
spray-on *adjective*
spray paint +s *noun*
spray-paint +s +ed
  +ing *verb*
spray skirt +s
spread
  spreads
  spread
  spread|ing
spread|abil|ity
spread|able
spread-eagle
  spread-eagles
  spread-eagled
  spread-eagling
spread-eagled
  adjective
spread|er +s
spread|sheet +s
Sprech|ge|sang
Sprech|stimme
spree +s
sprig
  sprigs
  sprigged
  sprig|ging
spright|li|ness
spright|ly
  spright|li|er
  spright|li|est
spring
  springs
  sprang or sprung
  sprung
  spring|ing
spring|board +s
Spring|bok +s (South
  African)
spring|bok (gazelle)
  plural spring|bok or
  spring|boks
spring|er +s
spring-fed

Spring|field (cities, US; municipality, Canada)
spring|form
spring|house +s
spring|i|er
spring|i|est
spring|i|ly
spring|i|ness
spring|less
spring|like
spring-loaded
spring roll +s
Spring|steen, Bruce (US singer-songwriter)
spring|tail +s
spring|time +s
spring water
springy
  spring|i|er
  spring|i|est
sprin|kle
  sprin|kles
  sprin|kled
  sprink|ling
sprink|ler +s
sprink|ling +s *noun*
sprint +s +ed +ing
sprint|er +s
sprit +s
sprite +s
sprit|sail +s
spritz
  spritz|es
  spritzed
  spritz|ing
spritz|er +s
spritzy
  spritz|i|er
  spritz|i|est
sprock|et +s
sprog +s
sprog|let +s
sprout +s +ed +ing
spruce
  • *noun*:
    plural **spruce** or
    spru|ces
  • *verb*
    spru|ces
    spruced
    spru|cing
  • *adjective*
    spru|cer
    spru|cest
spruce beer +s
Spruce Grove (city, Canada)
spruce|ly
spruce|ness
sprue +s
sprung *adjective*

spry
  spry|er
  spry|est
spry|ly
spud
  spuds
  spud|ded
  spud|ding
spudg|el +s
spu|mante +s
spume
  spumes
  spumed
  spum|ing
spu|moni
spumy
  spum|i|er
  spum|i|est
spun *adjective*
spunk
spunk|i|ly
spunk|i|ness
spunky
  spunk|i|er
  spunk|i|est
spur
  spurs
  spurred
  spur|ring
spurge
  spur|ges
spur gear +s
spur|i|ous
spur|i|ous|ly
spur|i|ous|ness
spur line +s
spurn +s +ed +ing
spur-of-the-moment *adjective*
spurred *adjective*
spurt +s +ed +ing
Sput|nik +s
sput|ter +s +ed +ing
sput|ter|er +s
sput|tery
spu|tum
  sputa
Spy (apple)
  Spys or **Spies**
spy
  spies
  spied
  spy|ing
spy|glass
  spy|glass|es
spy|master +s
squab +s
squab|ble
  squab|bles
  squab|bled
  squab|bling
squab|bler +s

squab|by
  squab|bi|er
  squab|bi|est
squad +s
squad|die +s
squad|dy (*use* squaddie)
  squad|dies
squad|ron +s
squal|id
squall +s +ed +ing
squally
squal|or
squa|ma
  squa|mae
squa|mate
Squa|mish (municipality, Canada; people, language)
  plural **Squa|mish**
squa|mose
squa|mous
squan|der +s +ed +ing
squan|der|er +s
square
  squares
  squared
  squar|ing
  squar|er
  squar|est
square-built
square dance
  square dan|ces
  square danced
  square dan|cing
square dan|cer +s
square-eyed
square-flipper
square|ly
square|ness
square-rigged
square sail +s
square-shouldered
square-toed
squar|ish
squar|rose
squash
  • (crush; suppress; sport; drink)
    squash|es
    squashed
    squash|ing
  • (fruit, plant)
    plural **squash** or
    squash|es
squash|berry
  squash|ber|ries
squash bug +s
squash|i|ly
squash|i|ness

squashy
  squash|i|er
  squash|i|est
squat
  squats
  squat|ted
  squat|ting
  squat|ter
  squat|test
squat|ter +s
squat|ty
  squat|ti|er
  squat|ti|est
squaw +s *offensive*
squaw|fish
  plural **squaw|fish** or
  squaw|fish|es
squawk +s +ed +ing
squawk|er +s
squaw root +s
squeak +s +ed +ing
squeak|er +s
squeak|i|ly
squeak|i|ness
squeaky
  squeak|i|er
  squeak|i|est
squeal +s +ed +ing
squeal|er +s
squeam|ish
squeam|ish|ly
squeam|ish|ness
squee|gee
  squee|gees
  squee|geed
  squee|gee|ing
squeez|able
squeeze
  squeez|es
  squeezed
  squeez|ing
squeeze|box
  squeeze|boxes
squeez|er
squelch
  squelch|es
  squelched
  squelch|ing
squelch|er +s
squelchy
squib
  squibs
  squibbed
  squib|bing
squib|ber +s
SQUID (detecting device)
  SQUIDs
squid (tentacled animal)
  plural **squid** or
  squids

squidgy
  squidg|i|er
  squidg|i|est
squid jig|ger +s
squid jig|ging
squiffed
squif|fy
  squif|fi|er
  squif|fi|est
squig|gle
  squig|gles
  squig|gled
  squig|gling
squig|gly
squill +s
squinch
  squinch|es
  squinched
  squinch|ing
squint +s +ed +ing
squint-eyed
squinty
  squint|i|er
  squint|i|est
squinty-eyed
squire
  squires
  squired
  squir|ing
squire|arch +s
squire|arch|ical
squire|archy
  squire|arch|ies
squire|ly (of or like a
  squire)
  [☞ squirrelly]
squirm +s +ed +ing
squirm|er +s
squirmy
  squirm|i|er
  squirm|i|est
squir|rel
  squir|rels
  squir|relled
  or squir|reled
  squir|rel|ling
  or squir|rel|ing
squir|rel cage +s
  (squirrel-cage when
  preceding a noun)
squir|rel fish
  plural squir|rel fish
  or squir|rel fish|es
squir|rel|ly (fidgety;
  eccentric)
squirt +s +ed +ing
squirt|er +s
squish
  squish|es
  squished
  squish|ing
squishy
  squish|i|er
  squish|i|est

squit|ters
squoosh
  squoosh|es
  squooshed
  squoosh|ing
squooshy
  squoosh|i|er
  squoosh|i|est
SRAM (static random
  access memory)
  SRAMs
Sri
Sri Lanka (country off
  India)
Sri Lan|kan +s
Sri|nagar (city, India)
SSHRC (Social
  Sciences and
  Humanities Research
  Council)
St. (saint)
  • For words, names
  & places beginning
  St. see Saint.
stab
  stabs
  stabbed
  stab|bing
Sta|bat Mat|er
stab|ber +s
stab|bing +s noun
sta|bile +s (sculpture)
  [☞ stable]
sta|bil|ity
  sta|bil|ities
sta|bil|iz|a|tion +s
sta|bil|ize
  sta|bil|iz|es
  sta|bil|ized
  sta|bil|iz|ing
sta|bil|iz|er +s
stable (steady, firm;
  building for horses)
  sta|bler
  sta|blest
  sta|bles
  sta|bled
  sta|bling
  [☞ stabile]
stable|boy +s
stable|man
  stable|men
stable|mate +s
sta|bling noun
stab|lish
  stab|lish|es
  stab|lished
  stab|lish|ing
stably
stac|cato +s
stack +s +ed +ing
stack|able
stacked adjective
stack|er +s

stack|yard +s
stacte
Stad|a|cona (former
  Iroquoian village)
stad|dle +s
stad|hold|er +s (use
  stadtholder)
stad|holder|ship +s
  (use
  stadtholdership)
sta|dium +s
stadt|hold|er +s
stadt|holder|ship +s
Staël, Ma|dame de
  (French writer)
staff
  • (pole; Music)
    staffs or staves
  • (personnel; provide
    with or work as staff;
    plaster)
    staffs
    staffed
    staff|ing
    [☞ staph]
Staf|fa (island, Inner
  Hebrides)
staffed adjective
staff|er +s
staff|ing noun
Staf|ford (town,
  England)
Staf|ford|shire
  (county, England)
staff room +s
stag +s
stag and doe +s
stage
  stages
  staged
  staging
stage|abil|ity
stage|able
stage|coach
  stage|coach|es
stage|craft
stage door John|ny
  stage door
  John|nies
stage fright
stage|hand +s
stage|head +s
stage-manage
  stage-manages
  stage-managed
  stage-managing
stage man|age|ment
stage man|ager +s
sta|ger +s
stage-struck
stage whis|per +s
  noun

stage-whisper +s
  +ed +ing verb
stage|worthi|ness
stage|worthy
sta|gey (use stagy)
  stagi|er
  stagi|est
stag|fla|tion
stag|ger +s +ed +ing
stag|ger|er +s
stag|ger|ing adjective
stag|ger|ing|ly
stag|horn +s
stag|hound +s
stagi|ly
stagi|ness
sta|ging +s noun
stag|nancy
stag|nant
stag|nant|ly
stag|nate
  stag|nates
  stag|nat|ed
  stag|nat|ing
stag|na|tion
stag's horn +s
  (= staghorn)
stagy
  stagi|er
  stagi|est
staid (sedate)
  [☞ stayed]
staid|ly
staid|ness
stain +s +ed +ing
stain|able
stain|er +s
stain|less
stair +s (step)
  [☞ stare]
stair|case +s
stair|head +s
stair|lift +s
stair|way +s
stair|well +s
staithe +s
stake (sharpened
  stick; mark off with
  stakes; claim; wager,
  risk; support; Horse
  Racing; Mormonism)
  stakes
  staked
  stak|ing
  [☞ steak]
stake|hold|er +s
stake out verb
  stakes out
  staked out
  stak|ing out
stake|out +s noun
stak|er
Sta|kha|nov|ism

Sta|kha|nov|ite +s
sta|lac|ti|form
sta|lac|tite +s
(hanging column)
sta|lac|tit|ic
Stalag +s
sta|lag|mite +s (rising
column)
sta|lag|mit|ic
stale
    stal|er
    stal|est
    stales
    staled
    stal|ing
stale-dated
stale|ly
stale|mate
    stale|mates
    stale|mated
    stale|mating
stale|ness
Stal|in (former name
    for Donetsk,
    Ukraine)
Stal|in, Jo|seph
    (Soviet leader)
Stal|in|grad (former
    name for Volgograd,
    Russia)
Stal|in|ism
Stal|in|ist +s
Stal|ino (former name
    for Donetsk,
    Ukraine)
stalk +s +ed +ing
    (stem; chimney;
    pursue, harass)
    [☞ stock]
stalked adjective
stalk|er +s (one who
    pursues or harasses
    another)
    [☞ stocker]
stalk-eyed
stalk|ing +s noun
    (harassment)
    [☞ stocking]
stalk|less
stalk|like
stalky (stalklike)
    stalk|i|er
    stalk|i|est
    [☞ stocky]
stall +s +ed +ing
    (delay; kiosk, booth;
    cubicle; choir seat)
    [☞ Staël, STOL]
stall-feed
    stall-feeds
    stall-fed
    stall-feeding
stall|hold|er +s
stal|lion +s

stal|wart
stal|wart|ly
stal|wart|ness
Stam|boul (former
    name for Istanbul,
    Turkey)
sta|men +s
stam|ina
stam|in|ate
stam|mer +s +ed
    +ing
stam|mer|er +s
stam|mer|ing|ly
stamp +s +ed +ing
stam|pede
    stam|pedes
    stam|ped|ed
    stam|ped|ing
stamp|er +s
stamp mill +s
stance
    stan|ces
stanch (stop the flow
    of: use staunch)
    stanch|es
    stanched
    stanch|ing
stan|chion +s +ed
    +ing
stand
    stands
    stood
    stand|ing
stand alone verb
    stands alone
    stood alone
    stand|ing alone
stand-alone adjective
stan|dard +s
standard-bearer +s
stan|dard|bred +s
stan|dard issue
    (standard-issue
    when preceding a
    noun)
stan|dard|iz|able
stan|dard|iz|a|tion
    +s
stan|dard|ize
    stan|dard|iz|es
    stan|dard|ized
    stan|dard|iz|ing
stan|dard|izer +s
stand by verb
    stands by
    stood by
    stand|ing by
standhy +s noun,
    adjective & adverb
standee +s
stand|er +s

stand in verb
    stands in
    stood in
    stand|ing in
stand-in +s noun
stand|ing +s noun &
    adjective
stand|ing
    eight-count +s
stand|ing room
    (standing-room
    when preceding a
    noun)
standing-room-only
Stan|dish, Myles (or
    Miles) (colonist at
    Plymouth)
stand off verb
    stands off
    stood off
    stand|ing off
stand-off +s (Rugby)
stand|off +s
    (deadlock;
    confrontation)
stand|off|ish
stand|off|ish|ly
stand|off|ish|ness
stand out verb
    stands out
    stood out
    stand|ing out
stand|out +s noun &
    adjective
stand|pipe +s
stand|point +s
stand still verb
    stands still
    stood still
    stand|ing still
stand|still +s noun
stand to verb
    stands to
    stood to
    stand|ing to
stand-to noun
stand up verb
    stands up
    stood up
    stand|ing up
stand-up +s adjective
    & noun
Stan|fields proprietary
Stan|ford, (Amasa)
    Le|land (US
    financier)
stan|hope +s
Stan|is|laus (patron
    saint of Poland)
Stan|is|lav|sky,
    Kon|stan|tin
    Serge|evich (Russian
    theatre director)
stank

Stan|ley (town,
    Falkland Islands;
    mountain, Congo–
    Uganda border)
Stan|ley, Fred|erick
    Ar|thur (Baron
    Stanley of Preston,
    16th Earl of Derby,
    governor general of
    Canada)
Stan|ley, Sir Henry
    Mor|ton (Welsh
    explorer)
Stan|ley Cup +s
Stan|ley Park (in
    Vancouver)
Stanley|ville (former
    name for Kisangani,
    Congo)
stan|nic
stan|nous
Stan|ton, Eliza|beth
    Cady (US feminist)
stan|za +s
stan|zaic
sta|pelia +s
sta|pes
    plural sta|pes
staph
    (staphylococcus)
staphyl|o|coc|cal
staphyl|o|coc|cus
staphyl|o|cocci
staple (paper fastener;
    principal element;
    Textiles)
    sta|ples
    sta|pled
    stap|ling
stap|ler +s
star
    stars
    starred
    star|ring
    [☞ Starr]
Stara Za|gora (city,
    Bulgaria)
star|board +s +ed
    +ing
star|burst +s
starch
    starch|es
    starched
    starch|ing
starch|er +s
starch|i|ly
starch|i|ness
starchy
    starch|i|er
    starch|i|est
star-crossed
star|dom
star|dust

stare (look fixedly)
  stares
  stared
  star|ing
  [☞ stair]
stared *past & past participle of* stare
  [☞ starred]
star|er +s
star|fish
  plural star|fish *or* star|fish|es
star|flower +s
star fruit
  plural star fruit
star|gaze
  star|gazes
  star|gazed
  star|gaz|ing
star|gazer +s
star|ing *conjugated form of* stare
  [☞ starring]
stark +er +est
stark|ers
stark|ly
stark|ness
star|less
star|let +s
star|light
star|like
Star|ling, Er|nest Henry (English physiologist)
star|ling +s
star|lit
Star of Beth|le|hem (*New Testament*)
star of Beth|le|hem (plant)
  plural stars of Beth|le|hem *or* star of Beth|le|hem
Star of David
  Stars of David
Starr, Myra Belle (US outlaw)
Starr, Ringo (Beatle)
starred (*past & past participle of* star; marked with stars)
  [☞ stared]
star|ri|ly
star|ri|ness
star|ring (*conjugated form of* star; in 'starring role' etc.)
  [☞ staring]
star|ry
  star|ri|er
  star|ri|est
starry-eyed
star shell +s

star|shine
star|ship +s
star-spangled
star-struck
star-studded
START (Strategic Arms Reduction Treaty)
start +s +ed +ing
start|er +s
star|tle
  star|tles
  star|tled
  start|ling
star|tled *adjective*
star|tle|ment
start|ler +s
start|ling *adjective*
start|ling|ly
start up *verb*
  starts up
  start|ed up
  start|ing up
start-up +s *noun & adjective*
star|va|tion
starve
  starves
  starved
  starv|ing
starve|ling +s
starv|ing *adjective*
star|wort +s
stash
  stash|es
  stashed
  stash|ing
Stasi
sta|sis
  sta|ses
stat +s
stat|able
state
  states
  stat|ed
  stat|ing
state|craft
stated *adjective*
state|hood
state|house +s
state|less
state|less|ness
state|let +s
state|li|ness
state|ly
  state|li|er
  state|li|est
state|ment +s
Stat|en Island (borough, US)
state of the art (state-of-the-art

when preceding a noun)
stater +s
state|room +s
States, the (the US)
state's evi|dence
state|side
states|man
  states|men
states|man|like
states|man|ly
states|man|ship
states|person +s
states|woman
  states|women
state|wide
stat|ic
stat|ic|al
stat|ic|ally
stat|ice +s (plant)
  [☞ status]
staticky
stat|ics
sta|tion +s +ed +ing
sta|tion|ari|ness
sta|tion|ary (not moving)
  [☞ stationery]
sta|tion|er +s
sta|tion|ery (writing materials)
  [☞ stationary]
sta|tion house +s
station-keeping
sta|tion mas|ter +s
sta|tion wag|on +s
stat|ism
stat|ist +s
sta|tis|tic +s
sta|tis|tical
sta|tis|tic|ally
sta|tis|ti|cian +s
sta|tis|tics
Sta|tius
sta|tor +s
Stats|Can
statu|ary
  statu|aries
stat|ue +s
stat|ued *adjective*
statu|esque
statu|esque|ly
statu|esque|ness
statu|ette +s
stat|ure +s
stat|ured
stat|us (position; standing)
  status|es
  [☞ statice]
stat|us quo
stat|us quo ante

stat|ute +s
statute-barred
statu|tor|i|ly
statu|tory
staunch (loyal, strong; stop the flow of)
  staunch|er
  staunch|est
  staunch|es
  staunched
  staunch|ing
staunch|ly
staunch|ness
Sta|vanger (city, Norway)
stave
  • (side plank; musical staff; *Prosody*; rung; puncture; crush)
  staves
  stove *or* staved
  stav|ing
  • (in 'stave off')
  staves
  staved
  stav|ing
staves
Stav|ro|pol
  • (territory & city, Russia)
  • (*former name for* Togliatti, Russia)
stay +s +ed +ing
stay-at-home +s *noun & adjective*
stayed *conjugated form of* stay
  [☞ staid]
stay|er +s
stay|sail +s
stay|stitch
  stay|stitch|es
  stay|stitched
  stay|stitch|ing
stay|stitch|ing *noun*
stay up *verb*
  stays up
  stayed up
  stay|ing up
stay-up +s *noun & adjective*
STD (sexually transmitted disease)
  STDs
Ste (Sainte)
  • For names & places beginning *Ste* see **Sainte.**
stead (in 'in a person's stead' *or* 'stand in good stead' etc.)
  [☞ steed]
stead|fast
stead|fastly

stead|fast|ness
stead|i|er +s *noun*
stead|i|ly
stead|i|ness
stead|ing +s
steady
  stead|i|er
  stead|i|est
  stead|ies
  stead|ied
  steady|ing
steady state (steady-state *when preceding a noun*)
steak +s (cut of meat)
  [☞ stake]
steak Diane +s
steak|ette +s
steak house +s
steak tar|tar +s (*use* steak tartare)
steak tar|tare +s
steal (pilfer etc.; sneak; easy task; bargain)
  steals
  stole
  stolen
  steal|ing
  [☞ steel, Steele, stele]
steal|er +s (one who steals)
  [☞ stelar]
stealth
stealth|i|ly
stealth|i|ness
stealthy
  stealth|i|er
  stealth|i|est
steam +s +ed +ing
steam bath +s
steam|boat +s
steamed *adjective*
steam|er +s
steam|ie +s *noun* (hot dog)
  [☞ steamy]
steam|i|ly
steam|i|ness
steam power *noun*
steam-powered *adjective*
steam|roll +s +ed +ing
steam|roll|er +s +ed +ing
steam room +s
steam|ship +s
steam table +s
steamy *adjective*
  steam|i|er

steam|i|est
  [☞ steamie]
stear|ate
stear|ic (derived from stearin)
  [☞ steric]
stear|in
stea|tite
stea|tit|ic
steato|pygia
steato|pygic
steato|pygous
steed +s (horse)
steel +s +ed +ing (metal; rail; harden; sharpen)
  [☞ steal, Steele, stele]
steel blue +s (steel-blue *when preceding a noun*)
steel-clad
Steele (mountain, Canada)
Steele, Sir Rich|ard (Irish writer)
Steele, Sir Sam|uel Ben|field (Cdn officer)
steel grey +s (steel-grey *when preceding a noun*)
steel|head
  plural steel|head or steel|heads
steel|head|er +s
steel|head|ing
steel|ie +s (marble; steelhead)
  [☞ steely, stele]
steel|i|ness
steel|maker +s
steel|making
Steel|town (Hamilton, Canada)
steel|work
steel|work|er +s
steel|works
  plural steel|works
steely (like steel)
  steel|i|er
  steel|i|est
  [☞ steelie, stele]
steel|yard +s
Steen, Jan Hav|icks|zoon (Dutch painter)
steen|bok (African dwarf antelope)
  plural steen|bok or steen|boks
  [☞ steinbock]

steep +er +est +s +ed +ing
steep|en +s +ed +ing
stee|ple
  stee|ples
  stee|pled
  steep|ling
steeple|chase +s
steeple|chas|er +s
steeple|chas|ing
stee|pled *adjective*
steeple|jack +s
steep|ly
steep|ness
steer +s +ed +ing (cattle; guide; guidance)
  [☞ stere]
steer|able
steer|age
steerage-way
steer|er +s
steer|ing *noun*
steers|man
  steers|men
steeve
  steeves
  steeved
  steev|ing
Stef|ans|son (island, Canada)
Stef|ans|son, Vilhjal|mur (Cdn explorer & ethnologist)
Stef|fens, (Jo|seph) Lin|coln (US journalist)
stego|saur +s (= stegosaurus)
stego|saur|us
  stego|saur|us|es
Stein, Ger|trude (US writer)
stein +s
Stein|bach (town, Canada)
  [☞ steinbock, steenbok]
Stein|beck, John Ernst (US novelist)
stein|bock (European ibex; *for* African dwarf antelope *use* steenbok)
  plural stein|bock or stein|bocks
Stein|em, Glo|ria (US feminist)
Stein|er, Ru|dolf (Austrian philosopher)

Stein|way, Henry Engel|hard (US piano maker)
stela (pillar)
  stelae
ste|lar (of a stele)
stele +s (*Botany*; *for* pillar *use* stela)
  [☞ steel, steal, Steele]
stel|lar (of stars; outstanding)
  [☞ Steller's jay, Steller's sea lion]
Stel|lar|ton (town, Canada)
stel|late
stel|lat|ed
Stel|len|bosch (town, South Africa)
Stel|ler's jay +s
  [☞ stellar]
Stel|ler's sea lion +s
  [☞ stellar]
stel|li|form
stel|lu|lar
stem
  stems
  stemmed
  stem|ming
stem|less
stem|let
stem|like
stem|ma
  stem|mata
stemmed *adjective*
stem|mer +s
stem|my
  stem|mi|er
  stem|mi|est
stem turn +s
stem|ware
stem|wind|er
stench
  stench|es
sten|cil
  sten|cils
  sten|cilled
  sten|cil|ling
Sten|dhal (French novelist)
Sten gun +s
Steno, Nico|laus (Danish geologist)
  [☞ Stheno]
steno +s
steno|og|raph|er +s
steno|graph|ic
steno|og|raphy
steno|o|sis
  steno|o|ses
steno|ot|ic
steno|type +s

steno|typ|ist +s
sten|tor|ian
step (pace; stair;
    measure; stage)
  steps
  stepped
  step|ping
  [☞ steppe]
Step|ana|kert
  (= Xankändi,
  Azerbaijan)
step|broth|er +s
step by step *adverb*
step-by-step *adjective*
step|child
  step|chil|dren
step|dad +s
step dance *noun*
  step dan|ces
step-dance *verb*
  step-dances
  step-danced
  step-dancing
step dan|cer +s
step-dancing *noun*
step|daugh|ter +s
step|fam|ily
  step|fam|ilies
step|father +s
steph|an|otis
  steph|an|otis|es
Ste|phen (first
  Christian martyr;
  patron saint of
  Hungary; English
  king)
  [☞ Stevens,
  Steffens,
  even-steven]
Ste|phen, Sir Les|lie
  (English biographer)
  [☞ Stevens,
  Steffens,
  even-steven]
Ste|phen|son, George
  (English engineer)
  [☞ Stevenson,
  Stefansson]
Ste|phen|son, Rob|ert
  (English engineer)
  [☞ Stevenson,
  Stefansson]
Ste|phen|ville (town,
  Canada)
step in *verb*
  steps in
  stepped in
  step|ping in
step-in +s *noun &*
  adjective
step|lad|der +s
step|less
step-like
step|mom +s

step|mother +s
step-parent +s
steppe +s (grassy
  plain)
stepped *adjective*
stepped-up *adjective*
step|per +s
step|ping stone +s
step|sis|ter +s
step|son +s
step|stool +s
step|wise
ste|radi|an +s
ster|cor|aceous
stere +s (unit of
  volume)
stereo +s
stereo|bate +s
stereo|chem|ical
stereo|chem|istry
stereo|graph +s
stereo|graph|ic
ster|eog|raphy
stereo|iso|mer +s
stereo|phon|ic
stereo|phon|ic|ally
ster|eoph|ony
ster|eop|sis
ster|eop|tic
ster|eop|ti|con +s
stereo|scope +s
stereo|scop|ic +s
stereo|scopic|ally
ster|eos|copy
  ster|eos|cop|ies
stereo|specif|ic
stereo|specif|ic|ally
stereo|speci|fi|city
stereo|tac|tic
stereo|taxic
stereo|taxis
stereo|type
  stereo|types
  stereo|typed
  stereo|typ|ing
stereo|typ|ic
stereo|typ|ical
stereo|typ|ical|ly
stereo|typy
ster|ic (atomic
  arrangement)
  [☞ stearic]
steric|al
steric|ally
ster|ile (infertile;
  aseptic)
  [☞ sterol]
ster|ile|ly
ster|il|ity
ster|il|iz|able
ster|il|iz|a|tion +s

ster|il|ize
  ster|il|iz|es
  ster|il|ized
  ster|il|iz|ing
ster|il|iz|er +s
ster|let +s
ster|ling (silver)
  [☞ Stirling]
Ster|lita|mak (city,
  Russia)
Stern, Isaac (US
  violinist)
  [☞ Sterne]
stern +er +est +s
sterna
ster|nal
stern drive +s
Sterne, Lau|rence
  (Irish novelist)
  [☞ Stern]
sterned
Stern Gang (Zionist
  group)
stern|ly
stern|most
stern|ness
stern|post +s
ster|num
  ster|nums or sterna
stern|way +s
stern|ward
stern|wards
stern|wheel|er +s
ster|oid +s
ster|oid|al
ster|ol +s (steroid
  alcohol)
ster|tor|ous
ster|tor|ous|ly
stet
  stets
  stet|ted
  stet|ting
stetho|scope
stetho|scop|ic
steth|os|copy
  steth|os|cop|ies
Stet|son +s
  proprietary
Stet|tler (town,
  Canada)
steve|dore
  steve|dores
  steve|dored
  steve|dor|ing
steve|dor|ing *noun &*
  adjective
Ste|vens, Thad|deus
  (US politician)
  [☞ Stephen,
  even-steven]
Ste|vens, Wal|lace
  (US poet)

  [☞ Stephen,
  even-steven]
Ste|ven|son, Adlai
  Ewing (US
  politician)
  [☞ Stephenson]
Ste|ven|son, Rob|ert
  Louis Bal|four
  (Scottish novelist)
  [☞ Stephenson]
stew +s +ed +ing
stew|ard +s +ed +ing
stew|ard|ess
  stew|ard|ess|es
stew|ard|ship
Stew|art (= Stuart,
  royal house of
  Scotland and
  England)
  [☞ Stuart Lake]
Stew|art, Jack|ie
  (Scottish racing
  driver)
  [☞ Stuart]
Stew|art, James
  Mait|land ('Jimmy')
  (US actor)
  [☞ Stuart]
Stew|art, Rod
  (English singer-
  songwriter)
  [☞ Stuart]
Stew|art Island (in
  New Zealand)
  [☞ Stuart Lake]
Stew|art River (in
  Canada)
  [☞ Stuart Lake]
stewed *adjective*
stew|pot +s
sthen|ic
Stheno +s (*Greek*
  Myth)
  [☞ Steno]
sticho|mythia
stick
  sticks
  stuck
  stick|ing
  [☞ Styx]
stick|ball
stick boy +s
stick|er +s +ed +ing
stick fig|ure +s
stick|handle
  stick|han|dles
  stick|han|dled
  stick|hand|ling
stick|hand|ler
stick|hand|ling *noun*
stick|i|er
stick|i|est
stick|i|ly
stick|i|ness

stick-in-the-mud
  sticks-in-the-mud
stickle|back +s
stick|ler +s
stick-like
stick on *verb*
  sticks on
  stuck on
  stick|ing on
stick-on *adjective*
stick pin +s
stick shift +s
stick-to-it-iveness
stick|um
stick up *verb*
  sticks up
  stuck up
  stick|ing up
stick|up +s *noun*
stick|weed
stick|work
sticky
  stick|i|er
  stick|i|est
  stick|ies
sticky|beak +s +ed
  +ing
Stieg|litz, Al|fred (US
  photographer)
stiff +er +est +s +ed
  +ing
stiff-arm +s +ed +ing
stiff|en +s +ed +ing
stiff|en|er +s
stiff|en|ing +s *noun*
stiff|ish
stiff|ly
stiff-necked
stiff|ness
stifle
  stifles
  stifled
  stif|ling
stif|ler +s
stif|ling *adjective*
stif|ling|ly
stig|ma
• (mark, blemish;
  Botany; *Entomology*)
  stig|mata or
  stig|mas
• (wound of Christ)
  stig|mata
stig|mat|ic
stig|ma|tist
stig|ma|tiz|a|tion +s
stig|ma|tize
  stig|ma|tiz|es
  stig|ma|tized
  stig|ma|tiz|ing
Sti|kine (river &
  former British
  territory, Canada)

stilb +s
stil|bene
stil|bes|trol
stile +s (steps over
  fence; part of
  panelling frame)
  [☞ **style**]
stil|etto +s
Stili|cho, Fla|vius
  (Roman general)
still +er +est +s +ed
  +ing
still|age +s
still|birth +s
still|born
still-hunt +s +ed
  +ing
still-hunter +s
still-hunting +s
still life
  still lifes
still|ness
still room +s
Still|son wrench
  proprietary
  Still|son wrench|es
stilly
stilt +s
stilt|ed
stilt|ed|ly
stilt|ed|ness
Still|ton *proprietary*
Still|well, Jo|seph
  War|ren ('Vin|egar
  Joe') (US general)
stimu|lant +s
stimu|late
  stimu|lates
  stimu|lat|ed
  stimu|lat|ing
stimu|lat|ing *adjective*
stimu|lat|ing|ly
stimu|la|tion +s
stimu|la|tive
stimu|la|tor +s
stimu|la|tory
stimu|lus
  stim|uli
sting
  stings
  stung
  sting|ing
sting|er +s
stin|gi|er
stin|gi|est
stin|gi|ly
stin|gi|ness
sting|ing *adjective*
sting|ing|ly
sting|less
sting|ray +s

stingy
  stin|gi|er
  stin|gi|est
stink
  stinks
  stank or stunk
  stunk
  stink|ing
stink bomb +s
stink|bug +s
stink|er +s
stink|horn +s
stink|i|er
stink|i|est
stink|ing *adjective &*
  adverb
stink|ing|ly
stink|ing wil|lie +s
stinko
stink|pot +s
stink|weed +s
stink|wood +s
stinky
  stink|i|er
  stink|i|est
stint +s +ed +ing
stipe +s
stiped
sti|pel +s
sti|pel|late
sti|pend +s
sti|pendi|ary
  sti|pendi|ar|ies
stipes[1] *plural of* stipe
sti|pes[2] (= stipe)
  stipi|tes
stipi|form
stipi|tate
sti|piti|form
stip|ple
  stip|ples
  stip|pled
  stip|pling
stip|pler +s
stip|pling *noun*
stipu|lar
stipu|late
  stipu|lates
  stipu|lated
  stipu|lat|ing
stipu|lated *adjective*
stipu|la|tion +s
stip|ule +s
stir
  stirs
  stirred
  stir|ring
stir|about
stir-crazy
stir-fry
  stir-fries
  stir-fried
  stir-frying

stirk +s
Stir|ling (surname;
  town, Scotland)
  [☞ **sterling**]
Stir|ling, James
  (Scottish
  mathematician)
Stir|ling, Sir James
  Frazer (English
  architect)
Stir|ling, Rob|ert
  (Scottish engineer)
stirps
  stir|pes
stir|rer +s
stir|ring +s *noun &*
  adjective
stir|ring|ly
stir|rup +s
stitch
  stitch|es
  stitched
  stitch|ing
stitch|er +s
stitch|ery
stitch|ing +s *noun*
stitch|less
stitch|wort +s
Stl'atl'imx
STM (scanning
  tunnelling
  microscope)
  STMs
stoa +s
stoat +s
sto|chas|tic
sto|chas|tic|ally
stock +s +ed +ing
  (supply; livestock;
  share; broth; origins;
  Grafting; flower;
  penal device; collar;
  rifle part; lathe part;
  brick; base, thick
  support; regularly
  available)
  [☞ **stalk**]
stock|ade
  stock|ades
  stock|ad|ed
  stock|ad|ing
stock boy +s
stock|breed|er +s
stock|breed|ing
stock|brok|er +s
stock|broker|age
stock|brok|ing
stocked *adjective*
stock|er +s (cattle;
  one who stocks
  shelves etc.; stock
  car)
  [☞ **stalker**]

stock|fish
plural stock|fish
stock|hold|er +s
stock|hold|ing
Stock|holm (capital of
Sweden)
stock|i|er
stock|i|est
stock|i|ly
stock|i|ness
stock|i|net (*use*
stockinette)
stock|i|nette
stock|ing +s *noun*
(clothing)
[☞ stalking]
stock|inged *adjective*
stock-in-trade
stock|ist +s
stock|job|ber +s
stock|job|bing
stock|less
stock|man
stock|men
stock|man|ship
stock mar|ket +s
stock|pile
stock|piles
stock|piled
stock|piling
stock|piler +s
Stock|port (town,
England)
stock|pot +s
stock|room +s
stock-still
stock-taking
Stockton-on-Tees
(town, England)
stocky (thickset)
stock|i|er
stock|i|est
[☞ stalky]
stock|yard +s
stodge
stodg|es
stodged
stodg|ing
stodg|i|ly
stodg|i|ness
stodgy (stuffy;
tedious; clumsy;
heavy & filling)
stodg|i|er
stodg|i|est
sto|gie +s (cigar, boot)
[☞ stodgy]
stogy (cigar, boot: *use*
stogie)
sto|gies
[☞ stodgy]

Stoic +s (Greek
philosophical
system)
stoic +s (indifferent to
pleasure or pain)
stoic|al (= stoic)
Stoic|ally (in a Stoic
manner)
stoic|ally (in a stoic
manner)
stoi|cheio|metric (*use*
stoichiometric)
stoi|chei|om|etry (*use*
stoichiometry)
stoi|chei|om|etries
stoi|chio|metric
stoi|chi|om|etry
stoi|chi|om|etries
Sto|icism (Stoic
system)
sto|icism (stoic
attitude)
Stoj|ko, Elvis (Cdn
figure skater)
stoke
stokes
stoked
stok|ing
stoked *adjective*
stoke|hold +s
stoke|hole +s
Stoke-on-Trent (city,
England)
Stok|er, Abra|ham
('Bram') (Irish
novelist)
stok|er +s
stokes
plural stokes
Sto|kow|ski, Leo|pold
An|toni Stan|is|law
Bole|slawa|wicz (US
conductor)
STOL (short takeoff
and landing aircraft)
STOLs
stole +s
stolen *adjective & past
participle of* steal
[☞ stollen]
stol|id
sto|lid|ity
stol|id|ly
stol|id|ness
stol|len (bread)
plural stol|len or
stol|lens
[☞ stolen]
Sto:lo
plural Sto:lo
sto|lon +s (branch)
sto|lon|ate
sto|lon|if|er|ous

stoma
sto|mata or sto|mas
stom|ach +s +ed
+ing
stom|ach ache +s
stomach-churning
stom|ach|er +s
stom|ach|ful +s
sto|mach|ic +s
stomal
sto|mata
sto|ma|tal
sto|ma|titis
sto|mato|logic|al
sto|ma|tol|o|gist +s
sto|ma|tol|ogy
stomp +s +ed +ing
stomp|er +s
Stone, Oli|ver (US
filmmaker)
stone
stones
stoned
ston|ing
Stone Age (Stone-
Age *when preceding a
noun*)
stone|boat +s
stone|chat +s
stone|crop +s
stone|cut +s
stone|cut|ter +s
stoned *adjective*
stone|fish
plural stone|fish
stone|fly
stone|flies
stone-ground
Stone|henge (historic
site, England)
stone|less
stone|mason +s
stone|mason|ry
Stone of Scone
ston|er +s
Stone sheep
plural Stone sheep
Stone's sheep (*use*
Stone sheep)
plural Stone's sheep
stone|wall +s +ed
+ing
stone|waller +s
stone|wall|ing *noun*
stone|ware
stone|wash
stone|wash|es
stone|washed
stone|wash|ing
stone|washed
adjective
stone|work
stone|work|er +s

stone|wort +s
Stoney (people &
language)
plural Stoneys or
Stoney
[☞ stony,
Stony Mountain,
Stony Plain]
stoney (of stones,
cold, expressionless,
broke, rigid: *use*
stony)
ston|i|er
ston|i|est
Stoney Creek (city,
Canada)
[☞ Stony Plain,
Stony Mountain]
ston|i|ly
ston|i|ness
stony (of stones; cold;
expressionless;
broke; rigid)
ston|i|er
ston|i|est
[☞ Stoney, Stoney
Creek]
stony-faced
Stony Moun|tain
(community,
Canada)
[☞ Stoney Creek]
Stony Plain (town,
Canada)
[☞ Stoney Creek]
stood
stooge
stoo|ges
stooged
stoo|ging
stook +s +ed +ing
stook|er +s
stook|ing *noun*
stool +s
stool|ie +s
stool pi|geon +s
stoop +s +ed +ing
(bend lower;
descend; porch)
[☞ stoup, stupe]
stoop|ball
stooped *adjective*
stop
stops
stopped
stop|ping
stop-action
stop-and-go
stop|cock +s
stope +s
Stopes, Marie
Char|lotte
Car|mi|chael

(Scottish birth control advocate)
stop-gap +s
stop-go
stop lamp +s
stop|light +s
stop-motion
stop|off +s
stop|over +s
stop|pable
stop|page +s
Stop|pard, Sir Tom (British dramatist)
stop-payment +s
stop|per +s +ed +ing
stop sign +s
stop valve +s
stop|watch
  stop|watch|es
stor|able
stor|age
stor|ax
  stor|ax|es
store
  stores
  stored
  stor|ing
store-bought
store|front +s
store|house +s
store|keep|er +s
store|man
  store|men
store owner +s
stor|er +s
store|room +s
store|wide
stor|ey +s (building level)
stor|eyed *adjective* (having designated number of storeys)
storied *adjective* (celebrated)
stork +s
storm +s +ed +ing
storm|bound
storm cloud +s
storm|i|ly
storm|i|ness
Stor|mont (suburb, Belfast)
storm|proof
storm-stayed
storm troop|er +s
stormy
  storm|i|er
  storm|i|est
Storn|o|way (opposition leader's residence; town, Scotland)

story (tale, article; *for* building level *use* storey)
  stor|ies
story|board +s
story|book +s
story|line +s
story|tell|er +s
story|tell|ing
sto|tin|ka
  sto|tin|ki
stoup +s (basin)
  [☞ stoop, stupe]
Stour (rivers, England)
stout +er +est
stout-hearted
stout-hearted|ly
stout-hearted|ness
stout|ish
stout|ly
stout|ness
stove +s
stove|pipe +s
stove|top +s
stove|wood
stow +s +ed +ing
stow|age +s
stow|away +s
Stowe, Har|riet Eliza|beth Bee|cher (US novelist)
stra|bis|mal
stra|bis|mic
stra|bis|mus
Strabo (Greek geographer)
Stra|chey, (Giles) Lyt|ton (English biographer)
Strad +s
strad|dle
  strad|dles
  strad|dled
  strad|dling
strad|dler +s
Stradi|vari, An|tonio (Italian violin maker)
Stradi|var|ius (instrument)
  Stradi|var|ius|es
strafe
  strafes
  strafed
  straf|ing
strag|gle
  strag|gles
  strag|gled
  strag|gling
strag|gler +s
strag|gly
  strag|gli|er
  strag|gli|est

straight +er +est +s (not bent or crooked; heterosexual; consecutive; directly; straight section; *Cards*)
  [☞ strait, Straits]
straight ahead *adverb*
straight-ahead *adjective*
straight-arm +s +ed +ing
straight arrow +s (straight-arrow *when preceding a noun*)
straight away *adverb*
straight|away +s *adjective & noun*
straight-backed
straight|edge +s
straight-eight +s
straight|en +s +ed +ing (make straight or tidy; in 'straighten out', 'straighten up')
  [☞ straiten]
straight|ened *adjective* (with bends or kinks removed; in 'straightened out')
  [☞ straitened]
straight|en|er +s
straight-faced
straight-facedly
straight|forward
straight|forward|ly
straight|forward|ness
straight|ish
straight|jacket +s +ed +ing (*use* straitjacket)
straight|laced (*use* straitlaced)
straight|ly (directly)
  [☞ straitly]
straight|ness (quality of being straight)
  [☞ straitness]
straight-out *adjective*
straight shoot|er +s
straight-shooting
straight-six
  straight-sixes
straight up *adverb*
straight-up *adjective*
straight|way
strain +s +ed +ing
strain|able
strained *adjective*
strain|er +s

strait +s (narrow channel; difficulty; restricted, strict)
  [☞ straight, Straits]
strait|en +s +ed +ing (restrict, make narrow)
strait|ened *adjective* (marked by poverty)
  [☞ straightened]
strait|jacket +s +ed +ing
strait|laced
strait|ly (strictly, severely)
  [☞ straightly]
strait|ness (strictness, severity)
  [☞ straightness]
Straits (language)
  [☞ straight]
strake +s
stra|mo|nium +s
strand +s +ed +ing
strand|ed *adjective*
strange
  stran|ger
  stran|gest
strange|ly
strange|ness
stran|ger +s
stran|gle
  stran|gles
  stran|gled
  stran|gling
strangle|hold +s
stran|gler
stran|gles
stran|gu|late
  stran|gu|lates
  stran|gu|lat|ed
  stran|gu|lat|ing
stran|gu|la|tion
stran|gur|ious
stran|gury
strap
  straps
  strapped
  strap|ping
strap|hang
  strap|hangs
  strap|hung
  strap|hang|ing
strap|hang|er +s
strap|less
strap|pado +s
strapped *adjective*
strap|per +s
strap|ping *adjective*
strap|py
Stras|bourg (city, France)
strata

strata|gem +s
strat|al
stra|tegic
stra|tegic|al
stra|tegic|ally
stra|tegics
strat|egist +s
strat|egize
  strat|egiz|es
  strat|egized
  strat|egiz|ing
strat|egy
  strat|egies
Strat|ford (city,
  Canada)
Stratford-upon-Avon
  (city, England)
strath +s
Strath|clyde (region,
  Scotland)
Strath|roy (town,
  Canada)
strath|spey +s
strat|i|fi|ca|tion
strat|ify
  strat|i|fies
  strat|i|fied
  strat|i|fy|ing
stra|tig|raph|er +s
strati|graph|ic
strati|graph|ical
strati|graph|ic|ally
stra|tig|raphy
strato|cirrus
strat|oc|racy
  strat|oc|ra|cies
strato|cumu|lus
strato|sphere
strato|spher|ic
strat|um
  strata
strat|us
Straus, Oscar (French
  composer)
  [☞ Strauss]
Strauss, Jo|hann
  (Austrian composers,
  father & son)
  [☞ Straus]
Strauss, Levi (US
  clothing
  manufacturer)
  [☞ Claude Lévi-
  Strauss, Straus]
Strauss, Rich|ard
  Georg (German
  composer)
  [☞ Straus]
Strauss|ian
Stra|vin|skian
Stra|vin|sky, Igor
  Fyodor|ovich

(Russian-born
  composer)
straw +s
straw|berry
  straw|ber|ries
straw|berry blond +s
  (strawberry-blond
  when preceding a
  noun)
straw|board
straw-colour +s
straw-coloured
straw|flower +s
straw man
  straw men
strawy
stray +s +ed +ing
stray|er +s
streak +s +ed +ing
streak|er +s
streak|i|ly
streak|i|ness
streak|ing noun
streaky
  streak|i|er
  streak|i|est
stream +s +ed +ing
stream bank +s
stream bed +s
stream|er +s
stream|less
stream|let +s
stream|line
  stream|lines
  stream|lined
  stream|lining
stream|lined adjective
stream of
  con|scious|ness
  noun
stream-of-
  conscious|ness
  adjective
stream|side +s
Streep, Mary Lou|ise
  ('Meryl') (US
  actress)
street +s
  [☞ Streit]
street|car +s
street cred
street|ed
street lamp +s
street legal
street light +s
street|proof +s +ed
  +ing
street|scape +s
street-smart
street smarts
street|walk|er +s
street|walk|ing
street|ward

street|wise
Strei|sand, Bar|bra
  (US actress & singer)
Streit, Mar|lene
  Stew|art (Cdn
  golfer)
strength +s
strength|en +s +ed
  +ing
strength|en|er +s
strength|less
strenu|os|ity
strenu|ous
strenu|ous|ly
strenu|ous|ness
strep
strep throat
strep|to|car|pus
  strep|to|car|puses
strep|to|coc|cal
strep|to|coc|cus
  strep|to|cocci
strep|to|kin|ase
strep|to|mycin
Strese|mann, Gus|tav
  (German statesman)
stress
  stress|es
  stressed
  stress|ing
stressed adjective
stressed out
  (stressed-out when
  preceding a noun)
stress|ful
stress|ful|ly
stress|ful|ness
stress|less
stres|sor +s
stretch
  stretch|es
  stretched
  stretch|ing
stretch|abil|ity
stretch|able
stretch|er +s
stretcher-bearer +s
stretch|i|ness
stretch marks
stretchy
  stretch|i|er
  stretch|i|est
streu|sel
strew
  strews
  strewed
  strewn or strewed
  strew|ing
strew|er +s
stria
  striae

stri|ate
  stri|ates
  stri|at|ed
  stri|at|ing
stri|at|ed adjective
stri|a|tion +s
strick|en adjective
  (afflicted; deleted)
Strick|land
  (mountain, Canada)
strict +er +est
strict|ly
strict|ness
stric|ture +s
stric|tured
stride
  strides
  strode
  strid|den
  strid|ing
stri|dency
stri|dent
stri|dent|ly
strid|er +s
stridu|lant
stridu|late
  stridu|lates
  stridu|lat|ed
  stridu|lat|ing
stridu|la|tion +s
strife +s
stri|gil +s
stri|gose
strik|able
strike
• (hit; act suddenly;
  work stoppage;
  reach a deal or
  balance; produce a
  spark, chord, coin,
  root or committee;
  take down a tent,
  flag, or set; fish)
  strikes
  struck
  strik|ing
• (afflict; overwhelm;
  in 'strike dumb' etc.)
  strikes
  struck
  struck or strick|en
  strik|ing
strike|bound
strike|break|er +s
strike|break|ing
strike out verb
  strikes out
  struck out
  strik|ing out
strike|out +s noun
strike pay
strik|er +s
strike-slip fault +s

strike zone +s
strik|ing *adjective*
strik|ing|ly
strik|ing|ness
Strind|berg, Johan
  Aug|ust (Swedish
  dramatist)
Strine
string
  strings
  strung
  string|ing
string bean +s
string|course +s
stringed *adjective*
strin|gency
  strin|gen|cies
strin|gendo
strin|gent
strin|gent|ly
string|er +s
string-figure game
  +s
string|halt
string|i|ly
string|i|ness
string|less
string|like
stringy
  string|i|er
  string|i|est
strip
  strips
  stripped
  strip|ping
stripe
  stripes
  striped
  strip|ing
striped *adjective*
strip|er +s
stripi|er
stripi|est
strip light +s
strip|ling +s
strip loin +s
strip mine +s *noun*
strip-mine *verb*
  strip-mines
  strip-mined
  strip-mining
strip min|ing *noun*
strip-o-gram +s
stripped-down
strip|per +s
strip search *noun*
  strip search|es
strip-search *verb*
  strip-searches
  strip-searched
  strip-search|ing
strip|tease +s
strip|teas|er +s

stripy
  stripi|er
  stripi|est
strive
  strives
  strove *or* strived
  striv|en
  striv|ing
striv|er +s
strobe
  strobes
  strobed
  strob|ing
stro|bila
  stro|bilae
stro|bile +s
stro|bilus
  stro|bili
strob|o|scope +s
strob|o|scop|ic
strob|o|scopic|al
strob|o|scopic|ally
strode
stro|gan|off +s
Stro|heim, Erich von
  (US filmmaker)
stroke
  strokes
  stroked
  strok|ing
stroke play
strok|er +s
stroll +s +ed +ing
stroll|er +s
stroll|ing *adjective*
stro|ma
  stro|mata
stro|matic
stro|mato|lite +s
Strom|boli (volcanic
  island,
  Mediterranean)
strong +er +est
strong-arm +s +ed
  +ing
strong|box
  strong|boxes
strong|hold +s
strong|ish
strong|ly
strong|man
  strong|men
strong-minded
strong-minded|ness
strong point +s
  (excellent feature)
  [☞ strongpoint]
strong|point +s
  (fortification)
  [☞ strong point]
strong|room +s
strong-willed
stron|tia

stron|tium
strontium-90
strop
  strops
  stropped
  strop|ping
stro|phe +s
stro|phic
strop|pi|ly
strop|pi|ness
stroppy
  strop|pi|er
  strop|pi|est
stroud +s
strove
strow
  strows
  strowed
  strown *or* strowed
  strow|ing
struck *adjective*
struc|tur|al
struc|tur|al|ism
struc|tur|al|ist +s
struc|tur|al|ly
struc|ture
  struc|tures
  struc|tured
  struc|tur|ing
struc|tured *adjective*
struc|ture|less
stru|del +s
strug|gle
  strug|gles
  strug|gled
  strug|gling
strug|gler +s
strug|gling *adjective*
strum
  strums
  strummed
  strum|ming
stru|ma
  stru|mae
strum|mer +s
stru|mose
  (= strumous)
stru|mous
strum|pet +s
strung
strung out (strung-
  out *when preceding a*
  noun)
strut
  struts
  strut|ted
  strut|ting
stru|thi|ous
strut|ter +s
strut|ting|ly
Struve, Otto (US
  astronomer)
strych|nic

strych|nine
Stu|art (royal house of
  Scotland and
  England)
  [☞ Stewart]
Stu|art, Charles
  Ed|ward (Bonnie
  Prince Charlie, the
  Young Pretender)
Stu|art, James
  Fran|cis Ed|ward
  (the Old Pretender)
Stu|art, Mary (Mary,
  Queen of Scots)
Stu|art Lake (in
  Canada)
  [☞ Stewart River,
  Stewart Island]
stub
  stubs
  stubbed
  stub|bing
stub|bi|er
stub|bi|est
stub|bi|ly
stub|bi|ness
stub|ble
stub|bled
stubble-jumper +s
stub|bly
stub|born
stub|born|ly
stub|born|ness
stub|by
  stub|bi|er
  stub|bi|est
  stub|bies
stuc|co
  stuc|coes
  stuc|coed
  stuc|co|ing
stuck *adjective*
stuck-up
stud
  studs
  stud|ded
  stud|ding
stud book +s
stud|ded *adjective*
stud|ding +s *noun &*
  adjective
stu|dent +s
student-at-law
  students-at-law
stu|dent|ship +s
stud|ied *adjective*
stud|ied|ly
stud|ied|ness
stu|dio +s
stu|di|ous
stu|di|ous|ly
stu|di|ous|ness

study
  stud|ies
  stud|ied
  study|ing
study hall +s
stuff +s +ed +ing
stuffed *adjective*
stuff|er
stuff gown +s
stuf|fi|ly
stuf|fi|ness
stuff|ing +s *noun*
stuf|fy
  stuf|fi|er
  stuf|fi|est
stul|ti|fi|ca|tion
stul|ti|fier +s
stul|ti|fy
  stul|ti|fies
  stul|ti|fied
  stul|ti|fy|ing
stul|ti|fy|ing *adjective*
stul|ti|fy|ing|ly
stum|ble
  stum|bles
  stum|bled
  stum|bling
stumble|bum +s
stum|bler +s
stum|bling|ly
stump +s +ed +ing
stump|age
stumped *adjective*
stump|er +s
stump|i|ly
stump|i|ness
stumpy
  stump|i|er
  stump|i|est
stun
  stuns
  stunned
  stun|ning
stung
stun gun +s
stunk
stunned *adjective*
stun|ner +s
stun|ning *adjective*
stun|ning|ly
stun|sail +s
stuns'l +s
  (= stunsail)
stunt +s +ed +ing
stunt|ed *adjective*
stunt|ed|ness
stunt|man
  stunt|men
stupa +s
stupe +s (stupid
  person)
  [☞ stoop, stoup]
stu|pe|fa|cient +s

stu|pe|fac|tion
stu|pe|fier +s
stu|pe|fy
  stu|pe|fies
  stu|pe|fied
  stu|pe|fy|ing
stu|pe|fy|ing *adjective*
stu|pe|fy|ing|ly
stu|pen|dous
stu|pen|dous|ly
stu|pen|dous|ness
stu|pid +er +est
stu|pid|ity
  stu|pid|ities
stu|pid|ly
stu|por +s
stu|por|ous
stur|di|ly
stur|di|ness
sturdy
  stur|di|er
  stur|di|est
stur|geon
  plural stur|geon or
  stur|geons
Stur|geon Falls
  (town, Canada)
Sturm und Drang
stut|ter +s +ed +ing
stut|ter|er +s
stut|ter|ing|ly
Stutt|gart (city,
  Germany)
Stuy|ve|sant, Peter
  (Dutch colonial
  governor)
sty (pigpen; eyelid
  swelling)
  sties
  stied
  sty|ing
stye +s (eyelid
  swelling: use sty)
  [☞ sty]
Sty|gian (*Greek Myth*)
sty|gian (dark,
  gloomy)
style (manner; fashion;
  stylus; *Botany*;
  Zoology)
  styles
  styled
  sty|ling
  [☞ stile]
style book +s
style|less
style|less|ness
styl|er +s
styl|et +s
styli
styl|ish
styl|ish|ly
styl|ish|ness

styl|ist +s
styl|is|tic
styl|is|tic|ally
styl|is|tics
styl|ite +s
styl|iz|a|tion +s
styl|ize
  styl|iz|es
  styl|ized
  styl|iz|ing
stylo|graph +s
stylo|graph|ic
styl|oid +s
sty|lus
  styli or sty|lus|es
sty|mie
  sty|mies
  sty|mied
  sty|mie|ing or
  stymy|ing
styp|tic +s
sty|rax
  sty|rax|es
sty|rene
Styria (state, Austria)
Styro|foam
  proprietary
Styx (*Greek & Roman
  Myth*)
suable
suasion
suasive
suave (charming;
  smooth)
  suav|er
  suav|est
  [☞ Soave]
suave|ly
suave|ness
suav|ity
  suav|ities
sub
  subs
  subbed
  sub|bing
sub|acid
sub|acid|ity
sub|acute
sub|adult +s
sub|agency
  sub|agen|cies
sub|agent +s
sub|alpine
sub|altern +s
sub|antarc|tic
sub|aqua|tic
sub|aque|ous
sub|aque|ous|ly
Sub|arctic *noun*
  (region south of the
  Arctic Circle)
sub|arctic *adjective* (of
  the Subarctic)

sub-assembly
  sub-assemblies
sub|atom|ic
sub|audi|tion +s
sub-basement +s
sub-branch
  sub-branch|es
sub|cat|egor|iz|a|tion
  +s
sub|cat|egor|ize
  sub|cat|egor|iz|es
  sub|cat|egor|ized
  sub|cat|egor|iz|ing
sub|cat|egory
  sub|cat|egor|ies
sub|cellu|lar
sub|class
  sub|class|es
sub|classi|fi|ca|tion
  +s
sub|clause +s
sub|clav|ian +s
sub|clinic|al
sub|com|mit|tee +s
sub|com|pact +s
sub|con|scious
  sub|con|scious|es
sub|con|scious|ly
sub|con|scious|ness
sub|contin|ent +s
sub|contin|ent|al
sub|con|tract +s +ed
  +ing
sub|con|tract|or +s
sub|con|trary
  sub|con|trar|ies
sub|corti|cal
sub|critic|al
sub|cultur|al
sub|cul|ture
  sub|cul|tures
  sub|cul|tured
  sub|cultur|ing
sub|cuta|neous
sub|cuta|neous|ly
sub|deacon +s
sub|diacon|ate +s
sub|direc|tory
  sub|direc|tor|ies
sub|div|ide
  sub|div|ides
  sub|div|id|ed
  sub|div|id|ing
sub|div|ision +s
sub|domin|ant +s
sub|duct +s +ed +ing
sub|duc|tion
sub|due
  sub|dues
  sub|dued
  sub|duing
sub|dued *adjective*
sub|dural

sub-edit +s +ed +ing
sub-editor +s
sub|family
  sub|fam|ilies
sub|floor +s
sub|floor|ing
sub|form +s
sub|freez|ing
sub|fusc
sub|gen|era
sub|gen|er|ic
sub-genre +s
sub|genus
  sub|gen|era
sub|glacial
sub|group +s
sub|head +s
sub|head|ing +s
sub|human +s
sub|jacen|cy
sub|jacent
sub|ject +s +ed +ing
sub|jec|tion
sub|ject|ive +s
sub|ject|ive|ly
sub|jec|tiv|ism
sub|jec|tiv|ist +s
sub|jec|tiv|ity
  sub|jec|tiv|ities
sub|ject|less
sub|join +s +ed +ing
sub judice
sub|ju|gate
  sub|ju|gates
  sub|ju|gat|ed
  sub|ju|gat|ing
sub|ju|ga|tion +s
sub|ju|ga|tor +s
sub|junc|tive +s
sub|king|dom +s
sub|lease
  sub|leas|es
  sub|leased
  sub|leas|ing
sub|lessee +s
sub|lessor +s
sub|let
  sub|lets
  sub|let
  sub|let|ting
sub|lethal
sub-lieuten|ant +s
sub|lim|ate
  sub|lim|ates
  sub|lim|at|ed
  sub|lim|at|ing
sub|lim|a|tion
sub|lime
  sub|lim|er
  sub|lim|est
sub|lime|ly
sub|lim|inal
sub|lim|inal|ly

sub|lim|ity
  sub|lim|ities
sub|lingual
sub|lit|tor|al
sub|lun|ary
sub|lux|a|tion +s
sub|machine gun +s
sub-margin|al
sub|ma|rine
  sub|ma|rines
  sub|ma|rined
  sub|ma|rin|ing
sub|marin|er
sub|maxil|lary
sub|medi|ant +s
sub|menu +s
sub|merge
  sub|mer|ges
  sub|merged
  sub|mer|ging
sub|merged *adjective*
sub|mer|gence
sub|merse
  sub|mers|es
  sub|mersed
  sub|mers|ing
sub|mer|sible +s
sub|mer|sion +s
sub|micro|scop|ic
sub|mini|ature
sub|mis|sion +s
sub|mis|sive
sub|mis|sive|ly
sub|mis|sive|ness
sub|mit
  sub|mits
  sub|mit|ted
  sub|mit|ting
sub|mit|ter +s
sub|mul|tiple +s
sub|net +s
sub|net|work +s
sub|normal
sub|normal|ity
sub|note|book +s
sub|nuclear
sub|ocean|ic
sub|optimal
sub|orbit|al
sub|order +s
sub|ordin|al
sub|ordin|ate
  sub|ordin|ates
  sub|ordin|at|ed
  sub|ordin|at|ing
sub|ordin|a|tion
sub|orn +s +ed +ing
sub|orn|a|tion
sub|par
sub|phylum
  sub|phyla
sub|plot +s

sub|poena
  sub|poenas
  sub|poenaed
  sub|poena|ing
sub|popu|la|tion +s
sub-post of|fice +s
sub|pro|gram +s
sub-region +s
sub-region|al
sub|rogate
  sub|rogates
  sub|rogat|ed
  sub|rogat|ing
sub|roga|tion
sub rosa *adverb*
sub-rosa *adjective*
sub|rou|tine +s
sub-Saharan
sub|scribe
  sub|scribes
  sub|scribed
  sub|scrib|ing
sub|scrib|er +s
sub|script +s
sub|scrip|tion +s
sub|sea
sub|sec|tion +s
sub|se|quence
  sub|se|quen|ces
sub|se|quent
sub|se|quent|ly
sub|serve
  sub|serves
  sub|served
  sub|serv|ing
sub|servi|ence
sub|servi|ency
sub|servi|ent
sub|servi|ent|ly
sub|set +s
sub-shrub +s
sub-shrubby
sub|side
  sub|sides
  sub|sid|ed
  sub|sid|ing
sub|sid|ence +s
sub|sidi|ary
  sub|sidi|aries
sub|sid|iz|a|tion +s
sub|sid|ize
  sub|sid|iz|es
  sub|sid|ized
  sub|sid|iz|ing
sub|sid|ized *adjective*
sub|sid|iz|er +s
sub|sidy
  sub|sid|ies
sub|sist +s +ed +ing
sub|sist|ence
sub|sist|ent
sub|soil +s +ed +ing
sub|soil|er +s

sub|sonic
sub|sonic|ally
sub|space +s
sub|special|ist +s
sub|special|ize
  sub|special|iz|es
  sub|special|ized
  sub|special|iz|ing
sub|special|ty
  sub|special|ties
sub|species
  plural sub|species
sub|specif|ic
sub|stance
  sub|stan|ces
sub|stance P
sub|stan|dard
sub|stan|tial
sub|stan|ti|al|ity
sub|stan|tial|ly
sub|stan|ti|ate
  sub|stan|ti|ates
  sub|stan|ti|at|ed
  sub|stan|ti|at|ing
sub|stan|ti|a|tion +s
sub|stan|tive
sub|stan|tive|ly
sub|station +s
sub|stitu|ent +s
sub|sti|tut|abil|ity
sub|sti|tut|able
sub|sti|tute
  sub|sti|tutes
  sub|sti|tut|ed
  sub|sti|tut|ing
sub|sti|tu|tion +s
sub|sti|tu|tion|al
sub|sti|tu|tion|ary
sub|sti|tu|tive
sub|strate +s
sub|strat|um
  sub|strata
sub|struc|tur|al
sub|struc|ture
sub|sume
  sub|sumes
  sub|sumed
  sub|sum|ing
sub|sump|tion +s
sub|sur|face +s
sub|system +s
sub-teen +s
sub|ten|ancy
sub|ten|ant +s
sub|tend +s +ed +ing
sub|ter|fuge
  sub|ter|fu|ges
sub|termin|al
sub|terran|ean
sub|terran|eous|ly
sub|text
sub|text|ual

subtil|ize
  subtil|iz|es
  subtil|ized
  subtil|iz|ing
sub|title
  sub|titles
  sub|titled
  sub|titling
sub|titled *adjective*
subtle (delicate; fine;
  understated; clever)
  subtler
  subtlest
subtle|ness
subtler *comparative of*
  subtle
  [☞ sutler]
subtle|ty
  subtle|ties
subtly
sub|tonic +s
sub|total +s
sub|tract +s +ed +ing
sub|trac|tion +s
sub|tract|ive
sub|trade +s
sub|tra|hend
sub|tropic|al
sub|tropics
sub|type +s
subu|late
sub|unit +s
sub|urb +s
sub|urban
sub|urban|ite +s
sub|urban|iz|a|tion
  +s
sub|urban|ize
  sub|urban|iz|es
  sub|urban|ized
  sub|urban|iz|ing
sub|urb|ia +s
sub|ven|tion +s
sub|ver|sion +s
sub|ver|sive +s
sub|ver|sive|ly
sub|ver|sive|ness
sub|vert +s +ed +ing
sub|vert|er +s
sub|way +s
sub|woof|er +s
sub-zero
sub|zone +s
suc|ceed +s +ed +ing
suc|ceed|er +s
suc|cès de scan|dale
  plural suc|cès de
  scan|dale
suc|cès d'estime
  plural suc|cès
  d'estime
suc|cès fou
  suc|cès fous

suc|cess
  suc|cess|es
suc|cess|ful
suc|cess|ful|ly
suc|cess|ful|ness
suc|ces|sion +s
suc|ces|sion|al
suc|ces|sive
suc|ces|sive|ly
suc|ces|sive|ness
suc|ces|sor +s
suc|cin|ate +s
suc|cinct
suc|cinct|ly
suc|cinct|ness
suc|cin|ic
suc|co|tash
Suc|coth (*use* Sukkot)
suc|cour (aid)
  [☞ Sukkur]
suc|cu|bus
  suc|cubi
suc|cu|lence
suc|cu|lent
suc|cu|lent|ly
suc|cumb +s +ed
  +ing
suc|cuss
  suc|cuss|es
  suc|cussed
  suc|cuss|ing
suc|cus|sion +s
such
such|like
suck +s +ed +ing
suck|er +s (one that
  sucks; gullible
  person; candy; fool)
  [☞ succour,
  Sukkur]
sucker-punch *verb*
  sucker-punches
  sucker-punched
  sucker-punching
suck|hole
  suck|holes
  suck|holed
  suck|hol|ing
suck|i|er
suck|i|est
suckle
  suckles
  suckled
  suck|ling
suck|ler +s
Suck|ling, Sir John
  (English writer)
suck|ling +s *noun*
suck up *verb*
  sucks up

sucked up
suck|ing up
suck-up +s *noun*
sucky
  suck|i|er
  suck|i|est
suc|ra|lose
Sucre (judicial capital
  of Bolivia)
Sucre, An|tonio José
  de (South American
  revolutionary &
  statesman)
suc|rose
suc|tion +s +ed +ing
suc|tor|ial
suc|tor|ian +s
Sudan (country &
  region, Africa)
Sudan|ese
  plural Sudan|ese
su|dar|ium
  su|dar|ia
suda|tor|ium
  suda|toria
suda|tory
  suda|tor|ies
Sud|bury (city,
  Canada)
sudd (floating
  vegetation)
  [☞ suds]
sud|den
sud|den death (*Sport*:
  sudden-death *when
  preceding a noun*)
sud|den|ly
sud|den|ness
Su|deten|land
  (region, Czech
  Republic)
sudor|if|er|ous
sudor|if|ic +s
Sudra (*Hinduism*)
suds (froth; lather;
  beer)
  suds|es
  sudsed
  suds|ing
  [☞ sudd]
suds|er +s
sudsy
  suds|i|er
  suds|i|est
Sue, Eu|gène (French
  novelist)
  [☞ Sioux, Soo,
  Sault Ste. Marie]
sue (*Law*; entreat)
  sues
  sued
  suing
  [☞ sou, xu]

sued *past & past
  participle of* sue
  [☞ pseud]
suede +s (leather,
  fabric)
suer +s (one who
  sues)
  [☞ sewer]
suet (animal fat)
Sueto|nius (Roman
  historian)
suety
Suez (canal & isthmus,
  Middle East)
suf|fer +s +ed +ing
suf|fer|able
suf|fer|ance
suf|fer|er +s
suf|fer|ing +s *noun*
suf|fice
  suf|fices
  suf|ficed
  suf|ficing
suf|fi|cien|cy
  suf|fi|cien|cies
suf|fi|cient
suf|fi|cient|ly
suf|fix
  suf|fixes
  suf|fixed
  suf|fix|ing
suf|fix|a|tion
suf|fo|cate
  suf|fo|cates
  suf|fo|cat|ed
  suf|fo|cat|ing
suf|fo|cat|ing
  adjective
suf|fo|cat|ing|ly
suf|fo|ca|tion +s
Suf|folk +s (county,
  England; sheep;
  horse)
Suf|folk Punch
  Suf|folk Punch|es
suf|fra|gan +s
suf|fra|gan|ship +s
suf|frage +s
suf|fra|gette +s
suf|fra|gism
suf|fra|gist +s
suf|fuse
  suf|fus|es
  suf|fused
  suf|fus|ing
suf|fu|sion +s
Sufi +s
Sufic
Suf|ism
sug|ar +s +ed +ing
sugar bush
  sugar bush|es
sugar cane +s

sugar-coat +s +ed +ing
sugar-coated *adjective*
sugar-coating +s *noun*
sugar cube +s
sugar daddy
  sugar dad|dies
sugar house +s
sugar|i|ness
sugar|ing *noun*
sugar|ing off
  (sugaring-off *when preceding a noun*)
sugar|less
sugar|loaf +s
Sugar Loaf Moun|tain (in Rio de Janeiro)
sugar lump +s
sugar maple +s
sugar-pea +s
sugar plum +s
sugar shack +s
sugar snap +s
sugary
sug|gest +s +ed +ing
sug|gest|er +s
sug|gest|ibil|ity
sug|gest|ible
sug|ges|tion +s
sug|gest|ive
sug|gest|ive|ly
sug|gest|ive|ness
Su|harto, Raden (Indonesian statesman)
Sui (Chinese dynasty)
sui|cid|al
sui|cid|al|ly
sui|cide
  sui|cides
  sui|cided
  sui|cid|ing
sui gen|er|is
sui juris
suint
suit +s +ed +ing (clothing; *Cards*; agree with)
  [☞ suite, suet]
suit|abil|ity
suit|able
suit|able|ness
suit|ably
suit|case +s
suit|case|ful +s
suit coat +s
suite +s (set of rooms, furniture, etc.; *Music*)
  [☞ sweet, suit]
suit|ed *adjective*

suit|ing +s *noun*
suit|or +s
suk +s (bazaar: *use* souk)
  [☞ sook]
Su|kar|no, Ach|mad (Indonesian statesman)
sukh +s (bazaar: *use* souk)
  [☞ sook]
Suko|tai (town, Thailand)
Suko|thai (= Sukhotai)
suki|yaki
Suk|kot
Suk|kur (city, Pakistan)
Sulai|ma|ni|ya (= Sulaymaniyah)
Sula|wesi (island, Indonesia)
Sulay|ma|ni|yah (city, Iraq)
sul|cate
sul|cus
  sulci
Sulei|man I (Ottoman sultan)
sul|fa +s (*use* sulpha)
sulfa|meth|ox|azole (*use* sulphamethoxazole)
sulfa|nil|a|mide (*use* sulphanilamide)
sul|fate (*use* sulphate)
  sul|fates
  sul|fat|ed
  sul|fat|ing
sul|fat|ed *adjective* (*use* sulphated)
sul|fa|tion (*use* sulphation)
sul|fide +s (*use* sulphide)
sul|fite +s (*use* sulphite)
sul|fon|a|mide +s (*use* sulphonamide)
sul|fon|ate (*use* sulphonate)
  sul|fon|ates
  sul|fon|at|ed
  sul|fon|at|ing
sul|fone +s (*use* sulphone)
sul|fon|ic (*use* sulphonic)
sul|fonyl|urea +s (*use* sulphonylurea)
sulf|ox|ide +s (*use* sulphoxide)

sul|fur +s (*use* sulphur)
sul|fur|eous (*use* sulphureous)
sul|fur|ic (*use* sulphuric)
sul|fur|iz|a|tion (*use* sulphurization)
sul|fur|ize (*use* sulphurize)
  sul|fur|iz|es
  sul|fur|ized
  sul|fur|iz|ing
sul|fur|ous (*use* sulphurous)
sul|fury (*use* sulphury)
sulk +s +ed +ing
sulk|er +s
sulk|i|ly
sulk|i|ness
sulky
  sulk|i|er
  sulk|i|est
  sulk|ies
Sulla (Roman general)
sul|lage
sul|len
sul|len|ly
sul|len|ness
Sul|li|van, Sir Ar|thur Sey|mour (English composer)
Sul|li|van, Ed|ward Vin|cent ('Ed') (US TV personality)
Sul|li|van, Louis Henri (US architect)
Sully, Maxi|mi|lien de Bé|thune, Duc de (French statesman)
sully
  sul|lies
  sul|lied
  sully|ing
Sully-Prudhomme, René Fran|çois Ar|mand (French poet)
sul|pha +s
sulpha|meth|ox|azole
sulpha|nil|a|mide
sul|phate
  sul|phates
  sul|phat|ed
  sul|phat|ing
sul|phat|ed *adjective*
sul|pha|tion
sul|phide +s
sul|phite +s
sul|phon|a|mide +s

sul|phon|ate
  sul|phon|ates
  sul|phon|at|ed
  sul|phon|at|ing
sul|phone +s
sul|phon|ic
sul|phonyl|urea +s
sulph|ox|ide +s
sul|phur +s
sul|phur|eous
sul|phur|ic
sul|phur|iz|a|tion
sul|phur|ize
  sul|phur|iz|es
  sul|phur|ized
  sul|phur|iz|ing
sul|phur|ous
sul|phury
Sul|pi|cian +s
sul|tan +s
sul|tana +s
sul|tan|ate +s
sul|tri|ly
sul|tri|ness
sul|try
  sul|tri|er
  sul|tri|est
Sulu (sea, Malay Archipelago)
sum (total)
  sums
  summed
  sum|ming
  [☞ some]
su|mac +s
su|mach +s (*use* sumac)
Su|ma|tra (island, Indonesia)
Su|ma|tran +s
su|ma|trip|tan
Sumba (Island, Indonesia)
Sum|bawa (island, Indonesia)
Sumer (ancient region, Asia)
Sumer|ian +s
sumi-e
summa
  sum|mae
sum|mabil|ity
sum|mable
summa cum laude
sum|mar|i|ly
sum|mar|i|ness
sum|mar|ist +s
sum|mar|iz|able
sum|mar|iz|a|tion +s
sum|mar|ize
  sum|mar|iz|es
  sum|mar|ized
  sum|mar|iz|ing

sum|mar|iz|er +s
sum|mary (brief
  account; without
  formalities)
sum|mar|ies
  [☞ summery]
sum|ma|tion +s
sum|ma|tion|al
sum|ma|tive
sum|mer +s +ed +ing
  [☞ Somers]
sum|mer|fal|low +s
  +ed +ing
sum|mer house +s
Sum|mer|land
  (municipality,
  Canada)
sum|mer|less
Sum|mer|side (city,
  Canada)
sum|mer stock +s
sum|mer|time +s
sum|mery
  (characteristic of
  summer)
  [☞ summary]
summing-up
  summings-up
sum|mit +s
sum|mit|eer +s
sum|mit|less
sum|mon +s +ed
  +ing (call; gather)
sum|mon|able
sum|mon|er +s
sum|mons (an order
  to appear in court;
  serve a summons to)
  sum|mons|es
  sum|monsed
  sum|mons|ing
sum|mum bonum
sumo
sump +s
sump pump +s
sump|ter +s
sump|tu|ary
sump|tu|os|ity
sump|tu|ous
sump|tu|ous|ly
sump|tu|ous|ness
Sum|qayit (city,
  Azerbaijan)
Sumy (city, Ukraine)
sun (star; sunbathe)
  suns
  sunned
  sun|ning
sun-baked
sun bath +s *noun*
sun|bathe *verb*
  sun|bathes

sun|bathed
sun|bath|ing
sun|bath|er +s
sun|beam +s
sun bear +s
sun|belt +s
sun|bird +s
sun|block +s
sun|bon|net +s
sun|burn
  sun|burns
  sun|burned
  or sun|burnt
  sun|burn|ing
sun|burned *adjective*
sun|burnt *adjective*
  (= sunburned)
sun|burst +s
sun|catch|er +s
Sunda (islands, Malay
  Archipelago)
sun|dae +s (ice
  cream)
sun dance +s
Sun|dar|bans (swamp,
  India & Bangladesh)
Sun|day +s
  [☞ sundae]
sun|deck +s
sun|der +s +ed +ing
Sun|der|land (city,
  England)
sun|dew +s
sun|dial +s
sun disc +s
sun dog +s
sun|down
sun|down|er +s
sun-drenched
sun|dress
  sun|dress|es
sun-dried
sun|drops
sundry
  sund|ries
sun|fish
  plural sun|fish or
  sun|fish|es
sun|flower +s
Sung (Chinese
  dynasty)
Sung, Al|fred (Cdn
  designer)
sung
sun|glass|es
sun god +s
sun hat +s
sunk *adjective*
sunk|en *adjective*
sunk|er +s
Sun King (Louis XIV
  of France)
sun-kissed

sun lamp +s
sun|less
sun|less|ness
sun|light
sun|like
sun|lit
Sunna (traditional
  Islamic law)
Sunni (branch of
  Islam)
  plural Sunni or
  Sun|nis
  [☞ sunny, sonny]
sun|ni|ly
sun|ni|ness
sunny (bright)
  sun|ni|er
  sun|ni|est
  [☞ sonny, Sunni]
sunny side up
sun par|lour +s
sun porch
  sun porch|es
sun|ray +s
sun|rise +s
sun|roof +s
sun|room +s
sun|screen +s
sun|set +s
sun|shade +s
sun|shine
Sun|shine Coast (of
  BC)
sun|shiny
sun|spot +s
sun|star +s
sun|stone +s
sun|stroke
sun|struck
sun|suit +s
sun|tan
sun|tanned
sun|tan|ning
sun|trap +s
sun-up
sun visor +s
sun|ward
sun|wards
Sun Yat-sen (Chinese
  statesman)
Sun Yixian
  (= Sun Yat-sen)
sup
  sups
  supped
  sup|ping
super +s
super|able
super|abound +s +ed
  +ing
super-absorb|ent
super|abun|dance
  super|abun|dan|ces

super|abun|dant
super|abun|dant|ly
super|add +s +ed
  +ing
super|addi|tion +s
super|annu|able
super|annu|ate
  super|annu|ates
  super|annu|at|ed
  super|annu|at|ing
super|annu|at|ed
  adjective
super|annu|a|tion
su|perb
super|bike +s
superb|ly
superb|ness
Super Bowl +s
  proprietary
super|bug +s
super|calen|der +s
  +ed +ing
super|cargo
  super|car|goes
super|charge
  super|char|ges
  super|charged
  super|char|ging
super|charged
  adjective
super|char|ger +s
super|cili|ary
super|cili|ous
super|cili|ous|ly
super|cili|ous|ness
super|class
  super|class|es
super|com|put|er +s
super|com|put|ing
super|con|duct|ing
super|con|duct|ive
super|con|duc|tiv|ity
super|con|duct|or
super|contin|ent +s
super|cool +s +ed
  +ing
super|critic|al
super-duper
super|ego +s
super|eleva|tion +s
super|eroga|tion
super|eroga|tory
super|family
  super|fam|ilies
super|fat|ted
super|feta|tion +s
super|ficial
super|ficial|ity
  super|ficial|ities
super|ficial|ly
super|ficial|ness
super|ficies
  plural super|ficies

super|fine
super|fluid
super|fluid|ity
super|fluity
  super|flu|ities
super|fluous
super|fluous|ly
super|fluous|ness
super G
  super G's
super|giant +s (star)
super giant slal|om +s
super|glue
  super|glues
  super|glued
  super|gluing or super|glue|ing
super|grass
  super|grass|es
super|group +s
super|heat +s +ed +ing
super|heat|er +s
super|hero
  super|heroes
super|hetero|dyne +s
super|high|way +s
super|human
super|human|ly
super|impose
  super|impos|es
  super|im|posed
  super|impos|ing
super|impos|ition +s
super|induce
  super|indu|ces
  super|induced
  super|indu|cing
super|induc|tion +s
super|intend +s +ed +ing
super|intend|ence
super|intend|ency
super|intend|ent +s
Su|peri|or (lake, N America)
su|peri|or
su|peri|or|ity
su|peri|or|ly
su|perla|tive
su|perla|tive|ly
su|perla|tive|ness
super|lumin|al
super|lun|ary
super|man
  super|men
super|mar|ket +s
super|minis|ter +s
super|model +s
super|mom +s
su|per|nal

su|per|nal|ly
super|natant +s
super|natur|al
super|natur|al|ism
super|natur|al|ist +s
super|natur|al|ize
  super|natur|al|izes
  super|natur|al|ized
  super|natur|al|izing
super|natur|al|ly
super|natur|al|ness
super|normal
super|normal|ity
super|nova
  super|novas or super|novae
super|numer|ary
  super|numer|aries
super|order +s
super|ordin|al
super|ordin|ate +s
super|oxide +s
super|phos|phate +s
super|physic|al
super|pose
  super|pos|es
  super|posed
  super|pos|ing
super|pos|ition +s
super|power +s
super|satur|ate
  super|satur|ates
  super|satur|at|ed
  super|satur|at|ing
super|satur|a|tion
super|scribe
  super|scribes
  super|scribed
  super|scrib|ing
super|script +s
super|scrip|tion +s
super|sede
  super|sedes
  super|seded
  super|seding
super|sedence
super|sedure
super|ses|sion +s
super|sonic
super|sonic|ally
super|sonics
super|star +s
super|star|dom
super|state +s
super|station +s
super|sti|tion +s
super|sti|tious
super|sti|tious|ly
super|sti|tious|ness
super|store +s
super|strat|um
  super|strata
super|struc|tur|al

super|struc|ture +s
super|tank|er +s
super|terres|trial
super|title +s
super|tonic +s
super|vene
  super|venes
  super|vened
  super|ven|ing
super|ven|ient
super|ven|tion +s
super|vise
  super|vises
  super|vised
  super|vising
super|vision
super|visor +s
super|visory
super|woman
  super|women
su|pin|ate
  su|pin|ates
  su|pin|at|ed
  su|pin|at|ing
su|pin|a|tion
su|pin|ator +s
su|pine +s
su|pine|ly
su|pine|ness
sup|per +s
sup|per|less
supper|time +s
sup|plant +s +ed +ing
sup|plant|er +s
sup|ple
  sup|pler
  sup|plest
  sup|ples
  sup|pled
  sup|pling
supple|jack +s
supple|ly (use supply)
sup|ple|ment +s +ed +ing
sup|ple|ment|al
sup|ple|ment|al|ly
sup|ple|men|tari|ly
sup|ple|ment|ary
sup|ple|men|ta|tion +s
supple|ness
sup|ple|tion +s
sup|ple|tive
sup|pli|ant
sup|pli|ant|ly
sup|pli|cant +s
sup|pli|cate
  sup|pli|cates
  sup|pli|cat|ed
  sup|pli|cat|ing
sup|pli|ca|tion +s
sup|pli|ca|tory

sup|pli|er
sup|ply[1] *verb & noun*
(provide; substitute; store)
  sup|plies
  sup|plied
  sup|ply|ing
supply[2] *adverb* (in a supple manner)
supply-side
supply-sider +s
sup|port +s +ed +ing
sup|port|abil|ity
sup|port|able
sup|port|ably
sup|port|er +s
sup|port|ing *adjective*
sup|port|ing|ly
sup|port|ive
sup|port|ive|ly
sup|port|ive|ness
sup|port|less
sup|pos|able
sup|pose
  sup|pos|es
  sup|posed
  sup|pos|ing
sup|pos|ed *adjective*
sup|pos|edly
sup|pos|ition +s
sup|pos|ition|al
sup|pos|itious
sup|pos|itious|ly
sup|pos|itious|ness
sup|posi|ti|tious
sup|posi|ti|tious|ly
sup|posi|ti|tious|ness
sup|posi|tory
  sup|posi|tor|ies
sup|press
  sup|press|es
  sup|pressed
  sup|press|ing
sup|pres|sant +s
sup|press|ible
sup|pres|sion +s
sup|pres|sive
sup|pres|sor +s
sup|pur|ate
  sup|pur|ates
  sup|pur|at|ed
  sup|pur|at|ing
sup|pur|a|tion +s
sup|pura|tive
supra
supra|nation|al
supra|nation|al|ism
supra|nation|al|ity
supra|orbit|al
supra|renal
su|prem|a|cism
su|prem|a|cist +s

su|prem|acy
  su|prem|a|cies
su|preme
  su|prem|er
  su|prem|est
su|preme|ly
su|premo +s
suq +s (bazaar: *use*
  souk)
  [☞ sook]
sura +s
Sura|baya (city,
  Indonesia)
sural
Surat (city, India)
sur|cease
  sur|ceas|es
  sur|ceased
  sur|ceas|ing
sur|charge
  sur|char|ges
  sur|charged
  sur|char|ging
sur|cin|gle +s
sur|coat +s
surd +s
sure
  surer
  sur|est
sure|fire
sure-footed
sure-footed|ly
sure-footed|ness
sure|ly (certainly)
  [☞ surly]
sure|ness
Sû|re|té
Sû|re|té du Qué|bec
sur|ety
  sur|eties
surety|ship
surf +s +ed +ing
  (waves; scan)
  [☞ serf]
sur|face
  sur|faces
  sur|faced
  sur|fa|cing
surface-active
sur|faced *adjective*
sur|facer +s
surface-to-air
surface-to-surface
surf|act|ant +s
surf|board +s
surf-cast
  surf-casts
  surf-cast
  surf-casting
surf-caster +s
surf-casting *noun*

sur|feit
  sur|feits
  sur|feit|ed
  sur|feit|ing
sur|feit|ed *adjective*
surf|er +s
surf-fishing
sur|ficial
surf|ing *noun*
surf|like
surfy
surge (rush; swell;
  increase)
  surges
  surged
  sur|ging
  [☞ serge]
sur|geon +s
sur|geon|fish
  plural sur|geon|fish
  or sur|geon|fish|es
sur|geon gen|er|al
  sur|geons gen|er|al
sur|geon's knot +s
sur|gery
  sur|ger|ies
sur|gical
sur|gical|ly
suri|cate +s
su|rimi
Suri|nam
  (= Suriname)
Suri|name (country,
  S America)
Suri|nam|er +s
Suri|nam|ese
  plural Suri|nam|ese
sur|li|ly
sur|li|ness
sur|ly (rude; hostile)
  sur|li|er
  sur|li|est
  [☞ surely]
sur|mise
  sur|mis|es
  sur|mised
  sur|mis|ing
sur|mount +s +ed
  +ing
sur|mount|able
sur|mul|let
  plural sur|mul|let or
  sur|mul|lets
sur|name
  sur|names
  sur|named
  sur|nam|ing
sur|pass
  sur|pass|es
  sur|passed
  sur|pass|ing
sur|pass|able
sur|pass|ing *adjective*

sur|pass|ing|ly
sur|plice +s
  (vestment)
sur|pliced
sur|plus (excess etc.)
  sur|plus|es
sur|plus|age +s
sur|prise
  sur|pris|es
  sur|prised
  sur|pris|ing
sur|prised *adjective*
sur|pris|ing *adjective*
sur|pris|ing|ly
sur|real (bizarre)
sur|real|ism (art
  movement)
sur|real|ist +s (of
  surrealism)
sur|real|is|tic
sur|real|is|tic|ally
sur|real|ity (surreal
  state)
sur|real|ly (in a
  surreal manner)
sur|rebut|tal +s
sur|rebut|ter +s
sur|rejoin|der +s
sur|ren|der +s +ed
  +ing
sur|rep|ti|tious
sur|rep|ti|tious|ly
sur|rep|ti|tious|ness
Sur|rey (city, Canada;
  county, England)
Sur|rey, Henry
  How|ard, Earl of
  (English courtier &
  poet)
sur|rey +s
sur|ro|gacy
sur|ro|gate +s
sur|round +s +ed
  +ing
sur|round|ing
  adjective
sur|tax
  sur|taxes
  sur|taxed
  sur|tax|ing
Sur|title +s
  proprietary
sur|tout +s
Surt|sey (island,
  Iceland)
sur|veil|lance +s
sur|vey +s +ed +ing
sur|vey|ing +s *noun*
sur|vey|or +s
sur|vey|or gen|er|al
  sur|vey|ors gen|er|al
sur|viv|a|bil|ity
sur|viv|able

sur|viv|al +s
sur|viv|al|ism
sur|viv|al|ist +s
sur|vive
  sur|vives
  sur|vived
  sur|viv|ing
sur|viv|or +s
sur|viv|or|ship
Surya (*Hinduism*)
sus (*use* suss)
  sus|ses
  sussed
  sus|sing
Susa
• (ancient city, Asia)
• (= Sousse, Tunisia)
  [☞ Sousa]
Susah (= Sousse,
  Tunisia)
  [☞ Susa, Sousa]
Su|sanna (*Apocrypha*)
sus|cept|ibil|ity
  sus|cept|ibil|ities
sus|cept|ible
sus|cept|ibly
sushi
sushi bar +s
sus|lik +s
sus|pect +s +ed +ing
sus|pect|ed *adjective*
sus|pend +s +ed +ing
sus|pend|er +s
sus|pense
sus|pense|ful
sus|pense|ful|ly
sus|pen|sible
sus|pen|sion +s
sus|pen|sive
sus|pen|sory
sus|pi|cion +s
sus|pi|cious
sus|pi|cious|ly
sus|pi|cious|ness
Sus|que|hanna (river,
  US)
suss
  suss|es
  sussed
  suss|ing
sussed *adjective*
Sus|sex (former
  county, England;
  dog; fowl)
Sussex|es
sus|tain +s +ed +ing
sus|tain|a|bil|ity
sus|tain|able
sus|tain|ably
sus|tained *adjective*
sus|tained-release
sus|tained yield
  (sus|tained-yield

when preceding a
noun)
sus|tain|er +s
sus|tain|ing adjective
sus|tain|ment
sus|ten|ance
su|sur|rant
su|sur|rat|ing
su|sur|ra|tion +s
su|sur|rous adjective
su|sur|rus noun
Suth|er|land, Don|ald
(Cdn actor)
Suth|er|land, Dame
Joan (Australian
soprano)
Sut|lej (river, India &
Pakistan)
sut|ler +s (army
provisioner)
[☞ subtler]
Sutra +s
sut|tee +s (widow's
self-immolation)
[☞ Sati]
Sut|ton Cold|field
(city, England)
su|tur|al
su|ture
su|tures
su|tured
su|tur|ing
su|tured adjective
su|ture|less
Suva (capital of Fiji)
Su|vorov, Alek|sandr
Vasily|evich
(Russian field
marshal)
Su|wan|nee (river, US)
Suyin, Han (British
writer)
su|zer|ain +s
su|zer|ainty
Su|zhou (city, China)
Su|zuki, David
Taka|yoshi (Cdn
scientist &
broadcaster)
Su|zuki (music
instruction)
Sval|bard (island
group off Norway)
svelte
Sven|gali +s
Sverd|lovsk (former
name for
Yekaterinburg,
Russia)
Sver|drup (island
group, Arctic
Archipelago)
Sve|tam|bara +s

swab
swabs
swabbed
swab|bing
Swabia (region,
Germany)
Swa|bian +s
swad|dle
swad|dles
swad|dled
swad|dling
swad|dled adjective
swad|dling clothes
swag
swags
swagged
swag|ging
swage
swa|ges
swaged
swa|ging
swag|ger +s +ed +ing
swag|ger|er +s
swag|ger|ing adjective
swag|ger|ing|ly
swag|man
swag|men
Swa|hili
plural Swa|hili
swain +s
swale +s
swal|low +s +ed +ing
swal|low|able
swal|low|er +s
swal|low|tail +s
swallow-tailed
swam
swami +s
Swam|mer|dam, Jan
(Dutch scientist)
swamp +s +ed +ing
swamped adjective
swamp|er +s
swamp|land +s
swamp maple +s
swampy
swamp|i|er
swamp|i|est
Swampy Cree
plural Swampy Cree
Swan (river, Australia)
Swan, Sir Jo|seph
Wil|son (English
physicist)
swan
swans
swanned
swan|ning
Swa|nee
(= Suwannee River,
US)
swank +er +est +s
+ed +ing

swanky
swan|ki|er
swan|ki|est
swan|like
swan neck +s
swan-necked
swan|nery
swan|ner|ies
swans|down
Swan|sea (city, Wales)
swan song +s
swap
swaps
swapped
swap|ping
SWAPO (South West
African People's
Organization)
swap|pable
swap|per +s
swa|raj
swa|raj|ist +s
sward +s (turf; lawn)
[☞ sword, sword
grass]
swarf
swarm +s +ed +ing
swarm|ing adjective
swart
swar|thi|ness
swarthy
swar|thi|er
swar|thi|est
swash
swash|es
swashed
swash|ing
swash|buck|ler +s
swash|buck|ling
swas|tika +s
SWAT (police)
swat (slap; swing at)
swats
swat|ted
swat|ting
[☞ swot]
swatch
swatch|es
swath (cleared strip;
in 'cut a swath')
swaths
[☞ swathe]
swathe (wrap, cover;
for cleared strip use
swath)
swathes
swathed
swath|ing
swath|er +s
swat|ter +s
sway +s +ed +ing
[☞ Sui]
sway-back +s

sway-backed
swayed conjugated
form of sway
[☞ suede]
Swazi
plural Swazi or
Swazis
Swazi|land (country,
Africa)
swear
swears
swore
sworn
swear|ing
swear|er +s
swear|ing noun
swearing-in
swearings-in
swear word +s
sweat (perspire etc.)
sweats
sweat|ed or sweat
sweat|ing
[☞ suite, sweet]
sweat|band +s
sweat bath +s
sweat|box
sweat|boxes
sweat|ed adjective
sweat|er +s
sweat|er coat +s
sweat|ered
sweat gland +s
sweat|i|er
sweat|i|est
sweat|i|ly
sweat|i|ness
sweat lodge +s
sweat|pants
sweat|proof
sweat|shirt +s
sweat|shop +s
sweat sock +s
sweat|suit +s
sweaty
sweat|i|er
sweat|i|est
Swede +s (Swedish
person)
swede +s (turnip)
Sweden (country,
Europe)
Sweden|borg,
Eman|uel (Swedish
theologian & mystic)
Sweden|borg|ian +s
swede saw +s
Swed|ish
sweep
sweeps
swept
sweep|ing
sweep|back +s

sweep|er +s
sweep|ing +s *adjective & noun*
sweep|ing|ly
sweep|ing|ness
sweep|stake +s
(= sweepstakes)
sweep|stakes
plural sweep|stakes
Sweet, Henry
(English philologist)
sweet +er +est +s
(sugary; sweet food)
[☞ suite]
sweet-and-sour
sweet|bread +s
sweet-brier +s
sweet|en +s +ed +ing
sweet|en|er +s
sweet|en|ing +s *noun*
sweet grass
sweet grass|es
sweet|heart +s
sweet|ie +s
sweet|ie pie +s
sweet|ing +s *noun*
sweet|ish
sweet|ly
sweet|meat +s
sweet|ness
sweet|sop +s
sweet talk *noun*
sweet-talk +s +ed +ing *verb*
sweet-talking *adjective*
sweet-tempered
sweet tooth +s
sweet wil|liam +s
swell
swells
swelled
swol|len or swelled
swell|ing
swell|ing +s *noun*
swel|ter +s +ed +ing
swel|ter|ing|ly
swept
swept-back
swept-wing
swerve
swerves
swerved
swerv|ing
swerv|er +s
Swift, Jona|than (Irish writer)
swift +er +est +s
Swift Cur|rent (city, Canada)
Swift|ian
swift|ie +s
swift|let +s

swift|ly
swift|ness
swig
swigs
swigged
swig|ging
swig|ger +s
swile +s
swil|er +s
swil|ing
swill +s +ed +ing
swill|er +s
swim
swims
swam
swum
swim|ming
swim|mable
swim|mer +s
swim|mer|et +s
swim|mer's ear
swim|ming *noun*
swim|ming|ly
swim|ming pool +s
swim|suit +s
swim|suit|ed
swim|wear
Swin|burne, Alger|non Charles (English poet)
swin|dle
swin|dles
swin|dled
swind|ling
swind|ler +s
Swin|don (town, England)
swine
• (pig)
plural swine
• (unpleasant person or thing)
plural swine or swines
swine|herd +s
swing
swings
swung
swing|ing
swing|beat
swinge
swin|ges
swinged
swinge|ing
swinge|ing *adjective & conjugated form of* swinge
swing|er +s
swing|ing *adjective & conjugated form of* swing
[☞ swingeing]
swing|ing|ly

swingle|tree +s
swing|man
swing|men
swing set +s
swing shift +s
swing-wing +s
swingy
swing|i|er
swing|i|est
swin|ish
swin|ish|ly
swin|ish|ness
swipe
swipes
swiped
swip|ing
swip|er +s
swirl +s +ed +ing
swirly
swirl|i|er
swirl|i|est
swish
swish|es
swished
swish|ing
swishy
swish|i|er
swish|i|est
Swiss
plural Swiss
Swiss Army knife
Swiss Army knives
Swiss cheese +s
(Swiss-cheese *when preceding a noun*)
[☞ Swiss cheese plant]
Swiss cheese plant +s
switch
switch|es
switched
switch|ing
switch|able
switch|back +s +ed +ing
switch|blade +s
switch|board +s
switched-on
switch|el
switch|er +s
switch|eroo +s
switch|gear *noun*
switch|grass
switch|grass|es
switch-hit
switch-hits
switch-hit
switch-hitting
switch hit|ter +s
switch-hitting *adjective*

switch|man
switch|men
switch over *verb*
switch|es over
switched over
switch|ing over
switch|over +s *noun*
swith|er +s +ed +ing
Switz|er|land
(country, Europe)
swiv|el
swiv|els
swiv|elled
swiv|el|ling
swiv|et
swiz (*use* swizz)
swiz|zes
swizz
swizz|es
swiz|zle
swiz|zles
swiz|zled
swiz|zling
swol|len *adjective*
swoon +s +ed +ing
swoony
swoon|i|er
swoon|i|est
swoop +s +ed +ing
swoosh
swoosh|es
swooshed
swoosh|ing
swop (*use* swap)
swops
swopped
swop|ping
sword +s (weapon)
[☞ sward]
sword|bear|er +s
sword|fern +s
sword|fish
plural sword|fish or sword|fish|es
sword grass
sword grass|es
sword-like
sword|play
swords|man
swords|men
swords|man|ship
sword stick +s
sword|tail +s
swore
sworn *adjective*
swot (study)
swots
swot|ted
swot|ting
[☞ swat]
swum
swung
sybar|ite +s

sybar|it|ic
sybar|it|ic|al
sybar|it|ic|al|ly
sybar|it|ism
syca|mine +s
syca|more +s (plane
  tree; maple; *Bible* fig
  tree)
syce +s
syco|more +s (*Bible*
  fig tree: *use*
  sycamore)
  [☞ sycamore]
sy|co|nium
  sy|co|nia
syco|phancy
syco|phant +s
syco|phant|ic
syco|phant|ic|ally
Syden|ham, Thom|as
  (English physician)
Syden|ham's chorea
Syd|ney (city,
  Australia;
  metropolitan area,
  Nova Scotia)
  [☞ Sidney]
Syd|ney Mines (urban
  community, Canada)
Sydney|sider +s
syen|ite
syen|itic
Syk|tyv|kar (city,
  Russia)
syl|lab|ary
  syl|lab|aries
syl|labi
syl|lab|ic
syl|lab|ic|ally
syl|labi|ca|tion
syl|lab|icity
syl|labi|fi|ca|tion
syl|lab|ify
  syl|labi|fies
  syl|labi|fied
  syl|labi|fy|ing
syl|lab|ize
  syl|lab|iz|es
  syl|lab|ized
  syl|lab|iz|ing
syl|la|ble
  syl|la|bles
  syl|la|bled
  syl|la|bling
syl|la|bled *adjective*
syl|la|bub +s
syl|la|bus
  syl|la|bus|es or
  syl|labi
syl|lep|sis
  syl|lep|ses
syl|lep|tic
syl|lep|tic|ally

syl|lo|gism +s
syl|lo|gis|tic
syl|lo|gis|tic|ally
syl|lo|gize
  syl|lo|giz|es
  syl|lo|gized
  syl|lo|giz|ing
sylph +s
sylph|like
sylva
  syl|vae or syl|vas
syl|van
Syl|van|us (woodland
  deity: *use* Silvanus)
sym|bi|ont +s
sym|bio|sis
  sym|bio|ses
sym|bi|ot|ic
sym|bi|ot|ic|ally
sym|bol (sign)
  sym|bols
  sym|bolled
  sym|bol|ling
  [☞ cymbal]
sym|bol|ic
sym|bol|ic|al
sym|bol|ic|al|ly
sym|bol|ism +s
sym|bol|ist +s
  (adherent of
  symbolism etc.)
  [☞ cymbalist]
sym|bol|is|tic
sym|bol|iz|a|tion
sym|bol|ize
  sym|bol|iz|es
  sym|bol|ized
  sym|bol|iz|ing
sym|bol|ogic|al
sym|bol|ogy
  sym|bol|o|gies
sym|met|ric
sym|met|ric|al
sym|met|ric|al|ly
sym|met|rize
  sym|met|riz|es
  sym|met|rized
  sym|met|riz|ing
sym|metry
  sym|met|ries
Sym|onds, John
  Ad|ding|ton (English
  writer)
Sy|mons, Ar|thur
  Wil|liam (English
  poet)
sym|path|ec|tomy
  sym|path|ec|to|mies
sym|pa|thet|ic
sym|pa|thet|ic|ally
sym|pa|thize
  sym|pa|thiz|es

sym|pa|thized
sym|pa|thiz|ing
sym|pa|thiz|er +s
sym|pa|thy
  sym|pa|thies
sym|pat|ico (*use*
  simpatico)
sym|pat|ric
sym|petal|ous
sym|phon|ic
sym|phon|ic|ally
sym|phon|ist +s
sym|phony
  sym|phon|ies
sym|phys|eal
sym|phys|ial
  (= symphyseal)
sym|phy|sis
  sym|phy|ses
sym|po|dial
sym|po|dium
  sym|po|dia
sym|po|sium
  sym|po|sia or
  sym|po|siums
symp|tom +s
symp|tom|atic
symp|tom|atic|ally
symp|tom|atol|ogy
symp|tom|less
syn|aer|esis (*use*
  syneresis)
  syn|aer|eses
syn|aes|the|sia (*use*
  synesthesia)
syna|gog|al
syna|gogic|al
syna|gogue +s
synal|lag|matic
syn|apse +s
syn|ap|sis
  syn|ap|ses
syn|ap|tic
syn|ap|tic|ally
syn|arth|ro|sis
  syn|arth|ro|ses
sync +s +ed +ing
  (synchronization;
  synchronize)
  [☞ sink, Cinque
  Ports]
syn|carp|ous
synch +s +ed +ing
  (synchronization,
  synchronize: *use*
  sync)
  [☞ sink, Cinque
  Ports]
syn|chro +s
syn|chro|cyclo|tron
syn|chro|mesh
  syn|chro|meshes
syn|chron|ic

syn|chron|ic|ally
syn|chron|icity
  syn|chron|icities
syn|chron|ism +s
syn|chron|is|tic
syn|chron|is|tic|ally
syn|chron|iz|a|tion
  +s
syn|chron|ize
  syn|chron|iz|es
  syn|chron|ized
  syn|chron|iz|ing
syn|chron|iz|er +s
syn|chron|ous
syn|chron|ous|ly
syn|chrony
  syn|chron|ies
syn|chro|tron +s
syn|clinal
syn|clinal|ly
syn|cline +s
synco|pal
synco|pate
  synco|pates
  synco|pat|ed
  synco|pat|ing
synco|pa|tion +s
synco|pa|tor +s
syn|cope +s
syn|cretic
syn|cre|tism +s
syn|cre|tist +s
syn|cre|tis|tic
syn|cre|tize
  syn|cre|tiz|es
  syn|cre|tized
  syn|cre|tiz|ing
syn|cytial
syn|cyt|ium
  syn|cytia
syn|dac|tyl
syn|dac|tyl|ism
syn|dac|tyl|ous
syn|dac|tyly
syn|desis
  syn|deses
syn|des|mo|sis
  syn|des|mo|ses
syn|detic
syn|dic +s
syn|dic|al
syn|dical|ism
syn|dical|ist +s
syn|di|cate
  syn|di|cates
  syn|di|cat|ed
  syn|di|cat|ing
syn|di|ca|tion +s
syn|di|ca|tor +s
syn|drome +s
syn|drom|ic
syne (since)
  [☞ sine]

syn|ec|doche +s
syn|ec|doch|ic
syn|ec|doch|ic|al
syn|ec|doch|ic|al|ly
syn|eco|logic|al
syn|ecol|ogy
syn|er|esis
  syn|er|eses
syn|er|get|ic
syn|er|gic
syn|er|gism +s
syn|er|gist +s
syn|er|gis|tic
syn|er|gis|tic|ally
syn|ergy
  syn|er|gies
syn|es|the|sia
syn|es|thet|ic
syn|gam|ous
syn|gamy
Synge, (Ed|mund)
  John Mil|ling|ton
  (Irish dramatist)
syn|od +s
syn|od|al
syn|od|ic
syn|od|ic|al
syno|nym +s
syno|nym|ic
syno|nym|ity
syn|onym|ous
syn|onym|ous|ly
syn|onym|ous|ness
syn|onymy
  syn|onym|ies
syn|op|sis
  syn|op|ses
syn|op|size
  syn|op|siz|es
  syn|op|sized
  syn|op|siz|ing
syn|op|tic +s
syn|optic|al
syn|optic|ally
syn|os|to|sis
syn|ovial
syn|ovitis
syn|tac|tic
syn|tac|tic|al
syn|tac|tic|ally
syn|tagm +s
  (= syntagma)
syn|tag|ma
  syn|tag|mas or
  syn|tag|mata
syn|tag|matic
syn|tag|matic|ally
syn|tax
synth +s
synth|ase +s
syn|the|sis
  syn|the|ses

syn|the|sist +s
syn|the|size
  syn|the|siz|es
  syn|the|sized
  syn|the|siz|ing
syn|thet|ase +s
syn|thet|ic +s
syn|thet|ic|al
syn|thet|ic|ally
syn|the|tist +s
  (= synthesist)
syn|the|tize
  (= synthesize)
  syn|the|tiz|es
  syn|the|tized
  syn|the|tiz|ing
syph
syph|ilis
syph|il|itic
syph|il|ize
  syph|il|iz|es
  syph|il|ized
  syph|il|iz|ing
syph|il|oid
sy|phon +s +ed +ing
  (use siphon)
sy|phon|age
sy|phon|al
sy|phon|ic
Syra|cuse (cities, Italy
  & US)
Syrah +s (wine)
  [☞ sera, sirrah]
Syr Darya
  (= Sirdaryo River)
Syria (country, Middle
  East)
Syr|iac
Syr|ian +s
syr|inga +s (mock
  orange; lilac)
  [☞ seringa]
syr|inge
  syr|in|ges
  syr|inged
  syr|in|ging
syr|in|geal
syr|in|ges plural of
  syringe & syrinx
syr|inx
  syr|inx|es or
  syr|in|ges
syr|phid +s
syr|up +s
syr|upy
sys|admin +s
sys|op +s
sys|tem +s
sys|tem|atic
sys|tem|atic|ally
sys|tem|atics
sys|tem|atism

sys|tem|atist +s
sys|tem|atiz|ation
sys|tem|atize
  sys|tem|atiz|es
  sys|tem|atized
  sys|tem|atiz|ing
sys|tem|atiz|er +s
sys|tem|ic
sys|tem|ic|ally
sys|tem|iz|a|tion +s
sys|tem|ize
  sys|tem|iz|es
  sys|tem|ized
  sys|tem|iz|ing
sys|tem|iz|er +s
sys|tem|less
sys|tole +s
sys|tol|ic
syzygy
  syzy|gies
Szcze|cin (city,
  Poland)
Sze|chuan
  • (Cooking)
  • (= Sichuan, China)
Sze|chwan
  (= Szechuan)
Szeged (city, Hungary)
Szell, George (US
  conductor)
Szent-Györgyi,
  Al|bert von
  Nagyra|polt (US
  biochemist)
Szi|lard, Leo (US
  physicist)

T

T
  • (letter; shape;
  T-shirt)
  T's
  • (tritium; tesla;
  thiamine; launch
  time)
  [☞ ti, tee, tea]
t (letter)
  t's
  [☞ ti, tee, tea]
t. (ton, tonne)
T4
  T4s
TA (teaching assistant)
  • noun
  TAs
  • verb
  TA's

TA'd
TA'ing
ta (thank you)
  [☞ taw, tau, Ptah]
tab
  tabs
  tabbed
  tab|bing
tab|ard +s
Ta|basco (state,
  Mexico; proprietary
  sauce)
tab|bing noun
tab|bou|leh +s
tabby
  tab|bies
tab|er|nacle +s
tab|er|nacled
tabes
tab|et|ic +s
tab|la +s
tab|la|ture +s
Table (mountain,
  South Africa)
table
  tables
  tabled
  tabling
tab|leau
  tab|leaux
tab|leau vi|vant
  tab|leaux vi|vants
table|cloth +s
table dance +s
table-dancer +s
table dan|cing
table d'hôte
  tables d'hôte
table|ful +s
table-hop
  table-hops
  table-hopped
  table-hopping
table lamp +s
table|land +s
table man|ners
table|mate +s
Table Moun|tain (in
  South Africa)
table saw +s
table|side
table|spoon +s
table|spoon|ful +s
tab|let +s
table talk
table|top +s
table|ware
tabling noun
tab|loid +s
ta|boo +s +ed +ing
  (designated as
  sacred or accursed;
  socially prohibited)

ta|bor +s
tab|or|et +s
tab|our|et +s (use taboret)
Tab|riz (city, Iran)
tabu +s (designated as sacred or accursed: use taboo)
[☞ taboo]
tabu|lar
tab|ula rasa
tab|ulae rasae
tabu|lar|ly
tabu|late
tabu|lates
tabu|lat|ed
tabu|lat|ing
tabu|la|tion +s
tabu|la|tor +s
tabun
tac (in 'tac team')
[☞ tach, tack]
taca|ma|hac +s
tacet (Music)
[☞ tacit]
tach +s (tachometer)
[☞ tac]
Taché, Alexandre-Antonin (Cdn archbishop)
Taché, Sir Étienne-Paschal (Cdn politician)
tach|ism
tach|isme (use tachism)
tach|ist +s
tach|iste +s (use tachist)
tachis|to|scope +s
tachis|to|scop|ic
tachis|to|scop|ic|ally
tacho +s (tachometer; tachograph)
[☞ taco]
tacho|graph +s
tach|om|eter +s
tachy|car|dia
tachyg|raph|er +s
tachy|graph|ic
tachy|graph|ical
tachyg|raphy
tachym|eter +s
tachy|on +s
tachyp|nea
tacit (implied without being stated)
[☞ tacet]
tacit|ly
taci|turn
taci|turn|ity
taci|turn|ly

Taci|tus (Roman historian)
tack +s +ed +ing (nail; stitch; course; rope; stickiness; saddle)
[☞ tach, tac]
tack|er +s
tack|ham|mer +s
tack|i|ly
tack|i|ness
tackle
tackles
tackled
tack|ling
tack|ler +s
tack|ling +s noun
tack room +s
tacky
tack|i|er
tack|i|est
taco +s (food)
[☞ tacho]
tacon|ite
tact
tac team +s
tact|ful
tact|ful|ly
tact|ful|ness
tac|tic +s
tac|tic|al
tac|tic|ally
tac|ti|cian +s
tac|tics
tac|tile
tac|til|ity
tact|less
tact|less|ly
tact|less|ness
tac|tual
tad
ta-da (= ta-dah)
ta-dah
Ta|dous|sac (village, Canada)
tad|pole +s
Ta|dzhik (use Tajik)
plural Ta|dzhiks or Ta|dzhik
Ta|dzhik|istan (= Tajikistan)
tae|dium vitae
Taegu (city, South Korea)
Tae|jon (city, South Korea)
tae kwon do
[☞ Tai Chi]
taf|feta +s
taff|rail +s
taffy
taf|fies
tafia +s

Taft, Wil|liam How|ard (US president)
tag
tags
tagged
tag|ging
Ta|gal|og
plural Ta|gal|og or Ta|gal|ogs
tag along verb
tags along
tagged along
tag|ging along
tag|along +s noun
Tag|an|rog (city, Russia)
tag day +s
tag end +s
ta|getes
tagged adjective
ta|gine +s (use tajine)
Tag|ish
plural Tag|ish or Tag|ish|es
taglia|telle
tag line +s
Tagli|oni, Marie (Italian dancer)
Ta|gore, Rab|in|dra|nath (Indian writer)
tag team +s (tag-team when preceding a noun)
Tagus (river, Europe)
ta|hi|ni
Ta|hi|ti (island, S Pacific)
Ta|hi|tian +s
Tahl|tan
plural Tahl|tan or Tahl|tans
tahr +s (mammal)
[☞ Thar]
tah|sil +s
Tai'an (city, China)
Tai Chi (martial art & callisthenics)
[☞ tae kwon do]
Tai Chi Chuan (= Tai Chi)
Tai|chung (city, Taiwan)
Ta'if (city, Saudi Arabia)
Taig +s offensive
tai|ga +s
tai|ko +s
tail +s +ed +ing (of an animal; end; follow; deviate;

diminish; Law)
[☞ tale]
tail|back +s
tail|board +s
tail|bone +s
tail|coat +s
tailed adjective
tail end +s
tail-ender +s
tail feath|er +s
tail fin +s
tail|gate
tail|gates
tail|gated
tail|gating
tail|gater +s
tail|hook +s
tail|ing +s noun
tail lamp +s
tail|less
tail light +s
tailor +s +ed +ing
[☞ Taylor]
tailored adjective
tailor|ing noun
tailor-made
tail|piece +s
tail|pipe +s
tail|plane +s
tail|race +s
tail|spin
tail|spins
tail|spun
tail|spin|ning
tail|stock +s
tail|water +s
tail|wheel +s
tail|wind +s
Tai|myr (peninsula, Russia)
Tai|nan (city, Taiwan)
Taine, Hip|po|lyte Adolphe (French writer)
Taino
plural Taino or Tai|nos
taint +s +ed +ing
taint|ed adjective
taint|less
tai|pan +s
Tai|pei (capital of Taiwan)
Tai|ping +s
Tai|wan (country, Asia)
Tai|wan|ese
plural Tai|wan|ese
Tai|yuan (city, China)
Ta'iz (city, Yemen)
Ta'izz (= Ta'iz)

Tajik
plural Ta|jiks or
Tajik
Ta|jik|istan (country,
Asia)
ta|jine +s
Taj Mahal
(mausoleum, India)
taka
plural taka
tak|able (*use*
takeable)
Tak|ak|kaw (waterfall,
Canada)
take
takes
took
taken
tak|ing
take|able
take away *verb*
takes away
took away
taken away
tak|ing away
take|away +s *noun*
take-charge *adjective*
take down *verb*
takes down
took down
taken down
tak|ing down
take|down +s *noun*
take-home +s
take-it-or-leave-it
adjective
taken *conjugated form*
of take
[☞ takin]
take-no-prisoners
adjective
take off *verb*
takes off
took off
taken off
tak|ing off
take|off +s *noun*
take out *verb*
takes out
took out
taken out
tak|ing out
take|out +s *noun*
take over *verb*
takes over
took over
taken over
tak|ing over
take|over +s *noun*
tak|er +s
take up *verb*
takes up
took up

taken up
tak|ing up
take-up +s *noun*
Taki|juq (lake,
Canada)
tak|in +s (animal)
[☞ taken]
tak|ing +s *adjective &*
noun
tak|ing|ly
Takla Makan
(= Taklimakan)
Tak|li|ma|kan (desert,
China)
Tako|radi (city,
Ghana)
tala +s
tal|aria
Tal|bot, Thom|as
(Cdn colonial
official)
Tal|bot, Wil|liam
Henry Fox (English
photography
pioneer)
talc
talcs
talced or talcked
talc|ing or talck|ing
tal|cum +s +ed +ing
talcy (like talc)
tale +s (story; total)
[☞ tail, *tales*]
tale-bearer +s
tale-bearing
Ta|leg|gio
tal|ent +s
tal|ent|ed
tal|ent|less
tales
• *singular noun* (writ
summoning jurors)
plural tales
• *plural noun* (list of
substitute jurors)
tales|man (person
summoned by a
tales)
tales|men
[☞ talisman]
tale-teller +s
tale-telling
tali *plural of* talus
[☞ thali, tally]
tali|pes
tali|pot +s
tal|is|man +s (lucky
charm)
[☞ talesman]
tal|is|man|ic
talk +s +ed +ing
(speak)
[☞ talc, tock]

talk|athon +s
talk|ative
talk|ative|ly
talk|ative|ness
talk back *verb*
talks back
talked back
talk|ing back
talk|back +s *noun*
talked-about
talk|er +s
talk|fest +s
talk|ie +s (movie with
sound)
[☞ talky, talcy]
talk|ing *adjective &*
noun
talking-to +s
talk show +s
talk time +s
talky (talkative,
verbose)
talk|i|er
talk|i|est
[☞ talkie, talcy]
tall +er +est
Tal|la|has|see (city,
US)
Tal|la|has|see|an +s
tall|boy +s
tall|er *comparative of*
tall
[☞ thaler]
Tal|ley|rand, Charles
Mau|rice de
full name **Charles**
Mau|rice de
Tal|leyrand-Périgord
(French statesman)
tall grass prair|ie +s
Tal|linn (capital of
Estonia)
Tal|lis, Thom|as
(English composer)
tal|lis
tal|lit|im
tall|ish
tal|lit (= tallis)
tal|lit|im
tal|lith (= tallis)
tal|li|thim
tall|ness
tal|low
tal|lowy
tall ship +s
tally (score, total)
tal|lies
tal|lied
tally|ing
[☞ thali]
tally|ho
• *noun*

tally|hos
• *verb*
tally|hoes
tally|hoed
tally|ho|ing
tally|man
tally|men
Tal|mud
Tal|mud|ic
Tal|mud|ic|al
Tal|mud|ist +s
Talon, Jean
(intendant of New
France)
talon +s
tal|oned
talus
• (ankle bone)
plural tali
• (*Geology*; sloping
side)
plural tal|us|es
tam +s
ta|male +s
ta|man|dua +s
tam|ar|ack +s
ta|mari
tam|ar|in +s (monkey)
tam|ar|ind +s (fruit
tree)
tam|ar|isk +s
Tamau|lipas (state,
Mexico)
Tambo, Oli|ver (South
African ANC
president)
tam|bour +s (drum;
shutter, door;
Needlework)
[☞ timbre]
tam|boura
tam|boured
tam|bour|ine +s
Tam|bov (city, Russia)
tam|bura +s (*use*
tamboura)
Tam|bur|laine
(= Tamerlane,
Mongol ruler)
tame
tamer
tamest
tames
tamed
taming
tame|ly
tame|ness
tamer +s
Tam|er|lane (Mongol
ruler)
Tam|il +s
Tamil|ian +s

Tamil Nadu (state, India)
Tam|many
Tam|muz (*Babylonian & Assyrian Myth*)
tammy
  tam|mies
tam-o'-shanter +s
tam|oxi|fen
tamp +s +ed +ing
Tampa (city, US)
Tampa Bay (inlet, US)
tamp|er[1] +s (tamping device)
tam|per[2] +s +ed +ing (meddle)
tam|per|er +s
tam|per|ing *noun*
tamper-proof
tamper-resist|ant
Tam|pi|co (city, Mexico)
tamp|ing *noun*
tam|pion
tam|pon +s
tam|pon|ade +s
tam-tam +s
Tam|worth (town, England)
tan
  tans
  tanned
  tan|ning
Tana (lake, Ethiopia)
tan|ager +s
Tana|na|rive (*former name for* Antananarivo, Madagascar)
tan|bark +s
Tan|cred (Norman soldier)
tan|dem +s
tan|door +s
tan|doori +s
Tang (Chinese dynasty)
tang +s
Tanga (city, Tanzania)
tan|ga +s
Tan|gan|yika (lake, Africa; *former name for* Tanzania)
tanged
tan|gelo +s
tan|gency
  tan|gen|cies
tan|gent +s
tan|gen|tial
tan|gen|tial|ly
tan|ger|ine +s
tan|gi|bil|ity
tan|gible

tan|gibly
Tan|gier (city, Morocco)
tang|i|er
Tan|giers (= Tangier)
tang|i|est
tang|i|ness
tangle
  tan|gles
  tan|gled
  tan|gling
tan|gled *adjective*
tan|gly
  tan|gli|er
  tan|gli|est
tango
  • *noun*
  tan|gos
  • *verb*
  tan|goes
  tan|goed
  tango|ing
tan|gram +s
Tang|shan (city, China)
Tan|guy, Yves (US painter)
tangy
  tang|i|er
  tang|i|est
tan|ist +s
tan|istry
tank +s +ed +ing
tan|ka +s
tank|age +s
tank|ard +s
tank car +s
tank|er +s
tank farm +s
tank|ful +s
tank|less
tank top +s
tan|nate +s
tanned *adjective*
tan|ner +s
tan|nery
  tan|ner|ies
Tann|häuser (German poet)
tan|nic
tan|nin +s
tan|ning *noun*
tan|nish
tan|noy +s *proprietary*
tansy
  tan|sies
tan|tal|ic
tan|tal|ite
tan|tal|iz|a|tion +s
tan|tal|ize
  tan|tal|iz|es
  tan|tal|ized
  tan|tal|iz|ing

tan|tal|iz|er +s
tan|tal|iz|ing *adjective*
tan|tal|iz|ing|ly
tan|ta|lum
Tan|ta|lus (*Greek Myth*)
tan|ta|lus
  tan|ta|lus|es
tan|ta|mount
tan|tivy
  tan|tiv|ies
tant mieux
tant pis
Tan|tra +s
Tan|tric
Tan|trism
Tan|trist +s
tan|trum +s
Tan|za|nia (country, Africa)
Tan|za|nian +s
Tao +s (*Taoism; Confucianism*)
  [☞ tau, Dou, dhow]
Taoi|seach
Tao|ism
Tao|ist +s
Tao|istic
tap
  taps
  tapped
  tap|ping
tapa +s (bar; cloth)
tapas (bar snacks)
tap dance
  tap dan|ces
  tap danced
  tap dan|cing
tap dan|cer +s
tap dan|cing *noun*
tape
  tapes
  taped
  taping
tape|able
tape deck +s
tape-delay
tape-delayed
tape meas|ure +s
tap|enade +s
tape play|er +s
taper +s +ed +ing (wick, candle; diminish in thickness)
  [☞ tapir]
tape-record +s +ed +ing *verb*
tape re|cord|er +s
tape re|cord|ing *noun*
taper|ing *adjective*
tap|est|ried

tap|estry
  tap|est|ries
ta|petum
  ta|peta or
  ta|pet|ums
tape|worm +s
tapho|nomic
ta|phon|omist +s
ta|phon|omy
tap-in +s
taping +s *noun*
tapi|oca
tapir +s (mammal)
  [☞ taper]
Ta|piri|sat (in 'Inuit Tapirisat of Canada')
tapir|oid +s
tapis
  plural tapis
tap|less
tap|pable
tapped-out
tap|per +s
tap|pet +s
tap|room +s
tap|root +s
tap|ster +s
tap water
tar (black substance; sailor)
  tars
  tarred
  tar|ring
  [☞ Thar Desert, tahr]
Tara (hill, Ireland)
tara|bish
tara|did|dle +s
tar|ama
tara|ma|sa|lata
Tara|naki (= Mount Egmont, New Zealand)
tar|an|tel|la +s
Tar|an|tino, Quen|tin Jer|ome (US filmmaker)
tar|an|tism
Ta|ran|to (city, Italy)
ta|ran|tula +s
Tar|awa (atoll, S Pacific)
tar baby
  tar babies
tar|boosh
  tar|boosh|es
tardi|grade +s
tard|i|ly
tard|i|ness
tardy
  tard|i|er
  tard|i|est

tare +s (plant; weight)
[☞ tear]
tar|ga +s
targe
  tar|ges
tar|get
  tar|gets
  tar|get|ed
  tar|get|ing
tar|get|able
tar|iff +s +ed +ing
Tarim (river, China)
Tar|king|ton,
  New|ton Booth (US
  writer)
Tar|kov|sky, An|drei
  Arsen|evich
  (Russian filmmaker)
tar|la|tan +s
Tar|mac *proprietary*
  (paving substance)
tar|mac (runway etc.;
  pave)
  tar|macs
  tar|macked
  tar|mack|ing
tar|mac|adam
Tarn (river, France)
tarn +s
tar|na|tion
tar|nish
  tar|nish|es
  tar|nished
  tar|nish|ing
tar|nish|able
taro +s (plant)
  [☞ tarot]
tarot +s (cards)
  [☞ taro]
tarp +s
tar|pan +s
tar|paper +s
tar|papered
tar|pau|lin +s
Tar|peia (Vestal
  Virgin)
Tar|peian Rock (in
  ancient Rome)
tar pit +s
tar|pon +s
Tar|quin[1] (Lucius
  Tarquinius Priscus,
  king of Rome)
Tar|quin[2] ('Tarquin
  the Proud', Lucius
  Tarquinius Superbus,
  last king of Rome)
tarra|did|dle +s (*use*
  taradiddle)
tar|ra|gon +s
tar|ri|er +s (one who
  tarries; *comparative*

of tarry)
  [☞ terrier]
tar|ri|ness
tar|ry
• (of or like tar)
  tar|ri|er
  tar|ri|est
• (linger)
  tar|ries
  tar|ried
  tarry|ing
  [☞ terry cloth,
  Terry]
tar|sal +s
tar sand +s
tarsi
tar|sier +s
Tar|sus (ancient city,
  Turkey)
tar|sus
  tarsi
tart +s +ed +ing +er
  +est
tar|tan +s
Tar|tar +s (people &
  language)
  [☞ tartare]
tar|tar +s (deposit on
  teeth and wine casks,
  in 'tartar sauce' &
  'tartar emetic')
  [☞ tartare]
tar|tare (in 'sauce
  tartare' & 'steak
  tartare')
  [☞ tartar, tartar
  sauce, tartar
  emetic]
Tar|tar|ean (of
  Tartarus)
  [☞ Tartarian]
tar|tar emet|ic
Tar|tar|ian (of the
  Tartars)
  [☞ Tartarean]
tar|tar|ic
tar|tar sauce +s
  [☞ tartare]
Tar|tarus (*Greek
  Myth*)
Tar|tary (historical
  region, Asia &
  E Europe)
tart|er *comparative of*
  tart
  [☞ tartar, tartare]
tart|i|er
tart|i|est
tart|i|ly
tart|i|ness
tart|let +s
tart|ly
tart|ness
tar|trate +s

tar|tra|zine
tar|tufo +s
tarty
  tart|i|er
  tart|i|est
Tasche|reau, Louis-
  Alexandre (Cdn
  politician)
Taser +s *proprietary*
Tashi lama +s
Tash|kent (capital of
  Uzbekistan)
task +s +ed +ing
task force +s
task|master +s
task|mis|tress
  task|mis|tress|es
Tas|man (sea,
  S Pacific)
Tas|man, Abel
  Jans|zoon (Dutch
  navigator)
Tas|man|ia (island &
  state, Australia)
Tas|man|ian +s
Tass
tas|sel
  tas|sels
  tas|selled
  tassel|ling
tas|selled *adjective*
Tasso, Tor|quato
  (Italian poet)
tast|able (*use*
  tasteable)
taste
  tastes
  tast|ed
  tast|ing
taste|able
taste bud +s
taste|ful
taste|ful|ly
taste|ful|ness
taste|less
taste|less|ly
taste|less|ness
taste|maker +s
tast|er +s
taste test +s *noun*
taste-test +s +ed
  +ing *verb*
tast|i|ly
tast|i|ness
tast|ing +s *noun*
tasty
  tast|i|er
  tast|i|est
tat
  tats
  tat|ted
  tat|ting
ta-ta

ta|tami
  plural ta|tamis or
  ta|tami
Tatar +s (= Tartar)
Tatar|stan (republic,
  Russia)
Tate, John Orley
  Allen (US poet &
  critic)
Tate, Nahum (Irish-
  born writer)
tater +s
Tatra +s (mountain
  range, Europe)
Tats|hen|shini (river,
  Canada)
tat|ter +s
tat|ter|de|mal|ion +s
tat|tered
tat|ter|sall +s
tat|tery
tat|tie +s (potato)
  [☞ tatty]
tat|ti|er
tat|ti|est
tat|ti|ly
tat|ti|ness
tat|ting +s
tat|tle
  tat|tles
  tat|tled
  tat|tling
tat|tler +s
tattle-tale +s
tat|too
  tat|toos
  tat|tooed
  tat|too|ing
tat|too|er +s
tat|too|ist +s
tatty (tattered;
  inferior; tawdry)
  tat|ti|er
  tat|ti|est
  [☞ tattie]
Tatum, Ar|thur (US
  pianist)
Tatum, Ed|ward
  Law|rie (US
  biochemist)
tau +s (Greek letter;
  cross; particle)
  [☞ Tao]
taught *past & past
  participle of* teach
  [☞ taut, tot]
taunt +s +ed +ing
taunt|er +s
taunt|ing|ly
Taun|ton (town,
  England)
taupe +s (colour)
  [☞ tope]

Taupo (lake, New Zealand)
Taupo|moana
(= Lake **Taupo**)
Tau|ranga (town, New Zealand)
Taur|ean +s
taur|ine
Taur|us (constellation; *Zodiac*; mountain range, Turkey)
[☞ **torus, Torres Strait**]
taut +er +est (tight; tense)
[☞ **taught, tot**]
taut|en +s +ed +ing
taut|ly
taut|ness
tau|tog
plural **tau|tog** or **tau|togs**
tauto|logic|al
tauto|logic|ally
tau|tol|o|gist +s
tau|tol|o|gize
tau|tol|o|giz|es
tau|tol|o|gized
tau|tol|o|giz|ing
tau|tol|o|gous
tau|tol|ogy
tau|tol|o|gies
tauto|mer +s
tauto|mer|ic
tauto|mer|ism
tav|ern +s
tav|erna +s
taw +s +ed +ing
(make into leather; *Marbles*)
[☞ **ta, tau, Ptah**]
tawd|ri|ly
tawd|ri|ness
tawd|ry
tawd|ri|er
tawd|ri|est
tawer +s
Taw|ney, Rich|ard Henry (English historian)
tawn|i|ness
tawny
tawn|i|er
tawn|i|est
Tawny Owl +s
(*Scouting*)
tawny owl +s
tax (levy; strain)
taxes
taxed
tax|ing
taxa
tax|able

tax-and-spend
tax|a|tion
tax cred|it +s
tax-credit|able
tax-deduct|ible
tax|er +s
taxes *plural of* **tax** & **taxis**
[☞ **taxis**]
tax-exempt
tax-free
taxi (cab; move airplane)
taxis
taxied
taxi|ing
taxi|cab +s
taxi|der|mal
taxi|der|mic
taxi|der|mist +s
taxi|dermy
taxi driv|er +s
taxi|meter +s
tax|ing *adjective*
taxis
• (*Surgery*; cell movement)
taxes
• *plural of* **taxi**
[☞ **taxes**]
taxi|way +s
tax|man
tax|men
Tax|ol +s *proprietary*
taxon
taxa
taxo|nomic
taxo|nomic|al
taxo|nomic|ally
tax|ono|mist +s
tax|ono|my
tax|ono|mies
tax|pay|er +s
tax|pay|ing
tax shel|ter +s
tax-sheltered
Tay (river, Scotland)
[☞ **Te Deum**]
tay|berry
tay|ber|ries
Tay|lor (surname)
[☞ **tailor**]
Tay|lor, Eliza|beth Rose|mond (US actress)
Tay|lor, Jer|emy (English churchman)
Tay|lor, Zach|ary (US president)
Tay|myr (= Taimyr Peninsula, Russia)
Tay–Sachs dis|ease

Tay|side (region, Scotland)
taz|za +s
t.b.a. (to be announced)
T-ball (game)
[☞ **tea ball**]
T-bar +s
Tbil|isi (capital of the Republic of Georgia)
T-bill +s
T-bone
T-bones
T-boned
T-boning
T-cell +s
Tchai|kov|skian
Tchai|kov|sky, Pyotr Ilich (Russian composer)
tchotch|ke +s
TCP/IP (Internet protocol)
TD (touchdown)
TDs
TDD (Telephone Device for the Deaf)
TDDs
te +s (musical note: *use* **ti**)
[☞ **tee, tea, ti, T**]
tea +s (evergreen shrub or tree; infusion; afternoon meal or reception)
[☞ **tee, ti, T**]
tea bag +s
tea ball +s (metal ball for tea leaves)
[☞ **T-ball**]
tea|berry
tea|ber|ries
tea bread +s
tea|cake +s
Teach, Ed|ward (Blackbeard, English pirate)
teach
teach|es
taught
teach|ing
teach|abil|ity
teach|able
teach|able|ness
teach|er +s
teach|er|age +s
teach|er|ish
teach|er|ly
teacher's aide +s
teachers' col|lege +s
teacher's pet +s
teach-in +s
teach|ing +s *noun*

tea cozy
tea coz|ies
tea|cup +s
tea|cup|ful +s
tea house +s
teak +s
tea|kettle +s
teak|wood
teal
• (duck)
plural **teal** or **teals**
• (colour)
plural **teals**
teal blue +s (teal-blue *when preceding a noun*)
tea leaf
tea leaves
team (*Sports*; group; match, combine)
teams
teamed
team|ing
[☞ **teem**]
team|mate +s
Team|ster +s
(member of the Teamsters union)
team|ster +s (one who drives a truck or team of animals)
team-teach
team-teaches
team-taught
team-teaching
team-teaching *noun*
team|work
tea party
tea par|ties
tea plant +s
tea|pot +s
tea|poy +s
tear[1] (rip)
tears
tore
torn
tear|ing
[☞ **tare**]
tear[2] +s +ed +ing
(liquid from eyes)
[☞ **tier, Tyr**]
tear away *verb*
tears away
tore away
torn away
tear|ing away
tear|away +s *noun*
tear|drop +s
tear duct +s
tear|er +s
tear|ful
tear|ful|ly
tear|ful|ness

tear gas *noun* (**tear-gas** *when preceding a noun*)
  tear gases
tear-gas *verb*
  tear-gases
  tear-gassed
  tear-gassing
tear|ing *adjective*
tear|jerk|er +s
tear-jerking
tear|less
tear|less|ly
tear off *verb*
  tears off
  tore off
  torn off
  tear|ing off
tear-off *adjective*
tea room +s
tear sheet +s
tear-stained
teary
tease
  teas|es
  teased
  teas|ing
  [☞ Tees River]
tea|sel +s +ed +ing
teas|er +s
tea shop +s
teas|ing|ly
tea|spoon +s
tea|spoon|ful +s
teat +s
tea time +s
tea towel +s
tea tree +s
  (Australasian flowering shrub; red-berried nightshade)
  [☞ ti tree]
tea|zel +s +ed +ing (*use* teasel)
tea|zle (*use* teasel)
  tea|zles
  tea|zled
  teaz|ling
tech +s
tech|ie +s (technical expert)
  [☞ techy, tetchy]
tech|i|er *comparative of* techy
  [☞ tetchier]
tech|i|est *superlative of* techy
  [☞ tetchiest]
tech|ne|tium
tech|nic +s
  (technology; technical methods &

details)
  [☞ technique]
tech|nic|al +s
tech|nic|al|ity
  tech|nic|al|ities
tech|nic|al|ly
tech|ni|cian +s
tech|ni|cist +s
Techni|color
  proprietary (*Film*)
techni|color (vivid colour; artificial brilliance)
techni|col|ored
techni|colour
  (= technicolor: vivid colour, artificial brilliance)
  [☞ Technicolor]
techni|col|oured
  (= technicolored)
tech|nique +s (execution, skill; method, procedure)
  [☞ technic]
techno
techno|babble
tech|noc|racy
  tech|noc|ra|cies
techno|crat +s
techno|crat|ic
techno|logic|al
techno|logic|ally
tech|nol|o|gist +s
tech|nol|o|gize
  tech|nol|o|giz|es
  tech|nol|o|gized
  tech|nol|o|giz|ing
tech|nol|ogy
  tech|nol|o|gies
techno|phile +s
techno|philia
techno|phil|ic
techno|phobe +s
techno|phobia
techno|phob|ic +s
techy (technical)
  tech|i|er
  tech|i|est
  [☞ techie, tetchy]
tec|ton|ic
tec|ton|ic|ally
tec|ton|ics
tec|tor|ial
tec|trix
  tec|tri|ces
Tecum|seh (Shawnee chief; town, Canada)
Ted +s (Teddy boy)
ted (spread hay etc. for drying)
  teds

  ted|ded
  ted|ding
ted|der +s
teddy
  ted|dies
teddy bear +s
Teddy boy +s
Te Deum +s
tedi|ous
tedi|ous|ly
tedi|ous|ness
tedi|um
tee (the letter *T*; *Golf*; *Football*; *Curling*; annoy; attack)
  tees
  teed
  tee|ing
  [☞ tea, ti, T]
tee-hee
  tee-hees
  tee-heed
  tee-heeing
teem +s +ed +ing (pour; abound, be full of)
  [☞ team]
teem|ing *adjective* (brimming; pouring)
  [☞ teaming]
teen +s
teen|age
teen|aged (= teenage)
teen|ager +s
teens
teen|sy
  teen|si|er
  teen|si|est
teensy-weensy
teeny
  teen|i|er
  teen|i|est
teeny|bop|per +s
teeny-weeny
tee off *verb*
  tees off
  teed off
  tee|ing off
tee-off +s *noun*
tee|pee +s
Tees (river, England)
  [☞ tease]
tee-shirt +s (*use* T-shirt)
Tees|side (region, England)
tee|ter +s +ed +ing
teeter-totter +s
teeth *plural of* tooth
teethe *verb*
  teethes

  teethed
  teeth|ing
teeth|er +s
teeth|ing *noun*
tee|total
  tee|to|talled
  tee|total|ling
tee|total|ism
tee|total|ler +s
tee|totum +s
teff
te|fil|lin
TEFL (teaching of English as a foreign language)
Tef|lon *proprietary* (non-stick coating)
Tegu|ci|galpa (capital of Honduras)
tegu|ment
tegu|ment|al
tegu|ment|ary
te-hee (= tee-hee)
  te-hees
  te-heed
  te-heeing
Teh|ran (capital of Iran)
Teil|hard de Char|din, Pierre (French Jesuit philosopher)
Te|jano +s
Te Kan|awa, Dame Kiri Jan|ette (New Zealand soprano)
tek|kie +s (technical expert: *use* techie)
  [☞ techy]
tek|tite
Tela|mon (*Greek Myth*)
tela|mon (*Architecture*)
  tela|mon|es
Tel Aviv (city, Israel)
Tel Aviv-Jaffa (= Tel Aviv)
tel|co +s
tele|bank|ing
tele|cast
  tele|casts
  tele|cast
  tele|cast|ing
tele|cast|er +s
tele|cine
tele|com
tele|com|muni|ca|tion +s
tele|com|mute
  tele|com|mutes
  tele|com|mut|ed
  tele|com|mut|ing
tele|com|mut|er +s

tele|com|mut|ing
  noun
tele|con|fer|ence
  tele|con|fer|en|ces
  tele|con|fer|enced
  tele|con|fer|en|cing
tele|con|fer|en|cing
  noun
Tele|fax *proprietary*
  Tele|fax|es
tele|film +s
tele|gen|ic
tele|gram +s
tele|graph +s +ed
  +ing
tele|graph|er +s
tele|graph|ese
tele|graph|ic
tele|graph|ic|ally
teleg|raph|ist *noun*
teleg|raphy
Tel|egu (*use* Telugu)
  plural Tel|egu or
  Tel|egus
tele|kin|esis
tele|kin|etic
Te|lema|chus (*Greek
  Myth*)
Tele|mann, Georg
  Phil|ipp (German
  composer)
tele|mark +s +ed
  +ing
tele|mar|ket|er +s
tele|mar|ket|ing
tele|medi|cine
tele|mes|sage
  tele|mes|sa|ges
tele|meter +s
tele|met|ric
telem|etry
teleo|logic
teleo|logic|al
teleo|logic|al|ly
tele|ol|o|gism +s
tele|ol|o|gist +s
tele|ol|ogy
  tele|ol|o|gies
tele|oper|at|ed
tele|oper|ation +s
tele|oper|ator +s
tele|ost +s
tele|path +s
tele|path|ic
tele|path|ic|ally
telep|a|thist +s
telep|a|thize
  telep|a|thiz|es
  telep|a|thized
  telep|a|thiz|ing
telep|athy

tele|phone
  tele|phones
  tele|phoned
  tele|phon|ing
tele|phon|er +s
tele|phon|ic
tele|phon|ic|ally
teleph|onist +s
teleph|ony
tele|photo +s
tele|port +s +ed +ing
tele|port|a|tion
tele|pres|ence
tele|print|er +s
tele|prompt|er +s
tele|sales
tele|scope
  tele|scopes
  tele|scoped
  tele|scop|ing
tele|scop|ic
tele|scop|ic|ally
tele|shop|ping
tele|text +s
tele|theatre +s
tele|thon +s
Tele|type +s
  proprietary noun
tele|type *verb*
  tele|types
  tele|typed
  tele|typ|ing
tele|type|writ|er +s
tel|evan|gel|ism
tel|evan|gel|ist +s
tele|vis|able
tele|vise
  tele|vis|es
  tele|vised
  tele|vis|ing
tele|vision +s
tele|visual
tele|visual|ly
tele|work +s +ed
  +ing
tele|work|er +s
tele|work|ing *noun*
telex
  tel|ex|es
  tel|exed
  tel|ex|ing
Tel|ford (town,
  England)
Tell, Wil|liam
  (legendary Swiss
  hero)
tell
  tells
  told
  tell|ing
tell|able
tell-all

Tell el-Amarna
  (archaeological site,
  Egypt)
Tel|ler, Ed|ward (US
  physicist)
tell|er +s
tell|er|ship +s
tell|ing *adjective*
tell|ing|ly
telling-off
  tellings-off
tell|tale +s
tel|lur|ate +s
tel|lur|ic
tel|lur|ide +s
tel|lur|ite +s
tel|lur|ium
tel|lur|ous
telly
  tel|lies
tel|net
  tel|nets
  tel|net|ted
  tel|net|ting
telo|mere +s
telo|phase +s
telos
tel|son +s
Tel|ugu
  plural Tel|ugu or
  Tel|ugus
Te|mag|ami (lake,
  Canada)
tem|blor +s
tem|er|ari|ous
tem|er|ari|ous|ly
tem|er|ity
Témis|ca|mingue,
  Lac (= Lake
  Timiskaming,
  Canada)
Témis|coua|ta (lake,
  Canada)
temp +s +ed +ing
tem|peh
tem|per +s +ed +ing
tem|pera +s (*Painting*)
  [☞ tempora,
  tempura]
tem|per|ament +s
tem|per|ament|al
tem|per|ament|al|ly
tem|per|ance
tem|per|ate
tem|per|ate|ly
tem|per|ate|ness
tem|per|ature +s
tem|pered *adjective*
tem|pest +s
tem|pes|tu|ous
tem|pes|tu|ous|ly
tem|pes|tu|ous|ness
tempi

Tem|plar
tem|plate +s
Tem|ple, Shir|ley (US
  actress)
Tem|ple, Sir Thom|as
  (governor of Nova
  Scotia)
Tem|ple, Sir Wil|liam
  (English statesman)
temple +s
tem|po
  tem|pos or tempi
tem|pora (in 'O
  tempora, O mores')
  [☞ tempura,
  tempera]
tem|por|al
tem|por|al|ity
  tem|por|al|ities
tem|por|al|ly
tem|por|ar|i|ly
tem|por|ar|i|ness
tem|por|ary
  tem|por|ar|ies
tem|por|iz|a|tion +s
tem|por|ize
  tem|por|iz|es
  tem|por|ized
  tem|por|iz|ing
tem|por|iz|er +s
tem|poro|
          man|dibu|lar
Tem|pra|nillo
tempt +s +ed +ing
tempt|abil|ity
tempt|able
temp|ta|tion +s
tempt|er +s
tempt|ing *adjective*
tempt|ing|ly
temp|tress
  temp|tress|es
tem|pura (*Japanese
  cooking*)
  [☞ tempora,
  tempera]
ten +s (number)
  [☞ Taine]
ten|abil|ity
ten|able
ten|able|ness
ten|ace +s (*Bridge*)
  [☞ tennis]
ten|acious
ten|acious|ly
ten|acious|ness
ten|acity
ten|acu|lum
  ten|acula
ten|ancy
  ten|an|cies

ten|ant +s +ed +ing
(renter)
[☞ Tennant, tenet]
ten|ant|able
ten|ant|less
ten|antry
tench
plural tench
Ten
Com|mand|ments
tend +s +ed +ing
tend|ance
[☞ tendency]
ten|dency
ten|den|cies
ten|den|tious
ten|den|tious|ly
ten|den|tious|ness
ten|der +s +ed +ing
+er +est
[☞ tenterhook]
ten|der|er +s
ten|der|foot
ten|der|foots or
ten|der|feet
tender-hearted
tender-hearted|ness
ten|der|ize
ten|der|iz|es
ten|der|ized
ten|der|iz|ing
ten|der|iz|er +s
ten|der|loin +s
ten|der|ly
ten|der|ness
ten|din|itis
ten|din|ous
ten|don +s
ten|don|itis (*use*
tendinitis)
ten|dril +s
Tene|brae
tene|brous
tene|ment +s
tene|ment|al
tene|ment|ary
Tene|rife (Canary
Island)
te|nes|mus
ten|et +s
(fundamental belief)
ten|fold
ten-four
10-gallon hat +s
Teng Hsiao-p'ing
(= Deng Xiaoping)
Ten|iers, David
(Flemish painter)
Ten|nant, Ver|on|ica
(Cdn ballet dancer)
[☞ tenant]

ten|ner +s (ten-dollar
bill)
[☞ tenor]
Ten|nes|sean +s
Ten|nes|see (state &
river, US)
Ten|niel, Sir John
(English illustrator)
ten|nis (racquet sport)
[☞ tenace]
ten|no +s
Tenny|son, Al|fred,
1st Baron (English
poet)
Tenny|son|ian
Te|noch|ti|tlán (Aztec
capital)
ten|on +s +ed +ing
tenon|er +s
tenor +s (*Music*; gist;
general course; *Law*)
[☞ tenner]
tenor|ist +s
tenor|man
tenor|men
teno|syno|vitis
ten|ot|omy
ten|ot|omies
ten|pin +s (bowling
pin; 10-pin bowling)
10-pin bowl|ing
ten|pin|ner +s
ten|rec +s
TENS (transcutaneous
electrical nerve
stimulation)
tense
tens|es
tensed
tens|ing
tens|er
tens|est
tense|less
tense|ly
tense|ness
tens|er *comparative of*
tense
[☞ tensor, Tensor
bandage]
ten|sile
ten|sil|ity
ten|sion +s +ed +ing
ten|sion|al
ten|sion|ally
ten|sion|er +s
ten|sion|less
ten|sity
ten|sor +s (muscle;
Math)
[☞ Tensor
bandage, tenser]
Ten|sor ban|dage
proprietary

ten|sor|ial
ten-speed +s
ten-spot +s
tent +s +ed +ing
ten|tacle +s
ten|tacled
ten|tac|u|lar
ten|tac|u|late
ten|ta|tive +s
ten|ta|tive|ly
ten|ta|tive|ness
tent|ed *adjective*
ten|ter +s
ten|ter|hook +s
tent flap +s
tent fly
tent flies
tenth +s
tenth|ly
tent|ing *noun*
tent-like
tent peg +s
tent pole +s
tenu|ity
tenu|ous
tenu|ous|ly
tenu|ous|ness
ten|ure +s
ten|ured *adjective*
tenure-stream
tenure-track
ten|uto +s
teo|calli +s
teo|sinte
Teo|tihua|cán
(ancient city,
Mexico)
tepal +s
te|pee +s (*use* teepee)
teph|ra +s
Tepic (city, Mexico)
tepid
tepid|ity
tepid|ly
tepid|ness
tep|pan|yaki
te|quila +s
tera|byte +s
tera|flop +s
ter|aph
ter|aph|im
tera|to|gen +s
tera|to|gen|ic
tera|to|gen|icity
tera|togeny
tera|to|logic|al
tera|tol|o|gist +s
tera|tol|ogy
tera|tol|o|gies
tera|toma +s
tera|watt +s
ter|bium

Ter Borch, Ger|ard
(Dutch painter)
Ter|borch, Ger|ard
(= Ter Borch)
terce (canonical hour)
[☞ terse]
ter|cel +s
ter|cen|ten|ary
ter|cen|ten|aries
ter|cen|ten|nial +s
ter|cet +s
tere|binth +s
ter|edo +s
Ter|ence (Roman
dramatist)
Ter|eng|ganu
(= Trengganu,
Malaysia)
ter|eph|thal|ic
Ter|esa (Mother
Teresa, missionary
nun)
Ter|esa of Ávila
(saint)
Ter|esa of Li|sieux
(= Thérèse of
Lisieux, saint)
Ter|esh|kova,
Val|en|tina
Vlad|i|mir|ovna
(Russian cosmonaut)
Tere|sina (city, Brazil)
ter|ete (smooth &
rounded)
[☞ terret, turret,
Tourette's
syndrome]
Ter|eus (*Greek Myth*)
ter|gi|ver|sate
ter|gi|ver|sates
ter|gi|ver|sat|ed
ter|gi|ver|sat|ing
ter|gi|ver|sa|tion +s
ter|gi|ver|sa|tor +s
teri|yaki
term +s +ed +ing
Ter|ma|gant +s
(character in
morality plays)
ter|ma|gant +s (ill-
tempered woman)
term|er +s (in 'first-
termer', 'long-
termer' etc.)
[☞ termor]
ter|min|able
ter|min|able|ness
ter|min|al +s
ter|minal|ly
ter|min|ate
ter|min|ates
ter|min|ated
ter|min|at|ing

ter|min|a|tion +s
ter|min|a|tion|al
ter|min|ator +s
ter|mi|ner
ter|mini
ter|min|o|logic|al
ter|min|o|logic|ally
ter|min|ol|o|gist +s
ter|min|ol|ogy
   ter|min|ol|o|gies
ter|minus
   ter|mini or
   ter|minus|es
ter|minus ad quem
ter|minus ante quem
ter|minus a quo
ter|minus post quem
ter|mit|arium
   ter|mit|aria
ter|mit|ary
   ter|mit|aries
ter|mite +s
term|less
term|ly
ter|mor +s (*Law*:
   holder of land etc.
   for a set term)
   [☞ termer]
term paper +s
tern +s (bird; set of
   three; prize)
   [☞ terne, turn]
tern|ary
tern|ate
tern|ate|ly
terne (metal)
   [☞ tern, turn]
ter|pene +s
Terp|sich|ore (*Greek
   & Roman Myth*)
terp|sich|or|ean
Ter|race (city,
   Canada)
ter|race
   ter|ra|ces
   ter|raced
   ter|ra|cing
ter|raced house +s
   (= terrace house)
ter|race house +s
ter|ra|cing *noun*
terra cotta +s
terra firma
terra|form +s +ed
   +ing
ter|rain +s (ground,
   landscape; *for*
   distinctive tectonic
   plate fragment *use*
   terrane)
terra in|cog|nita
   ter|rae in|cog|nitae

ter|rane +s
   (distinctive tectonic
   plate fragment)
   [☞ terrain]
Terra Nova (park,
   Canada)
ter|ra|pin +s
ter|rar|ium
   ter|rar|iums or
   ter|raria
ter|raz|zo +s
Terre|bonne (town,
   Canada)
Terre Haute (city, US)
ter|rene (earthy;
   earthly; terrestrial)
   [☞ terrine, tureen]
terre|plein +s
ter|res|trial +s
ter|res|trial|ity
ter|res|trial|ly
ter|ret +s (loop on a
   horse harness)
   [☞ terete, turret,
   Tourette's
   syndrome]
terre verte
ter|rible
ter|rible|ness
ter|ribly
ter|rico|lous
ter|rier +s (dog)
   [☞ tarrier]
ter|rif|ic
ter|rif|ic|ally
ter|ri|fier +s
ter|ri|fy
   ter|ri|fies
   ter|ri|fied
   ter|ri|fy|ing
ter|ri|fy|ing *adjective*
ter|ri|fy|ing|ly
ter|ri|gen|ous
ter|rine +s (pâté;
   vessel for this)
   [☞ terrene, tureen]
ter|ri|tor|ial
ter|ri|tor|ial|ity
ter|ri|tory
   ter|ri|tor|ies
ter|roir +s
Ter|ror (*French
   History*)
ter|ror +s
ter|ror|ism
ter|ror|ist +s
ter|ror|is|tic
ter|ror|ize
   ter|ror|iz|es
   ter|ror|ized
   ter|ror|iz|ing
terror-strick|en
terror-struck

Terry, Dame (Alice)
   Ellen (English
   actress)
   [☞ tarry]
terry (cloth)
   ter|ries
   [☞ tarry]
terry cloth +s (terry-
   cloth *when preceding
   a noun*)
terse (brief; curt)
   ters|er
   ters|est
   [☞ terce]
terse|ly
terse|ness
ter|tian
Ter|tiary (*Geology*)
ter|tiary
   ter|tiar|ies
ter|tium quid
Ter|tul|lian (early
   Christian theologian)
ter|va|lent
terza rima
ter|zet|to
   ter|zet|tos or
   ter|zet|ti
TESL (teaching of
   English as a second
   language)
Tesla, Nikola (US
   inventor)
tesla +s
Tesla coil +s
Tes|lin (lake, Canada)
TESOL (teaching of
   English to speakers
   of other languages)
TESSA (tax exempt
   special savings
   account)
   TESSAs
tes|sel|ate (*use*
   tessellate)
   tes|sel|ates
   tes|sel|at|ed
   tes|sel|at|ing
tes|sel|at|ed *adjective*
   (*use* tessellated)
tes|sel|a|tion +s (*use*
   tessellation)
tes|sel|late
   tes|sel|lates
   tes|sel|lat|ed
   tes|sel|lat|ing
tes|sel|lat|ed *adjective*
tes|sel|la|tion +s
tes|sera
   tes|serae
tes|ser|al
Tes|sin (= Ticino,
   Switzerland)
tes|si|tura

test +s +ed +ing
testa
   tes|tae
test|abil|ity
test|able
tes|ta|ceous
Test Act +s
tes|tacy
   tes|ta|cies
Tes|ta|ment (*Bible*)
tes|ta|ment +s
tes|ta|ment|ary
tes|tate
tes|ta|tor +s
tes|ta|trix
   tes|ta|tri|ces or
   tes|ta|trix|es
test ban +s
Test-Ban Treaty
test bed +s
test drive
   test drives
   test drove
   test driv|en
   test driv|ing
test driv|er +s
test|ed *adjective*
test|ee +s (one
   subjected to a test)
   [☞ testy, testes]
test|er +s
tes|tes *plural of* testis
test fire
   test fires
   test fired
   test firing
test flight +s
test-fly
   test-flies
   test-flew
   test-flown
   test-flying
tes|ticle +s
tes|ticu|lar
testi|fier +s
test|ify
   testi|fies
   testi|fied
   testi|fy|ing
test|i|ly
test|i|ness
testi|mon|ial
testi|mony
   testi|mon|ies
test|ing *noun*
tes|tis
   tes|tes
test mar|ket +s *noun*
test-market +s +ed
   +ing *verb*
tes|tos|ter|one
test pilot +s *noun*

test-pilot +s +ed
+ing *verb*
test spin +s
test tube +s (test-
tube *when preceding
a noun*)
tes|tu|do
tes|tu|dos or
tes|tu|di|nes
testy (irritable)
test|i|er
test|i|est
[☞ testee, testes]
tet|an|ic
tet|an|ic|ally
tet|an|ize
tet|an|iz|es
tet|an|ized
tet|an|iz|ing
tet|an|oid
teta|nus
tet|any
tetch|i|er *comparative
of* tetchy
tetch|i|est *superlative
of* tetchy
tetch|i|ly
tetch|i|ness
tetchy (irritable)
tetch|i|er
tetch|i|est
tête-à-tête +s
tête-bêche +s
teth|er +s +ed +ing
Tethy|an
Tethys (*Greek Myth*;
Astronomy; *Geology*)
Tet Of|fen|sive
Té|touan (city,
Morocco)
tetra
plural tetra or
tet|ras
tetra|chlor|ide
tetra|cyc|lic
tetra|cy|cline +s
tet|rad +s
tetra|ethyl lead
tetra|gon +s
tet|rag|on|al
tet|rag|on|al|ly
tetra|gram +s
Tetra|gram|ma|ton
tetra|hed|ral
tetra|hed|rite +s
tetra|hed|ron
tetra|hed|rons or
tetra|hedra
**tetra|hydro|
can|nabi|nol**
tet|ral|ogy
tet|ral|ogies
tet|ram|er|ous

tet|ram|eter
Tetra Pak +s
proprietary
tetra|plegia
tetra|plegic +s
tetra|ploid +s
tetra|ploidy
tetra|pod +s
tet|rarch +s
tetra|syllab|ic
tetra|sylla|ble
tetra|valent
tet|rode +s
tetro|do|toxin
tet|rox|ide +s
tet|ter +s
Tet|zel, Jo|hann
(German Dominican
friar)
Teu|ton +s (people)
Teu|ton|ic
Teu|toni|cism
Teu|ton|ic Knights
Tews|ley, Rob|ert
(English dancer)
Tex|ada (island,
Canada)
Tex|an +s
Texas (state, US)
Tex-Mex
text +s
text|book +s
text|book|ish
tex|tile +s
text|less
text|ual
text|ual|ism
text|ual|ist +s
text|u|al|ity
text|u|al|ities
text|ual|ly
tex|tur|al
tex|tur|al|ly
tex|ture
tex|tures
tex|tured
tex|tur|ing
tex|tured *adjective*
tex|ture|less
tex|tur|ize
tex|tur|iz|es
tex|tur|ized
tex|tur|iz|ing
tex|tur|ized *adjective*
tex|tur|ous
Tezel, Jo|hann
(= Tetzel)
TGV (*Train à Grande
Vitesse*)
TGVs
**Thack|eray, Wil|liam
Make|peace**
(English novelist)

Thai (of Thailand)
plural Thai or Thais
Thai|land (country &
gulf, Asia)
thal|amic
thal|amus
thal|ami
thal|as|saemia +s
(*use* thalassemia)
thal|as|semia +s
thal|as|sic
thal|as|so|ther|apist
+s
thal|as|so|ther|apy
thal|er +s (coin)
Thales (Greek
philosopher)
thali +s (Indian meal,
platter)
[☞ thalli]
Thalia (*Greek &
Roman Myth*)
thal|ido|mide
thal|li *plural of* thallus
[☞ thali]
thal|lic
thal|lium
thal|loid
thal|lous (of thallium)
[☞ thallus]
thal|lus (*Botany*)
thal|li
[☞ thallous]
thal|weg +s
Thames (rivers,
England & Canada)
than
thana|to|logic|al
thana|tol|o|gist +s
thana|tol|ogy
Thana|tos
thane +s
thane|dom +s
thank +s +ed +ing
thank|ful
thank|ful|ly
thank|ful|ness
thank|less
thank|less|ly
thank|less|ness
Thanks|giv|ing +s
(holiday)
thanks|giv|ing +s
thank you +s (thank-
you *when preceding a
noun*)
Thant, U (UN
secretary-general)
Thar (desert, India &
Pakistan)
[☞ tahr]
Tharp, Twyla (US
choreographer)

that
that|away
thatch
thatch|es
thatched
thatch|ing
thatched *adjective*
**Thatch|er, Mar|garet
Hilda** (British prime
minister)
thatch|er +s
Thatch|er|ism
Thatch|er|ite +s
thatch|ing *noun*
thauma|turge
thauma|tur|gic
thauma|tur|gic|al
thauma|tur|gist
thauma|turgy
thaw +s +ed +ing
the
the|ater +s (*use*
theatre)
theater-goer +s (*use*
theatre-goer)
theater-going (*use*
theatre-going)
theater-in-the-round
(*use* theatre-in-the-
round)
the|atre +s
theatre-goer +s
theatre-going
theatre-in-the-round
theatre|sports
theat|ric|al
theat|ric|al|ism
theat|ric|al|ity
theat|ric|al|iz|a|tion
theat|ric|al|ize
theat|ric|al|iz|es
theat|ric|al|ized
theat|ric|al|iz|ing
theat|ric|al|ly
theat|rics
Theb|an +s
thebe
plural thebe
Thebes (cities, Greece
& ancient Egypt)
theca
thecae
thec|ate
thé dan|sant
thés dan|sants
thee
theft +s
the|ine (caffeine)
their *adjective*
[☞ there, they're]
theirs
their|selves *informal*
(= themselves)

the|ism +s
the|ist +s
the|is|tic
the|is|tic|al
the|is|tic|ally
The|lon (river, Canada)
them
the|mat|ic
the|mat|ic|ally
thema|tiz|a|tion
thema|tize
  thema|tiz|es
  thema|tized
  thema|tiz|ing
theme
  themes
  themed
  them|ing
themed *adjective*
theme park +s
Them|is (*Greek Myth*)
The|mis|to|cles (Athenian statesman)
them|self
them|selves
then
the|nar +s
thence
thence|forth
thence|for|ward
theo|bro|mine
theo|cen|tric
theo|cen|trism
theoc|racy
  theoc|ra|cies
theo|crat +s
theo|crat|ic
theo|crat|ic|ally
Theoc|ri|tean
Theoc|ri|tus (Greek poet)
theod|i|cean
theod|icy
  theod|icies
theod|o|lite +s
theod|o|lit|ic
Theo|dora (Byzantine empress)
Theo|dor|akis, Mikis (Greek composer & politician)
Theo|doric (Ostrogothic king)
Theo|do|sius I (Roman emperor)
theo|gonic
theog|ony
  theog|o|nies
theo|lo|gian +s
theo|logic|al
theo|logic|ally
theol|o|gist +s

theol|o|gize
  theol|o|giz|es
  theol|o|gized
  theol|o|giz|ing
theol|ogy
  theol|o|gies
theoph|any
  theoph|an|ies
Theo|phras|tus (Greek philosopher)
theo|phyl|line
the|orb|ist +s
the|orbo +s
theor|em +s
theor|em|atic
theor|etic
theor|etic|al
theor|etic|al|ly
theor|eti|cian +s
theor|ist +s
theor|iz|a|tion +s
theor|ize
  theor|iz|es
  theor|ized
  theor|iz|ing
theor|iz|er +s
theory
  theor|ies
theo|soph|ic
theo|soph|ic|al
theo|soph|ic|ally
theos|o|phist +s
theos|o|phy
  theos|o|phies
The Pas (town, Canada)
Thera (Greek island)
thera|peut|ic
thera|peut|ic|al
thera|peut|ic|ally
thera|peut|ics
ther|apist +s
ther|ap|sid +s
ther|apy
  ther|apies
Thera|vada (*Buddhism*)
there (in that place)
  [☞ their, they're]
there|about (= thereabouts)
there|abouts
there|after
there|at
there|by
there|for (for the thing mentioned: 'liability therefor')
  [☞ therefore]
there|fore (for that reason)
  [☞ therefor]
there|from

there|in
there|in|after
there|in|to
there|of
there|on
there's
Ther|esa
  [☞ Teresa]
Thé|rèse of Li|sieux (saint)
there|to
there|to|fore
there|under
there|unto
there|upon
there|with
there|withal
theri|an|throp|ic
therio|morph|ic
therm +s
ther|mae
ther|mal +s
ther|mal|ly
ther|mic
thermi|dor
ther|mion +s
ther|mion|ic
ther|mion|ics
ther|mis|tor +s
ther|mit (= thermite)
ther|mite
thermo|chem|ical
thermo|chem|istry
thermo|cline +s
thermo|couple +s
thermo|dynam|ic
thermo|dynam|ic|ally
thermo|dynami|cist +s
thermo|dynam|ics
thermo|elec|tric
thermo|elec|tric|ally
thermo|elec|tri|city
thermo|gen|esis
thermo|gram +s
thermo|graph +s
thermo|graph|ic
therm|og|raphy
thermo|karst +s
thermo|labile
thermo|lumin|es|cence
thermo|lumin|es|cent
therm|oly|sis
therm|oly|tic
therm|om|eter +s
therm|om|et|ric
therm|om|et|ric|al
therm|om|etry
thermo|nuclear

Thermo|pane +s *proprietary*
thermo|phile +s
thermo|phil|ic
thermo|pile +s
thermo|plas|tic +s
Therm|opy|lae (ancient battle site, Greece)
thermo|regu|late
  thermo|regu|lates
  thermo|regu|lat|ed
  thermo|regu|lat|ing
thermo|regu|la|tion
thermo|regu|la|tory
Ther|mos *proprietary*
  Ther|mos|es
thermo|set
thermo|set|ting
thermo|sphere
thermo|stabil|ity
thermo|stable
thermo|stat +s
thermo|stat|ic
thermo|stat|ic|ally
thermo|tac|tic
thermo|taxic
thermo|taxis
thermo|trop|ic
thermo|trop|ism
thero|pod +s
the|saur|us
  the|saur|us|es or the|sauri
these
The|seus (*Greek Myth*)
thesis
  theses
thes|pian +s
Thes|pis (Greek poet)
Thes|sa|lía (= Thessaly)
Thes|sa|lian +s
Thes|sa|lon|ians
Thes|sa|lon|ica (= Thessaloníki)
Thes|sa|lon|íki (city, Greece)
Thes|saly (region, Greece)
theta +s
Thet|ford Mines (city, Canada)
Thetis (*Greek Myth*)
theur|gic
theur|gical
theur|gist +s
theur|gy
thew +s
thewy
  thew|i|er
  thew|i|est
they

they'd
they'll
they're (they are)
[☞ their, there]
they've
thia|min (use
thiamine)
thia|mine
thick +er +est +s
thick|en +s +ed +ing
thick|en|er +s
thick|en|ing +s noun
thick|et +s
thick|head +s
thick-headed
thick-headed|ness
thick|ish
thick|ly
thick|ness
thick|ness|es
thick|set
thick-skinned
thick-skulled
thick-witted
thief
thieves
Thiers, (Louis)
Adolphe (French
historian &
statesman)
thieve
thieves
thieved
thiev|ing
thiev|ery
thieves
thiev|ing adjective
thiev|ish
thiev|ish|ly
thiev|ish|ness
thigh +s
thigh bone +s
thigh-high
thigh-slapper +s
thigh-slapping
thig|mo|trop|ic
thig|mo|trop|ism
thill +s
thim|ble +s
thimble|berry
thimble|ber|ries
thimble|ful +s
thimble|rig
thimble|rigger +s
Thim|bu
(= Thimphu,
Bhutan)
thi|mero|sal
Thim|phu (capital of
Bhutan)

thin
thin|ner
thin|nest
thins
thinned
thin|ning
thine
thing +s
thing|a|ma|bob +s
thing|a|ma|jig +s
thing|ummy
thing|um|mies
thingy
thing|ies
thin|horn sheep
plural thin|horn
sheep
think
thinks
thought
think|ing
think|able
think|er +s
think|ing noun &
adjective
think piece +s
think-tank +s
thin|ly
thin|ner +s
thin|ness
thin|ness|es
thin|ning adjective
thin|nings
thin-skinned
Thin|su|late
proprietary
thiol +s
thio|pen|tal so|dium
thio|sul|fate +s (use
thiosulphate)
thio|sul|phate +s
thio|urea
third +s
third-best
third class (third-
class when preceding
a noun)
third de|gree (third-
degree when
preceding a noun)
third-genera|tion
third hand adverb
(heard it third hand)
third-hand adjective
(third-hand
information)
third|ly
third-rate
Third Reich
third-string
third-string|er +s
Third World
thirst +s

thirst|i|ly
thirst-quench|er +s
thirst-quench|ing
thirsty
thirst|i|er
thirst|i|est
thir|teen +s
Thir|teen Col|onies
(N American History)
thir|teenth +s
thir|ti|eth +s
thirty
thir|ties
thirty-eight +s
thirty-eighth +s
thirty-fifth +s
thirty-first +s
thirty-five +s
thirty|fold
thirty-four +s
thirty-fourth +s
thirty|ish
thirty-nine +s
Thirty-nine Arti|cles
thirty-ninth +s
thirty-one +s
thirty-second +s
thirty-seven +s
thirty-seventh +s
thirty-six
thirty-sixes
thirty-sixth +s
thirty|some|thing +s
thirty-third +s
30-30 (gun, cartridge)
30-30s
Thirty Thou|sand
Islands (in Canada)
thirty-three +s
thirty-two +s
Thirty Years War
this
Thisbe (Roman Myth)
this|tle +s
thistle|down
this-worldli|ness
this-worldly
thith|er
thixo|trop|ic
thix|otropy
tho' (= though)
thole
tholes
tholed
thol|ing
thole-pin +s
thol|os
thol|oi
Thom, Ron|ald James
(Cdn architect)
Thom|as (apostle)

Thom|as, Aud|rey
Grace (Cdn writer)
Thom|as, Dylan
Mar|lais (Welsh
poet)
Thom|as à Kem|pis
(German theologian)
Thom|as Aqui|nas
(saint)
Thom|as More
(English humanist
scholar & Lord
Chancellor)
Thom|as of
Ercel|doune
(Scottish poet)
Thom|as the
Rhym|er
(= Thomas of
Erceldoune)
Thom|ism
Thom|ist +s
Thom|is|tic
Thomp|son
• (city & river, Canada;
surname)
• (= Nlaka'pamux,
Aboriginal people &
language)
[☞ Thomson]
Thomp|son, Sir
Ben|ja|min (Count
Rumford, English
physicist)
Thomp|son, Daley
(English athlete)
Thomp|son, David
(Cdn fur trader &
explorer)
Thomp|son, Ed|ward
Pal|mer (English
historian & activist)
Thomp|son, Emma
(English actress)
Thomp|son, Fran|cis
(English poet)
Thomp|son, Sir John
Spar|row David
(Cdn prime minister)
Thomp|son|ian
Thom|son (surname)
[☞ Thompson]
Thom|son, Sir
George Paget
(English physicist)
Thom|son, James
(Scottish poets)
Thom|son, Sir
Jo|seph John
(English physicist)
Thom|son, Roy
Her|bert, 1st Baron
Thom|son of Fleet

(Cdn-born media entrepreneur)

Thom|son, Thom|as John ('Tom') (Cdn painter)

Thom|son, Vir|gil (US composer)

Thom|son, Sir Wil|liam (Lord Kelvin)

thong +s

thonged

Thor (*Scandinavian Myth*)

thor|acal

thor|acic

thora|cot|omy thora|cot|omies

thor|ax thor|ax|es or thor|aces

Thor|eau, Henry David (US poet)

Thor|eau|vian

thor|ium

Thorn (= Toruń, Poland)

thorn +s

thorn|apple +s

thorn|back +s

Thorn|dike, Dame Agnes Sybil (English actress)

Thorn|dike, Ed|ward Lee (US psychologist)

thorn|i|ly

thorn|i|ness

thorn|less

thorn|proof

thorn|tail +s

thorny thorn|i|er thorn|i|est

Thor|old (city, Canada)

thor|ough

thor|ough bass thor|ough bass|es

Thorough|bred +s (breed of racehorses descending from English mares & Arabian stallions)

thorough|bred +s (any purebred horse etc.)

thorough|fare +s

thorough|going

thorough|ly

thorough|ness

thorp +s (village)

Thorpe, James Fran|cis ('Jim') (US athlete)

thorpe +s (village: *use* thorp)

Thors|havn (= Tórshavn, capital of the Faeroe Islands)

Thor|vald|sen, Ber|tel (Danish sculptor)

Thor|wald|sen, Ber|tel (= Thorvaldsen)

those

Thoth (*Egyptian Myth*)

thou
• (you)
• (thousand)
   plural thou or thous

though

thought +s *noun*

thought|ful

thought|ful|ly

thought|ful|ness

thought|less

thought|less|ly

thought|less|ness

thought out (thought-out *when preceding a noun*)

thought-provok|ing

thought-wave +s

thou|sand *plural* thou|sands or thou|sand

thousand|fold

Thou|sand Island (salad dressing)

Thou|sand Islands (island groups, N America & Indonesia)

thou|sandth +s

Thrace (ancient country, Balkan Peninsula; region, Turkey & Greece)

Thra|cian +s

thral|dom (*use* thralldom)

Thrale, Mrs. (Hester Lynch Piozzi)

thrall

thrall|dom

thrash (lash, whip; scold; flail; sail against the wind; party; in 'thrash out'; *Music; for* separate grain by shaking or beating *use* thresh)

thrash|es

thrashed

thrash|ing

thrash|er +s (*Music;* one who flails etc.; songbird; *for* person or machine that threshes grain *use* thresher)
   [☞ thresher]

thrash metal (thrash-metal *when preceding a noun*)

thrashy thrash|i|er thrash|i|est

thread +s +ed +ing

thread|bare

thread|ed *adjective*

thread|er +s

thread|fin *plural* thread|fin or thread|fins

thread|like

Thread|needle Street (in London)

thread|worm +s

thready thread|i|er thread|i|est

threat +s

threat|en +s +ed +ing

threat|ened *adjective*

threat|en|ing *adjective*

threat|en|ing|ly

three +s

three-and-a-half +s (apartment)

three-bagger +s

three-base hit +s

three-card

three-chord

three-colour

three-coloured

three-cornered

3-D (three-dimensional)

three-day

three-decker +s

three-dimension|al

three-dimension|al|ity

three-dimensional|ize three-dimensional|iz|es three-dimensional|ized three-dimensional|iz|ing

three-dimension|al|ly

three|fold

three-handed

three-in-one

three-legged

three-line

three-martini lunch three-martini lunch|es

Three Mile Island (in the US)

three-on-one +s

three-on-three

three-peat +s +ed +ing

three|pence

three|penny

three-phase

three-piece +s

three-piecer +s

three-pitch

three-ply

three-point

three-point|er +s

three-prong

three-pronged

three-quarter +s

three-quarter back +s

three-ring

three score

three-sixty three-sixties

three|some +s

three-star

three strikes (US legislation)

three-way

three-wheel|er +s

thren|odic

thren|odist

thren|ody thren|odies

threo|nine

thresh (separate grain by beating or shaking; *for* lash, whip, *or* flail about *use* thrash)

thresh|es

threshed

thresh|ing
   [☞ thrash]

thresh|er +s (person or machine that threshes grain; shark)
   [☞ thrasher]

thresher|man thresher|men

thresh|ing floor

thresh|ing ma|chine +s

thresh|old +s

threw *past tense of*
  throw
  [☞ thru, through]
thrice
thrift +s
thrift|i|er
thrift|i|est
thrift|i|ly
thrift|i|ness
thrift|less
thrift|less|ly
thrift|less|ness
thrift shop +s (thrift-
  shop *when preceding
  a noun*)
thrift store +s (thrift-
  store *when preceding
  a noun*)
thrifty
  thrift|i|er
  thrift|i|est
thrill +s +ed +ing
thrilled *adjective*
thrill|er +s
thrill|ing *adjective*
thrill|ing|ly
thrill-seeker +s
thrill-seeking
thrips
  plural thrips
thrive
  thrives
  thrived or throve
  thrived or thriv|en
  thriv|ing
thriv|ing *adjective*
thro' (*in literary use*
  = through)
  [☞ throe, throw]
throat +s
throat|ed *adjective*
throat|i|ly
throat|i|ness
throaty
  throat|i|er
  throat|i|est
throb
  throbs
  throbbed
  throb|bing
throe +s (pang,
  anguish; in 'in the
  throes of')
  [☞ throw]
throm|bi
throm|bin +s
throm|bo|cyte +s
throm|bo|cyto|penia
throm|bo|cyto|penic
throm|bo|embol|ism
throm|bose
  throm|bos|es

throm|bosed
throm|bos|ing
throm|bo|sis
  throm|bo|ses
throm|bot|ic
throm|bus
  throm|bi
throne (chair, seat;
  heavenly being)
  thrones
  throned
  thron|ing
  [☞ thrown]
throne|less
throne room +s
Throne Speech
  Throne Speech|es
throng +s +ed +ing
thros|tle +s
throt|tle
  throt|tles
  throt|tled
  throt|tling
throt|tler +s
through (from one
  end to the other etc.)
  [☞ threw]
through|out
through|put
through|way +s
throve
throw (propel;
  confuse; host;
  deliberately lose;
  turn; light rug etc.;
  Geology)
  throws
  threw
  thrown
  throw|ing
  [☞ throe]
throw|able
throw away *verb*
  throws away
  threw away
  thrown away
  throw|ing away
throw|away +s
  adjective & noun
throw back *verb*
  throws back
  threw back
  thrown back
  throw|ing back
throw|back +s *noun*
throw|er +s
throw in *verb*
  throws in
  threw in
  thrown in
  throw|ing in
throw-in +s *noun*
thrown *past participle
  of* throw

throw rug +s
thru (*in commercial use*
  = through)
  [☞ threw]
thrum
  thrums
  thrummed
  thrum|ming
thrummed *adjective*
thrum|ming *noun*
thrush
  thrush|es
thrust
  thrusts
  thrust
  thrust|ing
thrust|er +s
Thu|cydi|des (Greek
  historian)
thud
  thuds
  thud|ded
  thud|ding
thud|ding|ly
Thug +s (*History*
  member of Indian
  criminal group)
thug +s (violent
  criminal; bully)
thug|gee
thug|gery
thug|gish
thug|gish|ly
thug|gish|ness
thuja +s
Thule (ancient
  northern land; Inuit
  culture; settlement,
  Greenland)
thul|ium
thumb +s +ed +ing
thumbed *adjective*
thumb index *noun*
  thumb in|dex|es
thumb-index *verb*
  thumb-indexes
  thumb-indexed
  thumb-indexing
thumb-indexed
  adjective
thumb|less
thumb|nail +s
thumb|print +s
thumb|screw +s
thumbs-down +s
thumb-sucker +s
thumb-sucking
thumbs-up +s
thumb|tack +s +ed
  +ing
thump +s +ed +ing
thump|er +s

thump|ing +s
  adjective & noun
thump|ing|ly
thun|der +s +ed +ing
Thun|der Bay (city,
  Canada)
thunder|bird +s
thunder|bolt +s
thunder|clap +s
thunder|cloud +s
thun|der|er +s
thunder|head +s
thun|der|ing *adjective*
thun|der|ing|ly
thun|der mug +s
thun|der|ous
thun|der|ous|ly
thunder|shower +s
thunder|storm +s
thunder|strik|ing
thunder|struck
thun|dery
thunk
  • *verb* (thud)
    thunks
    thunked
    thunk|ing
  • *jocular past & past
    participle of* think
**Thur|ber, James
  Gro|ver** (US
  humorist)
Thurber|esque
thur|ible +s
thur|ifer +s
Thur|in|gia (state,
  Germany)
Thurs|day +s
Thur|so (town,
  Scotland)
thus
thus|ly
Thut|mose (Egyptian
  kings)
thuya +s (*use* thuja)
thwack +s +ed +ing
thwaite +s
thwart +s +ed +ing
thy
Thy|es|tean
Thy|es|tes (*Greek
  Myth*)
thyme +s (herb)
thymi *plural of*
  thymus
thym|ic
thy|mi|dine
thy|mine
thy|mol
thy|mus
  thy|mus|es or thymi
thy|ris|tor +s
thy|roid +s

thyro|toxi|co|sis
thy|rox|in (*use*
   thyroxine)
thy|rox|ine
thyr|sus
   thyr|si
thy|self
ti +s (houseplant with
   edible roots; *Music*)
   [☞ tea, tee, T]
Tia|mat (*Babylonian
   Myth*)
Tian|an|men Square
   (in China)
Tian|jin (city, China)
ti|ara +s
ti|araed
Tiber (river, Italy)
Ti|ber|ias, Lake
   (= Sea of Galilee,
   Israel)
   [☞ Tiberius]
Ti|ber|ius (Roman
   emperor)
   [☞ Tiberias]
Ti|bes|ti (mountain
   range, Africa)
Tibet (region, Asia)
Tibet|an +s
Tibeto-Burman
tibia
   tib|iae or tib|ias
tib|ial
tibio|tar|sus
   tibio|tar|si
tic +s (twitch; in *tic
   douloureux*; quirk)
   [☞ tick]
Ticat +s
   (= Tiger-Cat)
tic dou|lou|reux
Ti|cino (canton,
   Switzerland)
tick +s +ed +ing
   (clicking sound;
   check mark; slight
   quantity; function;
   bug; in 'on tick';
   fabric, pillow
   covering)
   [☞ tic, tic
   douloureux]
tick-borne
ticked *adjective*
tick|er +s
ticker|tape
tick|et
   tick|ets
   ticket|ed
   ticket|ing
ticket|ed *adjective*
tick|et hold|er +s
ticket|less

tickety-boo
tick|ing *noun*
tick|lace +s
tickle
   tickles
   tickled
   tick|ling
tickle|ass (*use*
   ticklace)
   tickle|ass|es
tick|ler +s
tick|lish
tick|lish|ly
tick|lish|ness
tick|ly
tick-tack *Brit.*
   (*Gambling*)
tick-tack-toe +s (*use*
   tic-tac-toe)
tick-tock +s
tick-trefoil +s
ticky-tacky
tic-tac *Brit.* (*Gambling*:
   use tick-tack)
tic-tac-toe +s
tidal
tidal|ly
tidal wave +s
tid|bit +s
tiddledy|wink +s
   (= tiddlywink)
tid|dler +s
tid|dly
   tid|dli|er
   tid|dli|est
tiddly|wink +s
tide (of the sea etc.;
   trend; flow; in 'tide
   over')
   tides
   tided
   tiding
   [☞ tied]
tide|land +s
tide|less
tide line +s
tide|mark +s
tide pool +s
tide-waiter +s
tide|water +s
tide|way +s
tidi|ly
tidi|ness
tid|ings *plural noun*
tidy
   tidi|er
   tidi|est
   tidies
   tidied
   tidy|ing
tie (bind with rope)
   ties

tied
   tying
   [☞ Thai, tae kwon
   do, Tai Chi]
tie-back +s
tie|break +s
tie|break|er +s
tie|break|ing
tie clip +s
tied *adjective &
   conjugated form of*
   tie
   [☞ tide]
Tiede|mann
   (mountain, Canada)
tie down *verb*
   ties down
   tied down
   tying down
tie-down +s *noun*
tie-dye
   tie-dyes
   tie-dyed
   tie-dying
tie-dyed *adjective*
tie in *verb*
   ties in
   tied in
   tying in
tie-in +s *noun*
tie|less
tie-line +s
Tien Shan
   (mountains, Asia)
Tien|tsin (= Tianjin,
   China)
tie pin +s
Tiep|olo, Gio|van|ni
   Bat|tis|ta (Italian
   painter)
tier[1] +s (level;
   stratum)
   [☞ tear, Tyr]
tier[2] +s (person who
   ties)
   [☞ tire, Tyre]
tierce +s
tiered
Tier|ra del Fuego
   (island, S America)
tie stall +s (tie-stall
   *when preceding a
   noun*)
tie up *verb*
   ties up
   tied up
   tying up
tie-up +s *noun*
TIFF (Tagged Image
   File Format)
tiff +s
Tif|fany, Louis
   Comfort (US glass-
   maker)

tif|fany (lamp)
   tif|fan|ies
tif|fin +s
Tif|lis (*former name for*
   Tbilisi, Georgia)
tiger +s
Tiger-Cat +s (CFL
   team)
tiger cat +s
tiger eye +s (= tiger's
   eye)
tiger|ish
tiger|ish|ly
tiger's eye +s
tight +er +est
tight-arse +s
tight-arsed
tight-ass
   tight-asses
tight-assed
tight|en +s +ed +ing
tight end +s
tight|er *comparative of*
   tight
   [☞ titre]
tight-fisted
tight-fisted|ness
tight-fitting
tight-knit
tight-lipped
tight|ly
tight|ly knit
tight|ness
   tight|ness|es
tight|rope +s
tights
tight|wad +s
tight|wad|dery
Tiglath-pileser
   (Assyrian kings)
tig|lon +s
tigon +s
Ti|gray (province,
   Ethiopia)
Ti|gray|an +s
Tigre (= Tigray,
   Ethiopia)
Tigre|an +s
   (= Tigrayan)
tig|ress
   tig|ress|es
Tig|ris (river, Asia)
Tihwa (*former name
   for* Urumqi, China)
Tiju|ana (town,
   Mexico)
Tikal (ancient Mayan
   city, Guatemala)
tiki|nagan +s
tikka
'til (until)
   [☞ till]

ti|lapia
  plural ti|lapia or
  ti|lap|ias
Til|burg (city, the
  Netherlands)
Til|bury (port,
  England)
til|bury
  til|bur|ies
tilde +s
Til|den, Wil|liam
  Tatem (US tennis
  player)
tile
  tiles
  tiled
  tiling
  tiled *adjective*
tile|fish
  plural tile|fish or
  tile|fish|es
tiler +s
tiling +s *noun*
till +s +ed +ing (until;
  money drawer; plow
  land etc.; clay)
till|able
till|age
till|er +s +ed +ing
till|er|ing *noun*
Til|ley, Sir Sam|uel
  Leon|ard (Cdn
  politician)
  [☞ Tilly]
Til|lich, Paul
  Jo|han|nes
  (German-born
  theologian)
Till|son|burg (town,
  Canada)
Tilly, Count Johan
  Tser|claes von
  (Flemish soldier)
tilt +s +ed +ing
tilt|er +s
tilth
Tima|ru (town, New
  Zealand)
tim|bal +s
  (kettledrum)
  [☞ timbale]
tim|bale +s (*Food*;
  Latin American
  dance drum)
  [☞ timbal]
tim|ber +s (wood,
  trees, etc.)
  [☞ timbre]
tim|bered
tim|ber frame +s
timber-framed
tim|ber fram|er +s
tim|ber|ing

timber|jack +s
timber|land +s
timber|line +s
timber|man
  timber|men
tim|ber wolf
  tim|ber wolves
tim|bral (of a timbre)
  [☞ timbrel]
tim|bre +s (sound
  quality)
  [☞ timber]
tim|brel +s
  (tambourine)
  [☞ timbral]
Tim|buc|too
  (= Timbuktu)
Tim|buk|tu (town,
  Mali; remote place)
time (duration,
  multiplication, etc.)
  times
  timed
  tim|ing
  [☞ thyme]
time bomb +s
time cap|sule +s
time clock +s
time code +s
time-consum|ing
time frame +s
time-honored (*use*
  time-honoured)
time-honoured
time|keep|er +s
time|keep|ing
time lag +s
time-lapse
time|less
time|less|ly
time|less|ness
time|line +s
time|li|ness
time lock +s
time-locked
time|ly
  time|li|er
  time|li|est
time out +s
time|piece +s
timer +s
times
time saver +s
time-saving
time scale +s
time-sensitive
time-server +s
time-serving
time-share +s
time-sharing
time sheet +s
time-shift +s +ed
  +ing

time slot +s
time span +s
Times Square (in
  New York)
time switch
  time switch|es
time|table
  time|tables
  time|tabled
  time|tabling
time-tested
time travel
time travel|ler +s
time trial +s
time warp +s
time-waster +s
time-wasting
time-worn
time zone +s
timid
timid|ity
  timid|ities
timid|ly
timid|ness
tim|ing +s *noun*
Ti|misk|aming (lake,
  Canada)
Timi|şoara (city,
  Romania)
Tim|mins (city,
  Canada)
Timor (island, Malay
  Archipelago; sea,
  Indian Ocean)
Timor|ese
  plural Timor|ese
timor|ous
timor|ous|ly
timor|ous|ness
Tim|othy (saint)
tim|othy (grass)
tim|pani
tim|pan|ist +s
tin
  tins
  tinned
  tin|ning
tina|mou +s
Tin|ber|gen, Jan
  (Dutch economist)
Tin|ber|gen,
  Niko|laas (Dutch
  ethologist)
tinc|tor|ial
tinc|ture
  tinc|tures
  tinc|tured
  tinc|tur|ing
Tin|dal, Wil|liam
  (= Tyndale)
  [☞ Tyndall]

Tin|dale, Wil|liam
  (= Tyndale)
  [☞ Tyndall]
tin|der
tinder|box
  tinder|boxes
tin|dery
tine +s (prong)
  [☞ Tyne]
tinea
tined
tin|foil +s
Ting, Sam|uel Chao
  Chung (US physicist)
ting +s +ed +ing
tinge
  tin|ges
  tinged
  tinge|ing or tin|ging
tin|gle
  tin|gles
  tin|gled
  tin|gling
tin|gly
  tin|gli|er
  tin|gli|est
tin|horn +s
tini|er *comparative of*
  tiny
  [☞ tinnier]
tini|est *superlative of*
  tiny
  [☞ tinniest]
tini|ly (in a tiny way)
  [☞ tinnily]
tini|ness
  (diminutiveness)
  [☞ tinniness]
tin|ker +s +ed +ing
tin|ker|er +s
tin|ker|ing +s *noun*
Tin|ker|toy
  proprietary
tin|kle
  tin|kles
  tin|kled
  tink|ling
tin|kly
tin Liz|zie +s
tinned *adjective*
tin|ner +s
tin|nie +s *noun* (*use*
  tinny)
tin|ni|er *comparative*
  of tinny
tin|ni|est *superlative of*
  tinny
tin|ni|ly (in a tinny
  way)
tin|ni|ness (tinny
  condition)
tin|nitus

tin|ny (like tin)
tin|ni|er
tin|ni|est
tin|nies
Tin Pan Alley
tin plate *noun*
tin-plate *verb*
  tin-plates
  tin-plated
  tin-plating
tin-plated *adjective*
tin|pot
tin|sel
  tin|sels
  tin|selled
  or tin|seled
  tin|sel|ling
  or tin|sel|ing
tin|seled *adjective (use*
  tinselled)
tin|selled *adjective*
tin|sel|ly
Tinsel|town
  (Hollywood)
tin|sely (*use* tinselly)
tin|smith +s
tin|smith|ing
tin|snips
tin|stone
tint +s +ed +ing
Tin|tagel (village,
  England)
tint|ed *adjective*
tint|er +s
T-inter|sec|tion +s
tin|tin|nabu|la|tion
  +s
Tin|tor|etto (Italian
  painter)
tin|type +s
tin|ware
tiny (small)
  tini|er
  tini|est
  [☞ tinny]
tip
  tips
  tipped
  tip|ping
tipi +s (*use* teepee)
tip in *verb*
  tips in
  tipped in
  tip|ping in
tip-in +s *noun*
tip|less
tip off *verb*
  tips off
  tipped off
  tip|ping off
tip|off +s *noun*
tipped *adjective*
tip|per +s

Tip|per|ary (county,
  Republic of Ireland)
tip|pet +s
tip|ple
  tip|ples
  tip|pled
  tip|pling
tip|pler +s
Tip|poo Sahib
  (= Tipu Sahib,
  sultan of Mysore)
tippy
  tip|pi|er
  tip|pi|est
tippy|toe
  tippy|toes
  tippy|toed
  tippy|toe|ing
tip|sheet +s
tipsi|ly
tipsi|ness
tip|staff
  tip|staffs or
  tip|staves
tip|ster +s
tipsy
  tipsi|er
  tipsi|est
tipsy cake +s
tip|toe
  tip|toes
  tip|toed
  tip|toe|ing
tip-top +s
tip up *verb*
  tips up
  tipped up
  tip|ping up
tip-up +s *noun &*
  adjective
Tipu Sahib (sultan of
  Mysore)
ti|rade +s
tira|mi|sù
Tir|ana (capital of
  Albania)
Tir|anë (= Tirana)
tire (exhaust; wheel)
  tires
  tired
  tiring
  [☞ tier, Tyre]
tired *adjective*
tired|ly
tired|ness
Tiree (island, Inner
  Hebrides)
tire|less
tire|less|ly
tire|less|ness
Ti|resi|as (*Greek Myth*)
tire|some
tire|some|ly

tire|some|ness
Tîrgu Mureş (city,
  Romania)
Tir|ich Mir (mountain,
  Pakistan)
tiring *adjective*
Tir-nan-Og (*Irish
  Myth*)
Tir|pitz, Al|fred von
  (German admiral)
Tirso de Mol|ina
  (Spanish dramatist)
Tiru|chi|ra|palli (city,
  India)
'tis
tis|ane
Ti|siph|one (*Greek
  Myth*)
tis|sue +s
tis|suey
Tisza (river, Europe)
tit +s
Ti|tan +s (*Greek Myth;
  Astronomy*)
ti|tan +s (powerful
  person or thing)
titan|ate (salt of
  titanic acid)
Ti|tan|ia (fairy queen;
  Astronomy)
Ti|tan|ic (ship)
ti|tan|ic
ti|tan|ic|ally
titan|ite +s (mineral)
ti|tan|ium
titch
  titch|es
titch|ie (*use* titchy)
  titch|i|er
  titch|i|est
titchy
  titch|i|er
  titch|i|est
titer (concentration of
  a solution or
  antibody: *use* titre)
  [☞ tighter]
tit|fer +s
tit-for-tat
tith|able
tithe
  tithes
  tithed
  tith|ing
tith|ing +s *noun*
Tith|onus (*Greek
  Myth*)
titi +s (monkey)
  [☞ titty]
Ti|tian (Italian painter)
ti|tian (colour)
Titian|esque

Titi|caca (lake, Peru–
  Bolivia border)
tit|il|late
  tit|il|lates
  tit|il|lat|ed
  tit|il|lat|ing
tit|il|lat|ing *adjective*
tit|il|lat|ing|ly
tit|il|la|tion
titi|vate
  titi|vates
  titi|vat|ed
  titi|vat|ing
titi|va|tion +s
title
  titles
  titled
  titling
titled *adjective*
title|hold|er +s
title page +s
titlist +s
tit|mouse
  tit|mice
Tito (Yugoslav
  statesman)
Tito|grad (*former
  name for* **Podgorica**,
  Montenegrin capital)
Tito|ism
Tito|ist +s
ti|trat|able
ti|trate
  ti|trates
  ti|trat|ed
  ti|trat|ing
ti|tra|tion +s
titre +s (concentration
  of a solution or
  antibody)
ti tree +s (houseplant
  with edible roots)
  [☞ tea tree]
tit|ter +s +ed +ing
tit|tle +s
tittle-tattle
  tittle-tattles
  tittle-tattled
  tittle-tattling
tit|tup
  tit|tups
  tit|tupped
  or tit|tuped
  tit|tup|ping
  or tit|tup|ing
titty (breast; in 'tough
  titty')
  tit|ties
titu|ba|tion
titu|lar
titu|lar|ly
Titus (Roman
  emperor; saint)

Tiu (*Germanic Myth*)

tiz
  tiz|zes

tizz (*use* tiz)
  tizz|es

tizzy
  tiz|zies

T-joint +s

TKO (technical knockout)
- *noun*
  TKOs
- *verb*
  TKO's
  TKO'd
  TKO'ing

Tlax|cala (state & its capital, Mexico)

Tlax|calan +s

TLC (tender loving care)

Tlem|cen (city, Algeria)

Tlin|git
  plural Tlin|git *or* Tlin|gits

T-lympho|cyte +s

TNT (explosive)

T.O. (Toronto, Ontario)

to *preposition* & *adverb* (in 'go to bed' etc.; introducing an infinitive; in 'come to' etc.)
  [☞ too, two]

toad +s (amphibian)
  [☞ toed]

toad-eater +s

toad|flax
  toad|flax|es

toad-in-the-hole

toad|let +s

toad|stool +s

toady (obsequious person)
  toad|ies
  toad|ied
  toady|ing
  [☞ tody]

toady|ing *adjective*

toady|ish

toady|ism

to and fro *adverb*

to-and-fro *noun*
  tos-and-fros

toast +s +ed +ing

toast|er +s

toast|i|ness

toast|master +s

toast|mis|tress
  toast|mis|tress|es

toasty
  toast|i|er
  toast|i|est

To|bac|co (nation, language)

to|bac|co +s

to|bac|co|nist +s

To|bago (island, West Indies)

Toba|go|nian +s

to-be

Tobey, Mark (US painter)
  [☞ Toby]

Tobin, Brian Vin|cent (Cdn politician)

To|bique (river, Canada)

Tobit (*Apocrypha*)

to|bog|gan +s +ed +ing

to|bog|gan|er +s

to|bog|gan|ing *noun*

to|bog|gan|ist +s

To|bruk (city, Libya)

Toby (jug)
  Tob|ies
  [☞ Tobey]

To|can|tins (river & state, Brazil)

toc|cata +s

Toch|ar|ian

tock +s +ed +ing (hollow sound; clock noise)
  [☞ talk]

toco|pher|ol +s

Tocque|ville, Alex|is Charles Henri Mau|rice Clé|rel de (French writer)

toc|sin +s (alarm)
  [☞ toxin]

tod (in 'on one's tod')
  [☞ Todd]

to|day +s

Todd, Alex|an|der Ro|ber|tus, Baron (Scottish biochemist)

tod|dle
  tod|dles
  tod|dled
  tod|dling

tod|dler +s

toddler|hood

toddy
  tod|dies

to-do +s

tody (bird)
  to|dies
  [☞ toady]

toe (part of a foot etc.)
  toes
  toed
  toe|ing
  [☞ tow]

toe|cap +s

toe|clip +s

toed *adjective* (having a toe or toes)
  [☞ toad]

toe|hold +s

toe|less

toe loop +s

toe|nail +s +ed +ing

toe pick +s

toe|rag

toe|shoe +s

toff +s

tof|fee +s

toffee-apple +s

toffee-nosed

tofu

tofu bur|ger +s

tog
  togs
  togged
  tog|ging

toga +s

toga'd

togaed (*use* toga'd)

to|geth|er

to|geth|er|ness

tog|gery

tog|gle
  tog|gles
  tog|gled
  tog|gling

Togli|at|ti (city, Russia)

Togo (country, Africa)

Togo|lese
  plural Togo|lese

To|ho|ku (region, Japan)

toil +s +ed +ing (labour)

toile +s (*Textiles*)

toil|er +s

toi|let +s (bathroom fixture; in 'make one's toilet')

toi|letry
  toi|let|ries

toi|lette (in 'make one's toilette': *use* toilet)
  [☞ toilet]

toi|let train +s +ed +ing

toils

toil|some

toil|some|ly

toil-worn

toing and fro|ing

Tojo, Hi|deki (Japanese prime minister)

toka|mak +s

To|kay +s

toke
  tokes
  toked
  tok|ing

Tok|elau (W Pacific island group)

tok|en +s

token|ism

token|is|tic

Toku|ga|wa (shogunate)

Tokyo (capital of Japan)

Tokyo|ite +s

Tol|bu|khin (*former name for* Dobrich, Bulgaria)

told

tole (lacquered or enamelled metal)
  [☞ toll]

To|led|an +s

To|ledo (cities, Spain & US)

tol|er|abil|ity

tol|er|able

tol|er|able|ness

tol|er|ably

tol|er|ance +s

tol|er|ant

tol|er|ant|ly

tol|er|ate
  tol|er|ates
  tol|er|at|ed
  tol|er|at|ing

tol|er|a|tion

tol|er|ator +s

Tol|kien, John Ron|ald Reuel (English novelist)

Tolkien|esque

toll +s +ed +ing (charge; damage, cost; ring a bell)
  [☞ tole]

toll booth +s

toll-free

toll|gate
  toll|gates
  toll|gat|ed
  toll|gat|ing

toll|gat|ing *noun*

toll house +s (toll booth)

toll|house (cookie)

Tol|mie, Simon Fraser (Cdn politician)
Tol|pud|dle mar|tyrs
Tol|stoy, Leo (Russian writer)
Tolstoy|an
tolt +s
Tol|tec +s
Tol|tec|an
tolu
To|lu|ca (city, Mexico)
To|lu|ca de Lerdo (= Toluca)
tolu|ene
tolu|ic
tolu|ol
Tol|yat|ti (= Togliatti, Russia)
tom +s
  [☞ Thom]
toma|hawk +s +ed +ing
toma|til|lo +s
to|mato
  to|ma|toes
to|mato|ey
tomb +s
tom|bac
Tom|baugh, Clyde Wil|liam (US astronomer)
tom|bo|la +s (raffle)
tom|bo|lo +s (spit joining an island to mainland)
Tom|bouc|tou (= Timbuktu, Mali)
tom|boy +s
tom|boy|ish
tom|boy|ish|ly
tom|boy|ish|ness
tomb|stone +s
tom|cat
  tom|cats
  tom|cat|ted
  tom|cat|ting
tom|cod
  plural tom|cod
Tom Col|lins
  Tom Col|lins|es
Tom, Dick, and Harry
tome +s
to|men|tose
to|men|tous (= tomentose)
to|men|tum
  to|men|ta
tom|fool +s
tom|fool|ery
  tom|fool|eries

Tomis (ancient name for Constanţa, Romania)
  [☞ Thomas]
tommy
  tom|mies
tommy bar +s
tommy|cod
  plural tommy|cod
Tommy gun +s
tommy-rot
tomo|gram +s
tomo|graph|ic
tom|og|raphy
to|mor|row +s
tom|pion +s (use tampion)
Tomsk (city, Russia)
Tom Thumb +s
tom-tom +s
ton +s (various units of weight or volume; refrigerating power)
  [☞ tonne, tun]
tonal
ton|al|ity
  ton|al|ities
ton|al|ly
tondo
  tondi
Tone, (Theo|bald) Wolfe (Irish nationalist)
tone
  tones
  toned
  ton|ing
tone arm +s
tone-deaf
tone-deafness
tone|less
tone|less|ly
ton|eme +s
ton|emic
toner +s
tone-row +s
tong +s +ed +ing (guild; style hair; use tongs)
  [☞ tongue]
Tonga (country, S Pacific)
tonga +s
Ton|gan +s
Ton|ga|riro (mountain, New Zealand)
tongs (grasping tool)
tongue (Anatomy etc.)
  tongues
  tongued
  tonguing
  [☞ tung]

tongue-and-groove
tongued adjective
tongue-in-cheek
tongue-lashing +s
tongue|less
tongue-tie
tongue-tied
tongue twist|er +s
tongue-twisting
tonguing +s noun
tonic +s
tonic|ally
ton|icity
tonic sol-fa
toni|er
toni|est
to|night
tonka bean +s
Ton|kin (region & gulf, Vietnam)
Tonlé Sap (lake, Cambodia)
ton-mile +s
ton|nage +s
tonne +s (1,000 kg, a metric ton)
  [☞ ton, tun]
ton|neau +s
ton|om|eter +s
ton|sil +s
ton|sil|lar
tonsil|lec|tomy
  tonsil|lec|to|mies
ton|sil|litis
ton|sor|ial
ton|sure
  ton|sures
  ton|sured
  ton|sur|ing
ton|sured adjective
ton|tine +s
Ton|ton Ma|coute
  Ton|tons Ma|coutes
Tony +s (award)
tony
  toni|er
  toni|est
too adverb (in 'too much' etc.; as well)
  [☞ to, two]
too|dle
  too|dles
  too|dled
  tood|ling
toodle-oo
took past tense of take
  [☞ toque]
tool +s +ed +ing
  [☞ tulle]
tool|bar +s
tool belt +s
tool box
  tool boxes

tool|er +s
tool|ing noun
tool kit +s
tool|maker +s
tool|making
tool|push
  tool|push|es
tool|push|er +s
tool shed +s
toon +s (cartoon)
  [☞ tune]
toon|ie +s
toot +s +ed +ing
toot|er +s
tooth
 • noun
  teeth
 • verb
  tooths
  toothed
  tooth|ing
tooth|ache +s
tooth|brush
  tooth|brush|es
toothed adjective
tooth|i|er
tooth|i|est
tooth|i|ly
tooth|less
tooth|like
tooth|paste +s
tooth|pick +s
tooth pow|der +s
tooth|some
tooth|some|ly
tooth|some|ness
tooth|wort +s
tooth|y
  tooth|i|er
  tooth|i|est
too|tle
  too|tles
  too|tled
  toot|ling
too-too (extreme; excessively)
  [☞ tutu]
toots
toot|sie +s (foot; woman)
  [☞ Tutsi]
Too|woom|ba (town, Australia)
top
  tops
  topped
  top|ping
Top 40
topaz
  topaz|es
top-class
top|coat +s
top-down

top drawer +s (top-drawer *when preceding a noun*)
top-dress *verb*
  top-dresses
  top-dressed
  top-dressing
top dress|ing *noun*
tope (drink; grove; stupa; shark)
  topes
  toped
  top|ing
  [☞ taupe]
topee +s (pith helmet: *use* topi)
  [☞ topi]
To|peka (city, US)
top-end
toper
top-flight
top|gal|lant +s
top-grade
top-hamper +s
top hat +s
top-hatted
top-heavily
top-heaviness
top-heavy
To|phet
top-hole
to|phus
  tophi
topi
• (pith helmet)
  plural topis
• (antelope)
  plural topi or topis
topi|ar|ian +s
topi|ar|ist +s
topi|ary
  topi|aries
topic +s
top|ic|al
top|ic|al|ity
top|ic|al|ly
top|knot +s
top|less
top|less|ness
top-level
top|line +s *noun*
top-line *adjective preceding a noun*
top|loft|i|ness
top|lofty
top|mast +s
top|most
top-notch
top-notcher +s
topo +s
top-of-the-line
top-of-the-range
top|og|raph|er +s

topo|graph|ic
topo|graph|ic|al
topo|graph|ic|al|ly
top|og|raphy
  top|og|raph|ies
topoi
topo|logic|al
topo|logic|al|ly
top|ol|o|gist +s
top|ol|ogy
  top|ol|o|gies
topo|nym +s
topo|nym|ic
top|onymy
topos
  topoi
top|per +s
top|ping +s *noun & adjective*
top|ple
  top|ples
  top|pled
  top|pling
top|sail +s
top seed +s
top-seeded
top shelf
top|side +s
Top|sid|er +s *proprietary*
top|soil +s
top|spin +s
top|stitch
  top|stitch|es
  top|stitched
  top|stitch|ing
top|stitch|ing *noun*
Topsy
topsy-turvily
topsy-turviness
topsy-turvy
top up *verb*
  tops up
  topped up
  top|ping up
top-up +s *noun*
top|water
toque +s (knitted winter hat; woman's brimless hat; bonnet; chef's hat)
  [☞ La Tuque]
to|quilla +s
tor +s (hill)
  [☞ tore, torr]
Torah (*Judaism*)
Tor|bay (towns, England & Canada)
torc +s (necklace)
  [☞ torque]
torch
  torch|es

  torched
  torch|ing
torch|bear|er +s
tor|chère +s (tall stand for candlestick etc.; *for* floor lamp with upturned shade *use* torchiere)
tor|chi|ere +s (floor lamp with upturned shade)
  [☞ torchère]
torch|light
torch|lit
tor|chon +s
torchy
  torch|i|er
  torch|i|est
tore (*past tense of* tear; torus)
  [☞ tor, torr]
torea|dor +s
tor|ero +s
tor|eutic +s
tori *plural of* torus
  [☞ Tory, torii]
toric
torii (shrine gateway)
  plural torii
tor|ment +s +ed +ing
tor|ment|ed|ly
tor|men|til
Tor|men|tine (cape, Canada)
tor|ment|ing|ly
tor|ment|or +s
torn
  [☞ Thorn]
tor|nadic
tor|na|do (storm)
  tor|na|does
  [☞ tournedos]
Torn|gat (mountain range, Canada)
Tor|nio (river, Europe)
tor|oid +s
tor|oid|al
To|ron|to (city & islands, Canada)
To|ron|to|nian +s
tor|ose
tor|pedo
  tor|ped|oes
  tor|ped|oed
  tor|pedo|ing
torpedo-like
tor|pid
tor|pid|ity
tor|pid|ly
tor|pid|ness
tor|por +s
tor|por|ific

Tor|quay (town, England)
  [☞ torquey]
torque (*Mechanics*; increase; *for* necklace use torc)
  torques
  torqued
  tor|quing
Tor|que|mada, Tomás de (Spanish inquisitor)
tor|quey (producing much torque)
  [☞ Torquay]
torr (unit of pressure)
  plural torr
tor|re|fac|tion
tor|re|fy
  tor|re|fies
  tor|re|fied
  tor|re|fy|ing
tor|rent +s
tor|ren|tial
tor|ren|tial|ly
Tor|res (strait between Australia & New Guinea)
  [☞ Taurus, torus]
Tor|ri|cel|li, Evan|gel|ista (Italian mathematician & physicist)
Tor|ri|cel|lian
tor|rid
tor|rid|ity
tor|rid|ly
Tórs|havn (capital of the Faeroe Islands)
tor|sion +s
tor|sion|al
tor|sion|al|ly
torso +s
tort +s (*Law*)
torte +s (cake)
  [☞ tourtière]
tor|tel|lini
tort|fea|sor +s
torti|col|lis
tor|tilla +s
tor|tious
tor|tious|ly
tor|toise +s
tortoise-like
tor|toise|shell +s
Tor|tola (island, British Virgin Islands)
tor|trix
  tor|tri|ces
tor|tu|os|ity
  tor|tu|os|ities

tor|tuous (twisty, not direct)
  [☞ torturous]
tor|tuous|ly
tor|tuous|ness
tor|ture
  tor|tures
  tor|tured
  tor|tur|ing
tor|tur|er +s
tor|tur|ous (agonizing)
  [☞ tortuous]
tor|tur|ous|ly
Toruń (city, Poland)
torus (*Geometry*; *Architecture*; *Anatomy*; *Botany*)
  tori or torus|es
  [☞ Taurus, Torres Strait]
Tor|vill, Jayne (English skater)
Tory (*Politics*)
  Tor|ies
  [☞ tori, torii]
Tory|ism
Tos|ca|nini, Ar|turo (Italian conductor)
tosh
toss
  toss|es
  tossed
  toss|ing
toss|er +s
toss-up +s
tos|ta|da +s
tos|ta|do +s (= tostada)
tot (child; small amount of liquor etc.; add; accumulate)
  tots
  tot|ted
  tot|ting
  [☞ taught, taut]
total
  totals
  to|talled
  total|ling
to|tali|tar|ian +s
to|tali|tar|ian|ism
to|tal|ity
  to|tal|ities
total|iz|a|tion
total|iz|ator +s
total|ize
  total|iz|es
  total|ized
  total|iz|ing
total|iz|er +s
total|ly
Total Qual|ity Man|age|ment

tote
  totes
  toted
  toting
  [☞ Thoth]
tote bag +s
tote board +s
to|tem +s
to|tem|ic
totem|ism
totem|ist +s
totem|is|tic
totem pole +s
toter +s
tote road +s
t'other
to|tipo|tency
to|tipo|tent
tot lot +s
tot|ter +s +ed +ing
tot|ter|er +s
tot|ter|ing *adjective*
tot|tery
tou|can +s
touch
  touch|es
  touched
  touch|ing
touch|able
touch|ably
touch and go (touch-and-go *when preceding a noun*)
  touch and goes or touch and go's
touch down *verb*
  touch|es down
  touched down
  touch|ing down
touch|down +s *noun*
tou|ché (*Fencing*)
touched *adjective*
touch|er +s (one who touches)
  [☞ touché]
touch hole +s
touch|i|er
touch|i|est
touch|i|ly
touch|i|ness
touch|ing *adjective*
touch|ing|ly
touch|ing|ness
touch|less
touch|line +s
touch-me-not +s
touch|pad +s
touch screen +s
touch-sensitive
touch|stone +s
Touch-Tone *proprietary*

touch type
  touch types
  touch typed
  touch typ|ing
touch typ|ing *noun*
touch typ|ist +s
touch up *verb*
  touch|es up
  touched up
  touch|ing up
touch-up +s *noun*
touchy
  touch|i|er
  touch|i|est
touchy-feely
tough +er +est +s +ed +ing (strong; rough; difficult)
  [☞ tuff]
tough|en +s +ed +ing
tough|en|er +s
tough guy +s (tough-guy *when preceding a noun*)
tough|ie +s
tough|ish
tough|ly
tough-minded
tough-minded|ness
tough|ness
toughy (*use* toughie)
  tough|ies
Tou|lon (city, France)
Tou|louse (city, France)
Toulouse-Lautrec, Henri Marie Ray|mond de (French artist)
tou|pée +s
tour +s +ed +ing
  [☞ Tours]
tour|aco +s (*use* turaco)
tour de force
  tours de force
tour d'hori|zon
  tours d'hori|zon
tour en l'air
  tours en l'air
tour|er +s
Tour|ette's syn|drome
  [☞ turret, terret]
Tour|ette syn|drome (= Tourette's syndrome)
  [☞ turret, terret]
tour|ism
tour|ist +s
tour|is|tic
tour|is|tic|ally
tour|isty

tour|ma|line +s
Tour|nai (town, Belgium)
tour|na|ment +s
tour|ne|dos (cut of beef)
  plural tour|ne|dos
tour|ney
  tour|neys
  tour|neyed
  tour|ney|ing
tour|ni|quet +s
Tours (city, France)
tour|tière +s
tou|sle (mess up the hair; treat roughly)
  tou|sles
  tou|sled
  tous|ling
  [☞ tussle]
tousle-haired
Tous|saint L'Ouver|ture, Pierre Domi|nique (Haitian revolutionary leader)
tout +s +ed +ing
tout court
tout de suite
tout|ed *adjective*
tout|er +s
tou|ton +s (food)
  [☞ Teuton]
to|var|ich
  to|var|ich|es
to|var|ish (*use* tovarich)
  to|var|ish|es
tow +s +ed +ing (pull; in 'in tow'; *Skiing*; *Forestry*; *Textiles*)
  [☞ toe]
tow|able
tow|age
to|ward
to|wards
tow bar +s
tow|boat
tow-coloured
towel
  towels
  tow|elled
  towel|ling
towel|ette +s
towel|ling *noun*
tow|er +s +ed +ing
tow|ered *adjective*
tower|ing *adjective*
tower|ing|ly
tow|ery
tow|head +s
tow-headed
tow|hee +s

tow line +s
Town, Har|old
  Bar|ling (Cdn artist)
town +s
town|ee +s (use
  townie)
Townes, Charles
  Hard (US physicist)
town|home
town|house +s
town|ie +s
town|ish
town|less
town|let +s
town line +s
town|scape +s
towns|folk
Towns|hend, Pete
  (English musician)
town|ship +s
Town|ship|per +s
town|site +s
towns|man
  towns|men
towns|pcoplc
Towns|ville (resort,
  Australia)
towns|woman
  towns|women
town|ward
town|wards
tow|path +s
tow rope +s
tow truck +s
tox|emia
tox|em|ic
toxic
toxic|ally
toxi|cant
tox|icity
  tox|ici|ties
toxi|co|logic|al
toxi|col|o|gist +s
toxi|col|ogy
tox|in +s (poison)
  [☞ tocsin]
tox|oid +s
toxo|plas|mo|sis
toy +s +ed +ing
toy boy +s
toy|land
toy|like
Toyn|bee, Ar|nold
  Jo|seph (English
  historian)
toy|town
TPA (tissue
  plasminogen
  activator)
  TPAs
trabe|ate
trabe|ated

trabe|ation
tra|becu|la
  tra|becu|lae
tra|becu|lar
tra|becu|late
Trab|zon (city,
  Turkey)
trace
  traces
  traced
  tracing
trace|abil|ity
trace|able
trace|less
tracer +s
tracer|ied
tracery
  tracer|ies
trachea
  trach|eae
trach|eal
trach|eate
trach|eos|tomy
  (= tracheotomy)
  trach|eos|to|mies
trach|eot|omy
  trach|eot|omies
tra|choma
tra|choma|tous
trach|yte
trach|yt|ic
tracing noun
track +s +ed +ing
track|age
track|ball +s
tracked adjective
track|er +s
track|ing noun
track|lay|er +s
track-laying
track|less
track|less|ness
track light +s
track pants
track|side
track suit +s
track|way +s
tract +s
tract|abil|ity
tract|able
tract|able|ness
tract|ably
Tract|arian +s
Tract|arian|ism
trac|tate
trac|tion
trac|tion|al
trac|tive
trac|tor +s
tractor-trailer +s
trac|tor train +s
Tracy (town, Canada)

Tracy, Spen|cer (US
  actor)
trad
trad|able +s
trade
  trades
  traded
  trad|ing
trade|able +s (use
  tradable)
trade|craft
trade in verb
  trades in
  traded in
  trad|ing in
trade-in +s noun
trade|mark +s +ed
  +ing
trade|marked
  adjective
trade name +s
trade off verb
  trades off
  traded off
  trad|ing off
trade-off +s noun
trader +s
trad|es|can|tia +s
trade show +s
trades|man
  trades|men
trades|people
trades|woman
  trades|women
trade-weight|ed
trad|ing noun
trad|ition +s
trad|ition|al
trad|ition|al|ism +s
trad|ition|al|ist +s
trad|ition|al|is|tic
trad|ition|alize
  trad|ition|al|iz|es
  trad|ition|al|ized
  trad|ition|al|iz|ing
trad|ition|al|ly
tradition-bound
trad|ition|ist +s
trad|ition|less
tra|duce
  tra|duces
  tra|duced
  tra|ducing
tra|duce|ment +s
tra|ducer +s
Tra|fal|gar (battle site
  off Spain)
traf|fic
  traf|fics
  traf|ficked
  traf|fick|ing
traf|ficked adjective
traf|fick|er +s

traf|fic|less
traga|canth +s
tra|gedian +s (writer
  of tragedies; tragic
  actor)
tra|gedi|enne +s
  (tragic actress)
tra|gedy
  tra|ged|ies
tra|gic
tra|gic|al
tra|gic|ally
tragi|com|edy
  tragi|com|edies
tragi|comic
tragi|comic|ally
trago|pan +s
trahi|son des clercs
Trail (city, Canada)
  [☞ Traill]
trail +s +ed +ing
trail|blaz|er +s
trail-blazing
trail-breaker +s
trail-breaking
trail|er +s
trailer|able
trail|head +s
trail|ing adjective
Traill, Cath|ar|ine
  Parr (Cdn pioneer)
  [☞ Trail]
trail|side +s
train +s +ed +ing
train|abil|ity
train|able
Train à Grande
  Vi|tesse
  Trains à Grande
  Vi|tesse
train|band +s
train|ee +s
trainee|ship +s
train|er +s
train|ing noun &
  adjective
train|less
train|load +s
train|man
  train|men
train-mile +s
train|spot|ter +s
train|spot|ting
traipse
  traips|es
  traipsed
  traips|ing
trait +s
trai|tor +s
trai|tor|ous
trai|tor|ous|ly
Tra|jan (Roman
  emperor)

tra|jec|tory
tra|jec|tor|ies
Tra|lee (town, Ireland)
tram +s
tram|car +s
tram|line +s
tram|mel
tram|mels
tram|melled
or tram|meled
tram|mel|ling
or tram|mel|ing
tra|mon|tana +s
(wind)
tra|mon|tane +s (on
the other side of
mountains; foreign;
for wind *use*
tramontana)
tramp +s +ed +ing
tramp|er +s
tramp|ish
tram|ple
tram|ples
tram|pled
tramp|ling
tramp|ler +s
tram|po|line
tram|po|lines
tram|po|lined
tram|po|lin|ing
tram|po|lin|er +s
tram|po|lin|ist +s
trampy
tram|way +s
trance
tran|ces
tranced
tran|cing
trance|like
tranche +s
trank +s +ed +ing
tran|ny
tran|nies
tran|quil
tran|quil|ity
tran|quil|ize
tran|quil|iz|es
tran|quil|ized
tran|quil|iz|ing
tran|quil|izer +s
tran|quil|iz|ing
adjective
tran|quil|lize (*use*
tranquilize)
tran|quil|liz|es
tran|quil|lized
tran|quil|liz|ing
tran|quil|liz|er +s
(*use* tranquilizer)
tran|quil|liz|ing
adjective (*use*
tranquilizing)

tran|quil|ly
trans|act +s +ed +ing
trans|action +s
trans|action|al
trans|action|al|ly
trans|act|or +s
trans|alpine
Trans|alpine Gaul
(ancient region,
Europe)
trans|amin|ase +s
trans|atlan|tic
trans|atlan|tic|ally
trans|axle +s
trans|bor|der
trans|bound|ary
Trans-Canada *noun*
(highway)
trans-Canada
adjective
Trans-Canada
High|way
Trans|cau|casia
(region south of
Caucasus
mountains)
Trans|cau|casian
trans|ceiv|er +s
tran|scend +s +ed
+ing
tran|scend|ence +s
tran|scend|en|cy
tran|scend|en|cies
tran|scend|ent +s
tran|scen|dent|al
tran|scen|dent|al|ism
tran|scen|dent|al|ist
+s
tran|scen|dent|al|ize
tran|scen|dent|al|
iz|es
tran|scen|dent|al|
ized
tran|scen|dent|al|
iz|ing
tran|scen|dent|al|ly
(in a transcendental
manner etc.)
tran|scend|ent|ly (in
a transcendent
manner etc.)
trans|code
trans|codes
trans|cod|ed
trans|cod|ing
trans|coder +s
trans|contin|ent|al
+s
trans|contin|ent|al|ly
tran|scribe
tran|scribes
tran|scribed
tran|scrib|ing

tran|scrib|er +s
tran|script +s
tran|scrip|tion +s
tran|scrip|tion|al
tran|scrip|tion|al|ly
tran|scrip|tion|ist +s
tran|script|ive
trans|cultur|al
trans|cuta|neous
trans|der|mal
trans|duce
trans|du|ces
trans|duced
trans|du|cing
trans|du|cer +s
trans|duc|tion +s
tran|sect +s +ed +ing
tran|sec|tion +s
tran|sept +s
tran|sept|al
tran|sex|ual +s (*use*
transsexual)
tran|sex|u|al|ism (*use*
transsexualism)
tran|sex|u|al|ity (*use*
transsexuality)
trans fat +s
trans fatty acid +s
trans|fect +s +ed
+ing
trans|fec|tion +s
trans|fer
trans|fers
trans|ferred
trans|fer|ring
trans|fer|abil|ity
trans|fer|able
trans|fer|ase +s
trans|fer|ee +s
trans|fer|ence +s
trans|fer|or +s (*Law*)
[☞ transferrer]
trans|fer|ral +s
trans|fer|rer +s (*in
general use*)
[☞ transferor]
trans|fer|rin
trans|fer RNA
Trans|fig|ur|a|tion
(*Christianity*)
trans|fig|ur|a|tion +s
(*in general use*)
trans|figure
trans|fig|ures
trans|fig|ured
trans|fig|ur|ing
trans|finite
trans|fix
trans|fix|es
trans|fixed
trans|fix|ing
trans|fixion +s

trans|form +s +ed
+ing
trans|form|able
trans|form|a|tion +s
trans|form|a|tion|al
trans|form|a|tion|
ally
trans|form|a|tive
trans|form|er +s
trans|fuse
trans|fus|es
trans|fused
trans|fus|ing
trans|fusion +s
trans|genic
trans|gress
trans|gress|es
trans|gressed
trans|gress|ing
trans|gres|sion +s
trans|gres|sive
trans|gres|sor +s
tran|ship (*use*
transship)
tran|ships
tran|shipped
tran|ship|ping
tran|ship|ment +s
(*use* transshipment)
trans|histor|ic
trans|histor|ical
trans|hu|mance
tran|si|ence
tran|si|en|cy
tran|si|ent +s
tran|si|ent|ly
trans|illu|min|ate
trans|illu|min|ates
trans|illu|min|at|ed
trans|illu|min|at|ing
trans|illu|min|a|tion
+s
tran|sis|tor
tran|sis|tor|iz|a|tion
tran|sis|tor|ize
tran|sis|tor|iz|es
tran|sis|tor|ized
tran|sis|tor|iz|ing
tran|sit
tran|sits
tran|sit|ed
tran|sit|ing
tran|si|tion +s
tran|si|tion|al
tran|si|tion|ally
tran|si|tive +s
tran|si|tive|ly
tran|si|tive|ness
tran|si|tiv|ity
tran|si|tor|i|ly
tran|si|tor|i|ness
tran|si|tory
transit|way +s

Trans|jordan (*former name for* Jordan, Middle East)
Trans|jor|dan|ian +s
Trans|kei (former homeland, South Africa)
trans|lat|abil|ity
trans|lat|able
trans|late
  trans|lates
  trans|lat|ed
  trans|lat|ing
trans|la|tion +s
trans|la|tion|al
trans|la|tion|al|ly
trans|la|tor +s
trans|liter|ate
  trans|liter|ates
  trans|liter|at|ed
  trans|liter|at|ing
trans|liter|a|tion +s
trans|liter|ator +s
trans|lo|cate
  trans|lo|cates
  trans|locat|ed
  trans|locat|ing
trans|loca|tion +s
trans|lu|cence
trans|lu|cen|cy
  trans|lu|cen|cies
trans|lu|cent
trans|lu|cent|ly
trans|lunar
trans|mar|ine
trans|mem|brane
trans|mi|grant +s
trans|mi|grate
  trans|mi|grates
  trans|migrat|ed
  trans|migrat|ing
trans|mi|gra|tion +s
trans|mi|gra|tor +s
trans|migra|tory
trans|mis|si|bil|ity
trans|mis|sible
trans|mis|sion +s
trans|mis|sive
trans|mit
  trans|mits
  trans|mit|ted
  trans|mit|ting
trans|mit|table
trans|mit|tal
trans|mit|tance
trans|mit|ter +s
trans|mog|rifi|ca|tion +s
trans|mog|rify
  trans|mog|ri|fies
  trans|mog|ri|fied
  trans|mog|rify|ing
trans|mon|tane

trans|mut|abil|ity
trans|mut|able
trans|mu|ta|tion +s
trans|mu|ta|tion|al
trans|mu|ta|tion|ist +s
trans|mu|ta|tive
trans|mute
  trans|mutes
  trans|mut|ed
  trans|mut|ing
trans|mut|er +s
trans|nation|al +s
trans|nation|al|ly
trans|ocean|ic
tran|som +s
tran|somed
tran|sonic
trans-Pacif|ic
trans|par|ence
trans|par|en|cy
  trans|par|en|cies
trans|par|ent
trans|par|ent|ly
trans|par|ent|ness
trans|person|al
trans|pierce
  trans|pier|ces
  trans|pierced
  trans|pier|cing
tran|spir|able
tran|spir|a|tion
tran|spire
  tran|spires
  tran|spired
  tran|spir|ing
trans|plant +s +ed +ing
trans|plant|able
trans|plant|a|tion +s
trans|plant|er +s
tran|spond|er +s
trans|port +s +ed +ing
trans|port|abil|ity
trans|port|able
trans|por|ta|tion +s
trans|port|ed *adjective*
trans|port|er +s
trans|pos|able
trans|pos|al +s
trans|pose
  trans|pos|es
  trans|posed
  trans|pos|ing
trans|pos|er +s
trans|pos|ition +s
trans|pos|ition|al
trans|posi|tive
trans|put|er +s
trans|sex|ual
trans|sex|u|al|ism

trans|sex|u|al|ity
trans|ship
  trans|ships
  trans|shipped
  trans|ship|ping
trans|ship|ment +s
tran|sub|stan|ti|a|tion
tran|sud|a|tion
tran|suda|tory
tran|sude
  tran|sudes
  tran|sud|ed
  tran|sud|ing
trans|uran|ic
Trans|vaal (former province, South Africa)
trans|valu|a|tion +s
trans|value
  trans|val|ues
  trans|val|ued
  trans|valu|ing
trans|ver|sal +s
trans|ver|sal|ity
trans|ver|sal|ly
trans|verse
trans|verse|ly
trans|ves|tism
trans|ves|tite +s
Tran|syl|vania
Tran|syl|van|ian
trap
  traps
  trapped
  trap|ping
trap boat +s
trap door +s
trap door spi|der +s
trap|eze +s
trap|ez|ist +s
tra|pez|ium (*Geometry*)
  tra|pez|ia or
  tra|pez|iums
tra|pez|ius (*Anatomy*)
  tra|pezii
trap|ez|oid +s
trap|ez|oid|al
trap|line +s
trap|per +s
trap|pings
Trap|pist +s
trap|rock +s
traps
trap shoot|er +s
trap shoot|ing
trap skiff +s
trash
  trash|es
  trashed
  trash|ing
trash can +s

trashed *adjective*
trash|i|er
trash|i|est
trash|i|ly
trash|i|ness
trash talk *noun*
trash-talk +s +ed +ing *verb*
trash-talker +s
trash-talking *noun & adjective*
trashy
  trash|i|er
  trash|i|est
Trás-os-Montes (region, Portugal)
trat|tor|ia +s
trauma +s
trau|mat|ic
trau|mat|ic|ally
trauma|tism
trauma|tiz|a|tion
trauma|tize
  trauma|tiz|es
  trauma|tized
  trauma|tiz|ing
tra|vail +s +ed +ing
trav|el
  trav|els
  trav|elled
  trav|el|ling
trav|el|led *adjective*
trav|el|ler +s
trav|el|ler's cheque +s
trav|el|ler's joy +s
trav|el|ling *noun*
trav|el|ogue +s
travel-sick
trav|el sick|ness
Traven, Ben (US writer)
tra|vers|able
tra|ver|sal +s
tra|verse
  tra|vers|es
  tra|versed
  tra|vers|ing
tra|vers|er +s
trav|er|tine +s
trav|es|ty
  trav|es|ties
  trav|es|tied
  trav|esty|ing
tra|vois
  plural tra|vois
trawl +s +ed +ing (fish by towing a net or with a buoyed line; search through) [☞ troll]

trawl|er +s (boat used
  for trawling; one who
  trawls)
  [☞ troller]
trawl|er|man
  trawl|er|men
trawl line +s
trawl net +s
tray +s (carrying
  platform)
  [☞ trey, très]
tray|ful +s
treach|er|ous
treach|er|ous|ly
treach|er|ous|ness
treach|ery
  treach|eries
treacle
treacly
tread
  treads
  trod
  trod|den or trod
  trod|ding
tread|er +s
treadle
  treadles
  treadled
  tread|ling
tread|mill +s
trea|son
trea|son|able
trea|son|ably
trea|son|ous
treas|ure
  treas|ures
  treas|ured
  treas|ur|ing
treas|ur|er +s
treas|ur|er|ship
treas|ury
  treas|ur|ies
treas|ury bill +s
Treas|ury Board
treas|ury bond +s
Treas|ury Branch
  Treas|ury
  Branch|es
treat +s +ed +ing
treat|able
treat|er +s
treat|ing noun
trea|tise +s
treat|ment +s
treaty
  treat|ies
treaty In|di|an +s
treaty rights
Treb|bi|ano +s
Trebi|zond
  (= Trabzon, Turkey)

treble
  trebles
  trebled
  treb|ling
Treb|linka
  (concentration camp,
  Poland)
treb|ly
trebu|chet +s
treb|uck|et +s
  (= trebuchet)
tre|cent|ist +s
tre|cento
Tree, Sir Her|bert
  Draper Beer|bohm
  (English theatre
  manager)
tree
  trees
  treed
  tree|ing
tree|creep|er +s
treed adjective
tree fern +s
tree frog +s
tree house +s
tree hug|ger +s
tree|less
tree|less|ness
tree|like
tree|line
treen
tree|nail +s
tree spik|ing
tree toad +s
tree|top +s
tree trunk +s
tref
trefa
tre|foil +s
tre|foiled
trek
  treks
  trekked
  trek|king
Trek|ker +s
  (= Trekkie)
trek|ker +s
Trek|kie +s (Star Trek
  fan)
trel|lis
  trel|lis|es
  trel|lised
  trel|lis|ing
trema|tode +s
Trem|blant
  (mountain, Canada)
  [☞ Mont-
  Tremblant]
trem|ble
  trem|bles
  trem|bled
  trem|bling

trem|bling|ly
trem|bly
  trem|bli|er
  trem|bli|est
tre|men|dous
tre|men|dous|ly
tre|men|dous|ness
trem|olo +s
trem|or +s +ed +ing
tremu|lous
tremu|lous|ly
tremu|lous|ness
tre|nail +s (use
  treenail)
trench
  trench|es
  trenched
  trench|ing
tren|chan|cy
tren|chant
tren|chant|ly
trench coat +s
trench|er +s
trench|er|man
  trench|er|men
trench foot
trend +s +ed +ing
trend|i|ly
trend|i|ness
trend|oid +s
trend-setter +s
trend-setting
trendy
  trend|i|er
  trend|i|est
  trend|ies
Treng|ganu (state,
  Malaysia)
Trent (rivers, England
  & Canada; council)
trente-et-quarante
Trentino-Alto Adige
  (region, Italy)
Tren|to (city, Italy)
Tren|ton (cities, US &
  Canada)
Trent-Severn
  (waterway, Canada)
tre|pan
  tre|pans
  tre|panned
  tre|pan|ning
trep|an|a|tion +s
tre|pang +s
tre|pan|ning noun
treph|in|a|tion +s
tre|phine
  tre|phines
  tre|phined
  tre|phin|ing
trepi|da|tion +s
très (very)
  [☞ tray, trey]

tres|pass
  tres|pass|es
  tres|passed
  tres|pass|ing
tres|pass|er +s
tres|pass|ing noun
tress
  tress|es
  tressed
  tress|ing
tressed adjective
tressy
tres|tle +s
trestle|work
tre|vally
  tre|val|lies
Tre|vel|yan, George
  Mac|aulay (English
  historian)
Tre|vel|yan, Sir
  George Otto
  (English historian)
Trev|ino, Lee Buck
  (US golfer)
Tre|vith|ick, Rich|ard
  (English engineer)
trews (pants)
T. Rex
  T. Rexes
trey +s (Basketball; a
  three in cards or
  dice)
  [☞ tray, très]
tri|able
tri|acet|ate +s
tri|ac|tor +s
Triad +s (Chinese
  secret society)
triad +s
triad|ic
triad|ic|ally
tri|age
  tri|ages
  tri|aged
  tri|aging
trial
  trials
  trialled
  trial|ling
trial|ist +s
tri|angle +s
tri|angu|lar
tri|angu|lar|ity
tri|angu|lar|ly
tri|angu|late
  tri|angu|lates
  tri|angu|lat|ed
  tri|angu|lat|ing
tri|angu|la|tion +s
Tri|as|sic
tri|ath|lete +s
tri|ath|lon +s
tri|atom|ic

tri|axial
tri|axial|ity
tribal +s
tribal|ism +s
tribal|ist +s
tribal|is|tic
tribal|ly
tribe +s
tribes|man
  tribes|men
tribes|person
  tribes|people
tribes|woman
  tribes|women
tribo|elec|tric
tribo|elec|tri|city
tribo|logic|al
trib|olo|gist +s
trib|ol|ogy
tribo|lumin|es|cence
tribo|lumin|es|cent
tribu|la|tion +s
tri|bu|nal +s
trib|un|ate +s
trib|une +s
trib|une|ship +s
tribu|tary
  tribu|tar|ies
trib|ute +s
trice
tri|cen|ten|nial +s
tri|cep +s (*use*
  triceps)
  • Although *tricep* is
  becoming more
  common in informal
  use, *triceps* remains
  standard as the
  singular noun.
tri|ceps
  plural tri|ceps
tri|cera|tops
  tri|cera|topses
tri|chia|sis
tri|china
  tri|chinae
Trich|in|opoly
  (= Tiruchirapalli,
  India)
trich|in|osis
trich|in|ous
trich|ol|o|gist +s
trich|ol|ogy
trich|ome +s
tricho|mon|ad +s
tricho|monal
tricho|mon|iasis
  tricho|mon|iases
tricho|tom|ic
tri|chot|om|ous
tri|chot|om|ous|ly
tri|chot|omy
  tri|chot|om|ies

tri|chro|mat|ic
tri|chro|ma|tism
tri|city
  tri|cities
trick +s +ed +ing
trick|ery
  trick|eries
trick|i|er
trick|i|est
trick|i|ly
trick|i|ness
trickle
  trickles
  trickled
  trick|ling
trick|le down *verb*
  trick|les down
  trickled down
  trick|ling down
trickle-down *adjective*
  preceding a noun
trick or treat!
  interjection
trick-or-treat *noun &*
  verb
  trick-or-treats
  trick-or-treated
  trick-or-treating
trick-or-treater +s
trick|si|ly
trick|si|ness
trick|ster +s
trick|sy
  trick|si|er
  trick|si|est
tricky
  trick|i|er
  trick|i|est
tri|clin|ic
tri|col|or +s (*use*
  tricolour)
tri|col|ored (*use*
  tricoloured)
tri|col|our +s
tri|col|oured
tri|corn +s (*use*
  tricorne)
tri|corne +s
tri|cot +s
tri|cus|pid +s
tri|cycle
  tri|cycles
  tri|cycled
  tri|cyc|ling
tri|cyclic +s
tri|cyc|list +s
Tri|dent +s
  (submarine; missile)
tri|dent +s (spear)
tri|den|tate
Tri|den|tine
tri|duum
tried *adjective*

tried-and-true
tri|enni|al +s
tri|enni|al|ly
tri|enni|um
  tri|enni|ums or
  tri|ennia
Trier (city, Germany)
trier +s
Tri|este (city, Italy)
tri|facial
tri|fecta +s
tri|**fid** (split into three)
tri|fle
  tri|fles
  tri|fled
  trif|ling
trif|ler +s
trif|ling *adjective*
trif|ling|ly
tri|focal +s
tri|foli|ate
tri|for|ium
  tri|for|ia
tri|fur|cate
tri|fur|cat|ed
trig
  trigs
  trigged
  trig|ging
tri|gem|inal
trig|ger +s +ed +ing
trig|gered *adjective*
trig|ger|fish
  plural trig|ger|fish or
  trig|ger|fish|es
trigger-happy
Trig|lav (mountain,
  Slovenia)
tri|gly|cer|ide +s
tri|glyph +s
tri|glyph|ic
tri|glyph|ic|al
tri|gon +s
tri|gon|al
tri|gon|al|ly
trig|on|o|met|ric
trig|on|o|met|ric|al
trig|on|om|etry
tri|gram +s
tri|graph +s
tri|halo|methane +s
tri|hed|ral
trike +s
tri|lat|eral
tri|lat|eral|ism
tri|lat|eral|ist +s
tril|bied
tril|by
  tril|bies
tri-level
tri|light +s
tri|linear

tri|lingual
tri|lingual|ism
tri|liter|al
tri|lith +s
tri|lith|ic
tri|lith|on +s
trill +s +ed +ing
Tril|ling, Lionel (US
  critic)
tril|lion
  plural tril|lion or
  tril|lions
tril|lion|aire +s
tril|lionth +s
tril|lium +s
trilo|bite +s
tril|ogy
  tril|ogies
trim
  trims
  trimmed
  trim|ming
tri|maran +s
tri|mer +s
tri|mer|ic
tri|mes|ter +s
tri|mes|tral
tri|mes|trial
tri|meter +s
tri|meth|o|prim
trim|ly
trim|mer +s
trim|ming +s *noun*
trim|ness
trim-tab +s
Tri|murti (*Hinduism*)
trinal
Trin|coma|lee (port,
  Sri Lanka)
trine +s
**Trini|dad and
  To|bago** (country,
  West Indies)
Trini|dad|ian +s
Trini|tar|ian +s
  (*Christianity*)
trini|tar|ian +s (in
  three parts)
Trini|tar|ian|ism
tri|nitro|tolu|ene
tri|nitro|tolu|ol
Trin|ity (*Christianity*)
  Trin|ities
trin|ity (group of
  three)
  trin|ities
trin|ket +s
trin|ket|ry
tri|nom|ial +s
trio +s
tri|ode +s
trio|let +s

tri|ox|ide

trip
  trips
  tripped
  trip|ping

tri|part|ite

tripe +s

trip-hammer +s +ed +ing

trip-hop

triph|thong +s

triph|thong|al

tri|plane +s

tri|ple
  tri|ples
  tri|pled
  trip|ling

Tri|ple A (Triple-A *when preceding a noun*)

triple-decker +s

triple-double +s

Triple-E Sen|ate

trip|let +s

triple-team +s +ed +ing

tri|ple wham|my
  triple wham|mies

tri|plex
  tri|plex|es

trip|li|cate
  trip|li|cates
  trip|li|cat|ed
  trip|li|cat|ing

trip|li|ca|tion +s

trip|li|city
  trip|li|ci|ties

trip|loid +s

trip|loidy

trip|ly

trip|man
  trip|men

trip|meter +s

tri|pod +s

tri|pod|al

Trip|oli (cities, Libya & Lebanon)

trip|oli +s

Tri|pol|itan +s

Trip|oli|tania (coastal region, Libya)

Trip|oli|tan|ian +s

tri|pos
  tri|poses

trip|per +s

trip|ping *noun*

trip|ping|ly

trip|py
  trip|pi|er
  trip|pi|est

Trip|Tik +s *proprietary* (map)

[☞ triptych, tryptic]

trip|tych +s (artistic work in three segments etc.)
[☞ TripTik, tryptic]

Trip|ura (state, India)

trip|wire +s

tri|reme +s

tri|sac|char|ide +s

tri|sect +s +ed +ing

tri|sec|tion +s

tri|sect|or +s

tri-service

tri|shaw +s

tris|kai|deka|phobia

tri|skel|ion +s

tris|mus

tri|sodium phos|phate

tri|som|ic

tri|somy
  tri|som|ies

trisomy-21

Tris|tan (lover of Iseult)

Tris|tan da Cunha (S Atlantic island)

Tris|tan|ian +s

tri|state

triste (sad)
[☞ tryst]

trist|esse

Tris|tram (= Tristan, lover of Iseult)

tri|syllab|ic

tri|sylla|ble +s

trite
  trit|er
  trit|est

trite|ly

trite|ness

triti|at|ed

triti|a|tion

triti|cale

trit|ium

Tri|ton (*Greek Myth*; *Astronomy*)

tri|ton +s (mollusc; *Physics*)

tri|tone +s (*Music*)

trit|ur|able

trit|ur|ate
  trit|ur|ates
  trit|ur|at|ed
  trit|ur|at|ing

trit|ur|a|tion

trit|ur|ator +s

tri|umph +s +ed +ing

tri|umph|al

tri|umph|al|ism

tri|umph|al|ist +s

tri|umph|ant

tri|umph|ant|ly

tri|um|vir
  tri|um|virs or
  tri|um|viri

tri|um|vir|ate +s

tri|une

tri|unity
  tri|uni|ties

tri|valence

tri|valen|cy

tri|valent

Tri|van|drum (city, India)

triv|et +s

trivia

triv|ial

triv|ial|ity
  triv|ial|ities

triv|ial|iz|a|tion +s

triv|ial|ize
  triv|ial|iz|es
  triv|ial|ized
  triv|ial|iz|ing

triv|ial|ly

Triv|ial Pur|suit *proprietary*

triv|ium

tri|week|ly

tRNA (transfer RNA)
  tRNAs

Troad (ancient region, Asia Minor)

Tro|bri|and (island group, SW Pacific)

Tro|bri|and|er +s

tro|car +s

tro|chaic +s

tro|chan|ter +s

tro|chan|ter|ic

tro|chee +s

troch|lea
  troch|leae

troch|lear

tro|choid +s

tro|choid|al

trod

trod|den

trog
  trogs
  trogged
  trog|ging

trog|lo|dyte +s

trog|lo|dyt|ic

trog|lo|dyt|ic|al

tro|gon +s

troi|ka +s

Troi|lus (*Greek Myth*)

Trois-Pistoles (city, Canada)

Trois-Rivières (city, Canada)

Tro|jan +s

Tro|jan Horse (*Greek Myth*)

Tro|jan horse +s (undermining influence; *Computing*)

troll +s +ed +ing (fish by towing a baited line; in 'troll for': search for; sing; stroll; dwarf)
[☞ trawl]

troll|er +s (boat used for trolling; one who trolls)
[☞ trawler]

troll|ey +s

troll|ing mo|tor +s

troll|ish

troll|op +s

Trol|lope, An|thony (English novelist)

Trol|lop|ian

trolly (*use* trolley)
  troll|ies

trom|bone +s

trom|bon|ist +s

trom|mel +s

tromp +s +ed +ing
[☞ *trompe l'oeil*]

trompe l'oeil +s

Trom|sø (city, Norway)

Trond|heim (city, Norway)

Troon (town, Scotland)

troop +s +ed +ing (assemblage; soldiers; *Scouting*; throng)
[☞ troupe]

troop|er +s (soldier; police officer; troopship; resilient or hard-working person)
[☞ trouper]

troop|ship +s

trope +s

troph|ic

tropho|blast +s

tropho|blas|tic

tro|phy
  tro|phies

Trop|ic +s (of Cancer or Capricon; *Astronomy*)

trop|ic +s (tropical; in 'the tropics')

trop|ic|al

trop|ic|al|ly

trop|ism +s

tropo|logic|al
trop|ol|ogy
tropo|pause
tropo|sphere
tropo|spher|ic
trop|po (too much; in 'ma non troppo')
Tros|sachs (valley, Scotland)
Trot +s
trot
 trots
 trot|ted
 trot|ting
troth
trot|line +s
Trot|sky, Leon (Russian revolutionary)
Trot|sky|ism
Trot|sky|ist +s
Trot|sky|ite +s
trot|ter +s
trot|ting noun
trou|ba|dour +s
trouble
 troubles
 troubled
 troub|ling
troubled adjective
trouble-free
trouble|maker +s
trouble|making
Troubles (Irish political unrest)
trouble|shoot
 trouble|shoots
 trouble|shot
 trouble|shoot|ing
trouble|shoot|er +s
trouble|shoot|ing noun
trouble|some
trouble|some|ly
trouble|some|ness
troub|lous
trough +s
trounce
 troun|ces
 trounced
 troun|cing
troun|cing +s noun
troupe +s (company of actors or dancers)
 [☞ troop]
trouper +s (performer; for resilient or hard-working person use trooper)
 [☞ trooper]
trou|ser +s
trou|sered

trouser|less
trou|sers
trous|seau
 trous|seaux or trous|seaus
trout
 plural trout or trouts
trout|ing
trou|vaille +s
trou|vère +s
trove +s
trov|er +s
trow +s +ed +ing
Trow|bridge (town, England)
trow|el
 trow|els
 trow|elled
 trow|el|ling
Troy (ancient city, Asia Minor)
 [☞ Troyes]
troy (weight)
Troyes (town, France)
Troyes, Chré|tien de (French poet)
truan|cy
 truan|cies
tru|ant +s +ed +ing
truce
 tru|ces
Tru|cial States (former name for the United Arab Emirates)
truck +s +ed +ing
 [☞ Truk Islands]
truck|er +s
truck|ing noun
truckle
 truckles
 truckled
 truck|ling
truck|load +s
truck stop +s
trucu|lence
trucu|lent
trucu|lent|ly
Tru|deau, Pierre El|liott (Cdn prime minister)
Trudeau|mania
trudge
 trudges
 trudged
 trudg|ing
trudg|er +s
true (not false etc.)
 truer
 tru|est
 trues
 trued

tru|ing or true|ing
 [☞ trews]
true be|liev|er +s (true-believ|er when preceding a noun)
true-believ|ing
true-blue
true-born
true-false
true-heart|ed
true life (true-life when preceding a noun)
true|ness
True North (Canada)
true north (direction)
Truf|faut, Fran|çois (French filmmaker)
truf|fle +s
truf|fled
trug +s
tru|ism +s
tru|is|tic
Tru|jil|lo (city, Peru)
Tru|jil|lo, Rafael (Dominican president)
Truk (W Pacific islands)
trull +s
truly
Tru|man, Harry S. (US president)
Truman|esque
trump +s +ed +ing
trumped-up
trump|ery
 trump|eries
trum|pet +s +ed +ing
trum|pet|er +s
trun|cal
trun|cate
 trun|cates
 trun|cat|ed
 trun|cat|ing
trun|cat|ed adjective
trun|ca|tion +s
trun|cheon +s
trun|dle
 trun|dles
 trun|dled
 trund|ling
trunk +s
trunk|ful +s
trunk|ing
trunk|less
trunk line +s
trunk road +s
trun|nel +s
trun|nion +s
Truro (towns, Canada & England)

truss
 truss|es
truss|er +s
trust +s +ed +ing
trust|able
trust|bust|er +s
trust|bust|ing
trust|ed adjective
trust|ee +s (administrator of a trust)
 [☞ trusty]
trustee|ship +s
trust|er +s
trust|ful
trust|ful|ly
trust|ful|ness
trust fund +s
trust|i|er
trust|i|est
trust|i|ly
trust|i|ness
trust|ing adjective
trust|ing|ly
trust|ing|ness
trust|worthi|ness
trust|worthy
trusty (trustworthy; prisoner)
 trust|i|er
 trust|i|est
 trust|ies
 [☞ trustee]
Truth, So|jour|ner (US activist)
truth +s
truth|ful
truth|ful|ly
truth|ful|ness
Truth or Dare
try
 tries
 tried
 try|ing
try|ing adjective
try|ing|ly
try out verb
 tries out
 tried out
 try|ing out
try|out +s noun
tryp|ano|some +s
tryp|ano|som|ia|sis
 tryp|ano|som|ia|ses
tryp|sin +s
tryp|sino|gen
tryp|tic (of or pertaining to trypsin)
 [☞ triptych, TripTik]
tryp|to|phan
try|sail +s
try square +s

tryst +s +ed +ing
(lovers' meeting)
[☞ **triste**]
tsar +s (*use* **czar**)
tsar|dom (*use*
czardom)
tsar|evich (*use*
czarevich)
tsar|evich|es
tsar|ina +s (*use*
czarina)
tsar|ism (*use* **czarism**)
tsar|ist +s (*use*
czarist)
Tsar|it|syn (*former
name for* **Volgograd**,
Russia)
Tsavo (national park,
Kenya)
Tsaw|was|sen (town,
Canada)
tse|tse +s
T-shirt +s
T-shirt|ed
Tsilh|qot'in
plural **Tsilh|qot'in**
Tsim|shian
plural **Tsim|shian** or
Tsim|shians
Tsing|hai (= Qinghai,
China)
**Tsiol|kov|sky,
Kon|stan|tin
Eduard|ovitch**
(Russian
aeronautical
engineer)
Tsi|tsi|kamma Forest
(park, South Africa)
tsk
Tskhin|vali (capital of
South Ossetia)
tsk tsk *noun & interj.*
tsk-tsk +s +ed +ing
verb
T-square +s
TSR (*Computing*)
TSRs
tsu|nami +s
Tsu|shima (Japanese
island & battle)
Tsuu T'ina
plural **Tsuu T'ina**
Tswana (people; *for*
language *use*
Setswana)
plural **Se|tswa|na**
TTY (teletypewriter)
TTYs
Tua|motu
(archipelago, French
Polynesia)

Tua|reg
plural **Tua|reg** or
Tua|regs
tua|tara +s
Tuatha Dé Dan|aan
(*Irish Myth*)
tub
tubs
tubbed
tub|bing
tuba +s
tubal
tub|bable
tub|bi|ness
tubby
tub|bi|er
tub|bi|est
tube
tubes
tubed
tub|ing
tube|less
tube|like
tuber +s
tu|ber|cle +s
tu|ber|cu|lar
tu|ber|cu|la|tion +s
tu|ber|cu|lin +s
tu|ber|cu|lo|sis
tu|ber|cu|lous
tuber|ose[1] (of, like, or
covered with tubers)
tube|rose[2] (plant)
[☞ **tuberous**]
tuber|os|ity
tuber|os|ities
tu|ber|ous
(= tuberose[1]: of,
like, or covered with
tubers)
[☞ **tuberose**[2]]
tube|worm +s
tub|ful +s
tubi|fex
tub|ing +s *noun*
**Tub|man, Har|riet
Ross** (US
abolitionist)
**Tub|man, Wil|liam
Vacan|arat
Shad|rach** (Liberian
statesman)
tub-thumper +s
tub-thumping
Tu|buai (islands,
French Polynesia)
tubu|lar
tu|bule +s
tuck +s +ed +ing
[☞ **Tuk**]
tucka|more +s
tucker +s +ed +ing
tuck|ered *adjective*

tuck|et +s
tuck in *verb*
tucks in
tucked in
tuck|ing in
tuck-in +s *noun*
tuck|ing +s *noun*
tuck-point +s +ed
+ing
tuck-pointing +s
noun
tuck shop +s
Tuc|son (city, US)
'tude
Tudor +s (English
royal house)
Tudor|beth|an
Tues|day +s
tufa +s
• (porous limestone
around mineral
springs)
• (= tuff, consolidated
volcanic ash)
tufa|ceous (of tufa; *for*
of tuff *use*
tuffaceous)
tuff +s (consolidated
volcanic ash)
[☞ **tough**]
tuff|aceous (of tuff)
[☞ **tufaceous**]
tuf|fet +s
tuft +s +ed +ing
tuft|ed *adjective*
tuft|ing +s *noun*
tufty
tug
tugs
tugged
tug|ging
tug|boat +s
tug|ger +s
tug-of-war
tugs-of-war
tu|grik +s
tu|ition +s
tu|ition|al
Tuk (Tuktoyaktuk)
Tuk|toyak|tuk (town,
Canada)
Tula (city, Russia;
ancient city, Mexico)
tu|lar|aemia (*use*
tularemia)
tu|lar|aemic (*use*
tularemic)
tu|lar|emia
tu|lar|emic
tulip +s
tulip|wood
Tull, Jeth|ro (English
agriculturalist)

Tul|la|more (town,
Ireland)
tulle (net)
[☞ **tool**]
tul|li|bee
plural **tul|li|bee**
Tulsa (city, US)
tum +s
tum|ble
tum|bles
tum|bled
tum|bling
tum|ble down *verb*
tum|bles down
tum|bled down
tum|bling down
tumble|down
adjective
tum|ble dry
tum|ble dries
tum|ble dried
tum|ble dry|ing
tumble|home
tum|bler +s
tumbler|ful +s
Tum|bler Ridge
(municipality,
Canada)
tumble|weed +s
tum|brel +s
tum|bril +s (*use*
tumbrel)
tu|me|fa|cient
tu|me|fac|tion
tu|me|fy
tu|me|fies
tu|me|fied
tu|me|fy|ing
tu|mes|cence
tu|mes|cent
tu|mes|cent|ly
tumid
tumid|ity
tumid|ly
tummy
tum|mies
tumor +s (*use*
tumour)
tumor|i|gen|ic
tumor|i|gen|icity
tumor|ous
tu|mour +s
tump|line +s
tu|mu|lar
tu|mult +s
tu|mul|tu|ous
tu|mul|tu|ous|ly
tu|mul|tu|ous|ness
tu|mu|lus
tu|mu|li
tun (cask, vat; store
wine; capacity

measure equal to
210 imperial gallons)
tuns
tunned
tun|ning
[☞ ton, tonne]
tuna
• (fish)
plural tuna *or* tunas
• (pear)
plural tunas
tun|abil|ity
tun|able
tuna fish
Tunb Islands (in
Persian Gulf)
Tun|bridge Wells
(town, England)
tun|dish
tun|dish|es
tun|dra +s
Tun|dra Buggy
proprietary
Tun|dra Bug|gies
tune (*Music*, adjust,
etc.)
tunes
tuned
tun|ing
[☞ toon]
tune|ful
tune|ful|ly
tune|ful|ness
tune|less
tune|less|ly
tune|less|ness
tun|er +s
tune|smith +s
tune up *verb*
tunes up
tuned up
tun|ing up
tune-up +s *noun*
tung +s (tree)
[☞ tongue]
tung|state
tung|sten
tung|stic
tung|stous
Tun|gus
plural Tun|gus
Tun|gus|ka (rivers,
Siberia)
tunic +s
tuni|cate +s
tu|nicle +s
tun|ing +s *noun*
Tunis (capital of
Tunisia)
Tu|ni|sia (country,
North Africa)
Tu|ni|sian +s
tun|ket

tun|nel
tun|nels
tun|nelled
tun|nel|ling
tun|nel|ler +s
tun|nel vi|sion
Tun|ney, Gene (US
boxer)
tunny
plural tunny *or*
tun|nies
tup
tups
tupped
tup|ping
Tu|pelo (city, US)
tu|pelo +s
Tupi
plural Tupi *or* Tupis
Tupi-Guarani
plural Tupi-Guarani
or Tupi-Guaranis
tupik +s
tup|pence
(= twopence)
tup|penny
(= twopenny)
Tup|per, Sir Charles
(Cdn prime minister)
Tup|per|ware
proprietary
tuque +s (knitted
winter hat: *use*
toque)
[☞ toque]
tura|co +s
tur|ban +s
tur|baned
tur|bel|lar|ian +s
tur|bid
tur|bid|ity
tur|bid|ly
tur|bid|ness
tur|bin|ate
tur|bin|a|tion
tur|bine +s
tur|bit +s (pigeon)
[☞ turbot]
tur|bo +s
turbo|charge
turbo|char|ges
turbo|charged
turbo|char|ging
turbo|char|ger +s
turbo|diesel +s
turbo|fan +s
turbo|jet +s
turbo|prop +s
turbo|shaft +s
turbo|super|charger
+s

tur|bot (fish)
plural tur|bot
[☞ turbit]
tur|bu|lence +s
tur|bu|lent
tur|bu|lent|ly
Tur|co|man +s (*use*
Turkoman)
turd +s
tu|reen +s (soup-
serving vessel)
[☞ terrine,
terrene]
Tu|renne, Vi|comte
de (Henri de La Tour
d'Auvergne, French
soldier)
turf
turfs
tur|fan De|pres|sion
(low-lying area,
China)
turfy
tur|fi|er
tur|fi|est
Tur|genev, Ivan
Serge|evich (Russian
writer)
tur|ges|cence
tur|ges|cent
tur|gid
tur|gid|ity
tur|gid|ly
tur|gid|ness
tur|gor
Tur|got, Anne
Rob|ert Jacques
(French statesman)
Turin (city, Italy)
Tur|ing, Alan
Math|ison (English
mathematician)
tu|ris|ta +s
Turk +s
Tur|kana (people &
language; lake,
Kenya)
plural Tur|kana
Turk|estan (region,
Asia)
Tur|key (country)
[☞ Turki]
tur|key +s (bird etc.)
turkey|cock +s
Tur|key red +s
Turki (people &
language)
plural Turki
[☞ Turkey]
Turk|ic
Turk|ish
Turk|istan
(= Turkestan)

Turk|men
plural Turk|men *or*
Turk|mens
Turk|men|ia
(= Turkmenistan)
Turk|men|istan
(country, Asia)
Turko|man +s
(= Turkmen)
Turks and Cai|cos
Islands (in the
W Indies)
Turk's cap +s
Turk's head +s
Turku (city, Finland)
tur|meric +s
tur|moil +s
turn +s +ed +ing
(rotate, change,
chance etc.)
[☞ tern, terne]
turn about *verb*
turns about
turned about
turn|ing about
turn|about +s *noun*
turn around *verb*
turns around
turned around
turn|ing around
turn|around +s *noun*
turn|buckle +s
turn|coat +s
turn down *verb*
turns down
turned down
turn|ing down
turn|down +s *noun*
Tur|ner, John Napier
(Cdn prime minister)
Tur|ner, Jo|seph
Mal|lord Wil|liam
(English painter)
Tur|ner, Tina (US
singer)
turn|er +s
Tur|ner|esque
Tur|ner's syn|drome
or Tur|ner
syn|drome
turn|ery
turn|eries
turn|ing +s *noun*
tur|nip +s (vegetable)
[☞ turn-up]
tur|nipy
turn|key +s
turn off *verb*
turns off
turned off
turn|ing off
turn|off +s *noun*

turn of the cen|tury
(turn-of-the-
century *when*
preceding a noun)
turn on *verb*
  turns on
  turned on
  turn|ing on
turn-on +s *noun*
turn out *verb*
  turns out
  turned out
  turn|ing out
turn|out +s *noun*
turn over *verb*
  turns over
  turned over
  turn|ing over
turn|over +s *noun*
turn|pike +s
turn sig|nal +s
turn|sole +s
turn|stile +s
turn|stone +s
turn|table +s
turn up *verb*
  turns up
  turned up
  turn|ing up
turn-up +s *noun*
  (surprise; cuff)
  [☞ turnip]
tur|pen|tine
  tur|pen|tines
  tur|pen|tined
  tur|pen|tin|ing
tur|pi|tude
turps
tur|quoise +s
turr +s
tur|ret +s (tower;
  armoured enclosure;
  lathe attachment)
  [☞ terret,
  Tourette's
  syndrome]
tur|ret|ed *adjective*
tur|tle +s
turtle|dove +s
turtle|head +s
Tur|tle Island (North
  America)
turtle|neck +s
tur|tle shell +s *noun*
turtle|shell *adjective*
turves *rare plural of*
  turf
Tus|can +s
Tus|cany (region,
  Italy)
Tus|ca|rora
  plural Tus|ca|rora *or*
  Tus|ca|roras

tush
  tush|es
tush|ie +s
tushy (*use* tushie)
  tush|ies
tusk +s
tusked
tusk|er +s
tusky
tus|sah +s
tus|sive
tus|sle (scuffle,
  struggle)
  tus|sles
  tus|sled
  tus|sling
  [☞ tousle]
tus|sock +s
tus|socky
tus|sore +s
tut
  tuts
  tut|ted
  tut|ting
Tut|ankh|amen
  (pharaoh)
Tut|ankh|amun
  (= Tutankhamen)
Tu|tcho|ne
  plural Tu|tcho|ne *or*
  Tu|tcho|nes
tu|tel|age
tu|tel|ary
tu|tor +s
tu|tor|ial +s
tutor|ship +s
Tutsi (Bantu-speaking
  people)
  plural Tutsi *or*
  Tut|sis
  [☞ tootsie]
tut|ti +s
tutti-frutti +s
tut-tut
  tut-tuts
  tut-tutted
  tut-tutting
Tutu, Des|mond
  Mpilo (South African
  clergyman)
  [☞ too-too]
tutu +s (dancer's skirt)
  [☞ too-too]
Tu|va|lu (country,
  SW Pacific)
Tu|va|luan +s
tu-whit, tu-whoo +s
tux
  tuxes
tux|edo
  tux|edos *or*
  tux|edoes

Tux|tla Gu|tiér|rez
  (city, Mexico)
tuy|ère +s
Tuzla (town, Bosnia)
TV (television)
  TVs
TV din|ner +s
Tver (city, Russia)
twad|dle
  twad|dles
  twad|dled
  twad|dling
twad|dler +s
Twain, Mark (US
  writer)
twain
twang +s +ed +ing
twangy
  twang|i|er
  twang|i|est
'twas
twat +s
tway|blade +s
tweak +s +ed +ing
twee (dainty, quaint)
  tweer
  tweest
  [☞ Twi]
Tweed (river, Britain)
tweed +s
tweed|i|ly
tweed|i|ness
Tweedle|dum and
  Tweedle|dee
Tweeds|muir, Baron
  (John Buchan)
tweedy
  tweed|i|er
  tweed|i|est
twee|ly
tween +s (tween-ager)
'tween (between)
tween-age
tween-ager +s
'tween decks
twee|ness
tween|ie +s
tweet +s +ed +ing
tweet|er +s
tweeze
  tweez|es
  tweezed
  tweez|ing
tweez|ers
twelfth +s
Twelfth Day
twelfth|ly
Twelfth Night
twelve +s
twelve|fold
twelve|month +s
twelve-note
twelve-pack +s

12-step
12-stepper +s
12-stepping
twelve-tone
twen|ti|eth +s
twenty
  twen|ties
twenty-eight +s
twenty-eighth +s
twenty-fifth +s
twenty-first +s
twenty-five +s
twenty|fold
twenty-four +s
24 Sus|sex Drive
  (prime minister's
  residence)
twenty-fourth +s
twenty-nine +s
twenty-ninth +s
twenty-one +s
  (blackjack)
twenty-second +s
twenty-seven +s
twenty-seventh +s
twenty-six (26-ounce
  bottle of liquor)
  twenty-sixes
twenty-sixth +s
twenty|some|thing
  +s
twenty-third +s
twenty-three +s
20/20
twenty-twenty
  (= 20/20)
twenty-two +s (gun,
  cartridge)
.22 (gun, cartridge)
  .22s
'twere
twerp +s
twerpy
  twerp|i|er
  twerp|i|est
Twi (people)
  plural Twi *or* Twis
twi|bill +s
twice
twid|dle
  twid|dles
  twid|dled
  twid|dling
twid|dler +s
twid|dly
twig
  twigs
  twigged
  twig|ging
twigged *adjective*
twiggy
twi|light +s
twi|light|ed (= twilit)

twi|lit
twill +s (*Textiles*)
'twill (it will)
Twill|lin|gate (town, Canada)
twin
  twins
  twinned
  twin|ning
twin|berry
  twin|ber|ries
twin bill +s
twin-cam
Twin Cit|ies (specific pair of neighbouring cities)
twin city (each of two closely tied usu. international cities)
  twin cit|ies
twine
  twines
  twined
  twin|ing
twin-engine (= twin-engined)
twin-engined
twin|er +s
twin|flower +s
twinge
  twin|ges
  twinged
  twin|ging
twi-night
twink +s
Twink|ie +s
  proprietary (food)
twink|ie +s (wimp; effeminate man)
twin|kle
  twin|kles
  twin|kled
  twin|kling
twink|ler +s
twink|ling +s
  adjective & noun
twink|ly
twinky (wimp, effeminate man: *use* twinkie)
  twink|ies
  [☞ Twinkie]
twin|ning +s *noun*
Twins (constellation; Zodiac)
twin-screw
twin-set +s
twin|ship
twin-size
twin-sized (= twin-size)
twirl +s +ed +ing
twirl|er +s

twirly
twist +s +ed +ing
twist|able
twist|ed *adjective*
twist|er +s
twist-tie
  twist-ties
  twist-tied
  twist-tying
twisty
  twist|i|er
  twist|i|est
twit
  twits
  twit|ted
  twit|ting
twitch
  twitch|es
  twitched
  twitch|ing
twitch|er +s
twitch|i|ly
twitch|i|ness
twitchy
  twitch|i|er
  twitch|i|est
twit|ter +s +ed +ing
twit|ter|er +s
twit|tery
'twixt
two +s (number)
  [☞ to, too]
two-and-a-half +s (apartment)
two-bagger +s
two-base hit +s
two-bit
two bits
two-by-four +s
two cents' worth
two-cycle
2-D (two-dimensional)
two-dimen|sion|al
two-dimen|sion|al|ity
two-dimen|sion|al|ly
two-edged
two-faced
two|fer +s (two-for-one deal)
  [☞ two-four]
two-fisted
two|fold
two-four +s (case of 24 bottles of beer)
2,4-D (herbicide)
two-handed
two-hander +s
twoon|ie +s (*use* toonie)
two-on-one +s
two|pence
two|penny

two|penny-halfpenny
two-piece +s
two-piecer +s
two-ply
two-pronged
two-seater +s
two-sided
two|some +s
two-step
  two-steps
  two-stepped
  two-stepping
two-stroke
two-time
  two-times
  two-timed
  two-timing
two-timer +s
two-tone
'twould
two-way
two-wheel drive
two-wheeled
two-wheel|er +s
Ty|burn (former site of public hangings, England)
Tyche (*Greek Myth*)
  [☞ Tai Chi]
ty|coon +s
ty|coon|ery
tyee +s
tying
tyke +s
Ty|len|ol +s
  proprietary
Tyler, John (US president)
Tyler, Wal|ter ('Wat') (English revolutionary)
tym|pan
tym|pani (*use* timpani)
tym|pan|ic
tym|pan|ites
tym|pan|itic
tym|pa|num
  tym|pana *or* tym|pa|nums
Tyn|dale, Wil|liam (English translator of the Bible)
Tyn|dall (limestone)
Tyn|dall, John (Irish physicist)
Tyn|dar|eus (*Greek Myth*)
Tyne (river, England)
  [☞ tine]
Tyne and Wear (county, England)

Tyne|side (region, England)
Tyne|sider +s
Tyn|wald (legislative assembly, Isle of Man)
typal
type
  types
  typed
  typ|ing
Type A
  Type A's
Type B
  Type B's
type|cast
  type|casts
  type|cast
  type|cast|ing
type|cast|ing *noun*
typed *adjective*
type|face +s
type|script +s
type|set
  type|sets
  type|set
  type|set|ting
type|set|ter +s
type|set|ting *noun*
type|writ|er +s
type|writ|ing
type|writ|ten
ty|phoid
ty|phoid|al
Ty|phoid Mary +s
Ty|phon (*Greek Myth*)
ty|phon|ic
ty|phoon +s
ty|phous *adjective*
ty|phus *noun*
typ|ical
typ|ical|ity
typ|ical|ly
typi|fy
  typi|fies
  typi|fied
  typi|fy|ing
typ|ist +s
typo +s
typ|og|raph|er +s
typo|graph|ic
typo|graph|ic|al
typo|graph|ic|al|ly
typ|og|raphy
typo|logic|al
typo|logic|al|ly
typ|olo|gist +s
typ|ol|ogy
  typ|ol|o|gies
Tyr (*Scandinavian Myth*)
  [☞ Tyre]
tyra|mine

tyr|an|nical
tyr|an|nical|ly
tyr|an|ni|cid|al
tyr|an|ni|cide +s
tyr|an|nize
  tyr|an|niz|es
  tyr|an|nized
  tyr|an|niz|ing
tyr|an|no|saur +s
tyr|an|no|saur|us
  (= tyrannosaur)
  tyr|an|no|saur|us|es
tyr|an|nous
tyr|an|nous|ly
tyr|anny
  tyr|an|nies
ty|rant +s
Tyre (town, Lebanon)
  [☞ Tyr]
Tyr|ian +s
tyro +s
Tyrol (state, Austria;
  region, Alps)
Tyrol|ean
Tyrol|ese
  plural Tyrol|ese
Ty|rone (county,
  Northern Ireland)
tyro|sine
Tyr|rhene +s
Tyr|rhen|ian +s (Sea,
  Mediterranean;
  Etruscan)
Tyson, Mike (US
  boxer)
Tyu|men (city, Russia)
Tzad|dik
  Tzad|dik|im
tza|tziki
tze|dakah
tzim|mes
  plural tzim|mes

U

U
• (letter; shape)
  U's
• (Burmese man; in
  commercial use
  = you)
  [☞ ewe, yew, you]
u
• (letter)
  u's
• (micro)
  [☞ ewe, yew, you]
Uban|ghi Shari
  (former name for the
  Central African
  Republic)
Über|mensch
  Über|mensch|en
ubi|qui|tous
ubi|qui|tous|ly
ubi|qui|tous|ness
ubi|quity
  ubi|qui|ties
U-boat +s
Uc|cel|lo, Paolo
  (Italian painter)
ud|der +s (mammary
  gland of cows etc.)
  [☞ utter]
ud|dered adjective
UDI (unilateral
  declaration of
  independence)
  UDIs
Udine (city, Italy)
udon
UEFA (Union of
  European Football
  Associations)
Ufa (city, Russia)
UFFI (urea
  formaldehyde foam
  insulation)
UFO (unidentified
  flying object)
  UFOs
ufo|logic|al
ufolo|gist +s
ufol|ogy
Ugan|da (country,
  Africa)
Ugan|dan +s
Uga|rit (ancient city,
  Syria)
Uga|rit|ic
ugh
Ugli proprietary (fruit)
  Ug|lies
ugli|fi|ca|tion

ugli|fy
  ugli|fies
  ugli|fied
  ugli|fy|ing
ugli|ly
ugli|ness
  ugli|ness|es
ugly (unpleasant,
  repulsive, etc.)
  ugli|er
  ugli|est
  ug|lies
  [☞ Ugli]
Ug|rian +s
Ug|ric +s
uh
uh-huh
uh|lan +s
Uh|land, (Jo|hann)
  Lud|wig (German
  writer)
uh-oh
uh-uh
uil|lean pipes
Uist (either of two
  islands, Outer
  Hebrides)
Uj|jain (city, India)
U-joint +s
Ujung Pan|dang (city,
  Indonesia)
ukase +s
Uke +s
Ukie +s
Ukraine (country,
  Europe)
Ukrain|ian +s
uku|lele +s
Ulaan|baatar (= Ulan
  Bator, Mongolia)
Ulala (former name for
  Gorno-Altaisk,
  Russia)
Ulan Bator (capital of
  Mongolia)
Ulan|ova, Gal|ina
  Ser|geev|na (Russian
  dancer)
Ulan-Ude (city,
  Russia)
Ul|bricht, Wal|ter
  (East German
  statesman)
ul|cer +s
ul|cer|ate
  ul|cer|ates
  ul|cer|at|ed
  ul|cer|at|ing
ul|cer|a|tion +s
ul|cera|tive
ul|cered adjective
ul|cer|ous
ulema +s

Ul|has|nagar (city,
  India)
ul|lage
Ulm (city, Germany)
ulna
  ulnae
ulnar
Ul|pian (Roman jurist)
Ulsan (city, South
  Korea)
Ul|ster (region,
  Ireland)
ul|ster +s
Ulster|man
  Ulster|men
Ulster|woman
  Ulster|women
ul|ter|ior
ul|ter|ior|ly
ul|tim|acy
  ul|tim|acies
ul|tim|ate +s
ul|tim|ate|ly
ul|tim|ate|ness
ul|tima Thule
ul|ti|matum
  ul|ti|matums or
  ul|ti|mata
ul|timo
ul|timo|geni|ture
ul|tra +s
ultra|
  centri|fu|ga|tion
ultra|centri|fuge +s
ultra|fil|tra|tion
ultra-high
ultra|ism
ultra|ist +s
ultra|light +s
ultra-marathon +s
ultra-marathon|er
  +s
ultra|marine +s
ultra|micro|scope +s
ultra|micro|scop|ic
ultra|mon|tane +s
ultra|mon|tan|ism
ultra|mon|tan|ist +s
ultra|mun|dane
ultra|sonic
ultra|sonic|ally
ultra|sonics
ultra|sonog|raphy
ultra|sound +s
ultra|struc|tur|al
ultra|struc|ture +s
Ultra|suede
  proprietary
ultra|violet
ultra vires
ulu +s
ulu|lant

ulu|late
ulu|lates
ulu|lat|ed
ulu|lat|ing
ulu|la|tion +s
Ul|un|di (town, South
  Africa)
Ul|ya|nov, Vlad|i|mir
  Ilich (Lenin)
Ul|ya|novsk (former
  name for Simbirsk,
  Russia)
Ulys|ses (Roman
  Myth; space probe)
um
Umay|yad +s
  (Muslim dynasty)
um|bel +s (Botany)
  [☞ umbles]
um|bel|lar
um|bel|late
um|bel|lif|er +s
um|bel|lif|er|ous
um|bel|lule
um|ber +s
um|bil|ic|al +s
um|bil|ic|al|ly
um|bil|icate
um|bil|icus
  um|bil|ici
um|bles (offal)
  [☞ umbel]
umbo
  umbos or umbo|nes
umbo|nal
umbo|nate
umbra
  um|bras or um|brae
um|brage
um|bra|geous
um|bral
um|brel|la +s
um|brel|laed
um|brella-like
Um|bria (region, Italy)
Um|brian +s
Umeå (city, Sweden)
umi|ak +s
um|laut +s +ed +ing
Umm al Qai|wain
  (state & its capital,
  UAE)
ump +s +ed +ing
umph
um|pire
  um|pires
  um|pired
  um|pir|ing
ump|teen
ump|teenth
umpty

Um|tali (former name
  for Mutare,
  Zimbabwe)
Um|tata (city, South
  Africa)
'un (informal = one)
un|abashed
un|abash|ed|ly
un|abated
un|abated|ly
un|able
un|abridged
un|ab|sorbed
un|academ|ic
un|accent|ed
un|accept|abil|ity
un|accept|able
un|accept|ably
un|accom|mo|dat|ing
un|accom|pan|ied
un|account|abil|ity
un|account|able
un|account|able|ness
un|account|ably
un|account|ed
un|accus|tomed
un|accus|tomed|ly
un|achiev|able
un|acknow|ledged
un|ac|quaint|ed
un|adapt|able
un|adapt|ed
un|ad|dressed
un|ad|jacent
un|admit|ted
un|adorned
un|adul|ter|ated
un|adven|tur|ous
un|adven|tur|ous|ly
un|adver|tised
un|advis|able
un|advised
un|advis|ed|ly
un|advis|ed|ness
un|aesthet|ic
un|aesthet|ic|ally
un|affect|ed
un|affect|ed|ly
un|affect|ed|ness
un|affec|tion|ate
un|affili|ated
un|afford|able
un|afraid
un|aggres|sive
un|aid|ed
un|aired
un|alien|able
un|aligned
un|alike
un|allevi|ated
un|allied
un|allow|able

un|alloyed
un|alter|able
un|alter|able|ness
un|alter|ably
un|altered
un|ambigu|ous
un|ambigu|ous|ly
un|ambi|tious
un|ambi|tious|ly
un|ambi|tious|ness
un|ambiva|lent
un|ambiva|lent|ly
un-American
un-American|ism
un|ami|able
un|ampli|fied
Una|mu|no, Mi|guel
  de (Spanish writer)
un|amused
un|ana|lys|able (use
  unanalyzable)
un|ana|lysed (use
  unanalyzed)
un|ana|lyz|able
un|ana|lyzed
un|aneled
unan|im|ity
unani|mous
unani|mous|ly
unani|mous|ness
un|an|nounced
un|answer|able
un|answer|able|ness
un|answer|ably
un|an|swered
un|antici|pated
un|apolo|get|ic
un|apolo|get|ic|ally
un|appar|ent
un|appeal|able
un|appeal|ing
un|appeal|ing|ly
un|appeas|able
un|appeased
un|appetiz|ing
un|appetiz|ing|ly
un|appre|ci|ated
un|appre|cia|tive
un|appre|hend|ed
un|approach|abil|ity
un|approach|able
un|approach|able|
              ness
un|approach|ably
un|appro|pri|ated
un|approved
un|apt
un|apt|ly
un|apt|ness
un|argu|able
un|argu|ably
un|arm +s +ed +ing

un|armed adjective
un|articu|lated
un|ascer|tain|able
un|ascer|tained
un|ashamed
un|asham|ed|ly
un|asham|ed|ness
un|asked
un|asked-for
un|assail|abil|ity
un|assail|able
un|assail|able|ness
un|assail|ably
un|assert|ive
un|assert|ive|ly
un|assert|ive|ness
un|assigned
un|assim|il|able
un|assim|il|ated
un|assist|ed
un|associ|ated
un|assuage|able
un|assuaged
un|assumed
un|assum|ing
un|assum|ing|ly
un|assum|ing|ness
un|attached
un|attack|able
un|attain|able
un|attain|able|ness
un|attain|ably
un|attempt|ed
un|attend|ed
un|attract|ive
un|attract|ive|ly
un|attract|ive|ness
un|attrib|ut|able
un|attrib|ut|ably
un|attrib|ut|ed
un|audit|ed
un|authen|tic
un|authen|tic|ally
un|authen|ti|cated
un|author|ized
un|avail|abil|ity
un|avail|able
un|avail|able|ness
un|avail|ing
un|avail|ing|ly
un|avoid|abil|ity
un|avoid|able
un|avoid|able|ness
un|avoid|ably
un|avowed
un|awak|ened
un|aware
un|aware|ness
un|awares
un|awed
un|backed
un|baked

un|bal|ance
  un|bal|an|ces
  un|bal|anced
  un|bal|an|cing
un|bal|anced *adjective*
un|ban
  un|bans
  un|banned
  un|ban|ning
un|ban|ning +s *noun*
un|bar
  un|bars
  un|barred
  un|bar|ring
un|bear|able
un|bear|able|ness
un|bear|ably
un|beat|able
un|beat|en
un|beauti|ful
un|beauti|ful|ly
un|becom|ing
un|becom|ing|ly
un|becom|ing|ness
un|befit|ting
un|behold|en
un|beknown
  (= unbeknownst)
un|be|knownst
un|belief
un|believ|abil|ity
un|believ|able
un|believ|ably
un|believ|er +s
un|believ|ing
un|believ|ing|ly
un|belt|ed
un|bend
  un|bends
  un|bent
  un|bend|ing
un|bend|able
un|bend|ing *adjective*
un|bend|ing|ly
un|bend|ing|ness
un|biased
un|bibli|cal
un|bid|den
un|bind
  un|binds
  un|bound
  un|bind|ing
un|bleached
un|blem|ished
un|blessed
un|blest
  (= unblessed)
un|blink|ing
un|blink|ing|ly
un|block +s +ed +ing
un|blown
un|blush|ing
un|blush|ing|ly

un|bolt +s +ed +ing
un|bolt|ed *adjective*
un|bon|net +s +ed
  +ing
un|born
un|bosom +s +ed
  +ing
un|both|ered
un|bound *adjective*
un|bound|ed
un|bound|ed|ly
un|bound|ed|ness
un|bowed
un|brace
  un|braces
  un|braced
  un|bracing
un|branched
un|brand|ed
un|breach|able
un|break|able
un|breath|able
un|bridge|able
un|bridle
  un|bridles
  un|bridled
  un|brid|ling
un|bridled *adjective*
un|brok|en
un|brok|en|ness
un|bruised
un|buckle
  un|buckles
  un|buckled
  un|buck|ling
un|budge|able
un|build
  un|builds
  un|built
  un|build|ing
un|built *adjective*
un|bun|dle
  un|bun|dles
  un|bun|dled
  un|bund|ling
un|bund|ler +s
un|bur|den +s +ed
  +ing
un|bur|dened
  adjective
un|buried *adjective*
un|burned
un|burnt
  (= unburned)
un|bury
  un|buries
  un|buried
  un|bury|ing
un|busi|ness|like
un|but|ton +s +ed
  +ing
un|but|toned *adjective*
un|caged

un|called
un|called for
  (un|called-for *when*
  preceding a noun)
un-Canadian
un|canni|ly
un|canni|ness
un|canny
  un|canni|er
  un|canni|est
un|canon|ical
un|canon|ical|ly
un|cap
  un|caps
  un|capped
  un|cap|ping
un|cared-for
un|caring
un|carpet|ed
un|case
  un|cases
  un|cased
  un|casing
un|cashed
un|cata|logued
un|catch|able
un|caught
un|ceas|ing
un|ceas|ing|ly
un|celeb|rated
un|cen|sored (uncut)
un|cen|sured (not
  criticized)
un|cere|moni|ous
un|cere|moni|ous|ly
un|cere|moni|ous|
          ness
un|cer|tain
un|cer|tain|ly
un|cer|tainty
  un|cer|tain|ties
un|certi|fied
un|chain +s +ed +ing
un|chal|lenge|able
un|chal|lenge|ably
un|chal|lenged
un|chal|len|ging
un|change|abil|ity
un|change|able
un|change|able|ness
un|change|ably
un|changed
un|chan|ging
un|chan|ging|ly
un|chap|er|oned
un|char|ac|ter|is|tic
un|char|ac|ter|is|tic|
          ally
un|charged
un|charis|mat|ic
un|charit|able
un|charit|able|ness

un|charit|ably
un|chart|ed
un|char|tered
un|chaste
un|chaste|ly
un|chas|tened
un|chas|tity
un|checked
un|chival|rous
un|chival|rous|ly
un|chosen
un|chris|tian
un|chris|tian|ly
un|church
  un|church|es
  un|churched
  un|church|ing
un|churched *adjective*
un|cial +s
un|ci|form
un|cin|ate
un|circum|cised
un|circum|cision
un|civil
un|civil|ized
un|civil|ly
un|clad
un|claimed
un|clasp +s +ed +ing
un|classi|fi|able
un|classi|fied
uncle +s
un|clean
un|clean|li|ness
un|clean|ly
un|clean|ness
un|clear
un|cleared
un|clear|ly
un|clear|ness
un|clench
  un|clench|es
  un|clenched
  un|clench|ing
Uncle Sam
Uncle Tom +s
  offensive
un|climb|able
un|climbed
un|clip
  un|clips
  un|clipped
  un|clip|ping
un|cloak +s +ed +ing
un|clog
  un|clogs
  un|clogged
  un|clog|ging
un|close
  un|clos|es
  un|closed
  un|clos|ing

un|clothe
  un|clothes
  un|clothed
  un|cloth|ing
un|clothed *adjective*
un|cloud|ed
un|clut|tered
unco +s
un|coat|ed
unco guid
un|coil +s +ed +ing
un|collect|ed
un|col|ored (*use*
  uncoloured)
un|col|oured
un|combed
un|come|ly
un|com|fort|able
un|com|fort|able|
      ness
un|com|fort|ably
un|com|mer|cial
un|com|mit|ted
un|com|mon
un|com|mon|ly
un|com|mon|ness
un|com|muni|ca|tive
un|com|muni|ca|tive|
      ly
un|com|muni|ca|tive|
      ness
un|com|pen|sated
un|com|peti|tive
un|com|plain|ing
un|com|plain|ing|ly
un|com|plet|ed
un|compli|cated
un|compli|ment|ary
un|com|pound|ed
un|com|pre|hend|ing
un|com|pre|hend|
      ing|ly
un|com|prehen|sion
un|com|pressed
un|compro|mis|ing
un|compro|mis|ing|
      ly
un|compro|mis|ing|
      .ness
un|con|cealed
un|con|cern
un|con|cerned
un|con|cern|ed|ly
un|con|clud|ed
un|con|dition|al
un|con|dition|al|ity
un|con|dition|al|ly
un|con|di|tioned
un|con|fi|dent
un|con|fined
un|con|firmed
un|con|form|able

un|con|form|able|
      ness
un|con|form|ably
un|con|form|ity
  un|con|form|ities
un|con|gen|ial
un|con|nect|ed
un|con|nect|ed|ly
un|con|nect|ed|ness
un|con|quer|able
un|con|quer|ably
un|con|quered
un|con|scion|able
un|con|scion|ably
un|con|scious
un|con|scious|ly
un|con|scious|ness
un|con|secrat|ed
un|con|sent|ing
un|con|sid|ered
un|con|sol|able
un|con|sol|ably
un|con|sti|tu|tion|al
un|con|sti|tu|tion|
      al|ity
un|con|sti|tu|tion|
      al|ly
un|con|strained
un|con|straint
un|con|strict|ed
un|con|struct|ed
un|con|sumed
un|con|sum|mated
un|con|tain|able
un|con|tamin|ated
un|con|ten|tious
un|con|test|ed
un|con|test|ed|ly
un|contra|dict|ed
un|con|trived
un|con|trol|lable
un|con|trol|lable|
      ness
un|con|trol|lably
un|con|trolled
un|contro|ver|sial
un|contro|ver|sial|ly
un|contro|vert|ed
un|contro|vert|ible
un|con|ven|tion|al
un|con|ven|tion|
      al|ity
un|con|ven|tion|al|ly
un|con|vert|ed
un|con|vinced
un|con|vin|cing
un|con|vin|cing|ly
un|cooked
un|cool
un|co|opera|tive
un|co|opera|tive|ly
un|co|ordin|ated

un|cork +s +ed +ing
un|cor|rect|ed
un|cor|robor|ated
un|cor|rupt|ed
un|count|abil|ity
un|count|able
un|count|ably
un|count|ed
un|couple
  un|couples
  un|coupled
  un|coup|ling
un|coupled *adjective*
un|court|ly
un|couth
un|couth|ly
un|couth|ness
un|coven|ant|ed
un|cov|er +s +ed
  +ing
un|cov|ered *adjective*
un|create
  un|creates
  un|creat|ed
  un|creat|ing
un|creat|ed *adjective*
un|creat|ive
un|cred|it|ed
un|critic|al
un|critic|al|ly
un|cropped
un|cross
  un|cross|es
  un|crossed
  un|cross|ing
un|crowd|ed
un|crowned
un|crush|able
un|crushed
unc|tion +s
unc|tuous
unc|tuous|ly
unc|tuous|ness
un|culti|vated
un|cul|tured
un|curb +s +ed +ing
un|curbed *adjective*
un|cured
un|curl +s +ed +ing
un|cur|tailed
un|cur|tained
un|cut
un|dam|aged
un|dated
un|daunt|ed
un|daunt|ed|ly
un|daunt|ed|ness
un|dead
un|deceive
  un|deceives
  un|deceived
  un|deceiv|ing

un|decid|abil|ity
un|decid|able
un|decid|ed +s
un|decid|ed|ly
un|deciph|er|able
un|declared
un|decor|ated
un|defeat|ed
un|defend|ed
un|defiled
un|defin|able
un|defin|ably
un|defined
un|deliv|ered
un|demand|ing
un|demo|crat|ic
un|demo|crat|ic|ally
un|demon|strated
un|demon|stra|tive
un|demon|stra|tive|
      ly
un|demon|stra|tive|
      ness
un|deni|able
un|deni|ably
un|dent|ed
un|depend|able
under
under|achieve
  under|achieves
  under|achieved
  under|achiev|ing
under|achieve|ment
under|achiev|er +s
under|act +s +ed
  +ing
under|age
under|arm +s
under|belly
  under|bel|lies
under|bid
  under|bids
  under|bid
  under|bid|ding
under|bid|der +s
under|body
  under|bod|ies
under|boss
  under|boss|es
under|brush
under|capit|al|ize
  under|capit|al|iz|es
  under|capit|al|ized
  under|capit|al|iz|ing
under|card +s
under|car|riage +s
under|charge
  under|char|ges
  under|charged
  under|char|ging
under|class
  under|class|es
under|clothes

under|cloth|ing
under|coat +s
under|coat|ing +s
under|cook +s +ed
+ing
under|cooked
adjective
under|cover
under|croft +s
under|cur|rent +s
under|cut
under|cuts
under|cut
under|cut|ting
under|devel|oped
under|devel|op|ment
under|dog +s
under|done
under|draw|ing +s
under|dress
under|dress|es
under|dressed
under|dress|ing
under|edu|cated
under|empha|sis
under|empha|ses
under|empha|size
under|empha|siz|es
under|empha|sized
under|empha|siz|
ing
under|employed
under|employ|ment
under|esti|mate
under|esti|mates
under|esti|mated
under|esti|mat|ing
under|esti|ma|tion
+s
under|expose
under|expos|es
under|exposed
under|expos|ing
under|expo|sure +s
under|fed
under|floor
under|flow +s
under|foot
under|fund +s +ed
+ing
under|fund|ed
adjective
under|fund|ing +s
under-fur
under|garment +s
under|gird +s +ed
+ing
under|glaze +s
under|go
under|goes
under|went
under|gone
under|going

under|grad +s
under|gradu|ate +s
under|ground
Under|ground
Rail|road (*History*)
Under|ground
Rail|way
(= Underground
Railroad)
under|growth +s
under|hand +s +ed
+ing
under|hand|ed
adjective & adverb
Under|hill, Bar|bara
Ann (Cdn figure
skater)
Under|hill, Frank
Haw|kins (Cdn
political theorist)
under|lay
• (set something under
another; something
laid under another)
under|lays
under|laid
under|lay|ing
• *past tense of* underlie
[☞ underlie]
under|lay|ment +s
under|lie (lie or be
situated underneath;
be the basis of)
under|lies
under|lay
under|lain
under|lying
[☞ underlay]
under|line
under|lines
under|lined
under|lin|ing
under|ling +s
under|lin|ing +s *noun*
under|lip +s
under|lying *adjective*
under|manned
under|mine
under|mines
under|mined
under|min|ing
under|miner +s
under|most
under|neath
under|nour|ished
under|nourish|ment
under|pad +s
under|paid *adjective*
under|pants
under|part +s
under|pass
under|pass|es

under|pay
under|pays
under|paid
under|pay|ing
under|pay|ment +s
under|per|form +s
+ed +ing
under|per|form|ance
under|per|form|er +s
under|pin
under|pins
under|pinned
under|pin|ning
under|pin|ning +s
noun
under|plant +s +ed
+ing
under|play +s +ed
+ing
under|popu|lated
under|popu|la|tion
under|powered
under|price
under|prices
under|priced
under|pricing
under|priv|il|eged
under|rate
under|rates
under|rated
under|rat|ing
under|rated *adjective*
under-report +s +ed
+ing
under-represent +s
+ed +ing
under|ripe
under|score
under|scores
under|scored
under|scor|ing
under|sea
under|secre|tary
under|secre|tar|ies
under|sell
under|sells
under|sold
under|sell|ing
under|served
under|sexed
under-sheriff +s
under|shirt +s
under|shoot
under|shoots
under|shot
under|shoot|ing
under|shorts
under|shot *adjective*
under|side +s
under|signed
under|size
(= undersized)
under|sized

under|skirt +s
under|slung
under|sold
under|sow
under|sows
under|sowed
under|sown
under|sow|ing
under|staffed
under|staff|ing
under|stand
under|stands
under|stood
under|stand|ing
under|stand|abil|ity
under|stand|able
under|stand|ably
under|stand|er +s
under|stand|ing +s
noun & adjective
under|stand|ing|ly
under|state
under|states
under|stated
under|stat|ing
under|stated *adjective*
under|stated|ly
under|stated|ness
under|state|ment +s
under|stater +s
under|steer +s +ed
+ing
under|stood *adjective*
under|storey +s
under|story (*use*
understorey)
under|stories
under|study
under|studies
under|studied
under|study|ing
under|surface +s
under|take
under|takes
under|took
under|taken
under|tak|ing
under|taker +s
under|tak|ing +s
noun
under-the-counter
under|things
under|tone +s
under|took
under|tow +s
under|trick +s
under|use
under|uses
under|used
under|using
under|util|iz|a|tion
+s

under|util|ize
  under|util|izes
  under|util|ized
  under|util|iz|ing
under|util|ized
  adjective
under|valu|a|tion +s
under|value
  under|values
  under|valued
  under|valu|ing
under|vest +s
under|water
under|way
under|wear
under|weight
under|went
under|whelm +s +ed
  +ing
under|wing +s
under|wire +s
under|wired
under|wood
under|work +s +ed
  +ing
under|world +s
under|write
  under|writes
  under|wrote
  under|writ|ten
  under|writing
under|writer +s
un|descend|ed
un|deserved
un|deserv|ed|ly
un|deserv|ing
un|deserv|ing|ly
un|desir|abil|ity
un|desir|able +s
un|desir|able|ness
un|desir|ably
un|desired
un|detect|abil|ity
un|detect|able
un|detect|ably
un|detect|ed
un|deter|mined
un|deterred
un|devel|oped
un|deviat|ing
un|deviat|ing|ly
un|diag|nosed
undid
und|ies
un|differ|en|ti|ated
un|digest|ed
un|digni|fied
un|dilut|ed
un|dimin|ish|able
un|dimin|ished
un|dim|mable
un|dimmed

un|dine +s
un|diplo|mat|ic
un|diplo|mat|ic|ally
un|direct|ed
un|disci|pline
un|disci|plined
un|dis|closed
un|dis|cov|ered
un|dis|crim|in|at|ing
un|dis|guised
un|dis|guis|ed|ly
un|dis|mayed
un|dis|puted
un|dis|solved
un|dis|tin|guished
un|dis|trib|ut|ed
un|dis|turbed
un|divid|ed
undo
• *verb*
  un|does
  undid
  un|done
  un|doing
• *noun*
  undos
un|dock +s +ed +ing
un|docu|ment|ed
un|doing +s *noun*
un|domes|ti|cated
un|done *adjective*
un|doubt|ed
un|doubt|ed|ly
un|drained
un|dramat|ic
un|dramat|ic|ally
un|draped
un|dreamed of
  (undreamed-of *when*
  preceding a noun)
un|dreamt of
  (undreamt-of *when*
  preceding a noun)
un|dress
  un|dress|es
  un|dressed
  un|dress|ing
un|dressed *adjective*
un|drink|able
Und|set, Sig|rid
  (Norwegian novelist)
undue
un|dulant
un|dulate
  un|du|lates
  un|dulat|ed
  un|dulat|ing
un|dula|tion +s
un|dula|tory
un|duly
un|dyed
un|dying
un|earned

un|earth +s +ed +ing
un|earth|li|ness
un|earth|ly
un|ease
un|easi|ly
un|easi|ness
un|easy
  un|easi|er
  un|easi|est
un|eat|able
un|eaten
un|econom|ic
un|econom|ic|al
un|edify|ing
un|edify|ing|ly
un|edited
un|educ|able
un|edu|cated
un|elect|able
un|elect|ed
un|embar|rassed
un|embel|lished
un|emotion|al
un|emotion|al|ly
un|emphat|ic
un|emphat|ic|ally
un|employ|abil|ity
un|employ|able +s
un|em|ployed
un|employ|ment
un|en|closed
un|encum|bered
un|end|ing
un|end|ing|ly
un|end|ing|ness
un|en|dowed
un|endur|able
un|endur|ably
un|enforce|able
un|en|gaged
un-English
un|enjoy|able
un|enlight|ened
un|enlight|en|ing
un|enter|pris|ing
un|enthusi|as|tic
un|enthusi|as|tic|ally
un|envi|able
un|envi|ably
un|equal
un|equalled
un|equal|ly
un|equipped
un|equivo|cal
un|equivo|cal|ly
un|equivo|cal|ness
un|err|ing
un|err|ing|ly
UNESCO (United
  Nations Educational,
  Scientific, & Cultural
  Organization)

un|escort|ed
un|essen|tial +s
un|estab|lished
un|ethical
un|ethical|ly
un|even
un|even|ly
un|even|ness
un|event|ful
un|event|ful|ly
un|event|ful|ness
un|exam|ined
un|exampled
un|excep|tion|able
  (not objectionable;
  satisfactory)
  [☞ unexceptional]
un|excep|tion|able|
             ness
un|excep|tion|ably
un|excep|tion|al
  (not outstanding;
  ordinary)
  [☞
  unexceptionable]
un|excep|tion|al|ly
un|excit|able
un|excit|ing
un|exhaust|ed
un|expect|ed
un|expect|ed|ly
un|expect|ed|ness
un|expired
un|explain|able
un|explain|ably
un|explained
un|explod|ed
un|exploit|ed
un|explored
un|exposed
un|expressed
un|expur|gated
un|face|able
un|fading
un|fail|ing
un|fail|ing|ly
un|fair
un|fair|ly
un|fair|ness
un|faith|ful
un|faith|ful|ly
un|faith|ful|ness
un|falter|ing
un|falter|ing|ly
un|famil|iar
un|famili|ar|ity
un|fashion|able
un|fashion|ably
un|fasten +s +ed
  +ing
un|fastened *adjective*
un|father|ly

un|fathom|able
un|fathom|ably
un|fathomed
un|favor|able (use
  unfavourable)
un|favor|able|ness
  (use
  unfavourableness)
un|favor|ably (use
  unfavourably)
un|favour|able
un|favour|able|ness
un|favour|ably
un|fazed
un|feas|ibil|ity
un|feas|ible
un|feas|ibly
unfed
un|feel|ing
un|feel|ing|ly
un|feel|ing|ness
un|feigned
un|felt
un|femin|ine
un|fenced
un|ferment|ed
un|fertil|ized
un|fetter +s +ed +ing
un|fettered adjective
un|filial
un|filial|ly
un|filled
un|filtered
un|finish|able
un|finished
unfit
un|fit|ness
un|fit|ted
un|fit|ting
un|fixed
un|flag|ging
un|flag|ging|ly
un|flap|pabil|ity
un|flap|pable
un|flap|pably
un|flatter|ing
un|flatter|ing|ly
un|flavored (use
  unflavoured)
un|flavoured
un|fledged
un|fleshed
un|flinch|ing
un|flinch|ing|ly
un|focused
un|focussed (use
  unfocused)
un|fold +s +ed +ing
un|fold|ing +s noun
un|fold|ment
un|forced
un|forced|ly

un|ford|able
un|fore|see|able
un|fore|seen
un|forget|table
un|forget|tably
un|forgiv|able
un|forgiv|ably
un|forgiv|en
un|forgiv|ing
un|forgiv|ing|ly
un|forgiv|ing|ness
un|formed
un|formu|lat|ed
un|forth|coming
un|forti|fied
un|fortu|nate +s
un|fortu|nate|ly
un|found|ed
un|found|ed|ly
un|found|ed|ness
un|framed
un|free
un|free|dom
un|freeze
  un|freez|es
  un|froze
  un|frozen
  un|freez|ing
un|frequent|ed
un|friend|li|ness
un|friend|ly
  un|friend|li|er
  un|friend|li|est
un|frock +s +ed +ing
un|froze
un|frozen adjective
un|fruit|ful
un|fruit|ful|ly
un|fulfill|able
un|fulfilled
un|fulfill|ing
un|fulfill|ment
un|fulfil|ment (use
  unfulfillment)
un|fund|ed
un|funni|ness
un|funny
  un|funni|er
  un|funni|est
un|furl +s +ed +ing
un|furnished
un|fussi|ly
un|fussy
un|gain|li|ness
un|gain|ly
un|gallant
un|gallant|ly
Un|gava (peninsula,
  bay & former
  territory, Canada)
un|gener|ous
un|gener|ous|ly

un|genial
un|gentle
un|gentle|man|li|
               ness
un|gentle|man|ly
un|gently
un|gifted
un|glamor|ous
un|glazed
un|gloved
un|glued
un|godli|ness
un|godly
un|govern|able
un|govern|ably
un|grace|ful
un|grace|ful|ly
un|gracious
un|gracious|ly
un|gracious|ness
un|gram|mat|ic|al
un|gram|mat|ic|al|ity
  un|gram|mat|ic|
           al|ities
un|gram|mat|ic|al|ly
un|grasp|able
un|grate|ful
un|grate|ful|ly
un|grate|ful|ness
un|greased
un|ground|ed
un|grudging
un|grudging|ly
un|guard +s +ed
  +ing
un|guard|ed adjective
un|guard|ed|ly
un|guard|ed|ness
un|guent +s
un|guess|able
un|guid|ed
un|guis
  un|gues
un|gu|late +s
un|hallowed
un|ham|pered
un|hand +s +ed +ing
un|handi|ly
un|handi|ness
un|hand|some
un|handy
un|happi|ly
un|happi|ness
un|happy
  un|happi|er
  un|happi|est
un|harmed
un|har|moni|ous
un|harness
  un|harness|es
  un|har|nessed
  un|harness|ing

un|har|nessed
  adjective
un|hatched
un|health
un|health|ful
un|healthi|ly
un|healthi|ness
un|healthy
  un|healthi|er
  un|healthi|est
un|heard
un|heard of
  (unheard-of when
  preceding a noun)
un|heat|ed
un|heed|ed
un|heed|ing
un|heed|ing|ly
un|help|ful
un|help|ful|ly
un|herald|ed
un|hero|ic
un|hero|ic|ally
un|hesitat|ing
un|hesitat|ing|ly
un|hin|dered
un|hinge
  un|hinges
  un|hinged
  un|hinging
un|hinged adjective
unhip
un|histor|ical
un|histor|ical|ly
un|hitch
  un|hitch|es
  un|hitched
  un|hitch|ing
un|hit|table
un|holi|ness
un|holy
  un|holi|er
  un|holi|est
un|honored (use
  unhonoured)
un|honoured
un|hook +s +ed +ing
un|hoped for
  (unhoped-for when
  preceding a noun)
un|horse
  un|horses
  un|horsed
  un|horsing
un|human
un|hung
un|hurried
un|hurried|ly
un|hurt
un|hurt|able
un|husked
un|hygien|ic
un|hygien|ic|ally

un|hyphen|ated
Uni|ate +s
uni|axial
uni|axial|ly
uni|cameral
UNICEF (United
  Nations Children's
  Fund)
uni|cellu|lar
uni|corn +s
uni|cycle
  uni|cycles
  uni|cycled
  uni|cyc|ling
uni|cyc|list +s
un|ideal
un|ideal|ized
un|iden|ti|fi|able
un|iden|ti|fied
uni|dimen|sion|al
uni|direc|tion|al
uni|direc|tion|al|ity
uni|direc|tion|al|ly
uni|fi|ca|tion +s
Uni|fi|ca|tion Church
uni|fi|ca|tory
uni|fied adjective
uni|fi|er +s
uni|form +s +ed +ing
uni|formi|tar|ian +s
uni|formi|tar|ian|ism
uni|form|ity
  uni|form|ities
uni|form|ly
unify
  uni|fies
  uni|fied
  uni|fy|ing
uni|fy|ing adjective
un|ignor|able
uni|lat|eral
uni|lat|eral|ism
uni|lat|eral|ly
uni|lin|gual +s
uni|lin|gual|ism
uni|lin|gual|ist +s
uni|lin|gual|ly
un|illum|in|ated
un|illus|trated
uni|locu|lar
un|imagin|able
un|imagin|ably
un|imagina|tive
un|imagina|tive|ly
un|imagina|tive|ness
un|imagined
un|impaired
un|impas|sioned
un|impeach|able
un|impeach|ably
un|impeded
un|impeded|ly

un|import|ance
un|import|ant
un|impos|ing
un|impos|ing|ly
un|im|pressed
un|impres|sion|able
un|impres|sive
un|impres|sive|ly
un|impres|sive|ness
un|improved
un|incor|por|ated
un|infect|ed
un|inflam|mable
un|inflect|ed
un|influ|enced
un|influ|en|tial
un|inform|a|tive
un|informed
un|inhabit|able
un|inhabit|ed
un|inhibit|ed
un|inhibit|ed|ly
un|inhibit|ed|ness
un|initi|ated
un|injured
un|inspired
un|inspir|ing
un|inspir|ing|ly
un|instruct|ed
un|insu|lated
un|insur|able
un|insured
un|intelli|gent
un|intelli|gent|ly
un|intelli|gi|bil|ity
un|intelli|gible
un|intelli|gibly
un|intend|ed
un|inten|tion|al
un|inten|tion|al|ly
un|inter|est|ed
un|inter|est|ed|ly
un|inter|est|ed|ness
un|inter|est|ing
un|inter|est|ing|ly
un|inter|est|ing|ness
un|inter|pret|able
un|inter|pret|ed
un|inter|rupt|ed
un|inter|rupt|ed|ly
un|inter|rupt|ed|ness
un|inter|rupt|ible
uni|nucle|ate
un|invent|ive
un|invent|ive|ly
un|invent|ive|ness
un|investi|gated
un|invited
un|invited|ly
un|inviting
un|inviting|ly
un|involved

Union (US History)
union +s
union-buster +s
union-busting
Union Gov|ern|ment
  (Cdn History)
union|ism
Union|ist +s
  (advocate of political
  union)
union|ist +s
  (advocate or
  member of a labour
  union)
union|is|tic
union|iz|a|tion +s
union|ize (enter into a
  labour union)
  union|iz|es
  union|ized
  union|iz|ing
un-ionized (not
  ionized)
Union Jack +s (flag of
  the UK)
union jack +s (flag
  consisting of the
  union of a national
  flag)
Union Na|tio|nale
Union of Soviet
  So|cial|ist
  Re|pub|lics (former
  country)
Union Ter|ri|tory (in
  India)
Union Ter|ri|tor|ies
unip|ar|ous
uni|planar
uni|pod +s
uni|polar
uni|polar|ity
unique (unequalled)
  [☞ Unix, eunuch]
unique|ly
unique|ness
un|ironed
uni|serial
uni|sex
uni|sex|ual
uni|sex|u|al|ity
uni|sex|ual|ly
uni|son +s
un|issued
unit +s
uni|tard +s
Uni|tar|ian
Uni|tar|ian|ism
uni|tar|ily
uni|tar|ity
uni|tary

unite
  unites
  united
  uniting
United +s adjective &
  noun (of the United
  Church)
united adjective
United Arab
  Emir|ates (country,
  Middle East)
United Can|ada
  (Upper & Lower
  Canada 1841–67)
United Church of
  Can|ada
United Em|pire
  Loyal|ist +s
United King|dom
  (country consisting
  of England, Wales,
  Scotland & Northern
  Ireland)
united|ly
United Na|tions
United States
  (country, N America)
unit|hold|er +s
uni|tive
uni|tive|ly
unity
  uni|ties
uni|valent
uni|valve +s
uni|ver|sal +s
uni|ver|sal|ism
uni|ver|sal|ist +s
uni|ver|sal|is|tic
uni|ver|sal|ity
uni|ver|sal|iz|a|tion
uni|ver|sal|ize
  uni|ver|sal|iz|es
  uni|ver|sal|ized
  uni|ver|sal|iz|ing
uni|ver|sal|ly
Uni|ver|sal Prod|uct
  Code +s
uni|verse +s
uni|ver|sity
  uni|ver|si|ties
uni|vocal +s
uni|vocal|ity
uni|vocal|ly
Unix proprietary
  (Computing)
  [☞ eunuch]
un|joined
un|just
un|justi|fi|able
un|justi|fi|ably
un|justi|fied
un|just|ly
un|just|ness

un|kempt
un|kempt|ly
un|kempt|ness
un|kept
un|kill|able
un|kind +er +est
un|kind|ly
un|kind|ness
un|kink +s +ed +ing
un|knit
  un|knits
  un|knit|ted
  un|knit|ting
un|knot
  un|knots
  un|knot|ted
  un|knot|ting
un|know|abil|ity
un|know|able +s
un|know|ing
un|know|ing|ly
un|know|ing|ness
un|known +s
un|known|ness
Un|known Sol|dier
un|labelled
un|labored (use
  unlaboured)
un|laboured
un|lace
  un|laces
  un|laced
  un|lacing
un|lade (unload)
  un|lades
  un|laded
  un|laden
  or un|laded
  un|lading
  [☞ unlaid]
un|laden adjective
un|lady|like
un|laid
• adjective (not laid)
• past & past participle
  of unlay
  [☞ unlade]
un|lament|ed
un|lash
  un|lash|es
  un|lashed
  un|lash|ing
un|latch
  un|latch|es
  un|latched
  un|latch|ing
un|law|ful
un|law|ful|ly
un|law|ful|ness
un|lay (untwist)
  un|lays
  un|laid
  un|lay|ing

un|lead|ed
un|learn
  un|learns
  un|learned
  or un|learnt
  un|learn|ing
un|learned[1] adjective
  (that has not been
  learned; innate)
un|learn|ed[2] adjective
  (ignorant)
un|learn|ed|ly
un|learnt adjective
  (that has not been
  learned, innate: use
  unlearned)
un|leash
  un|leash|es
  un|leashed
  un|leash|ing
un|leav|ened
un|less
un|let|tered
un|liber|ated
un|licenced (use
  unlicensed)
un|licensed
un|light|ed
un|likable (use
  unlikeable)
un|like
un|like|able
un|like|li|hood
un|like|li|ness
un|like|ly
  un|like|li|er
  un|like|li|est
un|like|ness
  un|like|ness|es
un|lim|ber +s +ed
  +ing
un|limit|ed
un|limit|ed|ly
un|limit|ed|ness
un|lined
un|link +s +ed +ing
un|list|ed
unlit
un|liv|able
un|lived-in
un|load +s +ed +ing
un|load|er +s
un|lock +s +ed +ing
un|locked adjective
un|looked-for
un|loose
  un|loos|es
  un|loosed
  un|loos|ing
un|loos|en +s +ed
  +ing (= unloose)
un|lov|abil|ity
un|lov|able

un|loved
un|love|li|ness
un|love|ly
un|lov|ing
un|lov|ing|ly
un|lov|ing|ness
un|luck|i|ly
un|luck|i|ness
un|lucky
  un|luck|i|er
  un|luck|i|est
un|made adjective
un|make
  un|makes
  un|made
  un|making
un|man
  un|mans
  un|manned
  un|man|ning
un|man|age|able
un|man|age|able|
            ness
un|man|age|ably
un|man|aged
un|man|li|ness
un|man|ly
un|manned
un|man|nered
un|man|ner|li|ness
un|man|ner|ly
un|mapped
un|marked
un|market|able
un|married
un|mask +s +ed +ing
un|mask|er +s
un|match|able
un|match|ably
un|matched
un|matured
un|mean|ing
un|mean|ing|ly
un|mean|ing|ness
un|meant
un|measur|able
un|measur|ably
un|meas|ured
un|medi|ated
un|melodi|ous
un|melodi|ous|ly
un|melt|ed
un|memor|able
un|memor|ably
un|men|tion|abil|ity
un|men|tion|able +s
un|men|tion|able|
            ness
un|men|tion|ably
un|men|tioned
un|mer|chant|able
un|merci|ful

un|merci|ful|ly
un|merci|ful|ness
un|merit|ed
unmet
un|mind|ful
un|mind|ful|ly
un|mind|ful|ness
un|miss|able
un|mistak|abil|ity
un|mistak|able
un|mistak|able|ness
un|mistak|ably
un|mistake|abil|ity
  (use
  unmistakability)
un|mistake|able (use
  unmistakable)
un|mistake|able|ness
  (use
  unmistakableness)
un|mistake|ably (use
  unmistakably)
un|miti|gated
un|miti|gated|ly
un|mixed
un|modern|ized
un|modi|fied
un|modu|lated
un|mold +s +ed +ing
  (use unmould)
un|molest|ed
un|moor +s +ed +ing
un|mother|ly
un|moti|vated
un|mould +s +ed
  +ing
un|mount|ed
un|mourned
un|movable
un|move|able (use
  unmovable)
un|moved
un|moving
un|mown
un|muf|fle
  un|muf|fles
  un|muf|fled
  un|muf|fling
un|muf|fled adjective
un|music|al
un|music|al|ity
un|music|al|ly
un|music|al|ness
un|muti|lated
un|muz|zle
  un|muz|zles
  un|muz|zled
  un|muz|zling
un|name|able
un|named
un|natur|al
un|natur|al|ly

un|natur|al|ness
un|navig|abil|ity
un|navig|able
un|neces|sar|ily
un|neces|sar|i|ness
un|neces|sary
  un|neces|sar|ies
un|need|ed
un|nerve
  un|nerves
  un|nerved
  un|nerv|ing
un|nerv|ing *adjective*
un|nerv|ing|ly
un|notice|able
un|notice|ably
un|noticed
un|num|bered
UNO (United Nations
  Organization)
  UNOs
un|objec|tion|able
un|objec|tion|able|
             ness
un|objec|tion|ably
un|obliging
un|ob|scured
un|observ|able
un|observ|ant
un|observ|ant|ly
un|ob|served
un|observ|ed|ly
un|ob|struct|ed
un|obtain|able
un|obtru|sive
un|obtru|sive|ly
un|obtru|sive|ness
un|occu|pied
un|offend|ed
un|offend|ing
un|official
un|official|ly
un|oiled
un|opened
un|opposed
un|or|dained
un|ordin|ary
un|organ|ized
un|origin|al
un|origin|al|ity
un|origin|al|ly
un|orna|ment|al
un|orna|ment|ed
un|ortho|dox
un|ortho|dox|ly
un|ortho|doxy
  un|ortho|dox|ies
un|osten|ta|tious
un|osten|ta|tious|ly
un|osten|ta|tious|
             ness
un|owned

un|pack +s +ed +ing
un|pack|er +s
un|paged
un|paid
un|paint|ed
un|paired
un|palat|abil|ity
un|palat|able
un|palat|able|ness
un|paral|leled
un|pardon|able
un|pardon|able|ness
un|pardon|ably
un|parlia|ment|ary
un|pasteur|ized
un|patent|ed
un|patri|ot|ic
un|patri|ot|ic|ally
un|patron|iz|ing
un|patron|iz|ing|ly
un|paved
un|peeled
un|peg
  un|pegs
  un|pegged
  un|peg|ging
un|people
  un|peoples
  un|peopled
  un|peop|ling
un|per|ceived
un|percep|tive
un|percep|tiv|ely
un|percep|tive|ness
un|perfect|ed
un|perfor|ated
un|per|formed
un|per|fumed
un|person +s
un|persuad|able
un|persuad|ed
un|persua|sive
un|persua|sive|ly
un|per|turbed
un|perturb|ed|ly
un|philo|soph|ic
un|philo|soph|ic|al
un|philo|soph|ic|al|ly
un|physio|logic
un|physio|logic|al
un|physio|logic|al|ly
un|pick +s +ed +ing
un|picked *adjective*
un|pictur|esque
un|pin
  un|pins
  un|pinned
  un|pin|ning
un|pitied
un|pity|ing
un|pity|ing|ly
un|place|able

un|placed
un|planned
un|plant|ed
un|play|able
un|play|ably
un|pleas|ant
un|pleas|ant|ly
un|pleas|ant|ness
un|pleas|antry
  un|pleas|ant|ries
un|pleas|ing
un|pleas|ing|ly
un|ploughed (*use*
  unplowed)
un|plowed
un|plucked
un|plug
  un|plugs
  un|plugged
  un|plug|ging
un|plugged *adjective*
un|plumb|able
un|plumbed
un|poetic
un|poetic|al
un|point|ed
un|pol|ished
un|polit|ic
un|polit|ic|al
un|polit|ic|al|ly
un|pollut|ed
un|popu|lar
un|popu|lar|ity
un|popu|lar|ly
un|popu|lated
un|posed
un|pos|sessed
un|pow|ered
un|prac|tical
un|practi|cal|ity
un|prac|tical|ly
un|prac|ticed (*use*
  unpractised)
un|prac|tised
un|preced|ent|ed
un|preced|ent|ed|ly
un|predict|abil|ity
un|predict|able
un|predict|ably
un|predict|ed
un|preju|diced
un|premedi|tat|ed
un|premedi|tat|ed|ly
un|pre|pared
un|prepar|ed|ly
un|prepar|ed|ness
un|prepos|sess|ing
un|pre|scribed
un|present|able
un|pressed
un|pressur|ized
un|presum|ing

un|presump|tu|ous
un|pretend|ing
un|pretend|ing|ly
un|pretend|ing|ness
un|preten|tious
un|preten|tious|ly
un|preten|tious|ness
un|priced
un|primed
un|prin|cipled
un|prin|cipled|ness
un|print|able
un|print|ably
un|print|ed
un|priv|il|eged
un|prob|lem|at|ic
un|prob|lem|at|ic|
             ally
un|pro|cessed
un|product|ive
un|product|ive|ly
un|product|ive|ness
un|profes|sion|al
un|profes|sion|al|ly
un|profit|able
un|profit|able|ness
un|profit|ably
UNPROFOR (United
  Nations Protection
  Force)
un|progres|sive
un|promis|ing
un|promis|ing|ly
un|prompt|ed
un|pro|nounce|able
un|pro|nounce|ably
un|propi|tious
un|propi|tious|ly
un|prosper|ous
un|prosper|ous|ly
un|protect|ed
un|protect|ed|ness
un|protest|ing
un|protest|ing|ly
un|prov|abil|ity
un|prov|able
un|proved
un|proven
un|provid|ed
un|pro|voked
un|publi|cized
un|publish|able
un|pub|lished
un|punc|tual
un|punc|tu|al|ity
un|punc|tu|ated
un|punish|able
un|pun|ished
un|puri|fied
un|put|down|able
un|quali|fied
un|quali|fied|ly

un|quanti|fi|able
un|quanti|fied
un|quench|able
un|quench|ably
un|quenched
un|question|abil|ity
un|question|able
un|question|able|
        ness
un|question|ably
un|questioned
un|question|ing
un|question|ing|ly
un|quiet
un|quiet|ly
un|quiet|ness
un|quot|able
un|quote
un|quoted
un|ranked
un|ravel
  un|ravels
  un|ravelled
  un|ravel|ling
un|ravel|ment
un|reach|able
un|reach|able|ness
un|reach|ably
un|read
un|read|abil|ity
un|read|able
un|read|ably
un|readi|ly
un|readi|ness
un|ready
un|real (not real)
  [☞ unreel]
un|real|is|tic
un|real|is|tic|ally
un|real|ity
  un|real|ities
un|real|iz|able
un|real|ized
un|real|ly
un|reason
un|reason|able
un|reason|able|ness
un|reason|ably
un|reasoned
un|reason|ing
un|reason|ing|ly
un|recep|tive
un|recip|ro|cat|ed
un|reckoned
un|recog|niz|able
un|recog|niz|able|
        ness
un|recog|niz|ably
un|recog|nized
un|recon|ciled
un|recon|struct|ed
un|record|able

un|record|ed
un|recover|able
un|recyc|lable
un|redeem|able
un|redeem|ably
un|re|deemed
un|re|dressed
un|reel +s +ed +ing
  (unwind)
  [☞ unreal]
un|ref|ereed
un|refined
un|reflect|ing
un|reflect|ing|ly
un|reflect|ive
un|reflect|ive|ly
un|reflect|ive|ness
un|reformed
un|regard|ed
un|regen|er|acy
un|regen|er|ate +s
un|regen|er|ate|ly
un|regis|tered
un|regulat|ed
un|re|hearsed
un|re|inforced
un|relat|ed
un|relat|ed|ness
un|relaxed
un|released
un|relent|ing
un|relent|ing|ly
un|relent|ing|ness
un|reli|abil|ity
un|reli|able
un|reli|able|ness
un|reli|ably
un|relieved
un|reliev|ed|ly
un|remark|able
un|remark|ably
un|remarked
un|remem|ber|able
un|remem|bered
un|remit|ting
un|remit|ting|ly
un|remit|ting|ness
un|remorse|ful
un|remorse|ful|ly
un|remov|able
un|remuner|a|tive
un|repeat|abil|ity
un|repeat|able
un|repent|ant
un|repent|ant|ly
un|report|ed
un|rep|re|sent|a|tive
un|rep|re|sent|able
un|rep|re|sent|ed
un|re|pressed
un|request|ed
un|requit|ed

un|requit|ed|ly
un|requit|ed|ness
un|resent|ful
un|re|served
un|reserv|ed|ly
un|reserv|ed|ness
un|resist|ed
un|resist|ed|ly
un|resist|ing
un|resist|ing|ly
un|resist|ing|ness
un|resolv|able
un|resolved
un|resolv|ed|ly
un|resolv|ed|ness
un|respon|sive
un|respon|sive|ly
un|respon|sive|ness
un|rest
un|rest|ful
un|rest|ful|ly
un|rest|ing
un|rest|ing|ly
un|restored
un|restrained
un|restrain|ed|ly
un|restrict|ed
un|restrict|ed|ly
un|returned
un|revealed
un|reveal|ing
un|revised
un|reward|ed
un|reward|ing
un|rhymed
un|rhyth|mic
un|rhyth|mic|al
un|rhyth|mic|ally
un|ridable
un|ridden
un|riddle
  un|riddles
  un|riddled
  un|riddling
un|riddler +s
un|ride|able (use
  unridable)
un|rig
  un|rigs
  un|rigged
  un|rig|ging
un|right|eous
un|right|eous|ly
un|right|eous|ness
un|ripe
un|ripe|ness
un|rivalled
un|road|worthy
un|robe
  un|robes
  un|robed
  un|robing

un|roll +s +ed +ing
un|roman|tic
un|roman|tic|ally
un|roofed
un|rope
  un|ropes
  un|roped
  un|roping
un|round|ed
un|ruf|flable
un|ruf|fled
un|ruled
un|ruli|ness
un|ruly
  un|ruli|er
  un|ruli|est
UNRWA (United
  Nations Relief and
  Works Agency)
un|sad|dle
  un|sad|dles
  un|sad|dled
  un|sad|dling
un|safe
un|safe|ly
un|safe|ness
un|said *adjective*
un|salabil|ity (*use*
  unsaleability)
un|salable (*use*
  unsaleable)
un|salar|ied
un|sale|abil|ity
un|sale|able
un|salt|ed
un|salvage|able
un|salvage|ably
un|sancti|fied
un|sanc|tioned
un|sani|tary
un|satis|fac|tor|i|ly
un|satis|fac|tor|i|
        ness
un|satis|fac|tory
un|satis|fied
un|satis|fy|ing
un|satis|fy|ing|ly
un|satur|ated
un|satur|a|tion
un|saved
un|savor|i|ly (*use*
  unsavourily)
un|savor|i|ness (*use*
  unsavouriness)
un|savory (*use*
  unsavoury)
un|savour|i|ly
un|savour|i|ness
un|savoury
un|say
  un|says
  un|said
  un|say|ing

un|say|able
un|scal|able
un|scarred
un|scathed
un|scent|ed
un|sched|uled
un|scholar|li|ness
un|scholar|ly
un|schooled
un|scien|tif|ic
un|scien|tif|ic|ally
un|scram|ble
  un|scram|bles
  un|scram|bled
  un|scram|bling
un|scram|bler +s
un|scratched
un|screened
un|screw +s +ed
  +ing
un|script|ed
un|scrip|tur|al
un|scrip|tur|al|ly
un|scrupu|lous
un|scrupu|lous|ly
un|scrupu|lous|ness
un|seal +s +ed +ing
un|sealed
un|search|able
un|search|able|ness
un|search|ably
un|season|able
un|season|able|ness
un|season|ably
un|season|al
un|seasoned
un|seat +s +ed +ing
un|sea|worthi|ness
un|sea|worthy
un|secured
un|see|able
un|seed|ed
un|see|ing
un|see|ing|ly
un|seem|li|ness
un|seem|ly
  un|seem|li|er
  un|seem|li|est
un|seen
un|segre|gated
un|seiz|able
un|select|ed
un|select|ive
un|self|con|scious
un|self|con|scious|ly
un|self|cons|cious|
           ness
un|self|ish
un|self|ish|ly
un|self|ish|ness
un|sell|able
un|sensa|tion|al

un|sensa|tion|al|ly
un|senti|men|tal
un|senti|men|tal|ity
un|senti|ment|al|ly
un|separ|ated
un|serious
un|serious|ly
un|serious|ness
un|service|abil|ity
un|service|able
un|serviced
un|set
un|set|tle
  un|set|tles
  un|set|tled
  un|set|tling
un|set|tled *adjective*
un|settled|ness
un|set|tling *adjective*
un|set|tling|ly
un|sewn
un|sex
  un|sex|es
  un|sexed
  un|sex|ing
un|sexed *adjective*
un|sexy
  un|sexi|er
  un|sexi|est
un|shackle
  un|shackles
  un|shackled
  un|shack|ling
un|shaded
un|shak|abil|ity (*use*
  unshakeability)
un|shak|able (*use*
  unshakeable)
un|shak|ably (*use*
  unshakeably)
un|shake|abil|ity
un|shake|able
un|shake|ably
un|shaken
un|shaken|ly
un|shared
un|shaven
un|shaven|ness
un|sheathe
  un|sheathes
  un|sheathed
  un|sheath|ing
un|shed
un|shelled
un|shel|tered
un|shield|ed
un|ship
  un|ships
  un|shipped
  un|ship|ping
un|shock|abil|ity
un|shock|able
un|shock|ably

un|shod
un|shorn
un|shov|elled
un|shrink|abil|ity
un|shrink|able
un|sight|ed
un|sightli|ness
un|sightly
un|signed
un|sink|abil|ity
un|sink|able
un|sized
un|skil|ful
un|skil|ful|ly
un|skil|ful|ness
un|skilled
un|skill|ful (*use*
  unskilful)
un|skill|ful|ly (*use*
  unskilfully)
un|skill|ful|ness (*use*
  unskilfulness)
un|slak|able (*use*
  unslakeable)
un|slake|able
un|sleep|ing
un|sleep|ing|ly
un|sliced
un|sling
  un|slings
  un|slung
  un|sling|ing
un|smiling
un|smiling|ly
un|smoked
un|snap
  un|snaps
  un|snapped
  un|snap|ping
un|snarl +s +ed +ing
un|sociabil|ity
un|sociable
un|sociable|ness
un|sociably
un|social
un|social|ist
un|social|ly
un|soiled
un|sold
un|solicit|ed
un|solv|abil|ity
un|solv|able
un|solved
un|sophis|ti|cated
un|sophis|ti|cated|ly
un|sophis|ti|cated|
           ness
un|sophis|ti|ca|tion
un|sort|ed
un|sought
un|sound
un|sound|ed

un|sound|ly
un|sound|ness
un|soured
un|sown
un|sparing
un|sparing|ly
un|sparing|ness
un|speak|able
un|speak|able|ness
un|speak|ably
un|speak|ing
un|special|ized
un|specif|ic
un|speci|fied
un|spec|tacu|lar
un|spec|tacu|lar|ly
un|spent
un|spilled
un|spilt (*use*
  unspilled)
un|spirit|ual
un|spirit|u|al|ity
un|spirit|ual|ly
un|spoiled
un|spoilt (*use*
  unspoiled)
un|spoken
un|spon|sored
un|spool +s +ed +ing
un|sport|ing
un|sport|ing|ly
un|sports|man|like
un|spot|ted
un|sprayed
un|sprung
un|spun
un|stabil|ized
un|stable
un|stable|ness
un|stably
un|stained
un|stamped
un|starched
un|stated
un|steadi|ly
un|steadi|ness
un|steady
  un|steadi|er
  un|steadi|est
un|sterile
un|stick
  un|sticks
  un|stuck
  un|stick|ing
un|stiff|en +s +ed
  +ing
un|stiff|ened *adjective*
un|stint|ed
un|stint|ing
un|stint|ing|ly

un|stitch
  un|stitch|es
  un|stitched
  un|stitch|ing
un|stop
  un|stops
  un|stopped
  un|stop|ping
un|stop|pabil|ity
un|stop|pable
un|stop|pably
un|stop|per +s +ed
  +ing
un|strained
un|strap
  un|straps
  un|strapped
  un|strap|ping
un|stressed
un|string
  un|strings
  un|strung
  un|string|ing
un|struc|tured
un|strung *adjective*
un|stuck
un|studied
un|studied|ly
un|stuffy
un|stylish
un|sub|dued
un|sub|scribe
  un|sub|scribes
  un|sub|scribed
  un|sub|scrib|ing
un|sub|stan|tial
un|sub|stan|ti|ality
un|sub|stan|tial|ly
un|sub|stan|ti|ated
un|subtle
un|subtly
un|success
un|success|ful
un|success|ful|ly
un|suit|abil|ity
un|suit|able
un|suit|able|ness
un|suit|ably
un|suit|ed
un|sullied
un|summoned
un|sung
un|super|vised
un|support|able
un|support|ably
un|support|ed
un|support|ive
un|sure
un|sure|ly
un|sure|ness
un|surfaced
un|surpass|able
un|surpass|ably

un|surpassed
un|surprised
un|surpris|ing
un|surpris|ing|ly
un|surveyed
un|suscept|ibil|ity
un|suscept|ible
un|suspect|ed
un|suspect|ed|ly
un|suspect|ing
un|suspect|ing|ly
un|suspect|ing|ness
un|suspi|cious
un|suspi|cious|ly
un|sustain|able
un|sustain|ably
un|sustained
un|swayed
un|sweet|ened
un|swept
un|swerv|ing
un|swerv|ing|ly
un|sworn
un|symmet|ric|al
un|symmet|ri|cal|ly
un|sympa|thet|ic
un|sympa|thet|ic|ally
un|system|atic
un|system|atic|ally
un|taint|ed
un|talent|ed
un|tamable (*use*
  untameable)
un|tame|able
un|tamed
un|tan|gle
  un|tan|gles
  un|tan|gled
  un|tan|gling
un|tanned
un|tapped
un|tar|nished
un|tasted
un|taught
un|taxed
un|teach|able
un|tech|nic|al
un|tempered
un|tenabil|ity
un|tenable
un|tenable|ness
un|tenably
un|tenant|ed
un|tend|ed
un|ten|dered
un|tenured
Unter|mensch
  Unter|mensch|en
un|test|able
un|test|ed
un|tethered
un|thanked

un|thank|ful
un|thank|ful|ly
un|think|abil|ity
un|think|able
un|think|able|ness
un|think|ably
un|think|ing
un|think|ing|ly
un|thought
un|thread +s +ed
  +ing
un|threat|en|ing
un|thrift|i|ly
un|thrift|i|ness
un|thrifty
un|throne
  un|thrones
  un|throned
  un|thron|ing
un|tidily
un|tidiness
un|tidy
  un|tidier
  un|tidiest
un|tie
  un|ties
  un|tied
  un|tying
un|tied *adjective*
until
un|till|able
un|tilled
un|time|li|ness
un|time|ly
un|tinged
un|tiring
un|tiring|ly
un|titled
unto
un|told
un|touch|abil|ity
un|touch|able +s
un|touched
un|toward
un|trace|able
un|trace|ably
un|traced
un|tracked
un|trad|ition|al
un|trained
un|tram|melled
un|trans|formed
un|trans|lat|abil|ity
un|trans|lat|able
un|trans|lat|ably
un|trans|lat|ed
un|trav|elled
un|treat|able
un|treat|ed
un|trendy
un|tried
un|trimmed

un|trod|den
un|troubled
un|true
un|truly
un|trust|worthi|ness
un|trust|worthy
un|truth +s
un|truth|ful
un|truth|ful|ly
un|truth|ful|ness
un|tuck +s +ed +ing
un|tuned
un|turned
un|tutored
un|twine
  un|twines
  un|twined
  un|twin|ing
un|twist +s +ed +ing
un|tying
un|typ|ical
un|typ|ical|ly
un|usable
un|used
un|usual
un|usual|ly
un|usual|ness
un|utter|able
un|utter|ably
un|uttered
un|vaccin|at|ed
un|valued
un|van|quished
un|var|nished
un|vary|ing
un|vary|ing|ly
un|veil +s +ed +ing
un|veil|ing +s *noun*
un|venti|lat|ed
un|veri|fi|able
un|veri|fied
un|versed
un|viable
un|visit|ed
un|voiced
un|waged
un|walled
un|want|ed (not
  wanted)
  [☞ unwonted]
un|wari|ly
un|wari|ness
un|warlike
un|warned
un|warrant|able
un|warrant|ably
un|warrant|ed
un|wary
un|washed
un|watch|able
un|watched
un|watered

un|waver|ing
un|waver|ing|ly
un|weaned
un|wear|able
un|wearied
un|wearied|ly
un|weary|ing
un|weary|ing|ly
un|weathered
un|wed
un|wed|ded
un|weed|ed
un|weight +s +ed
  +ing
un|weight|ed
  adjective
un|welcome
un|welcome|ly
un|welcom|ing
un|well
un|whole|some
un|whole|some|ly
un|whole|some|ness
un|wield|i|ly
un|wield|i|ness
un|wieldy
  un|wield|i|er
  un|wield|i|est
un|will|ing
un|will|ing|ly
un|will|ing|ness
un|wind
  un|winds
  un|wound
  un|wind|ing
un|wink|ing
un|wink|ing|ly
un|win|nable
un|wisdom
un|wise
un|wise|ly
un|withered
un|wit|nessed
un|wit|ting
un|wit|ting|ly
un|wit|ting|ness
un|woman|ly
un|wont|ed (not
  customary or usual)
  [☞ unwanted]
un|wont|ed|ly
un|work|abil|ity
un|work|able
un|work|ably
un|worked
un|world|li|ness
un|world|ly
un|worn
un|worried
un|worthi|ly
un|worthi|ness

un|worthy
  un|worthi|er
  un|worthi|est
un|wound *adjective*
un|wound|ed
un|woven
un|wrap
  un|wraps
  un|wrapped
  un|wrap|ping
un|wrin|kled
un|writ|able
un|writ|ten
un|wrought
un|yield|ing
un|yield|ing|ly
un|yield|ing|ness
un|yoke
  un|yokes
  un|yoked
  un|yok|ing
unzip
  un|zips
  un|zipped
  un|zip|ping
up
  ups
  upped
  up|ping
up|along
up-and-comer +s
up-and-coming
Upani|shad +s
Upani|shad|ic
upas
  upas|es
up|beat +s
up|braid +s +ed +ing
up|braid|ing +s *noun*
up|bring|ing +s
UPC (Universal
  Product Code)
  UPCs
up|cast
  up|casts
  up|cast
  up|cast|ing
up|chuck +s +ed
  +ing
up-close-and-
  person|al
  adjective preceding a
  noun
up|com|ing
up|coun|try
up|court
up|dat|able
up|date
  up|dates
  up|dated
  up|dating
up|date|able (*use*
  updatable)

up|dated *adjective*
up|dater +s
Up|dike, John Hoyer
  (US writer)
up|draft +s
up|draught +s (*use*
  updraft)
up|end +s +ed +ing
up|field
up front *adverb* (*We*
  require $50 up front;
  Let's sit up front)
up|front *adjective* (*We*
  require an upfront
  payment of $50; She
  is honest and upfront)
up|grad|able (*use*
  upgradeable)
up|grade
  up|grades
  up|graded
  up|grading
up|grade|able
up|grader +s
up|growth +s
up|heav|al +s
up|heave
  up|heaves
  up|heaved
  up|heav|ing
up|hill +s
up|hold
  up|holds
  up|held
  up|hold|ing
up|hold|er +s
up|hol|ster +s +ed
  +ing
up|hol|ster|er +s
up|hol|stery
up ice
U-pick +s (farm,
  orchard)
  [☞ Yupik]
up-island
up|keep
up|land +s
up|lift +s +ed +ing
up|lift|er +s
up|lift|ing *adjective*
up|light +s
up|light|ing
up|link +s +ed +ing
up|linked *adjective*
up|load +s +ed +ing
up|market
upon
up|per +s
Upper Arrow (lake,
  Canada)
Upper Aus|tria (state,
  Austria)
Upper Can|ada

Upper Can|ad|ian +s
upper case (upper-
  case *when preceding*
  a noun)
upper class (upper-
  class *when preceding*
  a noun)
  upper class|es
upper|class|man
  upper|class|men
upper crust (upper-
  crust *when preceding*
  a noun)
upper|cut
  upper|cuts
  upper|cut
  upper|cut|ting
upper|most
Upper Volta (*former*
  name for Burkina
  Faso)
upper|works
uppish
uppish|ly
uppish|ness
uppiti|ness
uppity
uppity|ness (*use*
  uppitiness)
Upp|sala (city,
  Sweden)
up|raise
  up|rais|es
  up|raised
  up|rais|ing
up|raised *adjective*
up|right +s +ed +ing
up|right|ly
up|right|ness
up|rise
  up|rises
  up|rose
  up|risen
  up|ris|ing
up|ris|ing +s *noun*
up|river
up|roar +s
up|roar|ious
up|roar|ious|ly
up|roar|ious|ness
up|root +s +ed +ing
up|root|ed|ness
up|rose
up|rush
  up|rush|es
UPS (uninterruptible
  power supply)
  UPSs
upsa|daisy
  (= upsy-daisy)
up|scale

upset
  up|sets
  upset
  up|set|ting
up|set|ter +s
up|set|ting|ly
up|shift +s +ed +ing
up|shot +s
up|side +s
up|side down
  (upside-down *when*
  preceding a noun)
up|sides
up|si|lon +s
up|size
  up|siz|es
  up|sized
  up|siz|ing
up|slope
up|stage
  up|stages
  up|staged
  up|staging
up|stairs
up|stand|ing
up|start +s
up|state
up|stater +s
up|stream
up|stroke +s
up|surge +s
up|swept
up|swing +s
upsy-daisy
up|take +s
up|tempo
up|throw +s
up|thrust +s
up|tick +s
up|tight
up|time +s
up to date (up-to-
  date *when preceding*
  a noun)
up-to-the-minute
up|town
up|town|er +s
up|turn +s +ed +ing
up|ward
up|ward|ly
up|wards
up|well|ing +s
up|wind
Ur (ancient Sumerian
  city)
ura|cil
ur|aeus
  uraei
Ural +s (mountain
  range, Russia)
Ural-Altaic
Ural|ic

Ur|ania (*Greek &*
  Roman Myth)
Ur|an|ian
ur|an|ic
ur|an|ium
uran|og|raph|er +s
uran|o|graph|ic
uran|og|raphy
Ura|nus (*Greek Myth*;
  planet)
Urban (popes)
urban (of a city)
ur|bane (refined,
  suave)
ur|bane|ly
ur|ban|ism
ur|ban|ist +s
ur|ban|ite +s
ur|ban|ity
  ur|ban|ities
ur|ban|iz|a|tion +s
ur|ban|ize
  ur|ban|iz|es
  ur|ban|ized
  ur|ban|iz|ing
ur|ceo|late
ur|chin +s
Urdu
urea
urea for|mal|de|hyde
ureal (pertaining to
  urea)
  [☞ Uriel]
ur|emia
ur|emic
ur|eter +s
ur|eter|al
ur|eter|ic
ur|eth|ane +s
ur|ethra
  ur|eth|rae or
  ur|eth|ras
ur|eth|ral
ur|eth|ritis
Urey, Har|old
  Clay|ton (US
  chemist)
Urga (*former name for*
  Ulan Bator,
  Mongolia)
urge
  urges
  urged
  ur|ging
ur|gency
  ur|gen|cies
ur|gent
ur|gent|ly
ur|ger +s
ur|ging +s *noun*
Uriah (*Bible*)
uric

Uriel (angel)
  [☞ ureal]
urin|al +s
urin|aly|sis
  urin|aly|ses
urin|ary
urin|ate
  urin|ates
  urin|ated
  urin|at|ing
urin|a|tion
urine +s
urin|ous
URL (*Computing*)
  URLs
urn +s (vase, vessel)
  [☞ earn]
uro|chord +s
uro|genital
uro|logic
uro|logic|al
ur|ol|o|gist +s
ur|ol|ogy
uro|pygium +s
Ur|quhart, Sir
  Thom|as (Scottish
  writer)
Ur|quhart, Jane (Cdn
  writer)
Ursa Major
  (constellation)
Ursa Minor
  (constellation)
ur|sine
Ur|sula (saint)
Ur|su|line +s
urti|caria
Uru|guay (country,
  S America)
Uru|guay|an +s
Uruk (ancient city,
  Mesopotamia)
Urum|chi (= Urumqi)
Urum|qi (city, China)
urus
  plural urus|es
us
usabil|ity
usable
usage +s
usance +s
use
  uses
  used
  using
use|abil|ity (*use*
  usability)
use|able (*use* usable)
used *adjective*
use|ful
use|ful|ly
use|ful|ness
use|less

use|less|ly
use|less|ness
Use|net
user +s
user-definable
user-defined
user-friendli|ness
user-friendly
ush|er +s +ed +ing
  [☞ Ussher]
usher|ette +s
Usher of the Black
  Rod
  Ush|ers of the
  Black Rod
Ushu|aia (town,
  Argentina)
Üskü|dar (suburb of
  Istanbul, Turkey)
Us|pa|llata (mountain
  pass, Andes)
us|que|baugh
Ussher, James (Irish
  clergyman)
Us|ta|ba|kan|skoe
  (*former name for*
  Abakan, Russia)
Us|tasha (*use*
  Ustashe)
Us|tashas (*use*
  Ustashe)
Us|tashe (Croatian
  nationalist
  movement)
  [☞ Saint-Eustache]
Us|tashi (*use* Ustashe)
Us|ti|nov, Sir Peter
  Alex|an|der (English
  dramatist)
usual +s
usu|al|ly
usu|al|ness
usu|fruct
usu|fruc|tu|ary
Usum|bura (*former*
  name for
  Bujumbura,
  Burundi)
usur|er +s
usur|ious
usur|ious|ly
usurp +s +ed +ing
usurp|a|tion +s
usurp|er +s
usury
Utah (state, US)
Utah|an +s
Utahn +s (*use*
  Utahan)
Ute (people &
  language)
  plural Ute or Utes
ute +s

uten|sil +s
uter|ine
uter|itis
uter|us
  uter|us|es or uteri
U Thant (UN
  secretary-general)
Uther Pen|dragon
  (*Arthurian Legend*)
utile
utili|dor +s
utili|tar|ian +s
utili|tar|ian|ism
util|ity
  util|ities
util|iz|able
util|iz|a|tion +s
util|ize
  util|iz|es
  util|ized
  util|iz|ing
util|iz|er +s
ut|most
Uto-Aztecan
Uto|pia +s
Uto|pian +s
Uto|pian|ism
Utrecht (province &
  its capital, the
  Netherlands)
utri|cle +s
utric|u|lar
utric|u|lus
  utric|uli
Utri|llo, Mau|rice
  (French painter)
Ut|sire (island,
  Norway)
Uttar Pra|desh (state,
  India)
ut|ter +s +ed +ing
  (complete, absolute;
  say)
  [☞ udder]
utter|able
utter|ance +s
utter|er +s
utter|ly
utter|most
U-turn +s +ed +ing
UV (ultraviolet
  radiation)
  UVs
uvea +s
UV Index
uvula
  uvu|lae
uvu|lar +s
Ux|bridge (township,
  Canada)
ux|or|ial
ux|ori|cid|al
ux|ori|cide +s

ux|ori|ous
ux|ori|ously
ux|ori|ous|ness
Uz|bek +s
Uz|bek|istan (country,
  Asia)
Uzi +s (machine gun)

V

V
• (letter; shape)
  V's
• (volt, voltage;
  potential difference)
  [☞ vee]
v (letter)
  v's
  [☞ vee]
v.
• (verse; volume)
  vv.
• (versus; *vide*)
V-1 (rocket)
  V-1s
V-2 (rocket)
  V-2s
V6 (engine; vehicle)
  V6's
V8 (engine; vehicle)
  V8's
Vaal (river, South
  Africa)
  [☞ Waal]
Vaasa (city, Finland)
vac +s
va|cancy
  va|can|cies
va|cant
va|cant|ly
va|cat|able
va|cate
  va|cates
  va|cat|ed
  va|cat|ing
va|ca|tion +s +ed
  +ing
va|ca|tion|er +s
va|ca|tion|ist +s
vacation|land +s
vac|cin|al
vac|cin|ate
  vac|cin|ates
  vac|cin|at|ed
  vac|cin|at|ing
vac|cin|a|tion +s
vac|cin|ator +s
vac|cine +s

vac|cinia
vacil|late
  vacil|lates
  vacil|lat|ed
  vacil|lat|ing
vacil|lat|ing *adjective*
vacil|la|tion +s
vacil|la|tor +s
vacua
vacu|ity
  vacu|ities
vacu|ol|ar
vacu|ol|at|ed
vacu|ol|a|tion +s
vacu|ole +s
vacu|ous
vacu|ous|ly
vacu|ous|ness
vac|uum
• *noun* (vacuum
  cleaner)
  plural vac|uums
• *noun* (spaced devoid
  of matter)
  vac|uums or vacua
• *verb*
  vac|uums
  vac|uumed
  vac|uum|ing
VAD (Voluntary Aid
  Detachment)
  VADs
vade mecum +s
Vado|dara (city, India)
Vaduz (capital of
  Liechtenstein)
vaga|bond +s
vaga|bond|age
vagal
Vagan|ova,
  Agrip|pina
  Jacov|levna
  (Russian dance
  teacher)
va|gari|ous
va|gary
  va|gar|ies
vagi
va|gina
  va|ginas or va|ginae
va|gina den|tata
vagin|al
vagin|is|mus
vagin|itis
va|gran|cy
va|grant +s
va|grant|ly
vague
  vaguer
  vaguest
vague|ly
vague|ness
vaguish

vagus (*Anatomy*)
  vagi
  [☞ Las Vegas]
Vail (city, US)
vail +s +ed +ing
  (respectfully lower
  one's weapon or
  remove one's hat;
  submit)
  [☞ veil, vale]
vain +er +est
  (conceited; futile; in
  'in vain')
  [☞ vein, vane,
  Vane]
vain|glor|i|ous
vain|glor|i|ous|ly
vain|glor|i|ous|ness
vain|glory
vain|ly
vain|ness
vair
Vaish|nava +s
  (*Hinduism*)
Vais|ya +s (*Hinduism*)
va|lance +s (curtain)
  [☞ valence,
  Valens]
va|lanced
Val-Bélair (town,
  Canada)
Valde|mar
  (= Waldemar)
Val-d'Or (city,
  Canada)
vale +s (valley; in 'vale
  of tears')
  [☞ veil, vail, Vail]
val|edic|tion +s
val|edic|tor|ian +s
val|edic|tory
  val|edic|tor|ies
va|lence +s
  (*Chemistry*;
  Linguistics)
  [☞ valance,
  Valens]
Va|len|cia (region &
  its capital, Spain;
  city, Venezuela)
Va|len|ciennes
va|len|cy
  va|len|cies
Val|ens (Roman
  emperor)
  [☞ valance,
  valence]
Val|en|tine (saint)
val|en|tine +s
Val|en|tine's Day
Val|en|tin|ian (Roman
  emperors)

Val|en|tino, Ru|dolph (Italian-born actor)

Val|era, Eamon de (Irish statesman)

Val|er|ian (Roman emperor)

val|er|ian +s

Val|éry, (Am|broise) Paul Tous|saint Jules (French writer)

valet
valets
valeted
valet|ing

val|etu|din|ar|ian +s

val|etu|din|ar|ian| ism

val|gus
val|gus|es

Val|halla (Scandinavian Myth)

vali|ant

vali|ant|ly

valid

valid|ate
valid|ates
valid|at|ed
valid|at|ing

valid|a|tion +s

valid|ity

valid|ly

val|ine

val|ise +s

Val|ium proprietary

Val|kyrie +s (Scandinavian Myth)

Valla|do|lid (city, Spain; former name for Morelia, Mexico)

val|lecu|la
val|lecu|lae

val|lecu|lar

val|lecu|late

Valle d'Aosta (region, Italy)

Val|let|ta (capital of Malta)

val|ley +s

Val|ley East (town, Canada)

Val|ley Forge (historical encampment site, US)

Val|ley girl +s

val|lum
valla

Va|lois (French royal house)

Va|lois, Dame Nin|ette de (English ballet director)

valor (use valour)

valor|iz|a|tion +s

valor|ize
valor|iz|es
valor|ized
valor|iz|ing

valor|ous

valour

Val|pa|raíso (city, Chile)

valu|able +s

valu|ably

valu|ate
valu|ates
valu|at|ed
valu|at|ing

valu|a|tion

valu|ator +s

value
val|ues
val|ued
valu|ing

value added noun

value-added adjective preceding a noun

value-free

value|less

value|less|ness

valu|er +s

valv|ate

valve +s

valved

valve|less

val|vul|ar

val|vul|itis

vam|brace +s

va|moose
va|moos|es
va|moosed
va|moos|ing

vamp +s +ed +ing

vam|pire +s

vam|piric

vam|pir|ism

vamp|ish

vampy

Van (lake, Turkey)

van +s

van|ad|ate +s

van|ad|ic

van|ad|ium

van|ad|ous

Van Allen, James Al|fred (US physicist)

Van Allen belt +s

Van|brugh, Sir John (English dramatist & architect)

Van Buren, Mar|tin (US president)

Van|cou|ver (city, island & mountain, Canada)

Van|cou|ver, George (English navigator)

Van|cou|ver|ite +s

Van|dal +s (member of a Germanic tribe)

van|dal +s (destructive person)

Van|dal|ic

van|dal|ism

van|dal|is|tic

van|dal|ize
van|dal|iz|es
van|dal|ized
van|dal|iz|ing

Van de Graaff (generator)

Van|der|bijl|park (city, South Africa)

Van|der|bilt, Cor|nel|ius (US financier)

Van|der|haeghe, Guy (Cdn writer)

van der Waals, Jo|han|nes Did|er|ik (Dutch physicist)

van der Waals for|ces

Van Die|men's Land (former name for Tasmania)

Van Doos (the Royal 22e Régiment)

Van Dyck, Sir An|thony (Flemish painter)
[☞ Vandyke, Vandyke brown]

Van|dyke, Sir An|thony (= Van Dyck)

Van|dyke +s (beard; cape, collar; lace border point)
[☞ Van Dyck]

Van|dyke brown +s (Vandyke-brown when preceding a noun)

Vane, Sir Henry ('Harry') (English statesman & colonial administrator)

vane +s (weather vane; propeller blade; fin on a projectile; feather part; quadrant sight)
[☞ vain, vein]

vaned

Vän|ern (lake, Sweden)

Van Eyck, Jan (Flemish painter)

vang +s

Van Gogh, Vin|cent Wil|lem (Dutch painter)

van|guard +s

Van Horne, Sir Wil|liam Cor|nel|ius (Cdn railway official)

Van|ier (cities, Canada)

Van|ier, Georges-Philéas (Cdn governor general)

Van|ier, Jean (Cdn spiritual leader)

Van|ier Cup

van|illa +s

van|il|lin

Vanir (Scandinavian Myth)

van|ish
van|ish|es
van|ished
van|ish|ing

van|ity
van|ities

van Ley|den, Lucas (Dutch artist)

van|quish
van|quish|es
van|quished
van|quish|ing

van|quish|able

van|quish|er +s

Van|taa (city, Finland)

van|tage +s

van't Hoff, Jaco|bus Hen|dri|cus (Dutch chemist)

Vanu|atu (country, SW Pacific)

Vanu|atu|an +s

Van|zet|ti, Bar|tolo|meo (Italian-born anarchist)

vapid

vap|id|ity
vap|id|ities

vap|id|ly

vap|id|ness

vapor +s +ed +ing (use vapour)

vapor|able

vapor|er +s (use vapourer)

vap|or|etto
vap|or|etti or vap|or|ettos

vapor|ing noun (use vapouring)

vapor|ish (use vapourish)

vapor|iz|able
vapor|iz|a|tion +s
vapor|ize
  vapor|iz|es
  vapor|ized
  vapor|iz|ing
vapor|iz|er +s
vapor|ous
vapor|ous|ness
vapor|ware (use
  vapourware)
vapory (use vapoury)
va|pour +s +ed +ing
vapour|er +s
vapour|ing noun
vapour|ish
vapour|ware
va|poury
va|quero +s
VAR (value-added
  reseller)
VARs
var|ac|tor +s
Var|an|asi (city, India)
Var|an|gian +s
var|ec +s (seaweed)
  [☞ varix]
Va|rennes (town,
  Canada)
var|eny|ky
Var|ese (town, Italy)
Va|rèse, Edgard (US
  composer)
Var|gas, Getú|lio
  Dor|nel|les
  (Brazilian president)
Var|gas Llosa, Jorge
  Mario Pedro
  (Peruvian writer)
vari|abil|ity
vari|able +s
vari|able|ness
vari|ably
vari|ance
  vari|an|ces
vari|ant +s
vari|ate +s
vari|a|tion +s
vari|a|tion|al
vari|cella
vari|cella zos|ter
vari|ces
vari|co|cele +s
vari|col|ored (use
  varicoloured)
vari|col|oured
vari|cose (in 'varicose
  veins' etc.; swollen)
  [☞ verrucose]
vari|cosed
vari|cos|ity
var|ied
var|ied|ly

varie|gate
  varie|gates
  varie|gat|ed
  varie|gat|ing
varie|gat|ed adjective
varie|ga|tion +s
var|iet|al +s
var|iet|al|ly
var|iety
  var|ieties
Vari|focal +s
  proprietary
vari|form
va|rio|la
va|rio|lar
va|rio|lous
vari|om|eter +s
vari|orum +s
vari|ous
vari|ous|ly
vari|ous|ness
var|is|tor +s
varix (dilated vein;
  shell ridge)
  vari|ces
  [☞ varec]
var|let +s
var|let|ry
Var|ley, Fred|erick
  Hors|man (Cdn
  painter)
var|mint +s
Varna (city, Bulgaria)
var|na +s (Hinduism)
var|nish
  var|nish|es
  var|nished
  var|nish|ing
var|nish|er +s
Varro, Mar|cus
  Ter|en|tius (Roman
  satirist)
var|sity
Var|sol proprietary
Var|una (Hindu god)
varus
varve +s
varved
vary (diversify;
  fluctuate)
  var|ies
  var|ied
  vary|ing
  [☞ very]
vary|ing adjective
vary|ing|ly
vas (Anatomy)
  vasa
  [☞ vase]
Vas|ari, Gior|gio
  (Italian artist &
  biographer)

Vasco da Gama
  (Portuguese
  explorer)
vas|cu|lar
vas|cu|lar|ity
vas|cu|lar|iz|a|tion
vas|cu|lar|ize
  vas|cu|lar|iz|es
  vas|cu|lar|ized
  vas|cu|lar|iz|ing
vas|cu|lar|ly
vas|cu|lum
  vas|cu|la
vas def|er|ens
  vasa def|er|en|tia
vase +s (ornamental
  vessel)
  [☞ vas]
vas|ec|to|mize
  vas|ec|to|miz|es
  vas|ec|to|mized
  vas|ec|to|miz|ing
vas|ec|tomy
  vas|ec|to|mies
Vas|el|ine proprietary
  noun
vas|el|ine verb
  vas|el|ines
  vas|el|ined
  vas|el|in|ing
vaso|active
vaso|con|stric|tion
vaso|con|strict|ive
vaso|con|strict|or +s
vaso|dila|ta|tion
vaso|dila|tion
vaso|dila|tor +s
vaso|dila|tory
vaso|motor +s
vaso|pres|sin
vas|sal +s
vas|sal|age +s
vast +er +est
Väs|ter|ås (city,
  Sweden)
vast|ly
vast|ness
VAT (value-added tax)
  VATs
vat (tank; dyeing
  solution)
  vats
  vatted
  vat|ting
vatic
Vati|can (pope's
  palace)
Vati|can City (papal
  state)
Vati|can|ism
Vati|can|ist +s
Vati|can II (council)
vati|cin|al

vati|cin|ate
  vati|cin|ates
  vati|cin|at|ed
  vati|cin|at|ing
vati|cin|a|tion +s
vati|cin|ator +s
Vät|tern (lake,
  Sweden)
Vau|ban, Sébas|tian
  Le Pres|tre de
  (French military
  engineer)
Vaud (canton,
  Switzerland)
vaude|ville
vaude|vil|lian
Vaud|ois
  plural Vaud|ois
Vau|dreuil
  (municipality,
  Canada)
Vau|dreuil, Marquis
  de (Philippe de
  Rigaud de Vaudreuil,
  governor of
  Montreal & New
  France)
Vau|dreuil, Marquis
  de (Pierre de Rigaud
  de Vaudreuil de
  Cavagnial, governor
  general of New
  France)
Vaudreuil-Dorion
  (city, Canada)
Vaughan (city,
  Canada)
Vaughan, Henry
  (Welsh poet)
Vaughan, Sarah Lois
  ('Sassy') (US singer)
Vaughan Wil|liams,
  Ralph (English
  composer)
vault +s +ed +ing
  (Architecture;
  Gymnastics)
  [☞ volte]
vault|ed adjective
vault|er +s
vault|ing noun
vault|ing|ly
vaunt +s +ed +ing
vaunt|ed adjective
vaunt|er +s
vava|sour +s
Vavi|lov, Niko|lai
  Ivan|ovich (Soviet
  geneticist)
VC (Victoria Cross;
  Vice-Chairman,
  -Chancellor, -Consul
  etc.)
VCs

v-chip +s
VCR (video cassette recorder)
VCRs
VD (venereal disease)
VDs
VDT (video display terminal)
VDTs
VDU (video display unit)
VDUs
veal
plural **veal**
vealy
veal|i|er
veal|i|est
Veb|len, Thor|stein Bunde (US economist)
vec|tor +s +ed +ing
vec|tor|ial
vec|tor|iz|a|tion
vec|tor|ize
vec|tor|iz|es
vec|tor|ized
vec|tor|iz|ing
Veda +s (*Hinduism*)
[☞ **Vedda**]
Ve|dan|ta
Ve|dan|tic
Ve|dan|tist +s
VE day
Vedda (people)
plural **Vedda** or Ved|das
[☞ **Veda**]
ved|ette +s
Vedic
vee +s (letter; shape)
vee|jay +s (= VJ)
vee|na +s (*Music*)
[☞ **vena cava**]
veep +s
veer +s +ed +ing
veery
veer|ies
veg
• (vegetable)
plural **veg**
• (vegetate, laze)
veg|ges
vegged
veg|ging
Vega (star)
Vega Car|pio, Lope Felix de (Spanish dramatist)
veg|an +s
vegan|ism
Vegas (Las Vegas)
[☞ **vagus**]
vege|table +s

vege|tal
vege|tar|ian +s
vege|tar|ian|ism
vege|tate
vege|tates
vege|tat|ed
vege|tat|ing
vege|ta|tion +s
vege|ta|tion|al
vege|ta|tive
vege|ta|tive|ly
vege|ta|tive|ness
veg|gie +s
Vegre|ville (town, Canada)
vehe|mence
vehe|ment
vehe|ment|ly
vehicle +s
ve|hicu|lar
veil +s +ed +ing (cover; headdress of a bride or nun)
[☞ **vail, Vail, vale**]
veiled *adjective* (wearing a veil; disguised)
[☞ **vailed**]
veil|ing +s *noun* (fabric, veil)
[☞ **vailing**]
veil|less
vein +s +ed +ing (blood vessel; stripe in cheese or wood etc.; *Geology*; nervure of a wing or leaf; style)
[☞ **vain, vane, Vane**]
veined *adjective*
vein|ing +s *noun*
vein|less
vein|let +s
vein|like
veiny
vein|i|er
vein|i|est
vela *plural of* **velum**
[☞ **Vila, villa, Villa**]
ve|la|men
ve|la|mina
velar
Ve|láz|quez, Diego Rod|rí|guez de Silva y (Spanish painter)
Vel|cro *proprietary*
Vel|croes
Vel|croed
Vel|cro|ing
Vel|croed *adjective*
veld +s

veldt +s (*use* veld)
veli|ger +s
vel|lum +s (paper or parchment)
[☞ **velum**]
velo|cim|eter +s
vel|oci|pede +s
vel|oci|ped|ist +s
vel|oci|rap|tor +s
vel|ocity
vel|oci|ties
velo|drome +s
velour
ve|lou|té +s
velum (membrane, flap)
vela
[☞ **vellum**]
velu|tin|ous
vel|vet +s
vel|vet|ed
vel|vet|een +s
velvet|leaf +s
Vel|vet Revo|lu|tion (in Czechoslovakia)
vel|vet revo|lu|tion +s (*in general use*)
vel|vety
vena cava (*Anatomy*)
venae cavae
venal (open to corruption or bribery)
[☞ **venial**]
ve|nal|ity
ve|nal|ly
ven|a|tion +s
ven|a|tion|al
vend +s +ed +ing
Venda (former homeland, South Africa)
vend|ee +s
ven|det|ta
vend|ible
Ven|dôme
vend|or +s
ven|du +s
ven|eer +s +ed +ing
ven|eer|ing *noun*
vene|punc|ture +s (*use* venipuncture)
ven|er|abil|ity
ven|er|able
ven|er|able|ness
ven|er|ably
ven|er|ate
ven|er|ates
ven|er|at|ed
ven|er|at|ing
ven|er|a|tion
ven|er|ator +s
ven|ereal

ven|ereal|ly
ven|ery
vene|sec|tion +s
Ven|etia (region, Italy)
Ven|etian +s (of Venice; glass; red; window)
ven|etian +s (blind)
ven|etianed
Ven|eto (= Venetia)
Vene|zuela (country, S America)
Vene|zuelan +s
ven|geance
venge|ful
venge|ful|ly
venge|ful|ness
veni|al (pardonable)
[☞ **venal**]
veni|al|ity
veni|al|ly
Ven|ice (city, Italy)
Ven|ing Mein|esz, Felix An|dries (Dutch geophysicist)
veni|punc|ture +s
veni|son
Ven|ite +s
Venn dia|gram +s
ven|om +s
ven|omed
ven|om|ous
ven|om|ous|ly
ven|om|ous|ness
ven|os|ity
ven|ous (marked by veins)
[☞ **Venus**]
ven|ous|ly
vent +s +ed +ing
vent hole +s
venti|fact +s
venti|late
venti|lates
venti|lat|ed
venti|lat|ing
venti|la|tion
venti|la|tive
venti|la|tor +s
Ven|to|lin *proprietary*
ven|tral
ven|tral|ly
ven|tricle +s
ven|tri|cose
ven|tri|cu|lar
ven|trilo|quial
ven|trilo|quism
ven|trilo|quist +s
ven|trilo|quize
ven|trilo|quiz|es
ven|trilo|quized
ven|trilo|quiz|ing

ven|trilo|quy
ven|ture
  ven|tures
  ven|tured
  ven|tur|ing
Ven|tur|er +s
  (*Scouting*)
ven|tur|er +s
ven|ture|some
Ven|turi, Rob|ert
  Charles (US
  architect)
ven|turi +s
venue +s
ven|ule +s
Venus (*Roman Myth*;
  beautiful woman;
  planet)
  Venus|es
  [☞ venous]
Venus fly|trap +s
Venus|ian
ver|acious (truthful)
  [☞ voracious]
ver|acious|ly
  (truthfully)
  [☞ voraciously]
ver|acious|ness
  (truthfulness)
  [☞ voraciousness]
ver|acity
  (truthfulness)
  [☞ voracity]
Vera|cruz (state &
  city, Mexico)
ver|an|da +s
ver|an|dah +s (*use*
  veranda)
verb +s
ver|bal +s
ver|bal|ism +s
ver|bal|ist +s
ver|bal|is|tic
ver|bal|iz|a|tion +s
ver|bal|ize
  ver|bal|iz|es
  ver|bal|ized
  ver|bal|iz|ing
ver|bal|iz|er +s
ver|bal|ly
ver|batim
ver|bena +s
ver|bi|age
ver|bose
ver|bose|ly
ver|bose|ness
ver|bos|ity
ver|boten
Ver|chères
  (municipality,
  Canada)
Ver|chères, Marie-
  Madeleine Jar|ret

de (French-Canadian
  heroine)
ver|dan|cy
ver|dant
verd-antique
ver|dant|ly
ver|derer +s
Verdi, Giu|seppe
  For|tu|nino
  Fran|cesco (Italian
  composer)
Verdi|an +s
ver|dict +s
ver|di|gris
Ver|dun (city, Canada;
  battle site, France)
ver|dure
ver|dured
ver|dur|ous
Ver|eeni|ging (city,
  South Africa)
verge
  ver|ges
  verged
  ver|ging
ver|ger +s
ver|ger|ship +s
Ver|gil (= Virgil)
ver|idi|cal
ver|idi|cal|ity
ver|idi|cal|ly
veri|est
veri|fi|able
veri|fi|ably
veri|fi|ca|tion +s
veri|fi|er +s
ver|ify
  veri|fies
  veri|fied
  veri|fy|ing
Veri|gin, Peter
  Vasil|evich
  (Doukhobor leader)
veri|ly
veri|sim|ilar
veri|sim|ili|tude
ver|ism +s
ver|ismo
ver|ist +s
ver|is|tic
verit|able
verit|ably
véri|té (realism)
ver|ity (truth)
  ver|ities
ver|juice (*use* verjus)
ver|jus
Ver|khne|udinsk
  (*former name for*
  Ulan-Ude, Russia)
Ver|laine, Paul Marie
  (French poet)

Ver|meer, Jan (Dutch
  painter)
ver|meil
vermi|celli
vermi|cide +s
vermi|compost|er +s
vermi|compost|ing
ver|micu|lar
ver|micu|late
ver|micu|lat|ed
ver|micu|la|tion
ver|micu|lite
vermi|culture
vermi|form
vermi|fuge +s
Ver|mil|ion (mountain
  pass & river, Canada)
ver|mil|ion +s
ver|min
ver|min|ous
Ver|mont (state, US)
Ver|mont|er +s
ver|mouth +s
ver|nacu|lar +s
ver|nacu|lar|ism
ver|nacu|lar|ize
  ver|nacu|lar|iz|es
  ver|nacu|lar|ized
  ver|nacu|lar|iz|ing
ver|nacu|lar|ly
ver|nal
ver|nal|iz|a|tion
ver|nal|ize
  ver|nal|iz|es
  ver|nal|ized
  ver|nal|iz|ing
ver|nal|ly
Verne, Jules (French
  novelist)
ver|nier +s
ver|nis|sage +s
Ver|non (city, Canada)
Verny (*former name for*
  Almaty, Kazakhstan)
Ver|ona (city, Italy)
ver|onal
Vero|nese, Paulo
  (Italian painter)
Ver|on|ica (saint)
ver|on|ica +s
Ver|ra|zano,
  Gio|van|ni da
  (Italian navigator)
Ver|raz|zano,
  Gio|van|ni da
  (= Verrazano)
Ver|roc|chio, An|drea
  del (Italian artist)
ver|ruca
  ver|ru|cae or
  ver|ru|cas

ver|ru|cose (covered
  with warts)
  [☞ varicose]
ver|ru|cous
  (= verrucose)
  [☞ varicose]
Ver|sace, Gianni
  (Italian fashion
  designer)
Ver|sailles (palace,
  France)
ver|sant +s
ver|sa|tile
ver|sa|til|ity
verse
  verses
  versed
  vers|ing
versed *adjective*
  [☞ verst]
verse|let +s
vers|icle +s
versi|color (*use*
  versicolour)
versi|colour
ver|sicu|lar
versi|fi|ca|tion +s
versi|fi|er +s
versi|fy
  versi|fies
  versi|fied
  versi|fy|ing
ver|sion +s
ver|sion|al
vers libre
verso +s
verst +s (Russian
  measure of length)
  [☞ versed, wurst]
ver|sus
vert +s
ver|te|bra
  ver|te|brae
ver|te|bral
ver|te|brate +s
ver|tex
  ver|tices or
  ver|texes
ver|ti|cal +s
ver|ti|cal|ity
ver|ti|cal|ly
ver|ti|cil +s
ver|ti|cil|late
ver|ti|gin|ous
ver|ti|gin|ous|ly
ver|ti|go
vertu (interest in fine
  arts, *objets d'art*, in
  'object of vertu': *use*
  virtu)
  [☞ virtue]
ver|vain +s
verve

ver|vet +s
Ver|viers (town, Belgium)
Ver|woerd, Hen|drik Frensch (prime minister of South Africa)
Very +s (light; pistol)
very (extremely; in the fullest sense; real, actual)
veri|est
[☞ vary]
Very Rev|er|end
Vesa|lius, An|dreas (Flemish anatomist)
ves|ica +s
vesi|cal
vesi|cant +s
vesi|cate
vesi|cates
vesi|cat|ed
vesi|cat|ing
vesi|ca|tion +s
ves|icle +s
ves|icu|lar
ves|icu|late
ves|icu|la|tion +s
Ves|pa|sian (Roman emperor)
ves|per +s
ves|pers
ves|per|tine
ves|pi|ary
ves|pi|aries
ves|pine
Ves|pucci, Amer|igo (Italian explorer)
ves|sel +s
vest +s +ed +ing
Vesta (Roman Myth; asteroid)
vesta +s (match)
ves|tal +s
vest|ed adjective
Ves|ter|ålen (islands off Norway)
ves|tibu|lar
ves|ti|bule +s
ves|tige +s
ves|ti|gial
ves|ti|gial|ly
vest|ment +s
vest-pocket adjective preceding a noun
ves|tral
ves|try
ves|tries
vestry|man
vestry|men
ves|ture
ves|tures

ves|tured
ves|tur|ing
Vesu|vius (volcano, Italy)
vet
vets
vet|ted
vet|ting
vetch
vetch|es
vetch|ling +s
vet|er|an +s
vet|er|in|ar|ian +s
vet|er|in|ary
vet|er|in|ar|ies
vet|iver +s
veto
vetoes
vetoed
veto|ing
vetoer +s
vex
vexes
vexed
vex|ing
vex|a|tion +s
vex|a|tious
vex|a|tious|ly
vex|a|tious|ness
vexed adjective
vex|ed|ly
vexer +s
vexil|lo|logic|al
vexil|lol|o|gist +s
vexil|lol|ogy
vex|il|lum
vex|il|la
vex|ing adjective
vex|ing|ly
V-formation +s
via
[☞ Villa]
Via Appia
vi|abil|ity
vi|able
vi|ably
via dol|or|osa
via|duct +s
vial +s (vessel)
[☞ vile, viol, Weil, Weill]
via media
viand +s
vi|ati|cum
vi|atica
vibe +s
vi|bracu|lar
vi|bracu|lum
vi|bracu|la
vi|bran|cy
vi|brant
vi|brant|ly
vi|bra|phone +s

vi|bra|phon|ist +s
vi|brate
vi|brates
vi|brat|ed
vi|brat|ing
vi|bra|tile
vi|bra|tion +s
vi|bra|tion|al
vi|brato +s
vi|bra|tor +s
vi|bra|tory
vib|rio
vib|rios
vi|bris|sae
vi|bur|num +s
vic|ar +s
[☞ Vickers]
vic|ar|age +s
vicar apos|tol|ic
vic|ars apos|tol|ic
vicar-general
vicars-general
vic|ar|ial
vic|ar|iate +s
vic|ari|ous
vic|ari|ous|ly
vic|ari|ous|ness
vicar|ship +s
vice +s (sin, bad habit; in place of)
[☞ vise]
vice ad|miral +s
vice-chair +s
vice-chairman
vice-chairmen
vice-chairwoman
vice-chairwomen
vice-chancel|lor +s
vice|ger|ency
vice|ger|en|cies
vice|ger|ent +s
vice|less
vi|cen|nial
Vi|cen|za (city, Italy)
vice-presiden|cy
vice-presiden|cies
vice-president +s
vice-presiden|tial
vice-princi|pal +s
vice|regal
vice|regal|ly
vice|reine +s
vice|roy +s
vice|roy|al
vice|roy|al|ty
vice-skip +s
vice versa
Vichy (town & WWII regime, France)
vichys|soise +s
vicin|age +s
vicin|al

vicin|ity
vicin|ities
vi|cious (wicked, fierce)
vi|cious|ly (in a vicious manner)
vi|cious|ness (severity)
vicis|si|tude
vicis|si|tud|in|ous
Vick|ers, Jona|than Stew|art ('Jon') (Cdn tenor)
[☞ vicar]
Vicks|burg (battle site, US)
Vico, Giam|bat|tista (Italian philosopher)
Vico|nian
vic|tim +s
vic|tim|hood
vic|tim|iz|a|tion +s
vic|tim|ize
vic|tim|iz|es
vic|tim|ized
vic|tim|iz|ing
vic|tim|iz|er +s
vic|tim|less
vic|tim|ol|ogy
vic|tor +s
Vic|tor Em|man|uel II (king of Sardinia & Italy)
Vic|tor Em|man|uel III (king of Italy)
Vic|toria (English queen; city, lake, mountain & island, Canada; mountain & capital of Hong Kong; capital of the Seychelles; lake & waterfall, Africa; state, Australia)
Vic|toria, Tomás Luis de (Spanish composer)
vic|toria +s (carriage; water lily; plum)
Vic|toria de Dur|an|go (city, Mexico)
Vic|tor|ian +s
Vic|tor|iana
Vic|toria Nile (river, Africa)
Vic|tor|ian|ism +s
Vic|toria Ny|an|za (= Lake Victoria, Africa)
Vic|toria|ville (city, Canada)
vic|tor|ious

vic|tor|ious|ly
vic|tory
  vic|tor|ies
Vic|tro|la +s
  proprietary
vict|ual (food; eat,
  feed)
  vict|uals
  vict|ualled
  vict|ual|ling
vict|ual|ler +s
vi|cu|ña +s
vid +s
Vidal, Eu|gene
  Lu|ther ('Gore') (US
  writer)
vide
vide|licet
video
  vid|eos
  vid|eoed
  video|ing
video|cam +s
video cam|era +s
video cas|sette +s
video con|fer|ence
  +s
video con|fer|en|cing
video|disc +s
video game +s
vid|eog|raph|er +s
vid|eog|raphy
video-on-demand
video|phile +s
video|phone +s
video|tape
  video|tapes
  video|taped
  video|tap|ing
video|tex
  video|tex|es
video|text +s
  (= videotex)
vie
  vies
  vied
  vying
vi|elle +s
Vien|na (capital of
  Austria; sausage)
Vienne (city, France)
Vien|nese
  plural Vien|nese
Vien|tiane (capital of
  Laos)
Viet Cong
  plural Viet Cong
Viet|minh
  plural Viet|minh
Viet|nam (country,
  Asia)
Viet|nam|ese
  plural Viet|nam|ese

view +s +ed +ing
view|able
view|data
view|er +s
view|er|ship +s
view|find|er +s
view|ing +s *noun*
view|less
view|point +s
view|port +s
View Royal (town,
  Canada)
Vigée-Lebrun,
  (Marie Lou|ise)
  Élisa|beth (French
  painter)
vi|gesi|mal
vi|gesi|mal|ly
vigil +s
vigi|lance
vigi|lant (alert)
vigi|lante +s (self-
  appointed law
  enforcer)
vigi|lan|tism
vigi|lant|ly
Vi|gneault, Gilles
  (Cdn singer-
  songwriter)
vi|gne|ron +s
vi|gnette +s
vignet|ting
Vi|gnola, Gia|como
  Bar|ozzi da (Italian
  architect)
Vigny, Al|fred Vic|tor,
  Comte de (French
  writer)
Vigo (city, Spain)
Vigo, Jean (French
  filmmaker)
vigor (*use* vigour)
vig|or|ish
vig|or|less (*use*
  vigourless)
vig|or|ous
vig|or|ous|ly
vig|or|ous|ness
vig|our
vig|our|less
Vi|jaya|wada (city,
  India)
Vi|king +s
Vila (capital of
  Vanuatu)
  [☞ Villa, villa, vela]
vile (disgusting;
  shameful)
  viler
  vilest
  [☞ vial, viol, Weil,
  Weill]
vile|ly

vile|ness
vili|fi|ca|tion +s
vili|fi|er +s
vili|fy
  vili|fies
  vili|fied
  vili|fy|ing
Villa, Pan|cho
  (Mexican
  revolutionary)
  [☞ Vila, vela]
vil|la +s (house)
  [☞ vela]
vil|lage
  vil|la|ges
vil|la|ger +s
vil|la|gey
Villa|her|mosa (de
  San Juan
  Bau|tis|ta) (city,
  Mexico)
vil|lain +s (evil
  person)
  [☞ villein]
vil|lain|ous
vil|lain|ous|ly
vil|lainy
  vil|lain|ies
Villa-Lobos, Hei|tor
  (Brazilian composer)
vil|lan|elle +s
vil|lein +s (serf)
  [☞ villain]
vil|lein|age +s
Ville-Marie (*former
  name for* Montreal)
Ville|neuve, Gilles
  (Cdn race-car driver)
Ville|neuve, Jacques
  (Cdn race-car driver)
Vil|liers, George
  (Dukes of
  Buckingham)
Vil|lon, Fran|çois
  (French poet)
  [☞ villain, villein]
vil|los|ity
vil|lous *adjective*
vil|lus *noun*
  villi
Vil|ni|us (capital of
  Lithuania)
vim
vim|in|eous
Vimy Ridge (battle
  site, France)
vin|aceous
vin|ai|grette +s
vinar|ter|ta
vin|blas|tine
Vin|cent de Paul
  (saint)
Vin|cen|tian

Vinci, Leo|nar|do da
  (Italian artist &
  engineer)
vin|ci|bil|ity
vin|cible
vin|cris|tine
vin|cu|lum
  vin|cu|la
vin|da|loo +s
vin|di|cate
  vin|di|cates
  vin|di|cat|ed
  vin|di|cat|ing
vin|di|ca|tion +s
vin|di|ca|tor +s
vin|dic|tive
vin|dic|tive|ly
vin|dic|tive|ness
Vine, Bar|bara (Ruth
  Rendell)
vine +s
vin|egar +s
vin|egared
vin|egary
vin|ery
  vin|eries
vine|yard
vine|yard|ist +s
vini|cul|tur|al
vini|cul|ture
vini|cul|tur|ist +s
vini|er
vini|est
vi|nif|era
  plural vi|nif|era or
  vi|nif|eras
vini|fi|ca|tion
vini|fy
  vini|fies
  vini|fied
  vini|fy|ing
vining
Vin|land (region in
  N America visited by
  Vikings)
Vin|ni|tsa (*Russian
  name for* Vinnytsya)
Vin|ny|tsya (city,
  Ukraine)
vino
vin or|di|naire
  vins or|di|naires
vin|os|ity
vin|ous
Vin|son Mas|sif
  (mountain range,
  Antarctica)
vin|tage
  vin|ta|ges
vin|ta|ger +s
vint|ner +s

viny
  vini|er
  vini|est
vinyl +s
viol +s (*Music*)
  [☞ vial, vile]
vio|la +s
viol|able
viol|aceous
viola da brac|cio
  viole da brac|cio or
  viola da brac|cios
viola da gamba
  viole da gamba or
  viola da gam|bas
viola d'amore
  viole d'amore or
  viola d'amor|es
vio|late
  vio|lates
  vio|lat|ed
  vio|lat|ing
vio|la|tion +s
vio|la|tor +s
vio|lence
vio|lent
vio|lent|ly
vio|let +s
  [☞ Viollet-le-Duc]
vio|lin +s
vio|lin|ist +s
viol|ist +s
Viollet-le-Duc,
  Eu|gène
  Em|man|uel (French
  architect)
vio|lon|cellist +s
vio|lon|cello +s
VIP (very important
  person)
  VIPs
vi|per +s
viper|ine
viper|ish
viper-like
viper|ous
viper's bu|gloss
  viper's bu|gloss|es
viper's grass
  viper's grass|es
viper's nest +s
vir|ago +s
viral
viral|ly
Vir|chow, Ru|dolf
  Karl (German
  pathologist)
vir|elay +s
vir|eo +s
vir|es|cence
vir|es|cent
vir|gate
vir|ger +s (*use* verger)

Vir|gil (Roman poet)
Vir|gil|ian
Vir|gin (the Virgin
  Mary; Caribbean
  islands; *Zodiac*;
  constellation)
vir|gin +s
vir|gin|al
  • (of a virgin)
  • (= virginals:
  harpsichord)
  plural vir|gin|als
vir|gin|al|ist +s
vir|gin|al|ly
vir|gin|als
  (instrument)
  plural virginals
Vir|ginia +s (state,
  US; waterfall,
  Canada; tobacco,
  cigarette)
Vir|ginia
  Al|gon|quian
Vir|ginia Beach (city,
  US)
Vir|gin|ian +s
vir|gin|ity
Vir|gin Mary +s (the
  mother of Jesus;
  drink)
Vir|gin Queen (Queen
  Elizabeth I of
  England)
vir|gin's bower +s
Vir|go +s
  (constellation;
  Zodiac)
Vir|go|an +s
vir|gule +s
viri|des|cence
viri|des|cent
vir|id|ian +s
vir|ile
vir|il|ism
vir|il|ity
vir|il|iz|a|tion
vir|il|ize
  vir|il|iz|es
  vir|il|ized
  vir|il|iz|ing
vir|ion +s
vir|oid +s
viro|logic|al
viro|logic|al|ly
vir|ol|o|gist +s
vir|ol|ogy
virtu (interest in fine
  arts; *objets d'art*; in
  'object of virtu')
  [☞ virtue]
vir|tu|al
vir|tu|al|ity
vir|tu|al|ly

vir|tue +s (moral
  excellence; merit;
  chastity; heavenly
  being)
  [☞ virtu]
virtue|less
vir|tu|os|ic
vir|tu|os|ity
  vir|tu|os|ities
vir|tu|oso
  vir|tu|osi or
  vir|tu|osos
vir|tu|ous
vir|tu|ous|ly
vir|tu|ous|ness
viru|lence
viru|lent
viru|lent|ly
virus
  virus|es
visa
  visas
  visaed or visa'd
  visa|ing
vis|age +s
vis|aged
Vi|sakha|pat|nam
  (city, India)
vis-à-vis
vis|cacha +s
vis|cera
vis|cer|al
vis|cer|al|ly
vis|cid
vis|cid|ity
visco|elas|tic
visco|elas|ti|city
vis|com|eter +s
visco|met|ric
visco|met|ric|ally
vis|com|etry
Vis|conti, Lu|chino
  (Italian filmmaker)
vis|cose (viscous
  solution used to
  make cellulose fibres
  & rayon)
  [☞ viscous]
vis|cos|ity
  vis|cos|ities
vis|count +s
vis|count|cy
  vis|count|cies
vis|count|ess
  vis|count|esses
Vis|count Mel|ville
  Sound (in Canadian
  Arctic)
vis|cous (having a
  high viscosity;
  sticky)
  [☞ viscus, viscose,
  vicious]

vis|cous|ly
  (glutinously)
  [☞ viciously]
vis|cous|ness
  (viscosity)
  [☞ viciousness]
vis|cus (internal
  organ)
  vis|cera
  [☞ viscous,
  vicious]
vise (clamp)
  vises
  vised
  vis|ing
  [☞ vice]
Vise-Grip +s
  proprietary
vise|like
Vish|in|sky, An|drei
  Yanu|ary|evich
  (= Vyshinsky)
Vish|nu (*Hinduism*)
Vishnu|ism
visi|bil|ity
  visi|bil|ities
vis|ible
vis|ible|ness
vis|ibly
Visi|goth +s
Visi|goth|ic
vi|sion +s +ed +ing
vi|sion|al
vi|sion|ari|ness
vi|sion|ary
  vi|sion|ar|ies
vi|sion|less
vis|it
  vis|its
  vis|ited
  vis|it|ing
vis|it|able
vis|it|ant +s
Vis|it|a|tion (*New
  Testament*; feast)
vis|it|a|tion +s
vis|it|ing +s *noun &
  adjective*
vis|itor +s
visi|tor|ial
visi|tors' book +s
visor +s
vis|ored
visor|less
vista +s
Vis|tula (river, Poland)
vis|ual +s
visu|al|ity
vis|ual|iz|able
vis|ual|iz|a|tion +s
vis|ual|ize
  visual|iz|es

visual|ized
visual|iz|ing
vis|ual|ly
vital +s (essential;
  paramount; lively)
  [☞ victual, vittle]
vital|ism
vital|ist +s
vital|is|tic
vital|ity
vital|iz|a|tion
vital|ize
  vital|iz|es
  vital|ized
  vital|iz|ing
vital|ly
vita|min +s
vita|min|ize
  vita|min|iz|es
  vita|min|ized
  vita|min|iz|ing
Vi|tebsk (*Russian
  name for* Vitsebsk,
  Belarus)
vi|tel|lin *noun*
vi|tel|line *adjective*
vi|tel|lus
  vi|tel|lus|es
viti|ate
  viti|ates
  viti|at|ed
  viti|at|ing
viti|a|tion
viti|ator +s
viti|cul|tur|al
viti|cul|ture
viti|cul|tur|ist +s
Viti Levu (island, Fiji)
viti|ligo
Vi|toria (city, Spain)
Vi|tória (city, Brazil)
Vi|tosha (ski resort,
  Bulgaria)
vit|reous
vit|reous|ness
vitri|fi|able
vitri|fi|ca|tion
vitri|form
vitri|fy
  vitri|fies
  vitri|fied
  vitri|fy|ing
vi|trine +s
vit|ri|ol
vit|ri|ol|ic
Vit|ruv|ian
Vit|ruv|ius (Roman
  architect)
Vit|sebsk (city,
  Belarus)
vitta
  vit|tae
vit|tate

vittle +s *informal*
  (= victual, food)
  [☞ victual]
vi|tu|per|ate
  vi|tu|per|ates
  vi|tu|per|at|ed
  vi|tu|per|at|ing
vi|tu|per|a|tion +s
vi|tu|per|a|tive
vi|tu|per|ator +s
Vitus (saint)
viva +s (shout; long
  live)
viva (oral exam)
  vivas
  vivaed *or* viva'd
  vivaing
viv|ace +s
viv|acious
viv|acious|ly
viv|acious|ness
viv|acity
Viv|aldi, An|tonio
  Lucio (Italian
  composer)
viv|ar|ium
  viv|ar|iums *or*
  viv|aria
viva voce +s
viver|rid +s
vivid
vivid|ly
vivid|ness
vivi|fi|ca|tion
viv|ify
  vivi|fies
  vivi|fied
  vivi|fy|ing
vivi|par|ity
viv|ip|ar|ous
viv|ip|ar|ous|ly
viv|ip|ar|ous|ness
vivi|sect +s +ed +ing
vivi|sec|tion +s
vivi|sec|tion|al
vivi|sec|tion|ist +s
vivi|sect|or +s
vixen +s
vixen|ish
vixen|ly
Vi|yella +s *proprietary*
viz.
viz|ier +s
viz|ier|ate +s
viz|ier|ial
viz|ier|ship +s
VJ (video jockey)
  VJs
Vlach +s
Vladi|kav|kaz (city,
  Russia)
Vlad|i|mir (city,
  Russia)

Vlad|i|mir (the
  Great) (saint)
Vladi|vos|tok (city,
  Russia)
Vla|minck, Mau|rice
  de (French painter &
  writer)
vlei +s
Vlis|singen (port, the
  Netherlands)
Vlona (= Vlorë)
Vlorë (town, Albania)
VLT (video lottery
  terminal)
  VLTs
Vltava (river, Czech
  Republic)
V-neck +s
V-necked
V-neckline +s
vocab
voc|able +s
vo|cabu|lary
  vo|cabu|lar|ies
vocal +s
vo|cal|ic
vocal|ise +s *noun*
  (singing exercise;
  vocal passage)
  [☞ vocalize]
vocal|ism
vocal|ist +s
vocal|ity
vocal|iz|a|tion +s
vocal|ize *verb* (utter;
  sing; *Linguistics*)
  vocal|iz|es
  vocal|ized
  vocal|iz|ing
  [☞ vocalise]
vocal|iz|er +s
vocal|ly
vo|ca|tion +s
vo|ca|tion|al
vo|ca|tion|al|ism
vo|ca|tion|al|ize
  vo|ca|tion|al|iz|es
  vo|ca|tion|al|ized
  vo|ca|tion|al|iz|ing
vo|ca|tion|al|ly
voca|tive +s
vo|cif|er|ant +s
vo|cif|er|ate
  vo|cif|er|ates
  vo|cif|er|at|ed
  vo|cif|er|at|ing
vo|cif|er|a|tion +s
vo|cif|er|ator +s
vo|cif|er|ous
vo|cif|er|ous|ly
vo|cif|er|ous|ness
vo|coder +s
vod|ka +s

vogue +s
vo|guing
vo|guish
voice
  voices
  voiced
  voi|cing
voice box
  voice boxes
voice|less
voice|less|ly
voice|less|ness
voice mail
voice mail|box
  voice mail|boxes
voice-over +s
voice print +s
voicer +s
voi|cing +s *noun*
void +s +ed +ing
void|able
void|ance
void|ed *adjective*
void|ness
voila *interjection*
voile +s (material)
voir dire
Voj|vod|ina (province,
  Serbia)
volant
volar
vola|tile +s
vola|tile|ness
vola|til|ity
vola|til|iz|able
vola|til|iz|a|tion
vola|til|ize
  vola|til|iz|es
  vola|til|ized
  vola|til|iz|ing
vol-au-vent +s
vol|can|ic +s
vol|can|ic|ally
vol|can|icity
vol|can|ism
vol|cano
  vol|ca|noes
vol|cano|logic|al
vol|can|ol|o|gist +s
vol|can|ol|ogy
vole +s
Volga (river, Russia)
Vol|go|grad (city,
  Russia)
voli|tant
vol|ition
vol|ition|al
vol|ition|al|ly
voli|tive
volk
völk|isch
vol|ley +s +ed +ing

vol|ley|ball +s
vol|ley|er +s
Vol|ogda (city, Russia)
Volos (city, Greece)
Vol|scian +s
volt +s (*Electricity; for Fencing & Equestrian senses use* volte)
[☞ vault]
Volta (river, Africa)
[☞ *volte-face*]
Volta, Ales|san|dro Giu|seppe An|tonio Ana|sta|sio, Count (Italian physicist)
[☞ *volte-face*]
volt|age +s
vol|taic
Vol|taire (French writer)
volt|am|eter +s (measures electric charge)
[☞ voltmeter]
volt|am|met|ric
volt|am|metry
volte +s (*Fencing; Equestrian*)
[☞ volt, vault]
volte-face +s
volt|meter +s (measures electric potential in volts)
[☞ voltameter]
volu|bil|ity
vol|uble
vol|uble|ness
vol|ubly
vol|ume +s
vol|umed
volu|met|ric
volu|met|ric|ally
vo|lu|min|os|ity
vo|lu|min|ous
vo|lu|min|ous|ly
vo|lu|min|ous|ness
vol|um|ize
vol|um|iz|es
vol|um|ized
vol|um|iz|ing
vol|un|tar|i|ly
vol|un|tar|i|ness
vol|un|tar|ism
vol|un|tar|ist +s
vol|un|tary
vol|un|tar|ies
vol|un|tary|ism
vol|un|tary|ist +s
vol|un|teer +s +ed +ing
vol|un|teer|ing *noun*
vol|un|teer|ism

vo|lup|tu|ary
vo|lup|tu|aries
vo|lup|tu|ous
vo|lup|tu|ous|ly
vo|lup|tu|ous|ness
vol|ute +s
vol|uted
Volzh|sky (city, Russia)
vomer +s
vomit
vomits
vomit|ed
vomit|ing
vomit|er +s
vomi|tor|ium
vomi|toria
vomi|tory
vomi|tor|ies
VON (Victorian Order of Nurses)
VONs
[☞ Vaughan]
von Braun, Wern|her Mag|nus Max|imil|ian (German rocket designer)
Von Gencsy, Eva (Cdn dancer)
Von|ne|gut, Kurt (US writer)
von Neu|mann, John (US mathematician)
voo|doo
voo|doos
voo|dooed
voo|doo|ing
voo|doo|ism
voo|doo|ist +s
vor|acious (ravenous; insatiable)
[☞ veracious]
vor|acious|ly (ravenously; insatiably)
[☞ veraciously]
vor|acious|ness (ravenousness; insatiability)
[☞ veraciousness]
vor|acity (ravenousness; insatiability)
[☞ veracity]
Vor|arl|berg (state, Austria)
Vor|on|ezh (city, Russia)
Voro|shi|lov, Kliment Yefrem|ovich (Soviet statesman)

Voro|shi|lov|grad (*former name for* Luhansk, Ukraine)
Vor|ster, Bal|thazar Jo|han|nes ('John') (South African prime minister)
vor|tex
vor|tices *or* vor|texes
vor|ti|cal
vor|ti|cal|ly
vor|ti|cella +s
vor|ti|cism
vor|ti|cist +s
vor|ti|city
vor|ti|cose
Vosges (mountains, France)
vot|able
vo|tary
vo|tar|ies
vote
votes
voted
vot|ing
vote-getter +s
vote-getting
vote|less
vote of no con|fi|dence (= vote of non-confidence)
votes of no con|fi|dence
vote of non-confidence
votes of non-confidence
vot|er +s
vot|ers list +s
vo|tive
vouch
vouch|es
vouched
vouch|ing
vouch|er +s
vouch|safe
vouch|safes
vouch|safed
vouch|saf|ing
vous|soir +s
vow +s +ed +ing
vow|el +s
vow|elled
vowel|less
vowel-point +s
vox pop +s
vox pop|uli
voy|age
voy|ages
voy|aged
voy|aging

Voya|ger +s (space probes)
voya|ger +s (traveller; *for* canoeman employed by a fur-trading company *use* voyageur)
[☞ voyageur]
voya|geur +s (canoeman employed by a fur-trading company; outdoorsman, canoe tripper)
[☞ voyager]
voya|geur ca|noe +s
voya|geur sash
voya|geur sash|es
voya|ging *noun*
voy|eur +s
voy|eur|ism
voy|eur|is|tic
voy|eur|is|tic|ally
Vozne|sen|sky, An|drei Andrei|evich (Russian poet)
VP (vice-president)
VPs
vroom +s +ed +ing
V-shaped
V sign +s
V/STOL (vertical/short takeoff and landing aircraft)
V/STOLs
VTOL (vertical takeoff and landing aircraft)
VTOLs
VTR (videotape recorder)
VTRs
vug +s
vuggy
Vuil|lard, (Jean) Édouard (French artist)
Vul|can (*Roman Myth*)
vul|can|ism (*use* volcanism)
vul|can|ite
vul|can|iz|able
vul|can|iz|a|tion
vul|can|ize
vul|can|iz|es
vul|can|ized
vul|can|iz|ing
vul|can|ized *adjective*
vul|can|iz|er +s
vul|cano|logic|al (*use* volcanological)

vul|can|ol|o|gist +s
(*use* volcanologist)
vul|can|ol|ogy (*use*
volcanology)
vul|gar
vul|gar|ian +s
vul|gar|is
vul|gar|ism +s
vul|gar|ity
  vul|gar|ities
vul|gar|iz|a|tion +s
vul|gar|ize
  vul|gar|iz|es
  vul|gar|ized
  vul|gar|iz|ing
vul|gar|ly
Vul|gate (Bible)
vul|gate +s (any
  traditionally
  accepted text;
  colloquial speech)
vul|ner|abil|ity
  vul|ner|abil|ities
vul|ner|able
vul|ner|ably
vul|ner|ary
  vul|ner|aries
vul|pine
vul|ture +s
vul|tur|ine
vul|tur|ish
vul|tur|ous
vul|va +s
vul|val
vul|var (= vulval)
Vun|tut (national park,
  Canada)
Vyat|ka (town, Russia)
vying
Vysh|in|sky, An|drei
  Yanu|ary|evich
  (Soviet statesman)

W

W
• (letter)
W's
• (watt)
w (letter)
w's
Waac (*US & Brit.*
  Women's Army
  Auxiliary Corps
  member)
  Waacs
  [☞ WAC, CWAC]
Waaf (*Brit.* Women's
  Auxiliary Air Force
  member)
  Waafs
  [☞ WAF]
waah
Waal (river, the
  Netherlands)
WAC (*US* Women's
  Army Corps
  member)
  WACs
  [☞ Waac]
Wace, Rob|ert (Anglo-
  Norman poet)
wack +s (harmful;
  dull; a wacko)
  [☞ whack, wacke,
  Waac, WAC]
wacke +s (rock)
  [☞ wack, whack,
  Waac, WAC]
wacked *adjective*
  (wacked out: *use*
  whacked)
wacked out (wacked-
  out *when preceding a*
  noun; crazy,
  intoxicated,
  exhausted: *use*
  whacked out)
wack|i|ly
wack|i|ness
wacko (crazy, lunatic)
  wack|os
  [☞ whacko]
wacky
  wack|i|er
  wack|i|est
wad
  wads
  wad|ded
  wad|ding
wadable
wad|ding +s *noun*
Wad|ding|ton
  (mountain, Canada)

Wad|ding|ton,
  Mir|iam (Cdn poet)
wad|dle (walk)
  wad|dles
  wad|dled
  wad|dling
  [☞ wattle, wattle
  and daub]
wad|dler +s
wade
  wades
  waded
  wading
wade|able (*use*
  wadable)
wader +s
wadi +s
Wadi Halfa (town,
  Sudan)
wady (*use* wadi)
  wad|ies
  [☞ Wadi Halfa]
WAF (*US* Women in
  the Air Force
  member)
  WAFs
  [☞ Waaf]
wafer +s
wafer|board +s
wafer-thin
wafery
Waf|fle (*Cdn History*)
waf|fle
  waf|fles
  waf|fled
  waf|fling
Waf|fler +s (member
  of the Waffle)
waf|fler +s (one who
  wavers or
  equivocates)
waffly
waft +s +ed +ing
wag
  wags
  wagged
  wag|ging
wage
  wages
  waged
  waging
wage earn|er +s
wage-earning
wager +s +ed +ing
wager|ing *noun*
Wagga Wagga (town,
  Australia)
wag|gery
  wag|ger|ies
wag|gish
wag|gish|ly
wag|gish|ness

wag|gle
  wag|gles
  wag|gled
  wag|gling
wag|gly
Wag|ner, (Wil|helm)
  Rich|ard (German
  composer)
Wag|ner|ian +s
wag|on +s
wag|on|er +s
wag|on|ette +s
wag|on|load
wag|tail +s
Wa|habi +s (*use*
  Wahhabi)
Wa|ha|bism (*use*
  Wahhabism)
Wah|habi +s
Wah|ha|bism
wa|hine +s
wahoo
  plural wahoo or
  wa|hoos
wah-wah +s (*Music*)
waif +s
waif|ish
waif|like
Wai|kato (river, New
  Zealand)
Wai|ki|ki (resort,
  Honolulu)
wail +s +ed +ing (cry;
  complain; play music
  with intensity)
  [☞ whale, wale,
  Wales]
wail|er +s (one who
  cries)
  [☞ whaler]
wail|ing *conjugated*
  form of wail
  [☞ whaling]
wail|ing|ly
Wail|ing Wall
  (= Western Wall,
  Jerusalem)
wain +s (wagon)
  [☞ wane, Wayne]
wain|scot
  wain|scots
  wain|scot|ted
  or wain|scot|ed
  wain|scot|ting
  or wain|scot|ing
wain|scot|ing +s
  noun (*use*
  wainscotting)
wain|scot|ting +s
  noun
Wain|wright (town,
  Canada)
wain|wright +s

waist +s (part of the body; middle part) [☞ **waste**]
waist|band +s
waist|coat +s
waist-deep
waist|ed *adjective* (in 'high-waisted' etc.) [☞ **wasted**]
waist-high
waist|line +s
wait +s +ed +ing (be patient; serve; band; in 'lie in wait') [☞ **weight**]
wait-a-bit +s (plant)
wait|ed *conjugated form of* wait [☞ **weighted**]
wait|er +s
wait|ing *noun* (pause, delay) [☞ **weighting**]
wait-list +s +ed +ing
wait|person
  wait|persons or
  wait|people
wait|ress
  wait|ress|es
  wait|ressed
  wait|ress|ing
wait|ress|ing *noun*
wait staff +s
wait state +s
waive (renounce; forgo; relinquish rights to)
  waives
  waived
  waiv|ing
  [☞ **wave**]
waiv|er +s (act of waiving a right, player etc.) [☞ **waver**]
Waka|shan
wake
• (awaken)
  wakes
  woke or waked
  woken or waked
  waking
• (vigil)
  wakes
  waked
  waking
• (trail; 'in the wake of')
  wakes
Wake|field (town, England)
wake|ful
wake|ful|ly
wake|ful|ness

waken +s +ed +ing
waker +s
wake-robin +s
wake-up call +s
wakey-wakey
waking *adjective*
Waks|man, Sel|man Abra|ham (US microbiologist) [☞ **Waxman**]
Wal|achia (= Wallachia, former European principality)
Wal|ach|ian +s (= Wallachian)
Wal|cott, Derek Alton (West Indian writer)
Wal|de|mar I (king of Denmark)
Wal|den (town, Canada)
Wal|den|ses
Wal|den|sian +s
Wald|heim, Kurt (Austrian president)
Waldo, Caro|lyn (Cdn synchronized swimmer)
Wal|dorf (salad; school)
wale +s (*Textiles*; *Nautical*; basket strip; welt) [☞ **whale, wail**]
Wales (principality, UK)
Wa|łe|sa, Lech (Polish president)
walk +s +ed +ing (move on foot) [☞ **wok**]
walk|able
walk about *verb*
  walks about
  walked about
  walk|ing about
walk|about +s *noun*
walk|athon +s
Walk|em, George An|thony (Cdn politician)
Walk|er, Alice Mal|sen|ior (US writer)
Walk|er, Hiram (US-born Cdn distiller)
Walk|er, Hor|atio (Cdn painter)
walk|er +s
Walk|er|ton (town, Canada)
walk|ies

walkie-talkie +s
walk in *verb*
  walks in
  walked in
  walk|ing in
walk-in +s *adjective & noun*
walk|ing *noun & adjective*
Walk|man +s *proprietary*
walk on *verb*
  walks on
  walked on
  walk|ing on
walk-on +s *noun*
walk out *verb*
  walks out
  walked out
  walk|ing out
walk|out +s *noun & adjective*
walk over *verb*
  walks over
  walked over
  walk|ing over
walk|over +s *noun*
walk through *verb*
  walks through
  walked through
  walk|ing through
walk-through +s *noun & adjective*
walk up *verb*
  walks up
  walked up
  walk|ing up
walk-up +s *adjective & noun*
walk|way +s
Wal|kyrie (*Scandinavian Myth* = Valkyrie)
wall +s +ed +ing [☞ **Waal**]
wal|laby
  wal|la|bies
Wal|lace, Al|fred Rus|sel (English naturalist) [☞ **Wallis**]
Wal|lace, Sir Wil|liam (Scottish hero)
Wal|lace|burg (town, Canada)
Wal|lachia (former principality, Europe)
Wal|lach|ian +s
wal|lah +s
wal|la|roo +s
Wal|la|sey (town, England)
wall ball
wall|board +s

wall chart +s
wall|cov|er|ing +s
walled *adjective*
Wal|len|berg, Raoul (Swedish diplomat)
Wal|len|stein, Al|brecht Wen|zel Euse|bius von (Thirty Years War general)
Wal|ler, Ed|mund (English poet)
Wal|ler, Thom|as Wright ('Fats') (US musician & bandleader)
wal|let +s
wal|ley +s (*Figure Skating*) [☞ **wally**]
wall|eye
• (fish)
  plural wall|eye or wall|eyes
• (eye)
  plural wall|eyes
wall|eyed
wall|flower +s
wall hang|ing +s
wall-hung
wall|ing *noun*
Wal|lis, Sir Barnes Nev|ille (English inventor) [☞ **Wallace**]
Wal|lis and Fu|tuna (central Pacific islands)
wall-less
wall-mounted
Wal|loon +s
wal|lop +s +ed +ing
wal|lop|er +s
wal|lop|ing +s *noun & adjective*
wal|low +s +ed +ing
wal|low|er +s
wall|paper +s +ed +ing
wall plate +s
Wall Street (in New York)
Wall Street|er +s
wall-to-wall
wally (nerd)
  wal|lies
  [☞ **walley**]
wally|ball
wal|nut
Wal|pole (island, Canada)

Wal|pole, Hor|ace (4th Earl of Orford, English writer)
Wal|pole, Sir Hugh Sey|mour (British novelist)
Wal|pole, Sir Rob|ert (1st Earl of Orford, British prime minister)
Wal|pur|gis night +s
wal|rus
  wal|ruses
Wal|sall (city, England)
Walsh (mountain, N America)
Wal|sing|ham, Sir Fran|cis (English politician)
Wal|ter, Bruno (German-born conductor)
Wal|ter Mit|ty +s
Wal|ther von der Vogel|weide (German minnesinger)
Wal|ton, Er|nest Thom|as Sin|ton (Irish physicist)
Wal|ton, Izaak (English writer)
Wal|ton, Sir Wil|liam Tur|ner (English composer)
waltz
  waltz|es
  waltzed
  waltz|ing
waltz|er +s
Wal|vis Bay (town, Namibia)
Wam|pa|noag
  plural **Wam|pa|noag** or **Wam|pa|noags**
wam|pum
WAN (wide-area network)
  WANs
wan (pale)
  wan|ner
  wan|nest
  [☞ **won**]
wand +s
wan|der +s +ed +ing (move aimlessly)
wan|der|er +s (one who wanders)
wan|der|ing +s noun
wan|der|ing Jew +s (Medieval Legend; plant)

Wander|jahr
  Wander|jahre
wander|lust
wan|deroo +s
wane (decrease)
  wanes
  waned
  waning
  [☞ **wain, Wayne**]
waney
Wan|ga|nui (town, New Zealand)
Wang Ching-wei (= Wang Jing Wei)
Wang Jing Wei (Chinese revolutionary)
wan|gle
  wan|gles
  wan|gled
  wan|gling
wan|gler +s
wan|igan +s
wank +s +ed +ing
Wan|kel en|gine +s
wank|er +s
Wan|kie (former name for Hwange, Zimbabwe)
wanly
wanna
wanna|be +s
wan|ness
want +s +ed +ing (desire; need; lack)
  [☞ **wont**]
want|ed adjective (sought by the police)
  [☞ **wonted**]
want|ing adjective
wan|ton +s +ed +ing (arbitrary, motiveless; licentious; unrestrained; mischievous)
  [☞ **won ton**]
wan|ton|ly
wan|ton|ness
wapen|take +s
wap|iti
  plural **wap|iti** or **wap|itis**
war (fighting etc.)
  wars
  warred
  war|ring
War|beck, Per|kin (claimant to English throne)
war|bird +s

war|ble
  war|bles
  war|bled
  war|bling
war|bler +s
war|bly
war bon|net +s
war bride +s
War|burg, Otto Hein|rich (German biochemist)
war chest +s
war cloud +s
war cry
  war cries
Ward, Dame Bar|bara Mary, Baron|ess Jack|son (English conservationist)
Ward, Mrs. Hum|phry (English social campaigner)
Ward, Max|well Wil|liam (Cdn aviator)
ward +s +ed +ing (division; charge; protect; key notch)
war dance +s
war|den +s
war|den|ship +s
ward|er +s
ward-heeler +s
ward-heeling
ward|ress
  ward|ress|es
ward|robe +s
ward|room +s
ward|ship +s
ware (articles for sale; aware; beware)
  wares
  wared
  waring
  [☞ **wear, where, were**]
ware|house +s
ware|house|man
  ware|house|men
ware|hous|er +s
war|fare
war|farin
war game +s noun
war-game verb
  war-games
  war-gamed
  war-gam|ing
war-gam|ing noun
war|head +s
War|hol, Andy (US artist)
War|hol|ian
war|horse +s

wari|er comparative of **wary**
  [☞ **warrior**]
wari|est
wari|ly
wari|ness
waring conjugated form of **ware**
  [☞ **wearing, warring**]
war|like
war|lock +s
war|lord +s
war|lord|ism
warm +er +est +s +ed +ing (slightly hot, etc.)
warm-blooded
warm-blooded|ness
War Meas|ures Act
warmed-over
warm|er +s noun
warm-hearted
warm-hearted|ly
warm-hearted|ness
warm|ing noun & adjective
warm|ish
warm|ly
warm|ness
war|monger +s
war|monger|ing
warmth +s
warm up verb
  warms up
  warmed up
  warm|ing up
warm-up +s noun
warn +s +ed +ing (inform of danger; admonish)
  [☞ **worn**]
warn|er +s
warn|ing +s noun
warn|ing|ly
warp +s +ed +ing
warp|age
war paint +s
war|path +s
warped adjective
warp|er +s
war|plane +s
war|rant +s +ed +ing
war|rant|abil|ity
war|rant|able
war|rant|ably
war|ran|tee +s (person given a warranty)
  [☞ **warranty**]
war|rant|er +s
war|rant|or +s

war|ranty (guarantee, justification)
  war|ran|ties
  [☞ warrantee]
War|ren, Earl (US justice)
War|ren, Rob|ert Penn (US writer)
war|ren +s
war|ring adjective & conjugated form of war
  [☞ waring]
War|ring|ton (city, England)
war|rior +s (fighter)
  [☞ warier]
War|saw (capital of Poland)
war|ship +s (fighting ship)
war-surplus
wart +s (protuberance)
  [☞ wort]
wart|ed
wart|hog +s
war|time
war|torn
warty
  wart|i|er
  wart|i|est
war-weariness
war-weary
War|wick (city, England)
War|wick, Rich|ard Nev|ille, Earl of ('the Kingmaker')
War|wick|shire (county, England)
wary (cautious)
  wari|er
  wari|est
  [☞ wherry]
war zone +s
was
was|abi
Was|aga Beach (town, Canada)
wash
  wash|es
  washed
  wash|ing
Wash, the (inlet, England)
wash|abil|ity
wash|able
wash-and-wear
wash basin +s
wash|board +s
wash|cloth +s
wash|day +s

washed out (washed-out when preceding a noun)
washed up (washed-up when preceding a noun)
wash|er +s
washer|less
washer|man
  washer|men
washer|woman
  washer|women
wash house +s
wash|i|er
wash|i|est
wash|i|ly
wash|i|ness
wash|ing +s noun
Wash|ing|ton (US capital & state; town, England; mountain, Canada)
Wash|ing|ton, Booker Talia|ferro (US educator)
Wash|ing|ton, George (US president)
Wash|ing|ton|ian +s
washing-up
wash out verb
  wash|es out
  washed out
  wash|ing out
wash|out +s noun
wash|rag +s
wash|room +s
wash|stand +s
wash|tub +s
washy
  wash|i|er
  wash|i|est
wasn't
WASP offensive (White Anglo-Saxon Protestant)
  WASPs
wasp +s
WASP|ish (characteristic of WASPs)
wasp|ish (petulant)
wasp|ish|ly
wasp|ish|ness
wasp|like
wasp waist +s
wasp-waisted
WASPy
was|sail +s +ed +ing
was|sail|er +s
Was|ser|mann test +s

wast archaic conjugated form of be
  [☞ waste, waist]
wast|age
waste (squander; wither; garbage)
  wastes
  wast|ed
  wast|ing
  [☞ waist]
waste|basket +s
waste bin +s
wast|ed adjective (exhausted; intoxicated)
  [☞ waisted]
waste|ful
waste|ful|ly
waste|ful|ness
waste|land +s
waste|less
waste paper
waste|paper bas|ket +s
wast|er +s
waste stream +s
waste water +s
wast|rel +s
wat +s (Buddhist monastery)
  [☞ watt, wot]
watch
  watch|es
  watched
  watch|ing
watch|able
watch|band +s
watch cap +s
watch case +s
watch-chain +s
watch|dog
  watch|dogs
  watch|dogged
  watch|dog|ging
watch|er +s (one who watches)
  [☞ wotcher]
watch|ful
watch|ful|ly
watch|ful|ness
watch|keep|er +s
watch|keep|ing
watch|maker +s
watch|making
watch|man
  watch|men
watch|spring +s
watch|tower +s
watch|word +s
wat|er +s +ed +ing
water bag +s
water-based

Water Bear|er (constellation; Zodiac)
water|bed +s
water bird +s
water bomb|er +s
water bomb|ing
water-borne
water boy +s
water|buck +s
water bus
  water buses
Water Car|ri|er (constellation; Zodiac)
water|color +s (use watercolour)
water|color|ist (use watercolourist)
water|col|our +s
water|col|our|ist +s
water-cooled
water cool|er +s (water-cooler when preceding a noun)
water|course +s
water|craft
  plural water|craft
water|cress
water|er +s
water|fall +s
Water|ford (county & town, Ireland)
water|fowl
  plural water|fowl
water|fowl|er +s
water|fowl|ing
water|front +s
Water|gate (US political scandal)
water|gate +s (floodgate)
water glass (drinking glass)
  water glass|es
water|glass (chemical solution; underwater viewing device)
  water|glass|es
water|hen +s
water hole +s
water|i|ness
water|ing +s noun
watering hole
water|leaf +s
water|less
water lily
  water lil|ies
water|line +s
water|logged
water|log|ging
Wat|er|loo +s (Napoleonic battle;

decisive defeat; city, Canada)
water main +s
water|man
water|men
water|mark +s
water|melon +s
water meter +s
water mill +s
water park +s
Water Pik +s
proprietary
water pipe +s
water pis|tol +s
water|proof
water|proof|ness
water re|pel|lent +s
(water-repellent *when preceding a noun*)
water re|sist|ance
water-resist|ant
Wat|ers, Muddy (US singer & guitarist)
water|scape +s
water|shed +s
water|side +s
water ski +s *noun*
water-ski *verb*
water-skis
water-skied
water-skiing
water ski|er +s
water|slide +s
water snake +s
water sol|uble
(water-soluble *when preceding a noun*)
water-splash
water-splash|es
water sport +s
water|spout +s
water|tight
Water|ton Lakes (national park, Canada)
water|way +s
water|weed +s
water wheel +s
water wings
water|works
wat|ery
Wat|ford (town, England)
Watha|wur|ung
Wat|ling Street (in London, England)
Wat|son, James Dewey (US biologist)
Wat|son, John Broad|us (US psychologist)

Wat|son, Sheila (Cdn writer)
Wat|son Lake (lake & town, Canada)
Watson-Watt, Sir Rob|ert Alex|an|der (Scottish physicist)
Watt, James (Scottish engineer)
[☞ **Watts**]
watt +s (unit of power)
[☞ **wat, wot**]
watt|age +s
Wat|teau, (Jean) An|toine (French painter)
watt-hour +s
wat|tle (interlaced rods & twigs; Australian acacia; loose flesh on the throat or head)
wat|tles
wat|tled
wat|tling
[☞ **waddle**]
wat|tle and daub (wattle-and-daub *when preceding a noun*)
wat|tled *adjective*
watt|meter +s
Watts, Isaac (English hymn writer)
[☞ **Watt**]
Waugh, Eve|lyn Ar|thur St. John (English novelist)
wave (hand gesture; sway; undulation; surge; in 'wave aside', 'wave off')
waves
waved
wav|ing
[☞ **waive**]
wave|band +s
wave|form +s
wave|front +s
wave|guide +s
wave|length +s
wave|less
wave|let +s
wave|like
Wav|ell, Archi|bald Per|ci|val, 1st Earl (English field marshal)
wave|num|ber +s
wave pool +s
wav|er +s +ed +ing (falter; vacillate)
[☞ **waiver**]

waver|er +s
waver|ing|ly
wav|ery
wave train +s
wav|i|ly
wav|i|ness
wavy
wav|i|er
wav|i|est
Wawa (community, Canada)
wa-wa +s (*Music: use* wah-wah)
wax
waxes
waxed
wax|ing
wax|berry
wax|ber|ries
wax|bill +s
waxed paper
waxen
wax|er +s
wax|i|er
wax|i|est
wax|i|ly
wax|i|ness
wax|ing *noun*
Wax|man, Al|bert Sam|uel ('Al') (Cdn actor)
[☞ **Waksman**]
wax|palm +s
wax paper (= waxed paper)
wax|wing +s
wax|work +s
waxy
wax|i|er
wax|i|est
way +s (route; means, manner; very much; in 'make way', 'by the way' etc.)
[☞ **weigh, whey, Wei**]
way|bill +s
way|farer +s
way|far|ing
Way|land the Smith (*Scandinavian Myth*)
way|lay
way|lays
way|laid
way|lay|ing
way|lay|er +s
way|mark +s
Wayne, John (US actor)
[☞ **wane, wain**]
Wayne, John Louis ('John|ny') (Cdn

comedian)
[☞ **wane, wain**]
way-out *adjective*
way|point +s
way|side +s
way sta|tion +s
(minor railway station; stopping point; intermediate stage)
[☞ **weigh station**]
way|ward
way|ward|ly
way|ward|ness
WC (water closet)
WCs
we *plural of* I
[☞ **wee, whee**]
weak +er +est (feeble)
[☞ **week**]
weak|en +s +ed +ing
weak|en|er +s
weak|fish
plural weak|fish or weak|fish|es
weak|ish
weak-kneed
weak|li|ness
weak|ling +s
weak|ly (feebly; sickly)
weak|li|er
weak|li|est
[☞ **weekly**]
weak-minded
weak-minded|ly
weak-minded|ness
weak|ness
weak|ness|es
weak|side (*Football*)
weal +s (welt; prosperity)
Weald (region, England)
[☞ **wield**]
Weald|en
wealth
wealth|i|ly
wealthy
wealth|i|er
wealth|i|est
wean +s +ed +ing (accustom an infant to food; withdraw a person from a habit; young child)
[☞ **ween**]
wean|er +s (young animal)
[☞ **wiener**]
wean|ling +s
weapon +s

weap|oned
weapon|less
weap|on|ry
weapons-grade
wear
• (have on as clothing; erode, damage)
  wears
  wore
  worn
  wear|ing
• (*Nautical*)
  wears
  wore
  wear|ing
  [☞ ware, where, wier]
wear|abil|ity
wear|able
wear|er +s
weari|er
weari|est
weari|ly
weari|ness
wear|ing *adjective*
  (tiring; stressful)
  [☞ waring]
wear|ing|ly
weari|some
weari|some|ly
weari|some|ness
weary
  weari|er
  weari|est
  wear|ies
  wear|ied
  weary|ing
weary|ing|ly
wea|sel +s +ed +ing
  (mammal)
  [☞ Wiesel]
weasel|ly
weath|er +s +ed +ing
  (atmospheric conditions; expose to weather; survive; in 'keep a weather eye on', 'under the weather')
  [☞ whether, wether, bellwether]
weather-beaten
weather|board +s +ed +ing
weather|board|ing *noun*
weather-bound
weather|cock +s
weath|er|ing +s *noun*
weather|iz|a|tion
weather|ize
  weather|iz|es
  weather|ized
  weather|iz|ing

weath|er|li|ness
weath|er|ly
weather|man
  weather|men
weather|proof +s +ed +ing
weather|proofed *adjective*
weather|proof|ing *noun*
weather|strip
  weather|strips
  weather|stripped
  weather|strip|ping
weather|strip|ping *noun*
weather|tight
weath|er vane +s
weather-worn
weave
• (interlace strands to make fabric, baskets etc.; blend, devise)
  weaves
  wove
  woven or wove
  weav|ing
• (zigzag)
  weaves
  weaved or wove
  weaved or woven
  weav|ing
  [☞ we've]
Weav|er, Rob|ert
  (Cdn editor)
weav|er +s
weav|ing +s *noun*
Web (World Wide Web)
  [☞ Webb]
web
  webs
  webbed
  web|bing
Webb, (Mar|tha) Bea|trice (English economist)
Webb, Sid|ney James (Baron Passfield, English economist)
webbed *adjective*
Web|ber, An|drew Lloyd (= Lloyd Webber, Andrew: English composer)
  [☞ Weber]
web|bing +s *noun*
webby
  web|bi|er
  web|bi|est
Weber (surname)
  [☞ Lloyd Webber]
Weber, Carl Maria Fried|rich Ernst

von (German composer)
Weber, Ernst Hein|rich (German physiologist)
Weber, Max (German sociologist)
Weber, Wil|helm Ed|uard (German physicist)
weber +s (unit)
Weber|ian
Web|ern, Anton Fried|rich Ernst von (Austrian composer)
  [☞ Weyburn]
web-footed
Web page +s
Web site +s
Web|ster, Dan|iel (US politician)
Web|ster, John (English dramatist)
Web|ster, Noah (US lexicographer)
web|work +s
web|worm +s
wed (marry)
  weds
  wed|ded or wed
  wed|ding
we'd (we had; we would)
wed|ded *adjective*
Wed|dell (sea off Antarctica)
wed|ding +s *noun*
wedge
  wedg|es
  wedged
  wedg|ing
wedge|like
wedge-shaped
wedg|ie +s
Wedg|wood, Jo|siah (English potter)
Wedg|wood *proprietary* (pottery)
Wedg|wood blue +s (Wedgwood-blue *when preceding a noun*)
wed|lock
Wed|nes|day +s
wee
• (tiny)
  weer
  weest
• (urinate)
  wees
  weed
  wee|ing
  [☞ whee]

weed +s +ed +ing
weed|bed +s
weed|er +s
weed-grown
weed|i|ness
weed kill|er +s
weed|less
weed|line +s
weeds
weedy
  weed|i|er
  weed|i|est
week +s (7-day period)
  [☞ weak]
week|day +s
week|end +s
week|ender +s
week-long
week|ly (occurring each week; weekly publication)
  week|lies
  [☞ weakly]
week|night +s
ween +s +ed +ing (think, suppose)
  [☞ wean]
wee|nie +s (frankfurter; geek; penis)
  [☞ weeny]
ween|sy
  ween|si|er
  ween|si|est
weeny (tiny)
  wee|ni|er
  wee|ni|est
  [☞ weenie, wienie]
weep
  weeps
  wept
  weep|ing
weep|er +s
weep|ie +s (tearjerker)
  [☞ weepy]
weep|i|ly
weep|i|ness
weep|ing *noun & adjective*
weep|ing|ly
weepy (tearful; evoking tears; for tearjerker use weepie)
  weep|i|er
  weep|i|est
  weep|ies
weer *comparative of* wee
  [☞ weir, we're]
weest

wee|vil +s
wee|vily
wee-wee +s
weft +s
Weg|ener, Al|fred Lo|thar (German geologist)
Wehr|macht
Wei (Chinese dynasties)
Wei|fang (city, China)
wei|gela +s
weigh +s +ed +ing (measure heaviness; evaluate; in 'weigh anchor', 'weigh into') [☞ whey, way, Wei]
weigh|able
weigh|er +s
weigh in verb
  weighs in
  weighed in
  weigh|ing in
weigh-in +s noun
weigh sta|tion +s (for weighing a truck's cargo) [☞ way station]
weight +s +ed +ing (heaviness; importance; bias)
weight|ed adjective (having extra weight; loaded; biased) [☞ waited]
weight|i|er
weight|i|est
weight|i|ly
weight|i|ness
weight|ing +s noun (amount added to a salary) [☞ waiting]
weight|less
weight|less|ly
weight|less|ness
weight|lift|er +s
weight|lift|ing
weight loss (weight-loss when preceding a noun)
weight room +s
weighty
  weight|i|er
  weight|i|est
Weil, Si|mone (French writer)
Weill, Kurt (German composer)
Wei|mar (city, Germany; republic)
Wei|mar|aner +s

Wein|zweig, John Jacob (Cdn composer)
weir +s (dam; fish trap)
weird +er +est +s +ed +ing
weird|ly
weird|ness
  weird|ness|es
weirdo +s
weirdy
  weird|ies
Weis|mann, Aug|ust Fried|rich Leo|pold (German geneticist) [☞ Weizmann, Wiseman]
Weis|mann|ism
Weiss|mul|ler, Peter John ('John|ny') (US swimmer & actor)
Weiz|mann, Chaim Az|riel (Israeli president) [☞ Weismann, Wiseman]
Wel|and (Wayland the Smith) [☞ Welland]
welch (= welsh: default)
  welch|es
  welched
  welch|ing [☞ Welsh]
wel|come
  wel|comes
  wel|comed
  wel|com|ing [☞ Welkom]
wel|come|ly
wel|come|ness
wel|com|er +s
wel|com|ing adjective
wel|com|ing|ly
weld +s +ed +ing
weld|abil|ity
weld|able
weld|er +s
wel|fare
wel|far|ism
wel|far|ist +s
wel|kin
Wel|kom (town, South Africa)
well
• (satisfactory, satisfactorily)
  bet|ter
  best
• (shaft dug for water etc.; gush)

wells
welled
well|ing
well-
• Compound adjectives beginning with well, such as well aimed, are written as two separate words when following a verb, as in That shot was well aimed, but with a hyphen when preceding a noun they modify, as in That was a well-aimed shot.
we'll (we will; we shall)
Wel|land (city, canal & river, Canada) [☞ Weland]
well-being noun
Welles, (George) Orson (US filmmaker) [☞ Wells]
Welles|ian
well-formed|ness
well|head +s
well|house +s
well|lie +s (use welly)
Wel|ling|ton (capital of New Zealand; in 'beef Wellington')
Wel|ling|ton, 1st Duke of (British soldier & statesman)
wel|ling|ton +s (boot)
Wel|ling|ton|ian +s
well|ness
well-nigh
well off (well-off when preceding a noun)
Wells, Clyde (Cdn politician) [☞ Welles]
Wells, Her|bert George (English novelist) [☞ Welles]
Wells|ian
well|spring +s
well-thought-of
well thought out (well-thought-out when preceding a noun)
well-to-do
well-wisher +s
well-woman adjective

welly
  wel|lies
Wels|bach, Carl Auer von (Austrian chemist)
Welsh (of Wales)
welsh (default)
  welsh|es
  welshed
  welsh|ing
welsh|er +s
Welsh|man
  Welsh|men
Welsh|ness
Welsh rab|bit
Welsh rare|bit (= Welsh rabbit)
Welsh|woman
  Welsh|women
welt +s +ed +ing
Welt|an|schau|ung
  Welt|an|schau|ung|en
wel|ter +s +ed +ing
welter|weight +s
Welt|schmerz
Welty, Eu|dora (US writer)
Wemba-wemba
wen +s (cyst; rune) [☞ when]
Wen|ces|las ('Good King Wenceslas', 10th-c. Bohemian duke & saint; for king of Bohemia & Germany d.1419 use Wenceslaus)
Wen|ces|laus (1361–1419; king of Bohemia & Germany, Holy Roman emperor; for saint use Wenceslas)
wench
  wench|es
  wenched
  wench|ing
wench|er +s
Wend +s
wend +s +ed +ing
Wend|ic
Wend|ish
Wen-Do proprietary
Wendy house +s
Wens|ley|dale +s
went
wentle|trap +s
Wen|zhou (city, China)
wept
were conjugated form of be

[☞ weir, ware, where, whirr]
we're (we are)
weren't
were|wolf
  were|wolves
Wer|fel, Franz (Austrian novelist)
wer|geld +s (= wergild)
wer|gild +s
Wer|ner, Abra|ham Gott|lob (German geologist)
Wer|ner, Al|fred (French-born chemist)
wert archaic conjugated form of be [☞ wort]
Weser (river, Germany)
Wes|ley, Charles (English Methodist leader & hymn writer)
Wes|ley, John (English Methodist leader)
Wes|ley|an +s
Wes|ley|an|ism
Wes|sex (region & former kingdom, England)
Wessi +s
West, Ben|ja|min (US-born English painter)
West, Mae (US actress)
West, Na|than|ael (US novelist)
West, Dame Reb|ecca (English writer)
West (particular region; Bridge)
west (compass point; direction)
West Bank (region, Middle East)
West Bank|er +s
west|bound
West Brom|wich (town, England)
West End|er +s
west|er +s +ed +ing
west|er|ing adjective
west|er|ly
  west|er|lies
West|ern (of the Occident; of the N American West)

west|ern +s (in general use; Riding; sandwich; omelette)
west|ern|er +s
west|ern hemi|sphere
west|ern|iz|a|tion
west|ern|ize
  west|ern|iz|es
  west|ern|ized
  west|ern|iz|ing
west|ern|iz|er +s
west|ern|most
West|ern Wall (in Jerusalem)
West High|land white ter|rier +s
West|ie +s
west|ing +s noun
West|ing|house, George (US engineer)
West|lock (town, Canada)
West|mann (islands off Iceland)
West|meath (county, Ireland)
West|min|ster (borough, London; British Parliament; chimes)
West|mor|land (former county, England)
West|mount (city, Canada)
West|mount|er +s
west-northwest
Wes|ton, Wil|lard Gar|field (Cdn manufacturer)
Weston-super-Mare (resort, England)
West|phal|ia (former province, Germany)
West|phal|ian +s
West Point|er +s
west-southwest
West Van|cou|ver (municipality, Canada)
west|ward
west|wards
wet (damp; Politics; wimp)
  wet|ter
  wet|test
  wets
  wet or wet|ted
  wet|ting
  [☞ whet]

Wet|as|ki|win (city, Canada)
wet|back +s
wet bar +s
wet fly
  wet flies
weth|er +s (castrated ram)
  [☞ weather, whether, bellwether]
wet|land +s
wet look (wet-look when preceding a noun)
wetly
wet|ness
wet nurse +s noun
wet-nurse verb
  wet-nurses
  wet-nursed
  wet-nursing
wet|suit +s
Wet'suwet'en
  plural Wet'suwet'en
wettable
wet|ter comparative of wet
  [☞ whetter]
wet|ting noun
wet|tish
wet|ware
we've (we have)
Wex|ford (county & town, Ireland)
Wey|burn (city, Canada)
  [☞ Webern]
Wey|den, Ro|gier van der (Flemish painter)
Wey|mouth (town, England)
whack +s +ed +ing (slap; kill; attempt; 'out of whack')
  [☞ wack, wacke, Waac, WAC]
whacked adjective (= whacked out)
whacked out (whacked-out when preceding a noun: crazy; intoxicated; exhausted)
whack|er +s
whack|i|ly (use wackily)
whack|i|ness (use wackiness)
whack|ing adjective & adverb (very large)

whacko (interjection; for crazy, lunatic use wacko)
  whack|os
whacky (use wacky)
  whack|i|er
  whack|i|est
whale (animal; beat; in 'whale of a')
  whales
  whaled
  whal|ing
  [☞ wail, wale, Wales]
whale|back +s
whale|boat +s
whale|bone (baleen)
whale|man
  whale|men
whal|er +s (person who hunts whales; boat)
  [☞ wailer]
whale-watch
  whale-watches
  whale-watched
  whale-watching
whal|ing noun (the hunting of whales)
wham
  whams
  whammed
  wham|ming
wham-bam
whammy
  wham|mies
whang +s +ed +ing
Whan|ga|rei (city, New Zealand)
whan|gee +s
whap (slap)
  whaps
  whapped
  whap|ping
  [☞ wop]
wharf
  wharves or wharfs
wharf|age
wharf|in|ger +s
Whar|ton, Edith New|bold (US writer)
wharves
what
what|cha|callit +s
what|chama|callit +s
what-d'you-call-it +s
what|ever
what-if +s
what|not +s
what say
whats|it +s

what|so|ever
wheat +s
Wheat Board
wheat|ear +s
wheat|en
wheat germ
wheat grass
  wheat grass|es
wheat|meal
Wheat|stone, Sir
  Charles (English
  physicist)
Wheat|stone bridge
  +s
whee *interjection*
  [☞ wee]
whee|dle
  whee|dles
  whee|dled
  wheed|ling
wheed|ler +s
wheed|ling *adjective*
wheed|ling|ly
wheel +s +ed +ing
  (spinning disc)
  [☞ weal]
wheel|barrow +s
wheel|base +s
wheel|chair +s
wheel clamp +s
wheeled *adjective*
Wheel|er, Anne (Cdn
  filmmaker)
wheel|er +s
wheeler-dealer +s
wheeler-dealing
wheel|horse +s
wheel|house +s
wheel|ie +s
wheel|less
wheel-like
wheel-lock +s
wheel|man (cyclist;
  driver; helmsman)
  wheel|men
wheel of For|tune
wheels|man
  (helmsman)
  wheels|men
wheel|spin
wheel|wright +s
wheeze
  wheez|es
  wheezed
  wheez|ing
wheez|er +s
wheez|i|ly
wheez|i|ness
wheezy
  wheez|i|er
  wheez|i|est

Whel|an, Ed|ward
  (Cdn journalist &
  politician)
whelk +s
whelm +s +ed +ing
whelp +s +ed +ing
when +s (at which
  time)
  [☞ wen]
whence
whence|so|ever (from
  whatever place)
  [☞ whensoever]
when|ever
when|so|ever
  (whenever)
  [☞ whencesoever]
where (in which place)
  [☞ ware, wear,
  were]
where|abouts
where|after
where|as
where|at
where|by
where|fore +s
where|from
where|in
where|of
where|on
where|so|ever
where|to
where|upon
wher|ever
where|with
where|with|al
wher|ry (boat)
  wher|ries
  [☞ wary]
whet (sharpen;
  stimulate)
  whets
  whet|ted
  whet|ting
wheth|er
  conjunction (if)
  [☞ wether,
  weather,
  bellwether]
whet|stone +s
whet|ter +s (a thing
  that whets)
whew
whey (milk residue)
  [☞ weigh, Wei,
  way]
whey-faced
which *adjective* &
  pronoun
  [☞ witch, wych
  elm]
which|ever
which|so|ever

whick|er +s +ed +ing
  (whinny)
  [☞ wicker]
whid|ah +s (*use*
  whydah)
whiff +s +ed +ing
whif|fle
  whif|fles
  whif|fled
  whif|fling
whif|fler +s
whiffle|tree +s
whiffy
  whiff|i|er
  whiff|i|est
Whig +s (*Politics*)
Whig|gery
Whig|gish
Whig|gism
while (period of time;
  during the time that;
  whereas, although;
  pass time)
  whiles
  whiled
  whil|ing
  [☞ wile]
whiles *archaic*
  (= while)
  [☞ wile]
whil|om
whilst
whim +s
whim|brel +s
whim|per +s +ed
  +ing
whim|per|er +s
whim|per|ing|ly
whim|si|cal
whim|si|cal|ity
whim|si|cal|ly
whim|sy
  whim|sies
whim-wham +s
whin +s (shrub)
whin|chat +s
whine (wail,
  complain)
  whines
  whined
  whin|ing
whin|er +s
whiney (whining: *use*
  whiny)
  whin|i|er
  whin|i|est
  [☞ winey, whinny]
whing|ding +s (*use*
  wingding)
whinge
  whin|ges
  whinged

whin|ging
  or whinge|ing
whin|ger +s
whin|gey
whin|i|er (more
  whiny)
whin|i|est (most
  whiny)
whin|ing|ly
whinny (neigh)
  whin|nies
  whin|nied
  whinny|ing
whiny (whining)
  whin|i|er
  whin|i|est
  [☞ winey, whinny]
whip
  whips
  whipped
  whip|ping
whip-bird +s
whip|cord +s
whip hand
whip kick +s +ed
  +ing
whip|lash
  whip|lash|es
  whip|lashed
  whip|lash|ing
whip|less
whip-like
whipped *adjective*
whip|per +s
whipper-snapper +s
whip|pet
whip|pi|ness
whip|ping +s *noun*
whipple|tree +s
whip|poor|will +s
whippy
  whip|pi|er
  whip|pi|est
whip-round +s *noun*
whip|saw
  whip|saws
  whip|sawed
  whip|sawed
  or whip|sawn
  whip|saw|ing
whip snake +s
whip|stitch
  whip|stitch|es
  whip|stitched
  whip|stitch|ing
whip|stock +s
whip|worm
whir (hum, drone: *use*
  whirr)
  whirs
  whirred
  whir|ring

whirl +s +ed +ing
(spin; spinning
movement; try;
frantic state)
[☞ whorl]
whirl|er +s
whirli|gig +s
whirl|ing *adjective*
whirl|ing|ly
whirl|pool +s
whirl|wind +s
whirly|bird +s
whirr +s +ed +ing
(drone, hum)
whish (sound)
whish|es
whished
whish|ing
[☞ wish]
whisht (hush)
[☞ whist, wist]
whisk +s +ed +ing
whisk broom +s
whis|ker +s
whis|kered
whis|kery
whis|key +s (for Irish
& American whiskey
or bourbon)
whisky (for Cdn &
Scotch whisky)
whis|kies
whisky blanc +s
whisky-jack +s
whis|per +s +ed +ing
whis|per|er +s
whis|per|ing +s *noun*
whist (*Cards; for* hush
use whisht)
[☞ wist]
whist drive +s
whis|tle
whis|tles
whis|tled
whist|ling
whistle-blower +s
whistle-blowing
whistle|punk +s
Whist|ler (mountain &
resort, Canada)
Whist|ler, James
Ab|bott Mc|Neill
(US painter)
whist|ler +s
Whist|ler|ian
whis|tle stop +s
(whistle-stop *when
preceding a noun*)
Whit (of Whitsuntide)
[☞ Witt]
whit (the smallest
amount)
[☞ wit]

Whit|by (town,
Canada)
Whitchurch-
Stouff|ville
(town, Canada)
White (surname; river
& mountain pass,
Canada; sea, Russia)
[☞ Isle of Wight]
White, Pat|rick
Vic|tor Mar|tin|dale
(Australian novelist)
White, Rob|ert ('Bob')
(Cdn labour leader)
White, Ter|ence
Han|bury (English
novelist)
white (colour; person)
whiter
whit|est
whites
whited
whit|ing
[☞ wight]
white|bait
plural white|bait
white|beam +s
white|board +s
white bread +s *noun*
white-bread *adjective*
white|cap +s
white|capped
white coat +s (lab
coat)
white|coat +s (seal)
white-coated
white-collar
White|court (town,
Canada)
White En|sign +s
white|face
white-faced
White Fath|ers
White|field, George
(English preacher)
White|fish (bay,
Canada)
white|fish (lake &
river fish of trout
family)
plural white|fish or
white|fish|es
white fish (any fish
with pale flesh, e.g.
cod, haddock, plaice
etc.)
plural white fish or
white fish|es
white|fly
white|flies
White Fri|ar +s
White|hall (street in
London, England)

White|head, Al|fred
North (English
mathematician)
white|head +s
White|horse (city,
Canada)
white-hot
White House (US
presidential
residence; Russian
parliament building)
white-knuckle
white|ly
whit|en +s +ed +ing
whit|en|er +s
white|ness
whit|en|ing *noun*
white out *verb*
whites out
whited out
whit|ing out
white|out +s *noun*
white pages
white|paint|er +s
white|paint|ing
white paper +s
(government report)
White Pass (in
Canada)
white picket fence
+s (white-picket-
fence *when preceding
a noun*)
White River (in
Canada)
White Rock +s (city,
Canada; chicken)
white rose
White Rus|sia
(= Belarus)
White Rus|sian +s
(drink; Belarusian)
White Sands (national
monument, US)
White Sea (inlet,
Russia)
white-shoe
white|smith
white|tail +s
(= white-tailed
deer)
white-tailed deer +s
white|throat +s
white tie +s (white-
tie *when preceding a
noun*)
white trash (white-
trash *when preceding
a noun*)
white|wall +s
white|wash
white|wash|es

white|washed
white|wash|ing
white|wash|er +s
white|water
white-winged
white|wood +s
whit|ey +s *offensive* (a
white person)
[☞ whity]
whith|er (to what
place)
[☞ wither, withers]
whither|so|ever
whit|ing *noun*
• (fish)
plural whit|ing
• (ground chalk)
plural whit|ings
whit|ish
whit|low
Whit|man, Wal|ter
('Walt') (US poet)
Whit|man|esque
Whit|ney (mountain,
US)
Whit|ney, Eli (US
inventor)
Whit|ney, Sir James
Pliny (Cdn
politician)
Whit|sun
Whit Sun|day +s
Whit|sun|tide
Whit|ti|er, John
Green|leaf (US poet)
Whit|ting|ton, Sir
Rich|ard ('Dick')
(Lord Mayor of
London, England)
Whit|tle, Sir Frank
(English aeronautical
engineer)
whit|tle
whit|tles
whit|tled
whit|tling
whity (whitish)
[☞ whitey]
whiz (buzz; person
with exceptional
skill; urinate)
whiz|zes
whizzed
whiz|zing
whiz-bang +s
whiz kid +s
whizz (buzz, person
with exceptional
skill, urinate: *use*
whiz)
whizz|es
whizzed
whizz|ing

whizz-bang +s
(= whiz-bang)
whiz|zer +s
who *pronoun*
[☞ hoo]
whoa (stop)
who'd
who-does-what
who|dun|it +s
who|dun|nit +s (*use*
whodunit)
who|ever
whole +s (entire,
complete, etc.)
[☞ hole]
whole cloth *noun*
whole-cloth *adjective*
whole food
whole-grain
whole|heart|ed
whole|heart|ed|ly
whole|heart|ed|ness
whole-life
in|sur|ance
whole|meal
whole milk
whole|ness
whole note +s
whole rest +s
whole|sale
whole|saler +s
whole|some
whole|some|ly
whole|some|ness
whole-tone scale
whole wheat
whol|ism (*use* holism)
whol|ist +s (*use*
holist)
whol|is|tic (*use*
holistic)
whol|is|tic|ally (*use*
holistically)
wholly (entirely;
exclusively)
[☞ holy, holey,
Holi]
whom
whom|ever
whomp +s +ed +ing
whom|so
whom|so|ever
whoop +s +ed +ing
(shout; raspy breath;
in 'whoop it up', 'no
big whoop')
[☞ whup, hoop]
whoop-de-do +s
whoop-de-doo +s
(= whoop-de-do)
whoop|ee +s
whoop|er +s
whoop|ing cough

whoop|ing crane +s
whoop|ing swan +s
whoops *interjection*
whoop-up +s
whoosh
whoosh|es
whooshed
whoosh|ing
whop (slap: *use* whap)
whops
whopped
whop|ping
[☞ wop]
whop|per +s
whop|ping *adjective*
whore (prostitute;
womanize)
whores
whored
whor|ing
[☞ hoar, hoer]
whore|dom
whore|house +s
whore|master +s
whore|monger +s
whorer +s
whore|son +s
(disliked person)
whor|ish
whor|ish|ly
whor|ish|ness
whorl +s (coil; ring of
leaves; turn of a
spiral shell; on a
fingerprint)
[☞ whirl]
whorled *adjective*
whortle|berry
whortle|ber|ries
who's (who is)
whose (of or
belonging to whom
or which)
whose|so *possessive of*
whoso
whose|soever
possessive of
whosoever
whos|ever *possessive
of* whoever
whoso (whoever)
who|soever
(whoever)
who's who +s
whump +s +ed +ing
whup (whip, defeat)
whups
whupped
whup|ping
[☞ whoop]
why +s (for what
reason?;

explanation)
[☞ Wye, wye]
Why|alla (town, South
Africa)
why|dah +s
Wicca
Wic|can +s
Wich|ita (city, US)
wick +s +ed +ing
wick|ed +er +est
adjective
wicked|ly
wicked|ness
wick|er (braided twigs
used for baskets etc.)
[☞ whicker]
wicker|work
wick|et +s
wicket-keeper +s
wicki|up +s
Wick|liffe, John
(= Wycliffe)
Wick|low (county &
town, Ireland)
Wicks, Al|fred ('Ben')
(Cdn cartoonist)
Wic|lif, John
(= Wycliffe)
wid|der|shins
wide
wider
wid|est
wide-angle *adjective*
wide-area network
+s
wide awake *adjective*
wide|awake +s (hat)
wide-band
wide-bodied
wide-body
wide-bodies
wide boy +s
wide-eyed
wide|ly
wid|en +s +ed +ing
widen|er +s
wide|ness
wide|out +s *noun*
wide-ranging
wide-screen *adjective*
wide|spread
widg|eon +s
widg|et +s
widish
Wid|nes (town,
England)
wid|ow +s +ed +ing
wid|owed *adjective*
wid|ower +s
widow|hood
widow-maker +s
widow's mite +s

widow's peak +s
widow's walk +s
widow's weeds
width +s
width|ways
width|wise
Wiebe, Rudy Henry
(Cdn writer)
Wie|land, Joyce (Cdn
artist)
wield +s +ed +ing
[☞ Weald]
wield|er +s
wieldy
wield|i|er
wield|i|est
Wie|ner, Nor|bert (US
mathematician)
wie|ner +s
(frankfurter; geek;
penis)
[☞ weaner]
Wie|ner schnit|zel +s
wie|nie +s
(frankfurter, geek,
penis: *use* weenie)
[☞ weeny]
Wies|baden (city,
Germany)
Wie|sel, Elie
(Romanian-born
human rights
advocate)
[☞ weasel]
Wie|sen|thal, Simon
(Austrian-born
investigator of Nazi
crimes)
wife
wives
wife|hood
wife|less
wife|like
wife|li|ness
wife|ly
wig (hair; rebuke; in
'wig out')
wigs
wigged
wig|ging
[☞ Whig]
Wigan (town,
England)
wigeon +s (*use*
widgeon)
wigged *adjective*
wig|ging +s *noun*
wig|gle
wig|gles
wig|gled
wig|gling
wig|gler +s

wig|gly
  wig|gli|er
  wig|gli|est
Wight (island off
  S England)
  [☞ White]
wight +s *archaic*
  (person)
wig|less
**Wig|ner, Eu|gene
  Paul** (US physicist)
Wig|town|shire
  (former county,
  Scotland)
wig|wag
  wig|wags
  wig|wagged
  wig|wag|ging
wig|wam +s
Wil|ber|force
  (waterfall, Canada)
**Wil|ber|force,
  Wil|liam** (English
  social reformer)
wilco
wild +er +est +s
wild card +s
wild|cat +s
wild|cat|ter +s
wild-caught
**Wilde, Oscar Fin|gal
  O'Flaher|tie Wills**
  (Irish writer)
Wild|ean
wilde|beest
  plural **wilde|beest** or
  wilde|beests
Wild|er, Billy (US
  filmmaker)
**Wild|er, Thorn|ton
  Niven** (US writer)
wild|er[1] *comparative
  of* **wild**
wil|der[2] +s +ed +ing
  (lead astray;
  bewilder)
wil|der|ness
  wil|der|ness|es
wild|fire +s
wild|flower +s
wild|fowl
  plural **wild|fowl**
wild|ing +s *noun*
wild|ish
wild|life
wild|ling +s
wild|ly
wild|ness
wild type +s
Wild West
wild|wood +s

wile (trick; lure)
  wiles
  wiled
  wiling
  [☞ while]
wil|ful
wil|ful|ly
wil|ful|ness
Wil|helm (emperors of
  Germany)
Wil|hel|mina (queen
  of the Netherlands)
Wil|helms|haven
  (town, Germany)
wili|er
wili|est
wili|ness
Wilkes, Charles (US
  naval officer)
Wilkes, John (English
  journalist &
  politician)
Wilkes Land (region,
  Antarctica)
**Wil|kins, Sir (George)
  Hu|bert** (Australian
  explorer)
**Wil|kins, Mau|rice
  Hugh Fred|erick**
  (New Zealand-born
  biochemist)
will
  • *auxiliary verb*
  present will
  past would
  • (wish; impel;
  bequeath)
  wills
  willed
  will|ing
**Wil|lan, (James)
  Healey** (English-
  born Cdn composer)
willed *adjective*
Willem|stad (capital
  of the Netherlands
  Antilles)
will|er +s
wil|let
  plural **wil|let**
will|ful (*use* wilful)
will|ful|ly (*use*
  wilfully)
will|ful|ness (*use*
  wilfulness)
Wil|liam
  • (English, Scottish &
  British kings; English
  prince)
  • (= Wilhelm,
  emperors of
  Germany)

Wil|liam Henry
  (*former name for*
  Sorel, Canada)
**Wil|liam of
  Malmes|bury**
  (English chronicler)
Wil|liam of Occam
  (English philosopher)
Wil|liam of Ock|ham
  (= William of
  Occam)
Wil|liam of Or|ange
  (William III of Great
  Britain and Ireland)
Wil|liam Rufus
  (William II of
  England)
**Wil|liams, Hiram
  ('Hank')** (US singer-
  songwriter)
**Wil|liams, John
  Chris|to|pher**
  (Australian guitarist)
**Wil|liams, Theo|dore
  Sam|uel ('Ted')** (US
  baseball player)
**Wil|liams,
  Ten|nes|see** (US
  dramatist)
**Wil|liams, Wil|liam
  Car|los** (US writer)
Wil|liams|burg (city,
  US)
Wil|liams Lake (city
  & lake, Canada)
**Wil|liam the
  Con|quer|or**
  (William I of
  England)
wil|lie +s (= willy)
wil|lies (creeps)
will|ing *adjective*
**Wil|ling|don,
  Free|man Freeman-
  Thomas, 1st
  Mar|quess of**
  (governor general of
  Canada)
will|ing|ly
will|ing|ness
Wil|lis|ton Lake
  (reservoir, Canada)
will-less
will-o'-the-wisp +s
wil|low +s
wil|lowy
will|power
**Wills, Helen
  New|ing|ton** (US
  tennis player)
willy (penis)
  wil|lies
willy-nilly

Wil|mot, Mon|tagu
  (British colonial
  administrator)
Wil|son, Ber|tha (Cdn
  judge)
**Wil|son, Charles
  Thom|son Rees**
  (Scottish physicist)
Wil|son, Ed|mund
  (US writer)
**Wil|son, Ed|ward
  Os|borne** (US social
  biologist)
Wil|son, Ethel Davis
  (South African-born
  Cdn writer)
**Wil|son, (James)
  Har|old** (British
  prime minister)
**Wil|son, (Thom|as)
  Wood|row** (US
  president)
Wil|son|ian +s
wilt +s +ed +ing
Wil|ton +s
Wilt|shire (county,
  England)
wily
  wili|er
  wili|est
Wimble|don (district,
  London; *Tennis*)
wim|min (= womyn)
WIMP (hypothetical
  subatomic particle)
  WIMPs
wimp +s +ed +ing
wimp|ish
wimp|ish|ly
wimp|ish|ness
wim|ple
  wim|ples
  wim|pled
  wimp|ling
Wimpy +s
  (hamburger)
wimpy
  wimp|i|er
  wimp|i|est
win (be victorious;
  gain)
  wins
  won
  win|ning
  [☞ whin]
wince
  win|ces
  winced
  win|cing
win|cer +s
winch
  winch|es
  winched
  winch|ing

winch|er +s
Win|ches|ter +s
• (city, England; Computing)
• proprietary (rifle)
win|cing|ly
Winck|el|mann, Jo|hann Joa|chim (German art historian)
wind
• (curve, spiral, turn, coil)
  winds
  wound
  wind|ing
• (moving air; affect breathing)
  winds
  wind|ed
  wind|ing
• (sound a horn by blowing)
  winds
  wind|ed or wound
  wind|ing
wind|age
Win|daus, Adolf (German chemist)
wind|bag +s
wind|blown
wind|bound
wind|break +s
wind|break|er +s
wind|burn +s
wind|burned
wind|burnt (= windburned)
wind|cheat|er +s
wind chill +s
wind chill factor +s
wind chimes
wind down verb
  winds down
  wound down
  wind|ing down
wind-down +s noun
wind|ed adjective
wind|er +s
Win|der|mere (lake, England)
wind|fall +s
wind farm +s
wind|flower +s
wind gap +s
Wind|hoek (capital of Namibia)
wind|hover +s
wind|i|er
wind|i|est
wind|i|ly
wind|i|ness

wind|ing +s noun & adjective
wind|jam|mer +s
wind|lass
  wind|lass|es
  wind|lassed
  wind|lass|ing
wind|less
windle|straw +s
wind|mill +s +ed +ing
win|dow +s
win|dow box
  win|dow boxes
win|dowed
win|dow frame +s
win|dow|ing
win|dow|less
win|dow|pane +s
win|dow shade +s
win|dow shop
  win|dow shops
  win|dow shopped
  win|dow shop|ping
win|dow shop|per +s
window|sill +s
wind|pipe +s
wind power
wind|proof
wind|row +s
wind sail +s
Wind|scale (former name for Sellafield, England)
wind|screen +s
wind shear +s
wind|shield +s
wind|sock +s
Wind|sor (city & town, Canada; British royal house; chair)
wind|storm +s
wind|surf +s +ed +ing
wind|surf|er +s
wind|surf|ing noun
wind|swept
wind|throw
wind up verb
  winds up
  wound up
  wind|ing up
wind|up +s noun & adjective
Wind|ward (island group, Caribbean)
wind|ward
windy
  wind|i|er
  wind|i|est

wine (drink)
  wines
  wined
  wining
  [☞ whine]
wine bar
wine|berry
  wine|ber|ries
wine|bib|ber +s
wine|bib|bing
wine|glass
  wine|glass|es
wine grow|er +s
wine-growing
wine gum +s
wine|less
wine|maker +s
wine|making
wine|press
  wine|press|es
win|ery
  win|er|ies
Wine|sap +s
wine|skin +s
winey (like wine)
  winier
  winiest
  [☞ whiny]
wing +s +ed +ing
wing|back +s
wing|beat +s
wing-case +s
wing|ding +s
winged adjective
wing|er +s
wing|less
wing|let +s
wing-like
wing|man
  wing|men
wing nut +s
wing shoot|er +s
wing shoot|ing
wing shot +s
wing|span +s
wing|spread +s
wing tip +s (tip of a wing)
wing|tip +s (shoe)
wingy
  wing|i|er
  wing|i|est
winier comparative of winey
  [☞ whinier]
winiest superlative of winey
  [☞ whiniest]
Win|isk (river, Canada)
wink +s +ed +ing

win|kle
  win|kles
  win|kled
  wink|ling
winkle-picker +s
Wink|ler (town, Canada)
wink|ler +s
win|less
win|nable
Win|ne|bago
• (people, language)
  plural Win|ne|bago or Win|ne|bagos
• (camper)
  plural Win|ne|bagos
win|ner +s
winner's cir|cle +s
winner-take-all
win|ning +s noun
win|ning|est
win|ning|ly
Win|ni|peg (city, lake & river, Canada)
Win|ni|peg|ger +s
Win|ni|peg|osis (lake, Canada)
win|now +s +ed +ing (Agriculture; sort out)
win|now|er +s
wino +s (alcoholic)
  [☞ winnow]
win|some
win|some|ly
win|some|ness
Win|stan|ley, Ger|rard (English pamphleteer)
Win|ter, Sir James Spear|man (premier of Newfoundland)
win|ter +s +ed +ing
winter|berry
  winter|ber|ries
win|ter cress
win|ter|er +s
win|ter feed
  win|ter feeds
  win|ter fed
  win|ter feed|ing
winter|green +s
win|ter|i|er (= wintrier)
win|ter|i|est (= wintriest)
win|ter|i|ness (= wintriness)
win|ter|iz|a|tion
win|ter|ize
  win|ter|iz|es
  win|ter|ized
  win|ter|iz|ing
win|ter|ized adjective

winter|kill +s +ed
+ing
winter|killed *adjective*
win|ter|less
win|ter|ly
Win|ter|peg
(Winnipeg)
Win|ter|thur (town,
Switzerland)
winter|time
win|tery (= wintry)
win|ter|i|er
win|ter|i|est
Win|throp, John
(governor of the
Massachusetts Bay
Colony)
Win|throp, John
(governor of
Connecticut)
win|tri|ly
win|tri|ness
win|try
win|tri|er
win|tri|est
win-win
winy (like wine: *use*
winey)
winier
winiest
[☞ whiny]
wipe
wipes
wiped
wiping
wipe|able
wiped out *adjective*
wipe out *verb*
wipes out
wiped out
wiping out
wipe|out +s *noun*
wiper +s
Wir|ad|huri
wire
wires
wired
wir|ing
wire brush *noun*
wire brush|es
wire-brush *verb*
wire-brushes
wire-brushed
wire-brushing
wire cut|ter +s
wired *adjective*
wire grass
wire grass|es
wire-hair +s
wire-haired
wire|less
wire-puller +s
wire-pulling

wire-rimmed
wire rims
wire rope +s
wire strip|per +s
wire|tap
wire|taps
wire|tapped
wire|tap|ping
wire|tap|per +s
wire|tap|ping *noun*
wire-to-wire
wire|worm +s
wiri|ness
wir|ing +s *noun*
Wir|ral (peninsula,
US)
wiry
wiri|er
wiri|est
wis *archaic* (know
well)
wis|ses
wissed
wis|sing
[☞ whiz]
Wis|con|sin (state,
US)
Wis|con|sin|ite +s
Wis|dom (*Bible*)
wis|dom +s
wise
wiser
wis|est
wises
wised
wis|ing
wise|acre +s
wise|ass
wise|ass|es
wise|crack +s +ed
+ing
wise|crack|er +s
wise|crack|ing *noun*
& *adjective*
wise guy +s
wise|ly
Wise|man, Adele
(Cdn writer)
[☞ Weismann,
Weizmann]
wis|ent +s
wish (desire; request)
wish|es
wished
wish|ing
[☞ whish]
wish|bone +s
wish|er +s
wish|ful
wish-fulfill|ment
wish-fulfil|ment (*use*
wish-fulfillment)
wish|ful|ly

wish|ful|ness
wish list +s
wishy-washy
wisp +s
wisp|i|ly
wisp|i|ness
wispy
wisp|i|er
wisp|i|est
wist *past & past
participle of* wit
[☞ whist, whisht]
wis|taria +s (*use*
wisteria)
wis|teria +s
wist|ful
wist|ful|ly
wist|ful|ness
wit
• (humour;
intelligence; in 'at
one's wits' end',
'scare the wits out
of')
wits
• (know; in 'to wit')
wot
wist
wit|ting
[☞ whit, Witt]
witch (sorceress)
witch|es
witched
witch|ing
[☞ which, wych
elm]
witch|craft
witch doc|tor +s
witch|ery
witches' brew +s
witches' Sab|bath +s
witch|etty
witch|et|ties
witch|grass
witch ha|zel +s
witch hunt +s
witch-hunting
witch|ing *adjective* &
noun
witch|like
witchy
witch|i|er
witch|i|est
wit|ena|gemot +s
with (in the company
of; by means of; etc.)
[☞ withe]
with|al
with|draw
with|draws
with|drew
with|drawn
with|draw|ing

with|drawal +s
with|drawing-room
+s
with|drawn *adjective*
withe +s (willow
shoot)
with|er +s +ed +ing
(shrivel; decline)
[☞ whither]
wither|ing *adjective*
wither|ing|ly
with|ers (back of a
horse etc.)
wither|shins
with|hold
with|holds
with|held
with|hold|ing
with|hold|er +s
with|in
with it (with-it *when
preceding a noun*)
with|out
with|stand
with|stands
with|stood
with|stand|ing
withy
with|ies
wit|less
wit|less|ly
wit|less|ness
Wit|ness (Jehovah's
Witness)
Wit|ness|es
wit|ness
wit|ness|es
wit|nessed
wit|ness|ing
wits' end
Witt, Johan de (Dutch
politician)
[☞ Whit]
wit|ted *adjective*
Wit|ten|berg (town,
Germany)
wit|ter +s +ed +ing
Witt|gen|stein,
Lud|wig Josef
Jo|hann (Austrian-
born philosopher)
Witt|gen|stein|ian
wit|ti|cism +s
wit|ti|er *comparative
of* witty
[☞ Whittier]
wit|ti|ly
wit|ti|ness
wit|ting *adjective*
wit|ting|ly
witty
wit|ti|er
wit|ti|est

Wit|waters|rand (region, South Africa)
wi|vern +s (use wyvern)
wives
wiz (person with exceptional skill: use whiz)
wiz|zes
[☞ whiz, wis]
wiz|ard +s
wiz|ard|ly
wiz|ardry
wiz|en (= wizened)
wiz|ened
wo (stop: use whoa)
[☞ woe]
w/o (without)
woad
wob|ble
wob|bles
wob|bled
wob|bling
wob|bler +s
wob|bli|ness
Wob|bly (Industrial Workers of the World member)
Wob|blies
wob|bly
wob|bli|er
wob|bli|est
Wode|house, Sir Pel|ham Gren|ville (English-born US writer)
[☞ Woodhouse]
Wode|hous|ian
Woden (= Odin, Scandinavian god)
wodge +s
woe +s (grief)
[☞ whoa]
woe|begone
woe|ful
woe|ful|ly
woe|ful|ness
wog +s offensive
wog|gle +s
Wöh|ler, Fried|rich (German chemist)
wok +s (frying pan)
woke
woken
Wo|king (town, England)
wold +s
Wolf, Fried|rich Aug|ust (German scholar)
[☞ Wolfe, Woolf]

Wolf, Hugo Phil|ipp Jakob (Austrian composer)
[☞ Wolfe, Woolf]
wolf
• noun
wolves
• verb
wolfs
wolfed
wolf|ing
Wolf Cub +s (Scouting)
wolf cub +s
wolf-dog +s
Wolfe (island, Canada; surname)
[☞ Wolf, Woolf]
Wolfe, James (English general)
Wolfe, Thom|as Clay|ton (1900–38; US novelist)
Wolfe, Thom|as Ken|ner|ley ('Tom') (b.1931; US writer)
wolf|er +s
wolf|fish (fish)
plural wolf|fish or wolf|fish|es
[☞ wolfish]
wolf|hound +s
wolf|ish (like a wolf)
[☞ wolffish]
wolf|ish|ly
wolf|like
wolf pack +s
wolf|ram
wolf|ram|ite +s
Wolf River +s (apple)
wolfs|bane
Wolfs|burg (city, Germany)
wolf|skin
wolf's milk +s (plant)
Wolf|ville (town, Canada)
wolf whis|tle +s noun
wolf-whistle verb
wolf-whistles
wolf-whistled
wolf-whistling
wolf wil|low +s
Wol|las|ton, Wil|liam Hyde (English scientist)
Wol|las|ton (lake & peninsula, Canada)
Wol|lon|gong (city, Australia)
Woll|stone|craft, Mary (English writer)

Wolof
plural Wolof or Wol|ofs
Wolse|ley, Gar|net Jo|seph (British soldier)
Wol|sey, Thom|as (English cardinal & statesman)
Wol|ver|hamp|ton (city, England)
wol|ver|ine +s
wolves
woman
• noun
women
• verb
womans
womanned or womaned
woman|ning or woman|ing
woman|hood
woman|ish
woman|ish|ly
woman|ish|ness
woman|ism
woman|ist +s
woman|ize
woman|iz|es
woman|ized
woman|iz|ing
woman|iz|er +s
woman|kind
woman|less
woman|like
woman|li|ness
woman|ly
woman|power
womb +s
wom|bat +s
womb|like
women
women|folk
Women's In|sti|tute
women's lib
women's lib|ber +s
Women's Lib|er|a|tion (specific movement)
women's lib|er|a|tion (in general use)
women's move|ment
women's rights
women's room +s
women's shel|ter +s
women's stud|ies
Women's Suf|frage (specific movement)
women's suf|frage (in general use)
womens|wear
womyn (= women)

won
• past & past participle of win
• (Korean currency)
plural won
[☞ wan]
Won|der, Stev|ie (US singer-songwriter)
won|der +s +ed +ing (amazement; be curious or amazed)
[☞ wander]
won|der|er +s (one who wonders)
[☞ wanderer]
won|der|ful
won|der|ful|ly
won|der|ful|ness
won|der|ing adjective
won|der|ing|ly
won|der|land +s
won|der|ment +s
wonder-struck
wonder-worker +s
wonder-working
won|drous
won|drous|ly
wonk +s
wonk|ery
wonk|i|ly
wonk|i|ness
wonk|ish
wonk|ish|ness
wonky (shaky; irregular; dull)
wonk|i|er
wonk|i|est
[☞ Wankie]
wont (habit; accustomed)
wonts or wont
wont or wont|ed
wont|ing
[☞ want]
won't (will not)
wont|ed adjective (usual)
[☞ wanted]
won ton +s (dumpling)
[☞ wanton]
woo (court)
woos
wooed
woo|ing
[☞ Wu]
woo|able
Wood (mountain, Canada)
Wood, Mrs Henry (English novelist)
Wood, Henry Wise (Cdn farmer leader)

Wood, Nat|alie (US actress)
wood +s (timber, forest)
[☞ would]
wood|bine +s
wood bison
  plural wood bison
wood|block +s
wood|box
  wood|boxes
Wood Buf|falo (municipality & national park, Canada)
wood buf|falo
  plural wood buf|falo or wood buf|fa|loes
wood-burner +s
wood-burning
wood|carv|er +s
wood|carv|ing +s
wood chip +s
wood|chuck +s
Wood|cock, George (Cdn writer)
wood|cock
  plural wood|cock
wood|craft
wood|cut +s
wood|cut|ter +s
wood|cut|ting
wood|ed
wood|en
wooden-head +s
wooden-headed
wooden-headed|ness
wood|en|ly
wooden|ness
wood grain +s
Wood|house, Ar|thur Suth|er|land Pig|gott (Cdn scholar)
[☞ Wodehouse]
wood|i|er
wood|i|est
wood|i|ness
wood|land +s
Wood|land Cree
  plural Wood|land Cree or Wood|land Crees
wood|land|er +s
wood|less
wood|lot +s
wood|louse
  wood|lice
wood|man
  wood|men
wood|mouse
  wood|mice

wood|note +s
wood|peck|er +s
wood|pile +s
wood pulp
wood|rat +s
wood|ruff +s
wood|rush
  wood|rush|es
woods
wood screw +s
wood|shed
  wood|sheds
  wood|shed|ded
  wood|shed|ding
wood|sia +s
woods|i|er
woods|i|est
woods|man
  woods|men
woods|man|ship
wood|smoke
wood stain +s
Wood|stock (rock festival; city & town, Canada)
wood stove +s
Woods|worth, James Shaver (Cdn politician)
woodsy
  woods|i|er
  woods|i|est
wood tick +s
Wood|ward, Charles (Cdn merchant)
Wood|ward, Rob|ert Burns (US chemist)
wood|wind +s
wood|work
wood|work|er +s
wood|work|ing
wood|worm +s
woody
  wood|i|er
  wood|i|est
  wood|ies
wood|yard +s
woo|er +s
woof +s +ed +ing
woof|er +s
wool +s
wool|en +s (use woollen)
Woolf, (Adel|ine) Vir|ginia (English writer)
[☞ Wolf, Wolfe]
wool|gather +s
wool|gather|ing
wool|grow|er +s
wool|len +s
Wool|ley, Sir (Charles) Leon|ard

(English archaeologist)
[☞ woolly]
wool-like
wool|li|ness
wool|ly
  wool|li|er
  wool|li|est
  wool|lies
[☞ Woolley]
Wool|sack
wool|shed +s
Wool|worth, Frank Win|field (US merchant)
Woom|era (town, Australia)
woom|era +s
woosh (= whoosh)
  woosh|es
  wooshed
  woosh|ing
woozi|ly
woozi|ness
woozy
  woozi|er
  woozi|est
wop +s offensive (Italian)
[☞ whap]
Worces|ter (city, England)
Worces|ter|shire (former county, England; sauce)
word +s +ed +ing (term, expression)
[☞ ward]
word|age
word-blind
word-blindness
word|book +s
word-deaf
word-deafness
word game +s
word|i|er
word|i|est
word|i|ly
word|i|ness
word|ing +s noun
word|less
word|less|ly
word|less|ness
word-painting +s
WordPerfect proprietary
word-perfect adjective
word-picture +s
word|play
word-process
  word-process|es

word-processed
word-process|ing
word pro|cess|ing noun
word pro|ces|sor +s
word|smith +s
word-square +s
Words|worth, Dor|othy (English diarist)
Words|worth, Wil|liam (English poet)
Words|worth|ian +s
word wrap
wordy
  word|i|er
  word|i|est
wore conjugated form of wear
work +s +ed +ing
work|abil|ity
work|able
work|able|ness
work|ably
work|aday
work|ahol|ic +s
work|ahol|ism
work-bag +s
work-basket +s
work bee +s
work|bench
  work|bench|es
work|book +s
work|boot +s
work|box
  work|boxes
work|day +s
work|er +s
work|ers' com|pen|sa|tion
work|fare
work|flow +s
work|force +s
work|group +s
work|horse +s
work|house +s
work|ing +s noun & adjective
work|ing class (working-class when preceding a noun)
work-in-progress
  works-in-progress
work|less
work|load +s
work|man
  work|men
work|man|like
work|man|ship
Work|mate +s proprietary (table)
work|mate +s

work out *verb*
  works out
  worked out
  work|ing out
work|out +s *noun*
work|people
work|piece +s
work|place +s
work|room +s
work|sheet +s
work|shop
  work|shops
  work|shopped
  work|shop|ping
work-shy
work site +s
work|song +s
work|space +s
work|station +s
work sur|face +s
work table +s
work|top +s
work-to-rule +s
work up *verb*
  works up
  worked up
  work|ing up
work|up +s *noun*
work|wear
work|week +s
world +s
world beat
world-beater +s
world-class
world|er +s
world-famous
world|li|ness
world|ling +s
world|ly
  world|li|er
  world|li|est
worldly-minded
worldly-wise
world's fair +s
world-shaking
world view +s
world war +s
World War I
World War II
World War III
world-weariness
world-weary
world|wide
World Wide Web
worm +s +ed +ing
  (earthworm; crawl)
  [☞ **warm**]
worm|cast +s
worm cast|ing +s
worm-eaten
worm|er +s
worm|hole +s

worm|i|er
worm|i|est
worm|i|ness
worm|like
Worms (town,
  Germany; Diet)
worm|seed +s
worm's-eye view +s
worm|wheel +s
worm|wood +s
wormy
  worm|i|er
  worm|i|est
worn (*past participle of*
  wear; damaged by
  wear; exhausted)
  [☞ **warn**]
worn out (**worn-out**
  when preceding a
  noun)
wor|ried *adjective*
wor|ried|ly
wor|rier +s (one who
  worries)
  [☞ **warrior**]
wor|ri|ment +s
wor|ri|some
wor|ri|some|ly
worry
  wor|ries
  wor|ried
  worry|ing
worry|ing *adjective*
worry|ing|ly
worry|wart +s
worse
worsen +s +ed +ing
wor|ship (praise etc.)
  wor|ships
  wor|shipped
  wor|ship|ping
  [☞ **warship**]
wor|ship|ful
wor|ship|ful|ly
wor|ship|ful|ness
wor|ship|per +s
worst +s +ed +ing
  (most bad; get the
  better of)
  [☞ **wurst**]
worst-case *adjective*
  preceding a noun
worst|ed +s *noun &*
  adjective
wort +s (plant;
  Brewing)
  [☞ **wart, wert**]
worth
worth|i|er
worth|i|est
worth|i|ly
worth|i|ness

Wor|thing (town,
  England)
worth|less
worth|less|ly
worth|less|ness
worth|while
worth|while|ness
worthy
  worth|i|er
  worth|i|est
  worth|ies
wot *conjugated form of*
  wit
  [☞ **wat, watt**]
Wotan (= Odin,
  Scandinavian god)
wotch|er *interjection*
  [☞ **watcher**]
would *auxiliary verb*
  [☞ **wood**]
would-be
wouldn't (would not)
wouldst
wound
  • (injure) +s +ed +ing
  • *conjugated form of*
    wind
wound|ed *adjective*
Wound|ed Knee
  (massacre site, US)
wound|ed|ness
wound|ing|ly
wound|wort +s
wove
woven
wow +s +ed +ing
wow|ser +s
wrack +s +ed +ing
  (seaweed; wreckage;
  for clouds, injure or
  torture, *and in* 'rack
  and ruin' *use* rack)
  [☞ **rack**]
wraith +s
wraith|like
Wran|gel (island off
  Siberia)
wran|gle
  wran|gles
  wran|gled
  wran|gling
wran|gler +s
wran|gling +s *noun*
wrap (envelop; finish;
  crash a vehicle; *Word*
  Processing)
  wraps
  wrapped
  wrap|ping
  [☞ **rap**]
wrap|around +s *noun*
  & adjective

wrap-over +s *noun &*
  adjective
wrap|per +s
  (covering;
  packaging)
  [☞ **rapper**]
wrap|ping +s *noun*
wrap up *verb*
  wraps up
  wrapped up
  wrap|ping up
wrap-up +s *noun &*
  adjective
wrasse
  plural **wrasse** or
  wrasses
wras|sle (*use* rassle)
  wras|sles
  wras|sled
  wras|sling
Wrath (cape,
  Scotland)
wrath +s
wrath|ful
wrath|ful|ly
wrath|ful|ness
wrathy
wreak +s +ed +ing
  (cause, carry out; in
  'wreak havoc,
  revenge etc.')
  [☞ **reek, wreck**]
wreak|er +s
wreath +s *noun*
wreathe *verb*
  wreathes
  wreathed
  wreath|ing
wreck +s +ed +ing
  (destroy, ruin etc.)
  [☞ **reck, rec,
  wreak**]
wreck|age +s
wrecked *adjective*
wreck|er +s
wrecker's ball +s
Wren, Sir
  Chris|to|pher
  (English architect)
  [☞ **Rennes**]
Wren +s (Women's
  Royal Naval Service
  member)
  [☞ **Rennes**]
wren +s (bird)
wrench
  wrench|es
  wrenched
  wrench|ing
wrest +s +ed +ing
  (take forcibly; distort;
  tuning key)
  [☞ **rest**]

wres|tle
wres|tles
wres|tled
wrest|ling
wrest|ler +s
wrest|ling +s
wretch (unfortunate or wicked person)
wretch|es
[☞ retch]
wretch|ed *adjective*
wretch|ed|ly
wretch|ed|ness
wrig|gle
wrig|gles
wrig|gled
wrig|gling
wrig|gler +s
wrig|gly
Wright, Frank Lloyd (US architect)
Wright, Or|ville & Wil|bur (US aviation pioneers)
Wright, Rich|ard Na|than|iel (US writer)
wright +s (maker)
[☞ right, write, rite]
wring (squeeze, twist)
wrings
wrung
wring|ing
[☞ ring]
wring|er +s (for wringing water from clothes; in 'put through the wringer')
[☞ ringer]
wring|ing *adjective* (wet)
[☞ ringing]
wrin|kle
wrin|kles
wrin|kled
wrink|ling
wrin|kled *adjective*
wrink|ly
wrink|li|er
wrink|li|est
wrink|lies
wrist +s +ed +ing (lower forearm)
[☞ wrest]
wrist|band +s
wrist|let +s
wrist shot +s
wrist|watch
wrist|watch|es
wristy
writ +s (*Law*; archaic past participle of write)

writ|able (that can be written to)
write (put words on paper etc.; *Computing*)
writes
wrote
writ|ten
writ|ing
[☞ wright, right, rite]
write down *verb*
writes down
wrote down
writ|ten down
writ|ing down
write|down +s *noun*
write in *verb*
writes in
wrote in
writ|ten in
writ|ing in
write-in +s *adjective & noun*
write off *verb*
writes off
wrote off
writ|ten off
writ|ing off
write-off +s *noun*
writ|er +s (person who writes)
[☞ righter]
writer-in-residence
writers-in-residence
writer|ly
writer's block
writer's cramp +s
write up *verb*
writes up
wrote up
writ|ten up
writ|ing up
write-up +s *noun*
writhe
writhes
writhed
writh|ing
writ|ing +s *noun*
Writ|ings (the Hagiographa)
writ|ten
Wroc|ław (city, Poland)
wrong +er +est +s +ed +ing
wrong|doer +s
wrong|doing +s
wrong|er +s
wrong-foot +s +ed +ing
wrong|ful
wrong|ful|ly

wrong|ful|ness
wrong-headed
wrong-headed|ly
wrong-headed|ness
wrong|ly
wrong|ness
wrote past tense of write
[☞ rote]
wroth (angry)
wrought (archaic past & past participle of work; formed, shaped)
[☞ rot]
wrought iron (wrought-iron when preceding a noun)
wrung past participle of wring
[☞ rung]
wry (mocking, sardonic; disgusted; distorted)
wryer or wrier
wry|est or wri|est
[☞ rai, rye, Ray, Reye's syndrome]
wryly
wry neck (torticollis)
wry|neck +s (bird)
wry|ness
Wu (language)
[☞ woo]
Wuhan
Wu-hsi (= Wuxi, China)
wul|fen|ite +s
wunder|kind
plural **wunder|kinds** or **wunder|kin|der**
Wundt, Wil|helm (German psychologist)
Wup|per|tal (city, Germany)
wurst +s (sausage)
[☞ worst, verst]
Würz|burg (city, Germany)
wuss
wuss|es
wussy
wus|si|er
wus|si|est
wus|sies
Wuxi (city, China)
WWI (World War I)
WWII (World War II)
Wyan|dot (people; language)
plural **Wyan|dot** or **Wyan|dots**

Wyan|dotte
• (fowl)
plural **Wyan|dottes**
• (people, language: *use* Wyandot)
plural **Wyan|dotte** or **Wyan|dottes**
Wyatt, Sir Thom|as (English poet)
wych elm +s
Wych|er|ley, Wil|liam (English dramatist)
wych-hazel +s (*use* witch hazel)
Wyc|lif, John (= Wycliffe)
Wyc|liffe, John (English religious reformer)
Wyc|liff|ite +s
Wye (river, England & Wales)
wye +s (railway track)
Wyeth, An|drew New|ell (US painter)
wyn +s (= wen, rune)
[☞ whin, win]
Wyn|ette, Tammy (US singer)
Wyo|ming (state, US)
Wyo|ming|ite +s
WYSIWYG (*Computing*)
wy|vern +s

X

X
• (letter; shape, symbol; kiss; in "X's and O's")
X's
• (chromosome)
[☞ ex]
x (letter)
x's
[☞ ex]
X-acto *proprietary* (knife)
Xan|adu +s (idyllic place)
Xan|kän|di (city, Azerbaijan)
xan|than gum
xan|thate +s
xan|thic
xan|thine +s

Xan|thip|pe (Socrates' wife)
xan|tho|ma
  xan|tho|mas or
  xan|tho|mata
xan|tho|phyll
Xan|tip|pe
  (= Xanthippe)
Xavier, Fran|cis (saint)
X-C (cross-country)
X chromo|some +s
X-country (cross-country)
xebec +s
Xen|akis, Ian|nis (French composer & architect)
xeno|graft +s
xeno|lith +s
xeno|lith|ic
xenon
Xen|opha|nes (Greek philosopher)
xeno|phobe +s
xeno|phobia
xeno|phob|ic
Xeno|phon (Greek historian)
Xer +s
xeran|the|mum +s
xeric
xeri|scape +s
xeri|scap|ing
xero|derma
xero|graph|ic
xero|graph|ic|ally
xer|og|raphy
xer|oph|il|ous
xero|phyte +s
xero|phyt|ic
Xerox *proprietary noun*
  Xer|ox|es
xerox *verb*
  xer|ox|es
  xer|oxed
  xer|ox|ing
Xerxes I (king of Persia)
Xhosa
  plural **Xhosa** or **Xho|sas**
xi +s (fourteenth Greek letter)
  [☞ **psi**]
Xia|men (city, China)
Xian (city, China)
Ximen|es de Cis|ner|os, Fran|cis|co (= Jiménez de

Cisneros, Spanish statesman)
Xingú (river, S America)
Xi|ning (city, China)
Xin|ji|ang (region, China)
xiphi|ster|num
  xiphi|ster|nums or **xiphi|ster|na**
xiph|oid
Xmas
X-rated
X-ray +s +ed +ing
X's and O's
xu (Vietnamese monetary unit)
  plural **xu**
Xuth|us (*Greek Myth*)
Xu|zhou (city, China)
Xwe Nal Mewx (*use* Sne Nay Muxw)
  plural **Xwe Nal Mewx**
xylem
xylene +s
xyli|tol
xylo|graph +s
xylog|raphy
xyloph|a|gous
xylo|phone +s
xylo|phon|ist +s

Y

....

Y
• (letter; shape; YMCA, YWCA, YMHA, YWHA)
Y's
• (yen; chromosome)
  [☞ **wye, Wye**]
y (letter)
  y's
  [☞ **wye, Wye**]
ya (yes)
  [☞ **yeah, yaw, yea, yay**]
yacht +s +ed +ing
yacht|ie +s
yacht|ing *noun*
yachts|man
  yachts|men
yack +s +ed +ing
  (talk: *use* yak)
  [☞ **yak**]
yackety-yack +s +ed +ing

yaf|fle +s
Yafo (= Jaffa, Israel)
Yag|ara
ya|hoo +s
yahoo|ism
Yah|veh (= Yahweh)
Yah|vist (= Yahwist)
Yah|vis|tic
  (= Yahwistic)
Yah|weh (*Bible*)
Yah|wist
Yah|wis|tic
Yajur-Veda
yak (animal; talk)
  yaks
  yakked
  yak|king
yaki|tori
Ya|ku|tia (autonomous republic, Russia)
Ya|kutsk (city, Russia)
ya|kuza
  plural **ya|kuza**
Yale (university, US)
Yale, Elihu (English merchant)
y'all (you all)
  [☞ **yawl**]
Yalta (city, Ukraine; conference)
Yalu (river, Asia)
yam +s
Yama (*Hindu Myth*)
Yama|moto, Iso|roku (Japanese admiral)
yam|mer +s +ed +ing
yam|mer|er +s
Yam|ous|sou|kro (capital of the Ivory Coast)
Yan|cheng (city, China)
Yang, Chen Ning (US physicist)
yang
Yan|gon (*official name for* Rangoon, Burmese capital)
Yang|shao (Chinese civilization)
Yang|tze (river, China)
Yank +s (American)
yank +s +ed +ing
Yan|kee +s
Yan|tai (city, China)
Yaoun|dé (capital of Cameroon)
yap
  yaps
  yapped
  yap|ping
yap|ok +s

yap|per +s
yappy
  yap|pi|er
  yap|pi|est
Yard (Scotland Yard)
yard +s +ed +ing
yard|age +s
yard|arm +s
yard|bird +s
yard|er +s
yard|light +s
yard|master +s
yard sale +s
yard|stick +s
yard|work
Yar|mouth (town, Canada)
yar|mul|ka +s (*use* yarmulke)
yar|mul|ke +s
yarn +s +ed +ing
Yaro|slavl (city, Russia)
yar|row +s
yash|mak +s
yat|ter +s +ed +ing
yaw +s +ed +ing (*Nautical*)
yawl +s (*Nautical*)
  [☞ **y'all, yowl**]
yawn +s +ed +ing (sign of sleepiness)
  [☞ **yon**]
yawn|er +s
yawn|ing|ly
yawp +s +ed +ing
yawp|er +s
yaws
yay (hooray; this much, in 'yay big' etc.)
  [☞ **yea**]
Y chromo|some +s
yclept
ye
• (*plural of* thou)
• *pseudo-archaic* (= the)
yea +s (affirmative vote; yes; indeed; hooray)
  [☞ **yay, yeah, ye**]
Yea|ger, Charles El|wood ('Chuck') (US pilot)
  [☞ **jaeger**]
yeah (yes; in 'oh yeah?'; hooray)
  [☞ **yea, ye, yay**]
year +s
year|book +s
year-end +s
year|ling +s

year-long
year|ly
yearn +s +ed +ing
yearn|er +s
yearn|ing +s noun &
  adjective
yearn|ing|ly
year-round
yeast +s
yeast|i|ly
yeast|i|ness
yeast|less
yeast|like
yeasty
  yeast|i|er
  yeast|i|est
Yeats, Wil|liam
  But|ler (Irish poet)
Yeats|ian
yecch (= yech)
yecchy (= yechy)
yech
yechy
yee-haw
yeesh
yegg +s
Yekat|er|in|burg (city,
  Russia)
Yekat|er|ino|dar
  (former name for
  Krasnodar, Russia)
Yekat|er|ino|slav
  (former name for
  Dnipropetrovsk,
  Ukraine)
Yeliza|vet|pol (former
  name for Gäncä,
  Azerbaijan)
yell +s +ed +ing
yell|ing noun
Yel|low (river, China;
  sea between Korea &
  China)
yel|low +s +ed +ing
yellow-bellied
yellow-belly
yellow-billed
yellow|cake
yellow|hammer +s
Yellow|head
  (mountain pass,
  Canada)
yellow|ish
yel|low jack|et +s
Yellow|knife (city,
  Canada; people)
  plural Yellow|knife
  or Yellow|knives
Yellow|knifer +s
yellow|legs
  plural yellow|legs
yellow|ly
yellow|ness

Yel|low Pages
  proprietary
Yellow|stone (park,
  US)
yellow|throat +s
Yel|low
  Trans|par|ent +s
yellow|wood +s
yel|lowy
yelp +s +ed +ing
yelp|er +s
Yelt|sin, Boris
  Nikola|evich
  (Russian statesman)
Yemen (country,
  Arabian peninsula)
Yem|eni +s
Yem|en|ite +s
yen
• (Japanese monetary
  unit)
  plural yen
• (yearning)
  yens
  yenned
  yen|ning
Yeni|sei (river, Siberia)
yenta +s
yente +s (use yenta)
yeo|man
  yeo|men
yeo|man|ly
yeo|man|ry
  yeo|man|ries
yep
yerba maté
Yere|van (capital of
  Armenia)
yes
  yeses
Ye|senin, Ser|gey
  Alek|san|dro|vich
  (= Esenin, Russian
  writer)
ye|shiva +s
ye|shivah +s (use
  yeshiva)
yes-man
  yes-men
yes|ter|day +s
yes|ter|year +s
yet
yeti +s
Yev|tu|shenko,
  Yev|geni
  Alek|san|dro|vich
  (Russian poet)
yew +s (tree)
  [☞ ewe, U]
Y-fronts proprietary
Ygg|dra|sil
  (Scandinavian Myth)

YHVH
  (Tetragrammaton)
Yichun (city, China)
Yid +s offensive
Yid|dish
Yid|dish|er +s
Yid|dish|ism +s
yield +s +ed +ing
yield|er +s
yield|ing adjective
yield|ing|ly
yield|ing|ness
yikes
yin +s
Yin|chuan (city,
  China)
yin-yang
yip
  yips
  yipped
  yip|ping
yip|pee interjection
yip|pie +s noun
ylang-ylang +s
Ymir (Scandinavian
  Myth)
yo
yob +s
yob|bish
yob|bish|ly
yob|bish|ness
yobbo +s
yod +s
yodel
  yo|dels
  yo|delled
  or yo|deled
  yodel|ling
  or yodel|ing
yodel|er +s (use
  yodeller)
yodel|ler +s
yoga +s
yogh +s
yo|ghurt +s (use
  yogourt)
yogi +s
yogic
yog|ism
yo|gourt +s
yo|gurt +s (use
  yogourt)
Yog|ya|karta (city,
  Indonesia)
yo-heave-ho
Yoho (park, Canada)
yo-ho interjection
yo-ho-ho (= yo-ho)
yoke
• (harness etc.; bond;
  Aviation)
  plural yokes

• (pair)
  plural yoke or yokes
• (link, join)
  yokes
  yoked
  yok|ing
  [☞ yolk]
yokel +s
Yoko|hama (city,
  Japan)
yolk +s (egg part;
  suint)
  [☞ yoke]
yolked
yolk|less
yolk sac +s
yolky
Yom Kip|pur
  (Judaism)
yomp +s +ed +ing
yon (yonder)
  [☞ yawn]
yon|der
yoni +s
yonks
yoo-hoo +s +ed +ing
yore (in 'of yore')
  [☞ your, you're]
York (former name for
  Toronto; city,
  England; cape,
  Australia; English
  royal house)
York boat +s
York Fac|tory
  (historic site,
  Canada)
York|ist +s
York|shire (former
  county, England;
  pudding; terrier)
York|shire|man
  York|shire|men
York|shire|woman
  York|shire|women
York|ton (city,
  Canada)
Yor|uba
  plural Yor|ubas or
  Yor|uba
Yosem|ite (park, US)
Yoshkar-Ola (city,
  Russia)
you pronoun
  [☞ yew, ewe, U]
you-all
you'd (you had; you
  would)
you-know-what +s
you-know-who
you'll (you will; you
  shall)
  [☞ yule]

Young (surname)
[☞ **Jung**]

Young, Brig|ham (US Mormon leader)

Young, Den|ton True ('Cy') (US baseball player)

Young, Ed|ward (English writer)

Young, Sir John (Baron Lisgar, governor general of Canada)

Young, Les|ter Wil|lis (US saxophonist)

Young, Neil Per|ci|val (Cdn singer-songwriter)

Young, Thom|as (English physicist)

young +er +est

young blood +s

young|er *noun*

young|ish

young|ling +s

Young Pre|tend|er (Charles Edward Stuart, 'Bonny Prince Charlie')

young|ster +s

Young Turk +s (Turkish revolutionary; radical reformer generally)

young turk +s *offensive* (violent youth)

young 'un +s

youn|ker +s (youngster)
[☞ **Junker**]

your *possessive adjective*
[☞ **you're, yore**]

Your|cenar, Mar|guer|ite (French writer)

you're (you are)
[☞ **your, yore**]

yours

your|self
  your|selves

yous (= youse)

youse *informal pronoun*
[☞ **use**]

youth
  youths

youth|ful

youth|ful|ly

youth|ful|ness

you've (you have)

You|ville, Marie-Marguerite d' (saint)

yowl +s +ed +ing (wail, cry)
[☞ **yawl**]

yo-yo
• *noun & adjective*
  yo-yos
• *verb*
  yo-yoes
  yo-yoed
  yo-yoing

Ypres (battle site, Belgium)

yt|ter|bium

yt|tri|um

Yuan (Chinese dynasty)

yuan (Chinese monetary unit)
  plural yuan

Yuan Jiang (= Red River, China)

Yuan Shi Kai (Chinese statesman)

Yuca|tán (peninsula & state, Mexico)

yuc|ca +s

yuck +s +ed +ing (expression of disgust; messy thing; *for* laugh, fool around *use* **yuk**)

yucky
  yuck|i|er
  yuck|i|est

Yugo|slav +s

Yugo|slav|ia (country, Europe)

Yugo|slav|ian +s

yuk (laugh; fool around; *for* expression of digust; messy thing *use* **yuck**)
  yuks
  yukked
  yuk|king

yu|kata
  plural yu|kata

Yu|kawa, Hideki (Japanese physicist)

yukky (= yucky)
  yuk|ki|er
  yuk|ki|est

Yukon (territory & former district, Canada; river, N America; stove)

Yukon|er +s

Yukon Gold +s

yule (Christmas season)
[☞ **you'll**]

yule|tide

yum

yum|my
  yum|mi|er
  yum|mi|est

yum-yum

Yun|nan (province, China)

yup +s (yes; yuppie)

Yupik (people, language)
  plural **Yupik** or **Yu|piks**
[☞ **U-pick**]

yup|pie +s

yup|pie|dom

yup|pi|fi|ca|tion

yup|pi|fy
  yup|pi|fies
  yup|pi|fied
  yup|pi|fy|ing

yuppy (*use* **yuppie**)
  yup|pies

yurt +s

Yuz|ovka (former *name for* **Donetsk**, Ukraine)

Z

z
• (letter)
  Z's
• (atomic number)
  [☞ **zed, zee**]

z (letter)
  z's
  [☞ **zed, zee**]

zaba|glione +s

Zabrze (city, Poland)

Zaca|tecas (state & its capital, Mexico)

Zach|ar|ias (= Zechariah, father of John the Baptist)
[☞ **Zechariah**]

zaf|tig

zag
  zags
  zagged
  zag|ging

Zaga|zig (city, Egypt)

Zag|reb (capital of Croatia)

Zag|reus (*Greek Myth*)

Zag|ros (mountains, Iran)

zai|batsu
  plural zai|batsu

Zaire
• (*former name for* the Democratic Republic of the **Congo**)
• (= **Congo** River)

zaire +s (currency of Congo)

Zair|ean +s

Zair|ian +s (*use* Zairean)

Zako|pane (resort, Poland)

Zam|bezi (river, Africa)

Zam|bia (country, Africa)

Zam|bian +s

Zam|bo|anga (city, the Philippines)

Zam|boni +s *proprietary*

zam|in|dar +s

zan|i|ly

zan|i|ness

ZANU (Zimbabwe African National Union)

Zan|uck, Dar|ryl Fran|cis (US filmmaker)

zany
  zan|i|er
  zan|i|est
  zan|ies

Zan|zi|bar (island off Tanzania)

Zan|zi|bari +s

Zao|zhuang (city, China)

zap
  zaps
  zapped
  zap|ping

Zap|ata, Emil|iano (Mexican revolutionary)

zapa|teado +s

Zapo|rizh|zhya (city, Ukraine)

Zapo|tec
  plural **Zapo|tec** or **Zapo|tecs**

Zappa, Fran|cis Vin|cent ('Frank') (US singer-songwriter)

zap|pable

zap|per +s

zappy
  zap|pi|er
  zap|pi|est

ZAPU (Zimbabwe African People's Union)
Zaqa|ziq (= Zagazig, Egypt)
Zara|thus|tra (Zoroaster)
Zara|thus|tri|an +s
zar|eba +s
Zaria (city, Nigeria)
zar|iba +s (use zareba)
Zarqa (city, Jordan)
zar|zuela +s
zax
zaxes
[☞ **Sachs**]
zeal
Zea|land (island, Denmark)
[☞ **Zeeland**]
Zeal|ot +s (member of 1st-c. Jewish sect)
zeal|ot +s (fanatic)
zeal|ot|ry
zeal|ous
zeal|ous|ly
zeal|ous|ness
zebec +s (use xebec)
zebeck +s (use xebec)
Zeb|edee (New Testament)
zebra
plural **zebras** or **zebra**
zebrine
zebu +s
Zebu|lon (= Zebulun)
Zebu|lun (Bible)
Zech|ar|iah (prophet; father of John the Baptist)
zed +s (letter)
zeda +s
Zed|ekiah (Bible)
zedo|ary
zedo|aries
zee +s (letter; in 'catch some zees')
Zee|brugge (port, Belgium)
Zee|land (province, the Netherlands)
[☞ **Zealand**]
Zee|man, Pieter (Dutch physicist)
Zef|fi|rel|li, Fran|co (Italian director)
zein +s (Biochemistry)
Zeiss, Carl (German manufacturer of optical instruments)
Zeit|geist

zem|in|dar +s (use zamindar)
Zen
zen|ana +s
Zend +s
Zend-Avesta
Zen|ist +s
ze|nith +s
ze|nith|al
Zen|like
Zen|nist +s (= Zenist)
Zeno (of Cit|ium) (c. 335–c. 263 BC; Greek philosopher)
Zeno (of Elea) (fl. 5th c. BC; Greek philosopher)
zeo|lite +s
zeo|lit|ic
Zepha|niah (Bible)
zephyr +s
Zephyr|us (Greek Myth)
Zep|pelin, Fer|di|nand Adolf Aug|ust Hein|rich, Count von (German aviation pioneer)
Zep|pelin +s
Zer|matt (resort, Switzerland)
zero
• noun
zeros
• verb
zeroes
zeroed
zero|ing
zero grav|ity (zero-gravity when preceding a noun)
zero-sum
zeroth
zest +s
zest|er +s
zest|ful
zest|ful|ly
zest|ful|ness
zesty
zest|i|er
zest|i|est
zeta +s
zeug|ma +s
zeug|mat|ic
Zeus (Greek Myth)
Zeux|is (Greek painter)
Zhang|jia|kou (city, China)
Zhan|jiang (city, China)
Zhao Ziyang (Chinese statesman)

Zhda|nov (former name for **Mariupol**, Ukraine)
Zhe|jiang (province, China)
Zheng|zhou (city, China)
Zhen|jiang (city, China)
Zhong|shan (city, China)
Zhou (Chinese dynasty)
Zhou Enlai (Chinese statesman)
Zhu De (Chinese military leader)
Zhu|kov, Georgi Kon|stan|tin|ovich (Soviet military leader)
Zhyto|myr (city, Ukraine)
Zia ul-Haq, Muham|mad (president of Pakistan)
Zibo (city, China)
zi|dovu|dine
Zieg|feld, Flor|enz (US theatre manager)
zig
zigs
zigged
zig|ging
zig|gu|rat +s
zig|zag
zig|zags
zig|zagged
zig|zag|ging
zig|zag|ged|ly
zilch
zil|lion
plural **zil|lion** or **zil|lions**
zil|lion|aire +s
zil|lionth +s
Zim|babwe (country, Africa)
Zim|bab|wean +s
zinc
zinc|blende +s
zinced
zinco|graph +s
zinc|og|raphy
zine +s (magazine) [☞ **zein**]
Zin|fan|del +s
zing +s +ed +ing
zing|er +s

zingy
zing|i|er
zing|i|est
Zinne|mann, Fred (US filmmaker)
zin|nia +s
Zin|ov|iev, Grig|ori Yevse|evich (Russian revolutionary)
Zin|zen|dorf, Count Niko|laus Lud|wig von (Moravian Church founder)
Zion (Religion)
Zion|ism
Zion|ist +s
zip
zips
zipped
zip|ping
Zip code +s proprietary
zip gun +s
zip-lock
zip|per +s +ed +ing
zip|pered adjective
zip|pi|ly
zip|pi|ness
zippo
zippy
zip|pi|er
zip|pi|est
zip up verb
zips up
zipped up
zip|ping up
zip-up adjective
zir|con +s
zir|co|nia
zir|co|nium
Ziska, Jan (Bohemian soldier)
zit +s
zith|er +s
zith|er|ist +s
Žižka, Jan (= Ziska)
zizz
zizz|es
zizzed
zizz|ing
zloty
plural **zloty** or **zlotys**
Zo|di|ac +s proprietary (dinghy)
zo|di|ac +s
zo|di|ac|al
Zog I (Albanian king)
Zola, Émile Édouard Charles An|toine (French writer)
Zola|esque
zoll|ver|ein +s

zom|bie +s
zombie|like
zom|bi|fied *adjective*
zom|bi|fy
  zom|bi|fies
  zom|bi|fied
  zom|bi|fy|ing
zonal
zon|a|tion +s
zone
  zones
  zoned
  zon|ing
zon|ing *noun*
zonk +s +ed +ing
zoo +s
zoo|geo|graph|ic
zoo|geo|graph|ic|al
zoo|geo|graph|ic|ally
zoo|geog|raphy
zo|ogra|phy
zooid +s
zooid|al
zoo|keep|er
zo|ola|try
zoo|logic|al
zoo|logic|al|ly
zo|olo|gist +s
zo|ology
zoom +s +ed +ing
zoom lens
  zoom lens|es
zoo|morph|ic
zoo|morph|ism
zoono|sis
  zoono|ses
zoo|not|ic
zoo|phyte
zoo|phyt|ic
zoo|plank|ton
zoo|plank|ton|ic
zoo|spore +s
zoo|spor|ic
zoot suit +s
zoot-suited
zoot-suiter +s
zori +s
zor|il +s
zor|ille +s (*use* zoril)
Zorn, An|ders
  Leon|hard (Swedish
  artist)
Zoro|as|ter (Persian
  prophet)
Zoro|as|trian +s
Zoro|as|trian|ism
Zor|rilla y Moral,
  José (Spanish writer)
Zouave +s
Zoug (= Zug,
  Switzerland)
zouk

zounds
zowee (= zowie)
zowie
Zsig|mon|dy,
  Rich|ard Adolph
  (German chemist)
zuc|chet|to +s
zuc|chi|ni
  plural zuc|chi|ni or
  zuc|chi|nis
Zug (canton & city,
  Switzerland)
zug|zwang +s
Zuider Zee (inlet, the
  Netherlands)
Zuker|man, Pin|chas
  (Israeli violinist)
Zulu +s
Zulu|land
  (= KwaZulu, former
  South African
  homeland)
Zuni
  plural Zuni or Zunis
Zuñi (= Zuni)
  plural Zuñi or Zuñis
zuppa
  zup|pas or zuppe
zuppa di pesce
  (= zuppa)
  zuppe di pesce
Zur|ba|rán,
  Fran|cis|co de
  (Spanish painter)
Zur|ich (city,
  Switzerland)
Zweig, Ar|nold
  (German novelist)
Zweig, Stef|an
  (Austrian writer)
Zwick|au (city,
  Germany)
zwie|back
Zwing|li, Ul|rich
  (Swiss religious
  reformer)
Zwing|li|an +s
zwit|ter|ion +s
zwit|ter|ion|ic
Zwolle (town, the
  Netherlands)
Zwory|kin, Vlad|i|mir
  Kuz|mich (US
  inventor)
zy|deco
zygo|dac|tyl +s
zygo|dac|tyl|ous
zy|go|ma
  zygo|mata or
  zy|go|mas
zygo|mat|ic
zygo|morph|ic
zygo|morph|ous

zygo|spore +s
zy|gote +s
zy|got|ic
zy|got|ic|ally
zym|ase
zymo|logic|al
zym|olo|gist +s
zym|ol|ogy
zym|o|sis
zym|ot|ic
zym|urgy
zzz

The indispensable companion to
The Canadian Oxford Spelling Dictionary

GUIDE TO CANADIAN ENGLISH USAGE
Margery Fee and Janice McAlpine

Canadian English is a variety of English in its own right, with its own distinctive mix of features. Yet in the past Canadians wanting to find out about their language have often had to choose between British and American guides. The *Guide to Canadian English Usage* offers an alternative based on what Canadian writers actually do.

Drawing on a corpus of 12 million words of Canadian English, its 1750 entries provide comprehensive coverage of specifically Canadian questions as well as problems common to all English-speakers, including:

* Canadianisms (*acclamation, chesterfield, durum, pogey, tuque*)

* confusables (*baluster, banister; ecology, environment; tartan, plaid*)

* difficult expressions (*beg the question, home in on, toe the line, whet the appetite*)

* First Nations names (*Nootka* or *Nuu-chah-nulth*? *Ojibwa, Ojibway,* or *Anishnabe*?)

* foreign phrases (*ad nauseam, coup de grâce, hoi polloi*)

* grammar (agreement, dangling modifiers, sentence fragments, the subjunctive)

* inclusive language (disabilities; job titles; race, sexist language)

* punctuation (apostrophe, comma, italics, quotation marks)

* spelling (*centre* or *center*? *honour* or *honor*? *Quebecker* or *Quebecer*?)

* troublesome pronunciations (*asphalt, Arctic, schedule, vulnerable*)

Each entry explains the problem at hand, outlines a range of prescriptions, and then either recommends a particular usage or reviews the alternatives from which the now-informed reader can choose. Quotations from a wide range of sources illustrate both problems and solutions.

"Lucid, comprehensive, humane, practical and effective."
— Tom McArthur,
   Editor, *The Oxford Companion to the English Language*